THE
SCHOOLS
BOOK

The discriminating parents' guide
to independent secondary schools

General Editors
KLAUS BOEHM
JENNY LEES-SPALDING

Editors
J A CUDDON
JANE SHAW

M
PAPERMAC

First published 1988 by
PAPERMAC
a division of Macmillan Publishers Limited
4 Little Essex Street London WC2R 3LF
and Basingstoke

Associated companies in Auckland, Delhi,
Dublin, Gaborone, Hamburg, Harare, Hong
Kong, Johannesburg, Kuala Lumpur, Lagos,
Manzini, Melbourne, Mexico City, Nairobi,
New York, Singapore and Tokyo

ISBN 0-333-45557-6

A CIP catalogue record for this
book is available from the
British Library.

Typeset by Rowland Phototypesetting Ltd,
Bury St Edmunds, Suffolk
Printed and bound in Great Britain by
Cox & Wyman Ltd, Reading

Contents

Foreword

FOREWORD

The Schools Book is a consumer book. To be precise, it is a book for discriminating parents considering the purchase of independent secondary school education, who want to know as much as possible before making their shortlist of schools worth visiting. It makes no pretence of being a substitute for careful reading of school prospectuses, on-the-spot reconnaissance or discussion with school staff.

There was a time when independent secondary schools were easily chosen. Fathers *knew* that their old schools would provide the best education for their sons. Girls' education did not matter. All this has changed. Independent secondary schools themselves are changing rapidly. The school that Dad or Mum knew may no longer be recognisable in the school that it now is. And, according to some estimates, the majority of parents now choosing independent secondary education have not themselves experienced independent education.

There are two key characteristics about today's discriminating parents. One is that many retain a residual nervousness (in some cases terror!) of school teachers, coupled with a belief that teachers are always right. If you doubt this, stand outside a school on an open day and watch the skirts being adjusted and the ties straightened by those on their way in. The other is that most parents' immediate knowledge of today's schools is likely to be restricted – probably to what the schools want them to know, ie what they say about themselves in their own prospectuses.

Many independent schools are good at getting pupils through exams but what else do you want from a school for *your* child? Discriminating parents usually want to know the answers to a whole host of questions before making a shortlist; but at that stage they have little or no chance of grilling Heads or getting the answers to them all, even if they are prepared to risk being branded as 'difficult'. So, you need access to published information from which you can sensibly construct a shortlist. As parents, we found the existing information – much of it excellent, particularly from ISIS and SFIA – did not provide what we wanted to know to make our own shortlist of schools that we wanted to visit and assess.

Having set out to find out for ourselves, the full diversity of the independent schools became apparent. From our own personal standpoint we immediately spotted a wide divergence in school cultures. For example:

- Many schools seemed to dragoon pupils into chapel and on to the sports field, whether or not they show enthusiasm or aptitude, but in many other schools chapel and sports are optional.
- Many schools (particularly girls') still appear to be geographically and socially isolated – girls being allowed into the local town 2–4 times a term, with little contact with boys' schools or the local community.

Conversely, some schools allow pupils into the local town every day after school, with permission (all have graded rules, more relaxed for seniors; but some seniors are still more restricted than juniors at other schools).

- Some boys' schools teach eg bed-sitter cooking; many schools of all types have Young Enterprise groups and an immense range of other extra-curricular activities (ferreting, astronomy, wine making, helping local handicapped, etc); others appear to have nothing beyond tennis and netball or cricket and rugby.

- Some schools have under 10 pupils learning musical instruments and no musical groups in the school; others have 70–100% pupils learning musical instruments with a variety of orchestras, bands and pop groups flourishing in the school. We specifically asked schools about pupils who had gone on to play in pop groups after leaving school. It provoked a variety of responses – some honest (quite a number of pop singers and their managers were educated at independent schools), many schools answered only with a question mark or exclamation mark and one rang up to make sure the questionnaire was intended for independent schools.

- Attitudes to discipline vary greatly. It seemed to us crucial to know a school's approach to discipline before sending one's children into its care. The response of some Heads reinforced our belief that it was not a topic which parents would find easy discussing with many of them. We developed what we own are fairly crude questions about the punishments that were likely in two instances – one fairly minor, one obviously serious. Most schools answered these sensibly, occasionally with inspiration and reflecting a carefully considered policy. Some schools didn't answer, which is their right; we were surprised, though, at the Heads who didn't answer because it was 'irrelevant'.

Choosing the right school for your child is one of the most important decisions you will take. Look carefully at our School Profiles (but please read the detail about the data in the next section 'How To Use the Book'). Then make your shortlist, read the prospectus, visit the schools and talk to the staff.

We are very grateful for the help we have received from the Heads of the majority of schools described in this book. They have not only provided the information without which *The Schools Book* could not have been published, but in many cases wrote most encouraging and thoughtful letters explaining the problems faced by discriminating parents. We are also grateful to Bryan Reading for the cartoons. Our very special thanks go to James Tomlinson and to Gill Drake whose administration of the information collection and creation of the database has underpinned the entire editorial effort.

Klaus Boehm and Jenny Lees-Spalding
September 1988

How to use the Book

HOW TO USE THE BOOK

The Schools Book aims to help parents prepare a shortlist of schools from which to select the right school for *their* child. It is in three sections:

1. **HOW TO GO ABOUT IT A–Z** gives, in alphabetical order, a number of general points about choosing schools and terms which may need explaining, such as GCSE.

2. **SCHOOLS A–Z** contains over 550 profiles of schools, arranged in alphabetical order. Most entries are based on questionnaires completed by the schools – and returned to Heads for checking once drafted.

The top section gives key facts such as full name, address, senior pupils' fees, affiliation (eg to HMC or GPDST) and number of pupils *over 12*. The black dots [●] in the middle column indicate which pupils are accepted, eg boys, mixed sixth, day and boarding.

WHAT IT'S LIKE is a brief description (based on information from the school) written by the editors, designed to give you a flavour of the school.

SCHOOL PROFILE gives a range of facts about the school. In many cases, figures are approximations. Schools were asked to give average annual figures over three years but even so these may be expected to vary to some degree from year to year.

Pupils – usually the entry gives the number of pupils over 12 – broken down into day/boarding and boys/girls. We give the main intake ages to the school so it is possible to tell if it takes children earlier than 12, even though the number of pupils does not reflect the younger children.

Entrance – this indicates how the school decides which candidates to accept and whether there is any financial assistance available.

Parents – where they live and whether there are significant proportions in any professions.

Staff – name of Head, number, age and turnover of staff.

Academic work – which public exams pupils are prepared for and the number of passes per pupil. Most schools are moving from O-levels to GCSE; the retrospective information therefore refers to O-level passes, grades A–C. Scotland is different; read the Scottish entries with care and see 'Scotland' in 'How To Go About It'.

Senior pupils' non-academic activities – usually refers to pupils in the upper fifth and above. It won't give a complete picture of all that happens in a school but does give some comparative information by which to judge how much is going on other than passing A-levels. Remember that, in some day schools, pupils may do eg music outside the school; not all schools know what their pupils are doing in this respect.

Careers – not intended to map in detail what happens to all pupils when they leave a school but, again, to provide some general comparative information.

Uniform, houses/prefects/religion/social – all give various items of information to help judge the flavour of a school.

Discipline – We felt it was important to know what a school's attitude was to discipline. Whilst it is obvious that each case must be judged individually, we asked schools what they would *expect* by way of punishment in two cases – a relatively minor incident (failure to produce homework on a single occasion) and an obviously serious offence (smoking cannabis). We must emphasise that in this latter case we asked for punishment *other than* any police involvement and many schools answered the question hypothetically; do not assume that a school has a drugs problem simply because it has considered its reaction to the possibility!

Boarding – some facts about the way boarding is organised and when pupils are allowed out.

Alumni Association – how to get in touch with the person who runs the old boys'/girls' association.

Former Pupils – these are the school's selection.

3. **SPECIAL FEATURES INDEX** lists all the schools by county and gives some outline information based on the entry for the school in 'Schools A–Z'. This section is for guidance only. In particular:

- Financial help indicates any fee reductions you may be able to get. Asst places = assisted places; Schols = scholarships and LEA or MoD mean that the Local Education Authority or the Ministry of Defence offer grants to eligible pupils.
- Religion is that which predominates at the school. It does not imply that pupils are exclusively drawn from that denomination.
- Special strengths gives non-academic activities in which the school appears to be strong. It does not imply it is, say, a specialised music school.
- Special provisions similarly means there is some provision for, say, dyslexic pupils; not that the school is geared to pupils with such difficulties.

Please be sure to read fully the entries on schools in which you are interested.

MOUNT ST MARY'S COLLEGE

Spinkhill S31 9YL

Type:
Mount St Mary's College is an Independent Headmasters' Conference School. It is a Catholic school run by the Society of Jesus, which welcomes non Catholics.

Pupils:
The college is co-educational taking boarders, weekly-boarders, and day pupils. Entry is at 13+ into Form 3 and pupils leave after Advanced Levels. Those between 8 and 13 are accepted at our own preparatory school, from other preparaory schools, or the state sector. The Common Entrance Examination is taken for entry in order to place pupils in their right academic sets according to subject.

There is also an 'A' Level entry at 16+.

Situation:
In the country, just off junction 30 of the M1.
Station: St. Pancras for Chesterfield.
Close to the Derbyshire High Peak District and Sherwood Forest.

Educational Aims:
The aim of the College is to produce men and women to serve others. Education we define as "Learning plus Character Formation."
Learning is taking the natural academic ability of the pupil and by high standards of teaching achieving the maximum potential:
Character formation comes from the growth of an imposed discipline to self-discipline, learning team work through a wide variety of sports and Club activities, and sound moral and religious values.

Facilities:
Although a smaller school of under 400 the College has excellent academic facilities including specialist laboratories for Music, Science, Computers, and Languages. Sporting facilities include 23 acres of games fields, and indoor Sports Hall and all-weather tennis courts: and Clubs include Drama, Ham Radio, and Television.

For free prospectus:

Dial Eckington (Derbyshire) 43 33 88 and dictate name and address: 24 hour sevice.

How to go about it A–Z

HOW TO GO ABOUT IT

Abbreviations

AAA	Amateur Athletic Association	**CDT**	Craft Design Technology
ABRSM	Associated Board of the Royal Schools of Music	**CEE**	Common Entrance exam; Certificate of Extended Education
ad hoc	Latin for this or that particular purpose	**CERN**	Conseil (now Organisation) Européenne pour la Recherche Nucléaire
A-level	Advanced level examination		
Alumni	Latin for old boys/girls of a school	**Cert Ed**	Certificate of Education
APS	Assisted Places Scheme	**CHE**	College of Higher Education
ARCM	Associate of the Royal College of Music	**CIFE**	Conference for Independent Further Education
AS-level	Advanced Supplementary level	**CNAA**	Council for National Academic Awards
ATC	Air Training Corps	**CofE**	Church of England
ATI	Association of Tutors Incorporated	**CSV**	Community Service Volunteers
BA	Bachelor of Arts degree	**CSYS**	Certificate of Sixth-year Studies Examination
BAGA	British Amateur Gymnastics Association	**DES**	Department of Education and Science
BAYS	British Association of Young Scientists	**DipEd**	Diploma of Education
BBC	British Broadcasting Corporation	**D of E**	Duke of Edinburgh's Award Scheme
BEd	Bachelor of Education	**ECIS**	European Council of International Studies
BSc	Bachelor of Science		
c/ca	circa. (Latin for approximate)	**EFL**	English as a Foreign Language
Cantab	abbreviated Latin for Cambridge University	**eg**	Latin term meaning for example
		ESB	English Speaking Board
CCF	Combined Cadet Force	**FCA**	Fellow of the Institute of Chartered Accountants
CCSS	Conference of Catholic Secondary Schools		
		FT/PT	Full Time/Part Time

GAP	Gap Activity Projects	**OTC**	Officers' Training Corps
GBA	Governing Bodies Association	**Oxbridge**	Oxford and Cambridge Universities
GBGSA	Governing Bodies of Girls' Schools Association	**Oxon**	Abbreviated Latin for Oxford University
GCSE	General Certificate of Secondary Education	**pa**	per annum (Latin for each year)
GNSM	Graduate of Northern School of Music	**PE/PT**	Physical Education/Physical Training
GPDST	Girls' Public Day School Trust	**PGCE**	Postgraduate Certificate of Education
GSA	Girls' Schools Association	**PNEU**	Parents' National Educational Union
HMC	Headmasters' Conference	**RAD**	Royal Academy of Dance
Hons	Honours degree	**RADA**	Royal Academy of Dramatic Art
IAPS	Incorporated Association of Preparatory Schools	**RC**	Roman Catholic
IB	International Baccalaureat	**RE/RI/RS**	Religious Education/Religious Instruction/Religious Studies
i/c	In charge		
IQ	Intelligence quotient	**RSA**	Royal Society of Arts
ISAI	Independent Schools Association Incorporated	**SAT**	Stanford Achievement Tests
ISBA	Independent Schools Bursars' Association	**SCE**	Scottish Certificate of Education
ISCO	Independent Schools Careers Organisation	**S-grade**	Standard grade examination
ISIS	Independent Schools Information Service	**SHA**	Secondary Heads' Association
ISJC	Independent Schools Joint Council	**SHMIS**	Society of Headmasters of Independent Schools
LAMDA	London Academy of Music and Dramatic Art	**SRN**	State Registered Nurse
LEA	Local Education Authority	**Steiner schools**	Schools founded by Rudolf Steiner
LRAM	Licentiate of the Royal Academy of Music	**STEP**	Sixth Term Exam Paper (entrance exam for Cambridge University)
LSE	London School of Economics		
MA	Master of Arts	**UKCPU**	United Kingdom College, Polytechnic or University
N/A	Not applicable		
O-grade	Ordinary grade examination		

V, VI	Roman numerals five and six (sometimes used to mean fifth and sixth forms)	**wef**	with effect from
		Woodard schools	Group of schools administered by the Woodard Corporation
VDU	Visual Display Unit		
VSO	Voluntary Service Overseas		

Academic results

Often equated by schools with A-level exam results, although O-level/ GCSE results are held to be a better indication of overall academic ability and are used by some universities, including Oxbridge, as part of the admissions procedure. Independent schools use examination results as units of comparison with one another. Most will trot out O- and A-level pass rates without hesitation. Although many schools *are* as academic as they purport to be, percentage results should be treated with caution. Without actually lying, schools can wangle very impressive records. Some only present pupils for exams that they are almost sure to pass, while what officially counts as a pass won't necessarily be of any use for UKCPU entrance.

The exam statistics in *The Schools Book* are only meant as a very rough guide. If academic results are one of your main criteria you'll need to know a lot more. Ask to see a breakdown of results by grade and by subject: this will indicate possible strengths and weaknesses in teaching. Make sure that you see results for several years; last year may have been a fluke. Most importantly, remember that you're selecting the best school for your child, so there's no point in choosing an academic hothouse unless you honestly believe that you've got an academic high flier.

Aegrotat

(Latin for 'is sick'.) In universities it means a medical certificate of illness or a degree granted on it; in schools, permission, usually in writing, for a pupil to be excused from a class or sporting activity on grounds of illness or injury. The term 'an aegrotat' denotes the written permission, *or* the person who is ill or injured; hence 'Have you got an aegrotat?' and 'All aegrotats will go to the medical room'. It is standard practice for parents with children at day schools to send a note (and/or doctor's certificate) if they wish their child to be granted an aegrotat. (See Exeat.)

Affiliation

Nearly all of the schools in *The Schools Book* are affiliated to some sort of association of schools or heads (GSA, ISAI, etc). It isn't always clear exactly what such affiliation entails but a school or head will probably have been vetted before being accepted, so a degree of quality control and uniformity of aims is indicated.

After school

Most independent school-leavers go on to higher education. *The Schools Book* Profiles give some idea of where they do this or what they do if they don't. Schools can prepare their pupils for life after school in a variety of ways:

- Liaison with UKCPUs through open days; visits; holding copies of prospectuses in libraries and careers rooms; giving advice about UKCPU courses and the best A-levels to do.
- Liaison with business and industry through visiting lecturers and post A-level work experience.
- Responsibilities while at school: as prefects; on school magazines; running clubs and societies.
- Courses in life skills, such as car maintenance, typing, cookery.
- Year off between school and UKCPU; GAP, CSV.

Age at joining

The Schools Book is about secondary schools. Many of them have their own junior or prep departments so you may be able to find a school that will suit your child from the age of 5 until A-levels.

Circumstances such as moving into a new area may force a change of school; otherwise consider:

- How many years of school fees do you want to pay?
- When does the school have intakes (usually at 5, 7–8, 11–13 and into the sixth)? It's easier not to be the only new kid in the class.
- Moves during GCSE or A-level courses should be avoided.

A-levels

A-levels matter. Three good ones are needed to get into university or polytechnic, 2 for direct entry into professions like accountancy and the army. The A-level course is designed to take 2 years to complete – usually between the ages of 16 and 18. Some schools may allow their more academic pupils to take the exams after one year. Most schools help match A-level choices with what your child wants to do after school. Some A-levels (eg, general studies and art), aren't always acceptable for UKCPU entrance. Find out which subjects and – most important – combinations of subjects are available; some schools have an arts or science bias. Ask to look at results for the past few years. Will this school help your child to get what's needed?

Helpful reading: *Your Choice at A-Levels* (CRAC, Hobson's Press).

Allied schools

A group of 7 Church of England foundations established during the 1920s. Four of them are for girls, 3 for boys.

Alumni

Latin for 'foster children'; it means former pupils of a school. *The Schools Book* includes famous alumni listed by the schools – the range of these shows something of the ethos of the school even if it doesn't necessarily imply that it'll turn your child into a great rugby player, writer or spy.

Some girls' schools use the feminine form – alumnae – good Latin but not necessary in English.

Art

Often part of the curriculum for the first few years of secondary school. Most schools teach it up to A-level although some academic ones don't regard it as a suitable A-level for brighter pupils to do (it isn't always valid for UKCPU entrance). Schools often offer it as a non-examined interest subject during A-level courses; some make art facilities (often very extensive – including screen printing, pottery, dyeing) available to pupils at lunch-time and after school.

AS-levels

Advanced Supplementary Levels were introduced in 1987; the first exams will be sat in 1989. They're designed to broaden the sixth-form syllabus by allowing for more subjects to be studied in less depth than under the present A-level system. Two AS-levels are equivalent to 1 A-level and pupils can opt to replace 1 or more A-levels with AS-levels, either to complement their specialisation (eg, a language with sciences) or to broaden it (eg, maths for biologists).

They've been greeted enthusiastically by UKCPUs, many professional bodies and employers; currently 2 A-levels and 2 AS-levels are counted as equivalent to 3 A-levels for admission to most universities, while the CNAA general entry requirements now allow for 2 A-levels to be replaced by 4 AS-levels (subject to specific course requirements).

Each of the English and Welsh exam boards has an expanding list of subjects offered to AS-level; not all schools teach them yet.

Assisted Places Scheme

Under this scheme the government pays a proportion of the school fees of children whose parents can't afford them. Means-tested help is available for children from the age of 11 or in the sixth form, regardless of their current school.

There are 36,439 government-assisted places at about 375 schools in England, Scotland and Wales. These account for about 8½% of the total independent school population.

The schools in the scheme set their own selection criteria – usually an exam and an interview. Government-assisted places don't include boarding fees but some of the schools participating run their own schemes for pupils who want to board.

Apply directly to the schools of your choice (see the Special Features Index and the individual School Profiles). Further information and lists of participating schools from:

- **England** Department of Education and Science, Room 3/65, Elizabeth House, York Road, London SE1 7PH (tel: 01-934 9200/9210/9212).
- **Wales** Welsh Office Education Department, Cathays Park, Cardiff CF1 3NQ (tel: 0222 823347).
- **Scotland** Scottish Education Department, Room 3/14–16, New St Andrew's House, St James Centre, Edinburgh EH1 3SY (tel: 031 244 5338/5521/5519).

ATI

The Association of Tutors Incorporated is a club for private tutors and for the principals of independent tutorial colleges. Members are all qualified tutors.

Boarding schools

These range from schools where all the pupils board to day schools that have one or two boarding houses attached. A lot now offer weekly boarding. You'll *have* to think about boarding schools if there are no suitable day schools within reach. Make sure that your child is reasonably happy with the idea, particularly if there are problems at home.

As well as the same considerations for day school selection, you'll have to think about:

- Distance: most parents choose a boarding school that's within about 1½ hours' travelling time of home; if that's impossible, is there one close to grandparents, friends or relations?
- Schedule and extra-curricular activities: what's available, especially at weekends; how much of the day is scheduled and organised? Is it geared to boarders or day pupils? Are children free to pursue their own interests as well as those that the school regards as appropriate?
- Food: more important for boarders who can't rely on daily supplements from home. Check over the kitchens and look at some sample menus; what other food can they buy or keep?
- Meet the house staff and find out about the routine in the boarding houses. Are children expected to help with table-laying? What are dormitories and other rooms like? How much privacy do pupils have?
- Exeats: how many and for how long? What about if you want to take your child out of school at short notice, or before the end of term? Is weekly boarding available and how prevalent is it?
- What provision is there for ill children? Is there a nurse on the premises and a nearby doctor on call?

Boys' schools

Traditional boys' secondary schools take boys from the age of 13 although many have a junior year or two for boys of 11 and 12 and others have their own prep/junior department taking boys from 4 or 5.

The drawbacks of all-male schools are notorious, from mild lack of ease with women to rampant misogyny or homosexuality. These are exaggerated; attempts are made to counteract them, such as mixed activities with local girls' schools and female teaching staff. Many boys' schools take girls into the Sixth and several have become co-ed throughout.

Bullying

It happens and has a multitude of causes. If you think that your child is being bullied, tell the head. The problem may not be immediately soluble but a good head will find out what's going on and can advise you and your child on how to deal with it. If you get no help, or if your child continues to be unhappy at school, investigate further: you might have chosen the wrong school.

Bursaries

These are means-tested awards made by some schools to the children of parents who can't afford to pay full fees. Bursaries for new pupils are usually awarded on the outcome of an entrance or other exam. If you fall on hard times after your child has started at the school you may be able to get a bursary on the strength of the child's school record. Some schools offer fee reductions for the children of clergymen, service personnel or alumni or for second and subsequent siblings.

Careers

In 1941 George Orwell saw independent education as 'partly a sort of tax that the middle classes pay to the upper classes in return for the right to enter certain professions'. This can be modified for the 1980s when everybody needs some sort of tertiary education to get virtually anywhere.

Most schools concentrate on getting their pupils into higher education, leaving decisions about occupational choice for the future. Careers advice is more or less synonymous with higher education advice. It can include:

- A careers library, with UKCPU prospectuses.
- At least one part-time advisor to point pupils towards the next step if they know what they want to do, and towards some books if they don't.
- Careers fairs arranged amongst several schools – again the emphasis is often on higher education.
- Films and talks about careers options: the services, industry or, depending on the head's friends, careers in falconry or bookmaking.

- Some schools send pupils on short-term job placements with local industry during the holidays or after exams; at others, pupils take the initiative and establish miniature companies to sell tuck, stationery or cigarettes; write, design, edit and produce their own magazine.

Look at the careers room when you visit; ask the head about careers advice and counselling; when does it start? who visits? what do pupils do immediately after they leave school? School magazines with their lists of leavers' destinations (or intended destinations – often those given are dependent on A-level results) are also useful for this. In *The Schools Book*, schools list traditional leavers' careers. Some, for instance, turn out generation after generation of successful local professionals – good secure establishment stuff but is this right for your child?

CCF

In 1906 the War Office created a committee to consider the possibilities of military training units in schools and universities and in 1908 the first OTCs (Officers' Training Corps) were formed: a senior division in universities; a junior division in schools. Several universities and 100 schools joined at once. Later, the ATC (Air Training Corps) was founded. In 1948 the organisations were regrouped as the modern Combined Cadet Force.

CCFs have been scaled down over the last 20 years (largely because of expense). Nevertheless, a very large number of schools run one, and in co-ed schools girls are also members. Many schools have only one section (Army, Navy, RAF or Royal Marines). Several schools combine 2 and some have 3. Many CCFs have a band (drums, brass; in Scotland, bagpipes). In quite a lot of schools the CCF is compulsory for periods of a term, 6 months, 2 years, 3 years. Often a CCF depends on the enthusiasm, knowledge and dedication of a handful of members of staff.

Basic training will include foot drill, arms drill, tactics, weapon training, shooting (with .22 rifles), aircraft recognition, map-reading, camping, first aid, radio communications, signals, assault courses, survival techniques and so on.

Most CCFs have an annual camp which is based on some form of military installation. There are also manoeuvres (sometimes in conjunction with other schools) and there is usually an annual inspection by somebody suitably distinguished in the services.

CCF activities are closely associated with outdoor pursuits, with the Outward Bound Scheme and the Duke of Edinburgh's Award Scheme and miscellaneous forms of adventure training, and thus with such activities as orienteering, canoeing, flying, sailing, fell-walking, rock-climbing, skiing, cliff-scaling, gliding and parachuting. Some schools have commando- and SAS-type exercises (including yomping). A few schools run auxiliary units (eg coastguard, fire services) and these are likely to be run in conjunction with a CCF contingent.

Membership of the CCF appeals to those who enjoy teamwork, team spirit, discipline and self-discipline, physical and mental challenge and an element of adventure accompanied by some hazard. There are agreeable perks, too, such as visits to naval bases (perhaps a guided tour of a warship), visits to RAF bases where you may get a flight, and visits to army depots where you may sample the full hardware of modern warfare. Such excursions are usually extremely interesting and the professional units concerned take a lot of trouble to make them stimulating.

Checklists

There are thousands of points to consider when you're choosing a school. Here are a few:

- area and distance from home;
- single sex/co-ed/mixed Sixth;
- boarding or day;
- size of school/size of sixth;
- facilities for your child's interests;
- town or country;
- special provisions for dyslexia etc;
- fees – what can you afford;
- intake age; junior/prep school attached;
- good academic record;
- sporting/outward bound;
- musical/artistic/dramatic;
- religious policy, if necessary;
- any of your own priorities.

Choir schools

There are 37 schools in the UK attached to churches, cathedrals and college chapels, providing choristers for their choïrs. Of these, about 14 teach up to A-level, the rest are prep schools only. Although some of the

schools accept girls, the choirs do not. If your son is good at singing and enjoys it enough to spend a lot of his time singing at church services, he may be able to get part or all of his fees paid as a chorister at a choir school. This usually means passing a voice trial some time between the ages of 7 and 10.

Further information from the Choir Schools Association, Westminster Cathedral Choir School, Ambrosden Avenue, London SW1P 1QH (tel: 01-834 9247).

Choosing

Choosing a school means finding the right school for your child. You, the child and the school have to make the decisions. First work out a strategy.

- Dip into *The Schools Book* for a feel of what to expect from independent schools.
- Draw up your basic criteria: location; fees; co-ed/single-sex; day/boarding; intake age; range of curricular and extra-curricular activities.
- Find out which schools fit. Include any that you think may be interesting even if they don't adhere absolutely to your expectations of what the right school is.
- Get the prospectuses and magazines from these schools. Mention your child's age, sex, the intended year of entry and any special needs.
- Go to open days.
- Draw up a shortlist of schools to visit.
- Arrange to go to at least 3 day (5 boarding) schools by contacting the head. Unless you *and* your child are adamant about, eg, single-sex schools, visit a range – co-ed, single-sex; town, country, suburban; with or without boarding.
- Prepare for the visit, arrange to speak to the teaching staff, housemasters and housemistresses; draw up a list of points to investigate and questions to ask.
- After the visit, shortlist again and take your child on a second visit to 1 or 2 schools.
- Register your child for the right school; if this is a very competitive one, have a fall-back in mind.
- Prepare your child for the admissions procedure, Common Entrance, exams, special subjects, etc.
- **Then get your child in.**

CIFE

The Conference for Independent Further Education is a club for the principals of independent tutorial colleges which are regularly inspected to make sure that they are up to DES standard.

Classroom discipline

Most schools now realise that interesting presentation is a far more successful way of teaching than is rigorous discipline. However, there are still a few teachers (and schools) that follow the speak-only-when-I-tell-you-to-and-stand-up-when-I-enter-the-room approach, just as there are some whose classes regularly turn into brawls. Either is equally boring and frustrating for anybody with an interest in the subject. Find out what the school's general policy is on classroom discipline when you visit. Pick up as much as you can from pupils and parents about what individual teachers are like. How are disruptive pupils dealt with? Whose classes are the most interesting; most chaotic? etc.

Co-ed schools

Co-educational schools admit girls *and* boys. Their number is increasing as many single-sex schools (particularly boys' schools) are letting in the opposite sex; much of this is in response to market demand.

Some heads opt for a specific male:female ratio, others let one evolve. In schools that have always been co-ed, this tends to be about 50:50 with perhaps a slight preference towards girls; schools that used to be single-sex are usually still dominated by that sex.

Co-ed schools often have a wider range of activities because they are less affected by generalised beliefs such as boys don't sew and girls don't like electronics.

Common Entrance

Many independent secondary schools use the same entrance exam, called Common Entrance (CE). This can be taken in February, June and November by girls aged 11 and boys aged 13 (traditionally girls transfer to secondary school at a younger age). Many independent primary schools will arrange for pupils to sit CE, if necessary; if your child's school doesn't, contact the Common Entrance Examination Board, Ashley Lane, Lymington, Hampshire SO4 9YR (tel: 0590 75947). You should do this at least 10 weeks before the exam, and ideally a lot earlier than this to allow time to prepare for the exam.

Common Entrance is centrally set and administered but is marked by the participating schools who also set their own pass mark. Pupils are tested in English, maths, French, science, history, geography and RE; Latin and Greek are optional extras. You can ask to have papers sent on to another school if your child doesn't get into the first one. CE isn't always necessary; many schools set their own entrance test instead of, or as an alternative to, Common Entrance.

Community service

Some schools organise their pupils to help in the community outside the school. This is often offered as an alternative to sport for senior pupils – very occasionally it is compulsory.

In practice, school community service usually means visiting old people; talking to them, entertaining them and doing odd jobs for them like decorating and gardening. It may also involve work with children. Some schools, especially rural ones, take the notion of community service several steps beyond and organise local services such as mountain rescue and fire-fighting.

Computing

It's going to be increasingly difficult to get through life without some computer competence and schools with no computing facilities are rare. Most integrate the use of computers with the teaching of other subjects such as sciences, geography and maths, as well as offering it as a subject in its own right. Lists of computing equipment may mean little to you, but you can still find out how much help pupils are given with learning how and when to use them.

Corporal punishment

Still a delicate matter. It has long been banished from the maintained sector and is virtually unknown (at any rate officially) in independent schools. The vast majority of headmasters and headmistresses stress emphatically that it is never used. However, there is a kind of loophole. In special circumstances heads may administer it provided they have the full permission of the pupil's parents.

Nowadays it is more likely that teachers will suffer corporal punishment in the form of assault (with or without weapons) by a pupil or pupils. Recently, a London headmaster told his staff: 'You must not hit the boys.' Then he added: 'And the boys must not hit you.' Quite right.

CSV

Community Service Volunteers will arrange community work in the UK for anybody aged 16 or over for periods of 4 months to a year. This makes it an option for students between A-level and UKCPU. Volunteers get board, lodging and pocket money. Details from CSV, 237 Pentonville Road, London N1 9NJ (tel: 01-278 6601).

CSYS

Certificates of Sixth-year Studies are Scottish exams which some pupils sit the year after Highers. They are very roughly comparable with

A-levels but are often not recognised as such, especially south of the border. Higher or A-level results are more normally used for university entrance.

Curriculum

Latin for career – the course of study taught at school. For the first few years at secondary school, most pupils follow roughly the same curriculum: English, maths, a modern language (usually French), history, geography, some science, Latin, (sometimes) art, music and sport. At 14, they choose GCSE or O-Grade subjects in 7 or 8 subjects. This usually means having to commit themselves to some sort of arts or science bias.

By the time they come to decide which A-levels to do, they'll have to limit themselves to taking 3 or 4 subjects seriously (5 or 6 if they're doing Highers or AS-levels).

CV game

As well as a good school education and a degree, your children need to have an impressive CV (curriculum vitae) if they're going to be noticed by future employers. They can get some useful CV building bricks at school from:

- holding positions of responsibility such as being a prefect;
- organising and managing school clubs, societies and events;
- involvement with magazines or school productions;
- voluntary or community work;
- Duke of Edinburgh's Awards;
- work experience during holidays or at weekends (if it doesn't conflict with school work).

Dance

Most people with a future as professional dancers start very young. Ballet dancers have to begin intensive training at the age of 11. Specialist schools like the Royal Ballet School concentrate heavily on teaching dance. Otherwise it tends to be part of physical education; some, especially boys' schools, don't bother with it at all while others offer a wide range including folk, modern, ballet, ballroom. Some emphasise free movement while others still regard dancing as a social accomplishment.

Day schools

As well as finding a school that suits your child academically and socially, your choice of day school is limited by distance; it has to be within easy daily travelling distance, allowing for some after-school activities.

Find out how much of your child's time the school expects to control (attendance at sports matches, compulsory after-school activities, etc) as well as how many optional extras it arranges for those who are interested. Most boarding schools take day pupils. How well are they incorporated by boarders and the school? At some boarding schools day pupils are regarded as second-class citizens.

You probably also want to find a school where at least a few of your child's schoolfriends are within easy reach for weekends and holidays.

Direct Grant schools

Until 1975 when the scheme was phased out, direct grant schools offered free or subsidised education to a proportion of their pupils in exchange for a grant from the Department of Education and Science. Those schools are now either fully independent or fully maintained by their LEAs. GPDST and many grammar schools fell into this category.

Distance

Choose a day school that's close enough to home to allow your child to take part in after-school activities, and accessible by public transport: you may not mind driving a 7-year-old to school every day but what about a 16-year-old?

Boarders now tend to live within 1½ hours' travelling distance from home. This makes it easier for you to get to each other and also increases the likelihood of your child having at least a few schoolfriends within reach for holidays and weekends.

Drama

Although there are schools which specialise in drama (many of which also supply young actors for TV, West End and local theatre) professional actors emerge from many non-specialist schools, even though drama isn't often taught as a curriculum subject beyond the age of about 14. Most schools put on dramatic productions every year. Find out how many of these there are, who and how many participate, what sort of drama it is (Shakespeare, musical, comedy, Greek tragedy, etc). Are pupils involved as scene builders, wardrobe people, with publicity? Are there any drama clubs?

Drinking

Adults are *expected* to drink in moderation and, while buying alcohol in pubs or shops is illegal for under-18s, most children have the occasional drink long before this. Several boarding schools allow limited drinking of beer and wine in sixth-form clubs and bars. Although this stops alcohol from having quite the illicit appeal that drugs and cigarettes enjoy, it doesn't stop massive amounts of cheap wine and strange spirits from being consumed at any opportunity. If your child does occasionally appear to have had too much to drink with friends, the biggest problem is probably next day's hangover.

However, habitual heavy drinking is far worse for adolescents than for adults. Their bodies are less able to cope with vast quantities of alcohol and there is an increased likelihood of dependence. If teenagers are drinking heavily and regularly (especially if they're drinking alone) it could be a symptom of other problems. You should speak to your GP or consult Alcoholics Anonymous (local address in the telephone directory).

Drugs

On the whole, cannabis is the drug that schoolchildren are most likely to come across. Experimenting with the occasional joint is now a common part of growing up and you have to take a lot of cannabis before it will do any harm. For schoolchildren, the greatest risk isn't so much the damage that it might be doing to their bodies as the damage that it might do to their futures if they're caught. Expulsion seems to be fairly likely (although probably not always automatic) and any police involvement could be serious.

Hard drugs are a different story, although they are far less prevalent in schools. Their effects on the brain are more dramatic and less predictable; any use of hypodermic needles carries the added risk of infection. It can be difficult to tell if a teenager is on drugs because many of the classical symptoms of hard-drug users – dramatic mood swings, listlessness, unhealthy complexion, lack of money, etc – are exhibited by normal, undrugged teenagers. There are lots of sources of help and counselling for people who are having problems with drugs (often drugs misuse is a symptom of another underlying problem). If you're worried, speak to a sympathetic doctor or contact Families Anonymous, 310 Finchley Road, London NW3 7AG (tel: 01-731 8060).

You can help by not making drugs an unmentionable horror. Make sure that your children are aware of the legal and health risks involved, and remain approachable. You want to know as soon as possible if your child is in difficulty because of drugs.

Duke of Edinburgh's Award Scheme

'Designed as an introduction to leisure-time activities, a challenge to the individual to personal achievement, and as a guide to those people and organisations who are concerned about the development of our future citizens' (HRH the Duke of Edinburgh).

Duke of Edinburgh's Awards can be taken outside school but many independent schools offer them as an extra-curricular activity. There are 3 levels: bronze (taken from the age of 14+), silver (15+) and gold (16+). Awards are made on successful completion of a programme of community service, sport, adventure training and practical skills. Courses must be finished by the age of 24.

Further information from the scheme's headquarters: 5 Prince of Wales Terrace, Kensington, London W8 5PG (tel: 01-937 5205).

Dyslexia

People with dyslexia have difficulty organising letters, numbers, words and ideas; this leads to problems with reading, writing and learning and holds sufferers back. Many of the schools in *The Schools Book* give extra help to dyslexic children. This varies a lot in frequency and intensity from school to school so make sure that the provision at the schools you are interested in is suitable for your child's particular needs. You can contact the British Dyslexia Association, 98 London Road, Reading, RG1 5AU (tel: 0734 668271/2), or the Dyslexia Institute, 133 Gresham Road, Staines, Middlesex TW18 2AJ (tel: 0784 59498).

Eileen Simpson has described her experience of dyslexia in *Reversals* (Gollancz, 1980).

Educational change

The chances are that, whether you are paying fees or not, your child's schooldays will be affected at some stage by the introduction of new examinations/educational legislation. Policies that are designed to bring about long-term changes can be disruptive during their first years and may disorientate pupils, parents and teachers, making them feel as though they are guinea pigs performing capricious tasks at the whim of the Secretary of State for Education.

Although the final aim of the change *may* be good, it isn't necessarily a comfort to know that all of your child's contemporaries are putting up with the same disruption, nor do many parents take kindly to educational changes which are designed to benefit future generations when their own children's chances of entering higher education may be jeopardised by the stresses of initial confusion. GCSEs are the current novelty, designed to replace and simplify the old two-tier O-level/CSE system. The first exams were sat in 1988 so it's too early to tell what effect they're going to have. Children in London maintained schools are about to lose the ILEA and it's predicted that this will encourage even more London parents to consider independent schools.

EFL

Teaching of English as a Foreign Language (EFL) is provided at some boarding and a few day schools. Such schools may be better geared all round to the needs of children for whom English is a foreign language, or whose parents live abroad. However, because school demands very high levels of English comprehension, children in schools that don't offer a lot of extra help often pick it up quickly just because they have to.

Entrance exams

Schools that don't use Common Entrance usually set their own exams for main entry points (eg, at 5, 7, 11 or 13). These are often held in October, January or February for entry the following September, so approach the school well in advance. You may be able to get hold of some past papers.

You're advised not to subject your child to too many entrance exams. This is difficult in places like London where competition is fierce and you don't want to put all your eggs in one basket. Try not to enter your child for more than 2 or 3; that means applying to schools that really are right and, perhaps, choosing one that's less competitive than the others.

Equipment

Depending on the school and the child you'll have to buy a variety of equipment, from pencils to bagpipes. You can expect to have to provide things like a calculator, a dictionary (even if you aren't expected to buy other books), various bits and pieces for sport and any optional extras. Boarders will need more – civilian clothes, suitcases, towels, duvet, clock, lamp, games and hobbies stuff.

Exeat

Exeat is a Latin word meaning 'let him escape'. At school (especially boarding school) it is used to mean permitted time spent away from school during term. Most schools have a policy of allowing a certain number of overnight or weekend exeats a term – this can vary from any weekend to only one break at half-term. You'll have to decide which is the most appropriate for your child; if you live abroad, your child may be happier at a school that doesn't empty at weekends, whereas if you live within easy travelling distance of the school, weekly boarding may be possible.

Expulsion

The ultimate deterrent at most schools. Although used rarely, it is more common in the independent than the maintained sector. It's not the end of the world. It goes on to your child's academic record and may be picked up in the future, but it needn't blight any careers. The immediate problem may be finding another school; the present school might be willing to help with this (depending on why your child's being expelled in the first place). Some schools expel far more readily than others and it's worth finding out from the head when the last expulsion was, and why. You may think that your child's a saint but anybody can fall foul of authority.

Extra-curricular activities

Extra-curricular activities are interests, sports and hobbies arranged by the school which are not on the formal curriculum. These can cover a wide variety of pursuits – music lessons, clubs, Scouts, etc – and give children the opportunity to try out a range of different things. Alternatively there may be better or preferable facilities out of school.

Some schools insist that all pupils take part in some extra-curricular activity. Find out the range available and the timetable – which activities conflict? Try also to get some idea of numbers involved, especially in optional extras. Apathetic peers can be just as pressurising as active ones.

Extras

As well as fees, most schools make additional charges for things like lunch, books, laundry and extra tuition. At many schools these can amount to about £500 pa. Parents are sometimes charged for such surprising things as transport to away matches for school sports teams. Ask what's included in school fees and what you should expect to pay on top of that. Try to look at specimen termly bills which will show you how much the school really costs. This isn't always easy to do.

Fagging

It's unlikely that you'll find a school that still has a policy of allowing seniors to use younger pupils as unpaid skivvies and lavatory-seat warmers on cold days. Fagging has been replaced at many schools with a sort of school community service. This is more common in boarding schools where all pupils may be expected to help with, say, keeping dormitories and dining rooms tidy.

Fees

Most schools state their termly fees (annual figures, although far more relevant, look horrific). These range from about £350–£1100 per term for day pupils and from about £1100–£2300 for boarding – plus extras. On average, they go up about 11% pa but this may increase when VAT is imposed on new buildings, improvements, power and water for independent schools in April 1989.

You may be able to pay fees in monthly instalments; otherwise there are ways of alleviating some of the burden:

- endowment life assurance;
- lump sum payments in advance;
- school fees insurance firms;
- school fees loans.

Twenty per cent of children at fee-paying schools are subsidised through a government-assisted place or a bursary from the school (both are means-tested on your income); or by winning a scholarship. You may be eligible for a grant from the Ministry of Defence, the Foreign Office or your firm. Finally, some schools give reductions in fees for second and subsequent children or the children of, for example, the clergy or old pupils.

Find out how promptly school bills have to be settled. What happens if you're late? You can insure against your inability to pay through death, illness or redundancy and some schools have their own support schemes for parents who fall on hard times. Investigate these in advance.

Fees insurance

You may be able to insure that the school fees are paid in the event of your death, disability or redundancy. Some school fees remission schemes may also reimburse you if your child is absent from school through illness for a long time. Ask your insurance broker, ISIS or the British Insurance Brokers Association, 10 Bevis Marks, London EC3A 7NT (tel: 01-623 9043).

Food

Although children are unlikely to starve, many schools still fall short of providing a healthy diet and continue to serve up overcooked vegetables and stodgy puddings. Dynamic heads are unlikely to throw their energy into dietary improvements while they've got things like exam results and discipline to sort out. When you visit a school, ask to look round the kitchens and to see some sample menus. This is especially important for

boarders who can't top up the school's diet at home. Find out what other food is available (tuck shops, etc). Some day schools allow packed lunches; and senior boarders may have limited cooking facilities.

Most schools will cater for children with special diets – vegetarian, Moslem, Jewish – sometimes with little imagination.

Friends' schools

These are schools run by Quakers (the Society of Friends). They hold regular Quaker religious meetings which pupils may or may not have to attend and emphasise the importance of tolerance of other people and of responsibility to the community. Friends' schools accept non-Quaker pupils. Further information from the Friends' Schools Joint Council, Friends House, Euston Road, London NW1 2BJ (tel: 01-387 3601).

Froebel Method

An educational method associated with Friedrich Froebel (1782–1852) who adapted the child-centred ideals and principles of Rousseau and Johann Pestalozzi to the education of infants in Germany. It was Froebel who founded the *Kindergarten* and thus established the kind of infant and nursery schools which are now very common and in which children explore and discover the world through play, games, toys, shapes, music, stories, drawing and so on. He had a considerable influence on Montessori and his long-term influence has been profoundly beneficial.

GAP

Gap Activity Projects provides about 6 months' overseas voluntary work in schools, farms, hospitals and businesses for sixth-form students after leaving school and before UKCPU or career. Not all schools are members of GAP, but anyone can apply. Find out more from school or from the Secretary, GAP Activity Projects (GAP) Limited, 7 King's Road, Reading, Berkshire RG1 3AA (tel: 0734 594914).

GBA

The Governing Bodies Association is for representatives from the governing boards of independent boys' schools. Many of them are schools whose heads are members of HMC or SHMIS.

GBGSA

The Governing Bodies of Girls' Schools Association is for representatives from the governing bodies of independent girls' schools – many of these are schools whose heads are members of GSA.

GCSE

The General Certificate of Secondary Education was started in 1987, to replace O-levels and CSEs. The first exams were sat in 1988. Taken at 15 or 16, the GCSE is designed to be less academically elitist than the old system which divided pupils into those believed capable of getting O-levels and those who did CSEs. It aims to test the ability to apply what is learned to practical situations rather than merely the ability to remember and re-present course work. Exams are taken in a variety of subjects including physical education and arts options.

Getting in

Once you've found a school that's right, your child has to get through an admissions procedure. This will probably involve:

- a report from your child's current school;
- an interview;
- an entry test (the school's own or Common Entrance);
- possibly additional tests for scholarships, bursaries or government-assisted places.

Find out which of these apply and make sure your child knows about the requirements and is reasonably prepared. Also choose a school that your child has a good chance of getting into.

Gifted children

Gifted children may be held back and frustrated by their less able contemporaries. If your child is gifted in one or more areas – music, maths, painting, etc – contact the National Association for Gifted Children, 1 South Audley Street, London W1Y 5DQ (tel: 01-499 1188).

Girls' schools

Girls' secondary schools take pupils from the age of 11. Many have their own prep or junior schools attached and, while very few take boys into the Sixth, girls' schools sometimes admit boys into the prep and junior years.

Exoduses of pupils to boys' schools for the Sixth have led to many girls' schools competing with improved teaching and facilities and girls at good all-girls' schools, according to statistics, get better exam results than those at co-ed schools.

Most girls' schools share activities, events and sometimes classes with local boys' schools and have some male teaching staff. Recently several girls' schools have appointed male heads.

Governors

These are the people who sit on a board and are responsible for the school's success as a business. Their main job is to ensure that there's enough money to run the school (a large, well-endowed boarding school has an annual turnover of some £5 million); they also usually appoint new heads.

Governors also often air their views (sometimes reactionary) on more day-to-day aspects of the running of the school (discipline, for example). This is in the stated belief that the implementation of their suggested policies will help to improve the school's standing as a marketable product. Governors can be the bane of heads' lives. When you visit, ask the head about school/governor relations: some forward-looking heads may be held back by boards of governors.

GPDST

Founded in 1872, until 1975 the schools in the Girls' Public Day School Trust were direct grant grammar schools. Currently there are 25 member schools providing education for girls of 5–18. Further information from GPDST, 26 Queen Anne's Gate, London SW1H 9AN (tel: 01-222 9595).

Grapevines

Schools change frequently. Heads move every 5–10 years on average and there's a complete change of pupils every 6 years or so; gossip about schools dates quickly and a bad reputation lives longer and travels further than a good one ('That's the school where the First Eleven burnt down the cricket pavilion after losing a home match').

A parent with a child already at the school will be best able to give you the low-down on pupil/staff and parent/staff relations. Is that dynamic head really as active as it seems? Are pupils with your child's particular

interests and abilities encouraged? They may also give you and your child the chance to meet some other pupils and to decide what you think of them.

GSA

The Girls' Schools Association is a club for the headmistresses of girls' schools; very occasionally male heads of girls' schools are members. It is roughly the female equivalent of the HMC.

It brings out an annual reference book, *The Independent Schools Yearbook: Girls' Schools* (A & C Black).

Guardians

Guardians step in for half-terms, at school events or in emergencies if you can't yourself. Your child will need a guardian if you live overseas or a long way from school. You can get help with finding a guardian through the school or ISIS, but it's better to find someone your child knows and likes.

Handicaps

A mildly handicapped child, especially an intelligent one, may do better at an ordinary school than a special one. Speak to the head about this. Possible problems include:

- Mobility: most schools aren't built to be easy to get around for people with a mobility or visual handicap.
- Teaching which is geared towards pupils who can hear well.
- A mildly handicapped pupil will have to cope with being noticeably different from everybody else.

For those with more serious handicaps contact:

- **England**: Department of Education and Science, Schools Branch II (Special Education), Elizabeth House, 39 York Road, London SE1 7PH (tel: 01-934 9230/9240).

- **Wales**: Welsh Office Education Department, Cathays Park, Cardiff CF1 3NQ (tel: 0222 823347).

- **Scotland**: Scottish Education Department (Special Schools), New St Andrews House, St James Centre, Edinburgh EH1 3SY (tel: 031 556 8400).

- **Northern Ireland**: Department of Education for Northern Ireland, Schools I Division, Rathgael House, Balloo Road, Bangor, Northern Ireland BT19 2PR (tel: 0247 466311).

Heads

Choosing a school means choosing a head. Because heads tend to move on up their own career paths to better schools, they last (on average) only 8 years at each school but have terrific influence while they're there, so find out as much as you can about the head's policies, principles and obsessions when you visit the school.

A lot of the business of choosing a head falls back on instinct, but while you're visiting the school and talking to the head, consider:

- how well would you trust their judgement?
- how approachable are they?
- how compatible are their special interests and concerns with your child's interests and needs?
- do they seem willing to admit to problems and to be capable of doing something about them?

Heads usually have a lot of experience of teaching and children. This doesn't mean that they are infallible. Don't hesitate to let your child's head know if you honestly think that they are wrong, or anything else about the school for that matter. Cultivating an aura of authority is part of the job. Don't be put off.

Read *Letters from School* by John Rae (Collins, 1987), to remind yourself that heads are human.

Head boy/girl

This is the head prefect, often elected by the other prefects with varying degrees of staff involvement. It's a responsible position and can be a strain – the entire school knows who they are and they're expected to behave like a paragon (hell breaks loose if they don't). The pay-off might come when they start applying for some universities and jobs where head prefect experience is a useful item on your child's CV.

Highers

These are exams taken by Scottish pupils at the age of 16 or 17. Four or 5 good Higher grades are needed for a place at university. Highers are sat the year after O-grades, allowing students to go to university a year earlier than they do in England (this practice is decreasingly popular). Some UKCPUs south of the border still find Highers confusing. Many Scottish schools offer A-level syllabuses as well as Highers – possibly a better bet for sixth-formers who want to go south. Be wary of your child attempting a full quota of both. The syllabuses are quite different and studying for Highers can distract from A-level course work.

HMC

The Headmasters' Conference is a club for headmasters which was started in 1869 and now has some 200 members (plus associate members). The heads of some schools become members automatically; otherwise they have to apply and go through a vetting procedure. It is the headmaster rather than the school who is affiliated. Members meet from time to time to discuss topics of a roughly educational nature.

There is an annual book giving details of schools run by members of the HMC, *The Independent Schools Yearbook: Boys' Schools* (A & C Black).

Homosexuality

Not as prevalent in schools as it is supposed to have been in the past. This is probably mainly due to the less monastic or nunnish existence of most schoolchildren nowadays and to a more open attitude towards sexuality in general. Children in single-sex schools are far more likely to fear the possibility of being homosexual than to feel encouraged to be so. Nowadays, if somebody is homosexual, it is unlikely to be because that is the norm at school.

Housemasters/mistresses

Usually a member of the teaching staff, often one that is married. This is a prestigious position within the school, and for boarders the housemaster or housemistress is *in loco parentis*. Make sure you trust them and that they'll get on well with your child. While the head has a massive influence on the school, houses within a school can vary a lot according to the personality of the housemaster/mistress in charge.

This is the person you should contact if you're worried about your child's happiness or health.

Houses

A lot of schools separate their pupils into different 'houses' for competitive and/or pastoral purposes. These usually have roughly equal numbers from each year and, depending on how seriously the school takes the house system, they may have a senior pupil as head of house, distinguishing ties or badges, etc.

Pupils at some boarding schools sleep in separate houses. These can be divided as competitive houses or by some other method (eg, by age). The house is in the charge of a housemaster or mistress (usually a member of the teaching staff, and married) and some assistants. There will often be a resident nurse or matron and regular visits from a local

28

doctor. The pupils may eat in the house or in a central dining room shared with the rest of the school.

Independent schools

These are schools that are not maintained by local or national government and are financed by fees and endowments. They include so-called public schools and private schools and are theoretically more free than maintained ones to decide their own policies and priorities. It is this element of choice that makes independent schools increasingly attractive to parents.

More than 7% (approximately 444,000) of schoolchildren in the UK are educated at independent schools – 18% of the 16–18 age-group. The numbers are increasing by about 1% pa in spite of a decrease in school-age population. Approximately 57% are boys. 66% of the parents of these children were not, themselves, educated at independent schools.

International Baccalaureat

This is an entrance exam accepted by many universities throughout the world and offered at some 250 schools worldwide. Teaching for the International Baccalaureat is in English; 6 subjects are studied, 3 to higher level and 3 as subsidiaries including 2 languages, maths, 1 human science, 1 exact science and 1 subject of the candidate's choice. The course is followed for the last 2 or 3 years of secondary school.

The International Baccalaureat Office is at 15 route de Morillons, CH-1218 Grand-Saconnex, Geneva, Switzerland (tel: 022 9102 74).

Interviews

These always form part of the school selection procedure. They should be a two-way process, allowing you, your child and the head to decide if this is the right choice of school. Interviews aren't necessarily designed to find out how much Latin children know, nor how well they cope under pressure. Don't worry if your normally self-assured child dries up – heads should be used to that sort of thing and the interview will probably go much better when you aren't in the room.

ISAI

The Independent Schools Association Incorporated, founded in 1895, is a club for the heads of a variety of schools (co-ed, single-sex, day, boarding).

ISCO

The Independent Schools Careers Organisation provides training, advice and resources for careers advisors and departments at its 250 member schools. It can sometimes help individuals, too. Contact ISCO, 12a–18a Princess Way, Camberley, Surrey GU15 3SP (tel: 0276 21188) for further information.

ISIS

The Independent Schools Information Service acts as an intermediary for its 1300 prep and secondary member schools and parents who are trying to find a school. It also provides advice on financing school fees, and how to choose a school; ISIS itself doesn't recommend individual schools but it can tell you how to contact a school consultant. ISIS has several regional offices; details from the central office at 56 Buckingham Gate, London SW1E 6AG (tel: 01-630 8793).

ISJC

The Independent Schools Joint Council is an umbrella organisation that represents 9 other independent school associations. These are: HMC, SHMIS, GBA, GBGSA, GSA, IAPS, ISAI, ISIS and ISBA.

Late developers

Children develop at different rates; education systems don't always cater for this. If your child seems to be having problems keeping up with the rest of the class, investigate the possibility of learning difficulties. Find a school that caters for a wide range of ability. Some slow starters have turned out to be high-fliers (Einstein, for example). Other children do better once they're out of an environment where they're always at the bottom of the class.

Latin

Still taught in many schools and widely regarded by, among others, scientists and teachers of English and modern languages as a very useful training and intellectual discipline, especially in the learning of logical and precise expression and in sound grammatical usage, and also in the development of vocabulary. Tens of thousands of words in the English language derive from Latin. Much scientific nomenclature *is* Latin. It is easily verifiable that children with a sound knowledge of the language have a much richer vocabulary.

For many years the teaching of Latin has been revolutionised to make the language more accessible and entertaining. In fact, it can be fun. However, it remains a bugbear for many children largely because they find it difficult, and therefore it involves hard work. In actuality it is no more difficult than modern languages such as Serbian, and very much easier than, say, Finnish, Hungarian, Turkish and Chinese.

Learning difficulties

Intelligent parents sometimes find it difficult to admit that their children have learning problems. However, some children do. Reading problems are often the first to be noticed. You can get help with this from the Dyslexia Institute, 133 Gresham Road, Staines, Middlesex TW18 2AJ (tel: 0784 59498) or the child's school. (The Special Features Index will tell you which schools have provision for dyslexic pupils.)

If your child does seem to be having problems, speak to the school, or an educational or child psychologist. Find something that your child enjoys doing and is reasonably good at. Many academic failures from strongly academic schools flourish in other schools where they are exposed to practical or creative subjects (gardening, mechanics, music, sports, drama).

Life assurance

A fixed term or endowment life assurance policy can help with school fees if you set one up at least 8 years before you need it. This will give you a lump sum which you can use to pay fees in advance and benefit from the reductions in cost that lump-sum-in-advance fee payments allow.

Loans for school fees

If you've left it too late to arrange any other method of paying school fees you may be able to raise a school fees loan which you can pay back over a

few years after your child has left school. Make sure that it will allow for increases in fees, extras, etc and that the money is available when you need it. Also, don't over-commit yourself. Ask your bank manager or ISIS for details.

Lump-sum fee payment

Also called composition fee payment. Some schools arrange for you to pay school fees in advance by putting down a lump sum (from an endowment scheme, for instance). This gives you a reduction in fees. The amount of the lump sum depends on how much you need per term for fees, for how many terms, and how far in advance you put it down – the earlier the better. Obviously, you need to have quite a lot of spare capital for this and you also need to have a pretty good idea that the school you have selected is the right school for your child. Most schemes allow you to transfer to another school if you find out that it's not, but check first.

If you don't have the capital yourself, you may be able to get it from somebody else (grandparents, perhaps). They should check first with an accountant or insurance broker, though, because any payments that they make may be subject to capital transfer tax.

Maintained schools

Ninety-three per cent of schoolchildren in the UK go to maintained schools. These are schools where parents don't have to pay fees because they get full financial support from local or national government. They are not included in *The Schools Book*.

Matching

Finding the right independent secondary school for your child involves matching your child's needs with the education provided by the school at an affordable price. Your main considerations should be:

- Academic: your child will probably be best suited to a school where he or she is above average but won't be bored by too slow a pace, and where the range of subjects seems to match the child's existing interests while allowing for new ones to develop.
- Social: what are the other children like? What are the most popular curricular and extra-curricular activities? What about other parents – do you think they may share some of your beliefs?
- Discipline: match this roughly to what your child is used to and can cope with. Find a regimen that isn't going to conflict too strongly with the one at home. Children ought to be given more autonomy as they get older.
- Non-academic activities: particularly important at boarding school. Are there facilities for your child's existing interests with room for variety: Duke of Edinburgh's Award, pottery, fencing, sailing, etc?

Are pupils given time to pursue interests other than those offered by the school?

- Routine: again, especially important at boarding school where school-enforced routine lasts all day. An impressive array of organised weekend activities might mean that children have no time to themselves. Do organised extra-curricular activities complement your child's existing interests and commitments or will they conflict?

Mixed Sixths

Since Marlborough introduced the idea in 1968, many boys' schools have started to take girls into their sixth forms for A-levels (a very few girls' schools do the same for boys). Roughly speaking, the benefits are thought to be that, while girls are given access to better facilities and teaching, boys are stimulated by the influx of ambitious, intelligent females at this stage. Some headmasters speak of the civilising influence girls have on boys. Questionable, but there *can* be advantages for both boys and girls, especially from single-sex schools where they aren't used to seeing each other in day-to-day life.

Montessori schools

An educational method associated with Maria Montessori (1870–1952), Italy's first woman doctor. Initially she worked in Rome with feeble-minded children and later with normal children (aged 3–7). She invented auto-didactic furniture and apparatus to exercise children's physical mechanisms and extend their capacity to assess length, size, weight, shape, colour and texture. The method was championed by progressive educationalists and is still widely used, though it is not so popular in Britain where the Froebel method is preferred. The Dottoressa's methods and doctrines can be applied until the age of 18, but most Montessori schools are nursery with a few taking pupils to the age of 10.

Music

Provisions for music vary greatly in the independent sector. A handful of schools have virtually none; others have a massive commitment which involves, say, two-thirds of the pupils learning an instrument. The vast majority of schools have a certain amount of music as an integral part of the curriculum. Most schools have a choir and some sort of orchestra. A lot of schools have 2 or more choirs plus 2 or 3 orchestras (and, perhaps, a pop group or jazz group). Much depends on the enthusiasm and dedication of the director of music and the staff, and also, of course, on the policy and interests of the head. Most schools have full-time music staff and visiting teachers (in some instances a dozen or more). Choir schools and those which are closely associated with cathedrals tend to provide a lot of music and have choristers who sing in the cathedral.

Many schools make excellent provision for individual tuition (at a

price) in a variety of instruments. This may include the opportunity to hire instruments. Lessons at school may be more convenient and are often fitted into the school day on a rota. Many school choirs, orchestras, pop groups and other groups give regular performances. Quite often they give public performances. Choirs and orchestras go on tour in Britain and overseas. There are numerous links with national youth orchestras, choirs and music schools.

Some non-specialist schools have a tradition of sending pupils into careers in music and have an impressive collection of musicians, pop stars and promoters among their alumni (see the School Profiles). Others encourage music as an extra-curricular interest.

Specialist music schools cater specifically for the needs of musically gifted children who have a future as professional musicians. Although some also have a wide range of A-level options, the vast majority of leavers go on to music school. Children at music schools tend to spend most of their free time in musical activities.

Narrowing down

Choosing the right school is a process of elimination; start wide, with plenty of time. This may get harder as the field narrows and you have to make decisions that are more and more specific – a wide range of extra-curricular activities versus strong ties with a school in France? You'll end up with one school eventually.

Objectives

Like any business, schools advertise their aims and objectives – often in a few succinct words in the prospectus about realisation of the individual's potential. Although there seems to be little to take exception to in this, a neatly stated objective should be treated with caution: what happens to those who don't fit the mould (ie, artists at a highly academic school)? Is the school actually living up to the promise of its objective?

It is helpful to have an idea of the school's priorities. Although children's determination will probably allow them to succeed anyway, it's easier if there's some support from school for their chosen field. Reading between the lines of prospectuses, magazines and *The Schools Book* can give you some clue as to what the school actually achieves. Look at school-leavers' first destinations; range of non-academic activities; exam results. Has the school listed any traditional careers? Does all this match what you think your child needs from school?

O-grades

Roughly speaking, the Scottish equivalent of GCSE (or O-levels). Scottish pupils often sit O-grades only in those subjects that they aren't going to continue to Higher or A-level. This means that some of the ablest Scottish pupils will have only 3 or 4 O-grades. Bear that in mind when you read Scottish School Profiles in *The Schools Book*.

Old pupils

Most schools have associations of ex-pupils who keep in touch with each other and the school. Past pupils are called old boys/girls or alumni (alumnae at more classically minded girls' schools). They can be useful to the school when it needs to raise cash for new facilities or wants somebody to talk to the Sixth about careers in commerce, the arts, etc. Pupils who have just left school may be a useful source of inside information on the school. They could have joined the alumni association for a variety of reasons:

- Old school tie: the school has some useful old pupils to tap in the careers market.
- They enjoyed their schooldays.
- Many alumni associations exist because of sporting ties.
- They don't have much else going on in their lives.
- They are professional old boys whose alma-maternal/umbilical cords are never severed.

O-levels

Although these have now been replaced by GCSEs, *The Schools Book* gives O-level results (where available) in the School Profiles because the first GCSEs weren't sat until summer 1988. O-level passes are counted as being Grade C or above (anything below that doesn't count as a pass for UKCPU admission).

Open days

Most schools have open days when prospective parents can visit and see what the school and some of the staff look like. A bit like a living prospectus, open days give you the opportunity to see the facilities for science, sports, art, music, eating, sleeping, etc and to look at classrooms (at their best) and noticeboards. You may be able to have a few words with a member of staff or to ask a few general questions. Open days are helpful; make full use of them both to find out about the individual school and to build up a general impression of the range of what independent schools have to offer.

Outings

Most schools arrange some of these; often related to classwork. Visits to museums, factories, nature reserves, theatre productions and trips abroad are usually a stimulating addition to normal school routine. Other outings are recreational; some schools have their own outdoor-pursuit centres, arrange ski-ing holidays, sailing, riding, community service, giving children the chance to develop new interests. Find out what outings the school arranges; school magazines often publish pupils' accounts of these.

Overseas parents

If you live overseas and are sending your child to school in Britain:

- You'll have to appoint a guardian. This can be a friend or relation with whom the child can stay at half-terms and for exeats; who is on call for emergencies and who can help to arrange travel home for holidays. Choose someone your child knows and likes, who is responsible and fun, and who lives within easy travelling distance of school. If you really can't come up with anyone yourself, some schools help with lists of suitable guardians.
- If English isn't your child's first language, arrange for some initial coaching. Survival at school requires very fluent English but many school-age children are able to pick it up quickly once they're there, regardless of the amount of help they're given. Schools with their own

EFL provisions may be better able to deal with non-native English speakers. Look for EFL provision in the Special Features Index.

- Make sure that the school is aware of, and can arrange for, any immunisation that your child may need before going home for the holidays.
- Choose a school where there are other pupils with parents overseas. What provisions are made at weekends and over half-term for those who can't go home? What transport to the airport does the school arrange?

Parents

Meet other parents while you're choosing a school. Do you have anything in common with them? Why did they think that this school was right for their child? What do they think is good about it and what would they like to change? How involved are they in what goes on at the school?

Parents' associations

Increasingly important; the role of parents' associations varies. A lot depends on how much parental involvement the head can cope with but, on the whole, there is a move towards allowing and encouraging more. School parents' associations can:

- have representatives on the board of governors;
- act as pressure groups on the head; presenting complaints or suggestions;
- organise and provide parent volunteers for school outings and holidays;
- help with fund-raising, selling second-hand uniform, books, etc.

They're more likely to be effective if the head and parents get on with one another.

Parents' meetings

These are when you meet your child's teachers for a progress report. Most schools invite you to at least one a year. They also provide a chance for you to assess the teachers and to raise any minor questions or concerns. For anything pressing, don't wait; make an appointment immediately to speak to the teacher or the head.

Parents separating

Let the school know what's going on. This is probably not the time to change your child's school unless absolutely unavoidable. If your child's at boarding school, make sure that you keep in closer touch than usual. Don't expect your children to do anything to make life any easier for you. If they *have* any sympathy with, or understanding of, what's going on, they may do their best to hide it.

PNEU

The Parents' National Educational Union was founded in 1887 by Charlotte Mason to encourage a wider interest in the education and training of children. There are now 40 member schools. Most are prep, but a few teach up to 15-year-olds. Further information from the Secretary, PNEU, Strode House, 44–50 Osnaburgh Street, London NW1 3NN (tel: 01-387 9228).

Prefects

These are senior pupils; usually chosen by the staff and head after some consultation with pupils. Prefects can be responsible for:

- organising inter-house and inter-school games calendars;
- helping with crowd control at school functions;
- showing prospective parents around;
- keeping an eye on younger pupils, especially in boarding houses.

In some areas of employment and higher education, prefect experience is a useful attribute for a school-leaver to have.

Increasingly, the system emphasises responsibility rather than superiority but, although prefects no longer expect to be allowed to beat younger pupils as they may have been in the past, they are usually given privileges and badges of office in recognition of their service to the school.

Prep schools

Traditional prep or preparatory schools take day or boarding pupils from the age of 7 or 8 until they start at secondary school (11 for girls, 13 for boys). Some have links with specific secondary schools; these are mentioned in the School Profiles. Many of the secondary schools in *The*

Schools Book have their own prep schools or departments (sometimes called junior) attached. This may make it harder to get your child straight into the secondary department from other schools; conversely, acceptance at the prep school doesn't always guarantee a place at the secondary school without passing an entrance test.

Private schools

These are strictly privately-owned schools; there are very few of them. The term is often used to describe those independent schools that are not regarded as public schools.

Progressive schools

Many of the practices and theories initiated by progressive schools from the end of the last century onwards have been adopted by others, so don't expect anything too revolutionary or liberal. Progressive schools tended to put the emphasis on community atmosphere and were less affected by the hangovers of Victorian public school values, such as unquestioning deference to authority and the status quo, than were many other schools. Now most of them are co-ed and many offer a wide range of non-academic activities including farming, gardening, adventure training and community service. Schools that have been regarded as progressive include Friends' schools, Round Square Conference schools and several others, including Bedales and Millfield.

Prospectuses

It is pretty well essential to get a prospectus. These vary enormously, from being totally inadequate 4-page leaflets which look as if they've been cobbled together by the school's media research officer, to 60-page brochures, with elegant text and beautiful photographs, created by

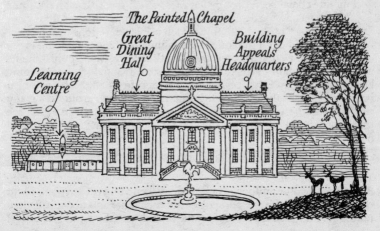

highly professional PR firms and first-class printers. There is sometimes a noticeable correspondence between the quality of a prospectus and the quality and name/reputation of a school. Crummy provincial schools that nobody's ever heard of provide crummy prospectuses; the most distinguished schools (but not all) provide high-gloss, extremely detailed brochures.

Prospectuses should be perused thoroughly and with caution. Not infrequently they are out-of-date. In any case, their aim is to present all or most of the best features of a school. They are *advertisements*. They do not, therefore, dwell on emetic food, pederastic staff, the nymphomaniac matron, or cannabis behind the cricket pavilion, or, indeed, any of the other shortcomings which, from time to time, surface in even the best-run establishments.

An original prospectus is rare for the very good reason that it is extremely difficult to produce a truthful and persuasive portrait of so complex a microcosm as a school. Too often they contain standard and cliché-ridden waffle about developing potential and producing well-rounded individuals in a caring environment. Nevertheless, a close study of a prospectus (including the essential reading between the lines) can be rewarding and can provide quite a lot of information. This has to be considered in conjunction with the obligatory visit to the school.

Public schools

The exact definition of a public school is unclear. Usually it is used to refer to schools with heads who are members of the HMC or GSA. Public schools are subdivided into major and minor, depending on the viewpoint and the alma mater of whoever is using the expression.

Punishments

Although some of the archaic, petty, time-wasting punishments such as writing lines have been dropped at most schools, nearly all have some sort of penal code for dealing with nonconforming and unruly pupils. Some still regard beating children as defensible if it is done by a head or housemaster. Find out the scale of punishments (some schools are cagey about this). How often are they meted out and why? Many punishments involve deprivation of free time in detention, manual work (sweeping leaves, picking up litter, sometimes referred to as hard labour) or, at boarding schools, the system of gating. For more serious offences many schools suspend pupils for a week or so. This could punish you more than your child if your schedule is built round not having children at home all day.

Pupils

Assessing the other pupils is important. When you visit a school, try to observe how friendly the pupils are with each other and to you. Do they reflect the impression you have of the school? Are they interested in all those extra-curricular activities or is high attendance at clubs and societies a result of coercion? No matter how impressed you may be by their beautiful behaviour and smart appearance, ask yourself how well would your child get on with them?

Pupils can also be a valuable source of information about the school. Find out what they like or don't like about the school. What would they change if they could? Show them the prospectus and see what comments it provokes.

Pupil/staff relations

Fortunately you're unlikely to come across any child molesters on the staff of a school. You should try and see as many of the staff as possible and assess how they and the pupils treat each other. Good, enthusiastic teaching is very stimulating. You may be able to see some classes in action when you visit. What's the atmosphere like? Better still, how do pupils and staff treat each other at school sports days and plays, when they're out of the formal setting of school? Do they seem to like each other?

Questions

Write down all the questions that occur to you about the schools on your shortlist, from how many pupils go on to Oxbridge to how often can they change their socks. Try to gather as many of the answers as possible from prospectuses, school magazines, the pupils and parents you meet, and observation when you visit. Keeping direct questioning of the staff and head to a minimum gives you more time to concentrate on summing them up. However, some things need to be asked outright. An evasive response can often answer a question just as well as a straightforward reply.

Range of schools

Investigate a range of schools to test your assumptions; you might find that a school of 1000 provides more individual attention than one of 200 or that the nearest girls' school has the best science facilities in the area.

Go to as many open days as possible and get a good background on which to base decisions about what's right for your child.

Try to investigate 4 or 5 schools fully (ie, arrange a meeting with the head) before making any final decisions. Investigate:

- co-ed and single-sex schools;
- town, suburban, country;
- long-established and new;
- big and small.

Regimental schools

Links (informal and formal) between some regiments and schools have built up over generations, often as a result of endowments. This doesn't mean that the schools involved are exclusively populated with embryonic army officers or the children of army officers. Links exist between:

- Harrow and the Coldstream Guards;
- Winchester and the Greenjackets;
- Shrewsbury and the Light Infantry;
- Ampleforth and the Parachute Regiment;
- Downside and the 17th/20th.

Registration

Once you've found the right school you'll have to register your child for entrance tests and interviews. The school's prospectus will tell you how. Usually it means filling in a form with details of your child's name, age, address and current school. You may have to pay a non-returnable registration fee – more common if the school is heavily subscribed.

Some schools are so over-subscribed that you're recommended to register your child's name several years before entry (occasionally you can do this at birth), so investigate well in advance. Registration does not guarantee entry; your child will still have to pass through the school's entry procedure, so have a back-up school in mind.

It's difficult to match a school to a new-born baby and, if this is what you've done, make absolutely sure that it *is* the right school before automatically embarking on the entry procedure.

Religion

During the last 25 years the ecumenical movement has had considerable and beneficial effects. There is much less bigotry, much more tolerance. Racial integration has had a profound effect and nowadays most schools are ecumenically disposed towards those of miscellaneous faiths and members of minority sects and those who are of no particular persuasion. But it is unusual to find a school which has any specific attitude towards, say, agnostics, gnostics, atheists and heretics.

Provisions for religious instruction and worship vary greatly. Most schools point out that they are non-denominational. Schools which have a clearly prescribed policy make it clear that they are willing to accept pupils of any persuasion or none. In the vast majority of schools Muslims, Hindus, Jews et al are allowed to opt out from any arrangements for Christians and have exemption from attendance at prayers, etc. Several schools provide facilities and opportunities for non-Christians to follow their own religious practices.

Nearly all schools appear to have religious education of *some* kind on the curriculum. There is a widespread tendency to make RE a study of world religions so that children get an idea of what inspires people of different faiths, and also an idea of practice, custom, law, convention, tradition and so forth.

A very large number of British schools are Church of England foundations of one kind and another and thus follow, to varying degrees, Protestant/Anglican practice. Some make a token subscription to this in the form of a prayer and perhaps a hymn at assembly, and occasional attendance at chapel. Others make a certain amount of worship compulsory. A lot of schools have a chaplain (or two) available. Candidates are prepared for confirmation. Cathedral schools (Protestant) and those which have close traditional links with a cathedral all lay quite a lot of stress on religious education and regular worship.

Methodist, Quaker and Presbyterian schools tend to have a clearly defined policy and give considerable attention to religious worship and instruction.

The Roman Catholic schools, administered by the Benedictines, the Christian Brothers and other Orders, and by various teaching Orders of nuns, have the clearest, most definite and comprehensive policies. The intention is to educate and nurture children in the Faith so that they become devout and mature Christians. Thus, there is considerable stress on religious instruction and on worship according to the liturgy of the Church. This involves regular attendance at high and low Mass on Sundays and Holidays of Obligation, the taking of the sacraments, attendance at prayers, benediction, vespers, saying the Angelus and so on. Catholic schools also run retreats. Theology and philosophy are taught up to GCSE and A-level. In many schools these are a compulsory part of the curriculum; and in some schools all pupils are obliged to take public exams in religious education.

Many people think that it is not a bad thing for children to be brought up according to *some* religious doctrine and set of beliefs rather than with a diluted form of 'liberal' Christianity or the vague and superficial study of different faiths and world 'movements'. If it matters to you that your child receives definite religious instruction and has the opportunity of worship and of cultivating a spiritual life then, clearly, you must investigate what is available. For example, some chaplains (and others in control of RE) pay a lot of attention to the teachings of the Old Testament and comparatively little to those of the New.

Reports

Reports come in a wide variety of formats; virtually every school has its own. They are usually sent 2 or 3 times a year. Basically a report comprises a grade mark on each taught subject. In addition there will probably be a comment from any or all of the following: head teacher, housemaster/mistress, tutor, form teacher, deputy head, games teacher. Some schools provide commodious reports in which there is much detail. Quite often there is so little space allotted to each subject that only 10–15 words of comment are possible. Reports which bear subject comments such as 'satis.', 'more effort needed', 'a good term's work', 'could work harder' *and nothing else* are the product of inefficiency, ignorance or laziness (or, conceivably, mere weariness). Whatever the reason, they should not be accepted. Remember that you are paying a large sum of money for your child's education and you are entitled, at the very least, to a thorough report. In other words – complain. Make sure you get your money's worth with a detailed report which goes into your child's merits and shortcomings. Teaching staff should always be prepared to answer any questions and discuss any problems you may have.

Right school for your child

This will not necessarily be the one you wish *you'd* gone to, nor the one that's right for your other children, or the most prestigious that you can afford. The right school will be the one your child fits into most easily without having to be forced into a mould, and will provide:

- good teaching and results in your child's best subjects;
- a range of subject combinations at GCSE and A-level that your child will benefit from;
- motivation to develop extra-curricular interests;
- an environment that your child will feel at home in.

The strengths and interests of a 5-, 7- or 11-year-old aren't always obvious. Selecting is a process of elimination. Reject those schools that are obviously wrong – not academic enough, too traditional, not enough music – before looking more carefully at the possible ones.

Round Square Conference

Named after the Round Square which is one of the buildings at Gordonstoun School in Morayshire where this association started. There are 14 member schools from all over the world which follow the educational theories and methods of Kurt Hahn, the founder of Gordonstoun, who placed much importance on the value of outward bound and community service activities.

Routine

Anybody who is trying to co-ordinate the movements of hundreds of children and teenagers with the demands of a curriculum that requires their attendance at classes has to work to a rigid schedule. School days are timetabled to the minute. In an attempt to make this less stultifying,

some schools operate a timetable over a 6- or 7-day cycle so that Monday doesn't always start with double maths. Senior pupils may be granted some autonomy in private study periods.

At boarding schools routine can stretch throughout the day, ending with set supper- and bed-times and baths according to a rota, and even into the weekend with organised trips to the local town on Saturday afternoons after playing sport for the school in the morning. This sort of routine is far more restricting than any that adults are likely to come up against and it won't necessarily foster self-motivation or the ability to use time properly when what you do, and when you do it, are not externally enforced. Many children need to have some time to fill themselves with reading, talking to their friends, playing tennis, painting, catching up on homework, or doing nothing. This means that your child may well be better at a school with a range of really optional extras than at one where every hour is filled from a list of permissible options.

Rules

Ask to see a copy of the school rules for pupils. (There will be a set for you as well, which may look like a particularly repressive contract of employment with strict instructions to inform the school of the least departure from your child's normal routine, and so on.) These indicate how much restriction the school places on its pupils and show how important traditions are, eg, perhaps only sixth-formers may walk on the grass. How much control does the school try to exert over its pupils when they aren't in school? How difficult would it be to take your child out of school for a few days because of some wonderful holiday opportunity or a family occasion? A lot of schools don't publicise their policies on issues like smoking, drinking and drugs because they don't want to imply that these are frequent problems.

Some children flourish in a fairly regimented environment, others find it a strain to be constantly bumping up against authority. Find a school where the level of insistence on conforming to rules matches what you think your child's own instinct is.

Scholarships and exhibitions

Some pupils can have all or a proportion of their fees paid by a scholarship or exhibition which is awarded by the school on the strength of the pupil's potential, usually judged by exam or test. Depending on the school, scholarships can be given for musical or academic ability, to choristers, for prowess at sport, etc at various ages. They are awarded irrespective of parental income. See the Special Features Index for schools with scholarships.

School consultants

These are people who give advice on suitable schools for your child. They may be worth considering if you really don't know where to begin in matching school and child (and if you're sure that your child needs an independent school). Consultants are often paid a retainer membership fee by schools who want to be recommended. Get advice about reputable consultants from ISIS.

School councils

The idea is that pupil representatives from every form or perhaps from only senior forms, should meet the staff to discuss issues such as food, discipline, school outings, and to air grievances. Some heads and staff at independent schools do not warm to this democratisation.

School magazines

Many schools will send you one when you ask for the prospectus. Like prospectuses, magazines are geared towards creating a good impression; they vary a lot in size and quality of production but most give you *some* idea of what's going on in the school. How much involvement do the pupils have in the magazine contents and production? How many trips and excursions are reported? What are leavers going to do and where – which UKCPUs, etc? Leavers' first destinations are important. (News of alumni may not be quite as relevant – many people lose touch with their schools.) What sort of drama, music and sport are the pupils doing? Do only one or two members of staff seem to be arranging all the extra-curricular activities? Does one pupil seem to excel at everything, making you wonder what the others are up to?

The pupils of some schools bring out their own unofficial magazine; these aren't usually written with a view to impressing parents and are difficult to get hold of through official channels. If you manage to track one down, it should give an impression of the concerns of the more vociferous (and critical?) pupils, and makes a good counterbalance to the official version.

Scotland

A slightly different system operates in Scottish maintained schools. Some Scottish independent schools follow the Scottish system, others stick to the English one, and others a hybrid of the two.

While English and Welsh pupils are doing GCSEs, Scots are doing O-grades which are followed a year later by Highers and CSYS a year after that. Traditionally, Scottish students went to university after Highers when they were 17; some still do.

Service children

The Ministry of Defence gives grants towards the day or boarding fees of the children of armed service personnel. You can find out more from your local Service Education Unit or from Service Children's Education Authority, Court Road, Eltham, London SE9 1YU (tel: 01-854 2242, x4206).

Setting

Some schools split children into teaching groups for each subject according to ability judged on performance in exams and class.

The advantages are that classes of similar ability are easier to teach, prevent quick learners from being held back and allow slower ones to move at a less pressured pace.

The disadvantages are that children can be held back by being wrongly setted and that often the best teachers and facilities may automatically go to the more able sets.

Sex

Depending on where they are, most schoolchildren don't have the opportunity to indulge in active sex lives, but they do think and talk about sex a lot. (It was once claimed that sixth-form boys thought, albeit fleetingly, about sex an average of eight times an hour.) *The Schools Book* doesn't attempt to assess the sex education provision of individual schools, because, firstly, a straightforward account of human copulation and reproduction, such as is provided on many school sex education courses, isn't necessarily the most relevant way of finding out about sex – it can confuse rather than clarify; secondly, it's difficult to measure sex education as it crops up in other subjects and classroom discussions.

Many parents find it difficult to think of their children as being sexually active and adolescents sometimes resent what they see as parental interference in their personal lives. However, it's worth braving the mutual embarrassment; while the repercussions of an unplanned pregnancy are as traumatic and lasting as ever, AIDS has made ignorance an even greater danger than it was before. There are lots of books about sex around; you could try *Sex with Paula Yates* (Sphere, 1987) and *Clare Rayner's Body Book* (Deutsch, 1982) to start with.

In the meantime, you can find out about the school's attitude towards sex – relationships between pupils of the same or different ages; homosexuality; pupils bringing soft porn to school. At boarding schools you may also want to find out whether girls and boys are allowed into each other's bedrooms; are they discouraged from forming close relationships?

S-grades

These are very gradually replacing O-grades in Scotland – the first S-grade courses were started in 1984 and the last will be introduced in 1989; not all schools adopted them at once. Currently they run alongside O-grades which are being phased out as S-grades take over.

The exams are designed to test a wider range of ability than O-grades – subjects are broken down into different elements such as application and understanding, and assessment is based on exams and set classwork during the course.

SHMIS

The Society of Headmasters of Independent Schools is a club for the headmasters of small independent boarding schools. It was established in 1961 because membership of the HMC was full. Some headmasters are members of both.

Siblings

Very often siblings are automatically sent to the same school. This has advantages; younger siblings have a familiar face around from day one,

it's convenient for them to have roughly the same daily and holiday routine, and some schools reduce the fees for second and subsequent children. However, siblings can have very different educational needs so make sure that the school matches *all* of them.

Sickness

If you keep your child away from school due to illness, inform the school at once and let them know what's wrong; this is especially important if it's infectious or will curtail your child's activities after going back to school.

School isn't necessarily any more dangerous than home but accidents happen. You should leave home and office telephone numbers with the school and be very specific about when and where you can be contacted. This can save much anxiety to frantic teachers and distraught parents. If for any reason you can't be contacted, arrange to have a friend standing by to step in if your child is ill or has an accident at school.

Find out what facilities for sick or injured children there are on the premises. Is there a resident SRN? a sick-room (especially relevant for boarding schools)? How far away is the nearest hospital?

You can insure school fees against long absences from school due to illness; speak to an insurance broker about this or contact ISIS.

Single-sex schools

Although it may be an artificial environment, some children are happier in all girls' or all boys' schools and a lot of the heavyweights (academically and socially) have remained single-sex. (Many boys' schools, however, now take girls into the Sixth.)

Academically, girls from single-sex schools appear to get better exam results than those from co-ed schools. The reverse is true of boys. (Exam results from boys' schools with mixed Sixths are seldom broken down by sex because the influx of intelligent girls into the school usually boosts A-level results and averages.)

Most schools make some attempt to introduce the opposite sex at some stage. Many team up with a brother or sister school (often one that was founded at about the same time to be just that) and share facilities, activities, productions and outings. They may also join forces for A-levels or in the prep/junior department.

Sixth form

Overall, only about 22% of pupils in the UK stay on at school after they are 16. However, the majority (approximately 58%) of independent schoolchildren stay on after GCSE (18% of the 16–18-year-old school population is at independent school as against 7% overall).

The sixth form lasts for two years (lower and upper). Some leave after one year, having done additional GCSEs or other qualifications (secretarial, City and Guilds, etc); others stay for two, doing A-level courses.

When schools state the size of their sixth forms they usually include both years; *The Schools Book* gives the size of the upper sixth, A-level year at the beginning of each school entry.

Size of school

Secondary independent schools with sixth forms range in size from about 120 pupils to about 1200. Just as some people are happier in the bustle of large cities than they are in small towns, some children prefer a certain size of school. Consider the facilities and subjects offered; there may be more going on at a large school and possibly better, newer facilities, but there isn't always a bigger range. In general, large schools are probably better able to accommodate a wider range of academic ability than are small ones.

Smoking

Still prevalent in schools in spite of massive anti-smoking campaigns from heads and the government. In general, if children get through school without smoking they'll probably never start but peer pressure and the need to flaunt authority makes this difficult. (Many of those who don't smoke have parents who do.)

Making children aware of the dangers doesn't seem to stop them; teenagers regard themselves as immortal and don't appreciate how difficult giving up can be. One headmaster recommends massive parental bribes for not smoking before they're 21 (£500–£1000 was the going rate in the mid 80s). Schools with an 'expulsion for smoking' policy have been known to have to step down when the entire sixth form is caught. There is a lot of anti-smoking information from pressure groups such as ASH (Action on Smoking and Health), 5–11 Mortimer Street, London W1 (tel: 01-637 9843).

Special needs

Some schools make provision for children with special needs due to, for example, mild handicap, learning or language difficulties. Some of these are listed in the Special Features Index. For listings of specialist schools contact:

- **England**: Department of Education and Science, Schools Branch II (Special Education), Elizabeth House, 39 York Road, London SE1 7PH (tel: 01-934 9230/9240).

- **Wales**: Welsh Office Education Department, Cathays Park, Cardiff CF1 3NQ (tel: 0222 823347).

- **Scotland**: Scottish Education Department (Special Schools), New St Andrews House, St James Centre, Edinburgh EH1 3SY (tel: 031 556 8400).

- **Northern Ireland**: Department of Education for Northern Ireland, Schools I Division, Rathgael House, Balloo Road, Bangor, Northern Ireland BT19 2PR (tel: 0247 466311).

Sports and games

There is much emphasis on sports and games in independent schools. In many, 5 or 6 afternoons a week (plus other times) are devoted to them and most schools have excellent facilities on site or nearby (including an increasing number of sports halls). Even so, performances at national and international level remain poor and the facilities that are provided in schools are inferior to those available in many other countries.

Many schools run sports and games on a voluntary basis and nowadays (fortunately) it is rare to find a school which insists on everyone taking part in official sports and games regardless of ability, physique and inclination.

The principal and most popular field games are: rugby union, cricket, hockey, soccer, lacrosse, handball, softball, rounders and forms of baseball. Some Irish schools provide hurling and Gaelic football. The main court games are: lawn tennis, hard-court tennis, badminton, basketball, squash, rackets, volleyball, and croquet; plus, at Eton, Rugby and Winchester, fives. A few schools provide real tennis.

Of the course games, golf is easily the most popular. Quite a lot of schools have 9-hole courses on their estates, or have access to courses nearby.

Athletics are very popular and most schools can provide a full range of field and track events (not a few schools have all-weather running tracks). Cross-country running is very popular.

Some martial arts are also common and popular and include judo, karate, kendo and kung-fu. Fencing is also popular, but boxing appears to be a thing of the past.

Target sports (eg, archery, clay-pigeon shooting, rifle-shooting – small and full-bore – and pistol-shooting) are available in quite a lot of schools and are linked with activities in the CCF.

Water sports (especially water polo, surfing, canoeing, sailing, rowing and diving) are always popular. Schools situated near the sea, a river or lake tend to make good use of water.

Gymnastic sports are extremely popular and most schools have good facilities for these.

Some schools (particularly girls' schools) can provide riding and some show-jumping.

Outdoor pursuits are often closely associated with sport (or are sports in their own right), and include sailing, canoeing, ski-ing, rock-climbing, fell-walking, cliff-scaling, gliding and parachuting. A few schools even manage to have their own packs of beagles. Country schools (especially those in Scotland and the North of England) have a very full range of outdoor pursuits/sports including outdoor-pursuit centres which pupils can visit for a few days at a time. Such activities have links with various enterprises in the Duke of Edinburgh's Award Scheme. The *mens sana in corpore sano* philosophy – no doubt a continuation of the Victorian cult of athletic prowess and muscle-bound Christianity – is still widespread and many schools see team and individual sports and games as valuable character-building influences. Most schools have a hard core of dedicated sports/games enthusiasts on the staff (some headmasters are fanatics) who are qualified to coach, referee and umpire and who are prepared to devote an enormous amount of time and effort to their chosen activity. The majority of schools run sports and games on a competitive basis, with inter-house competitions and numerous fixtures with other schools.

Whether or not all this is a good thing is another issue. The amount of time and effort given to sports and games is often a matter of contention among school staffs. Clashes of interest are frequent. Parents are well advised to think carefully about what their child might be exposed to – or deprived of.

Staff

You'll probably get a list of staff and their credentials with the prospectus. You can investigate them further when you visit. What is the male:female ratio? Which departments have the largest teaching staff? How old are they (or do they seem)? The average pupil:staff ratio is about 11:1 or 12:1, but this varies a lot and you're probably more interested in the range of sizes for teaching groups. What do you think your child will make of the staff, and how interesting would *you* find them? Can you find out how long they've served? *The Schools Book* gives the annual staff turnover – this is usually about 5–10%. When it's low, is this because the staff are good, happy teachers or because they're inert?

Starting out

Before your child's first day at a new school, check:

- what time the new pupils are expected to get there;
- what time the day ends; or, at a boarding school, when the first exeat is;

- that you've got all the necessary equipment and uniform.

Try to introduce your child to some of the other pupils in the class so that there'll be someone familiar on the first day.

Stealing

Theft is inherent and pretty well inevitable in all institutional life. In any school, at any given moment, there is likely to be a thief or two about. Petty pilfering (of pens, watches, calculators, cash and items of clothing) is especially frequent in day schools (the swag can be got away easily). In a school, life is often easy for the petty thief because pupils are so extraordinarily careless about their belongings, especially on games days. Changing-rooms are easy targets. In most schools, easily portable valuables are collected before games, but many pupils forget to hand them in. Parents are much to blame for the scale of the problem because they are extremely lax about naming children's property. **Mark everything that can be marked**.

Don't send your child to school with large amounts of cash or other valuables. If this can't be avoided, hand it over to a member of staff for safekeeping (make sure your child knows which one). Also, find out what locker and other facilities for protection there are, where bicycles can be stored and so on. Bicycles should always be chained and locked. If you think your child has had something stolen you should immediately contact the head, the form teacher and anyone else relevant.

Steiner schools

Schools whose teaching follows the philosophy of Rudolf Steiner who placed great emphasis on the development of the individual and believed that spiritual truth was human rather than in some way divine. The first Steiner school opened in Germany in 1914; subsequently they were closed by the Nazis in 1938. Currently there are about 200 worldwide. Many of them are prep only but a few (included in *The Schools Book*) teach up to A-level.

Further details from the Secretary, Steiner Schools Fellowship, c/o Elmfield School, Love Lane, Stourbridge, West Midlands DY8 2EA (tel: 0384 394633).

Streaming

A form of internal organisation in which pupils are grouped across the curriculum by such criteria as age, intelligence, ability and aptitude (or a combination of two or more of these). It is largely based on achievement in the three Rs. It starts in primary schools and extends into selective secondary education. An alternative pattern of mixed ability exists in many schools. Streaming is to be distinguished from setting, a system by which pupils are grouped for particular subjects (eg, maths, modern languages) according to ability.

Subjects offered

Check what GCSE and A-level subjects the school offers. Even more important, what subject combinations are possible? Because of the early specialisation demanded by A-levels, many pupils have to opt for an exclusively arts or science bias at the age of 16. Some schools don't have the facilities to offer teaching in a combination of both areas.

Touring the school

You'll find out a lot about a school from observation when you visit.

- Go during term-time.
- Observe the pupils. What do they look like? How do they react to what you ask (even if it's just 'Where's the head's study?')? Do they seem friendly, alert, interested?
- What about staff? what age range? how interested and interesting do they seem?
- Look at noticeboards. What's going on; who's involved? Sports, drama, talks, films, out-of-school visits, volunteers for community work or to help with school events? Are pupils honoured for achievements or are there lists of the latest suspensions?
- Look at classroom displays. Do they cover a range of interests and are they stimulating? Have the pupils done them themselves or do they look as though they've been pinned there in the vague hope that someone will look at them?
- Buildings: how impressive are they? How comfortable are they to work and live in? What are the facilities like? How consistently good or bad are they? (your child may not be among those using the new physics lab).

- Boarding accommodation: how stark, over-crowded or otherwise, are the dormitories and bathrooms? Can you believe that normal children live here happily?
- Don't be put off by discreet graffiti in pupils' lavatories and on desks – that's universal; spray paint on the swimming-pool wall isn't, though.

Trinity Group

A group of schools founded c.1978. Basically a consultative body, it comprises 17 schools in London and the south which collaborate to avoid clashes over entrance exams and to deal with applications. The head-masters confer periodically to pool their experiences and knowledge of administrative matters. Heads of departments hold annual conferences to discuss matters of mutual interest.

Tutorial colleges

Sometimes called crammers, they can be day or boarding and are nearly always co-ed. Tutorial colleges usually take students from the age of 16 for A-levels or additional GCSEs; many also coach for other exams: International Baccalaureat, Royal Society of Arts, Higher National Diploma. Fees are often charged according to the number of subjects studied. Because their youngest students are the age of a school's oldest pupils, tutorial colleges tend to have fewer rules, making them a good option for sixth-formers who have had enough of school discipline and tradition. The CIFE or the ATI can provide lists of qualified tutorial colleges.

Uniform

Most independent schools have a uniform. Often it won't have changed for a long time. This usually means buying a special tie and blazer; skirts/trousers, shirts, shoes, jumpers, even knickers, in the right colour. In addition you may need to buy special sports equipment and clothes, school colours for sports teams, summer clothes, formal dress (kilts if it's a Scottish school), coats, macks, smocks for art, etc. Schools will let you know where to buy the uniform, including any second-hand sources, before your child joins. Some are more demanding than others about what will or will not do. Uniforms can set you back by hundreds of pounds.

Value for money

As more and more parents opt for independent education, often at the expense of family holidays, costs continue to rise at a higher rate than inflation. ISIS gives the 1987/88 average annual fees for day schools as £2055 and for boarding as £4866. At the current annual rate of increase in school fees (11%) that means that 5 years of independent education costs approximately £13,148 for day and £31,134 for boarding school, so make

sure that you're getting what you and your child want and need for this.

One alternative is to move to an area where you're happy in the maintained sector and come within the catchment area of the right school for your child.

Visiting the school

This is an absolute must. These are arranged through the school and are your chance to see what the school is like. Try to visit at least four or five schools.

- Go during term time to get some idea of how the school operates and arrange to speak to any members of staff who are particularly relevant to your child's need (housemaster or mistress, teaching staff for best subjects).
- Try and speak to pupils or the prefect who shows you round. What do they do in their free time, how enthusiastic are they about curricular and extra-curricular activities?
- Speak to the head – this is the most influential person in the school.
- Look at timetables, exam results, facilities and menus.
- Ask all the questions you still have: what happens if a child is taken ill? What careers advice is there? What extras are you charged for?
- Make a final shortlist of 1 or 2 schools to visit again with your child. Some schools arrange for prospective pupils to spend a day at school during term-time.

Everyone you meet will be trying to impress. Be fair, but critical. This isn't the time to put the head's back up by attacking his methods, but just because a policy has been adopted for the 600 pupils of the school it doesn't mean that it's right for your child.

Voluntary-aided schools

These are voluntary in so far as they have been founded by a voluntary religious body (eg, the Church of England or the Roman Catholic Church) and aided in that they are supported by public funds. The LEA meets the running costs. Repairs and three-quarters of improvements are paid for out of national funds. The rest is covered by the religious body. The voluntary body has the right to choose staff and decide on what religious education may be given. There are not many voluntary-aided schools today and most of them are church schools.

Woodard schools

Canon Woodard founded 10 boys' schools during the 1840s and 1850s. These are all Anglican foundations. Membership has increased to 26 schools, including some for girls, sharing extra-curricular activities and events with each other.

Young Enterprise Scheme

The Young Enterprise Scheme will advise and help school students who want to set up their own mini-companies at school. Further information from Young Enterprise, Robert Hyde House, Bryanston Square, London W1H 7LN (tel: 01-724 7641).

Schools
A-Z

ABBOTS BROMLEY

School of St Mary & St Anne
Rugeley
Staffordshire WS15 3BW
Telephone number 0283 840232

Co-ed   Pupils 260
Boys   Upper sixth Yes
● Girls   Termly fees:
Mixed sixth   Day £1200
● Day   Boarding £1790
● Boarding   Woodard; GSA;
GBGSA

Head Mrs B Harbron (4 years)
Age range 11–18, own prep from age 7; entry by own exam
Music and art scholarships, bursaries for clergy daughters. Founded 1874.

ABINGDON

Abingdon School
Abingdon
Oxfordshire
OX14 1DE
Telephone number 0235 21563

Co-ed   Pupils 730
● Boys   Upper sixth Yes
Girls   Termly fees:
Mixed sixth   Day £920
● Day   Boarding £1830
● Boarding   HMC; GBA;
BSA

WHAT IT'S LIKE

One of the oldest schools in England, its foundation appears to precede its first mention (in 1256) in the records of Abingdon Abbey to which it was attached for several centuries. Boarders were taken at least as early as 1272. In 1576 it moved to a new site and was re-endowed by John Royse of the Mercers' Company. It was rebuilt on its present site near the centre of Abingdon in 1870. Further buildings have been added in recent years, including a sports hall and a technology centre. The school is now very well equipped and has about 30 acres of fine playing fields and gardens. The school is Anglican by tradition and the chapel is a focus of its corporate life. Much of the organisation is centred on a tutorial system and considerable stress is put on the importance of parental involvement. A broad, general academic education is provided and versatility is preferred to over-specialisation. All pupils take foundation courses in art, music and technology. Teaching is done in a moderately traditional style. In recent years some 80% of all pupils have gone on to higher education, of whom a quarter have won places to Oxbridge. Music is particularly strong with about half the boys taking instrumental or vocal lessons. A wide variety of sports and games is available (including rowing) and standards are high. There is also a plentiful range of extra-curricular activities and a large and flourishing voluntary CCF. Some commitment to local community services and the Duke of Edinburgh's Award Scheme. Ample use is made of the cultural amenities of Oxford 6 miles away.

SCHOOL PROFILE

Head M StJ Parker (13 years)
Age range 11–18; entry by common entrance and own exam
Assisted places. Music, art and design and common entrance scholarships.

ACKWORTH

Ackworth School
Barnsley Road
Pontefract
West Yorkshire 4FL 7LT
Telephone number 0977 611401

Enquiries/application to the Head

- Co-ed
  Boys
  Girls
  Mixed sixth
- Day
- Boarding

Pupils 387
Upper sixth 40
Termly fees:
Day £1038
Boarding £1790
SHMIS

WHAT IT'S LIKE

Founded in 1779 in the village of Ackworth (4 miles from Pontefract). It is blessed with an estate of 270 acres, including a school farm. The surroundings are delightful and the fine buildings include a superb Georgian block (1758–63). There are many modern facilities and new buildings. The pupils (it has a school council) play a considerable part in the running of the school and there are strong bonds with the local community. As it is a Quaker foundation the pattern of life has as its basis the belief of Friends that religion and life are one. It stresses the traditional values of 'courtesy, service and academic rigour'. All boarders attend Meeting for Worship in the manner of the Society of Friends. It being a small school, a 'family' atmosphere prevails and this is much encouraged.

SCHOOL PROFILE

Pupils Total over 12, 387. Day 132 (boys 49, girls 83); Boarding 255 (boys 139, girls 116). Entry age, 11 and into sixth. 6% are children of former pupils.
Entrance Common entrance and own entrance exam used. Oversubscribed for day pupils. Keen on musical entrants. Parents are expected to buy text books in the sixth form. 35 scholarships/bursaries available (including music), £2,500–£600.
Parents 15+% in industry or commerce. 10+% live within 30 miles, 10+% live overseas.
Staff Head Mr G R McKee, in post for 17 years. 41 full time staff, 2 part time. Annual turnover 5%. Average age 41.
Academic work GCSE and A-levels. Average size of upper fifth 75; upper sixth 40. *O-levels*: on average, 31 pupils in upper fifth pass 1–4 subjects; 23, 5–7 subjects; 27 pass 8+ subjects. *A-levels*: on average, 5 pupils in the upper

sixth pass 1 subject; 8, 2 subjects; 13, 3 subjects and 8 pass 4 subjects. On average, 18 take science/engineering A-levels; 9 take arts and humanities; 11 a mixture. *Computing facilities*: full scale Information Technology Unit with 25 stations networked. Provision for dyslexia via local institute. EFL teacher.

Senior pupils' non-academic activities *Music*: 141 learn a musical instrument, 35 up to Grade 6, 3 accepted for music courses, 56 in school orchestra, 90 in school choir, 12 in chamber choir, 12 in brass group, 2 in City of Sheffield Youth Orchestra. *Drama and dance*: 70 in school productions, 80 in junior plays, 50 in Drama Workshops, 9 in Recorder Group, 12 in Folk Dance. 1 accepted for Drama/Dance School. *Art*: 6 take art as non-examined subject; 63 take O-level art; 6 A-level art; 3 accepted for Art School; 20 attend art workshops. *Sport*: Soccer, hockey, cricket, athletics, tennis, swimming, squash, netball, rounders available. 253 take non-compulsory sport. 75 take exams in eg gymnastics, swimming. 17 represent county/country (hockey, athletics, netball). *Other*: 75 take part in local community schemes. 29 have bronze Duke of Edinburgh's Award, 19 silver and 9 gold. 10% enter voluntary schemes after leaving school. Other activities include aeromodelling, natural history, gym, needlework, fabric printing, art workshop, cookery, badminton, electronics, weight training, canoeing, sailing, CDT workshops, pottery, drama, folk dance, art studies, aerobics, jazz.

Careers 2 full time and 4 part time careers advisors. Average number of pupils accepted for *arts and humanities degree courses* at Oxbridge, 1; other universities, 10; polytechnics, or CHE, 3. *science and engineering degree courses* at Oxbridge, 1; other universities, 8; medical schools, 1; polytechnics or CHE, 4. *BEd*, 2. *other general training courses*, 2. Average number of pupils going straight into careers in industry, 4; civil service, 2.

Uniform School uniform worn throughout.

Houses/prefects Competitive houses. No prefects, all sixth formers share duties. Head boy and girl, heads of houses, appointed by the Head and house staff after consultation with sixth formers. School Council.

Religion Religious worship is encouraged. All boarders attend Meeting for Worship in the manner of the Society of Friends.

Social Membership of Riding for Disabled Association. Membership of local Music Society. Ski-ing and trips to cultural centres abroad. Travel scholarships are awarded to sixth formers. Pupils allowed to bring bicycle/horse to school (bicycles encouraged); cars with special permission. Meals formal. School shop. No tobacco/alcohol allowed.

Discipline Pupils failing to produce homework once might expect to have to produce to a deadline; those caught smoking cannabis could expect to be expelled.

Boarding All sixth form in single or double studies, most of rest in bedrooms of 6 or less. Pupils divided into different single-sex houses by age group. 45–90 in each house. Resident qualified medical staff. Central dining rooms. Pupils can provide and cook their own snacks. 3 exeats each term. Visits to the local town allowed.

Alumni association is run by John Davies, 17 Ongar Road, Writtle, Chelmsford, Essex, CM1 3NA.

Former pupils Richard Denby (President, The Law Society); Prime Minister of Nepal; numerous academics.

ADCOTE

Adcote School
Little Ness
Near Shrewsbury
Shropshire SY4 2JY
Telephone number 0939 260202

Enquiries/application to the Headmistress

Co-ed
Boys
● Girls
Mixed sixth
● Day
● Boarding

Pupils 140
Upper sixth 6
Termly fees:
Day £1050
Boarding £1770
GSA

WHAT IT'S LIKE

Founded in 1907, it occupies a neo-Tudor grade-one listed building (1879) in a glorious landscaped parkland with a view to the Briedden and south Shropshire hills. An extremely comfortable and well-equipped establishment, a proportion of pupils' parents are on overseas contracts or serving abroad. It provides full travel arrangements for such pupils. It also welcomes a few foreign girls. Being a small school a very friendly and 'family' atmosphere prevails. It gives a sound academic education and a wide range of extra curricular activities in a disciplined and caring community.

SCHOOL PROFILE

Pupils Total 140. Day 75; Boarding 65. Entry age, from 7–sixth form.
Entrance Admission by school's own day of assessment. Not oversubscribed. No special skills or religious requirements. Parents expected to buy text books for A-level pupils. Scholarships/bursaries available for sixth form.
Staff Head Mrs S B Cecchet, in post for 9 years. 14 full time staff, 5 part time. Low turnover.
Academic work GCSE and A-levels. Average size of upper fifth 25; upper sixth 6. *Computing facilities*: 9 computers. Computer Studies a curriculum subject throughout the school. Dyslexia and EFL provisions.
Senior pupils' non-academic activities *Music*: Some pupils learn a musical instrument up to Grade 6 or above and play/sing in school instrumental group/choir and in orchestras/choirs with local HMC schools. *Drama and dance*: Some pupils take part in school productions and to Grade 6 in ESB; others take part in drama productions at neighbouring HMC schools, and participate in the Chester and Cheshire Festivals. Some accepted for Drama School. *Art*: Some pupils take as a non-examined subject, at GCSE and at A-level. Some are accepted for Art School. Some belong to eg the photographic club, ceramic/art club. *Sport*: Lacrosse, netball, gym, dance, tennis, rounders and athletics available. Pupils take part in non-compulsory sport. Some represent county in junior lacrosse team. Other activities include riding, judo and swimming. Driving lessons available.
Careers Careers department; school is member of ISCO. Some pupils go on to degree courses at universities, polytechnics, or CHE.
Uniform School uniform worn except in the sixth form.
Houses/prefects Competitive houses. Prefects and head girl appointed by staff; head of house and house prefects elected by school.
Religion School assembly compulsory. Boarders attend local C of E or RC church.
Social Music, drama and lectures (careers and subject) with local HMC

schools. Organised trips abroad and exchange systems with schools abroad. Pupils allowed to bring own car or bicycle to school. Some meals are formal, others self service. School shop sells books, tuck, uniforms.

Discipline No corporal punishment. Pupils failing to produce homework could expect to have to do it.

Boarding Sixth formers have single or twin study bedrooms, others in rooms of 4–8. No Houses. Resident qualified nurse. Central dining room. Pupils not allowed to provide or cook their own food. Exeats – weekly boarding available. Visits to the local town allowed for seniors.

ALDENHAM

Aldenham School
Elstree
Hertfordshire HD6 3AJ
Telephone number 09276 6131

Enquiries/application to the Headmaster

Co-ed	Pupils 360
• Boys	Upper sixth 65
Girls	Termly fees:
• Mixed sixth	Day £1530
• Day	Boarding £2430
• Boarding	HMC

WHAT IT'S LIKE

Founded in 1597, it occupies its original site, extending now to 135 acres of grounds, playing fields and farm land in the Hertfordshire green belt. Though only 15 miles from London's centre it possesses the 'singular Woods, Underwoods, Hedgerowes, Trees and Ponds, Waters and Fishings in . . . the same P'emysses' described by Richard Platt, the brewer and founder. It retains firm ties with the Worshipful Company of Brewers. Many brewing organisations are generous benefactors. The original Elizabethan buildings were demolished in 1825. Handsome buildings dating from mid-19th century now have numerous modern additions making it very well equipped. The house system operates and it is strong on pastoral and tutorial care and community service. It is very much a Christian foundation and Christian ideals are evident in its structure and life. Theology is taught to all pupils. Being a small school, it enjoys a 'family' atmosphere and there are strong ties with the local community. The school seeks the all round development of its pupils within an environment setting high standards of achievement and mutual responsibility.

SCHOOL PROFILE

Pupils Total, 360. Day 110 (all boys); Boarding 250 (boys 215, girls 35). Entry age, 13+, boys; into the sixth form, boys and girls. 10% are children of former pupils.

Entrance Common entrance and own entrance test used. Oversubscribed. Pupils skilled in sport, music and art welcomed. All religions welcome but attendance at C of E worship is compulsory. Parents expected to buy text books after GCSE level. 35 assisted places. 18 means tested scholarships/bursaries, £1600–£300 per term.

Parents 15+% are doctors, lawyers, etc; 15+% in industry or commerce. 60+% live within 30 miles; 10+% live overseas.

Staff Head M Higginbottom, in post for 5 years. 34 full time staff, 8 part time. Annual turnover 3–4%.

Academic work GCSE and A-levels. Average size of upper fifth 70; upper sixth 65. *O-levels*: on average, 28 pupils in upper fifth pass 1–4 subjects; 22, 5–7 subjects; 20 pass 8+ subjects. *A-levels*: on average, 14 pupils in the upper sixth pass 1 subject; 16, 2 subjects; 26, 3 subjects and 5 pass 4 subjects. On average, 25% take science/engineering A-levels; 50% take arts and humanities; 25% a mixture. Computing, electronics and technology are offered to GCSE/A-level. *Computing facilities*: Lab with 20 BBC-2 computers. All boys take computing in first two years. Extra tuition in English available.

Senior pupils' non-academic activities *Music*: 60 learn a musical instrument, 15 to Grade 6 or above, occasional pupil accepted for Music School; 25 in school orchestra, 30 in choir; 2 in county orchestra. *Drama and dance*: 30+ in school productions; 40 in House productions. *Art*: 10+ take as non-examined subject; 6–10 take A-level. 3–4 accepted for Art School. 10 belong to eg photographic club. *Sport*: Soccer, hockey, cricket, athletics, tennis, fives, squash, fencing, judo, karate, badminton, netball, lacrosse, rounders available. Most pupils take part in non-compulsory sport. Most major games have county representatives; swimming, soccer and cricket for country. Strong school tradition in team games. *Other*: 12 take part in local community schemes. 24 have bronze Duke of Edinburgh's Award, 12 have silver, 3 have gold. 20 junior and 30 senior pupils take part in CCF. Occasional pupils work for national charities. Other activities include a computer club, driving, electronics, chess, stamps, debating etc.

Careers 3 part time careers advisors and Housemasters. Average number of pupils accepted for *arts and humanities degree courses* at Oxbridge, 2; other universities, 9; polytechnics or CHE, 9. *science and engineering degree courses* at Oxbridge, 3; other universities, 5; medical schools, 2; polytechnics or CHE 3. *other general training courses*, 5. Average number of pupils going straight into careers in armed services, 2; the church, 1; industry, 2; the City, 6; insurance/advertising/computing/retail, 6.

Uniform School uniform worn throughout.

Houses/prefects Non-competitive houses. Prefects, head boy, head of house and house prefects appointed by the Head.

Religion Religious worship is compulsory.

Social Involvement in local competitions, joint events etc with local schools. Organised trips abroad and exchange systems eg ski-ing, sailing, geography, language. Day boys allowed to bring own car. Meals self service. School shop. No tobacco allowed; sixth form bar for over 17s.

Discipline No corporal punishment. Pupils failing to produce homework once might expect to be reported to Tutor/Housemaster; those caught smoking cannabis on the premises could expect expulsion.

Boarding Few pupils have own study bedroom; most are in dormitories of 6 or more. Accommodation houses are mixed sex in the sixth form. Resident qualified nurse. Central dining room. Pupils can provide and cook some food. Exeats every Sunday and two weekends a term. Half-day visits to the local town allowed.

Alumni association is run by J K Waddell, Aldenham School, Elstree, Hertfordshire.

Former pupils Bishops of Winchester and Exeter; Lord Justice Kerr; Sir Richard Vincent; N Durden-Smith.

ALICE OTTLEY

The Alice Ottley School		Co-ed	Pupils 565
The Tything		Boys	Upper sixth Yes
Worcester	●	Girls	Termly fees:
Worcestershire WR1 1HW		Mixed sixth	Day £775
Telephone number 0905 27061	●	Day	Boarding £1525
	●	Boarding	GSA; GBGSA

Head Miss C Sibbit (2 years)
Age range 11–18; own junior school nearby. Entry by common entrance or own exam
Scholarships available.

ALLEYN'S

Alleyn's School	●	Co-ed	Pupils 920
Townley Road		Boys	Upper sixth 128
Dulwich		Girls	Termly fees:
London SE22 8SU		Mixed sixth	£1080
Telephone number 01-693 3422	●	Day	HMC
		Boarding	

Enquiries/application to the Headmaster

WHAT IT'S LIKE

Founded in 1619, endowed by Edward Alleyn the Elizabethan actor-manager, it occupies a single site in South London on 26 acres of fine grounds and playing fields. Very accessible on public transport. The main buildings date from 1887. Numerous additions (especially since 1961) provide excellent facilities of all kinds to a school which, academically and intellectually, is one of the foremost in southern England. A first-rate traditional education is provided, and it is strong in music, drama and art. As a C of E foundation there is a certain emphasis on religious education, but of an ecumenical kind. Particular attention is given to pupils with individual needs, including those with slight physical handicaps. It is highly regarded in the locality where it enjoys vigorous support.

SCHOOL PROFILE

Pupils Total over 12, 920 (boys 459, girls 461). Entry age, 11+, 13+ and into sixth. 5% are children of former pupils.
Entrance Own entrance exam used. Oversubscribed. No special skills or religious requirements; any welcomed. Parents not expected to buy text-

books. 196 assisted places. 15 scholarships/bursaries available, two-thirds to one-third fees.

Parents 100% live within 30 miles.

Staff Head D A Fenner, in post for 12 years. 80 full time staff, 2 part time. Annual turnover 5–6%. Average age 39.

Academic work Pupils prepared for GCSE and A-levels. Average size of fifth, 125; upper sixth, 128. *O-levels*: on average, 18 pupils in upper fifth pass 1–4 subjects; 45, 5–7 subjects; 70 pass 8+ subjects. *A-levels*: on average, 10 pupils in the upper sixth pass 1 subject; 17, 2 subjects; 58, 3 subjects and 13 pass 4 subjects. On average, 36 take science/engineering A-levels; 60 take arts and humanities; 32 a mixture. Theatre Studies is offered to GCSE/A-level. *Computing facilities*: 12 station BBC network; 6 stand-alone BBC and six for teaching. DEC PDP 11, running 5 terminals; 2 Apple Mac word processors for administration.

Senior pupils' non-academic activities *Music*: 300 learn a musical instrument, 50 up to Grade 6 or above, 2 accepted for Music School; 120 pupils each in school orchestra/choir; 1 in National Youth Orchestra. *Drama and dance*: 40 in school productions; 2 accepted for Drama School. *Art*: 35 take GCSE; 12 take A-level; 3 accepted for Art School. 10 belong to eg photographic club. *Sport*: Football, hockey, cricket, athletics, tennis, swimming, rugby-fives, badminton, basketball, fencing, judo, netball, gymnastics available. 100 take non-compulsory sport. 10 take exams eg in gymnastics, swimming. 9 represent county (gym, swimming, hockey, netball, football, athletics, cross-country). *Other*: 25 take part in local community schemes. 24 have bronze Duke of Edinburgh's Award and 24 have gold. 5 enter voluntary schemes after leaving school. Other activities include computer, bridge and chess clubs, debating society, CCF.

Careers 5 part time careers advisors. Average number of pupils accepted for *arts and humanities degree courses* at Oxbridge, 6; other universities 40; polytechnics or CHE, 10. *science and engineering degree courses* at Oxbridge, 5; other universities, 20; medical schools, 3; polytechnics or CHE, 3. *BEd*, 2. *other general training courses*, 12. Average number of pupils going straight into careers in armed services, 3; industry, 6; the City, 8; civil service, 5. Strong tradition of pupils taking up acting careers.

Uniform School uniform worn, except sixth form.

Houses/prefects Competitive houses. Prefects, head boy/girl (School Captain), head of house (House Captain) and house prefects appointed by the Headmaster in consultation with housemasters. School Council.

Religion Assemblies broad Anglican. Parents may withdraw pupils.

Social Occasional joint careers conferences, general election debates with other schools. Regular organised holiday visits to eg Russia; exchanges with French and German schools. Pupils allowed to bring own car/bicycle/motorbike to school. Meals self service. School shop. No tobacco/alcohol allowed.

Discipline No corporal punishment. Detentions are given for bad work and bad behaviour; those caught in possession of illegal drugs on the premises can expect expulsion.

Alumni association is run by P J Reeve, 33 Carver Road, London SE24.

Former pupils Julian Glover; Simon Ward, John Stride (actors); Stuart Blanch, former Archbishop of York.

ALL HALLOWS (DITCHINGHAM)

All Hallows	Co-ed	Pupils 99
Ditchingham	Boys	Upper sixth 10
Bungay	● Girls	Termly fees:
Suffolk NR35 2DU	Mixed sixth	Day £950
Telephone number 0986 2133	● Day	Boarding £1505
	● Boarding	GSA; SHA
Enquiries/application to the Headmistress		

WHAT IT'S LIKE

Founded in 1864 by the Church of England community which bears its name. It is a single-site purpose-built school in delightful countryside on the edge of the village of Ditchingham, very near Bungay and Beccles (both of historical interest) and 10 miles from Norwich. It has large grounds and beautiful gardens. The original house has been extended and many first-rate modern facilities provided (including refectory, libraries, common rooms, study-bedrooms, gymnasium, heated swimming pool and dormitories). There is a high staff/pupil ratio. It is deliberately a small 'family' school and, because of its links with the convent importance is attached to Christian worship and values.

SCHOOL PROFILE

Pupils Total over 12, 99. Day 49; Boarding 50. Entry age, 5 and into sixth form. 10% are children of former pupils. Own prep school of 70 provides more than 20%.

Entrance Own entrance exam used. Not oversubscribed. No special skills or religious requirements. Parents not expected to buy text books. Scholarships/bursaries are available on application, up to 50% of fees.

Parents 15+% in industry or commerce; 15+% in farming; 15+% in the Church. 30+% live within 30 miles; up to 10% live overseas.

Staff Head Miss A C Harris, in post for 4 years. 13 full time staff, 11 part time. Low annual turnover. Average age 35.

Academic work GCSE and A-levels. Average size of upper fifth 30, upper sixth 10; career sixth 7. *O-levels*: on average, 16 pupils in upper fifth pass 1–4 subjects; 11, 5–7 subjects; 4 pass 8+ subjects. *A-levels*: on average, 2 pupils in the upper sixth pass 1 subject; 2, 2 subjects; 4, 3 subjects. On average, 4 take science/engineering A-levels; 4 take arts and humanities; 2 a mixture. *Computing and office training facilities*: BBC and RML computers, plus trained computer staff. Some EFL provision. Weekly work experience for career sixth.

Senior pupils' non-academic activities *Music*: 5 learn one or more musical instruments in school, 2 to Grade 6 or above, 1 accepted for Music School; 8 in school orchestra, 20 in choir. *Drama and dance*: 20 pupils participate in school productions; 2 accepted for Drama Schools. *Art*: 14 pupils take GCSE art; 1 A-level; 2 accepted for Art School. *Sport*: Horse riding, canoeing, tennis, hockey, netball, swimming, gymnastics, rounders, athletics available. 24 take non-compulsory sport. 35 take exams in eg gymnastics, swimming. 2 represent county (hockey). *Other*: 18 take part in local community schemes. 20 have bronze Duke of Edinburgh's Award. Other activities include a computer club, animal club, German speaking club, learning to drive, self defence, life saving, first aid.

Careers 1 full time, 1 part time careers advisors. Average number of pupils accepted for *arts and humanities degree courses* at universities, 5; polytechnics or CHE, 3. *science and engineering degree courses* at universities, 2. *other general training courses*, 10. On average, 1 pupil goes straight into a career in armed services.

Uniform School uniform worn except in sixth form.

Houses/prefects Competitive houses. No prefects; Head girl appointed by the Head; head of houses by Head and school. School Food Committee.

Religion Compulsory religious worship.

Social Lectures, theatre visits, dances, shared classes (woodwork and cookery) with local schools. Organised trips abroad and exchanges. Pupils allowed to bring own car to school. Meals formal. School shop. No tobacco or alcohol allowed.

Discipline Maintained by carefully structured pastoral care system culminating in the Headmistress. Expulsion would result from any evidence of drugs.

Boarding Senior girls have own study bedroom, others share. Separate sixth form house. Resident qualified nurse; doctor on call. Central dining room. Sixth formers can provide and cook own food in. 2 fixed exeats most terms, others on request. Visits to the local town allowed (Saturdays) 14+.

Alumni association is run by Miss A C Harris, c/o the School.

Former pupils Rosemary Harris (actress).

ALLHALLOWS (LYME REGIS)

Allhallows School
Rousdon
Lyme Regis
Dorset
DT7 3RA

Telephone number 0297 20444

- Co-ed
  Boys
  Girls
  Mixed sixth
- Day
- Boarding

Pupils 290
Upper sixth Yes
Termly fees:
Day £980
Boarding £2100
HMC

WHAT IT'S LIKE

The date of foundation is unknown but it was well established by 1524. It occupies an unusually magnificent site on the Devon–Dorset coast, near Lyme Regis, which comprises 350 acres of playing fields, agricultural land and a nature reserve. The cliffs below are geologically unique in the south. The fine buildings are a combination of the old and brand new. There are 7 houses (a separate house for 50 girls) with 45 boys in each. The environment is healthy and invigorating and very well suited to outdoor pursuits. The staff:pupil ratio is about 1:11. A sound general education is provided and results are very good. The sixth form is large (about 130 pupils) and many leavers go on to further education. About half proceed to degree or equivalent courses; about a third go to the services, agriculture and further education colleges. The school has considerable strength in music, drama and art. Quite a lot of pupils go on to art college. There is a fine range of sports and games and standards are high. Outdoor pursuits include fishing, abseiling, climbing and canoeing. There is much emphasis on hobbies. One afternoon a week all junior pupils must join one or more of the activities on offer: bird watching, entomology, auto-engineering, carpentry, judo, chess and so forth. The CCF contingent is large and service for 2 years is compulsory. There is also an auxiliary coast-guard cliff rescue team trained by the local coastguards. The school is rather unusual in possessing an astronomical observatory, a meteorological satellite and a video-film unit. There is a big commitment to local community services.

SCHOOL PROFILE

Head Peter Larkman (5 years)
Age range 13–18; entry by common entrance or interview
8% of pupils are from overseas. Academic, music, art and service scholarships.

AMPLEFORTH

Ampleforth College
York YO6 4ER
Telephone number 043 93 224

Enquiries/application to the Headmaster

Co-ed
● Boys
Girls
Mixed sixth
Day
● Boarding

Pupils 620
Upper sixth 120
Termly fees:
Boarding £2330
HMC

WHAT IT'S LIKE

Established at Ampleforth in 1802, the school adjoins the Benedictine monastery and abbey of St Laurence in a stretch of magnificent Yorkshire countryside a mile from the local village. The monastic community are the 'descendants' of the monks who, in 1608, founded a monastery at Dieulouard in Lorraine. The headmaster and some of the teaching staff are monks. The main purpose is to educate Catholics in their faith and in all branches of learning. The boarding houses are scattered over a big site and provide comfortable accommodation. Many first-rate modern facilities. A very good education is given and academic results are excellent (60–70% university entrants each year). An unusually strong music staff; musical activities play a major role in the life of the school. Games and outdoor pursuits are very popular; standards are high. As it's a Catholic school discipline is somewhat tighter than elsewhere and the way of life is marginally more ascetic and rigorous. The preparatory department is at Gilling Castle, two miles from the College.

SCHOOL PROFILE

Pupils Total over 12, 620. Entry age, 10+, 13+ and into the sixth form. About 30% are children of former pupils.
Entrance Common entrance and own entrance exam used. No special skills required but should be Roman Catholic. 12–14 scholarships, up to half fees. Also a number of bursaries.

Parents 15+% are doctors, lawyers etc; 15+% in industry and commerce. Up to 10% live within 30 miles; up to 10% live overseas.

Staff Head Reverend D L Milroy, in post for 8 years. 90 full time staff, 7 part time.

Academic work GCSE and A-levels. Average size of upper fifth 120; upper sixth 120. *O-levels*: on average, 75 pupils in upper fifth pass 1–4 subjects; 45, 5–7 subjects (all took 3 to 6 the previous year). *A-levels*: on average, 10 pupils in the upper sixth pass 1 subject; 20, 2 subjects; 80, 3 subjects and 10 pass 4 subjects. On average, 30 take science/engineering A-levels; 70 take arts and humanities; 20 a mixture. Electronic systems, Portuguese and Modern Standard Chinese are offered to GCSE and/or A-level. *Computing facilities*: An ECO-network of BBC micros plus several free-standing micros in use in maths classroom. Special provisions for eg mild handicap, learning difficulties and EFL.

Senior pupils' non-academic activities *Music*: 178 learn a musical instrument, 26 up to Grade 6 or above, 4 accepted to read music at university; 90 in school orchestra, 104 in choir. *Drama and dance*: 50 take part in school productions. 15 take GCSE Drama; 15 sixth form take History of Theatre; 25 take other drama/dance exams. 2 a year accepted for drama/dance schools; 2 go on to work in theatre; 2 into National Youth Theatre. *Art*: 35 take as non-examined subject; 22 take A-level. 6 accepted for art school; 5 for architectural school. 20 take art as a leisure activity; 45 belong to eg photographic club. *Sport*: Rugby, cricket, hockey, tennis, swimming, squash, badminton available. 300 take part in non-compulsory sport. 12 take bronze medallion life saving; 60 BAGA gymnastic awards. 6 represent county (cricket, rugby); 4 represent country (cricket, rugby under-19). *Other*: School has links with Cheshire Homes, Children's Home and other local needs. 10 pupils have bronze Duke of Edinburgh's Award, 10 have silver and 8 gold. 12 have Red Cross Adult, 12 Youth certificates. Other activities include debating societies, historical bench, archaeological society, modern languages, bridge, chess and computer clubs.

Careers 1 full time, 1 part time careers advisor. Average number of pupils accepted for *arts and humanities degree courses* at Oxbridge, 10; other universities, 50; polytechnics or CHE, 20. *science and engineering degree courses* at Oxbridge, 4; other universities, 12; medical schools, 2. BEd, 2. *other general training courses*, 5. Average number of pupils going straight into careers in armed services, 8; industry, 7; the City, 2; civil service, 1; other, 4.

Uniform None, though jacket and tie required (suit on Sundays).

Houses/prefects Competitive houses. Prefects and head boy – appointed by the Headmaster; head of house and house prefects – appointed by Housemasters.

Religion Compulsory religious worship.

Social Theatrical and choral productions and debates with other schools. Regular exchanges with 2 schools in France and Germany. Schola Tours; ski-ing, climbing etc abroad. Pupils allowed to bring own bicycle to school. Meals formal. School shop. No alcohol/tobacco allowed.

Discipline No corporal punishment. All punishments are dependent on circumstances.

Boarding 20% have own study bedroom, 20% share with 2–3; 60% are in dormitories of 6 or more. Houses of 60+. Local doctor and resident nursing staff. No central dining room – boys eat in own Houses. Sixth form can provide and cook some own food. 2 weekend exeats each term and half term in the autumn. Visits to local towns allowed.

Alumni association is run by The Secretary, The Ampleforth Society, Ampleforth Abbey, York YO6 4ER.

ARDINGLY

Ardingly College
Ardingly
Haywards Heath
West Sussex RH17 6SQ
Telephone number 0444 892 577

Enquiries/application to the Registrar

- Co-ed
  Boys
  Girls
  Mixed sixth
- Day
- Boarding

Pupils 471
Upper sixth 85
Termly fees:
Day £1830
Boarding £2340
Woodard

WHAT IT'S LIKE

Founded in 1858, it lies in one of the most beautiful parts of Sussex on a big estate. At the heart of its handsome buildings is the chapel. As a Woodard school it caters for and appeals to those seeking a C of E education. It has its own junior school, a mix of boarding/day co-ed and the aim is very much to be a 'family' school. One of its prides is the fine pastoral system based on individual tutors for each pupil. It offers a good all-round education, music, art and drama, the CCF and a very well-organised house system; plus a lot of emphasis on outdoor activities. Practical skills are encouraged. It has a reputation for good teaching and a highly creditable academic record.

SCHOOL PROFILE

Pupils Total over 13, 471. Day 113 (boys 64, girls 49); Boarding 358 (boys 273, girls 85). Entry age, 13+, 14+ and into sixth form. Own Junior School provides 30%. 7% are children of former pupils.

Entrance Common entrance and own entrance exam used. No special skills but pupils expected to be in sympathy with aims and ethos of C of E. Approx 25 scholarships/bursaries, full fees to instrumental tuition fees.

Parents 30+% live within 30 miles; 10+% live overseas.

Staff Head J W Flecker, in post for 7 years. 65 full time staff, 25 part time. Annual turnover 10%. Average age 32.

Academic work GCSE and A-levels. Average size of upper fifth 100; upper sixth 85. *O-levels*: on average, 30 pupils in upper fifth pass 1–4 subjects; 30, 5–7 subjects; 40 pass 8+ subjects. *A-levels*: on average, 10 pupils in the upper sixth pass 1 subject; 20, 2 subjects; 50, 3 subjects and 5 pass 4 subjects. On average, 15 take science/engineering A-levels; 40 take arts and humanities; 30 a mixture of both. Archaeology is offered to A-level. *Computing facilities*: Specialist computer room – UNIX system. Several micros. Two main computers each with 8 terminals and 24 Nimbus. PASCAL, 'C' and PROLOG available.

Senior pupils' non-academic activities *Music*: 200 learn a musical instrument, 72 up to Grade 6 or above, 2 accepted for Music School; 50 in school orchestra, 55 in choir, some in pop group. Chamber music, choral society and band available. *Drama and dance*: 150–200 participate in school productions. 2 accepted for Drama Schools; 2 go on to work in theatre. *Art*: Many take as non-examined subject; 32 take GCSE; 24 A-level. 7 accepted for Art School. *Sport*: Soccer, rugby, hockey, tennis, cricket, netball, volleyball, squash, swimming, cross-country, athletics, sailing, lacrosse available. 30 take part in non-compulsory sport. 1 representation at Public Schools' soccer. *Other*: Numerous other activities including chess, learning to drive, computers.

Careers 4 part time careers advisors and 1 professional consultant. Average number of pupils accepted for *arts and humanities degree courses* at Oxbridge, 2; other universities, 11; polytechnics or CHE, 5. *science and engineering degree courses* at Oxbridge, 3; other universities, 11; medical schools, 1; polytechnics or CHE, 5. *BEd*, 1. *other general training courses*, 8. Average number of pupils going straight into careers in armed services, 3; the church, 1; industry, 5; the City, 5; civil service, 1; music/drama, 3; other, 10.

Uniform School uniform worn except in sixth form.

Houses/prefects Competitive houses. Prefects, head boy/girl, head of house and house prefects – appointed after consultation.

Religion Compulsory religious studies and chapel attendance.

Social Continuous contact with local schools. Exchange with schools in Toulouse (annual), and Heidelberg (sporadic). Many other organised trips abroad. Day pupils allowed to bring own car/bicycle to school. Meals self service. School shop. No tobacco allowed; alcohol in supervised bar.

Discipline No corporal punishment. Pupils failing to produce homework once might expect to be asked why; those caught smoking cannabis on the premises could expect instant expulsion.

Boarding 40% have own study bedroom or share with 1 other; 60% in dormitories of 6 or more. Houses of 50, single-sex, except for new Upper Sixth House. 2 resident qualified nurses. Central dining room. Pupils can provide and cook some own food. 2–5/24 hour exeats each term, plus half term (3–5 days) and days out. Visits to the local town allowed when free, to 6.30 (4.30 in winter).

Alumni association R C Munyard, FCA, c/o Touche Ross & Co, Hill House, 1 Little New Street, London EC4A 3TR.

Former pupils Terry Thomas; Dr Hayes (Director of National Portrait Gallery); Cdr Longhurst (potential astronaut); Ian Hislop (Private Eye); Stephen Oliver (composer); Andrew Bowden and T Gorst (MPs).

ARNOLD

Arnold School	● Co-ed	Pupils 594
Lytham Road	Boys	Upper sixth 95
Blackpool	Girls	Termly fees:
Lancashire FY4 1JG	Mixed sixth	Day £679
Telephone number 0253 46391	● Day	Boarding £1360
	● Boarding	HMC
Enquiries/application to the Headmaster		

WHAT IT'S LIKE

Founded in 1896, situated in Blackpool half a mile from the sea. It has adequate buildings and nearby playing fields. Considerable expansion in recent years has provided good up-to-date facilities. The aim is to inculcate 'lasting values of service, loyalty and self-discipline' in the belief that these are increasingly vital. Religious worship is encouraged and religious assemblies are compulsory. It is strong on music and in general has a reputation for sound traditional academic training, and its records are creditable. Throughout its life it has played a prominent part in the life of the Fylde and Blackpool. Strong back-up from old Arnoldians. A bonus is the outdoor pursuits centre at Glenriding, described as 'a classroom in the Lake District'.

SCHOOL PROFILE

Pupils Total over 12, 594. Day 538 (boys 337, girls 201); Boarding 56 (boys 30, girls 26). Entry age, 11+ and into the sixth. Own Junior School provides 40%. 10% are children of former pupils.

Entrance Common entrance and own entrance exam used. Oversubscribed. No special skills or religious requirements. Parents not expected to buy text books. 55 assisted places. 8 scholarships/bursaries, £300–£800.

Parents 15% in hotel/tourism. 60+% live within 30 miles; up to 10% live overseas.

Staff Head J A B Kelsall, in post for 1 year. 57 full time staff, 4 part time. Annual turnover 2%. Average age 43.

Academic work GCSE and A-levels. Average size of upper fifth 100; upper sixth 95. *O-levels*: on average, 4 pupils in upper fifth pass 1–4 subjects; 47, 5–7 subjects; 50 pass 8+ subjects. *A-levels*: on average, 7 pupils in the upper sixth pass 1 subject; 11, 2 subjects; 15, 3 subjects and 49 pass 4 subjects. On average, 50 take science/engineering A-levels; 30 take arts and humanities; 5 mixture of both. Law A-level offered. *Computing facilities*: Computer room (16 BBCs – networked), 8 departmental computers, one Weatherstat Satellite Dish. Specialist dyslexic teacher.

Senior pupils' non-academic activities *Music*: 130 learn a musical instrument, 10 up to Grade 6 or above, 2 accepted for Music School; 40 in school orchestra, 6 in school pop group, 80+ in choir, 20 in wind band, 14 in dance band; others in Lancashire Schools Symphony Orchestra, wind band and dance band. 30 play in pop groups; 2 in hit parade. One manager of Sex Pistols/co-founder of Virgin Records. *Drama and dance*: 140 in school productions. 60 in outside productions. 1 accepted for drama/dance school; 2 go on to work in the theatre. *Art*: 4 take as non-examined subject; 16 GCSE; 6 A-level; 3 A-level photography. 3 accepted for Art School; 2 for architecture. 7 take ceramics allied to CDT. Ceramics option available. *Sport*: Rugby, hockey, netball, cricket, athletics, cross-country, squash, swimming, badminton, golf, tennis available. 150 take non-compulsory sport. 30 take exams in life saving. Many represent county (athletics, hockey, rugby, badminton). 1 Cambridge Blue, 1 England rugby international. *Other*: 35 take part in local community schemes (6th form games option). 67 have bronze Duke of Edinburgh's Award, 23 have silver and 20 gold. 3 enter voluntary schemes after leaving school. Other activities include a computer club, chess club, book-shop, CCF, CDT club.

Careers 1 full time and 3 part time careers advisors. Average number of pupils accepted for *arts and humanities degree courses* at Oxbridge, 3; other universities, 16; polytechnics or CHE, 4. *science and engineering degree courses* at Oxbridge, 5; other universities, 22; medical schools, 3; polytechnics or CHE, 8. *other general training courses*, 3. Average number of pupils going straight into careers in armed services, 4; industry/commerce, 8; civil service, 2; music/drama, 1; other, 8.

Uniform School uniform worn throughout.

Houses/prefects Competitive houses. Prefects, head boy/girl, head of house and house prefects – appointed by the Head and school.

Religion Encouraged (religious assemblies are compulsory).

Social Debates, concerts, visits etc with local schools. Organised trips abroad for French, German, geology, geography; hockey tour of Holland, rugby tour of Canada. Pupils allowed to bring own car/motorbike/bicycle to school. Meals self service. School shop. No tobacco/alcohol allowed.

Discipline No corporal punishment. Pupils failing to produce homework once might expect a homework detention. Those caught smoking cannabis on the premises could expect expulsion.

Boarding 17% have own study bedroom, 73% share; 10% are in dormitories of 6+. Houses, of 15–36, are divided by age group, single sex. Resident qualified nurse. Central dining room. Pupils can provide and cook own food. 3 weekend exeats each term. Visits to the local town allowed.

Alumni association is run by J M Hartley, 97–99 Central Drive, Blackpool FY1 5EE.

Former pupils David Ball (Soft Cell); Chris Lowe (Pet Shop Boys); J Armfield; G Eastham; Sir Walter Clegg MP; Peter Boydell QC; T Graveney; Stanley Matthews (Junior tennis).

Arts Educational (London)

The Arts Educational Schools
Cone Ripman House
14 Bath Road
London W4
Telephone number 01-994 9366

Enquiries/application to the Registrar

- Co-ed
- Boys
- Girls
- Mixed sixth
- Day
- Boarding

Pupils 160
Upper sixth Yes
Termly fees:
Day £1132

WHAT IT'S LIKE

Founded in 1919, it occupies a single site in a pleasant residential area of West London. Well-designed buildings and good facilities. It is a school for the specific training of boys and girls in the performing arts. There is a balanced curriculum in academic and vocational disciplines in the performing arts for pupils aged 11–16. It also offers post-16 courses, a 3-year dance course, a 3-year musical theatre course, a 2-year creative arts A-level course, a 3-year adult drama course and a 1-year postgraduate acting course for mature students. Naturally, everyone is involved in dance, music and drama. There is a large staff of 42 for 160 pupils, plus 120 visiting teachers. Societies, extra-curricular activities and frequent participation in national events concerned with the performing arts. The Arts Educational Schools at both London and Tring are run by the same Trust.

SCHOOL PROFILE

Pupils Total, 160 (boys 32, girls 128). Entry age, 11, and into sixth.

Entrance Own entrance exam used based on national tests. Not oversubscribed. Special skills in dance and drama required; no religious requirements. Some assisted places. 6 scholarships/bursaries, up to full fees.

Parents 60+% live within 30 miles.

Staff Head Peter Fowler, in post for 2 years. 42 full time staff, 120 part time. Annual turnover (part time) 10%. Average age 40.

Academic work GCSE and A-levels. Average size of upper fifth 32, in small teaching groups. *O-levels*: on average, 24 pupils in upper fifth pass 1–4 subjects; 8 pass 5–7 subjects. *Computing facilities* available in maths department, and for administrative staff.

Senior pupils' non-academic activities *Music*: 80 learn a musical instrument, 5 to Grade 6 or above; 20 in school orchestra, all sing in school choirs; many in English National Opera chorus and perform on radio and TV. *Drama and dance*: Whole school participates in productions; many take up to Grade 6 in ESB, RAD etc; 90% accepted for Drama and Dance schools. Many dance with London Festival Ballet and other major companies and on film and television. *Art*: 19 take GCSE art. *Sport*: Local leisure centre used.

Careers Most pupils go into careers in music and drama.

Uniform School uniform worn except in sixth.

Houses/prefects No competitive houses. Prefects, head boy and girl, selected by staff.

Religion No compulsory worship.

Social Organised local events occasionally. Pupils allowed to bring own bicycle to school. Meals self service. No tobacco/alcohol allowed.

Discipline No corporal punishment. Pupils failing to produce homework or committing other infringements might expect a black mark or detention.

Former pupils Large number of well-known names including Julie Andrews; Claire Bloom; Leslie Crowther; Nigel Havers; Glynis Johns; Margaret Lockwood; Sarah Miles; Jane Seymour; Antoinette Sibley; Teresa Jarvis; Seth Gilber; Catherine Becque; Finola Hughes; Sarah Brightman; Josephine Campbell.

ARTS EDUCATIONAL (TRING)

The Arts Educational Schools
Tring Park
Tring
Hertfordshire HP23 5LX
Telephone number 044 282 4255

Co-ed
Boys
● Girls
Mixed sixth
● Day
● Boarding

Pupils 320
Upper sixth Yes
Termly fees:
Day £918
Boarding £1545
SHMIS

Head Mrs M I Jack (35 years)
Age range 9–18; entry by audition and test
Specialises in dance and drama training. Sister school in Chiswick, London.

ASHFORD

Ashford School
East Hill
Ashford
Kent TN24 8PB
Telephone number 0233 625171

Enquiries/application to the Headmistress

Co-ed
Boys
● Girls
Mixed sixth
● Day
● Boarding

Pupils 482
Upper sixth 60
Termly fees:
Day £839
Boarding £1466
GSA

WHAT IT'S LIKE

Founded in 1898, it occupies 23 acres of very pleasant grounds in the town, together with land bordering the Stour. The oldest building is the 16th-century Alfred House. Expansion has incorporated neighbouring houses and much accommodation is now purpose-built. There are many excellent modern facilities and results are good. It is strong on music and drama and has a well-organised house system. Being an urban school it has plentiful local ties and is well supported by the community. There is a pronounced sense of service to the town (eg helping the handicapped and elderly et al).

SCHOOL PROFILE

Pupils Total over 12, 482. Day 287; Boarding 195. Entry age, 11 and into sixth. Own junior school provides 50%. 4–5% are children of former pupils.
Entrance Own entrance exam used. Oversubscribed in some areas. No special skills or religious requirements. Parents expected to buy sixth form text books. 41 assisted places. 4–6 scholarships/bursaries (including 1 music) £839–£420.
Parents 15+% are doctors, lawyers, farmers, etc; 15+% in industry or commerce. 30+% live within 30 miles; 10+% live overseas.
Staff Head Mrs A T D Macaire, in post for 3 years. 50 full time staff, 6 part time (plus music). Annual turnover 4%. Average age 44.
Academic work GCSE and A-levels. Average size of upper fifth 86; upper sixth 60 (and expanding). *O-levels*: on average, 10 pupils in upper fifth pass 1–4 subjects; 29, 5–7 subjects; 47 pass 8+ subjects. *A-levels*: on average, 6

pupils in the upper sixth pass 1 subject; 12, 2 subjects; 24, 3 subjects and 6 pass 4 subjects. On average, 15 take science/engineering A-levels; 20 take arts and humanities; 13 a mixture. Ancient Greek offered to GCSE/A-level. *Computing facilities*: 4 BBC Bs and 10 BBC B+s in computer centre and 2 printers (+ 2 old Research 3802). 1 BBC in the science wing (plus printer, plotters, 2nd processor, bit-stick, modem). Special provisions on an ad hoc basis for dyslexia etc.

Senior pupils' non-academic activities   *Music*: 131 learn a musical instrument, 11 up to Grade 6 or above, 2 involved in music after leaving; 21 in school orchestra, 90 in choir, 13 in band, 10 in recorder groups. *Drama and dance*: 25–30 in school productions; 10 to Grade 6 in ESB; 2 accepted for Drama Schools, 1 each into alternative theatre and TV. Private lessons taken by 25–30, 50 in House drama competitions, 15 in eg Kent Festival. *Art*: 5 take as non-examined subject; 25 take GCSE; 8, A-level; 4 accepted for Art School, 1 for history of art at university. *Sport*: Hockey, netball, swimming, tennis, rounders, athletics, squash, badminton, trampolining, judo, ballet, dance, modern dance, gym available. 75+ take non-compulsory sport. (50 go horse-riding etc outside school). 40+ in school teams. 20+ take exams. 4 represent county (squash, tennis, hockey, swimming). *Other*: 60+ take part in local community schemes. 150 have bronze Duke of Edinburgh's Award, 7 have silver and 28, gold. 20 enter voluntary schemes after leaving. Other activities include a computer club, debating and public speaking (various competitions), bridge club (inter-school matches), science club, outdoor pursuits, riding at weekends, visits etc.

Careers 1 full time advisor and fortnightly careers talks. Average number of pupils accepted for *arts and humanities degree courses* at Oxbridge, 2; other universities, 9; polytechnics or CHE, 6. *science and engineering degree courses* at Oxbridge, 3; other universities, 8; medical school, 3. BEd, 2. *other general training courses*, 9. Average number of pupils going straight into careers in armed services, 1; industry, 1; the City, 1; civil service, 1; music/drama, 1–2. Traditional school careers include medicine, engineering, veterinary surgery.

Uniform School uniform worn except in sixth form.

Houses/prefects Competitive houses. Prefects, 2 head girls (one day, one boarding), head of house and house prefects elected by girls, staff and Head.

Religion Compulsory, non-denominational Christian-based assembly and religious education. Borders attend Parish Church. Confirmation classes available.

Social Many joint events with local schools, eg productions and debates, local guitar orchestra, host discos, formal sixth form supper dance etc. Annual ski trip, Mediterranean cruise; many others eg Russia and Israel in 1988. Pupils allowed to bring own car/motorbike to school. Meals self service. No tobacco/alcohol allowed.

Discipline No corporal punishment. Pupils failing to produce homework once might expect a reprimand; those caught smoking cannabis on the premises can expect to be expelled.

Boarding 16% have own study bedroom, 20% share, 38% are in dormitories of 6 or more. Houses, of 45–60, are the same as competitive houses. Resident qualified nurse. Weekly doctor's surgery. Central dining room. Sixth formers can provide and cook own food. Exeats each term: 2 weekends, 3 single days, half-term. Visits to the local town allowed (accompanied to 13; daily in sixth).

Alumni association is run by Mrs A Preisig, Impkins Farm, Charing, Ashford, Kent.
Former pupils Pamela Armstrong (ITV newscaster).

ASHVILLE

Ashville College
Harrogate
North Yorkshire HG2 9JR
Telephone number 0423 66358

Enquiries/application to the Headmaster

- Co-ed
  Boys
  Girls
  Mixed sixth
- Day
- Boarding

Pupils 391
Upper sixth 60
Termly fees:
Day £888
Boarding £1633
HMC

WHAT IT'S LIKE

Founded in 1877 by the United Methodist Free Church, it has incorporated two other non-Conformist schools: Emfield College and New College. It owns a fine estate of 45 acres 600 feet above sea level on the south side of the spa town. During the 1970s extensive additions were made and it now possesses many excellent facilities. It is kept fairly small deliberately to 'preserve the benefits of life in a family community'. Religious services are compulsory but the religious 'ethos' is ecumenical. Culturally, there is close rapport with the town; and there is a good deal of emphasis on outdoor activities (eg fishing, fell walking and rock climbing). Its academic record is very sound and it has a distinguished reputation in Harrogate.

SCHOOL PROFILE

Pupils Total over 12, 391. Day 250 (boys 146, girls 104); Boarding 141 (boys 110, girls 31). Entry age, 7, 11, 13 and into sixth. Own junior school provides 20%.
Entrance Common entrance and own entrance exam used. Sometimes oversubscribed. No special skills or religious requirements but school is methodist. Parents not expected to buy text books. 106 scholarships/bursaries, £585–£163.
Parents 15+% in industry or commerce. 60+% live within 30 miles; up to 10% live overseas.
Staff Head M H Crosby, in post for 1 year. 44 full time staff, 13 part time. Annual turnover 5%. Average age about 40.
Academic work GCSE and A-levels. Average size of upper fifth 66; upper sixth 60. *O-levels*: on average, 24 pupils in upper fifth pass 1–4 subjects; 21, 5–7 subjects; 20 pass 8+ subjects. *A-levels*: on average, 7 pupils in the upper sixth pass 1 subject; 8, 2 subjects; 7, 3 subjects and 15 pass 4 subjects. On average, 11 take science/engineering A-levels; 22 take arts and humanities; 8 a mixture. *Computing facilities*: Computer Room with 12 BBC computers and some in other departments. Links with the Dyslexia Institute in Harrogate; help for occasional foreign students with linguistic difficulties.
Senior pupils' non-academic activities *Music*: 120 learn a musical instrument, 4 up to Grade 6 or above; 45 in school orchestra, 110 in choir. *Drama*

and dance: 150 in school productions. 1 accepted for Drama School, 1 to work in theatre. 30 in workshop production, 2 take Guildhall acting exam. *Art*: 200 take as non-examined subject; 20 GCSE; 10 A-level; 5 accepted for Art School, 2 for architecture and degrees with art component. 20 take recreational art. *Sport*: Rugby, hockey, cricket, tennis, squash, badminton, swimming, karate, judo, netball, basketball, sailing available. 80% take non-compulsory sport. 4 represent county (rugby, cricket, squash, sevens). 50 in university teams. *Other*: 20 take part in local community schemes. 60 are taking bronze Duke of Edinburgh's Award, 1 has silver. 1 works for Leprosy Centre and national charity after leaving. Other activities include a computer club, chess, horse-riding, art, archery, sub aqua, war games, ski-ing.

Careers Two part time careers advisors. Average number of pupils accepted for *arts and humanities courses* at Oxbridge, 1; other universities, 9; polytechnics or CHE, 4. *science and engineering degree courses* at Oxbridge, 2; other universities, 9; medical schools, 2; polytechnics or CHE, 3. *other general training courses*, 5. Average number of pupils going straight into careers in armed services, 1; industry, 8; the City, 1; civil service, 2; music/drama, 1; other, 3.

Uniform School uniform worn throughout.

Houses/prefects Competitive houses. Prefects, head boy and girl, head of houses appointed by the Head.

Religion Compulsory worship.

Social Joint Sixth Form Society with Harrogate Ladies' College. Organised trips abroad. Pupils allowed to bring own car with school approval. Meals self service. School shops for tuck and clothing. No tobacco/alcohol allowed.

Discipline No corporal punishment. Pupils failing to produce homework more than once might expect a prep detention; those caught smoking cannabis on the premises would be suspended, probably expelled.

Boarding Sixth form have own study bedroom or share with 2 or 3. Houses, of approximately 45 are single sex. Resident qualified nurses. Central dining room. Pupils can provide and cook own food. 3 exeats each term (2 nights) plus half term. Visits to the local town allowed on Saturday mornings.

Alumni association is run by Mr R Search, Cherry Tree Farm, Gill Lane, Kearby, Nr Wetherby.

Former pupils Alastair Burnett.

ASSUMPTION

Assumption School	Co-ed	Pupils 158
Reeth Road	Boys	Upper sixth 20
Richmond	● Girls	Termly fees:
North Yorkshire DL10 4EP	Mixed sixth	Day £900
Telephone number 0748 2117	● Day	Boarding £1615
	● Boarding	GSA
Enquiries to the Headmistress		
Applications to the Admissions Secretary		

81

WHAT IT'S LIKE

Founded in 1850 by Sisters of the Assumption, who have been responsible for the development of its ethos and character. Religious education (Catholic) is integral to its aim and spirit. It lies on a single site in splendid countryside, conveniently near the old and most interesting town of Richmond in the Swale Valley. The main accommodation consists of handsome 19th-century buildings. There are many up-to-date facilities. The junior school is combined. It provides a sound education and the results are good. Music is strongly encouraged. A fair number of girls are involved in local community schemes.

SCHOOL PROFILE

Pupils Total over 12, 158. Day 60; Boarding 98. Entry age, 8, 11 and into sixth. Own junior school provides 20%. 10% are children of former pupils.

Entrance Own entrance exam used. Not oversubscribed. No special skills or religious requirements. 2 scholarships, two-thirds tuition fees.

Parents 15+% in armed services, 15+% in farming and 15+% in industry or commerce. 30+% live within 30 miles; 10+% live overseas.

Staff Head Mrs J Coulthard. 15 full time staff, 12 part time. Average age 40.

Academic work GCSE and A-levels. Average size of upper fifth 30; upper sixth 20. *O-levels*: on average, 5% pupils in upper fifth pass 1–4 subjects; 25%, 5–7 subjects; 70% pass 8+ subjects. *A-levels*: on average, 10% pupils in the upper sixth pass 1 subject; 40%, 2 subjects; 40%, 3 subjects and 10% pass 4 subjects. On average, 13 take science/engineering A-levels; 24 take arts and humanities A-levels; 8 a mixture of both. *Computing facilities*: Computer department. Computer studies from juniors to fourth form. Specialist teachers for both dyslexia and EFL.

Senior pupils' non-academic activities *Music*: 16 learn a musical instrument, 10 up to Grade 6 or above. I accepted for music school, 1 to Marlborough on sixth form music scholarship. 12 in school orchestra; 20 in choir; 8 in flute ensemble. *Drama and dance*: 24 in school productions; 1 accepted for Drama School. *Art*: 10 take GCSE; 3 A-level; 3 accepted for Art School. *Sport*: Hockey, netball, trampolining, badminton, gymnastics available. 30 take non-compulsory sport. 4 pupils represent county (hockey, badminton). *Other*: 45 take part in local community schemes. 12 have bronze Duke of Edinburgh's Award; 8 silver and 1 gold. Other activities include a debating society, guitar club, driving lessons outside school hours. Specialist member of staff available for weekend outdoor activities, ie canoeing, hiking etc.

Careers 1 full time and 2 part time careers advisors. Average number of pupils accepted for *arts and humanities degree courses* at universities, 4; polytechnics or CHE, 4. *science and engineering degree courses* at Oxbridge, 1; other universities, 2; medical schools, 1; polytechnics or CHE, 1. *BEd*, 1. *other general training courses*, 1. Average number of pupils going straight into careers in industry, 1; music/drama, 1; other, 3.

Uniform School uniform worn except in sixth form.

Houses/prefects Competitive houses Prefects, head girl, house prefects elected by the school. School Council.

Religion Religious worship compulsory.

Social Debates and discos with other local schools. Exchange system with

France, Spain, Germany. Language and ski-ing trips abroad. Pupils allowed to bring own car/bicycle to school. Meals self service. No tobacco/alcohol allowed.

Discipline No corporal punishment. Pupils failing to produce homework once might expect extra homework; those caught smoking cannabis on the premises would be expelled.

Boarding Sixth have own study bedroom; dormitories have individual cubicles. Resident qualified nurse. Central dining room. 2 weekend exeats each term. Visits to the local town allowed but never alone.

Alumni association is run by Mrs J Scothern, c/o Assumption School, Richmond, North Yorkshire.

ATHERLEY

The Atherley School	Co-ed	Pupils 340
Hill Lane	Boys	Upper sixth 15
Southampton	● Girls	Termly fees:
Hampshire SO9 1GR	Mixed sixth	Day £789
Telephone number 0703 772898	● Day	GSA; CSCoLtd;
	Boarding	SHA
Enquiries/application to the Headmistress		

WHAT IT'S LIKE

Opened in 1926 and governed by the Church Schools Company Ltd, it lies on a 5-acre site on the edge of Southampton Common. Since 1972 there has been considerable modernisation. Its facilities are more than adequate. A principal objective is to provide a sound education in basic subjects.

SCHOOL PROFILE

Pupils Total over 12, 340. Entry age, 4, 11, and into sixth form. Own junior school provides 20+%.

Entrance Own entrance exam used. Not oversubscribed. No special skills or religious requirements but is a Church of England school. Parents not expected to buy text books. 5–6 scholarships/bursaries, £550–£230.

Parents All live within 30 miles.

Staff Head Miss M E Taylor, first year in post. 31 full time staff, 12 part time. Annual turnover 3%.

Academic work GCSE, A-levels and RSA/Pitman Secretarial (results not available). Computing facilities: 10 PET, 2 Acorn. Provision for dyslexia, mild visual handicaps and EFL.

Senior pupils' non-academic activities *Sport*: Lacrosse, netball, tennis, rounders, athletics, badminton, table tennis, gymnastics available. *Other*: Pupils take part in the Duke of Edinburgh's Award Scheme (bronze and silver). Other activities include a computer club, drama, choir, orchestra, chess, science club, recorders, guitar club, debating club, Christian societies, individual instrumental tuition.

Careers 1 careers advisor. Average number of pupils accepted for *arts and humanities degree courses* at universities, 5; polytechnics or CHE, 2. *science* *and engineering degree courses* at Oxbridge, 2; other universities, 4. *BEd*, 4. *other general training courses*, 5.

Uniform School uniform worn except in sixth.

Houses/prefects Competitive houses. Prefects, head girl and head of house – elected by the staff and senior pupils.

Religion Encouraged.

Social Public speaking, games, BAYS with local schools. Organised trips abroad. Pupils allowed to bring own car/bicycle to school. Meals formal. School shop selling uniform. No tobacco/alcohol allowed.

Discipline No corporal punishment. Pupils failing to produce homework once might expect to lose house points; those caught smoking on the premises could expect to be suspended, pending further action.

Alumni association is run by Mrs R Kitcatt.

AUSTIN FRIARS

Austin Friars School
Carlisle
Cumbria CA3 9PB
Telephone number 0228 28042

Enquiries/application to the School Secretary

- Co-ed
  Boys
  Girls
  Mixed sixth
- Day
- Boarding

Pupils 251
Upper sixth 29
Termly fees:
Day £772
Boarding £1414
SHMIS

WHAT IT'S LIKE

Founded in 1951, it is situated on the outskirts of Carlisle, at its highest point, overlooking the River Eden. The grounds are spacious and the buildings are handsome. The sixth form residential area is in a comfortable house additional to the main site. A Catholic school, it is run by priests of the Order of St Augustine. A community of Sisters lives in a convent in the grounds. The entire philosophy of the school is pervaded by ideals inspired by religious values. Thus, religious education is an integral part of the curriculum. Discipline is firm. Trustworthiness and self-discipline are deemed vital. A sound education is provided and there is a good range of sports and activities. A fair commitment to local community schemes and the Duke of Edinburgh Award Scheme.

SCHOOL PROFILE

Pupils Total over 12, 251. Day 153 (boys 132, girls 21); Boarding 98 (all boys). Entry age, 11, 13 and into sixth, boys; 11 and into sixth, girls. 2% are children of former pupils.

Entrance Common entrance and own entrance exam used. Sometimes oversubscribed. No special skills or religious requirements but is predominantly Catholic. Parents not expected to buy books. May soon have assisted places. 13 scholarships available (8 boarders, 5 day), £942–£257.

Parents 15+% are doctors, lawyers, etc; 15+% in industry or commerce. 60+% live within 30 miles; up to 10% overseas.

Staff Head Reverend Thomas Lyons, in post 7 years. 27 full time staff, 3 part time. Annual turnover 6%. Average age 44.

Academic work GCSE and A-levels. Average size of upper fifth 45; upper sixth 29. *O-levels*: on average, 9 pupils in upper fifth pass 1–4 subjects; 10, 5–7 subjects; 23 pass 8+ subjects. *A-levels*: on average, 3 pupils in the upper sixth pass 1 subject; 5, 2 subjects; 6, 3 subjects and 17 pass 4 subjects. On average, 12 take science/engineering A-levels; 10 take arts and humanities A-levels; 7 a mixture of both. *Computing facilities*: SJ network; with hard disk serving 12 BBC micros in computer room and 3 for staff and administration. English lessons for non native speakers; some dyslexic provision.

Senior pupils' non-academic activities *Music*: 10 learn a musical instrument, 3 up to Grade 6 or above; 10 in school orchestra, 10 in choir, 5 in school pop group. *Drama and dance*: 20 in school productions; 5 take LAMDA exams. *Art*: 20 take GCSE; 6 A-level; 4 accepted for Art School. 12 in photographic club. *Sport*: Rugby, cricket, athletics, basketball, netball, hockey, gymnastics, swimming, cross country, tennis, badminton, rowing, sailing, canoeing available. 40 take non-compulsory sport. 10 take exams eg in gymnastics, swimming. 20 represent county (rugby, cricket, tennis). *Other*: 40 take part in local community schemes. 20 have bronze Duke of Edinburgh's Award, 20 silver. Other activities include a computer club, girls' keep-fit, judo, chess, debating society, public-speaking.

Careers 1 full time careers advisor. Average number of pupils accepted for *arts and humanities degree courses* at universities, 5; polytechnics or CHE, 5. *science and engineering degree courses* at universities, 5; medical schools, 3; polytechnics or CHE, 2. *BEd*, 2. Average number of pupils going straight into careers in armed services, 2; the church, 1; industry, 2.

Uniform School uniform worn except in sixth form.

Houses/prefects 3 competitive houses. Prefects, head boy, head of house and house prefects appointed by the Head and Housemasters.

Religion Assembly compulsory four days a week. All encouraged to attend Mass during the week; Sunday Mass compulsory for boarders.

Social Public speaking competitions, choral works, careers conventions with other local schools. Organised trips abroad to eg France, Russia. Pupils allowed to bring own car/bicycle/motorbike to school. Lunch self-service; other meals formal. School tuck shop (run by 6th form) and clothing shop (by parents). No tobacco allowed; alcohol on supervised social occasions.

Discipline Pupils failing to produce homework once might expect to receive extra work; those caught smoking cannabis on the premises could expect expulsion.

Boarding 10% have own study bedroom, 30% share doubles; 60% are in dormitories cf 6 or more, divided by age. Weekly visit by local GP, resident qualified nurse. Central dining room. Exeats each term: 1 week (autumn and summer) and 2 days (spring and autumn). Visits to the local town allowed on Saturday afternoons.

BADMINTON

Badminton School
Westbury on Trym
Bristol BS9 3BA
Telephone number 0272 623141

Enquiries/application to the Headmaster

Co-ed
Boys
● Girls
Mixed sixth
● Day
● Boarding

Pupils 275
Upper sixth 40
Termly fees:
Day £1150
Boarding £2050
GSA

WHAT IT'S LIKE

Founded in 1858, agreeably sited on the outskirts of Bristol near the Downs and in spacious grounds. 'The style of the school is a combination of discipline and warmth.' Staff–pupil relationships are mature and friendly, based on 'principles of courtesy and mutual respect'. All pupils are encouraged to work hard and play hard. The all-rounder is encouraged. Good on music and the creative arts. There is an emphasis on 'thinking people' and 'exceptional talent'. The dull and mediocre are not particularly welcome. It has a reputation for good teaching and a distinguished academic record. Full advantage is taken of the facilities of the City and its university.

SCHOOL PROFILE

Pupils Total over 12, 275. Day 75; Boarding 200. Entry age, 7, 11, 12, 13 and into sixth. Own prep school provides more than 20%. 10% are children of former pupils.

Entrance Common entrance and own entrance exam used. Oversubscribed. Special skills in music, science, sport, languages, art looked for. No religious requirements. Parents expected to buy text books. 20 scholarships/bursaries, £3000–£600.

Parents 25+% are doctors, lawyers, etc; 25+% in industry or commerce. 30+% live within 30 miles, 10+% live overseas.

Staff Head Mr C J T Gould, in post for 7 years. 30 full time staff, 10 part time. Annual turnover 5%. Average age 39.

Academic work GCSE and A-levels. Average size of upper fifth 50; upper sixth 40. *O-levels*: on average, 3 pupils in upper fifth pass 1–4 subjects; 10, 5–7 subjects; 35 pass 8+ subjects. *A-levels*: on average, 1 pupil in the upper sixth passes 1 subject; 4, 2 subjects; 31, 3 subjects and 4 pass 4 subjects. On average, 20 take science/engineering A-levels; 20 take arts and humanities; 5 a mixture. Spanish offered to GCSE/A-level. *Computing facilities*: 2 rooms, 24 computer installations and wide range of facilities to emphasise literacy/experience (no computer science exams).

Senior pupils' non-academic activities *Music*: 200 learn a musical instrument, 40 up to Grade 6 or above, 8 take GCSE, 4 take A-level, 2 accepted for Music School, 2 for music degrees; 100 in school orchestras, 4 in CASO, 100 in ensembles, 100 in main choir, 40 in middle choir, 12 in special choir; 3 in National Youth Orchestras. *Drama and dance*: 50 in school productions, 100 perform in House plays, 40 go on to Grade 6 in ESB, RAD etc, 20 take Guildhall exams. 1 accepted for Drama School. *Art*: 250 take as non-examined subject; 30 GCSE; 12 A-level. 4 accepted for Art School, 4 for degree courses, 6 for history of art; 30 belong to photographic club, 30 to Sunday art club. *Sport*: Hockey, netball, volleyball, badminton, tennis, squash, short-tennis, aerobics, rounders, golf, fencing, self-defence, judo, yoga, jazz dancing, skating, swimming, diving, ballet, gymnastics, athletics, riding, ski-ing available. 200 take non-compulsory sport. 120 take exams in eg gymnastics, swimming, judo, self-defence. 15 represent county (hockey, riding, tennis, swimming, synchronised swimming, fencing). *Other*: 10 take part in local community schemes. 12 participate in survival weekends, 50 in activity weekends. 12 take first aid. 3 enter voluntary schemes after leaving school. Other activities include two computer clubs, driving, politics, science, art, photography, design, first aid, maths association, classical club, historical society, drama, public speaking, debating society, bookshop, fundraising, social service.

Careers 1 full time careers advisor. Average number of pupils accepted for *arts and humanities degree courses* at Oxbridge, 2; other universities, 10; polytechnics or CHE, 4. *science and engineering degree courses* at Oxbridge, 4; other universities, 8; medical schools, 4; polytechnics or CHE, 4. *BEd*, 2. *other general training courses*, 2.

Uniform School uniform worn except in sixth form.

Houses/prefects Competitive houses; head girl and head of house elected. School Council.

Religion Worship not compulsory but encouraged.

Social Joint events including Bristol Schools Debating; Choral/Orchestral with Clifton; Science Society with Clifton; debates, socials, sports. Organised exchanges to France, Spain, Germany. Ski-ing trips abroad and expeditions to Italy, Iceland, Paris, Madrid. Pupils allowed to bring own car/bicycle to school. Lunch formal with grace. Other meals self service. 2nd-hand uniform shop. No tobacco/alcohol allowed.

Discipline No corporal punishment. Firm approach to discipline. Pupils failing to produce homework once might expect report/detention; those caught with drugs could expect instant expulsion.

Boarding 20% have own study bedroom, 30% share; 10% in dormitories of 6+. Houses, of approx 35–50, divided by age. Qualified medical staff available. Central dining room. Sixth form can provide own breakfasts. 2 exeats each term (1 night) plus half term. Weekend visits to the local town allowed but never alone; reporting back in person.

Alumni association is run by Miss Leila Eveleigh, Yew Tree Farm, Winford, Bristol.

Former pupils Dame Iris Murdoch, Indira Ghandi, Polly Toynbee, Dame Margaret Miles among others.

BANCROFT'S

Bancroft's School
Woodford Green
Essex IG8 0RF
Telephone number 01-505 4821

Enquiries/application to the Headmaster

● Co-ed
Boys
Girls
Mixed sixth
● Day
Boarding

Pupils 600
Upper sixth 100
Termly fees:
Day £972
HMC; SHA

WHAT IT'S LIKE

Founded in 1737, it occupied its present premises in Woodford about 100 years ago. There are long-standing links with the Company of Drapers. The main buildings are handsome Victorian architecture and most of the later structures blend in sympathetically. The school is well equipped with excellent modern facilities. The playing fields are nearby. Some religious worship in the Anglican tradition. A well-run school with vigorous local support, it provides good teaching and the academic standards are high. About 45–50 leavers proceed to university each year. A wide range of sports and games and considerable achievements (a very large number of county representatives and some internationals). A certain amount of commitment to local community schemes and a most impressive record in the Duke of Edinburgh's Award Scheme.

SCHOOL PROFILE

Pupils Total over 12, 600 (boys 300, girls 300). Entry age, 11 and into the sixth. 5% are children of former pupils.

Entrance Common entrance and own entrance exam used. Oversubscribed. No special skills or religious requirements. Parents not expected to buy text books. 70 assisted places. Some scholarships/bursaries (including music scholarship), £2916 pa.

Parents 60+% live within 30 miles.

Staff Head Dr P C D Southern, in post for 3 years. 53 full time staff, 2 part time. Annual turnover 5%. Average age 33.

Academic work GCSE and A-levels. Average size of upper fifth 100; upper sixth 90. *O-levels*: on average, 8 pupils in upper fifth pass 1–4 subjects; 12, 5–7 subjects; 80 pass 8+ subjects. *A-levels*: on average, 5 pupils in upper sixth pass 1 subject; 15, 2 subjects; 73, 3 subjects; 7 pass 4 subjects. On average, 45 take science/engineering A-levels; 45 take arts and humanities; 10 take a mixture. *Computing facilities*: Computer laboratory with 20 computers.

Senior pupils' non-academic activities *Music*: 75 learn a musical instrument, 22 to Grade 6 or above, 2 accepted for Music School; 30 in school orchestra, 50 in school choir, 5 in school pop group; 3 in National Youth Orchestra. *Drama and dance*: 85 in school productions. 3 take grade 6 in ESB, RAD etc. 1 accepted for Drama School. *Art*: 30 take as non-examined subject; 15 take GCSE; 13 take A-level. 3 accepted for Art School. *Sport*: Rugby, hockey, athletics, netball, tennis, cricket, badminton, squash, gymnastics, trampolining, swimming and golf available. 150 take non-compulsory sport. 30 take exams. 30 represent county, 4 represent country. *Other*: 15 take part in local community schemes. 35 have bronze Duke of Edinburgh's Award, 33 silver and 15 have gold. 3 enter voluntary schemes after leaving school. Other activities include clubs for a large variety of activities including chess and computers.

Careers 2 part time careers advisors. Average number of pupils accepted for *arts and humanities degree courses* at Oxbridge, 5; other universities, 18; polytechnics or CHE, 5. *science and engineering degree courses* at Oxbridge, 7; other universities, 17; polytechnics or CHE, 10. *other general training courses*, 5. Average number of pupils going straight into careers in the armed services, 3; the church, 1; industry, 7; the City, 10; the civil service, 1; music/drama, 1; other, 4.

Uniform School uniform worn throughout.
Houses/prefects Competitive houses. Prefects, head boy/girl, head of house and house prefects – appointed by the Headmaster. School Council.
Religion Chapel/assemblies. Special Catholic and Jewish assemblies.
Social Lectures organised by departments. French and German exchanges plus other trips abroad. Pupils allowed to bring own car/bike to school. Meals self service. School shop. No tobacco/alcohol allowed.
Discipline No corporal punishment. Pupils failing to produce homework once might expect detention; those caught smoking cannabis on the premises might expect expulsion.
Alumni association run by The Secretary, P J Denhard Esq, Lower Flat, 20 Kendall Road, Beckenham, Kent BR3 4PZ.
Former pupils Dennis Quilley; Sir Neil Macfarlane MP; Prof Sir Frederick Warner; Fred Emery.

BANGOR GRAMMAR

Bangor Grammar School	Co-ed	Pupils 890
College Avenue	• Boys	Upper sixth Yes
Bangor	Girls	Termly fees:
County Down BT20 5HH	Mixed sixth	not known
Telephone number 0247 473734	• Day	GBA; HMC
	Boarding	

Head T W Patton (9 years)
Age range 11–18, own prep from age 5; entry by own exam

BARNARD CASTLE

Barnard Castle School	Co-ed	Pupils 470
Barnard Castle	• Boys	Upper sixth 70
Durham DL12 8UN	Girls	Termly fees:
Telephone number 0833 37119	• Mixed sixth	Day £772
Enquiries/application to the Headmaster	• Day	Boarding £1442
	• Boarding	HMC

WHAT IT'S LIKE

The present foundation dates from 1883, derived, partially, from St John's Hospital (founded in the 13th century by John Baliol, whose widow founded the Oxford College). It is on a fine site in the Teesdale countryside on the outskirts of Barnard Castle. The grounds adjoin those of the Bowes Museum. The main Victorian building is used for admin and accommodation; all the teaching is done in purpose-built classrooms. In the last 25 years there has been much modernisation and development. Facilities are now excellent.

The new (1984) Design Technology Centre is outstanding. Strong on music, drama and sport. Very good academic record and plentiful university entrants. Chapel assembly on all weekdays; compulsory Sunday chapel for boarders. Vigorous local support and commitment to the community. Altogether a well run and flourishing establishment.

SCHOOL PROFILE

Pupils Total over 12, 470. Day 215 (boys 200, girls 20); Boarding 260 (boys 240, girls 20). Entry age, 11, 13, boys; into sixth boys and girls. Own Prep School provides over 50%.

Entrance Common entrance and own entrance exam used. Not heavily oversubscribed. No special skills or religious requirements. Parents not expected to buy text books. Scholarships/bursaries available, variable value.

Staff Head F S McNamara. 42 full time staff, 4 part time, plus music staff. Small annual turnover.

Academic work GCSE and A-levels. Average size of upper fifth 85; upper sixth 65–70. Exam results revealed to prospective parents. On average, 30 take science/engineering A-levels; 30 take arts and humanities; 10 a mixture. *Computing facilities*: Computer lab with 12 machines, 2 teaching monitors and business machines; 10 machines in various academic/admin department (BBC 'B', disc drivers, colour monitors and printers).

Senior pupils' non-academic activities *Music*: 100+ learn a musical instrument, 10 up to Grade 6 or above; 37 in school orchestra, 65 in choir, 16 in jazz ensemble, 5 in school pop group, 12 in woodwind ensemble; 1 organ scholar; 3 play in pop groups after leaving. *Drama and dance*: 60–70 in school productions. 1 goes on to work in theatre. *Art*: 20 take as non-examined subject in art club; 20 GCSE; 5 A-level; 2 accepted for Art School; 1 for architecture degree. 20 belong to photographic club. *Sport*: Rugby, cricket, squash, swimming, hockey, cross-country, athletics, tennis, basketball, badminton, soccer, judo, canoeing available. Sport is compulsory. 60–80 participate regularly in inter-school sport at 5th year or above. 19 represent county (rugby, cricket, hockey, squash, cross-country, athletics); 1 represents country (rugby). *Other*: 12 take part in local community schemes. 35 are taking gold Duke of Edinburgh's Award. 1 enters voluntary scheme after leaving school. Other activities include a computer club, photography (good darkroom facilities), archery, public speaking, CCF, pottery, technology, various musical activities, car maintenance, drama, horse riding, model making, role playing, model railway.

Careers 4 part time careers advisors. Average number of pupils accepted for *arts and humanities degree courses* at Oxbridge, 2; other universities, 13; polytechnics or CHE, 7. *science and engineering degree courses* at Oxbridge, 3; other universities, 18; medical schools, 3; polytechnics or CHE, 4. *BEd*, 1. *other general training courses*, 1. Average number of pupils going straight into careers in armed services, 4; industry, 1; the City, 4; other, 1.

Uniform School uniform worn throughout.

Houses/prefects Competitive houses. Prefects, head boy/girl, head of house and house prefects appointed by the Head and housemasters.

Religion Compulsory Sunday Chapel for boarders. Chapel assembly all weekdays.

Social Organised trips abroad. Pupils allowed to bring own bicycle to school;

cars as privilege. Meals self service, few formal. School tuck and stationery shops. No tobacco/alcohol allowed.

Discipline No corporal punishment. Pupils failing to produce homework once would be dealt with according to circumstances; those caught smoking or possessing cannabis on the premises could expect to be expelled.

Boarding 10% have own study bedroom, 50% share; 40% in dormitories of 6+. Houses of 60–70. Resident qualified medical staff. Central dining room. Pupils can provide and cook some own food. 2 exeats a term (1.5 days), plus half term. Visits to the local town allowed at housemaster's discretion.

Alumni association is run by K C N G King, Barnard Castle School.

Former pupils Lord Mills (PC, KCB, Minister of Power in 1959); Geoffrey Smith (TV gardening expert); Craig Raine (poet); Kevin Whately (actor); Bentley Beetham (climber – Everest Expedition 1924); Sir Edward Mellanby, GBE, KCB, FRS (Secretary of MRC); Rory Underwood, Robert Andrew and Tom Danby (rugby internationals); Brian Patterson, Ian Nuttall, Peter Verow (squash internationals); Geoff Turner (international athlete); Kim Hamilton (international modern pentathlete); George Macaulay (test cricketer).

BASTON

Baston School	Co-ed	Pupils 194
Hayes	Boys	Upper sixth 20
Bromley	● Girls	Termly fees:
Kent BR2 7AB	Mixed sixth	Day £780
Telephone number 01-462 1010	● Day	Boarding £1425
Enquiries/application to the Headmaster	● Boarding	ISAI

WHAT IT'S LIKE

Founded in 1933, it has a very pleasant 14-acre site of playing fields, gardens and orchards, on the edge of broad common land in the green belt on the southern outskirts of Bromley. Many of its facilities are purpose built and of a high order (providing comfortable accommodation for the boarders). Well equipped for games and outdoor activities. It gives a sound traditional education and has a good academic record. Strong in music, drama, arts and crafts. Plentiful use is made of the amenities of a capital city. A congenial school with a friendly informal atmosphere. The preparatory department is on the same site.

SCHOOL PROFILE

Pupils Total over 12, 194. Day 161; Boarding 33. Entry age, 3, 4, 5, 11 and into sixth form. Own junior school provides 20+%.

Entrance Own entrance exam used. Oversubscribed. No special skills or religious requirements. Parents expected to buy sixth form text books only. 3 scholarships/bursaries, £780–£78 per term.

Parents 60+% live within 30 miles; up to 10% live overseas.

Staff Head C R Wimble. 23 full time staff, 17 part time. Annual turnover, 3%.

Academic work GCSE and A-levels. Average size of upper fifth 40; upper

sixth 20. *O-levels*: on average, 16 pupils in upper fifth pass 1–4 subjects; 13, 5–7 subjects; 11 pass 8+ subjects. *A-levels*: on average, 4 pupils in the upper sixth pass 1 subject; 3, 2 subjects; 12, 3 subjects and 1 passes 4 subjects. On average, 8 take science/engineering A-levels; 8 take arts and humanities; 4 a mixture. Business studies offered to GCSE/A-level. *Computing facilities*: 5 BBC B/Master, 3 Amstrad 1512. EFL provision.

Senior pupils' non-academic activities *Music*: 12 learn a musical instrument, 7 up to Grade 6 or above, 1 accepted for Music School; 9 in school orchestra, 21 in choir; 1 in National Youth Orchestra. *Drama and dance*: 25 in school productions. *Art*: 2 take as non-examined subject; 25 GCSE; 8 A-level. 4 accepted for Art School. *Sport*: Lacrosse, netball, gymnastics, squash, tennis, athletics, swimming available. 35 take non-compulsory sport. 8 pupils represent county (lacrosse, tennis); 1 represents country (lacrosse). *Other*: Activities include computer and art clubs, music, drama, sport.

Careers 2 full time careers advisors. Average number of pupils accepted for *arts and humanities degree courses* at universities, 3; polytechnics or CHE, 2. *science and engineering degree courses* at universities, 4; medical schools, 1; polytechnics or CHE, 2. *BEd*, 3. *other general training courses*, 2. Average number of pupils going straight into careers in the City, 1; other, 2.

Uniform School uniform worn, except in sixth form.

Houses/prefects Competitive houses. Prefects, head girl, head of house and house prefects – appointed by staff.

Religion Assemblies compulsory.

Social Organised trips abroad; ski trips, exchange visits to France and Germany, Russian trips, educational cruises. Upper sixth allowed to bring own car to school. Meals self service. No tobacco/alcohol allowed.

Discipline No corporal punishment. Pupils failing to produce homework once might expect admonishment; those caught smoking cannabis on the premises could expect expulsion.

Boarding 5% own study bedroom, 95% share with 2–5. No resident medical staff. Central dining room. Pupils can provide and cook own food. 3 weekend exeats each term. Weekend visits to local town allowed.

Alumni association is run by Mrs J C Wimble, c/o the School.

Former pupils Carol Thatcher.

BATH HIGH

Bath High School	Co-ed	Pupils 400
Hope House	Boys	Upper sixth 45
Lansdown	● Girls	Termly fees:
Bath	Mixed sixth	Day £620
Avon BA1 5ES	● Day	GSA; GPDST
Telephone number 0225 22931	Boarding	

WHAT IT'S LIKE

Founded in 1872 and a member of the Girls' Public Day School Trust, it occupies beautiful Georgian buildings in Lansdown. There is a large terraced garden and fine views over the city. Games facilities are nearby. There have been extensive modern additions in the last 25 years and the facilities are good. A junior school and a senior school are combined. There are about 550 pupils altogether: 150 (ages 4–10) in the junior section and 400 (ages 11–18) in the senior section. A large sixth form of about 100. A good general education is provided and academic standards are high. A high proportion of pupils go on to university each year. Music, drama and art are all strong. Full use is made of Bath's cultural amenities. Much time and care is devoted to careers advice. A good range of sports and games is provided and standards are very creditable. There is a wide variety of clubs and societies and considerable commitment to local community services.

SCHOOL PROFILE

Head Miss Margaret Winfield (3 years)
Age range 11–18, own junior from age 5; entry by own exam
Assisted places and scholarships available.

BATLEY GRAMMAR

Batley Grammar School	Co-ed	Pupils 617
Carlinghow Hill	● Boys	Upper sixth 75
Batley	Girls	Termly fees:
West Yorkshire WF17 0AD	● Mixed sixth	£693.30
Telephone number 0924 474980	● Day	GBA
Enquiries/application to the Headmaster	Boarding	

WHAT IT'S LIKE

Founded in 1612, it lies on the outskirts of Batley near the countryside. Playing fields adjoin it. The buildings are of Yorkshire stone and brick. They are well appointed and all the modern facilities are first class. Recent developments include spacious labs and a sixth form centre. It has remained very much a grammar school in the old tradition of such establishments and provides a sound education which produces consistently creditable results. Strong in music. Vigorous local support and commitment to the community.

SCHOOL PROFILE

Pupils Total, 617. Entry age, 11+ and into sixth. Girls into sixth from September 1988. 5% are children of former pupils.
Entrance Own entrance exam used. Oversubscribed. No special skills or religious requirements. Parents not expected to buy text books. 247 assisted places. 5–10 scholarships/bursaries pa, full to 25% fees.
Parents 100% live within 30 miles.
Staff Head C S Parker, in post for 2 years. 41 full time staff, 4 part time. Annual turnover 0–1%. Average age 39.
Academic work GCSE and A-levels. Average size of upper fifth 100; upper sixth 75. *O-levels*: on average, 15 pupils in upper fifth pass 1–4 subjects; 20, 5–7 subjects; 55 pass 8+ subjects. *A-levels*: on average, 4 pupils in the upper

sixth pass 1 subject; 12, 2 subjects; 22, 3 subjects and 30 pass 4 subjects. On average, 27 take science/engineering A-levels; 31 take arts and humanities; 12 a mixture. *Computing facilities*: 16 station computer room with hard disk storage; others in individual departments.

Senior pupils' non-academic activities   *Music*: 115 learn a musical instrument, 25 up to Grade 6 or above, 45 in school orchestra/bands, 15 in percussion and recorder groups, 10 play in pop group, 14 members of local brass bands, 20 in county orchestra. *Drama and dance*: 30 in school productions. 1 accepted for Drama/Dance School, 1 to work in theatre. *Art*: 40 take GCSE; 4 A-level. 4 accepted for Art School. *Sport*: Soccer, cricket, cross-country, basketball, athletics, tennis, wind-surfing, sailing, squash, badminton available. 90 take non-compulsory sport. 6 represent county (cricket, cross-country, rugby), 1 in national youth swimming, 1 England final trials, hockey, 2 England 16/18 group rugby. *Other*: 30 take part in local community schemes. 42 have silver Duke of Edinburgh's Award, 35 have gold. 230 in voluntary CCF. Other activities include a computer club, drama, chess club, choir, orchestra, three bands, ski-ing, junior walking club, railway club, French film club, light engineering society, community service group, Christian fellowship.

Careers 2 part time careers advisors. Average number of pupils accepted for *arts and humanities degree courses* at Oxbridge, 2; other universities, 9; polytechnics or CHE, 10. *science and engineering degree courses* at Oxbridge, 2; other universities, 12; medical schools, 2; polytechnics or CHE, 10. *BEd*, 2. *other general training courses*, 2. Average number of pupils going straight into careers in armed services, 3; industry, 10; banking, 4; civil service, 3; music/drama, 2; other, 2.

Uniform School uniform worn throughout.

Houses/prefects Competitive houses. Prefects, head boy, head of house and house prefects appointed by the Head or housemasters.

Religion Morning assembly unless parents request exclusion.

Social Local road safety quiz organised by seniors; British Association of Young Scientists meetings. Girls from local school in plays. 2 organised ski trips; 1 to Greece/Italy. Pupils allowed to bring own car/bicycle to school with head's permission. Meals self service. No tobacco/alcohol allowed.

Discipline No corporal punishment. Pupils failing to produce homework once might initially expect extra work; Saturday detention for repeated offences.

Alumni association is run by Mr A Allen, Parkroyd, 9 Lewisham Street, Morley.

Former pupils Sir Stanley Rouse (President FIFA); Sir Willie Morris (Ambassador to Egypt); Professor Norman Franklin (Chairman UKAE); Joseph Priestley (discovered oxygen).

BATTLE ABBEY

Battle Abbey School	Co-ed	Pupils 120
Battle	Boys	Upper sixth 6
East Sussex TN33 0AD	● Girls	Termly fees:
Telephone number 04246 2385	Mixed sixth	Day £1040
	● Day	Boarding £1670
Enquiries/application to the	● Boarding	GSA
Headmaster's Secretary		

WHAT IT'S LIKE

Founded at Bexhill in 1912, it moved to its present site in 1922 and thus enjoys the privilege of being housed in within one of the most remarkable buildings in Britain (set in 52 acres of fine parkland). As part of a valuable ancient monument it is maintained to the highest standards of the Department of the Environment. It is very comfortable and civilised and has excellent modern facilities. It offers a good all-round education in a 'family' atmosphere and has all the advantages of a small school. Most girls learn a musical instrument, all take art as a non-examined subject, take part in a non-compulsory sport, and everyone, if at all possible, is involved in dramatic productions. Academic results are very good. Its major strength lies with girls who lack self-confidence and who might sink without trace in a larger establishment. At Battle Abbey they can be 'big fish in a small pond'; there are no 'also-rans'. They produce confident young women from sometimes the most unlikely of pupils. The house system is competitive in work, conduct, deportment and sport. High standards of conduct and deportment are expected and achieved.

SCHOOL PROFILE

Pupils Total over 12, 120. Day 25; Boarding 95. Entry age, 11 and into sixth. 5% are children of former pupils.

Entrance Common entrance and own entrance exam used. Oversubscribed. No special skills or religious requirements, although school is Christian. Parents expected to buy A-level text books. 1 scholarship a year, full tuition fees.

Parents 15+% in armed services.

Staff Head D J A Teall, in post for 6 years. 15 full time staff, 12 part time. Low annual turnover. Average age 45.

Academic work GCSE and A-levels, CEE. Average size of upper fifth 25; upper sixth 6. Exam information not available. On average, 50% take science/engineering A-levels; 45% take arts and humanities; 5% a mixture. *Computing facilities*: Two computer centres, with BBC micros. EFL and specialist teaching for mild dyslexia and other learning difficulties.

Senior pupils' non-academic activities *Music*: Most learn a musical instrument, 6 up to Grade 6 or above; 15 in school orchestra, 30 in choir, 8 in madrigal group. *Drama and dance*: All pupils participate in musical school productions; 30 in others. 2 up to Grade 6 ESB etc or above. 2 accepted for Drama/Dance Schools. *Art*: All take as non-examined subject; 12 GCSE; 5 A-level. 2 accepted for Art School. *Sport*: Hockey, netball, rounders, swimming, tennis, athletics, cross-country, badminton, volley ball, squash available. All take non-compulsory sport. 2 take exams in eg gymnastics, swimming. 2 represent county (cross country, athletics). *Other*: 15 take part in local community schemes. Other activities include computer club, driving, judo, photography, dance (modern, ballroom and tap) and riding.

Careers 2 part time careers advisors. Average number of pupils accepted for *arts and humanities degree courses* at universities, 1; polytechnics or CHE, 1. *science and engineering degree courses* at universities, 1; polytechnics or CHE, 2. *other general training courses*, 10. Average number of pupils going straight into careers in armed services, 2; few into industry; music/drama, 2.

Uniform School uniform worn except in sixth form.

Houses/prefects Competitive houses. Prefects, head of house and house prefects appointed by the Head or housemistresses. School Council.

Religion Christian morning assembly compulsory. Boarders attend Sunday Church (non-Christians excused).

Social Regular social functions with Eastbourne College and Tonbridge School. Organised trips to France and Germany, ski-ing. 8 week exchange for 3 girls with a school in Australia. No bicycles but pupils allowed to bring own horse to school. Meals formal. Sixth formers may smoke in designated room, and have wine for 18th birthdays.

Discipline No corporal punishment. Pupils failing to produce homework once might expect extra work and an 'order mark' (counting against their house); those caught smoking cannabis on the premises could expect to be expelled without hesitation.

Boarding Upper sixth have own study bedroom, lower sixth share; others in dormitories of 5. Resident qualified SRN nurse. Central dining room. Seniors can provide and cook own food. 2 weekend exeats per term, half-term and 4 Sundays. Visits to the local town allowed.

Alumni association is run by Mrs M Steward, c/o the School.

BEARWOOD

Bearwood College	Co-ed	Pupils 321
Bear Wood	● Boys	Upper sixth 29
Wokingham	Girls	Termly fees:
Berkshire RG11 5BG	Mixed sixth	Day £1200
Telephone number 0734 786915	● Day	Boarding £2050
	● Boarding	
Enquiries/application to the Headmaster		

WHAT IT'S LIKE

Founded in 1827, as the Royal Merchant Navy School, it is now under the Queen's patronage and its president is the Duke of Edinburgh. The main building is a handsome neo-Renaissance mansion on a splendid estate of 500 acres with lakes, riding school and golf course. The more recent buildings are well appointed and comfortable. The ethics and general tenor of the college encourage the growth of the individual. Organisation is directed towards self-discipline and leadership by example. Basically it is a C of E school but it takes all denominations. Academic education is sound and results very creditable. A good deal of emphasis on leisure pursuits. Many extra-curricular activities available. Boarding accommodation is comfortable and there are good relationships between staff and pupils.

SCHOOL PROFILE

Pupils Total over 12, 321. Day 67; Boarding 254. Entry age, 11, 13 and into sixth.

Entrance Common entrance and own entrance exam used. Well subscribed. No special skills. School is C of E but takes all denominations. Parents expected to pay £15 per term for books. 16–25 scholarships/bursaries, at the Headmaster's discretion and for children of deceased Merchant Navy personnel, £2050 per term.

Parents 15+% are doctors, lawyers, etc, 15+% in industry or commerce. 30+% live within 30 miles, 10+% live overseas.

Staff Head The Hon Martin C Penney, in post for 7 years. 30 full time staff, 5 part time. Annual turnover under 1%. Average age 38.

Academic work GCSE and A-levels. Average size of fifth 75; upper sixth 29. *O-levels*: on average, 35 pupils in fifth pass 1–4 subjects; 25, 5–7 subjects; 15 pass 8+ subjects. *A-levels*: on average, 6 pupils in the upper sixth pass 1 subject; 11, 2 subjects; 12, 3 subjects. On average, 12 take science/engineering A-levels; 12 take arts and humanities; 5 a mixture. Spanish, Portuguese, Japanese, Chinese and Arabic are offered to GCSE/A-level as extras. *Computing facilities*: Computing department equipped with 18 BBC computers and hard disc. EFL and provision for mild dyslexia.

Senior pupils' non-academic activities *Music*: 44 learn a musical instrument, 16 up to Grade 6 or above; 15 in school orchestra, 13 in choir, 12 in school pop group, 8 in school jazz group, 7 in brass ensemble, 3 in baroque group; 1 in Reading Youth Orchestra, 2 in Berkshire Youth Jazz Orchestra. *Drama and dance*: 30+ in school productions, 120+ in house plays. *Art*: 34 take GCSE; 4 A-level. 1 or 2 accepted for Art School. *Sport*: Archery, squash, badminton, soccer, rugby, cricket, swimming, cross country, athletics, tennis, croquet available. Many take non-compulsory sport. 7 represent county (cricket, rugby, athletics, including National Youth Champion at Hurdles). *Other*: Other activities include a computer club, sailing, golf, riding, chess, war games, angling, karate, dry ski-ing, fencing, team shooting, CCF, drama.

Careers 1 full time and 6 part time careers advisors. Average number of pupils accepted for *arts and humanities degree courses* at universities, 5; polytechnics or CHE, 5. *science and engineering degree courses* at universities, 5; polytechnics or CHE, 6. *other general training courses*, 25. Average number of pupils going straight into careers in armed services, 1. Strong tradition of ex-pupils going into commerce and industry.

Uniform School uniform worn, variation allowed in sixth form.

Houses/prefects Competitive houses. Prefects, head boy, head of house and house prefects appointed by the Head or housemasters.

Religion Daily Chapel. Other denominations can attend own place of worship on Sundays.

Social Compete locally at all sports and chess. Annual local collection for King George VI Fund for Sailors. Activity Club travel extensively eg to Alaska. Pupils allowed to bring own bicycle/horse to school. Meals self service. School tuck and uniform shops. No tobacco allowed. Limited alcohol (beer or lager) for 17+.

Discipline No corporal punishment. Pupils failing to produce homework once might expect a verbal warning; those caught smoking cannabis on the premises could expect dismissal.

Boarding 15% have own study bedroom, 70% share (2–5); 15% are in dormitories of 6 or more. Houses, of approximately 60 are the same as competitive houses. Resident medical staff; separate sanatorium. Central dining room. Sixth formers can cook snacks. 3 Sundays and 2 weekend exeats a term. Visits to the local town allowed with housemaster's permission.

Alumni association is run by J N Hedley, c/o the College.

Former pupils Francis Scarfe (Academic).

BEDALES

Bedales School	● Co-ed	Pupils 405
Petersfield	Boys	Upper sixth 75
Hampshire GU32 2DG	Girls	Termly fees:
Telephone number 0730 63286	Mixed sixth	Day £1714
	● Day	Boarding £2438
Enquiries/application to Registrar for	● Boarding	HMC
Admissions		

WHAT IT'S LIKE

Opened in 1893 (one of the very first co-ed schools in Britain), it has a splendid site of 150 acres in East Hampshire, 16 miles from the sea, on a hill overlooking the Rother valley. Civilised and comfortable buildings in beautiful grounds. The Memorial Library is one of the best school libraries in Britain. It was founded as a 'pioneer school' by J H Badley who developed it as a reformed version of his contemporary public schools. His reforms involved a serious commitment to the arts and crafts, rural skills and work out of doors as well as to academic study. Always progressive in the best sense, it is a product of its dissenting origins and idealistic drives; a school within a supporting community, believing strongly in itself and what it has to offer and resistant to orthodoxies and bureaucracies. It is a 'one-off' school with a unique character. Very strong on art, drama, dance and crafts – and music, which has a central position in the life of the school. A feature is the Outdoor Work Department where pupils maintain a large tree nursery, grow fruit, keep poultry, build their own barns and run it as a profit-making concern. Very much a 'family' atmosphere, relaxed, informal, friendly; informal personal relationships between pupils and staff. Very good academic results.

SCHOOL PROFILE

Pupils Total over 13, 405. Day 58 (boys 21, girls 37); Boarding 347 (boys 166, girls 181). Entry age, 3–7, 8, 11 (junior schools), 13 and sixth (senior school). Own junior school provides approximately 50%.

Entrance Own entrance exam used. Oversubscribed. School looks for pupils with a broad base – academic, art, music, design etc with potential for six or more GCSEs, 3 A-levels. Parents expected to buy a few text books. 5 assisted places in each year of sixth form only. Means tested scholarships/bursaries available.

Parents Up to 10% live within 30 miles; 15% live overseas.

Staff Head E A M MacAlpine, in post for 7 years. 41 full time staff, 6 part time.

Academic work GCSE and A-levels. Average size of upper fifth 80; upper sixth 75. *O-levels*: average number of O-levels passed 7.5. Average number of A-levels passed – fractionally under 3. On average, 12 take science/engineering A-levels; 43 take arts and humanities; 23 a mixture. Part-time dyslexic teacher. *Computing facilities*: Network of 16 Nimbus computers and shared printers which can be expanded; 6 BBCs and 3 Thorn EMI Liberators.

Senior pupils' non-academic activities *Music*: 250 learn a musical instrument, 70 up to Grade 6 or above; 55 in school orchestra; 100 in school choir; usually some in various youth orchestras; 2 pupils accepted for higher education in music. Music is compulsory in first year of senior school. *Drama and dance*: 80 in school productions; 40 in other productions; 3 accepted for Drama Schools. *Art*: 150 take as non-examined subject; 90 GCSE; 35 A-level; 10 accepted for Art School. Art and design is compulsory in first year of senior school. *Sport*: Football, hockey, cricket, tennis, basketball, volleyball, swimming, athletics, netball, badminton, gymnastics, minor games, trampolining, health-related fitness, squash, weight training, cross country, outdoor pursuits available. *Other*: 30 pupils take part in voluntary service in the village. Some 12 enter voluntary schemes after leaving school. Years 3 and 4 camp in Wales and Dartmoor. Participation in Schools Partnership Worldwide.

Careers 1 part time careers advisor. All pupils go on to higher and further education. 75–80% to university and polytechnic; 20%–30% to art, design, music college etc.

Uniform School uniform not worn.

Houses/prefects No competitive houses. Head boy/girl but no prefects. Sixth form committee. Boarding house committees and central committee.

Religion No compulsory worship.

Social Organised trips abroad include visits to CERN, Spain, ski trips etc. Meals self service. School shop.

Discipline No corporal punishment. Anyone caught buying, bringing in or consuming drugs will be expelled. Pupils punished for smoking and drinking.

Boarding Small dormitories; sixth formers can be in ones or twos. One large boys' house, one large girls' and two small out houses; all single sex. Resident qualified nurse/doctor. Central dining room. Pupils can provide and cook own food. Exeats allowed on all but 3 weekends a term.

Alumni association is run by T W Slack, c/o the School.

BEDFORD

Bedford School
Burnaby Road
Bedford MK40 2TU
Telephone number 0234 53436

Enquiries/application to the Registrar

Co-ed   Pupils 900
● Boys   Upper sixth 140
Girls   Termly fees:
Mixed sixth   Day £1200
● Day   Boarding £2058
● Boarding   HMC

WHAT IT'S LIKE

Founded in 1552, it lies in 50 acres of peaceful and extensive grounds in the centre of Bedford. All but two boarding houses are on site; two within 5 minutes' walk. The main school building was gutted by fire in 1979. All has been rebuilt and, over the last 30 years, there have been many modern additions. Its facilities are now excellent. It provides continuous education for boys from 7–18 with an unusual mix of local day and international boarders. Strong in all academic disciplines with first-rate exam results (70-odd university entrants each year). Also very good at athletics, games and rowing. It has a fine range of extra-curricular activities, plus CCF, community service unit and outdoor pursuits. Vigorous local support, good back-up from alumni.

SCHOOL PROFILE

Pupils Total over 12, 900. Day 590; Boarding 310. Entry age, 7, 8, 11, 13 and a few into sixth. Own prep school provides 50%. 15% are children of former pupils.

Entrance Common entrance and own entrance exam used. Oversubscribed. No special skills or religious requirements. Parents expected to buy text books. 76 assisted places. 32 scholarships plus means tested bursaries for boys resident in Bedfordshire, full fee remission – £300.

Parents 15+% are doctors, lawyers, etc; 15+% in industry or commerce. 30+% live within 30 miles; 10+% live overseas.

Staff Head M E Barlen, in post for 1 year. 107 full time staff, 8 part time. Annual turnover 9%. Average age 35.

Academic work GCSE and A-levels. Average size of upper fifth 160; upper sixth 140. *O-levels*: on average, 8 pupils in upper fifth pass 1–4 subjects; 9, 5–7 subjects; 107 pass 8+ subjects. *A-levels*: on average, 7 pupils in the upper sixth pass 1 subject; 17, 2 subjects; 89, 3 subjects and 12 pass 4 subjects. On average, 60 take science/engineering A-levels; 60 take arts and humanities; 20 a mixture. *Computing facilities*: 40+ BBC computers netted into central hard disk facility.

Senior pupils' non-academic activities *Music*: 80 learn a musical instrument, 30 up to Grade 6 or above, 2 accepted for Music School, 5 play in pop groups; 80 in school orchestra, 70 in choir, 5 in school pop group, 30 in chamber groups; 30 in County Youth Orchestras; 2 in National Youth Orchestra; 20 in adult orchestras. *Drama and dance*: 100+ in school productions. *Art*: All take as non-examined subject; 20 take GCSE; 10 A-level. 4 accepted for Art School. 30 belong to eg photographic club. *Sport*: Cricket, hockey, rowing, rugby, athletics, badminton, basketball, boxing, canoeing, croquet, cross country, fives, fencing, jujitsu, shooting, soccer, squash, swimming, table tennis, tennis, sub-aqua, water polo, weight training, golf, mountaineering available. 200+ take non-compulsory sport. 30+ represent county/country (rowing, rugby, hockey, athletics, shooting, cricket). *Other*: 150 take part in local community schemes. 30 have bronze Duke of Edinburgh's Award, 10 have silver and 3 gold. Boys' charities committee raised £4000 last year. Other activities include computer club, driving lessons, strong bridge and chess clubs, printing, quiz club, CCF, stamp club, photography, wine and beer making, fish-keeping, debating.

Careers 4 part time careers advisors. Average number of pupils accepted for *degree courses* at Oxbridge, 14; other universities, 55; medical schools, 6; polytechnics or CHE, 20. Average number of pupils going straight into careers in armed services, 8; the church, 1; industry, 4; the City, 5; music/drama, 1; other, 10.

Uniform School uniform worn throughout.

Houses/prefects Competitive houses. Prefects, head boy, head of house and house prefects appointed by the Head. Various advisory committees. Paid fagging in boarding houses.

Religion Compulsory assembly and chapel on Sunday for boarders (unless parents object on valid religious grounds).

Social Joint debates, choral productions, theatrical productions, dances with sister schools. Numerous organised trips abroad. Pupils allowed to bring own car/bicycle/motorbike to school with permission. Meals formal. School shop. No tobacco allowed. Limited beer for over 18's at weekends.

Discipline No corporal punishment. Punishments depend upon individual cases and personalities. Those caught smoking cannabis on the premises should expect severe punishment.

Boarding Upper sixth have own study bedroom. Senior pupils divided into 6 houses of 50, parallel to competitive houses. Resident qualified nurse. Central dining room. Pupils can provide and cook some own food. 2 weekend exeats per term plus half term (up to 1 week). Visits to local town allowed.

Alumni association is run by Arthur Nightall, OB Club Office, 10 Glebe Road, Bedford MK40 2PL.

BEDFORD HIGH

The High School	Co-ed	Pupils 830
Bromham Road	Boys	Upper sixth Yes
Bedford	● Girls	Termly fees:
Bedfordshire MK40 2BS	Mixed sixth	Day £780
Telephone number 0234 60221	● Day	Boarding £1530
	● Boarding	GSA

Head Mrs D M Willis (1 year)
Age range 7–18; entry by own exam
Bursaries, means-tested.

BEDFORD MODERN

Bedford Modern School	Co-ed	Pupils 822
Maulon Lane	• Boys	Upper sixth 114
Bedford MK41 7NT	Girls	Termly fees:
Telephone number 0234 64331	Mixed sixth	Day £733
	• Day	Boarding £1365
Enquiries to the Headteacher	• Boarding	HMC; IAPS
Application to the Admissions Secretary		

WHAT IT'S LIKE

One of the Harpur Trust schools of Bedford, sharing in the endowment made to Bedford by Sir William Harpur in 1566. In 1974 the school moved to entirely new buildings on the northern outskirts of the town. It is a 50-acre wooded hill site with spacious playing fields. The new school is extremely well equipped in every respect and includes sophisticated facilities for sport. Teaching and academic standards are of a high order; 60-odd pupils go to university each year. Not a few pupils go into agriculture and industry. Strong in music, it has a wide variety of clubs and societies. A very flourishing school with strong local support.

SCHOOL PROFILE

Pupils Total over 12, 822. Day 757; Boarding 65. Entry age, 7, 8, 9, 11, 13 and into sixth. Own junior school provides 20+%.

Entrance Common entrance and own entrance exam used. Oversubscribed. No special skills or religious requirements. Parents not expected to buy text books. 135 assisted places. 30 bursaries pa (income related for inhabitants of Bedfordshire) £10–full fee remission.

Parents 60+% live within 30 miles; up to 10% live overseas.

Staff Head P J Squire, in post for 10 years. 79 full time staff, 2 part time. Annual turnover 5–10%. Average age 40.

Academic work GCSE and A-levels. Average size of upper fifth 140; upper sixth 114. *O-levels*: on average, 17 pupils in upper fifth pass 1–4 subjects; 38, 5–7 subjects; 83 pass 8+ subjects. *A-levels*: on average, 10 pupils in the upper sixth pass 1 subject; 20, 2 subjects; 75, 3 subjects and 8 pass 4 subjects. On average, 70 take science/engineering A-levels; 40 take arts and humanities; 15 a mixture. *Computing facilities*: Computing room, BBC microcomputers, 3802 and Acorns. Some help for dyslexia, other mild handicaps and EFL where possible.

Senior pupils' non-academic activities *Music*: 94 learn a musical instrument; 40 in school orchestra, 10 in dance band, 15 in wind band, 16 in chamber group, 10 in school choir. *Drama and dance*: 40 in school productions. 1 in County Youth Theatre; 4 had auditions for National Youth Theatre. *Art*: 32 take GCSE, 17 A-level. 3 accepted for Art School, 1 for School of Architecture. 5 belong to eg photographic club. *Sport*: Rugby, football, cricket, rowing, athletics, cross-country, swimming, water polo, squash, badminton, table tennis, shooting, fencing, fives, tennis available. 250 take non-compulsory sport. 12 take GCSE theory and practice of physical education. 20 represent county (rugby, cricket, athletics, tennis, table tennis); 7 represent country (rowing, rugby, shooting, cricket, table tennis). *Other*: 40 have bronze Duke of Edinburgh's Award, 6 have silver and 4 gold. Other activities include computer club, many other clubs and societies, music in particular.

Careers 5 part time careers advisors. Average number of pupils accepted for *arts and humanities degree courses* at Oxbridge, 5; other universities, 25; polytechnics or CHE, 10. *science and engineering degree courses* at Oxbridge, 5; other universities, 30; medical schools, 7; polytechnics or CHE, 7. *other general training courses*, 15. Average number of pupils going straight into careers in armed services, 3; industry, 12; the City, 3; civil service, 2. Many ex pupils go into agriculture; many into industry, post degree.

Uniform School uniform worn throughout.

Houses/prefects Competitive houses. Prefects, head boy, head of house – appointed by the Head after consultation with staff and sixth form. School Council.

Religion C of E assemblies (compulsory for those not specifically withdrawn). Optional communion services.

Social Debates, concerts, plays with other local schools. About 15 organised trips abroad each year, including French and German exchanges. Pupils allowed to bring own car/bicycle/motorbike/horse to school. Meals self service. School shop. No tobacco/alcohol allowed.

Discipline No corporal punishment. Pupils failing to produce homework once might expect a warning or imposition; those caught smoking cannabis on the premises could expect to be suspended.

Boarding One house only. Central dining room. Exeats at half term and weekends as necessary. Visits to the local town allowed, as requested.

Alumni association is run by A G Underwood, c/o the School.

Former pupils Keith Speed MP; R E G Jeeps; Vice Admiral Sir Ted Horlick; Major General Keith Burch; Richard Janko (Professor of Classics, University of Los Angeles); Nicholas Lloyd (Editor *Daily Express*); Professor E Cochin.

BEDGEBURY

Bedgebury School	Co-ed	Pupils 306
Goudhurst	Boys	Upper sixth 30
Kent TN17 2SH	● Girls	Termly fees:
Telephone number 0580 211221	Mixed sixth	Day £1100
	● Day	Boarding £1856
Enquiries/application to the Headmistress	● Boarding	GSA

WHAT IT'S LIKE

Founded in 1860, it lies in the Kentish Weald and consists of two establishments 6 miles apart. The Lower School at Hawkhurst is accommodated in the fine Victorian and Georgian houses of Lillesden and Collingwood which have delightful grounds. The Upper School occupies a fine 17th century country house in Bedgebury Park – a superb estate of 250 acres. Excellent modern accommodation and facilities are available, including a business school. A pleasant friendly atmosphere prevails. Staff:pupil ratio of 1:7. The main aim is to achieve the all-round development of each girl and bring out her best. A sound general education is provided and results are creditable. Some 5–10 leavers go on to university each year; most go on to degree courses. Very strong art, music and drama departments. An excellent range of sports and games. Activities are plentiful and include riding for many pupils. There are big stables and 38 horses and ponies are available. Some local community service work and an impressive record in the Duke of Edinburgh's Award Scheme.

SCHOOL PROFILE

Pupils Total over 12, 306. Day 46; Boarding 260. Entry age, 8–13 and into sixth. Own junior school provides over 20%. Under 5% are children of former pupils.

Entrance Own entrance exam used. Not oversubscribed. A variety of skills (music, riding, art, academic) looked for; a C of E school but other religions accepted. Parents not expected to buy text books. 10–15 scholarships/bursaries pa, 10% day fees to 66% boarding fees.

Parents 10+% live within 30 miles, 10+% live overseas.

Staff Head Mrs M E A Kaye, in post for 1 year. 44 full time staff, 13 part time. Annual turnover 10–15%.

Academic work GCSE, A-levels, City & Guilds Fashion Diploma, RSA and Pitmans. Average size of upper fifth 60; upper sixth 30. *O-levels*: on average, 23 pupils in upper fifth pass 1–4 subjects; 20, 5–7 subjects; 20 pass 8+ subjects. *A-levels*: on average, 4 pupils in the upper sixth pass 1 subject; 7, 2 subjects; and 11, 3 subjects. On average, 5 take science/engineering A-levels; 6 take arts and humanities; 14 a mixture. Ceramics offered to GCSE/A-level. *Computing facilities*: 2 computer rooms and computers in several classrooms. Provision for individual tuition in EFL and for dyslexic pupils (2 and 3 full time staff respectively).

Senior pupils' non-academic activities *Music*: 34 learn a musical instrument, 18 to Grade 6 or above, 1 accepted for Music School; 9 in school orchestra, 18 in school choir, 2 in school jazz group. *Drama and dance*: 80 in school productions. 10 take up to Grade 6 in ESB, RAD. *Art*: 60 take as non-examined subject; 34 take GCSE; 15 A-level; 14 history of art; 15 fashion and design; 2 ceramics. 5 accepted for Art School. 30 belong to eg photographic club. *Sport*: Tennis, lacrosse, netball, badminton, volleyball, basketball, table tennis, swimming, rounders, athletics, gymnastics, trampolining, cross country, judo, fencing, self-defence available; golf and squash off-site. 140 take non-compulsory sport. 100 take sport exams; 30 tennis; 100 athletics. Some pupils represent county (lacrosse reserves, hockey, tennis), 1 represents region (cross country). *Other*: 6 take part in local community schemes. 31 have bronze Duke of Edinburgh's Award and 18 gold. Other activities include a computer club, riding (38 horses and ponies available), sailing, driving lessons.

Careers Deputy Head acts as careers advisor; other senior staff also advise. Average number of pupils accepted for *arts and humanities degree courses* at universities, 3; polytechnics, art college or CHE, 6. *science and engineering degree courses* at Oxbridge, 1; other universities, 5; medical schools, 1; polytechnics or CHE, 2. *other general training courses*, 8.

Uniform School uniform worn except the sixth.

Houses/prefects Competitive houses. Prefects, head girl and heads of houses – appointed after election. School Council.

Religion Compulsory daily assembly; Sunday church, Chapel (Catholics go to own church; Muslims may have own instruction).

Social Joint musical (possibly drama) activities with Bethany School. Debates and drama workshops, discos with other schools. Exchanges with France and Germany. Pupils allowed to bring own car/horse to school. Meals mostly self-service. School shop. No tobacco/alcohol allowed.

Discipline No corporal punishment. Pupils failing to produce homework once might expect to produce it next day; those caught smoking cannabis on the premises may expect expulsion.

Boarding 25% have own study bedroom, 75% share with 2 or 3. Houses divided by age. 4 resident qualified nurses. Central dining rooms on each site. Sixth formers can provide and cook own food. 2 weekend exeats each term, more by special arrangement. Visits to local town allowed; sixth may go to London for weekends.

Alumni association run by Mrs Chippindale, Wintons, Peasmarch, Rye, E Sussex.

Former pupils Virginia Holgate (3 day eventer).

BELFAST ACADEMY

Belfast Royal Academy
7 Cliftonville Road
Belfast BT14 6JL
Telephone number 0232 740423

Enquiries/application to the Headmaster

- Co-ed
- Boys
- Girls
- Mixed sixth
- Day
- Boarding

Pupils 1263
Upper sixth 164
Termly fees:
Day £500
HMC

WHAT IT'S LIKE

Founded in 1785 (the oldest school in the city), its new premises were opened in 1880 in north Belfast. The neo-Gothic buildings of that period have received extensive additions and modernisation now providing excellent facilities. It is non-denominational. The fees of 95% of pupils are paid by the local authority. A very high standard of teaching and consistently good results (well over 100 university entrants per year). Many pupils go into medicine, dentistry and engineering. Very strong in music, drama and sport. Substantial commitment to local community schemes and Duke of Edinburgh Award Scheme.

SCHOOL PROFILE

Pupils Total 1263 (boys 596, girls 667). Entry age, 11+ and into sixth. 30% are children of former pupils.

Entrance Admission by test set by the Department of Education. Oversubscribed. Academic competence required; no religious requirements. Parents not expected to buy text books. No scholarships/bursaries available; 95% of pupils have fees paid by LEA.

Parents 15+% are doctors, lawyers, etc; 15+% in industry or commerce. 60+% live within 30 miles.

Staff Head W M Sillery, in post for 8 years. 77 full time staff, 12 part time. Annual turnover 5%. Average age 40.

Academic work GCSE and A-levels. Average size of upper fifth 195; upper sixth 164. *O-levels*: on average, 22 pupils in upper fifth pass 1–4 subjects; 66, 5–7 subjects; 101 pass 8+ subjects. *A-levels*: on average, 17 pupils in the upper sixth pass 1 subject; 24, 2 subjects; 105, 3 subjects and 12 pass 4 subjects. On average, 65 take science/engineering A-levels; 60 take arts and humanities; 39 a mixture. *Computing facilities*: 15 networked BBC 'B' using AMCOM-E-NET in computer room; 3 stand-alone BBC 'B'; 3 BBC Master 128; 2 RML 380Z; 6 RML Nimbus.

Senior pupils' non-academic activities *Music*: 45 learn a musical instrument, 10 up to Grade 6 or above; 40 in school orchestra, 65 in choir, 4 in school pop group; 15 in area youth orchestras; 12 go on to university orchestra/choir. *Drama and dance*: 75 act in school productions (120 backstage). 10 take GCSE drama; 12 in 'Studio' plays etc. 1 accepted for Drama School, 1 to work in theatre. *Art*: 3 take as non-examined subject; 36 take GCSE; 13 A-level. 3 accepted for Art School. *Sport*: Hockey, rugby, tennis, badminton, swimming, squash, netball, cross country, cricket, athletics, sailing, basketball, volleyball, judo, orienteering and Olympic gymnastics available. 235 take non-compulsory sport. 30 take life-saving exams. 23 represent Ulster (athletics, rugby, swimming, tennis, rifle shooting). *Other*: 80 take part in local community schemes. 57 have bronze Duke of Edinburgh's Award, 58 have silver and 85 gold. Other activities include computer club, chess, community service, Christian Union, ATC, rifle shooting, Girl Guides, dramatic society, electronics society.

Careers 4 part time careers advisors. Average number of pupils accepted for *arts and humanities degree courses* at Oxbridge, 3; other universities, 36; polytechnics or CHE, 3. *science and engineering degree courses* at Oxbridge, 7; other universities, 66 (including medical schools); polytechnics or CHE, 4. *BEd*, 4. *other general training courses*, 8. Average number of pupils going straight into careers in armed services, 1; the church, 1; industry, 8; civil service, 6; other, 17. Best pupils go into medicine and engineering.

Uniform School uniform worn throughout.

Houses/prefects Competitive houses. Prefects, head boy and girl, head of house and house prefects elected by pupils.

Religion Morning assembly is compulsory, unless exclusion requested by a parent.

Social Youth club for handicapped children organised with community service group of neighbouring grammar school. Annual ski trip to France or Austria, visit to Paris and at least one other trip abroad. Pupils allowed to bring own car/bicycle/motorbike to school. Meals self service. School tuck shop. No tobacco/alcohol allowed.

Discipline No corporal punishment. Pupils failing to produce homework once might expect a scolding or extra work. Smoking cannabis would entail permanent exclusion.

Alumni association is run by Mr R D Reid, 1 Orchard Close, Cherryvalley Park, Belfast BT5 6PN (boys) and Mrs D Elliott, 3 Old Station Road, Craigavad, Co. Down (girls).

Former pupils Sir Francis Evans (soldier and diplomat); Archbishop John Armstrong; Archbishop Robin Eames; Major-General Eric Girdwood; Rear Admiral Dudley Gurd; John Cole, Douglas Gageby (journalists); Jack Kyle (sportsman).

BELMONT HOUSE

Belmont House School
Sandringham Avenue
Newton Mearns
Glasgow G77 5DU
Telephone number 041 639 2922

Enquiries/application to the Headmaster

Co-ed
• Boys
Girls
Mixed sixth
• Day
Boarding

Pupils 200
Upper sixth 18
Termly fees:
Day £750
IAPS

WHAT IT'S LIKE

Founded in 1929, it is suburban single-site, 7 miles from the centre of Glasgow. The main building is a mansion of the Broom estate. Playing fields are nearby and the surroundings are pleasant. Good facilities are available. The school stresses the fact that it fosters an intimate caring attitude in the classroom with maximum individual attention so that a pupil can reach his academic potential in preparation for adult life. Academic standards are good and 5–10 pupils go on to university each year. The school prides itself on its tutorial service: all members of staff stay on for an extra hour one day per week to give extra help for those who may need it. Not a great deal of music or drama. Adequate range of sports, games and activities. No community services, no Duke of Edinburgh's Award Scheme.

SCHOOL PROFILE

Pupils Total over 12, 200. Entry age, 4, 10, 12 and into the sixth. 10% are children of former pupils.

Entrance Own entrance exam used. Oversubscribed sometimes. No special skills or religious requirements. Parents not expected to buy text books (book rental scheme). 15 assisted places pa. No bursaries/scholarships.

Parents 15+% are doctors, lawyers, etc; 15+% in industry or commerce. 60+% live within 30 miles.

Staff Head J Mercer, in post for 16 years. 22 full time staff, 3 part time. Annual turnover less than 5%. Average age 40.

Academic work O-grade, S-grade, Highers, CSYS. Average size of upper fifth 28; upper sixth 18. *O-grade*: on average, 12 pupils pass 1–4 subjects; 5, 5–7 subjects; 14 pass 8+ subjects. *Highers*: on average, 9 pupils pass 1 or 2 subjects; 2, 3 subjects; 9, 4 subjects; 9 pass 5 subjects. On average, 11 take science/engineering Highers; 11 take arts and humanities; 7 take a mixture. *Computing facilities*: Computers in chemistry, physics, English, modern languages and geography departments. A bank of networked computers in mathematics. Basic English support for non-native speakers.

Senior pupils' non-academic activities *Music*: 6 learn a musical instrument, 4 play in pop group. *Drama and dance*: 12 in school productions. 1 takes Grade 6 in ESB, RAD etc. 1 accepted for Drama School. *Art*: 6 take art as non-examined subject; 8 take O-grade; 7 take Higher. 2 accepted for Art School. *Sport*: Rugby, cricket, skiing, canoeing, swimming, orienteering, basketball, squash, tennis, curling, golf, athletics and shooting available. All take non-compulsory sport. Most take exams. 8 represent county/country (rugby, rowing, badminton). *Other*: Some enter voluntary schemes or work for national charities after leaving school. Other activities include a computer club, chess club, debating club, model making, shooting, hill walking, wind surfing.

Careers 2 part time advisors. Average number of pupils accepted for *arts and humanities degree courses* at universities, 4; polytechnics or CHE, 3. *science and engineering degree courses* at universities, 4; medical schools, 1; polytechnics or CHE, 1. Average number of pupils going straight into careers in the armed services, 1; the church, 1; industry, 2; the civil service, 1; retail, 4. Traditional school careers are accountancy and business studies.

Uniform School uniform worn throughout.

Houses/prefects Competitive houses. Prefects, head boy – appointed by Head and staff; head of house and house prefects – elected by pupils.

Religion School prayers held each morning; Rabbi visits weekly for Jewish pupils.

Social Debates with local girls' schools or in national competitions. Inter school Trivial Pursuits competition hosted and organised by Belmont. 1 continental ski trip and 1 sightseeing trip organised annually. Pupils allowed to bring own car/bike/motorbike to school. Meals, formal. No tobacco/alcohol allowed.

Discipline Corporal punishment only allowed via Headmaster. Pupils failing to produce homework once might expect to rewrite it with additional work; those caught smoking cannabis on the premises might expect expulsion.

Former pupils Lord Goold (Chairman of Scottish Conservative Party); Sandy Carmichael (most capped Scottish Rugby Forward).

BELVEDERE

The Belvedere School
16 Belvidere Road
Princes Park
Liverpool L8 3TF
Telephone number 051 727 1284

Enquiries/application to the Headmistress

Co-ed
Boys
● Girls
Mixed sixth
● Day
Boarding

Pupils 555*
Upper sixth 40
Termly fees:
Day £695
GPDST
*whole school

WHAT IT'S LIKE

It has been an important part of Liverpool life since it opened in 1880 as Liverpool High School and aims to have a wide social spread of pupils. Somewhat unusual in site and structure since it occupies four large Victorian houses (3 scheduled) in Belvidere Road, overlooking Prince's Park. The grounds are agreeable: gardens, lawns, trees. Extensive additions in the last 25 years include a new science block and a gymnasium/hall. The junior school is combined nearby. A pleasantly friendly atmosphere prevails. Music, drama, art and a variety of extra-curricular activities are much encouraged and academic results are good. Religious practice is also encouraged. Fees are low.

SCHOOL PROFILE

Pupils Total 555. Entry age, 4+, 7+, 11+ and into sixth. 5% are children of former pupils.

Entrance Own entrance exam used. Not oversubscribed. No special skills (other than academic potential) or religious requirements. Parents not expected to buy text books. 159 assisted places. A number of bursaries and at least 1 scholarship pa, value varies.

Parents 15+% in industry or commerce; 15+% are doctors, lawyers etc. 60+% live within 30 miles.

Staff Head Miss S Downs, in post for 16 years. 35 full time staff, 8 part time. Annual turnover 5%.

Academic work GCSE and A-levels. Average size of upper fifth 70, upper sixth 40. *O-levels*: on average, pupils pass 8 or 9 subjects. *A-levels*: on average, pupils pass 3–4 subjects. On average, 16 take science/engineering A-levels; 18 take arts and humanities; 6 a mixture. *Computing facilities*: Computer dept with RML 380Z, Atari 800 XL, Amstrad 6128 and Amstrad PCW 8256 for GCSE and A-level courses.

Senior pupils' non-academic activities *Music*: 40 learn a musical instrument, 8 up to Grade 6 or above, 1 accepted for Music School; 1 now works in stage entertainment; 20 in school orchestra, 20 in choir; 8 in local orchestras or wind band. *Drama and dance*: Many in school productions. 2 up to Grade 6 Guildhall exam. 10 have regular drama lessons. 3 accepted for Drama Schools; 1 now works in theatre. *Art*: 5 take A-level; all lower sixth attend history of art talks. 1 accepted for Art School; 4 into foundation art course. Art room open for interested pupils at lunchtime. *Sport*: Lacrosse, netball, rounders, tennis, volleyball, gymnastics, trampolining, swimming, athletics, table tennis, basketball available. 15 take non-compulsory sport. 5 represent county (lacrosse). *Other*: 40 have bronze Duke of Edinburgh's Award, 12 have silver and 10 gold. Other activities include computer club, chess club, debating society, Christian fellowship, young enterprise, choir, orchestra plus various subject groups.

Careers 1 part time careers advisor. Average number of pupils accepted for *arts and humanities degree courses* at universities, 10; polytechnics or CHE, 5. *science and engineering degree courses* at Oxbridge, 4; other universities, 10; medical schools, 4; polytechnics or CHE, 10. *BEd*, 3. Average number of pupils going straight into careers in armed services, 1; industry, 2; civil service, 5; music/drama, 2.

Uniform School uniform worn except in sixth.

Houses/prefects No houses. No prefects; head girl and deputies elected by school and staff.

Religion All attend assembly.

Social Debates and occasional musical events with local schools. Trips abroad arranged each year. Pupils allowed to bring own car/bicycle. Meals self service. No tobacco/alcohol allowed.

Discipline Punishment appropriate to offence. Detention is given for continuous unsatisfactory work.

Alumni association is run by Miss Eirilys Owen.

Former pupils Dame Rose Heilbron (High Court Judge); Alyson Bailes (Diplomatic Service); Muriel St Clare Byrne (writer).

BEMBRIDGE

Bembridge School
Hillway
Bembridge
Isle of Wight PO35 5PH
Telephone number 0983 872101

Enquiries/application to the Headmaster

- Co-ed   Pupils 166
- Boys   Upper sixth 22
- Girls   Termly fees:
- Mixed sixth   Day £864
- Day   Boarding £1560
- Boarding   SHMIS

WHAT IT'S LIKE

Founded in 1919 by J Howard Whitehouse, it has a stunningly beautiful site of 100 acres of fields and woodlands on the easternmost tip of IOW, overlooking Whitecliffe Bay and Culver Cliff. Whitehouse was an educational pioneer and the first to establish the basic core of the modern curriculum now generally accepted. He also endowed the school with a priceless collection of original works by John Ruskin and his contemporaries. Special interests and ability in any non-academic field are strong qualifications for entry. It was one of the first British schools to introduce creative activities into the formal curriculum and much emphasis is put on the development of the individual by encouraging particular skills and enthusiasms. It is ideally suited to environmental studies, for geography, geology and natural history. Outdoor pursuits are very popular (the school is one of the oldest members of the Duke of Edinburgh Award Scheme). Also strong in music and art. Its academic record is highly creditable. In general its life is based on Christian values (daily prayers, chapel services, traditional Anglican teaching).

SCHOOL PROFILE

Pupils Total over 12, 166. Day 26 (boys 19, girls 7); Boarding 140 (boys 114, girls 26). Entry age, 7+, 13 and into sixth. Own junior department provides over 36%. 2% are children of former pupils.

Entrance Common entrance and own entrance exam used. No special skills or religious requirements. Parents expected to buy text books. No assisted places. 6 scholarships (academic, art, music and day pupils) value up to half fees; bursaries for children of service personnel.

Parents 15+% in armed services. 10+% live within 30 miles; 10+% live overseas.

Staff Head J High, in post for 2 years. 25 full time staff, 16 part time (including 12 music). Annual turnover 4%. Average age 38.

Academic work GCSE and A-levels. Average size of upper fifth 45; upper sixth 22. *O-levels*: on average, 20 pupils in fifth pass 1–4 subjects; 19, 5–7 subjects; 4 pass 8+ subjects. *A-levels*: on average, 8 pupils in upper sixth pass 1 subject; 6, 2 subjects; 8 pass 3 subjects. On average, 5 take science/engineering A-levels; 9 take arts and humanities; 8 a mixture. *Computing facilities*: Computer studies to GCSE/A-level. Well equipped computer classroom. Computers in most academic departments. Specific Learning Difficulties Unit and individual coaching available.

Senior pupils' non-academic activities *Music*: All learn a musical instrument, 10 up to Grade 6 or above; 30 in school orchestra, 40 in choir, 13 in pop group. *Drama and dance*: 50 in school productions. *Art*: 12 take as non-examined subject; 12 GCSE; 4 A-level. 1 accepted for Art School. 10 belong to photographic club, 12 take pottery. *Sport*: Rugby, football, netball, hockey, squash, rounders, basketball, tennis, volleyball, cricket, archery, swimming, sailing, windsurfing, shooting, riding, canoeing, 9-hole golf course available. All take non-compulsory sport. 12 take life saving exams. 7 represent county (athletics, cricket). *Other*: 50 have bronze Duke of Edinburgh's Award, 8 have silver and 2 gold. Other activities include computer club. Two afternoons a week devoted to a wide range of activities.

Careers 1 full time careers advisor. Member of ISCO. Average number of pupils accepted for *arts and humanities degree courses* at Oxbridge, 1; other universities, 4; polytechnics or CHE, 6. *science and engineering degree courses* at Oxbridge, 1; other universities, 4; medical schools, 1; polytechnics or CHE, 6. *other general training courses*, 2. Average number of pupils going straight into careers in armed services, 3; industry, 4. Many pupils join the armed services.

Uniform School uniform worn, modified in sixth.

Houses/prefects Competitive houses. Prefects, head boy/girl, head of house and house prefects appointed by the Headmaster or Housemaster.

Religion Morning chapel compulsory unless parents request otherwise.

Social Joint Sixth Form Society and occasional social functions with local schools. Organised ski trip abroad. Senior pupils allowed to bring own bicycle to school. Meals formal. School tuck and uniform shops. No tobacco allowed. Sixth formers allowed alcohol on supervised social occasions.

Discipline No corporal punishment. Pupils failing to produce homework once might expect a reprimand or detention. Gating for smoking or consumption of alcohol. Expulsion for possession or use of drugs.

Boarding 25% have own study bedroom, 40% share 3 to a room; 35% in dormitories of 6+. Houses, of approximately 50 are single sex and the same as competitive houses. Resident qualified nurse. Central dining room. 2 weekend exeats a term and half-term. Weekly visits to local town allowed.

Alumni association is run by Mr J Dearden, Bembridge School, Bembridge, Isle of Wight.

Former pupils Sir Robin Day; Dingle Foot; Frank Hilton QC HE; Sir Richard Parsons; Gen Sir Peter Whiteley; Richard Studt and Paul Gregory (musicians).

BENENDEN

Benenden
Cranbrook
Kent TN17 4AA
Telephone number 0580 240592

Enquiries/application to the Registrar

Co-ed
Boys
● Girls
Mixed sixth
Day
● Boarding

Pupils 398
Upper sixth 53
Termly fees:
Boarding £2150
GSA

WHAT IT'S LIKE

Founded in 1923 by three mistresses from Wycombe Abbey, the main building is a neo-Elizabethan mansion (built in 1862) in enormous gardens designed in the 19th century, set in 240 acres of parkland and woods in one of the loveliest regions of Kent. Numerous recent developments and excellent facilities. Exceptionally well equipped for sports, games and recreations. Socially, a middle- and upper-class school, its academic standards are high and it is strong in art, music, drama and dance. Religious life is based on Christian principles and following Anglican practice (the Archbishop of Canterbury is the Visitor). It enjoys flourishing links with the local community. Seniors help and visit the elderly in the neighbourhood. Girls are encouraged to make friends in the local community and entertain parish friends on Sundays. Local voluntary organisations call on the school. There is liaison with local boys' schools for debates, dances and musical entertainment.

SCHOOL PROFILE

Pupils Total 398. Entry age, 11, 12, 13 and few into sixth. 10% are children of former pupils.

Entrance Common entrance and own entrance exam used. Oversubscribed. No special skills or religious requirements. Parents expected to buy text books. 9 open academic, 2 music and 1 art scholarships, 80%–10% of fees.

Parents 15+% in industry or commerce; 15+% are doctors, lawyers etc. 10+% live within 30 miles; 20+% live overseas.

Staff Head Mrs Gillian du Charme, in post for 3 years. 45 full time staff, 38 part time. Annual turnover 8. Average age 40.

Academic work GCSE and A-levels. Average size of upper fifth 70; upper sixth 53. *O-levels*: on average 9.9% pupils in upper fifth pass 1–4 subjects; 23%, 5–7 subjects; 67.6% pass 8+ subjects. *A-levels*: on average, 9% pupils in upper sixth pass 1 subject; 19%, 2 subjects; 60.4%, 3 subjects and 8% pass 4 subjects. On average, 8 take science/engineering A-levels; 33 take arts and humanities; 12 a mixture. *Computing facilities*: ECONET system with BBC micro computers. Some special help available for pupils with EFL or eg dyslexia, or mild handicaps.

Senior pupils' non-academic activities *Music*: 185 learn a musical instrument, 20 up to Grade 6 or above; 40 in school orchestra, 200 in choirs, 20 in school pop group. *Drama and dance*: 40–120 in school productions. 40–100 in workshops; 60 in House plays; 20–200 in competitions. 200 take LAMDA exams. 1–2 accepted for Drama Schools; 2–6 work in theatre; 12 involved in university drama; 30 in amateur groups. *Art*: 30 take as non-examined subject; 12 GCSE; 3 A-level. 2–3 accepted for Art School. 15 belong to photographic club; 20 in others. *Sport*: Lacrosse, netball, basketball, badminton, fencing, judo, riding, rounders, squash, swimming, table tennis, tennis, ballet, golf, gymnastics, keep fit, modern dance, sailing, self-defence, tap dancing, trampolining, volleyball available. 99% take non-compulsory sport. 100 take exams eg BAGA (gymnastics), swimming – bronze medal and resuscitation. 20 represent county, region or country (junior) at lacrosse. *Other*: 28 take part in local community schemes. 30 have bronze Duke of Edinburgh's Award, 6 silver. Other activities include computer club, Young Enterprise (2 companies).

Careers 1 full time and 1 part time careers advisors. Average number of pupils accepted for *arts and humanities degree courses* at Oxbridge, 2; other universities, 14; polytechnics or CHE, 4. *science and engineering degree courses* at Oxbridge, 2; other universities, 10; polytechnics or CHE, 3. *BEd*,

2. *other general training courses*, 10. Average number of pupils going straight into careers in the City, 1; music/drama, 1; other, 1.

Uniform School uniform worn throughout.

Houses/prefects Competitive houses. Prefects, head girl (appointed by the Head). Head of house and house prefects elected by upper school and staff. School Council.

Religion Morning prayers, Sunday church service, weekday Communion.

Social Ad hoc joint functions with several local schools, eg drama and singing. Organised trips abroad eg ski-ing or to Italy or Greece. Senior pupils allowed to bring own bicycle to school. Lunch formal, other meals self service. School shop. No tobacco allowed. A glass of wine allowed for sixth formers in weekly social club (supervised).

Discipline No corporal punishment. Pupils failing to produce homework once might expect work to be marked down or supervised to get it done; those caught smoking cannabis on the premises could expect expulsion.

Boarding 46 have own study bedroom, 28 share with 1 or 2; 200 are in dormitories of 6+ (many cubicled). Pupils in accommodation houses, 50–64 per house. Two resident qualified nurses, doctor on call. Central dining room. Sixth formers can provide and cook own food. Termly exeats: 2 (1.5 days) and half term (4 or 5 days minimum). Visits to the local town allowed, but never alone.

Alumni association is run by The Seniors' Secretary, c/o the School.

Former pupils The Princess Royal.

BERKHAMSTED (BOYS)

Berkhamsted School
Castle Street
Berkhamsted
Hertfordshire HP4 2BE
Telephone number 04427 3236

Enquiries/application to the Headmaster's secretary

Co-ed   Pupils 575
● Boys   Upper sixth 90
   Girls   Termly fees:
   Mixed sixth   Day £1100
● Day   Boarding £1924
● Boarding   HMC

WHAT IT'S LIKE

Founded in 1541 by John Incent, Dean of St Paul's, it is in the centre of the old and agreeable country town and thus an integral part of it. The original school building, the Tudor Hall, forms part of School House. The rest comprises pleasant 19th-century buildings, plus many modern extensions. All-round facilities are excellent. Its outlook is Anglican in the 'broad tradition' and it provides a very good all-round education with highly creditable exam results (40–50 university entrants per year). Very strong in music, art, CCF, community service and Duke of Edinburgh Award Scheme. Plentiful use is made of the Chiltern countryside for outdoor pursuits. As the preparatory department is nearby it provides continuity from 7–18 if desired. There is close co-operation with Berkhamsted School for Girls (under the same board of governors). There is flexibility between day and boarding. Day-boys come from a defined catchment area, so the school is quite local, but not parochial because of the boarding element which is strongly international (25% of boarders are 'British Overseas', 25% foreign). The school is 'passionately committed to the concept of all-roundness' and discourages specialisation in any activity. The aim is to turn out generally well-educated all-rounders.

SCHOOL PROFILE

Pupils Total over 12, 575. Day 455; Boarding 120. Entry age, 7+, 10+, 13+ and into sixth. Berkhamsted Prep and Junior provide over 50%.

Entrance Common entrance exam, NFER tests and own entrance exam used. Oversubscribed. No special skills (favours all-rounders). No religious requirements but this is an Anglican school. Parents expected to buy text books. 5 assisted places pa. 10–12 scholarships/bursaries, up to full fees.

Parents 15+% in industry or commerce. 60+% live within 30 miles; up to 10% live overseas.

Staff Head C J Driver, in post for 5 years. 53 full time staff, 9 part time. Annual turnover 5%. Average age 39.

Academic work GCSE, A-levels, S-levels. Average size of upper fifth 100; upper sixth 90. *O-levels*: on average, 5 pupils in upper fifth pass 1–4 subjects; 35, 5–7 subjects; 60 pass 8+ subjects. *A-levels*: on average, 5 pupils in upper sixth pass 1 subject; 5, 2 subjects; 52, 3 subjects and 13 pass 4 subjects. On average, 25 take science/engineering A-levels; 40 take arts and humanities; 25 a mixture. Ceramics offered to GCSE, CDT to A-level. *Computing facilities*: 14 Apple II's linked by Ominet with Corvus storage and 6 BBC Masters with individual disc drive; plus variety of computers in departments. EFL and extra English provisions.

Senior pupils' non-academic activities *Music*: 100 learn a musical instrument, 20 up to Grade 6 or above; 40 in school orchestra, 30 in choir, 10 in school pop group, 30 in wind group, 8 in brass group, 60 in choral society. Some of school in youth choral groups and orchestras; 6 in pop group; Oxbridge Choral Scholarships. *Drama and dance*: 17 in school productions; 7 in House plays. 1 accepted for university drama course; 1 now working in theatre; 3 in local dramatic society. *Art*: 30 take as non-examined subject; 45 GCSE; 9 A-level. 4 accepted for Art School. 20 belong to eg photographic club; 10 to ceramics workshop; 30 take arts topics; 1 now working in product design. *Sport*: Rugby, cricket, swimming, athletics, Eton fives, squash, tennis, volleyball, basketball, weight training, rowing, canoeing, cycling, cross country, hockey, association football, fencing available. Sport compulsory for all. Some represent county (canoeing, rowing, swimming, shooting, rugby, cricket, athletics, squash, golf, tennis). *Other*: 35 have silver Duke of Edinburgh's Award, 20 gold. 173 in CCF (140 Army, 33 Navy). Other activities include computer club, music, drama, chess, bridge, maths society, economics society, history society, debating and public speaking, ceramics, art.

Careers 2 part time careers advisors. Average number of pupils accepted for *arts and humanities degree courses* at Oxbridge, 4; other universities, 26; polytechnics or CHE, 8. *science and engineering degree courses* at Oxbridge, 5; other universities, 13; medical schools, 1; polytechnics or CHE, 2. *other general training courses*, 7 (including HNDs, art etc). Average number of pupils going straight into careers in armed services, 3; industry, 4; the City, 2.

Uniform School uniform worn throughout.

Houses/prefects Competitive houses. Prefects, head boy, head of house and house prefects – appointed by the Headmaster, after consulting Housemasters and other prefects. No personal fagging, some collective responsibilities.

Religion Chapel attendance compulsory, but parents' 'conscience clause'.

Social Close co-operation with Berkhamsted Girls' School, especially in music, drama, Chapel, social activities. Organised trips abroad for modern languages, ski-ing, classics, CCF, history. Day pupils allowed to bring own car/bicycle/motorbike to school. Meals self service (formal occasionally). School shops for sports clothes, second hand clothing, stationery. No tobacco/alcohol allowed.

Discipline No corporal punishment. Pupils failing to produce homework once might expect a ticking-off; those caught smoking cannabis on or off the premises could expect expulsion.

Boarding 15% have own study bedroom, 60% share 2–4; 25% are in dormitories of 6+. Houses of approximately 45–55. Resident SRN and visiting school medical officer. Central dining room. Pupils can sometimes provide and cook own food. Termly exeats: 2 weekends and half-term. Visits to the local town allowed as requested.

Alumni association is run by Michael Horton, The President, Old Berkhamstedian Association, c/o The Bursary, Berkhamsted School.

Former pupils Antony Hopkins (musician); Air Vice Marshal Sir David Parry Evans (airman); Mr Justice Michael Coombe (judge); Alexander Goehr (composer, 1987 Reith Lectures); Richard Maybey (writer and naturalist); Sir Kenneth Cork (accountant, former Lord Mayor of London); Tarn Hodder (chairman, Hockey Association); Alex Grinsdell (President RFU); Michael Meacher MP (Labour); Keith Mans MP (Conservative); John Bly (antique dealer and broadcaster); Michael van Straten (naturopath and broadcaster); Robin Knox-Johnston (explorer).

BERKHAMSTED (GIRLS)

Berkhamsted School for Girls
King's Road
Berkhamsted
Hertfordshire HP4 3BG
Telephone number 04427 2168

Co-ed
Boys
• Girls
Mixed sixth
• Day
• Boarding

Pupils 550
Upper sixth Yes
Termly fees:
Day £878
Boarding £1596
GSA

Head Miss V E M Shepherd (8 years)
Age range 5–18, entry by own exam
Scholarships available including music.

BETHANY

Bethany School
Goudhurst
Cranbrook
Kent TN17 1LB
Telephone number 0580 211273

Enquiries/application to the Headmaster

Co-ed
● Boys
Girls
Mixed sixth
● Day
● Boarding

Pupils 252
Upper sixth 30
Termly fees:
Day £1245
Boarding £1865
SHMIS

WHAT IT'S LIKE

Founded on its present site in 1866 by the Rev J J Kendon, a Baptist minister. Thereafter it was run as a small 'family' school until 1948 by members of the minister's family. It remains a small school with a family atmosphere and the chapel is at the centre of its life. Services are in the evangelical tradition and every effort is made to relate religious teaching to daily modern life. The school has a delightful rural setting and its buildings comprise houses round the village green of Curtisden Green, near Goudhurst. A large staff allows a most favourable staff:pupil ratio of about 1:9. Academic results are good and about 12 pupils go on to degree courses each year. There is considerable commitment to music, drama and art. A large variety of sports and games is provided and there are the usual extra-curricular activities.

SCHOOL PROFILE

Pupils Total over 12, 252. Day 45; Boarding 207. Entry age, 11, 13 and into the sixth. 5% are children of former pupils.

Entrance Common entrance and own entrance exam used. Sometimes oversubscribed. No special skills or religious requirements. Parents not expected to buy text books. 10 scholarships/bursaries, 50%–10% of fees.

Parents 30+% live within 30 miles; up to 10% live overseas.

Staff Head W M Harvey, appointed 1988. 27 full time staff, 3 part time. Annual turnover 2%. Average age 43.

Academic work GCSE and A-levels. Average size of upper fifth 55; upper sixth 30. *O-levels*: on average, 22 pupils in upper fifth pass 1–4 subjects; 12, 5–7 subjects; 18 pass 8+ subjects. *A-levels*: on average, 11 pupils in upper sixth pass 1 subject; 9, 2 subjects; 10, 3 subjects and 3 pass 4 subjects. On average, 19 take science/engineering A-levels; 10 take arts and humanities; 5 a mixture. *Computing facilities*: 16 computers, others in classrooms. Dyslexic unit for pupils with good IQ.

Senior pupils' non-academic activities *Music*: 65 learn a musical instrument, 10 to Grade 6 or above; 20 in school orchestra, 40 in choir, 6 in school pop group. *Drama and dance*: 12–30 in school productions. 1 goes on to work in theatre. *Art*: 15 take as non-examined subject; 14 GCSE; 6 A-level. 3 accepted for Art School. 14 belong to eg photographic club. *Sport*: Rugby, cross country, swimming, tennis, athletics, badminton, basketball, squash, rifle shooting, indoor cricket nets, soccer, hockey available. 70 take non-compulsory sport; 11 take GCSE PE. 5 represent county/country (rugby, cross-country). *Other*: 12 have bronze Duke of Edinburgh's Award. Other activities include a computer club, chess club, driving lessons etc.

Careers 1 full time careers advisor. Average number of pupils accepted

116

for *arts and humanities degree courses* at universities, 3; polytechnics or CHE, 6. *science and engineering degree courses* at universities, 5; medical schools, 2; polytechnics or CHE, 7. *other general training courses*, 3. Average number of pupils going straight into careers in armed services, 4; industry, 7; the City, 5; civil service, 3; music/drama, 2; farming, 4.

Uniform School uniform worn except the sixth.

Houses/prefects Competitive houses. Prefects, head boy, head of house and house prefects – appointed by Head and housemasters. School Council.

Religion Compulsory religious worship.

Social Discos, lectures, choral events with girls' schools. Rugby, ski-ing, cycling, natural history trips abroad. Pupils allowed to bring own bike to school. Meals self service. School tuckshop. No tobacco allowed, some alcohol in presence of staff.

Discipline Corporal punishment abolished in 1987. Pupils failing to produce homework once might expect a warning.

Boarding 15 have own study bedroom, 35 share with 1 other, the rest are in dormitories mostly of 4. Houses, of approximately 15–60, divided by age. Resident qualified nurses, doctor in village. Central dining room. 2 overnight exeats per term plus 3 days, after chapel. Weekend visits to village allowed.

Alumni association run by P S Holmes Esq, Secretary, c/o the School.

Former pupils Lord Stamp.

BIRKENHEAD

Birkenhead School
55 Shrewsbury Road
Birkenhead
Wirral
Merseyside L43 2JA
Telephone number 051 652 4014

Co-ed
● Boys
Girls
Mixed sixth
● Day
Boarding

Pupils 500
Upper sixth Yes
Termly fees:
Day £675
HMC

WHAT IT'S LIKE

Founded in 1860 and soon established as the leading boys' school in the locality. It has pleasant late Victorian and modern buildings on an estate of some 50 acres. The principal playing fields are central. Others lie two minutes' walk away. There have been many additions and improvements to facilities in the last 20 years. The school is organised in 3 departments: the prep with over 200 pupils (aged 4–11); the junior school of 180 boys (aged 11–13) and the senior school of 500 boys (aged 13–19). There is a favourable staff:pupil ratio, especially in the sixth form. A good general education is given and academic results are highly creditable. Quite a large number of pupils go on to university each year. The school has a strong Christian tradition and prayers are held each morning in the chapel. The music, drama and art departments are very active. A good range of sports and games in which high standards are attained. There is also a wide variety of extra-curricular activities and a flourishing CCF contingent.

SCHOOL PROFILE

Head J A Gwilliam (25 years)
Age range 13–19, own prep from age 4; entry by own exam
Assisted places and scholarships available.

BIRKENHEAD HIGH

Birkenhead High School	Co-ed	Pupils 759
86 Devonshire Place	Boys	Upper sixth 90
Birkenhead	● Girls	Termly fees:
Merseyside L43 1TY	Mixed sixth	Day £622
Telephone number 051 652 5777	● Day	GPDST
	Boarding	
Enquiries/application to the Headmistress		

WHAT IT'S LIKE

Founded in 1901, it is single-site in a quiet, pleasant, residential district. The junior school is nearby. There have been many modern developments and additions to its late Victorian buildings. A high standard of teaching to a traditional curriculum. 75–80% go into Higher Education (not a few go into medicine and the law). A distinguished school with vigorous local support, it is fundamentally Christian in ethos. A friendly, informal atmosphere in which plenty of freedom is given to sixth formers who play a considerable part in running the school. A wide range of sport and games, numerous societies and clubs. Very strong indeed in music and drama. Substantial commitment to local community schemes and to the Duke of Edinburgh Award Scheme.

SCHOOL PROFILE

Pupils Total over 12, 759. Entry age, 4, 7, 11 and into sixth. Own junior school supplies over 20%. 5% are children of former pupils.
Entrance Own entrance exam used. Oversubscribed. No special skills or religious requirements. Parents not expected to buy text books. 40 assisted places pa. Some scholarships/bursaries available.
Parents 15+% in industry or commerce; 15+% are doctors, lawyers etc. 60+% live within 30 miles.
Staff Head Mrs Kathleen Irving, in post for 2 years. 57 full time staff, 19 part time.
Academic work GCSE and A-levels. Average size of upper fifth 111; upper sixth 90. *O-levels*: on average, 8 pupils in upper fifth pass 1–4 subjects; 26, 5–7 subjects; 75 pass 8+ subjects. *A-levels*: on average, 6 pupils in the upper sixth pass 1 subject; 10, 2 subjects; 14, 3 subjects; 50 pass 4 subjects and 4 pass 5 subjects. On average, 38 take science/engineering A-levels; 27 take arts and humanities; 25 a mixture. Greek and Russian are offered to GCSE/A-level. *Computing facilities*: 10 – RM Nimbus PC; 4 – BBC.
Senior pupils' non-academic activities *Music*: 150 learn a musical instrument, 50 up to Grade 6 or above; 1 now plays in a pop group; 3 accepted at universities and colleges for music degrees; 40 in school orchestra, 100 in

choir, 20 in wind ensemble, 4 in string quartet. *Drama and dance*: 60–80 in school productions; 20 in drama clubs, 36 produce school drama festival; 1 takes Guildhall Grade 6, 14 GCSE drama. 2 accepted for Drama Schools; 4–10 outside auditions; 20 enter drama festivals; 1 entered playwriting competition. *Art*: 58 take GCSE; 9 A-level. 6 accepted for Art School; 2 for architecture. 18 in eg photographic club. *Sport*: Lacrosse, hockey, netball, tennis, rounders, badminton, trampolining, gymnastics, dance, athletics, volleyball, table tennis, swimming, squash, archery available. 100 take non-compulsory sport. 10 take exams eg judo; 40 GCSE; 20 trampolining. 25 represent county (lacrosse, netball, hockey, tennis, badminton, gymnastics, squash, swimming). *Other*: 100+ take part in local community schemes. 45 have bronze Duke of Edinburgh's Award, 20 have silver and 7 gold. Other activities include computer, history, geography, modern languages, classical, biology, chemistry, political debating and St Vincent de Paul societies, Christian Union, orchestra, 2 choirs, wind ensemble, renaissance band, guitar club, gym, dance, badminton, volleyball, squash, table tennis clubs and trampolining group.

Careers 1 full time careers advisor plus help from pastoral staff. Average number of pupils accepted for *arts and humanities degree courses* at Oxbridge, 3; other universities, 19; polytechnics or CHE, 6. *science and engineering degree courses* at Oxbridge, 4; other universities, 18; medical schools, 9; polytechnics or CHE, 6. *BEd*, 4. *other general training courses*, 14. Average number of pupils going straight into careers in industry, 2; the City, 2; other, 4. Traditional school careers: medicine and law.

Uniform School uniform worn except in sixth.

Houses/prefects Competitive houses. No prefects. Head girl and 3 deputies, head of house – elected by the school.

Religion Christian morning assembly.

Social Debates and joint theatrical productions with local boys' independent school. Organised trips abroad. Pupils allowed to bring own car/bicycle/motorbike to school. Meals self service. No tobacco/alcohol allowed.

Discipline No corporal punishment. Pupils failing to produce homework once might expect a reprimand.

Former pupils Patricia Routledge (actress and singer); Ann Bell (actress); Judith Collins (first Woman Curator of the Tate Gallery); Janet McNeill (novelist, especially of children's books).

Bishop Challoner

Bishop Challoner School	Co-ed	Pupils 235
228 Bromley Road	• Boys	Upper sixth 15
Shortlands	Girls	Termly fees:
Kent BR2 0BS	• Mixed sixth	Day £695
Telephone number 01-460 3546	• Day	ISAI
	Boarding	
Enquiries/application to the Headmaster		

119

WHAT IT'S LIKE

Founded in 1946 by two local parish priests, it is single-site and semi-rural on 4.5 acres and combines junior and senior schools. In 30 years there have been numerous extensions to the original house to provide good modern facilities. A sound education is given and academic attainments are creditable. The majority of pupils are Roman Catholic. Thus, assemblies are religious, Mass is said regularly and the curriculum incorporates religious instruction, including theology and philosophy. Latin compulsory for all boys in the first two years in the senior school.

SCHOOL PROFILE

Pupils Total over 12, 235. Entry age, 4, 11 and into sixth; girls into sixth from September 1988. Own junior school provides approximately 50%. 5% are children of former pupils.

Entrance Own entrance exam used. Oversubscribed at junior level. No special skills or religious requirements but majority are Roman Catholic. Parents not expected to buy text books. 6 scholarships/bursaries available, £695–£347.

Parents 15+% in industry or commerce; 15+% are doctors, lawyers etc. 60+% live within 30 miles.

Staff Head Terence Robinson, in post for 3 years. 27 full time staff, 4 part time. Annual turnover 1%. Average age 40.

Academic work GCSE and A-levels. Average size of upper fifth 40; upper sixth 15. *O-levels*: on average, 30% pupils in upper fifth pass 1–4 subjects; 20%, 5–7 subjects; 10% pass 8+ subjects. *A-levels*: on average, 1 pupil in the upper sixth passes 1 subject; 2, 2 subjects; 9, 3 subjects. On average, 8 take science/engineering A-levels; 5 take arts and humanities; 2 a mixture. *Computing facilities*: Computer room with 8 BBC micros. Facilities for GCSE and A-level computer studies.

Senior pupils' non-academic activities *Music*: 8 learn a musical instrument. *Drama and dance*: 30 in school productions. *Art*: 12 take GCSE; 4 A-level. 1 accepted for Art School. 2 belong to eg photographic club. *Sport*: Soccer, rugby, athletics, basketball, tennis, cricket, fencing available. 50 take non-compulsory sport. *Other*: 10 take part in local community schemes. Other activities include computer, chess and fishing clubs and choir.

Careers 2 part time careers advisors. Average number of pupils accepted for *arts and humanities degree courses* at universities, 2; *science and engineering degree courses* at Oxbridge, 1; other universities, 3; polytechnics or CHE, 5. Average number of pupils going straight into careers in armed services, 5; the church, 1; industry, 5; the City, 5; civil service, 2; music/drama, 2.

Uniform School uniform worn except in sixth.

Houses/prefects No competitive houses. Prefects and head boy appointed by the Head after consulting school. School Council.

Religion All attend religious assemblies. Regular Mass for Catholics.

Social Organised trips abroad for ski-ing, classics, adventure etc. Pupils allowed to bring own car/bicycle/motorbike/horse to school. Meals formal. School tuck shop. No tobacco/alcohol allowed.

Discipline No corporal punishment. Pupils failing to produce homework once might expect loss of free time to do the work; those caught smoking cannabis on the premises could expect expulsion.

BISHOP'S STORTFORD

Bishop's Stortford College
Maze Green Road
Bishop's Stortford
Hertfordshire CM23 2QZ
Telephone number 0279 57911

Co-ed   Pupils 360
● Boys   Upper sixth Yes
   Girls   Termly fees:
● Mixed sixth   Day £1440
● Day   Boarding £2020
● Boarding   HMC

WHAT IT'S LIKE

The college was founded in 1868, mainly by Nonconformists in East Anglia, and was then primarily intended for the education of Nonconformists. It was reconstituted in 1904 and now accepts members of all Christian denominations. It has a fine site on high ground on the edge of the pleasant town, next to open countryside, with gardens and grounds covering 100 acres. The buildings are agreeable and well equipped. At their centre stands an impressive Memorial Hall (erected in 1921). The school is divided into junior and senior sections and the organisation of each is largely separate. Religious instruction and worship are inter-denominational. Overall there is a favourable staff:pupil ratio of about 1:10. Academic standards are high and results are impressive. The vast majority of sixth formers go on to universities or colleges of higher education. Music is very strong indeed throughout the school, and so is drama. There is a good deal of collaboration between the music and drama departments. There is a good range of sports and games and these are pursued to quite a high level. A plentiful variety of extra-curricular activities is available.

SCHOOL PROFILE

Head S G G Benson (4 years)
Age range 13–18; own prep from age 7; entry by common entrance or own exam
Scholarships and assisted places available, plus awards for sons of Free Church ministers.

BLACKHEATH HIGH

Blackheath High School
Wemyss Road
Blackheath
London SE3 0TF
Telephone number 01-852 1537

Co-ed   Pupils 371
   Boys   Upper sixth Yes
● Girls   Termly fees:
   Mixed sixth   Day £684
● Day   GPDST; GSA
   Boarding

Head Mrs H E Webber Williams (10 years)
Age range 11–18, own junior from age 4; entry by own exam
Scholarships, bursaries and assisted places available.

BLOXHAM

Bloxham School
Bloxham
Near Banbury
Oxfordshire OX15 4PE
Telephone number 0295 720206

Co-ed   Pupils 345
● Boys   Upper sixth Yes
Girls   Termly fees:
● Mixed sixth   Day £1420
● Day   Boarding £2115
● Boarding   Woodard; HMC

Head Mr M W Vallance (6 years)
Age range 13–18; entry by common entrance or own test
7 scholarships and bursaries plus art and music scholarships. Founded 1860.

BLUNDELL'S

Blundell's School
Tiverton
Devon EX16 4DN
Telephone number 0884 252543

Co-ed   Pupils 480
● Boys   Upper sixth Yes
Girls   Termly fees:
● Mixed sixth   Day £1250
● Day   Boarding £2100
● Boarding   HMC

WHAT IT'S LIKE

Founded and endowed in 1604 at the sole charge of the estate of Peter Blundell, clothier of Tiverton, by Sir John Popham. In 1882 it moved to its present site on the outskirts of Tiverton. The site comprises a fine estate of 100 acres of beautiful gardens and playing fields and other grounds. Its pleasant and well-equipped buildings provide good facilities and comfortable accommodation. The school maintains a Christian tradition and Anglican practice; all pupils are expected to attend weekday morning chapel and the school service on Sundays. In the lower school the life and teaching of Christ is the main area of religious study. The curriculum includes exploration of other faiths, the Old Testament and moral issues. A large staff allows a staff:pupil ratio of about 1:8. Academic standards are high and results impressive. A lot of pupils go on to university and other forms of further education. The school has always been strong in music and a good music centre provides excellent facilities. There are a choir, 3 orchestras, wind and jazz bands, rock bands and brass ensemble. Music is studied by all pupils on entry to the school. Drama is also very strong. There are house plays, inter-house drama competitions and at least one major school play per year. Art, crafts and technology are also flourishing fields of work and study. A wide variety of sports and games is available and standards are high. Many clubs and societies cater for most conceivable needs. Every Tuesday afternoon is set aside for specifically non-sporting activities. There is a large CCF (Army, Navy and RAF section). Everyone who enters the school in the lower and middle fifth forms does a year's service. Activities include climbing, canoeing, abseiling, flying, sailing and expeditions on Dartmoor and

Exmoor. Adventure training is popular and the school has its own centre on Dartmoor. There is an unusually big commitment to local community service.

SCHOOL PROFILE

Head A J D Rees (8 years)
Age range 13–18; entry by common entrance or own exam
Academic, musical and artistic scholarships available, 50 in all.

BOLTON (BOYS)

Bolton School Boys' Division	Co-ed	Pupils 990
Chorley New Road	● Boys	Upper sixth 120
Bolton	Girls	Termly fees:
Lancashire BL1 4PA	Mixed sixth	Day £796
Telephone number 0204 40202	● Day	HMC
Enquiries/application to the Headmaster	Boarding	

WHAT IT'S LIKE

Originally founded in 1524, endowed by Robert Lever in 1641 and re-endowed in 1913 by Sir W H Lever (later Viscount Leverhulme). It comprises impressive and very large buildings with a huge hall, plus recent additions, which lie to the NW of Bolton in an urban residential area, a mile from the town centre on an estate of 32 acres. The prep and junior departments are nearby. The boys' and girls' divisions are in the same building and though the organisation of the two divisions provides basically single-sex schools there are many opportunities for boys and girls to meet and co-operate in the running of societies etc. A broad traditional education is given, academic standards are high (in any one year 90 or more pupils go on to university) and it has a high reputation far beyond Bolton. There are 300 assisted-place pupils and fees are astonishingly low. Though non-denominational, Christian beliefs are encouraged. A good deal of emphasis on health and fitness. Its outdoor activities centre in the Pennines is used a lot.

SCHOOL PROFILE

Pupils Total over 12, 990. Entry age, 8, 9, 11 and into sixth. Own junior school provides over 20%.
Entrance Own entrance exam used. Oversubscribed. No special skills or religious requirements. Parents not expected to buy text books. 300 assisted places. 1 music bursary, £250 towards music tuition.
Parents 60+% live within 30 miles.
Staff Head A W Wright, in post for 5 years. 66 full time staff, 4 part time. Annual turnover 3%. Average age 37.
Academic work GCSE and A-levels. Average size of upper fifth 120; upper sixth 120. *O-levels*: on average, 4 pupils in upper fifth pass 1–4 subjects; 10, 5–7 subjects; 105 pass 8+ subjects. *A-levels*: on average, 3 pupils in upper sixth pass 1 subject; 8, 2 subjects; 30, 3 subjects and 80 pass 4 subjects. On

average, 60 take science/engineering A-levels; 40 take arts and humanities; 20 a mixture. Technology offered to GCSE/A-level. *Computing facilities*: Computer studies laboratory, BBC/Network system and computers in main departments. School has a lift system for wheelchair users.

Senior pupils' non-academic activities *Music*: 250 learn a musical instrument, 50 up to Grade 6 or above; 45 in school orchestra, 130 in choir, 20 in jazz group, 25 in concert brass band; 6 in Bolton or other local youth orchestras; 4 university organ scholars. *Drama and dance*: 100 participate in school productions. 3 now work in theatre. *Art*: 120 take as non-examined subject; 26 GCSE; 10 A-level. 3 accepted for Art School. 15 in eg photographic club. *Sport*: Soccer, rugby, cricket, cross country, athletics, swimming, basketball, volleyball, hockey, badminton, tennis available. 300+ take non-compulsory sport. 12 represent county (soccer, rugby, athletics, cross country). *Other*: 10 take part in local community schemes. 30 have bronze Duke of Edinburgh's Award, 10 have silver and 10 gold. 2 enter voluntary schemes after leaving school, 1 works for national charity. Other activities include computer club, camps, outdoor pursuits base near Sedbergh, treks, large and flourishing scout group with new purpose built HQ.

Careers 1 full time and 3 part time careers advisors, plus 2 careers secretaries. Average number of pupils accepted for *arts and humanities degree courses* at Oxbridge, 8; other universities, 37; polytechnics or CHE, 7. *science and engineering degree courses* at Oxbridge, 7; other universities, 37; medical schools, 10; polytechnics or CHE, 3. *BEd*, 1. Average number of pupils going straight into careers in armed services, 1; industry, 5; retail/banking, 5.

Uniform School uniform worn except in sixth.

Houses/prefects Competitive houses. Prefects, head boy (appointed by Head), head of house and house prefects (elected by staff and school).

Religion Compulsory Christian assembly.

Social Girls' division of same foundation adjacent; joint drama, music, opera, debating society, Christian Union, swimming team. Organised German and French exchanges each year; Russian visit every other year; school trips to Rhineland, classical sites in Europe, weekend to Boulogne; 4 weeks in central southern Europe or Asia each summer (trek camp); 3 ski trips each winter. Pupils allowed to bring own car/bicycle/motorbike to school. Meals formal. School shop. No tobacco/alcohol allowed.

Discipline No corporal punishment. Pupils failing to produce homework once might expect evening detention; those caught smoking cannabis on the premises could expect immediate and indefinite suspension.

Alumni association is run by N Slater, Hon Sec, Old Boltonians Association, c/o the School.

Former pupils Sir Robert Haslam (chairman of National Coal Board); Nigel Short (chess champion); Sir Geoffrey Jackson (British ambassador to Uruguay); Ian McKellen (actor).

BOLTON (GIRLS)

Bolton School Girls' Division
Chorley New Road
Bolton
Lancashire BL1 4PB
Telephone number 0204 40201

Co-ed   Pupils 760
Boys   Upper sixth Yes
● Girls   Termly fees:
Mixed sixth   Day £775
● Day   GSA; GBGSA
Boarding

WHAT IT'S LIKE

Founded in 1877, it moved to other premises in 1891 and to its present site in 1928. The boys' and girls' divisions are a single foundation, provided for by Lord Leverhulme. It has an excellent site of 32½ acres on the western side of Bolton and a mile from its centre. The handsome sandstone buildings are set among lawns, playing fields and woodland. They are extremely well equipped with a fine library and spacious hall and overall are dignified and comfortable. Many additions and improvements have been made in the last 25 years. Most of the facilities are shared by the boys' school. Recent improvements include an indoor sports complex. The school also has a field study centre in Cumbria, and a nearby 18 acre site for the Leverhulme centre. Academically it is a high powered and well-run school which has a notable reputation in the locality and further afield. Results are consistently good and each year 80% of pupils go on to take degree courses, including a number at Oxbridge. A very efficient careers advice service is provided for all pupils. Music, drama and art are extremely strong and involve a large number of pupils, who reach high levels of achievement. A wide range of sports and games is available and the school has had many representatives at county, regional and national level (especially in lacrosse). Numerous clubs and societies cater for extra-curricular needs. The school organises regular expeditions in Britain and abroad and pupils also have a big commitment to local community services and the Duke of Edinburgh's Award Scheme.

SCHOOL PROFILE

Head Mrs M A Spurr (9 years)
Age range 11–18, own prep from age 5; entry by own exam
Many activities shared with Bolton Boys' Division, joint prep from 5–8.
Assisted places.

BOOTHAM

Bootham School
York YO3 7BU
Telephone number 0904 23636

Enquiries/application to the Headmaster

● Co-ed   Pupils 271
Boys   Upper sixth 40
Girls   Termly fees:
Mixed sixth   Day £1173
● Day   Boarding £1889
● Boarding   HMC

WHAT IT'S LIKE

Founded in 1823, a Quaker Foundation (The Society of Friends), it has an agreeable site of 10 acres just outside York's medieval walls and a few minutes' walk from the City centre. Playing fields adjoin it. A number of Georgian houses constitute the core; there are numerous modern extensions and facilities. It has most of the advantages of being a comparatively small school. Full use is made of the City's amenities (several excellent museums, the theatre and art gallery). Quaker beliefs underlie the daily life of pupils and staff but those of other persuasions are welcome. Strong in music, art and the sciences. A fair number of pupils (20–30 per year) go on to university. Most seniors take part in a variety of local community schemes and there is vigorous local support.

SCHOOL PROFILE

Pupils Total over 12, 271. Day (boys 71, girls 74); Boarding 126 (boys). Entry age, 11, 13 and into sixth. 10% are children of former pupils.

Entrance Common entrance and own entrance exam used. Not oversubscribed. No special skills or religious requirements. Parents not expected to buy text books. 12 scholarships, entrance awards and bursaries according to need as far as possible, value half fees to eighth fees.

Parents 15+% in industry or commerce, 15+% are doctors and lawyers etc. 30+% live within 30 miles; up to 10% live overseas.

Staff Head J H Gray, in post for 16 years. 26 full time staff, 10 part time. Annual turnover 3%. Average age 40.

Academic work GCSE and A-levels. Average size of upper fifth 40; upper sixth 40. *O-levels*: on average, 9 pupils in upper fifth pass 1–4 subjects; 16, 5–7 subjects; 10 pass 8+ subjects. *A-levels*: on average, 6 pupils in upper sixth pass 1 subject; 6, 2 subjects; 11, 3 subjects and 10 pass 4 subjects. On average, 14 take science/engineering A-levels; 16 take arts and humanities; 4 a mixture. *Computing facilities*: room equipped with 8 BBC computers; 2 departmental computers; 2 common room (pupils) computers; 1 computer for use by staff. Special provisions: dyslexic pupils attend York Branch of Dyslexic Institute; specialist EFL teacher gives supervision, counsel and extra English lessons to Anglo-Chinese pupils.

Senior pupils' non-academic activities *Music*: 50 learn a musical instrument, 25 up to Grade 6 or above, 1 accepted for Music School; 32 in school orchestra, 18 in choir, 7 in pop group; 45 in other musical activities; 4 in local orchestra. *Drama and dance*: 40 in school productions. *Art*: 110 take as non-examined subject; 18 GCSE; 4 A-level. 2 accepted for Art School; 1 for architecture. 20 belong to eg photographic club. *Sport*: Football, hockey, cricket, tennis, swimming, squash, badminton, netball, volleyball, self defence, fencing, athletics, rowing available. All pupils take non-compulsory sport. 3 represent county (hockey, swimming, bridge). *Other*: Most seniors take part in local community schemes. Other activities include computer and chess clubs; eligible pupils can learn to drive. Leisure hour activities are structured and regarded as very important, wide range available.

Careers 1 full time careers advisor. Average number of pupils accepted for *arts and humanities degree courses* at Oxbridge, 2; other universities, 5; polytechnics or CHE, 6. *science and engineering degree courses* at Oxbridge, 2; other universities, 12; medical schools, 2; polytechnics or CHE, 6. *other general training courses*, 8. Average number of pupils going straight into

careers in the City, 1; other, 10. Traditional school careers in the sciences.
Uniform School uniform worn except in the sixth.
Houses/prefects Competitive houses for sport, music and speech-making. Prefects, head boy/girl, head of house and house prefects – elected by the school. There is a Communications Group.
Religion Quakerism (The Society of Friends).
Social Joint drama productions with sister school, The Mount, York. Organised exchanges abroad with school in West Germany; ski-ing trips and language trips abroad. Pupils allowed to bring own car/bicycle/motorbike to school. Meals usually self service, few special meals formal. No tobacco/alcohol allowed.
Discipline No corporal punishment. Pupils failing to produce homework once might expect 'Columns' (writing out words from a dictionary) or 'Gating' (staying within the School campus); those caught smoking cannabis on the premises could expect suspension and likely expulsion.
Boarding 50% of sixth formers have own study bedroom, 50% share (with 1); very few pupils are in dormitories of 6+. Houses divided by age. Resident qualified nurse/doctor. Central dining room. Pupils can provide and cook own food. 2 weekend exeats each term. Visits to the local town allowed as required.
Alumni association is run by The Secretary, O.Y.S.A., c/o the School.
Former pupils A J P Taylor (historian).

Box Hill

Box Hill School
Mickleham
Dorking
Surrey RH5 6EA
Telephone number 0372 373382

Enquiries/application to the Headmaster's Secretary

- Co-ed
- Boys
- Girls
- Mixed sixth
- Day
- Boarding

Pupils 278
Upper sixth 25
Termly fees:
Day £1135
Boarding £1935
SHMIS; ISAI; GBA

WHAT IT'S LIKE

Founded in 1959, the main building is a handsome Victorian mansion (plus purpose-built modern facilities) situated in 40 acres of delightful bosky grounds, with big playing fields, next to the village of Mickleham in whose life the school plays an active part. It belongs to The Round Square Conference and is run on the principles of Kurt Hahn, founder of Salem and Gordonstoun. It thus has close international links with schools in Europe, USA, Canada, India and Australia. There is an annual conference at one of the sister schools. Sixth formers do project work in Indian villages in association with schools in India. They have an efficient system of exchanges and post A-level attachments. A wide range of activities and expeditions is operated in the belief that all pupils may excel at something and will develop through challenging experiences. Drama, music and art are regarded as particularly important. The staff includes a dyslexia specialist and a specialist in teaching English as a second language.

SCHOOL PROFILE

Pupils Total, 278. Day 87 (boys 55, girls 32); Boarding 191 (boys 116, girls 75). Entry age, 11, 13 and into sixth form.

Entrance Common entrance and own entrance exam used. Not oversubscribed. Good music or art and an ability to contribute to school life looked for. No religious requirements. Parents expected to buy some A-level text books. Assistance for 8–10 entering the sixth form, £300–£250 per term.

Parents 15+% in industry or commerce. 30+% live within 30 miles; 20% live overseas.

Staff Head Dr Rodney Atwood, in post for 1 year. 22 full time staff, 21 part time. Annual turnover 5%.

Academic work GCSE and A-levels. Average size of upper fifth 55; upper sixth 25. *O-levels*: on average 33 pupils in upper fifth pass 1–4 subjects; 10, 5–7 subjects; 2 pass 8+ subjects. *A-levels*: on average, 7 pupils in upper sixth pass 1 subject; 9, 2 subjects; 7 pass 3 subjects. On average, 7 take science/engineering A-levels; 13 take arts and humanities; 5 a mixture. Spanish is offered to GCSE/A-level. *Computing facilities*: Computer room equipped with 12 Apple computers with full word processing facilities. Other departments have their own computers including staffroom and sixth form centre. *Special provisions*: Qualified dyslexia specialist and a qualified teacher of English as a second language.

Senior pupils' non-academic activities *Music*: 70 pupils learn a musical instrument. *Drama and dance*: 45 in school plays. Whole school participates in annual internal drama competition scripted and directed by the pupils. *Art*: 3 take A-level. 15 belong to eg photographic club. *Sport*: Soccer, cricket, tennis, athletics, swimming, netball, hockey, volleyball, riding, squash, badminton, karate, judo, fencing, table tennis, climbing (expeditions and indoor climbing wall) available. Over 100 take non-compulsory sport. Over 50 take exams eg gymnastics, swimming. Others do karate, judo, life saving (St John Ambulance). Some represent county (athletics). *Other*: 12 have bronze Duke of Edinburgh's Award, 6 have silver and 2 have gold. All pupils raise money, help old people, the local primary school, the Talking Newspaper for the Blind, etc. Other activities include a computer club (part of the electronics club); St John Ambulance first aid, bee-keeping, conservation work, pony care.

Careers 3 part time careers advisors. Average number of pupils accepted for *arts and humanities degree courses* at universities, 9; polytechnics or CHE, 6. *science and engineering degree courses* at Oxbridge, 1; other universities, 5. *other general training courses*, 7 (a number go into agricultural training courses). Average number of pupils going straight into careers in armed services, 1; industry, 3; the City, 1; music/drama, 2; other, 5.

Uniform School uniform worn throughout.

Houses/prefects Competitive houses. Prefects, head boy and girl, head of house and house prefects – elected by senior prefect body. School Council.

Religion Non-denominational service every Sunday from which parents may request exemption.

Social Sixth form conference and careers conference to which other schools are invited. Organised trips to Germany; mountaineering trips to Alps; well developed exchanges. Meals formal on Sundays and sixth form dinners; self service at other times. School shops selling books and tuck. No tobacco/alcohol allowed.

Discipline No corporal punishment. Pupils failing to produce homework would be expected to do it; those caught smoking cannabis on the premises could expect expulsion.

Boarding 2% have own study bedroom, 68% share (1–4); 30% are in dormitories of 6 or more. Single sex houses, of approximately 35–50, divided by age. 2 resident SRNs, 2 non-resident school doctors. Central dining room. Pupils can provide and cook own food. 4 weekend exeats each term plus half term. Visits to the local town allowed.

Alumni association is run by Mr Nicholas Booth, Box Hill School Association Secretary, c/o the School.

BRADFIELD

Bradfield College
Reading
Berkshire RG7 6AR
Telephone number 0734 744203

Enquiries/application to the Headmaster's secretary

Co-ed
● Boys
Girls
● Mixed sixth
● Day
● Boarding

Pupils 515
Upper sixth 94
Termly fees:
Day £1836
Boarding £2450
HMC

WHAT IT'S LIKE

Founded in 1850, it became well known by 1900 as one of the leading independent schools in southern England. In effect the school *is* the village of Bradfield and vice versa; a very attractive village of brick-and-half-timber and brick-and-flint houses in one of the prettiest regions of Berkshire. The total grounds cover about 200 acres. Its accommodation is excellent (comfortable small dormitories) and has outstandingly good facilities in general (including a modern design centre, an electronics centre, a TV studio and a satellite tracking equipment). It is a C of E foundation and Christian values are embodied in the life of the school, but those of other denominations are very welcome. High academic standards (50–60 university entrants per year). Strong in sport and games and very strong in music and drama. It is unusual in having an open-air Greek theatre where plays *in Greek* are performed every three years. Other strengths are the large CCF unit (much emphasis on adventure training and leadership skills), plentiful outdoor activities plus recreations such as fly-fishing on the Pang and sailing on the gravel pits at Theale. A point is made of keeping close contacts with industry, with 'attachments' for all lower sixth pupils.

SCHOOL PROFILE

Pupils Total 515. Day 42 (boys 28, girls 14); Boarding 473 (boys 462, girls 11). Entry age, boys 13+, boys and girls into sixth. 14% are children of former pupils.

Entrance Common entrance exam plus Bradfield Scholarship examination used. Oversubscribed. No special skills required, but any are taken into account. No religious requirements. Parents expected to buy text books at sixth form level. 3 assisted places at sixth form level only. 15 scholarships/bursaries, 80%–10% of fees.

Parents 15+% in industry or commerce, 15+% are doctors, lawyers etc. 10+% live within 30 miles; up to 10% live overseas.

Staff Head P B Smith, in post for 3 years. 53 full time staff, 21 part time. Annual turnover 10%. Average age 35.

Academic work GCSE and A-levels. Average size of upper fifth 100; upper sixth 94. *O-levels*: on average, 4 pupils in upper fifth pass 1–4 subjects; 46, 5–7 subjects; 50 pass 8+ subjects. *A-levels*: on average, 4 pupils in upper sixth pass 1 subject; 8, 2 subjects; 70, 3 subjects and 8 pass 4 subjects. On average, 32 take science/engineering A-levels; 32 take arts and humanities; 30 a mixture. Electronic systems offered at A-level. *Computing facilities*: Computers in every academic department; computer-aided design; full computing room; well-equipped electronics room.

Senior pupils' non-academic activities *Music*: 120 learn a musical instrument, 30 up to Grade 6 or above. 5 take A-level music, 5 accepted for music degrees; 60 in orchestra, 60 in choir. *Drama and dance*: 200 in school productions. 4 accepted for Drama/Dance schools. *Art*: 20 take as non-examined subject; 12 GCSE; 8 A-level. 4 accepted for art school. 40 belong to eg photographic, architectural and art appreciation clubs. *Sport*: Football, hockey, cricket, tennis, athletics, shooting, swimming, sailing, golf, basketball, judo, karate, cross country, fives, squash, water polo, fly-fishing, clay-pigeon shooting, fencing available. Virtually all take non-compulsory sport. Pupils represent county at various sports. *Other*: 50 take part in local community schemes. 15 have bronze Duke of Edinburgh's Award, 15 have silver and 15 gold. Other activities include a computer club, chess club, 30 societies, electronics club, design centre, CCF.

Careers 5 full time and 1 part time careers advisors. Average number of pupils accepted for *arts and humanities degree courses* at Oxbridge, 5; other universities, 25; polytechnics or CHE, 10. *science and engineering degree courses* at Oxbridge, 5; other universities, 20; medical schools, 6; polytechnics or CHE, 10. *other general training courses*, 1. Average number of pupils going straight into careers in armed services, 5; industry, 1; the City, 1; civil service, 1; music/drama, 1.

Uniform School uniform worn throughout.

Houses/prefects Prefects, head boy, head of house and house prefects appointed by the Head in consultation with staff and pupils.

Religion Attendance at school Chapel, once on Sunday, twice per week for morning prayers.

Social Many joint theatrical and choral productions with local girls' schools. Organised holiday expeditions, several per year. French school exchange. Pupils allowed to bring own bicycle to school. Meals self service. School shop. No tobacco allowed. School bar for 17 year olds.

Discipline No corporal punishment. Pupils failing to produce homework once would be asked to do it; those caught smoking cannabis on the premises could expect to be expelled.

Boarding 30% have own study bedroom, 30% share 1–3; 30% are in dormitories of 6 or more. Houses, of approximately 60–65. Resident qualified medical staff. Central dining room. Pupils can provide and cook own food. Up to 4 weekend exeats per term. Visits to the local town allowed for sixth form.

Alumni association is run by J B Johnson, c/o the College.

Former pupils Richard Adams (author); David Owen (politician).

BRADFORD (BOYS)

Bradford Grammar School
Keighley Road
Bradford
West Yorkshire BD9 4JP
Telephone number 0274 542492

Enquiries/application to the Headmaster

Co-ed
● Boys
Girls
● Mixed sixth
● Day
Boarding

Pupils 898
Upper sixth 132
Termly fees:
Day £766
HMC

WHAT IT'S LIKE

It existed c1548 and was incorporated by royal charter in 1662. A mile from the centre of Bradford, it comprises four main buildings on a 20-acre site: the Clock House, a 17th-century manor house for the juniors; the handsome senior school (opened in 1949); the Kenneth Robinson Building (1974); and the Edward Clarkson Library and Information Technology Centre (1988). Its overall amenities are first-rate. The two principles of discipline laid down are: firstly, that pupils are expected to know what is and what is not good conduct and to do nothing likely to bring themselves and their school into disrepute; secondly, that study is a discipline in itself. It provides a sound, traditional education in many branches of learning, including not only Classics and Information Technology but also economics and electronics systems and sets very high all-round standards. It enjoys strong local loyalties and support and in fact has long been one of the most distinguished schools in Britain with remarkable academic records: in any one year 30 pupils may go on to Oxbridge and 100 to other universities. Fees are astonishingly low by modern levels.

SCHOOL PROFILE

Pupils Total over 12, 898 (boys 850, girls 48). Entry age, 11, boys, directly into sixth boys and girls. 10% are children of former pupils.

Entrance Own entrance exam used. Oversubscribed. No special skills or religious requirements. Parents not expected to buy text books. 30 assisted places. 5 scholarships/bursaries, up to £1000 pa.

Parents 15+% in industry or commerce; 15+% are doctors, lawyers etc. 60+% live within 30 miles.

Staff Head D A G Smith, in post for 14 years. 76 full time staff, 7 part time. Annual turnover 4%. Average age 35.

Academic work GCSE and A-levels. Average size of upper fifth 125; upper sixth 132. *O-levels*: on average, 8 pupils in upper fifth pass 1–4 subjects; 38, 5–7 subjects; 78 pass 8+ subjects. *A-levels*: on average, 7 pupils in upper sixth pass 1 subject; 16, 2 subjects; 103, 3 subjects and 3 pass 4 subjects. On average, 59 take science/engineering A-levels; 50 take arts and humanities; 32 a mixture. *Computing facilities*: Purpose built Infotech block opens 1988.

Senior pupils' non-academic activities *Music*: 200 learn a musical instrument, 30 up to Grade 6 or above, 3 accepted for music school; 60 in orchestra, 40 in choir, 100 participate in brass, wind group, strings; 1 in National youth orchestra. *Drama and dance*: 100 in school productions. *Art*: 10 take GCSE, 10 A-level. 3 accepted for art school. *Sport*: Athletics, badminton, basketball, cross country, cricket, fencing, hockey, lawn tennis, rugby football, rowing, squash, swimming, water polo, fencing, aikido, outdoor pursuits, table tennis available. 350 take non-compulsory sport. Pupils represent county (rugby, cricket, cross country, athletics, squash, hockey). *Other* activities include a computer club, venture scouts, CCF, archaeological society, chess, debating society, drama, ski club, voluntary action group, theatre club.

Careers 4 part time careers advisors. Average number of pupils accepted for *arts and humanities degree courses* at Oxbridge, 20; other universities, 55; polytechnics or CHE, 10. *science and engineering degree courses* at Oxbridge, 10; other universities, 45; medical schools, 10; polytechnics or CHE, 10. Average number of pupils going straight into careers in armed services, 2; the church, 1; industry, 5; other, 5.

Uniform School uniform worn except in sixth.

Houses/prefects No competitive houses. Prefects and head boy/girl appointed by the Head.

Religion School prayers.

Social No organised local events. Organised trips abroad. Meals self service. School shop. No tobacco/alcohol allowed.

Discipline No corporal punishment. Pupils failing to produce homework once might expect a detention; those caught smoking cannabis on the premises could expect expulsion.

Alumni association is run by Mr S R Matthews, President: BGS Old Boys' Association, c/o the School.

Former pupils Dennis Healey; David Hockney; Sir Maurice Hodgson and others.

BRADFORD (GIRLS)

Bradford Girls' Grammar School	Co-ed	Pupils 590
Squire Lane	Boys	Upper sixth 60
Bradford	● Girls	Termly fees:
West Yorkshire BD9 6PB	Mixed sixth	Day £637
Telephone number 0274 545395	● Day	GSA
	Boarding	
Enquiries to the Headmistress		
Applications to the Registrations Secretary		

WHAT IT'S LIKE

Founded in 1876, it comprises fine, solid, well-equipped buildings and excellent up-to-date facilities on 17 acres of pleasant grounds, playing fields and woodland, in an urban residential area near the city centre. It has its own sixth-form college on site. Its academic standards and reputation are high and its pupils very motivated (a large number of university entrants: 30–40 per year). It is especially strong in music and drama and enjoys vigorous local community support as well as support from alumni. The fees are surprisingly low.

SCHOOL PROFILE

Pupils Total, 590. Entry age, 11 and into sixth form. Own junior school provides over 20%. 10–15% are children of former pupils.

Entrance Own entrance exam used. Oversubscribed. No special skills or religious requirements. Parents not expected to buy text books. 60 assisted places. Scholarships and bursaries available according to need.

Parents 15+% in industry or commerce; 15+% are doctors, lawyers etc. 60+% live within 30 miles.

Staff Head Mrs L J Warrington, in post for 1 year. 45 full time staff, 16 part time. Annual turnover 5–10%. Average age 35–40.

Academic work GCSE and A-levels. Average size of upper fifth 90 (planned to increase to 110); upper sixth 60 (planned to increase to 90). *O-levels*: on average, 5 pupils in upper fifth pass 1–4 subjects; 30, 5–7 subjects; 55 pass 8+ subjects. *A-levels*: on average, 3 pupils in the upper sixth pass 1 subject; 9, 2 subjects; 48 pass 3 subjects. On average, 50% take science/engineering A-levels; 50% take arts and humanities; very few take a mixture. *Computing facilities*: Class set Acorn Electrons and BBC B's in physics, chemistry, geography, business studies careers; masters in computer studies, business studies. Computer studies taught as examination subject and taken by all in 2nd year.

Senior pupils' non-academic activities *Music*: 200+ learn a musical instrument, 20–30 up to Grade 6 or above; 60 in orchestra; 120 in choir, others in madrigals, string quartet, wind quintet etc; 3 in Leeds, Calderdale and Kirklees orchestras; 10 in other activities in musicals, church, choral groups etc. *Drama and dance*: 150 in school productions. 4 take O-level drama in sixth form. *Art*: 10 take A-level art. 5 accepted for art school. *Sport*: Hockey, netball, rounders, tennis, swimming, volleyball, athletics throughout, badminton, squash, self-defence, fencing available in sixth form. 200+ take non-compulsory sport. 27 represent county (hockey, netball). *Other*: 20+ take part in local community schemes. All forms organise annual event in aid of charity. Other activities include a computer club, drama societies, dance club, choir, orchestra, madrigal group, history society, horse riding club etc.

Careers 3 part time careers advisors. Average number of pupils accepted for *arts and humanities degree courses* at Oxbridge, 3; other universities, 14; polytechnics or CHE, 5. *science and engineering degree courses* at Oxbridge, 3; other universities, 14; medical schools, 6; polytechnics or CHE, 7. *BEd*, 2. *other general training courses*, 4.

Uniform School uniform worn except in sixth.

Houses/prefects No competitive houses. Prefects, President of Junior Common Room – elected by school and staff. School Council.

Religion Daily act of worship compulsory except in sixth form or unless withdrawn by parents.

Social Occasional careers conventions and debating society joint with other schools. Organised trips: 2nd year to France and exchanges with France, Germany and Spain. Pupils allowed to bring own car/bicycle/motorbike to school in sixth form only. Meals self service. School shop. No tobacco/alcohol allowed.

Discipline No corporal punishment. Pupils failing to produce homework once might expect a deadline if there was no good reason; those caught smoking cannabis on the premises could expect expulsion.

BRENTWOOD

Brentwood School
Ingrave Road
Brentwood
Essex CT15 8AS
Telephone number 0277 214580

Enquiries/application to the Headmaster

Co-ed
● Boys
● Girls
● Mixed sixth
● Day
● Boarding

Pupils 830
Upper sixth 120
Termly fees:
Day £975
Boarding £1708
HMC

WHAT IT'S LIKE

Founded in 1558, it occupies a single site in an urban area (not too urban) with extensive gardens and 60 acres of playing fields. It is architecturally pleasing (the old 'Big School' built in 1568 is still in use) and there have been many modern developments. Facilities are now first rate. The standard of teaching is high and a large number of leavers proceed to university. Some of its main strengths lie in music, drama and art, and there is a flourishing CCF. It enjoys good local support. A boys' school with a mixed sixth; from September 1988, girls will be admitted from 11 but educated separately to GCSE. The sixth form will remain co-ed.

SCHOOL PROFILE

Pupils Total, 830. Day 690 (boys 660, girls 30); Boarding 140 (boys). Entry age, 11 and into the sixth (girls admitted at age 11 from 1988). Own prep school provides over 20% of pupils. 10% are children of former pupils.

Entrance Common entrance and own entrance exam used. Oversubscribed. Music and fluency in second language looked for at entry. No religious requirements but Protestant tradition. Parents not expected to buy text books. Assisted places. 12 scholarships pa, bursaries as required – £2916 –£330.

Parents 15+% in industry or commerce; 15+% are doctors, lawyers etc. More than 60% live within 30 miles.

Staff Head J A E Evans, in post for 7 years. 66 full time staff, 5 part time. Annual turnover approx 2%. Average age 35.

Academic work GCSE and A-level. Average size of upper fifth 130; upper sixth 120. *O-levels*: on average, 27 pupils in upper fifth pass 1–4 subjects; 35, 5–7 subjects; 57 pass 8+ subjects. *A-levels*: on average, 15 pupils in upper sixth pass 1 subject; 22, 2 subjects; 67, 3 subjects and 9 pass 4 subjects. On average, 40 take science/engineering A-levels; 60 take arts and humanities; 20 a mixture. Electronic systems and ancient history are offered to GCSE/A-level. *Computing facilities*: Computer lab with 16 BBCs, 3 Amstrads, 2 Apples (Sinclair Spectrums in reserve). Subsidiary EFL classes offered.

Senior pupils' non-academic activities *Music*: 100 learn a musical instrument, 30 to Grade 6 or above. 1 accepted for Music School. 10 play in pop group beyond school; 75 in orchestra, 75 in choir, 50 in pop group. *Drama and dance*: 50 in school productions; 2 accepted for Drama/Dance Schools. *Art*: 50 take as non-examined subject; 32 take GCSE; 11, A-level; 16, Art History; 6, AS level; 2 or 3 go on to study art including history of art degree courses. 24 belong to photographic club; 80 in general studies and short courses. *Sport*: Rugby, football, basketball, volleyball, cricket, squash, fencing, swimming, badminton, (netball), athletics, cross-country, tennis available. 60 take part in school team practices each week. 15 take exams in gymnastics, swimming, 20 take fencing, lifesaving. 36 represent country/district/county (fencing, rugby, soccer, athletics, swimming, cross-country). *Other*: 30 take part in local community schemes. 100 in CCF. Other activities include a computer club, chess club, archery, athletics, life saving, art, brass ensemble, bridge, Chapel choir, choral choir, Christian Union, community service, rifle club.

Careers 2 part time advisors and 8 senior Housemasters. Average number of pupils accepted for *arts and humanities degree courses* at Oxbridge, 4; other universities, polytechnics or CHE, 33. *science and engineering degree courses* at Oxbridge, 5; other universities, 23; medical schools, 6; polytechnics or CHE, 15. Some go on to training courses eg secretarial, City & Guilds, nursing etc. Average number of pupils going straight into careers in the armed services, 3; industry, 12; the City, 15; civil service, 1; music/drama, 1; other, 8. Traditional school careers are medicine and engineering.

Uniform School uniform worn throughout.

Houses/prefects Competitive houses. Prefects, head boy, head of house and house prefects – appointed by the Head. School Council.

Religion Regular chapel (C of E) encouraged but not compulsory.

Social Debates, historical society, drama, foreign exchange visits, county sports of various kinds. Organised trips to Germany, France, USA and ESU scholars both ways. Pupils allowed to bring own car/bike to school. Self service meals. School shop. No tobacco/alcohol allowed.

Discipline No corporal punishment. Pupils failing to produce homework once might expect a warning; those caught smoking cannabis on the premises could expect expulsion.

Boarding 40% have own study bedroom, 40% share; 20% are in dormitories of 6+. Houses, of 25–50, divided mainly by age groups. Resident qualified medical staff. Central dining room. Pupils can provide and cook own food. Exeats: 8 days over 3 terms. Visits to local town allowed with Housemaster's permission.

Alumni association run by Mr P Clements, Secretary, 8 Shenfield Gardens, Hutton, Essex CM13 1DT.

Former pupils Hardy Amies (1919–27); Robin Day (TV); H Whittaker (Almanac); Jack Straw (MP); Bishop Griggs of Ludlow; Bishop Adams late of Barking; Air Marshal Sir John Rogers.

BRIGHTON COLLEGE

Brighton College	• Co-ed	Pupils 500
Eastern Road	Boys	Upper sixth 100
Brighton	Girls	Termly fees:
East Sussex BN2 2AL	Mixed sixth	Day £1415
Telephone number 0273 697131	• Day	Boarding £2150
Enquiries/application to the Headmaster	• Boarding	HMC

WHAT IT'S LIKE

Founded in 1845, it stands on high ground in the Kemp Town district of Brighton and enjoys handsome buildings (the school chapel, which is in regular use, is especially striking) in beautiful gardens. Ample playing fields. Well over a million pounds have been spent in the last ten years on major developments. The teaching is of a high standard and academic results are impressive (some 40 university entrants per year). It is a good all-round school, with plenty of regard for the less talented. Strong in music, art and drama; also in sports and games. It possesses a wide range of clubs and societies and there is considerable involvement in local community schemes. Full use is made of the cultural amenities of Brighton.

SCHOOL PROFILE

Pupils Total, 500. Day 352 (boys 330, girls 22); Boarding 148 (boys 110, girls 38). Entry age, 13, and into the sixth. Own junior school provides about 60%. Approx 20% are children of former pupils.

Entrance Common entrance exam used. Oversubscribed. Pupils who have a positive contribution to make in any sphere are welcomed. No religious requirements but the College is a Christian (C of E) foundation. Parents expected to buy text books. 20 assisted places. 14 scholarships/bursaries, full fees to 10% of fees.

Parents 15+% in industry or commerce; 15+% are doctors and lawyers etc. More than 60% live within 30 miles; up to 10% live overseas.

Staff Head J D Leach, in post for 1 year. 45 full time staff, 10 part time. Annual turnover 4% (very stable). Average age 39.

Academic work GCSE and A-levels. Average size of upper fifth 93; upper sixth 100. *O-levels*: on average, 18 pupils in upper fifth pass 1–4 subjects; 23, 5–7 subjects; 52 pass 8+ subjects. *A-levels*: on average, 9 pupils in upper sixth pass 1 subject; 19, 2 subjects; 63 pass 3 subjects or more. On average, over one-third take science/engineering A-levels; one-third take arts and humanities; well under one-third a mixture. Geology is offered to A-level. *Computing facilities*: 16 workstation RML NIMBUS network. BBC 'B' stations in departments. Laser printer, computer graphics. Newly built computer laboratories.

Senior pupils' non-academic activities *Music*: 75 learn a musical instrument, 26 to Grade 6 or above. 1 accepted for Music School; 1 to university; 1–2 to polytechnic. 25 in school orchestra, 48 in school choir, 21 in band, 14 in ensembles; 7 play in Brighton Youth Orchestra, 2 in East Sussex Youth Orchestra. *Drama and dance*: All pupils are encouraged to take part in drama productions, musicals and concerts. *Art*: 50 take as non-examined subject; 18 take GCSE; 16, A-level. 5 accepted for Art School. *Sport*: Rugby, hockey, cricket, netball, tennis, volleyball, soccer, golf, squash, swimming, judo, fencing, badminton, basketball available. Some sport is compulsory (unless health reasons preclude); 12 take life saving. 23 represent county (hockey, cricket, rugby, athletics, swimming). *Other*: 70 take part in local community schemes. 2 have silver Duke of Edinburgh's Award, 5 have gold. Other activities include a computer club, alternative forum, auto club, Christian forum, computer science, debating, dialectic, economics/politics, history, industrial, law, literary/play reading, mathematical, medical, modern languages, music appreciation, philosophy, photography, physics, chemistry, biology, astronomy, sketch club, sports, travel, chess, electronics and radio, experimental science, junior debating, rock society, archives, weight training.

Careers 2 full time advisors. Average number of pupils accepted for *arts and humanities degree courses* at Oxbridge, 3; other universities, 21; polytechnics or CHE, 12. *science and engineering* at Oxbridge, 3; other universities, 12; medical schools, 4; polytechnics or CHE, 5. *BEd*, 4. *other general training courses*, 6. Average number of pupils going straight into careers in the armed services, 4; industry, 4; the City, 2; civil service, 2; music/drama, 2; other, 6.

Uniform School uniform worn including in the sixth.

Houses/prefects Competitive houses. Prefects, head boy/girl, head of house and house prefects – appointed by the Headmaster and Housemaster/mistress.

Religion Religious worship compulsory, College Chapel or own place of worship for those of non C of E persuasion.

Social Public speaking competitions, concerts, participation in Brighton Festival, Challenge of Industry Conference. Organised trips abroad. Pupils allowed to bring own car/bike/motorbike to school (with permission from the Headmaster). Meals self service. School shop. No tobacco allowed; limited bar in sixth form club.

Discipline No corporal punishment. Pupils failing to produce homework once might expect a 'Yellow Paper' signed by the Housemaster; those caught smoking cannabis on the premises could expect expulsion.

Boarding 20% have own study bedroom, 40% share; 40% are in dormitories of 6+. Houses, of 50–60. Resident matron, doctor visits daily. Central dining room. Pupils can provide and cook own snacks. Weekend exeats, by arrangement. Visits to the local town allowed.

Alumni association run by Mrs H Williamson, Brighton College, Eastern Road, Brighton.

Former pupils George Sanders (actor); Prof Noel Odell (mountaineer and Cambridge Professor); John Worsley (artist); Rt Rev T J Bavin (Bishop of Portsmouth); Rear Admiral P G V Dingemans (Falklands); Sir Michael Hordern (actor); Sir Vivien Fuchs (explorer); Sir Humphrey Edwardes-Jones (Air Commodore); Macdonald Hobley (TV presenter); Sir Robert Alexander QC; Jonathan Palmer (doctor and Formula 1 racing driver).

BRIGHTON HIGH

Brighton and Hove High School	Co-ed	Pupils 750
The Temple	Boys	Upper sixth Yes
Montpelier Road	● Girls	Termly fees:
Brighton	Mixed sixth	Day £622
East Sussex BN1 3AT	● Day	Boarding £1866
Telephone number 0273 734112	● Boarding	GPDST; GSA

Head Mrs J B E Wells (10 years)
Age range 5–18; entry by own exam
Scholarships, bursaries and 35 assisted places pa.

BRIGIDINE CONVENT

Brigidine Convent	Co-ed	Pupils 275
King's Road	Boys	Upper sixth 17
Windsor	• Girls	Termly fees:
Berkshire SL4 2AX	Mixed sixth	Day £595
Telephone number 0753 863779	• Day	GBGSA
	Boarding	
Enquiries/application to the Headmistress		

WHAT IT'S LIKE

Established at Windsor in 1948 it lies on a single site near Windsor Great Park and combines kindergarten, junior and senior schools in comfortable and civilised buildings amidst pleasant grounds. Teachers are lay as well as convent sisters. Life is firmly based on Roman Catholic education in many aspects of school life: classroom, liturgy, assembly, Mass, retreats. Discipline is fairly tight. Strong on pastoral organisation, music and extra-curricular activities.

SCHOOL PROFILE

Pupils Total over 12, 275. Entry age, 11 and into sixth. 2% are children of former pupils.

Entrance Own entrance exam used. Oversubscribed. No special skills. Roman Catholic school but other denominations accepted. Parents not expected to buy text books. 2 bursaries pa to RC girls living in the parish, £1785.

Parents 60+% live within 30 miles.

Staff Head Mrs M B Cairns, in post for 1 year. 21 full time staff. 21 part time. Annual turnover 5%. Average age 44.

Academic work GCSE and A-levels. Average size of upper fifth 58; upper sixth 17. *O-levels*: on average, 22 pupils in upper fifth pass 1–4 subjects; 17, 5–7 subjects; 15 pass 8+ subjects. *A-levels*: on average, 1 pupil in upper sixth passes 1 subject; 6, 2 subjects; 7, 3 subjects and 1 passes 4 subjects. On average, 3 take science/engineering A-levels; 10 take arts and humanities; 5 a mixture. *Computing facilities*: 12 BBC 'B'; 1 RS1 computer. Special provisions for EFL, dyslexic and mildly visually handicapped pupils.

Senior pupils' non-academic activities *Music*: 14 learn a musical instrument, 3 to Grade 6 or above. 1 accepted for Music School. 6 in school orchestra, 15 in choir. *Drama and dance*: 55 in school productions; others in general dance; 40 pupils to Grade 6 in ESB, RAD etc. 3 accepted for Drama Schools. 20 enter competitions; 2 go on to work in the theatre. *Art*: 28 take GCSE art; 6 A-level. 2 accepted for Art School. *Sport*: Hockey, tennis, badminton, rounders, baseball, basketball, squash, cricket, football, volleyball, netball, Newcombe ball available. 20 take non-compulsory sport. 3 take exams eg gymnastics, swimming. *Other*: Activities include a computer club, Aikido, debating society, keep fit.

Careers 3 part time advisors. Average number of pupils accepted for *arts and humanities degree courses* at universities, 4; polytechnics or CHE, 3. *science and engineering degree courses* at Oxbridge, 1; other universities, 3; polytechnics or CHE, 3. *BEd*, 2. *other general training courses*, 12. Average

number of pupils going straight into careers in industry, 1; civil service, 1; music/drama, 2.
Uniform School uniform worn throughout.
Houses/prefects Competitive houses. Prefects, head girl, head of house and house prefects elected by the school. School Council.
Religion Compulsory RC worship.
Social Organised events with other local schools; organised trips abroad and exchange systems. No tobacco/alcohol allowed.
Discipline No corporal punishment. Pupils failing to produce homework once might expect a reprimand; those caught smoking cannabis on the premises could expect suspension.
Former pupils Lady Mayoress of London.

BRISTOL CATHEDRAL

Bristol Cathedral School
College Square
Bristol BS1 5TS
Telephone number 0272 291872

Co-ed
● Boys
Girls
● Mixed sixth
● Day
Boarding

Pupils 460
Upper sixth Yes
Termly fees:
Day £747
CSA; HMC

WHAT IT'S LIKE

The origins of the school are in the Grammar School of St Augustine's Abbey founded in 1140. It was refounded by Henry VIII in 1542 and is Bristol's only royal foundation. It stands in the cathedral precinct and the buildings span 800 years of architectural history. The main classrooms are on the original site of the old Abbey School. There have been many modern developments and facilities are very good. A first class liberal education is provided and results are most creditable. Not a few pupils go on to university each year. Because of the close links with the cathedral (which is the school's chapel) there is considerable emphasis on religious education in the Anglican tradition. There are about 440 boys; and 25 girls (in the sixth form). The staff:pupil ratio is about 1:13. The art, drama and music departments are extremely strong and the school is quite famous for its range of musical activities. A standard range of sports and games is available and there is a fair variety of extra-curricular activities, clubs, societies etc. Work experience is undertaken by nearly all members of the fifth form and the school has close links with a wide range of commercial and industrial concerns in and about the city. Full use is made of the city's cultural amenities.

SCHOOL PROFILE

Head C S Martin (9 years)
Age range 10–18; girls into sixth; entry by own exam
25+ assisted places pa; music, academic and instrumental scholarships.

BRISTOL GRAMMAR

Bristol Grammar School
University Road
Bristol BS8 1SR
Telephone number 0272 736006

Enquiries/application to the Headmaster

- Co-ed
  Boys
  Girls
  Mixed sixth
- Day
  Boarding

Pupils 836
Upper sixth 130
Termly fees:
Day £826
HMC

WHAT IT'S LIKE

Founded in 1532, it lies in Tyndall's Park, to the north-west side of Bristol next door to the university. Its core consists of handsome Victorian buildings (especially the Great Hall) and there have been many developments in the last 15 years. It now has one of the best school libraries in England. It enjoys a high reputation academically and has played a major part in the educational life of the City. Flourishing local ties and back-up from the community and from Old Bristolians. An exceptional number of activities (over 100) on offer each week. Though a big school it has a very friendly atmosphere and much is done to maintain high standards of pastoral care through the house system and year Head/Form tutor organisation.

SCHOOL PROFILE

Pupils Total over 12, 836. Boys 625, girls 211. Entry age, 11, 12, 13 and into the sixth form. Own lower school provides over 20%. Less than 2% are children of former pupils.

Entrance 11+ entrance exam used. Oversubscribed. No special skills or religious requirements. Parents not expected to buy text books. School has Government and Governors Schemes for 350 assisted places. 7 scholarships/bursaries, 50% to 20% fees.

Parents 15+% in industry or commerce; 15+% are doctors, lawyers etc. More than 60% live within 30 miles.

Staff Head Charles Martin, in post for 2 years. 67 full time staff, 8 part time. Annual turnover 10%. Average age 38.

Academic work GCSE and A-levels. Average size of fifth 144; upper sixth 130. *O-levels*: on average, 10 pupils in fifth pass 1–4 subjects; 37, 5–7 subjects; 80 pass 8+ subjects. *A-levels*: on average, 6 pupils in upper sixth pass 1 subject; 21, 2 subjects; 95 pass 3 subjects. On average, 45 take science/engineering A-levels; 50 take arts and humanities; 35 a mixture. Russian and Greek are offered to GCSE/A-level. *Computing facilities*: 16 station BBC network plus 8 individual BBC computers.

Senior pupils' non-academic activities *Music*: 150 learn a musical instrument, 20 to Grade 6 or above, 2 accepted for Music School, 10 play in pop group beyond school; 80 in school orchestra, 150 in school choir, 15 in pop group; 1 in National Youth Orchestra; 6 in County Orchestra. *Drama and dance*: 116 participate in school plays; 80 in house productions. *Art*: 337 take as non-examined subject; 13 take A-level. 4 accepted for Art School. 20 belong to photographic club. *Sport*: Cricket, rugby, soccer, hockey, netball, athletics, cross-country, bowls, golf, fives, volleyball, ski-ing, squash, badminton, swimming, weight-training, judo, gym club, fencing available. 70 take non-compulsory sport. 56 represent county/country (rugby, hockey, cricket, swimming, athletics, golf, tennis, skiing, fencing). *Other*: 60 take part in local community schemes. 10 enter voluntary schemes after leaving school. Other activities include a computer club. Compulsory Weekly Activities Scheme up until fifth year offers 100 different options ranging from cookery, glass engraving to ice-skating and wind-surfing. 70% of sixth formers continue to participate voluntarily in the scheme.

Careers 5 part time advisors. Average number of pupils accepted for *arts and humanities degree courses* at Oxbridge, 14; other universities, 30; polytechnics or CHE, 15. *science and engineering* at Oxbridge, 6; other universities, 26; medical schools, 9; polytechnics or CHE, 7. BEd, 3. *other general training courses*, 1. Average number of pupils going straight into careers in the armed services, 1; the City, 6; other, 4. Traditional school careers are in medicine.

Uniform School uniform worn throughout.

Houses/prefects 6 competitive houses. Prefects, head boy/girl, head of house and house prefects – appointed by the Head in consultation with staff. School Council.

Religion No compulsory religious worship.

Social Regular local, area and national debating competitions and joint competitions with neighbouring schools. Regular exchanges to USA, Bordeaux, Hanover. Trips to France, Russia, Italy and Greece. Pupils allowed to bring own bike/motorbikes to school. Meals self service. Second-hand uniform shop. No tobacco/alcohol allowed.

Discipline No corporal punishment. Punishment for pupils failing to produce homework would depend on circumstances; those caught smoking cannabis on the premises could expect expulsion.

Alumni association run by Michael L Booker MA, c/o Bristol Grammar School.

Former pupils Lord Franks (British Ambassador to USA, Provost of Worcester College, Oxford); Tom Graveney (Test cricketer and commentator); Robert Lacey (author); Brian Barron (BBC correspondent); Clive Ponting (ex Civil Servant); Fred Wedlock (entertainer); General Tunbu Osman (CinC, Malaysian Army); Geoffrey Cutter (Welsh hockey international and Olympic team manager); Rt Rev Peter Nott (Bishop of Norwich); John Currie (rugby international and selector); Canon G A Ffrench-Beytagh (Anti-apartheid churchman); Dr Basil Greenhill (Director, Maritime Museum, Greenwich); G H Heath-Grace (organist); Dave Prowse (film star [Darth Vader] and Body Culture); Prof Keith Robbins (historian); Sir Richard Sheppard (architect); David Drew (ballet).

BROMLEY HIGH

Bromley High School
Blackbrook Lane
Bickley
Bromley
Kent BR1 2TW
Telephone number 01-468 7981

Co-ed
Boys
• Girls
Mixed sixth
• Day
Boarding

Pupils 530
Upper sixth 50
Termly fees:
Day £684
GPDST; GSA

WHAT IT'S LIKE

Founded in 1883 by the Girls' Public Day School Trust. Originally situated in the middle of Bromley. In 1981 it moved to Bickley to occupy new purpose-built buildings in spacious grounds. Upper and junior schools are combined. Facilities are very good. The total number of pupils is roughly 690, and there is a sixth form of about 120 pupils. Entrants come from a wide area, including Bromley, Bickley, Beckenham, Chislehurst, Petts Wood and Orpington. The school aims to provide a good all-round education, and to foster an enquiring mind and an independent spirit – plus worthwhile habits in work and leisure, and a responsive attitude to the needs and demands of society. Drama, music and art are quite strong. There is a decent range of sports and games and extra-curricular activities.

SCHOOL PROFILE

Head Mrs A B Schofield (4 years)
Age range 11–18, own junior from age 4; entry by own exam
Assisted places and 3 scholarships pa.

BROMSGROVE

Bromsgrove School
Bromsgrove
Worcestershire B61 7DU
Telephone number 0527 32774

- Co-ed
- Boys
- Girls
- Mixed sixth
- Day
- Boarding

Pupils 560
Upper sixth Yes
Termly fees:
Day £1089
Boarding £1717
HMC

Head T M Taylor (2 years)
Age range 8–18; entry by own exam or common entrance
Some scholarships, exhibitions and bursaries.

BROWN & BROWN

Brown & Brown Tutorial College
20 Warnborough Road
Oxford OX2 6JA
Telephone number 0865 36511

Enquiries/application to the Head

- Co-ed
- Boys
- Girls
- Mixed sixth
- Day
- Boarding

Pupils 97
Upper sixth 37
Termly fees:
Day £600–£900
per subject
Boarding £840
plus tuition
CIFE; Association
of Tutors

WHAT IT'S LIKE

Founded in 1971, it lies in central North Oxford, near the University Parks and close to St Hugh's College and St Antony's College. The surroundings are pleasant and the accommodation provided locally is comfortable. Despite being such a small establishment there is considerable activity in music, drama and art – and even sport. The pupils also have membership of various university societies. The intensive teaching and tutoring is of a high standard and the vast majority of pupils go on to a university. It is a well-run establishment with a high reputation.

SCHOOL PROFILE

Pupils Total 97. Day 30 (boys 14, girls 16); Boarding 67 (boys 35, girls 32). Entry age, 15.

Entrance Not oversubscribed. No special skills or religious requirements. Parents expected to buy some text books. 5 scholarships/bursaries available, 10% of fees.

Parents 15+% in the armed services; 15+% are doctors and lawyers etc. 10+% live within 30 miles; up to 10% live overseas.

Staff Head Mrs C H Brown, in post for 12 years. 18 full time staff, 43 part time. Annual turnover 2%. Average age 38.

Academic work GCSE and A-levels. Average size of upper fifth 7; upper sixth 37. *O-levels*: on average, 1 pupil in upper fifth passes 1–4 subjects; 4, 5–7 subjects; 1 passes 8+ subjects. *A-levels*: on average, 3 pupils in upper sixth pass 1 subject; 26, 2 subjects; 7, 3 subjects and 1 passes 4 subjects. On average, 40% take science/engineering A-levels; 40% take arts and humanities; 20% a mixture. Communication studies; non-European languages (eg Chinese, Arabic) are offered to GCSE/A-level. *Computing facilities*: BBC Amstrad. Dyslexic and EFL provision.

Senior pupils' non-academic activities *Music*: 20 learn a musical instrument, 10 to Grade 6 or above. *Drama and dance*: 60 in college productions; 20 study up to Grade 6 in ESB, RAD etc; 10 accepted for Drama/Dance Schools or other. *Art*: 20 take GCSE; 18, A-level; 10 accepted for Art School. *Sport*: Rugby, football, hockey, squash, swimming, running, cricket available. 60 take non-compulsory sport. 5 take exams eg gymnastics, swimming etc. 2 represent county/country. *Other*: 20 have bronze and silver Duke of Edinburgh's Award, 10 gold. 5 enter voluntary schemes or work for national charities after leaving college. Other activities include a computer club, drama, debating, punting.

Careers 1 full time and 3 part time advisors. Average number of pupils accepted for *degree courses* at Oxbridge, 2; other universities, 30; medical schools, 2; polytechnics or CHE, 7. *other general training courses*, 1. Average number of pupils going straight into careers in the armed services, 7; industry, 2; the City, 2; civil service, 2; music/drama, 1.

Uniform School uniform not worn.

Houses/prefects No competitive houses, prefects or head boy/girl. School Council.

Social Membership of university societies, eg Oxford Union. Organised trips abroad. Pupils allowed to bring own car/bike/motorbike to school. Meals self service. Pupils allowed tobacco but not alcohol.

Discipline No corporal punishment. Pupils failing to produce homework once might expect a warning; those caught smoking cannabis on the premises could expect expulsion.

Boarding 95% have own study bedroom, 5% share with 1. Pupils divided into houses for sleeping, 1–15 in each, usually single sex. Central dining room. Pupils can provide and cook own food occasionally. 1 long weekend exeat each term. Visits to local town allowed.

BRUTON (SUNNY HILL)

Bruton School for Girls	Co-ed	Pupils 440
Sunny Hill	Boys	Upper sixth 55
Bruton	● Girls	Termly fees:
Somerset BA10 0NT	Mixed sixth	Day £750
Telephone number 0749 812277	● Day	Boarding £1350
Enquiries/application to the School Registrar	● Boarding	GSA

WHAT IT'S LIKE

Founded in 1900, it has a fine 40-acre rural site on the edge of the small town of Bruton in a beautiful part of Somerset with views of the Quantocks and the Mendips. Bath and Bristol are easily accessible and full use is made of their cultural facilities. The school is commonly known as 'Sunny Hill'. Its buildings are pleasant and very well equipped and facilities are good. It serves the local community (which gives good support) and represents all sections of society. Boarders come from all over the British Isles and overseas. Its declared aims are to provide a full, well-balanced education, while at the same time developing musical, artistic and dramatic talents. There is a strong commitment to local community schemes and to the Duke of Edinburgh's Award Scheme.

SCHOOL PROFILE

Pupils Total over 12, 440. Day 244; Boarding 195. Entry age, 11+ and into the sixth. Own junior school provides over 20%. 8% are children of former pupils.

Entrance Own entrance exam used. Oversubscribed. No special skills or religious requirements. Parents not expected to buy text books. 25 assisted places. 3 scholarships/bursaries, 75% to 30% of tuition.

Parents 15+% in the armed services. 60+% live within 30 miles; up to 10% live overseas.

Staff Head Mrs J M Wade, second year in post (previously Deputy Headmistress). 42 full time staff, 10 part time. Annual turnover 5%. Average age 42.

Academic work GCSE and A-levels. Average size of upper fifth 84; upper sixth 55. *O-levels*: on average, 13 pupils in upper fifth pass 1–4 subjects; 31, 5–7 subjects; 40 pass 8+ subjects. *A-levels*: on average, 9 pupils in upper sixth pass 1 subject; 15, 2 subjects; 24, 3 subjects and 2 pass 4 subjects. On average, 17 take science/engineering A-levels; 18 take arts and humanities, 20 a mixture. *Computing facilities*: suite of 12 BBC computers plus computer in science department. EFL provisions.

Senior pupils' non-academic activities *Music*: 150 learn a musical instrument, 38 to Grade 6 or above. 1 accepted for Music School; 2 for degree courses. 28 in school orchestra, 110 in school choir, 3 in Somerset Youth Orchestra. *Drama and dance*: 50 in school productions; 100 in informal productions; 90 take LAMDA exams; 1 onto degree course. *Art*: 10 take as non-examined subject; 20 take GCSE; 2, A-level; 2 accepted for Art School; 10 belong to photographic club. *Sport*: Hockey, netball, cross-country, athletics, tennis, rounders, swimming, gymnastics available. 200 take non-compulsory sport. 30 take exams eg gymnastics, swimming. 23 represent county/country (hockey, netball, athletics). *Other*: 20 take part in local community schemes. 60 have bronze Duke of Edinburgh's Award, 20 have silver. Other activities include a computer club, music, art, drama and charity work. Driving lessons also available.

Careers 2 part time advisors. Average number of pupils accepted for *arts and humanities degree courses* at Oxbridge, 1; other universities, 9; polytechnics or CHE, 3. *science and engineering degree courses* at Oxbridge, 1; other universities, 10; medical schools, 2; polytechnics or CHE, 5. *BEd*, 2. *other general training courses*, 12. Average number of pupils going straight into careers in the civil service, 1; banking/accountancy, 3. A tradition in engineering careers.

Uniform School uniform worn except in the sixth.

Houses/prefects Competitive houses. Head girl appointed. Head of house and house prefects.

Religion Daily assembly. All boarders attend Church on Sundays.

Social Many brothers attend King's School, Bruton. Joint social events are arranged. Local schools are invited to sixth form functions. Organised trips abroad. Pupils allowed to bring own bikes to school. Meals self service. School shop. No tobacco/alcohol allowed.

Discipline Pupils failing to produce homework once might expect to do a repeat; those caught smoking cannabis on the premises would expect instant expulsion.

Boarding 44 have own study bedroom, 20 share (double rooms); 90 are in dormitories of 6+. Houses, of 32–65, divided by age group. Resident qualified medical staff. Central dining room. Sixth formers can provide and cook own food. Number of exeats each term varies with age. Visits to the local town allowed.

Alumni association run by Mrs Joy Howard, c/o the School.

BRYANSTON

Bryanston School	• Co-ed	Pupils 648
Blandford	Boys	Upper sixth 140
Dorset DT11 0PX	Girls	Termly fees:
Telephone number 0258 52411	Mixed sixth	Day £1534
Enquiries/application to the Admissions Secretary	• Day	Boarding £2300
	• Boarding	HMC

WHAT IT'S LIKE

Founded in 1928, it lies in a magnificent 400-acre estate just outside Blandford Forum, bordering a 2.5-mile stretch of the Stour in one of the most beautiful parts of England. For splendour of setting it probably has no equal among schools. The main building matches the surroundings: a huge palatial country house in red brick banded with Portland stone, designed by Shaw and completed in 1897. An example of monumental classicism, its main corridor is 100 yards long. This is the heart of the school. Some of the satellite buildings are, by comparison, somewhat plain and functional but they are well designed and exceptionally well equipped. There is also an open-air Greek theatre (built by the pupils), an observatory and the Coade Hall which contains a theatre with an auditorium seating 600 (far better equipped than many professional theatres). The teaching is well known to be excellent and academic standards are high (80–90 pupils go to university each year). There is much emphasis on creativity, on the development of individual talents; also on self-discipline, self-motivation, self-organisation and finding out how to find out on your own. It has long since been outstanding for its commitment to music; 450 pupils learn a musical instrument and there are many musical events. The drama and art departments are also very strong. At least 15 plays a year are produced, and the Arts Centre brings in some 20 professional musical and dramatic productions to Coade Hall each year (eg the Amadeus Quartet, the RSC). Sport and games appear to be compulsory for virtually everyone but there is a 'gentlemanly' and 'laid back' attitude towards these. However, the old-fashioned 'amateur' approach in no way affects the high standards that are attained. There is strong back-up from the old boys' association and a substantial commitment to local community activities and the Duke of Edinburgh's Award Scheme.

SCHOOL PROFILE

Pupils Total 648. Day 24 (boys 14, girls 10); Boarding 624 (boys 404, girls 220). Entry age, 13 and into the sixth. 25% are children of former pupils.

Entrance Common entrance and own entrance exam used. Oversubscribed. No special skills or religious requirements. Parents expected to buy text books. 20 scholarships/bursaries, 66% to 15% of fees.

Parents 15+% in industry or commerce; 15+% are doctors, lawyers etc; 15+% in the armed services; 15+% in theatre, media and music. Up to 10% live within 30 miles; 10+% live overseas.

Staff Head T D Wheare, in post for 4 years. 65 full time staff, 36 part time. Annual turnover 10%. Average age 40.

Academic work GCSE and A-levels. Average size of upper fifth 120; upper sixth 140. *O-levels*: on average, 10% pupils in upper fifth pass 1–4 subjects; 10%, 5–7 subjects; 80% pass 8+ subjects. *A-levels*: on average, 1% pupils in upper sixth pass 1 subject; 1%, 2 subjects; 90%, 3 subjects and 3% pass 4 subjects. On average, 40% take science/engineering A-levels; 56% take arts and humanities; 4% a mixture. *Computing facilities*: Extensive BBC network. Pupils with eg mild dyslexia are catered for without special provisions.

Senior pupils' non-academic activities *Music*: 450 learn a musical instrument, 100 to Grade 6 or above. 10 accepted for Music School. 60 in school orchestra, 60 in school choir, 5 in school pop group; 2 in National Youth Orchestra; 10 in county youth orchestra. *Drama and dance*: 120 in school productions; 80 in other; 50 take Grade 6 in ESB, RAD etc. 4 accepted for Drama/Dance Schools. *Art*: 300 take as non-examined subject; 40 take GCSE; 40 A-level. 15 accepted for Art School; 60 belong to photographic club. *Sport*: Rugby, hockey, cricket, tennis, rowing, athletics, netball, swimming, canoeing, lacrosse, cross-country, archery, squash, badminton, fencing available. 250 take non-compulsory sport, 640 compulsory. 5 take exams eg in gymnastics and swimming. 20 represent county/country (rugby, athletics). *Other*: 100 take part in local community schemes. 50 have bronze Duke of Edinburgh's Award, 20 have silver and 1 gold. Other activities include a computer club, driving, chess, film, bell ringing, philately, astronomy, clay pigeon shooting, soccer, reptiles, jazz.

Careers 1 full time and 12 part time advisors. Average number of pupils accepted for *arts and humanities degree courses* at Oxbridge, 12; other universities, 50; polytechnics or CHE, 10. *science and engineering degree courses* at Oxbridge, 6; other universities, 20; medical schools, 11; polytechnics or CHE, 3. *other general training courses*, 3. Average number of pupils going straight into careers in the armed services, 4; industry, 4. Traditional school careers are in medicine.

Uniform School uniform not worn.

Houses/prefects Prefects, head boy and girl, head of house and house prefects – elected by the school and appointed by the Head.

Religion Religious worship encouraged but not compulsory.

Social Very few organised local events. Regular exchanges with a German school, regular visits to France and Italy, ski-ing trips. Pupils allowed to bring own bike to school. Meals self service. School shop. Alcohol allowed for the upper sixth.

Discipline No corporal punishment. No punishment for failing to produce homework once; those caught smoking cannabis on the premises could expect expulsion.

Boarding 20% have own study bedroom, 20% share (in 2's); less than 60% are in dormitories of up to 6. Houses, of 55, divided by age group and single sex. Resident qualified nurse. Central dining room. Pupils can provide and cook some of own food. 4 weekend exeats each term. Visits to local town allowed – any age, twice a week on average.

Alumni association run by W E Potter, c/o the School.

Former pupils Sir Terence Conran; Jasper Conran; Lucien Freud; Fred Sanger OM; John Eliot Gardner; Mark Elder.

BUCHAN

The Buchan School	Co-ed		Pupils 120
Castletown	Boys		Upper sixth Yes
Isle of Man	● Girls		Termly fees:
Telephone number 0624 822526	Mixed sixth		Day £718
	● Day		Boarding £1435
	● Boarding		GSA; BSA

Head J N Pinkney (2 years)

Age range 11–19, own prep from age 4; entry by own exam including for pupils of own prep

Scholarships available. Isle of Man Board of Education boarding places.

BUCKINGHAM

Buckingham College
Hindes Road
Harrow
Middlesex HA1 1SH
Telephone number 01-427 1220

Enquiries/application to the Secretary

Co-ed   Pupils 137
● Boys   Upper sixth 10
Girls   Termly fees:
● Mixed sixth   Day £735
● Day
Boarding

WHAT IT'S LIKE

Founded in 1936 it is single site in a pleasant urban residential area conveniently placed for public transport. It has agreeable buildings which are well-equipped. The lower school is on a separate site at Northwick Park. The sixth form was re-opened in 1986. There is emphasis on the basic principles of Christian conduct, courtesy and a sense of duty to the community. A sound general education is provided and results are creditable. A handful of pupils proceed to university each year. The number will no doubt increase as the sixth form burgeons. Adequate music, drama and art. An adequate range of sports, games and extra-curricular activities. Some commitment to local community services and the Duke of Edinburgh's Award Scheme.

SCHOOL PROFILE

Pupils Total over 12, 137. Entry age, 11 and into the sixth; girls into the sixth from 1988. Own lower school provides over 20%. 5% are children of former pupils.

Entrance Own entrance exam used. Oversubscribed. No special skills or religious requirements. Parents expected to buy sixth form text books. 3 sixth form scholarships/bursaries, from one-third fees.

Parents 15+% in industry or commerce. 60+% live within 30 miles; up to 10% live overseas.

Staff Head D F T Bell, in post for 1 year. 13 full time staff, 8 part time. Annual turnover 12½%. Average age 35.

Academic work GCSE and A-levels. Average size of upper fifth 30; upper sixth 10. *O-levels*: on average, 14 pupils in upper fifth pass 1–4 subjects; 14, 5–7 subjects; 9 pass 8+ subjects. *A-levels* (sixth form re-opened 1986): on average, 1 pupil in upper sixth passes 1 subject; 2, 2 subjects and 2 pass 3 subjects. On average, 10 take arts and humanities. *Computing facilities*: lab with BBC system. Provision for mild visual handicap, EFL and dyslexia.

Senior pupils' non-academic activities *Music*: 2 learn a musical instrument to Grade 6 or above, 2 accepted for Music School; 12 in school choir. *Drama and dance*: 6 in school productions. 1 accepted for Drama School. *Art*: 4 take GCSE. 1 accepted for Art School. *Sport*: Soccer, table tennis, swimming, athletics, badminton, cricket, tennis available. 12 take non-compulsory sport. 4 pupils represent county/country (judo, athletics, swimming). *Other*: Some take part in local community schemes. Some have bronze Duke of Edinburgh's Award. Some go on to work for national charities. Other activities include computer club, chess, electronics, crafts.

Careers 1 part time advisor. Average number of pupils accepted for *arts and humanities degree courses* at universities, 3; polytechnics or CHE, 3. Average

number of pupils going straight into careers in the City, 3; civil service, 1; music/drama, 1. Majority of pupils enter the commercial world.
Uniform School uniform worn except the sixth.
Houses/prefects Competitive houses. Prefects, head boy, head of house – appointed by Head.
Religion Worship encouraged.
Social Participation in E Ivor Hughes music festival and Rotary public speaking competition. Annual trips abroad. Pupils allowed to bring own bike/car. Meals self service. School shop. No tobacco/alcohol allowed.
Discipline Corporal punishment (Headmaster only). Pupils failing to produce homework once might expect admonition; those caught smoking cannabis on the premises might expect suspension.
Alumni association run by J Musgrove.
Former pupils John Timpson.

BURGESS HILL

Burgess Hill School for Girls	Co-ed	Pupils 304
Keymer Road	Boys	Upper sixth 35
Burgess Hill	● Girls	Termly fees:
West Sussex RH15 0AQ	Mixed sixth	Day £1020
Telephone number 044-46 41050	● Day	Boarding £1790
Enquiries/application to the Registrar	● Boarding	GSA

WHAT IT'S LIKE

Founded in 1906, it combines junior and senior schools on a single 12.5 acre site on the highest point of Burgess Hill in well-kept gardens, plus ample playing fields. To the original Victorian houses have been added many modern facilities: assembly hall, labs, gym, music school, art complex and a business and computer studies centre. It is now very well equipped. Boarders are well cared for in comfortable accommodation. All religious assemblies are compulsory; the Anglican tradition prevails. The school is motivated by a strong belief in the merits of single-sex education, and the declared aim is to get the majority of leavers into higher education. Very strong in drama. Extensive involvement in local community schemes. Vigorous local support.

SCHOOL PROFILE

Pupils Total over 11, 304. Day 254; Boarding 50. Entry age, 11+ and into the sixth. 5% are children of former pupils.
Entrance Own entrance exam used. Oversubscribed in certain areas. No special skills or religious requirements. Parents expected to buy text books in sixth form only. 17 scholarships/bursaries, half fees to £150 pa.
Parents 15+% in industry or commerce; 15+% are doctors, lawyers etc. 60+% live within 30 miles; up to 10% live overseas.
Staff Head Mrs B H Webb, in post for 8 years. 33 full time staff, 29 part time. Annual turnover 1%. Average age 30.

Academic work GCSE and A-levels. Average size of upper fifth 67; upper sixth 35. *O-levels*: on average, 10% pupils in upper fifth pass 5–7 subjects; 90% pass 8+ subjects. *A-levels*: on average, 2% pupils in upper sixth pass 1 subject; 6%, 2 subjects; 92%, 3 subjects. On average, 10 take science/engineering A-levels; 10 take arts and humanities; 5 a mixture. GCSE Business Information Technology offered. *Computing facilities*: Six assorted BBC Acorn computers; six printers; 15 disc drives and one IBM compatible. *Special provisions*: Dyslexia; EFL for A-level students.

Senior pupils' non-academic activities *Music*: 20 learn a musical instrument, 10 to Grade 6 or above. 1 accepted for Music School. 22 in school orchestra, 35 in school choir, 10 in chamber group; 2 in West Sussex CYO. *Drama and dance*: 100 in school productions; 14 NEA; 5 GCSE; 2 Guildhall; 40 ESB Grade 2. 3 accepted for Drama/Dance school; 2 go on to work in theatre. *Art*: 10 take GCSE art; 6 A-level; 16 take art history. 3 accepted for Art School. 20 belong to art club; 30 to pottery club. *Sport*: Tennis, hockey, netball, rounders, badminton, basketball, volleyball, squash, swimming, short-tennis available. 160 take non-compulsory sport. 120 take exams in swimming and gymnastics; 12 take fencing exams. 6 represent county/country (netball, athletics, fencing). *Other*: 100 take part in local community schemes. Other activities include a computer club, stamp club, judo, gardening, calligraphy, aerobics, gym and dance clubs, art and craft clubs, fencing and sailing clubs, BAYS, social services, debating society.

Careers 2 part time advisors. Average number of pupils accepted for *arts and humanities degree courses* at Oxbridge, 2; other universities, 8; polytechnics or CHE, 3. *science and engineering degree courses* at Oxbridge, 1; other universities, 4; medical schools, 2. *BEd*, 2. *other general training courses*, 2.

Uniform School uniform worn except in the sixth.

Houses/prefects Competitive houses. Prefects, head girl, head of house and house prefects – appointed by the Head. School Council.

Religion Assembly is compulsory. Church attendance compulsory for Anglican boarders.

Social Joint debates, matches, discos, with local boys' Public Schools. Organised ski trip, biennial Classics trip, history trip to Soviet Union, field trips, German/French exchanges. Sixth form allowed to bring own car to school. Meals self service. School tuckshop. No tobacco/alcohol allowed.

Discipline No corporal punishment. Pupils caught smoking, drinking or any involvement with drugs would be asked to leave.

Boarding 3 houses, 9–18, divided by age group. Central dining room. 2 weekend exeats each term. Visits to the local town allowed.

Alumni association run by Miss J Anthony, Pine Court, Beacon Road West, Crowborough, East Sussex.

BURY GRAMMAR (BOYS)

Bury Grammar School for Boys	Co-ed	Pupils 550
Tenterden Street	● Boys	Upper sixth 75
Bury	Girls	Termly fees:
Lancashire BL9 0HN	Mixed sixth	Day £621
Telephone number 061 797 2700	● Day	HMC
	Boarding	
Enquiries/application to the Headmaster		

WHAT IT'S LIKE

Founded early 17th century, re-endowed in 1726. After World War II a new boys' school was erected near the original buildings in the town. It combines junior and senior schools and is purpose-built with every desirable amenity including swimming pool and spacious playing fields. The school has many active Christians among masters and boys, but is non-denominational and welcomes pupils of many faiths. It has a well-established tradition of good teaching and highly creditable results. Very well equipped workshops and technology department (many pupils go on to become professional engineers). Flourishing ties with local community and good mutual support. Strong in sport and games; also outdoor pursuits in the Lake District.

SCHOOL PROFILE

Pupils Total over 12, 550. Entry age, 11 and into the sixth. Own junior department provides over 20%.

Entrance Own entrance exam used. Oversubscribed. No special skills or religious requirements. Parents not expected to buy text books. 30 assisted places. 1 Kay Scholarship per year.

Parents 100% live within 30 miles.

Staff Head J Robson, in post for 19 years. 43 full time staff, 4 part time. Annual turnover 3%. Average age 42.

Academic work GCSE and A-levels. Average size of upper fifth 94; upper sixth 75. *O-levels*: on average, 8 pupils in upper fifth pass 1–4 subjects; 28, 5–7 subjects; 57 pass 8+ subjects. *A-levels*: on average, 7 pupils in upper sixth pass 1 subject; 7, 2 subjects; 10, 3 subjects and 51 pass 4 subjects. On average, 25 take science A-levels; 26 take arts and humanities; 24 a mixture. *Computing facilities*: Computer suite.

Senior pupils' non-academic activities *Music*: 40 learn a musical instrument, 12 to Grade 6 or above; 1 accepted for Music School; 23 in school orchestra; 60 in choral society. *Drama and dance*: 30 in school productions; 1/2 in Manchester Youth; occasional pupil accepted for Drama/Dance Schools. *Art*: 76 take as non-examined subject; 10–15 take GCSE; 5–8, A-level. 3–4 accepted for Art School. *Sport*: Soccer, rugby, cricket, tennis, hockey, basketball, badminton, swimming, cross-country, athletics available. Large numbers train for team membership. 23 pupils represent county/country (cricket, golf, table-tennis, ski-ing, soccer, swimming, rugby, triathlon). *Other*: 20 take part in local community schemes. 14 have bronze Duke of Edinburgh's Award, 5 silver. Other activities include a computer club, chess club (frequent matches), Young Enterprise, bird-watching, CCF (strong contingent – army only), hiking.

Careers 2 part time careers advisors. Average number of pupils accepted for *arts and humanities degree courses* at Oxbridge, 2–3; other universities, 20; polytechnics or CHE, 10. *science and engineering degree courses* at Oxbridge, 2–3; other universities, 20; medical schools, 2–3; polytechnics or CHE, 8. *other general training courses*, 1. Average number of pupils going straight into careers in the armed services, 1; industry, 3; other, 3. A large number of ex pupils become chartered engineers.

Uniform School uniform worn throughout up to fifth year.

Houses/prefects Competitive houses. Prefects, head boy, head of house – appointed.

Religion Morning assembly compulsory.

Social Joint productions with Bury Grammar School for Girls. French, German and ski trips, exchange with a school in Cologne. Pupils allowed to bring own bikes to school. Meals self service. School shop. No tobacco/alcohol allowed.

Discipline No corporal punishment. Great care is taken to suit the punishment of offenders to the character and age of each individual.

Alumni association run by Mr J T Grundy, 11 Hebburn Drive, Bury BL8 1ED.

Former pupils David Trippier (MP, Under Secretary of State at the Dept of Environment); Alistair Burt (MP, PPS to Kenneth Baker).

BURY GRAMMAR (GIRLS)

Bury Grammar School (Girls)	Co-ed	Pupils 780
Bridge Road	Boys	Upper sixth 90
Bury BL9 0HH	● Girls	Termly fees:
Telephone number 061 797 2808	Mixed sixth	Day £621
Enquiries/application to Miss J M Lawley	● Day	GSA
	Boarding	

WHAT IT'S LIKE

Founded in 1884, it lies a few minutes from the town centre and close to the rail and bus stations. The main school is housed in a handsome Edwardian building (to which there have been many fine modern additions), surrounded by ample playing fields. A Christian foundation, it has connections with Bury parish church but is ecumenical in spirit. All pupils follow a course of religious education and philosophy throughout the school. The standard of teaching is good and some 60 girls go on to university. Almost all pupils pursue some form of higher education. There are good facilities for art, music and drama. There is a strong tradition of achievement in games and athletics; plus many clubs and societies. Vigorous local support. Extensive work is done on behalf of national charities.

SCHOOL PROFILE

Pupils Total over 12, 780. Entry age, 4, 8/9, 10/11 and into the sixth. Own junior school provides over 20%. 10% are children of former pupils.

Entrance Own entrance exam used. Oversubscribed. No special skills or religious requirements. Parents not expected to buy text books. 35 assisted places. 1 Kay Scholarship per year, full fees.

Parents 15+% in industry or commerce; 15+% are doctors, lawyers etc. 100% live within 30 miles.

Staff Head Miss J M Lawley, in post for 2 years. 48 full time staff, 14 part time.

Academic work GCSE and A-levels. Average size of upper fifth 120; upper sixth 90. *O-levels*: on average, 20 pupils in upper fifth pass 5–7 subjects; 100 pass 8+ subjects. *A-levels*: on average, 15 pupils in the upper sixth pass 2 subjects; less than 10, 3 subjects and the remainder pass 4 or 5 subjects. On average, 50 take science/engineering A-levels; 20 take arts and humanities; 20 a mixture. *Computing facilities*: GCSE, AS and A-level computing are taught. 2 fully equipped computer rooms and several portable computer systems; computers are used across the curriculum. Special provisions through outside agencies, for minor learning problems.

Senior pupils' non-academic activities *Music*: 47 learn a musical instrument, 25+ to Grade 6 or above, 3 accepted for Music School; 30 in school orchestra, 65 in school choir; 3 play in National Youth Orchestra, 17 in Bury Youth Orchestra, 30+ in Bury Music Centre. School choirs take part in music festivals in England and abroad. *Drama and dance*: 20+ in school productions; 18 in year plays. 1 accepted for Drama/Dance School; 3 to Manchester Youth Theatre. *Art*: 16 take as non-examined subject; 63 take GCSE; 7 A-level; 6 GCSE pottery. 6 accepted for Art School. *Sport*: Clubs: Hockey (50), netball (70), badminton (80), swimming (30), tennis (60), rounders (100+), gymnastics (4). 248 take RLSS exams. 1 represents north-west at gymnastics; 4+ represent county (swimming, diving). Other activities include a computer club, chess and many other clubs and activities.

Careers 4 part time advisors. Average number of pupils accepted for *arts and humanities degree courses* at Oxbridge, 3; other universities, 25; polytechnics or CHE, 8. *science and engineering degree courses* at Oxbridge, 3; other universities, 40; medical schools, 10; polytechnics or CHE, 8. *BEd*, 5. *other general training courses*, 2 or 3. Average number of pupils going straight into careers in the armed services, 2; industry, 1 or 2; civil service, 1 or 2; music/drama, 1.

Uniform School uniform worn except in the sixth.

Houses/prefects No competitive houses or prefects. Head girl – elected. School Council.

Religion Compulsory religious study and philosophy throughout the school.

Social All concerts, plays and societies are joint with BGS Boys. Both schools share common room facilities. Pupils allowed to bring own car/bike/motorbike to school. Meals self service. School tuckshop. No tobacco/alcohol allowed.

Discipline No corporal punishment. Pupils failing to produce homework would be expected to hand it in the next day; those involved in drugs or smoking could expect immediate suspension. Anyone with drugs on the premises could expect expulsion.

Former pupils Victoria Wood.

BUSH DAVIES

Bush Davies Schools Ltd
Charters Towers
East Grinstead
Sussex RH19 2JS
Telephone number 034 287 227

- Co-ed
  Boys
  Girls
  Mixed sixth
- Day
- Boarding

Pupils 287
Upper sixth Yes
Termly fees:
Day £1200
Boarding £1700

Head Paul Leopold-Kimm
Age range 11–19
Specialist dance and drama school; entry by audition and test for pupils with promise. 5% of pupils are from overseas.

CAMPBELL COLLEGE

Campbell College
Belfast BT4 2ND
Telephone number 0232 63076

Enquiries/application to the Headmaster

- Co-ed
- Boys
  Girls
  Mixed sixth
- Day
- Boarding

Pupils 420
Upper sixth 85
Termly fees:
Day £802
Boarding £1794
HMC

WHAT IT'S LIKE

Founded in 1894 to give a liberal Protestant education similar to that in English and Scottish public schools. The College (and its prep dept, Cabin Hill) lies on the north-east outskirts of Belfast, five miles from the City centre, on a splendid 100-acre estate with fine trees, an ornamental lake and superb playing fields; a tranquil and beautiful setting. An excellent all-round education is provided and results are very good (40–50 university entrants per year). Strong in music and drama and outstanding in sport and games. A flourishing and large CCF with a pipe band. Social services are extensive. Though basically a Protestant foundation it is ecumenical.

SCHOOL PROFILE

Pupils Total, 420. Day 345; Boarding 75. Entry age, 13+ and into the sixth. Own preparatory school provides over 20% of pupils. 40% are children of former pupils.
Entrance Common entrance exam used. No special skills or religious requirements. Books supplied by LEA 4 scholarships/bursaries, £75–£1000.
Parents 15+% are doctors, lawyers, etc; 15+% in industry or commerce. 30+% live within 30 miles; up to 10% live overseas.
Staff Head Dr R J I Pollock, in post for 1 year. 40 full time staff, 14 part time. Annual turnover 1%. Average age 39.
Academic work GCSE and A-levels. Average size of upper fifth 91; upper sixth 85. *O-levels*: on average, 8 pupils in upper fifth pass 1–4 subjects; 44, 5–7 subjects; 33 pass 8+ subjects. *A-levels*: on average, 3 pupils in upper

sixth pass 1 subject; 14, 2 subjects; 55, 3 subjects and 8 pass 4 subjects. On average, 45 take science/engineering A-levels; 23 take arts and humanities; 17 a mixture. Spanish offered to GCSE/A-level. *Computing facilities*: City & Guilds Certificate in computer competence offered in Lower Sixth. Computer studies at A-level taught. Network system with 12 BBC computers. Provision for dyslexia; some private English tuition; special English classes for Chinese pupils.

Senior pupils' non-academic activities *Music*: 51 learn a musical instrument, 12 to Grade 6 or above. 5 accepted for Music School; 10 play in pop group beyond school, 40 in school orchestra, 80 in school choir, 15 in pop group, 10 in jazz orchestra, 1 in National Youth Orchestra, 5 in Studio Symphony, 1 Pro Corda (Senior). *Drama and dance*: 30 in school productions; 70 in house drama; 2 accepted for Drama/Dance schools; 2 go on to work in theatre. *Art*: 9 take GCSE art; 6, A-level. 1 accepted for Art School; 2 for graphic/furniture design; 1 for architecture; 33 belong to photographic club; 3 belong to pottery club. *Sport*: Rugby football, hockey, cricket, cross-country, athletics, lawn tennis, sailing, squash, swimming, shooting, golf available. 50 take non-compulsory sport (badminton, squash), 20 (swimming). 13 represent county/country (rugby football, hockey, sailing, golf, squash, swimming, three-day eventing). *Other*: 5 enter voluntary schemes and 5 work for national charities after leaving school. Other activities include a computer club, archery club, badminton, basketball, bridge club, chess club, choir, orchestra, CCF, croquet club, dramatic society, debating society, geological society, historical society, mountaineering club, music society, natural history society, photographic society, pipe band, social services group.

Careers 4 part time advisors. Average number of pupils accepted for *arts and humanities degree courses* at Oxbridge, 4; other universities, 12; polytechnics or CHE, 4. *science and engineering degree courses* at Oxbridge, 3; other universities, 32; medical schools, 6; polytechnics or CHE, 8. *BEd*, 1. *other general training courses*, 11. Average number of pupils going straight into careers in the armed services, 2; the church, 1; industry, 7; civil service, 4; music/drama; 2; other, 5.

Uniform School uniform worn throughout.

Houses/prefects Competitive houses for sport, drama, music etc. Prefects, head prefect, head of house and house prefects – appointed by the Headmaster. Sixth Form Committee.

Religion Morning prayers. For boarders – school, family and parish services.

Social Dramatic productions, carol service, senior citizens' Christmas party run by social services group. Organised trips to France, Germany and ski-ing parties to Austria, etc. Pupils allowed to bring own car/bike/motorbike to school. Meals self service. School shop. No tobacco/alcohol allowed.

Discipline No corporal punishment. Pupils failing to produce homework once might expect to have to copy out poetry; those caught smoking cannabis on the premises could expect expulsion.

Boarding All sixth form have own study bedroom. Others in dormitories of 6+. Houses, of approximately 37–38, are the same as competitive houses. Resident matron and assistant. Central dining room. 2 weekends and half-term week exeats each term. Visits to local town allowed in sixth form, usually once a week.

Alumni association is run by C F Gailey Esq, c/o the College.

Former pupils Michael Gibson (rugby, captained Ireland, British Lions); Iain Johnstone (BBC interviewer and producer – interviewed President Reagan); Mark Lambert (Royal Shakespeare actor and film star).

CANFORD

Canford School
Wimborne
Dorset BH21 3AD
Telephone number 0202 882411

Co-ed
● Boys
Girls
● Mixed sixth
● Day
● Boarding

Pupils 536
Upper sixth Yes
Termly fees:
Day £1540
Boarding £2220
HMC; Allied

WHAT IT'S LIKE

Founded in 1923, it has a magnificent site in an enclosed park of 300 acres on the edge of Canford Heath in Dorset 2 miles from Wimborne Minster and 8 miles from Bournemouth. The oldest part of the buildings is the fine medieval hall known as John of Gaunt's Kitchen which is all that survives of the medieval Canford Manor. The present house was added in 1825 and remodelled in 1845. There are beautiful gardens and splendid playing fields. The northern boundary of the grounds is formed by the River Stour. Since its foundation there have been many additions to the buildings. Facilities – which are excellent – include a fine art and design centre, an indoor theatre and an open-air theatre and rifle range. There are approximately 480 boys in the school and 50 girls (sixth form only). They are taught by a staff of about 60 full timers giving a very favourable staff:pupil ratio. The school is divided into upper and lower departments. The boarding house system operates. A full range of academic subjects is provided and results are good. Each year quite a large number of pupils go to university. Religious education is quite an important part of the curriculum and is taught to all forms throughout the school. Services (C of E) are held in the Norman church of Canford Magna which stands in the school grounds. Music, drama and art are strong. Games and sports are also very strong and the facilities are unusually good. Swimming, sailing and golf (there is a 9-hole course in the grounds) are readily available and the school also has one of the few real tennis (or royal tennis) courts in the country. A wide variety of hobbies and extra-curricular activities are available. There is a flourishing CCF contingent (army, navy and air force). Pupils are encouraged to take part in local community services. All boys, in their first year, do a three-term course of initiative training which includes first aid, camp craft, map reading, canoeing and preparation for the Duke of Edinburgh's Award scheme.

SCHOOL PROFILE

Head M M Marriott (12 years)
Age range 13–18; entry by common entrance or own exam
13+ scholarships (academic, art and music) available pa.

CARMEL COLLEGE

Carmel College
Mongewell Park
Wallingford
Oxfordshire
Telephone number 0491 37505

Enquiries/application to the Headmaster

- Co-ed
  Boys
  Girls
  Mixed sixth
- Day
- Boarding

Pupils 300
Upper sixth 34
Termly fees:
Day £1355
Boarding £2500
SHMIS

WHAT IT'S LIKE

Founded in 1948 by Rabbi Kopul Rosen, it opened at Greenham Common, Newbury and in 1953 moved to Mongewell Park near Wallingford on the Thames. The mansion house is the focal point of a large and beautiful estate. Excellent modern facilities and accommodation. It is a Jewish public school committed to cultivating a love and appreciation of Jewish practice, learning and culture. It offers a 'total Jewish environment' within which Judaism is of prime importance. All pupils attend morning services and they are required to have Tefillin and Siddurim. Attendance at Shabbat service is compulsory for all. Everyone is encouraged to take part in the Synagogue ritual by taking service and reading from the weekly Parashah. A large staff allows a staff:pupil ratio of roughly 1:5. Academic standards are high and results are good. Some 20–25 pupils go on to university each year. Hebrew and Jewish studies are an important part of the curriculum. Strong music, art and drama (there is an amphitheatre as well as a synagogue). A good range of sport and games. Rowing is quite strong. A plentiful range of extra-curricular activities. Business and entrepreneurial training is included as an activity.

SCHOOL PROFILE

Pupils Total over 12, 300. Day 14 (boys 8, girls 6); Boarding 286 (boys 208, girls 78). Entry age, 11, 13 and into sixth. 10% are children of former pupils.

Entrance Own entrance exam used. Oversubscribed. No special skills but required to be Jewish. Parents expected to buy text books. 91 assisted places. 120 scholarships/bursaries, £7000 to £500 pa.

Parents 15+% are doctors, lawyers, etc; 15+% in industry or commerce. Up to 10% live within 30 miles; 10+% live overseas.

Staff Head P Skelker, in post for 4 years. 60 full time staff, 15 part time. Annual turnover 5%. Average age 40.

Academic work GCSE and A-levels. Average size of upper fifth 58; upper sixth 34. *O-levels*: on average, 13 pupils in upper fifth pass 1–4 subjects; 20, 5–7 subjects; 25 pass 8+ subjects. *A-levels*: on average 4 pupils in the upper sixth pass 1 subject; 8, 2 subjects; 13, 3 subjects; 1 passes 4 subjects. On average, 14 take science/engineering A-levels; 17 take arts and humanities; 3 take a mixture. Hebrew and Jewish studies are offered to GCSE/A-level. *Computing facilities*: Computer lab – BBC equipment, Amstrads and RM Nimbus. Provisions for dyslexia/slow learning and EFL.

Senior pupils' non-academic activities *Music*: 40 learn a musical instrument, 27 to Grade 6 or above, 1 accepted for Music School; 13 in school orchestra, 27 in school choir, 4 in school pop group; 10 go on to play in pop group. *Art*: 20 take as non-examined subject; 52 take GCSE; 8 take A-level. 2

accepted for Art School, 1 to take B/Tech; 12 belong to photographic club, 26 in art club. *Sport*: Soccer, rowing, netball, hockey, tennis, athletics, judo, rounders, horse-riding, cricket, squash, swimming, basketball and dance available. 70 take non-compulsory sport. 80 take exams. 2 represent county/country (rowing). Other activities include a computer club, debating society, Young Enterprise Scheme, current affairs society, Israel Society.

Careers 1 full time and 1 part time advisor. Average number of pupils accepted for *arts and humanities degree courses* at Oxbridge, 4; other universities, 12; polytechnics or CHE, 6. *science and engineering degree courses* at Oxbridge, 2; other universities, 4; medical schools, 3; polytechnics or CHE, 2. *other general training courses*, 10. Average number of pupils going straight into careers in the City, 2; music/drama, 1; other, 3. Traditional school careers are law and medicine.

Uniform School uniform worn except the sixth.

Houses/prefects Competitive houses. Prefects, head boy and girl, head of house and house prefects – appointed by the Head after consultation with the staff. School Council.

Religion Compulsory attendance at religious service daily.

Social Many visits from local groups who wish to find out about Judaism. Organised trips abroad. Pupils allowed to bring own horse to school. Meals self service, formal on Sabbath. School shop. No tobacco/alcohol allowed (apart from wine on Sabbath).

Discipline No corporal punishment. Pupils failing to produce homework once might expect detention; those caught smoking cannabis on the premises will be expelled.

Boarding 5% have own study bedroom, 75% share with 1 other; 15% are in dormitories of 6 or more. Single-sex houses, of 26–80, divided by age group. Resident qualified medical staff. Central dining room. 2 weekend exeats each term. Visits to local town allowed.

Alumni association is run by Mr A Barr-Taylor, Carmel College.

Former pupils Roland Joffe; Gary Davis; Prof Edward Lutwak; Dr Raymond Dirck; Rabbi Dr Abraham Levy; Stephen Frankel.

CASTERTON

Casterton School	Co-ed	Pupils 300
Kirkby Lonsdale	Boys	Upper sixth 40
Carnforth	● Girls	Termly fees:
Lancashire LA6 2SG	Mixed sixth	Day £1067
Telephone number 05242 71202	● Day	Boarding £1767
	● Boarding	GSA
Enquiries/application to the Headmaster		

WHAT IT'S LIKE

Founded in 1823, established at Casterton in 1833, it stands in its own grounds of 50 acres on the outskirts of the village. The surroundings are very beautiful. Handsome solid buildings, excellent modern facilities, comfortable boarding accommodation. A sound traditional education is provided. Its religious life is based on Anglican practice and the village parish church is used regularly for worship. A happy, friendly place with a 'family' atmosphere, it is strong in music and drama and the Duke of Edinburgh's Award Scheme. Plentiful use is made of the superb Cumbrian countryside for outdoor pursuits (riding, fell walking, canoeing, camping). The junior school is adjacent (the Brontë sisters attended Casterton in 1824).

SCHOOL PROFILE

Pupils Total over 12, 300. Day 40; Boarding 260. Entry age, 8–14 and into the sixth. 2% are children of former pupils.

Entrance Own entrance exam used. No special skills or religious requirements but the school is Anglican. Parents not expected to buy text books. 43 assisted places. 48 scholarships/bursaries, £1000–£300.

Parents 15+% in industry or commerce. 10+% live within 30 miles; 10+% live overseas.

Staff Head G Vinestock, in post for 4 years. 40 full time staff, 10 part time. Annual turnover 6%. Average age 41.

Academic work GCSE and A-levels. Average size of upper fifth 55; upper sixth 40. *O-levels*: on average, 6 pupils in upper fifth pass 1–4 subjects; 13, 5–7 subjects; 36 pass 8+ subjects. *A-levels*: on average, 4 pupils in upper sixth pass 1 subject; 5, 2 subjects; 16, 3 subjects and 9 pass 4 subjects. On average, 30 take science/engineering A-levels; 48 take arts and humanities; 28 a mixture. *Computing facilities*: 8 BBC micros centrally, 2 Archimedes; and science dept (1); junior school (1); and separate commerce/word processing unit. Special provisions for mild dyslexia.

Senior pupils' non-academic activities *Music*: 175 learn a musical instrument, 25 to Grade 6 or above, 1 goes on to university/college of music; 32 in school orchestra, 37 in school choir, 28 in wind band; 5 in Cumbria Youth Orchestra. *Drama and dance*: 25 in school productions 34 take Associated Board, 5 Theatre Arts, Ballet. 1 accepted for Drama/Dance School. *Art*: 20 take GCSE; 7 A-level. 2 per year accepted for Art School. 15 belong to photographic club. *Sport*: Netball, tennis, swimming, athletics, rounders, hockey, volleyball, badminton, trampolining, table tennis, gymnastics, subaqua diving, canoeing, cross-country, yoga available. Pupils represent county (hockey, netball, swimming, athletics, tennis). *Other*: 5 take part in local community schemes. 47 have bronze Duke of Edinburgh's Award, 26 have silver and 15 have gold. Other activities include a computer club, public speaking, choral society, video, cookery, Young Enterprise, electronics, driving lessons.

Careers 4 part time advisors. Average number of pupils accepted for *arts and humanities degree courses* at Oxbridge, 1; other universities, 7; polytechnics or CHE, 6. *science and engineering degree courses* at Oxbridge, 1; other universities, 6; polytechnics or CHE, 5. *other general training courses*, 2. Average number of pupils going straight into careers in the civil service, 1.

Uniform School uniform worn throughout.

Houses/prefects Competitive houses. Prefects, head girl, head of house and house prefects – appointed by the Head.

Religion Compulsory Anglican services.

Social Theatre performances, Young Enterprise, Debates and many social events with other schools. Organised trips to France, Australia and ski-ing trips. Pupils allowed to bring own bike. Meals formal. School shop. No tobacco/alcohol allowed.

Discipline No corporal punishment. Pupils failing to produce homework once rewrite it; involvement with drugs would lead to expulsion.

Boarding 10% have own study bedroom, 35% share (1–3). Houses of 20–45 (separate sixth form houses). Resident SRN. Central dining room. Sixth form can cook own food at weekends. 2 weekend exeats each term. Visits to the local town allowed at weekends.

Alumni association run by Mrs M Crisp, c/o the School.

CATERHAM

Caterham School	Co-ed	Pupils 430
Harestone Valley	● Boys	Upper sixth Yes
Caterham	Girls	Termly fees:
Surrey CR3 6YA	● Mixed sixth	Day £964
Telephone number 0883 43028	● Day	Boarding £1755
	● Boarding	HMC; GBA

WHAT IT'S LIKE

Founded in 1811 in Lewisham, it moved to Caterham in 1884. It stands in 80 acres of delightful grounds among the North Downs just inside the green belt. The prep school has its own buildings and staff. The senior school has very pleasant modern buildings and excellent facilities. It has strong links with the United Reform Church. Christian worship and religious studies are an important part of its life. The aim is to provide a broad education based on Christian principles and practice. There are about 420 boys and 25 day girls divided into three boarding and four day houses. The accommodation is very good. A broad general education is provided, academic standards are high and results are most creditable. The drama, music and creative arts departments are strong. A wide variety of sports and games is available and standards are high. There are numerous clubs and societies for extra-curricular activities.

SCHOOL PROFILE

Head Mr S R Smith (14 years)

Age range 13–18, own prep from age 8; entry by common entrance or own exam

Some scholarships available.

CAWSTON COLLEGE

Cawston College
Cawston
Norwich NR10 4JD
Telephone number 0603 871204

Co-ed	Pupils 150
• Boys	Upper sixth No
Girls	Termly fees:
Mixed sixth	Day £905
• Day	Boarding £1575
• Boarding	Woodard

Head J F Berry
Age range 11–17; entry by own exam
Special department for boys with specific learning problems.

CHANNING

Channing School
Highgate
London N6 5HF
Telephone number 01-340 2328

Enquiries/application to the Headmistress

Co-ed	Pupils 242
Boys	Upper sixth 25
• Girls	Termly fees:
Mixed sixth	Day £1050
• Day	
Boarding	

WHAT IT'S LIKE

Founded in 1885 for 'the daughters of Unitarian ministers and others'. It occupies the large 18th century building now known as Channing, Highgate Hill. The present school is a combination of old and modern buildings which have been adapted and improved over the years. The senior school occupies a 3½ acre site with fine views over London and Essex; the junior school has a nearby site of 2½ acres. There are pleasant gardens and playing fields. A broad, general education is provided with a good spread of subjects up to GCSE and a wide range of A-level subjects. A large staff permits a most favourable staff:pupil ratio of 1:11. Academic results are good; 15 or so girls go on to university each year (quite a high proportion for a small school). The music and drama depts are reasonably active. Sports and games are well catered for and there is a fair variety of extra-curricular activities. A substantial commitment to local community services (a quarter of the school).

SCHOOL PROFILE

Pupils Total over 12, 242. Entry age, 5, 11 and into the sixth. Own junior school provides over 20%. 5% are children of former pupils.
Entrance Own entrance exam used. Oversubscribed. No special skills or religious requirements. Parents not expected to buy text books. Scholarships for academic merit, bursaries for music and cases of financial need.
Parents 15+% are doctors, lawyers etc; 15+% in industry or commerce. 60+% live within 30 miles.
Staff Head Mrs I R Raphael, in post for 3½ years. 30 full time staff, 14 part time.

161

Academic work GCSE and A-levels. Average size of upper fifth 48; upper sixth 25. *O-levels*: on average, 41 pupils in upper fifth pass 5–7 subjects; 6 pass 8+ subjects. *A-levels*: on average, 3 pupils in the upper sixth pass 2 subjects and 22, 3 subjects. On average, one-third take science/engineering A-levels; one third take arts and humanities; one-third a mixture. *Computing facilities*: Computer room with 13 computers.

Senior pupils' non-academic activities *Music*: 75 learn a musical instrument, 35 in school orchestra, 35 in choir. *Drama and dance*: 30 in school productions. *Art*: 10 take A-level. 2 accepted for Art School. *Sport*: Hockey, netball, tennis, rounders, gymnastics, dance, trampolining, fencing, badminton available. 150 take non-compulsory sport. 150 BAGA acrobatic awards. Occasional pupils represent county (tennis). *Other*: 60 take part in local community schemes. New Duke of Edinburgh's Award scheme.

Careers 1 part time careers advisor. Average number of pupils accepted for *arts and humanities degree courses* at Oxbridge, 3; other universities, 6; polytechnics or CHE, 3. *science and engineering degree courses* at Oxbridge, 2; other universities, 4; medical schools, 1; polytechnics or CHE, 2. *BEd*, 3. *other general training courses*, 3. Average number of pupils going straight into careers in music/drama, 1.

Uniform School uniform worn except the sixth.

Houses/prefects No competitive houses or prefects. Head girl. School Council.

Religion Compulsory school assembly and RE classes.

Social Some organised local events and trips abroad. Pupils allowed to bring own bike to school. Meals self service. No tobacco/alcohol allowed.

Discipline No corporal punishment.

Alumni association run by Mrs M Banks, 57 Fordington Road, London N6 4TH.

CHARMANDEAN

Charmandean School	Co-ed	Pupils 83
Tile House	Boys	Upper sixth Yes
Lillingstone Dayrell	● Girls	Termly fees:
Buckinghamshire MK18 5AN	Mixed sixth	Day £756
Telephone number 028 06 204	● Day	Boarding £1381
	● Boarding	ISAI

Head Mr and Mrs Askew (12 years)
Age range 11–18, own prep from age 8; entry by own exam
Sixth form scholarships.

CHARTERHOUSE

Charterhouse
Godalming
Surrey GU7 2DN
Telephone number 0483 426222

Enquiries/application to the Headmaster

Co-ed   Pupils 700
● Boys   Upper sixth 160
Girls   Termly fees:
● Mixed sixth   Day £2133
● Day   Boarding £2585
● Boarding   HMC

WHAT IT'S LIKE

Founded in 1611, on the site of a Carthusian monastery established in London in 1371, it moved in 1872 to Godalming. It stands in a superb estate of 200 acres on a plateau above the River Wey with fine views south and south-west. With its towers and spires and its blend of neo-Gothic and neo-Tudor buildings in stone and brick, it presents an almost emblematic image of the traditional English public school. There is a number of modern buildings as well and the whole place is superbly equipped with virtually every facility that one might expect and hope for. The teaching is well known to be excellent and a first-rate education is provided. The majority of Carthusians proceed to university (ie 140–150 each year). It also has the advantages of exceptionally good libraries, a museum, an art studio, a design and technology centre and the new Ben Travers Theatre which is better equipped than many professional theatres. Very strong in music, drama and art. Numerous productions and performances each year. Outdoor pursuits are various and popular. There is an impressive range of extra-curricular activities. There is even a school farm. The CCF, scouts and social services (locally and in London) are vigorously supported. There is a strong sporting tradition and wide range of sports and games; there are fixtures against the leading schools. A nine-hole golf course was recently opened.

SCHOOL PROFILE

Pupils Total 700. Day 24 (boys 18, girls 6); Boarding 676 (boys 612, girls 64). Entry age, boys 13; boys and girls into the sixth. 13% are children of former pupils.

Entrance Common entrance and own entrance exam for Foundation Scholarship. Oversubscribed. Academic ability (and sound character) looked for. No religious requirements. Parents not expected to buy text books. 10 assisted places (sixth form only). 21 academic, 7 music, 4 art scholarships at 16+ and 13+, values range from full fees to £500. Also awards for sons of lawyers, sons of CAPS teachers and for classics. Awards may be supplemented by bursaries in case of financial need.

Parents 15+% in industry or commerce. 30+% live within 30 miles; 10+% live overseas.

Staff Head P J Attenborough, in post for 6 years. 79 full time staff, 2 part time (plus music staff). Annual turnover 3%. Average age 41.

Academic work GCSE and A-levels. Average size of upper fifth 120; upper sixth 160. *O-levels*: on average, 3 pupils in upper fifth pass 1–4 subjects; 15, 5–7 subjects; 105 pass 8+ subjects. *A-levels*: on average, 5 pupils in upper sixth pass 1 subject; 11, 2 subjects; 123, 3 subjects and 16 pass 4 subjects. On average, 55 take science/engineering A-levels; 63 take arts and humanities; 36

a mixture. Arabic project offered (for non-Arabic speakers). *Computing facilities*: Network of 16 BBC computers in computer room and a further 16 stand-alone BBCs in various academic departments.

Senior pupils' non-academic activities   *Music*: 300 learn a musical instrument, 100 to Grade 6 or above. 100 in school orchestra, 100 in choir, brass band and jazz band; 3 accepted for Music School; 3 go on to read music at university. *Drama and dance*: 100 in school productions, 150 in House plays, foreign language plays (French, German, Spanish) etc; 1 accepted for Drama/Dance School. *Art*: 250 take as non-examined subject; 24 take GCSE; 10 A-level; 6 A-level History of Art. 5 accepted for Art School; 1 for architecture; 2 take degrees in History of Art; 2 go into other art training; 50 belong to photographic club. *Sport*: Cricket, soccer, hockey, tennis, squash, fives, racquets, athletics, cross-country, swimming, shooting, rugby, water polo, fencing, lacrosse (girls), sailing, golf, canoeing, rowing, riding, climbing, windsurfing available. 400 take non-compulsory sport. 24 represent county/country (shooting, swimming, golf, soccer, hockey, tennis). *Other*: 40 take part in local community schemes. 13 have bronze Duke of Edinburgh's Award; 2 work for national charities after leaving school. Other activities include bridge, debating, farm, forestry, historical buildings, magical, motor, opera, railway, photography, ballroom dancing, antique film, astronomical, recording, art, politics, economics, natural history, play reading, science, stamps, stratagem, driving lessons etc.

Careers 20 part time advisors. Average number of pupils accepted for *arts and humanities degree courses* at Oxbridge, 17; other universities, 80 (4 overseas); polytechnics or CHE, 10. *science and engineering degree courses* at Oxbridge, 10; other universities, 38; medical schools, 3; polytechnics or CHE, 6. *other general training courses*, 1. Average number of pupils going straight into careers in the armed services, 4; industry, 1; the City, 2; music/drama, 4; other, 7.

Uniform School uniform worn throughout.

Houses/prefects Competitive houses. Prefects (monitors), head boy, head of house and house prefects (house monitors) – appointed.

Religion Charterhouse is a Christian foundation; religious worship compulsory.

Social Organised trips abroad annually. Pupils allowed to bring own bike to school. Meals formal. Four shops. Senior pupils allowed alcohol, no tobacco.

Discipline Corporal punishment not used (although not formally abolished). Pupils failing to produce homework once might expect a warning, or time extended and extra imposition; those caught smoking cannabis on the premises would expect expulsion.

Boarding 81% have own study bedroom, 11% share with 1 other. Houses, of approximately 65. Resident qualified nurses. 3 central dining rooms. Pupils can provide and cook own food. Half term exeats only. Visits to local town allowed.

Alumni association is run by Major M G P Chignell, c/o the School.

Former pupils Peter May; James Prior; John Wakeham; William Rees-Mogg; Max Hastings; Peter Gabriel; Jonathan King; Ian Wallace; Don Cupitt; Jonathan Dimbleby; David Dimbleby; Gerald Priestland; David Hicks; Simon Raven; Dick Taverne; Graham Seed; Nicholas Henson; Lord Donaldson; Mr Justice (Oliver) Popplewell; Bishop Whinney; C J Swallow; David Miller; Sir Ronald Millar; Frederick Raphael; Peter de Savary.

CHARTERS-ANCASTER

Charters-Ancaster College
Hastings Road
Bexhill-on-Sea
East Sussex TN40 2NP
Telephone number 0424 211092

Enquiries/application to the Headmistress

Co-ed
Boys
● Girls
Mixed sixth
● Day
● Boarding

Pupils 182
Upper sixth 20
Termly fees:
Day £850
Boarding £1650
GSA; GBGSA

WHAT IT'S LIKE

The result of an amalgamation in 1986 of two long-established local schools (Ancaster House and Charters Towers), it comprises senior and junior schools in separate buildings close to each other on the outskirts of Bexhill-on-Sea. Basically Christian in ethos, it is a multi-national school which regards United Nations Day as one of the most important in the calendar. It has cosmopolitan links with Europe, USA and Australia. A sound traditional education is provided and it is strong in music, drama and extra-curricular activities. Flourishing local support and involvement with the Bexhill community.

SCHOOL PROFILE

Pupils Total over 12, 182. Day 82; Boarding 100. Entry age, 3 onwards and into sixth. 1% are children of former pupils.

Entrance Common entrance and own entrance exam used. Not oversubscribed. No special skills or religious requirements. Parents not expected to buy text books. 4 scholarships, £850–£230 per term. Discount for serving HM Forces children.

Parents 15+% in industry or commerce. 30+% live within 30 miles; 30+% live overseas.

Staff Head Mrs S Chapman, in post for 4 years. 32 full time staff, 29 part time. Annual turnover 4–5%. Average age 45.

Academic work GCSE and A-levels. Average size of upper fifth 40; upper sixth 20. *O-levels*: on average, 10% pupils in upper fifth pass 1–4 subjects; 80%, 5–7 subjects; 10% pass 8+ subjects. *A-levels*: on average, 40% pupils in upper sixth pass 1 subject; 30%, 2 subjects; 15%, 3 subjects and 5% pass 4 subjects. On average, 50% take science/engineering A-levels; 10% take arts and humanities; 40% a mixture. *Computing facilities*: 12 BBC computers on Econet system, plus 6 individual. Teaching for dyslexics and EFL coaching.

Senior pupils' non-academic activities *Music*: 28 learn a musical instrument, 8 to Grade 6 or above. 3 accepted for Music School. 10 in school orchestra, 20 in choir, 12 in folk group, 2 in National Youth Orchestra, 3 in National Youth Choir, 3 in East Sussex Youth Orchestra; 8 in other choirs beyond school. *Drama and dance*: 20 in school productions; 25 in drama workshops/clubs. 5 take Grade 6 in ESB, RAD etc; 5 New Era; 3 accepted for Drama/Dance Schools; 5 in dance/drama festivals beyond school. *Art*: 16 take as non-examined subject; 17 take GCSE; 3, A-level. 4 accepted for Art School. 15 belong to photographic club; 8 to pottery club. *Sport*: Hockey, netball, swimming, gymnastics, athletics, tennis, rounders, stoolball are all curricular, with squash, riding, badminton, self-defence, karate, judo, trampolining available, as clubs or extras. 6 take non-compulsory sport; 12+ belong to martial arts clubs; 5 take exams eg gymnastics, swimming; 8 represent county/country (hockey, lacrosse, swimming, tennis, gymnastics). *Other*: 10 take part in local community schemes. 3 have bronze Duke of Edinburgh's Award; 4 work for national charities beyond school. Other activities include a computer club, astronomy, volleyball, jazz dance, self-defence, karate, judo, Young Enterprise; also driving, sailing, sixth form only.

Careers 1 full time and 2 part time advisors. Average number of pupils accepted for *degree courses* at universities, 7; medical schools, 4; polytechnics or CHE, 10. *other general training courses*, 20. Traditional school careers are in the sciences and medicine.

Uniform School uniform worn excepting in the sixth.

Houses/prefects Competitive houses. Prefects, head girl, head of house and house prefects. School Council.

Religion Compulsory non-denominational assembly. Boarders attend nearby churches and there is a period set aside on Sundays for non-Christians to study devotional books.

Social Debates, public speaking, outings, parties/discos with other schools. Chamber choir European tour, hockey squad training in Holland, exchanges with French families, link-exchanges with Australia and USA available. Pupils allowed to bring own car/bike to school. Meals self service. School shops sell tuck, books, second-hand uniform; school bank. No tobacco/alcohol allowed.

Discipline No corporal punishment. Those caught smoking cannabis on the premises could expect expulsion.

Boarding 20% have own study bedroom, 25% share (double study). Houses, of approximately 40, divided by age group. Resident SRN. Central dining room. Sixth formers can provide and cook own food. 3 weekend and half term exeats each term. Visits to local town allowed.

Alumni association is run by Mrs J Smith, Elm Cottage, Chilsham Lane, Herstmonceux, East Sussex.

Former pupils Lady Havers.

CHEADLE HULME

Cheadle Hulme School
Claremont Road
Cheadle Hulme
Cheadle
Cheshire SK8 6EF
Telephone number 061 485 4142

- Co-ed
  Boys
  Girls
  Mixed sixth
- Day
- Boarding

Pupils 600
Upper sixth 120
Termly fees:
Day £835
Boarding £1735
HMC

Enquiries/application to the Headmaster

WHAT IT'S LIKE

Founded in 1855, formerly the Manchester Warehousemen and Clerks' Orphan school. Urban, single-site, near Manchester in 80-acre grounds. The original Victorian building has been recently modernised. Extensive additions over the years. The boarding block is very spacious and comfortable. The junior school is nearby. An excellent academic education is given (80–90 university entrants per year) and nearly every pupil goes on to higher education. Altogether a well-run establishment, particularly strong in music, art and drama.

SCHOOL PROFILE

Pupils Total over 12, 600. Day 540 (boys 270, girls 270); Boarding 60 (boys 30, girls 30). Entry age, 7, 8, 11 and into the sixth.

Entrance Own entrance exam used. Oversubscribed. No special skills or religious requirements. Parents not expected to buy text books. 20 assisted places. 4 scholarships/bursaries for excellence in music or drama, 1 for boarding, full fees to £500.

Parents 15+% in industry or commerce; 15+% are doctors, lawyers etc. 60+% live within 30 miles; up to 10% live overseas.

Staff Head D Colin Firth, in post for 12 years. 71 full time staff, 9 part time. Annual turnover 5%. Average age 45.

Academic work GCSE and A-levels. Average size of upper fifth 120; upper sixth 120. *O-levels*: on average, 12 pupils in upper fifth pass 1–4 subjects; 26, 5–7 subjects; 82 pass 8+ subjects. *A-levels*: on average, 6 pupils in upper sixth pass 1 subject; 6, 2 subjects; 20, 3 subjects and 85 pass 4 subjects. On average, 50 take science/engineering A-levels; 50 take arts and humanities; 20 a mixture of both. *Computing facilities*: Computer room with 15 terminals; micros in all major departments.

Senior pupils' non-academic activities *Music*: 200 learn a musical instrument, 30 up to Grade 6 or above. 3 or 4 per year accepted for Music School; 1 or 2 read music at university. 80 in school orchestra, 80 in choir, 2 in National Youth Orchestra. *Drama and dance*: 30 in school productions; 1 or 2 accepted for Drama/Dance Schools. *Art*: 20 take as non-examined subject; 30 take GCSE; 6 A-level. 2 or 3 accepted for Art School. 15 belong to photographic club. *Sport*: Rugby, hockey, lacrosse, cross-country, netball, swimming, tennis, cricket, athletics, badminton, fencing, archery available. Sport is compulsory. 12 represent county; 1 or 2 represent country. Other activities include a computer club, electronics, beekeeping, chess and many others.

Careers 7 part time advisors. Average number of pupils accepted for *arts and humanities degree courses* at Oxbridge, 8; other universities, 25; polytechnics or CHE, 15. *science and engineering degree courses* at Oxbridge, 8; other universities, 25; medical schools, 6; polytechnics or CHE, 15. BEd, 2. *other general training courses*, 4. Average number of pupils going straight into careers in the armed services, 1. Virtually all go on to higher education before starting a career.

Uniform School uniform worn throughout.

Houses/prefects No competitive houses. Prefects, head boy/girl, head of boarding house and house prefects – appointed by the Head on advice. School Council.

Religion No compulsory religious worship.

Social No organised events with other schools. Many organised trips to France, Germany, Italy/Greece, skiing each year. Pupils allowed to bring own car/bike/motorbike to school. Meals self service. No tobacco/alcohol allowed.

Discipline No corporal punishment. Pupils failing to produce homework once might expect a verbal reprimand; those caught smoking cannabis on the premises could expect suspension, then expulsion.

Boarding 30% have own study bedroom, 30% share (with 1 other); 10% are in dormitories of 6+. Houses divided by age group, single sex. Resident medical staff. Central dining room. Many weekend exeats. Visits to local town allowed most weekends.

Alumni association run by Mr D H James, 32 Woodfield Road, Cheadle Hulme, Cheadle, Cheshire SK8 7JS.

CHELTENHAM (BOYS)

Cheltenham College
Bath Road
Cheltenham
Gloucestershire GL53 7LD
Telephone number 0242 513540

Enquiries/application to the Headmaster

Co-ed   Pupils 569
● Boys   Upper sixth 120
Girls   Termly fees:
● Mixed sixth   Day £1785
● Day   Boarding £2380
● Boarding   HMC

WHAT IT'S LIKE

Founded in 1841, it has a fine site in the town centre. Handsome Victorian buildings in beautiful gardens and playing fields. In the period 1973–88 a great many developments and modernisations were achieved and the facilities are now excellent. It is a C of E foundation and chapel services and some Sunday services are compulsory. However, it is fully ecumenical. Academic standards are high and results good. About 70% of leavers go on to university each year (15–20 to Oxbridge). Music is very strong and plays a large part in the lives of many pupils. There are joint musical activities with the Ladies' College. Drama is also strong and there are regular productions in the big classical theatre. The arts and crafts centre is a particularly active one. There are fine facilities for sports and games and the College achieves a high standard in these. A plentiful range of extra-curricular activities, clubs, societies and so on. A very energetic community scheme serves the town. Wherever possible all college facilities are made available to the town and other schools. One of the school's aims is to maintain a tradition of service to a modern industrial society. A feature is the thriving 'Industrial Link' organisation.

SCHOOL PROFILE

Pupils Total over 12, 569. Day 184 (boys 161, girls 23); Boarding 385 (boys 357, girls 28). Entry age, boys, 13+; girls and boys into the sixth. Own junior school provides over 20%. 17% are children of former pupils.

Entrance Common entrance and own sixth form scholarship or entry tests used. Oversubscribed. Motivation looked for; C of E foundation but fully ecumenical. Parents expected to buy seniors' text books. 20 scholarships/bursaries (for 16+, 13+), 80–10% of fees.

Parents 15+% in industry or commerce. 30+% live within 30 miles; up to 10% live overseas.

Staff Head R M Morgan, in post for 10 years. 56 full time staff, 4 part time. Annual turnover 3%. Average age 34.

Academic work GCSE, A-levels. Average size of upper fifth 106; upper sixth 120. *O-levels*: on average, 90+% pass rate. *A-levels*: on average, 90+% in the upper sixth pass 1–3 subjects; 2 pass 4 subjects. On average, 40% take science/engineering A-levels; 40% take arts and humanities; 20% a mixture. *Computing facilities*: rated by *The Times* recently to be one of the best in the country.

Senior pupils' non-academic activities *Music*: Tuition in many instruments to GCSE/A-level; choral society, chapel choir, orchestra, string orchestra, wind and big bands, small and close harmony ensembles, madrigal group. *Drama and dance*: 7–8 annual productions in fully equipped theatre. *Art*: New Art School with lecture theatre, darkrooms, pottery, printmaking; department open at all times. *Sport*: Rugby, hockey, tennis, squash, rackets, rowing, athletics, fives, swimming, shooting (small bore indoor range, use of 600 yd outdoor military range), badminton, basketball available; opportunities for golf, canoeing, sailing, orienteering, climbing and camping. School represented in cross-channel relay race (winners in fastest recorded time). *Other*: Fifth formers upwards take part in local community schemes. Duke of Edinburgh's Award Scheme. Wide range of societies and activities includes bridge, chess, computer club, debating, drama, Young Enterprise, mountaineering, music, opera, technology (micro-electronics and design), CCF.

Careers 12 full time careers advisors. 'Industrial Link' scheme. On average, 70+% pupils accepted for degree courses.

Uniform School uniform worn throughout.

Houses/prefects Competitive houses. Prefects, senior prefect (head boy), head of house and house prefects – appointed by Head.

Religion Compulsory daily chapel.

Social Musical links with Ladies' College. Industrial link with Boston and Tokyo. Pupils allowed to bring own bike to school. Meals self service. School shop. No tobacco, limited beer for upper sixth only in licensed club.

Discipline No corporal punishment. Pupils failing to produce homework once might expect 'sides'; taking or handling drugs leads to automatic expulsion.

Boarding Sixth form have own study bedroom; juniors in dormitories of 6+. Houses, of approximately 70, are same as competitive houses and single sex. Resident matron in each house. Central dining room. Pupils can provide and cook snacks in houses. 2 termly exeats. Visits to local town allowed.

Former pupils Nigel Davenport; Lindsay Anderson; Patrick White; Major General Sir Jeremy Moore.

CHELTENHAM (GIRLS)

The Cheltenham Ladies' College
Bayshill Road
Cheltenham
Gloucestershire GL50 3EP
Telephone number 0242 520691

Co-ed
Boys
● Girls
Mixed sixth
● Day
● Boarding

Pupils 840
Upper sixth Yes
Termly fees:
Day £1420
Boarding £2120
GSA; BSA

WHAT IT'S LIKE

Founded in 1853 and a pioneer of the belief that the education of girls is every bit as important as that of boys, it opened in 1854 at Cambray House and in 1873 occupied fine new buildings at Bayshill. This is a very agreeable quarter of Cheltenham comprising Regency and early Victorian houses. There have been many additions since to provide a school which is well equipped by any standards and in which a civilised and sophisticated atmosphere prevails. The main buildings contain over 120 rooms, plus three halls and a very big and well-stocked library. The Princess Hall seats 1500 people. A new large building was opened in 1970 to provide a sixth form college. There are 7 junior boarding houses, each accommodating 60–70 girls, and 4 sixth form houses. The day girl centre takes 150 pupils. Religious services or prayers (in the Anglican tradition) are held every morning and all girls are expected to attend. Girls attend Sunday service at local churches. Very high-powered academically, the college has a huge, well-qualified staff of over 150 (the music department alone has over 30 members). No other school in Britain has a larger staff. This permits a staff:pupil ratio of 1:5.5 (a ratio probably unmatched in Britain). Academic standards are very high indeed (quite a lot of girls read Classics) and results are consistently outstanding. Some 80% of girls stay on to take A-levels. About 60% of leavers proceed to University (many to Oxbridge) and 30% go on to other places of further education. Music, drama, and art are all extremely strong and very high standards are continuously achieved. Facilities for sports and games are first-rate and a wide variety of sports and games is available. Again, very high standards are attained and the college has produced many representatives at county, regional and national level (especially in hockey, lacrosse, squash and gymnastics). The college also has a big commitment to local community services and has participated successfully in the Duke of Edinburgh's Award Scheme.

SCHOOL PROFILE

Head Miss Enid Castle (1 year)
Age range 11–18; entry by common entrance, scholarship or own exam
5 grants of ⅙–⅔ fees.

CHERWELL TUTORS

Cherwell Tutors
Greyfriars
Paradise Street
Oxford OX1 1LD
Telephone number 0865 242670

Enquiries to the Secretary
Application to the Headmaster

- Co-ed   Pupils 140
- Boys   Upper sixth 120
- Girls   Termly fees:
- Mixed sixth   Day £2000
- Day   Boarding £3000
- Boarding   BAC; CIFE

WHAT IT'S LIKE

Founded in 1973, the central administration premises lie at Greyfriars in the centre of the city. The halls of residence are ten minutes by bike. Accommodation is scattered round the town. It is a private tutorial college offering only individual tuition supplemented by group seminars and department meetings. It has its own newly equipped and modern science laboratory on site. Most of its leavers go on to university. The standards of teaching are high and it is a most reputable establishment.

SCHOOL PROFILE

Pupils Total 140. Day 20 (boys 12, girls 8); Boarding 120 (boys 70, girls 50). Entry age, 16–18.

Entrance Admission by interview only. No special skills or religious requirements. Parents expected to buy text books. 3 scholarships/bursaries available, £100–£500.

Parents 15+% in private business. Up to 10% live within 30 miles; 10+% live overseas.

Staff Head P J Gordon. 50 full time staff, 70 part time. Annual turnover 5%. Average age 30.

Academic work GCSE, A-levels, EFL exams. Average size of upper fifth 20; upper sixth 120. *O-levels*: on average, 17 pupils in upper fifth pass 1–4 subjects; 3 pass 5–7 subjects. *A-levels*: on average, 10 pupils in upper sixth pass 1 subject; 20, 2 subjects; 50 pass 3 subjects. On average, 10 take science/engineering A-levels; 20 take arts and humanities; 10 a mixture. Any subject, or combination of subjects taught to A-level. *Computing facilities*: Research machines. Nimbus computer. *Special provisions*: dyslexic help available. EFL teachers.

Senior pupils' non-academic activities *Music*: 5 learn a musical instrument, 2 in school pop group. *Art*: 5 take GCSE, 5 A-level. 2 accepted for Art School. *Sport*: College teams: football, rugby, table tennis, tennis, squash, fencing, karate, keep fit and most sports available nearby. 40 take non-compulsory sport. 3 represent county/country. *Other activities*: social club.

Careers 2 part time advisors. Average number of pupils accepted for *arts and humanities degree courses* at Oxbridge, 2; other universities, 40. *science and engineering degree courses* at Oxbridge, 1; other universities, 20. *other general training courses*, 4. Average number of pupils going straight into careers in the armed services, 4; industry, 2; the City, 1; other, 3. Traditional school careers are medicine, law, management.

Uniform School uniform not worn.

Houses/prefects No competitive houses or prefects.

Religion No compulsory religious worship.

Social Sports fixtures with other local schools. No organised trips abroad. Pupils allowed to bring own car/bike/motorbike to school. Meals self service. Pupils allowed tobacco/alcohol only in non-academic areas.

Discipline No corporal punishment. Pupils failing to produce homework once might expect an oral reprimand; those caught smoking cannabis on the premises could expect parental notification.

Boarding 70% have own study bedroom, 30% share (with 1 other). 3 halls of residence (16–20) plus family accommodation (1–5), divided by age group and mixed. Local doctor. No central dining room. Pupils can provide and cook own food. Any number of weekend exeats, plus one long weekend. Visits to the local town allowed.

Former pupils Some overseas royalty; children of MPs and famous businessmen.

CHETHAM'S

Chetham's School of Music
Long Millgate
Manchester M3 1SB
Telephone number 061 834 9644

Enquiries/application to the Headmaster or Headmaster's Secretary

- Co-ed
  Boys
  Girls
  Mixed sixth
- Day
- Boarding

Pupils 242
Upper sixth 50
Termly fees:
Day £2466
Boarding £3185
SHMIS

WHAT IT'S LIKE

Founded in 1653, it lies in the centre of Manchester in its own grounds. The buildings are well designed and well equipped. The boarding accommodation is comfortable. It has been a specialist music school since 1969. It is possible to study any musical instrument, keyboard, guitar or voice. All entrants who have been resident in this country for at least two years prior to admission qualify automatically for the DES aided-pupil scheme (a separate scheme similar to the AP scheme but covering boarding, travel and uniform where required). Pupils normally study one first-study instrument (or voice or composition) and one second study. They are also prepared for national public exams and results are good (10–15 university entrants per year). There is a fair range of sport and games and other recreations.

SCHOOL PROFILE

Pupils Total over 12, 242. Day 45 (boys 34, girls 11); Boarding 201 (boys 69, girls 132). Entry age, 7–18. Own prep school provides over 20%.

Entrance Admission only by audition. Oversubscribed. Musical potential looked for; no religious requirements. Parents not expected to buy text books. Government Aided Pupil Scheme for all entrants resident in UK for at least 2 years prior to entry, means tested, value up to £9555 pa plus travel and uniform grants.

Parents 10+% live within 30 miles; up to 10% live overseas.

Staff Head John Vallins, in post for 13 years. 42 full time staff, 88 part time. Annual turnover 5%. Average age 40 (very approx).

Academic work GCSE, A-levels, ABRSM. Average size of upper fifth 37; upper sixth 50. *O-levels*: on average, 14 pupils in upper fifth pass 1–4 subjects; 22 pass 5–7 subjects. *A-levels*: on average, 11 pupils in upper sixth pass 1 subject; 21, 2 subjects; 14, 3 subjects and 4 pass 4 subjects. On average, 1 takes science/engineering A-levels; 37 take arts and humanities; 12 a mixture. Music and practical music are offered to A-level. *Computing facilities*: A computer room with six machines – plans for a larger room and six more machines.

Senior pupils' non-academic activities *Music*: 140 learn a musical instrument, 140 to Grade 6 or above; 110 in school orchestras, 140 in choirs, 6 in school pop group; 10 in National Youth Orchestra; about 60% accepted for Music College; 5 play in pop group beyond school. *Drama and dance*: 40 in school productions. *Art*: 10 take GCSE; 5 A-level. *Sport*: Swimming, squash, badminton, table-tennis, trampolining, netball, rounders, weight-training, running, aerobics, five-a-side football available. 50 take non-compulsory sport. *Other activities* include a computer club. Intensive musical studies predominate (orchestras, choirs, ensemble work, lunchtime concerts etc), including daily practice.

Careers 2 full time advisors (both also teach music). Average number of pupils accepted for *arts and humanities degree courses* at Oxbridge, 6; other universities, 3; polytechnics or CHE (mainly music colleges), 34. *science and engineering degree courses* at Oxbridge, 3; other universities, 1. *other general training courses*, 1. Average number of pupils going straight into careers in the armed services, 1. Traditional school careers are in the field of music.

Uniform School uniform worn throughout.

Houses/prefects No competitive houses. Prefects, head boy/girl, head of house and house prefects – appointed by the Head/Second Master/Heads of Houses.

Religion Weekly (non-denominational) service in Manchester Cathedral except for those who specifically opt out. Sunday service is encouraged. RCs have their own weekly instruction or service.

Social No organised local events. Organised choral/orchestral tours (about 1 per year); ski-ing, individual or group competitions. Pupils allowed to bring own car/bike to school. Meals self service. School tuckshop. No tobacco/alcohol allowed.

Discipline No corporal punishment. Pupils failing to produce homework once might expect a reprimand, extra work; those caught smoking cannabis on the premises could expect expulsion.

Boarding 39% share (2 to a room); 18% (3); 9% (4); 29% (6). Houses, of approximately 50 are single sex. Resident nurse plus day-time nurse, 3 visiting doctors. Central dining room. Pupils can provide and cook own food in Houses. Any number of weekend exeats. Visits to the local town allowed.

Alumni association is run by The Chairman, Chetham's Association, c/o Chetham's School of Music.

Former pupils Peter Donohoe, Stephen Hough and Anna Markland (all pianists); Grant Llewellyn (conductor); Mike Lindup (Pop group – Level 42); John Mundy (BBC TV announcer).

CHIGWELL

Chigwell School
Chigwell
Essex IG7 6QF
Telephone number 01-500 1396

Enquiries/application to the Headmaster or Admissions Secretary

Co-ed
● Boys
Girls
● Mixed sixth
● Day
● Boarding

Pupils 378
Upper sixth 60
Termly fees:
Day £1101
Boarding £1645
HMC

WHAT IT'S LIKE

Founded in 1629, it is well positioned since it lies in fine open countryside in Chigwell village on a delightful 50-acre estate, only 10 miles from central London. Architecturally it makes a most satisfying unit and the original 17th-century buildings are still in use. It has many excellent modern facilities. The junior school is combined. A sound general education is provided (40–50 university entrants per year). It is Christian in its ideals and inspiration. Considerable strengths are music and art (they look for ability in these subjects in candidates). A good range of extra-curricular activities and high standards in sport and games.

SCHOOL PROFILE

Pupils Total over 12, 378. Day 330 (boys 310, girls 20); Boarding 48 (boys 40, girls 8). Entry age boys, 7, 11, 13; directly into the sixth form, boys and girls. Own junior school provides over 20% of pupils. 10% are children of former pupils.

Entrance Own entrance exam used. Very few pupils admitted by common entrance. Oversubscribed. Pupils with special skills in music and art looked for. No religious requirements. Parents expected to buy text books. 60 assisted places. 6 scholarships/bursaries, full fees to 25% of fees.

Parents 15+% in industry or commerce. More than 60% live within 30 miles; up to 10% live overseas.

Staff Head B J Wilson, in post for 16 years. 44 full time staff, 18 part time (music). Annual turnover 10%. Average age about 40.

Academic work GCSE and A-levels. Average size of upper fifth 70; upper sixth 55–60. *O-levels*: on average, 12 pupils in upper fifth pass 1–4 subjects; 17, 5–7 subjects; 33 pass 8+ subjects. *A-levels*: on average, 2 pupils in upper sixth pass 1 subject; 20, 2 subjects; 25, 3 subjects and 4 pass 4 subjects. On average, 23 take science/engineering A-levels; 23 take arts and humanities; 4 a mixture. CDT and pottery are offered to GCSE. *Computing facilities*: A large laboratory specifically for computers. About 20 BBC Acorn B computers on an Econet system. Special provision for EFL.

Senior pupils' non-academic activities *Music*: 100 learn a musical instrument, 15 to Grade 6 or above. 20 in school orchestra, 20 in school choir, 6 in pop group, 25 in ensemble; 2 in Essex Youth Orchestra; 15 in Church choir; 1 accepted for Music School; 2 take up music as a career. *Drama and dance*: 50 in school productions. *Art*: 22 take GCSE art, 10 pottery, 12 CDT; 8 A-level. 3 (average) accepted for Art School; 3 for BTEC. *Sport*: Soccer, athletics, cricket, badminton, swimming, squash, cross-country, rugger, hockey, basketball, tennis available. 100 take non-compulsory sport. 3 represent county/

country (soccer, cricket). *Other*: 6 take part in local community schemes. 10 have bronze Duke of Edinburgh's Award. Other activities include a computer club, inter-house chess, Scouts, drama, music, learning to drive.

Careers 2 part time advisors. Average number of pupils accepted for *arts and humanities degree courses* at Oxbridge, 3; other universities, 20; polytechnics or CHE, 4. *science and engineering degree courses* at Oxbridge, 3; other universities, 20; medical schools, 3; polytechnics or CHE, 4. *other general training courses*, 4. Average number of pupils going straight into careers in the armed services, 1; industry, 4; the City, 6; civil service, 2; music/drama, 2.

Uniform School uniform worn throughout.

Houses/prefects Competitive houses. Prefects, head boy, head of house and house prefects – appointed.

Religion All pupils attend Chapel but opting out possible on conscientious grounds.

Social Occasional joint musical functions with other schools. 8 or more organised trips abroad/exchange systems each year. Pupils allowed to bring own car/bike/motorbike to school. Meals self service. School shop. No tobacco/alcohol allowed.

Discipline No corporal punishment. Pupils failing to produce homework once might expect a warning or additional work; those caught smoking cannabis on the premises could expect expulsion.

Boarding 40% share (2 or 3); 60% are in dormitories of 6+. Houses, same as competitive houses. Resident qualified nurse. Central dining room. Pupils can provide and cook own food. Exeats every weekend. Visits to the local town allowed.

Former pupils Professor Bernard Williams (previously Provost of King's College, Cambridge); Michael Thomas CMG, QC (Attorney General of Hong Kong).

CHRIST COLLEGE

Christ College	Co-ed		Pupils 320
Brecon	● Boys		Upper sixth Yes
Powys LD3 8AG	Girls		Termly fees:
Telephone number 0874 3359	● Mixed sixth		Day £1220
	● Day		Boarding £1610
	● Boarding		HMC

Head Mr S W Hockey (6 years)
Age range 11–19; entry by own exam or common entrance
7 scholarships plus music scholarships and bursaries.

CHRISTIAN BROTHERS'

Christian Brothers' Grammar School	Co-ed	Pupils 1140
Glen Road	● Boys	Upper sixth 150
Belfast BT11 8NR	Girls	Termly fees:
Telephone number 0232 615321	Mixed sixth	Day £400
Enquiries/application to Rev Br D Gleeson	● Day	
	Boarding	

WHAT IT'S LIKE

Founded in 1866, it has two sites: one in the centre of Belfast, the other in the suburbs. It is a Roman Catholic foundation but pupils of all faiths are admitted. Religious worship is encouraged. There is strong emphasis on hard work and academic excellence, hence the phenomenal number of university entrants (500 in the period 1980–84). Very strong indeed in art; music and drama flourish. Vigorous participation in local community schemes. Fees are very low.

SCHOOL PROFILE

Pupils Total over 12, 1140. Entry age, 11+ and into the sixth. 40% are children of former pupils.

Entrance Own selection procedure used. Oversubscribed. No special skills or religious requirements but school is a Catholic foundation. Parents not expected to buy text books. Scholarships/bursaries available.

Parents 15+% in industry or commerce; 15+% are doctors, lawyers etc. 60+% live within 30 miles.

Staff Head Rev D R Gleeson, appointed 1988. 73 full time staff, 7 part time. Annual turnover 4%. Average age 36.

Academic work GCSE and A-levels. Average size of upper fifth 180; upper sixth 150. *O-levels*: on average, 20 pupils in upper fifth pass 1–4 subjects; 100, 5–7 subjects; 60 pass 8+ subjects. *A-levels*: on average, 20 pupils in upper sixth pass 1 subject; 30, 2 subjects; 90, 3 subjects and 10 pass 4 subjects. On average, 90 take science/engineering A-levels; 30 take arts and humanities; 30 a mixture. *Computing facilities*: Network of 15 4802 Research Machines – most departments have free-standing computers.

Senior pupils' non-academic activities *Music*: 80 learn a musical instrument, 30 to Grade 6 or above; 40 in school orchestra, 40 in choir; 10 play in pop group beyond school. *Drama and dance*: 120 participate in school productions. 6 accepted for Drama/Dance schools. *Art*: 400 take art as non-examined subject; 20 take GCSE; 12 A-level. 4 accepted for Art School. 60 belong to photographic club. *Sport*: Football, hurling, basketball, swimming, water-polo, weight-training, badminton, handball, ski-ing, athletics, cross-country available. 300 take non-compulsory sport. 4 pupils represent county/country (basketball, chess). *Other*: 50 take part in local community schemes. 30 enter voluntary schemes after leaving school. Other activities include a computer club, chess club and driving lessons.

Careers 1 full time and 3 part time careers advisors. Average number of pupils accepted for *degree courses* at Oxbridge, 4; other universities, 95; medical schools, 8; polytechnics or CHE, 12. Average number of pupils going straight into careers in the church, 3; industry, 15; the City, 5; civil service, 5.

Traditional school careers are medicine, dentistry, pharmacy, law, business administration.

Uniform School uniform worn except in the sixth.

Houses/prefects No competitive houses. Prefects, head boy – elected. School Council.

Religion Religious worship encouraged.

Social Peace and Reconciliation Inter Schools Movement (PRISM). Strong debating society – All-Ireland Champions many times. Organised trips to Europe, Eastern Bloc, USA and Canada. Pupils allowed to bring own car/bike/motorbike to school. Meals self service. Senior pupils allowed tobacco, no alcohol.

Discipline No corporal punishment. Pupils failing to produce home-work once might expect a warning; those caught smoking cannabis on the premises could expect expulsion.

Alumni association run by Mr J Johnston, President, 287 Antrim Road, Belfast.

Former pupils Rev Dr P Walsh (Auxiliary Bishop of Down and Connor); Bernard Davey; Professor Vincent McBriarty (Trinity College Dublin).

CHRIST'S COLLEGE

Christ's College
4 St Germans Place
Blackheath
London SE3 0NJ
Telephone number 01-858 0692

Enquiries/application to the School
Secretary

Co-ed   Pupils 173
• Boys   Upper sixth 16
Girls   Termly fees:
Mixed sixth   Day £655
• Day   Boarding £1245
• Boarding   ISJC; ISAI

WHAT IT'S LIKE

Founded in 1823, there are two main school houses (one Georgian and one Victorian) on one of the finest sites in London looking across 200 acres of Blackheath. It has five acres of private grounds. The Anglican tradition prevails but it is religiously tolerant. Music and drama taken to form three. The teaching is sound and there are EFL provisions throughout the school. No great range of sport, games or extra-curricular activities.

SCHOOL PROFILE

Pupils Total over 12, 173. Day 50; Boarding 123. Entry age, 4 and into the sixth. Own junior school provides over 50%. 8% are children of former pupils.

Entrance Common entrance or interview plus school reports used. Not oversubscribed. No special skills or religious requirements. Parents expected to buy text books. 2 full fees scholarships, usually awarded to existing pupils in need.

Parents 15+% in industry or commerce; 15+% are doctors, lawyers etc. 60+% live within 30 miles; up to 40% live overseas.

Staff Head D Engelheart-Knight, in post for 16 years. 17 full time staff, 10 part time. Annual turnover 5%. Average age 30+.

Academic work GCSE, A-level, JMB Test in English. Average size of fifth 50;

upper sixth 16. *O-levels*: on average, 37 pupils in fifth pass 1–4 subjects; 10, 5–7 subjects; 3 pass 8+ subjects. *A-levels*: on average, 3 pupils in upper sixth pass 1 subject; 4, 2 subjects; 7, 3 subjects and 2 pass 4 subjects. On average, 12 take science/engineering A-levels; 2 take arts and humanities; 2 a mixture. *Computing facilities*: 12 computers. *Special provision*: EFL.

Senior pupils' non-academic activities *Music*: 4 learn a musical instrument, 1 to Grade 6 or above. 16 in school choir. *Art*: Up to form five take as non-examined subject; 5 take GCSE; 4 A-level. 10 belong to photographic club. *Sport*: Football, cricket, tennis, basketball, volleyball, athletics, judo, cross-country, swimming available. Sport is compulsory. 2 represent county/country (athletics, judo). *Other*: 3 work for national charities after leaving school. Other activities include a computer club; driving lessons; chess, modelling and Roamers' clubs, horseriding, karate.

Careers 1 part time advisor. Average number of pupils accepted for *arts and humanities degree courses* at university, 1. *science and engineering degree courses* at Oxbridge, 1; other universities, 5; medical schools, 5; polytechnics or CHE, 2. Average number of pupils going straight into careers in the armed services, 1; the City, 1; civil service, 3; music/drama, 1. Traditional school careers are medicine, engineering.

Uniform School uniform worn throughout.

Houses/prefects Competitive houses. Prefects, head boy, appointed by the Head.

Religion Religious worship encouraged. There are many religious denominations in the school; all respect each other's point of view.

Social Discos with local girls' school. Infrequent trips abroad (many pupils are from overseas). Pupils not allowed to bring own car/bike/motorbike to school. Meals formal. School tuckshop. No tobacco/alcohol allowed.

Discipline Corporal punishment allowed. Pupils failing to produce homework once might expect detention; those caught smoking cannabis on the premises would be removed from school.

Boarding 25 share with 1 or 2 others, 25 share (3–5 to a room); 10 dormitories of 6+. Houses, of approximately 75, divided by age group. Resident qualified nurse. Central dining room. Sixth formers can provide and cook own food. 4 weekend exeats each term. Visits to local town allowed, but not alone.

Alumni association run by Mr M J Beaver, 27 Goddington Road, Rochester, Kent ME2 3DD.

CHRIST'S HOSPITAL

Christ's Hospital	• Co-ed	Pupils 700
Horsham	Boys	Upper sixth 110
West Sussex RH13 7YP	Girls	Termly fees:
Telephone number 0403 52547	Mixed sixth	(means tested –
	Day	see below)
Enquiries/application to the Admissions Officer	• Boarding	HMC

WHAT IT'S LIKE

Founded in 1552 by King Edward VI for children in need. In September 1985 the boys' school at Horsham and the girls' at Hertford joined to form one co-educational boarding school. Originally the boys' school had moved out of London in 1902 and a complete new school was built on an estate of 1200 acres. The buildings and campus are splendid and facilities are first-rate. Among other things there is a very good careers centre, a fine library and a purpose-built theatre which seats 500. It has been described as 'an extraordinary school for the children of ordinary people' and it is an apt description. Worship in the Anglican tradition is compulsory (within the 1944 Act) and the Chapel is central to the school life. The school is an extremely well run establishment with high standards of teaching and distinguished academic results. The staff:pupil ratio is 1:9. About 60–65 pupils go on to university each year. There is great strength in the music and drama departments. The school is famous for its bands. Numerous dramatic entertainments are staged each year. Also very strong in games and sport. A wide variety of activities is available. The CCF has a big contingent and scout group is very active. The school's record in the Duke of Edinburgh's Award Scheme is phenomenal and is almost certainly the best in the country (48 bronze, 45 silver, 72 gold).

SCHOOL PROFILE

Pupils Total over 12, 700. Boys 510, girls 190. Entry age, 10–11 only. 5% are children of former pupils.

Entrance Own entrance exam used. Oversubscribed. Music and drama skills looked for. No special religious requirements. Parents not expected to buy text books. 80% of all costs are funded from the Hospital's endowments according to parental income which, in most cases, must not exceed £17,500 gross at date of entry. Maximum value £5700 pa. The original charitable intention is still very strongly maintained. Children are assessed on grounds of need as well as ability.

Parents 30+% live within 30 miles; less than 1% live overseas.

Staff Head R C Poulton, in post for 1 year. 90 full time staff, 40 part time. Annual turnover 6%. Average age 41.

Academic work GCSE and A-levels. Average size of upper fifth 120; upper sixth 110. *O-levels*: on average, 12 pupils in upper fifth pass 1–4 subjects; 31, 5–7 subjects; 77 pass 8+ subjects. *A-levels*: on average, 6 pupils in upper sixth pass 1 subject; 16, 2 subjects; 80, 3 subjects; 8 pass 4 subjects. On average, 35 take science/engineering A-levels; 52 take arts and humanities; 23 take a mixture. GCSE drama and A-level Archaeology, Latin, Greek, Russian offered. *Computing facilities*: Computer centre with admin machine and micros. All laboratories and most departments have their own micros. Provision for mild dyslexia.

Senior pupils' non-academic activities *Music*: 145 learn a musical instrument, 70 to Grade 6 standard or above, 9 take A-level, 5 accepted for Music School, 2 gain choral scholarships, 2 now play in pop groups; 46 in school orchestra, 85 in school choir, 40 in school pop and jazz groups, 53 in concert band, 19 in show band; 18 in holiday music courses, 24 in holiday choir tours. *Drama and dance*: 100 in school productions, 100 in house plays, 30 in departmental plays. 2 accepted for Drama Schools, 2 go on to work in theatre; 11 take GCSE drama, 40 take drama classes and 20 take dance classes. *Art*: 90 take as non-examined subject; 15 take GCSE; 12 take A-level. 10 accepted for Art School. *Sport*: Association football, rugby football, hockey, cricket, swimming, shooting, netball, athletics, tennis, squash rackets available. 260

take non-compulsory sport. 2 take exams. 4 represent county/country (rugby, cricket, hockey). *Other*: 40 take part in local community schemes. 48 have bronze Duke of Edinburgh's Award, 45 have silver and 72 have gold. 5 enter voluntary schemes after leaving school. Other activities include a computer club, chess, debating, drama, music (military band, orchestra, many chorus), CCF, cycling.

Careers 6 part time advisors. Average number of pupils accepted for *arts and humanities degree courses* at Oxbridge, 12; other universities, 26; polytechnics or CHE, 14. *science and engineering degree courses* at Oxbridge, 6; other universities, 18; medical schools, 4; polytechnics or CHE, 6. *BEd*, 1. *other general training courses*, 2. Average number of pupils going straight into careers in the armed services, 4; industry, 1; the City, 2.

Uniform Distinctive school uniform worn throughout, provided by the school.

Houses/prefects Competitive houses. Prefects, head boy/girl, head of house and house prefects – appointed by Headmaster and/or housemaster/mistress.

Religion Chapel (C of E) compulsory.

Social No organised local events. Organised trips abroad and exchange systems. Pupils allowed to bring own bike to school. Meals formal. School shop. No tobacco allowed, pupils over 17 may join sixth form club and buy beer and wine.

Discipline No corporal punishment. Pupils failing to produce homework once might expect a warning.

Boarding 2% have own study bedroom, 20% share with others; 78% are in dormitories of 6+. Houses, of approx 50–60, same as competitive houses and single-sex. Resident qualified nurses and doctor. Central dining room. Pupils can provide and cook own food. No exeats. Visits to local town allowed for over 14s.

Alumni association run by Dr J R A Kennedy, CH Club, c/o Hospital.

Former pupils John Snow; Stuart Holland; Lord Stewart; Keith Douglas; Air Cmdr E M Donaldson; Bryan Magee.

CHURCHER'S

Churcher's College
Petersfield
Hampshire GU31 4AS
Telephone number 0730 63033

Co-ed
● Boys
Girls
● Mixed sixth
● Day
● Boarding

Pupils 480
Upper sixth Yes
Termly fees:
Day £917
Boarding £1770
HMC; SHMIS

Head G W Buttle appointed 1988
Age range 11–18; entry by common entrance or own exam
Bursaries and 19 assisted places pa.

CITY OF LONDON (BOYS)

City of London School
Queen Victoria Street
London EC4V 3AL
Telephone number 01-353 0046

Enquiries to the Headmaster
Application to the Admissions Secretary

Co-ed
● Boys
Girls
Mixed sixth
● Day
Boarding

Pupils 715
Upper sixth 120
Termly fees:
Day £1165
HMC

WHAT IT'S LIKE

The original foundation dates from 1442. The first school building opened in 1837 and the school moved to its present brand-new and very fine buildings in 1986. These occupy a superb riverside site, near Blackfriars with St Paul's vista as the eastern boundary. Its various terraces and open spaces command fine views of St Paul's and of the river from Tower Bridge to Westminster. The new buildings are outstandingly well equipped and comfortable in every respect. The playing fields are at Grove Park. A high standard of academic excellence is aimed at and achieved. 20% of leavers go to Oxbridge; 70% to other universities, polytechnics and medical schools. The study of medicine is a vigorous tradition. There is also a strong tradition of musical excellence (the choristers of the Temple Church and the Chapel Royal, St James's, are all pupils). Drama and art also flourish. Sport and games are compulsory and standards are high. A substantial commitment to local community schemes.

SCHOOL PROFILE

Pupils Total over 12, 715. Entry age, 10, 11, 13 and into the sixth.
Entrance Own entrance exam used. Oversubscribed. No special skills or religious requirements. Parents not expected to buy text books. 25 assisted places. 15 scholarships (academic, music) full fees to one-third fees. Choral bursaries, two-thirds fees.
Parents 60+% live within 30 miles.
Staff Head J M Hammond, in post for 4 years. 74 full time staff, 3 part time. Annual turnover 3%.
Academic work GCSE and A-levels. Average size of upper fifth 135; upper sixth 120. *O-levels*: on average, 90% of pupils pass between 5–8 subjects. *A-levels*: on average, 8% of pupils pass 2 subjects; 90% pass 3 subjects. *Computing facilities*: Some 40 computers in Computer Centre, Maths Centre and other departments.
Senior pupils' non-academic activities *Music*: 65 learn a musical instrument, 35 to Grade 6 or above, 1 accepted for Music School, 1 Cambridge Organ scholar, 1 ARCO; 34 in school orchestra, 21 in choir; 8 in other orchestras. *Drama and dance*: 40 in school productions. *Art*: 65 take GCSE; 12 A-level. 2–3 accepted for Art School. 15 participate in out of school activities. *Sport*: Cricket, football, rugby, athletics, tennis, rowing, fencing, squash, judo, karate, table-tennis, swimming, water-polo, shooting, sailing, cross-country, volleyball, basketball, badminton, indoor hockey available. 20 in senior sixth take non-compulsory sport; compulsory for the remainder. 2 represent country at fencing; 9 represent county (cricket,

water-polo). *Other*: 75 take part in local community schemes. 4 have bronze Duke of Edinburgh's Award.

Careers 20% of leavers go on to degree courses at Oxbridge and 70% to other universities/polytechnics/colleges. Traditional school careers are in medicine, law, engineering.

Uniform School uniform worn except in the sixth.

Houses/prefects Competitive houses. Prefects, head boy, head of house and house prefects – elected. School Council.

Religion No compulsory worship.

Social There are several joint functions with City of London School for Girls. Several organised trips and an exchange with a school in Hamburg. Pupils allowed to bring own bike to school. Meals self service. No tobacco/alcohol allowed.

Discipline No corporal punishment. Pupils failing to produce homework once might expect detention; those caught smoking cannabis on the premises could expect expulsion.

Alumni association is run by G A Coulson, 11 Mapleton Close, Bromley, Kent.

Former pupils H H Asquith; Kingsley Amis; Denis Norden; Mike Brearley.

CITY OF LONDON (GIRLS)

City of London School for Girls
Barbican
London EC2Y 8BB
Telephone number 01-628 0841

Enquiries/application to the Admissions Secretary

Co-ed
Boys
● Girls
Mixed sixth
● Day
Boarding

Pupils 543
Upper sixth 71
Termly fees:
Day £850
GSA

WHAT IT'S LIKE

Founded in 1894, it is urban, single-site with some open spaces. A very well equipped establishment in a lively and stimulating environment. A sound education is given and 30 or so leavers proceed to university each year. The music and art departments are especially strong (the majority of the school are involved in musical activities) and there is a fair range of clubs and societies. As the school is in the Barbican there are numerous opportunities for trips to the theatre, art galleries, museums and so forth. The Corporation of London provides further opportunities for girls to watch and take part in a variety of civic functions.

SCHOOL PROFILE

Pupils Total over 12, 543. Entry age, 11+ and into the sixth. Small proportion are children of former pupils.

Entrance Own entrance exam used. Oversubscribed. No special skills or religious requirements. Parents not expected to buy text books. 104 assisted places. 3 scholarships/bursaries up to full fees.

Parents 15+% in industry or commerce; 15+% are doctors, lawyers, etc. 60+% live within 30 miles.

Staff Head Mrs V E France, in post for 1 year. 54 full time staff, 12 part time.
Academic work GCSE and A-levels. Average size of upper fifth 80; upper sixth 71. *O-levels*: on average, 4 pupils in upper fifth pass 1–4 subjects; 19, 5–7 subjects; 61 pass 8+ subjects. *A-levels*: on average, 6 pupils in upper sixth pass 1 subject; 18, 2 subjects; 41, 3 subjects and 4 pass 4 subjects. On average, 26 take science/engineering A-levels; 27 take arts and humanities; 22 a mixture. Russian offered to GCSE/A-level. *Computing facilities*: Computer room with 12 BBC B micros and staff micro. Level 3 40 megabyte Winchester network. 3 character printers. School will help with special provisions where possible.
Senior pupils' non-academic activities *Music*: 334 learn a musical instrument, 100 to Grade 6 or above. 1 or 2 accepted for Music School; 6 senior exhibitions at various colleges; 94 in school orchestra, 131 in choir, 4 in Barbershop, 4 in National Youth Choir, 4 in Finchley Children's Choir, 10 in other local orchestra, 3 in ENO children's chorus. *Drama and dance*: 25 in school productions; 11 in recreational activity (sixth option); 30 in speech and drama lessons; 8 to Guildhall School, 12 LAMDA medals; 1–2 go to drama courses at university or college. *Art*: 250 take as non-examined subject; 30 take GCSE; 8, A-level. 10 in life drawing classes; 40 in recreational activity art clubs; 4 accepted for Art School; 1 for history of art; 1 for architecture. *Sport*: Netball, volleyball, basketball, gymnastics, swimming, hockey, judo, self-defence, fencing, badminton, multi-gym, tennis, rounders, athletics available. 60 take non-compulsory sport; 100 take exams eg gymnastics, swimming; BAGA Gym Awards, ASA Survival and Bronze Medallion Awards, Fencing and Judo Awards. 35 represent county/country (tennis, tumbling, gymnastics); P/E at college/university (1), Oxford Blue (1). *Other*: 60 take part in local community schemes. Duke of Edinburgh's Award Scheme just started. Whole school supports national charities. Other activities include a computer club, pre-driver training courses, political society, debating clubs, theatre club, play-reading society, film club.
Careers 2 part time advisors. Average number of pupils accepted for *arts and humanities degree courses* at Oxbridge, 7; other universities, 12; polytechnics or CHE, 4. *science and engineering degree courses* at Oxbridge, 4; other universities, 9; medical schools, 5; polytechnics or CHE, 3. BEd, 2. *other general training courses*, 6. Traditional careers are in medicine, law, engineering.
Uniform School uniform worn except in the sixth.
Houses/prefects No competitive houses or prefects. Head girl – nominated and elected by staff and sixth form. School Council.
Religion Daily act of worship for all.
Social Joint concerts, theatrical productions, fund raising and social activities with City of London School. Organised exchanges to France/Germany, trips to USSR, Italy and Greece. Meals self service. No tobacco/alcohol allowed.
Discipline No corporal punishment. Pupils failing to produce homework once might expect a warning and firm deadline; those caught smoking cannabis on the premises could expect expulsion.
Alumni association run by Mrs Jane Cresswell, 19 Hazlewood Grove, Sanderstead, Surrey CR2 9DW.
Former pupils Anne Farrell (actress); Clare Rayner; Katharine Dyson (D'Oyley Carte); Elizabeth Emmanuel (dress designer).

CITY OF LONDON FREEMEN'S

City of London Freemen's School	● Co-ed	Pupils 344
Ashtead Park	Boys	Upper sixth Yes
Ashtead	Girls	Termly fees:
Surrey KT21 1ET	Mixed sixth	Day £1055
Telephone number 0372 277933	● Day	Boarding £1579
	● Boarding	HMC; SHMIS

WHAT IT'S LIKE

Founded in 1854, it moved to Ashtead Park in 1926 where it stands in 57 acres of splendid parkland, playing fields and woodlands, between Epsom and Leatherhead. The main building is a magnificent 18th century house (formerly home of the Howard family). Conversion and modernisation have provided good facilities. A steady expansion programme has gone on for the last 30 years. The house system operates and there are two boarding houses (one for girls, one for boys) which provide comfortable accommodation. Over 50% of parents have taken out Freedom of the City and about 40% of the present pupils have a brother or sister currently at the school. Thus, with its Foundation, Corporation patronage and City connections the school has a flourishing family and community element. The declared aims are to promote the spiritual, academic and social development of all to the fullest extent in an atmosphere of hard work, self-criticism, loyalty and enthusiasm. A sound general education is provided and academic standards and results are highly creditable. Each year about 50% of leavers go on to university. The school is particularly strong in music and drama. The art department is also a flourishing organisation. A good range of sports and games is available for boys and girls and quite high standards are achieved. There are many clubs and societies for extra-curricular activities, of which one of the most popular is the Duke of Edinburgh's Award Scheme which has had a number of successes. There is also active commitment to local community services in the parish among the senior pupils.

SCHOOL PROFILE

Head Mr D C Haywood (1 year)
Age range 13–18, own prep from age 8; entrance by common entrance or own exam
Some scholarships available (including one music).

CLAYESMORE

Clayesmore School	● Co-ed	Pupils 324
Iwerne Minster	Boys	Upper sixth 45
Blandford Forum	Girls	Termly fees:
Dorset DT11 8LL	Mixed sixth	Day £1615
Telephone number 0747 811217	● Day	Boarding £2295
	● Boarding	SHMIS

Enquiries/application to Mr D J Beeby

WHAT IT'S LIKE

Founded in 1896, it was formerly in London, Pangbourne and Northwood Park. In 1933 it moved to its present site, the former seat of Lord Wolverton on the edge of the pretty village of Iwerne Minster. The impressive house has large gardens and a 62-acre estate, surrounded by beautiful Dorset countryside. Extensive modern additions provide first-rate facilities. The playing fields are on the estate. There is some compulsory worship in the Anglican tradition. A staff:pupil ratio of 1:10. Academic standards are high and results good. Some 10–15 leavers go on to university each year. Very active music, art and drama depts. A good reputation for sports and games (a large number of representatives at county level). A lively CCF and considerable emphasis on outdoor pursuits for which the environment is ideal. Some commitment to local community services and an impressive record in the Duke of Edinburgh's Award Scheme.

SCHOOL PROFILE

Pupils Total 324. Day 63 (boys 30, girls 33); Boarding 261 (boys 148, girls 113). Entry age, 13+ and into the sixth. Own prep school provides over 35%. 3% are children of former pupils.

Entrance Common entrance and own tests used. Not oversubscribed. No special skills or religious requirements. Services are C of E but all denominations and faiths are welcome. Text books supplied. Applied to join Assisted Places Scheme. Up to 20 scholarships/bursaries pa, £324 pa to full fees.

Parents 15+% in the armed services. 30+% live within 30 miles; 10+% live overseas.

Staff Head D J Beeby, in post for 2 years. 34 full time staff, 6 part time. Annual turnover 8%. Average age 40.

Academic work GCSE and A-levels. Average size of upper fifth 80; upper sixth 45. *O-levels*: on average, 44 pupils in upper fifth pass 1–4 subjects; 21, 5–7 subjects; 12 pass 8+ subjects. *A-levels*: on average, 9 pupils in the upper sixth pass 1 subject; 7, 2 subjects; 10, 3 subjects; 6 pass 4 subjects. On average, 15 take science/engineering A-levels; 15 take arts and humanities; 11 take a mixture. *Computing facilities*: Computer studies classroom, open out of class time for interested pupils. Provision for remedial English, maths and EFL.

Senior pupils' non-academic activities *Music*: 80 learn a musical instrument, 12 up to Grade 6 or above, 1 accepted for Music School; 20 in school orchestra, 20 in school choir, 6 in school pop group, 10 in chamber music group, 1 taken junior recital certificate, 2 in National Youth Orchestra. *Drama and dance*: 40 in school productions. *Art*: 36 take as non-examined subject; 58 take GCSE; 6 take A-level, 5 take A-level History of Art. 2 or 3 each year accepted for Art School; a few pupils go into BTEC courses at 16+. 8 belong to eg photographic clubs. *Sport*: Rugby football, hockey, netball, soccer, squash, swimming, cross-country, badminton, judo, lacrosse, athletics, cricket, tennis, golf and sailing available. 120 take non-compulsory sport. 60 take exams. 20 represent county (hockey, rugby, cricket, athletics). *Other*: 25 take part in local community schemes. 43 have bronze Duke of Edinburgh's Award, and 18 have silver. Other activities include debating and public speaking.

Careers 4 part time advisors. Average number of pupils accepted for *arts and humanities degree courses* at Oxbridge, 1; other universities, 5; polytechnics or CHE, 6. *science and engineering degree courses* at Oxbridge, 1; other universities, 5; polytechnics or CHE, 2. *BEd*, 1. *other general training courses*, 8. Average number of pupils going straight into careers in the armed services, 2; industry, 1; the City, 2; other, 1.

Uniform School uniform worn except the sixth.

Houses/prefects Competitive houses. Prefects, head boy and girl, head of house and house prefects – appointed by the Head.

Religion Compulsory daily Chapel service; longer service on Sunday.

Social Community Service Group regularly in debating, public speaking and general knowledge competitions. Regular exchanges organised by Modern Languages department; visits abroad by games teams, choirs etc. Pupils allowed to bring own bike to school. Meals self service. School shop. No tobacco allowed. Sixth form bar twice a week.

Discipline No corporal punishment. Pupils failing to produce homework once might expect to repeat it or do additional work; those caught smoking cannabis on the premises might expect expulsion.

Boarding 6 sixth formers have own study bedroom, 6 share; one-third in dormitories of 6+. Houses, of approximately 55, same as competitive houses, single-sex. Resident SRN. Central dining room. Pupils can provide and cook own food. Two weekend exeats each term. Visits to local town allowed once a week.

Alumni association is run by N Zelle Esq, 25 Whitehall Gardens, London W3.

CLIFTON

Clifton College
32 College Road
Clifton
Bristol BS8 3JH
Telephone number 0272 735945

Enquiries/application to the Registrar

- Co-ed   Pupils 631
- Boys   Upper sixth 110
- Girls   Termly fees:
- Mixed sixth   Day £1600
- Day   Boarding £2350
- Boarding   HMC

WHAT IT'S LIKE

Founded in 1862, incorporated by Royal Charter in 1877, it became a prominent public school very quickly and was one of the first major public schools to move towards co-education at all levels. It is fortunate in its situation above the city, on the edge of Clifton Downs and near open country. Its handsome buildings are neo-Tudor and neo-Gothic and stand in beautiful grounds. Much money has been spent and its facilities are exceptionally good. It has a modern theatre and two superb libraries (as well as house libraries). The prep department is nearby. An unusual feature is that one of the boarding houses is reserved for boys of Jewish faith. Religious worship is compulsory for Jews at their synagogue. For others, some Christian services are compulsory. It provides a thoroughly good and liberal education and academic standards are high (60–70 university entrants per year). Very strong indeed in music and drama. A very high standard in games and sports. Numerous extra-curricular activities and a strong CCF. A big commitment to local community schemes and the Duke of Edinburgh's Award Scheme. Much use is made of Bristol's cultural amenities.

SCHOOL PROFILE

Pupils Total 631. Day 194 (boys); Boarding 437 (boys 389, girls 48). Entry age, 13 and into the sixth. Own prep school provides over 20%. About 15% are children of former pupils.

Entrance Common entrance and own entrance exam used. Oversubscribed. No special skills or religious requirements. Parents expected to buy text books. 34 assisted places. 24 scholarships/bursaries, for academic, artistic and musical excellence, to £5750 pa.

Parents 15+% are doctors, lawyers, etc; 15+% in industry or commerce. 30+% live within 30 miles; 10+% live overseas.

Staff Head S D Andrews, in post for 12 years. 66 full time staff, 8 part time. Annual turnover 4%. Average age 42.

Academic work GCSE and A-levels. Average size of upper fifth 130; upper sixth 110. *O-levels*: on average, 21 pupils in upper fifth pass 1–4 subjects; 41, 5–7 subjects; 68 pass 8+ subjects. *A-levels*: on average, 8 pupils in the upper sixth pass 1 subject; 12, 2 subjects; 70, 3 subjects; 20 pass 4 subjects. On average, 35 take science/engineering A-levels; 50 take arts and humanities; 25 a mixture. Latin, Greek, Spanish and Russian are offered to GCSE/A-level. *Computing facilities*: Computing centre with 16 BBC Apple Computers. Computers are available and in increasing use throughout the school. Professional EFL instruction provided.

Senior pupils' non-academic activities *Music*: 200 learn a musical instrument, 65 to Grade 6 or above, 2 accepted for Music School; 45 in school orchestra, 45 in wind band, 100 in school choir, 15 in 3 school pop groups, 15 in jazz band, 20 in barber shop/a capella; 1 in National Youth Orchestra, 6 in county orchestra. *Drama and dance*: 60 in school productions. 1 or 2 per year accepted for Drama/Dance schools. 300 in house drama festival. *Art*: 25 take as non-examined subject; 52 take GCSE; 12 take A-level, 8 take history of art (A-level). 6 accepted for Art School, 1 for architectural college. 20 in extra art, 25 in extra pottery groups, 20 belong to photographic club. *Sport*: Rugby football, association football, hockey, cricket, rowing, athletics, cross-country, netball, tennis, lacrosse, sailing, badminton, volleyball, basketball, fives, squash, racquets, fencing, tetrathlon, weight training, trampolining, aerobics, swimming, water polo and gymnastics available. 280 take non-compulsory sport. 2 or 3 represent county (rugby, hockey, cricket, athletics). 2 1987 Young England cricketers. *Other*: 60 take part in local community scheme. 20 have bronze Duke of Edinburgh's Award and 20 have silver. Other activities include a computer club, rock climbing, chess, country dancing, arctic expeditions and CCF.

Careers 1 full time and 4 part time advisors. Average number of pupils accepted for *arts and humanities degree courses* at Oxbridge, 9; other universities, 31; polytechnics or CHE, 20. *science and engineering degree courses* at Oxbridge, 8; other universities, 16; medical schools, 7; polytechnics or CHE, 6. *other general training courses*, 12. Average number of pupils going straight into careers in the armed services, 5; the church, 2; industry, 14; the City, 4; music/drama, 3; sports, 2. Traditional school careers are: law, accountancy, business administration, engineering and the media.

Uniform School uniform worn throughout.

Houses/prefects Competitive houses. Prefects, head boy/girl, head of house and house prefects – appointed by the headmaster, after consultation. Limited fagging.

Religion For Jewish pupils attendance at Synagogue is compulsory. For Christians some Chapel services are compulsory, others are voluntary.

Social School debates, co-productions of plays, including modern language play, subject conferences in the school theatre with other local schools. Strong connection with an earthquake damaged school in Mexico City; organised trips there. Exchanges with France and Germany. Pupils allowed to bring own car/bike to school. Meals self service. School shop selling stationery. No tobacco/alcohol allowed.

Discipline No corporal punishment. Pupils failing to produce homework once might expect detention. Those caught smoking cannabis on the premises would have specific circumstances considered before disciplinary action taken.

Boarding 25% have own study bedroom, 45% share with others; 30% are in dormitories of 6 or more. Houses, of approximately 60, are the same as competitive houses and are single-sex. School doctor visits daily, two qualified nurses in sanatorium. Central dining room. Pupils can provide and cook their own food. 1 Saturday night exeat plus half term each term. Visits to the local town allowed with permission.

Alumni association is run by H G Edwards Esq OBE, Old Clifton Society, c/o the College.

Former pupils Lord Clyde Hewlett and Lord Patrick Jenkin (Politicians); Michael Redgrave, Trevor Howard, John Cleese, and John Houseman (the stage); Sir David Willcocks and Joseph Cooper (music); Mark Tully, David Bunavia and Stephen Pile (the media).

CLIFTON HIGH

Clifton High School for Girls	Co-ed	Pupils 569
College Road	Boys	Upper sixth 60
Clifton	● Girls	Termly fees:
Bristol BS8 3JD	Mixed sixth	Day £720
Telephone number 0272 730201	● Day	Boarding £1450
Enquiries/application to Mrs J D Walters	● Boarding	GSA

WHAT IT'S LIKE

Founded in 1877, it has a fine site in the middle of the Georgian village of Clifton, near the Downs and the Suspension Bridge. Handsome buildings and agreeable surroundings. The facilities and accommodation are first-class. Religious worship, non-denominational, is compulsory and religious studies are taught throughout the school. The school has a long standing reputation for providing an excellent education. Results are very good. Each year some 30 pupils go on to university. There are extremely strong music, drama and art depts involving a large number of pupils. Also a good range of games and sports (many representatives at county level). Plentiful activities are available. There is a great commitment to social services and the school has a fair record in the Duke of Edinburgh's Award Scheme. Full use is made of Bristol's cultural amenities.

SCHOOL PROFILE

Pupils Total over 12, 569. Day 475; Boarding 94. Entry age, 10–11 and into the sixth. Own junior department provides over 50%. 5% are children of former pupils.

Entrance Own entrance exam used. Oversubscribed. Skills in sport, music and art are looked for. No religious requirements. Parents not expected to buy text books. 52 assisted places. 43 scholarships, up to full fees.

Parents 15+% are doctors, lawyers, etc; 15+% in industry or commerce. 60+% live within 30 miles; up to 10% live overseas.

Staff Head Mrs J D Walters, in post for 3 years. 50 full time staff, 26 part time. Annual turnover 5–10%. Average age 35.

Academic work GCSE and A-levels. Average size of upper fifth 75; upper sixth 60. *O-levels*: on average, 7 pupils in upper fifth pass 1–4 subjects; 34, 5–7 subjects; 34 pass 8+ subjects. *A-levels*: on average, 2 pupils in the upper sixth pass 1 subject; 10, 2 subjects; 30, 3 subjects; 5 pass 4 subjects. On average, 45% take science/engineering A-levels; 45% take arts and humanities; 10% take a mixture. Greek, Italian, Fashion and Fabrics are offered to GCSE/A-level. *Computing facilities*: Computer centre with 15 computers, plus others in departments.

Senior pupils' non-academic activities *Music*: 210 learn a musical instrument, 15 to Grade 6 or above, 12 take GCSE/O-level, 3 A-level; 30 in school orchestra, 130 in school choir, 30 in wind band. *Drama and dance*: 50+ in school productions, 100+ in house plays, clubs etc; 4 or 5 take Guildhall, LAMDA exams, 4 or 5 take AO course in Theatre Arts in sixth form. 2 accepted for Drama Schools, 2 or 3 accepted for university or FE courses in drama. Some old girls working in theatre. *Art*: 19 take as non-examined subject; 48 GCSE; 24 A-level. 5 applying for Art School. *Sport*: Hockey, netball, tennis, swimming, rounders and athletics are available. Sport is compulsory. 60 teams and extra curricular sport, 18 take fencing, 40 take self defence, outdoor pursuits and riding. 1 or 2 take exams in gymnastics; some have skating certificates and life saving. 10 represent county (swimming, hockey, netball, tennis, athletics). *Other*: 14 take part in bronze Duke of Edinburgh's Award, 9 have silver and 13 gold. Other activities include a computer club, woodwork, technology club, Christian Union, art club.

Careers 1 full time advisor. Average number of pupils accepted for *arts and humanities degree courses* at Oxbridge, 2; other universities, 12; polytechnics or CHE, 8. *science and engineering degree courses* at Oxbridge, 1; other universities, 8; medical schools, 2; polytechnics or CHE, 6. *BEd*, 4. *other general training courses*, 2. Average number of pupils going straight into careers in the armed services, 1; the civil service, 1; other, 2.

Uniform School uniform worn except in sixth.

Houses/prefects Competitive houses. Prefects, head girl, head of house and house prefects – appointed by staff and school. School Council.

Religion Non-denominational religious worship compulsory.

Social Debates, plays, choral performances with Clifton College. Organised trips to France, Russia, Spain and Italy. School exchanges with Toulouse.

Pupils allowed to bring own bike to school. Meals self service. Second-hand clothes shop. No tobacco/alcohol allowed.

Discipline No corporal punishment. Pupils failing to produce homework once might expect detention; those caught smoking cannabis on the premises would be expelled.

Boarding Sixth form share bedrooms or have individual studies; 60 in dormitories of 6+. 2 houses, senior 60, junior 40. Central dining room. Pupils can provide and cook own food. Exeats most weekends. Visits to village allowed daily; Bristol Centre at weekends.

Alumni association is run by Mrs J Huckman, 3, Pitch and Pay Park, Sneyd Park, Bristol BS9 1NJ.

Former pupils Jo Durie, Mary Renault.

COBHAM HALL

Cobham Hall
Cobham
Nr Gravesend
Kent DA12 3BL
Telephone number 0474 82 3371

Enquiries/application to the School
Secretary

Co-ed
Boys
● Girls
Mixed sixth
● Day
● Boarding

Pupils 284
Upper sixth 33
Termly fees:
Day £1725
Boarding £2585
GSA; GBGSA

WHAT IT'S LIKE

It opened as an independent public school for girls in 1962 and is a member of the Round Square Conference. Thus its aims are based on the pioneering ideals of Kurt Hahn. The main building was once the home of the Earls of Darnley, a very fine example of an Elizabethan country mansion which contains some work by Inigo Jones. Some 18th century developments include designs by James Wyatt. It lies in a superb site of 140 acres of landscaped gardens and parkland in the countryside. There are modern extensions. Overall, the facilities are first class and accommodation for boarders is very comfortable. The senior girls live in a modern house set apart from the rest of the school. The house system operates and there is an efficient tutorial system. The school is international and also interdenominational. The standards of teaching are high and academic results are good. Music, drama, dance and art play an important part in the life of the school. All girls take dance as a cultural subject. Sport and games are well catered for and standards are high. There is a plentiful range of extra-curricular activities. Many of the senior girls are involved in voluntary community services locally and help local organisations in their spare time. Some participation in the Duke of Edinburgh's Award Scheme.

SCHOOL PROFILE

Pupils Total over 12, 284. Day 25; Boarding 259. Entry age, 11 and into the sixth. 1 child of former pupil.

Entrance Own entrance exam used. Oversubscribed. All-rounders looked for; no religious requirements. Parents not expected to buy text books. Scholarships/bursaries, 50%–30% of fees.

Parents 15+% in industry or commerce. 10+% live within 30 miles; 10+% live overseas.

Staff Head Miss Susan Cameron, in post for 3 years. 36 full time staff, 19 part time. Annual turnover 9%. Average age 40.

Academic work GCSE and A-levels. Average size of upper fifth 45; upper sixth 33. *O-levels*: on average, 20 pupils in upper fifth pass 1–4 subjects; 33, 5–7 subjects; 10 pass 8+ subjects. *A-levels*: on average, 7 pupils in the upper sixth pass 1 subject; 13, 2 subjects; 10, 3 subjects and 1 passes 4 subjects. On average, 9 take science/engineering A-levels; 19 take arts and humanities; 3 a mixture. Latin, Classical Civilisation, Greek offered to GCSE/A-level. *Computing facilities*: Nimbus, Network, BBC Bs in depts. Provision for dyslexia, mild visual handicap and EFL.

Senior pupils' non-academic activities *Music*: 124 learn a musical instrument, 14 to Grade 6 or above, 2 accepted for Music School; 18 in school orchestra, 65 in choir; clarinet quartet; regular concerts and inter-house music festivals. *Drama and dance*: 40 in school productions; 300 in other. 9 take GCSE dance; 30 Associated Board Grade 6 upwards. 2 go on to work in theatre. *Art*: 10 take as non-examined subject; 79 GCSE; 17 A-level. 3 accepted for Art School. 10 belong to photographic club; 25 to art clubs; 24 make jewellery. *Sport*: Swimming, tennis, netball, hockey, cross-country, rounders, athletics, squash, trampolining, gymnastics, yoga, aerobics, self-defence, badminton, life saving, riding, weight training, ski-ing, judo available. 100% take compulsory sport, 50% take non-compulsory; 35–40% take exams. *Other*: 120 take part in local community schemes. 22 have bronze Duke of Edinburgh's Award, 23 have silver and 10 gold. Many enter voluntary schemes on leaving; at least 4 work for national charities. Other activities include computer, driving, cookery, pottery, toy making, dress, French and Spanish clubs.

Careers 1 full time careers advisor. Average number of pupils accepted for *arts and humanities degree courses* at universities, 10; polytechnics or CHE, 5. *science and engineering degree courses* at Oxbridge, 1; other universities, 2; medical schools, 3. *other general training courses*, 8. Average number of pupils going straight into careers in the City, 1. Traditional school careers are medicine and art foundation.

Uniform School uniform worn except the sixth.

Houses/prefects Competitive houses. Prefects, head girl, head of house and house prefects – elected by the school. School Council.

Religion All religions welcomed.

Social General knowledge quizzes, debates, joint musical productions, sixth form dances and discos with other schools. Trips to Russia, America, France, Spain, Italy, Egypt; exchanges with America, Switzerland, Germany, France, Spain, India. Pupils allowed to bring own bike/horse/car to school. Meals self service. School shop. No tobacco/alcohol allowed.

Discipline No corporal punishment. Pupils failing to produce homework once might expect detention and work re-done at weekend under supervision (at discretion of staff concerned); those caught smoking cannabis on the premises might expect expulsion.

Boarding Sixth form have own study bedroom. Houses, of approximately 60, are of mixed ages. Resident qualified nurse. Central dining room. Seniors can provide and cook own food. 2 termly exeats. Visits to local town allowed at weekends.

Alumni association run by Miss C Cawston, 73 Warner Road, London SE5 9NE.

Former pupils Jane How; Taryn Power; Ramina Power.

COLERAINE

Coleraine Academical Institution
Castlerock Road
Coleraine
Londonderry BT51 3LA
Telephone number 0265 4331

Enquiries/application to the Headmaster

Co-ed
● Boys
Girls
Mixed sixth
● Day
● Boarding

Pupils 985
Upper sixth 120
Termly fees:
Day £325
Boarding £908
HMC

WHAT IT'S LIKE

Founded in 1859, it is semi-rural and single-site in 70 acres of playing fields and grounds on the outskirts of Coleraine with a view over beautiful landscapes and the lower reaches of the River Bann. There has been much expansion since 1955. A well-run school with high academic standards (70 plus university entrants last year), it aims to provide a full and thorough instruction in all branches of a liberal education. Music and drama are strong departments and there is a good range of sports, games, clubs, societies etc. A fair commitment to local community schemes and the Duke of Edinburgh's Award Scheme.

SCHOOL PROFILE

Pupils Total, 985. Day 770; Boarding 215. Entry age, 12 and into the sixth. About 30% are children of former pupils.

Entrance Very few admitted by common entrance. Not oversubscribed. Above average IQ expected. No religious requirements. Parents not expected to buy text books. Sons of clergymen given 10% reduction of fees.

Parents Up to 10% of boarders' parents live within 30 miles; 60+% live overseas.

Staff Head R S Forsythe, in post for 4 years. 63 full time staff, 6 part time. Annual turnover 5%. Average age 40.

Academic work GCSE and A-levels. Average size of upper fifth 170; upper sixth 120. *O-levels*: on average, 15 pupils in upper fifth pass 1–4 subjects; 25, 5–7 subjects; 80 pass 8+ subjects. *A-levels*: on average, 5 pupils in upper sixth pass 1 subject; 15, 2 subjects; 90, 3 subjects and 10 pass 4 subjects. On average, 80 take science/engineering A-levels; 20 take arts and humanities; 20 a mixture. *Computing facilities*: network system for school; administration totally on computer. EFL provision.

Senior pupils' non-academic activities *Music*: 60 learn a musical instrument, 5 to Grade 6 or above. 40 in school orchestra, 80 in school choir. *Drama and dance*: 100 in school productions; 1 accepted for Drama School. *Art*: 50 take GCSE art, 20 A-level; 10 accepted for Art School. 30 belong to photographic club. *Sport*: Rugby, cricket, athletics, swimming, cross-country, tennis, squash, badminton, rowing, sailing, angling, canoeing available. 300 take non-compulsory sport, 10 take exams. 17 represent county/country (rugby football, badminton, athletics, table tennis, cross-country). *Other*: 40 take part in local community schemes. 30 have bronze Duke of Edinburgh's Award, 12 have silver and 10 gold. Other activities include a computer club, chess club, bridge club, debating society, dramatics, stamp club, school bank, community services, scouts, scripture union.

Careers 4 part time advisors. Average number of pupils accepted for *arts and humanities degree courses* at Oxbridge, 1; other universities, 10; polytechnics or CHE, 3. *science and engineering degree courses* at Oxbridge, 3; other universities, 60; medical schools, 10; polytechnics or CHE, 27. *BEd*, 2. *other general training courses*, 5. Average number of pupils going straight into careers in the armed services, 4; the church, 2; industry, 4; the City, 1; civil service, 2; music/drama, 1.

Uniform School uniform worn throughout.

Houses/prefects Competitive houses. Prefects, head boy, head of house and house prefects – elected by staff and sixth form.

Religion Religious worship is encouraged.

Social Joint schools' community service group, debating society meet together, girls assist in drama. Ski trip, modern language trip and rugby tour each year. Pupils allowed to bring own car to school. Meals formal in boarding school, self service in day school. School shop. No tobacco/alcohol allowed.

Discipline No corporal punishment. Pupils failing to produce homework once might expect to do it by the following day; those caught smoking cannabis on the premises could expect expulsion.

Boarding 25% have own study bedroom, 60% are in dormitories of 6+. Houses, of approximately 30/40, divided by age group. Resident qualified nurse. Central dining room. Pupils can provide and cook own food. 2 day exeats 3–5 times a term depending on term length. Visits to local town allowed.

Former pupils Air Marshal Sir George Beamish.

COLFE'S

Colfe's School	Co-ed	Pupils 568
Horn Park Lane	● Boys	Upper sixth 74
London SE12 8AW	Girls	Termly fees:
Telephone number 01-852 2283/4	● Mixed sixth	Day £905
Enquiries/application to the Registrar	● Day	HMC; IAPS
	Boarding	

WHAT IT'S LIKE

Founded in 1652, it moved from its original site below Blackheath to new purpose-built premises in 1964: a single urban site with 18 acres of pleasant grounds and playing fields. It retains strong links with the Leathersellers' Company and its official visitor is Prince Michael of Kent who takes a close interest in the school. A C of E foundation, worship and religious instruction are encouraged. A very good general and academic education is provided and results are impressive. About 30 leavers proceed to university each year. There is a tremendously strong music dept involving a great many people, also much strength in drama and art. An excellent range of sports and games is available and high standards are attained. A good range of extra-curricular activities.

SCHOOL PROFILE

Pupils Total over 12, 568 (boys 525, girls 43). Entry age, from 7+ but mainly 11+, boys; boys and girls into the sixth. Own junior school provides over 50%. 3% are children of former pupils.

Entrance Common entrance and own entrance exam used. Oversubscribed. Candidates who are strong academically, and in sports and music looked for. No religious requirements. Parents not expected to buy text books. 222 assisted places. 30 scholarships/bursaries pa, from two-thirds fees to £450.

Parents 15+% in industry or commerce. 60+% live within 30 miles.

Staff Head V S Anthony, in post for 11 years. 55 full time staff, 18 part time. Annual turnover minimal. Average age 36.

Academic work GCSE and A-levels. Average size of upper fifth 90; upper sixth 74. *O-levels*: on average, 22 pupils in upper fifth pass 1–4 subjects; 23, 5–7 subjects; 45 pass 8+ subjects. *A-levels*: on average, 9 pupils in the upper sixth pass 1 subject; 14, 2 subjects; 34, 3 subjects; 11 pass 4 subjects. On average, 23 take science/engineering A-levels; 34 take arts and humanities; 16, a mixture. *Computing facilities*: Network of 14 BBC Master Computers, plus various individual departmental BBC Masters. Provision for mild dyslexia may be arranged.

Senior pupils' non-academic activities *Music*: 200 learn a musical instrument, 20 take orchestra and 15 organ and piano to Grade 6 or above, 3 accepted for Music School; 70 in school orchestra, 160 in school choir, 10 in 2 school pop groups, 40 in senior band, 20 in wind ensemble; 30 in local youth orchestras; 15 go into university choirs/orchestras; 1 to pop group. *Drama and dance*: 120 in school productions, 20 take GCSE drama, 10/12 take A-level. 2/3 go on to work in the theatre. *Art*: 120 take as non-examined subject; 40 take GCSE; 20 A-level. 2 accepted for Art School. *Sport*: Cricket, tennis, golf, swimming, football, rugby, squash, athletics, judo, sailing, hockey, netball, basketball, badminton, table tennis, windsurfing, cross-country, outdoor pursuits, climbing, abseiling, canoeing, orienteering and fell-walking available. 7 represent county/country (rugby). *Other*: 3 take part in local community schemes. 2 have gold Duke of Edinburgh's Award, 20 have Barnardo's award. Other activities include a computer club and clubs for technology, chess, ATC, crafts, badminton, comics, photography, art, Christian Union, modelling, war games and ski-training.

Careers 2 part time advisors. Average number of pupils accepted for *arts and humanities degree courses* at Oxbridge, 3; other universities, 10; polytechnics or CHE, 4. *science and engineering degree courses* at Oxbridge, 2; other universities, 15; medical schools, 4; polytechnics or CHE, 4. Average number of pupils going straight into careers in the armed services, 1; industry, 1; the City, 14; the civil service, 1; other, 3.

Uniform School uniform worn throughout.

Houses/prefects Competitive houses. Prefects and head boy/girl – appointed by the Head and staff.

Religion Worship encouraged.
Social From time to time large scale choral productions with other schools.
Organised trips to France, Germany, USA, Russia, Egypt, Romania, Switzerland. Some meals formal, some self service. School shop. No tobacco/alcohol allowed.
Discipline No corporal punishment. Pupils failing to produce homework once might expect rebuke; those caught smoking cannabis on the premises might expect expulsion.
Former pupils Eric Ambler; Henry Williamson; sundry ambassadors.

COLSTON'S (BOYS)

Colston's School	Co-ed	Pupils 340
Stapleton	● Boys	Upper sixth 52
Bristol BS16 1BJ	Girls	Termly fees:
Telephone number 0272 655207	● Mixed sixth	Day £1100
	● Day	Boarding £1825
Enquiries/application to the Headmaster	● Boarding	HMC; SHMIS

WHAT IT'S LIKE

Founded in 1710, it is single-site at Stapleton in the northern outskirts of Bristol. There are 30 acres of good grounds and playing fields and the main building is the former palace of the Bishop of Bristol. There have been numerous modern developments and facilities are of a high standard. The preparatory department is nearby. A sound education is provided and not a few leavers (15–20) proceed to university. It being a C of E school chapel is quite an important part of school life; all denominations are welcome. There are flourishing music, art and drama departments. There is a substantial commitment (nearly 50% of pupils) to their own local community schemes. Full use is made of the cultural and other amenities of Bristol.

SCHOOL PROFILE

Pupils Total, 340. Day 250 (boys 243, girls 7); Boarding 90 (boys 80, girls 10). Entry age, 13+ boys; boys and girls into the sixth. Own prep school provides over 20%. 5% are children of former pupils.
Entrance Common entrance and own entrance exam used. Oversubscribed. Any special ability is taken into account. No religious requirements. Parents not expected to buy text books. 90 assisted places. 8 scholarships/bursaries, full fees to £300 per term.
Parents 15+% in industry or commerce; 15+% are doctors, lawyers, etc. 30+% live within 30 miles; 11–30% live overseas.
Staff Head S B Howarth, first year in post. 28 full time staff, 5 part time. Annual turnover 5%. Average age 40.
Academic work GCSE and A-levels. Average size of upper fifth 69; upper sixth 52. *O-levels*: on average, 25 pupils in upper fifth pass 1–4 subjects; 23, 5–7 subjects; 21 pass 8+ subjects. *A-levels*: on average, 6 pupils in upper sixth pass 1 subject; 7, 2 subjects; 23, 3 subjects and 4 pass 4 subjects. On average, 14 take science/engineering A-levels; 23 take arts and humanities; 7

a mixture. Accounting offered to GCSE. *Computing facilities*: 10 Amstrad (IBM compatible), 2 Apple, 6 BBC model D. Dyslexia Unit for limited numbers.

Senior pupils' non-academic activities *Music*: 34 learn a musical instrument, 10 to Grade 6 or above; 1 accepted for Music School; 23 in school orchestra, 20 in choir, 6 in pop group. *Drama and dance*: 40–50 participate in school productions. 10 in local productions; 1 goes on to work in theatre. *Art*: 50 take GCSE; 6–8 A-level. 2 accepted for Art School. 10 belong to photographic club. *Sport*: Rugby, hockey, cross-country, rugby fives, cricket, tennis, swimming, squash, volleyball, badminton available. Sport is compulsory. 80% also take part in non-compulsory sport. About 30–40 represent county/country (rugby, hockey, cricket, cross-country, tennis, squash, badminton). *Other*: 130 take part in our own local community schemes. Other activities include a computer club, chess, walking, climbing, CCF (RAF and Army) and driving lessons.

Careers 3 part time advisors. Average number of pupils accepted for *arts and humanities degree courses* at Oxbridge, 1; other universities, 8; polytechnics or CHE, 7. *science and engineering degree courses* at Oxbridge, 2; other universities, 7; medical schools, 2; polytechnics or CHE, 5. *BEd*, 1. *other general training courses*, 2. Average number of pupils going straight into careers in armed services, 5; industry, 1; the City, 1; banking, insurance, estate agency etc, 16.

Uniform School uniform worn throughout.

Houses/prefects Competitive houses. Prefects, head boy, head of house and house prefects – appointed by the Head.

Religion Religious worship compulsory.

Social Choir, choral society and plays with Colston's Girls' School. Organised French and German exchanges. Pupils allowed to bring own bike to school; cars – day pupils only. Meals self service. School shop. No tobacco/alcohol allowed.

Discipline No corporal punishment. Pupils failing to produce homework once might expect to do it by the following day; those caught smoking cannabis on the premises could expect expulsion.

Boarding 15% have own study bedroom, 20% share (with 1 other); 50% are in dormitories of 6+. Houses, of 45–50, same as competitive houses. Resident qualified nurse. Central dining room. Pupils can provide and cook own food. Exeats each term: 2 for 13–16, 4 for 16–18. Visits to the local town allowed by arrangement with Housemaster.

Alumni association run by J Cook, Dean Lodge, Iron Acton, Bristol.

Former pupils Professor Peter Mathias (Master of Downing College, Cambridge); Chris Broad (England cricketer); Alan Morley and Austin Sheppard (England rugby players); John Mason (*Daily Telegraph* rugby correspondent); Simon Mugglestone (International athlete).

COLSTON'S (GIRLS)

Colston's Girls' School
Cheltenham Road
Bristol BS6 5RD
Telephone number 0272 424328

Enquiries/application to Mrs L Harrison, Secretary

Co-ed
Boys
● Girls
Mixed sixth
● Day
Boarding

Pupils 640
Upper sixth 65
Termly fees:
Day £705
GSA

WHAT IT'S LIKE

Founded in 1891, urban, inner city and single-site. The original buildings form the nucleus of the modern school and have been extensively augmented to provide very good facilities. Every girl is treated as an individual and encouraged to discover her own strengths and gifts so that she can further them. The teaching is good and so are the results (20 or so university entrants per year). Religious education is Christian but non-denominational. A fair range of standard sports, games and activities. There is a big commitment to music and drama. The Duke of Edinburgh's Award Scheme is popular.

SCHOOL PROFILE

Pupils Total over 12, 640. Entry age, 10, 11 and into the sixth (and when vacancies occur). 25% are children of former pupils.

Entrance Own entrance exam used. Fully subscribed. No special skills required. C of E foundation, but all denominations welcome. Parents not expected to buy text books. 150 assisted places. 60 scholarships (music and sixth form) and school assisted places, variable value.

Parents 15+% in industry or commerce; 15+% are doctors, lawyers, etc; 15+% in the church. More than 60% live within 30 miles.

Staff Head Miss A C Parkin, in post for 7 years. 37 full time staff, 25 part time. Annual turnover 4%. Average age 30–40.

Academic work GCSE and A-levels. Average size of upper fifth 105; upper sixth 65. *O-levels*: on average, 20 pupils in upper fifth pass 1–4 subjects; 40, 5–7 subjects; 50 pass 8+ subjects. *A-levels*: on average, 5 pupils in upper sixth pass 1 subject; 18, 2 subjects; 40, 3 subjects and 2 pass 4 subjects. On average, 45% take science/engineering A-levels; 45% take arts and humanities; 10% a mixture. Russian offered to GCSE/A-level. *Computing facilities*: 10 BBC Master.

Senior pupils' non-academic activities *Music*: 140 learn a musical instrument, 60 to Grade 6 or above, 3 accepted for Music School; 70 in school orchestra, 100 in choir, 40 in chamber group; 1 in National Youth Orchestra, 6 in county orchestra, 25 in senior schools orchestras, 1 in youth choir. *Drama and dance*: Between 50–100 in school productions. *Art*: 30 take GCSE; 12 A-level. 6 accepted for Art School. *Sport*: Dance, gymnastics, hockey, squash, badminton, aerobics, athletics, weight training, swimming available. All sport compulsory. 200 take exams eg gymnastics, swimming. 6 represent county/country (athletics, hockey, netball, swimming). *Other*: 40 have bronze Duke of Edinburgh's Award, 10 have silver and 2 have gold.

Other activities include a computer club, drama clubs, electronics, music groups, dance club.

Careers 1 part time advisor. Average number of pupils accepted for *arts and humanities degree courses* at Oxbridge, 2; other universities, 10; polytechnics or CHE, 4. *science and engineering degree courses* at Oxbridge, 2; other universities, 8; medical schools, 4; polytechnics or CHE, 3. *BEd*, 3. *other general training courses*, 6. Average number of pupils going straight into careers in the armed services, 1; industry, 6.

Uniform School uniform worn except in the sixth.

Houses/prefects Competitive houses. Prefects, head girl, house captains – elected by the school.

Religion Religious worship encouraged. Voluntary attendance at religious services in church once a term.

Social Debates, choir, drama productions dance with other schools. Organised trips to Russia, Germany, Austria, France, Spain, Italy, Greece. A few pupils allowed to bring own car/bike/motorbike to school. Meals self service. Small tuckshop. No tobacco/alcohol allowed.

Discipline No corporal punishment. Pupils failing to produce homework once might expect a discussion with staff member; those caught smoking cannabis on the premises could expect expulsion.

COMBE BANK

Combe Bank School Educational Trust Ltd	Co-ed	Pupils 250
Sundridge	Boys	Upper sixth 16
Sevenoaks	● Girls	Termly fees:
Kent TN14 6AD	Mixed sixth	Day £980
Telephone number 0959 63720	● Day	Boarding £1680
Enquiries/application to the Secretary	● Boarding	GSA

WHAT IT'S LIKE

Founded in 1868, it passed to the Educational Trust in 1972 and is housed in a superb Palladian country mansion (an historic building) built in 1720 and set in 27 acres of beautiful parkland. The prep school is nearby. It is Roman Catholic but accepts all denominations. Christian doctrine and training is central to the curriculum; the syllabus is ecumenical. It caters for all abilities and talents; recently very strong in music and quite strong in drama. There is a fair range of sports, games and activities and the standard in games is high. Vigorous participation in local community schemes.

SCHOOL PROFILE

Pupils Total over 12, 250 (all day; weekly boarding available from September 1988). Entry age, 3, 11, 12 and into the sixth. Own prep school provides over 40% of pupils. Small number are children of old pupils.

Entrance Own entrance exam used. Not oversubscribed. No special skills or religious requirements; any special skills (eg music) an advantage. School is a Roman Catholic foundation although only 30% pupils are Catholic. Parents expected to buy some text books. No assisted places yet. Some scholarships/ bursaries are available.

Parents 60 + % live within 30 miles.

Staff Head Mrs A J K Austin, in post for 6 years. 18 full time staff, 14 part time. Annual turnover 10%. Average age about 40.

Academic work GCSE and A-levels. Average size of upper fifth 43; upper sixth approx 16. *A-levels*: on average, 1 pupil in the upper sixth passes 1 subject; 7, 2 subjects; 6, 3 subjects. On average, 50% take science/engineering A-levels. *Computing facilities*: BBC Bs, computer studies room, computers in careers and secretarial studies. Special provision for dyslexic pupils.

Senior pupils' non-academic activities *Music*: 180 learn a musical instrument, 15 to Grade 6 or above. 30 in school orchestra, 100 in school choir, 20 in wind, 20 in recorder, 10 in string groups. *Drama and dance*: Large number in school productions; a few take Guildhall exams. *Art*: 3 or 4 take as a non-examined subject, 10 take GCSE; 2–6 A-level. 30 belong to pottery and sculpture clubs. *Sport*: Hockey, netball, rounders, athletics, cross-country running, swimming, badminton, volleyball are available. 100 take non-compulsory sport. *Other*: 40 take part in local community schemes. 30 have bronze Duke of Edinburgh's Award, 15 have silver and 5 gold. Other activities include a computer club, pottery and craft, calligraphy, judo, trampoline and music.

Careers 1 part-time advisor. Average number of pupils accepted for *arts and humanities degree courses* at universities, 2; polytechnics or CHE, 2. *science and engineering degree courses* at universities, 2; medical schools, 1; polytechnics or CHE, 1. *BEd*, 1. *other general training courses*, 3. Average number of pupils going straight into careers in industry, 1–2; the City, 2; music/drama, 1; other 2.

Uniform School uniform worn except in the sixth.

Houses/prefects Competitive houses. Prefects, head girl, head of house and house prefects – head girl appointed after discussion by staff. School Council.

Religion Religious worship encouraged; very occasional compulsory services.

Social Young Enterprise, voluntary service (with all Sevenoaks schools), choir with schools and local choirs, Ernest Reed concerts. Ski trip, French exchange, German exchange, Russian trip, hockey tour to Zimbabwe. Pupils allowed to bring own car/bike to school. Meals self service. School shop sells second-hand uniform. No tobacco/alcohol allowed.

Discipline No corporal punishment. Pupils failing to produce homework once might expect to have to repeat it; those caught smoking cannabis on the premises could expect immediate suspension, almost certain expulsion.

Alumni association run by Mrs M Roffey, c/o the School.

COMMONWEAL LODGE

Commonweal Lodge
Woodcote Lane
Purley
Surrey CR2 3HB
Telephone number 01-660 3179

Enquiries/application to the Headmistress

Co-ed   Pupils 120
Boys   Upper sixth 3
● Girls   Termly fees:
Mixed sixth   Day £790
● Day   GSA
Boarding

WHAT IT'S LIKE

Founded in 1916, it lies on the west side of Purley in an agreeable residential area with four acres of private grounds. The buildings are purpose-designed and have good facilities. The lower junior school is nearby. Its general aim is to educate girls to use their individual abilities – mentally, physically, spiritually. Sound standards and values based on Christian principles are fostered. Assembly and religious education are an integral part of the life. Sport, games and extra-curricular activities are adequate.

SCHOOL PROFILE

Pupils Total over 12, 120. Entry age, 5 and into the sixth. Own prep school provides over 20% of pupils.
Entrance Own entrance exam used. Not oversubscribed. No special skills or religious requirements. Parents not expected to buy text books. No assisted places. 3 scholarships/bursaries.
Parents 15+% in industry or commerce. More than 60% live within 30 miles.
Staff Head Miss J M Brown, in post for 6 years. 17 full time staff, 13 part time. Annual turnover 6–10%. Average age 40.
Academic work GCSE and A-levels. Average size of upper fifth 25; upper sixth 3. *O-levels*: on average, 7 pupils in upper fifth pass 1–4 subjects; 15, 5–7 subjects; 3 pass 8+ subjects. *A-levels*: on average, 3 pupils in upper sixth pass 2 subjects. On average, 1 takes arts and humanities; 2 a mixture of both arts and sciences. *Computing facilities*: 8 BBC micros, 2 Acorns, 2 Pet Commodore. Special provisions made for pupils who are eg dyslexic, or for EFL.
Senior pupils' non-academic activities *Music*: 3 learn a musical instrument, 2 to Grade 6 or above, 2 in school groups, 3 in school choir. *Art*: 3 take as non-examined subject, 15 take GCSE. *Sport*: Tennis, swimming, rounders, netball, lacrosse, badminton, volleyball and gymnastics available. 15 take non-compulsory sport. *Other*: Activities include music, drama and art clubs and choirs.
Careers 1 full time advisor. Average number going on to *general training courses*, 40. Average number of pupils going straight into careers in the armed services, 2; industry, civil service, 2; music/drama, 2.
Uniform School uniform worn except in the sixth.
Houses/prefects Competitive houses. Prefects, head girl, head of house and house prefects – appointed by the Head and the school.
Religion Religious worship is encouraged.
Social No regular events with local schools. Trips to France and Germany, ski parties and Mediterranean cruises. Pupils allowed to bring own car/bike/motorbike to school. Meals self service. No tobacco/alcohol allowed.

Discipline No corporal punishment. Pupils failing to produce homework once might expect a warning; those caught smoking cannabis on the premises could expect suspension – probably expulsion.

Alumni association run by The Old Knots Secretary, Mrs Kate Blair, Rosemount, Grosvenor Road, Godalming, Surrey.

Former pupils Jacqueline du Pré (cellist); Alex Hildred (archaeologist); Angharad Rees (actress); Yvonne Sintes (first woman airline pilot).

COVENTRY

Coventry School
Warwick Road
Coventry
West Midlands CV3 6AQ
Telephone number 0203 73442

- Co-ed   Pupils 1688
  Boys   Upper sixth Yes
  Girls   Termly fees:
  Mixed sixth   Day £630
- Day   GBA; HMC
  Boarding

Head R Cooke (14 years)
Age range 11–18, own prep from age 7; entry by own exam
Bursaries.

CRAIGHOLME

Craigholme School
72 St Andrew's Drive
Glasgow G41 4HS
Telephone number 041 427 0375

Enquiries/application to the Secretary
or Headmistress

Co-ed   Pupils 300
Boys   Upper sixth 50
- Girls   Termly fees:
  Mixed sixth   Day £665
- Day   SHA
  Boarding

WHAT IT'S LIKE

Founded in 1894, it has handsome well-equipped premises in a pleasant residential suburb of Glasgow. The playing fields are on the Pollok estate a few minutes away. The infant and primary departments are combined. Excellent facilities are provided. Religious worship is compulsory. Academic standards are high and results good. About 20–25 pupils proceed to university each year. There is a tremendously strong music dept (300 pupils learn an instrument), and also much strength in drama (a third of the school being engaged in productions each year). Sports and games are also of a high standard and quite a lot of pupils represent the school at county level. A plentiful range of extra-curricular activities. Many enterprising trips and expeditions at home and abroad are organised. The school's record in the Duke of Edinburgh's Award Scheme is outstanding.

SCHOOL PROFILE

Pupils Total over 12, 300. Entry age, 5. Own junior school provides over 90%.

Entrance Own entrance exam used. Oversubscribed in the senior school. No special skills or religious requirements. Parents expected to buy text books. 20 assisted places. 2–4 Packer Bursaries – partial assistance with fees, means tested.

Parents 15+% in industry or commerce; 15+% are doctors, lawyers etc. More than 60% live within 30 miles.

Staff Head Miss I W McNeillie, in post for 13 years. 40 full time staff, 6 part time. Annual turnover 2 or 3. Average age 40.

Academic work O-grade, Highers, CSYS. Average size of fourth 50; fifth 50. *O-grade*: on average, 7 pupils pass 1–4 subjects; 14, 5–7 subjects; 29 pass 8+ subjects. *Highers*: on average, 6 pupils pass 1 subject; 7, 2 subjects; 18, 3–4 subjects and 19 pass 5–6 subjects. On average, 24 pupils take Highers in the broad area of science and engineering; 13 take arts and humanities; 37 a mixture. *Computing facilities*: A large new computing department – BBC micros and Amstrad machines.

Senior pupils' non-academic activities *Music*: 300 learn a musical instrument, Grade 3 to Grade 6 or above; 100 in school orchestra; 3 in Independent Schools Orchestra; 20 in brass ensemble; 2 in Strathclyde Orchestra; 10 in Glasgow Schools Orchestra; 100 in carol singing choir. *Drama and dance*: Approximately 200 participate in school productions and musicals. *Art*: 24 take O-grade; 8 Higher; 2 CSYS. 2 accepted for Art School; 1 for architecture; 3 for design (various); personal sketchbooks are encouraged. Visits arranged to art galleries and current exhibitions. *Sport*: Hockey (9 teams), tennis, athletics, netball, volleyball, badminton, gymnastics, dance/keep-fit/yoga, recreational swimming, tukido and curling (as requested) available. 84 take non-compulsory sport. 5 pupils represent county/country (tennis, hockey, golf, equestrian). *Other*: Some work for national charities and 5 at Oxfam shops. 39 have bronze Duke of Edinburgh's Award, 19 have silver and 15 have gold. 14 take first aid course with St Andrew's Ambulance Association. Other activities include a stamp club, debating society, public speaking, German and French clubs. Work experience programme in summer term for 36.

Careers 1 part time advisor. Careers convention every 2 or 3 years. Work experience programme in summer term for some senior girls. Average number of pupils accepted for *arts and humanities degree courses* at universities, 12; polytechnics or CHE, 10. *science and engineering degree courses* at universities, 10; medical schools, 1; polytechnics or CHE, 2. *BEd*, 3. *other general training courses*, 8. Average number of pupils going straight into careers in banking, 2; secretarial work, 2.

Uniform School uniform worn throughout.

Houses/prefects Competitive houses. Head girl (appointed by staff), head of house and house prefects (elected). School Council.

Religion Compulsory morning assembly three days a week. Separate Jewish assembly once a week.

Social Joint disco for charity with local schools. Frequent organised trips abroad (at least one annually) including ski-ing, France, Germany, Russia and Pompeii. Pupils allowed to bring own car/bike to school. Meals self service. No tobacco/alcohol allowed.

Discipline No corporal punishment. Pupils failing to produce homework once might expect extra homework; those caught smoking cannabis on the premises could expect suspension or expulsion.

Alumni association run by Mrs Clare Giles, 46 Hamilton Avenue, Glasgow G41.

Former pupils Jane Will (nurse) Scotswoman of the Year 1981; Susan Wighton (nurse) Scotswoman of the Year 1987.

CRANBORNE CHASE

Cranborne Chase School
Wardour Castle
Tisbury
Salisbury, Wiltshire SP3 6RH
Telephone number 0747 870464

Enquiries/application to the Head's Secretary

Co-ed
Boys
● Girls
Mixed sixth
● Day
● Boarding

Pupils 140
Upper sixth 20
Termly fees:
Day £895
Boarding £2150
GSA

WHAT IT'S LIKE

Founded in 1946 at Crichel House. In 1960 it moved to its present site of Wardour Castle (near Salisbury), a superb grade 1 listed country house in Palladian style designed for Lord Arundell in the 1760s. It lies in a delightful estate of 50 acres and has excellent modern facilities. It has all the advantages of a small school and enjoys a staff:pupil ratio of 1:8. It has a high reputation for its pastoral care and a very efficient tutor system. Each pupil is helped to achieve her best over as wide an area as possible. A happy, family atmosphere prevails. Academic standards are high and the teaching is good. About 60% of leavers go on to university. The school is especially strong in the arts. Art and music involve a great many people and all are involved in drama. Productions are of a very high standard. Each year the dramatic society performs in France, and in 1987 toured China with a play. There is a good range of sports and games and plentiful extra-curricular activities.

SCHOOL PROFILE

Pupils Total over 12, 140. Currently all board. Entry age, 11, 12, 13 and into the sixth.

Entrance Common entrance and own entrance exam used. Not oversubscribed. No special skills or religious requirements. Parents expected to buy text books for GCSE courses onwards. Scholarships/bursaries – academic, music, drama and art – 50% to 20% fees.

Parents 15+% are doctors, lawyers, etc; 15+% in theatre, media etc; 15+% in the armed services. Up to 10% live within 30 miles; 10+% live overseas.

Staff Head Mrs M Simmons, in post for 5 years. Average age of staff 40.

Academic work GCSE and A-levels. Average size of upper fifth 35; upper sixth 20. *O-levels*: on average, 10% of upper fifth pass 1–4 subjects; 40%, 5–7 subjects; 50% pass 8+ subjects. *A-levels*: on average, 10% of upper sixth pass 1 subject; 40%, 2 subjects; 50% pass 3 subjects. Some take arts and humanities A-levels; some take a mixture of arts and science. Theatre studies are offered to GCSE/A-level. *Computing facilities*: 3 computers in Maths department, 1 in English. Provision for dyslexia.

Senior pupils' non-academic activities *Music*: 75% learn a musical instrument; 25% in school orchestra, 25% in school choir. *Drama and dance*: 100% in school productions. 5% take Grade 6 ESB, RAD etc. 10% accepted for Drama/Dance schools. *Art*: 80% take as non-examined subject; 60% take GCSE; 50% take A-level. 40% accepted for Art School. 20% belong to eg photographic club. *Sport*: Tennis, athletics, gymnastics, swimming, netball and hockey available. 50% take non-compulsory sport. A few represent county at cross-country running. Other activities include a computer club, driving lessons; several lively arts clubs including photography, pottery, screen printing; drama at all levels.

Careers 1 member of staff is i/c careers; all others participate. On average, 60% accepted for universities, 40% for polytechnics or CHE. 1 pupil has gone into journalism. Tradition of pupils going into the broad field of arts.

Uniform School uniform not worn.

Houses/prefects Competitive houses. No head girl. All first year sixth form serve as prefects. School Council.

Religion Compulsory religious worship 4 times a week.

Social Organised local events. Theatre exchange with French school. Trip organised to China. Pupils allowed to bring own bike to school. Meals formal. School shop.

Discipline No corporal punishment. The few rules are applied strictly. Certain offences result in immediate expulsion.

Boarding All sixth formers have own study bedroom, fifth form share; others in dormitories of 6+. Central dining room. Sixth form can provide and cook own food. 2 overnight exeats each term, 4 for sixth form. Visits to local town allowed for everyone. Visits to Salisbury for seniors.

Alumni association run by Miss Ginny Russell, Grange Cottage, East Hanney, Wantage, Oxfordshire OX12 0HQ.

CRANBROOK COLLEGE

Cranbrook College	Co-ed	Pupils 104
34 Mansfield Road	● Boys	Upper sixth 4
Ilford	Girls	Termly fees:
Essex IG1 3BD	Mixed sixth	Day £530
Telephone number 01-554 1757	● Day	ISAI
	Boarding	
Enquiries/application to the Headmaster		

WHAT IT'S LIKE

Founded in 1896, it is the only school of its type in Ilford and is sited in a quiet residential quarter near the station. By current standards fees are low.

SCHOOL PROFILE

Pupils Total over 12, 104. Main entry age, 5. Own junior department provides majority of pupils.

Entrance Own entrance exam used. No special skills or religious requirements. Parents not expected to buy text books.

Parents 60+% live within 30 miles.

Staff Head G T Reading, in post for 11 years. 13 full time staff, 7 part time.

Academic work GCSE and A-levels. Average size of upper fifth 19; upper sixth 4. *O-levels*: on average, 6 pupils in upper fifth pass 1–4 subjects; 6, 5–7 subjects; 6 pass 8+ subjects. *A-levels*: on average, 1 pupil in upper sixth passes 1 subject; 1, 2 subjects; 1, 3 subjects – all in arts and humanities. *Computing facilities*: 3 computers.

Senior pupils' non-academic activities *Sport*: Cricket, football, athletics, swimming, cross-country, squash, badminton, tennis, table tennis, basketball available. Other activities include a computer club.

Uniform School uniform worn throughout.

Houses/prefects Competitive houses. Prefects, head boy – appointed by Head.

CRANBROOK

Cranbrook School
Waterloo Road
Cranbrook
Kent TN17 3JD
Telephone number 0580 712163

- Co-ed   Pupils 730
   Boys   Upper sixth Yes
   Girls   Termly fees:
   Mixed sixth   Day Free
- Day   Boarding £920
- Boarding   Woodard;
    SHMIS

Head P A Close, first year of appointment
Age range 13–18; entry by common entrance

CRANLEIGH

Cranleigh School
Cranleigh
Surrey GU6 8QQ
Telephone number 0483 273997

   Co-ed   Pupils 550
- Boys   Upper sixth Yes
   Girls   Termly fees:
- Mixed sixth   Day £1640
- Day   Boarding £2350
- Boarding   HMC; GBA

WHAT IT'S LIKE

Founded in 1865 as a boys' boarding school it became partly co-educational in 1971 with the admission of girls to the sixth form. It has a splendid site in 200 acres of Surrey farmland near the small town of Cranleigh. The buildings are very pleasant and well appointed. During the last 15 years there has been considerable expansion and the school is now extremely well equipped by any standards. The prep school is on the main campus. The chapel was built as the central point of the school and the policy is to maintain Christian values as a way of life. There is quite a lot of emphasis on worship and instruction in the Anglican tradition. It is an extremely well run, energetic and purposeful school which displays considerable enterprise in many fields. A large staff allows a staff:pupil ratio of about 1:9. Academic standards are high and results consistently good. A large number of pupils go on to university each year. There are particularly good facilities for science, computer studies, electronics and technology. For many years Cranleigh has maintained a high reputation for music. There are as many as 25 visiting music teachers. There are several choirs and several orchestras and at least a quarter of the school learns an instrument. It is no less strong in drama. There are a lot of productions each year, including house plays and regular plays in French and German. Experimental entertainment is presented in the open-air theatre. First-rate facilities are available for art, pottery and printing. The school also has a long-standing reputation for its achievements in games and sports, of which there is a big range available including sailing and golf (there is a 9-hole course on the estate). Numerous clubs and societies cater for most needs. A large and active voluntary CCF provides adventure training and trips abroad to military units. There is also a fire brigade section. Field trips and expeditions overseas are frequent and there are regular scientific expeditions to Iceland. Travel grants are available to allow pupils to carry out their own projects. The school has a substantial commitment to local community services; especially through the physically handicapped/able bodied course, a residential event at the school. There has been considerable success in the Duke of Edinburgh's Award Scheme.

SCHOOL PROFILE

Head Mr Anthony Hart (4 years)
Age range 13–18; own prep; entry by common entrance
Assisted places, music and academic scholarships available.

CROFT HOUSE

Croft House School	Co-ed	Pupils 216
Shillingstone	Boys	Upper sixth 15
Blandford	● Girls	Termly fees:
Dorset DT11 0QS	Mixed sixth	Day £1320
Telephone number 0258 860295	● Day	Boarding £1900
	● Boarding	GSA
Enquiries/application to the Headmistress		

WHAT IT'S LIKE

Started in 1941 by Colonel and Mrs Torkington in their own house (in the village of Shillingstone) to provide education for their daughter and the daughters of friends. Thus began the tradition of a small family school which has been preserved. It has a very pleasant environment and there have been considerable extensions. It is C of E by foundation but other persuasions are welcomed. A sound education is provided. The music and drama departments are very active and there is a good range of sports, games and other activities.

SCHOOL PROFILE

Pupils Total, 216. Day 23; Boarding 193. Entry age, 11, 12, 13 and into the sixth. Fewer than 5% are children of former pupils.

Entrance Own entrance exam used. Early application advised. C of E foundation but other persuasions welcomed. Parents expected to buy sixth form text books. 5 major scholarships and some bursaries (riding, academic, art, music, sixth form), up to 40% of fees. Oversubscribed.

Parents 15+% in the armed services. 10+% live within 30 miles; 10+% live overseas.

Staff Head Mrs E A Rawlinson, in post for 3 years. 26 full time staff, 8 part time. Annual turnover 6%. Average age 30–35.

Academic work GCSE and A-levels. Average size of fifth 40+; upper sixth 15. *O-levels*: on average, 13 pupils in upper fifth pass 1–4 subjects; 20, 5–7 subjects; 5 pass 8+ subjects. *A-levels*: on average, 2 pupils in upper sixth pass 1 subject; 4, 2 subjects; 5 pass 3 subjects. On average, 30% take science/engineering A-levels; 45% take arts and humanities; 45% a mixture. Drama offered to GCSE/A-level. *Computing facilities*: Computer room (6 units). *Special provisions*: Limited individual tuition.

Senior pupils' non-academic activities *Music*: Music is important; many girls play or sing. *Drama and dance*: Drama GCSE and A-level popular. Many drama competitions and major school productions. *Art*: Many take as non-examined subject. Pottery, screen-printing, batik etc also available. A few accepted for Art School. *Sport*: Hockey, netball, tennis, swimming, athletics, badminton, rounders available. Everyone takes sport. *Other*: Pupils take part in local community schemes, Duke of Edinburgh's bronze and silver Awards. Other activities include a computer club, riding, judo, dance (modern), ballet, bellringing (church).

Careers 1 full time advisor. Average number of pupils accepted for *arts and humanities degree courses* at universities, 2; polytechnics or CHE, 2. *science and engineering degree courses* at universities, 2. *BEd*, 3. *other general training courses*, 4. Average number of pupils going straight into careers in industry, 2.

Uniform School uniform worn except in the sixth.

Houses/prefects Competitive houses. Prefects, head girl, head of house and house prefects – appointed by staff discussion.

Religion Anglican religious worship encouraged.

Social Choral society; Christian Union; Gilbert & Sullivan; dances, etc with local schools. Organised trips abroad. Pupils allowed to bring own bike to school. Meals semi-formal. School tuck shop and stationery shop. No tobacco/alcohol allowed.

Discipline No corporal punishment.

Boarding Most sixth form have own study bedroom, others share with one other; 20% are in dormitories of 6+. Houses, 100–20 pupils. Resident qualified medical staff. Central dining room. 3 exeats each term (4 in sixth form). Visits to the local town rarely allowed except for seniors.

CROHAM HURST

Croham Hurst School
79 Croham Road
Croydon
Surrey CR2 7YN
Telephone number 01-680 3064

Enquiries to the Headmistress's Secretary
Application to the Head

Co-ed
Boys
• Girls
Mixed sixth
• Day
Boarding

Pupils 598
(whole school)
Upper sixth 35
Termly fees:
Day £777
GSA

WHAT IT'S LIKE

Founded in 1897, it is single-site and semi-rural and stands on a slope facing Croham Hurst, on the verge of woodlands, parkland and the green belt. Altogether it is a pleasant environment with gardens and playing fields. The buildings are comfortable and well appointed and there are plentiful modern facilities. The junior school is nearby. Basically a Christian foundation, it provides a sound academic training (about 15 university entrants per year) and is particularly strong in music.

SCHOOL PROFILE

Pupils Total 598. Entry age, 4, 7, 11 and into the sixth. Own junior department provides over 20%. 20–30% are children of former pupils.

Entrance Own entrance exam used. No special skills or religious requirements. Parents not expected to buy text books. 16 scholarships/bursaries, 100–25% fees.

Parents 60+% live within 30 miles.

Staff Head Miss J M Shelmerdine, in post for 2 years. 35 full time staff, 15 part time. Annual turnover less than 10%. Average age 35.

Academic work GCSE and A-levels. Average size of upper fifth 55; upper sixth 35. *O-levels*: on average, 3–6 pupils in upper fifth pass 1–4 subjects; 20–25, 5–7 subjects; 20–25 pass 8+ subjects. *A-levels*: on average, 1–3 pupils in upper sixth pass 1 subject; 3–6, 2 subjects; 15–20, 3 subjects and 3–5 pass 4 subjects. On average, 10–15 take science/engineering A-levels; 10–15 take arts and humanities; 5–6 a mixture. *Computing facilities*: 3 computers in junior school. Computer room with 8 computers in senior school. Specialist tuition available for dyslexia and EFL.

Senior pupils' non-academic activities *Music*: 200 learn a musical instrument, 12–15 in school orchestras, wind bands, etc, 50–60 in school choir. *Art*: 10–20 take GCSE; 6 A-level; 6 A-level textiles. 3 accepted for Art School. *Sport*: Lacrosse, netball, tennis, rounders, athletics, basketball available. *Other*: Activities include a computer club, drama.

Careers 1 full time careers advisor. Average number of pupils accepted for *arts and humanities degree courses* at Oxbridge, 1–2; other universities, 6–8; polytechnics or CHE, 3–5. *science and engineering degree courses* at Oxbridge, 1–2; other universities, 6–8; medical schools, 1–3; polytechnics or CHE, 3–5. BEd, 5. *other general training courses*, 3–5. Average number of pupils going straight into careers in the church, 1–2; civil service, 1–2; music/drama, 1–2.

Uniform School uniform worn except in the sixth.

Houses/prefects Competitive houses. No prefects. Head girl and head of house – elected by the school. School Council.
Religion Christian assembly compulsory.
Social Debates. Joint theatre productions with Whitgift Boys' School. Exchange trips to Germany and France; ski trips. Pupils allowed to bring own car/bike/motorbike to school. Meals self service.
Discipline No corporal punishment. Pupils failing to produce homework once would have no punishment.
Alumni association run by Mrs M Carter Pegg, Whyteacre, 16 Manor Way, South Croydon, Surrey.

CROOKHAM COURT

Crookham Court School	Co-ed	Pupils 98
Newbury	● Boys	Upper sixth –
Berkshire RG15 8DQ	Girls	not at present
Telephone number 0635 63090	Mixed sixth	Termly fees:
	● Day	Day £745
Enquiries/application to the Headmaster	● Boarding	Boarding £1470

WHAT IT'S LIKE

Founded in 1961 in a Victorian mansion set in 18 acres 5 miles from Newbury. Teaching is in small groups (6–19) up to GCSE. Some A-levels are offered for those staying on; first sixth form started in 1988. The school specialises in providing for boys of average ability or brighter children lacking the confidence to cope with a highly competitive school. It has provision for dealing with specific learning problems, remedial help is given with English, maths and EFL. Many pupils are from overseas.

SCHOOL PROFILE

Pupils Total over 11, 98. Day 12; Boarding 86. Entry age, 11–13.
Entrance Not oversubscribed. No special skills or religious requirements. Parents expected to buy senior text books. Service bursaries available. ✎
Parents 30+% in the armed services; 15+% in industry or commerce. 20+% live within 30 miles; 10+% live overseas.
Staff Principal S P Cadman, in post for 15 years. Head M L Gold. 9 full time staff, 8 part time. Annual turnover 10–15%. Average age 42.
Academic work GCSE. A-levels from 1988. Average size of upper fifth 25. *O-levels*: on average, 12 pupils in upper fifth pass 1–8 subjects; 3 pass 5–7 subjects. Theatre studies offered to GCSE. *Computing facilities* are limited. Computer studies GCSE taken by arrangement with Newbury College. *Special provisions*: strong EFL department, dyslexia specialist.
Senior pupils' non-academic activities *Music*: 12 learn a musical instrument; 40 in school choir. *Drama and dance*: 40 in school productions. *Art*: 8 take GCSE; occasionally other exams taken. *Sport*: Soccer, hockey, rugby, cricket, tennis, basketball, volleyball, croquet, archery, table tennis, snooker, judo, karate, swimming, squash, badminton, canoeing available. Most pupils take non-compulsory sport. Several take exams in swimming. Occa-

sional pupil represents county at sport. *Other*: Pupils occasionally take part in local community schemes. Other activities include a computer club, fishing, gardening, chess, woodwork, pottery/art; large and flourishing Army Cadet Force who enjoy a wide range of outdoor pursuits.

Careers 2 part time advisors. Most pupils continue education after leaving either at the end of GCSE or after an extra (lower sixth) year. Many pupils go into the armed services.

Uniform School uniform worn, modified in the sixth.

Houses/prefects Competitive houses. Prefects, head boy, head of house and house prefects – appointed by the Head. School Council.

Religion 2 compulsory Chapels (inter-denominational) each week. 2 additional chapels for Christians (majority).

Social Occasional debates with local schools. Organised exchange visits for French pupils, skiing trips annually. Pupils allowed to bring own bike to school. Meals self service. School shop. No tobacco/alcohol allowed.

Discipline Very limited corporal punishment (Head only). Pupils failing to produce homework once might expect to have to do it; those caught smoking cannabis on the premises could expect suspension certainly, if not expulsion.

Boarding Head boy has own study bedroom, seniors share (3 or 4); 60% are in dormitories of 6+, divided by age. Resident trained, but unqualified nurse. Central dining room. Pupils can provide and cook own food. Exeats depending on age and circumstances. Visits to local town allowed.

Alumni association run by Russel Gardner, c/o the School.

CROYDON HIGH

Croydon High School for Girls	Co-ed	Pupils 643
Old Farleigh Road	Boys	Upper sixth 92
Selsdon	• Girls	Termly fees:
South Croydon	Mixed sixth	Day £789
Surrey CR2 8YB	• Day	GPDST
Telephone number 01-657 0123	Boarding	

Enquiries/application to the Headmistress

WHAT IT'S LIKE

Founded in 1874, it moved to its present site on the outskirts of Croydon in 1966. This comprises a purpose-built and extremely well-equipped and comfortable establishment in beautiful landscaped grounds. The teaching is well known to be very good and standards are high (60+ university entrants per year). It is particularly strong in music and in games (especially netball and hockey). Big commitment to local community schemes and the Duke of Edinburgh's Award Scheme.

SCHOOL PROFILE

Pupils Total over 12, 643. Entry age, 5, 7, 9, 11 and into the sixth. 10% are children of former pupils. Own junior department provides over 60%.

Entrance Own entrance exam used. Oversubscribed. Good academic ability required; no religious requirements. Parents not expected to buy text books. 24 assisted places pa. 4 scholarships pa (11+ and sixth form), 33–50% fees. **Parents** 100% live within 30 miles.

Staff Head Miss A M Mark, in post for 8 years. 58 full time staff, 24 part time. Annual turnover up to 10%.

Academic work GCSE and A-levels. Average size of upper fifth 108; upper sixth 92. *O-levels*: on average, 3 pupils in upper fifth pass 1–4 subjects; 23, 5–7 subjects; 82 pass 8+ subjects. *A-levels*: on average, 4 pupils in upper sixth pass 1 subject; 12, 2 subjects; 62, 3 subjects and 14 pass 4 subjects. On average, 28 take science/engineering A-levels; 30 take arts and humanities; 34 a mixture. *Computing facilities*: range of RML and BBC computers.

Senior pupils' non-academic activities (Figures refer to pupils of 15+.) *Music*: 100 learn a musical instrument, 60 to Grade 6 or above. 5 accepted for Music School, 6 for university. 50 in school orchestra, 80 in school choir, 20 in wind band; 20 in Croydon Youth Philharmonic Orchestra, 20 in Croydon Wind Bands. *Drama and dance*: 25–30 in school productions. 12 take drama GCSE; 30 take Associated Board Exams. 2 accepted for Drama/Dance Schools; 3–4 take drama as a university subject; 3 entered competitions. *Art*: 38 take GCSE art; 9 A-level, 10 Liberal Study (sixth form). 2 accepted for Art School. 6 belong to photographic club, 34 of fourth year take art option. *Sport*: Hockey, netball, tennis, swimming, synchro-swimming, cricket, athletics, cross-country, badminton, squash, table tennis, volleyball, gymnastics, sports acrobatics available. 188 take non-compulsory sport. 50 take exams, eg gymnastics, swimming. 17 national netball and hockey players in last 25 years. Many play at club and county level and for university in many sports. *Other*: 85+ take part in local community schemes. 40 have bronze Duke of Edinburgh's Award, 25 have silver and 5 gold. All participate in School's annual Guild of Charity fund-raising effort. Other activities include a computer club, Young Enterprise, a wide range of music and drama, sporting clubs and other subject based clubs, chess and bridge clubs.

Careers 2 part time advisors. Average number of pupils accepted for *arts and humanities degree courses* at Oxbridge, 8; other universities, 22; polytechnics or CHE, 8. *science and engineering degree courses* at Oxbridge, 5; other universities, 24; medical schools, 3; polytechnics or CHE, 5. BEd, 5. *other general training courses*, 8. Average number of pupils going straight into careers in banking, insurance, etc, 4.

Uniform School uniform worn except in the sixth.

Houses/prefects No competitive houses. Prefects and 2 head girls – elected by school. School Council.

Religion Compulsory regular school assemblies.

Social Joint sixth form society with Trinity Boys' School. Exchange trips, educational courses, study trips, and ski trips abroad. Meals self service. School tuck shop and second-hand uniform shop. No tobacco/alcohol allowed.

Discipline No corporal punishment. Pupils failing to produce homework might expect letter home at 3rd instance; those caught smoking cannabis on the premises could expect automatic suspension.

Alumni association run by Mrs M Knight, c/o the School.

Former pupils Baroness Seear; Marion Roe; Jill Tweedie; Jane Drew; Wendy Savage; Jacqueline du Pré.

CULFORD

Culford School
Bury St Edmunds
Suffolk IP28 6TX
Telephone number 028 484 615

Enquiries/application to the Headmaster

- Co-ed
- Boys
- Girls
- Mixed sixth
- Day
- Boarding

Pupils 501
Upper sixth 75
Termly fees:
Day £1160
Boarding £1785
HMC

WHAT IT'S LIKE

Founded in 1881, it has a splendid site 4 miles north of Bury St Edmunds. The main building is Culford Hall, a fine and palatial 18th-century mansion (formerly the seat of Earl Cadogan) in 400 acres of beautiful gardens and parkland. Numerous modern extensions, including several new and comfortable boarding houses. It is a Methodist foundation but all denominations are welcome. The school has a deep-rooted respect for tradition in teaching methods, manners and behaviour and sees education as something that goes on outside as well as in the classroom. It seeks to establish a partnership with parents and expects pupils to work hard and make the most of their abilities whether they are outstanding academically or not. Strong emphasis on sense of community. The music and drama departments are very vigorous and there are many outdoor pursuits (including angling and clay-pigeon shooting). There are close social service ties with Bury Youth Aid. The junior school is also in the park.

SCHOOL PROFILE

Pupils Total over 12, 501. Day 235 (boys 124, girls 111); Boarding 266 (boys 149, girls 117). Entry age, 8, 11, 13 and into the sixth. Own prep school provides over 20%. 15% are children of former pupils.

Entrance Common entrance and own entrance exam used. Oversubscribed. No special skills or religious requirements. Parents not expected to buy text books. 50 assisted places. 4 scholarships/bursaries up to 75% fees.

Parents 15+% in industry or commerce; 15+% in the armed services. 30+% live within 30 miles; 10+% live overseas.

Staff Head D Robson, in post for 16 years. 67 full time staff, 6 part time. Annual turnover 5%. Average age 41.

Academic work GCSE and A-levels. Average size of upper fifth 100; upper sixth 75. *Computing facilities*: Econet terminal in each classroom of main teaching block. Computer room with 12 terminals. Computers in other departments. Special provisions for dyslexia, EFL etc.

Senior pupils' non-academic activities Music, drama, art and sport.

Careers 3 part time advisors. Average number of pupils accepted for *arts and humanities degree courses* at Oxbridge, 4; other universities, 12; polytechnics or CHE, 3. *science and engineering degree courses* at medical schools, 3; polytechnics or CHE, 1. *other general training courses*, 5. Average number of pupils going straight into careers in the armed services, 2; the City, 1.

Uniform School uniform worn throughout.

Houses/prefects Competitive houses. Prefects, head boy and girl, head of house and house prefects – nominated by pupils, appointed by the Head.

Religion Religious worship compulsory.

Social Some organised local events and trips abroad. Pupils allowed to bring own car/bike/motorbike to school. Meals self service. School shop. No tobacco/alcohol allowed.

Discipline No corporal punishment.

Boarding Most share study bedrooms; none are in dormitories of 6+. Houses of varying size, divided by age group, single sex. Resident qualified medical staff. Central dining room. Pupils can provide and cook own food. 2 exeats each term. Visits to the local town allowed.

Alumni association run by Roland Beaney, Orchard House, Larters Lane, Middle Wood Green, Stowmarket, Suffolk.

Former pupils Sir David Plastow (Chief Executive, Vickers plc); Admiral Sir Derek Reffell; John Motson (sports commentator).

DAME ALICE HARPUR

The Dame Alice Harpur School	Co-ed	Pupils 830
Cardington Road	Boys	Upper sixth Yes
Bedford MK42 0BX	● Girls	Termly fees:
Telephone number 0234 40871	Mixed sixth	Day £641
	● Day	GSA
	Boarding	

Head Miss S M Morse (18 years)
Age range 11–18, own prep from age 7; entry by own exam
Bursaries and assisted places.

DAME ALLAN'S (BOYS)

Dame Allan's Boys' School	Co-ed	Pupils 420
Fowberry Crescent	● Boys	Upper sixth 52
Fenham	Girls	Termly fees:
Newcastle upon Tyne NE4 9YJ	Mixed sixth	Day £733
Telephone number 091 2750 608	● Day	HMC
Enquiries/application to the Headmaster	Boarding	

WHAT IT'S LIKE

Founded in 1705, established at Fenham in 1926 and occupied new buildings on an urban site (with playing fields attached) in 1935. It is an Anglican foundation with a fair amount of emphasis on worship and very close links with the cathedral church of St Nicholas. It aims to provide a sound general education and results are good (30+ university entrants per year). Music is an important part of the school life. There are plentiful societies and a decent range of games, sports and activities. Quite a lot of involvement in local community schemes, charities (fund-raising) and in the Duke of Edinburgh's Award Scheme.

SCHOOL PROFILE

Pupils Total over 12, 420. Entry age, 10/11 and into the sixth. Fair proportion are children of former pupils (many old pupils leave the area).

Entrance Own entrance exam used. Oversubscribed. Academic ability and broad interests looked for; no exclusive religious requirements. Parents not expected to buy text books. 23 assisted places pa. 8 scholarships pa of half fees; bursaries according to need.

Parents 15+% in industry or commerce. 60+% live within 30 miles.

Staff Principal T A Willcocks, since September 1988. 28 full time staff, 2 part time. Annual turnover 3–7%. Average age 41.

Academic work GCSE, AS-levels and A-levels. Average size of upper fifth 64; upper sixth 52. *O-levels*: on average, 9 pupils in upper fifth pass 1–4 subjects; 15, 5–7 subjects; 40 pass 8+ subjects. *A-levels*: on average, 2 pupils in upper sixth pass 1 subject; 3, 2 subjects; 8, 3 subjects and 27 pass 4 subjects. On average, 18 take science/engineering A-levels; 22 take arts and humanities; 14 a mixture. *Computing facilities*: 5 departmental computers (BBC with colour monitors) for teaching purposes (simulation, statistics, data processing, etc); computer room with 10 computers/monitors/printers for computer studies/information technology (with Teletext, Modem and Control Applications).

Senior pupils' non-academic activities *Music*: 9 learn a musical instrument, 5 to Grade 6 or above. 1 accepted for music degree (university), 2 choral scholarships, 1 university instrumental award. 5 in school orchestra, 20 in school choir both shared with Dame Allan's Girls'; 4 in school pop group, 2 in brass ensemble, 3 in string quartet with younger pupils; 1 in National Children's Youth Orchestra; 2 in Northern Junior Philharmonic; 1 on chamber music course in USA. *Drama*: 25 in school productions. *Art*: 10 take art as non-examined subject, 20 take GCSE; 7 A-level; 2 AS-level. 2 accepted for Art School; 2 for architecture. 25 belong to photographic club. *Sport*: Cricket, tennis, golf, swimming, rugby, athletics, cross-country, orienteering, table tennis, badminton available. 140 take non-compulsory sport. 18 represent county/country (cricket, rugby, athletics/running, tennis). *Other*: 20 take part in local community schemes. 18 have silver Duke of Edinburgh's Award and 21 have gold. 2 enter voluntary schemes after leaving school. Other activities include a computer club, chess, philately, Christian Fellowship, debating, science society (BAYS), mountain walking, skiing, Action Aid (sponsoring schools in the Gambia).

Careers 11 part time advisors. Membership of ISCO. Average number of pupils accepted for *arts and humanities degree courses* at Oxbrige, 2–3; other universities, 12; polytechnics or CHE, 7. *science and engineering degree courses* at Oxbridge, 2–3; other universities, 11; medical schools, 3; polytechnics or CHE, 4. *BEd*, 1. *other general training courses*, 4. Average number of pupils going straight into careers in the armed services, 1; banking, 2; retail management, 1. Traditional school careers are engineering, medicine, law, accountancy.

Uniform School uniform worn throughout.

Houses/prefects Competitive houses. Prefects, head boy – appointed by the Head in consultation with staff and sixth form. School Council.

Religion Morning assembly compulsory unless parents request otherwise.

Social Joint events with neighbouring Girls' School on same foundation – choir and orchestra, drama productions. Christian Fellowship. Sponsored walks. Exchanges and organised trips to France and Germany. Pupils allowed to bring own car/bike/motorbike to school. Meals self service. No tobacco/alcohol allowed.

Discipline Corporal punishment not needed; no discipline problem. Pupils failing to produce homework once might expect to produce it in spare time; suspension/expulsion for serious offences (rarely used).

Alumni association run by W F Armstrong, Hon Sec Dame Allan's Old Boys' Assoc, c/o the School.

Former pupils Ian La Frenais (TV); Sir David Lumsden (Royal Academy of Music); Sir Michael Scott (Royal Commonwealth Society); Prof A E Bell (Kew Gardens); Dr R Laws (British Antarctic Survey); Graham Rose (Journalism/Gardening); Fenwick Allison and Colin White (England Rugby XV); Captain Ridley (Commodore Cunard Line).

DAME ALLAN'S (GIRLS)

Dame Allan's Girls' School	Co-ed	Pupils 440
Fowberry Crescent	Boys	Upper sixth Yes
Fenham	• Girls	Termly fees:
Newcastle upon Tyne NE4 9YJ	Mixed sixth	Day £696
Telephone number 091 275 0708	• Day	GSA
	Boarding	

Head T A Willcocks (first year in post)
Age range 10–19; entry by own exam
8 scholarships and 20 assisted places.
Oversubscribed.

DANIEL STEWART'S

Daniel Stewart's and Melville College	Co-ed	Pupils 788
Queensferry Road	• Boys	Upper sixth Yes
Edinburgh EH4 3EZ	Girls	Termly fees:
Telephone number 031 332 7925	Mixed sixth	Day £772
	• Day	Boarding £1492
	• Boarding	HMC

Head R M Morgan (11 years)
Age range 12–18, own prep from age 3; entry by own exam
7 scholarships and bursaries also assisted places. Twinning with Mary Erskine School, shared prep.

DAUNTSEY'S

Dauntsey's School
West Lavington
Devizes
Wiltshire SN10 4HE
Telephone number 038 081 2446

Enquiries/application to the Headmaster

- Co-ed
- Boys
- Girls
- Mixed sixth
- Day
- Boarding

Pupils 580
Upper sixth 95
Termly fees:
Day £1260
Boarding £2084
HMC

WHAT IT'S LIKE

Founded in 1542, it lies on 100 acres of fine estate in West Lavington, a pleasant village in the Vale of Pewsey, five miles south of Devizes. The junior school is in an attractive manor house nearby, with its own estate. It is a Christian foundation, but ecumenical in spirit and practice, and aims to provide a sound education avoiding undue specialisation. Standards of teaching are high and academic results are impressive (55 or more university candidates per year). Very strong tradition in music; pretty strong in drama and art. It enjoys a good reputation for sport and games and there are many activities (including outdoor pursuits).

SCHOOL PROFILE

Pupils Total over 11, 580. Day 340 (boys 190, girls 150); Boarding 240 (boys 130, girls 110). Entry age, 10–11, 13 and into the sixth. 15% are children of former pupils.

Entrance Common entrance and own entrance exam used. Oversubscribed. No special skills or religious requirements. Parents not expected to buy text books. 55 assisted places. Flexible number of scholarships/bursaries, £1260–£150 per term.

Parents 15+% in industry or commerce; 15+% in the armed services; 15+% are doctors, lawyers, etc. 50+% live within 30 miles; up to 10% live overseas.

Staff Head C R Evans, in post for 3 years. 60 full time staff, 18 part time. Annual turnover 5%. Average age 38.

Academic work GCSE and A-levels. Average size of upper fifth 90; upper sixth 95. *O-levels*: on average, 35 pupils in upper fifth pass 1–4 subjects; 15, 5–7 subjects; 40 pass 8+ subjects. *A-levels*: on average, 5 pupils in upper sixth pass 1 subject; 10, 2 subjects; 45, 3 subjects and 35 pass 4 subjects. On average, 40 take science/engineering A-levels; 32 take arts and humanities; 23 a mixture. *Computing facilities*: 30 units, BBC computers/Archimedes/Apple Macintosh. Special provisions for dyslexia, mild visual handicaps, EFL etc.

Senior pupils' non-academic activities *Music*: 250 learn a musical instrument, 73 to Grade 6 or above. 3 accepted for Music School. A few play in pop groups and many play in college/amateur orchestras or sing in choirs after leaving; 84 in school orchestra, 130 in school choir, 6 in school pop group, 20 in brass groups, 20 in wind group; 5 in Wiltshire Youth Concert Orchestra. *Drama and dance*: 84 in school productions. 1 accepted for Drama/Dance School. *Art*: 56 take GCSE; 22 A-level. 4 accepted for Art School; 4 for architecture. 15 belong to photographic club; 20 to art club and 6 D of E pottery. *Sport*: Rugby, cricket, hockey, tennis, athletics, swimming, netball, badminton, cross-country, golf, gymnastics, taekwendo, sailing, canoeing

216

available. 100 take non-compulsory sport. 10 take exams, eg gymnastics, swimming. 30 represent county/country (rugby, hockey, netball, athletics, tennis, swimming). *Other*: 10 take part in local community schemes. 6 have bronze Duke of Edinburgh's Award, 6 have silver and 2 gold. 4 enter voluntary schemes after leaving school. Other activities include a computer club, Moonrakers (outward bound organisation), sailing club with 56' gaff cutter for ocean cruising, adventure club (mountaineering, canoeing, expeditions, etc).

Careers 1 full time and 5 part time advisors. Average number of pupils accepted for *arts and humanities degree courses* at Oxbridge, 4; other universities, 17; polytechnics or CHE, 9. *science and engineering degree courses* at Oxbridge, 6; other universities, 25; medical schools, 4; polytechnics or CHE, 5. *BEd*, 3. *other general training courses*, 7. Average number of pupils going straight into careers in the armed services, 4; industry, 2; the City, 2; civil service, 1; other, 5.

Uniform School uniform worn except in the sixth.

Houses/prefects Competitive houses. Prefects, head boy and girl, head of house and house prefects – appointed by the Head and house staff.

Religion Christian non-denominational assembly compulsory.

Social Regular visits abroad, ski trips, climbing/adventure club expeditions, ocean sailing, French and German exchange. Day pupils allowed to bring own car/bike/motorbike to school. Meals self service. School shop. No tobacco allowed; alcohol only in sixth form club.

Discipline No corporal punishment. Pupils failing to produce homework once might expect to have to do it; those caught smoking cannabis on the premises could expect expulsion.

Boarding 30% have own study bedroom, 70% share with one other. 3 junior, 6 senior houses, of approximately 64, single sex. Resident qualified sister. Central dining room. Pupils can provide and cook own food. Exeats on request. Visits to local town allowed.

Alumni association run by H J Hodges, c/o the School.

Former pupils Desmond Morris; Rev Awdry (Thomas the Tank Engine); Prof Barnes Wallis.

DEAN CLOSE

Dean Close School	● Co-ed	Pupils 420
Cheltenham	Boys	Upper sixth Yes
Gloucestershire	Girls	Termly fees:
GL51 6HE	Mixed sixth	Day £1400
Telephone number 0242 522640	● Day	Boarding £2200
	● Boarding	HMC

WHAT IT'S LIKE

Founded in 1866 and one of the earliest fully co-educational independent schools, it has an agreeable site on the south-west edge of Cheltenham. The main building is a handsome example of late Victorian architecture and the modern additions fit in well. Boarding accommodation is comfortable and teaching facilities are good. There are 9 houses which are separate units of accommodation in most respects. Teaching and chapel services are in accordance with the Church of England and the school's evangelical tradition is maintained. Attendance is compulsory at normal chapel services. A sound general education is provided by a large staff. A third of the school are members of the sixth form. Most of them go on to further education and a place at university is the aim of most sixth formers. There is a strong tradition of choral and instrumental music. The choir makes regular visits to sing in cathedrals and churches and gives other public performances. Drama is also strong and much use is made of the open-air theatre, built with the boys' assistance. A large variety of sports and games is available and the facilities for these are first-rate. Standards of performance are high. More than 90 clubs and societies cater for virtually every conceivable extra-curricular activity. There are also a scout group and a big CCF. The school has a considerable commitment to the Duke of Edinburgh's Award Scheme and the sixth formers run a large and active social services unit. The cultural amenities of Cheltenham are frequently made use of.

SCHOOL PROFILE

Head C J Bacon (9 years)
Age range 12–18; entry by common entrance
Own junior school. 8% of pupils are from overseas. Scholarships, bursaries and music awards.

DENSTONE

Denstone College
Uttoxeter
Staffordshire ST14 5HN
Telephone number 0889 590484

Enquiries to the Headmaster's Secretary
Application to the Headmaster

- Co-ed
  Boys
  Girls
  Mixed sixth
- Day
- Boarding

Pupils 364
Upper sixth 60
Termly feees:
Day £1540
Boarding £2118
HMC; Woodard

WHAT IT'S LIKE

Founded in 1868, a Woodard school, it stands five miles north of Uttoxeter, in open hilly countryside on 70 acres of very pleasant grounds. The main building is Victorian. Numerous modern extensions provide excellent up-to-date facilities of all kinds. The standard of teaching is high and the results are good. For a comparatively small school it sends a goodly number of pupils to university (some 20 per year). It is particularly strong in music and drama and has a very impressive range of clubs and societies. Vigorous participation in the Duke of Edinburgh's Award Scheme. The declared aim is to encourage pupils to develop their individual talents – to the extent of awarding scholarships to any outstanding talent which contributes to the life of the school. Its pupils speak enthusiastically of it and parents comment on the relaxed courteous relationships between pupils and staff. A friendly hard-working school where high standards of manners are maintained without any rigid formality or oppression.

SCHOOL PROFILE

Pupils Total 364. Day 106 (boys 65, girls 41); Boarding 258 (boys 173, girls 85). Entry age, 13 and into the sixth. Own prep school (Smallwood Manor) provides 20+%. 5–10% are children of former pupils.

Entrance Common entrance and own entrance exam used. Oversubscribed for girls' boarding places. Special skills required for scholarships only. No religious requirements but pupils expected to attend C of E services. Parents expected to buy sixth form text books; buy-back scheme operates. 100 assisted places. 78 scholarships (academic, instrumental, choral, sporting, art and any other useful talent, eg drama) and bursaries (for children of clergy, servicemen) – up to ⅔ fees.

Parents 15+% in industry or commerce; 15+% in farming. 30+% live within 30 miles; up to 10% live overseas.

Staff Head R M Ridley, in post for 2 years. 39 full time staff, 4 part time. Annual turnover 8%. Average age 42.

Academic work GCSE and A-levels. Average size of upper fifth 80; upper sixth 60. *O-levels*: on average, 30 pupils in upper fifth pass 1–4 subjects; 25, 5–7 subjects; 29 pass 8+ subjects. *A-levels*: on average, 14 pupils in upper sixth pass 1 subject; 15, 2 subjects; 26, 3 subjects and 3 pass 4 subjects. On average, 17 take science/engineering A-levels; 24 take arts and humanities; 19 a mixture. *Computing facilities*: 12 BBC B computers, 2 PC compatible. Special provisions for eg dyslexia, EFL, on small scale.

Senior pupils' non-academic activities *Music*: 100 learn a musical instrument, 32 to Grade 6 or above. 2 accepted for Music School. 70 in school orchestra, 80 in school choir; 1 in National Youth Orchestra; 35 in Schola Cantorum (chapel choir: visits cathedrals, makes TV, radio and private recordings; foreign tours). *Drama and dance*: 50 in school productions, 12–30 in small productions, drama training in first two years. 1 accepted for Drama/Dance Schools. *Art*: 20 take as non-examined subject; 28 take GCSE art; 17 A-level art/ceramics. 15 belong to photographic club, etc. *Sport*: Rugby, hockey, Association football, fives, squash, cricket, athletics, cross-country, orienteering, shooting, fencing, riding, netball, rounders, swimming, table tennis, trampolining, badminton available. Many take non-compulsory sport. 15 have specialist training for swimming, 12 have top-class cricket coaching. 13 represent county/country (rugby, hockey, athletics, squash, cricket). *Other*: 30 have bronze Duke of Edinburgh's Award, 30 silver and 20 gold. 2 members of British Schools' Exploring Society Expeditions. Other activities include a computer club, driving club, chess, bridge, scenery construction, war-gaming and whatever is a current staff enthusiasm. The CCF (which is voluntary – alternatives are D of E or outward bound training) is popular.

Careers 2 part time advisors. Average number of pupils accepted for *arts and humanities degree courses* at Oxbridge, 2; other universities, 9; polytechnics or CHE, 11. *science and engineering degree courses* at Oxbridge, 1; other universities, 11; medical schools, 1; polytechnics or CHE, 3. BEd, 1. *other general training courses*, 2. Average number of pupils going straight into careers in the armed services, 6; industry, 8; the City, 1; music/drama, 1; other, 11.

Uniform School uniform worn throughout.

Houses/prefects Competitive houses. Prefects, head boy/girl, head of house and house prefects – appointed by Head in consultation with staff.

Religion Attendance at Chapel compulsory (Tue–Fri, simple service; Sunday Sung Eucharist for boarders).

Social Foreign tours by Schola Cantorum; expeditions abroad for climbing/ hill-walking; annual skiing holiday; school exchanges; CCF camp abroad. Pupils allowed to bring own bike to school. Meals self service. School tuck, general equipment and uniform shops. No tobacco allowed; alcohol allowed only in sixth form bar.

Discipline No corporal punishment.

Boarding 10% have own study bedroom, 55% share (with 1 or 3 others); 35% in dormitories of 6+. Houses, of approximately 60, single sex, same as competitive houses (boys), divided by age group (girls). Resident qualified nurse. Central dining room. Pupils can provide and cook own food. 2 28-hour exeats each term and half term. Visits to local town allowed.

Former pupils Quentin Crisp (entertainer); Geoffrey Smith (Political columnist, *The Times*); Alistair Hignell (sportsman); John Makepeace (furniture designer).

DITCHAM PARK

Ditcham Park School	• Co-ed	Pupils 195
Petersfield	Boys	Upper sixth No
Hampshire GU31 5RN	Girls	Termly fees:
Telephone number 0730 85659	Mixed sixth	Day £930
	• Day	ISAI
	Boarding	

Head Mrs P M Holmes (12 years)

Age range 11–16, own prep from age 5; entry by interview
2 scholarships pa. Remedial and dyslexia departments. No A-levels offered. Oversubscribed.

DOLLAR ACADEMY

Dollar Academy	• Co-ed	Pupils 739
Dollar	Boys	Upper sixth Yes
Clackmannanshire FK14 7DU	Girls	Termly fees:
Telephone number 02594 2511	Mixed sixth	Day £694
	• Day	Boarding £1512
	• Boarding	GBA; HMC;
		ISBA

Head L Harrison (4 years)

Age range 12–18, own prep from age 5; entry by own exam

DOUAI

Douai School
Upper Woolhampton
Reading
Berkshire RG7 5TH
Telephone number 0734 713114

Enquiries/application to the Headmaster

Co-ed
● Boys
Girls
Mixed sixth
● Day
● Boarding

Pupils 302
Upper sixth 45
Termly fees:
Day £1210
Boarding £1923
HMC

WHAT IT'S LIKE

Founded in 1615 in Paris, the school and the Benedictine community moved to the present site in 1903. Its handsome buildings lie in a setting of considerable beauty and comprise 200 acres, bordered by fields and woodlands on the southern edge of the Berkshire Downs, overlooking the Kennet valley. The school adjoins the Benedictine monastery and its abbey church. It is run by monks (the Head is a monk) as well as lay staff and the pupils are brought up in the Benedictine tradition of learning and service to God and the community in which they live. It is a popular school because it is comparatively small and well located and there is a strong atmosphere of community. It is very well equipped with every modern facility (including comfortable boarding accommodation) and has particularly fine playing fields. The teaching is of a high standard and results are very creditable (25–30 university entrants per year). There is much emphasis on physical fitness and games and sports are important. Music, drama and art are flourishing. Very good facilities for such activities as light engineering, electronics and woodwork. There is a strong tradition of participation in community service and an impressive record in the Duke of Edinburgh's Award Scheme.

SCHOOL PROFILE

Pupils Total, 302. Day 24; Boarding 278. Entry age, 11/13 and into the sixth. 8% are children of former pupils.

Entrance Common entrance and own entrance exam used. Oversubscribed. No special skills required; most pupils are Roman Catholics, other Christians welcome. Parents not expected to buy text books. 10 scholarships/bursaries, £1797–£800.

Parents 15+% in the armed services; 15+% are doctors, lawyers, etc. 25% live within 30 miles; 25% live overseas.

Staff Head Rev Geoffrey Scott, in post since 1987. 35 full time staff, 15 part time. Annual turnover 5%. Average age 41.

Academic work GCSE and A-levels. Average size of upper fifth 55; upper sixth 45. *O-levels*: on average, 8 pupils in upper fifth pass 1–4 subjects; 16, 5–7 subjects; 30 pass 8+ subjects. *A-levels*: on average, 4 pupils in upper sixth pass 1 subject; 7, 2 subjects; 18, 3 subjects and 14 pass 4 subjects. On average, 14 take science/engineering A-levels; 26 take arts and humanities; 6 a mixture. Photography offered to GCSE/A-level. *Computing facilities*: 9-station Nimbus Network, 4 BBC, 3 RML 480Z, 3 RML 380Z, 26 Amstrad PCW 8256. *Special provisions*: For dyslexia and EFL.

Senior pupils' non-academic activities *Music*: 32 learn a musical instrument, 6 to Grade 6 or above. 11 in school orchestra, 11 in school choir, 8 in school pop group; 1 in National youth choir. *Drama and dance*: 30 in school productions, 10 in informal productions. *Art*: 3 take as non-examined subject; 25 take GCSE art, 8 A-level; 7 A-level photography. 2 accepted for Art School; 1 for photography course; 20 belong to photographic club. *Sport*: Rugby, soccer, cricket, fencing, swimming, badminton, squash, hockey, sailing, canoeing, tennis, judo, athletics, cross-country, kung-fu, multi-gym available. 60 take non-compulsory sport. 25 take exams in athletics, gymnastics and swimming; 8 represent county/country (rugby, athletics). *Other*: 8 take part in local community schemes. 14 have bronze Duke of Edinburgh's Award, 32 silver and 10 gold. 12 help with handicapped children's pilgrimage to Lourdes. Other activities include a computer club, driving lessons, chess club, debating, amateur politics, bookbinding.

Careers 1 part time advisor. Average number of pupils accepted for *arts and humanities degree courses* at Oxbridge, 3; other universities, 13; polytechnics or CHE, 10. *science and engineering degree courses* at Oxbridge, 2; other universities, 9; medical schools, 2; polytechnics or CHE, 3. Average number of pupils going straight into careers in the armed services, 3; the City, 2; other, 3.

Uniform School uniform worn throughout.

Houses/prefects Competitive houses. Prefects, head boy, head of house and house prefects – appointed after consultation with staff and boys.

Religion Compulsory Sunday mass; other religious events available during week.

Social Debates with other boys' and girls' schools, dances and other social functions. Regular ski trips, art trips, sporting tours. Exchanges with Germany and France. Meals self service. School shop. No tobacco/alcohol allowed.

Discipline No corporal punishment.

Boarding Upper sixth have own study bedroom, fifth and lower sixth in cubicles; others are in dormitories of 6+. Houses are administrative (65 in each), not residential. 4 SRNs in rotation; doctor visits daily. Central dining room. 2 weekend exeats each term and half term. Visits to local town allowed for fifth form and above.

Alumni association run by Godfrey Linnett, 26 Den Road, Shortlands, Bromley, Kent.

DOVER COLLEGE

Dover College	• Co-ed	Pupils 370
Dover	Boys	Upper sixth Yes
Kent CT17 9RH	Girls	Termly fees:
Telephone number 0304 205969	Mixed sixth	Day £1370
	• Day	Boarding £2080
	• Boarding	HMC; GBA

WHAT IT'S LIKE

Founded in 1871 and granted a royal charter by George V in 1923, it has a fine site in Dover on the grounds formerly occupied by the medieval Priory of St

Martin, some of whose monastic buildings survive and are occupied by the school. The refectory (c.1130) is the school dining hall, the Guest hall is the chapel and the Gatehouse contains the headmaster's study and offices. The college Close is surrounded by the ancient buildings. There have been numerous improvements and extensions in recent years and the school is now very well equipped. Accommodation for boarders is comfortable. The junior school is a separate establishment at Westbrook House, Folkestone. The college tries to order its life according to Christian principles and also to provide ample opportunity for Christian worship and study of the Christian faith. Quite a large staff permits a staff:pupil ratio of about 1:10. A sound general education is provided and results are consistently creditable. A good many leavers go on to university or some other place of further education. Music plays an important part in the school's life. There are an orchestra, a choir and various ensembles and bands. Drama is also strong and there are several productions each year, plus a house drama festival. Art and technology are well provided for. A wide range of sports and games is available, and there are good playing fields 10 minutes' walk away on the edge of the town. Some 40 clubs and societies cater for most extra-curricular needs. There is some emphasis on adventure training and outdoor pursuits and there are regular trips to Ullswater. The college has a lot of international and, particularly, European contacts and there are close ties with similar schools in France and West Germany. This cosmopolitan element is beneficial.

SCHOOL PROFILE

Head Mr J K Ind (7 years)

Age range 13–19; own junior from age 3; entry by common entrance or own exam. 30% of pupils are foreign nationals

Scholarships and bursaries for music, art, academic and general.

DOWNE HOUSE

Downe House		Co-ed	Pupils 435
Cold Ash		Boys	Upper sixth Yes
Newbury	●	Girls	Termly fees:
Berkshire RG16 9JJ		Mixed sixth	Day £1330
Telephone number 0635 200286	●	Day	Boarding £2050
	●	Boarding	GSA

WHAT IT'S LIKE

Founded by Miss Olive Wills in 1907 in Darwin's home, Downe House, in Kent. It moved to its present site in 1922. This is a very beautiful site indeed of 100 acres in the village of Cold Ash, on a wooded ridge 5 miles north of Newbury. Extensive modernisation has taken place over the years and facilities are now first-rate. There are about 435 pupils, of whom 40 are day girls. The senior school takes girls from 12–18; the 11-year-olds live in two separate boarding houses. There are 4 houses of a mixed age range. When girls reach their second year in the sixth form they move to York House where they live in double and single study bedrooms. The accommodation is very civilised. Life in the sixth form is planned to provide a transition between school and further education. Girls are given a greater degree of independence. The school has its own chapel which all are required to attend daily. Scripture is a compulsory subject throughout the school. A full range of academic subjects is taught, the teaching is very good and so are the results. A high proportion of the sixth form go on to university. The school is very strong indeed in music; the art and drama departments are very active. There are excellent sports and games facilities and a wide range of extra-curricular activities.

SCHOOL PROFILE

Head Miss S E Farr (10 years)
Age range 11–18; entry by common entrance
Scholarships including music scholarships available.

DOWNSIDE

Downside School	Co-ed	Pupils 481
Stratton-on-the-Fosse	• Boys	Upper sixth 100
Bath	Girls	Termly fees:
Somerset BA3 4RJ	Mixed sixth	Day £1338
Telephone number 0761 232206	• Day	Boarding £2026
	• Boarding	HMC; English
Enquiries/application to the Headmaster		Benedictine

WHAT IT'S LIKE

Founded in 1606 at Douai. At the time of the French Revolution the monks of the community were obliged to flee to England and were accommodated at Acton Burnell near Shrewsbury. In 1814 the school was removed to Downside where the English Benedictine community of St Gregory became established. It lies at the foot of the Mendip Hills in splendid Somerset countryside, 12 miles from Bath. Handsome buildings and excellent modern facilities make a compact campus. The monastery and its Abbey Church are a part of it. Superb playing fields, gardens and grounds surround it. The aim of the school is to help each boy to become fully Catholic and adult. The monastic influence is strong. The headmaster and the housemasters are monks. There are 15–20 monks on the teaching staff. The staff:pupil ratio is 1:7. A good general education is provided and results are very creditable. Not a few pupils go on to university. The music and art departments are active and much use is made of the purpose-built theatre for a wide range of dramatic productions. The school is strong in sports and games (about 20 are available). A very large number of societies and clubs (about 40) cater for extra-curricular activities.

SCHOOL PROFILE

Pupils Total 481. Day 11; Boarding 470. Entry age, 13 and into the sixth. 40–50% are children of former pupils.
Entrance Common entrance and own entrance exam used. Not oversub-

scribed. No special skills required. Roman Catholicism required. Parents not expected to buy text books. 10 scholarships pa for art, music, maths, and for sixth form entrants, up to £4000 pa. Bursaries available at discretion of headmaster.

Parents Up to 10% live within 30 miles; 10+% live overseas.

Staff Head Dom Philip Jebb, in post for 7 years. 76 full time staff, 16 part time. Annual turnover 4%.

Academic work GCSE and A-levels. Average size of upper fifth 90; upper sixth 100. O-level and A-level results not available. On average, 20 take science/engineering A-levels; 45 take arts and humanities; 25 take a mixture. Portuguese, Russian, Italian and theology are offered to GCSE/A-level. Provisions for EFL, dyslexia, mild visual, aural or physical handicap and special dietary needs.

Senior pupils' non-academic activities *Sport*: Rugby, soccer, hockey, cricket, tennis, athletics, squash, fencing, golf, judo, basketball, swimming, archery and cross-country available. Other activities include a computer club, driving, horse riding, chess, cookery and local history.

Careers 2 part-time advisors.

Uniform School uniform worn throughout.

Houses/prefects Houses. Prefects, head boy, head of house and house prefects – appointed by the Head.

Religion Mass on Sunday; house service once a week; morning and evening prayers, all compulsory.

Social Choral society production with St Antony's-Leweston. Occasional theatrical productions and debates with local comprehensive schools. Organised trips abroad for skiing, various sports tours, exchange with Austrian and Irish schools. Pupils allowed to bring own bike to school. Meals self service. School shop. No pupils allowed tobacco.

Discipline No corporal punishment. Pupils failing to produce homework once might expect to be kept from the Sunday film; those caught smoking cannabis on the premises might expect expulsion.

Boarding All sixth formers have own study bedroom. Others are in dormitories of 6+. Houses of approximately 60. Resident qualified nursing staff on site 24 hrs a day, doctor visits twice a day. Central dining room. 1 weekend exeat each term. Weekend visits to the local town allowed for sixth form unsupervised.

Alumni association is run by Dom Martin Salmon, c/o the School.

Former pupils Richard Stokes (Privy Seal); Lord Rawlinson (former Attorney General).

DUCHY GRAMMAR

The Duchy Grammar School
Tregye
Truro
Cornwall TR3 6JH
Telephone number 0872 862289

Enquiries/application to the Headmaster

- Co-ed   Pupils 104
- Boys   Upper sixth 4
- Girls   Termly fees:
- Mixed sixth   Day £690
- Day   Boarding £1350
- Boarding

WHAT IT'S LIKE

Founded in 1982, it lies on a single site of eight acres in pleasant countryside 4 miles from Truro. The central building is Tregye, a small 19th-century country house. A sound general education is provided and its ethos is intended to reflect the values of the former Cathedral School from which it derives. There are good modern facilities and comfortable boarding accommodation. A more than adequate range of sport, games and extra-curricular activities is provided.

SCHOOL PROFILE

Pupils Total over 12, 104. Roughly 50% day; 50% boarding. Boy:girl ratio of 3:1. Entry age, 7 and into the sixth. Own junior department provides over 20%.

Entrance Not oversubscribed. No special skills or religious requirements. Parents not expected to buy text books. 6 scholarships/bursaries, 33–75% tuition fees.

Parents 60+% live within 30 miles; up to 10% live overseas.

Staff Head Michael Fuller, in post for 2 years. 14 full time staff, 7 part time. Annual turnover 5%. Average age 41.

Academic work GCSE and A-levels. Average size of upper fifth 18; upper sixth 4. *O-levels*: on average, 8 pupils in upper fifth pass 1–4 subjects; 7, 5–7 subjects; 3 pass 8+ subjects. *A-levels*: on average, 1 pupil in upper sixth passes 1 subject; 1, 2 subjects; and 2 pass 3 subjects. On average, 2 take science/engineering A-levels; 2 take arts and humanities. Nautical studies offered to GCSE. *Computing facilities*: 4 micros. *Special provisions*: EFL course.

Senior pupils' non-academic activities *Music*: 20 learn a musical instrument, 6 to Grade 6 or above. 8 in school orchestra, 34 in school choir. *Drama and dance*: 25 in school productions. *Art*: 12 take GCSE art. *Sport*: Soccer, rugby, netball, basketball, volleyball, hockey, squash, tennis, athletics, swimming, cricket, sailing, canoeing, snorkelling available. 12 take non-compulsory sport. *Other*: 4 take part in local community schemes. 10 have bronze Duke of Edinburgh's Award and 2 have silver. Other activities include a computer club, chess club, electronics club, horse riding, recorder consort, puppet theatre, hiking (10 Tors expedition), drama (annual Shakespeare production).

Careers 1 full time careers advisor. Average number of pupils accepted for *arts and humanities degree courses* at universities, 1; polytechnics or CHE, 1. *other general training courses*, 2. Average number of pupils going straight into careers in industry, 4; other, 14.

Uniform School uniform worn throughout.
Houses/prefects Competitive houses. Prefects, head boy/girl, head of house and house prefects – appointed by the Head. School Council.
Religion Daily assembly.
Social Debates with other local sixth forms. Joint visit to France each autumn with local state school. 5-day French visit. 7-day ski-ing trip. Pupils allowed to bring own car/bike/motorbike to school. Meals formal. School shop. No tobacco/alcohol allowed.
Discipline Corporal punishment with parental permission. Pupils failing to produce homework once might expect immediate after-school detention; those caught smoking cigarettes on the premises could expect talk in presence of parents and suspension; expulsion for subsequent offences.
Boarding 3% have own study bedroom, 57% share (3); 40% are in dormitories of 6+. Central dining room. Pupils allowed to provide and cook food and drink. 2 weekend exeats each term. Visits to local town allowed at weekends.
Alumni association Just being launched.

DUKE OF YORK'S

Duke of York's Royal Military School	Co-ed	Pupils 398
Dover	● Boys	Upper sixth 40
Kent CT15 5EQ	Girls	Termly fees:
Telephone number 0304 203012	Mixed sixth	Boarding £200
Enquiries/application to the Headmaster	Day	GBA
	● Boarding	

WHAT IT'S LIKE

Founded in 1803, the modern establishment is purpose-built, rural, in about 150 acres of pleasant parkland 2 miles from Dover. Its president is the Duke of Kent and the governing body consists of 15 commissioners some of whom are appointed by the monarch. Though largely financed by the Ministry of Defence it is a school not a military unit. About 15% of leavers enter the services and those who wish to do so are given every help and encouragement. However the school aim is to offer a broad, traditional grammar boarding school education. Standards are high and academic results are good. In religious terms it is in the 'main stream' of Anglican practice. Sports and games are well supported; high standards are expected and attained. There is an impressive range of extra-curricular activities. The military ethos survives in a large and active CCF; membership of which is compulsory from the third form.

SCHOOL PROFILE

Pupils Total over 12, 398 (boarding). Entry age, 11 and into the sixth. Very few are children of former pupils.
Entrance Own entrance exam used. Ability to benefit from a grammar boarding education looked for. Only sons of army personnel of at least 4 years' service (serving or retired) admitted; must accept the Christian ethos

of the school. Parents not expected to buy text books. School is largely financed by MoD, hence low fees; free places may be offered in cases classed as 'compassionate'.

Parents Up to 10% live within 30 miles; 30+% live overseas.

Staff Head Lieutenant Colonel C F P Horsfall, in post for 1 year. 48 full time staff. Part time music and modern language conversationalists. Annual turnover 5%.

Academic work GCSE, A-levels and BTEC National Diplomas. Average size of upper fifth 75; upper sixth 40. *O-levels*: on average, 18 pupils in upper fifth pass 1–4 subjects; 17, 5–7 subjects; 34 pass 8+ subjects. *A-levels*: on average, 6 pupils in upper sixth pass 1 subject; 6, 2 subjects; 16, 3 subjects and 8 pass 4 subjects. On average, 22 take science/engineering A-levels; 2 take arts and humanities; 14 a mixture. BTEC National Diplomas in Engineering and in Business and Finance; close to 100% pass rate. *Computing facilities*: Very extensive, include computer science, information technology and technology blocks.

Senior pupils' non-academic activities *Music*: 3 learn a musical instrument; 3 in school orchestra, 3 in school choir, 5 in school jazz group; occasional A-level students. *Drama and dance*: 10 in school productions. *Art*: 11 take GCSE art/ceramics, 1 takes A-level art. 5 belong to photographic club. *Sport*: Major school (representative) sports are rugby, hockey, cricket, athletics and swimming. 60 take non-compulsory sport; swimming and life saving awards. On average 4–8 per year (more with rugby and hockey team group) represent county (swimming, water polo, rugby, hockey). *Other*: 115 take part in CCF (compulsory from third until upper sixth). All pupils must take part in activities (1 or 2) twice a week: art, astronomy, ballroom dancing, badminton, bridge, business club, canoeing, chess, choir, choral society, Christian Union, classical music, climbing, computers, dance band, debating society, drama, indoor football, fishing, gymnastics and trampoline, gardening, horse riding, judo, languages, library, life saving, meteorology, modelling, plastic and metal work, model railway, orchestra, photography, pottery, philately, quizzes, science, shooting (.22 and .303), amateur radio and electronics, table tennis, war gaming, water polo, weight training, woodwork.

Careers 1 part time advisor. More than 50% go on to degree courses. On average 15% go into the armed services.

Uniform School uniform worn throughout.

Houses/prefects Competitive houses. Prefects, head boy, head of house and house prefects – appointed by the Head.

Religion Compulsory Sunday services.

Social Drama, musical, debates, industrial conferences with local girls' grammar school. Skiing and language trips abroad. Meals – some formal, some self service. School shop. No tobacco/alcohol allowed.

Discipline No corporal punishment. Pupils failing to produce homework once might expect extra work; firm disciplinary policy in respect of any habits that endanger health.

Boarding Sixth form have own study bedroom, forms 1–5 share (with 1 other). 8 houses of between 70 and 55, divided by age group. Resident qualified nurse. Non-resident doctor. Central dining room. 1 exeat each term (winter term, 1 week; others: long weekend). Visits to local town allowed on request.

Alumni association run by A Sadler, President and Secretary of the Old Boys Association, 'Birnham', 1 Bush Road, Fetcham, Leatherhead, Surrey KT22 9SX.

DULWICH

Dulwich College		Co-ed	Pupils 1430
Dulwich		• Boys	Upper sixth Yes
London SE21 7LD		Girls	Termly fees:
Telephone number 01-693 3601		Mixed sixth	Day £1070
		• Day	Boarding £2140
		• Boarding	GBA; HMC;
			BSA

WHAT IT'S LIKE

Founded by Edward Alleyn, the Elizabethan actor-manager. In 1619 a licence was granted for his 'College of God's Gift' at Dulwich. In 1857 Alleyn's College was reconstituted by a special Act of Parliament. The upper part of the foundation was thereafter known as Dulwich College and moved to its present site in 1870. It has very handsome, patrician buildings (designed by Charles Barry the younger) set on a big expanse of splendid playing fields in one of the most agreeable residential districts of London. Since the late 1940s extensive building programmes have enormously improved the facilities and the college is now one of the best equipped schools in the country. A notable feature is the Picture Gallery (designed by Sir John Soane) which contains a priceless collection of paintings, some of which were originally assembled for King Stanislas of Poland. Another is the Wodehouse Library which houses some 30,000 books, plus 40,000 books and documents published before 1800. The library contains a record and cassette section and a paperback bookshop. The college is divided into 3 sections: lower, middle and upper. There are 4 comfortable boarding houses for 140 boarders. Some pupils are weekly boarders. There is some emphasis on religious worship and practice in the Anglican tradition. This includes daily assemblies and a special school service once a term. Religious instruction is part of the curriculum for all pupils up to and including the fifth form. Thereafter sixth formers do further work in the philosophy of religion. Academically, the college is very high powered indeed and in this respect (as in many others) is one of the most distinguished in Britain. Academic studies are extremely well run by a large and very well qualified staff (the staff:pupil ratio is about 1:11) who consistently produce outstanding results. Each year 150–160 pupils go on to university (including 30 or more to Oxbridge). Hardly any other school in Britain matches such a record. Music plays an important part in the life of the school. A 250 strong choir undertakes major works in regular concerts at the Festival Hall and the Fairfield Hall. There are several orchestras and smaller instrumental groups. Drama involves a very large number of pupils throughout the school. There are numerous productions each year. Art is no less strong. An extremely well-equipped art school produces work of a high order. The design and technology centre has sophisticated workshops for engineering, boatbuilding and cabinet making. There is also a first-class computer centre. A wide variety of sports and games is available. Games are compulsory on certain afternoons for all who are fit. The huge multi-purpose sports hall is in constant use. On average about 500 boys go to it daily. Standards in sports and games are very high indeed and the college has produced many representatives at county, regional and national level. There are 3 scout troops and a venture scout unit which organise many expeditions abroad and in Britain. A large and very active CCF contingent (which had its origins in 1877 and thus 40 years before OTCs were created) shows much enterprise. There is also a very big voluntary service unit which may involve up to 250 boys at a time and which has 150 regular clients in the locality. About 50 clubs and societies form the College Union and these cater for every conceivable need.

SCHOOL PROFILE

Head A C F Verity (2 years)
Age range 8–18; entry by own exam and interview
Up to 40 scholarships, including music and art. Also 58 assisted places pa.

DUNDEE HIGH

High School of Dundee
Euclid Crescent
Dundee DD1 1HU
Telephone number 0382 29921

Enquiries/application to the Rector

- Co-ed
  Boys
  Girls
  Mixed sixth
- Day
  Boarding

Pupils 748
Upper sixth 90
Termly fees:
Day £678
HMC

WHAT IT'S LIKE

Founded in 1239 by the Abbot of Lindores. The main buildings are very striking: neo-classical/Georgian erected in 1832–34. Excellent modern facilities are provided. The playing fields are about a mile away. The school enjoys a very strong corporate life and spirit and has a high reputation, with vigorous local support. Academically high-powered, it produces consistently excellent results. About 70–75 pupils go on to university each year. Notably strong in music, drama and art. There is a very large number of extra-curricular activities and many of these are carried to high levels of achievement. Sports and games are also of a high standard and the school produces many representatives at county level. The record in the Duke of Edinburgh's Award Scheme is impressive.

SCHOOL PROFILE

Pupils Total over 12, 748 (boys 357, girls 391). Entry age, 5, 12 and into the sixth. Own junior school provides over 20%. 20% are children of former pupils.
Entrance Own entrance exam used. Oversubscribed in some forms. Good average ability looked for. No religious requirements. Parents expected to buy text books. 150 assisted places. 30 scholarships/bursaries, half fees–£200.

Parents 15+% in industry or commerce; 15+% are doctors, lawyers, etc. 60+% live within 30 miles.

Staff Head R Nimmo, in post for 11 years. 80 full time staff, 7 part time. Annual turnover 5%. Average age 40.

Academic work O-grade, Highers and CSYS. Average size of upper fifth 140; upper sixth 90. *O-grade*: on average, 20 pupils in upper fifth pass 5–7 subjects; 120 pass 8+ subjects. *Highers*: on average, 19 pupils pass 1 subject; 19, 2 subjects; 17, 3 subjects and 73 pass 4 subjects. On average, 66 take science/engineering CSYS-levels; 66 take arts and humanities; 8 a mixture. *Computing facilities*: Two computer laboratories.

Senior pupils' non-academic activities *Music*: 70 learn a musical instrument, 40 to Grade 6 or above, 4 accepted for Music School; 23 in school orchestra, 115 in choir, 6 in pop group, 24 in folk group; 6 in National Youth Orchestra. *Drama and dance*: 60 in school productions. 30 take Grade 6 in ESB, RAD etc. 2 accepted for Drama/Dance Schools; 1 goes on to work in theatre. *Art*: 30 take as non-examined subject; 24 take O-grade; 11 Higher. Approx 2 or 3 accepted for Art School. *Sport*: Rugby, hockey, cricket, tennis, athletics, netball, golf, swimming, squash available. 320 take non-compulsory sport. 12 take exams eg gymnastics, swimming. 18 pupils represent county (hockey, rugby, cricket). *Other*: 12 take part in local community schemes. 25 have silver Duke of Edinburgh's Award, 12 have gold. 5 enter voluntary schemes after leaving school. Other activities: a wide variety of extra-curricular activities in terms of clubs (several computer clubs), hobbies and leisure interests (41 at the last count).

Careers 5 part time advisors, plus an Industrial Liaison Officer. Average number of pupils accepted for *arts and humanities degree courses* at Oxbridge, 2; other universities, 38; polytechnics or CHE, 13. *science and engineering degree courses* at Oxbridge, 3; other universities, 31; medical schools, 11; polytechnics or CHE, 31. *BEd*, 2. *other general training courses*, 17. Average number of pupils going straight into careers in the armed services, 2; industry, 7. Traditional school careers are in medicine and law/accountancy.

Uniform School uniform worn throughout.

Houses/prefects Competitive houses. Prefects, head boy and girl – elected by staff and pupils. School Council.

Religion Weekly school assembly and end-of-term services.

Social Debates, ESU, United Nations, Press and Journal with other local schools. Organised exchanges with Spain and Germany; trips to France, Belgium; ski trips; rugby/hockey tours to Canada. Meals self service. School tuck and thrift shops. No tobacco/alcohol allowed.

Discipline No corporal punishment. Pupils failing to produce homework once might expect to write it out twice for next day; those caught smoking cannabis on the premises could expect expulsion.

Alumni association run by Harvey Findlay, 8 Abercrombie Street, Barnhill, Dundee.

Former pupils Sir Robert Lickley (designer of the Harrier jet); Lord Perry (former Principal of the Open University); Sir David Anderson (designer of Forth Road Bridge); Sir Alan Peacock (former Principal of Independent University); Lord Fulton (former Principal of Sussex University); Chris Rae (sports commentator); Bill Hamilton (BBC newscaster).

DUNOTTAR

Dunottar School	Co-ed	Pupils 370
High Trees Road	Boys	Upper sixth Yes
Reigate	● Girls	Termly fees:
Surrey RH2 7EL	Mixed sixth	Day £680
Telephone number 0737 61945	● Day	GSA
	Boarding	

WHAT IT'S LIKE

Founded in 1926, it lies high on the North Downs on the south side of Reigate and Redhill and has handsome buildings in very pleasant surroundings with beautiful gardens and playing fields. Modern facilities for teaching are very good and the accommodation is comfortable. A non-denominational but specifically Christian school, it puts some emphasis on the need for religious studies and there are daily assemblies with a religious element. A happy and efficient working atmosphere is maintained by the encouragement of common sense, an insistence on self-discipline and good manners. A large staff allows a staff:pupil ratio of 1:10. Academic standards and results are good and quite a high proportion of girls go on to university and other places of further education. There is a strong sport and games tradition and good standards are achieved. A plentiful variety of extra-curricular activities is provided and the school participates successfully in the Duke of Edinburgh's Award Scheme.

SCHOOL PROFILE

Head Miss J Burnell (3 years)
Age range 7–18; entry by own exam or common entrance
4 scholarships at age 11 and some in the sixth form.

DURHAM

Durham School	Co-ed	Pupils 371
Durham City DH1 4SZ	● Boys	Upper sixth 70
Telephone number 0385 47977	Girls	Termly fees:
	● Mixed sixth	Day £1535
Enquiries/application to the Headmaster's	● Day	Boarding £2302
secretary	● Boarding	HMC

WHAT IT'S LIKE

One of the oldest schools in England and always closely associated with the diocese of Durham. As the Bishop's School it was reorganised and re-endowed by Cardinal Langley in 1414 and refounded in 1541 by Henry VIII. It has occupied its present site since 1842 and enjoys a magnificent position below the west towers of the cathedral. During the last 15 years over a million pounds has been spent in providing first-class modern facilities for a wide range of activities. It is physically compact with playing fields nearby and makes full use of the advantages of an ancient cathedral and university city. A strong Anglican tradition prevails and religious worship is compulsory. A high standard of education is provided (staff ratio of 1:10) and some 70% of leavers proceed to university. Strong in music, drama and art and local community services. Very strong in sport, with players at county and international level.

SCHOOL PROFILE

Pupils Total, 371. Day 136 (boys 131, girls 5); Boarding 235 (boys 212, girls 23). Entry age boys, 11, 13; boys and girls into the sixth. Few are children of former pupils.

Entrance Common entrance and own entrance exam used. Oversubscribed. No special skills or religious requirements but school is C of E foundation. Scholarships/bursaries available.

Parents 60+% live within 30 miles; up to 10% live overseas.

Staff Head M A Lang, in post for 5 years. 36 full time staff, 8 part time. Annual turnover 10%. Average age – young.

Academic work GCSE and A-levels. Average size of upper fifth 68; upper sixth 70. *O-levels*: on average pupils pass 7 subjects. *A-levels*: on average pupils pass 3.25 subjects. *Computing facilities*: Computer lab with 20 BBC Masters. Computers in most departments. Special provisions for EFL, dyslexia etc.

Senior pupils' non-academic activities *Music*: 30% of school learn a musical instrument, 20 to Grade 6 or above. 50 in school orchestra, 50 in school choir, 7 in school pop group. *Drama and dance*: 40 in school productions. *Art*: All pupils take as non-examined subject, 20 take GCSE, 7 A-level. 2 accepted for Art School. 20 belong to photographic club. *Sport*: Athletics, rugby, rowing, swimming, cross-country, squash, fives, shooting, basketball, badminton, tennis, hockey, netball available. All pupils take non-compulsory sport. 3 represent country (rugby, rowing, riding), 16 senior county rugby players. *Other*: Some pupils take part in local community schemes. Duke of Edinburgh's Bronze and Silver Awards. Other activities include a computer club, highland cattle society, chess club, bridge club, archaeology, model building, railway society, rambling society, music society, debating society.

Careers 1 full time advisor. On average, proportion of pupils accepted for *degree courses* at Oxbridge, 10%; other universities, 60%; polytechnics or CHE, 10%, medical schools, 5%. A few go on to *other general training courses*. Average number of pupils going straight into careers in the armed services, 6–7; the church, 1; industry, some; the City, a few; civil service, a few.

Uniform School uniform worn throughout.

Houses/prefects Competitive houses. Prefects, head boy/girl, head of house and house prefects – appointed by the Head.

Religion Religious worship compulsory.

Social Many organised trips abroad. Meals self service. School shop. No tobacco/alcohol allowed.

Discipline No corporal punishment. Pupils failing to produce homework once might expect repeat work; those caught smoking cannabis on the premises could expect expulsion.

Boarding Some share study bedroom with one other; most are in dormitories of 6+. Houses, of approximately 60, same as competitive houses, single sex. Resident qualified nurse. Central dining room. Pupils can provide and cook own food. 2 weekends and 3 Sunday exeats each term. Visits to local town allowed.

Alumni association run by D Baty, c/o the School.

DURHAM HIGH

Durham High School	Co-ed	Pupils 260
Farewell Hall	Boys	Upper sixth 30
Durham DH1 3TB	● Girls	Termly fees:
Telephone number 0385 43226	Mixed sixth	Day £710
Enquiries/application to the Head	● Day	
	Boarding	

WHAT IT'S LIKE

Founded in 1884, its aim is to give a sound general education within a Christian framework (it is a Church school), but all faiths are accepted. In 1968 it moved to a new purpose-built school at Farewell Hall on the southern edge of Durham – a semi-rural site. The junior school is combined. Academic results are promising (15–20 university entrants per year) and the school enjoys a good local reputation. A fair range of sports, games and extra-curricular activities is available.

SCHOOL PROFILE

Pupils Total over 12, 260. Entry age, 11 and into the sixth. Own junior department provides over 20%.

Entrance Own entrance exam used. Often oversubscribed. No special skills or religious requirements. Parents expected to buy some text books. 3 scholarships/bursaries pa, up to 75% of fees.

Parents 60+% live within 30 miles.

Staff Head Miss B E Stephenson, in post for 9 years. 20 full time staff, 11 part time. Annual turnover 5%. Average age 45.

Academic work GCSE and A-levels. Average size of upper fifth 45; upper sixth 30. *O-levels*: on average, 3 pupils in upper fifth pass 1–4 subjects; 12, 5–7 subjects; 30 pass 8+ subjects. *A-levels*: on average, 2 pupils in upper sixth pass 1 subject; 5, 2 subjects; 20, 3 subjects and 3 pass 4 subjects. On average, 10 take science/engineering A-levels; 16 take arts and humanities; 4 a mixture. *Computing facilities*: 10 BBC machines. Computers are part of the curriculum. *Special provisions*: EFL in exceptional circumstances.

Senior pupils' non-academic activities *Music*: 20 to Grade 6 or above; 2 in National Youth Orchestra. *Drama and dance*: 50 take up to Grade 6 (LAMDA, Guildhall) elocution and acting; 1 accepted for Dance/Drama School. *Art*: 10 take as non-examined subject; 15 take GCSE art; 5 A-level. 3 accepted for Art School. *Sport*: Hockey, netball, tennis, rounders, swimming, badminton, squash, golf, rowing available. 10 take non-compulsory sport. 3 represent county (hockey). *Other*: 15 have silver Duke of Edinburgh's Award and 10 have gold. Other activities include a drama club, music, karate.

Careers 1 part time advisor. Average number of pupils accepted for *arts and humanities degree courses* at Oxbridge, 1; other universities, 9; polytechnics or CHE, 1. *science and engineering degree courses* at Oxbridge, 2; other universities, 7; medical schools, 2; polytechnics or CHE, 2. *BEd*, at polytechnics or CHE, 2. *other general training courses*, 1. Straight into careers, 3.

Uniform School uniform worn except in the sixth.

Houses/prefects Competitive houses. Head girl, appointed by the Head with consultation; head of house and house prefects – elected.

Religion Daily Christian worship.

Social Organised trips abroad. Pupils allowed to bring own car to school. Meals self service. No tobacco/alcohol allowed.

Discipline No corporal punishment.

Alumni association run by Headmistress (Chairman) and Mrs K Hankey (Secretary) c/o the School.

EALING COLLEGE

Ealing College Upper School
83 The Avenue
London W13 8JS
Telephone number 01-997 4346

Enquiries/application to the Headmaster or Secretary

Co-ed
● Boys
  Girls
● Mixed sixth
● Day
  Boarding

Pupils 320
Upper sixth 30
Termly fees:
Day £695

WHAT IT'S LIKE

Founded in 1820, it is single-site in a residential urban area with good public transport facilities. It comprises pleasant, modern and well-equipped buildings with recent extensions. It provides a sound general education and its declared philosophy is to maximise the potential of each individual whatever their innate ability. A reasonable range of sport and games for which local grounds are used.

SCHOOL PROFILE

Pupils Total, 320 (boys 310, girls 10). Entry age boys, 11, 12, 13; boys and girls into the sixth. Very few are children of former pupils.

Entrance Own informal tests may be set. Sometimes oversubscribed. No special skills or religious requirements. Parents expected to buy text books beyond form 3. Occasional scholarships/bursaries for sixth form entrants with exceptional O-level results.

Parents 60+% live within 30 miles; up to 10% live overseas.

Staff Head B Webb, in post for 3 years. 23 full time staff, 3 part time. Annual turnover 4%. Average age 35–40.

Academic work GCSE and A-levels. Average size of upper fifth 60; upper sixth 30. *O-levels*: on average, 29 pupils in upper fifth pass 1–4 subjects; 18, 5–7 subjects; 5 pass 8+ subjects. *A-levels*: on average, 8 pupils in upper sixth pass 1 subject; 6, 2 subjects; 11, 3 subjects and 1 passes 4 subjects. On average, 10 take science/engineering A-levels; 7 take arts and humanities; 13 a mixture. Law offered to A-level. *Computing facilities*: Comprehensive system of BBC micros and Amstrad PCs in computer room; computers used by other departments. *Special provisions*: extra English language tuition available for overseas students.

Senior pupils' non-academic activities *Music*: 10 learn a musical instrument, 5 to Grade 6 or above. 15 in school choir. *Drama and dance*: Small number in school productions. Occasional pupil accepted for Drama School. *Art*: 15 take GCSE; 3, A-level. Occasional pupil accepted for Art School. *Sport*: Football, rugby, cricket, athletics, swimming, cross-country, badminton, tennis, squash, basketball, table tennis, karate available. 30 take non-compulsory sport (mainly football, cricket, tennis, squash, table tennis, badminton, karate). 2 represent county/country (karate and hockey). *Other*: Small number take part in local community schemes. Other activities include a computer club, chess and debating.

Careers 1 part time careers advisor. Average number of pupils accepted for *arts and humanities degree courses* at universities, 4; polytechnics or CHE, 2. *science and engineering degree courses* at universities, 6; medical schools, 2; polytechnics or CHE, 3.

Uniform School uniform worn except in the sixth.

Houses/prefects Competitive houses. Prefects, head boy/girl – appointed by the Head. School Council.

Religion No compulsory worship; religious studies is part of the curriculum.

Social Occasional debates with local schools. Annual ski trip and trips to France. Meals self service. School canteen. No tobacco/alcohol allowed.

Discipline No corporal punishment. Pupils failing to produce homework once might expect detention; those caught smoking cannabis on the premises could expect expulsion.

EASTBOURNE

Eastbourne College	Co-ed	Pupils 560
Eastbourne	● Boys	Upper sixth Yes
East Sussex BN21 4JX	Girls	Termly fees:
Telephone number 0323 37655	● Mixed sixth	Day £1550
	● Day	Boarding £2100
	● Boarding	GBA; HMC

WHAT IT'S LIKE

Founded in 1867 by the 8th Duke of Devonshire, it has an excellent site in the residential area of Eastbourne with elegant buildings and fine grounds and gardens. It is a few minutes' walk from the station, a modern shopping centre and two theatres. The sea front is 400 yards away and the South Downs are within easy reach. The school is divided into 5 boarding houses, 3 day-boy houses and a sixth form house for girls. Accommodation is comfortable. The college sets out to be a Christian school and its pupils are expected to attend instruction in Christian beliefs and chapel services. There are also voluntary services. The choir plays an important part in the worship of the school. The emphasis on Christianity extends to a more than usual amount of local community services through an organisation called Action Care. Large numbers of pupils (the Social Commandos) assist old and elderly residents and also entertain them with plays, concerts and other social events. A large staff allows a staff:pupil ratio of about 1:9. There is a very large sixth form. The teaching is good and academic standards and results are consistently high. A large number of leavers go on to university, quite a lot of them to Oxbridge. The music, drama and art departments are all strong and work closely together, forming an integral part of the academic and social life of the school. The choir and orchestra often give public performances with professional musicians. Many plays of quality are put on each year in the purpose-built theatre; and in the very well-equipped art school work of a high standard is produced. The technology, electronics and computer departments are also very active. The college has long had a high reputation for excellence in sports and games and there is a wide range of these including golf and sailing. There have been many representatives at county, regional and national levels. A large CCF shows great enterprise and there is considerable emphasis on adventure training and expedition. Numerous clubs and societies cater for most needs.

SCHOOL PROFILE

Head C J Saunders (7 years)
Age range 13–18; entry by common entrance
Scholarships, including music and art. Links with St Andrew's prep school, 8–13.

ECCLES HALL

Eccles Hall School
Quidenham
Norwich NR16 2PA
Telephone number 095 387 217

Co-ed
● Boys
Girls
Mixed sixth
● Day
● Boarding

Pupils 155
Upper sixth No
Termly fees:
Day £885
Boarding £1740
ISAI

Head S A Simington (3 years)
Age range 10–16; entry by interview and test
Special department for boys with specific learning problems.

EDGBASTON HIGH

Edgbaston High School for Girls
Westbourne Road
Edgbaston
Birmingham B15 3TS
Telephone number 021 454 5831

Co-ed   Pupils 540
Boys   Upper sixth Yes
● Girls   Termly fees:
Mixed sixth   Day £730
● Day   GSA
Boarding

WHAT IT'S LIKE

Founded in 1876, it comprises a nursery department, a prep school and a senior school on a 4-acre site (plus 8 acres of playing fields) 2 miles from the centre of Birmingham. In recent years the school has been completely rebuilt and is very well equipped. Additions include a sixth form block, pavilion and art block. The teaching is good and academic standards are high. A number of girls go on to university each year. Music is particularly strong and most girls learn an instrument. Art and drama are also strong. There is a good range of sports and games (the standards are high) and a plentiful variety of extra-curricular activities.

SCHOOL PROFILE

Head Mrs S J Horsman (1 year)
Age range 11–18; own prep from age 3; entry by own exam

EDGEHILL

Edgehill College
Bideford
Devon EX39 3LY
Telephone number 02372 71701

Enquiries/application to the Admissions Secretary

Co-ed   Pupils 321
Boys   Upper sixth 40
● Girls   Termly fees:
Mixed sixth   Day £845
● Day   Boarding £1610
● Boarding   GSA

WHAT IT'S LIKE

Founded in 1884, this Methodist foundation is single-site in the splendid countryside of North Devon, overlooking Bideford and the Torridge estuary. Its five elegant houses and other buildings form part of an estate of 50 acres in a peaceful and healthy spot. Comfortable accommodation and excellent modern facilities. The junior and nursery departments are attached. A Christian school, it worships in Bideford Methodist church and there are quite a lot of activities associated with the church. A sound education is provided and a fair number of leavers go to university (15–20 per year). The music and drama departments are flourishing and there is a good range of extra-curricular activities.

SCHOOL PROFILE

Pupils Total over 12, 321. Day 200; Boarding 121. Entry age, 11+ and into the sixth.

Entrance Common entrance and own entrance exam used. Oversubscribed. No special skills or religious requirements. Parents not expected to buy text books. 20 assisted places pa. Scholarships/bursaries, up to full fees.

Parents 30+% live within 30 miles; up to 10% live overseas.

Staff Head Mrs E M Burton, in post for 1 year. 27 full time staff, 8 part time. Annual turnover 8%.

Academic work GCSE and A-levels. Average size of upper fifth 75; upper sixth 40. *O-levels*: on average, 17 pupils in upper fifth pass 1–4 subjects; 20, 5–7 subjects; 19 pass 8+ subjects. *A-levels*: on average, 4 pupils in upper sixth pass 1 subject; 6, 2 subjects; and 30, 3 subjects. On average, 10 take science/engineering A-levels; 15 take arts and humanities; 15 a mixture. *Computing facilities*: Computer studies room. GCSE computer studies. *Special provisions*: Extra lessons with specialist staff for eg dyslexic pupils or for EFL.

Senior pupils' non-academic activities *Music*: 160 learn a musical instrument, 22 to Grade 6 or above. 1 accepted at university to study music. 16 in school orchestra (string group), 66 in school choir, 5 in school pop group, 16 in wind band, 3 in brass group; 4 in Bideford Youth Orchestra; 6 in Devon County Youth Choir; 2 in Cornwall County Youth Orchestra; several play in local town bands, sing in church choirs or play organ in church. *Drama and dance*: 60 in school productions; some take GCSE drama or A-level theatre studies. Several have gone on to do drama studies at higher education, some in county youth theatre. *Art*: 52 take GCSE; 13 A-level; 3 AO-level art history. 6 belong to photographic club; usually approx 20 involved in societies; 10 in ceramic society. *Sport*: Hockey, netball, volleyball, badminton, squash, tennis, archery, swimming, cross-country, athletics, gymnastics available. 40 take non-compulsory sport; 20 take exams. 5 represent county (hockey). *Other*: 8 take part in local community schemes. 40 have bronze Duke of Edinburgh's Award, 14 silver and 6 gold. Each form/house supports a charity. Other activities include a computer club, driving lessons and horse riding.

Careers 2 part time advisors. Average number of pupils accepted for *arts and humanities degree courses* at universities, 12; polytechnics or CHE, 5. *science and engineering degree courses* at Oxbridge, 2; other universities, 6; medical schools, 1; polytechnics or CHE, 3. *other general training courses*, 10. Average number of pupils going straight into careers in the armed services, 2; music/drama, 2.

Uniform School uniform worn except in the sixth.

Houses/prefects Competitive houses. Prefects, head girl, head of house and house prefects – elected by the school. School Council.

Religion Sunday morning worship. Morning assembly. Christian Union.

Social Joint choir, theatrical productions and film society with brother school, Shebbear. Organised trips abroad. Meals self service. School shop. No tobacco/alcohol allowed.

Discipline No corporal punishment.

Boarding Houses, of 50–60, same as competitive houses, plus separate sixth form house. Resident qualified nurse. Central dining room. Pupils can provide and cook own food. Two weekend exeats each term. Visits to local town allowed.

Former pupils Debbie Thrower.

EDINBURGH ACADEMY

The Edinburgh Academy
42 Henderson Row
Edinburgh EH3 5BL
Telephone number 031 556 4603

Enquiries/application to the Registrar
or Rector

Co-ed
● Boys
  Girls
● Mixed sixth
● Day
● Boarding

Pupils 559
Upper sixth 95
Termly fees:
Day £1040
Boarding £2100
HMC

WHAT IT'S LIKE

Founded in 1824 (Sir Walter Scott was one of the founding spirits and presided at the opening ceremony). The upper school buildings include the handsome original hall. All the modern facilities are spacious and first rate and the playing fields are a short walk from the school. The Academy is well known as one of the outstanding British schools, a civilised establishment which provides an extremely thorough, broad education. It is non-denominational within the Christian tradition. There are monthly school services and, for boarders, compulsory local church attendance. The Academy has a tradition of academic excellence – it enjoys a staff:pupil ratio of 1:11 and achieves high standards of scholarship and excellent results. It caters best for boys and girls with university ambitions and facilities are particularly good for experimental science and art. No subject is weak. Several pupils study Greek and Latin and each year, 75–80 leavers go on to university. The drama, art and music departments are all very strong. High standards are also attained in sport and games of which there is a wide range including hailes, curling and riding. There is also a wide variety of extra-curricular activities and considerable emphasis on outdoor pursuits (the Academy has its own field centre in the Highlands). The CCF contingent is unusually strong (compulsory at 14½ and six terms' service are required). The Academy also has a good record in the Duke of Edinburgh's Award Scheme. Much use is made of Edinburgh's cultural amenities.

SCHOOL PROFILE

Pupils Total over 12, 559. Day 495 (boys 472, girls 23); Boarding 64 (boys 59, girls 5). Entry age, boys, 10½–11½; boys and girls into the sixth. Own prep school provides over 70%. 14% are children of former pupils.

Entrance Own entrance exam or common entrance used. Oversubscribed at certain levels. No special religious requirements; pupils should immediately be able to receive all teaching in English. Parents are billed for text books. 7 assisted places pa. 5 scholarships/bursaries (academic, art or music), ½ day fees plus ¼ boarding fees if required.

Parents 15+% are doctors, lawyers etc; 15+% in industry or commerce. 60+% live within 30 miles; up to 10% live overseas.

Staff Head (Rector) L E Ellis, in post for 11 years. 56 full time staff, 5 part time plus 11 part time music staff. Annual turnover 2%. Average age 43.

Academic work GCSE, A-levels and Highers. Average size of upper fifth 97; upper sixth 95. *O-levels*: on average, 14 pupils in upper fifth pass 1–4 subjects; 14, 5–7 subjects; 65 pass 8+ subjects. *Highers*: on average, 24 pupils pass 1 subject; 24, 2 subjects; 22, 3 subjects; 30, 4 subjects; 38 pass 5+ subjects. *A-levels*: on average, 11 pupils in upper sixth pass 1 subject; 16, 2 subjects; 24 pass 3+ subjects. On average, 26 take science/engineering A-levels; 28 take arts and humanities; 7 a mixture. All Higher candidates take a mixture. *Computing facilities*: 15 BBC micros, 1 Apricot, 1 Vela, network disc sharing facilities. Provision for extra English tuition, one to one; learning support in small groups.

Senior pupils' non-academic activities *Music*: 54 learn a musical instrument, 28 to Grade 6 or above; 27 in school orchestra, 24 in school choir, 11 in dance band; 6 in Edinburgh Youth Orchestra; 4 sing in cathedral and church choirs. *Drama and dance*: 60 in school productions. 2 accepted for Drama/Dance Schools; 2 go on to work in theatre. *Art*: 20 take as non-examined subject; 27 take GCSE; 19 A-level; 21 Higher. 5 accepted for Art School; 3 to study architecture; 1 for art history; 2 joint art course. 20 belong to photographic club; 35 to art society. *Sport*: Rugby, soccer, cross-country, cricket, athletics, tennis, sailing, canoeing, shooting, badminton, squash, curling, fencing, fives, golf, hockey, ski-ing, hailes, judo, horse-riding available. 200 take non-compulsory sport. 15 represent county/country (athletics, fencing, cricket, squash). *Other*: 35 have bronze Duke of Edinburgh's Award, 18 have silver and 15 gold. Other activities include a computer club, pipe band, chess, reel club, art, photography, bridge, expeditions during holidays, canal cruising.

Careers 4 part time careers advisors. Average number of pupils accepted for *arts and humanities degree courses* at Oxbridge, 4; other universities, 32; polytechnics or CHE, 11. *science and engineering degree courses* at Oxbridge, 7; other universities, 25; medical schools, 9; polytechnics or CHE, 7. *BEd*, 1. *other general training courses*, 1. Average number of pupils going straight into careers in armed services, 2; the church, 1; industry, 1; the City, 1; civil service, 1; music/drama, 2; careers overseas. 1. Traditional school careers are engineering, law, accountancy, medicine, Army (5 Army scholars, 86–87).

Uniform School uniform worn throughout.

Houses/prefects Competitive houses. Prefects (called Ephors), head boy and girl, head of house and house prefects – elected by school and appointed by Rector.

Religion Morning prayers for whole school; school services once a month; compulsory local church attendance for boarders.

Social Regular joint productions, debates, Burns suppers, reel club with St George's School for Girls. Organised trips and exchange systems with school abroad. Pupils allowed to bring own bike to school (car may be parked nearby with permission). Meals formal. School shop (books and stationery). No tobacco/alcohol allowed.

Discipline No corporal punishment. Pupils failing to produce homework once might expect a request via parents; those caught smoking cannabis on the premises may expect automatic expulsion.

Boarding 18 have own study bedroom, 5 share, 2 dormitories of 6+. Houses, of up to 35, single sex over 13. 2 resident qualified nurses plus 4 matrons. Central dining room. Pupils can provide and cook own food. 2 weekend exeats and half term each term. Visits to city allowed.

Alumni association run by Mr J M Martin, Secretary, Edinburgh Academical Club, c/o the Academy.

Former pupils Magnus Magnusson; Gordon Honeycombe; Paul Jones; Lord Cameron of Lochbroom; Giles Gordon; David Caute; Vice-Admiral Jock Slater; Ian Vallance; Ian Glen.

ELIZABETH COLLEGE

Elizabeth College
Guernsey
Channel Islands
Telephone number 0481 26544

Enquiries to the Principal's secretary
Application to the Bursar

Co-ed
● Boys
Girls
Mixed sixth
● Day
● Boarding

Pupils 557
Upper sixth 68
Termly fees:
Day £420
Boarding £1170
HMC

WHAT IT'S LIKE

Founded in 1563 by royal charter of Queen Elizabeth, it is one of the original HMC schools. It comprises an upper school and a lower school. The former lies on a hill overlooking the town and harbour of St Peter Port. The playing fields are on 2 sites of about 20 acres. A well-equipped establishment with plentiful modern resources. Religious worship is compulsory. A sound basic education is given and results are good (30–35 university entrants per year). A good range of games, sports and activities provided. Strong in music and drama. It has an active community service unit, a voluntary CCF and takes part in the Duke of Edinburgh's Award Scheme.

SCHOOL PROFILE

Pupils Total over 12, 557. Day 492; Boarding 65. Entry age, 7–16 but not into the fifth. Many are children of former pupils.

Entrance Common entrance and own entrance exam used. Not oversubscribed. No special skills or religious requirements. Parents not expected to buy text books. Gibson Fleming scholarships for boarders, up to full fees.

Parents 15+% in industry or commerce. 60+% live within 30 miles; up to 10% live overseas.

Staff Head R A Wheadon, in post for 16 years. 46 full time staff. 1 part time. Annual turnover less than 4%. Average age 40.

Academic work GCSE and A-levels. Average size of fifth 90; upper sixth 68. *O-levels*: on average, 90 pass 8+ subjects. *A-levels*: on average, 66 pass 3 subjects. On average, 68 take a mixture of both science and arts A-levels. *Computing facilities*: 16 BBC B type computers econetted together.

Senior pupils' non-academic activities *Music*: 60% learn a musical instrument, 10% to Grade 6 or above. 50% in school orchestra(s), wind band, brass band etc, 6% in school choir; 5% in Guernsey Youth Orchestra; 5% play in pop group. *Drama and dance*: 20% in school productions. 1% accepted for Drama Schools, 1% go on to work in theatre. *Art*: 10% take as non-examined subject, 30% take GCSE; 2% A-level. 1% accepted for Art School. 4% belong to photographic club. *Sport*: Football, hockey, tennis, squash, basketball, athletics, cross-country, swimming, shooting, sailing, archery, badminton, fencing and golf available. 80% take non-compulsory sport. 10% take exams in life saving, AAA Five star awards and fencing. 10% represent county/country at sport. *Other*: 10% take part in local community schemes. 30% have bronze Duke of Edinburgh's Award, 20% silver and 5% gold. 35% take part in CCF. Other activities include a computer club, sixth form society, theatre, electronics, literary, debating, chess, geography, film.

Careers 1 full time advisor. Average number of pupils accepted for *arts and* *humanities degree courses* at Oxbridge, 3; other universities, 10; polytechnics or CHE, 5. *science and engineering degree courses* at Oxbridge, 3; other universities, 10; medical schools, 4; polytechnics or CHE, 5. *BEd*, 1. Average number of pupils going straight into careers in armed services, 5; the church, 1; other, eg industry, civil service, 20.

Uniform School uniform worn throughout.

Houses/prefects Competitive houses. Prefects, head boy, head of house and house prefects – appointed by Principal.

Religion Christian worship compulsory.

Social Debates, joint theatre, ski trips, music occasions with local schools. Trips to France, Germany. Exchanges with Germany. Pupils allowed to bring own car/bike/motorbike to school. School tuck and book shops. No tobacco/alcohol allowed.

Discipline No corporal punishment. Pupils failing to produce homework once might expect a caution and explanation of the system; those caught smoking cannabis on the premises could expect expulsion.

Boarding 15% share with 1 or 2 others; 85% in dormitories of 6+. Resident qualified nurse. Central dining room. Pupils can provide and cook own food. Exeats as required (not overnight). Visits to local town allowed at housemaster's discretion.

Alumni association run by C P Meinke, Clifton House, Clifton Street, St Peter Port, Guernsey.

Former pupils Air Chief Marshal Sir Peter Le Cheminant (Lt Governor of the Baliwick of Guernsey, 2 I/C NATO forces Europe) + 4 Victoria Crosses.

ELLESMERE

Ellesmere College	Co-ed	Pupils 420
Ellesmere	● Boys	Upper sixth Yes
Shropshire SY12 9AB	Girls	Termly fees:
Telephone number 069 1712321	● Mixed sixth	Day £1420
	● Day	Boarding £2020
	● Boarding	HMC; Woodard

WHAT IT'S LIKE

Founded in 1884, it is one of the schools of the Society of Saints Mary and John of Lichfield, the Midland division of the Woodard Corporation, and is one of the original schools founded by Canon Woodard. It has a magnificent site of about 70 acres in beautiful Shropshire countryside (the main campus is surrounded by fields) with views across the North Shropshire plain to the Breidden Hills and the Berwyns. The school is so planned that all pupils and staff live under one roof. Its solid and elegant buildings stand amidst trees, lawns and gardens. There have been many improvements and additions in recent years and facilities are now first-rate. At the centre of the school life is the chapel where 'the community offers its common life to God and from it receives the incentive to fulfil its vocation'. The majority of pupils are Church of England but those of other denominations are welcome. There is considerable emphasis on religious instruction and worship in the Anglican tradition.

A large and well-qualified staff allows a staff:pupil ratio of about 1:10. Stress is put on the need for solitary private study. Academic standards are high and results consistently good. A lot of leavers go on to universities. The college has a very strong musical tradition and possesses two of the finest organs in the country. Drama and art are also strong and extensive use is made of the new arts centre, designed for drama, dance, film, music and art exhibitions. Artists of international repute in all these fields are invited regularly. The facilities are also used by the local community. All pupils are expected to take part in games and sports of which there is a wide variety and first-class facilities. Outdoor pursuits, for which the environment is ideal, including mountaineering, sailing and canoeing. The college has its own field centre near Betws-y-Coed for climbing and expeditions. All pupils are expected to join one of the following: training unit, CCF, venture scouts, social services. Groups are prepared for the Duke of Edinburgh's Award Scheme and much social work is done in the local community. Numerous clubs and societies cater for most extra-curricular needs.

SCHOOL PROFILE

Head New appointment in 1988
Age range 11–18; entry by common entrance or own exam. 5% of pupils are from overseas
Scholarships, bursaries and exhibitions available (including music, art and sons of clergy).

ELMHURST

Elmhurst Ballet School	● Co-ed		Pupils 233
Heathcote Road	Boys		Upper sixth Yes
Camberley	Girls		Termly fees:
Surrey GU15 2HS	Mixed sixth		Day £1250
Telephone number 0276 65301	● Day		Boarding £1710
	● Boarding		GSA

WHAT IT'S LIKE

Founded early in the 20th century, Elmhurst gradually evolved to its present position as a leading centre for training in dance and drama and has an international reputation. It has very pleasant premises and gardens in Camberley and excellent modern facilities, including a purpose-built 200 seat theatre. Religious education is an important part of the school's life. The school is basically C of E but other denominations are welcome. Services are held in the chapel. A full academic programme for GCSE and A-levels is provided and results are good. The main emphasis, of course, is on drama and dance. A highly qualified staff give instruction on all aspects of dance. The school has a number of large modern studios. Classical ballet (including Cecchetti), modern and contemporary dance, pas de deux, jazz, tap as well as Spanish and National are taught. Pupils are entered for exams in speech and drama. Theatre studies are also taught as a GCSE and A-level subject. Naturally, music is a very strong part of the school life. A standard range of sports and games is vailable. Entrance fees (in addition to termly ones) are £900 for pupils living overseas and £450 for pupils living in the UK.

SCHOOL PROFILE

Head Jeffrey Skitch (7 years)
Age range 9–19; entry by dancing audition
Selected A-levels offered.

ELTHAM COLLEGE

Eltham College
Grove Park Road
London SE9 4QF
Telephone number 01-857 1455

Enquiries/application to the Headmaster

Co-ed
● Boys
Girls
● Mixed sixth
● Day
● Boarding

Pupils 470
Upper sixth 75
Termly fees:
Day £1029
Boarding £2194
HMC

WHAT IT'S LIKE

Founded in 1842, originally for the sons of missionaries, it occupies a single suburban site of 25 acres, in handsome buildings (formerly those of the Royal Navy School). Its sister school, Walthamstow Hall, is in Sevenoaks. It remains loyal to its Christian foundation. The junior school is attached and 95% of junior pupils spend 11 years at the school. In terms of its size it has a most impressive record of university entrants (60 per year; nearly 40 in the last two years to Oxbridge). Very strong indeed in musical activities and in drama (new performing arts centre just completed). Excellent all-round facilities are provided. Standards in sports and games are high and there is a substantial commitment to local community service.

SCHOOL PROFILE

Pupils Total over 12, 470. Day 445 (boys 409, girls 36); Boarding 25 (boys). Entry age boys, 7, 8 and 11; boys and girls into the sixth. Own junior school provides about 60%. 10% are children of former pupils.
Entrance Own entrance exam used. Oversubscribed. Special skills welcome. No religious requirements but Christian (non-denominational) foundation emphasised. Parents not expected to buy text books. 102 assisted places in total. 19 scholarships/bursaries, 66–33% fees.
Parents 15+% in industry or commerce; 15+% in theatre, media, music, etc; 15+% are doctors, lawyers, etc.; 90+% live within 30 miles; up to 10% live overseas.
Staff Head Dr C D Waller, in post for 5 years. 49 full time staff, 9 part time. Annual turnover 5%. Average age 34.
Academic work GCSE, AS and A-levels. Average size of upper fifth 75; upper sixth 75. *O-levels*: on average, 10 pupils in upper fifth pass 1–4 subjects; 15, 5–7 subjects; 50 pass 8+ subjects. *A-levels*: on average, 5 pupils in upper sixth pass 1 subject; 10, 2 subjects; 45, 3 subjects and 14 pass 4 subjects. On average, 30% take science/engineering/maths A-levels; 30% take arts and humanities; 40% a mixture. Portuguese, geology and 5 different

sorts of maths are offered to A-level; Russian studies and Science in Society to AO-level. *Computing facilities*: An excellent computing room – GCSE and A-level computer studies are popular. Most academic departments have their own computer. *Special provisions*: access to specialists if problems emerge while at the school.

Senior pupils' non-academic activities   *Music*: 175 learn a musical instrument, 20 to Grade 6 or above. 1 accepted for Music School. 45 in school orchestra(s), 160 in school choir(s), 12 in school pop group, 30 in senior concert band; 46 in local orchestras; 8 play in pop group after leaving. Annual tour of cathedrals (eg Salisbury, Gloucester). *Drama and dance*: 50–150 in school productions; 1 or 2 accepted for Drama Schools. *Art*: 19 take as non-examined subject, 16 take GCSE; 16 A-level. 2 or 3 accepted for Art School. 25 belong to photographic club. *Sport*: Rugby, cricket, tennis, swimming, some hockey and soccer, badminton, squash, golf, cross-country, athletics available. All pupils take non-compulsory sport. 10% take exams. 17 represent county (rugby, cricket, swimming); 2 represent country (rugby, swimming). *Other*: 78 take part in local community schemes. D of E award scheme recently relaunched. 20 work for national charities. Other activities include a computer club, CDT, chess, International Society, College Society (distinguished speakers are invited), debating, public speaking, film, astronomical (observatory on site), printing, Christian Union.

Careers 1 full time advisor, assisted by sixth form tutors. Average number of pupils accepted for *arts and humanities degree courses* at Oxbridge, 9; other universities, 20; polytechnics or CHE, 5. *science and engineering degree courses* at Oxbridge, 9; other universities, 25; medical schools, 6; polytechnics or CHE, 5. *other general training courses*, 2. Average number of pupils going straight into careers in the armed services, 2; the church, 1; industry, 4; the City, 5; civil service, 2; music/drama, 2. Traditional school careers are medicine, engineering, the City.

Uniform School uniform worn throughout.

Houses/prefects Competitive houses. Prefects, head boy/girl, head of house and house prefects – elected by the school, appointed by the Head. School Council.

Religion Daily chapel compulsory.

Social Debates, conferences, dances, discos regularly shared with other local schools. 6 partner schools in France and Germany. Approximately 100 exchanges annually. Pupils allowed to bring own car/bike/motorbike to school. Meals formal. No tobacco/alcohol allowed.

Discipline No corporal punishment. Pupils failing to produce homework once might expect either a 40-minute detention or a double homework; those engaged in any drug-connected activities could expect expulsion. Constant contact between school and home actively encouraged and practised.

Boarding 25% have own study bedroom, 75% share with maximum of 3. Two houses, 18 and 7, divided by age group, single sex. Central dining room. Senior pupils can provide and cook own food. Exeats, very flexible. Visits to the local town allowed.

EMANUEL

Emanuel School
Battersea Rise
Wandsworth
London SW11 1SH
Telephone number 01-870 4171

Enquiries/application to Headmaster

Co-ed
● Boys
Girls
Mixed sixth
● Day
Boarding

Pupils 660
Upper sixth 65
Termly fees:
Day £896
HMC

WHAT IT'S LIKE

Founded in Westminster in 1594 by Lady Dacre (two of whose descendants are members of the governing body) it moved to Wandsworth in 1883 where it occupies a 10-acre site next to Wandsworth Common, just off the south circular and a few minutes' walk from Clapham Junction. There are many fine trees, lawns and big playing fields (there are other playing fields at Raynes Park) and, considering the site is less than 5 miles from the West End, it is surprisingly rich in fauna (including foxes). The main building is a handsome example of mid-Victorian architecture. Recent developments include excellent labs and two new classroom blocks. Facilities are good. The school is interdenominational and ecumenical; worship in the Anglican tradition is encouraged. There is a staff:pupil ratio of 1:13. Academic standards are high and results are good (especially in maths and the sciences). Twenty or more pupils go on to university each year. The music department is particularly strong (the choir is well known) and there is considerable strength in drama and art. The CDT centre is a very active and successful part of school life. A wide range of sports and games is available and standards are high, especially in rowing. Emanuel is one of the best rowing schools in Britain (its boat house is at Barnes Bridge) and has produced 5 Olympic oarsmen and over 50 international 'vests'. A flourishing CCF is RAF-based. A fair range of extra-curricular activities is provided and much use is made of London's cultural amenities. Rapidly rising roll (514 in 1984, 750 in 1988).

SCHOOL PROFILE

Pupils Total over 12, 660. Entry age, 10+, 11+, 13+ and into the sixth. 2% are children of former pupils.
Entrance Common entrance and own entrance exam used. Oversubscribed. Music and sport skills looked for; no religious requirements. Parents not expected to buy text books. 322 assisted places. 82 scholarships/bursaries, full fees to £100.
Parents 15% in industry or commerce. 60+% live within 30 miles.
Staff Head P F Thomson, in post for 4 years. 60 full time staff, 5 part time. Annual turnover 8%. Average age 35–40.
Academic work GCSE and A-levels. Average size of upper fifth 108; upper sixth 65. *O-levels*: on average, 33 pupils in upper fifth pass 1–4 subjects; 33, 5–7 subjects; 38 pass 8+ subjects. *A-levels*: on average, 9 pupils in upper sixth pass 1 subject; 16, 2 subjects; 21, 3 subjects and 5 pass 4 subjects. On average, 27 take science/engineering A-levels; 33 take arts and humanities; 5 a mixture. Russian, Polish offered to GCSE/A-level. *Computing facilities*:

Computer room with 25 BBC Masters; computer club room; machines in science department and CDT.

Senior pupils' non-academic activities *Music*: 75 learn a musical instrument, 10 to Grade 6 or above, 2 accepted for Music School; 27 in school orchestra, 52 in choir, 200 in house groups and inter-school pop groups. *Drama and dance*: 30–40 in school productions, 50–60 in other productions. 3 accepted for Drama School. 1 enters competitions, 2–3 go on to work in theatre. *Art*: 310 take as non-examined subject; 30 take GCSE; 10 A-level. 2 accepted for Art School. *Sport*: Rowing, rugby, cricket, soccer, tennis, badminton, golf, squash, table tennis, athletics, soft-ball, gymnastics available. Sport compulsory for all. Large number represent county/country eg in cricket, rugby, and rowing (50 internationals). *Other*: 10 take part in local community schemes. Other activities include active computer, chess and French clubs; debating, war games, dramatic societies, CCF.

Careers 1 full time and 1 part time advisor. Average number of pupils accepted for *arts and humanities degree courses* at Oxbridge, 3; other universities, 4; others to polytechnics or CHE. *science and engineering degree courses* at Oxbridge, 3; other universities, 12; medical schools, 4; others to polytechnics or CHE. *BEd*, 1.

Uniform School uniform worn throughout.

Houses/prefects Competitive houses. Prefects, head boy, head of house and house prefects – appointed by Head after consultation with staff.

Religion Compulsory assembly/chapel (Muslims exempt if parents wish); communion services.

Social Joint cultural events with local girls' schools. 3–4 trips abroad pa; exchange with French schools. Pupils allowed to bring own car/bike/motorbike to school. Meals self service. No tobacco/alcohol allowed.

Discipline No corporal punishment. Pupils failing to produce homework once might expect reprimand or detention; those caught smoking cannabis on the premises might expect an enquiry with subsequent suspension or expulsion, depending on circumstances.

Former pupils Stuart Surridge (cricketer); Michael Aspel (TV presenter); Leslie Henson (actor); Sir Denis Noble FRS; N F Simpson (dramatist).

EMBLEY PARK

Embley Park School	Co-ed	Pupils 180
Romsey	● Boys	Upper sixth 16
Hampshire SO51 6ZE	Girls	Termly fees:
Telephone number 0794 512206	● Mixed sixth	Day £1175
	● Day	Boarding £1780
Enquiries/application to the Headmaster's secretary, Mrs Jeanne de la Cuona	● Boarding	ISAI

WHAT IT'S LIKE

Founded in 1946, it is housed in a neo-Tudor mansion (formerly the family home of Florence Nightingale). It is in 70 acres of private park, including wild gardens, woodland and a lake, surrounded by splendid countryside bordering the New Forest. Altogether a delightful and healthy environment. It has all the advantages of a small school and takes boys of a wide ability range. The ethos and regime is basically that of a boarding school but there is an increasing number of day pupils. The sixth form is expanding. Very good modern facilities. Drama and art are quite strong, and there is strong emphasis on games and activities – which form part of every afternoon's curriculum. For a small school it has a phenomenal record of success in the Duke of Edinburgh's Award Scheme.

SCHOOL PROFILE

Pupils Total over 12, 180. Day 75; boarding 105 (boys). Entry age boys, 11+/13+ and into the sixth. Day girls will be accepted into the sixth from 1988.

Entrance Common entrance and own entrance exam used. Oversubscribed. No special skills or religious requirements. Parents expected to buy some text books. Academic/sporting scholarships and bursaries, £890–£585. Also bursaries for the children of services, clergy and teachers.

Parents 60% in industry or commerce; 15+% in the armed services. 30+% live within 30 miles; 10+% live overseas.

Staff Head D F Chapman, in post since Sept 1987. 15 full time staff, 5 part time. Annual turnover 5%. Average age 39.

Academic work GCSE, AS and A-levels. Average size of upper fifth 40; upper sixth 16. *O-levels*: on average, 20 pupils in upper fifth pass 1–4 subjects; 16, 5–7 subjects; 4 pass 8+ subjects. *A-levels*: on average, 5 pupils in upper sixth pass 1 subject; 3, 2 subjects; 3, 3 subjects and 2 pass 4 subjects. On average, 5 take science/engineering A-levels; 2 take arts and humanities; 8 a mixture. *Computing facilities*: Computer centre (BBC × 12). Special provisions for dyslexia and EFL.

Senior pupils' non-academic activities *Music*: 6 learn a musical instrument; 20 in school choir; 1 plays in pop group. *Drama and dance*: 20 in school productions, 60 in other drama/dance-related activities. *Art*: 6 take as non-examined subject; 25 take GCSE; 2, A-level. 1 accepted for Art School. 10 belong to photographic club. *Sport*: Cricket, tennis, golf, swimming, football, rugby, squash, athletics, karate, basketball, table tennis available. 70 take non-compulsory sport. 20 take exams. 4 represent county/country (cricket, rugby, squash). *Other*: 18 take part in local community schemes. 60 have bronze Duke of Edinburgh's Award, 20 silver and 7 gold. Other activities include a computer club, riding, shooting, fishing, drama, chess, debating, philately, canoeing, driving lessons etc. All pupils participate in activities programme on non-games afternoon.

Careers 1 part time advisor. Average number of pupils accepted for *arts and humanities degree courses* at universities, 2; polytechnics or CHE, 2. *science and engineering degree courses* at universities, 2; polytechnics or CHE, 3. *other general training courses*, 3. Average number of pupils going straight into careers in the armed services, 2; industry, 15; the City, 1; civil service, 1.

Uniform School uniform worn throughout.

Houses/prefects Competitive houses. Prefects, head boy, head of house and house prefects – appointed by housemaster and Headmaster.

Religion Some compulsory religious worship, other is encouraged.

Social Disco – 3 local girls' schools invited. Skiing trips (France/Switzerland), cultural exchanges (France), canoeing (France). Pupils allowed to bring own car/bike/motorbike/horse to school. Meals formal. School shop. No tobacco/ alcohol allowed.

Discipline No corporal punishment. Pupils failing to produce homework once might expect to re-do work, be detained, gated or put on housemaster's report; those caught smoking cannabis on the premises could expect expulsion.

Boarding 4% have own study bedroom (all sixth have studies), 50% are in dormitories of 6+. Houses, of approximately 30, same as competitive houses, single sex. Resident matron (SRN). Central dining room. Pupils can provide and cook own food. 5 weekend exeats each term. Visits to local town allowed occasionally and where necessary (15+).

Alumni association run by R Bell, Hon Secretary, 3 Windbrook Meadow, Stratton St Margaret, Swindon, Wiltshire.

EOTHEN

Eothen School	Co-ed Pupils 200
3 Harestone Hill	Boys Upper sixth 10
Caterham	● Girls Termly fees:
Surrey CR3 6SG	Mixed sixth Day £879
Telephone number 0883 43386	● Day GSA; Church School
	Boarding
Enquiries/application to the Headmistress	

WHAT IT'S LIKE

Founded in 1892, it belongs to the Church Schools' Company and occupies a pleasant wooded site of six and a half acres near the middle of Caterham, 2 minutes from the station. The junior school adjoins the main school in its own grounds. It has a good range of modern facilities and provides good teaching and a sound general education. There is a fair amount of musical and dramatic activity. Sport and games are well provided for.

SCHOOL PROFILE

Pupils Total over 12, 200. Entry age, 3–12 and into sixth. Own prep school provides over 20%. 5% are children of former pupils.

Entrance Own entrance exam used. Not oversubscribed. No special skills or religious requirements although the school belongs to the Church Schools Company (an Anglican body). Parents not expected to buy text books. Scholarships/bursaries are available and are means-tested, 20%–75% of fees.

Parents 60+% live within 30 miles.

Staff Head Miss D C Raine, in post for 15 years. 23 full time staff, 13 part time. Annual turnover 5%. Average age 45.

Academic work GCSE and A-levels. Average size of upper fifth 35; upper sixth 10. *O-levels*: on average, 11 pupils in upper fifth pass 1–4 subjects; 12, 5–7 subjects; 11 pass 8+ subjects. *A-levels*: on average, 1 pupil in upper sixth passes 1 subject; 3, 2 subjects; 7, 3 subjects and 1 passes 4 subjects. On average, 2 take science/engineering A-levels; 3 take arts and humanities; 5 a mixture. *Computing facilities*: 9 computers. Mildly dyslexic pupils given some extra help; preparation for EFL certificates.

Senior pupils' non-academic activities *Music*: 20 learn a musical instrument, 6 to Grade 6 or above, occasional pupil accepted for Music School. 5 in school orchestra, 20 in school choir; 1 in Croydon Wind Band, 1 in Sutton Schools Orchestra. *Drama and dance*: Numbers in school productions vary; occasional pupil accepted for Drama School or goes on to work in theatre. *Art*: 40 take GCSE; 2 or 3 A-level. Senior pupils can take Life Drawing classes. Occasional pupils accepted for Art School. Others go on to window dressing or theatrical costume design. *Sport*: Netball, lacrosse, tennis, rounders, short tennis, pop lacrosse, badminton, volleyball, basketball, gymnastics, athletics, judo, swimming available. 50 take non-compulsory sport. Occasionally pupils have represented county (judo, swimming, hurdles). *Other*: 8 have bronze Duke of Edinburgh's Award, 4 have silver and 2 gold. Some pupils enter voluntary schemes after leaving school. Other activities include a computer club, sixth form pre-driving course and electronics club.

Careers 1 part time careers advisor. Average number of pupils accepted for *arts and humanities degree courses* at universities, 2; polytechnics or CHE, 1. *science and engineering degree courses* at Oxbridge, 1; other universities, 1. *BEd*, 2. *other general training courses*, 2. Average number of pupils going straight into careers in industry, 1; the City, 2.

Uniform School uniform worn except in sixth.

Houses/prefects Competitive houses. All sixth formers act as prefects. Head girl appointed by the Head after consultation with staff and sixth form; house captains elected by school.

Religion Daily general assembly.

Social General studies lectures with Caterham School for Boys. Trips to France and Amsterdam and ski-ing. Pupils allowed to bring own car/bicycle to school. Meals self service. School shop selling second-hand uniform, run by parents. No tobacco/alcohol allowed.

Discipline No corporal punishment. Pupils failing to produce homework more than once might expect warning; those caught smoking on the premises could expect parents to be asked to see Head.

Alumni association is run by Mrs M Gabain, c/o the School.

Former pupils Imogen Holst; Richard Hughes; Dame Albertine Winner (co-founder of St Christopher's Hospice); Beroe Bicknell KC.

EPSOM COLLEGE

Epsom College	Co-ed	Pupils 643
Epsom	● Boys	Upper sixth 145
Surrey KT17 4JQ	Girls	Termly fees:
Telephone number 03727 23621	● Mixed sixth	Day £1500
	● Day	Boarding £2150
Enquiries/application to the Headmaster	● Boarding	HMC

WHAT IT'S LIKE

Founded in 1853, it has a fine site of 80 acres close to open countryside on Epsom Downs, 15 miles south of London. The main buildings are handsome

Victorian architecture; the modern ones fit in well. Considerable modernisation and extension in recent years. Now very well equipped with every facility. It is a school which expects pupils to aim for high academic standards and at the same time to be fully involved in the general life of an active community. The teaching is well known to be good and the standards are high (90–100 university entrants per year). There is a long-standing tradition of leavers studying medicine. A wide range of sport and games (again standards are high), plus many clubs and societies. Very strong in music and drama. A substantial commitment to local community schemes. As a C of E school, religious worship is encouraged.

SCHOOL PROFILE

Pupils Total, 643. Day 257 (boys 242, girls 15); Boarding 386 (boys 335, girls 51). Entry age, 13, boys; boys and girls into sixth. 10% are children of former pupils.

Entrance Common entrance and own entrance exam used. Oversubscribed. No special skills or religious requirements. Parents not expected to buy text books. 10 assisted places. 30 scholarships/bursaries for academic, all-rounder, music and art, 80% to 5% of fees.

Parents 15+% in industry or commerce; 15+% are doctors, lawyers, etc. 30+% live within 30 miles; up to 10% live overseas.

Staff Head Dr J B Cook, in post for 6 years. 62 full time staff, 20 part time. Annual turnover 5%. Average age 38.

Academic work GCSE and A-levels. Average size of upper fifth 120; upper sixth 145. *O-levels*: on average, 5 pupils in upper fifth pass 1–4 subjects; 35, 5–7 subjects; 80 pass 8+ subjects. *A-levels*: on average, 3 pupils in upper sixth pass 1 subject; 12, 2 subjects; 110, 3 subjects and 20 pass 4 subjects. On average, 70 take science/engineering A-levels; 50 take arts and humanities; 25 a mixture. *Computing facilities*: well equipped computer studies department. Many computers in other departments. Special help available for mild disabilities.

Senior pupils' non-academic activities *Music*: 250 learn a musical instrument, 50 to Grade 6 or above, 3 accepted for Music School; 100 in school orchestra/band, 85 in school choir; 1 in National youth orchestra. *Drama and dance*: 250 participate in school or house productions. Exams in drama and dance not offered. *Art*: 30 take as non-examined subject; 30 take GCSE, 25 take A-level. 5 accepted for Art School. 60 belong to photographic club. *Sport*: Rugby, cricket, hockey, soccer, athletics, tennis, squash, badminton, cross-country, golf, shooting, chess, bridge, netball, lacrosse, sailing, riding, swimming, sailboarding, fencing, gymnastics, volleyball, basketball, archery and rounders available. 500 take non-compulsory sport. Exams in sport not offered. 20 represent county/country (rugby, cricket, hockey, shooting, athletics, swimming, squash, tennis, golf). *Other*: 50 take part in local community schemes. 100 have bronze Duke of Edinburgh's Award, 50 have silver and 2 gold. Other activities include a computer club and 25 non-sporting clubs and societies.

Careers 3 part time careers advisors. Average number of pupils accepted for *arts and humanities degree courses* at Oxbridge, 4; other universities, 35; polytechnics or CHE, 5. *science and engineering degree courses* at Oxbridge, 10; other universities, 45; medical schools, 30; polytechnics or CHE, 10. *BEd*, 2. *other general training courses*, 2. Average number of pupils going straight into careers in armed services, 3; the church, 1; industry, 1; the City, 2; other, 2. Medicine is traditional school career.

Uniform School uniform worn throughout.

Houses/prefects Competitive houses. Prefects, head boy/girl and head of house appointed by the Head or Housemaster.

Religion Worship compulsory except for practising members of non-Christian religions.

Social Debates, intellectual and sporting competitions. Average of 5 trips abroad a year. Pupils allowed to bring own car/bicycle/motorbike to school. Meals self service. School shop. Sixth formers allowed beer on supervised occasions. No tobacco allowed.

Discipline No corporal punishment. All breaches of discipline dealt with according to the circumstances.

Boarding 10% have own study bedroom, 50% share; 30% are in dormitories of 6 or more. Houses, of approximately 60, are single sex. Two resident qualified nurses. Central dining room. Pupils can provide and cook own food. Exeats each weekend or each 3 weeks. Visits to the local town allowed.

Alumni association is run by Mrs P Benson, c/o the College.

Former pupils Graham Sutherland; John Piper.

Eton

Eton College
Eton
Windsor
Berkshire SL4 6DB
Telephone number 0753 869991

Enquiries/application to the Registrar

Co-ed   Pupils 1260
• Boys   Upper sixth 250
Girls   Termly fees:
Mixed sixth   Boarding £2585
Day   HMC
• Boarding

WHAT IT'S LIKE

Founded in 1440 by Henry VI for the worship of God, and for the training of young men to the service of Church and State. His aim was to have 70 so trained, first at Eton, then at King's College, Cambridge. These were his Scholars. He also provided for other boys to come from any part of the realm to be taught at Eton, paying for their own maintenance. In Henry's time, or shortly afterwards, most of the school's ancient buildings were completed. These include the chapel, the cloisters, the lower school, College Hall and part of College. Building and rebuilding have gone on ever since. The whole architectural complex constitutes an urbane and civilised enclave. The numerous premises are scattered in the town of Windsor and thus there is a close 'town and gown' relationship. There are beautiful gardens and playing fields and the school is one of the best-equipped in existence. There are several excellent libraries: the College library has a remarkable collection of rare books and manuscripts. There is considerable emphasis on religious instruction. Worship during a boy's time in the school is designed to meet his spiritual needs at each stage of his development. Academically Eton is very high-powered indeed. A large and very well-qualified staff permits a staff:

pupil ratio of 1:9. Academic results are outstanding. Each year 205–210 pupils (more than any other school in Britain) go on to university; this figure includes 65–70 to Oxbridge. It is immensely strong in music (600 boys learn an instrument) and also in drama. The purpose-built Farrer theatre is in constant use and the English department has a drama studio in the Caccia Schools. In the course of a year there may be 20 main productions and house plays. The art department is also extremely strong. There is a very wide range of sports and games (including the Eton wall game and the Eton field game, both peculiar to the college) in which very high standards are achieved (a very large number of representatives at county and national level). At any one time 50 or more clubs and societies are active and these cater for every conceivable need. The school has its own newspaper (The Eton College Chronicle) which has been published regularly each half since 1863. There is a substantial commitment to local community services, plus the Eton-Dorney project for conferences, discussion and social work involving disadvantaged children from elsewhere, and the Eton Action fund-raising organisation. The CCF and the Police Cadet unit are very well supported.

SCHOOL PROFILE

Pupils Total, 1260. Entry age, 13+ and into the sixth. 45% are children of former pupils.

Entrance Common entrance used following preliminary entrance exam at age 10. Oversubscribed. No special skills or religious requirements, although school is C of E. Parents expected to buy a few senior text books. 155 scholarships (academic, music, junior, sixth form), full fees to £250 per term; 120 bursaries.

Parents 15+% are doctors, lawyers etc; 15+% in industry or commerce. 30+% live within 30 miles; up to 10% live overseas.

Staff Head W E K Anderson, in post for 8 years. 136 full time staff, 6 part time. Annual turnover 6%. Average age mid thirties.

Academic work GCSE and A-levels. Average size of upper fifth 250; upper sixth 250. *O-levels*: on average, 10 pupils in upper fifth pass 5–7 subjects; 240 pass 8+ subjects. *A-levels*: on average, 6 pupils in upper sixth pass 1 subject; 19, 2 subjects; 160, 3 subjects and 65 pass 4 subjects. On average, 34 take science/engineering A-levels; 149 take arts and humanities; 67 a mixture. Russian, Portuguese offered to GCSE/A-level. *Computing facilities*: Two computer rooms; 1 or more in most departments.

Senior pupils' non-academic activities *Music*: Occasional pupil accepted for Music School; 2/3 organ/choral awards to Oxbridge. *Drama and dance*: 360 in 20 school productions pa; 100 house drama competition. 6 take A-level Drama; 1 accepted for Drama School. *Art*: 350 take as non-examined subject; 40 take GCSE; 25, A-level. 6 accepted for Art School. *Sport*: Soccer, rugby, cricket, rowing, squash, rackets, fives, swimming, judo, aikido, basketball, fencing, athletics, shooting, tennis, golf, badminton, Eton Field Game, Eton Wall Game available. 1100 take non-compulsory sport, 400 take exams (sub-aqua, gymnastics, life-saving, survival swimming). 36 pupils represent county; 17, country (rowing, swimming, water polo, rugby, cricket, athletics, golf, fencing, fives, shooting). *Other*: 130 take part in local community schemes. Other activities include computer club, social service, political, Keynes, art, history societies, CCF, beagles.

Careers 4 part time advisors. Average number of pupils accepted for *arts* *and humanities degree courses* at Oxbridge, 43; other universities, 105; polytechnics or CHE, 10. *science and engineering degree courses* at Oxbridge, 22; other universities, 35; medical schools, 3; polytechnics or CHE, 5. Average number of pupils going straight into careers in armed services, 10%; 2–3% in industry, the City, music/drama, other.

Uniform School uniform worn throughout.

Houses/prefects Competitive houses. Prefects, head boy, head of house and house prefects.

Religion Compulsory religious assembly unless parents request otherwise.

Social 4-day exchanges with certain comprehensive schools. French, Spanish and German exchanges; 1- or 2-person exchanges with USA, Japan; occasional trips to Russia, Malawi, Australia etc. Meals formal in some houses, self service in the remainder. Some alcohol allowed for senior boys; no tobacco.

Discipline No corporal punishment. Pupils failing to produce homework once might expect extra work; those caught smoking cannabis on the premises might expect rustication or expulsion.

Boarding All have own study bedroom. Houses, of approximately 50, are the same as competitive houses. Resident qualified nurse and doctor. Central dining room (for half houses). Pupils can provide and cook own food within limits. 1 exeat per term (week in autumn term, weekend in other 2 terms). Visits to local town allowed.

Alumni association run by N J T Jaques Esq, c/o the College.

Former pupils Alec Douglas-Home; Harold Macmillan; Douglas Hurd; Lord Hailsham; Sir Robert Armstrong; Anthony Powell; Lord Carrington; Robin Leigh-Pemberton; Archbishop of York.

ETON HOUSE

Eton House School
Southchurch Lawn
Thorpe Bay
Essex SS3 0PY
Telephone number 0702 582553

Enquiries/application to the Headmaster

Co-ed
● Boys
Girls
Mixed sixth
● Day
Boarding

Pupils 30
Upper sixth 3
Termly fees:
Day £455
ISAI

WHAT IT'S LIKE

Founded in 1898, it has an agreeable rural site on the outskirts of Southend-on-Sea in 26 acres of attractive grounds with a lake and woodlands. Well equipped with modern facilities, the school is well known for its high standards of discipline. Good manners and academic excellence are encouraged. The music department is flourishing and there is a fair range of basic games, clubs, societies etc. It has a strong Old Boys' association which organises a careers advisory panel through which pupils are put in touch with old boys for personal and direct advice about their future.

SCHOOL PROFILE

Pupils Total over 12, 30. Entry age, 5–6 or 10–11. Own prep school provides 20+%. 5% are children of former pupils.

Entrance NFER entrance exam used. Usually oversubscribed. No special skills or religious requirements. Parents expected to buy text books. Occasional scholarships/bursaries.

Parents 60+% live within 30 miles.

Staff Principal Mr S H Tomlinson since 1926. Pastoral Headmaster, Mr T R Sharp; Academic Headmaster, Mr J Pendegrass. 6 full time staff, 5 part time. Annual turnover 1 every few years.

Academic work GCSE and A-levels. Average size of upper fifth 25; upper sixth 3. *O-levels*: on average, 5 pupils in upper fifth pass 1–4 subjects; 15, 5–7 subjects; 5 pass 8+ subjects. *A-levels*: this is school's first A-level form. *Computing facilities*: 4 BBC and 1 'mini' computer. Help given for mildly handicapped as appropriate.

Senior pupils' non-academic activities *Music*: 2/3 learn a musical instrument; 60 in school choir (including juniors). *Art*: 10 take as non-examined subject; 10 take GCSE art; 2 take A-level art. 1 accepted for Art School. 12 belong to photographic club. *Sport*: Association football, cricket, gymnastics, tennis and judo available. 10 take non-compulsory sport. 12 take exams in eg gymnastics. 1 represents county/country (diving). *Other*: Other activities include a computer club, chess club with outside court, philatelic society, debating society and photographic society.

Careers 1 full time careers advisor. This is school's first A-level year; no pupils have gone onto degree courses as yet. Average number of pupils going straight into careers in industry, 7; the City, 7; civil service, 1; other, 2.

Uniform School uniform worn throughout.

Houses/prefects Competitive houses. Prefects and head boy; head of house – elected by the house.

Religion Religious worship is compulsory.

Social Gymnastic and sporting events with all local schools eg debating, chess, art competitions. Ski holidays and other trips abroad on various occasions. Pupils allowed to bring own bicycle to school. Meals formal. School shop. No tobacco/alcohol allowed.

Discipline Corporal punishment possible but rare. Pupils failing to produce homework might expect to repeat the work in own time; those caught smoking cannabis on the premises judged upon circumstances.

Alumni association is run by Mr D W Davy, MBIM, c/o the School.

Former pupils CO for logistics in the Falkland campaign; a member of the Mastermind Team; a consultant haematologist.

EWELL CASTLE

Ewell Castle		Co-ed	Pupils 320
Church Street	•	Boys	Upper sixth 30
Ewell		Girls	Termly fees:
Surrey	•	Mixed sixth	Day £880
Telephone number 01-393 1413	•	Day	SHMIS; GBA
Enquiries/application to the Headmaster		Boarding	

WHAT IT'S LIKE

Founded in 1926, the main building is a castellated mansion in 15 acres of gardens and playing fields which were once part of Nonsuch Park (the grounds of Henry VIII's Nonsuch Palace). Altogether a pleasant environment in the Surrey green belt. There have been extensive modern additions and facilities are good. The co-educational junior school has a separate site close by. An interdenominational school, it is not narrowly academic. Its sporting record is good and it has a well-organised pastoral system. High standards of discipline are expected.

SCHOOL PROFILE

Pupils Total over 12, 320 (boys 317, girls 3). Entry age, 3 upwards, boys; girls directly into the sixth.

Entrance Common entrance and own entrance exam used. Moderately oversubscribed. No special skills or religious requirements. Parents not expected to buy text books. Some scholarships/bursaries available, up to 75% of fees.

Parents 30+% in industry or commerce. 60+% live within 30 miles.

Staff Head R A Fewtrell, in post for 5 years. 41 full time staff. Annual turnover 5%. Most staff under 40.

Academic work GCSE and A-levels. Average size of upper fifth 72; upper sixth 30. *O-levels*: 30% pass 7+ subjects. *A-levels*: on average, 3 pupils in upper sixth pass 1 subject; 4, 2 subjects; 15, 3 subjects and 2 pass 4 subjects. On average, 12 take science/engineering A-levels; 6 take arts and humanities; 6 a mixture. *Computing facilities*: 20 BBC micros – used both in Computer Studies and in CDT and Science. Some limited extra teaching for those not native English speakers.

Senior pupils' non-academic activities *Music*: 30 learn a musical instrument, 2 up to Grade 6 or above. About 6 play in orchestras. Some 6 continue their interest in music beyond school. *Drama and dance*: School productions; exams not offered. *Art*: 20 take GCSE; 10 take A-level; 1–2 pa accepted for Art School. 50 belong to eg photographic club. *Sport*: Rugby, soccer, cricket, tennis, fencing, squash, cross country, athletics, swimming available. Compulsory to 5th year. Most of sixth form take part in non-compulsory sport. 6 represent county/country (squash, cricket, rugby). *Other*: Some take part in local community schemes. Other activities include a computer club, bridge, rifle club, Army Cadet Force, railway club.

Careers 2 part time careers advisors. Average number of pupils accepted for *arts and humanities degree courses* at universities, 1; polytechnics or CHE, 3. *science and engineering degree courses* at universities, 7; polytechnics or

CHE, 2. *BEd*, 1. *other general training courses*, 1. Fifth year leavers – about 30% go on to technical and sixth form colleges and the rest into employment.
Uniform School uniform worn throughout.
Houses/prefects Competitive houses. Prefects and head boy appointed by head.
Religion Religious worship is compulsory unless exempted by parental request.
Social Joint theatrical ventures with local girls' school. Rugby, ski-ing trips abroad. French Exchange with Avignon. Pupils allowed to bring own car/bicycle/motorbike to school. Meals self service. School tuck shop. No tobacco/alcohol allowed.

EXETER

Exeter School
Exeter
Devon EX2 4NS
Telephone number 0392 73679

Enquiries to the Headmaster
Application to the Headmaster's
  secretary

Co-ed   Pupils 614
● Boys   Upper sixth 110
  Girls   Termly fees:
● Mixed sixth   Day £830
● Day   Boarding £1530
● Boarding   HMC

WHAT IT'S LIKE

Founded in 1633, it stands in 27 acres of pleasant grounds within a mile of the City centre. It has occupied its present site since 1880 and most of its well-designed buildings date from that time. There have been many recent additions and it now enjoys first-rate facilities. A C of E school its moral and spiritual life depends on a general acceptance of Christian values. There is emphasis on encouragement to the individual, on self-discipline and self-motivation. A well-run school with high all-round standards and impressive academic results (90 university entrants per year). There is a massive involvement in music and drama. A very good range of games and sports (high standards attained) and outdoor activities (eg adventure training on Dartmoor). The school has always been closely involved with the life of the City and its university and it has a substantial commitment to local community schemes.

SCHOOL PROFILE

Pupils Total over 12, 614. Day 610 (boys 594, girls 16); Boarding 4 (boys). Entry age, 11, 12, 13, boys; into the sixth boys and girls. Exeter Prep school provides over 20%. 15% are children of former pupils.
Entrance Common entrance and own entrance exam used. Oversubscribed. No special skills required but sport and the arts help. No particular religious persuasion required, but Christians fit most easily. Parents not expected to buy text books. 30 assisted places. 4+ scholarships/bursaries, 10–100% fees.
Parents 10+% are doctors. 60+% live within 30 miles; up to 10% live overseas.

Staff Head G T Goodall, in post for 9 years. 50 full time staff, 10 part time. Annual turnover 6%. Average age 37.

Academic work GCSE and A-levels. Average size of upper fifth 100; upper sixth 110. *O-levels*: on average, 3 pupils in upper fifth pass 1–4 subjects; 23, 5–7 subjects; 70 pass 8+ subjects. *A-levels*: on average, 7 pupils in upper sixth pass 1 subject; 14, 2 subjects; 64, 3 subjects and 15 pass 4 subjects. On average, 55% take science/engineering A-levels; 35% take arts and humanities; 10% a mixture. *Computing facilities*: Computer in every major department. Computer laboratory with 20 computers.

Senior pupils' non-academic activities *Music*: 300 learn a musical instrument, 30 up to Grade 6 or above, 3 accepted for Music School; 7 orchestras with a total of 200 pupils, 100 in school choir, 30 in school pop group (joint with St Margaret's School); 1 in National Youth Orchestra, 4 in county orchestra. *Drama and dance*: 200 in school productions; 3 in NYMT. 6 accepted for drama schools and degree courses, 2 to work in theatre. *Art*: 20 take as non-examined subject; 20 take GCSE, 12 take A-level. 2 accepted for Art School. 20 belong to eg photographic club. *Sport*: Hockey, cross country, cricket, athletics, tennis, swimming, squash, badminton, basketball, golf, canoeing, volleyball available. 150–200 take non-compulsory sport. 50 or more pupils represent county (cricket, squash, golf, tennis, rugby, badminton, athletics, hockey, basketball, running). *Other*: 60 take part in local community schemes. 10 have bronze Duke of Edinburgh's Award, 6 have silver and 3 have gold. Other activities include a computer club, 20 or more clubs from debating to classics or chess.

Careers 2 full time and 1 part time careers advisors. Average number of pupils accepted for *arts and humanities degree courses* at Oxbridge, 6; other universities, 30; polytechnics or CHE, 5. *science and engineering degree courses* at Oxbridge, 12; other universities, 40; medical schools, 8–10; polytechnics or CHE, 10. *BEd*, 2. Average number of pupils going straight into careers in armed services, 6–8; industry, 8–10; music/drama, 2 or 3. Tradition of pupils going into engineering and medicine.

Uniform School uniform worn except in the sixth form.

Houses/prefects Competitive houses. Prefects, head boy, head of house and house prefects – appointed by the Head and the school.

Religion Morning assemblies in chapel, 11–16 year olds.

Social Joint sixth form lessons and theatrical productions with local girls' school. Annual trips abroad. Exchanges to Rennes and Hildesheim, Soviet Union and USA. Pupils allowed to bring own car/bicycle/motorbike to school. Meals self service. School shop. No tobacco/alcohol allowed.

Discipline No corporal punishment. Pupils failing to produce homework once might expect detention; if caught smoking cannabis on the premises punishment would depend on whether it was repeated.

Boarding Sixth formers have own study bedroom, others share, 2–3. One boarding house of 60 pupils. No resident medical staff. Central dining room. Pupils can provide and cook own food. Exeats at weekends and half term. Visits to the local town allowed.

Alumni association is run by D Mullins, c/o the School.

Former pupils MPs, bishops, TV commentators, actors, conductors, generals, explorers, scientists and so on. Former CinC NATO NW Europe and Commandant of the Parachute Regiment.

FARLINGTON

Farlington School
Strood Park
Horsham
West Sussex RH12 3PN
Telephone number 0403 54967

Enquiries/application to the Headmistress

Co-ed
Boys
● Girls
Mixed sixth
● Day
● Boarding

Pupils 210
Upper sixth 11
Termly fees:
Day £1100
Boarding £1800
GSA

WHAT IT'S LIKE

Founded in 1896, it lies in delightful grounds and gardens in a large park. The main building, formerly a country house, is part Jacobean and part Georgian. Other handsome buildings are nearby. New facilities were added in 1980 and a programme for 1988–89 will provide further classrooms and sixth form facilities. A sound general education is provided and results are creditable. About 8 leavers go on to university each year. The music, games and art depts are very active. A good range of sport, games and activities. Excellent record in the Duke of Edinburgh's Award Scheme.

SCHOOL PROFILE

Pupils Total over 12, 210. Day 148; Boarding 62. Entry age 9, 11 and into the sixth.
Entrance Own entrance exam used. Oversubscribed. No special religious requirements. Likes girls who have active extra-curricular interests (music, sport). Parents not expected to buy text books. 6 scholarships/bursaries pa, half to one-third fees.
Parents 60+% live within 30 miles; up to 10% live overseas.
Staff Head Mrs P Metham, in post for 1 year. 26 full time staff, 27 part time. Annual turnover 5%. Average age 45.
Academic work GCSE and A-levels. Average size of upper fifth 44; upper sixth 11. *O-levels*: on average, 16 pupils in upper fifth pass 1–4 subjects; 12, 5–7 subjects; 14 pass 8+ subjects. *A-levels*: on average, 2 in upper sixth pass 1 subject; 2, 2 subjects; 3 pass 3 subjects. On average, 2 take science/engineering A-levels; 7 take arts and humanities; 2 a mixture. *Computing facilities*: 7 BBC B computers on a level II Econet network, 1 Commodore PET. Limited dyslexia provision for otherwise able girls.
Senior pupils' non-academic activities *Music*: 50 learn a musical instrument, 20 up to Grade 6 or above. 5 accepted for Music School; 20 in school orchestra, 50 in school choir, 15 in wind band. *Drama and dance*: 15 in school productions, 20 take LAMDA exams. 1 accepted for Drama/Dance school; 25 take extra speech and drama. *Art*: 20 take as non-examined subject; 20 take GCSE; 4, A-level; 2 accepted for Art School. 15 belong to photographic club. *Sport*: Hockey, netball, volleyball, rounders, tennis, athletics, swimming, dance, gym, running, ice skating, riding, ballet, judo, gliding, ski-ing available. 15 take non-compulsory sport. 20 take sailing, windsurfing, riding etc. 10 take exams. 2 represent county (hockey, tennis). *Other*: 5 take part in local community schemes. 22 have bronze Duke of Edinburgh's Award, 16 have silver and 5 gold. 2 work for national charities. Other activities include computer, art and typing clubs.

Careers 1 full time advisor. Average number of pupils accepted for *arts and humanities degree courses* at universities, 3; polytechnics or CHE, 1; *BEd*, 2. *other general training courses*, 20.

Uniform School uniform worn except the sixth.

Houses/prefects Competitive houses. Prefects, head girl, head of house and house prefects, elected by staff and pupils. School Council.

Religion Short religious assembly each day, juniors 1 period of RS per week; seniors 1 period of ethics.

Social Joint concerts, mainly choral, with neighbouring schools such as Cranleigh, Hurstpierpoint. Annual ball and discos. Organised trips to France, art trips to Italy, ski holidays in Alps, individual exchanges. Pupils allowed to bring own car/bike/motorbike to school. Some meals self service. No school shop but frequent sales of goods for charity. No tobacco/alcohol allowed.

Discipline No corporal punishment. Pupils failing to produce homework once might expect discussion with the subject teacher; those caught smoking cannabis on the premises should expect suspension, parental involvement and likely expulsion.

Boarding 5% have own study bedroom, 12% share with others; 70% are in dormitories of 6 or more. Houses are divided as for competitive purposes. Resident qualified nurse. Central dining room. 2 weekend exeats each term. Visits to the local town allowed for 14/15 upwards.

Alumni association is run by Mrs P Murphy, Farlington School.

FARNBOROUGH HILL

Farnborough Hill Convent College	Co-ed	Pupils 435
Farnborough	Boys	Upper sixth 38
Hampshire GU14 8AT	● Girls	Termly fees:
Telephone number 0252 545197	Mixed sixth	Day £878
Enquiries to the Headmistress	● Day	GSA
	Boarding	

WHAT IT'S LIKE

Founded in 1889 by the Religious of Christian Education, the school was favoured by the ex-Empress Eugenie. After her death and that of Prince Victor Napoleon the trustees of the college bought her estate of Farnborough Hill (in 1927). The whole school is established in the Empress's former home. This lies in the highest part of Hampshire on an estate of parklands and gardens covering 35 acres. Four school blocks and a chapel have been added, to make a very agreeable campus. It is Roman Catholic and the primary purpose is to provide an education which will help girls to become mature and committed Christians. Preference is given to Roman Catholics. Others must subscribe to the school's value system. Mass and assembly are compulsory. Exam results are good. There is a wide range of sports and games and a variety of clubs and societies.

SCHOOL PROFILE

Pupils Total over 12, 435. Entry age, 11 and into the sixth. 1% are children of former pupils.

Entrance Common entrance, APS and own tests used. Usually oversubscribed. No special skills required. Preference given to Roman Catholics, others must subscribe to value system of school. Parents not expected to buy text books. Assisted places and bursaries available.

Parents 15+% in industry or commerce; 15+% are doctors, lawyers, etc.

Staff Head Sister Sylvia Cousins, in post for 5 years. 28 full time staff, 23 part time. Annual turnover 8–10%.

Academic work GCSE and A-levels. Average size of fifth 75; upper sixth 38. *Computing facilities*: recently upgraded; network being installed. Mildly dyslexic pupils admitted.

Senior pupils' non-academic activities Many pupils involved in music and drama. *Sport*: Hockey, netball, basketball, volleyball, badminton, tennis, cross-country, athletics, gymnastics, swimming, lacrosse, archery (also, outside school for sixth form, squash, windsurfing, riding; plus popmobility, keep-fit, ballroom dancing) available. Other activities include a computer club, fund-raising through house system, drama, sports, art workshops, strong choral tradition.

Careers 1 full time careers advisor.

Uniform School uniform worn except in the sixth form.

Houses/prefects Houses competitive only for sports and an annual quiz. Prefects, head girl, head of house (house captain) appointed by the Head after consultation with staff and senior pupils.

Religion School Masses and assemblies compulsory.

Social Debates with other schools; oratorio with other schools and parents and other adult contacts; dances for sixth form. Regular visits abroad, exchanges with France, Spain, Germany. Pupils allowed to bring own car/bicycle to school. School meals or sandwiches. School shop. No tobacco/alcohol allowed.

Discipline Various sanctions imposed according to misdemeanour. Detentions may be given outside school hours. Suspension reserved for serious offences.

Alumni assocation is run by Miss Kim Hasty (Secretary), FHOGA.

FARRINGTON

Farringtons Girls' School	Co-ed	Pupils 241
Chislehurst	Boys	Upper sixth 30
Kent BR7 6LR	● Girls	Termly fees:
Telephone number 01-467 5586	Mixed sixth	Day £977
	● Day	Boarding £1785
Enquiries to the Headmistress	● Boarding	GBSA

WHAT IT'S LIKE

Founded in 1911, it lies in 22 acres of fine wooded parkland in the green belt on the borders of Kent and 12 miles south-east of central London. The buildings are well designed, comfortable and pleasant to look at. Every modern facility is provided and the boarding accommodation is comfortable. The junior and senior schools are combined so education can be continuous from 5–18. A Christian atmosphere is fostered; the chapel is central both physically and spiritually. A good all-round education is given and exam results are good; 12–20 pupils go on to university. The music and drama departments are flourishing. A good range of sports and games and a fair commitment to the Duke of Edinburgh Award Scheme.

SCHOOL PROFILE

Pupils Total over 12, 241. Day 73; boarding 168. Entry age, 11, and into the sixth. Own Junior School provides over 70%.

Entrance Own entrance exam and, rarely, common entrance exam used. Sometimes oversubscribed. No special skills or religious requirements. Parents expected to buy text books after year 3. 4 bursaries, from full fees to fractional fees.

Parents 15+% in industry or commerce. 10+% live within 30 miles; 30+% live overseas.

Staff Head Mrs B J Stock, in post for 1 year. 30 full time staff, 12 part time. Annual turnover 2%. Average age 35.

Academic work GCSE, A-levels and CEE. Average size of upper fifth 50; upper sixth 30. *O-levels*: on average, 20 pupils in upper fifth pass 1–4 subjects; 20, 5–7 subjects; 7 pass 8+ subjects. *A-levels*: on average, 7 pupils in upper sixth pass 1 subject; 6, 2 subjects; 10, 3 subjects and 2 pass 4 subjects. On average, 10 take science/engineering A-levels; 18 take arts and humanities; 2 a mixture. *Computing facilities*: computer room, club, sixth form course, timetabled years 1–3. Dyslexic tuition and extra English for non native English speakers available.

Senior pupils' non-academic activities *Music*: 24 learn a musical instrument, 8 up to Grade 6 or above, 1 accepted for Music School; 5 in school orchestra, 44 in school choir. *Drama and dance*: 23 take ballet or modern/tap dancing; 3 take ballet exams. *Art*: 25 take GCSE; 11 take A-level, 6 take History of Art; 3 accepted for Art School, 1 for University course. *Sport*: Lacrosse, tennis, netball, squash, judo, trampolining, dry ski-ing, gymnastics and athletics available. Most take non-compulsory sport. 30–40 take exams in gymnastics, swimming, trampolining, and 30 in ski-ing. 8 represent county (lacrosse). *Other*: 36 have bronze Duke of Edinburgh's Award, 9 silver. Other activities include a computer club.

Careers 1 part time careers advisor. Average number of pupils accepted for *arts and humanities degree courses* at Oxbridge, 1; elsewhere, 6. *science and engineering degree courses*: 6; medical schools 1. *other general training courses*, 2. Average number of pupils going straight into careers in armed services, 2; the City, 1; welfare, 1. Traditional school careers are in engineering/maths.

Uniform School uniform worn except in the sixth form.

Houses/prefects Competitive houses. Prefects, head girl and head of house elected by the upper sixth and appointed by the Head. School Council.

Religion Religious attendance compulsory.

Social Joint musical productions with Eltham College. Organised trips abroad. Pupils allowed to bring own car/bicycle to school. Meals self service. School shop. No tobacco/alcohol allowed.

Discipline No corporal punishment. Pupils failing to produce homework once might expect to repeat it twice; those caught smoking cannabis on the premises could expect expulsion.

Boarding Houses divided by age group. Qualified nurse. Central dining room. Pupils can provide and cook own food. 2 exeats per term of 2 days. Visits to the local town allowed for years 4 upwards, Saturday afternoons.

Alumni association is run by Miss Kathleen Hargreaves, c/o the School.

FELIXSTOWE

Felixstowe College
Maybush Lane
Felixstowe
Suffolk IP11 7NQ
Telephone number 0394 284269

Enquiries/application to
Mrs P Dangerfield (Registrar)

Co-ed Pupils 294
Boys Upper sixth 37
● Girls Termly fees:
Mixed sixth Day £1136
● Day Boarding £1865
● Boarding GSA

WHAT IT'S LIKE

Founded in 1929, it is a single site and right by the sea, within fairly easy range of Ipswich and Norwich. Many of the school buildings were originally family homes. A continuous programme of modernisation and extension has gone on to create a compact and well-equipped campus with spacious playing fields and agreeable gardens. All girls attend chapel and religious studies and the life of the chapel is an important part of the school. A friendly and happy 'family' atmosphere prevails. The education is sound and broad-based. Exam results are good and a fair number of pupils (12–20) go on to university each year. Very strong indeed in music (almost everyone is involved); pretty strong in drama. A fair and standard range of sport, games and extra-curricular activities. Substantial commitment to local community services, and a remarkable record in the Duke of Edinburgh's Award Scheme.

SCHOOL PROFILE

Pupils Total over 12, 294. Day 28; Boarding 266. Entry age, 11 and into sixth. 10% are children of former pupils.

Entrance Common entrance exam used. Sometimes oversubscribed. No special skills required. Church of England foundation; other religions accepted. Parents not expected to buy text books. Some scholarships/bursaries; full fees to one sixth fees.

Parents 15+% are farmers; 15+% in Armed Services; 15+% are doctors, lawyers, etc. 30+% live within 30 miles; 10+% live overseas.

Staff Head Mrs A F Woodings. 43 full time staff, 9 part time. Annual turnover 10%. Average age 39.

Academic work GCSE and A-levels. Average size of upper fifth 64; upper sixth 37. *O-levels*: on average, 17 pupils in upper fifth pass 1–4 subjects; 19, 5–7 subjects; 16 pass 8+ subjects. *A-levels*: on average, 10 pupils in upper

sixth pass 1 subject; 6, 2 subjects; 10, 3 subjects and 9 pass 4 subjects. On average, 19 take science/engineering A-levels; 15 arts and humanities; 6 a mixture. *Computing facilities*: fully-equipped computer room with nine BBC microcomputers with disc drives; 4 printers. Some EFL provision.

Senior pupils' non-academic activities *Music*: 189 learn a musical instrument, 57 up to Grade 6 or above, 8 take GCSE, 3 A-level, 1 accepted for Music School, 1/2 accepted for teacher training (music), 36 in school orchestra, 40 in school choir, 6 in school pop group, 13 in wind ensemble, 16 in string ensemble, 15 in Gilbert and Sullivan group, 3 in Suffolk Schools Orchestra, 1 in National Children's Wind Orchestra of Great Britain; 8/10 in London-based choral societies. *Drama and dance*: 27 in school productions; 36 in speech and drama lessons, 39 public speaking course, 49 in ISTD dance (modern, tap and ballet); 34 take LAMDA exams, 31 ISTD Dance Exam; 1 accepted for Drama School, 5 for Dance School. *Art*: 3 take as non-examined subject, 40 take GCSE, 10 A-level, 12 history of art. 2/3 go on to degree courses in history of art; 2/3 accepted for Art School. *Sport*: Hockey, tennis rounders, swimming, netball, trampolining, golf, badminton, clay pigeon shooting available. 120 take non-compulsory sport. 4–5 pupils represent county (junior) at hockey. *Other*: 42 take part in local community schemes. 50 have bronze Duke of Edinburgh's Award, 20 have silver and 20, gold. Other activities include computer club, chess club, debating society, gym club, bible study groups, bridge club, country dancing, madrigal society.

Careers 8 part time careers advisors. Average number of pupils accepted for *arts and humanities degree courses* at Oxbridge, 1; other universities, 9; polytechnics or CHE, 6. *science and engineering degree courses* at Oxbridge, 1; other universities, 4; medical schools, 5; polytechnics or CHE, 2. BEd, 1. *other general training courses*, 7. Average number of pupils going straight into careers in armed services, 1; industry, 2; music/drama, 1.

Uniform School uniform worn throughout.

Houses/prefects Competitive houses. Prefects, head girl, head of house and house prefects – appointed by the Head and pupils.

Religion Religious worship compulsory.

Social Combined choir performances, community service, lectures, sixth form dances with local schools. Organised trips abroad. Sixth formers allowed to bring own bicycle. Meals self service. School bookshop. No tobacco/alcohol allowed.

Discipline No corporal punishment. Pupils failing to produce prep once receive a reprimand; smoking results in gating or suspension; those caught smoking cannabis on the premises could expect expulsion.

Boarding Seniors have own study bedroom, or share with 3; 16% are in dormitories of 6+. 8 houses, of 14–69, divided by age group. Resident qualified nurse. Central dining room. Seniors cook own food. Termly exeats: half term plus 2 weekends (juniors); flexible weekends (sixth form). Visits to the local town allowed.

Alumni association is run by Mrs J Copland, Boundary House, North Waltham, Basingstoke, Hants RG25 2BG.

FELSTED

Felsted School	Co-ed	Pupils 490
Dunmow	● Boys	Upper sixth 110
Essex CM6 3LL	Girls	Termly fees:
Telephone number 0371 820258	● Mixed sixth	Day £1740
Enquiries/application to the Headmaster	● Day	Boarding £2207
	● Boarding	HMC

WHAT IT'S LIKE

Founded in 1564, it lies in the village of Felsted in beautiful countryside. A number of the original 16th-century buildings are still in use. Many modern developments. Architecturally the whole school is extremely pleasing and it has splendid grounds covering some 70 acres. Virtually every conceivable modern facility is provided, including comfortable boarding accommodation. It is a C of E school and all pupils attend the various services in chapel. An excellent all-round education is given and a large number of leavers proceed to university (12% to Oxbridge; 55% to other universities). The music, drama and art departments are strong and there is a very good range of sports and games (in which high standards are achieved, especially in hockey). Many extra-curricular activities. Substantial commitment to local community services and participation in the Duke of Edinburgh Award Scheme.

SCHOOL PROFILE

Pupils Total over 12, 490. Day 23 (boys); Boarding 470 (boys 410, girls 60). Entry age, 13, boys; into the sixth, boys and girls. Own prep school provides 20+%. 15% are children of former pupils.

Entrance Common entrance and own entrance exam used. No special skills or religious requirements. Parents expected to buy text books in sixth form only. 38 assisted places. 16 scholarships/bursaries, full fees–10% of fees.

Parents 10+% live within 30 miles; up to 10% live overseas.

Staff Head E J H Gould, in post for 5 years. 49 full time staff, 2 part time. Annual turnover 6%. Average age 40.

Academic work GCSE and A-levels. Average size of upper fifth 90; upper sixth 110. Average pupil gains 7.5 O-levels; 2.5 A-levels. *Computing facilities*: Econet covering the school, based on BBC machines – all pupils involved.

Senior pupils' non-academic activities *Music*: Significant number learn a musical instrument. AB exams, Grade 8 taken in a range of instruments. Orchestras, chamber groups, choir, choral society; some pupils reach National Youth Orchestra and win choral scholarships. Each year pupils are in Essex Youth Orchestra. Music is compulsory part of curriculum in 1st year. *Drama and dance*: Drama on the curriculum (compulsory in 1st year) but no A-level. Regular school, house and year group productions. *Art*: Art and history of art to A-level. Well-supported as examined and extra-curricular subject. Compulsory part of the curriculum in 1st year. *Sport*: Rugby, football, cricket, hockey, squash, swimming, cross country running, tennis, athletics, shooting, fencing, badminton, netball and others. Sports Hall related activities available. All pupils take athletic exercise, from fitness programmes to specialised coaching in a range of sports. Regular county representation. Higher/national selection gained by some. *Other*: Duke of Edinburgh's Award Scheme available. Contributions are made to local community activities. Other activities include computer club and wide range of (40) society/club activity based on the Bury, a special house for societies and spare time activities.

Careers 3 part time careers advisors. On average 12% of pupils go on to Oxbridge; 55% to other universities; 15% to polytechnics or CHE; 9% to further education (non-degree); rest to direct employment. Large range of degree courses followed, engineering prominent.

Uniform School uniform worn except in the sixth.

Houses/prefects Prefects. No fagging but community duties for juniors.

Religion Daily chapel, pupils may be exempted at parents' request.

Social Meals self service. School shop sells clothing, sports equipment and tuck. No tobacco allowed; sixth form bar at weekends (wine and beer).

Discipline No corporal punishment.

Boarding 66% in studies of 1 or 2. Houses, same as competitive houses, are single sex, up to 60 pupils. Resident SRNs; daily doctor's surgery. Central dining room. 2 weekend exeats per term, plus half term.

FERNHILL

Fernhill School
Fernbrae Avenue
Fernhill, Rutherglen
Glasgow G73 4SG
Telephone number 041 634 2674

Enquiries/application to the Head

Co-ed   Pupils 165
Boys   Upper sixth 30
● Girls   Termly fees:
Mixed sixth   Day £550
● Day
Boarding

WHAT IT'S LIKE

Founded in 1972, it is a single site of 9 acres in the southern outskirts of Rutherglen, high above Glasgow and overlooking the Cathkin Braes and a golf course; an altogether pleasant and healthy environment. It has good accommodation. A Roman Catholic school but other denominations are welcome. Attendance at religious services in school is compulsory. Its declared priorities are the training of the intellect and will according to Christian principles, the development of habits of hard work, the fostering of good social relationships and success in study. A sound education is given and results are good (10–12 university entrants per year, a high proportion for a small school). Strong in music, art and drama. A decent range of games, sports and activities.

SCHOOL PROFILE

Pupils Total, 165. Entry age, 12 and into the sixth. Own primary department provides over 50%.

Entrance Own entrance exam used. Oversubscribed. No special skills; School is Roman Catholic but other denominations accepted. Parents not expected to buy text books. 45 assisted places.

Parents 15+% are doctors, lawyers etc; 15+% in industry or commerce. 60+% live within 30 miles.

Staff Head Mrs E M Fitzpatrick, in post for 10 years. 7 full time staff, 7 part time. Annual turnover low. Average age 43.

Academic work O grade, Highers and A-levels. Average size of fourth year 32; fifth year 30. *O grades*: on average, 3 pupils in fourth year pass 1–4 subjects; 15, 5–7 subjects; 14 pass 8+ subjects. *Highers*: on average, 2 pupils in fifth year pass 1 subject; 3, 2 subjects; 5, 3 subjects; 12, 4 subjects; 8 pass 5 or more subjects. On average, 11 take arts and humanities Highers; 19 take a mixture of science and arts. *Computing facilities*: one small computing room.

Senior pupils' non-academic activities *Music*: 30 learn a musical instrument, 4 to Grade 6 or above; 30 in school choir, 15 in ensembles. *Drama and dance*: 40 in school productions; 16 in Scottish country dance display teams. 2 take up to Grade 6 in ESB, RAD etc. 1 goes on to work in theatre. *Art*: 60 take as non-examined subject; 16, O-grade; 5, Higher. 2 accepted for Art School. *Sport*: Hockey, netball, tennis, badminton, volleyball, swimming available. 60 take non-compulsory sport. 3 pupils represent county/country (athletics, hockey). Other activities include chess – regional and national competitions; public speaking – regional competitions.

Careers 1 part time careers advisor. Average number of pupils accepted for *arts and humanities degree courses* at Oxbridge, 1 or 2; other universities, 6; polytechnics or CHE, 2. *science and engineering degree courses* at universities, 4; medical schools, 3; polytechnics or CHE, 3. *BEd*, 2. *other general training courses*, 3. Average number of pupils going straight into careers in civil service, 1; art, 2; banking, 2; nursing, 2.

Uniform School uniform worn, modified in sixth.

Houses/prefects Competitive houses. Prefects, head girl, head of house and house prefects elected by staff and school.

Religion Attendance at services compulsory; participation not.

Social Chess, debates, hockey, swimming competitions with local schools; occasional trips abroad. Pupils allowed to bring own car/bike/motorbike to school. Meals self service. No tobacco/alcohol allowed.

Discipline No corporal punishment. Pupils failing to produce homework once might expect a warning; parents of those caught smoking cannabis on the premises would be interviewed.

Alumni association run by Mrs L McLay, Deputy Head.

FETTES

Fettes College	● Co-ed	Pupils 468
Carrington Road	Boys	Upper sixth 105
Edinburgh EH4 1QX	Girls	Termly fees:
Telephone number 031 332 2281	Mixed sixth	Day £1465
	● Day	Boarding £2180
Enquiries/application to Registrar	● Boarding	HMC; GBA; ISBA

WHAT IT'S LIKE

Founded in 1870 under the will of Sir William Fettes, twice Lord Provost of Edinburgh. It occupies a splendid estate of 100 acres a mere 1½ miles from the centre of the city. The main building is a Victorian Gothic extravaganza, spired, turreted and pinnacled. Since 1945 there have been extensive additions. Boarding accommodation and facilities are good. The junior school is in the college grounds. The college has a Christian approach but is non-denominational. There are Anglican and Presbyterian chaplains and there is some emphasis on religious instruction and worship. A distinguished and well-run school with a friendly atmosphere, in which great attention is given to individual needs. Its declared aim is to provide a balanced and challenging education in the belief that each pupil is accepted for what he or she is and that this includes an unknown potential for becoming something greater not only in terms of assessable ability but also in terms of development as a person. Pupils are encouraged to aim at and achieve the very highest standard of which they are capable. A large staff permits a staff:pupil ratio of 1:8. Academic standards are high and results are excellent. Sixty or more leavers go on to university each year. Very strong indeed in music, art and drama. Excellent range of sports and games (high standards); equally good range of extra-curricular activities. The CCF (founded 1908) is a large and particularly active contingent. Much emphasis on specialist skills and arduous training. The college has a big commitment to community service and a splendid record in the Duke of Edinburgh's Award Scheme. Copious use is made of Edinburgh's cultural amenities.

SCHOOL PROFILE

Pupils Total over 12, 468. Day 80 (boys 48, girls 32); Boarding 388 (boys 224, girls 164). Entry age, 10½, 13½ and into the sixth. 17% are children of former pupils.

Entrance Common entrance and own entrance exam used. Any special skills welcome; no religious requirements. Parents buy text books on a sale or return basis; branch of university bookshop on campus. 28 assisted places. 15 scholarships/bursaries, full fees to £500.

Parents 15+% are doctors, lawyers etc; 15+% in industry or commerce. 10+% live within 30 miles; 10+% live overseas.

Staff Head M T Thyne, appointed September 1988. 62 full time staff, 8 part time. Annual turnover 5%. Average age 40.

Academic work GCSE, A-levels, Highers. Average size of upper fifth 85; upper sixth, 105. *O-levels*: on average, 20 pupils in the upper fifth pass 1–4 subjects; 40, 5–7 subjects; 25 pass 8+ subjects. *A-levels*: on average, 15 pupils in upper sixth pass 1 subject; 60, 2 subjects; and 65 pass 3 subjects. On average, 40 take science/engineering A-levels; 60 take arts and humanities; 5 a mixture. 25 subjects in all offered to GCSE/A-level. *Computing facilities*: 14 station BBC Econet level 2 computer room; 7 other stand alone BBC within academic departments; 1 Ferranti 20 MB PC and 1 Amstrad 512 KB for admin office. Provision for dyslexia and EFL.

Senior pupils' non-academic activities *Music*: 50 learn a musical instrument, 15 to Grade 6 or above, 25 in school orchestra, 100 in choir; 2 in Scottish National Youth Orchestra, 3 in Edinburgh Youth Orchestra. *Drama and dance*: 25 in school productions, 50 in house plays; 100, other drama. 3 take to Grade 6 in ESB, RAD etc; 25 take private lessons. 3 accepted for Drama/Dance

Schools. *Art*: 140 take as non-examined subject; 30 GCSE; 12 A-level. 6 accepted for Art School; 1 for university fine art course. 12 belong to photographic club, 12 take ceramics. *Sport*: Rugby, hockey, lacrosse, swimming, shooting, fencing, squash, fives, badminton, basketball, netball, cross-country running and ski-ing, athletics, cricket, tennis, soccer, sailing, canoeing, climbing available. 60 take non-compulsory sport. 10 take swimming exams; 6, fencing. 3 pupils represent county/country (cricket, squash, rugby). *Other*: 40 take part in local community schemes. 50 have bronze Duke of Edinburgh's Award, 30 have silver and 16 gold. Other activities – computer club, bell-ringing, chess, CCF, sub-aqua, climbing, ski mountaineering, driving lessons, country dancing, political society and many others.

Careers 4 part time careers advisors. Average number of pupils accepted for *arts and humanities degree courses* at Oxbridge, 5; other universities, 30; polytechnics or CHE, 7. *science and engineering degree courses* at Oxbridge, 5; other universities, 20; medical schools, 5; polytechnics or CHE, 5. *BEd*, 8. *other general training courses*, 6. Average number of pupils going straight into careers in armed services, 3; the church, 1; industry, 2; the City, 1; civil service, 1; music/drama, 1.

Uniform School uniform worn including the sixth.

Houses/prefects Competitive houses. Prefects, head boy/girl, head of house and house prefects – appointed by Head on recommendation of housemaster/mistress and senior prefects.

Religion Daily interdenominational chapel services.

Social Joint careers talks and historical society with other local schools. Organised expeditions to eg Norway, Greenland, Kashmir; exchanges with 3 Canadian, 1 American, 1 German and 1 Australian schools. Meals self service. School shop. No tobacco allowed; alcohol occasionally.

Discipline Corporal punishment abolished years ago. Pupils failing to produce homework once might expect to complete it in their spare time; those caught smoking cannabis on the premises may expect expulsion.

Boarding 12% have own study bedroom, 12% share; 30% are in dormitories of 6+. Houses, of approximately 50–65, mostly same as competitive houses, single sex. Resident qualified medical staff. Central dining room. Pupils can provide and cook own food to a limited extent. 4 Sunday exeats or 2 weekends each term. Visits to the local town allowed.

Alumni association is run by G D C Preston, c/o the College.

Former pupils Iain Macleod; Selwyn Lloyd; Lord Fraser of Kilmorack; Lord Drumalbyn; Tilda Swinton; General John Learmont; Tony Blair MP.

FOREST SCHOOL

Forest School	Co-ed	Pupils 750
College Place	● Boys	Upper sixth Yes
Near Snaresbrook	● Girls	Termly fees:
London E17 3PY	● Mixed sixth	Day £1050
Telephone number 01-520 1744	● Day	Boarding £1529
	● Boarding	HMC; GBA

WHAT IT'S LIKE

Founded in 1834 as 'The Forest Proprietary School', it became Forest School in 1847, and in 1947 attained charitable status and became a public school. It has a big campus in an open part of Epping Forest. In effect, three schools share this campus: the boys' school, divided into senior and junior departments (about 375 junior boys and 400 seniors); and the girls' school with about 280 pupils. The latter has its own block for teaching girls up to age 16. The sixth form is co-educational. The original Georgian building is used for dormitories, libraries, recreation rooms and offices. There have been many additions since 1950, including a theatre and a sports hall. Excellent playing fields cover the 27 acres. Religious worship is in accordance with Anglican faith and practice. All pupils are required to attend daily services in chapel. A broad general education is provided for GCSE and A-level. Academic standards and results are high and a large proportion (35–40) of pupils proceed to university each year, including a number to Oxbridge. The music, drama and art departments are strong. A good range of sports and games is available. All pupils are expected to take part in these. Standards in hockey, cricket, soccer and rowing are high. Extra-curricular activities are numerous. There is a big commitment to local community services. Full use is made of the cultural amenities of London.

SCHOOL PROFILE

Head Mr J C Gough (5 years)
Age range 11–18 (girls), 7–18 (boys); entry by common entrance or own exam Some scholarships available (including music) and assisted places.

FORT AUGUSTUS

Fort Augustus Abbey School	Co-ed	Pupils 76
Fort Augustus	● Boys	Upper sixth 12
Inverness-shire PH32 4DB	Girls	Termly fees:
Telephone number 0320 6232	Mixed sixth	Day £960
Enquiries/application to the Headmaster	● Day	Boarding £1570
	● Boarding	GBA; HAS

WHAT IT'S LIKE

Founded in 1880. The Benedictine Abbey was founded in 1876 as a successor to two much older monasteries: the Abbey of St James of the Scots in Ratisbon on the Danube (founded c1100), and the English Abbey of SS Adrian and Denys at Lamspring near Hanover (founded 1645). The monastery, abbey and school have a magnificent site, on the position of the old redcoat fort, at the southern end of Loch Ness. The buildings are fine examples of late Victorian architecture and the whole complex constitutes a grade 1 listed building. The present school accommodation (which can take up to 150 boys) comprises the original main school block of 1878, a new wing opened in 1960 and a block taken over from the monastery in 1969. New developments are under way. Facilities are very good. It has all the advantages of a very small school and there are 11 teaching staff for 76 boys. Some 75% of the pupils are

Roman Catholics. Doctrine according to the Church is taught throughout the school and some religious services are compulsory. Some of the school's declared aims are: to give an all-round education, physical and mental, academic and spiritual; to produce a young adult who is a gentleman and a Christian; to turn out responsible citizens who are alive to the challenges facing them in the world and the Church. Academic standards are high and about 25% of leavers go on to university each year. There is considerable strength in music, drama and art. Most pupils are involved in sport and games. There is a good range of activities, with quite a lot of emphasis on outdoor pursuits for which the highland environment is ideal. The CCF contingent is particularly strong.

SCHOOL PROFILE

Pupils Total 76 (all boarders, although day pupils welcome). Entry age, from 11½ to 16. 10% are children of former pupils.

Entrance By interview and school report. Not oversubscribed. No special skills or religious requirements, but 75% of pupils are Roman Catholic. Parents expected to buy text books. 25 assisted places.

Parents 15+% in industry or commerce; 15+% are doctors, lawyers etc. Up to 10% live within 30 miles; 10+% live overseas.

Staff Head T E Delepine, appointed July 1988. 11 full time staff, 6 part time. Annual turnover 10%. Average age 45.

Academic work O-grade, Highers, CSYS. Average size of upper fifth 20; upper sixth 12. *O-grade*: on average, 7 pupils in upper fifth pass 1–4 subjects; 9, 5–7 subjects; 4 pass 8+ subjects. *Highers*: on average, 4 pupils pass 1 subject; 3, 2 subjects; 3, 3 subjects and 2 pass 4 subjects. Every pupil passes 2 subjects by upper sixth. On average, 25% take science/engineering Highers; 20% take arts and humanities; 40% a mixture. *Computing facilities*: BBC computers, O-grade computing offered.

Senior pupils' non-academic activities *Music*: 7 learn a musical instrument. *Drama and dance*: 25 participate in school productions. *Art*: 10 take O-grade; 5 Higher. *Sport*: Rugby, hockey, cricket, athletics, golf available. 50% take non-compulsory sport. *Other*: Other activities include a computer club, sailing, chess, bridge, photography, piping.

Careers 1 part time advisor. Average number of pupils accepted for *arts and humanities degree courses* at universities, 2; polytechnics or CHE, 2. *science and engineering degree courses* at universities, 2; medical schools, 1; polytechnics or CHE, 2. *other general training courses*, 1. Average number of pupils going straight into careers in the armed services, 1; industry, 1.

Uniform School uniform worn throughout.

Houses/prefects Competitive houses. Prefects, head boy, head of house and house prefects – appointed by the Head.

Religion Mass and evening service every Sunday is compulsory. Weekday worship encouraged.

Social Meals self service. School shop. Senior boys allowed some tobacco and alcohol on the premises.

Discipline No corporal punishment. Pupils failing to produce homework once might expect to have to produce it in free time; those caught smoking cannabis on the premises could expect to be admonished, given manual tasks for several days; parents would be informed; a further offence would bring expulsion.

Boarding 12–15% have own study bedroom, 35% share (3); 50% are in dormitories of 6+. Houses, of approximately 40, same as competitive houses. Resident matron. Central dining room. 2 weekend exeats each term. Visits to local town allowed.

Alumni association run by Rev M B Seed, The Abbey, Fort Augustus, Inverness-shire PH32 4DB.

FRAMLINGHAM

Framlingham College	● Co-ed	Pupils 472
Framlingham	Boys	Upper sixth 78
Woodbridge	Girls	Termly fees:
Suffolk IP13 9EY	Mixed sixth	Day £1125
Telephone number 0728 723 789	● Day	Boarding £1755
	● Boarding	HMC
Enquiries/application to the Headmaster's Secretary		

WHAT IT'S LIKE

Founded in 1864, it has a splendid rural site on a hill overlooking the ruins of Framlingham Castle and the town below. There are 50 acres of gardens and playing fields. The well-designed buildings are very well equipped and provide comfortable boarding accommodation. It has a particularly fine technology and activities centre. Religious worship in the Anglican tradition is encouraged. Very strong indeed in music, drama and art. The academic standards are high and exam results are consistently good. Some 45–50 university entrants per year. Excellent range of sports and games in which high standards are achieved.

SCHOOL PROFILE

Pupils Total, 472. Day 143 (boys 78, girls 65); Boarding 329 (boys 271, girls 58). Entry age, 13 and into sixth. Own junior school, Brandeston Hall, provides over 20%. 10% are children of former pupils.

Entrance Common entrance and own entrance exam used. Oversubscribed. No special skills or religious requirements but school is C of E. Parents not expected to buy text books. 6–8 scholarships/bursaries, £3000–£250 pa.

Parents 30+% live within 30 miles; 10+% live overseas.

Staff Head L I Rimmer, in post for 16 years. 45 full time staff, 3 part time, plus music staff. Annual turnover 10–12%. Average age 30–35.

Academic work GCSE and A-levels. Average size of upper fifth 110; upper sixth 78. *O-levels*: on average, 43 pupils in upper fifth pass 1–4 subjects; 35, 5–7 subjects; 27 pass 8+ subjects. *A-levels*: on average, 10 pupils in upper sixth pass 1 subject; 21, 2 subjects; 36, 3 subjects and 4 pass 4 subjects. On average, 20 per year take science/engineering A-levels; 39 take arts and humanities; 19 a mixture. *Computing facilities*: Computer room (18 Econet stations) with other classrooms linked in. Special provisions for pupils who are dyslexic, mildly handicapped etc.

Senior pupils' non-academic activities *Music*: 120 learn a musical instru-

ment, 30 up to Grade 6 or above, 1 accepted for Music School; 40 in school orchestra, 100 in school choir(s). *Drama and dance*: 35 in school productions; 20 in other; 1 accepted for Drama School, 1 now works in theatre. *Art*: 52 take GCSE, 30 take A-level. 6 accepted for Art School. 25 belong to eg photographic club. *Sport*: Hockey, rugby, netball, cricket, cross-country, athletics, sailing, shooting (.303, .22, clay pigeon), squash, badminton, archery, gymnastics, multiple indoor games, swimming, tennis, canoeing, golf, rounders available. 150 take non-compulsory sport. 10 take exams in eg gymnastics or swimming. 12 represent county (rugby, hockey, cricket). *Other*: 10 take part in local community schemes. 12 have silver Duke of Edinburgh's Award and 2 have gold. 4 enter voluntary schemes after leaving school. Other activities include computer club, driving, chess, bridge, cookery, pottery, printing, wood and metal work, ballroom dancing, modelling, debating, etc.

Careers 11 part time careers advisors. Average number of pupils accepted for *arts and humanities degree courses* at Oxbridge, 1; other universities, 30; polytechnics or CHE, 10. *science and engineering degree courses* at Oxbridge, 1; other universities, 15; medical schools, 2; polytechnics or CHE, 5. *BEd*, 2. *other general training courses*, 4. Average number of pupils going straight into careers in armed services, 4; the church, 1; industry, 3; the City, 1; civil service, 2; music/drama, 1; other, 6.

Uniform School uniform worn throughout, different in sixth.

Houses/prefects Competitive houses. Prefects, head boy/girl, head of house and house prefects – appointed by Head.

Religion Religious worship (C of E) encouraged.

Social Debates (occasional), choral productions, dances, religious events with other local schools. Organised trips abroad. Pupils allowed to bring own car/bicycle/motorbike to school. Meals self service. School shop. No tobacco allowed; limited alcohol allowed for upper sixth.

Discipline Corporal punishment allowed. Pupils failing to produce homework once would have to do it as soon as possible; those caught smoking cannabis on the premises could expect expulsion.

Boarding 20–25% have own study bedroom, 55–60% share with 1–3, 15–20% in dormitories of 6+. Houses, of approximately 55–60 (single sex) are same as competitive houses. Resident qualified nurse. Central dining room. Pupils can provide and cook own food. 2–3 exeats each term – not normally overnight. Weekly visits to the local town allowed.

Alumni association is run by V Bromage, 51 Park Road, Aldeburgh, Suffolk.

Former pupils Gen Sir Patrick Howard Dobson; N F Borrett; J F Larter; A Hancock.

Francis Holland (Regent's Park)

Francis Holland School
Clarence Gate
London NW1 6XR
Telephone number 01-723 0176

Co-ed
Boys
● Girls
Mixed sixth
● Day
Boarding

Pupils 360
Upper sixth Yes
Termly fees:
Day £840
GSA; GBGSA

WHAT IT'S LIKE

The Francis Holland (C of E) schools were founded by Canon Francis J Holland. The first was opened in 1878 in Baker Street, London, and transferred in 1915 to its present building at Clarence Gate, near Regent's Park. There has been a continuous programme of modernisation and the facilities in its fine buildings are excellent. There are about 350 day girls (ages 11–18). A sophisticated school with high academic standards, it produces first-rate results. A large number of pupils go on to university. Religious teaching is based on the principles of the Church of England. There is much emphasis on music throughout the school. The drama and art departments are very strong and active. Regent's Park provides good facilities for sports and games, in which standards are also high. There is a good range of extra-curricular activities. Full use is made of the cultural amenities of the capital.

SCHOOL PROFILE

Head Mrs P Parsonson (first year in post)
Age range 11–18; entry by own exam
A few scholarships available.

Francis Holland (Sloane Square)

Francis Holland School
39 Graham Terrace
Westminster
London SW1W 8JF
Telephone number 01-730 2971

Enquiries/application to the Head

Co-ed
Boys
● Girls
Mixed sixth
● Day
Boarding

Pupils 180
Upper sixth 27
Termly fees:
Day £987
GSA

WHAT IT'S LIKE

The Francis Holland (Church of England) Schools Trust was founded in 1878. This school opened in 1881 in Eaton Terrace and transferred to its present site in 1884. This is very near Sloane Square in central London. It has close links with its sister school in Clarence Gate, Regent's Park. The junior school shares the main site. It has handsome buildings which have been well adapted to modern needs. A strong local and family tradition prevails. Its position makes possible a wide use of London's amenities for outings of all kinds. The teaching is good and academic results are creditable. There is a strong music dept and drama is popular. Some sport and games take place on the school site, otherwise local sports centres and Battersea Park are used.

SCHOOL PROFILE

Pupils Total over 12, 180. Entry age, 4+, 5+, 11+ and into the sixth. Own junior school provides over 50%.

Entrance Own entrance exam used. Oversubscribed. No special skills; C of E school but all denominations accepted. Parents expected to buy text books. Bursaries available. 5 scholarships, $\frac{1}{12}$–$\frac{1}{2}$ fees.

Parents Drawn from a wide range of professions: medicine, law, banking, the Church, the academic world, the theatre etc. 60+% live within 30 miles.

Staff Head Mrs J A Anderson, in post for 6 years. 20 full time staff, 7 part time.

Academic work GCSE and A-levels. Average size of upper fifth 30; upper sixth 27. *O-levels/GCSE*: most pupils take 8–9 subjects. *A-levels*: most pupils take 3 subjects; usually a mixture of science and arts. *Computing facilities*: Computer room with BBC micros. EFL and dyslexic help for exams.

Senior pupils' non-academic activities *Music*: Many learn musical instruments. There is a school orchestra, a choir, a woodwind ensemble, a string group, and some girls help with junior musical events. *Sport*: Tennis, hockey, netball, gymnastics, swimming available. *Other* activities include a computer club, clubs for drama, debating, pottery and aerobics, inter-form play competitions, ballet, Scottish dancing, fencing.

Careers 1 careers advisor. Membership of ISCO and NACCW.

Uniform School uniform worn except in sixth.

Houses/prefects Competitive houses. Head girl, head of house and house prefects – elected by school and staff. School Council.

Social Organised trips abroad, ski-ing, history of art to Italy, France and Spain, also Greece. Meals self service. No tobacco/alcohol allowed.

Discipline No corporal punishment.

FRENSHAM HEIGHTS

Frensham Heights School		
Rowledge	● Co-ed	Pupils 270
Farnham	Boys	Upper sixth Yes
Surrey GU10 4EA	Girls	Termly fees:
Telephone number 025 125 2134	Mixed sixth	Day £1370
	● Day	Boarding £2290
	● Boarding	GBA; SHMIS; HMC

WHAT IT'S LIKE

Founded in 1925 as part of a progressive movement to promote co-education and democratic and informal relationships between teachers and pupils. The stress is on non-competitive and non-punitive attitudes and methods. The school is deliberately kept small and is non-denominational. The buildings are grouped round a handsome Edwardian house in a fine position overlooking the valley of the River Wey. The site comprises 150 acres of beautiful gardens and wooded parkland. Boarding accommodation is comfortable and the school is well equipped with modern teaching facilities. Academic standards are high and a large staff allows a staff:pupil ratio of 1:8. A sound general education is provided. Results are good and quite a large number of pupils go on to universities and other places of further education each year. All pupils in the first three years study art, ceramics, craft, music, drama and dance. Drama and music are particularly strong. When they enter the fourth form they must choose two subjects among these. Physical education and games are compulsory in the first five years. Older pupils are not obliged to take part in games and sports in which they have no interest. A standard range of sports and games is provided and there is a plentiful variety of extra-curricular activities.

SCHOOL PROFILE

Head Alan L Pattinson (15 years)
Age range 11–18; entry by own exam or common entrance
Scholarships for art, drama, academic work and music.

FRIENDS' (ANTRIM)

The Friends' School	• Co-ed	Pupils 870
Lisburn	Boys	Upper sixth 105
Antrim	Girls	Termly fees:
Northern Ireland BT28 3BH	Mixed sixth	Day £283
Telephone number 08462 2156	• Day	Boarding £550
Enquiries/application to the Headmaster	• Boarding	Quaker

WHAT IT'S LIKE

Founded in 1774, a Quaker school, its site is on Prospect Hill near the centre of the town. The grounds are spacious and provide ample playing areas for 1000 pupils. Since 1960 there has been extensive development and modernisation. Excellent boarding accommodation and good up-to-date facilities of all kinds. Pupils are taken from a wide range of religious backgrounds and a general form of Christian worship is practised. Academic attainments are high (50–60 university entrants per year). Very strong musically. A good range of games and sports. A remarkable record in the Duke of Edinburgh's Award Scheme.

SCHOOL PROFILE

Pupils Total over 12, 870. Day 807 (boys 379, girls 428); Boarding 63 (boys 40, girls 23). Entry age, 4+, 11+ and into sixth. Own junior school provides 20+%. 25% are children of former pupils.
Entrance Common entrance rarely used; usually own exam. Sometimes oversubscribed. Good academic ability required; no religious requirements.

Parents of fee-paying pupils expected to buy text books. Tuition fees paid for all grammar school 'qualified' pupils resident in Northern Ireland.

Parents 60+% live within 30 miles; up to 10% live overseas.

Staff Head A G Chapman, in post for 18 years. 62 full time staff, 5 part time. Annual turnover 3–4%. Average age 40.

Academic work GCSE and A-levels. Average size of upper fifth 129; upper sixth 105. *O-levels*: on average, 22 pupils in upper fifth pass 1–4 subjects; 41, 5–7 subjects; 64 pass 8+ subjects. *A-levels*: on average, 15 pupils in upper sixth pass 1 subject; 23, 2 subjects; 53, 3 subjects and 11 pass 4 subjects. On average, 37 take science/engineering A-levels; 47 take arts and humanities, 34 a mixture. *Computing facilities*: 15-station Econet computer network. 6 other computers based in individual departments. *Special provisions*: EFL coaching available. Access to local authority facilities for children with handicaps.

Senior pupils' non-academic activities *Music*: 125 learn a musical instrument, 40 to Grade 6 or above, 2 accepted for Music School, 4 in pop group. 80 in school orchestra, 200 in choir, 15 in school pop group; 1 in National Youth Orchestra. *Drama and dance*: 30 in school productions, 25 in other; 1 accepted for Drama School. *Art*: 35 take GCSE; 27 take A-level; 5 accepted for Art School. 5 belong to eg photographic club. *Sport*: Rugby, hockey, cricket, tennis, athletics, badminton, squash, netball, swimming, soccer available. 150 take non-compulsory sport. 25 take exams, eg swimming, gymnastics. 7 pupils represent county (rugby, hockey, soccer, ski-ing). *Other*: 18 take part in local community schemes. 37 have bronze Duke of Edinburgh's Award, 19 have silver and 43 have gold. 10 enter voluntary schemes after leaving school. Other activities include computer club, chess club, debating society, scripture union, swimming and lifesaving (own pool), ski-ing (on artificial slope and tours).

Careers 4 part time careers advisors. Average number of pupils accepted for *arts and humanities degree courses* at Oxbridge, 1; other universities, 25; polytechnics or CHE, 4. *science and engineering degree courses* at Oxbridge, 1; other universities, 29; medical schools, 5; polytechnics or CHE, 6. *BEd*, 2. *other general training courses*, 10. Average number of pupils going straight into careers in armed services, 3; the church, 1; industry, 4; civil service, 3; music/drama, 1.

Uniform School uniform worn throughout.

Houses/prefects Competitive houses for sport. Prefects (volunteer), head boy/girl (appointed) and heads of house (elected). School Council.

Religion General Christian worship with bible teaching, prayer and praise.

Social Link with a school in the Republic of Ireland (Co-operation North), joint lectures with a local grammar school. Frequent ski trips and cultural visits to Europe. Pupils allowed to bring own bicycle to school. Lunch self service; meals for boarders formal. School milk bar. No tobacco/alcohol allowed.

Discipline No corporal punishment. Pupils failing to produce homework once might expect to do it after school; those caught smoking cannabis on the premises could expect expulsion.

Boarding 10% share a study bedroom with 1 other. 2 houses, single sex. Resident qualified nurse; doctor on call. Central dining room. Pupils can provide and cook own food at weekends. Saturday and Sunday afternoon exeats. Visits to local town allowed.

Alumni association is run by Mrs F MacLeod, Friends' School OS Association, c/o the School.

FRIENDS' (GREAT AYTON)

Friends School
High Green
Great Ayton
Middlesbrough TS9 6BN
Telephone number 0642 722141

Enquiries/application to the Headmaster

- Co-ed
  Boys
  Girls
  Mixed sixth
- Day
- Boarding

Pupils 173
Upper sixth 13
Termly fees:
Day £795
Boarding £1715
GBA (Quaker)

WHAT IT'S LIKE

Founded in 1841, it has a fine site of 60 acres of beautiful grounds in the shadow of the North Yorkshire moors, 9 miles south of Middlesbrough. The attractive buildings are very well equipped with modern facilities. A Quaker school (though 85% of the pupils are not Quakers) it lays stress on the need for self-discipline and the creation of a calm, well-ordered community. A lively and purposeful establishment it is interested in academic success and gets good results. Strong in music, drama and art. There is an excellent range of sports and games and these are pursued with enthusiasm and in a spirit of vigorous competition. A wide variety of extra-curricular activities is provided. Considerable commitment to local community schemes and national charities.

SCHOOL PROFILE

Pupils Total 173. Day 135 (boys 75, girls 60); Boarding 38 (boys 23, girls 15). Entry age, 7+, onwards according to vacancies. 15% are children of former pupils.

Entrance Common entrance and own entrance exam used. No special skills or religious requirements; 15% come from Quaker backgrounds. Parents expected to buy only very few specialist sixth form text books. Various scholarships/bursaries.

Parents 15+% in industry or commerce; 15+% are doctors, lawyers, etc. 60+% live within 30 miles; up to 10% live overseas.

Staff Head D G Cook, in post for 3 years. 20 full time staff, 14 part time. Annual turnover 10%. Average age 40.

Academic work GCSE and A-levels. Average size of upper fifth 35; upper sixth 13. *O-levels*: on average, 12 pupils in upper fifth pass 1–4 subjects; 18, 5–7 subjects; 5 pass 8+ subjects. *A-levels*: on average, 2 pupils in upper sixth pass 1 subject; 1, 2 subjects; 2, 3 subjects and 6 pass 4+ subjects. On average, 60% take science/engineering A-levels; 20% take arts and humanities; 20% a mixture. *Computing facilities*: lab of BBC Bs. Main laboratories also computerised. Special provisions made particularly for English as a second language.

Senior pupils' non-academic activities *Music*: 10 learn a musical instrument, 8 up to Grade 6 or above, 2 accepted for Music School, 2 play in pop group; 10 in school orchestra, 10 in school choir; 1 in National Youth Orchestra, 3 in county orchestra. *Drama and dance*: 30 in school productions. Occasional pupil works in theatre. *Art*: 10 take as non-examined subject; 20 take GCSE, 3 take A-level. 5 belong to eg photographic club. 2–3 accepted for Art School. *Sport*: Football, hockey, netball, tennis, cricket, athletics, swimming, cross-country, rounders, badminton, gymnastics/trampolining available. 10 take exams in sport. 5 represent county (basketball, tennis). Sport is compulsory. *Other*: 20 take part in local community schemes. 5 have bronze Duke of Edinburgh's Award. Many work for national charities. Other activities include computer club, hiking/outward-bound, drama (own theatre), music and art/pottery/textiles.

Careers 1 full time careers advisor. Average number of pupils accepted for *arts and humanities degree courses* at universities, 2; polytechnics or CHE, 2. *science and engineering degree courses* at universities, 5; medical schools, 1; polytechnics or CHE, 2. *BEd*, 1. *other general training courses*, 15. Average number of pupils going straight into careers in armed services, 1; other, 3.

Uniform School uniform worn except in sixth.

Houses/prefects 3 competitive houses. No prefects, all sixth form shares responsibilities. Head boy/girl appointed by the head after consultation. Heads of houses appointed by houses.

Religion Daily assemblies compulsory.

Social Support village events, local (and distant) charities and take part in competitions eg public speaking. 2 organised trips abroad annually. Pupils allowed to bring own car/bicycle/motorbike to school. Meals formal. School shops (food and second-hand uniform). No tobacco/alcohol allowed.

Discipline No corporal punishment. Pupils failing to produce homework once will produce it next morning.

Boarding 33% have own study bedroom, 66% share with 1 other; not in houses. Resident qualified nurse. Central dining room. Pupils can provide and cook some food. Termly exeats; half term, 2 set weekends and according to individual circumstances. Visits to local town allowed for pupils of 14 and above.

Former pupils Allan Gilmour (actor); David Holden (murdered reporter).

FRIENDS' (SAFFRON WALDEN)

Friends' School
Mount Pleasant Road
Saffron Walden
Essex CB11 3EB
Telephone number 0799 25351

Enquiries/application to the Head

- Co-ed
  Boys
  Girls
  Mixed sixth
- Day
- Boarding

Pupils 274
Upper sixth 30
Termly fees:
Day £1085
Boarding £1816
SHMIS

WHAT IT'S LIKE

Founded in 1702, it is single-site and on the edge of the countryside. It has handsome well-equipped buildings in delightful grounds. Saffron Walden itself is a most attractive country town in a beautiful part of Essex. Christian worship in the Quaker tradition is compulsory. A good all-round education is provided and the facilities are first-rate. Though a small school it sends a large number of pupils to university (20 per year). Very strong indeed in music (virtually everyone is involved) and drama. A good range of games, sports and activities. It has the bonus of a Young Farmers' Club with a 35-acre estate.

SCHOOL PROFILE

Pupils Total over 12, 274. Day 120 (boys 52, girls 68); Boarding 154 (boys 73, girls 81). Entry age, 11 and into sixth. 5% are children of former pupils.

Entrance Own entrance exam used. Not oversubscribed. No special skills or religious requirements. Parents not expected to buy text books. 80 assisted places. Up to 4 sixth form awards and Quaker bursaries, up to half fees.

Parents 50+% live within 30 miles; up to 10% live overseas.

Staff Head J C Woods, in post for 19 years. 30 full time staff, 4 part time. Annual turnover 5%. Average age 40.

Academic work GCSE and A-levels. Average size of upper fifth 60; upper sixth 30. *O-levels*: on average, 15 pupils in upper fifth pass 1–4 subjects; 40, 5–7 subjects; 15 pass 8+ subjects. *A-levels*: on average, 5 pupils in upper sixth pass 1 subject; 5, 2 subjects; 12, 3 subjects and 3 pass 4 subjects. On average, 10 take science/engineering A-levels; 10 take arts and humanities; 10 a mixture. Theatre Studies offered at A-level. *Computing facilities*: Adequate. *Special provisions*: support for English.

Senior pupils' non-academic activities *Music*: 120 learn a musical instrument, 5 to Grade 6 or above, 1 accepted for Music School, 1 in pop group; 40 in school orchestra, 30 in school choir, 6 in school pop group; 1 in Essex Youth Orchestra. *Drama and dance*: 50 in school productions; 2 accepted for Drama School. *Art*: 25 take GCSE, 8 take A-level. 3 accepted for Art School. 5 belong to eg photographic club. *Sport*: Soccer, rugby, hockey, cricket, athletics, tennis, swimming and netball available. 200 take non-compulsory sport. 6 pupils represent county (cricket, hockey, athletics). *Other*: 10 take part in local community schemes. 2 have gold Duke of Edinburgh's Award. 10 enter voluntary schemes after leaving school, 5 work for national charities. Other activities include a computer club, scouts, young farmers and chess.

Careers 1 full time and 12 part time careers advisors. Average number of pupils accepted for *arts and humanities degree courses* at universities, 7; polytechnics or CHE, 7. *science and engineering degree courses* at universities, 7; medical schools, 2; polytechnics or CHE, 7. *other general training courses*, 10.

Uniform School uniform worn except in sixth.

Houses/prefects Competitive houses. No prefects. Head boy/girl – elected by the school. School Council.

Religion Religious worship compulsory.

Social Organised local events and trips abroad. Pupils allowed to bring own bicycle to school. Meals self service. School shop. No tobacco/alcohol allowed.

Discipline No corporal punishment. Pupils failing to produce homework once might expect detention; those caught smoking cannabis on the premises could expect suspension.

Boarding Accommodation divided by age; middle school single sex, sixth form and junior mixed. Resident qualified nurse. Central dining room.

Pupils can provide and cook own food. Exeats, any weekend. Visits to local town allowed daily.
Former pupils Tom Robinson; Ralph Erskine; Eric Beale; Deborah Norton; Matthew Evans.

FULNECK (BOYS)

Fulneck Boys' School
Pudsey
West Yorkshire LS28 8DT
Telephone number 0532 571864

Enquiries/application to the Headmaster

Co-ed
● Boys
Girls
Mixed sixth
● Day
● Boarding

Pupils 260
Upper sixth 28
Termly fees:
Day £770
Boarding £1455
SHMIS

WHAT IT'S LIKE

Founded in 1753, established by the Moravian Church (Unitas Fratrum) for the education of its own ministers and missionaries. The Moravian Church claims to be the oldest Protestant church and Comenius himself presided over the original school of Fulneck, in Moravia. Essentially a Christian establishment its aim is to provide an education which will enable a pupil to lead a full life, of varied interest and abundant in opportunity for service. Religious education is quite an important part of the curriculum. It has well-designed buildings which stand in a semi-rural site on the side of a valley in the green belt near Leeds and Bradford. It has good modern facilities and extensive grounds and playing fields. A sound traditional education is given and results are good (15–20 university entrants per year). Quite strong in music, drama and art. A fair range of sports, games and activities. Very creditable results in the Duke of Edinburgh Award Scheme.

SCHOOL PROFILE

Pupils Total over 11, 260. Day 220; Boarding 40. Entry age, 8–13 and into sixth. Own junior school provides 20+%. 15% are children of former pupils.
Entrance Common entrance and own entrance exam used. Not oversubscribed. No special skills or religious requirements. Parents not expected to buy text books.
Parents 15+% in industry or commerce; 15+% in Armed Services. 60+% live within 30 miles; up to 10% live overseas.
Staff Head I D Cleland, in post for 7 years. 25 full time staff, 7 part time. Annual turnover 7%. Average age 41.
Academic work GCSE and A-levels. Average size of upper fifth 50; upper sixth 28. *O-levels*: on average, 10 pupils in upper fifth pass 1–4 subjects; 30, 5–7 subjects; 10 pass 8+ subjects. *A-levels*: on average, 1 pupil in upper sixth passes 1 subject; 2, 2 subjects; 11, 3 subjects and 14 pass 4 subjects. On average, 42% take science/engineering A-levels; 28% take arts and humanities; 30% a mixture. *Computing facilities*: Computing laboratory; computers in maths and sciences.
Senior pupils' non-academic activities *Music*: 55 learn a musical instrument, 5 to Grade 6 or above; 25 in school orchestra, 20 in choir, 3 in school

pop group; 5 in other pop group. *Drama and dance*: 20 in school productions. *Art*: 10 take as non-examined subject; 25 take GCSE; 3 A-level. 2 accepted for Art School. 20 belong to eg photographic club. *Sport*: Rugby, tennis, cricket, golf, badminton, sailing, athletics, cross country available. 70 take non-compulsory sport. 5 represent county (rugby, athletics, tennis, sailing). *Other*: 20 take part in local community schemes. 20 have bronze Duke of Edinburgh's Award, 15 silver and 10 gold. Most enter voluntary schemes after school; a few work for national charities. Other activities include a computer club, chess, theatre workshop, outward-bound type holidays.

Careers 3 part time careers advisors. Average number of pupils accepted for *arts and humanities degree courses* at universities, 8; polytechnics or CHE, 2. *science and engineering degree courses* at universities, 10; medical schools, 2; polytechnics or CHE, 6. *other general training courses*, 2. Average number of pupils going straight into careers in armed services, 3; the church, 1; industry, 1; civil service, 1.

Uniform School uniform worn except in sixth.

Houses/prefects Competitive houses. Prefects, head boy – appointed by the Head, staff and pupils.

Religion Compulsory Chapel once a week, prayers on other 4 days.

Social Close links, at sixth form, with Fulneck Girls' School for music and drama. Usually 1–3 foreign trips + Yorkshire–France, Yorkshire–Germany Exchange. Pupils allowed to bring own car/bicycle to school. Meals self service. No tobacco/alcohol allowed.

Discipline No corporal punishment. Pupils failing to produce homework once might expect a reprimand; those caught smoking cannabis on the premises could expect automatic suspension and probably expulsion.

Boarding 10% have own study bedroom; 90% are in dormitories of 6+. No resident qualified medical staff. Central dining room. Sixth form can provide and cook own food. Weekend exeats as required. Saturday visits to local town allowed.

Former pupils include one prime minister; one Nobel prize winner; Sir Frank Cooper (ex Permanent Secretary, MOD).

FULNECK (GIRLS)

Fulneck Girls' School
Fulneck
Pudsey
West Yorkshire LS28 8DS
Telephone number 0532 570235

Co-ed — Pupils 438
Boys — Upper sixth Yes
• Girls — Termly fees:
Mixed sixth — Day £685
• Day — Boarding £1297
• Boarding — GSA; Moravian

Head Miss R A Stephenson (6 years)
Age range 4–18; entry by own exam
Moravian school. Shared sixth form with Fulneck Boys'.

GATEWAYS

Gateways School
Harewood
Leeds LS17 9LE
Telephone number 0532 886345

Enquiries to the Headmistress
Application to Secretary

Co-ed
Boys
● Girls
Mixed sixth
● Day
Boarding

Pupils 193
Upper sixth 9
Termly fees:
Day £620
GSA

WHAT IT'S LIKE

Founded in 1941, it is sited in the delightful village of Harewood, 4 miles from Leeds and Harrogate. It incorporates the quondam dower house of the Harewood estate which lies in beautiful surroundings and is a conservation area. Very good modern facilities and accommodation. The prep department is in separate buildings within the school grounds. It has the advantage of being a fairly small school where pupils get individual encouragement and reach a high level of personal achievement. Emphasis is placed on initiative, and education for leadership. Girls are given the opportunity to take serious responsibility for their courses and the development of the school. The sixth form has been reconstituted and is expected to expand rapidly over the next few years. Academic standards are creditable. A few girls go on to university each year. An adequate range of sport, games and activities. A good record in the Duke of Edinburgh's Award Scheme.

SCHOOL PROFILE

Pupils Total over 12, 193. Entry age, 4, 11, 13 and into the sixth. Own junior school provides over 20%. 5% are children of former pupils.

Entrance Own entrance exam used. Sometimes oversubscribed. No special skills or religious requirements. Parents not expected to buy text books. 8 scholarships/bursaries, £100 per term.

Parents 15+% are doctors, lawyers etc; 15+% in industry or commerce. 60+% live within 30 miles.

Staff Head Miss L M Brown, in post for 4 years. 27 full time staff, 2 part time. Annual turnover 2%. Average age 38.

Academic work GCSE and A-levels. Average size of upper fifth 38; upper sixth 9. *O-levels*: on average, 6 pupils in upper fifth pass 1–4 subjects; 29, 5–7 subjects; 6 pass 8+ subjects. *A-levels*: on average, 1 pupil in the upper sixth passes 1 subject; 2, 2 subjects; 1, 3 subjects and 1 passes 4 subjects. On average, 1 takes science/engineering A-levels; 3 take arts and humanities; 1 a mixture. *Computing facilities*: Computer room and single computers in other areas. Extra help for mild cases of dyslexia.

Senior pupils' non-academic activities *Music*: 100 learn a musical instrument, 3 choirs, 1 in county orchestra. Biennial music festival. *Drama and dance*: 25 in school productions; 4, other. *Art*: 12 take as non-examined subject; 12 take GCSE; 3, A-level; 3 accepted for Art School. *Sport*: Lacrosse, netball, gymnastics, trampolining, athletics, golf, table tennis, volleyball, badminton, rounders available. 30 take non-compulsory sport. *Other*: 38 have bronze Duke of Edinburgh's Award, 5 have silver; 2 enter voluntary schemes after leaving school. Other activities include computer, card, walking and two drama clubs.

Careers 1 part time careers advisor. Average number of pupils accepted for *arts and humanities degree courses* at universities, 2; polytechnics or CHE, 2. *other general training courses*, 10. Average number of pupils going straight into careers in trade and commerce, 3.

Uniform School uniform worn except the sixth.

Houses/prefects Competitive houses. Prefects and head girl appointed by headmistress. School Council.

Religion Religious worship encouraged.

Social Local school debating and public speaking competitions. Organised trips abroad. Pupils allowed to bring own car to school. Meals self service. No tobacco/alcohol allowed.

Discipline No corporal punishment. Pupils failing to produce homework once might expect a reprimand; those caught smoking cannabis on the premises might expect a serious talk and warning, then a close watch.

Alumni association run by Mrs Swift, c/o the School.

GEORGE HERIOT'S

George Heriot's School
Lauriston Place
Edinburgh EH3 9EQ
Telephone number 031 229 7263

Enquiries/application to the Headmaster

- Co-ed
  Boys
  Girls
  Mixed sixth
- Day
  Boarding

Pupils 1434*
Upper sixth 130
Termly fees:
Day £785
HMC
*whole school

WHAT IT'S LIKE

Founded in 1659 by George Heriot, an Edinburgh jeweller and banker and goldsmith to James VI and I, for the fatherless sons of burgesses. It has very elegant buildings and fine grounds in the centre of Edinburgh. The original building has been preserved and comprises the chapel, council room, common room, class rooms and school offices. In the last 100 years a succession of developments has produced excellent facilities. A Junior School building was completed in 1983. Further developments began in 1987. Non-denominational, Heriot's is deeply rooted in the Scottish tradition and its pupils come from far afield and from a wide variety of social backgrounds. The playing fields are at Goldenacre. Academically high-powered, it produces consistently good results and sends some 75 pupils on to university each year. Very strong music and flourishing drama. Virtually all sports and games are available and high standards are achieved. A CCF contingent, plus a scout troop, a cub pack, guides and brownies. Some 50 clubs and societies cater for an unusually wide range of extra-curricular activities. There is much emphasis on outdoor pursuits and a fine record in the Duke of Edinburgh's Award Scheme.

SCHOOL PROFILE

Pupils Total (including primary school), 1434. (Boys 898, girls 56). Entry age, throughout primary school, Form 1 (12+) and into the sixth. Own Junior School provides over 20%. 25% are children of former pupils.

Entrance Own entrance exam used. Oversubscribed. No special skills or religious requirements. Parents expected to buy text books. 220 assisted places. 30 scholarships and 70 foundationers.

Parents 15+% in education; 15+% are doctors, lawyers etc; 15+% in industry or commerce. 60+% live within 30 miles.

Staff Head Mr K P Pearson, in post for 5 years. 93 full time staff, 5 part time. Annual turnover 3%. Average age 35.

Academic work O-grade, Highers, CSYS. Average size of upper fifth 170; upper sixth 130. *O-grade*: on average, 146 pupils in upper fifth pass 1–4 subjects; many pupils by-pass O-grade and go straight on to Higher courses. *Highers*: on average, 11 pupils pass 1 subject; 24, 2 subjects; 22, 3 subjects; 31, 4 subjects; 29, 5 subjects; 33 pass 6 subjects. On average, 60% take science/engineering Highers; 30% take arts and humanities; 10% a mixture. *Computing facilities*: a network of 23 BBC micros with a 40 megabyte file server and 2 printers; facilities also in other departments. Provision for dyslexia and EFL.

Senior pupils' non-academic activities *Music*: 250 learn a musical instrument, 20 to Grade 6 or above, 3 accepted for Music School; 125 in school orchestra, 300 in choir, 20 in pop group; 5 in National Youth Orchestra. *Drama and dance*: 40–60 in school productions. 1 or 2 accepted for Drama/Dance Schools. *Art*: 5 take as non-examined subject; 23 O-grade; 12 Higher. 1 accepted for Art School, 1 for architecture courses, 2 to foundation courses. 8 belong to photographic club, 6 to art club. *Sport*: Virtually all sports available. 260 take non-compulsory sport. 17 pupils represent county/ country (rugby, hockey, rowing, shooting, fencing). *Other*: 8 take part in local community schemes. 82 have bronze Duke of Edinburgh's Award, 61 have silver and 56 gold. 41 work for national charities. Other activities include a computer club and 50 other clubs and activities.

Careers 2 part time careers advisors. Average number of pupils accepted for *arts and humanities degree courses* at Oxbridge, 2; other universities, 32. *science and engineering degree courses* at Oxbridge, 2; other universities, 29; medical schools, 6. *other general training courses*, 23. Average number of pupils going straight into careers in armed services, 3; industry, 1; the City, 10; music/drama, 1; other, 10. Traditional school careers are accountancy, business, law, medicine.

Uniform School uniform worn throughout.

Houses/prefects Competitive houses. Prefects, head boy and girl and house captains elected by upper school.

Religion Compulsory morning assembly with broad Christian element.

Social Music, inter-school and ESU debating with other schools; own school theatrical production. Many organised trips abroad including Canada, Greece, Majorca, Zimbabwe, and school French exchange. Pupils allowed to bring own bike to school. Meals self service; tuck shop. No tobacco/alcohol allowed.

Discipline No corporal punishment. Pupils failing to produce homework once might expect a written exercise or detention; those caught smoking cannabis on the premises might expect expulsion.

Former pupils Lord Mackay (Lord Chancellor); several ex-Lord Provosts of Edinburgh; former Chief Constable of Lothian and Borders Police; Robert Urquhart, Paul Young and Roy Kinnear (actors); many well-known sporting figures including Kenneth Scotland, Andrew Irvine and Iain Milne.

GEORGE WATSON'S

George Watson's College
Colinton Road
Edinburgh EH10 5EG
Telephone number 031 477 7931

Enquiries/application to the Principal

- Co-ed
- Boys
- Girls
- Mixed sixth
- Day
- Boarding

Pupils 1255
Upper sixth 175
Termly fees:
Day £772
Boarding £1442
HMC

WHAT IT'S LIKE

Founded in 1741, it moved to its present site in 1932. The George Watson's Ladies' College and the boys' college were amalgamated in 1974. The site is on the outskirts of the city and playing fields are nearby. The impressive buildings are very well equipped with modern facilities. It is a school with a distinguished record of achievement where excellent teaching is provided and academic standards are high. The bulk of the pupils are local. Its declared objectives are to enable pupils to live their lives to the full, to understand the world they live in, to be active in serving other people and to commit themselves to causes with open-eyed and critical awareness. It caters for individualists. About 100–110 of its pupils go on to university each year (70-plus of them to Scottish universities). There are immensely strong music, drama and art depts involving a very large number of pupils. A wide variety of sports and games are available (including curling) and high standards are achieved. (A very large number of county and international representatives.) About 30 clubs and societies cater for most extra-curricular activities. There is a big commitment to local community schemes, an active scout group and considerable emphasis on outdoor pursuits. (There is a fine outdoor centre at Glen Isla.) The college's record in the Duke of Edinburgh's Scheme is outstanding (one of the best in Britain) with 65 bronze, 47 silver and 30 gold.

SCHOOL PROFILE

Pupils Total over 12, 1255. Day 1184 (boys 644, girls 540); boarding 71 (boys 42, girls 29). Entry age, 3, 5, 12 and into the sixth. Own junior school provides over 20%. 25% are children of former pupils.

Entrance Own entrance exam used. Oversubscribed. No special skills or religious requirements. Parents expected to buy text books. 237 assisted places. 11 scholarships/bursaries, £450 to £1000.

Parents 15+% are doctors, lawyers, etc, 15+% in industry or commerce. 60+% live within 30 miles; up to 10% live overseas.

Staff Head F E Gerstenberg, in post for 2 years. 128 full time staff, 12 part time. Annual turnover 5%. Average age 44.

Academic work O-grade, Highers and CSYS. Average size of upper fifth 220; upper sixth 175. *O-grade*: on average, 109 pupils in 4th or 5th year pass 1–4 subjects; 91, 5–7 subjects; 1 passes 8+ subjects. *Highers*: on average, 22 pupils in 5th form pass 1 subject; 25, 2 subjects; 37, 3 subjects; 117 pass 4 or more subjects. On average, 35 take science/engineering Highers; 35 take arts and humanities; 150 take a mixture. Russian and Italian are offered to Highers. *Computing facilities*: most departments have computers. Expanding department teaches from first year upwards. Strong remedial unit with 4 full time staff.

Senior pupils' non-academic activities   *Music*: 286 learn a musical instrument, 14 to Grade 6 or above; 2 accepted for Music School, 160 in school orchestra, 120 in school choir, 20 in jazz band, 40 in other various music groups, 30 in Barbershop choir, 45 in ensemble choir, 15 in local youth orchestra, 1 in National Youth Orchestra for Scotland. *Drama and dance*: 250–300 in school productions, 80 in house productions, 9 accepted for Drama/Dance schools, 2 go on to work in theatre. *Art*: Most take as non-examined subject, 49 take O-grade, 20 take Higher, 2 accepted for Art School, 4 go on to architecture, 1 to textiles, 30 belong to photographic club, 50 in sketch club. *Sport*: Angling, athletics, badminton, basketball, cricket, cross-country, curling, fencing, golf, gymnastics, hockey, orienteering, rowing, rugby, sailing, ski-ing, squash, table tennis, tennis and volleyball available. 700 take non-compulsory sport. 15 take exams, 38 pupils represent county/country in variety of sports. *Other*: 56 take part in local community schemes. 65 have bronze Duke of Edinburgh's Award, 47 have silver and 30 have gold. Variety of other activities including a computer club.

Careers 3 part time advisors. Average number of pupils accepted for *arts and humanities degree courses* at Oxbridge, 3; Scottish universities, 43; other universities, 16; polytechnics or CHE, 30. *science and engineering degree courses* at Oxbridge, 4; Scottish universities, 30; other universities, 12; medical schools, 10; polytechnics or CHE, 16. *BEd*, 3. *other general training courses*, 10. Average number of pupils going straight into careers in the armed services, 2; the church, 1; industry, 12; the civil service, 1; music/drama, 1; other, 12. Traditional school careers are medicine, accountancy, law and academic.

Uniform School uniform worn throughout.

Houses/prefects Competitive houses. Prefects, head boy and girl, head of house and house prefects – elected by pupils, confirmed by Head. School Council.

Religion Morning assembly compulsory.

Social Some co-operation with other Merchant Company schools (Daniel Stewarts, Mary Erskine) otherwise large enough to be self-sufficient. Exchanges with France, Germany, Spain, Italy, United States and many other organised trips abroad. Day pupils allowed to bring own car/bike/motorbike to school. Meals self service. School shop sells second-hand clothing. No tobacco/alcohol allowed.

Discipline No corporal punishment. Pupils failing to produce homework once might expect to do it within 24 hours. Parents of those caught smoking cannabis on the premises would be asked to withdraw the pupil; if parents refused, pupil would be expelled.

Boarding Half share with 1 or 2 others; others in dormitories of 6+. Resident qualified nurse. Central dining room. Pupils can provide and cook some own food. Exeats any weekend. Visits to local town allowed.

Alumni association run by Duncan McGregor, Myreside Pavilion, Myreside Road, Edinburgh.

Former pupils Malcolm Rifkind; David Steele; Gavin Hastings (Rugby); Scott Hastings (Rugby); Alison Kinnaird (Clarsach); David Johnstone (Rugby); Eric Anderson (Head of Eton); Martin Bell (Ski); Magda Sweetland (Novelist).

GIGGLESWICK

Giggleswick School
Giggleswick
Settle
North Yorkshire BD24 0DE
Telephone number 072 92 3545

Enquiries/application to the Headmaster

- Co-ed   Pupils 314
- Boys   Upper sixth 55
- Girls   Termly fees:
- Mixed sixth   Day £1498
- Day   Boarding £2242
- Boarding   HMC

WHAT IT'S LIKE

Founded in 1512, it moved to its present site in 1869 on the edge of the village. This is a superb position overlooking the Ribble valley in North Yorkshire and a mile west of the market town of Settle. It has handsome buildings and the accommodation is very comfortable. The junior school is at Catteral Hall and continuous education is available from 8–18. The school prides itself on its happy atmosphere and offers an excellent all round education. High importance is attached to personal courtesy and the school aims to develop 'the whole person' whilst having proper regard for the importance of helping all pupils to achieve their best personal academic potential. Prayers and morning service, in the Anglican tradition, are compulsory. The teaching is well known to be good and exam results are first rate. Some 35–40 university entrants per year (a very high proportion for a school of 314). Music, drama and art are strong departments. Considerable strength in games and sport. A wide range of outdoor pursuits is provided (including fell walking, orienteering, rock-climbing, canoeing, mountaineering and pot-holing). There are flourishing community service projects and numerous successes in the Duke of Edinburgh's Award Scheme.

SCHOOL PROFILE

Pupils Total 314. Day 48 (boys 21, girls 27); Boarding 266 (boys 164, girls 102). Entry age, 13 and into sixth. Catteral Hall provides 20+%. 9% are children of former pupils.

Entrance Common entrance, interviews and other methods used. Oversubscribed for girls. Anglican foundation but other faiths and convictions welcomed. Parents not expected to buy text books. No assisted places at present. 18 scholarships/bursaries available – academic, music, art, general distinction and continuation, full fees to 25% of fees.

Parents 15+% in industry or commerce. Up to 10% live within 30 miles; up to 10% live overseas.

Staff Head P Hobson. 35 full time staff, 12 part time. Annual turnover 4%. Average age 41.

Academic work GCSE and A-levels. Average size of upper fifth 65; upper sixth 55. *O-levels*: on average, 6 pupils in upper fifth pass 1–4 subjects; 34,

5–7 subjects; 25 pass 8+ subjects. *A-levels*: on average, 5 pupils in upper sixth pass 1 subject; 12, 2 subjects; 16, 3 subjects and 22 pass 4 subjects. On average, 22 take science/engineering A-levels; 19 take arts and humanities; 14 a mixture. *Computing facilities*: 17 keyboard room with BBC machines, 6 other departments have computers and are on joint network to CS dept.

Senior pupils' non-academic activities *Music*: 95 learn a musical instrument, 26 up to Grade 6 or above; 28 in school orchestra, 63 in concert band, 36 in choir; 1 accepted for Music School. *Drama and dance*: 65 in school productions; 3 accepted for Drama/Dance Schools. *Art*: 11 take as non-examined subject, 20 take GCSE, 18 take A-level, 6 belong to eg photographic club; 1 art history; 5 accepted for Art School, 2 foundation course, 1 architecture. *Sport*: Rugby, soccer, cricket, athletics, tennis, hockey, swimming, squash, fives, athletics, cross country, gym, karate, rounders, netball, basketball, badminton and golf available. 6 represent county (rugby union, athletics). *Other*: 50 have bronze Duke of Edinburgh's Award, 12 have silver and 6 gold. Other activities include a computer club, chess club, fishing, outward-bound, motor club, driving lessons, etc.

Careers 5 part time careers advisors. Average number of pupils accepted for *arts and humanities degree courses* at Oxbridge, 2; other universities, 15; polytechnics or CHE, 9. *science and engineering degree courses* at Oxbridge, 2; other universities, 16; medical schools, 2; polytechnics or CHE, 6. *BEd*, 3. *other general training courses*, 4. Average number of pupils going straight into careers in armed services, 6; industry, 6; the City, 4; civil service, 2; music/drama, 1.

Uniform School uniform worn except in sixth.

Houses/prefects Competitive/pastoral houses. Prefects and head boy/girl appointed by Head; head of house and house prefects, appointed by housemasters.

Religion House prayers and morning services are compulsory.

Social Rugby, hockey and ski trips abroad, foreign language visits to stay with families (Easter 1988, combined cricket, music and drama trip to Australia). Pupils allowed to bring own bicycle to school. Meals self service. School shop (school uniform, sports equipment and tuck). Sixth form club serves limited amounts of beer and wine with parents' permission and staff supervision. No tobacco allowed.

Discipline No corporal punishment. Pupils failing to produce homework once might expect extra work; anyone found in possession of drugs would be expelled (this has not arisen).

Boarding 30% have own study bedroom, 50% in doubles; rest in dormitories of 4–6. Houses, approximately 40–60. Doctor visits regularly. Resident SRN Matron with an assistant. Central dining room. Pupils can provide and cook own snacks. 2 weekend exeats each term and half term. Visits to local town allowed at set times.

Alumni association is run by D E W Morgan, Secretary OG Society, c/o Giggleswick School.

Former pupils Judges Christopher Oddie and Roger Hunt; Sir Douglas Glover; Sir Anthony Wilson; Richard Whiteley; Keith Duckworth.

GLASGOW ACADEMY

The Glasgow Academy
Colebrooke Street
Glasgow G12 8HE
Telephone number 041 334 8558

Enquiries/application to the Rector

Co-ed   Pupils 550
● Boys   Upper sixth 90
Girls   Termly fees:
Mixed sixth   Day £705
● Day   HMC
Boarding

WHAT IT'S LIKE

Founded in 1846, it is single site (with its own junior department) in the west end of the city. A compact campus with handsome buildings in the classical Victorian manner. Very good modern facilities. The academy has a high reputation academically and produces consistently good results. Between 65–70 leavers go on to university each year. Music, drama and art are quite strong. A wide range of sports and games in which high standards are attained. A good variety of extra-curricular activities, and a promising record in the Duke of Edinburgh's Award Scheme.

SCHOOL PROFILE

Pupils Total 550. Entry age, 4½–5½ etc and into the sixth. Own junior department provides over 20%. 30% are children of former pupils.

Entrance Own entrance exam used. Sometimes oversubscribed. No special skills or religious requirements. Parents expected to buy text books. 40 assisted places. Various scholarships/bursaries, up to £350.

Parents 15+% are doctors, lawyers etc; 15+% in industry or commerce. 60+% live within 30 miles.

Staff Head C W Turner, in post for 5 years. 57 full time staff, 7 part time. Annual turnover 2%. Average age 40.

Academic work O-grade, Highers, A-levels. Average size of upper fifth 90; upper sixth 90. *O-grades*: most boys go straight to Highers. *Highers*: on average, 30 pupils pass 1–2 subjects; 50, 3–4 subjects and 60 pass 5+ subjects. On average, 40% take science/engineering Highers; 40% take arts and humanities; 20% a mixture. *Computing facilities*: Computer room with 15 BBC computers; each department has its own computer and VDU.

Senior pupils' non-academic activities *Music*: 12 learn a musical instrument, 8 to Grade 6 or above; 4 in school orchestra, 19 in choir, 6 in pop group. *Drama and dance*: 50 in school plays; 60 in pantomime; 50 in musicals. *Art*: 30 take O-grade; 5 A-level; 26 Higher. 3 accepted for Art School. 4 belong to photographic club, 6 to printing. *Sport*: Rugby, cricket, athletics, tennis, indoor racquets, shooting, swimming, sports hall games, ski-ing, sailing, canoeing available. 200 take non-compulsory sport including sub-aqua, soccer, basketball, curling, squash, climbing, badminton. 20 take RLSS exams; 8 sub-aqua; 10 sailing; 20 ski-ing. 9 represent county/district (rugby, windsurfing); 1 represents country (ski-ing). *Other*: 5 take part in local community schemes. 18 have bronze Duke of Edinburgh's Award, 10 have silver and 6 gold. Other activities include a very active computer club, public speaking, debating, chess, SU, bridge, mountaineering, rock climbing.

Careers 4 part time careers advisors. Average number of pupils accepted for *arts and humanities degree courses* at Oxbridge, 4; other universities, 30; polytechnics or CHE, 10. *science and engineering degree courses* at Oxbridge, 4; other universities, 30; medical schools, 15; polytechnics or CHE, 10. *other general training courses*, very few. Average number of pupils going straight into careers in armed services, 2; industry, 5; the City, 2; civil service, 2; music/drama, 1; other, 5. Traditional school careers are accountancy, law, medicine.

Uniform School uniform worn throughout.

Houses/prefects Competitive houses. Prefects, head boy, head of house and house prefects – appointed by the Rector.

Religion Compulsory morning assembly for all except Jews.

Social Debates, Young Enterprise Scheme, drama, some games (eg hockey), dances with other local schools. Organised trips to France, Greece, Crete; ski-ing at Christmas and Easter. Pupils allowed to bring own car/bike to school. Meals self service but formal seating. School shops (tuck, sports equipment and stationery). No tobacco/alcohol allowed.

Discipline No corporal punishment. Pupils failing to produce homework once might expect to do it or detention; those caught smoking cannabis on the premises might expect expulsion.

Alumni association run by The President, Glasgow Academical Club, New Anniesland, Helensburgh Drive, Glasgow.

Former pupils Lord Reith (BBC Governor General); Jeremy Isaacs (Channel 4 TV); Iain Vallance (Chairman, British Telecom); Robert McLennan, MP; Lord Gould (Chairman, Scottish Conservatives); Donald Dewar, MP; John Beattie (Scotland, British Lions).

GLASGOW HIGH

The High School of Glasgow
637 Crow Road
Glasgow G13 1PL
Telephone number 041 954 9628

Enquiries/application to Mr R G Easton

• Co-ed   Pupils 486
Boys   Upper sixth 70
Girls   Termly fees:
Mixed sixth   Day £800
• Day   HMC
Boarding

WHAT IT'S LIKE

Founded in 1124 as the Grammar School of Glasgow and closely associated with the cathedral. It was closed in 1976. The new independent co-educational High School came into being the same year as a result of a merger involving the Former Pupil Club of the old High School and Drewsteignton School in Bearsden. The senior school has modern purpose-built premises at Anniesland on the western outskirts of the city next to 23 acres of playing fields. The junior school is in the former Drewsteignton School buildings about 3 miles away. The school is non-denominational. Its academic standards are high and results are good. About 50 pupils go on to university each year. Music and drama are quite strong. It has a good record in games and sports (a lot of representatives at county level) and an excellent range of activities. An impressive list of awards in the Duke of Edinburgh's Award Scheme. Full use is made of the city's cultural amenities.

SCHOOL PROFILE

Pupils Total over 12, 486 (boys 266, girls 220). Entry age, 10–11, 11–12 and when vacancies occur. Own junior school (entry age 4) provides over 60%. 10% are children of former pupils.

Entrance Own entrance exam used. Oversubscribed. Academic potential and ability to contribute to life of school is looked for. No religious requirements but school has a Christian background. Parents not expected to buy text books. 58 assisted places. 5 scholarships/bursaries per annum, full fees to £300.

Parents 15+% in industry or commerce, 15+% are doctors, lawyers etc. More than 60% live within 30 miles.

Staff Head R G Easton, in post for 4 years. 38 full time staff, 7 part time. Annual turnover 5%. Average age 39.

Academic work O-grade, Highers, CSYS. Average size of upper fifth 87; upper sixth 70. *O-grades*: on average, 6 pupils in upper fifth pass 1–4 subjects; 25, 5–7 subjects; 56 pass 8+ subjects. *Highers*: on average, 4 pupils in upper sixth pass 1 subject; 9, 2 subjects; 12, 3 subjects; 18, 4 subjects; 37 pass 5 subjects. All pupils take a mixture of science/engineering and arts and humanities Highers. *Computing facilities*: Fully equipped computer laboratory.

Senior pupils' non-academic activities *Music*: 35 learn a musical instrument, 15 to Grade 6 or above; 20 in school orchestra, 30 in choir, several in instrumental groups; 5 play in pop group beyond school. *Drama and dance*: 80 in school productions. 1 goes on to work in theatre. *Art*: 15 take O-grade; 19 Higher. 1 accepted for Art School. 6 belong to photographic club. *Sport*: Rugby, hockey, athletics, cricket, tennis, badminton, basketball, netball, volleyball, swimming, cross-country running, golf, gymnastics, orienteering, canoeing, sailing and ski-ing available. 150 take non-compulsory sport. 10 represent county (rugby, hockey, swimming, athletics, cross-country, orienteering). *Other*: 6 take part in local community schemes. 25 have bronze Duke of Edinburgh's Award, 15 have silver and 8 gold. 4 work for national charities beyond school. Other activities include a computer club, literary and debating, historical and zoological societies, satellite-tracking, chess, bridge, stamp club, Scripture Union, explorers' club (hill walking and sailing).

Careers 3 part time advisors. Average number of pupils accepted for *arts and humanities degree courses* at Oxbridge, 2; other universities, 18; polytechnics or CHE, 10. *science and engineering degree courses* at Oxbridge, 2; other universities, 22; medical schools, 4; polytechnics or CHE, 6. *other general training courses*, 4. Average number of pupils going straight into careers in the armed services, 2; industry, 3; the City, 2; music/drama, 2; other, 2.

Uniform School uniform worn throughout.

Houses/prefects Competitive houses. Prefects, head boy or girl (school captain), deputy (vice-captain), head of house and house prefects – voting by senior pupils and staff used by Head in making appointments.

Religion Morning assembly (non-denominational).

Social Debating and public-speaking competitions. Joint Scripture Union meetings. Usually two organised trips abroad per annum. Pupils allowed own car/bike/motorbike to school. Meals self service. No school shop but some items of uniform are sold. No tobacco/alcohol allowed.

Discipline No corporal punishment. Pupils failing to produce homework once might expect additional work.

Alumni association run by R M Williamson, Secretary, 34 First Avenue, Glasgow G44 3UA.

Former pupils Sir Henry Campbell-Bannerman, Andrew Bonar Law (Prime Ministers); Viscount James Bryce (Diplomat); Sir Norman Macfarlane (Chairman of Guinness).

GLENALMOND

Glenalmond College
Perthshire PH1 3RY
Telephone number 073 888 205

Enquiries/application to the Warden

Co-ed   Pupils 385
• Boys   Upper sixth 75
Girls   Termly fees:
Mixed sixth   Boarding £2450
Day   HMC; GBA
• Boarding

WHAT IT'S LIKE

Founded in 1841 as Trinity College by Mr W E Gladstone and others, it stands in magnificent countryside, 10 miles west of Perth, beside the River Almond on the edge of the Highlands. It has an estate of about 250 acres, with beautiful gardens and playing fields. A very healthy environment. The main buildings are grouped round two quadrangles and belong to the Victorian collegiate style, with neo-Tudor features, towers and turrets. There have been many modern developments, including a superb sports complex, a purpose-built theatre, concert hall, art school, and design and technology centre. The chapel, built by the Episcopalian founders, is one of the finest in the country. Religious education forms part of the curriculum and all denominations attend chapel. A succession of gifted headmasters has ensured a very active, energetic school with an enthusiastic commitment to all enterprises. Academic standards are high and results consistently good. About 40–45 pupils go on to university each year. Music is very strong and plays a central part in school life. The theatre, which seats 400, is in regular use. Art is also strong. There is a wide range of sports and games and the college has long had a reputation for excellence in these (a large number of representatives at county and national level). A very wide range of clubs and societies cater for most needs. Golf, ski-ing, salmon fishing, rock-climbing, sailing and canoeing are also available. There is a large CCF with its own pipe band. A substantial commitment to local community services and a promising record in the Duke of Edinburgh's Award Scheme.

SCHOOL PROFILE

Pupils Total, 385. Entry age, 12+, 13+ and into the sixth. 12–15% are children of former pupils.

Entrance Common entrance and own entrance tests used. Oversubscribed. No special skills or religious requirements. Parents expected to buy some text books. 36 assisted places. 63 scholarships (for academic and musical excellence) and bursaries (in cases of genuine need), 100%–10% of fees.

Parents 15+% in the armed services; 15+% are doctors, lawyers etc; 15+% in industry or commerce. 10+% live within 30 miles; up to 10% live overseas.

Staff Head (Warden) S R D Hall, in post for 1 year. 41 full time staff, 7 part time. Annual turnover up to 5%. Average age 30–35.

Academic work Pupils prepared for GCSE, A-levels, O grades and Highers. Average size of fifth 77; upper sixth 75. *O-levels*: on average, 14 pupils in fifth pass 1–4 subjects; 35, 5–7 subjects; 28 pass 8+ subjects. *A-levels*: on average, 2 pupils in upper sixth pass 1 subject; 20, 2 subjects; 48, 3 subjects and 5 pass 4 subjects. On average, 20 take science/engineering A-levels; 30 take arts and humanities; 25 a mixture. *Computing facilities*: Network of 14 BBC monitors plus 8 BBC Bs, 1 master dedicated to CAD, 1 master to CHC lathe, 1 admin machine.

Senior pupils' non-academic activities *Music*: 60 learn a musical instrument, 10 to Grade 6 or above, 1 accepted for Music School; 17 in school orchestra, 25 in choir, 6 in chamber choir, 14 in brass group; 2 in Edinburgh Youth Orchestra, 2 Perth Symphony Orchestra. *Drama and dance*: 50 in school and 90 in house productions; 25 take part in drama evening; 20 in revue. 2 accepted for Drama/Dance Schools; 2 go on to work in theatre. *Art*: Many take as non-examined subject; 1 GCSE; 7 O-grade; 4 Higher; 3 A-level art; 2 history of art. 3 apply for Art School. 8 belong to photographic club; 4 to other clubs. *Sport*: Rugby, hockey, cricket, tennis, squash, athletics, swimming, golf (own course), fly-fishing (own river), basketball, badminton, shooting, rock/snow/ice climbing, sailing, curling, sub-aqua available. 18 take life-saving exams. 11 represent county (cricket, rugby); 5 represent country (cricket, rugby, eventing, tetrathlon). *Other*: 15 take part in local community schemes. 5 have gold Duke of Edinburgh's Award. Other activities include a computer club, debating, design, electronics, technology, pipe band.

Careers 1 full time and 4 part time careers advisors. Average number of pupils accepted for *arts and humanities degree courses* at Oxbridge, 5; other universities, 21; polytechnics or CHE, 7. *science and engineering degree courses* at Oxbridge, 4; other universities, 11; medical schools, 1; polytechnics or CHE, 1. Average number of pupils going straight into careers in armed services, 8; industry, 3; the City, 3; music/drama, 3; other, 2. Traditional school career is the law.

Uniform School uniform worn throughout.

Houses/prefects Competitive houses. Prefects, head boy, head of house and house prefects appointed by the Warden and housemasters.

Religion Compulsory attendance at chapel services.

Social Public speaking competitions, theatrical productions, and some dances with local schools. Ski-ing trips abroad; 1987 Kashmir expedition (some boys climbed to over 20,000 ft). Pupils allowed to bring own bike to school. Meals formal. School shops (tuck and sports equipment). No tobacco/ alcohol allowed.

Discipline Firm but not oppressive. No corporal punishment. Pupils failing to produce homework once might expect extra work or detention; any involvement with drugs results in immediate expulsion.

Boarding 20% have own study bedroom, 20% share with 1 or 2; 15% are in dormitories of 6+; remainder in cubicles. 6 houses, of 60–65, same as for competitive purposes. 2 resident qualified nurses. Central dining room for 4 houses. Pupils can provide and cook own food. 2 weekend exeats each term plus half term. Visits to local town allowed.

Alumni association run by W H Rankin, St Barbara's, Glenalmond, Perth PH1 3RX.

Former pupils Sandy Gall (TV newscaster); Sir David Wilson (Governor, Hong Kong); David Leslie and David Sole (Scottish rugby internationals); Lord Sanderson of Bowden and Alick Buchanan-Smith (politicians).

GODOLPHIN

Godolphin School	Co-ed	Pupils 315
Milford Hill	Boys	Upper sixth Yes
Salisbury	• Girls	Termly fees:
Wiltshire SP1 2RA	Mixed sixth	Day £1115
Telephone number 0722 333059	• Day	Boarding £1875
	• Boarding	GSA; BSA;
		ISBA

WHAT IT'S LIKE

The original foundation is based on the will of Elizabeth Godolphin made in 1726. The school was started on a small scale late in the 18th century and in 1890 moved to its present site in the outskirts of Salisbury. The premises comprise agreeable modern buildings in gardens with playing fields nearby. There are four boarding houses and the accommodation is comfortable. The day girls are divided into two houses. There are approximately 300 girls (aged 11–18) of whom 200 are boarders and the rest day girls. It is a C of E foundation and some religious services and prayers are compulsory. On Sundays pupils worship in one of various churches in the city or in the cathedral. A broad general education is provided and results are good. A large staff allows a favourable staff:pupil ratio of about 1:10. There are very active music, drama and art departments. About 50% of the girls learn one or more instruments. There are regular dramatic productions. The school is well equipped with sporting facilities, including a modern sports hall. There is a fair range of extra-curricular activities.

SCHOOL PROFILE

Head Miss E A S Hannay (8 years)
Age range 11–18; entry by common entrance
Scholarships and bursaries.

GODOLPHIN AND LATYMER

Godolphin and Latymer	Co-ed	Pupils 700
Iffley Road	Boys	Upper sixth 100
Hammersmith	● Girls	Termly fees:
London W6 0PG	Mixed sixth	Day £998
Telephone number 01-741 1936	● Day	GSA
Enquiries/application to the Headmistress	Boarding	

WHAT IT'S LIKE

Founded in 1905 (formerly the Godolphin school for boys, built in 1861). It is single-site and urban on 4 acres of grounds with playing fields attached. Extensive additions have been made to the original Victorian buildings and facilities are first rate. Religious worship in the Anglican tradition is encouraged. A well-run and academically high-powered school which gets very good results. Some 65–70 pupils go on to university each year. Very strong indeed in music, drama and art. There is a massive commitment among the pupils. An excellent record in games and sports (a wide variety offered) and an impressive number of clubs and societies.

SCHOOL PROFILE

Pupils Total, 700. Entry age, 11 and into the sixth. 5% are children of former pupils.

Entrance Own entrance exam used. Oversubscribed. No special skills or religious requirements. Parents not expected to buy text books. 170 assisted places. Some bursaries and a music scholarship (½ fees).

Parents 15+% are doctors, lawyers, etc; 15+% in industry or commerce; 15+% in theatre, media, music, etc. 60+% live within 30 miles.

Staff Head Miss Margaret Rudland, in post for 2 years. 48 full time staff, 17 part time.

Academic work GCSE and A-levels. Average size of upper fifth 100; upper sixth 100. *O-levels*: on average, 10 pupils in upper fifth pass 1–4 subjects; 10, 5–7 subjects; 80 pass 8+ subjects. *A-levels*: on average, 1 pupil in upper sixth passes 1 subject; 17, 2 subjects; 65, 3 subjects; 17 pass 4 subjects. On average, 20 take science/engineering A-levels; 30 take arts and humanities; 50 take a mixture. Russian offered to GCSE/A-level. *Computing facilities*: network of BBC Micros, several individual computers in departments.

Senior pupils' non-academic activities *Music*: 200+ learn a musical instrument, 50 to Grade 6 or above, 1 accepted for Music School; 100 in school orchestra, 160 in school choir. *Drama and dance*: 200+ in school productions. 1 accepted for Drama School, 1 gone on to work in theatre. *Art*: 300 take art as non-examined subject; 50 take GCSE; 20 take A-level art; 25 take A-level History of Art. 5 accepted for Art School or fine art degrees, 8 taking Art History degrees. 10 belong to eg photographic club. *Sport*: Netball, tennis, hockey, athletics, gymnastics, dance, basketball, badminton, fencing and squash available. 75 take non-compulsory sport. 6 pupils represent county (hockey) and 1 country (fencing). *Other*: 3 enter voluntary schemes after leaving school, 1 works for a national charity. Other activities include a computer club, and many other clubs and societies.

Careers 4 part time advisors. Average number of pupils accepted for *arts and humanities degree courses* at Oxbridge, 7; other universities, 38; polytechnics or CHE, 5. *science and engineering degree courses* at Oxbridge, 5; other universities, 17; medical schools, 4; polytechnics or CHE, 4. *BEd*, 2. *other general training courses*, 1. Average number of pupils going straight into careers in the City, 1; music/drama, 1; other, 6. Traditional school careers are law, medicine.

Uniform School uniform worn except the sixth.

Houses/prefects No competitive houses or prefects. Head girl and team of Deputies – elected by the school. School Forum.

Religion Religious worship encouraged; morning assembly for whole school.

Social Joint orchestra with Latymer Upper School. Trips to France, Germany and Italy. Senior pupils allowed to bring own bike to school. Meals self service. School shop. No tobacco/alcohol allowed.

Discipline Pupils failing to produce homework once might expect advice.

GORDONSTOUN

Gordonstoun School
Elgin
Morayshire IV30 2RF
Telephone number 0343 380445

Enquiries/application to the Headmaster

- Co-ed
- Boys
- Girls
- Mixed sixth
- Day
- Boarding

Pupils 470
Upper sixth 90
Termly fees:
Day £1526
Boarding £2376
HMC

WHAT IT'S LIKE

Founded in 1934 by Kurt Hahn from Salem. It began in two historic houses: Gordonstoun House and the famous 17th century 'Round Square'. In 1951 part of the school moved to Altyre. In 1960 an intensive building programme enabled the school to re-unite. There was further expansion and development in the 1970s and thereafter and it is now one of the best-equipped schools in the country. The complex lies on a 150-acre estate in magnificent countryside which includes a mile of the Moray Firth foreshore. The prep school is at Aberlour House, 20 miles away on the banks of the River Spey. There are beautiful gardens and playing fields at both. The school's motto is, appropriately, 'Plus est en vous' (There is more in you than you think). Hahn's celebrated triple view of education – the Ionian, Spartan and Platonic – have made a basis for a philosophy of education which is exemplified in Gordonstoun life. It aims to produce balanced men and women who know the value of working hard but 'who have tried their hands at boats as well as books'. It strives for all-round development and lays emphasis on skill, enterprise, a sense of adventure and compassion. There is much emphasis, too, on self-reliance and responsibility to oneself as well as to others. Hahn's vision of a school as a place where international understanding should be fostered has also become part of the Gordonstoun way of life. A fifth of the school come from overseas (8% of pupils have English as their second language) and exchanges are made regularly with schools in Australia, New Zealand, Canada, France and Germany. All are expected to attend chapel services. A large staff allows a staff:pupil ratio of 1:9. The teaching is very good and academic standards are high. Results are consistently impressive and 55–60 pupils go on to university each year. Music and drama are very strong indeed and high standards are achieved in performance. A wide range of sports and team games with a high level of attainment and plenty of fixtures. There are also outdoor pursuits, including ski-ing, wind-surfing, gliding, game shooting, fishing, canoeing and rock-climbing and all pupils do a course in seamanship and some expeditions. Not surprisingly the school has a remarkable record in the Duke of Edinburgh's Award Scheme. Many pupils are also involved in a fire service, a coastguard unit, plus mountain rescue and inshore rescue units. There is also an Air Training Corps and a large community service unit.

SCHOOL PROFILE

Pupils Total, 470. Day 20 (boys 9, girls 11); Boarding 450 (boys 255, girls 195). Entry age, 13 and into the sixth. Aberlour House provides 20–25%. Approx 5% are children of former pupils.

Entrance Common entrance and own scholarship exams used. No special skills or religious requirements but abilities in different areas will always be helpful. Parents not expected to buy text books. 21 assisted places. 25 scholarships/bursaries pa, full fees to £850 pa.

Parents 22% live within 100 miles; 20% live overseas.

Staff Head M B Mavor, in post for 10 years. 54 full time staff, 18 part time. Annual turnover 2–3%. Average age 38.

Academic work GCSE and A-levels; also centre for SAT and Achievement Test for US colleges. Average size of upper fifth 100; upper sixth 90. On average, 45 take science/engineering A-levels and 45 take arts and humanities A-levels. A-level design offered. *Computing facilities*: 16 station research machines Nimbus network. 12 BBC computers and various microcomputers.

Senior pupils' non-academic activities *Music*: 187 learn a musical instrument, 80 to Grade 6 or above, 2 accepted for Music School; 64 in school orchestra, 40 in school choir, 20 in various ensembles; 2 in National Youth Orchestra, Scotland, 6 in Grampian Symphony Orchestra. *Drama and dance*: 150 pa in school opera/light musical/serious drama/revue productions. Occasional acceptances for Drama/Dance Schools, 2–3 for drama at university. 2 pa for National Youth Theatre. *Art*: 45 take as non-examined subject; 18 GCSE; 10 A-level. 4 accepted for Art School; 2, other art courses. 40 belong to art project, 20 to art society. *Sport*: All usual games plus ski-ing, windsurfing, gliding, game shooting, fishing, canoeing, orienteering and rock climbing. All pupils do a course in seamanship and go on expeditions. More than 250 take non-compulsory sport. More than 50 take exams. 3 represent county/country in rugby; also cross-country and downhill ski-ing, athletics. *Other*: 64 take part in local community schemes. 67 have bronze Duke of Edinburgh's Award, 13 have silver and 23 gold. Participation also in fire service, 24; community service, 55; coastguards, 20; mountain rescue, 45; inshore rescue, 39. Other activities include a computer club, a wide variety of clubs, projects and societies; music and drama are of a very high standard.

Careers 2 part time careers advisors. Average number of pupils accepted for *degree courses* at Oxbridge, 4; other universities, 45; overseas universities, 8; medical schools, 4; polytechnics or CHE, 13. *other general training courses*, 10. Average number of pupils going straight into careers in armed services, 5; the City, 2; other, 1.

Uniform School uniform worn throughout.

Houses/prefects Prefects, head boy/girl, head of house and house prefects. School Council.

Religion Services are non-denominational and pupils are expected to attend.

Social Many games fixtures and debates with other schools. Exchanges with schools in Germany, USA, Australia, France; trips abroad for ski-ing and with rugby, squash teams and orchestra. Pupils allowed to bring own bike to school. Meals self service. School shop. No tobacco/alcohol allowed.

Discipline No corporal punishment.

Boarding Houses, of approximately 55–60, are single sex. Resident qualified medical staff. Central dining room. Pupils can on occasion provide and cook their own food. Weekend exeats and visits to local town allowed.

Alumni association run by G Neil Esq (Chairman), The Gordonstoun Association, 25 Grosvenor Street, London W1X 9FE.

GRANGE, THE

The Grange School
Bradburns Lane
Hartford
Northwich, Cheshire CW8 1LR
Telephone number 0606 74007

Enquiries to the Headmaster's Secretary
Application to the Admissions Secretary

- Co-ed   Pupils 400+
  Boys   Upper sixth Yes
  Girls   Termly fees:
  Mixed sixth   Day £600
- Day   ISAI
  Boarding

WHAT IT'S LIKE

Founded in 1933 as a kindergarten/prep school. In 1978, as a result of vigorous local and parental support, a grammar school was built and this venture has been a resounding success. The school has pleasant modern buildings with 13 acres of sports grounds. In the last 10 years a million pounds have been spent on building programmes and facilities are now first-rate. A busy, purposeful school where academic results in the sixth form are already burgeoning. About 75–80% of the sixth form go on to university or polytechnic. There are active music, drama and art depts. A good range of games and sports, plus extra-curricular activities. A promising record in the Duke of Edinburgh's Award Scheme.

SCHOOL PROFILE

Pupils Total over 12, 400+ (boys 200, girls 200). Entry age, 11 and into the sixth. Own prep school provides over 60%.

Entrance Own entrance exam used. Oversubscribed. No special skills or religious requirements.

Parents 75+% in industry or commerce. 90+% live within 30 miles.

Staff Head E Scott Marshall, in post for 11 years. 40 full time staff, 12 part time.

Academic work GCSE and A-levels. *Computing facilities*: 11 BBC Model 'B'; 1 RML 380E; 2 Commodore 32K Pets; 4 Printers; 1 Modem; extensive range of other peripherals and software.

Senior pupils' non-academic activities *Music*: 50 learn a musical instrument, 12 to Grade 6 or above; 40 in school orchestra, 32 in school choir, 4 in string quartet, 6 in brass group; 2 in National Children's Orchestra, 5 in local youth orchestra, 2 in 'Bessies' Brass Band. *Drama and dance*: 18 in school productions, 30 in house plays. 10 Grade 6 in ESB, RAD etc. 2 accepted for Drama Schools. *Art*: 45 take as non-examined subject; 8 take A-level. 2 accepted for Art School. *Sport*: Football, rugby, hockey, netball, athletics, tennis, rounders and cricket available. All take part in non-compulsory sport. *Other*: 12 have silver Duke of Edinburgh's Award, 16 have gold. Other activities include a computer club, art, bookshop, chess, bridge, debating, drama, electronics, mathematics clubs.

Careers 4 part time advisors. 10% go on to Oxbridge; 70–80% to other universities.

Uniform School uniform worn except in sixth.

Houses/prefects Competitive houses. Prefects, head boy/girl, head of house and house prefects – appointed by Headmaster and staff.

Religion Regular religious worship.

Social Organised trips abroad, regular exchange with French school. Pupils allowed to bring own car/bike/motorbike to school. Meals self service. Clothing shop. No tobacco/alcohol allowed.

GREENACRE

Greenacre School	Co-ed	Pupils 279
Sutton Lane	Boys	Upper sixth 20
Banstead	● Girls	Termly fees:
Surrey SM7 3RA	Mixed sixth	Day £535
Telephone number 0732 353820	● Day	Boarding £1125
Enquiries/application to the Headmistress	● Boarding	

WHAT IT'S LIKE

Founded in 1938, it is single-site on the edge of the green belt in pleasant surroundings. Most of the buildings are converted houses plus purpose-built accommodation. Facilities are good. A sound general education is provided and results are creditable. Between 5 and 10 leavers go on to university each year. A high proportion of the girls are involved in music, drama and art. An adequate range of games and sports and adequate activities. No local community services and no Duke of Edinburgh's Award Scheme.

SCHOOL PROFILE

Pupils Total 279. 5% are children of former pupils.
Entrance Own entrance exam used. Oversubscribed. No special skills or

religious requirements. Parents not expected to buy text books. 1 Founder scholarship pa at 11+ for half day fees. Several sixth form scholarships and bursaries; 10% reduction for service children.

Parents 15+% are doctors, lawyers, etc; 15+% in industry or commerce. 60+% live within 30 miles; up to 10% live overseas.

Staff Head Miss R E Haggerty, in post for 11 years. Annual turnover 5%.

Academic work GCSE and A-levels. Average size of upper fifth 50; upper sixth 20. *O-levels*: on average, 20 pupils in upper fifth pass 1–4 subjects; 14, 5–7 subjects; 21 pass 8+ subjects. *A-levels*: on average, 2 in the upper sixth pass 1 subject; 4, 2 subjects; 14 pass 3 subjects. On average, 20% take science/engineering A-levels; 60% take arts and humanities; 20%, a mixture. Photography offered to GCSE. *Computing facilities*: 10 BBC series B computers, 1 380Z. EFL teacher.

Senior pupils' non-academic activities *Music*: 40% learn a musical instrument, 4% to Grade 6 or above; 20% in school orchestra, 30% in school choir; 1 Choral Award to Cambridge, 1 post O music scholarship. *Drama and dance*: 60% in school productions. 1 accepted for Drama/Dance school. 30% do speech and drama exams. *Art*: 60% take as non-examined subject; 5% take GCSE; 20% of sixth form take A-level. 20% of sixth form accepted for Art School. 5% belong to photographic club. *Sport*: Lacrosse, netball, tennis, rounders, swimming, golf, squash and badminton are available. 20% take non-compulsory sport. Some represent county/country (lacrosse, squash, netball). Some pupils work for national charities, other activities include a computer club, drama and music being the strongest societies.

Careers 1 part time advisor. Average number of pupils accepted for *arts and humanities degree courses* at Oxbridge, 1; other universities, 4; polytechnics or CHE, 1. *science and engineering degree courses* at universities, 2; medical schools, 1; polytechnics or CHE, 2. *BEd*, 4. *other general training courses*, 10. Average number of pupils going straight into careers in police, 1; banking, 1.

Uniform School uniform worn except fifth and sixth.

Houses/prefects Competitive houses. Prefects, head girl, head of house and house prefects – elected by the school. School Council.

Religion Worship compulsory.

Social No organised local events. Many organised trips abroad. Pupils allowed to bring own car/bike/motorbike to school. Some meals formal, some self service. No tobacco/alcohol allowed.

Discipline No corporal punishment. Pupils failing to produce homework once might expect a sharp word; those caught smoking cannabis on the premises might expect parental involvement and expulsion.

Boarding No dormitories of 6 or more. Houses, of approximately 17 and 21, are divided by age. Central dining room. Sixth form pupils can provide and cook their own food. 2–3 exeats each term. Visits to the local town allowed on Saturdays.

GRENVILLE COLLEGE

Grenville College
Bideford
North Devon EX39 3JR
Telephone number 02372 72212

Co-ed   Pupils 350
● Boys   Upper sixth Yes
Girls   Termly fees:
Mixed sixth   Day £875
● Day   Boarding £1735
● Boarding   SHMIS; GBA;
                 Woodard

Head Dr D C Powell-Price (13 years)
Age range 10–18; entry by common entrance or own exam
Bursaries and scholarships. Dyslexia and EFL provisions.

GRESHAM'S

Gresham's School
Holt
Norfolk NR25 6EY
Telephone number 0263 713271

● Co-ed   Pupils 470
Boys   Upper sixth Yes
Girls   Termly fees:
Mixed sixth   Day £1480
● Day   Boarding £2180
● Boarding   HMC

WHAT IT'S LIKE

Founded in 1555 by Sir John Gresham. The endowments were placed under the management of the Fishmongers' Company with which the school retains close associations. It enjoys a fine position in one of the most beautiful parts of England, a few miles from the sea near Sheringham. There are delightful grounds of about 50 acres and some 90 acres of woodland as well. All the buildings except the Old School House (1870) are 20th century. Since 1964 there have been extensive developments and accommodation and facilities are now excellent. There are five boys' boarding houses and one girls' house. The policy is to increase the number of girls. It is a C of E foundation and a good deal of attention is given to religious instruction. However, all denominations are accepted. Academic standards are high and results are very good. About 50–75 per cent of leavers go on to university each year, the majority to Cambridge. A wide variety of sports and games are available and the facilities for these are first-rate. Music and drama are an important part of the school's life and there is considerable strength in these fields. A very good range of extra-curricular activities. The CCF contingent is strong and there is a good deal of emphasis on outdoor pursuits. The prep school and pre-prep school are affiliated. At present there are about 335 boys and 75 girls in the senior school.

SCHOOL PROFILE

Head Mr H R Wright (3 years)
Age range 13–19; entry by common entrance
4 scholarships and 5 assisted places pa, plus music scholarships.

GROSVENOR HIGH

Grosvenor High School
Grosvenor Place
London Road
Bath
Avon BA1 6AX
Telephone number 0225 314458

- Co-ed   Pupils 160
- Boys   Upper sixth No
- Girls   Termly fees:
- Mixed sixth   Day £590
- Day
- Boarding

Enquiries/application to the Headmaster

WHAT IT'S LIKE

Founded in 1915, moved to its present site in 1954. Own prep school takes pupils of 8–11, main school teaches up to GCSE. Many pupils transfer to other schools for A-levels. Separate unit within the school caters for children with specific learning difficulties, liaising with external consultant psychologists and tailoring the timetable to suit the individual child. Parents of children using the unit are charged an extra fee. The school operates a branch of the Midland Bank (staffed by pupils).

SCHOOL PROFILE

Pupils Total 160. Boys 80, girls 80. Entry age, 11. Own junior school provides over 20%. 10% are children of former pupils.

Entrance Not oversubscribed. No special skills or religious requirements. Parents not expected to buy text books. 2 scholarships, £100 per term to half fees.

Parents 40% in industry or commerce. 60+% live within 30 miles.

Staff Head R H Side, in post for 4 years. 8 full time staff, 4 part time, plus 3 music staff. Annual turnover 1. Average age 35–40.

Academic work GCSE and AEB basic tests. Average size of upper fifth 35. *O-levels*: on average, 20 pupils in upper fifth pass 1–4 subjects; 15, 5–7 subjects. *Computing facilities*: Amstrads – 5 in computer studies room and various BBC 'B's in classrooms, including dyslexic unit. Nimbus network installed 1988–89. Special provision for pupils with learning difficulties, mainly dyslexia, and EFL. Foreign students accepted on a termly basis.

Senior pupils' non-academic activities *Music*: 28 learn a musical instrument; 12 take GCSE. 34 in choir. *Drama and dance*: 40 in school productions; 1 accepted for Drama School, 1 for Dance School; 20 enter competitions (Mid Somerset Festival). *Art*: All take GCSE. *Sport*: Wide range of sports and activities all played and coached at Bath University. 6 represent county (swimming, athletics). *Other*: 16 have bronze Duke of Edinburgh's Award. Other activities include computer, robotics and science clubs. Gymnastics, sailing, judo, craft. YHA trips, activity days out and weekend camps. School Council runs many activities and own bank account.

Careers 2 part time advisors. Approximately 23 pa go to other schools for A-levels. *general training courses*, 12. Average number of pupils going straight into careers in the armed services, 2; banks and finance houses, 3.

Uniform School uniform worn throughout.

Houses/prefects Competitive houses. Prefects, head boy and girl – appointed after written application and interview. School Council.

Religion Compulsory morning assembly.
Social Organised French trips at Easter. Annual ski trip abroad or Scotland. Pupils allowed to bring own bike to school. All pupils bring own lunch. School shop. No tobacco/alcohol allowed.
Discipline No corporal punishment. Pupils failing to produce homework once might expect a detention. Conduct report for minor offences. Work report in conjunction with parental co-operation.

GUILDFORD HIGH

High School for Girls
London Road
Guildford
Surrey GU1 1SJ
Telephone number 0483 61440

Co-ed
Boys
● Girls
Mixed sixth
● Day
Boarding

Pupils 452
Upper sixth Yes
Termly fees:
Day £875
CSCL; GSA

Head Miss J E Dutton (11 years)
Age range 11–18, own prep from age 5; entry by own exam. Sixth form scholarships.

HABERDASHERS' ASKE'S (BOYS)

The Haberdashers' Aske's School
Butterfly Lane
Elstree
Borehamwood
Hertfordshire WD6 3AF
Telephone number 01 207 4323

Co-ed
● Boys
Girls
Mixed sixth
● Day
Boarding

Pupils 945
Upper sixth 150
Termly fees:
Day £1122
HMC

Enquiries to the School Secretary
Applications to the Admissions Secretary

WHAT IT'S LIKE

Founded in 1690 by the Worshipful Company of Haberdashers; the original buildings were opened at Hoxton in 1692. In 1898 it moved to new buildings in Hampstead and in 1947 a prep school was opened at Mill Hill. The whole school moved to Elstree in 1961. Thirteen years later the Haberdashers' Aske's School for Girls moved to the adjoining site. The two now occupy fine grounds and playing fields in green belt country covering about 104 acres. With the exception of the original building (Aldenham House) all were purpose-built. The result is a fine modern school with splendid facilities. Standards of teaching are high and a large number of pupils go on to further education (110–120 university entrants per year). Very strong in music, drama and art. Also has much strength in sports and games. There are no fewer than 48 clubs and societies providing as many different activities. Extra-curricular activities are shared with the Girls' School. Excellent results in the Duke of Edinburgh's Award Scheme.

SCHOOL PROFILE

Pupils Total over 12, 945. Entry age, 7, 11 and into sixth. Own prep school provides 30+%. 4% are children of former pupils.

Entrance Common entrance sometimes used; usually own entrance exam. Oversubscribed. No special skills or religious requirements. Parents not expected to buy text books. 40 assisted places pa. 12 bursaries (including at least one for music), £1000–£600.

Parents 15+% in industry or commerce; 15+% are doctors, lawyers, etc. 60+% live within 30 miles.

Staff Head K Dawson, in post for 1 year. 94 full time staff, 22 part time. Annual turnover 8%. Average age 39.

Academic work GCSE and A-levels. Average size of upper fifth 150; upper sixth 150. *O-levels*: average pupil passes 8.8. *A-levels*: on average, 2 pupils in the upper sixth pass 1 subject; 6, 2 subjects; 121, 3 subjects and 20 pass 4. On average, 65 take science/engineering A-levels; 45 take arts and humanities; 40 a mixture. Arabic and Chinese offered. *Computing facilities*: 3 specialist rooms in computing department, ample hardware and good software. Increasing use of computing in other departments. Network of micros in prep school. Qualified assistance for few dyslexic pupils.

Senior pupils' non-academic activities *Music*: 480 learn a musical instrument, 180 to Grade 6 or above; 1 accepted for Music School, 2 in pop group; 100 in school orchestra, 80 in choir; 1 in National Youth Orchestra. *Drama and dance*: 60 in school productions; 2 accepted for Drama Schools, 2 to work in theatre. *Art*: 120 take as non-examined subject; 40 take GCSE, 10 take A-level, 5 take AS-level. 3 accepted for Art School. 15 belong to photographic club, 20 to art club after school, 10 to poster group, 10 to typography group, 5 to stage group. *Sport*: Archery, athletics, badminton, basketball, cricket, cross country, fencing, football, golf, hockey, rugby, sailing and sailboarding, shooting, squash, swimming, table tennis, tennis, volleyball and water-polo available. 180–200 take non-compulsory sport. 6 take exams in lifesaving. 9 pupils represent county (rugby, hockey, cricket). *Other*: 70 have silver Duke of Edinburgh's Award and 5 gold. Other activities include a computer club and 48 others – wide variety.

Careers 6 part time careers advisors. Average number of pupils accepted for *arts and humanities degree courses* at Oxbridge, 21; other universities, 37; polytechnics or CHE, 6. *science and engineering degree courses* at Oxbridge, 19; other universities, 38; medical schools, 9; polytechnics or CHE, 2. *BEd*, 2. *other general training courses*, 2. Average number of pupils going straight into careers in armed services, 3; industry, 1; the City, 2; music/drama, 2.

Uniform School uniform worn except in sixth.

Houses/prefects Competitive houses. Prefects, head boy, head of house and house prefects – appointed after consultation. Sixth Form Committee.

Religion Daily assemblies.

Social Extra-curricular activities shared with sister girls' school. Organised trips to Europe and USA. Pupils allowed to bring own car/bicycle/motorbike to school. Meals self service. School shop. No tobacco/alcohol allowed.

Discipline No corporal punishment. Pupils failing to produce homework

once might expect extra work; those caught smoking cannabis on the premises could expect exclusion from school pending enquiry and consultation with parents.

Alumni association is run by Jeremy Gibb, Secretary, Old Haberdashers' Association, c/o the School.

Former pupils Michael Green (Carlton Communications Group – Thames Television, LWT etc); Nicholas A Serota (Director: Tate Gallery); Rt Hon Leon Brittan PC, QC, MP.

HABERDASHERS' ASKE'S (GIRLS)

Haberdashers' Aske's School for Girls
Aldenham Road
Elstree
Hertfordshire WD6 3BT
Telephone number 01-953 4261

Enquiries/application to the Admissions
Secretary

Co-ed   Pupils 712
Boys   Upper sixth 112
● Girls   Termly fees:
Mixed sixth   Day £693
● Day   GSA
Boarding

WHAT IT'S LIKE

Founded in 1690, in 1974 it moved to Aldenham estate which is semi-rural and comprises 43 acres of fine park and woodland. A single-site school with first-rate modern facilities. Religious worship is compulsory. Academic standards are very high and results first-class. About 75–80 leavers go on to university each year (including 15 or more to Oxbridge). Immensely strong in music, drama and art. A very good range of games and sports in which high standards are achieved (several representatives at county and national level). A wide variety of activities are available. The school has an outstanding record in the Duke of Edinburgh's Award Scheme.

SCHOOL PROFILE

Pupils Total over 12, 712. Entry age, 5, 7, 11, and into the sixth. Own junior school provides over 20%. 1 or 2% are children of former pupils.

Entrance Own entrance exam used. Oversubscribed. All special skills welcomed. Parents not expected to buy text books. 127 assisted places. 6–10 scholarships/bursaries, for academic skills, £650 to £350.

Parents 15+% are doctors, lawyers, etc; 15+% in industry or commerce. 60+% live within 30 miles.

Staff Head Mrs S Wiltshire, in post for 13 years. 62 full time staff, 20 part time. Annual turnover 10–12%. Average age 39.

Academic work GCSE and A-levels. Average size of upper fifth 120; upper sixth 112. *O-levels*: on average, 2 pupils in upper fifth pass 1–4 subjects; 14, 5–7 subjects; 104 pass 8+ subjects. *A-levels*: on average 5 pupils in the upper sixth pass 1 subject; 8, 2 subjects; 95, 3 subjects; 4 pass 4 subjects. On average, 50% take science/engineering A-levels; 45% take arts and humanities; 5% a mixture. *Computing facilities*: Computer studies centre and individual provision in certain departments and lower school.

Senior pupils' non-academic activities *Music*: 173 learn a musical instrument, 110 to Grade 6 or above, 38 take GCSE, 22 take A-level, 2 accepted for Music School, 4 to Royal School of Music; 2 take university degree, 70 in school orchestra, 110 in school choir, 6 in school pop group, 30 in chamber ensembles; 1 in National Youth Orchestra, 28 in outside choirs, 18 in LEA choir/orchestra, 5 in County Youth Orchestra, 9 in Jewish Youth Club. 27 continue instrument lessons. *Drama and dance*: 30–50 in school productions, 10 in other. *Art*: 33 take GCSE, 5 take A-level. 4 accepted for Art School. *Sport*: Lacrosse, netball, rounders, tennis, trampolining, badminton, swimming, fencing, table tennis, keep fit, golf and riding available. 125 take non-compulsory sport. 14 take exams. 7 represent county (lacrosse, squash, tennis, hockey); 3 represent country in swimming. 33 take skiing trip. *Other*: 94 have bronze Duke of Edinburgh's Award, 38 have silver and 6 gold. Other activities include a computer club, bridge, chess, community service, science, electronics, debating and public speaking, cultural society, modern languages, Christian Union, school magazine and Young Enterprise.

Careers 1 full time advisor. Average number of pupils accepted for *arts and humanities degree courses* at Oxbridge, 9; other universities, 33; polytechnics or CHE, 6. *science and engineering degree courses* at Oxbridge, 5; other universities, 27; medical schools, 5; polytechnics or CHE, 5. *BEd*, 1. *other general training courses*, 4. Average number of pupils going straight into careers in industry, 2; music and drama, 3.

Uniform School uniform worn except the sixth.

Houses/prefects No competitive houses. Prefects and head girl elected by school. School Council.

Religion Compulsory worship.

Social Debates, quizzes and many extra-curricular activities with brother school next door. Organised trips abroad. Pupils allowed to bring own car/bike to school. Meals self-service. School shop. No tobacco/alcohol allowed.

Discipline No corporal punishment. Pupils failing to produce homework once might expect a warning; those caught smoking cannabis on the premises might expect expulsion.

HABERDASHERS' MONMOUTH

Haberdashers' Monmouth School for Girls	Co-ed	Pupils 510
Hereford Road	Boys	Upper sixth Yes
Monmouth	● Girls	Termly fees:
Gwent NP5 3XT	Mixed sixth	Day £800
Telephone number 0600 4214	● Day	Boarding £1420
	● Boarding	GSA

Head Miss Helen L Gichard (2 years)
Age range 11–18, own prep from age 7; entry by own exam
Scholarships.

HAILEYBURY

Haileybury and Imperial Service College
Hertford SG13 7NU
Telephone number 0992 463353/462352

Enquiries/application to the Registrar

Co-ed
● Boys
Girls
● Mixed sixth
● Day
● Boarding

Pupils 690
Upper sixth 155
Termly fees:
Day £1600
Boarding £2500
HMC

WHAT IT'S LIKE

Founded in 1862, it lies in a beautiful estate of 500 acres of countryside and playing fields. By any school standards the buildings are magnificent. The main buildings, quadrangle and terrace front were designed by William Wilkins in 1806 for the East India College where, for 50 years, students of the East India Company were educated. In 1874 one of the Haileybury housemasters became head of the United Services College at Westward Ho!. This later moved to Windsor and became the Imperial Service College. In 1942 Haileybury and the ISC combined. The school maintained the tradition of 'imperial service' well into the 1950s. The original main quadrangle forms the centre of the school and round it are the domed Romanesque chapel, the library, council chamber and six houses. There have been many additions since the beginning of this century and the overall facilities are first-class. The religious education aims to prepare pupils for adult membership of the C of E and some chapel services are compulsory. A large staff allows a staff:pupil ratio of about 1:10. The teaching is very good, academic standards are high and results are excellent. Some 85–90 leavers go on to university each year, 20–25 of these to Oxbridge. The music department is one of the strongest in the country (about 260 pupils learn an instrument, there are several orchestras and choirs, a concert band and a pop group). Drama is also extremely strong and there are many productions each year. The art and design centre is very active and work of high quality is achieved. A wide variety of sports and games is provided (including real tennis) and the school is well-known for its successes (numerous representatives at county and national levels). A good deal of emphasis on outdoor pursuits. A large and flourishing CCF and an impressive record in the Duke of Edinburgh's Award Scheme.

SCHOOL PROFILE

Pupils Total, 690. Day 110 (boys 100, girls 10); Boarding 580 (boys 490, girls 90). Entry age, boys, 13; boys and girls into the sixth. Own junior school in Windsor provides over 20%. 35% are children of former pupils.

Entrance Common entrance and own entrance exam used. Oversubscribed. No special skills required; C of E school but others accepted. Parents expected to buy text books. 15 scholarships (academic, music and art) and bursaries (by arrangement), full fees to £600.

Parents 30+% live within 30 miles; up to 10% live overseas.

Staff Head D J Jewell, in post for 1 year. 70 full time staff, 10 part time.

Academic work GCSE and A-levels. Average size of upper fifth 110; upper sixth 155. *O-levels*: on average, 7.7 passes per candidate. *A-levels*: on average, 10 pupils in upper sixth pass 1 subject; 22, 2 subjects; 100, 3 subjects and 10 pass 4 subjects. On average, 40% take science/engineering A-levels; 40%

take arts and humanities; 20% a mixture. Medieval and Ancient History offered to A-level; Spanish, GCSE and A-level; Russian GCSE. *Computing facilities*: Technology centre with fully equipped computer room; computers in most departments. EFL provision.

Senior pupils' non-academic activities *Music*: 258 learn a musical instrument, 120 to Grade 6 or above, 4 accepted for Music School; 1 Oxbridge organ scholarship, 6 accepted to read music at university; 56 in school orchestra, 170 in choir, 8 in pop group, 60 in concert band. *Drama and dance*: One-third in school productions, remainder in small group productions. About 20 former pupils now professional actors. *Art*: 50 take as non-examined subject; 24 GCSE; 15 A-level; 16 History of Art. 6 accepted for Art School. 30 belong to photographic club. *Sport*: Rackets, tennis, squash, fives, basketball, badminton, hockey, football, rugby, cricket, archery, windsurfing, sailing, canoeing, lacrosse, netball, trampolining, weight training, athletics, cross country, golf, swimming, scuba diving, real tennis, judo, fencing available. All take non-compulsory sport as well as compulsory. Many pupils have represented county/country in all sports. *Other*: 55 take part in local community schemes. 30 have bronze Duke of Edinburgh's Award, 10 have silver and 4 gold. 3 enter voluntary schemes after leaving. Other activities include a computer club, chess, bridge, stamp collecting, woodwork, electronics, metalwork and plastics, technical drawing, printing, photography, calligraphy, ceramics.

Careers 2 part time careers advisors and 1 Services advisor. Average number of pupils accepted for *arts and humanities degree courses* at Oxbridge, 13; other universities, 42; polytechnics or CHE, 12. *science and engineering degree courses* at Oxbridge, 8; other universities, 24; medical schools, 5; polytechnics or CHE, 2. *other general training courses*, 1. Average number of pupils going straight into careers in armed services, 2; industry, 2; the City, 5; civil service, 1; music/drama, 1.

Uniform Modified school uniform worn throughout.

Houses/prefects Competitive houses. Prefects, head boy/girl, head of house and house prefects – appointed by Head.

Religion Daily chapel compulsory; also one Sunday service.

Social Geography field trips abroad, expeditions to Himalayas, cricket tours to Australia and Barbados, skiing etc. Some sixth form day pupils allowed to bring own car to school. Meals formal. School tuck and games equipment shops. No tobacco allowed; licensed sixth form bar sells wine and beer to 17+.

Discipline No corporal punishment. Pupils failing to produce homework once might expect detention.

Boarding A few sixth formers have own study bedroom, nearly all other pupils are in dormitories. Houses, of approximately 50, same as competitive houses and single sex. Resident qualified nurse and doctor. Central dining room. Pupils can provide and cook own food. 2 weekend exeats each term, and half term. Visits to local town allowed with housemaster's permission.

Alumni association run by Bill Tyrwhitt-Drake Esq, 1 Lodge Lane, Bexley, Kent DA5 1DJ.

Former pupils Clement Attlee (former PM); Stirling Moss (racing driver); Alan Ayckbourn (playwright); Max Robertson (sports commentator); Michael Bonallack (golfer); Simon MacCorkindale (actor); Lord de Freitas (Parliamentarian); Denis Mack Smith (historian).

HAMILTON LODGE

Hamilton Lodge School for Deaf Children
Walpole Road
Brighton
East Sussex BN2 2ET
Telephone number 0273 682362

- Co-ed
  Boys
  Girls
  Mixed sixth
- Day
- Boarding

Pupils 35
Upper sixth Yes
Termly fees:
Day £2325
Boarding £3100

Head Miss M M Moore (9 years)
Age range 7–18.
Many pupils' fees paid by their LEA.

HAMMOND

Hammond School
Hoole Bank House
Mannings Lane
Hoole Bank
Chester CH2 2PB
Telephone number 0244 28542

- Co-ed
  Boys
  Girls
  Mixed sixth
- Day
- Boarding

Pupils 120
Upper sixth No
Termly fees:
Day £640
Boarding £1770
ISAI

Head Sybil Elliott
Age range 11–16; entry by own exam and dance audition.
Grant-aided by most LEAs. Specialises in classical ballet training. No A-levels offered.

HAMPTON

Hampton School
Hanworth Road
Hampton
Middlesex TW12 3HD
Telephone number 01-979 5526

Enquiries/application to the Headmaster

Co-ed
- Boys
  Girls
  Mixed sixth
- Day
  Boarding

Pupils 750
Upper sixth 115
Termly fees:
Day £880
HMC

WHAT IT'S LIKE

Founded in 1557, endowed by the will of Robert Hammond, which provided for a school room beside the parish church and for a master's salary. The present buildings, which are on a single site in a suburban area, with adjoining playing fields, date from 1939. Recent extensions and developments provide good facilities and accommodation. It is very well equipped. Staffing allows a ratio of 1:14 pupils. Academic standards are high and results are good. Some 60–70 university entrants per year. An extremely strong music dept (a fine music centre was opened in 1978) and about 230 pupils learn an instrument. Considerable strength in drama and art. A high reputation in games and sports; especially rowing at which the school excels. A large number of county and international representatives in sports and games. There is a flourishing CCF and the school has a promising record in the Duke of Edinburgh's Award Scheme.

SCHOOL PROFILE

Pupils Total over 12, 750. Entry age, 11, 13 and into the sixth. 5% are children of former pupils.

Entrance Common entrance and own entrance exam used. Oversubscribed. No special skills or religious requirements. Parents not expected to buy text books. 150 assisted places. 8 scholarships/bursaries, £880 to £250.

Parents 15+% are doctors, lawyers, etc; 15+% in industry or commerce; 15+% in the armed services, 15+% in the Church; 15+% in the theatre, media, music etc. 60+% live within 30 miles.

Staff Head G G Able, in post from April 1988. 65 full time staff, 5 part time. Annual turnover 8–10%. Average age 38.

Academic work GCSE and A-levels. Average size of upper fifth 135; upper sixth 115. *O-levels*: on average, 11 pupils in upper fifth pass 1–4 subjects; 25, 5–7 subjects; 99 pass 8+ subjects. *A-levels*: on average, 6 pupils in the upper sixth pass 1 subject; 10, 2 subjects; 18, 3 subjects; 80 pass 4 subjects. On average, 33⅓% take science/engineering A-levels; 33⅓% take arts and humanities; 33⅓%, a mixture. Technology and theatre studies offered to GCSE/A-level. *Computing facilities*: Network of 15 RM Nimbus; 6 BBC; DEC PDP 11/34 mini. Some ad hoc help given for dyslexia or EFL.

Senior pupils' non-academic activities *Music*: 230 learn a musical instrument, 30 up to Grade 6 or above, 1 accepted for Music School; 55 in school orchestra, 80 in school choir, 50 in wind bands; 4 or 5 go on to play in pop group. *Drama and dance*: 70 in school productions. Some pupils accepted for Drama/Dance schools. *Art*: 20 sixth-formers take as non-examined subject; 25 take GCSE; 10 take A-level. 4–6 accepted for Art School. 10 belong to photographic club. *Sport*: Rugby, football, cricket, rowing, basketball, volleyball, tennis, table tennis, squash, swimming, athletics and cross-country available. 650 take non-compulsory sport. 12 represent country (rugby, rowing); 20 represent county (rugby, football, cricket, tennis). *Other*: 10 take part in local community schemes. 12 have bronze Duke of Edinburgh's Award, 6 have silver and 2 gold. 1 or 2 enter voluntary schemes after leaving school. Other activities include bridge, chess, war-games, debating and discussion, electronics, and whole range of subjects, societies and clubs, CCF (Army, RAF), adventure including climbing, camping, canoeing, expeditions at home and overseas.

Careers 5 part time advisors. Average number of pupils accepted for *arts and humanities degree courses* at Oxbridge, 6; other universities, 18; polytechnics or CHE, 3. *science and engineering degree courses* at Oxbridge, 12; other universities, 22; medical schools, 6; polytechnics or CHE, 8. BEd, 1. *other general training courses*, 6 (mostly HND). Average number of pupils going straight into careers in the armed services, 3; the church, 1–2; industry, 3; the City, 2; civil service, 2; other, 12.

Uniform School uniform worn throughout.

Houses/prefects No competitive houses. All upper sixth act as prefects. Head boy and 10 senior prefects.

Religion One traditional religious assembly per week, two Church services per year.

Social Drama (including joint A-level theatre studies), music, debates etc. with The Lady Eleanor Holles School. Exchanges with Konstanz (Germany), Orange (France). Skiing trips, expeditions etc. Pupils allowed to bring own bike/motorbike to school. Meals self service. School shop selling limited range of tuck. No tobacco/alcohol allowed.

Discipline No corporal punishment. Pupils failing to produce homework once might expect reprimand or perhaps lunch time detention; those caught smoking cannabis on the premises might expect expulsion.

Alumni association is run by C E Ledger Esq, 10 Garden Close, Hampton, Middlesex (Telephone: 01-979 4995).

HARROGATE COLLEGE

Harrogate Ladies' College	Co-ed	Pupils 350
Clarence Drive	Boys	Upper sixth 40+
Harrogate	● Girls	Termly fees:
North Yorkshire HG1 2QG	Mixed sixth	Day £1210
Telephone number 0423 504543	● Day	Boarding £1815
	● Boarding	GSA
Enquiries/application to the Headmistress		

WHAT IT'S LIKE

Founded in 1893, it has a most agreeable site in a quiet residential area (the Duchy estate) a few minutes' walk from the town centre and from the countryside. Harrogate itself is a pleasant and civilised town and the school's houses (7 formerly privately owned) are set in gardens. The college has an academic bias but aims to provide a very good all-round education for girls of above average and average intellectual ability. Though there are day pupils great attention is given to create a happy and purposeful resident community. The boarding accommodation is comfortable and every modern facility is provided. A C of E school (it has its own chapel) there is a certain emphasis on religious instruction and daily worship. The teaching is good and so are results (20 plus university entrants per year). Very strong in music (virtually everyone is involved). Substantial successes in the Duke of Edinburgh Award Scheme. Strong support in the local community where the school enjoys a high reputation.

SCHOOL PROFILE

Pupils Total over 12, 350. Day 44; Boarding 306. Entry age, 11 and into sixth. 4% are children of former pupils.

Entrance Own entrance exam used. Oversubscribed. No special skills or religious requirements. Parents not expected to buy text books (but pay a small hire charge). Up to 40 assisted places. 50+ scholarships/bursaries, 33%–25% of fees.

Parents 15+% in industry or commerce. 30+% live within 30 miles; 20% live overseas.

Staff Head Mrs J C Lawrance, in post for 14 years. 42 full time staff, 20 part time. Annual turnover 4%. Average age 40.

Academic work GCSE and A-levels. Average size of upper fifth 70–80; upper sixth 40+. *O-levels*: on average, 8 pupils in upper fifth pass 1–4 subjects; 24, 5–7 subjects; 43 pass 8+ subjects. *A-levels*: on average, 6 pupils in the upper sixth pass 1 subject; 9, 2 subjects; 12, 3 subjects and 8 pass 4 subjects. On average, 10 take science/engineering A-levels; 14 take arts and humanities; 18 a mixture. *Computing facilities*: 12 station laboratory – RML 480Z (12 machines), 2 380Z machines. BBC computers in careers library, maths and science depts. Specialist help available at dyslexia centre and for deaf pupils.

Senior pupils' non-academic activities *Music*: 200 learn a musical instrument, 10 to Grade 6 or above; some take GCSE and A-level; 2 accepted for Music School; 40 in school orchestra, 80 in choir, 20 in wind band, 15 in brass group, house music competitions; 1 in National Youth Orchestra, 5 in local youth orchestra. *Drama and dance*: 1 major school production each year, house drama, and public speaking competitions; 8 take to Grade 6 ESB. 1–2 accepted for Drama School. *Art*: 20 take GCSE, 5 A-level. 2–3 accepted for Art School. 15 in photographic club, 15 in ceramic club; CDT taught throughout. *Sport*: Netball, lacrosse, gymnastics, swimming, athletics, squash, tennis, badminton, volleyball, basketball, aerobics, yoga available. Many take non-compulsory sport. Many take exams, eg lifesaving. Pupils represent county (athletics, tennis, swimming, lacrosse). *Other*: 18 take part in local community schemes. 30 have bronze Duke of Edinburgh's Award, 20 have silver and 2–3 gold. 2–3 enter voluntary schemes after leaving school. 12 work for national charities. Other activities include a computer club, drawing, riding, amateur radio, maths, debating, sixth form society, British Association of Young Scientists, first aid, French club, guides, ballet, dancing, car maintenance.

Careers 2 full time careers advisors. Average number of pupils accepted for *arts and humanities degree courses* at Oxbridge, 1–2; other universities, 11; polytechnics or CHE, 12. *science and engineering degree courses* at Oxbridge, 1–2; other universities, 6; medical schools, 2; polytechnics or CHE, 2. *BEd*, 2. *other general training courses*, 4–6. Average number of pupils going straight into careers in armed services, 2; industry, 1–2; civil service, 1–2; other 2–3.

Uniform School uniform worn except in sixth.

Houses/prefects Competitive houses. Prefects, head girl, head of house and house prefects – appointed by staff. There is a committee of form representatives.

Religion Daily assembly and Sunday C of E services compulsory.

Social British Association of Young Scientists, sixth form society, industry conference etc with Ashville College (boys). Annual trips to France and Germany. Recent choir concerts in Russia and Czechoslovakia. Meals formal. School shop for small items. No tobacco/alcohol allowed.

Discipline Pupils failing to produce work once might expect more. Abuse of freedoms means restriction of privileges. Courtesy and consideration for others regarded as essential.

Boarding 50% have study bedroom, most shared with one other. Houses, of approximately 40–45 are divided by age. 2 resident qualified nurses. Central dining room. Upper sixth can provide and cook some food. 2 weekend exeats each term. Visits to local town allowed.

Alumni association is run by Mrs E Wheatcroft, Westfield Farm, North Wheatley, Retford DN22 9DU.

Former pupils Diane Leather (athlete); Henrietta Shaw (1st woman Cambridge cox); Sheila Burnford (writer – *The Incredible Journey*).

HARROW

Harrow School
Harrow-on-the-Hill
Harrow
Middlesex HA1 3HW
Telephone number 01-422 2196

Enquiries/application to the Registrar
or individual housemasters

Co-ed   Pupils 765
● Boys   Upper sixth 160
Girls   Termly fees:
Mixed sixth   Day £1860
● Day   Boarding £2480
● Boarding   HMC

WHAT IT'S LIKE

Founded in 1572 under a royal charter of Queen Elizabeth, its buildings are scattered over Harrow-on-the-Hill across some 360 acres. This superb environment includes a lake, a conservation area, a golf course and a sizeable farm. Ten million pounds have been spent in the last 7 years to create first-class accommodation and first-class facilities of every conceivable kind. The school has a notable reputation for its teaching and all-round academic achievements (90–100 university entrants each year, including 25–30 to Oxbridge). Very strong indeed in music and drama. Also a high standard in sport and games. Numerous extra-curricular activities. Substantial involvement with local schools and local community services.

SCHOOL PROFILE

Pupils Total 765, Day 5 (must reside on Harrow Hill); Boarding 760. Entry age, 13 and into sixth. 28–30% are children of former pupils.

Entrance Common entrance used. Oversubscribed. No special skills or religious requirements. Parents not expected to buy text books. 17–20 scholarships/bursaries, full fees – 10% fees.

Parents 15+% in industry or commerce, 15+% are doctors, lawyers etc; 15+% in armed services. 10+% live within 30 miles; up to 10% live overseas.

Staff Head I D S Beer, in post for 7 years. 79 full time staff, 36 part time. Annual turnover 3%. Average age 39.

Academic work GCSE and A-levels. Average size of upper fifth 150; upper sixth 160. *O-levels*: on average, 10 pupils in upper fifth pass 1–4 subjects; 30, 5–7 subjects; 120 pass 8+ subjects. *A-levels*: on average, 8 pupils in upper sixth pass 1 subject; 12, 2 subjects; 118, 3 subjects and 20 pass 4 subjects. On average, 59 take science/engineering A-levels; 78 take arts and humanities; 23 a mixture. Arabic offered to GCSE/A-level. Way of Life Course for all sixth formers. *Computing facilities*: Nimbus networks (one in CDT; one in computing centre). Computers in separate depts/classrooms/labs, boarding houses etc. Computing exams compulsory for all pupils.

Senior pupils' non-academic activities *Music*: 285 learn a musical instrument, 35 to Grade 6 or above, 4 accepted for Music School. 170 in school orchestras, 120 in choir, 20 in pop group; 2 in National Youth Orchestra. *Drama*: 100 in school productions, 250 in house productions, 50 in individual productions. *Art*: 225 take as non-examined subject; 50 take GCSE; 20 take A-level; 20 take history of art. 8 accepted for Art School. 25 belong to eg photographic club. *Sport*: Rugby, Harrow football, soccer, cricket, shooting (various), swimming, athletics, tennis, golf, archery, badminton, volleyball, basketball, Eton fives, rackets, squash, fencing, karate, cross country, show jumping available. 400 take non-compulsory sport. 31 pupils represent county/country (rugby, cricket, fencing, athletics, gymnastics, swimming). *Other*: 40 take part in local community schemes. 10 enter voluntary schemes after leaving school. Other activities include driving lessons, chess, bridge, farming, business companies.

Careers 10 part time careers advisors. Average number of pupils accepted for *arts and humanities degree courses* at Oxbridge, 13; other universities, 40; polytechnics or CHE, 6. *science and engineering degree courses* at Oxbridge, 15; other universities, 26; medical schools, 5; polytechnics or CHE, 5. Average number of pupils going straight into careers in armed services, 10; the church, 1; industry, 6; the City, 4; music/drama, 2; other, 28.

Uniform School uniform worn throughout.

Houses/prefects Competitive houses. Prefects (monitors), head boy, head of house and house prefects (monitors) – appointed by the head/masters/senior boys. Communal fagging; no personal fagging.

Religion Holy Communion and morning prayer every day; 2/3 services on Sunday. 2 C of E chaplains, 1 RC chaplain, 1 Jewish doctor.

Social Society meetings open to other local schools; exchanges with local comprehensive school, schools in Germany, France. Joint choral works, plays with local girls' schools, etc. Community service with girls' school, other local schools and in conjunction with NSPCC. Visits to London for concerts, plays etc. Trips this year to Jordan (scientific expedition), China, Greece, Australia, Austria, France, Egypt. Lunch formal, others self-service. School shops sell clothes, books, tuck and photographic items. No tobacco allowed; sixth form club over 17 is licensed.

Discipline No corporal punishment. Pupils failing to produce homework once might expect to repeat it plus extra work; those caught smoking cannabis on the premises could expect expulsion.

Boarding 60% have own study bedroom, 40% share with one other. Houses, of approximately 58–70. Resident qualified nurse. Central dining room. Pupils can use house kitchens for snacks. 2 Sunday exeats per term and half term. Visits to local town allowed with housemaster's permission.

Alumni association is run by J F Leaf, c/o Harrow School.

Former pupils Churchill; King Hussein; Crown Prince Hassan; Nehru; Lord Monckton; Duke of Westminster; Sir Keith Joseph; Earl of Lichfield; Sir William Deedes; Sir Robin Butler; Alexander of Tunis; Sir John Clark, etc.

HATHEROP CASTLE

Hatherop Castle School	Co-ed	Pupils 85
Hatherop	Boys	Upper sixth 4
Cirencester	● Girls	Termly fees:
Gloucestershire GL7 3NB	Mixed sixth	Day £920
Telephone number 0285 75206	● Day	Boarding £1800
Enquiries/application to the Headmaster	● Boarding	GBGSA; ISAI

WHAT IT'S LIKE

Founded in 1927 in Cambridge, it moved to its present site in 1946. This comprises what was formerly a semi-fortified Tudor country house (some parts survive from Tudor times) in a 30-acre estate in splendid Cotswold countryside. It is a delightful environment and the school provides very civilised accommodation. It has all the advantages of a small school (only 85 pupils) and a friendly and happy atmosphere prevails. The staff:pupil ratio is 1:7. A sound general education is provided and results are creditable. Everyone is involved in music and drama. A good range of games and sports and a fair variety of activities. All boarders are engaged in local community services.

SCHOOL PROFILE

Pupils Total over 12, 85. Day, 14; Boarding, 71. Entry age, 10, 11 and into the sixth. 25% are children of former pupils.

Entrance Common entrance and own entrance exam used. Not oversubscribed. No special skills or religious requirements. Parents not expected to buy text books. 5 scholarships/bursaries pa, half fees to 10%.

Parents 15+% in farming; 15+% in industry or commerce. 10+% live within 30 miles; up to 10% live overseas.

Staff Head Mr Brian Forster, in post for 3 years. 15 full time staff, 6+ part time. Annual turnover 5%. Average age 40.

Academic work Pupils prepared for GCSE, A-levels, RSA, Pitman and Associated Board of Music. Average size of upper fifth 20; upper sixth 4. *O-levels*: on average, 9 pupils in upper fifth pass 1–4 subjects; 8, 5–7 subjects; 3 pass 8+ subjects. *A-levels*: Just started to teach A-level courses. Drama offered to GCSE/A-level. *Computing facilities*: Spectrum (48k) printers, Amstrad word processors.

Senior pupils' non-academic activities *Music*: 75 learn a musical instrument, 2 up to Grade 6 or above; 18 in school orchestra, 50 in school choir. *Drama and dance*: 50 in school productions, all girls take drama, 20 take GCSE. *Art*: 12 take GCSE. 15 in art club. *Sport*: Hockey, netball, tennis, swimming, rounders, squash, gymnastics and badminton are available. All take non-compulsory sport. 40 take exams. *Other*: All boarders take part in local community schemes. Other activities include knitting, drama and gymnastic clubs.

Careers 1 part time advisor. Average number of pupils accepted for *general training courses*, 6. Most pupils go on to sixth form at other schools.

Uniform School uniform worn on formal occasions only.

Houses/prefects Competitive houses. No prefects.

Religion No form of worship compulsory.

Social Organised trips abroad. Pupils allowed to bring own car/bike to school. Meals formal. School shop. No tobacco/alcohol allowed.

Discipline No corporal punishment. Pupils failing to produce homework once might expect to repeat it. Those caught smoking cannabis on the premises might expect expulsion.

Boarding 10% have own study bedroom, others share with up to 5. Resident qualified medical staff. Central dining room. Pupils can provide and cook own food. 2 weekend exeats each term. Visits to the local town allowed for seniors only, 2 or 3 times a term.

Former pupils Nancy Mitford; Rachel & Tracy Ward (actresses); Arabella Pollen (designer).

HEADINGTON

Headington School	Co-ed	Pupils 530
Oxford OX3 7TD	Boys	Upper sixth Yes
Telephone number 0865 62711	● Girls	Termly fees:
	Mixed sixth	Day £850
	● Day	Boarding £1570
	● Boarding	GSA; GBGSA

WHAT IT'S LIKE

Founded in 1916 by a group of people with a vision of a school that would provide a Christian education for girls. It is a C of E foundation. The buildings and playing fields occupy an agreeable site of 20 acres on Headington Hill, a mile from the city centre. The main building was opened in 1930. Since then there have been considerable extensions to provide excellent facilities. In the senior school there are about 500 girls (nearly half of them boarders aged 10 upwards) with some 120 girls in the sixth form. The prep department (on a separate site with a boarding house) is in walking distance and can take 130 pupils. A broad general education is provided and results are good. Pastoral care and careers guidance are efficiently run. Quite a large number of pupils come from overseas. There is an adequate range of games and sports (tennis is particularly well catered for). A good variety of clubs and societies.

SCHOOL PROFILE

Head Miss E M Tucker (6 years)

Age range 10–18, own prep from age 4; entry by common entrance or own exam. Early registration recommended.

Scholarships and bursaries available.

HEATHFIELD (ASCOT)

Heathfield School
London Road
Ascot
Berkshire SL5 8BQ
Telephone number 0344 882955

Co-ed
Boys
● Girls
Mixed sixth
Day
● Boarding

Pupils 200
Upper sixth Yes
Termly fees:
Boarding £2300
GSA

WHAT IT'S LIKE

Founded in 1899 with the object of giving girls a sound education within a religious framework. The buildings consist of a handsome late Georgian house in delightful and peaceful grounds of 34 acres near Swinley Forest and Englemere Pond. The teaching facilities are good and boarding accommodation very comfortable. The upper sixth live in their own purpose built bungalow where they are encouraged to cater for themselves. It is a strictly C of E foundation of Anglican worship. The chapel is physically and spiritually at the heart of the school. A well-balanced academic education is provided and standards are high. At A-level a 100% pass rate is expected. Quite a lot of pupils proceed to university each year. Very strong pastoral care system. Considerable strength in music, drama and art. Games and sports are well catered for and there are many extra-curricular activities. Frequent trips are made to London for cultural purposes.

SCHOOL PROFILE

Head Mrs S E Watkins (6 years)
Age range 11–18; entry by common entrance

HEATHFIELD (PINNER)

Heathfield School
Beaulieu Drive
Pinner
Middlesex HA5 1NB
Telephone number 01-868 2346

Enquiries/application to the Headmistress

Co-ed
Boys
● Girls
Mixed sixth
● Day
Boarding

Pupils 250
Upper sixth 19
Termly fees:
Day £789
GSA; GBGSA;
GPDST

WHAT IT'S LIKE

Founded in 1900 in Harrow, it has a 9-acre site (including playing fields) with pleasant buildings. Well positioned for public transport. It has good up-to-date facilities and provides a strong all-round education. The music and drama departments are strong. A reasonable range of games, sports and extra-curricular activities.

SCHOOL PROFILE

Pupils Total over 12, 250. Entry age, 7, 11 and into sixth. Own junior school provides 20+%. 1% are children of former pupils.

Entrance Own entrance exam used. Oversubscribed. No special skills or religious requirements. Some scholarships/bursaries.

Parents 15+% in industry or commerce, 15+% are doctors, lawyers, etc. 60+% live within 30 miles.

Staff Head Mrs J Merritt, in post for 1 year. 25 full time staff, 11 part time. Annual turnover 7%.

Academic work GCSE and A-levels. Average size of upper fifth 52; upper sixth 19. *O-levels*: on average, 16 pupils in upper fifth pass 1–4 subjects; 20, 5–7 subjects; 17 pass 8+ subjects. *A-levels*: on average, 2 pupils in upper sixth pass 1 subject; 8, 2 subjects; 6 pass 3 subjects. On average, 5 take science/engineering A-levels; 10 take arts and humanities; 3 a mixture. *Computing facilities*: 5 BBC and 1 380Z computers.

Senior pupils' non-academic activities *Music*: 154 learn a musical instrument, 10 to Grade 6 or above, 30 in school orchestra, 48 in choir, 6 in string group, 8 in recorder group; 6 in LEA Music School. *Drama and dance*: 90 in school productions. *Art*: 3 take A-level; 2 accepted for Art School. *Sport*: Rounders, tennis, athletics, lacrosse, netball available. 4 represent county at lacrosse. *Other*: Sixth form take part in local community schemes. 2 have bronze Duke of Edinburgh's Award and 2 have silver. Other activities include a computer club, social service volunteers, public speaking group, drama group, discussion group.

Careers 1 part time careers advisor. Average number of pupils accepted for *arts and humanities degree courses* at Oxbridge, 1; other universities 6; polytechnics or CHE, 2. *science and engineering degree courses* at universities, 4; polytechnics or CHE, 2. *BEd*, 1. *other general training courses*, 2. On average 2 pupils go straight into industry.

Uniform School uniform worn except in sixth.

Houses/prefects Competitive houses. Prefects, head girl, head of house and house prefects – elected by upper part of school.

Religion Daily assembly.

Social Social service volunteers with local boys' school. 2nd year go to France, 3rd year exchange with school in Paris. Occasional trips to Spain. Pupils allowed to bring own car/bicycle/motorbike to school. Meals self service. School tuck shop. No tobacco/alcohol allowed.

Discipline No corporal punishment. Pupils failing to produce homework once might expect reprimand by head; those caught smoking cannabis on the premises could expect parents to be involved immediately.

Alumni association is run by Mr Howard Gross, c/o the School.

HEREFORD CATHEDRAL

Hereford Cathedral School
Old College
29 Castle Street
Hereford HR1 2NN
Telephone number 0432 273757

Enquiries/application to the Headmaster

- Co-ed
  Boys
  Girls
  Mixed sixth
- Day
- Boarding

Pupils 529
Upper sixth 85
Termly fees:
Day £850
Boarding £1487
HMC

WHAT IT'S LIKE

There is no record of a foundation date but by 1384 a school had been long established and it is a fair presumption that some form of educational establishment had always adjoined the cathedral (founded in the 7th century). Hereford is one of the most beautiful cathedral cities in England and the school is situated right next to the cathedral and housed in a variety of fine buildings of different periods in lovely gardens very near the Wye. Large playing fields are nearby. It is a C of E foundation and religious instruction and worship are an essential part of its life. The school uses the cathedral for many services and the cathedral choristers are members of the school. Naturally, music plays a very important part in the curriculum. There is extensive participation in musical festivals. Academic standards are high and results are good. Sports and games flourish and there is a fine range of extra-curricular activities.

SCHOOL PROFILE

Pupils Total over 12, 529. Day 447 (boys 235, girls 212); Boarding 82 (boys 50, girls 32). Entry age, 11+ and into sixth. Own prep school provides 20+%.

Entrance Common entrance and own entrance exam used. Oversubscribed. No special skills required. All pupils attend Christian worship. Parents not expected to buy text books. 40 assisted places. 5 scholarships/bursaries.

Parents 60+% live within 30 miles; up to 10% live overseas.

Staff Head Dr Howard Tomlinson. 42 full time staff, 8 part time. Annual turnover 5%.

Academic work GCSE and A-levels. Average size of upper fifth 100; upper sixth 85. *O-levels*: on average, 75 pupils in upper fifth pass 8+ subjects. *A-levels*: on average, 60 pupils in upper sixth pass 3 subjects. On average, 40 take science/maths A-levels; 40 take arts and humanities; 5 a mixture. *Computing facilities*: Extensive.

Senior pupils' non-academic activities All pupils take a full part in a range of activities. *Sport*: Rugby, cricket, rowing, hockey, netball, tennis, squash and outward bound pursuits available. Other activities include a computer club.

Uniform School uniform worn throughout.

Houses/prefects Competitive houses. Prefects, head boy/girl, head of house and house prefects – appointed by the Head and House masters/mistresses. School Council.

Religion Daily services at the cathedral.

Social School participates in many Hereford festivals (3 Choirs, etc). Organised trips abroad. Pupils allowed to bring own car/bicycle to school. Meals self service. School shop. No tobacco/alcohol allowed.

Discipline No corporal punishment.

Boarding 20% have own study bedroom, 20% share. Houses, of approximately 30, are the same as competitive houses, divided by age group and single sex. Resident medical staff. Central dining room. Pupils can provide and cook own food. Exeats as required – some weekly boarding. Visits to local town allowed in daylight.

Former pupils Kingsley Martin; Godfrey Winn; Sir David Roberts; Peter and Dick Richardson; Paul Thorburn; Alec Rowe; Air Marshal Sir Geoffrey Dhenin.

HETHERSETT OLD HALL

Hethersett Old Hall School	Co-ed		Pupils 202
Hethersett	Boys		Upper sixth Yes
Norwich NR9 3DW	• Girls		Termly fees:
Telephone number 0603 810390	Mixed sixth		Day £805
	• Day		Boarding £1405
	• Boarding		GSA; ISAI

WHAT IT'S LIKE

Founded in 1928 at Hellesdon House near Norwich, it moved to its present site in 1938. The main building is a fine early Georgian house set in beautiful gardens and grounds. It and its associated buildings have been modernised and enlarged. Boarders have comfortable accommodation in the main house. There is an open-air stage and a play-house. Sports and games facilities are good. The school is affiliated to the Church of England, but girls of other denominations are accepted. Each day starts with morning prayers for all and religious instruction is part of the curriculum at all levels. Girls are encouraged to develop Christian attitudes and ideals in their relationships. It has many of the advantages of being a small school and a happy 'family' atmosphere prevails. There is considerable strength in music (which is much encouraged) and also in drama and art. A standard range of sports and games is available and there is a good variety of extra-curricular activities.

SCHOOL PROFILE

Head Mrs V M Redington
Age range 11–18, own prep from age 8; entry by own exam.

HIGHGATE

Highgate School	Co-ed	Pupils 620
North Road	● Boys	Upper sixth 100
Highgate	Girls	Termly fees:
London N6 4AY	Mixed sixth	Day £1305
Telephone number 01-340 1524	● Day	Boarding £2270
Enquiries/application to the Headmaster	● Boarding	HMC

WHAT IT'S LIKE

Founded in 1565, the main buildings are in Highgate Village and many of the houses in the village form part of the school, creating a very agreeable environment. The oldest buildings are late Victorian. Since 1928 there has been steady expansion which has provided new and better facilities. It is now extremely well equipped by any standards. It takes boys who have skills and talents they can contribute to the community. The education is for responsibility to the individual, to the individual's talents and abilities – plus responsibility to fellow human beings. It is well known for its good teaching and high academic attainments (60–70 university entrants per year). Music is strong. Very wide range of sports and games (high standards are achieved). An outstanding record in the Duke of Edinburgh's Award Scheme.

SCHOOL PROFILE

Pupils Total, 620. Day 495; Boarding 125. Entry age, 12–13 and into sixth. Own junior school provides 55–60%. 3% are children of former pupils.

Entrance Common entrance and own entrance exam used. Oversubscribed. No special skills or religious requirements but school is a C of E foundation. Parents expected to buy text books. 21 assisted places. 8 scholarships, 2 music awards, art award, 30 bursaries, up to full fees.

Parents 15+% in industry or commerce; 15+% are doctors, lawyers, etc. 60+% live within 30 miles; very few live overseas.

Staff Head R C Giles, in post for 14 years. 55 full time staff, 2 part time. Annual turnover 3%.

Academic work GCSE and A-levels. Average size of upper fifth 125; upper sixth 100. *O-levels*: on average, 15 pupils in upper fifth pass 1–4 subjects; 30, 5–7 subjects; 80 pass 8+ subjects. *A-levels*: on average, 2 pupils in upper sixth pass 1 subject; 6, 2 subjects; 80, 3 subjects and 6 pass 4 subjects. On average, 29 take science/engineering A-levels; 32 take arts and humanities; 38 a mixture. *Computing facilities*: Computer room: 14 BBC As, 3 BBC Bs, 1 RML 380Z, 2 printers. Also 4 BBC Bs, 1 BBC Master 128 and 5 printers in science departments.

Senior pupils' non-academic activities *Music*: 80 learn a musical instrument, 20 to Grade 6 or above; 20 in school orchestra with girls from Channing, 30 in choir, 10 in pop groups, school dance band. *Drama*: 25 in school productions. *Art*: 20 take as non-examined subject, 25 take GCSE; 8 take A-level. 15 belong to eg photographic club, 10 take printing, pottery; entire sixth form take history of art. *Sport*: Football, rugby, Eton fives, cross country running, athletics, cricket, swimming, basketball, fencing, golf, gymnastics, hockey, sailing, shooting, squash, tennis, water polo, canoeing, life-saving, skiing, weight training available. 250 take non-compulsory sport. All take exams in swimming, survival. 14 represent county, 5 represent country (Eton fives, fencing); 2 represent independent schools (soccer). *Other*: 30 take part in local community schemes. 50 have bronze Duke of Edinburgh's Award, 50 have silver and 30+ gold. Other activities include a computer club, chess club, chemistry society, school press, various historical, literary and debating societies, philatelic, zoological, astronomical societies, orchestras, bands, choirs (incl chapel choir).

Careers 2 part time careers advisors. Average number of pupils accepted for *arts and humanities degree courses* at Oxbridge, 9; other universities, 30; polytechnics or CHE, 10. *science and engineering degree courses* at Oxbridge, 6; other universities, 20; medical schools, 6; polytechnics or CHE, 5. *art college* 3. *HND course* 5. Average number of pupils going straight into careers in armed services, 1; industry, 2; the City, 3; music/drama, 1.

Uniform School uniform worn throughout.

Houses/prefects Competitive houses. Prefects, head boy, head of house and house prefects – appointed by the Head. Sixth Form Committee.

Religion Religious worship compulsory.

Social Sixth form general studies, drama, music with other local schools. Exchange with school in Paris. Annual skiing and trips to Mediterranean (cruise), Greece, Italy, Russia (every other year). Pupils allowed to bring their own car/bicycle/motorbike to school. Lunch formal; others self service. School shop. No tobacco/alcohol allowed.

Discipline No corporal punishment. Pupils failing to produce homework once might expect to be judged according to circumstances; those caught smoking cannabis on the premises could expect expulsion.

Boarding 28% have own study bedroom, 13% share with one other, 5% with two others; 41% are in dormitories of 6 or more. Houses of around 40, are the same as competitive houses. Resident qualified nurse. Central dining room. Pupils can provide and cook own food. Exeats every weekend. Visits to local town allowed.

Alumni association is run by M J Gadsden, 2 Park Avenue, St Albans AL1 4PB.

Former pupils Anthony Crosland; John Rutter; Howard Shelley; John Tavener; The Warden of All Souls; 2 Lord Justices of Appeal; Lord Garner, Bishop of Manchester; Martin Gilbert; Anthony Green RA; Patrick Procter RA; Roland Culver; Robin Ellis; Barry Norman; Robin Ray; Geoffrey Palmer; Philip Harben; Mike Ockrent; Christopher Morahan.

Holy Child Senior

Holy Child Senior School		Co-ed	Pupils 250
Sir Harry's Road		Boys	Upper sixth Yes
Edgbaston		● Girls	Termly fees:
Birmingham B15 2UR		Mixed sixth	Day £760
Telephone number 021 440 4103		● Day	Boarding £1260
		● Boarding	GBGSA; GSA

Head Miss J M Johnson (1 year)
Age range 11–18; own prep from age 3; entry by own exam. Weekly boarding only.
Scholarships and bursaries.

Holy Trinity (Bromley)

Holy Trinity Convent School		Co-ed	Pupils 320
81 Plaistow Lane		Boys	Upper sixth 40
Bromley		● Girls	Termly fees:
Kent BR1 3LL		Mixed sixth	Day £638
Telephone number 01-460 1712		● Day	GSA; GBGSA
		Boarding	

Enquiries/application to the Headmistress

WHAT IT'S LIKE

Founded in 1886, by a small group of Trinitarian Sisters, it moved in 1888 to 'Freelands', a big 18th-century mansion in a landscaped park of 15 acres. Since 1913 the school has expanded at regular intervals to provide increasingly up-to-date facilities and accommodation. It is now very well equipped. It has its own kindergarten and preparatory department. Pupils are predominantly Roman Catholic but others are accepted. Religious worship is compulsory and the school's prime aim is to develop the spiritual life of its pupils. Catholic doctrine is central to the teaching, and life is allied to the calendar and liturgy of the Church. A sound general education is provided and standards are high. A fair commitment to local community schemes.

SCHOOL PROFILE

Pupils Total over 12, 320. Entry age, 11 and into sixth. Own prep school provides 60%. 6.6% are children of former pupils.
Entrance Own entrance exam used. Oversubscribed. No special skills required. Most pupils are Roman Catholic but others are accepted. Parents not expected to buy text books. No assisted places yet. 3 scholarships/bursaries, full fees to ⅓ fees.
Parents 15+% in industry or commerce; 15+% are doctors, lawyers, etc. 60+% live within 30 miles.
Staff Head Sister Bernadette, in post for 2 years. 40 full time staff, 7 part time. Annual turnover 11.6%. Average age 43.

Academic work GCSE and A-levels. Average size of fifth 58; upper sixth 40. *O-levels*: on average, 6 pupils in fifth pass 1–4 subjects; 22, 5–7 subjects; 24 pass 8+ subjects. *A-levels*: on average, 8 pupils in upper sixth pass 1 subject; 14, 2 subjects; 14, 3 subjects and 2 pass 4 subjects. On average, 33% take science/engineering A-levels; 33% take arts and humanities; 33% a mixture. History of art and theatre studies are offered to A-level. *Computing facilities*: 10 BBC, 6 Horizons.

Senior pupils' non-academic activities *Music*: 120 learn a musical instrument, 80 to Grade 6 or above; 35 in school orchestra, 60 in choir. *Drama and dance*: 30–40 in school productions; 30 entered competitions. *Art*: 20 take GCSE art; 6 take A-level. 2 accepted for Art School. *Sport*: Hockey, netball, gym, dance, swimming, tennis, rounders, athletics and other minor games available. 160 take non-compulsory sport. 2 represent county (hockey). *Other*: 40 take part in local community schemes. Other activities include computer, science, art, chess and debating clubs.

Careers 1 full time careers advisor. Average number of pupils accepted for *arts and humanities degree courses* at Oxbridge, 1; other universities, 5. *science and engineering degree courses* at Oxbridge, 2; other universities, 5; medical schools, 2. *BEd*, 3. *other general training courses*, 3. Average number of pupils going straight into careers in the City, 3; civil service, 1; other, 12.

Uniform School uniform worn throughout.

Houses/prefects Competitive houses. Prefects, head girl, head of house and house prefects – appointed by Head in consultation with staff.

Religion Religious worship compulsory.

Social No organised functions with local schools. Trips to France, skiing, Venice/Rome. Pupils allowed to bring own car/bicycle/motorbike to school. Meals self service. No tobacco/alcohol allowed.

Discipline No corporal punishment. Pupils failing to produce homework once might expect a warning; those caught smoking cannabis on the premises could expect expulsion.

HOWELL'S (DENBIGH)

Howell's School	Co-ed	Pupils 300
Denbigh	Boys	Upper sixth Yes
Clwyd	● Girls	Termly fees:
North Wales LL16 3EN	Mixed sixth	Day £1250
Telephone number 074 571 3631	● Day	Boarding £1900
	● Boarding	GSA; GBGSA

WHAT IT'S LIKE

Its origins date from 1540 when Thomas Howell bequeathed 12,000 gold ducats to the Drapers' Company. In 1852 an act of parliament authorised the trust to build two girls' schools in Wales. Howell's School, Denbigh was opened in 1859. The Drapers' Company provides considerable support. It has very pleasant mellow grey stone buildings in delightful grounds and gardens some 20 miles from Snowdonia. A very healthy environment amidst splendid countryside. Predominantly a boarding school, it enjoys comfortable accommodation and excellent modern facilities of all kinds. The prep department (for 7–10 year olds) is next to the senior school. The school aims to teach the essentials of the Christian way of life and religious education (in the Anglican tradition) is part of the curriculum. It has a high academic reputation and the large staff allows a staff:pupil ratio of 1:9. The teaching is extremely good and results are first rate. About 75% of leavers go on to university each year (about 15% of these to Oxbridge). The music, drama and art departments are strong and there is a superb arts and crafts complex. Howell's is also very well equipped for sports and games and has one of the best sports halls in the country. Standards are high and quite a few girls have played hockey at county and national level. A good range of extra-curricular activities is provided.

SCHOOL PROFILE

Head Mr John H Delany (2 years)
Age range 11–18, own prep from age 7; entry by own exam.
Assisted places, scholarships and bursaries available.

HOWELL'S (LLANDAFF)

Howell's School
Llandaff
Cardiff CF5 2YD
Telephone number 0222 562019

Enquiries/application to the School Secretary

Co-ed
Boys
● Girls
Mixed sixth
● Day
● Boarding

Pupils 558
Upper sixth 59
Termly fees:
Day £732
Boarding £1588
GPDST

WHAT IT'S LIKE

Founded in 1860, it has an urban site on a wooded ridge overlooking Cardiff. The main building is a fine example of mid-Victorian Gothic. Some of the accommodation is in converted Edwardian houses. Excellent modern facilities. A sound education in the grammar school tradition is provided, and Welsh is optionally taught as a first and as a second language. Academic standards are high and results good. Some 30–35 leavers proceed to university each year. Very strong in music and drama. A good range of games and sports in which high standards are achieved. A plentiful range of activities. Some involvement in local community schemes.

SCHOOL PROFILE

Pupils Total over 11, 558. Day 517, Boarding 41. Entry age, 11+ and into the sixth. Own junior school provides over 20%. A significant number are children of former pupils.
Entrance Own entrance exam used. Oversubscribed for day girls. No special skills or religious requirements. Parents not expected to buy text books. 190 assisted places. 16 scholarships/bursaries, £4284 to £100 pa.

Parents 15+% are doctors, lawyers, etc; 15+% in industry or commerce. 60+% live within 30 miles; up to 10% live overseas.

Staff Head Miss J P Turner, in post for 10 years. 41 full time staff, 13 part time. Annual turnover 5%.

Academic work GCSE and A-levels. Average size of upper fifth 80; upper sixth 59. *O-levels*: on average, 9 pupils in upper fifth pass 1–4 subjects; 20, 5–7 subjects; 54 pass 8+ subjects. *A-levels*: on average, 4 pupils in the upper sixth pass 1 subject; 8, 2 subjects; 45 pass 3 subjects. On average, 21 take science/engineering A-levels; 24 take arts and humanities; 12, a mixture. Welsh (first and second language) offered to GCSE/A-level. *Computing facilities*: Network of 14 RM Nimbus, BBC B or Master in most subject areas.

Senior pupils' non-academic activities *Music*: 55% learn a musical instrument (10% learn 2 or 3), most to Grade 6 or above, 2–3 accepted for Music School; 90 in school orchestra, 100 in school choir, 1 in National Youth Orchestra, 30 in county orchestras and choirs. No school pop group but many pupils form small groups on own initiative. *Drama and dance*: 50% in school productions, some take Grade 6 in ESB, RAD etc; occasionally accepted for Drama/Dance schools. About 15% take out-of-school drama. *Art*: 20 take GCSE; 5 take A-level. 2 or 3 accepted for Art School, 1 or 2 take fine arts at university, 15 belong to photographic club. *Sport*: Lacrosse, hockey, netball, table tennis, badminton, squash, tennis, cricket, rounders, athletics and swimming available. Many take non-compulsory sport. 25 have RLSS Bronze awards, 10, Merit, and 5 teacher's certificate. *Other*: 30 take part in local community schemes. Many enter voluntary schemes after leaving school. Several work for national charities. Other activities include a computer club, Young Enterprise firms, debating, school book shop (run by pupils).

Careers 2 full time advisors. Average number of pupils accepted for *arts and humanities degree courses* at Oxbridge, 2 or 3; other universities, 15–25; polytechnics or CHE, 1 or 2. *science and engineering degree courses* at Oxbridge, 3 or 4; other universities, 15–25; medical schools, 5–8; polytechnics or CHE, 3–5. *BEd*, 3–5. 1–2 to secretarial courses; 2–3 to nursing. Traditional school careers are medicine and law.

Uniform School uniform worn except the sixth.

Houses/prefects Competitive houses. Prefects, head girl, head of house and prefects. School Council.

Social Meals self-service. School shop. No tobacco/alcohol allowed.

Boarding Weekly boarding available. Pupils are divided by age into different houses. 1 weekend exeat each half term.

Alumni association is run by Miss J L Davies, 6 Maynard Court, Fairwater Road, Llandaff, Cardiff.

Former pupils Baroness Jean McFarlane (Prof of Nursing); Dr Anne-Rosalie David (Egyptologist); Audrey Bates (Sport); Trudy Fraser (dress designer); Elaine Morgan (playwright).

HULL HIGH

Hull High School for Girls
Tranby Croft
Anlaby
Hull
Humberside
Telephone number 0482 657016

Co-ed   Pupils 260
Boys   Upper sixth Yes
● Girls   Termly fees:
Mixed sixth   Day £730
● Day   Boarding £1100
● Boarding   CSCL; GSA

Head Miss C M B Radcliffe (12 years)
Age range 11–18, own prep from age 4; entry by own exam
A few scholarships. Weekly boarding only.

HULME GRAMMAR (BOYS)

The Hulme Grammar School for Boys
Chamber Road
Oldham
Lancashire OL8 4BX
Telephone number 061 624 4497

Enquiries/application to the Headmaster
(Bursar for financial enquiries)

Co-ed   Pupils 620
● Boys   Upper sixth 75
Girls   Termly fees:
Mixed sixth   Day £725
● Day   HMC
Boarding

WHAT IT'S LIKE

Founded in 1611, reconstituted in 1887, it occupies a residential urban site with its own playing fields. Some annexes are outside the main buildings many of which date from 1895. Many modern additions provide very good facilities. The girls' school is on the same site and there is collaboration in cultural activities. High standards of discipline and behaviour are expected. The teaching and academic attainments are highly creditable (40 plus university entrants per year). Strong in music, games and sports (a lot of county and national representatives). Also strong on outdoor pursuits. Vigorous participation in local community schemes.

SCHOOL PROFILE

Pupils Total over 12, 620. Entry age, 11 and into sixth. Own prep school provides 20+%.
Entrance Own entrance exam used. Oversubscribed. No special skills or religious requirements. Parents not expected to buy text books. 220 assisted places. 6 scholarships/bursaries pa, £800–£200.
Parents 60+% live within 30 miles; up to 10% live overseas.
Staff Head G F Dunkin, in post for 1 year. 53 full time staff, 3 part time. Annual turnover 1%. Average age 35.
Academic work GCSE and A-levels. Average size of upper fifth 97; upper sixth 75. *O-levels*: on average, 8 pupils in upper fifth pass 1–4 subjects; 24, 5–7 subjects; 65 pass 8+ subjects. *A-levels*: on average, 4 pupils in upper

sixth pass 1 subject; 6, 2 subjects; 12, 3 subjects and 45 pass 4 or 5 subjects. On average, 36 take science/engineering A-levels; 16 take arts and humanities; 16 a mixture. All take A-level general studies. *Computing facilities*: Computer room with Econet facility; several computers in separate departments. Ad hoc provisions for EFL, dyslexia etc.

Senior pupils' non-academic activities *Music*: 30 learn a musical instrument, 8–10 to Grade 6 or above; 2 accepted for Music School; 8 in school orchestra, 20 in choir, 10 in brass ensemble; 4 in brass bands, 2 in local orchestras; occasionally pupils play in National Youth Orchestra, National Youth Brass Band and pop groups. *Drama and dance*: 10–12 in school productions; 12 in drama group. *Art*: 8 take as non-examined subject, 14 take GCSE; 4 take A-level. 3 accepted for Art School. *Sport*: Soccer, cricket, athletics, hockey, basketball, badminton, swimming, gymnastics, volleyball, tennis, table-tennis available. 85% take non-compulsory sport. Over 70 play for competition teams at inter-school level; at least 1 international pa (usually soccer), 10 county players (various sports). *Other*: 50 take part in local community schemes. 1 per year may work for national charity. Other activities include a computer club, debating, chess and cinema clubs, sixth form discussion group.

Careers 1 full time and 1 part time careers advisors. Average number of pupils accepted for *arts and humanities degree courses* at Oxbridge, 4; other universities, 13; polytechnics or CHE, 9. *science and engineering degree courses* at Oxbridge, 4; other universities, 14; medical schools, 7; polytechnics or CHE, 4. *other general training courses*, 5. Average number of pupils going straight into careers in armed services, 2; industry, 1; the City, 1; other (insurance, banking, retail), 8. Traditional school careers are in medicine (especially academic).

Uniform School uniform worn throughout.

Houses/prefects Competitive houses. Prefects, head boy, head of house and house prefects – appointed by combination of nominations and elections.

Religion Religious worship not compulsory.

Social Girls' school on same site so some co-operation in music and drama, especially chamber choir. Skiing trip, visits to Austria, and French and German exchange visits annually. Pupils allowed to bring own car to school. Meals self service. No tobacco/alcohol allowed.

Discipline Very limited corporal punishment. Pupils failing to produce homework once might expect lines; those caught smoking cannabis on the premises could expect suspension.

Alumni association is run by Mr P Savic (Secretary, OBA), 16 Walden Avenue, Oldham OL4 2PW.

Former pupils John Stapleton (TV journalist and presenter); Jack Tinker (*Daily Mail* drama critic); Andy Kershaw (TV pop music presenter); Sir Arthur Armitage (Master of Queens and Vice-Chancellor of Cambridge).

HULME GRAMMAR (GIRLS)

The Hulme Grammar School for Girls
Chamber Road
Oldham
Lancashire OL8 4BX
Telephone number 061 624 2523

Enquiries/application to the Headmistress

Co-ed
Boys
● Girls
Mixed sixth
● Day
Boarding

Pupils 460
Upper sixth 51
Termly fees:
Day £665
GSA

WHAT IT'S LIKE

Founded in 1895, it has an urban site and the main building adjoins the boys' school. The prep department is nearby. A short distance away are the lower sixth form house and a separate building housing art and computer studies. The buildings are well appointed within and facilities are up-to-date. The school is non-denominational but religious education is considered to be an important part of the curriculum, and daily worship and prayers are compulsory. Academic results are good. Most girls go on to higher education and 25–30 proceed to university each year. There is a strong music department and a good range of sports and games and extra-curricular activities. Some commitment to local community services. An outstanding record in the Duke of Edinburgh's Award Scheme.

SCHOOL PROFILE

Pupils Total over 12, 460. Entry age, 11 and into the sixth. Estcourt, school's prep department, provides over 20%.

Entrance Own entrance exam used. Oversubscribed. No special skills or religious requirements. Parents not expected to buy text books. 35 assisted places pa. Bursaries offered, value varies annually.

Parents 60+% live within 30 miles; up to 10% live overseas.

Staff Head Mrs Alison Groom, in post for 3 years. 35 full time staff, 7 part time. Annual turnover 5%. Average age 40.

Academic work GCSE and A-levels. Average size of upper fifth 61; upper sixth 51. *O-levels*: on average, 3 pupils in upper fifth pass 1–4 subjects; 5, 5–7 subjects; 53 pass 8+ subjects. *A-levels*: on average, 2 pupils in upper sixth pass 1 subject; 4, 2 subjects; 10, 3 subjects and 33 pass 4 subjects. On average, 17 take science/engineering A-levels; 22 take arts and humanities; 12 a mixture. *Computing facilities*: Information Technology room shared with boys' school; network of 14 machines; plus computers in some departments.

Senior pupils' non-academic activities *Music*: 90 learn a musical instrument, 6 to Grade 6 or above; 50 in school orchestra, 100 in choirs. *Drama and dance*: 10 in joint productions with boys' school. *Art*: 1–5 take as non-examined subject; 24 take GCSE; 5 A-level. *Sport*: Hockey, netball, tennis, rounders, badminton, table tennis, trampolining, swimming available. 100 take non-compulsory sport; many take life-saving bronze medallion. 5/6 have represented county (hockey). *Other*: 10–20 take part in local community schemes. 45 have bronze Duke of Edinburgh's Award, 35 have silver and 29 gold. Other activities include a computer club, Christian Fellowship, Young Enterprise, Community Action.

Careers 1 part time careers advisor. Average number of pupils accepted

for *arts and humanities degree courses* at Oxbridge, 4; other universities, 12; polytechnics or CHE, 5. *science and engineering degree courses* at Oxbridge, 1; other universities, 10; medical schools, 2–3; polytechnics or CHE, 4. *BEd*, 1. *other general training courses*, 2–3. Average number of pupils going straight into careers, 2–3.

Uniform School uniform worn throughout.

Houses/prefects No competitive houses. Prefects and head girl – elected by staff and senior pupils.

Religion Compulsory daily morning prayers.

Social Debates, drama, choral performances with brother school. Annual skiing holiday, regular French and German exchanges, frequent foreign visits to eg Florence, Venice, Rome, also educational cruises. Pupils allowed to bring own car/bike/motorbike to school. Meals self service. School tuckshops organised occasionally by pupils for charity. No tobacco/alcohol allowed.

Discipline No corporal punishment. Pupils failing to produce homework once might expect talk with form mistress, lunchtime detention if poor reason; those caught smoking cannabis on the premises might expect to be given medical/social help and to be expelled.

Alumni association c/o Headmistress.

Former pupils Olwen Hufton (Professor of History, Reading University).

Hunmanby Hall

Hunmanby Hall School	Co-ed		Pupils 164
Hunmanby	Boys		Upper sixth 21
Filey	● Girls		Termly fees:
North Yorkshire YO14 0JA	Mixed sixth		Day £975
Telephone number 0723 890666	● Day		Boarding £1820
	● Boarding		GSA

Enquiries to the Headmistress
Application to the Headmistress's Secretary

WHAT IT'S LIKE

Founded in 1928, it has a semi-rural single site in a bracing environment near the coast. The heart of the school is the Old Hall of the Mitford family, in an estate of 50 acres of fine parkland with big woodlands. It is a Methodist foundation and the development of pupils' spiritual life is important. Much of the modern school is purpose-built and it is very well equipped. It provides good teaching and a sound education. In terms of its size it has an impressive record of university entrants. Very strong indeed in music. Drama also flourishes. Good pastoral care. Traditionally there has been a big commitment to the Duke of Edinburgh's Scheme and pupils have gained an exceptional number of medals.

SCHOOL PROFILE

Pupils Total over 12, 164. Day 50; Boarding 114. Entry age, from 5 and into sixth. Own prep school provides 20+%.

Entrance Own entrance exam used. Not oversubscribed. No special skills. Methodist school, but accepts pupils from other denominations. Parents not expected to buy text books. 9 scholarships/bursaries, £500–£100.

Parents 30+% live within 30 miles; 10+% live overseas.

Staff Head Miss J Rutherford, in post for 2 years. 27 full time and 4 part time staff.

Academic work GCSE and A-levels. Average size of upper fifth 55; upper sixth 21. *O-levels*: on average, 18 pupils in upper fifth pass 1–4 subjects; 14, 5–7 subjects; 17 pass 8+ subjects. *A-levels*: on average, 6 pupils in upper sixth pass 1 subject; 2, 2 subjects; 4, 3 subjects and 7 pass 4 subjects. On average, 6 take science/engineering A-levels; 10 take arts and humanities; 9 a mixture. Theatre studies offered to A-level. *Computing facilities*: Micros – 14 BBC Model B; 3 Apple II; 1 Opus II, all with disc drives. Printers – 4 dot matrix; 1 thermal. Two computer rooms. *Special provisions*: Staff trained in remedial teaching and EFL.

Senior pupils' non-academic activities *Music*: 117 learn a musical instrument, 10 up to Grade 6 or above, 1 accepted to university to read music; 40 in school orchestra, 86 in choir(s), 10 in string groups, 45 in recorder groups, 25 in wind band; 6 in local orchestras. *Drama and dance*: 34 in school productions; 8 in festivals; 5 take A-level theatre studies. 12 take LAMDA and 2 Guildhall examinations. 2 accepted for Drama School. *Art*: 16 take GCSE, 4–6 take A-level. 3 accepted for Art School, others go to university (fine art, landscape architecture). 12 belong to eg photographic club, 15–20 belong to art club. *Sport*: Hockey, netball, tennis, swimming, volleyball, badminton, basketball, table tennis, rounders, gymnastics, aerobics, athletics, trampolining, cricket available. 25 take non-compulsory sport, 4 take riding lessons, 10 aerobics. 10 have bronze medallion life-saving exams. 8 represent district (hockey, netball, tennis). *Other*: 14 take part in local community schemes. 37 have bronze Duke of Edinburgh's Award, 30 have silver and 22 gold. 38 have St John Public First Aid Certificate. Other activities include a computer club and driving lessons.

Careers 1 part time careers advisor. Average number of pupils accepted for *arts and humanities degree courses* at Oxbridge, 1; other universities, 4; polytechnics or CHE, 6. *science and engineering degree courses* at universities, 3; medical schools, 2; polytechnics or CHE, 5. *BEd*, 2. *other general training courses*, most fifth and lower sixth form leavers. Average number of pupils going straight into careers in armed services, 1–2; civil service, 1–2.

Uniform School uniform worn except in sixth form.

Houses/prefects Competitive houses. Prefects, head girl, head of house and house prefects – appointed by sixth form and staff. School Council.

Religion Religious worship encouraged. Methodist church each Sunday during term time.

Social Organised local events, joint functions with other schools and trips abroad. Pupils allowed to bring own bicycle to school. Meals self service. No tobacco/alcohol allowed.

Discipline No corporal punishment. Pupils failing to produce homework once might expect to have to produce it within 24 hrs.

Boarding Sixth formers have own study bedroom, fifth formers share; others in dormitories of 6+. Resident qualified nurse. Central dining room. Sixth form can provide and cook own food. Two weekend exeats a term. Visits to local town allowed occasionally.

Alumni association is run by Mrs Rachel Webster, Mowbray Hill, Bedale, North Yorkshire.
Former pupils Frances Bennett (Director, Child Poverty Action Group 1987).

HUNTERHOUSE

Hunterhouse College	Co-ed	Pupils 692
Finaghy	Boys	Upper sixth 100
Belfast BT10 0LE	● Girls	Termly fees:
Telephone number 0232 612293	Mixed sixth	Day £273
Enquiries/application to the Headmistress	● Day	Boarding £813
	● Boarding	Voluntary
		Grammar

WHAT IT'S LIKE

Founded in 1865, formerly called Princess Gardens, it amalgamated with Ashleigh House school in 1987. One of the oldest grammar schools for girls in N. Ireland, it lies in a beautiful 37-acre estate of wooded parkland, gardens and playing fields 4 miles south of the centre of Belfast. The main building is a large elegant country house, formerly one of the 'linen mansions'. The purpose-built teaching and recreational accommodation dates from 1967. Excellent facilities and accommodation. The Prep dept is on the same site. A cheerful relaxed, but orderly, family atmosphere prevails. The pursuit of excellence is the prime aim. Academically strong (30–33% of pupils go on to university). Fairly strong music, art and drama depts. Very good range of sport, games and activities. Big commitment to local community schemes and education for international understanding. An impressive record in the Duke of Edinburgh's Award Scheme.

SCHOOL PROFILE

Pupils Total over 12, 692. Day 592; Boarding 100. Entry age, 11+ and into the sixth.
Entrance Oversubscribed (in boarding). No special skills or religious requirements – welcome all-rounders. Parents expected to buy text books. No assisted places.
Parents 15+% in industry or commerce. 60+% live within 30 miles; 10+% live overseas (including GB).
Staff Head Miss D E M Hunter, in post for 5 years. 50 full time staff, 10 part time. Annual turnover 2%. Average age 37.
Academic work GCSE and A-levels. Average size of upper fifth 120; upper sixth 100. *O-levels*: most pupils take 9. *A-levels*: on average, 10+ pupils in upper sixth pass 1 subject; 30+, 2 subjects; 30+, 3 subjects; 4–5 pass 4 subjects. On average, 16 take science/engineering A-levels; 44 take arts and humanities; 26 a mixture. *Computing facilities*: Network of BBC machines and others. Total of 15 machines. Teachers qualified to teach EFL. Needs of individual children are met.
Senior pupils' non-academic activities *Music*: 12 learn a musical instru-

ment, 4 to Grade 6 or above; 6 take GCSE, 4 take A-level music, 2 accepted for degree in music; 10 in school orchestra, 14 in school choir, 6 in wind band, 15 in choral groups, 2 in string training orchestra. *Drama and dance*: 20–30 in school productions. 24 to Grade 6 in ESB, RAD etc, 26 take other exams, 13 take GCSE Drama & Theatre Arts; 26 in musical festivals. *Art*: 23 take as non-examined subject; 27 take GCSE; 24 take A-level. 5 accepted for Art School. 28 belong to art club. 10 on community project. *Sport*: Hockey, netball, tennis, squash, badminton, table tennis, golf, riding, swimming, athletics, gymnastics, judo, karate and ice-skating available. 74 take non-compulsory sport. 1 umpires hockey. 11 represent county (hockey, swimming, athletics, badminton); 1 Commonwealth Games athlete. *Other*: 59 take part in local community schemes. 29 have bronze Duke of Edinburgh's Award, 15, silver; 5, gold. 100 in voluntary schemes in sixth form. 20 work for national charities. Other activities include two computer clubs, bridge, photography, debating, public speaking, SU, stage craft + make-up club, mini-company (an in-school commercial venture), work experience programme and work shadowing.

Careers 2 part time advisors. Average number of pupils accepted for *arts and humanities degree courses* at universities, 20%; polytechnics or CHE, 20%. *science and engineering degree courses* at Oxbridge, 1%; other universities, 7–10%; medical schools, 1%; polytechnics or CHE, 10%. *BEd*, 4–5%. *other general training courses*, 20%. Average number of pupils going straight into careers in the armed services, 1%; other, 10%.

Uniform School uniform worn except the sixth.

Houses/prefects Competitive houses (in sport and music). No prefects; head girl and house captains – elected by the staff and upper sixth. School Council.

Religion Boarders attend church (if Christian). Morning assembly is Christian but non-denominational.

Social Regular inter-school debates, sports, fund raising for charities etc. Modern language trips, group and individual exchanges usually under auspices of Central Bureau for Educational Visits and Exchanges. Ski-trips. Pupils allowed to bring own car to school. Meals formal for boarders, self service for dayschool. School shop, tuck and second-hand uniforms. No tobacco/alcohol allowed.

Discipline No corporal punishment. Pupils failing to produce homework once might expect verbal reprimand. Those caught smoking or with cannabis on the premises should expect the school to take an extremely serious view.

Boarding Most are in dormitories of 6+. Houses, of 50, divided by age group. Resident nurse sometimes. Central dining room. Overseas pupils can provide and cook own food. Weekly boarding available. Visits to local town allowed.

Alumni association is run by The President, c/o Hunterhouse College.

Former pupils Miss Kathleen Robb (former matron Victoria Hospital, Belfast); Miss Suzanne Lowry (*Observer* Journalist); Miss Judith Rodgers (British Universities Record Holder in 100m hurdles).

HURN COURT

Hurn Court School
Christchurch
Dorset BH23 6AB
Telephone number 0202 35812

Co-ed
● Boys
Girls
Mixed sixth
● Day
● Boarding

Pupils 150
Upper sixth No
Termly fees:
Day £810
Boarding £1420
ISAI

Head J D Clark (2 years)
Age range 10–18; entry by interview.
Open to pupils with specific learning difficulties, dyslexia or below average IQs. No A-levels offered.

HURSTPIERPOINT

Hurstpierpoint College
Hurstpierpoint
Hassocks
West Sussex BN6 8JS
Telephone number 0273 833636

Enquiries/application to the Headmaster

Co-ed
● Boys
Girls
Mixed sixth
● Day
● Boarding

Pupils 422
Upper sixth 65
Termly fees:
Day £1770
Boarding £2280
Woodard

WHAT IT'S LIKE

A Woodard school, founded in 1849, it has a totally rural 100-acre site in beautiful Sussex countryside, 2 miles from Hurstpierpoint village and 10 miles north of Brighton. Its very attractive buildings are in the collegiate style. The original ones form two pleasant quadrangles. Many additions in the last 25 years. It has the advantage of being a small, compact, unified campus. Everything, including playing fields, is easily accessible. It is pledged to C of E tradition and practice and the large chapel is used a lot. Religious worship is compulsory part of the time. A friendly and relaxed atmosphere prevails and there are manifold opportunities for leisure as well as learning. The standards of teaching and academic attainment are high (some 25 university entrants per year). A high standard also in sport and games. Plentiful extra-curricular activities. Very strong in music, arts and crafts and drama. A big and flourishing CCF (the first such unit to be formed in England).

SCHOOL PROFILE

Pupils Total, 422. Day 38; Boarding 384. Entry age, 13+ and into sixth. Own junior school provides 80+%. 4% are children of former pupils.
Entrance Common entrance exam used. Oversubscribed. No special skills required. Pupils expected to be C of E. Parents not expected to buy text books. 20 scholarships/bursaries, 66%–25% of fees.

Parents 15+% in industry or commerce. 60+% live within 30 miles; 10+% live overseas.

Staff Head S A Watson, in post for 2 years. 41 full time staff, 19 part time. Annual turnover 5%. Average age 40.

Academic work GCSE and A-levels. Average size of upper fifth 85; upper sixth 65. *O-levels*: on average, 16 pupils in upper fifth pass 1–4 subjects; 29, 5–7 subjects; 45 pass 8+ subjects. *A-levels*: on average, 8 pupils in upper sixth pass 1 subject; 14, 2 subjects; 35, 3 subjects and 2 pass 4 subjects. On average, 16 take science/engineering A-levels; 25 take arts and humanities; 19 a mixture. *Computing facilities*: 10 station network of BBC computers connected to a Winchester to be centred in a new CDT centre containing Atari computers.

Senior pupils' non-academic activities *Music*: 105 learn a musical instrument, 25 to Grade 6 or above, 2 or 3 accepted for Music School; 42 in school orchestra, 36 in school choir, 8 in jazz group, others in choral society and small choir/ensembles; 4 in county youth orchestra. *Drama and dance*: 80 in school productions, up to 7 house plays and musicals pa each involving 20–60. *Art*: 80 take as non-examined subject, 26 take GCSE, 6 take A-level; 3 accepted for Art School. 15 belong to art club, 15 take metal, craft, plastics and pottery. *Sport*: Rugby, hockey, cricket, athletics, squash, tennis, fencing, cross country, shooting, swimming (heated indoor pool), water polo, basketball, badminton available (new £½m sports hall). 140 take non-compulsory sport. 6 take exams in lifesaving. 1 international schoolboy shooter, 15 represent county (rugby, hockey, cricket). *Other*: 8 have bronze Duke of Edinburgh's Award, 1 has silver and 2 have gold. Other activities include computer, bridge, chess and engineering clubs, clay pigeon shooting, natural history society, scholars' lecture society, debating, money raising for charity, war games, learning to drive.

Careers 2 part time careers advisors. Average number of pupils accepted for *arts and humanities degree courses* at Oxbridge, 2; other universities, 6; polytechnics or CHE, 7. *science and engineering degree courses* at Oxbridge, 3; other universities, 9; medical schools, 4; polytechnics or CHE, 5. Average number of pupils going straight into careers in armed services, 4; industry, 2; the City, 8; civil service, 2; music/drama, 2; other, 6.

Uniform School uniform worn throughout.

Houses/prefects Competitive houses. Prefects and head boy appointed by Head. Head of house and house prefects by Housemaster. School Council.

Religion 2 week day and 1 Sunday service compulsory; other services voluntary.

Social Theatrical and musical functions with Roedean, St Michael's Petworth, Farlington, Burgess Hill School for Girls. German school exchange annually; annual trips to Rome, Venice, Dieppe, Holland and India (every 4 years), Rugby XV to S. France, Vancouver. Pupils allowed to bring own bicycle to school. Meals self service. School shop. No tobacco allowed. There is a sixth form bar.

Discipline No corporal punishment. Pupils failing to produce homework once might expect warning; those caught smoking cannabis on the premises could expect expulsion.

Boarding 26% have own study bedroom, 9% share; 65% are in dormitories of 6+. 7 houses, of approximately 60, are same as competitive houses. Resident qualified nurse. Central dining room. Prefects can provide and cook own food. Exeats every Sunday for the day and every second Saturday night. Visits to local town (Burgess Hill) allowed daily; Brighton for special reasons. **Former pupils** Lord Plummer of Marylebone; Sir Brian Cartledge (UK Ambassador Moscow); Sir Derek Day (High Commissioner in Canada); Michael York (actor); Richard Page (MP).

HUTCHESON'S

Hutcheson's Grammar School	● Co-ed	Pupils 1073
21 Beaton Road	Boys	Upper sixth 190
Glasgow G41 4NW	Girls	Termly fees:
Telephone number 041 423 2933	Mixed sixth	Day £660
Enquiries/application to the Rector	● Day	HMC
	Boarding	

WHAT IT'S LIKE

Founded in 1641, it occupied its present site (pleasant, quiet and in a residential area, 3 miles from the city centre) in 1959. The premises are well-equipped. Academically it is a very high-powered school with outstanding results. Recent surveys suggest that it is pre-eminent in Scotland and among the most successful schools in Britain. Latterly it has sent 160–170 candidates on to university each year. Only a handful of schools in Britain match this achievement. Very strong indeed in music, drama and art. Equally strong in sports and games (a large number of representatives at county and national level). A good range of extra-curricular activities. Some commitment to local community services.

SCHOOL PROFILE

Pupils Total over 12, 1073. Entry age, 5, 9, 12 and into the sixth. Own junior dept provides over 20%.

Entrance Own entrance exam used. Oversubscribed. No special skills or religious requirements. Parents expected to buy text books. Some scholarships/bursaries available.

Parents 15+% are doctors, lawyers etc; 15+% in industry or commerce. 60+% live within 30 miles.

Staff Head (Rector) David R Ward, in post for 2 years. 108 full time staff, 8 part time. Annual turnover negligible.

Academic work Highers and A-levels. Average size of upper fifth 190; upper sixth 190. *Computing facilities*: Computer lab with 12 stations and a printer on an Econet system, 2 stand-alone machines with disc drives and shared printer, Plotmate, Buggy and Prestel link; 2 further Econet stations in one Physics lab; chemistry, biology and classics departments have 1 computer each.

Senior pupils' non-academic activities *Music*: 350 learn a musical instrument, 30 to Grade 6 or above, 4 accepted for Music School; 80 play in school orchestra, 250 in school choir; 1 plays in National Youth Orchestra, 4 in National Youth Orchestra of Scotland. *Drama and dance*: 150 in annual opera/musical/dramatic production. *Art*: 15 take as non-examined subject;

25 take Higher. 1 accepted for Art School. *Sport*: Boys: rugby, cricket, athletics. Girls: hockey and netball. Rowing, squash, badminton, table tennis, swimming, curling, canoeing also available. 160 take non-compulsory sport. 10 take swimming exams. 16 represent county/country (rugby, tennis, golf, cricket). *Other*: 20 take part in local community schemes. Other activities include a computer club, Scripture Union, gardening.

Careers 2 full time careers advisors. Average number of pupils accepted for *arts and humanities degree courses* at Oxbridge, 3; other universities, 100; polytechnics or CHE, 30. *science and engineering degree courses* at Oxbridge, 3; other universities, 60; medical schools, 15; polytechnics or CHE, 10. *other general training courses*, 15. Average number of pupils going straight into careers in armed services, 6; industry, 2; the City, banks and insurance, 6; civil service, 4; music/drama, 2; other, 10. Popular school careers are medicine, law, accountancy, engineering.

Uniform School uniform worn throughout.

Houses/prefects Competitive houses. Prefects and head boy/girl – elected by the staff. School Council.

Religion Morning assembly 4 mornings each week involving reading, prayer, hymn.

Social English Speaking Union debates with local schools. October trip to Paris; skiing trip to Switzerland; exchange with Kassel (Germany) for 20 pupils. Pupils allowed to bring own car/bike/motorbike to school. Meals self service. No tobacco/alcohol allowed.

Discipline No corporal punishment.

Alumni association run by, Boys: Geoffrey Forbes, Forbes & Co, 180 West Regent Street, Glasgow 1. Girls: Mrs Margaret Anderson, 11 Tavistock Drive, Glasgow 43.

Former pupils Ken Bruce (Radio 2 presenter); Ally Scott (Rangers footballer); Sir William Wilfred Morton (former Head of Britain's Customs and Excise); Ronald Laing (psychologist); Maev Alexander (TV That's Life); Sir Kenneth Carmichael McDonald (Deputy Secretary of State, Ministry of Defence); Russell Hillhouse (Permanent Under Secretary of State, Scottish Office).

HUYTON

Huyton College	Co-ed	Pupils 190
Blacklow Brow	Boys	Upper sixth 20
Huyton	● Girls	Termly fees:
Liverpool L36 5XQ	Mixed sixth	Day £816
Telephone number 051 489 4321	● Day	Boarding £1852
	● Boarding	GSA; GBSA
Enquiries/application to the Headmistress		

WHAT IT'S LIKE

Founded in 1894, it has a self-contained urban site 6 miles from Liverpool. The core of the school is Huyton Hall, a handsome 19th-century building set in 20 acres of private gardens and playing fields. A continuous programme of extension and modernisation has provided excellent up-to-date facilities for work and games. The prep school adjoins the main school. A sound general education is provided. Religious teaching and church services are based on the doctrines of the Church of England, but the school is ecumenical.

SCHOOL PROFILE

Pupils Total over 12, 190. Day 165; Boarding 25. Entry age, 2½ onwards including into sixth. Own junior department provides 20+%.

Entrance Common entrance and own entrance exam used. No special skills required. C of E School, but others accepted. Parents expected to buy text books in sixth form. Scholarships/bursaries (including Service). Special allowance for daughters of clergy. College aid scheme in cases of hardship.

Parents 60+% live within 30 miles; 2% live overseas.

Staff Head Miss Wendy E Edwards. 22 full time staff, 19 part time including 15 music staff. Annual turnover less than 2%.

Academic work GCSE and A-levels. Also Commercial Studies course.

Senior pupils' non-academic activities *Music*: School orchestras, choirs, chamber groups, wind band, string group; pupils prepared for Music School. *Drama and art*: Pupils can be prepared for Drama and Art School. *Sport*: Lacrosse, netball, tennis, rounders, athletics, swimming, badminton, volleyball, gymnastics, judo, educational dance available. School enters Aberdare cup (tennis) and National Schools Lacrosse Tournament.

Careers Pupils go onto degree courses, further education, or secretarial or administrative careers.

Uniform School uniform worn except in sixth.

Houses/prefects Competitive houses. Prefects and house prefects.

Religion Compulsory worship.

Social Termly social with Liverpool College. Visits to France, Germany and Greece.

Boarding Boarding houses (mixed ages) same as competitive houses, plus sixth form house. Sixth formers can provide and cook own food.

HYMERS

Hymers College	Co-ed	Pupils 556
Hymers Avenue	● Boys	Upper sixth 90
Hull HU3 1LW	Girls	Termly fees:
Telephone number 0482 43555/48257	● Mixed sixth	Day £605
	● Day	HMC
Enquiries/application to the Headmaster	Boarding	

WHAT IT'S LIKE

Founded in 1893, it is single-site and urban. Decent, solid, late Victorian and Edwardian buildings are situated on a 35-acre estate of the former Hull botanic gardens, ½ a mile from the centre of the city. There has been a lot of recent development and very good facilities are provided. Firm discipline and high academic standards are insisted on and the need for full parental involvement in the school is considerably stressed. The teaching and results are good, and between 70 and 80 pupils go on to university/polytechnic each year. The music, drama and art depts are impressively active and a large number of people are engaged. High standards prevail in sport and games (there are a lot of county representatives). A plentiful range of extra-curricular activities and some emphasis on outdoor pursuits. A distinguished record in the Duke of Edinburgh's Award Scheme.

SCHOOL PROFILE

Pupils Total over 12, 556. (Boys 518, girls 38.) Entry age, boys, 8, 9, 11 and 13; boys and girls into the sixth. Own junior school provides over 20%. 10–15% are children of former pupils.

Entrance Common entrance and own entrance exam used. Oversubscribed. No special skills or religious requirements. Parents not expected to buy text books. 135 assisted places. Scholarships/bursaries at all points of entry, full fees to £360.

Parents 15+% are doctors, lawyers, etc; 15+% in industry or commerce. 60+% live within 30 miles.

Staff Head B G Bass, in post for 5 years. 51 full time staff, 6 part time staff. Turnover 5%. Average age 35–40.

Academic work GCSE and A-levels. Average size of upper fifth 90; upper sixth 90. *O-levels*: on average, 5 pupils in upper fifth pass 1–4 subjects; 10, 5–7 subjects; 75 pass 8+ subjects. *A-levels*: on average, 2 pupils in the upper sixth pass 1 subject; 5, 2 subjects; 73, 3 subjects; 10 pass 4 subjects. On average, 35 take science/engineering A-levels; 50 take arts and humanities; 5 take a mixture. Business studies and accountancy offered to GCSE. *Computing facilities*: 15 station computer room; computers in all science, geography and economics depts. CAD in CDT centre.

Senior pupils' non-academic activities *Music*: 65 learn a musical instrument, 45 to Grade 6 or above, 2 accepted for Music School; 50+ in school orchestra, 55 in school choir, 12+ in school jazz group, others in various chamber groups; 20+ in local youth & city orchestras. *Drama and dance*: 120 in school productions. 1 in National Youth Theatre. *Art*: 60 take as non-examined subject; 60 take GCSE; 4 take A-level. 2 accepted for Art School. 50 belong to art club. *Sport*: Rugby, cricket, tennis, squash, basketball, fencing, athletics, rowing, badminton, hockey, cross-country, orienteering and swimming available. 280 take non-compulsory sport. 10 represent county (rugby, cricket). *Other*: 80 have bronze Duke of Edinburgh's Award, 30 have silver and 6 have gold. Other activities include a computer club, chess, stamps, war-games, debating, Christian Union, photography, angling, bridge, outdoor pursuits (walking, climbing and camping).

Careers 4 part time advisors. Average number of pupils accepted for *arts and humanities degree courses* at Oxbridge, 5; other universities, 25; polytechnics or CHE, 10. *science and engineering degree courses* at Oxbridge, 5; other universities, 20; medical schools, 5; polytechnics or CHE, 15. *BEd*, 3. Average number of pupils going straight into careers in the church, 1; industry, 2–3; civil service, 2–3; other, 4–5.

Uniform School uniform worn throughout.

Houses/prefects No competitive houses. Prefects, head boy/girl – appointed by Head in consultation with staff and senior prefects.

Religion Daily assembly for whole school.

Social No organised functions with other schools. Organised trips abroad. Pupils allowed to bring own car/bike/motorbike to school. Meals self-service. School tuck shop. No tobacco/alcohol allowed.

Discipline No corporal punishment. Pupils failing to produce homework once might expect detention; those caught smoking cannabis on the premises might expect expulsion.

Alumni association is run by Mr J R Fewlass, 10 Hall Walk, Welton, Brough, North Humberside.

IPSWICH

Ipswich School	Co-ed	Pupils 620
Henley Road	● Boys	Upper sixth Yes
Ipswich	Girls	Termly fees:
Suffolk IP1 3SG	● Mixed sixth	Day £900
Telephone number 0473 55313	● Day	Boarding £1360
	● Boarding	GBA; HMC

Head Dr J M Blatchly (16 years)

Age range 11–19, own prep from age 7; entry by own exam or common entrance. 4% from overseas.

Scholarships, including for music, and assisted places.

IPSWICH HIGH

Ipswich High School	Co-ed	Pupils 420
Westerfield Road	Boys	Upper sixth 55
Ipswich	● Girls	Termly fees:
Suffolk IP4 2UH	Mixed sixth	Day £622
Telephone number 0473 52213	● Day	GSA; GPDST
	Boarding	

Enquiries/application to the Headmistress

WHAT IT'S LIKE

Founded in 1878, it moved in 1907 to its present urban site in a residential area of North Ipswich. There are 9 acres of playing fields nearby. It has pleasant buildings. Numerous modern additions including a fine library. Junior school on the same site. Its social spread is wide and it provides a good all-round education, with the emphasis on development of individual talents and the education of 'the whole person'. There is a big commitment to music; intensive dramatic activities. Overall standards are high, with some 30 university entrants per year. Good range of sports and games. Everyone does some voluntary service in the district from age 15 or 16.

SCHOOL PROFILE

Pupils Total over 12, 420. Entry age, 4½, 7, 11 and into sixth. Own junior school provides 20+%.

Entrance Own entrance exam used. Oversubscribed. No special skills or religious requirements. Parents not expected to buy text books. 29 assisted places. 3–4 scholarships awarded on academic merit, ½, ⅓ or ¼ of fees; bursaries subject to means test.

Parents 60+% live within 30 miles.

Staff Head Miss P M Hayworth, in post for 17 years. 34 full time staff, 17 part time (plus 13 for 'extras'). Annual turnover very small.

Academic work GCSE and A-levels. Average size of upper fifth 60; upper sixth 55. *O-levels*: most pupils entered for 9 subjects. High pass rate. *A-levels*: on average, 2 pupils in upper sixth pass 1 subject; 4, 2 subjects; 45, 3 subjects and 4 pass 4 subjects. On average, 18–20 take science/engineering A-levels; 18–20 take arts and humanities; 18–20, a mixture. *Computing facilities*: Specialist computer room, with a network of machines plus computers in laboratories and geography room.

Senior pupils' non-academic activities *Music*: 80 learn a musical instrument, 50 to Grade 6 or above; 3 accepted for Music School, 45 in school orchestra, 90 in school choirs; 12 in Suffolk Youth Orchestra, 14 in Suffolk Schools Choir. *Drama and dance*: Sometimes almost everyone participates in annual school play and four drama competitions; 12 to Grade 6 in ESB, RAD, etc; 1 or 2 accepted for Drama Schools. *Art*: 40 take as non-examined subject; 30 take GCSE; 10 take A-level. 6 belong to eg photographic club. 4–5 accepted for Art School. *Sport*: Hockey, tennis, netball, rounders, volleyball, squash, swimming, athletics available. Most take non-compulsory sport. 20 take exams in eg swimming. 10 represent county (hockey, tennis, netball) or country (athletics). *Other*: All 15–16 year old pupils do local voluntary service. Duke of Edinburgh's Award Scheme available for all. Other activities include chess, debating, Christian Union, games club, business/industry club, young enterprise scheme. Pupils allowed to use computers in their free time.

Careers 3 part time careers advisors. Average number of pupils accepted for *arts and humanities degree courses* at Oxbridge, 3; other universities, 10; polytechnics or CHE, 2. *science and engineering degree courses* at Oxbridge, 3; other universities, 14; medical/veterinary schools, 3; polytechnics or CHE, 4. *BEd*, 4. *other general training courses*, 5. Average number of pupils going straight into careers in industry, 1; the City, 1.

Uniform School uniform worn except in sixth.

Houses/prefects No competitive houses. All sixth form are prefects. Head girl elected by sixth form and staff. School Council.

Religion Daily assembly involves worship. Parents may withdraw their children if they wish.

Social Occasional debates and shared lectures or musical performances with local schools. Annual exchange with schools in Chevreuse and Hamburg. Annual History of Art visits to France or Italy, and skiing trips. Pupils allowed to bring own car/bicycle to school. Meals self service. Tuck shop at break. Second-hand uniform sales organised by parents. No tobacco/alcohol allowed.

Discipline No corporal punishment. Cases of pupils failing to produce homework once would be judged on their merits; those caught smoking cannabis on the premises could expect expulsion in most cases.

ITALIA CONTI

Italia Conti Academy of Theatre Arts
23 Goswell Road
London EC1M 7BB
Telephone number 01-608 0044

- Co-ed
  Boys
  Girls
  Mixed sixth
- Day
  Boarding

Pupils 340
Upper sixth Yes
Termly fees:
Day £1250
ISAI

Head C K Vote (12 years)
Age range 9–21; entry by audition
Specialist dance and drama school.

JAMES ALLEN'S

James Allen's Girls' School
East Dulwich Grove
London SE22 8TE
Telephone number 01-693 1181

Enquiries to the Headmistress/Admissions
Secretary
Application to the Admissions Secretary

Co-ed
Boys
- Girls
  Mixed sixth
- Day
  Boarding

Pupils 604
Upper sixth 103
Termly fees:
Day £990
GSA

WHAT IT'S LIKE

Founded in 1741, one of three schools of the Alleyn's College foundation and
the oldest girls' school in London. Commonly known as 'JAGS', it moved in
1886 to its present site of 22 acres in the pleasant inner London suburb of
Dulwich. There have been massive additions since 1978 to provide excellent
modern facilities. Interdenominational, it puts some stress on the inculcation
of Christian ethics. Its declared aims are to encourage and promote: enthusiasm; a concern for others; a willingness to apply intelligence as a way of life;
confidence and independence of mind; the pursuit of excellence (whatever
the undertaking). A popular school, it is well known for its good teaching
and academic achievements (30 or more university entrants per year). There
is a big commitment to music and drama (it has its own theatre designed to
professional standards). Collaboration with Dulwich College in cultural
enterprises. An unusually wide range of sporting and games activities. Also
strong in extra-curricular activities.

SCHOOL PROFILE

Pupils Total over 12, 604. Day 600; Boarding 4. Entry age, 11+ and into the
sixth. James Allen's Lower School provides over 25%. Very few are children
of former pupils.
Entrance Own entrance exam used. Oversubscribed. No special skills or
religious requirements. Parents expected to buy some sixth form text books.
150 assisted places. 17 scholarships/bursaries, from 66–33% fees.

Parents 15+% are doctors, lawyers, etc. 60+% live within 30 miles.

Staff Head Mrs B C Davies, in post for 4 years. 54 full time staff, 17 part time. Annual turnover 10%. Average age 35.

Academic work GCSE and A-levels. Average size of upper fifth 106; upper sixth 103. *O-levels*: on average, 4 pupils in upper fifth pass 1–4 subjects; 27, 5–7 subjects; 72 pass 8+ subjects. *A-levels*: on average, 1 pupil in upper sixth passes 1 subject; 9, 2 subjects; 42, 3 subjects and 7 pass 4 subjects. On average, 30% take science/engineering A-levels; 40% take arts and humanities; 30% a mixture. Theatre studies and philosophy offered to A-level; Arabic and Japanese for Cambridge Proficiency Certificate in lower sixth. *Computing facilities*: Two computing rooms: one with 15 BBCs, one with six of varied makes. Most science departments have own computers. *Special provisions*: Limited provision for dyslexia.

Senior pupils' non-academic activities *Music*: 150 learn a musical instrument, 25 to Grade 6 or above. 2 accepted for Music School. 56 in school orchestra, 25 in school choir, 8 in school pop group, 12 in wind, 3 play in pop group; 8 in youth orchestras. *Drama and dance*: 60 in school productions, 16 take ESB speech and drama lessons; 80 take ESB exams in public speaking. 2 accepted for Drama/Dance School, 2 for university courses. *Art*: 10 take as non-examined subject; 60 take GCSE art; 20, A-level. 6 accepted for Art School; 20 belong to photographic club. *Sport*: Hockey, netball, tennis, rounders, athletics, squash, volleyball, basketball, fencing, table tennis, indoor hockey, weight-training, keep fit, gymnastics, dance, swimming, self-defence, canoeing, sailing, gliding, riding available. 100 take non-compulsory sport. 50 take exams. 10 represent county/country (hockey, badminton, netball, athletics, fencing, tennis). *Other*: 30 have bronze Duke of Edinburgh's Award and 10 silver. Other activities include a computer club, chess, debating, orator's contest, poetry workshop, polyglots society, literary society, history society, French club, library club.

Careers 4 part time advisors. Average number of pupils accepted for *arts and humanities degree courses* at Oxbridge, 6; other universities, 13; polytechnics or CHE, 2. *science and engineering degree courses* at Oxbridge, 2; other universities, 10; medical schools, 6; polytechnics or CHE, 1. *BEd*, 2. *other general training courses*, 2. Average number of pupils going straight into careers in the City or banking, 3; music/drama, 2; art (foundation courses), 5.

Uniform School uniform worn except in the sixth.

Houses/prefects Houses. 10 prefects, head girl and head of house – elected by sixth form. School Council.

Religion Interdenominational assembly 4 times a week; emphasis on Christian ethics. Non-Christians can be exempted at parents' request.

Social Dulwich College is brother school: semi-integrated general studies in upper sixth; joint theatre productions and some societies; Japanese and Arabic in lower sixth a joint venture. Windsurfing, skiing and adventure trips abroad. Trips and exchanges to France, Germany, Italy, Russia, USA, Egypt, Greece. Pupils allowed to bring own bike to school. Meals self service. School uniform shop. No tobacco/alcohol allowed.

Discipline No corporal punishment. Pupils failing to produce homework once might expect detention mark (3 = ½ hour detention); those caught smoking cannabis on the premises could expect suspension, possibly expulsion.

Alumni association run by Mrs Brenda Hillier, 27 Beechwood Rise, Edgebury, Chislehurst, Kent BR7 6TF.
Former pupils Anita Brookner and Lisa St Aubin de Teran (authors).

JEWISH HIGH

Jewish High School for Girls	Co-ed	Pupils 138
Beth Malkah	Boys	Upper sixth Yes
Radford Street	● Girls	Termly fees:
Salford	Mixed sixth	Day £675
Lancashire M7 0NT	● Day	
Telephone number 061 792 2118	Boarding	

Head Rabbi M I Young
Age range 11–18; entry by test in Jewish studies, English and maths.
Founded in 1956 to provide a Jewish education for girls.

JOHN LYON

The John Lyon School	Co-ed	Pupils 490
Middle Road	● Boys	Upper sixth Yes
Harrow	Girls	Termly fees:
Middlesex HA2 0HN	Mixed sixth	Day £830
Telephone number 01-422 2046	● Day	HMC; GBA
	Boarding	

Enquiries to the Headmaster
Application to the Headmaster's Secretary

WHAT IT'S LIKE

Founded in 1868, it has agreeable premises on the west side of Harrow Hill amidst gardens. There are spacious playing fields nearby. There have been substantial additions and improvements over the years, especially in the 1970s and 1980s. The school is now well equipped. Some religious education is provided weekly for all pupils throughout the school. There are regular school assemblies. A sound general education is given and this includes Latin in the second year. Academic results are good and a large number of pupils go on to universities, including Oxbridge. Music and drama are quite strong. A fair range of sports and games is provided and there is a plentiful variety of extra-curricular activities.

SCHOOL PROFILE

Total number of pupils, 490. Entry age, 11+, 13+ and into sixth.
Parents expected to buy text books. 118 assisted places. Scholarships at 11 and 13 entry.
Head Revd T J Wright, in post 1 year. 37 full time staff, 3 part time.

KELLY COLLEGE

Kelly College
Tavistock
Devon PL19 0HZ
Telephone number 0822 3005

Co-ed   Pupils 340
● Boys   Upper sixth Yes
Girls   Termly fees:
● Mixed sixth   Day £1220
● Day   Boarding £2100
● Boarding   GBA; HMC

WHAT IT'S LIKE

Founded in 1877 by Admiral Kelly, it has a magnificent site above the River Tavy on the edge of one of the most beautiful parts of Dartmoor and thus in a very healthy and invigorating environment. The pleasant market town of Tavistock is nearby. There are 4 boys' boarding houses and a new boarding house for girls in the sixth form. Many additions and improvements have been made in recent years and there are plans for further developments. The school is already very well equipped and even has an Outward Bound briefing room and training centre. Numbers are kept low as a matter of policy and the large and well qualified staff allows a most favourable staff:pupil ratio of 1:8. A sound general education is provided in a friendly and happy atmosphere. Academic results are good. Music, drama and art are all strong. The college has unusually fine playing fields and sports facilities and there is a lot of emphasis on sports and games. High standards are attained and there have been a number of representatives at county, regional and national level. There are many clubs and societies for extra-curricular activities, which include fishing (salmon and trout), riding and printing. Every pupil is taught art and carpentry. The CCF is large, with Royal Navy, Army and Royal Marine sections. The college has maintained its nautical connections and there are close links with the Navy in Dartmouth and Devonport. There is a large number of Outward Bound activities, for which the locality is ideal. Overseas trips and expeditions are a regular feature.

SCHOOL PROFILE

Head Christopher Hirst (3 years)
Age range 11–18; entry by common entrance or own exam.
17 art, music, science, naval and all-rounder scholarships. Plus exhibitions and bursaries.

KELVINSIDE

Kelvinside Academy
33 Kirklee Road
Glasgow G12 0SW
Telephone number 041 357 3376

Enquiries/application to the Rector

Co-ed   Pupils 420
● Boys   Upper sixth 55
Girls   Termly fees:
Mixed sixth   Day £819
● Day   HMC; HAS;
Boarding   GBA

WHAT IT'S LIKE

Founded in 1878, it has a fine site with very handsome buildings in a pleasant urban residential area. Ample playing fields are three-quarters of a mile away. It has its own junior department incorporated. Excellent modern facilities of all kinds are provided. One of Scotland's leading schools, it is strongly academic with a high standard of teaching and consistently good results. About 35–40 leavers go on to university each year. The music and drama departments are extremely active. There is a big range of sports and games (the school has produced a large number of international and county representatives). An equally good range of activities. There is a flourishing CCF and considerable emphasis on outdoor pursuits (the school has a base in the Cairngorms for skiing, hill-walking and field studies).

SCHOOL PROFILE

Pupils Total over 12, 420. Entry age, 4½ onwards, including into the sixth. Own junior school provides over 50%. Approx 20% are children of former pupils.

Entrance Own entrance exam used. Oversubscribed. Must have academic ability and fluent English; no religious requirements. Parents expected to buy text books. 50 assisted places. 4 scholarships/bursaries pa, £300–£100.

Parents 25+% in industry or commerce; 25+% are doctors, lawyers, etc. 90+% live within 30 miles.

Staff Head J H Duff, in post for 7+ years. 44 full time staff, 3 part time. Annual turnover 4%. Average age 37.

Academic work O-grade, Highers, A-level and CSYS. Average size of upper fourth 75; fifth 75; sixth 55. *O-grades*: on average, 8 pupils in upper fourth pass 1–4 subjects; 67 pass 5–7 subjects. *Highers/CSYS/A-levels*: on average, 2 pupils pass 1 subject; 6, 2 subjects; 12, 3 subjects and 110 pass 4 subjects. All take a mixture of science/engineering and arts and humanities – at least one Higher will be chosen from each area. *Computing facilities*: Computer laboratory on network system. Prestel. Provision for mildly handicapped pupils.

Senior pupils' non-academic activities *Music*: 30 learn a musical instrument, 5 to Grade 6 or above, 1 every 3 or 4 years accepted for Music School; 16 in school orchestra, 20+ in choir, 6 in pop group, 12 in pipe band; 10 in Strathclyde Schools orchestra and concert band. *Drama and dance*: 100 in school productions (including lighting and stage staff). 1 accepted for Royal Ballet school; occasionally pupils go on to work in theatre. *Art*: 5 take as non-examined subject; 25 take O-grade; 20 Higher. 2 accepted for Art School. *Sport*: Rugby football, cricket, athletics, shooting (full and small bore), cross-country running, golf, tennis, sailing, curling, skiing, badminton, hill walking and climbing, windsurfing, canoeing, swimming, squash, basketball, volleyball, wrestling, gymnastics available. 300+ take non-compulsory sport. Approx 5 take exams. 14 represent Scotland and 20+ Glasgow/West (rugby, cricket, golf, athletics, shooting, cross-country running, badminton, squash, tennis, swimming). *Other*: 20 take part in local community schemes. 2 have silver Duke of Edinburgh's Award. Other activities include a computer club, CCF, chess, debating, Scripture Union, model railway club, business games, 'Dungeons and Dragons', electronics society and many others.

Careers 3 full time and 1 part time advisors. Average number of pupils accepted for *arts and humanities degree courses* at Oxbridge, 1; other universities, 17; polytechnics or CHE, 5. *science and engineering degree courses* at Oxbridge, 2; other universities, 17; medical schools, 5; polytechnics or CHE, 5. *BEd*, 1. *other general training courses*, 10. Average number of pupils going straight into careers in the armed services, 2; industry, 5; banking, 4. Many go on to law, accountancy or medicine.

Uniform School uniform worn throughout.

Houses/prefects Competitive houses. Prefects, head boy, head of house and house prefects – appointed by the Rector.

Religion Daily morning assembly – non-Christians in senior school may opt out. Timetabled RE classes – all attend.

Social Joint debates, mixed badminton team, social functions with local schools. Organised rugby and cricket tours, ski trips, 'interest' trips eg Israel/France, CCF camps with BAOR, some exchanges. Pupils allowed to bring own car/bike/motorbike to school. Meals self service. School tuck shop. No tobacco/alcohol allowed.

Discipline Corporal punishment exists in theory (Rector and Deputy only); rarely used. Pupils failing to produce homework once might expect extra work or detention; those caught smoking cannabis on the premises could expect expulsion.

Alumni association run by John A Welsh, Secretary, Kelvinside Academical Club, 18 Grange Road, Bearsden, Glasgow G61.

Former pupils Sir T Risk (Governor of Bank of Scotland); Sir Hugh Fraser (Lord Fraser); Colin Mackay (TV political commentator) and many leading figures in the professions.

KENT COLLEGE (TUNBRIDGE WELLS)

Kent College
Pembury
Tunbridge Wells
Kent TN2 4AX
Telephone number 089 282 2006

Enquiries/application to the Headmaster

Co-ed
Boys
● Girls
Mixed sixth
● Day
● Boarding

Pupils 302
Upper sixth 40
Termly fees:
Day £1045
Boarding £1765
GSA

WHAT IT'S LIKE

Founded in 1886, a Methodist foundation, it stands in 75 acres of fine parkland half a mile from the village. The main building is Hawkwell Place, a country mansion. There are numerous modern additions and a good range of facilities. Some emphasis on religious worship and education; daily morning prayers are integral to the school's life. High standards of behaviour are expected. A sound general education is provided and there is a very wide variety of extra-curricular activities.

SCHOOL PROFILE

Pupils Total 302. Day 126; Boarding 176. Entry age, 11 and into the sixth. 5% are children of former pupils.

Entrance Common entrance and own entrance exam used. No special skills required. Methodist foundation but now interdenominational. Parents not expected to buy text books. No assisted places yet. 7 scholarships pa plus various bursaries.

Parents 15+% in industry or commerce; 15+% are doctors, lawyers, etc; 15+% in the armed services. 30+% live within 30 miles; 10+% live overseas.

Staff Head Rev John Barrett, in post for 5 years. 29 full time staff, 16+ part time. Annual turnover 5%. Average age 35–40.

Academic work GCSE and A-levels. Average size of upper fifth 68; upper sixth 40. *O-levels*: on average, 70% pass 5+ subjects. Pupils take up to 9 subjects out of a possible 20. On average, 40% take science/engineering A-levels; 40% take arts and humanities; 20% a mixture. *Computing facilities*: Computer room. *Special provisions*: Tutorial help for mild dyslexia.

Senior pupils' non-academic activities *Sport*: Netball, hockey, tennis, rounders, swimming, athletics, badminton, gymnastics, trampolining available. Full range of other activities including a computer club.

Careers 2 full time advisors.

Uniform School uniform worn except in the sixth.

Houses/prefects Competitive houses. Prefects, head girl, head of house and house prefects – elected by the school. School Council.

Religion Morning assembly and Sunday worship compulsory.

Social Some organised trips abroad. Pupils allowed to bring own car to school. Meals self service. School shop. No tobacco/alcohol allowed.

Discipline Firm but unobtrusive.

Boarding Houses are divided by age group. Resident qualified medical staff. Central dining room. Variable exeats each term. Visits to local town allowed.

KILGRASTON

Kilgraston School Convent of
   The Sacred Heart
Bridge of Earn
Perthshire PH2 9BQ
Telephone number 0738 812257

Co-ed   Pupils 220
Boys   Upper sixth Yes
• Girls   Termly fees:
Mixed sixth   Day £740
• Day   Boarding £1430
• Boarding

Head Sister B Farquharson (1 year)
Age range 8–18
Scholarships/bursaries/assisted places.

KING ALFRED (BRIDGWATER)

King Alfred School
Edington Manor
Bridgwater
Somerset TA7 9JL
Telephone number 0278 722248

	Co-ed	Pupils 40
•	Boys	Upper sixth Yes
	Girls	Termly fees:
	Mixed sixth	Day £600
•	Day	Boarding £1190
•	Boarding	ISAI

Head K G Bick (7 years)
Age range 11–18; entry by own interview.
Scholarships for seniors.

KING ALFRED (HAMPSTEAD)

King Alfred School
Manor Wood
North End Road
London NW11 7HY
Telephone number 01-455 9601

Enquiries/application to the Admissions
Secretary

	Co-ed	Pupils 250
•	Boys	Upper sixth 16
	Girls	Termly fees:
	Mixed sixth	Day £1104
•	Day	GBA
	Boarding	

WHAT IT'S LIKE

Founded in 1898, it is single-site, urban, in 6 acres of woodland gardens on the edge of Hampstead Garden suburb. Strictly undenominational. It is kept deliberately small and enjoys a high staff:pupil ratio (1:9.5). A good university record: 10 plus entrants per year. It provides a good range of sport and games and extra-curricular activities.

SCHOOL PROFILE

Pupils Total over 12, 250 (boys 130, girls 120). Entry age, 4+ and into the sixth. Own junior department provides over 80%. 5–7% are children of former pupils.
Entrance Own entrance exam, 2 day visit and interview used. Oversubscribed. No special skills or religious requirements. Parents expected to buy text books. 5 sixth form bursaries, subject to means.
Parents 15+% in industry or commerce. Almost all live within 30 miles.
Staff Head Francis Moran, in post for 4 years. 38 full time staff, 15 part time. Annual turnover 5–10%. Average age youngish.
Academic work GCSE and A-levels. Average size of upper fifth 37; upper sixth 16. *O-levels*: on average, 15 pupils in upper fifth pass 1–4 subjects; 15, 5–7 subjects; 7 pass 8+ subjects. *A-levels*: on average, 3 pupils in upper sixth pass 1 subject; 3, 2 subjects; 9, 3 subjects. On average, 6 take science/engineering A-levels; 6 take arts and humanities; 4 a mixture. *Computing facilities*: Purpose-built computer lab; facilities for computer graphics in

technology; computers in some science labs. *Special provisions*: Strong remedial department for students with various degrees of handicap.

Senior pupils' non-academic activities *Music*: 6 learn a musical instrument, 2 to Grade 6 or above. 5 play in pop group after school; 3 in school orchestra, 13 in school pop group. *Drama and dance*: 9 in school productions; 2 accepted for Drama/Dance Schools, 1 goes on to work in theatre. *Art*: 11 take as non-examined subject, 14 take GCSE; 6, A-level; 3 accepted for Art School; 9 belong to photographic club. *Sport*: Football, netball, volleyball, basketball, table tennis, badminton, cricket, tennis, rounders, squash, gymnastics, American football, five-a-side, weights available. 7 take non-compulsory sport. *Other*: 1 pupil has bronze Duke of Edinburgh's Award. Other activities include computer clubs, animal club, bulletin editorial group, French club, explorers, maths, chess, puppet theatre.

Careers 1 part time advisor. Average number of pupils accepted for *arts and humanities degree courses* at Oxbridge, 1; other universities, 5; polytechnics or CHE, 1. *science and engineering degree courses* at universities, 5; medical schools, 1; polytechnics or CHE, 2. *other general training courses*, 7. Average number of pupils going straight into careers in the armed services, 1; the City, 2; civil service, 1; music/drama, 1.

Uniform School uniform not worn.

Houses/prefects No competitive houses. Prefects – elected by the school. School Council.

Religion No compulsory worship.

Social Organised trips abroad. Pupils allowed to bring own car/bike/motorbike to school. No tobacco/alcohol allowed.

Discipline No corporal punishment. Pupils failing to produce homework once would have no punishment; those caught smoking cannabis on the premises would be given professional help.

Alumni association is run by Mrs X Bowlby, Boundary House, Wyldes Close, London NW11.

Former pupils Anthony Pleeth, Janet Craxton and Pamela Moisewitch (musicians); Maggie Norden (radio); Zoe Wannamaker, Stacey Tendeter, Catherine Harrison (actresses); Mamoun Hassan (films).

KING EDWARD VI (BIRMINGHAM)

King Edward VI High School for Girls	Co-ed	Pupils 472
Edgbaston Park Road	Boys	Upper sixth 75
Birmingham B15 2UB	● Girls	Termly fees:
Telephone number 021 472 1834	Mixed sixth	Day £808
Enquiries/application to the Headmistress	● Day	GSA
	Boarding	

WHAT IT'S LIKE

Founded in 1883, it moved to its present urban site in Edgbaston (next to the boys' school) in 1940. Purpose-built and well-equipped, it has spacious playing fields. Non-denominational, it enjoys good teaching and high academic achievement. Plentiful collaboration with the neighbouring boys' school. Quite strong in music, drama and art. A good range of sport, games and extra-curricular activities. Some commitment to local community schemes.

SCHOOL PROFILE

Pupils Total over 12, 472. Entry age, 11 and into the sixth.

Entrance Own entrance exam used. Oversubscribed. No special skills or religious requirements. Parents not expected to buy text books. 185 assisted places. 25 scholarships/bursaries, 100–25% fees.

Parents 60+% live within 30 miles; none live overseas.

Staff Head Miss E W Evans, in post for 11 years. 39 full time staff, 7 part time. Annual turnover 4%. Age range 22–60.

Academic work GCSE and A-levels. Average size of upper fifth 76; upper sixth 75. *O-levels*: on average, 1 pupil in upper fifth passes 1–4 subjects; 7, 5–7 subjects; 68 pass 8+ subjects. *A-levels*: on average, 2 pupils in upper sixth pass 1 subject; 2, 2 subjects; 7, 3 subjects and 56 pass 4 subjects. *Computing facilities*: Specialist room and machines throughout the school.

Senior pupils' non-academic activities   *Sport*: Gymnastics, hockey, netball, tennis, rounders, dance, fencing, badminton, squash, rackets, swimming, athletics, lacrosse, basketball, volleyball, golf, self-defence, aerobics available. A wide variety of other activities including community service.

Careers Normally all pupils go on to further or higher education; most to universities.

Uniform School uniform worn except in the sixth.

Houses/prefects Competitive houses. School Council.

Social Many joint activities with brother school (King Edward's School). Organised trips abroad. Pupils allowed to bring own car/bike to school. Meals self service. School shop. No tobacco/alcohol allowed.

Discipline No corporal punishment.

KING EDWARD VI (SOUTHAMPTON)

King Edward VI School	Co-ed	Pupils 940
Kellett Road	● Boys	Upper sixth Yes
Southampton	Girls	Termly fees:
Hampshire SO9 3FP	● Mixed sixth	Day £800
Telephone number 0703 704561	● Day	GBA; HMC;
	Boarding	

Head C Dobson (17 years)
Age range 11–19; entry by own exam.
Scholarships, bursaries and 40 assisted places pa.

KING EDWARD VII (LYTHAM)

King Edward VII School
Lytham St Anne's
Lancashire FY8 1DT
Telephone number 0253 736459

Enquiries/application to the Headmaster

Co-ed
● Boys
Girls
Mixed sixth
● Day
Boarding

Pupils 550
Upper sixth 57
Termly fees:
Day £650
HMC

WHAT IT'S LIKE

Founded in 1908, it has a 40-acre site by the seaside, close to sandhills and dunes. It is semi-rural and suburban in an open and bracing position. Non-denominational, it has good facilities and playing fields. The standards of teaching are high and results are good (40 university entrants per year). It collaborates with its sister school Queen Mary. Adequate sports and games. Use is made of an outdoor pursuit centre at Ribblehead in the Dales. Some community service and participation in the Duke of Edinburgh's Award Scheme.

SCHOOL PROFILE

Pupils Total over 12, 550. Entry age, 7, 8, 11+, 13 and into the sixth. Own junior school (of 90 pupils) provides over 20%.

Entrance Common entrance and own entrance exam used. Oversubscribed. Overall academic ability required. No religious requirements. Parents not expected to buy text books. 30 assisted places pa. 1 or 2 open scholarships pa, 50% fees. 5 or 6 bursaries, 27.5% fees.

Parents Virtually all live within 30 miles.

Staff Head D Heap, in post for 6 years. 45 full time staff, 4 part time. Annual turnover 7%. Average age 38.

Academic work GCSE and A-levels. Average size of upper fifth 84; upper sixth 57. *O-levels*: on average, 20 pupils in upper fifth pass 1–4 subjects; 34, 5–7 subjects; 29 pass 8+ subjects. *A-levels*: on average, 4 pupils in upper sixth pass 1 subject; 7, 2 subjects; 11, 3 subjects; 32 pass 4 subjects. On average, 17 take science/engineering A-levels; 20 take arts and humanities; 19, a mixture. *Computing facilities*: BBC Micros Econet interfaced and Hewlett Packards, Zeus, mainframe link.

Senior pupils' non-academic activities Include computer clubs, chess club, driving club, aviation society, caving, canoeing and fell-walking clubs.

Careers 2 part time advisors. Average number of pupils accepted for *arts and humanities degree courses* at Oxbridge, 3; other universities, 16; polytechnics or CHE, 5; *science and engineering degree courses* at Oxbridge, 2; other universities, 11; medical schools, 2; polytechnics or CHE, 3. Average number of pupils going straight into careers in the armed services, 6; the church, 1; industry, 7; the City (banking & commerce generally), 15; the civil service, 4; music/drama, 1; other, 8.

Uniform School uniform worn throughout.

Houses/prefects Competitive houses. Prefects, head boy, head of house and house prefects – appointed by the Head after consultation.

Religion Normal school assemblies, non-denominational.

Social Many activities with sister school, Queen Mary. Organised trips abroad. Pupils allowed to bring own car/bike/motorbike to school. Meals self-service. School shop. No tobacco/alcohol allowed.

Discipline Corporal punishment currently under review.

Alumni association is run by M Nield, 9 Cambridge Road, Ansdell, Lytham St Anne's.

Former pupils Sir Alan Leslie (Past Pres, Law Soc.); Lawrence Libbert (Judge); Ian Anderson (of Jethro Tull); Peter Shaffer (playwright); Sir Peter Harrop KCB (Permanent Secretary DOE).

KING EDWARD'S (BATH)

King Edward's School
North Road
Bath
Avon BA2 6HU
Telephone number 0225 64313

Enquiries/application to the Admissions Secretary

Co-ed   Pupils 580
- Boys   Upper sixth 73
   Girls   Termly fees:
- Mixed sixth   Day £681
- Day   HMC
   Boarding

WHAT IT'S LIKE

Founded in 1552 by royal charter of Edward VI, the school occupied its present premises in 1961 which lie on a fine site of 14 acres on the southern slope of the city, just below the university. The Old Building (c1830) houses part of the school, but there are many new buildings from 1961. Modern facilities and accommodation are first-class. There is a high standard of teaching and academic achievement (30 plus university entrants per year) and the music, art and drama departments are very strong. A good range of sports and games and much emphasis on outdoor pursuits. Full use is made of the city's cultural amenities and also those of Bristol.

SCHOOL PROFILE

Pupils Total over 12, 580 (boys 545, girls 35). Entry age, boys, 11 and 13; boys and girls, into the sixth form. Own junior school provides 20+%. 5% are children of former pupils.

Entrance Own entrance exam used. Oversubscribed. No special skills or religious requirements. Parents not expected to buy text books. 18 assisted places. 2 sixth form scholarships, £1000 pa. Bursaries according to need.

Parents 60+% live within 30 miles.

Staff Head J P Wroughton, in post for 6 years. 45 full time staff, 2 part time. Annual turnover 5%. Average age 37.

Academic work GCSE and A-levels. Average size of upper fifth 90; upper sixth 73. *O-levels*: on average, 8 pupils in upper fifth pass 1–4 subjects; 31, 5–7 subjects; 48 pass 8+ subjects. *A-levels*: on average, 10 pupils in the sixth pass 1 subject; 11, 2 subjects; 37, 3 subjects and 9 pass 4 subjects. On average, 36 take science/engineering A-levels; 26 arts and humanities; 18 a mixture. *Computing facilities*: An Econet system in the Computer Centre with 30 terminals on the network plus 6 computers in subject rooms.

Senior pupils' non-academic activities *Music*: 45 learn a musical instrument, 8 to Grade 6 or above. 1 accepted for Music School. 25 in school orchestra, 90 in school choir, 6 in school pop group, 5 in wind band, 40 in string ensembles; 1 in Avon Schools' Orchestra, 8 in Bath Society of Young Musicians. *Drama and dance*: 30 in school productions, 12 in public speaking classes; 1 goes on to work in theatre. The school organises an annual arts festival. *Art*: 30 take as non-examined subject; 70 take GCSE; 30 A-level; 12 printmaking option; 6 pottery option; 4 accepted for Art School, 3 for architecture courses; 12 belong to art club. *Sport*: Rugby, hockey, cricket, tennis, athletics, badminton, squash, swimming, soccer, cross country, orienteering, golf available. All senior pupils play sport. About 10 represent county (rugby, athletics, hockey, cricket, badminton, squash or golf). 2 represent England (golf and showjumping). *Other*: 6 take part in local community schemes. 30 have bronze Duke of Edinburgh's Award, 6 silver and 12 gold. Other activities include a computer club and societies: astronomical, chess, Christian Union, wargames, radio-controlled cars, craft/design/technology, ornithology, wildlife, outdoor pursuits, rock climbing, skiing. For sixth form – car maintenance, bedsit cookery, typing, word-processing, photography, Arts Society, English Society, theatre club.

Careers 1 part time advisor. Average number of pupils accepted for *arts and humanities degree courses* at Oxbridge, 4; other universities, 8; polytechnics or CHE, 8. *science and engineering degree courses* at Oxbridge, 4; other universities, 16; medical schools, 3; polytechnics or CHE, 10. *BEd*, 1. *other general training courses*, 2. Average number of pupils going straight into careers in the armed services, 4; industry, 1; civil service, 1; music/drama, 1; other, 1.

Uniform School uniform worn except in the sixth form.

Houses/prefects Competitive houses. Prefects, elected by staff, after poll of school. Head boy/girl – appointed by the Head. School Improvements Committee can make suggestions.

Religion Morning assembly compulsory; voluntary communion services twice a term.

Social Pupils belong to joint Sixth Form Societies (eg Economics, Science) and the Bath Society of Young Musicians with other local schools. Exchange visits to France and Germany; expeditions to a community in Kenya; four ski trips a year; music tours abroad. Pupils allowed to bring own car/bike to school. Meals self service. School shop. No tobacco/alcohol allowed.

Discipline No corporal punishment. Pupils failing to produce homework once might expect extra work during the lunch break; those caught smoking cannabis on the premises could expect expulsion.

Alumni association is run by Mr H M Kenwood, c/o the School.

Former pupils Viscount Simon, Chancellor of Exchequer 1937–40 and Lord Chancellor 1940–45.

KING EDWARD'S (BIRMINGHAM)

King Edward's School
Edgbaston Park Road
Birmingham B15 2UA
Telephone number 021 472 1672

Enquiries/application to the Chief Master

Co-ed   Pupils 750
• Boys   Upper sixth 100
Girls   Termly fees:
Mixed sixth   Day £810
• Day   HMC
Boarding

WHAT IT'S LIKE

Founded in 1552 by royal charter of Edward VI, it moved from the City centre to its present site at Edgbaston in 1936 to occupy a purpose-built establishment of pleasing design in a big area of parkland and spacious playing fields. The site is shared with King Edward's High School for Girls and there is plenty of collaboration between them. High academic standards are needed for entry. Academically it is one of the leading schools in England. 90% of all pupils go on to university; 30–40% to Oxbridge. It is strong in music, drama and the visual arts and has an excellent all-round record in sports and games.

SCHOOL PROFILE

Pupils Total over 11, 750. Entry age, 11+, 13+ and into the sixth.

Entrance Own entrance exam used. Oversubscribed. A high academic standard required for entry. No religious requirements. Parents not normally expected to buy text books. 280 assisted places. Up to 20 academic, music and art scholarships, full fees to £200.

Parents 90+% live within 30 miles.

Staff Head (Chief Master) Martin Rogers. 57 full time staff, 1 part time. Annual turnover 5%.

Academic work GCSE and A-levels. Average size of upper fifth 100; upper sixth 100. *O-levels*: on average, 1 pupil in upper fifth passes 1–4 subjects; 3, 5–7 subjects; 96 pass 8+ subjects. *A-levels*: on average, 2 pupils in upper sixth pass 2 subjects; 4, 3 subjects and 91 pass 4 subjects. On average, 45% take science/engineering A-levels; 45% take arts and humanities; 10% a mixture. *Computing facilities*: A well equipped computer laboratory. Computers in most departments.

Senior pupils' non-academic activities Music, drama and the visual arts are strong and flourishing.

Careers Over 90% of all pupils attend universities. They are encouraged to spend a year between school and university, preferably working abroad. Over a third of all boys go to Oxford or Cambridge.

Uniform School uniform worn throughout.

Houses/prefects School prefects.

Social No tobacco/alcohol allowed.

Discipline No corporal punishment. Any contact with drugs would result in expulsion.

KING EDWARD'S (WITLEY)

King Edward's School Witley
Godalming
Surrey GU8 5SG
Telephone number 042 879 2572

Enquiries to the Head
Application to the Head's Secretary

- Co-ed
  Boys
  Girls
  Mixed sixth
- Day
- Boarding

Pupils 509
Upper sixth 54
Termly fees:
Day £1310
Boarding £1780
HMC

WHAT IT'S LIKE

Founded in 1553 by King Edward VI, it was formerly at the Bridewell Palace and in 1867 moved to its present splendid site of 100 wooded acres near the Surrey/Sussex/Hampshire borders where it is easily accessible by road and rail. It retains strong links with the City and the Lord Mayor of London. The Bridewell Foundation is well-endowed and several million pounds have been spent on facilities in the last 20 years. Now extremely well equipped in every respect. Pupils come from a wide social background. It is a C of E school and there is pronounced emphasis on religious instruction, and worship in its fine Victorian Gothic chapel. Academically it is quite distinguished and sends 20 or more pupils to university each year. The music and art departments are tremendously strong. There is a good range of sport, games and activities and the school has an outstanding record in the Duke of Edinburgh's Award Scheme.

SCHOOL PROFILE

Pupils Total, 509. Day 113 (boys 63, girls 50); Boarding 396 (boys 196, girls 200). Entry age, 11+, 13 and into the sixth. Very few are children of former pupils.

Entrance Own entrance exam used. Not oversubscribed. No special skills required. Pupils required to be C of E. Parents not expected to buy text books. 15 assisted places. Boarding bursaries, a few small Forces bursaries, sixth form scholarship – £400–£1740.

Parents 15+% in industry or commerce; 15+% are doctors, lawyers, etc; 15+% in the armed services. 30+% live within 30 miles; 10+% live overseas.

Staff Head R J Fox. 46 full time staff, 21 part time. Annual turnover 5%. Average age 40.

Academic work GCSE and A-levels. Average size of upper fifth 100; upper sixth 54. *O-levels*: on average, 18 pupils in upper fifth pass 1–4 subjects; 24, 5–7 subjects; 48 pass 8+ subjects. *A-levels*: on average, 5 pupils in upper sixth pass 1 subject; 9, 2 subjects; 11, 3 subjects and 22 pass 4 subjects. On average, 18 take science/engineering A-levels; 22 arts and humanities; 12 a mixture. *Computing facilities*: Several BBC computers; taught to GCSE and used in activities.

Senior pupils' non-academic activities *Music*: 72 learn a musical instrument or study singing, 27 to Grade 6 or above. 1 accepted for Music School; 3 for university music courses. 29 in school orchestra, 30+ in school choir, 2 in pop group, 10 in flute choir and saxophone and guitar group; 1 in Surrey Wind Orchestra, 6 in Holiday Youth Orchestra. *Drama and dance*: 30 in school productions. *Art*: 203 take as non-examined subject; 30–40 take

GCSE; 12 study GCSE after school; 12+, A-level art (with art history); 40–50 take general studies in several media; 4–6 accepted for Art School; 52 in art clubs. *Sport*: Soccer, hockey, basketball, tennis, rounders, netball, swimming, squash, cricket, athletics, canoeing, shooting, badminton, etc available. Most take non-compulsory sport. 10 represent county/country (athletics, swimming). *Other*: 50 have bronze Duke of Edinburgh's Award; 4 silver and 17 gold. Other activities include a computer club, outside driving teachers, aerobics, pottery, cooking, etc.

Careers 2 full time advisors. Average number of pupils accepted for *arts and humanities degree courses* at universities, 10; polytechnics or CHE, 15. *science and engineering degree courses* at Oxbridge, 2; other universities, 11; medical schools, 2; polytechnics or CHE, 14. *BEd*, 4. *other general training courses*, 10. Average number of pupils going straight into careers in the armed services, 3; the church, 2; industry, 2; the City, 3; music/drama, 3.

Uniform School uniform worn throughout.

Houses/prefects Competitive houses. Prefects, head boy and girl, head of house and house prefects – elected by school, approved by Head. School Council.

Religion Religious worship compulsory.

Social Debates, contests, etc with other local schools. Organised trips to France and Germany. Pupils allowed to bring own bike to school. Meals self service. School shop. No tobacco/alcohol allowed.

Discipline No corporal punishment. Pupils failing to produce homework once might expect detention; those caught smoking cannabis on the premises could expect expulsion.

Boarding All sixth formers have own study bedroom, all fifth formers share with one other; only juniors are in dormitories of 6+. Houses, of approximately 55, same as competitive houses, single sex. Resident qualified nurse. Central dining room. One overnight exeat every 3 weeks. Visits to local town allowed at weekends.

Alumni association run by Mr P Whittle, c/o the School.

KING'S COLLEGE (WIMBLEDON)

King's College School
South Side
Wimbledon Common
London SW19 4TT
Telephone number 01-947 9311

Enquiries/application to the Head Master

Co-ed
● Boys
Girls
Mixed sixth
● Day
Boarding

Pupils 650
Upper sixth 125
Termly fees:
Day £1100
HMC

WHAT IT'S LIKE

Founded in 1829, originally in the Strand, it moved to its present site at the end of the 19th century and occupies 17 acres of pleasant grounds on the south side of Wimbledon Common in a very pleasant residential area. Good playing fields; a further 15 acres of fields at West Barnes Lane. Junior and senior schools share the same campus. Well-designed and comfortable buildings provide first-rate facilities. High standards are expected in work and behaviour. Integrity and tolerance are regarded as important qualities. A well-run school, it has strong academic traditions: a quarter of the leavers go to Oxbridge; three-quarters of the rest go to other universities. Very strong music, drama and art depts. A very good range of sports and games (high standards are achieved) and a large number of activities. There is considerable emphasis on outdoor pursuits and the CCF is a flourishing contingent.

SCHOOL PROFILE

Pupils Total, 650. Entry age, 13+ and into the sixth. Own junior school provides over 60%.

Entrance Common entrance used. Oversubscribed. Academic scholarships for music, classics, and modern languages. C of E school but boys not required to be of any particular persuasion. Parents expected to buy text books but there is a loan scheme. 9 assisted places pa. Up to 12 scholarships, 100% to 10% of fees.

Parents 15+% in the theatre, media, music etc; 15+% are doctors, lawyers; 15+% in industry or commerce. 60+% live within 30 miles; up to 10% live overseas.

Staff Head R M Reeve, in post for 8 years. 60 full time staff, 3 part time. Annual turnover 5%. Average age not known.

Academic work GCSE and A-levels. Average size of upper fifth 130; upper sixth 125. On average, 50 take science/engineering A-levels; 60 take arts and humanities; 10 take a mixture. *Computing facilities*: 30 BBC computers of various sorts, mostly networked using Amcom E-Net.

Senior pupils' non-academic activities *Music*: 166 learn a musical instrument, 104 to Grade 6 or above; 60 in school orchestra, 32 in school choir, 40 in wind band; 2 in Stoneleigh Orchestra. *Drama and dance*: 75 in school productions. 1 accepted for Drama/Dance Schools; 1 now works in theatre. *Art*: 10 take as non-examined subject; 110 take GCSE; 10 take A-level. 4 accepted for Art School. *Sport*: Rugby, hockey, cricket, athletics, archery, badminton, basketball, cross-country, fencing, golf, rowing, sailing, shooting, soccer, squash, swimming, table tennis and tennis available. 300 take non-compulsory sport. 100 take exams eg swimming. 22 represent county (rugby, hockey, cricket and cross-country). *Other*: Chess, computer, debating, English and history societies.

Careers Average number of pupils going straight into careers in the armed services, 8; the church, 2.

Uniform School uniform worn throughout.

Houses/prefects Competitive houses. Prefects, head boy, head of house and house prefects – recommended by committee of housemasters for approval by Head Master. School Council.

Religion 3 religious assemblies plus one divinity period per week. Opting out is possible.

Social Joint debating union with Wimbledon High School for Girls. Girls recruited from local schools for theatrical productions. Trips and exchanges abroad. Pupils allowed to bring own car/bike/motorbike to school. Meals self service. School shop. No tobacco/alcohol allowed.

Discipline No corporal punishment. Pupils failing to produce homework

once might expect a prefect-supervised period at lunchtime; those caught smoking cannabis on the premises might expect to be asked to leave.
Alumni association is run by Alan Wells, Secretary, Old King's Club.
Former pupils Roy Plomley; Alvar Liddell; Jimmy Edwards; Richard Pascoe.

KING'S HIGH (WARWICK)

The King's High School for Girls
Smith Street
Warwick CV34 4HJ
Telephone number 0926 494485

Co-ed   Pupils 540
Boys   Upper sixth Yes
● Girls   Termly fees:
Mixed sixth   Day £670
● Day   GSA; GBGSA
Boarding

Head Mrs J M Anderson (1 year)
Age range 11–18; entry by own exam.
35 assisted places pa.

KING'S (BRUTON)

King's School
Bruton
Somerset BA10 0ED
Telephone number 074 981 3326

Enquiries/application to the Headmaster

Co-ed   Pupils 329
● Boys   Upper sixth 51
Girls   Termly fees:
● Mixed sixth   Day £1635
● Day   Boarding £2290
● Boarding   HMC

WHAT IT'S LIKE

Founded in 1519, it occupies the original site in a very pretty small town (2000 inhabitants). The old school house (1519) is still in use. Modern buildings provide very good accommodation and the school is well-equipped with modern facilities. Delightful playing fields adjoin it by the parish church. There are strong, long standing links with the town and the parish. A balanced all-round education is provided within a strong Christian framework. Academic results are good and some 70% of leavers go on to university, polytechnic or college of higher education. The music, drama and art departments are very active. A good range of games and sports (a number of representatives at county level). A big commitment to local community schemes.

SCHOOL PROFILE

Pupils Total 329. Day 36 (boys); Boarding 293 (boys 270, girls 23). Entry age, boys 13; boys and girls into the sixth. Own junior school provides over 50%. 7% are children of former pupils.
Entrance Common entrance; other exam rarely used. Oversubscribed. No

special skills or religious requirements but expected to attend C of E services. Parents not expected to buy text books. 8 scholarships/bursaries, from full fees to £245.

Parents 15+% in industry or commerce. 30+% live within 30 miles.

Staff Head A H Beadles, in post for 3 years. 32 full time staff. Annual turnover 3. Average age 41.

Academic work GCSE and A-levels. Average size of upper fifth 65; upper sixth 51. *O-levels*: on average, 8 pupils in upper fifth pass 1–4 subjects; 36, 5–7 subjects; 21 pass 8+ subjects. *A-levels*: on average, 5 pupils in the upper sixth pass 1 subject; 17, 2 subjects; 30, 3 subjects; 3 pass 4 subjects. On average, 25 take science/engineering A-levels; 30 take arts and humanities; 8 a mixture. *Computing facilities*: BBC Micro system. Provision for dyslexia.

Senior pupils' non-academic activities *Music*: 130 learn a musical instrument, 12 up to Grade 6 or above; 25 in school orchestra, 30 in school choir. *Drama and dance*: 120–160 in school productions. *Art*: 130 take as non-examined subject; 35 take GCSE; 4 take A-level. 25 belong to photographic club. *Sport*: Rugby, hockey, cricket, athletics, cross-country, tennis, swimming, basketball, judo, badminton, squash, fives, gymnastics, soccer, volleyball, indoor hockey and soccer available. 8 pupils represent county/country (athletics, hockey). *Other*: 35 take part in local community schemes. Other activities include a computer club, canoeing, pot holing, chess, riding, driving etc.

Careers 6 part time advisors. Approximately 70% of upper sixth go on to degree courses.

Uniform School uniform worn throughout.

Houses/prefects Competitive houses. Prefects, head boy/girl, head of house and house prefects – appointed by the Head and housemaster.

Religion Compulsory C of E services on Wednesday and Sunday.

Social Many organised local events, trips and exchanges abroad. Meals self service. School shop. No pupils allowed tobacco/alcohol.

Discipline No corporal punishment. Pupils failing to produce homework once would be treated according to teacher; those caught smoking cannabis on the premises might expect expulsion.

Boarding 15% have own study bedroom. 25% share with others, 60% are in dormitories of 6+. Houses, of approximately 55–65, are the same as competitive houses and are single-sex. Resident qualified nurse and 2 doctors in town. Central dining room. Some pupils can provide and cook their own food. 1 weekend exeat each term. Visits to the local town allowed.

Alumni association is run by J Tyndall, Threeways.

KING'S (CANTERBURY)

The King's School
Canterbury
Kent CT1 2ES
Telephone number 0227 475501

Enquiries/application to the Headmaster

Co-ed
● Boys
Girls
● Mixed sixth
● Day
● Boarding

Pupils 713
Upper sixth 140
Termly fees:
Day £1715
Boarding £2450

WHAT IT'S LIKE

Founded in 597, the school was first a part of the 6th century Benedictine monastery. It has been associated with the cathedral for most of its life. Nearly all the buildings are in the cathedral precincts or at St Augustine's Abbey nearby. Many of them date from the middle ages, some belong to the 16th and 17th centuries. Thus, the school is blessed with an unusually civilised environment and some of the finest architecture in England. Modern facilities are first-class and include exceptionally good libraries. A very well run school, it reveals high standards in virtually every enterprise. Religious worship and instruction form an important part of the curriculum. Academically it is high-powered and achieves excellent results. Some 100–110 leavers go on to university each year (45–50 of them to Oxbridge: very few schools achieve a better ratio). The music in the school is of outstanding quality and vigour. Drama is also very strong. Each year the school presents its own festival of music and drama which is attended by thousands. A wide variety of sports and games is available and standards are very high. Thirty or more clubs and societies cater for most extra-curricular activities. There is a flourishing CCF contingent and considerable emphasis on outdoor pursuits. A fine record in the Duke of Edinburgh's Award Scheme.

SCHOOL PROFILE

Pupils Total, 713. Day 133 (boys 110, girls 23); Boarding 580 (boys 502, girls 78). Entry age, 13+ boys; boys and girls into the sixth.

Entrance Common entrance and own sixth form entrance exam used. Sometimes oversubscribed. No special skills or religious requirements. Various academic, art and music awards for up to full fees.

Parents 15+% are doctors, lawyers etc; 15+% in industry or commerce.

Staff Head Canon A C J Phillips, in post for 2 years. 80 full time staff, 5 part time. Annual turnover 2%.

Academic work GCSE and A-levels. Russian offered to GCSE/A-level. *Computing facilities*: Extensive in computer department and CDT centre.

Senior pupils' non-academic activities *Sport*: Rugby, soccer, tennis, rowing, swimming, basketball, hockey, fencing, lacrosse, netball available. *Other*: Some pupils take part in local community schemes; some participate in Duke of Edinburgh's Award scheme. Other activities include a computer club, music, drama, crafts, debating, gardening, writing and literary appreciation, chess, printing, CCF etc.

Careers 4 part time careers advisors. Average number of pupils accepted for *arts and humanities degree courses* at Oxbridge, 34; other universities, 44;

polytechnics or CHE, 3. *science and engineering degree courses* at Oxbridge, 12; other universities, 26; polytechnics or CHE, 6.

Uniform School uniform worn throughout.

Houses/prefects Competitive houses. Prefects, head boy, head of house and house prefects – appointed by headmaster and housemasters. Various school committees.

Religion Compulsory attendance at cathedral or other religious establishments on alternate Sundays.

Social Concerts, debates, dances, quiz programmes with other schools. Organised trips abroad. Pupils allowed to bring own bike to school. Meals self service. School shop. No tobacco/alcohol allowed.

Discipline No corporal punishment.

Boarding Pupils divided into single sex houses, of approximately 55. Resident qualified medical staff. Central dining room. Pupils can provide and cook own food on a small scale. Half term plus weekend exeats as required. Visits to local town allowed.

Alumni association run by Lt Col C B Manning-Ross, 14 The Avenue, Colchester, Essex CO3 3PA.

KING'S (CHESTER)

The King's School
Wrexham Road
Chester CH4 7QL
Telephone number 0244 671800

Enquiries/application to the Headmaster

Co-ed   Pupils 370
● Boys   Upper sixth 60
Girls   Termly fees:
Mixed sixth   Day £544 (1986)
● Day   HMC
Boarding

WHAT IT'S LIKE

Founded in 1541, it was originally in the cathedral precinct. In 1960 it moved to a semi-rural site on the Wrexham Road, 1 mile from the city. This is an agreeable purpose-built establishment in 32 acres of grounds and playing fields. The junior school is combined. A C of E foundation, worship and religious instruction are of some importance. Very strong in music and drama. The academic ability is high and results are good (some 50 university entrants per year). A good range of sports and games and numerous extra-curricular activities. Quite a big commitment to local community services.

SCHOOL PROFILE

Pupils Total over 12, 370. Entry age, 8, 9, 11 and into the sixth. Own junior school provides over 20%. Some are children of former pupils.

Entrance Own entrance exam used. Oversubscribed. Pupils should have all-round intellectual ability. Anglican foundation but all denominations and creeds accepted. Parents not expected to buy text books. 100 assisted places. Several means-tested scholarships/bursaries.

Parents 15+% are doctors, lawyers etc. 90+% live within 30 miles.

Staff Head A R D Wickson, in post for 7 years. 31 full time staff, 2 part time. Annual turnover 5%. Average age 26–50.

Academic work GCSE and A-levels. Average size of upper fifth 60+; upper sixth 60+. Most pass at least 7 O-levels and 3 A-levels. On average, 35 take science/engineering A-levels; 15 take arts and humanities; 10, a mixture. *Computing facilities*: A well-equipped computer room; several departments have their own computers. Mildly visually handicapped pupils are assimilated into normal teaching groups.

Senior pupils' non-academic activities *Music*: 100–150 learn a musical instrument, 10 up to Grade 6 or above, 1 or 2 accepted for Music School, 40 in school orchestras; 60 in school choirs. *Drama and dance*: Many in school productions. *Art*: About 6 take GCSE, 2 or 3 take A-level. 2 or 3 accepted for Art School. *Sport*: Rowing, soccer, hockey, basketball, table tennis, squash, swimming, athletics, cross-country, cricket, tennis available. Large numbers take non-compulsory sport. Several represent county/country (rowing, cricket, football). *Other*: 30 take part in community schemes. Lively chess club.

Careers 1 part time advisor. Average number of pupils accepted for *arts and humanities degree courses* at Oxbridge, 4; other universities, 12; polytechnics or CHE, 2. *science and engineering degree courses* at Oxbridge, 7; other universities, 25; medical schools, 2; polytechnics or CHE, 1. *BEd*, 1. Average number of pupils going straight into careers in the armed services, 4; other, 3 or 4.

Uniform School uniform worn throughout.

Houses/prefects No competitive houses. All sixth form perform prefectorial duties. Head boy appointed by the Headmaster with sixth form advice. Sixth form Council.

Religion Daily services and 4 cathedral services a year, plus voluntary communion services in school and cathedral.

Social A variety of activities with Queen's School eg debating society, Christian Union, Gilbert & Sullivan. Regular trips and exchanges abroad. Meals self service. No tobacco/alcohol allowed.

Discipline Corporal punishment not ruled out. Pupils failing to produce homework once might expect a talking to; those caught smoking cannabis on the premises would be asked to leave immediately.

Former pupils Ronald Pickup; Nicholas Grace; others in academic or medical spheres.

KING'S (ELY)

The King's School
Ely
Cambridgeshire CB7 4DB
Telephone number 0353 662824

Enquiries/application to the Admissions Secretary or Headmaster's Secretary

- Co-ed
  Boys
  Girls
  Mixed sixth
- Day
- Boarding

Pupils 420
Upper sixth 70
Termly fees:
Day £1485
Boarding £2330
HMC

WHAT IT'S LIKE

Founded in 970, refounded in 1541 by Henry VIII, it has a superb position on the edge of one of the most beautiful cathedral cities in Europe. Much of the school is housed in the buildings of the old Benedictine monastery and these are of great architectural and historical interest. They include Prior Crauden's chapel, the 14th-century monastic barn (now the school dining hall), the Porta (gateway of the monastery) which is now the art centre, and the Norman undercroft of the school house which contains the library. Since 1960 there has been a massive development and modernisation programme which has included the creation of the Hayward Theatre. Facilities and accommodation are excellent. The school combines a kindergarten and a junior school, thus providing continuous education from 4–18. Ely is C of E orientated and pupils are expected to attend services unless conscience precludes. A high standard of teaching prevails and results are very good (45–55 university entrants per year). Very strong indeed in music, and quite strong in drama. A fair range of sports and games (standards are high). A lot of emphasis on outdoor pursuits and adventure training. Full use is made of the City's facilities, and those of Cambridge a few miles away.

SCHOOL PROFILE

Pupils Total, 420. Day 240 (boys 140, girls 100); Boarding 180 (boys 100, girls 80). Entry age, 13 and into the sixth. Own junior school provides 75%. 5–10% are children of former pupils.

Entrance Common entrance and own entrance exam used. Oversubscribed. No special skills required. Church of England orientated school; pupils are expected to attend a school service unless conscience precludes. Parents expected to buy text books. 50 scholarships/bursaries, 5%–33% fees.

Parents 30+% live within 30 miles; up to 10% live overseas.

Staff Head H Ward, in post for 18 years. 45 full time staff, 4 part time. Annual turnover 5–10%. Average age 35–40.

Academic work GCSE and A-levels. Average size of upper fifth 95; upper sixth 70. *O-levels:* on average, 30 pupils in upper fifth pass 1–4 subjects; 26, 5–7 subjects; 33 pass 8+ subjects. *A-level*: average pupil passes 2.28. On average, 45% take science/engineering A-levels; 45% take arts and humanities; 10% a mixture. *Computing facilities*: Computing centre, supported largely by Pye Foundation. *Special provisions*: for eg dyslexia, EFL, so long as pupils are able to take a proper part in the normal life of the school.

Senior pupils' non-academic activities *Music*: 200 learn a musical instrument, 30 to Grade 6 or above. 1 accepted for Music School. 25 in school orchestra(s), 40 in school choir, 10 in school pop group; occasional pupil in National Youth Orchestra. *Drama and dance*: 15–20 in school productions, 80–100 in house and form plays; 1 accepted for Drama/Dance School. *Art*: 10 take GCSE; 3–4, A-level. 1–2 accepted for Art School. *Sport*: Rugby, hockey, cricket, athletics, rowing, tennis, girls' hockey, netball, rounders, sailing, swimming, squash, badminton, golf available. 10–12 represent county/country (rowing, rugby, cricket, hockey). *Other*: 25 have bronze Duke of Edinburgh's Award. Other activities include a computer club, chess club, driving lessons can be arranged.

Careers 34 part time advisors (including 30 house tutors). Average number of pupils accepted for *arts and humanities degree courses* at Oxbridge, 3–5; other universities, 17–20. *science and engineering degree courses* at Oxbridge, 3–5; other universities, 17–20.

Uniform School uniform worn on formal occasions; school dress on other occasions.

Houses/prefects Houses predominantly pastoral. Prefects, head of school and deputies, head of house and house prefects – appointed by the Headmaster or housemaster/mistress. Sixth form committee.

Religion 2 morning services per week. Sunday service for boarders.

Social Annual French exchange. Pupils allowed to bring own car/bike/motorbike to school. Some meals formal, some self service. School book and tuck shops. No tobacco/alcohol allowed.

Discipline No corporal punishment. Pupils failing to produce homework once will be asked to re-do it; detention and work-force for persistent minor offences; suspension for 1 week if more serious.

Boarding 3 or 4 in each house have own study bedroom; most share with 2 or 3 others; few in dormitory of 6+. Houses, of 40–50, same as competitive houses, single sex. Resident qualified nurse; local doctor. Central dining room. Pupils can provide and cook own snacks. Exeats each weekend. Weekly boarding is an option. Visits to local town allowed out of school time.

Alumni association is run by Hon Sec, Old Elean's Club, c/o the School.

KING'S (GLOUCESTER)

The King's School
Pitt Street
Gloucester GL1 2BG
Telephone number 0452 21251

Enquiries/application to the Headmaster

- Co-ed
- Boys
- Girls
- Mixed sixth
- Day
- Boarding

Pupils 424
Upper sixth 45
Termly fees:
Day £980
Boarding £1655
SHMIS; CSA

WHAT IT'S LIKE

The first reference to some kind of school attached to the cathedral dates from 1072. The present school was refounded by Henry VIII in 1541. It lies in the cathedral close in the middle of Gloucester and is a pleasant combination of ancient and modern buildings. Good up-to-date facilities. It provides a sound general education in the context of the Christian faith. The cathedral is the spiritual and cultural centre of the school. Most days begin with worship in it. Its strong music dept has for its core the cathedral choristers who get free tuition. The drama dept is also active. Academically, results are good and some 20 leavers go on to university. A decent range of games and sports and an adequate number of clubs and societies. Quite a good record in the Duke of Edinburgh's Award Scheme.

SCHOOL PROFILE

Pupils Total over 12, 424. Day 328 (boys 280, girls 48); Boarding 96 (boys). Entry age, 4+, 11+, 13+ and into the sixth. Own junior school provides over 20%. 12% are children of former pupils.

Entrance Common entrance and own entrance exam used. Oversubscribed.

Musical skills looked for. Parents expected to buy text books. 15 scholarships, for choristers, academic and music, 40% to full fees.

Parents 15+% in industry or commerce; 15+% are farmers. 60+% live within 30 miles; 11–30% live overseas.

Staff Head Rev Alan C Charters, in post for 5 years. 42 full time staff, 8 part time. Annual turnover 2%. Average age 40.

Academic work GCSE and A-levels. Average size of upper fifth 65; upper sixth 45. *O-levels*: on average, 17 pupils in upper fifth pass 1–4 subjects; 22, 5–7 subjects; 27 pass 8+ subjects. *A-levels*: on average, 4 pupils in the upper sixth pass 1 subject; 11, 2 subjects; 14, 3 subjects; 2 pass 4 subjects. On average, 13 take science/engineering A-levels; 7 take arts and humanities; 12 take a mixture. *Computing facilities*: Computer centre (compulsory course in 3rd form), computers in departments. Dyslexia provisions.

Senior pupils' non-academic activities *Music*: 53 learn a musical instrument, 15 up to Grade 6 or above, 2 accepted for Music School; 22 in school orchestra, 50 in school choir, 12 in madrigal group, 6 in school pop group; 1 in National Youth Orchestra, 1 ARCO, FRCO, 1 organ scholar, 3 choral scholars. *Drama and dance*: 15 in school productions, 30 in theatre workshops. *Art*: 15 take as non-examined subject; 6 take A-level; 4–5 accepted for Art School. 8 belong to photographic club. *Sport*: Rugby, hockey, rowing, cricket, athletics, cross-country, squash, tennis, basketball, netball, and rounders available, plus badminton and soccer. 50–60 take non-compulsory sport. 7–8 represent county/country (rugby, cross-country, hockey). *Other*: 15 have bronze Duke of Edinburgh's Award, 6 have silver and 1, gold. 3–4 enter voluntary schemes after leaving school. Other activities include computer and chess clubs, literary and debating society, theatre workshop, astronomy society and numerous smaller clubs.

Careers 1 part time advisor. Average number of pupils accepted for *arts and humanities degree courses* at Oxbridge, 2; other universities, 7; polytechnics or CHE, 5. *science and engineering degree courses* at Oxbridge, 4; other universities, 4; medical schools, 1; polytechnics or CHE, 2. *BEd*, 2. Average number of pupils going straight into careers in the armed services, 7; industry, 2; the civil service, 1; banking/insurance, 8.

Uniform School uniform worn throughout.

Houses/prefects Competitive houses. Prefects, head boy/girl, head of house and house prefects – appointed by the Head and housemasters. School Council.

Religion Compulsory daily worship in Cathedral. Sunday morning service. Voluntary participation in Cathedral services.

Social Joint theatre workshops with local girls' independent school; choral society productions with girls' grammar schools; dances/discos with local girls' schools. Annual choir trip to Brittany, exchange with France (Metz), European trip (Moscow in 1988); Pyrenees annual climbing holiday. Pupils allowed to bring own car/bike/motorbike to school. Meals formal. School shop. No tobacco/alcohol allowed.

Discipline No corporal punishment. Pupils failing to produce homework once might expect to complete it by the next day; those caught smoking cannabis on the premises would be asked to leave.

Boarding Sixth formers have own study bedroom, 4th and 5th share with 1 or 2 others; only one dormitory has 6+. Houses, of approximately 36, are divided by age and are single-sex. Resident nurse and doctor. Central dining room. Pupils can provide and cook a small amount of their own food. 2 exeats of 24 hours each term. Visits to the local town allowed.

Alumni association is run by C J Ashby, c/o the School.

Former pupils Terry Biddlecombe (champion jockey); Sir Herbert Brewer (organist).

KING'S (MACCLESFIELD)

The King's School
Cumberland Street
Macclesfield
Cheshire SK10 1DA
Telephone number 0625 22505

Enquiries/application to the School
Secretary

Co-ed   Pupils 850
● Boys   Upper sixth 110
   Girls   Termly fees:
● Mixed sixth   Day £825
● Day   HMC
   Boarding

WHAT IT'S LIKE

Founded in 1502, re-established in 1552 by Royal Charter of Edward VI. In 1855 it moved to its present urban site, spread across 2 roads. It has handsome buildings and the new buildings include a very large library and a fine science block. The playing fields are on two sites and the junior school is combined. A well-run and strongly academic school, it lays considerable stress on the encouragement of pupils to develop confidence in their own judgement and to develop their own particular interests to the full in a secure and supportive environment. The active involvement of parents is much encouraged. Academic standards are in fact high and many leavers (70–80 per year) go on to university. Very strong in music, drama and art. Wide range of sports and games (again standards are high) and activities. Substantial commitment to local community schemes.

SCHOOL PROFILE

Pupils Total over 12, 850 (boys 800, girls 50). Entry age, 11+, boys; boys and girls into the sixth. 10% are children of former pupils.

Entrance Common entrance and own entrance exam used. Oversubscribed. Welcomes all talents. No religious requirements. Parents not expected to buy text books. 35 assisted places. 5 scholarships/bursaries pa, £300 to £100.

Parents 15+% in industry or commerce. 60+% live within 30 miles.

Staff Head A G Silcock, in post since September 1987. 74 full time staff, 14 part time. Annual turnover 2%. Average age late thirties.

Academic work GCSE and A-levels. Average size of upper sixth 110. Exam results not provided. *Computing facilities*: One lab, with roughly 20 machines; various in several departments. Some special teaching provisions when necessary.

Senior pupils' non-academic activities *Music*: 97 learn a musical instrument, 37 up to Grade 6 or above, 2/3 accepted for Music School; 36 in school orchestra, 34 in school choir, 4 in school pop group; 3 in National Youth Orchestra, 18 in local orchestras/bands. *Drama and dance*: 30 in school productions; 20 take GCSE; 20 in theatre arts, 12 in Revue, 22 in general studies. 1 in National Youth Theatre. *Art*: 55 take GCSE; 12 take A-level. 2 accepted for Art School. 10 in recreational art, 10 belong to eg photographic club, 10 in art club. Most A-level art pupils are placed in foundation courses. *Sport*: Rugby, hockey, cricket, soccer, athletics, cross-country, swimming, badminton, tennis, squash, table tennis, sailing, orienteering, hill-walking, rock-climbing, caving, abseiling, basketball, netball, canoeing available. 300 take non-compulsory sport. 51 represent county (rugby, hockey, swimming, athletics, cricket, tennis and table tennis). *Other*: 20–30 take part in local community schemes. Activities include a computer club, chess, ornithology, railways, debating, DIY, car maintenance, aviation, Christian Union, botany, historical society.

Careers 2–3 part time advisors. Average number of pupils accepted for *arts and humanities degree courses* at Oxbridge, 6; other universities, 25; polytechnics or CHE, 15; *science and engineering degree courses* at Oxbridge, 8; other universities, 30; medical schools, 15; polytechnics or CHE, 20. *BEd*, 15. *other general training courses*, 8–10. Average number of pupils going straight into careers in the armed services, 2; the church, 1; industry, 2–3; the City, 1; the civil service, 1; music/drama, 2.

Uniform School uniform worn except the sixth.

Houses/prefects No competitive houses. Prefects and head boy appointed by the Head. School Council.

Religion C of E worship encouraged.

Social No organised events with local schools. 5–6 foreign trips and exchanges per year. Pupils allowed to bring own car/bike/motorbike to school. Meals self service. School shop. No tobacco/alcohol allowed.

Discipline No corporal punishment. Pupils failing to produce homework once might expect to explain why; those caught smoking cannabis on the premises would probably expect expulsion.

Alumni association is run by P R Mathews, c/o the school.

Former pupils Alan Beith; Christian Blackshaw; Forbes Robinson; Steve Smith; Hewlett Johnson; Sir Arthur Smith Woodward; A A Golds; G G Hulme; F N Golding; E A Wrigley; Comm J R Porter; F E Knowles; G N Sanderson; C Booth; A Garner; R J Johnson; R J Hewitt etc, etc.

KING'S (ROCHESTER)

King's School	Co-ed	Pupils 400
Rochester	● Boys	Upper sixth 70
Kent ME1 1TD	Girls	Termly fees:
Telephone number 0634 43913	● Mixed sixth	Day £1019
	● Day	Boarding £1699
Enquiries/application to the Headmaster	● Boarding	HMC

WHAT IT'S LIKE

There was probably a cathedral school early in the 7th century; the present school dates from 1542 and has a fine site in the precinct of the cathedral, close by the castle and very near the Medway. The older buildings are very agreeable and there has been considerable expansion and modernisation since 1955 to produce excellent modern facilities. Naturally there are strong links with the cathedral and its life. Religious instruction is important in the curriculum. Attendance at services and chapel is compulsory. Academic standards are good and a large number (45–50) of leavers go on to university each year. Strong music, art and drama depts. A wide range of sports and games (high standards achieved) and a good range of activities. A vigorous CCF and a lively commitment to local community services.

SCHOOL PROFILE

Pupils Total over 12, 400. Day 339 (boys 310, girls 29); Boarding 61 (boys 60, girls 1). Entry age, 5, 8, 13+ boys; boys and girls into the sixth. Own junior school provides over 50%. 50% are children of former pupils.

Entrance Common entrance and own entrance exam used. No special skills or religious requirements. Parents not expected to buy text books. 54 assisted places. 99 scholarships/bursaries, £500 to £33 per term.

Parents 15+% are doctors, lawyers, etc; 15+% in industry or commerce. 60+% live within 30 miles; up to 10% live overseas.

Staff Head Dr I R Walker, in post for 2 years. 50 full time staff, 12 part time. Annual turnover 2%. Average age 35.

Academic work GCSE and A-levels. Average size of upper fifth 75; upper sixth 70. *O-levels*: on average, 10 pupils in upper fifth pass 1–4 subjects; 30, 5–7 subjects; 35 pass 8+ subjects. *A-levels*: on average 8 pupils in the upper sixth pass 1 subject; 12, 2 subjects; 50 pass 3 subjects. On average, 25 take science/engineering A-levels; 30 take arts and humanities; 15 take a mixture. Greek offered to GCSE. *Computing facilities*: NIMBUS.

Senior pupils' non-academic activities *Music*: 60 learn a musical instrument, 40 up to Grade 6 or above. 3 accepted for Music School, 30 in school orchestra, 28 in school choir, 15 in instrument groups, 2 in Kent Youth Orchestra, 1 in Rochester Arts Orchestra, 2 play in pop group. *Drama and dance*: 120 in school productions. 1 accepted for Drama/Dance school. 1 entered competitions. *Art*: 60 take as non-examined subject; 20 take GCSE; 10 take A-level. 2 accepted for Art School, 3 for foundation course. 10 belong to photographic club. *Sport*: Boys; Rugby, hockey, cricket, fencing, rowing, athletics, basketball, badminton, squash, tennis available. Girls; Hockey, netball, rowing and tennis. Most take non-compulsory sport. 5 represent county/country (rugby, hockey, cricket). *Other*: 30 take part in local community schemes. 1 enters volunteer scheme after leaving school. Other activities include a computer club, debating, geographical, art, historical, Christian Fellowship, chess, technical, ornithology and science societies.

Careers 1 full time and 3 part time advisors. Average number of pupils accepted for *arts and humanities degree courses* at Oxbridge, 3; other universities, 20; polytechnics or CHE, 7. *science and engineering degree courses* at Oxbridge, 2; other universities, 20; medical schools, 3; polytechnics or CHE, 10. *other general training courses*, 2. Average number of pupils going straight into careers in the armed services, 4; industry, 5; the City, 3; music/drama, 1. Traditional school careers are medicine, law and accountancy.

Uniform School uniform worn throughout.

Houses/prefects Competitive houses. Prefects, head boy/girl, head of house and house prefects – appointed by the Head.

Religion Compulsory C of E services and chapel.

Social No organised local events. Organised trips to France and Germany. Pupils allowed to bring own car/bike to school. Meals self service. School shop. No tobacco/alcohol allowed.

Discipline No corporal punishment. Pupils failing to produce homework once might expect a verbal warning; anyone involved with drugs can expect expulsion.

Boarding 20% have own study bedroom, 80% share with others. Houses, of approximately 60 and 30, divided by age group 12+ and under 12, and are single-sex. Resident qualified nurse. Central dining room. Pupils can provide and cook own food. 4 weekend exeats each term. Visits to the local town allowed after school.

Alumni association is run by Mr R Hale, 7 Quarry Hill, Sevenoaks, Kent TN15 0HH.

Former pupils John Selwyn Gummer.

KING'S (TAUNTON)

King's College
South Road
Taunton
Somerset TA1 3DX
Telephone number 0823 272708

Co-ed
● Boys
Girls
● Mixed sixth
● Day
● Boarding

Pupils 470
Upper sixth Yes
Termly fees:
Day £1520
Boarding £2050
HMC; Woodard

WHAT IT'S LIKE

Its historical links go back to the medieval grammar school which was refounded by Bishop Fox of Winchester in 1522. In 1869 it was moved from what are now the municipal buildings in Taunton to its present site half a mile south of the city. It is the oldest school in the Western Division of the Woodard Corporation, and stands in a well wooded and spacious setting of 110 acres. There are fine playing fields and splendid views of the Blackdown and Quantock Hills. All told, a very attractive and civilised environment. The junior school is housed in Pyrland Hall, a handsome Georgian mansion north of the city. There is a pre-prep school at King's House. The senior school has about 465 boys, including 50 day boys. There are 40 girl boarders in the sixth form. A lot of excellent facilities have been added in recent years and the school is very well-equipped. The chapel and its services are an important part of school life and there is a good deal of emphasis on religious education. A full range of academic subjects is available, the teaching is good and standards and results are high. A large proportion of leavers go on to university each year. Music and drama are very strong. Full use is made of two fully equipped theatres. There is an excellent art and design centre which produces impressive results. Much use is made, too, of a sophisticated video production unit. Facilities for sports and games are first-rate and there is a high standard of performance. Many clubs and societies cater for most extra-curricular activities. The CCF is a flourishing contingent and there is a good deal of emphasis on outdoor pursuits. A large number of pupils are involved in local community services.

SCHOOL PROFILE

Head R S Funnell, first year in post
Age range 13–18, own prep from age 7; entry by common entrance
Scholarships, including for music and science, available.

KING'S (WORCESTER)

The King's School	Co-ed	Pupils 644
Worcester WR1 2LH	● Boys	Upper sixth 130
Telephone number 0905 23016	Girls	Termly fees:
	● Mixed sixth	Day £889
Enquiries to the Headmaster	● Day	Boarding £1506
Application to the Headmaster's Secretary	● Boarding	HMC

WHAT IT'S LIKE

Refounded in 1541 by Henry VIII, it comprises an enclave of very fine buildings grouped round College Green on the south side of the Cathedral and on the banks of the Severn. The oldest structure is the 14th-century College Hall. There are many 17th, 18th and 19th-century buildings and a large number of modern ones, all in fine grounds and gardens. The Junior School occupies separate premises, St Albans, in its own grounds near the main school. Academic standards are very high and the teaching is good (110–120 leavers go on to further education; 14–18 of them to Oxbridge). Basic Christian ethics and doctrine are taught and the Cathedral is an important part of the school's life. A very strong music dept which gains much from its association with the Cathedral. Strong, too, in art and drama (6 or 7 productions each year). Excellent sport and games and an enormous range of activities. The CCF is especially vigorous. A fair commitment to local community schemes and to the Duke of Edinburgh's Award Scheme.

SCHOOL PROFILE

Pupils Total over 12, 644. Day 514 (boys 451, girls 63); Boarding 130 (boys 110, girls, 20). Entry age, boys, 8, 9, 11 and 13; boys and girls into the sixth. Own junior school provides more than 20%.
Entrance Own entrance exam used, some admission by common entrance. Oversubscribed. No special skills or religious requirements. Parents not expected to buy text books. 34 assisted places pa. 20 scholarships/bursaries, full fees to £450.
Parents 60+% live within 30 miles; up to 10% live overseas.
Staff Head Dr J M Moore, in post for 4 years. 61 full time staff, 7 part time. Annual turnover 7%.
Academic work GCSE and A-levels. Average size of upper fifth, 98; upper sixth, 130. *O-levels*: on average, 4 pupils in upper fifth pass 1–4 subjects; 50, 5–7 subjects; 40 pass 8+ subjects. *A-levels*: on average, 1 pupil in upper sixth passes 1 subject; 5, 2 subjects; 110, 3 subjects; 8 pass 4 subjects. On average, 40/50 take science/engineering A-levels; 40/50 take arts and humanities; 20/30 take a mixture. *Computing facilities*: Computers in each department plus the computer room. Provisions for mild sight handicap and very slight dyslexia.

Senior pupils' non-academic activities   *Music*: 300 learn a musical instrument, a lot to Grade 6 or above, a few accepted for Music School, some go on to play in pop group; 90 in school orchestra, 100 in school choir, 8–14 in school pop group; occasional pupil in National Youth Orchestra, 22 choristers in cathedral choir. Much other musical activity.   *Drama and dance*: Many pupils in school productions, 9 productions a year, school/house/group plays.   *Art*: Many take as non-examined subject; 30 take GCSE; 8 take A-level. A few accepted for Art School. 20 belong to eg photography club.   *Sport*: Rugby, football, hockey, rowing, cricket, athletics, badminton, canoeing, cross-country running, fencing, fives, sailing, squash, swimming and tennis available. Very many take non-compulsory sport. Some take exams. A lot of pupils represent county/country (eg rugby, cricket, rowing, canoeing, tennis, fencing).   *Other*: 10–20 take part in local community schemes. 20+ have silver Duke of Edinburgh's Award, 5 have gold. Some enter voluntary schemes after leaving school. Other activities include a computer club, craft workshop, swimming club, nature club, chess club, .22 rifle shooting, model engineering, drama workshop, wind band, Christian Union, literary society, Keys Society, debates, printing, ice skating, rock climbing, cinema club, theatre visits, golf, basketball, dry skiing, rounders, sub-aqua and confirmation classes.

Careers 4 part time advisors. 100 pupils go on to degree courses, with 14–18 to Oxford and Cambridge. *other general training courses*, 1–2. Average number of pupils going straight into careers in the armed services, 4–5; industry, a few; the City, a few.

Uniform School uniform worn except upper sixth.

Houses/prefects Pastoral rather than competitive houses. Prefects, head boy/girl, head of house and house prefects – appointed by the Head.

Religion Worship is encouraged.

Social No organised local events. French/German exchanges, skiing trips, geography field trips, other trips to Italy, France and Spain. Pupils allowed to bring own car/bike/motorbike to school. Some meals formal, some self service. School shop. No tobacco/alcohol allowed.

Discipline No corporal punishment.

Boarding Seniors in own or shared studies; juniors in dormitories of 6 or more. Houses, of approximately 40, are pastoral units, divided by age group, single-sex. Resident qualified nurse. Central dining room. Pupils can provide and cook their own food. Regular exeats usually of 36 hours. Visits to local town allowed.

Alumni association is run by Mr R Craze, c/o School.

KINGSLEY

The Kingsley School	Co-ed	Pupils 340
Beauchamp Avenue	Boys	Upper sixth Yes
Leamington Spa	● Girls	Termly fees:
Warwickshire CV32 5RD	Mixed sixth	Day £700
Telephone number 0926 25127	● Day	Boarding £1360
	● Boarding	GSA

Head Miss E C Fairhurst (11 years)
Age range 11–18, own junior from age 4; entry by own exam.
4 scholarships pa.

KINGSTON GRAMMAR

Kingston Grammar School	● Co-ed	Pupils 460
70 London Road	Boys	Upper sixth Yes
Kingston upon Thames	Girls	Termly fees:
Surrey KT2 6PY	Mixed sixth	Day £880
Telephone number 01-546 5875	● Day	HMC
	Boarding	

Head Mr A B Creber (1 year)
Age range 11–18; entry by common entrance and own exam.
Scholarships, bursaries, assisted places.

KINGSWOOD

Kingswood School	● Co-ed	Pupils 454
Lansdown	Boys	Upper sixth 90
Bath	Girls	Termly fees:
Avon BA1 5RG	Mixed sixth	Day £1400
Telephone number 0225 311 627	● Day	Boarding £2160
	● Boarding	

Enquiries/application to the Headmaster

WHAT IT'S LIKE

Founded in 1748 by John Wesley who created its first curriculum and compiled its first text books. It has a particularly splendid position on the slopes of Lansdown Hill, overlooking Bath. The main buildings are Victorian Gothic (1851) and these remain the heart of the modern school which has a vast campus of 218 acres. Many new buildings have been added, including a Georgian mansion, a big library, a sixth form centre, a superb sports hall, and Art and CDT centres. In these very civilised surroundings, the facilities and accommodation are first class. Though ecumenical, the school retains especially strong links with the Methodist Church. An excellent academic education is given and results and standards are high: more than 50 university entrants per year (a high ratio for a school of this size). Very strong music and art departments. An exceptionally fine range of sports, games, clubs, societies and extra-curricular activities. Strong commitment to local community services and an impressive record in the Duke of Edinburgh's Award Scheme. The prep school, Prior's Court, is near Newbury, Berkshire.

SCHOOL PROFILE

Pupils Total over 12, 454. Day 126 (boys 67, girls 59); Boarding 328 (boys 204, girls 124). Entry age, 11, 13 and into the sixth. Prior's Court (own prep school) provides over 20%. 11% are children of former pupils.

Entrance Common entrance and own entrance exam used. Oversubscribed. No special skills or religious requirements, but school has strong links with the Methodist Church. Parents not expected to buy text books. 37 assisted places. 6 scholarships/bursaries pa, 33–25% fees.

Parents 30+% live within 30 miles; 10+% live overseas.

Staff Head G M Best, in post for 1 year. 46 full time staff, 4 part time. Annual turnover 5% (including retirement). Average age 40.

Academic work GCSE, AS and A-levels. Average size of upper fifth 85; upper sixth 85. *O-levels*: on average, 17 pupils in upper fifth pass 1–4 subjects; 20, 5–7 subjects; 48 pass 8+ subjects. *A-levels*: on average, 13 pupils in upper sixth pass 1 subject; 13, 2 subjects; 39, 3 subjects and 11 pass 4 subjects. On average, 35 take science/engineering A-levels; 30 arts and humanities; 14 a mixture. *Computing facilities*: Computer room (Mackintosh System). *Special provisions*: Visiting specialists offer help with special needs, including dyslexia.

Senior pupils' non-academic activities *Music*: 140 learn a musical instrument, 20 to Grade 6 or above. 2 accepted for Music School; 1 choral/organ scholar. 50 in school orchestra, 70 in school choir, 10 in school pop group, 8 in jazz/swing and 30 in wind bands. *Drama and dance*: 60 participate in school productions; 20 in informal theatre; 1 accepted for Drama/Dance Schools, 1 goes on to work in theatre. *Art*: 24 take as non-examined subject, 34 take GCSE art, 15, A-level, 22, A-level history of art. 6 accepted for Art School, 2 for university fine art courses, 4, history of art and 1, architecture; 20 belong to photographic club. *Sport*: Archery, athletics, badminton, basketball, cricket, cross-country, golf, hiking, hockey, horse-riding, karate, multi-gym, netball, orienteering, rounders, rugby, sailing, self-defence, shooting, squash, swimming, tennis, trampolining, volleyball, windsurfing available. 200 take non-compulsory sport. 25 represent county/country (rugby, hockey, cricket, tennis, cross-country, athletics, orienteering). *Other*: 20 take part in local community schemes. 25 have bronze Duke of Edinburgh's Award, 20, silver and 15, gold. 2 are D of E Award Panel Members; 10 enter voluntary schemes after leaving school, 5 work for national charities. Other activities include 3 computer clubs, astronomy, bridge, CB radio, canal group, chess, Christian Fellowship, community service, current affairs, dance, debating, drama, electronics, film, history, law, model making, model railway, printing, video making, wargames and many others.

Careers 3 part time advisors. Average number of pupils accepted for *arts and humanities degree courses* at Oxbridge, 4; other universities, 25; polytechnics or CHE, 4. *science and engineering degree courses* at Oxbridge, 6; other universities, 17; medical schools, 6; polytechnics or CHE, 11. *BEd*, 6. *other general training courses*, 3. Average number of pupils going straight into careers in the armed services, 2; the church, 1; industry, 2; the City, 1; music/drama, 1; commerce/banking, 2.

Uniform School uniform worn except in the sixth.

Houses/prefects Competitive houses. Prefects, head boy/girl, head of house and house prefects – appointed by the Head.

Religion Daily morning assembly (religious) for all. Sunday service for boarders.

Social Local schools joint cricket tour abroad, choral production (annually), debating competitions and joint sixth form activities occasionally. Annual ski trip abroad. Occasional small group trips (history, art, visit to Taize, etc); annual exchange with German school. Pupils allowed to bring own car to school. Meals self service. School shop. No tobacco/alcohol allowed.

Discipline No corporal punishment. Pupils failing to produce homework once might be required to produce it within 24 hours; those caught smoking cannabis on the premises could expect expulsion.

Boarding All sixth form share (2 or 3); 50% are in dormitories of 6+. Houses, of approximately 40, 2 junior, 7 senior, single sex. Resident qualified nurse, visiting doctor. Central dining room. Pupils can provide and cook own snacks. 2 weekend exeats each term plus some day exeats. Visits to local town allowed.

Alumni association run by Mr W B Mountford, c/o the School.

KING WILLIAM'S

King William's College
Castletown
Isle of Man
Telephone number 0624 822551

- Co-ed
  Boys
  Girls
  Mixed sixth
- Day
- Boarding

Pupils 350
Upper sixth Yes
Termly fees:
Day £1330
Boarding £1900
HMC

Head P K Bregazzi (9 years)
Age range 8–19; entry by common entrance or own exam
Bursaries (services) and scholarships, including for music.

KIRKHAM GRAMMAR

Kirkham Grammar School
Ribby Road
Kirkham
Preston
Lancashire PR4 2BH
Telephone number 0772 684264

Enquiries/application to the Headmaster

- Co-ed   Pupils 500
- Boys   Upper sixth 45
- Girls   Termly fees:
- Mixed sixth   Day £675
- Day   Boarding £1255
- Boarding   SHMIS

WHAT IT'S LIKE

Founded in 1549, it occupies an agreeable 20-acre rural site in the Fylde close to Kirkham. The main school buildings date from 1910, but there have been many additions since the 1930s. A programme of expansion is still under way. Accommodation and facilities are now very good. It retains old and traditional links with the Drapers' Company and provides a traditional grammar school education. Results are good. Kirkham sets out to be a Christian school and to prepare its pupils for a Christian life in the world. A well-organised establishment, it has a purposeful and motivated atmosphere. Very strong music and drama departments. An impressive range of sport, games and activities.

SCHOOL PROFILE

Pupils Total over 11, 500. Day 420 (boys 220, girls 200); Boarding 80 (boys 40, girls 40). Entry age, 11 and into the sixth form. About 4% are children of former pupils.

Entrance Own entrance exam used. No special skills or religious requirements. Parents not expected to buy text books. 10 assisted places pa. 10 scholarships/bursaries, ½ fees to £100 per term.

Parents 15+% in industry or commerce; 15+% are doctors, lawyers, etc. 60+% live within 30 miles; up to 10% live overseas.

Staff Head M J Summerlee, in post for 16 years. 39 full time staff, 3 part time. Annual turnover 3%. Average age 35.

Academic work GCSE and A-levels. Average size of upper fifth 85; upper sixth 45. *O-levels*: on average, 26 pupils in upper fifth pass 1–4 subjects; 21, 5–7 subjects; 17 pass 8+ subjects. *A-levels*: on average, 8 pupils in upper sixth pass 1 subject; 10, 2 subjects; 8, 3 subjects and 16 pass 4 subjects. On average, 25 take science/engineering A-levels; 15 take arts and humanities; 20 a mixture. *Computing facilities*: Computer room with 8 computers. Special provisions for eg dyslexia.

Senior pupils' non-academic activities *Music*: 58 learn a musical instrument, 8 to Grade 6 or above. 28 in school orchestra(s), 150 in school choir(s); 1 on RSCM Cathedral course; 2 in RSCM cathedral singers; 2 in Lancashire School Training Orchestra; 1 finalist in national electronic organ championships. *Drama and dance*: 60 in school productions; 20 in junior workshop; 23 in GCSE drama course; 21 to Grade 6 and above in LAMDA; 12 in dance class; 200 (years 1–3) take drama once a week. 1 goes on to work in theatre. *Art*: 30 take GCSE; 7 A-level. 4 accepted for Art School; 2 for architecture courses. 20 belong to photographic club. *Sport*: Badminton, squash, athletics, cricket, tennis, rugby, swimming, netball, hockey, gymnastics, dance available. 100 take non-compulsory sport. Some take exams in gymnastics and swimming. 11 represent county (tennis, swimming, rugby, squash); some county champions; 1 represents country at rugby plus 7 in trials. *Other*: 10 take part in local community schemes. 6 enter voluntary schemes after leaving school; 20 work for national charities. Other activities include a computer club, angling society (local fishing), fell-walking society, electronics, bridge club, astronomical society, natural history.

Careers 3 full time and 2 part time advisors. Average number of pupils accepted for *arts and humanities degree courses* at Oxbridge, 1; other universities, 16; polytechnics or CHE, 10. *science and engineering degree courses* at Oxbridge, 2; other universities, 14; medical schools, 4; polytechnics or CHE, 6. *BEd*, 2. *other general training courses*, 10. Average number of pupils going straight into careers in the armed services, 3; the church, 1; industry, 6; the City, 1; civil service, 1; music/drama, 3; other, 6.

Uniform School uniform worn throughout.

Houses/prefects Competitive houses. Prefects, head boy/girl, head of house and house prefects – appointed by the Head or housemasters.

Religion Church of England worship encouraged.

Social No organised events with local schools. Trips to Germany and France. Pupils allowed to bring own car/bike/motorbike to school. Meals self service. School shop. No tobacco/alcohol allowed.

Discipline No corporal punishment. Pupils failing to produce homework once might expect a second chance. Detention system operates.

Boarding 40% have own study bedroom, 20% share with one other; 40% are in dormitories of 6+. Resident qualified medical staff. Central dining room. One weekend exeat every 3 weeks. Visits to local town allowed.

Alumni association run by David Stirzaker, 112 Thorn Court, Salford M6 5EL.

Former pupils Prof E R Laithwaite (Imperial College, London); David W H Walton, PhD (Director of Research British Antarctic Survey); Graham Clark (English National Opera).

LADIES' COLLEGE (GUERNSEY)

The Ladies' College		Co-ed	Pupils 340
Les Gravées		Boys	Upper sixth Yes
St Peter Port	●	Girls	Termly fees:
Guernsey		Mixed sixth	Day £320
Channel Islands	●	Day	GSA; GBGSA
Telephone number 0481 21602		Boarding	

Head Miss J Honey (12 years)
Age range 11–18, own prep from age 3; entry by own exam.
50% of pupils on direct grant which still operates in Guernsey.

LADY ELEANOR HOLLES

The Lady Eleanor Holles School	Co-ed	Pupils 600
Hanworth Road	Boys	Upper sixth Yes
Hampton	● Girls	Termly fees:
Middlesex TW12 3HF	Mixed sixth	Day £820
Telephone number 01-979 1601	● Day	GBGSA; GSA
	Boarding	

Head Miss E M Candy (7 years)
Age range 11–18, own prep from age 7; entry by own exam.
Foundation bursaries and scholarships.

LANCING

Lancing College	Co-ed	Pupils 555
Lancing	● Boys	Upper sixth Yes
West Sussex BN15 0RW	Girls	Termly fees:
Telephone number 07917 452213	● Mixed sixth	Day £1530
	● Day	Boarding £2250
	● Boarding	HMC; Woodard

WHAT IT'S LIKE

Founded in 1848 by the Rev Nathaniel Woodard and the first of the Woodard schools. It has a splendid site by any standards on a spur of the South Downs overlooking the sea to the south and the Weald to the north. The superb grounds comprise about 550 acres and include the college farm. The main buildings – handsome examples of the collegiate style of architecture – are grouped round two main quadrangles. There have been many improvements and developments in recent years, including a music school, a sixth form residence, a sports hall, study bedrooms and a new theatre. The boys are comfortably accommodated in 8 houses; the girls have 2 purpose-built boarding houses. Lancing is intended primarily for Church of England boys but boys of other Christian denominations may be accepted. The college has a magnificent chapel which is used a great deal. There is considerable emphasis on religious instruction and worship. A large and well-qualified staff allows a staff:pupil ratio of about 1:11. A broad general education is provided. Academic standards are high and results consistently good. Over 85% of pupils go on to higher education; about 70% go to universities and 20% to Oxbridge. Music and art are an important part of the education of all pupils. Quite a lot of dramatic work is also done. A good range of sports and games is available and standards are high. There is also a fair variety of extra-curricular activities. The flourishing CCF contingent contains Army, Naval and RAF sections. The college also has a farming group which helps to run the school farm. There is a particularly active social services organisation which helps the local community and also people in the Camberwell district of London.

SCHOOL PROFILE

Head J S Woodhouse (7 years)
Age range 13–18; entry by common entrance.
30 scholarships and exhibitions pa.

LANGLEY

Langley School
Langley Park
Nr Loddon
Norwich NR14 6BJ
Telephone number 0508 20210

Enquiries/application to the Admissions
Secretary

Co-ed   Pupils 172
● Boys   Upper sixth 11
Girls   Termly fees:
● Mixed sixth   Day £989
● Day   Boarding £1904
● Boarding   GBA

WHAT IT'S LIKE

Founded in 1910 in St Giles, Norwich, in 1946 it moved to Langley Park and was renamed. Langley Hall – between Norwich and the pleasant town of Beccles – is a handsome red-brick Georgian mansion in Palladian style and is a Grade I listed building. Modern classrooms, laboratories, a computer and resources centre and an indoor sports hall and workshops are set in 50 acres of grounds which provide for a range of sports. It has good facilities and comfortable accommodation. The staff:pupil ratio is 1:11. The aim of the school is to provide a full education, academically, socially and culturally, to encourage the average pupil to develop his or her talents and own personality, to use time wisely, to achieve a high standard of self discipline and to draw out and train the qualities of leadership. Some 25 clubs and societies cater for most needs. The CCF is strong with an army and naval section. Langley Junior School is in Norwich.

SCHOOL PROFILE

Pupils Total over 12, 172. Day 87 (boys 85; girls 2); Boarding 85 (boys 84; girls 1). Entry age, boys, 11, 12 and 13; boys and girls into the sixth. Parents expected to buy text books in sixth form. Prizes for Direct Entry Examination and university entrance, some bursaries, boarding discounts for service families.
Parents 30+% live within 30 miles; 10+% live overseas.
Staff Head C D Young, in post for 22 years. 16 full time staff, 9 part time. Annual turnover 5%. Average age 43.

LA RETRAITE

La Retraite School	Co-ed	Pupils 250
Campbell Road	Boys	Upper sixth Yes
Salisbury	• Girls	Termly fees:
Wiltshire SP1 3BQ	Mixed sixth	Day £650
Telephone number 0722 333094	• Day	GSA
	Boarding	

Head Mrs M Paisey
Age range 11–18, own prep from age 3; entry by own exam
RC pupils of 'grammar ability' on Wiltshire LEA grants.

LA SAGESSE

La Sagesse Convent High School	Co-ed	Pupils 350
North Jesmond	Boys	Upper sixth 30
Newcastle upon Tyne NE2 3RJ	• Girls	Termly fees:
Telephone number 091 281 3474	Mixed sixth	Day £698
	• Day	GSA
Enquiries/application to the Headmistress	Boarding	

WHAT IT'S LIKE

Founded in 1912, it is run by the Sisters of La Sagesse (an order founded at La Rochelle in 1703). The premises lie on the fringe of the city overlooking Jesmond Dene. It is single-site (with 9 acres of grounds) but housed in 5 buildings. Sports facilities are available on site. A Roman Catholic foundation. Religious education is compulsory at all levels. Most pupils are Christian but currently 12 different religious denominations are represented. A sound general academic education is provided and results are good (20 plus university entrants per year). Some music, drama and art. An adequate range of sport, games, clubs and societies. Some involvement in local community schemes.

SCHOOL PROFILE

Pupils Total 350. Entry age, 11+ and into the sixth. Own junior department provides 20%. 5% are children of former pupils.
Entrance Own entrance exam used. Not oversubscribed. No special skills or religious requirements. Parents not expected to buy text books. 175 assisted places. 6 scholarships/bursaries per year, ⅓ fees.
Parents 15+% are doctors, lawyers, etc; 15+% in industry or commerce. 60+% live within 30 miles.
Staff Head Sister Pauline, in post for 20 years. 29 full time staff, 4 part time. Annual turnover 2%. Average age 47.
Academic work GCSE and A-levels. Average size of upper fifth 60; upper sixth 30. *O-levels*: on average, 26% pupils in upper fifth pass 1–4 subjects; 37%, 5–7 subjects; 37% pass 8+ subjects. *A-levels*: on average, 14% pupils

in upper sixth pass 1 subject; 25%, 2 subjects; 50% pass 3 subjects. On average, 25% take science/engineering A-levels; 25% take arts and humanities; 50%, a mixture. *Computing facilities*: Computer room with 11 computers. Dyslexia teacher visits each week.

Senior pupils' non-academic activities *Music*: 50 learn a musical instrument; 40 in school orchestras, 70 in school choirs; 1 in National Youth Orchestra. *Drama and dance*: 80 in school productions. 1 takes Grade 6 in ESB, RAD etc. 2 accepted for Drama/Dance schools, 2 went to work in theatre, several teams entered competitions. *Art*: 10 take GCSE; 3 take A-level. 2 accepted for Art School. *Sport*: Netball, hockey, tennis, badminton, swimming, squash, rounders available. 15 take non-compulsory sport. 10 take exams. 3 represent county/country (tennis, hockey, badminton). *Other*: 20 take part in local community schemes. 2 enter voluntary schemes after leaving school, 2 work for national charities. Other activities include computer club, dance, drama, gym, debating society, typing course in sixth form.

Careers 1 part time advisor. Average number of pupils accepted for *arts and humanities degree courses* at Oxbridge, 1; other universities, 10; polytechnics or CHE, 5. *science and engineering degree courses* at Oxbridge, 1; other universities, 10; medical schools, 3. *BEd*, 2. *other general training courses*, 3. Average number of pupils going straight into careers in the civil service, 1; music/drama, 2.

Uniform School uniform worn, except the sixth.

Houses/prefects Competitive houses. Prefects, head girl, head of house and house prefects – appointed by the school. School Council.

Religion School prays together twice a week (RC).

Social Public speaking and geographical quiz with other local schools. Language and skiing trips abroad, individual sixth formers visit Spain and France. Pupils allowed to bring own car/bike to school. Meals, most bring own food. School shop. No tobacco/alcohol allowed.

Discipline No corporal punishment. Pupils failing to conform to acceptable standards of behaviour are warned.

LATYMER UPPER

Latymer Upper School	Co-ed	Pupils 1000
King Street	• Boys	Upper sixth Yes
London W6 9LR	Girls	Termly fees:
Telephone number 01-741 1851	Mixed sixth	Day £920
	• Day	GBA; HMC
	Boarding	

WHAT IT'S LIKE

Founded by the will of Edward Latymer in 1624, the modern school lies between King Street and the Thames in Hammersmith in west London. In 1969 an extensive rebuilding programme was started and in 1981 there began the modernisation of the older buildings. Now a well equipped school, it has playing fields about 1½ miles away. A sound general education is provided and academic standards are high. A large number of pupils go on to further education and many of these take degree courses at universities. Drama and music are strong and all boys are encouraged to take part in musical activities. There is a good deal of collaboration with the Latymer and Godolphin girls' school. Many sports and games are provided and standards of achievement are high. Latymer runs scouts, cubs and a venture scout unit and takes part in the Duke of Edinburgh's Award Scheme. A lot of camps, expeditions and field courses are organised.

SCHOOL PROFILE

Head M Pavey, first year in post.
Age range 9–18; entry by own exam.
Assisted places.

LAUREL BANK

Laurel Bank School	Co-ed	Pupils 242
4 Lily Bank Terrace	Boys	Upper sixth 50
Glasgow G12 8RX	● Girls	Termly fees:
Telephone number 041 339 9127	Mixed sixth	Day £830
Enquiries/application to the Headmistress	● Day	
	Boarding	

WHAT IT'S LIKE

Founded in 1903, it moved to its present site in 1919. This consists of converted terraced houses in the west end of the city and near the university. The nursery, junior school and senior school are combined. Good modern facilities are provided. Religious education is given throughout the school. Academic standards are high and results good. About 30 pupils go on to university each year. Strong in drama, music and art. Considerable strength in sports and games and high standards. A promising record in the Duke of Edinburgh's Award Scheme. Plentiful use is made of the cultural amenities of Glasgow.

SCHOOL PROFILE

Pupils Total over 12, 242. Entry age, 4–5 and into the sixth. A number are children of former pupils.
Entrance Own entrance exam used. Not oversubscribed. No special skills or religious requirements. Parents expected to buy text books. 60+ assisted places. 6 scholarships/bursaries, half fees to £100.
Parents 15+% are in industry or commerce, 15+% are doctors, lawyers, etc. 90+% live within 30 miles.
Staff Head Miss L G Egginton, in post for 4 years. 35 full time staff, 8 part time. Annual turnover, 5%. Average age, early 40s.
Academic work O-grades, Highers, CSYS; A-levels on request. Average size of fourth (O-grade) year 50; fifth (Higher) year 50. *Computing facilities*: BBC; computing lab; sundry departmental based computers. Some provision for learning difficulties.

Senior pupils' non-academic activities *Music*: 36 learn a musical instrument, 8 to Grade 6 or above; 14 in school orchestra, 11 in choir, 7 in wind band; 2 in Glasgow Schools wind group, 2 in Glasgow Schools orchestra, 1 Junior RSAM, 4 Junior SNO choir, 6 in Dunbartonshire wind band. *Drama and dance*: Many participate in school productions. *Art*: 8 take art as non-examined subject; 16 take O-grade; 8 H-grade; 3 other exams. 2 accepted for Art School; 6 go on to art-based HND courses. 6 belong to art club. *Sport*: Badminton, gymnastics, netball, short tennis, table tennis, trampoline, volleyball, hockey available. Athletics and tennis main sports in summer and the school successfully competes annually in schools (Glasgow and Scottish) athletics and swimming competitions, and all West District Hockey Tournaments. 50 take non-compulsory sport – skiing, squash, aerobics. 3 pupils represent county at hockey. *Other*: 6 have bronze Duke of Edinburgh's Award, 8 have silver and 2 have gold. Other activities include a computer club, chess, drama, debating and public speaking.

Careers 2 part time advisors. Average number of pupils accepted for *arts and humanities degree courses* at Oxbridge, 1; other universities, 38; polytechnics or CHE, 22. *science and engineering degree courses* at universities, 6; medical schools, 2; polytechnics or CHE, 2. *BEd*, 2. *other general training courses*, 3. Average number of pupils going straight into careers in industry, 1; the City, 1.

Uniform School uniform worn throughout.

Houses/prefects Competitive houses. Prefects, head girl, head of house and house prefects – elected by the school. School Council.

Religion Morning assembly (other religions may opt out).

Social Mixed badminton, debates, social events, shared conferences. Organised tours abroad, especially skiing. Meals self service. Stationery may be bought at school office. No tobacco/alcohol allowed.

Discipline No corporal punishment. Pupils failing to produce homework once might expect a warning; those caught smoking cannabis on the premises could expect expulsion (after consideration of all circumstances).

Alumni association run by Miss Margaret Cathcart, Orotara, Knockbuckle Road, Kilmalcolm, Renfrewshire PA13.

Former pupils Frances Cairncross (Editor of *Economist*); Paddy Higson (film producer); Sally Magnusson (TV presenter); Gudrun Ure (actress – Supergran).

LAVANT HOUSE

Lavant House School	Co-ed	Pupils 155*
Lavant	Boys	Upper sixth 7
Chichester	• Girls	Termly fees:
West Sussex PO18 9AB	Mixed sixth	Day £970
Telephone number 0243 527211	• Day	Boarding £1635
	• Boarding	GSA; GBSA;
Enquiries/application to the Headmistress		AHIS
		*whole school

WHAT IT'S LIKE

Founded in 1952, the main building is Lavant House, formerly the property of the Duke of Richmond, in a pleasant estate of 15 acres. It is a small school with a happy family atmosphere and has many of the advantages of being small. The modern facilities are good. A sound general education is provided and there is considerable emphasis on character values. Academic results are creditable and 5–10 leavers go on to university each year. Virtually everyone is involved in music. There is some drama and art. A good range of games and sports and plentiful activities. A promising record in the Duke of Edinburgh's Award Scheme.

SCHOOL PROFILE

Pupils Total (including under 12) 155. Day 98; Boarding 57. Entry age, 8, 11 and into the sixth. Own junior school provides more than 80%.

Entrance Common entrance and own entrance exam used. Not oversubscribed. No special skills or religious requirements. Parents expected to buy certain GCSE English text and some A-level books. 6 scholarships/bursaries, £500 to £250.

Parents 15+% in industry or commerce. 60+% live within 30 miles; up to 10% live overseas.

Staff Head Mrs B M Gay, in post for 1 year. 9 full time staff, 11 part time. Annual turnover 10%.

Academic work GCSE and A-level. Average size of upper fifth 20; upper sixth 7. *O-levels*: on average, 7 pupils in upper fifth pass 1–4 subjects; 6, 5–7 subjects; 6 pass 8+ subjects. *A-levels*: on average 1 pupil in the upper sixth passes 1 subject; 2, 2 subjects; 3 pass 3 subjects. On average, 1 takes science/engineering A-levels; 6 take arts and humanities; 1 a mixture. *Computing facilities*: 8 BBC Masters and printers in purpose-built room. Extra tuition available for dyslexic pupils.

Senior pupils' non-academic activities *Music*: 62 learn a musical instrument, 1 up to Grade 6 or above; 90 in 3 school choirs. *Drama and dance*: 10 in school productions, 6 take LAMDA exams. 1 accepted for Drama School. 4 entered competitions. *Art*: 15 take GCSE; 2 take A-level; 7 take A-level History of Art. *Sport*: Lacrosse, netball, swimming, athletics, tennis, squash, badminton, volleyball, gymnastics, rounders and cricket available. All girls take part in sport. 2 represent county/country (lacrosse). *Other*: Sixth form take part in local community schemes. 20 have bronze Duke of Edinburgh's Award, 9 have silver. Other activities include a computer club.

Careers 1 part time advisor. Average number of pupils accepted for *arts and humanities degree courses* at university, 2; polytechnics or CHE, 2. *science and engineering degree courses* at university, 1; polytechnics or CHE, 1. *BEd*, 2.

Uniform School uniform worn except the sixth.

Houses/prefects Competitive houses. Prefects, head girl, head of house and house prefects – appointed by Head and staff.

Religion Religious worship at assembly, 3 times per week. Attendance at church on Sunday for boarders, or service in school. Carol Service; Confirmation.

Social Debates, sixth form dances and dinner parties with other schools. Organised trips abroad. Pupils allowed to bring own car/bike/horse to school. Meals self service. School shop. No tobacco allowed.

Discipline No corporal punishment. Pupils failing to produce home-work once might expect a warning; those caught smoking cannabis on the premises might expect expulsion.

Boarding 4 have own study bedroom, 41 share with others, 12 are in dormitories of 6 or more. Resident qualified medical staff. Central dining room. Upper sixth can provide and cook their own food. 4 weekend, 4 days and half term exeats each term. Visits to local town allowed.

LAWNSIDE

Lawnside School	Co-ed	Pupils 150
Albert Road South	Boys	Upper sixth Yes
Malvern	● Girls	Termly fees:
Worcestershire WR14 3AJ	Mixed sixth	Boarding £1830
Telephone number 06845 5504	Day	GSA; GBGSA
	● Boarding	

Head Miss D M M Stewart (17 years)
Age range 11–18; entry by common entrance.
6 scholarships (including music) pa; allowances for children of forces and clergy.

LEEDS GRAMMAR

Leeds Grammar School	Co-ed	Pupils 1100
Moorland Road	● Boys	Upper sixth Yes
Leeds LS6 1AN	Girls	Termly fees:
Telephone number 0532 433417	Mixed sixth	Day £720
	● Day	HMC
	Boarding	

Head B W Collins (2 years)
Age range 10–19, own prep from age 8; entry by own exam.

LEEDS HIGH

Leeds Girls' High School	Co-ed	Pupils 580
Headingley Lane	Boys	Upper sixth 55
Leeds LS6 1BN	● Girls	Termly fees:
Telephone number 0532 744000	Mixed sixth	Day £772
	● Day	GSA
Enquiries/application to the Admissions Secretary	Boarding	

WHAT IT'S LIKE

Founded in 1876, it has elegant and well-equipped buildings on 8 acres of pleasant grounds with lawns and gardens 2 miles from the city centre. The junior department, Ford House, is 3 minutes' walk away. The prep department, Rose Court, is on the same site as the High School. The teaching is good and academic standards are high, each year a number of pupils go on to Oxbridge and other universities. Music, drama and art are strong and the Elinor Lupton centre provides excellent facilities for work in these subjects. There are also very good facilities for sports and games of which there is a wide range. Extra-curricular activities are well catered for.

SCHOOL PROFILE

Pupils Total number of pupils 580. Entry age, 4, 11 and into sixth.
Entrance Own entrance exam used. Oversubscribed. No special skills or religious requirements. 20 assisted places pa. Scholarships and bursaries available.
Staff Head Miss B A Randall, in post 10 years. 54 full time staff, 15 part time. Average turnover 5%.

LEGAT BALLET

The Legat Ballet School
Mark Cross
Crowborough
East Sussex
Telephone number 089 285 2353

Enquiries/application to the Director

- Co-ed
  Boys
  Girls
  Mixed sixth
- Day
- Boarding

Pupils 95
Upper sixth 15
Termly fees:
Day £965
Boarding £1595

WHAT IT'S LIKE

Founded in 1939, it occupies a former seminary in 54 acres of beautiful park and farm land 6 miles from Tunbridge Wells. It is the only boarding school in England offering Russian-style ballet training. From an academic point of view, the intake is truly comprehensive. The classes are small and the aim of the very experienced and dedicated staff is to enable every pupil to achieve their academic potential. In the sixth form most pupils are aiming at a professional dance career and this precludes the majority from taking A-levels. Leavers who fail to get a position in a ballet company should have obtained a diploma enabling them to teach.

SCHOOL PROFILE

Pupils Total over 12, 95. Day 8 (girls); Boarding 87 (boys 13, girls 74). Entry age, 10+ onwards including into the sixth.
Entrance Entry by ballet audition. Not oversubscribed. Ballet skills required. Parents are not expected to buy text books. Scholarships/bursaries, for pupils with outstanding potential at ballet, by negotiation with the director, from £1,595 to £400.
Parents 15+% in the theatre, media, music etc. 30+% live within 30 miles; up to 10% live overseas.

Staff Head Mrs J D Bilitch, in post for 2 years. Director Derek Westlake. 6 full time staff, 20 part time. Annual turnover 1–2. Average age 40.

Academic work GCSE and A-levels. Average size of upper fifth 12; upper sixth 15. *O-levels*: on average, 8 pupils in upper fifth pass 1–4 subjects; 4 pass 5–7 subjects. *A-levels*: on average, 2 pupils in the upper sixth pass 1 subject. On average 66% take arts and humanities A-levels. Provision for dyslexic pupils, those with learning difficulties and EFL.

Senior pupils' non-academic activities *Music*: 50 learn a musical instrument; 20 in school orchestra, 20 in school choir. *Drama and dance*: All fifth and sixth forms in school productions. 2 accepted for Drama/Dance schools (Royal Ballet), 9 placed in ballet or dance companies, 2 teaching ballet. 30 doing LAMDA drama exams, 12 passed advanced and 1 professional standards (with honours) with the society of Russian Style Ballet Schools. *Art*: 12 take GCSE; 5 take A-level. 1 accepted for Art School, 6 are following a course in creative art & theatre related studies. *Sport*: Swimming, tennis and badminton available. Other activities include tap, contemporary and jazz dance.

Careers 3 part time advisors: 2 ballet & dance, 1 academic & teaching. Average number of pupils accepted for *degree courses* at polytechnics or CHE, 1. *other general training courses*, 1. *Ballet and dance companies*, 9. Traditional school careers are in ballet and dance.

Uniform School uniform worn.

Houses/prefects No competitive houses. Prefects and head girl – appointed by the Head. Annual meetings of school with the Director.

Religion Morning assembly. Classes 1–4 expected to attend C of E or Catholic Church on Sundays.

Social No organised local events. Day trips to France. Pupils allowed to bring own bike/motorbike to school. Formal lunch and supper, self-service breakfast and tea. School shop selling tuck and second-hand clothes. No tobacco/alcohol allowed.

Discipline No corporal punishment. Pupils failing to produce homework once might expect to produce it on the following day; those caught smoking cannabis on the premises might expect expulsion.

Boarding 10% have own study bedroom, 10% share with 1 other; 50% in dormitories of 6 or more. Separate wing for boys. Resident qualified nurse. Central dining room. Sixth form can provide and cook their own food. Half-term (week) and 2 or 3 weekend exeats per term. Visits to Tunbridge Wells allowed.

LEICESTER GRAMMAR

Leicester Grammar School	• Co-ed	Pupils 414
Applegate	Boys	Upper sixth 55
Leicester LE1 5LB	Girls	Termly fees:
Telephone number 0533 21221	Mixed sixth	Day £630
	• Day	SHA
Enquiries/application to the Headmaster	Boarding	

WHAT IT'S LIKE

Founded in 1981 as a direct result of the loss of the City's grammar schools through reorganisation. It is housed in two late Victorian buildings in the cathedral precinct in the middle of Leicester. These buildings have been extensively modernised to provide up-to-date facilities. The school's growth has been remarkable: from an original 90 pupils to 535 in seven years: a success story which reflects much credit on those involved – and the needs of the community. The curriculum is geared to the academic rather than the average pupil (good staff ratio of 1:16) and fees are kept low. Exceptionally strong departments in music, drama and art. A good standard of general education is provided. A fair range of games, sports (civic amenities are used) and activities. The school enjoys vigorous local support and it has a substantial commitment to local community schemes.

SCHOOL PROFILE

Pupils Total over 12, 414 (boys 212, girls, 202). Entry age, 10+ and into the sixth.

Entrance Common entrance and own entrance exam used. Oversubscribed. No special skills or religious requirements. Open to all faiths. Parents not expected to buy text books. Assisted places from 1989. 7/8 scholarships/bursaries pa up to full fees.

Parents 15+% in industry or commerce. 60+% live within 30 miles.

Staff Head John Eagle Higginbotham, in post for 7 years. 35 full time staff, 12 part time. Annual turnover 4%. Average age 34.

Academic work GCSE and A-levels. Average size of upper fifth 84; upper sixth 55. *O-levels*: on average, 2 pupils in upper fifth pass 1–4 subjects; 15, 5–7 subjects; 67 pass 8+ subjects. School is too new for any average A-level results pattern to have emerged. On average, 29 take science/engineering A-levels; 21 take arts and humanities; 5 take a mixture. Greek and Russian are offered to GCSE/A-level. *Computing facilities*: new computer lab with RMA NIMBUS.

Senior pupils' non-academic activities *Music*: 154 learn a musical instrument, 56 up to Grade 6 or above; 36 in school orchestra, 65 in school choir, jazzband, 24 in school pop groups; 1 in National Youth Orchestra, 10 in Leicestershire Schools orchestras. *Drama and dance*: 205 in school productions. *Art*: 275 take as non-examined subject; 36 take GCSE; 10 take A-level. 24 belong to eg photographic club and 26 in sketch club. *Sport*: Rugby, football, hockey, basketball, netball, tennis, cricket, athletics, squash and badminton available. 255 take non-compulsory sport. *Other*: 65 take part in local community schemes. Other activities include a computer club, gymnastics, dance band, fitness club, chess, bridge, table tennis and dramatic society.

Careers 5 part time advisors. In view of the school's recent foundation, the first pupils have just reached the top of the school and no pattern has emerged.

Uniform School uniform worn except the sixth.

Houses/prefects No competitive houses. Prefects, head boy and girl, head of house and house prefects – appointed by the Headmaster in consultation with staff and prefects.

Religion Daily assembly, monthly Cathedral services for all.

Social Pupils take part in local competitions for debating and academic activities (eg science, geography, classical reading). French, German exchanges, classical tours and ski trips abroad. Pupils allowed to bring own bike to school. Meals self service. School shop. No tobacco/alcohol allowed.

Discipline No corporal punishment. Pupils failing to produce homework once might expect detention. Those caught smoking cannabis on the premises might expect expulsion.

Alumni association is run by C L Duckworth, 12 Plantation Avenue, Leicester.

LEICESTER HIGH

Leicester High School for Girls	Co-ed	Pupils 250
454 London Road	Boys	Upper sixth Yes
Leicester LE2 2PP	● Girls	Termly fees:
Telephone number 0533 705338	Mixed sixth	Day £700
	● Day	GBGSA; GSA;
	Boarding	ISAI

Head Mrs D Buchan (6 years)
Age range 10–18, own prep from age 6; entry by own exam.
Scholarships including music.

LEIGHTON PARK

Leighton Park School	Co-ed	Pupils 360
Shinfield Road	● Boys	Upper sixth 60
Reading	Girls	Termly fees:
Berkshire RG2 7DH	● Mixed sixth	Day £1500
Telephone number 0734 872065	● Day	Boarding £2145
Enquiries/application to the Headmaster	● Boarding	HMC; Quaker

WHAT IT'S LIKE

Founded in 1890, it is not far from the middle of Reading but enjoys a most peaceful environment of 70 acres of lovely wooded grounds, formerly the estates of two large country houses. Some of the well-designed school buildings are 19th-century, some 20th. The junior school is combined and the facilities are excellent. A Quaker school, it lays considerable emphasis on Quaker philosophy and adheres to the principles and practice of Quakerism which, of its nature, is ecumenical and tolerant. The teaching is good and academic standards are high (over 70% of the sixth form proceed to university; ie about 35–45 candidates per year, 15% of these to Oxbridge). Extremely strong in music; good drama and art. High level in sports and games (a lot of representatives of county standard). Much emphasis on outdoor pursuits and adventure training. Big commitment to local community services (a lot of post-school voluntary work). Wide range of activities, including an unusual number of hobby interests, and an impressive record in the Duke of Edinburgh's Award Scheme.

SCHOOL PROFILE

Pupils Total, 360. Day, 92 (boys 90, girls 2); Boarding, 268 (boys 230, girls 38). Entry age, boys 11 and 13; directly into the sixth form boys and girls. 10% are children of former pupils.

Entrance Common entrance and own entrance exam used. Fully subscribed. Pupils must be in top 25% of ability range; no religious requirements. Parents only expected to buy text books sometimes in sixth form. 50 scholarships/bursaries, 75%–25% of fees.

Parents 15+% in industry or commerce. 30+% live within 30 miles; 10+% live overseas.

Staff Head John A Chapman, in post for 2 years. 37 full time staff, 25 part time. Annual turnover 7%. Average age 35–40.

Academic work GCSE and A-levels. Average size of fifth 60; upper sixth 60. *O-levels*: on average, 8 pupils in fifth pass 1–4 subjects; 38, 5–7 subjects; 14 pass 8+ subjects. *A-levels*: on average, 3 pupils in upper sixth pass 1 subject; 9, 2 subjects; 45, 3 subjects and 3 pass 4 subjects. On average, 15 take science/engineering A-levels; 15 take arts and humanities; 30 a mixture. *Computing facilities:* A computer teaching room; scattered computers, including in boarding houses. Technological development on the way.

Senior pupils' non-academic activities *Music*: 165 learn a musical instrument, 25 to Grade 6 or above, 2–4 pa accepted for Music School, 10–20 play in pop group beyond school; 25 in school orchestra; 20 in choir; 10 in pop group, 60+ in brass, jazz and big bands; 2 in National Youth Orchestra; 10 in local orchestras. *Drama and dance*: 50 in school productions. 2 take to Grade 6 in ESB, RAD etc. 2–3 accepted for Drama/Dance Schools. *Art*: 20 take GCSE; 12, A-level. 2–3 accepted for Art School; 2–3 accepted for foundation art courses. 20 belong to printing club or others. *Sport*: Rugby, soccer, basketball, canoeing, athletics, cross-country, swimming, tennis, cricket, hockey, squash, golf available. 180 take non-compulsory sport. 20 represent county/country at various sports. *Other*: 20 take part in local community schemes. 20 have bronze Duke of Edinburgh's Award, 10 have silver and 5 gold. 20 enter voluntary schemes after leaving school; 30 work for national charities eg Amnesty. Other activities include a computer club and 58 other hobbies/interests.

Careers 1 careers teacher assisted by 8 tutors. Average number of pupils accepted for *arts and humanities degree courses* at Oxbridge, 4; other universities, 15; polytechnics or CHE, 5. *science and engineering degree courses* at Oxbridge, 4; other universities, 15; medical schools, 4; polytechnics or CHE, 5. Average number of pupils going straight into careers in the armed services, 1–2; industry, 1–2; music/drama, 1–2.

Uniform School dress code followed throughout.

Houses/prefects Competitive houses. Prefects, head boy/girl, head of house and house prefects – appointed by the Head and school. School Council.

Religion Some compulsory worship in the Quaker manner.

Social Regular conferences at sixth form level and discos with other schools, also Challenge of Industry events. Organised trips abroad and exchange systems. Meals formal. School shop. No tobacco/alcohol allowed.

Discipline No corporal punishment. Pupils failing to produce homework once might expect extra prep or detention work; those caught smoking cannabis on the premises would be asked to leave.

Boarding 10% have own study bedroom, 20% share; 20% are in dormitories of 6+. Houses, of approximately 65–75, same as competitive houses, mixed age. Resident qualified medical staff. Pupils can provide and cook own food. Weekly exeats, if required. Visits to the local town allowed.

Former pupils Michael Foot; David Lean; Richard Rodney Bennett; Laurence Gowing; Lord Caradon; Bishop Newbigin.

LEYS, THE

The Leys School	Co-ed	Pupils 384
Cambridge CB2 2AD	● Boys	Upper sixth 80
Telephone number 0223 355327	Girls	Termly fees:
	● Mixed sixth	Day £1605
Enquiries/application to the Headmaster	● Day	Boarding £2160
	● Boarding	

WHAT IT'S LIKE

Founded in 1875, it has a compact site on the edge of the city, bounded by common land on two sides and close to the river. The main buildings are late Victorian and very pleasing, and lie in 50 acres of delightful grounds and playing fields. Modern extensions provide excellent facilities, including a big design and technology centre. It is a Methodist foundation but interdenominational. A large staff allows a staff:pupil ratio of about 1:9. An informal and friendly atmosphere characterises the school. The standard of teaching is high (there is a particularly good tutorial system) and results are good. About 40 leavers go on to university each year. Very strong in music, drama and art. A wide range of sport and games and a very good variety of activities. Plentiful use is made of the cultural amenities of Cambridge. A substantial commitment to local community schemes and an outstanding record in the Duke of Edinburgh's Award Scheme.

SCHOOL PROFILE

Pupils Total, 384. Day 76 (boys 74, girls 2); Boarding 308 (boys 277, girls 31). Entry age, 13+ boys; boys and girls into the sixth. St Faith's School, Cambridge provides over 20%. 12% are children of former pupils.

Entrance Common entrance and own entrance exam used. Oversubscribed (for sixth form girls' places). Fairly high academic attainment and extra-curricular interests looked for. No special religious requirements, Methodist foundation with ecumenical tradition. Parents expected to buy text books. 7 assisted places. 18 scholarships/bursaries, 50% to 10% of fees.

Parents 15+% are doctors, lawyers, etc; 15+% in industry or commerce. 30+% live within 30 miles; up to 10% live overseas.

Staff Head Timothy Beynon, in post for 2 years. 45 full time staff, 8 part time. Annual turnover 5%. Average age 40.

Academic work GCSE, A- and S-levels. Average size of upper fifth, 80; upper sixth, 80. *O-levels*: on average, 10 pupils in upper fifth pass 1–4 subjects; 16, 5–7 subjects; 54 pass 8+ subjects. *A-levels*: on average, 3 pupils in the upper sixth pass 1 subject; 15, 2 subjects; 51, 3 subjects; 6 pass 4 subjects. On average, 17 take science/engineering A-levels; 35 take arts and humanities; 23 take a mixture. *Computing facilities*: Computer department equipped with 10 BBC A, 6 BBC B, 10 BBC Master, 3 Archimedes. Computers in most other departments. Dyslexia or EFL provision for those who have reached minimum academic requirements.

Senior pupils' non-academic activities *Music*: 72 learn a musical instrument, 21 up to Grade 6 or above; 40 in school orchestra, 20 in school choir, 3 in school pop group; 2 in county orchestra, 1 in National Children's Orchestra, 1 in jazz band. *Drama and dance*: 105 in school productions, 20 in house plays, 65 in first year activities. 25, GCSE; 8, A-level. 3 accepted for Drama/Dance schools, 2 go on to work in theatre. *Art*: 175 take as non-examined subject; 30 take GCSE; 16 take A-level. 4 accepted for Art School; 4 for architecture; 1 for textiles; 2 for graphic design. 25 belong to photographic club; 50 calligraphy and mixed crafts. Ceramics included for senior year group. *Sport*: Rugby, football, cricket, hockey, squash, water-polo, swimming, fencing, soccer, tennis, athletics, shooting, sailing, rowing, canoeing, cross-country running, clay-pigeon shooting available. 240 take part in compulsory sport. 105 in rugby; 75, hockey; 75, cricket; 14, water polo; 6, squash; 24, tennis. 2 pupils represent county/country (cricket). *Other*: 40 take part in local community schemes. 32 have bronze Duke of Edinburgh's Award, 48 have silver and 10 gold. Other activities include a computer club, debating and public speaking, local history society, philosophical society, science society, Christian Union, etc.

Careers 1 full time and 2 part time advisors. Average number of pupils accepted for *arts and humanities degree courses* at Oxbridge, 4; other universities, 21; polytechnics or CHE, 11. *science and engineering degree courses* at Oxbridge, 5; other universities, 13; medical schools, 4; polytechnics or CHE, 2. Average number of pupils going straight into careers in the armed services, 2; industry, 3; the City, 2; agriculture, 2. Former pupils enter a wide range of careers.

Uniform School uniform worn, modified in the sixth.

Houses/prefects Competitive houses. Prefects, head boy/girl, head of house and house prefects – appointed by the Head or Housemasters.

Religion Services on Wednesdays and Sundays, 'religious' assembly on Fridays.

Social Organised local events include inter-school debates and public speaking competitions (eg ESU); combined choral concerts; schools challenge (inter-schools quiz contests). Visits to classical sites abroad, cultural visits (art and art history); individual language exchanges; ski trips, walking holidays in Alps; choir tours. Pupils allowed to bring own bike to school. Meals self service. School shop. No tobacco/alcohol allowed.

Discipline No corporal punishment. Pupils failing to produce homework once might expect work to be re-done and seen by the Housemaster; those caught smoking cannabis on the premises can expect expulsion.

Boarding 30% have own study bedroom, 25% share with others; 45% are in dormitories of 6 or more. Houses, of approximately 50–65 (boys), 33 (girls), are the same as competitive houses (girls sixth form only), and are single-sex. Resident qualified medical staff. Central dining room. Pupils can provide and cook their own food. Two exeats each term. Visits to the local town allowed once or twice a week.

Alumni association is run by The Secretary of the OLU: Mr P R Chamberlain, c/o the School. Editor of the OL Directory: Mr M Howard (same address).

Former pupils Sir Alastair Burnet (ITN Editor); Martin Bell (BBC TV correspondent); J G Ballard (fiction writer); Richard Heffer (actor).

LICENSED VICTUALLERS' (SLOUGH)

Licensed Victuallers' School
Slough
Berkshire SL1 1XP
Telephone number 0753 71623

Enquiries/application to the Headmaster's Secretary

- Co-ed
  Boys
  Girls
  Mixed sixth
- Day
- Boarding

Pupils 691
Upper sixth Yes
Termly fees:
Day £957
Boarding £1767
ISAI

WHAT IT'S LIKE

Founded in 1803, it moved from London to Slough in 1921, and benefited from royal patronage from the accession of William IV in 1830. The premises in Slough are being vacated and the school is to be relocated at Ascot where a completely new school is being built. This should open in about 1989–1990. The school continues to cater for boys and girls of all abilities. This was the Founders' intention and the existing and planned buildings are designed for this purpose. The junior department is to provide a firm grounding for younger pupils in the basic skills of numeracy and literacy with the gradual introduction of specialist subjects. Musical, artistic and sporting development is also regarded as important and children are introduced to a variety of activities from an early age. In the senior department pupils are in mixed-ability classes in the first instance and this arrangement is maintained in pastoral tutor groups. There is no general streaming but within each faculty there is a facility for setting arrangements independent of other subject areas which allows pupils to be placed in groups working at the same level of attainment. The programme is gradually narrowed to specialisation but all follow a programme of English, maths, French, science, humanities, creative studies and PE to age 16. The underlying aim of the educational approach is to encourage self-motivation, to stimulate children to produce their best and to compete with others whilst ensuring that they develop confidence by maintaining steady progress on courses of study continually adjusted to their needs. All are prepared for GCSE at 16+ or earlier. The sixth form courses include GCE A and AS levels and one-year mature GCSE courses.

SCHOOL PROFILE

Pupils Total, 691. Day 525 (boys 397, girls 128); Boarding 166 (boys 108, girls 58). Entry age, 4, 8, 13 and into the sixth.

Entrance Parents expected to buy senior text books. Scholarships/bursaries available.
Staff Head F A D Bland, in post for 16 years. 64 full time staff, 8 part time. Annual turnover 5%.
Academic work GCSE and A-levels.

LIME HOUSE

Lime House School
Holm Hill
Dalston, Carlisle
Cumbria CA5 7BX
Telephone number 0228 710 225

Enquiries/application to the Chairman of
the Board of Governors

- Co-ed
  Boys
  Girls
  Mixed sixth
- Day
- Boarding

Pupils 150
Upper sixth 25
Termly fees:
Day £675
Boarding £1500
ISAI

WHAT IT'S LIKE

Founded in 1899 at Wetheral, it moved in 1947 to its present site near Dalston where it lies in 25 acres of its own very agreeable grounds which are surrounded by a large private estate. The main building (a fine country house built in 1638) has been extensively modernised to provide good accommodation. Other facilities and buildings are nearby. It has all the advantages of a small school and enjoys a high staff:pupil ratio. Strong music, art and drama depts. A fair range of sports, games and activities. Some commitment to local community schemes and the Duke of Edinburgh's Award Scheme.

SCHOOL PROFILE

Pupils Total over 12, 150. Day 40 (boys 20, girls 20); Boarding 110 (boys 70, girls 40). Entry age, 4+ and into the sixth. Own junior school provides 20+%. 12% are children of former pupils.
Entrance Common entrance and own entrance exam used. Not oversubscribed. No special skills or religious requirements. Parents not expected to buy text books. No assisted places. 12 scholarships/bursaries per year.
Parents 15+% in industry or commerce; 15+% in the armed services. 10+% live within 30 miles; 10+% live overseas.
Staff Head N A Rice, in post for 5 years. 40 full time staff, 8 part time. Annual turnover 1%. Average age 36.
Academic work GCSE and A-levels. Average size of upper fifth, 40; upper sixth, 25. *O-levels*: on average, 6 pupils in upper fifth pass 1–4 subjects; 30, 5–7 subjects; 4 pass 8+ subjects. *A-levels*: on average, 5 pupils in the upper sixth pass 1 subject; 20 pass 2 subjects. An even spread across science/engineering, and arts/humanities A-levels. Chinese, technical drawing, Dutch, pottery, PE offered to GCSE/A-level. *Computing facilities*: 20 interlinked Spectrums with disc drives, 12 BBC B interlinked into Prestel, 6 Comador PCS. Dyslexic unit; some EFL provision.
Senior pupils' non-academic activities *Music*: 60% learn a musical instrument, 31% to Grade 6 or above; 20% in school orchestra, 20% in school choir. *Drama and dance*: All in school productions. 2–3 accepted for Drama/

Dance schools per year. *Art*: 12% take as non-examined subject; 15 take GCSE; 4 take A-level. 4–6 accepted for Art School per year. 20 belong to eg photographic club. *Sport*: All sports available. 50% take non-compulsory sport. 20% take exams eg swimming. Some represent county (hockey, football, rugby, athletics, netball, swimming, golf, tennis). *Other*: Pupils involved in local community schemes, and Duke of Edinburgh's Award, at all levels. Pupils enter voluntary schemes after leaving school. Other activities include a computer club, driving instruction, skiing, chess and train clubs.

Careers 1 full time and 1 part time advisor. Average number of pupils accepted for *arts and humanities degree courses* at universities, 3; polytechnics or CHE, 3. *other general training courses*, 12. Average number of pupils going straight into careers in the armed services, 20–25; industry, 11; the City, 2; the civil service, 4; music/drama, 1.

Uniform School uniform worn throughout.

Houses/prefects Competitive houses. Prefects, head boy/girl, head of house and house prefects – appointed by the Head, School Governors and the School.

Religion Religious worship compulsory.

Social No organised events with local schools. Organised trips abroad. Pupils allowed to bring own car/bike/motorbike to school. Some meals formal, some self service. School shop. No tobacco/alcohol allowed.

Discipline Corporal punishment by Deputy Head or S.H. Mistress. Pupils failing to produce homework once might expect detention; those caught smoking on the premises might expect corporal punishment.

Boarding Fifth and sixth formers have own bedroom, most others share with 2 others; 10% are in dormitories of 6 or more. Houses, of approximately 38, are divided by age group and sex. Resident qualified nurse. Central dining room. 1 termly exeat of three days plus half term. Visits to local town allowed.

Former pupils Michael Rodd; James Fox.

LIVERPOOL COLLEGE

Liverpool College	Co-ed	Pupils 520
Mossley Hill	● Boys	Upper sixth 60
Liverpool L18 8BE	Girls	Termly fees:
Telephone number 051 724 1563	● Mixed sixth	Day £769
	● Day	Boarding £1422
Enquiries/application to the Headmaster	● Boarding	HMC

WHAT IT'S LIKE

Founded in 1840, it moved to its present premises at Mossley Hill in the 1930s. It is single-site and suburban in 26 acres of grounds and playing fields in a pleasant area. The buildings are mostly modern and well-equipped. Three schools (preparatory, lower and upper) are combined. A C of E foundation (but thoroughly ecumenical) it has high academic standards and good results (35-plus university entrants per year). Strong in music, games and sports. The CCF is very active. Some participation in local community schemes, and quite a lot in the Duke of Edinburgh's Award Scheme. The school has a good reputation and enjoys vigorous local support.

SCHOOL PROFILE

Pupils Total over 12, 520. Day 490 (boys 460, girls 30); Boarding (weekly only) 30 (boys). Entry age, boys 5+ or 11+; girls and boys, into the sixth. Own junior school provides over 20%. 15% are children of former pupils.

Entrance Own entrance exam used. Oversubscribed (though not all pass exam). No special skills or religious requirements. Parents expected to buy text books in sixth form only. 175 assisted places. 8 scholarships/bursaries, £100 to half fees; plus 4 music scholarships and bursaries pa, up to half fees.

Parents 15+% in industry or commerce; 15+% are doctors and lawyers etc. 60+% live within 30 miles.

Staff Head R V Haygarth, in post for 9 years. 50 full time staff, 2 part time. Annual turnover 5%. Average age 41.

Academic work GCSE and A-levels. Average size of upper fifth 80; upper sixth 60. *O-levels*: on average, 15 pupils in upper fifth pass 1–4 subjects; 25, 5–7 subjects; 40 pass 8+ subjects. *A-levels*: on average, 2 pupils in upper sixth pass 1 subject; 9, 2 subjects; 45, 3 subjects and 4 pass 4 subjects. On average, 20 take science/engineering A-levels; 20 take arts and humanities; 20 a mixture. *Computing facilities*: A fully equipped computer science room and computers in some departments.

Senior pupils' non-academic activities *Music*: 100+ learn a musical instrument, 10 to Grade 6 or above. 1 accepted for music school; some play in pop group beyond school. 40 in school orchestra, 50+ in choir; 5 in local youth orchestra. *Drama and dance*: 150 in school productions; 1 accepted for Drama/Dance School. *Art*: 400+ take as non-examined subject; 20 take GCSE; 5, A-level. 2 accepted for Art School; 10+ belong to photographic club. *Sport*: Rugby, cricket, hockey, athletics, cross-country, tennis, swimming, badminton, golf, cycling available. 50 in lower school take swimming exams. 11 represent county/country (rugby, hockey, tennis). *Other*: 15 take part in local community schemes. 30 have bronze Duke of Edinburgh's Award, 10 have silver. Other activities include a computer club, plus over 20 different societies, debating especially strong.

Careers 6 part time advisors. Average number of pupils accepted for *arts and humanities degree courses* at Oxbridge, 2; other universities, 12; polytechnics or CHE, 4. *science and engineering degree courses* at Oxbridge, 3; other universities, 18; medical schools, 4; polytechnics or CHE, 4. *BEd*, 1. *other general training courses*, 1. Average number of pupils going straight into careers in the armed services, 1; industry, 2; music/drama, 1. Traditional school career, medicine.

Uniform School uniform worn throughout.

Houses/prefects Competitive and pastoral houses. All sixth formers have prefectorial duties. Head boy/girl, head of house and house prefects – appointed by the Head and Common Room.

Religion A C of E foundation. All pupils attend unless parents wish them not to.

Social No organised events with local schools. Organised trips abroad. Pupils allowed to bring own car/bike/motorbike to school. Meals self service. No tobacco/alcohol allowed.

Discipline No corporal punishment. Pupils failing to produce homework once might expect detention; those caught smoking cannabis on the premises could expect probable expulsion.
Boarding (only weekly) All have studies; 12 are in dormitories of 6+ in 1 House. Resident qualified nurse. Central dining room. Pupils can provide and cook own food. Visits to local town allowed.
Alumni association run by The Bursar, c/o the College.

LLANDOVERY

The College	● Co-ed	Pupils 250
Llandovery	Boys	Upper sixth Yes
Dyfed SA20 0EE	Girls	Termly fees:
Telephone number 0550 20315	Mixed sixth	Day £953
	● Day	Boarding £1595
	● Boarding	HMC

WHAT IT'S LIKE

Founded and endowed by Dr Thomas Phillips in 1848, it has a fine site amidst magnificent countryside in the small market town of Llandovery. The extensive grounds and playing fields run alongside 2 miles of the River Towy. It was founded to provide a classical and liberal education in which the Welsh language and the study of Welsh literature and history were to be cultivated. The original buildings are handsome and well appointed and there have been a number of good additions and improvements. It is now very well equipped. There is some emphasis on religious instruction and worship. There is a daily morning service for all. Sunday services are compulsory. English and Welsh are used in worship. Academically – as in other respects – Llandovery is one of the most distinguished schools in Wales (and, indeed in Britain). The staff:pupil ratio is about 1:10. Academic standards are high and results consistently good. A lot of pupils go on to universities, including a number to Oxbridge. Welsh is compulsory for all boys in the first two years and special provision is made for beginners. All are expected to study Latin and music. Greek may be started in the third year. The college is particularly strong in music and drama and most of its 250 pupils are involved in these. An arts festival is normally held in each Lent term. There is an annual programme of visiting artists. Sports and games are compulsory and the college has an outstanding record in these (especially rugby), with many representatives at county, regional and national level. There is considerable emphasis on outdoor pursuits which include fishing, canoeing and fell-walking. The college has taken part in the Duke of Edinburgh's Award Scheme with some success. All boys are expected to join the strong CCF for one year when aged 14. A large number of pupils take part in a well-organised local community service programme.

SCHOOL PROFILE

Head Dr R Brinley Jones (12 years)
Age range 11–18; entry by common entrance and own exam.

LOMOND

Lomond School
Stafford Street
Helensburgh
Dunbartonshire G84 9SX
Telephone number 0436 2476

Enquiries/application to the Headmaster

- Co-ed
  Boys
  Girls
  Mixed sixth
- Day
- Boarding

Pupils 302
Upper sixth 45
Termly fees:
Day £785
Boarding £1815

WHAT IT'S LIKE

Founded in 1977 as a result of the amalgamation of Larchfield School for Boys (1845) and St Bride's School for Girls (1895). It has an agreeable split site in the upper part of Helensburgh, a dormitory town a few miles from Loch Lomond and 40 minutes' drive from Glasgow. The three main buildings are quite near each other and have pleasant gardens. The staff:pupil ratio is 1:8. Academic standards are high and results very good. About 20 or more pupils go on to university each year (90% of sixth form go on to degree courses). The music, drama and art departments are all strong. There is a high standard of public performance in drama and music. Sports and games are well catered for (a large number of representatives at county and national level). An unusually wide range and large number of extra-curricular activities (about 70 are on offer). Good facilities for outdoor pursuits and adventure training for which the neighbouring environment is ideal. Some commitment to local community schemes and an outstanding record in the Duke of Edinburgh's Award Scheme.

SCHOOL PROFILE

Pupils Total over 12, 302. Day 246 (boys 111, girls 135); Boarding 56 (boys 26, girls 30). Entry age, 5 and into the sixth. Own junior school provides over 20%.

Entrance Own entrance exam used. Oversubscribed in some areas. No special skills or religious requirements. Parents not expected to buy text books. 44 assisted places. 15 scholarships/bursaries, £730–£387.

Parents 15+% are doctors, lawyers etc. 60+% live within 30 miles; up to 10% live overseas.

Staff Head A D Macdonald, in post for 2 years. 41 full time staff, 8 part time. Annual turnover less than 10%.

Academic work O-grades, Highers, A-levels. Average size of upper fifth 52; upper sixth 45. *O-grades*: on average, 3 pupils in upper fifth pass 1–4 subjects; 44 pass 5–7 subjects. *A-levels*: on average, 4 pupils in upper sixth pass 1 subject; 6, 2 subjects; 6 pass 3 subjects. (Many pupils take Highers instead.) On average, 6 take science/engineering A-levels; 10 take arts and humanities; 16 a mixture. *Computing facilities*: Computer lab, 10 BBC micros with Econet system. Specialised help in cases of need.

Senior pupils' non-academic activities *Music*: 6–7 learn a musical instrument to Grade 6 or above; 20–30 in school orchestra, 40–50 in school choir, 5 in school pop group. *Drama and dance*: 20–30 in school productions. 5 productions pa. *Art*: 25 take O-grade; 2–3 A-level; 12 Higher. 2–3 accepted for Art School. 10 belong to eg photographic club. *Sport*: Rugby, hockey, athletics, tennis, squash, golf, sailing, badminton, table tennis, swimming, cricket, netball available. Over 75% participate in team games. 50 take swimming tests. 12 represent county/country (rugby, hockey, athletics, tennis, squash, sailing). *Other*: 8–10 take part in local community schemes. 50 have bronze Duke of Edinburgh's Award, 20 have silver and 20 gold. Other activities include a computer club, square dancing, dog training, electronics, chess, bridge, microwave cookery, rifle shooting, first aid, piping, strategic simulations, 3D art, soft toy making, car maintenance, knitting, keep fit, architectural studies.

Careers 2 part time careers advisors plus external advisor. Average number of pupils accepted for *arts and humanities degree courses* at universities, 11; polytechnics or CHE, 12. *science and engineering degree courses* at Oxbridge, 1; other universities, 9; medical schools, 2; polytechnics or CHE, 7. *other general training courses*, 2–3. Average number of pupils going straight into careers in armed services, 1; the City, 1–2.

Uniform School uniform worn throughout.

Houses/prefects Competitive houses. Prefects, head boy/girl, head of house and house prefects – elected by Head and school.

Religion Religious worship encouraged.

Social No organised events with local schools. Exchange visits to France and Germany. Pupils allowed to bring own car/bike/motorbike to school. Meals self service. School shop. No tobacco/alcohol allowed.

Discipline No corporal punishment. Pupils failing to produce homework once might expect extra prep; those caught smoking cannabis on the premises will be expelled.

Boarding 10% have own study bedroom, 20% share; remainder in dormitories of 6+. Houses, of approximately 30, single sex. Resident qualified nurse and doctor. Central dining room. Pupils can provide and cook own food. 2 exeats of 2 days each term. Visits to local town allowed.

Alumni association run by Mrs P Norman, Secretary, Lomond Society, c/o the School.

LONGRIDGE TOWERS

Longridge Towers School
Berwick upon Tweed
Northumberland TD15 2XH
Telephone number 0289 307584

Enquiries/application to the Headmaster's Secretary

- Co-ed
  Boys
  Girls
  Mixed sixth
- Day
- Boarding

Pupils 142
Upper sixth 3
Termly fees:
Day £825
Boarding £1625
ISAI; SHA

WHAT IT'S LIKE

Founded in 1983, it occupies an impressive Victorian mansion on a fine estate of 80 acres in very beautiful surroundings. A good staff:pupil ratio of 1:11. It provides a sound general education and results are creditable. A few pupils go on to university. There is some music and quite a lot of drama and art. A good range of sports and games and a fair range of other activities. A promising record in the Duke of Edinburgh's Award Scheme.

SCHOOL PROFILE

Pupils Total over 12, 142. Day 104 (boys 40, girls 64); Boarding 38 (boys 22, girls 16). Entry age, 4–16 if places available. Own junior school provides over 60%.

Entrance Common entrance and own entrance exam used. Not oversubscribed. Tests in English and maths looked for at entry. Parents not expected to buy text books. 6 scholarships pa, to half fees. Scholarships, bursaries and concessions for children of HM Forces, £275–£50 per term.

Parents 15+% in the armed services; 15+% in industry or commerce; 15+% are farmers. 60+% live within 30 miles; 10+% live overseas.

Staff Head Dr M J Barron, in post for 5 years. 20 full time staff, 3 part time. Annual turnover 10%. Average age 35.

Academic work GCSE, A-levels and Highers. Average size of upper fifth 28; upper sixth 3. *O-levels*: on average, 8 pupils in upper fifth pass 1–4 subjects; 3, 5–7 subjects; 3 pass 8+ subjects. *Computing facilities*: 10 BBC computers with Econet.

Senior pupils' non-academic activities *Music*: 6 learn a musical instrument; 15 in school choir; 1 goes on to play in pop group. *Drama and dance*: 50 in school productions. *Art*: 3 take as non-examined subject; 25 take GCSE; 2/3 take A-level. 2/3 accepted for Art School. *Sport*: Athletics, tennis, cricket, rounders, swimming (own pool), rugby, hockey, netball, cross-country, archery, rowing, and gymnastics available. 20 take non-compulsory sport. 50 take exams. 2 represent county/country (athletics). *Other*: 15 have bronze Duke of Edinburgh's Award, 5 have silver. 1 works for national charity. Other activities include a computer club, gym, country dancing, first aid, judo, statistics, chess, squash and shooting.

Careers 1 full time and 1 part time advisor. Average number of pupils accepted for *arts and humanities degree courses* at university, 1; polytechnics or CHE, 1. *other general training courses*, 20. Average number of pupils going straight into careers in the armed services, 6; industry, 3. The traditional school career is farming.

Uniform School uniform worn except the sixth.

Houses/prefects Competitive houses. Prefects, head boy (School Captain), head of house and house prefects – appointed by head after consultation with staff.

Religion Morning prayers held Mon–Thurs. Service in school chapel each Sunday.

Social Performance of Verdi opera in Edinburgh with other schools; debating with Merchiston School. Regular trips abroad eg Morgins (Switzerland). Some meals self service. School tuck shop for boarders and book shop for all. No tobacco/alcohol allowed.

Discipline No corporal punishment. Pupils failing to produce homework once might expect a verbal warning; those caught smoking cannabis on the premises would be expelled.

Boarding 5% have own study bedroom, 85% share with others, 10% are in dormitories of 6 or more. Houses, of approximately 20 for girls and 30 for boys, are single sex. Resident matron. Central dining room. Four weekend exeats each term. Visits to the local town allowed.

Alumni association is run by Alister Blades, c/o the School.

LORD WANDSWORTH

Lord Wandsworth College
Long Sutton
Basingstoke
Hampshire RG25 1TB
Telephone number 0256 862482

Enquiries/application to the Headmaster's
Secretary or Foundation Registrar

Co-ed   Pupils 310
• Boys   Upper sixth 50
    Girls   Termly fees:
• Mixed sixth   Day £1450
• Day   Boarding £1920
• Boarding   HMC

WHAT IT'S LIKE

Founded in 1920 and endowed by Lord Wandsworth. It has very agreeable buildings in a beautiful part of Hampshire on an estate of 1000 acres. One could hardly hope for a better position or finer surroundings. Early links between the school and agriculture have now virtually disappeared but the rural environment remains a strong feature of the school. It is extremely well equipped in a 'village' environment and provides a sound education. Academic results are highly creditable. An Anglican foundation, religious education and attendance at chapel is more or less compulsory. The staff: pupil ratio is good – 1:11. There is a strong CCF and a good range of games, sports and activities. Day fees are high.

SCHOOL PROFILE

Pupils Total over 12, 310. Day, 270; Boarding, 40. Entry age, boys 11 and 13 and into the sixth; girls into sixth form from 1988.

Entrance Common entrance and own entrance exam used. Oversubscribed. No special skills or religious requirements. Parents not expected to buy text books. 75 assisted places. 26 scholarships and Foundation Awards for sons of widows, widowers or single parents, one-third to full fees.

Parents 30+% live within 30 miles; up to 10% live overseas.

Staff Head G A G Dodd, in post for 6 years. 35 full time staff, 3 part time. Annual turnover 1 or 2. Average age 38.

Academic work GCSE, A-levels. On average, upper fifth 74; upper sixth 50.

Senior pupils' non-academic activities *Sport*: Hockey, rugby, cricket, athletics, cross-country, swimming, tennis, badminton, squash, shooting, golf available. *Other*: Activities include a computer club, Duke of Edinburgh's Award Scheme, community service project, sixth form society.

Careers 1 full time advisor.

Uniform School uniform worn throughout.

Houses/prefects Mildly competitive houses. Prefects, head boy, head of house and house prefects – appointed by the Head and Housemaster in consultation with senior pupils.

Religion Worship compulsory.

Social Many dramatic and choral functions, dances/discos with local girls' schools. Organised trips abroad and exchange systems. Meals self service. School shop. No tobacco allowed; some beer in sixth form centre.

Discipline No corporal punishment.

Boarding Houses of 75 pupils (including day). Resident qualified nurse. Central dining room. Exeats each term. Visits to the local town allowed.

Alumni association The Old Sternian Association, c/o the School.

LORETTO

Loretto School	Co-ed	Pupils 300
Musselburgh	● Boys	Upper sixth 70
Midlothian EH21 7RE	Girls	Termly fees:
Telephone number 031 665 5003	● Mixed sixth	Day £1470
Enquiries/application to the Headmaster	● Day	Boarding £2350
	● Boarding	HMC

WHAT IT'S LIKE

Founded in 1827 by the Rev Thomas Langhorne, it was bought in 1862 by Hely Hutchinson Almond, a distinguished scholar of strong and unconventional convictions. He built up the school and was its head until he died in 1903. Since then it has become one of the most distinguished schools in Britain. It has a fine site on the outskirts of the small town of Musselburgh on the Firth of Forth, 6 miles from Edinburgh. This comprises 80 acres of lawns, trees and playing fields. The junior school is a separate unit on the same site. The buildings are handsome, especially Pinkie House – an historic building (partly because of its connections with the Battles of Prestonpans and Pinkie). Many recent developments have produced excellent facilities (including good boarding accommodation). An interdenominational school, chapel plays an important part in its life. The policy has always been to keep the school small and pupils are expected to give their loyalty and make a general all-round contribution. They are given authority and responsibility from an early age. There is a staff:pupil ratio of 1:9. Academic standards are high and results consistently good. There are 40–45 university entrants per year (a high proportion for a school of this size). Very strong in music, drama and art. Much use is made of the cultural amenities of Edinburgh. Loretto has long had a reputation for excellence in sports and games of which there is a wide variety. Many clubs and societies cater for most conceivable extra-curricular needs. There is a very strong CCF (compulsory for every boy for at least 3 years) with its own Pipes and Drums. Physical fitness and regular exercise are high priorities and there is an emphasis on adventure training. A substantial commitment to local community services. An outstanding record in the Duke of Edinburgh's Award Scheme.

SCHOOL PROFILE

Pupils Total 300. Day 10 (boys); Boarding 386 (boys 350, girls 36). Entry age, 13, boys; boys and girls into the sixth. Own junior school provides up to 20%. 25% are children of former pupils.

Entrance Common entrance, own entrance and scholarship exams used. Oversubscribed at most levels. General all-round contribution looked for; non-denominational. Parents expected to buy some specialist sixth form text books. 22 assisted places. Various scholarships/bursaries pa, from full fees to £1000.

Parents 15+% are doctors, lawyers etc.; 15+% in industry or commerce. A number live overseas.

Staff Head Rev Norman W Drummond, in post for 4 years. 31 full time staff, 4 part time.

Academic work GCSE and A-levels. Average size of upper fifth 50; upper

sixth 70. *O-levels*: on average, 5 pupils in upper fifth pass 1–4 subjects; 20, 5–7 subjects; 20 pass 8+ subjects. *A-levels*: on average, 3 pupils in the upper sixth pass 1 subject; 10, 2 subjects; 56, 3 subjects and 4 pass 4 subjects. On average, 22 take science/engineering A-levels; 26 take arts and humanities; 25 a mixture. *Computing facilities*: Computer centre in new Industry and Business Centre; departmental computers/word processors. Provision for mild dyslexia; cystic fibrosis.

Senior pupils' non-academic activities *Music*: 87 learn a musical instrument, 22 to Grade 6 or above, 1 diploma candidate, 1–2 accepted for Music School, 2 go on to play in pop group; 31 in school orchestra, 35 in chamber choir, whole school regularly sings as a choir in chapel, 7 in pop group, 5 in jazz band, 25 in concert band, 16 in pipe band, 1 in Edinburgh Youth Orchestra. *Drama and dance*: New award-winning theatre; 3 full length productions annually, several others. *Art*: 50 take as non-examined subject; 20 take GCSE, 10 take A-level. 2 accepted for Art School, 1 for course in architecture, landscape architecture or photography. 10 belong to eg photographic club. *Sport*: Rugby, cricket, hockey, tennis, golf, squash, fives, badminton, athletics, lacrosse, fencing, swimming, curling, cycling, horse riding, miniature range and clay pigeon shooting, sailing, skiing available. 120 take non-compulsory sport. 43 take exams. 8 represent county/country (rugby, hockey, cricket). *Other*: 65 take part in local community schemes. 54 have gold Duke of Edinburgh's Award. 14 enter voluntary schemes after leaving, 5 work for national charities. Other activities include computer club, art and crafts, debating, chess, bridge, Scottish country dancing, industrial and political societies.

Careers 2 part time advisors. Average number of pupils accepted for *arts and humanities degree courses* at Oxbridge, 2; other universities, 22; polytechnics or CHE, 14. *science and engineering degree courses* at Oxbridge, 2; other universities, 18; medical schools, 4; polytechnics or CHE, 7. Average number of pupils going straight into careers in armed services, 2; the City, 1; industry and business, 2.

Uniform School uniform worn throughout.

Houses/prefects No competitive houses. Prefects, head boy (head of school), head of house/room/table (graduated system of responsibility) and house prefects – appointed by Head and Housemasters. Committees for eg messing, charities. Regular leadership seminars on service and management.

Religion Sunday Chapel and mid-week services compulsory.

Social Joint community service committee with Musselburgh Grammar School; involved with local club for disabled. Sharing of school and local facilities eg sports hall, swimming pool, squash club, theatre. Carol service for town. Some organised trips abroad. Pupils allowed to bring own bike to school (summer term). Meals formal. School shop. No tobacco/alcohol allowed.

Discipline No corporal punishment. Pupils failing to produce homework once might expect to do it in their own time and detention; rigorous framework of discipline leading to suspension and expulsion for the most serious of offences.

Boarding 25% have own study bedroom, lower sixth girls share; 75% are in dormitories of 6+. Houses, of approximately 60 (boys), 36 (girls) are single sex. Resident qualified sanatorium sister. Central dining room. 2 overnight exeats each term plus half term. Visits to local town (Musselburgh) at specific times allowed according to age.

Former pupils Jim Clark (motor racing); Sir Hector Laing (Chairman, United Biscuits); Sir Denis Forman (Chairman, Granada TV); Sandy Carmichael (Scotland XV – 50 caps); Peter Fraser, QC (Solicitor General for Scotland); Michael Mavor (Headmaster, Gordonstoun); David McMurray (Headmaster, Oundle); Norman Lamont MP; Nicholas Fairbairn, QC MP; Professor John Hunter (Grant Professor of Dermatology, Edinburgh University); Professor I M Murray-Lyon (Consultant Physician and Gastroenterologist, Charing Cross Hospital).

LOUGHBOROUGH HIGH

Loughborough High School	Co-ed	Pupils 530
Burton Walks	Boys	Upper sixth Yes
Loughborough	● Girls	Termly fees:
Leicestershire LE11 2DU	Mixed sixth	Day £650
Telephone number 0509 212 348	● Day	Boarding £1150
	● Boarding	GBGSA; GSA

WHAT IT'S LIKE

The school is part of the foundation originally provided by Thomas Burton who, in 1495, endowed a chantry with which was connected a grammar school for boys. The foundation was extended to girls in 1849. The upper girls' school was at Rectory Place and moved to its present site in 1880. There are spacious and very pleasant grounds on the edge of the town. There have been many modern additions to the late Victorian buildings and facilities are now excellent. Religious instruction is non-denominational but the school has a Christian basis and all pupils are expected to attend RE lessons and prayers. The aim is to provide an academic education of the traditional grammar school type in a disciplined atmosphere of steady work. Standards are high and results good. Some 50 girls go on to university each year. The school is very strong in music, drama and art. There are also high standards in sport and games (not a few representatives at county and international level). There is a full range of extra-curricular activities. A big commitment to local community schemes and quite an impressive record in the Duke of Edinburgh's Award Scheme.

SCHOOL PROFILE

Head Miss J E L Harvatt (10 years)
Age range 11–18; entry by own exam. Own junior school shared with Loughborough Grammar School. Weekly boarding only.
Scholarships, bursaries and assisted places.

LUBAVITCH (BOYS)

Lubavitch House School
126 Stamford Hill
Hackney
London N16 5RP
Telephone number 01-800 0022

Co-ed   Pupils 60
● Boys   Upper sixth Yes
Girls   Termly fees:
Mixed sixth   Day £450
● Day   ISAI
Boarding

Head M H Sufrin (6 years)
Age range 11–18, own prep from age 2; entry by own exam.
Scholarships.

LUBAVITCH (GIRLS)

Lubavitch House School
107–115 Stamford Hill
Hackney
London N16 5RP
Telephone number 01-800 0022

Co-ed   Pupils 108
Boys   Upper sixth Yes
● Girls   Termly fees:
Mixed sixth   Day £445
● Day   ISAI
Boarding

Head Rabbi S Lew (12 years)
Age range 11–18, own junior from age 2; entry by own exam.
Scholarships.

LUCKLEY-OAKFIELD

Luckley-Oakfield School
Luckley Road
Wokingham
Berkshire RG11 3EU
Telephone number 0734 784175

Co-ed   Pupils 290
Boys   Upper sixth Yes
● Girls   Termly fees:
Mixed sixth   Day £950
● Day   Boarding £1500
● Boarding   GSA; GBGSA

Head Mr Richard C Blake (4 years)
Age range 11–18; entry by own exam.
Some scholarships.

MAGDALEN COLLEGE SCHOOL

Magdalen College School
Oxford OX4 1DZ
Telephone number 0865 242191

Co-ed	Pupils 500
● Boys	Upper sixth Yes
Girls	Termly fees:
Mixed sixth	Day £810
● Day	Boarding £1580
● Boarding	CSA; GBA; HMC

WHAT IT'S LIKE

Founded in 1478 by William of Waynflete as part of Magdalen College. It was a distinguished school in Tudor times and produced some famous grammarians. William Tyndale was a pupil and so, in all probability, were Thomas More and Richard Hooker. Cardinal Wolsey was one of its Masters. Formerly, the famous choristers had their own school but from 1849 became part of the college in the School House. It has fine buildings and grounds not far from Magdalen Bridge and is well equipped with up-to-date facilities. A wide range of subjects is provided for a sound general education. Academic standards and results are consistently good and 50 or more pupils go on to universities each year. Music is very strong, and there is some strength, too, in art and drama. A good range of sports and games is provided on the large playing fields surrounded by the River Cherwell. Standards in sports and games are quite high. There is also a plentiful variety of extra-curricular activities.

SCHOOL PROFILE

Head W B Cook (16 years)
Age range 11–18; entry by common entrance or own exam.
5+ scholarships pa (including music); 24 assisted places pa. Bursaries.

MAIDENHEAD

Maidenhead College
1 College Avenue
Maidenhead
Berkshire SL6 6AW
Telephone number 0628 28225

Enquiries/application to Mrs E Marsden

Co-ed	Pupils 164
Boys	Upper sixth 11
● Girls	Termly fees:
● Mixed sixth	Day £851
● Day	
Boarding	

WHAT IT'S LIKE

Founded c1900 it occupies a 4.5 acre site in central Maidenhead with pleasant buildings and gardens. A nursery and kindergarten are combined. It is a Roman Catholic school with a multi-denominational outlook. Facilities are good. There is emphasis on solid work and sound learning and results are very creditable. A number of leavers proceed to university. Flourishing music, drama and art departments. A range of games, sports and extra-curricular activities are available.

SCHOOL PROFILE

Pupils Total over 12, 164 girls. Entry age girls, 3–18; boys are welcome in the sixth form. Own junior school provides over 20%.

Entrance Own entrance exam used. Oversubscribed. No special skills or religious requirements. Parents not expected to buy text books. 1–4 scholarships/bursaries, up to full fees.

Parents 15+% in the armed services; 15+% in industry or commerce; 15+% are doctors, lawyers, etc. More than 60% live within 30 miles.

Staff Head Mrs E Marsden, in post for 1 year. 24 full time staff, 14 part time. Annual turnover 10%. Average age 40.

Academic work GCSE and A-levels. Average size of upper fifth 44; upper sixth 11. *O-levels*: on average, 18 pupils in upper fifth pass 1–4 subjects; 13, 5–7 subjects; 9 pass 8+ subjects. *A-levels*: on average, 3 pupils in upper sixth pass 1 subject; 4, 2 subjects; 3 pass 3 subjects. On average, 2 take science/engineering A-levels; 6 take arts and humanities; 3 a mixture. *Computing facilities*: 7 BBC computers model B, with word processor, 4 disk drives – 40 track, 7 monitors, printer. Special tuition available for eg EFL, mildly dyslexic pupils.

Senior pupils' non-academic activities *Music*: 20 learn a musical instrument, 4 to Grade 6 or above; 1 accepted for Music School; 10 in school choir; 1 gone on to play in pop group. *Drama and dance*: 50 participate in school productions; 40 in other workshop activities; 20 LAMDA; 23 take GCSE in theatre arts; 3–4 accepted for Drama/Dance Schools; 2 belong to local drama groups. *Art*: 12 take GCSE; 4 A-level; 1 sculpture D of E; 2 accepted for art foundation courses; 5 belong to school oil painting group. *Sport*: Netball, hockey, tennis, swimming, rounders, athletics, gymnastics available. 26 take non-compulsory sport. 2 take exams eg gymnastics, swimming; 8 take dance grades. 5 represent county/region (hockey, netball). *Other*: Pupils take part in local community schemes and some work for national charities beyond school. Other activities include a computer club, gym club, theatre workshops.

Careers 1 part time advisor. Average number of pupils accepted for *arts and humanities degree courses* at polytechnics or CHE, 1. *science and engineering degree courses* at universities, 5; medical schools, 1. *BEd*, 1. *other general training courses*, 14. Average number of pupils going straight into careers in industry, 1; other, 1.

Uniform School uniform worn except in the sixth.

Houses/prefects Competitive houses. Prefects, head girl, head of house and house prefects – elected by the school, confirmed by the Head.

Religion All Roman Catholics expected to attend regular termly masses.

Social Inter school sports matches. Organised trips abroad. Pupils allowed to bring own car/bike/motorbike to school. Meals self service. No tobacco/alcohol, makeup or jewellery allowed.

Discipline No corporal punishment. Pupils failing to produce regular homework might expect detention; those caught smoking on the premises could expect suspension.

MALVERN (BOYS)

Malvern College	Co-ed	Pupils 602
Malvern	• Boys	Upper sixth 120
Worcestershire WR14 3DF	Girls	Termly fees:
Telephone number 06845 3497	Mixed sixth	Day £1560
Enquiries/application to the Registrar	• Day	Boarding £2150
	• Boarding	HMC

WHAT IT'S LIKE

Founded in 1865 it has one of the most beautiful and civilised settings in England. The elegant, well-appointed buildings are arranged in a horse-shoe around the grounds on an eastern slope of the Malvern Hills, with magnificent views over the Severn Valley and the Vale of Evesham. It has first-class facilities of every kind, including excellent boarding accommodation. The town is 10 minutes' walk away and the College benefits greatly from its position by a town which has become an important centre of education. It also benefits through close co-operation with the four independent girls' boarding schools in the area. The aims of the house system and the tutorial arrangements are to ensure that each boy learns to live in a community and develops his potential. It is an Anglican foundation and boys are obliged to attend certain chapel services. Academic standards are very high. Results are first-rate and 85 or more leavers go on to university each year. It is very strong indeed in music (230+ learn an instrument), drama and art. Also very strong in sport and games. All take part in a sporting programme (compulsory), but there are a large number of options. The CCF is compulsory for 1 year, then optional. Adventure training is compulsory in the lower sixth. There is a substantial commitment to local community services for the old, disabled and homeless. A fine record in the Duke of Edinburgh's Award Scheme (25 golds).

SCHOOL PROFILE

Pupils Total 602. Day 42; Boarding 560. Entry age, 13 and into the sixth. 13% are children of former pupils.

Entrance Common entrance and own entrance exam used. Oversubscribed. No special skills or religious requirements. Parents expected to buy text books. 58 assisted places. 20 scholarships/bursaries, £5000–£500.

Parents 15+% are doctors, lawyers etc. Up to 10% live within 30 miles; up to 10% live overseas.

Staff Head R de C Chapman, in post for 5 years. 67 full time staff, 10 part time.

Academic work GCSE and A-levels. Average size of upper fifth 120; upper sixth 120. *O-levels*: on average, 11 pupils in upper fifth pass 1–4 subjects; 27, 5–7 subjects; 81 pass 8+ subjects. *A-levels*: on average, 7 pupils in upper sixth pass 1 subject; 12, 2 subjects; 55, 3 subjects and 37 pass 4 subjects. On average, 33 take science/engineering A-levels; 50 take arts and humanities; 29 a mixture. CDT is offered to GCSE/A-level; electronics to A-level. *Computing facilities*: 12 BBC Bs & Masters in Science School and other BBCs in departments. 12 Apple Macintosh in main school, more in departments.

Senior pupils' non-academic activities *Music*: 232 learn a musical instru-

ment, 50 to Grade 6 or above, 3 accepted for Music School; 3 Cambridge choral scholars; 80 in school orchestra, 100 in choir. *Drama and dance*: 50 in school productions; 100 in House plays. *Art*: 50 take GCSE; 30 A-level. 2–10 accepted for Art School. *Sport*: Soccer, rugby and cricket are major games; also athletics, cross-country running, squash, lawn tennis, rackets, fives, hockey, swimming, sailing, rifle shooting, golf, badminton, fencing, gymnastics, judo available. Sport is compulsory with large number of options. 20 take exams eg gymnastics, swimming. *Other*: 50 take part in local community schemes. 25 have gold Duke of Edinburgh's Award. About 5 enter voluntary schemes beyond school. Other activities include a computer club, adventure training, chess, natural history, science, debating, language, architecture, music societies.

Careers 7 part time advisors, headed by a teaching careers master. Average number of pupils per year accepted for *arts and humanities degree courses* at Oxbridge, 12; other universities, 55; polytechnics or CHE, 12. *science and engineering degree courses* at Oxbridge, 6; other universities, 15; medical schools, 6; polytechnics or CHE, 3. *BEd*, 2. *other general training courses*, 1. Average number of pupils going straight into careers in the armed services, 5; industry, 1; the City, 2; music/drama, 3; other, 1. Consistently good numbers go into medicine, law and business.

Uniform School uniform worn throughout.

Houses/prefects Competitive houses. Prefects and head boy – appointed by the Head; head of house and house prefects – appointed by Housemasters.

Religion Some compulsory chapel services.

Social Joint general studies classes, debates, dances, discos, plays, concerts with local schools. Organised trips abroad (eg to USA). Exchanges with French/German pupils on individual basis. Pupils allowed to bring own bike to school. Meals formal. School shop. Sixth form bar. No smoking.

Discipline No corporal punishment.

Boarding 40% have own study bedroom, 60% are in dormitories of 6+. Houses, of approximately 60, same as competitive houses. Resident qualified nurse, doctor on call. No central dining room. Pupils can provide and cook own food at times. 2 weekend exeats each term plus half term. Visits to the local town allowed.

Alumni association run by G H Chesterton, c/o the School.

Former pupils Bernard Weatherill (Speaker of the House of Commons).

Malvern (Girls)

Malvern Girls' College	Co-ed	Pupils 479
Avenue Road	Boys	Upper sixth 80
Malvern	● Girls	Termly fees:
Worcestershire WR14 3BA	Mixed sixth	Day £1280
Telephone number 0684 892288	● Day	Boarding £1920
	● Boarding	HMC; GSA
Enquiries/application to the Registrar		

WHAT IT'S LIKE

Founded in 1893, it has a splendid site at the foot of the Malvern Hills in the town. Eight school houses are scattered near the main buildings. It is extremely well equipped with modern facilities, not least its fine libraries and resources centre. Worship and prayer in the Anglican tradition are encouraged and there is considerable emphasis on religious instruction. There is a high standard of teaching and academic standards and results are excellent. About 35–40 pupils go on to university each year. It is tremendously strong in music and 390–400 girls learn an instrument. Also a big commitment to drama. Games and sports are of a high standard and in 1987 alone there were 40–50 representatives at county and district level. A plentiful range of extra-curricular activities and quite a lot of emphasis on outdoor pursuits. Full use is made of Malvern's cultural and festival events.

SCHOOL PROFILE

Pupils Total over 12, 479. Day 51; Boarding 428. Entry age, 11+, 12+, 13+ and into the sixth.

Entrance Common entrance and own scholarship exam used. Oversubscribed. No special skills or religious requirements but majority C of E. Parents expected to buy some text books. 10 scholarships/bursaries (including music scholarship), ⅔ to ⅓ fees.

Parents 15+% are doctors, lawyers, etc; 15+% in industry or commerce; 15+% in armed services. 10+% live within 30 miles; 10+% live overseas.

Staff Head Dr V B Payne, in post for 2 years. 46 full time staff, 23 part time. Annual turnover 5%.

Academic work GCSE and A-levels. Average size of upper fifth 82; upper sixth 80. *O-levels*: on average, 25 pupils in upper fifth pass 5–7 subjects; 57 pass 8+ subjects. *A-levels*: on average, 3 pupils in upper sixth pass 1 subject; 3, 2 subjects; 43, 3 subjects; 32 pass 4 subjects. On average, 26 take science/engineering A-levels; 42 take arts and humanities; 12 take a mixture. Excellent computing facilities.

Senior pupils' non-academic activities *Music*: 394 learn a musical instrument, 112 to Grade 6 or above; 132 in school orchestra, 74 in school choir, 32 in school pop group. *Drama and dance*: Middle school performs in house plays competition annually. Sixth form annual production with local boys' public school. *Art*: 20 take as non-examined subject; 3 take GCSE; 11 take A-level. 5 accepted for Art School. *Sport*: Lacrosse, hockey, netball, swimming, squash, badminton, golf, tennis, athletics, rounders, cricket, aerobics, volleyball, basketball, table tennis, dance, gymnastics and fencing available. 120 take non-compulsory sport. 45 represent county/district (lacrosse, hockey, swimming, tennis, athletics). *Other*: Pupils have bronze, silver and gold Duke of Edinburgh's Award. Other activities include outdoor pursuits eg (canoeing, climbing and walking).

Careers 5 part time advisors. Average number of pupils accepted for *arts and humanities degree courses* at Oxbridge, 4; other universities, 23; polytechnics or CHE, 2. *science and engineering degree courses* at Oxbridge, 1; other universities, 10; medical schools, 6; polytechnics or CHE, 1. *BEd*, 3. *other general training courses*, 9. Law and medicine are popular careers, but a wide variety of professions is embraced and encouraged.

Uniform School uniform worn except the sixth.

Houses/prefects No competitive houses. Prefects, head girl, head of house and house prefects – appointed by Head after consultation with staff. School Council.

Religion Worship encouraged.

Social Joint choral and theatrical productions with Malvern College. Debating societies, sixth form general studies with local schools participating. Organised trips abroad. Sixth form allowed to bring own bike to school. Meals formal; self service in sixth. School shop sells books and secondhand uniform. No tobacco/alcohol allowed.

Discipline No corporal punishment. Pupils caught smoking cannabis on the premises might expect instant dismissal.

Boarding 15% have own study bedroom, 85% share with 1, 2 or 3 others. 9 houses, of 40–60, including 2 sixth form houses. 2 resident qualified nurses. Sixth form can provide and cook own food. Half term plus 2 weekend or 6 day exeats each term. Visits to local town allowed.

Alumni association is run by the Old Girls' Secretary, Mrs P Wilkinson, Syke House, Saddleworth Road, Greelland, Halifax.

MANCHESTER GRAMMAR

The Manchester Grammar School	Co-ed	Pupils 1444
Rusholme	● Boys	Upper sixth 200
Manchester M13 0XT	Girls	Termly fees:
Telephone number 061 224 7201	Mixed sixth	Day £830
Enquiries/application to the High Master's Secretary	● Day	HMC; GBA
	Boarding	

WHAT IT'S LIKE

Founded in 1515 by Hugh Oldham, Bishop of Exeter. In 1931 it moved from its original site in Long Millgate to Fallowfield and grew to nearly 1450 boys, its present size. The original buildings have been constantly added to and facilities are first-class. The playing fields are adjacent and the whole area covers 28 acres. As its founder intended, it is a predominantly academic school and has long been one of the most distinguished in the country. Each year over 200 boys join it from widely differing backgrounds and from a wide area of the north-west. Intellectually and academically very high-powered, its results are consistently fine. Each year 160 or more pupils go on to university (about 60 to Oxbridge). Almost all the other leavers go on to some form of further education. Religious worship is encouraged and religious studies form a fundamental part of the curriculum. Very strong in music, drama and art. An excellent range of games and sports in which high standards are attained. There is an immense range of out-of-school activities – many carried to remarkable levels of achievement. Considerable emphasis on outdoor pursuits; the school owns two sites (one in Cheshire and one near Grasmere) where these are followed; in addition several other camp sites are used each year. Local community schemes are active. One of the most outstanding features of the school is its vigorous corporate life, and its prestige is enhanced by its very high reputation locally and far afield.

SCHOOL PROFILE

Pupils Total, 1444. Entry age, 11. 5% are children of former pupils.

Entrance Common entrance and own entrance exam used. Oversubscribed. High ability in English and number looked for; no religious requirements. Parents not expected to buy text books. 290 assisted places. Bursaries, on scale similar to DES AP scheme.

Parents 15+% are in industry or commerce. 60+% live within 30 miles; very few live overseas.

Staff Head J G Parker, in post for 3 years. 104 full time staff, 10 part time. Annual turnover 5%. Average age 35.

Academic work GCSE and A-levels. Average size of upper fifth 210; upper sixth 200. *O-levels*: on average, 10 pupils in upper fifth pass 1–4 subjects; 140, 5–7 subjects; 60 pass 8+ subjects. *A-levels*: on average, 2 pupils in upper sixth pass 1 subject; 5, 2 subjects; 180, 3 subjects and 3 pass 4 subjects. On average, 90 take science/engineering A-levels; 100 take arts and humanities; 10 a mixture. Greek, Russian offered to GCSE/A-level. *Computing facilities*: Microcomputer lab, minicomputer.

Senior pupils' non-academic activities *Music*: 60 learn a musical instrument. 40 in school orchestra, 100 in choir. *Drama and dance*: 30 in school productions. *Art*: 10 take as non-examined subject. 40 take GCSE, 6 A-level. 2 accepted for Art School; 15 in eg photographic club. *Sport*: Soccer, rugby, cross-country, swimming, squash, badminton, cricket, tennis, athletics available. 120 take non-compulsory sport; 10 take exams. 10 represent county/country (soccer, rugby, cricket, cross-country, badminton). *Other*: 30 take part in local community schemes; 5 work for national charities after leaving. Other activities include chess, camping, fell walking, trekking.

Careers 6 part time advisors. Average number of pupils accepted for *arts and humanities degree courses* at Oxbridge, 30; other universities, 45; polytechnics or CHE, 20. *science and engineering degree courses* at Oxbridge, 25; other universities, 45; medical schools, 12; polytechnics or CHE, 13. *BEd*, 5. Average number of pupils going straight into careers in armed services, 5; industry, 5.

Uniform School uniform worn except the sixth.

Houses/prefects No competitive houses. Prefects, head boy – appointed by High Master. Sixth Form Committee.

Religion Religious worship encouraged.

Social Joint society meetings, productions, other activities with local schools. Trips abroad, exchange systems. Pupils allowed to bring own car/bike/ motorbike to school. Meals self service. No tobacco/alcohol allowed.

Discipline No corporal punishment. Pupils failing to produce homework once might expect verbal warning; those caught smoking cannabis on the premises might expect suspension/expulsion.

Alumni association run by Mr W T Hall, c/o school.

Former pupils Sir William Barlow; Lord Sieff; Lord Winstanley; Lord Tordoff; Lord Lever; Ben Kingsley; Robert Powell; John Ogdon; Robert Bolt; Sir Joseph Cantley.

MANCHESTER HIGH

Manchester High School for Girls	Co-ed	Pupils 730
Grangethorpe Road	Boys	Upper sixth Yes
Rusholme	• Girls	Termly fees:
Manchester M14 6HS	Mixed sixth	Day £720
Telephone number 061 224 0447	• Day	GBGSA; GSA
	Boarding	

Head Miss M M Moon (5 years)
Age range 11–18, own prep from age 4; entry by own exam.
Assisted places, scholarships and bursaries are available.

MANCHESTER JEWISH GRAMMAR

Manchester Jewish Grammar School	Co-ed	Pupils 130
Charlton Avenue	• Boys	Upper sixth Yes
Prestwich	Girls	Termly fees:
Greater Manchester M25 8PH	Mixed sixth	Day £670
Telephone number 061 773 1789	• Day	
	Boarding	

Head P Pink (12 years)
Age range 10–18; entry by own exam.
Fees based on parental income; Greater Manchester council bursaries available.

MARLBOROUGH

Marlborough College	Co-ed	Pupils 885
Marlborough	• Boys	Upper sixth 200
Wiltshire SN8 1PA	Girls	Termly fees:
Telephone number 0672 52684	• Mixed sixth	Day £1676
	• Day	Boarding £2235
Enquiries/application to the Registrar	• Boarding	HMC;
		(SHA/BSA)

WHAT IT'S LIKE

Founded in 1843 as a school 'for the Sons of Clergy of the Church of England', it has a delightful setting on the edge of one of the most agreeable country market towns in southern England. The Marlborough Downs lie to the north, Savernake Forest to the east, and the Kennet runs through the school grounds. Its elegant and well-appointed buildings lie amidst fine lawns and gardens. Very large playing fields adjoin them. All facilities are of a high standard. It pioneered the admission of girls into the sixth form in 1968 (now 101 boarders) and the first intake of girls at 13 may be in September 1989. One of the most distinguished schools in the country, it is said to combine strenuous activity with relaxed personal relations. In line with the terms of its foundation, there is quite a lot of emphasis on Anglican worship and instruction and worship is encouraged. Some services are compulsory. A great range of choice of subjects and different combinations for A-level. A very large full-time staff (plus 20 part-timers) allows a ratio of 1:9 pupils. Academic standards are extremely high and results are consistently impressive. Between 165 and 170 leavers go on to university each year (one of the highest proportions in Britain) and on average 30 of these go to Oxbridge. Tremendously strong involvement in music (400+ pupils learn an instrument). Very strong also in the art department. Numerous dramatic productions involving 250–300 pupils. There are 33 different sports and games on offer and the college has an outstanding record in these (especially hockey) with many county and national representatives. A phenomenal range of extra-curricular activities is provided: clubs and societies cater for virtually everyone's needs. The CCF is a flourishing contingent. Outdoor pursuits (eg fishing, orienteering) are encouraged and the college owns a pack of beagles. There is a very substantial commitment to local community schemes. The Duke of Edinburgh's Award Scheme is to be started soon.

SCHOOL PROFILE

Pupils Total, 885. Day 3 (boys 2, girls 1); Boarding 882 (boys 781, girls 101). Entry age, boys, 13 and into the sixth; girls into the sixth (13 in near future). About 20% are children of former pupils.

Entrance Common entrance used and own exam for sixth form entrance. Oversubscribed. No special skills but students are encouraged in extra-curricular activities; no religious requirements but is an Anglican foundation. Parents expected to buy text books. Large number of scholarships/bursaries, depending on quality of candidates; special scholarships for art, music and technology, up to 100% of fees.

Parents 10+% live overseas.

Staff Head David Cope, in post for 2 years. 95 full time staff, 20 part time. Annual turnover 6%. Average age 38.

Academic work GCSE and A-levels. Average size of upper fifth 155; upper sixth 200. *O-levels*: on average, 5 pupils in upper fifth pass 1–4 subjects; 12, 5–7 subjects; 138 pass 8+ subjects. *A-levels*: on average, 7 pupils in upper sixth pass 1 subject; 22, 2 subjects; 140, 3 subjects and 32 pass 4 subjects. On average, 46 take science/engineering A-levels; 86 take arts and humanities; 75 a mixture. Arabic (UCLEs) in sixth, also Latin, Greek, Russian offered to GCSE/A-level. *Computing facilities*: 14 station Econet of BBC masters, 14 station network of RML Nimbus PCs, 25 Standdone BBC, 6 PC compatibles, 2 DEC series 11 minis. Diagnosis and special tuition for dyslexic pupils.

Senior pupils' non-academic activities *Music*: 410 learn a musical instrument, 180 to Grade 6 or above, 100 play in 3 school orchestras, 170 in choir, 35 in school pop group, also jazz group and 100 in wind and brass bands; 21 music scholars, 1 exhibitioner, 20 take singing lessons; 4 accepted for Music School, 4 play in pop group, 4 to conservatoire, 3 to study music at university. *Drama and dance*: 60 in school productions, 200 others participate. *Art*: Whole school takes as non-examined subject, 60 take GCSE, 50 A-level (no failures), 420 attend upper school art lectures; 30 in eg photographic club; 20 accepted for Art School; 12 to foundation courses. *Sport*: Cricket, rugger, soccer, hockey, athletics, squash, fencing, rackets, cross-country, tennis, basketball, badminton, fives, gymnastic skills, canoeing, climbing, swimming, judo, shooting, volleyball, water polo, table tennis, archery, golf, weight training available among others. Approx 500 take non-compulsory sport, all do some compulsory. 36 pupils represent county (rugby, hockey, tennis, athletics, swimming, cricket, fencing). *Other*: 140 take part in local community schemes. Other activities include a computer club, driving lessons, Duke of Edinburgh's Award Scheme to start soon. 40 other diverse clubs and societies eg languages, wine making, philosophy, literature.

Careers 4 part time careers advisors. Average number of pupils accepted for *arts and humanities degree courses* at Oxbridge, 15; other universities, 100, polytechnics or CHE, 10. *science and engineering degree courses* at Oxbridge, 15; other universities, 35; medical schools, 6; polytechnics or CHE, 5. Average number of pupils going straight into careers in armed services, 8; the church (via university), 2; the City, 2. Traditional school careers are varied, most to engineering, design, business studies, economics, languages, higher education courses.

Uniform School uniform worn by lower school.

Houses/prefects Prefects, head boy/girl, head of house and house prefects – appointed by the Head. School Council.

Religion Religious worship encouraged, a few compulsory services each term.

Social 'Day School' organised periodically with St John's Comprehensive, Third World Development link with The Gambia. A number of trips abroad and exchanges. Pupils allowed to bring own bike to school. Meals self service. School shop. No tobacco allowed; some supervised house bars.

Discipline No corporal punishment. Pupils failing to produce homework once might expect a warning, maybe extra work; those caught smoking cannabis on the premises can expect expulsion.

Boarding About 220 have own study bedroom, about 310 share with 1 other, 355 are in dormitories of 3. Houses, of about 60, divided by age, mixed sex. 3 qualified nurses in sanatorium; doctor local. Central dining room. Pupils can provide and cook own food. 2 weekend exeats each term plus half term. Afternoon visits to local town allowed.

Alumni association run by John Thompson, c/o the college.

Former pupils Captain Mark Phillips; Sir John Betjeman; Norris McWhirter; The Hon Peter Brooke; Lord Hunt; Norman Del Mar; Sir Nicholas Goodison; Julian Pettifer; Chris De Burgh.

MARY ERSKINE'S

The Mary Erskine School
Ravelston
Edinburgh EH4 3NT
Telephone number 031 337 2391

Co-ed · Pupils 675
Boys · Upper sixth Yes
● Girls · Termly fees:
Mixed sixth · Day £770
● Day · Boarding £1500
● Boarding · GSA

Head R M Morgan (10 years)
Age range 12–18, own prep from age 5 shared with Daniel Stewart's and Melville College; entry by own exam.
4 scholarships and some bursaries.

MARYMOUNT

Marymount International School
George Road
Kingston upon Thames
Surrey KT2 7PE
Telephone number 01-949 0571

Enquiries/application to the Admissions Officer

Co-ed · Pupils 194
Boys · Upper sixth 45
● Girls · Termly fees:
Mixed sixth · Day £1675
● Day · Boarding £2842
● Boarding

WHAT IT'S LIKE

Founded in 1955, it derives from an educational movement inaugurated by the Roman Catholic Institute of the Religious of the Sacred Heart of Mary in Beziers which established international schools in four continents. Known as Marymount schools; the first was in New York. This one in Surrey, like its sister schools in Rome and Paris, has as its goal the provision of continuity in the academic careers of students whose education has been interrupted by family moves abroad. Many pupils have parents in the diplomatic corps. Representatives of 40 nations are currently on the roll at Kingston. Its 7-acre campus of pleasant grounds lies on the outskirts of the town. The original main building is a mock-Tudor private house. Recent buildings adjoin it. It is extremely well equipped and provides very comfortable boarding accommodation. The academic curriculum is designed to meet the needs of an international student body and it provides a wide selection of courses at all levels. It enjoys an excellent staff:pupil ratio of 1:10. High academic standards are achieved and for such a small school there is an impressive number of university entrants (35+ per year). It has compulsory religious study programmes which include the study of world religions: a multi-faith approach. The school maintains strong international links with educational bodies and with other Marymount schools. Its cosmopolitanism is pervasive and very constructive.

SCHOOL PROFILE

Pupils Total 194. Day 96; Boarding, 98. Entry age, 12–16. 1% are children of former pupils.

Entrance Not oversubscribed. Good working knowledge of English required; no religious requirements. Parents expected to buy some specialist text books. Limited financial help at Principal's discretion.

Parents 15+% are from the diplomatic service; 15+% in industry or commerce. 30+% live within 30 miles; 30+% live overseas.

Staff Head Sister Breda Shelly, in post for 4 years. 23 full time staff, 3 part time. Annual turnover 4%. Average age 38.

Academic work International Baccalaureate. Average size of upper fifth (10th grade) 40; upper sixth (12th grade) 45. School offers no external examination at 16 years. Twelfth grade students sit for IB Diploma and IB Certificate (Higher and Subsidiary level) exams. 24 pupils gained full IB Diploma; 20 IB certificates at subsidiary and higher level. The IB programme covers 6 subjects to be chosen from 5 subject areas including science, maths, arts, humanities. School will arrange tutorials in Arabic, Urdu, Japanese, Dutch etc for native speakers in preparation for IB. *Computing facilities*: laboratory with 10 BBC and Apple computers. Computer studies is a compulsory part of all student programmes in first 3 years. *Special provisions*: EFL.

Senior pupils' non-academic activities *Music*: 13 learn a musical instrument, 3 take voice training; 1 takes IB higher level music. 1 accepted for Music School every 2 years. *Drama and dance*: 100 in school productions; 15 in Independent Schools Theatre Association; 1 accepted for Drama/Dance Schools every few years. *Art*: 25 take as non-examined subject; 6 take IB HL; 3 accepted for Art School; 6 belong to eg photographic club. *Sport*: Badminton, basketball, volleyball, softball, soccer, tennis available. 100 take non-compulsory sport; 60 in ISST & AIST tournaments as varsity and junior varsity basketball, volleyball and soccer teams. *Other*: 50 take part in local community schemes. Other activities include various once-a-week club activities, occasional discos, film evenings and other social activities.

Careers 2 part time careers advisors. Average number of pupils accepted for *arts and humanities degree courses* at Oxbridge, 1; other universities, 25; polytechnics or CHE, 1. *science and engineering degree courses* at universities, 12; medical schools, 2; polytechnics or CHE, 2. *other general training courses*, 2.

Uniform School uniform worn throughout.

Houses/prefects No competitive houses. Student Council elected by the school.

Religion Compulsory religious studies programme includes study of world religions: a multi-faith approach. Students are encouraged to bear witness to their own faith and to learn to respect and understand the beliefs of others.

Social Drama, sports and maths competitions with other European Council of International Schools members all over Europe; sports tournaments with other members of London American-International Schools Sports Tournament Association; participate in the Model United Nations in The Hague. Annual educational tours week in February in which all students participate. Several destinations each year eg Russia, Egypt, Turkey, France, Italy, Austria. Pupils allowed to bring own bike to school. Meals self service. School tuckshop. No tobacco/alcohol allowed.

Discipline No corporal punishment. Punishment for pupils failing to produce homework dependent on individual teachers; those caught smoking cannabis on the premises could expect immediate expulsion.

Boarding 100% share with 1 or 2. Qualified nurse during school hours, then on call; as is school doctor. Central dining room. Pupils can provide and cook snacks. Exeats any weekend. Visits to local town allowed, but not alone.

Alumni association run by Sister Mary Catherine Walsh, c/o the School.

MAYFIELD

Mayfield College	Co-ed	Pupils 200
Mayfield	● Boys	Upper sixth 20
East Sussex TN20 6PL	Girls	Termly fees:
Telephone number 0435 872041	Mixed sixth	Day £1355
Enquiries/application to the Headmaster	● Day	Boarding £2070
	● Boarding	ISAI

WHAT IT'S LIKE

Founded in 1868 it has a fine site of 40 acres in the Sussex weald, a mile from Mayfield. Agreeable buildings and good modern facilities. A sound education is provided and results are creditable (10 plus university entrants per year). Adequate music, drama and art. Good range of games and sports. Some commitment to local community schemes and some participation in the Duke of Edinburgh's Award Scheme.

SCHOOL PROFILE

Pupils Total, 200. Day, 100; Boarding, 100. Entry age, 10–11 and directly into the sixth form. 5% are children of former pupils.

Entrance Common entrance and own entrance exam used. Not oversubscribed. No special skills or religious requirements. Parents not expected to buy text books. Scholarships, up to 50% of fees, awarded on results of competitive examination. Bursaries, in cases of special need, are income-related.

Parents 15+% in industry or commerce. 31–60% live within 30 miles; 10+% live overseas.

Staff Head G Briscoe, in post for 6 years. 24 full time staff, 2 part time. Annual turnover 8%. Average age 41.

Academic work GCSE and A-levels. Average size of upper fifth 36; upper sixth 20. *O-levels*: on average, 13 pupils in upper fifth pass 1–4 subjects; 11, 5–7 subjects; 7 pass 8+ subjects. *A-levels*: on average, 4 pupils in upper sixth pass 1 subject; 5, 2 subjects; 5, 3 subjects and 2 pass 4 subjects. On average, 5 take science/engineering A-levels; 6 take arts and humanities; 8 a mixture. *Computing facilities*: Network of RM Nimbus machines. Tuition and experience is available through all age groups. *Special provisions*: EFL and assistance for dyslexics of good ability.

Senior pupils' non-academic activities *Music*: 12 learn a musical instrument, 1 or 2 to Grade 6 or above; 20 in school choir, 6 in school pop group. *Drama and dance*: 25 in school productions. *Art*: 15 take GCSE; 2, A-level. 1 accepted for Art School. *Sport*: Team games: rugby, soccer, cricket, basketball; racquet sports: tennis, squash, badminton; water sports: swimming, canoeing, sailing; individual sports: athletics, fencing, archery available. 50 take non-compulsory sport. 12 represent county (rugby, athletics). *Other*: 10 take part in local community schemes. 6 have bronze Duke of Edinburgh's Award. Other activities include a computer club, debating, choral singing.

Careers 2 part time advisors. Average number of pupils accepted for *arts and humanities degree courses* at universities, 4; polytechnics or CHE, 6. *science and engineering degree courses* at universities, 6; polytechnics or CHE, 2. Average number of pupils going straight into careers in industry, 4; commerce, 10.

Uniform School uniform worn except in the sixth.

Houses/prefects Competitive houses. Prefects, head boy, head of house and house prefects – appointed after consultation.

Religion Compulsory daily assembly for all. One service of worship midweek for all Christians and Sunday mass.

Social Sports fixtures, debates, music and drama, socials with local schools. Visits to France (to support language studies), ski-ing (once a year), sports camp in Majorca (once a year). Pupils allowed to bring own car/motorbike to school. Meals self service. School shop. No tobacco/alcohol allowed.

Discipline No corporal punishment. Pupils failing to produce homework once might expect a detention; those caught smoking cannabis on the premises could expect suspension, leading to probable expulsion.

Boarding Prefects have own study bedroom, all other sixth formers share with one other; 8 in each dormitory cubicle. House dormitories of 25, subdivided into cubicles divided by competitive houses and age group. Resident SRN. Central dining room. 2 weekend exeats each term. Visits to the local town allowed.

Alumni association run by M R Cullnane, 31 Rosemont Road, Acton, London W3.

MAYNARD

The Maynard School	Co-ed	Pupils 450
Denmark Road	Boys	Upper sixth Yes
Exeter	● Girls	Termly fees:
Devon EX1 1SJ	Mixed sixth	Day £720
Telephone number 0392 73417	● Day	GBA; GBGSA
	Boarding	

Head Miss F Murdin (8 years)
Age range 10–18, own prep from age 7; entry by own exam.

MERCHANT TAYLORS' (CROSBY)

Merchant Taylors' School
Crosby
Liverpool L23 0QP
Telephone number 051 928 3308

Enquiries/application to the Secretary

Co-ed
● Boys
Girls
Mixed sixth
● Day
Boarding

Pupils 555
Upper sixth 88
Termly fees:
Day £820
HMC

WHAT IT'S LIKE

Founded in 1620 by John Harrison, citizen and Merchant Taylor of London, it moved to its present site in 1878. This is urban and well-equipped with modern facilities. A separate junior school is attached to the main school. Academic standards are high and results are good (50–55 university entrants per year). Strong music, drama and art departments. Good range of sports and games (high standards and a lot of county representatives) plus activities. Some participation in the Duke of Edinburgh's Award Scheme.

SCHOOL PROFILE

Pupils Total over 12, 555. Entry age, 7, 11, 13 and into the sixth. Own junior department provides over 20%. 20–25% are children of former pupils.

Entrance Own entrance exam used. Oversubscribed. No special skills or religious requirements. Parents not expected to buy text books. 185 assisted places. 50 grants, to full fees.

Parents 15+% in industry or commerce, 15+% are doctors, lawyers, etc. More than 60% live within 30 miles.

Staff Head S J R Dawkins, in post for 2 years. 48 full time staff, 10 part time. Annual turnover 7%. Average age 40.

Academic work GCSE and A-levels. Average size of upper fifth 109; upper sixth 88. *O-levels*: on average, 11 pupils in upper fifth pass 1–4 subjects; 25, 5–7 subjects; 73 pass 8+ subjects. *A-levels*: on average, 6 pupils in upper sixth pass 1 subject; 9, 2 subjects; 14, 3 subjects and 59 pass 4 subjects. On average, 50 take science/engineering A-levels; 25 take arts and humanities; 13 a mixture. Russian is offered to GCSE; philosophy to A-level. *Computing facilities*: An SJ Research MDFS Econet with 24 BBC Master stations, plus 6 stand alone BBC Bs, PRESTEL subscriber, MIMAC IP. *Special provisions*: dyslexic, visually handicapped and partially deaf pupils can be catered for.

Senior pupils' non-academic activities *Music*: 45 learn a musical instrument, 20 to Grade 6 or above, 1 accepted for Music School; 31 in school orchestra, 35 in choir, 10 in pop group; 4 in Merseyside youth orchestra. *Drama and dance*: 70 in school productions; 50 in house plays; 10 in lower sixth play; 12 sixth form drama course. *Art*: 24 take as non-examined subject; 3–6 take GCSE; 1, A-level; art history is a compulsory short course for general studies. Rarely is a student accepted for Art School. *Sport*: Rugby, hockey, rowing, cross-country, swimming, tennis, cricket, softball, basketball, table tennis, golf, sailing, wind-surfing available. 60 take exams eg gymnastics, swimming. 20 represent county/country (rugby, hockey). *Other*: 6 have silver Duke of Edinburgh's Award, 2 have gold. Other activities include a computer club, CCF (voluntary), Scouts; societies: Amnesty; Arts: Christian, classical, debating, economics, railway, science, French play reading.

Careers 2 part time advisors. Average number of pupils accepted for *arts and humanities degree courses* at Oxbridge, 8; other universities, 19; polytechnics or CHE, 9. *science and engineering degree courses* at Oxbridge, 6; other universities, 21; medical schools, 7; polytechnics or CHE, 6. *other general training courses*, 8. Average number of pupils going straight into careers in the armed services, 1; industry, 1; the City, 1; music/drama, 1.

Uniform School uniform worn throughout.

Houses/prefects Competitive houses. Prefects, head boy, head of house and house prefects – appointed by the Head.

Religion Non-denominational Christian assemblies involve prayers and readings and RS classes explain (amongst other things) the meaning and purpose of Christian worship. Parents may 'opt out'; very few do.

Social Drama, music, several societies with sister girls' school. Organised trips abroad. Pupils allowed to bring own car/bike/motorbike to school. Meals formal. School shop. No tobacco/alcohol allowed.

Discipline No corporal punishment. Pupils failing to produce homework once might expect a verbal warning; those caught smoking cannabis on the premises would be expelled.

Alumni association run by R R R Fisher, 25 Little Crosby Road, Crosby, Liverpool L23.

MERCHANT TAYLORS' (GIRLS)

Merchant Taylors' School for Girls	Co-ed	Pupils 464
Crosby	Boys	Upper sixth 60
Liverpool L23 5SP	● Girls	Termly fees:
Telephone number 051-924 3140	Mixed sixth	Day £735
Enquiries/application to the Headmistress	● Day	GSA
	Boarding	

WHAT IT'S LIKE

Founded in 1888, it is suburban, single-site, in the centre of Crosby which is on the coast, 10 miles from Liverpool and 12 from Stockport. Its well designed and pleasant buildings lie in gardens, with playing fields nearby. The junior school is close. It is non-denominational. There are strong traditional links with Merchant Taylors' Boys' School Crosby, especially in cultural activities. It is a well run school with high academic standards and very good results. Nearly all girls do A-levels. Each year some 30 pupils go on to university. The music department is extremely strong. There is a good range of sports, games and extra-curricular activities. In the sixth form there is a very substantial commitment to local community services.

SCHOOL PROFILE

Pupils Total over 12, 464. Entry age, 4, 11+ and into the sixth. Own junior school provides over 30%. More than 50% are children of former pupils.

Entrance Own entrance exam used. Oversubscribed. No special religious requirements, music and sports skills looked for. Parents not expected to buy text books. 164 assisted places. 6–7 scholarships/bursaries, depending upon parents' income.

Parents 15+% are doctors, lawyers, etc, 15+% in industry or commerce. More than 60% live within 30 miles.

Staff Head Miss E J Panton, in post since Sept 1988. 46 full time staff, 30 part time. Annual turnover 3%. Average age 38.

Academic work GCSE and A-levels. Average size of upper fifth 80; upper sixth 60. *O-levels*: on average, 2 pupils in upper fifth pass 5–7 subjects; 78 pass 8+ subjects. *A-levels*: on average, 2 pupils in upper sixth pass 1 subject; 4, 2 subjects; 16, 3 subjects; 38 pass 4 subjects. On average, 25 take science A-levels; 20 take arts and humanities; 15 take a mixture. *Computing facilities*: 2 computer rooms.

Senior pupils' non-academic activities *Music*: Very many learn a musical instrument, 10–12 to grade 6, 1–2 accepted for Music School; brass and wind ensembles in school, 2 orchestras of about 50 each, 3 school choirs; 1 or 2 in National Youth Orchestra, several in local youth orchestras, several enter local music festivals. *Drama and dance*: Number in school productions depends; Some grade of ESB taken in first–third forms – also some teaching in speech and drama. 4 or 5 known to enter local dance competitions. *Art*: 10 take GCSE; 5 or 6 take A-level. 3 accepted for Art School. *Sport*: Swimming, hockey, netball, tennis, athletics are available. Sixth form use a sports centre. 2 or 3 represent county (athletics, hockey, swimming, tennis). *Other*: Voluntary service is a sixth form option. Other activities include a computer club, gymnastics, science, history, computing and drama.

Careers 2 part time staff advisors. Average number of pupils accepted for *arts and humanities degree courses* at Oxbridge, 3; other universities, 12; polytechnics or CHE, 2; *social science degree courses*, 13. *science and engineering degree courses* at Oxbridge, 3; other universities, 8; medical schools, 4 or 5; polytechnics or CHE, 2. *BEd*, 2 or 3. *other general training courses*, 3 or 4. Average number of pupils going into careers in the civil service, 2 or 3; music/drama, 1 or 2. Retail management training. Traditional school careers are medicine and law.

Uniform School uniform worn, modified in sixth.

Houses/prefects No house system or prefects – school affairs run by sixth form committees. Head girl and 2 deputies, elected by staff and seniors, election confirmed by Head. School Council.

Religion Compulsory, non-denominational morning assembly.

Social Work closely with brother school Merchant Taylors' Boys' School. Regular trips abroad, though not in exchange. Pupils allowed to bring own car/bike/motorbike to school. Meals self service. Tuck facilities at break. No tobacco/alcohol allowed.

Discipline No corporal punishment. Pupils failing to produce homework once might expect to be kept in to do it; those caught smoking cannabis on the premises might expect immediate suspension until facts were verified.

Alumni association is run by Mrs S Duncan, Fairhaven, Serpentine South, Blundellsands, Liverpool L23 6UQ.

Former pupils Beryl Bainbridge.

MERCHANT TAYLORS' (NORTHWOOD)

Merchant Taylors' School
Sandy Lodge
Northwood
Middlesex HA6 2HT
Telephone number 09274 21850

Enquiries/application to the Headmaster

Co-ed   Pupils 740
• Boys   Upper sixth 120
Girls   Termly fees:
Mixed sixth   Day £1365
• Day   Boarding £2100
• Boarding   HMC

WHAT IT'S LIKE

Founded in 1561 by the Merchant Taylors' Company, its first headmaster was Richard Mulcaster. It moved to its present premises at Sandy Lodge in 1933 where it occupies a superb 300-acre estate of gardens, wooded grounds and lakes. The Merchant Taylors' Company continues to support the school financially. The handsome, well-equipped brick buildings are dominated by the Great Hall. Facilities are excellent and the libraries outstanding. It provides a highly academic and competitive environment and results are consistently impressive (85-plus university entrants each year). Music, drama and art are all very well supported. A wide range of games and sports is available and standards are high. Also a wide range of activities including a very big CCF and a flourishing Scout group. A fair commitment to local community services and a fine record in the Duke of Edinburgh's Award Scheme.

SCHOOL PROFILE

Pupils Total 740. Day 665; Boarding 75. Entry age, 11+, 13+ and into the sixth. York House, Rickmansworth; St John's, Northwood; Orley Farm, Harrow provide over 20% of pupils.

Entrance Common entrance (at 13) and own entrance exam (at 11 and for scholarships at 13) used. Oversubscribed. Excellence in all fields is welcomed. No religious requirements. Parents not expected to buy text books. 20 assisted places pa. 14 scholarships (including 2 music) pa. Various bursaries available in case of need, up to two-thirds day fees.

Parents 15+% in industry or commerce; 15+% are doctors, lawyers, etc. 60+% live within 30 miles; 10+% live overseas.

Staff Head D J Skipper, in post for 7 years. 56 full time staff, 14 part time. Annual turnover 8%. Average age 40.

Academic work GCSE and A-levels. Average size of upper fifth 130; upper sixth 120. *O-levels*: on average, 12 pupils in upper fifth pass 1–4 subjects; 31, 5–7 subjects; 96 pass 8+ subjects. *A-levels*: on average, 10 pupils in upper sixth pass 1 subject; 20, 2 subjects; 81, 3 subjects and 6 pass 4 subjects. On average, 45 take science/engineering A-levels; 41 take arts and humanities; 32 a mixture. Ancient Greek and Russian are offered to GCSE/A-level. *Computing facilities*: A computer centre with 14 computers. Almost every department uses computers. *Special provisions*: academically suitable 'Wornock' children accepted (medical advice sought as appropriate). Pupils must be able to cope with teaching in English without remedial help.

Senior pupils' non-academic activities *Music*: 70 learn a musical instrument, 25 to Grade 6 or above; 45 in school orchestra; 20 in choir; 12 in pop group; 1 in National Youth Orchestra. *Drama and dance*: 30 participate in school productions; 100+ in House plays; 1 accepted for Drama/Dance School; 1 competes in ice dancing. *Art*: 26 take GCSE; 12 A-level. 3 accepted for Art School. 1 belongs to photographic club. *Sport*: Athletics, badminton, basketball, chess, cricket, cross-country, canoeing, fencing, fishing (fly and coarse), fives, golf, hockey, judo, multigym, rock climbing, rugby, sailing, shooting, soccer, squash, swimming, table tennis, tennis, volleyball, windsurfing available. 40% take non-compulsory sport. 2 represent country (golf, ice dance); 6 represent county (rugby, athletics, cricket). *Other*: 36 take part in local community schemes. 25 have bronze Duke of Edinburgh's Award, 25 have silver. 30 in scouts. 10 enter voluntary schemes after leaving school. Other activities include a computer club; driving lessons.

Careers 7 part time careers advisors. Average number of pupils accepted for *arts and humanities degree courses* at Oxbridge, 8; other universities, 35; polytechnics or CHE, 24. *science and engineering degree courses* at Oxbridge, 8; other universities, 34; medical schools, 9; polytechnics or CHE, 23. Average number of pupils going straight into careers in armed services, 1; the church, occasionally; industry, 2; the City, 2; other, 10.

Uniform School uniform worn throughout.

Houses/prefects Competitive houses. Prefects, head boy, head of house and house prefects – appointed by the Head and Housemasters after consultation.

Religion Daily assembly.

Social Choral works, concerts, debates, drama, field work, careers conventions, industrial conferences, academic lectures with local schools. Organised French/German exchanges; German orchestral exchange visit. Ski trips. Sports tours. Pupils allowed to bring own car/bike/motorbike to school. Meals self service. School shop. No tobacco/alcohol allowed.

Discipline No corporal punishment. Pupils failing to produce homework once might expect to have to do it by the following day; those caught smoking cannabis on the premises could expect expulsion.

Boarding 25 have own study bedroom, 36 share (2); 17 are in dormitories (12, 5). 1 House. Resident qualified nurse; doctor visits regularly and is always on call. Central dining room. Pupils can provide and cook their own food. 3 weekend exeats each term. Visits to the local town allowed in sixth form.

Alumni association is run by N J Foley, Chairman OMT Society, St Benets, Northfield Avenue, Pinner, Middlesex.

Former pupils Rt Rev Donald Coggan; Reginald Maudling; Michael Peschardt; Lyn Chadwick.

MERCHISTON

Merchiston Castle School	Co-ed	Pupils 300
Colinton	● Boys	Upper sixth 63
Edinburgh EH13 0PU	Girls	Termly fees:
Telephone number 031 441 1567/1722	Mixed sixth	Day £1480
Enquiries to the Headmaster	● Day	Boarding £2300
Applications to the Registrar	● Boarding	HMC

WHAT IT'S LIKE

Founded in 1833 in the centre of Edinburgh, it moved in 1930 to Colinton House and the ruins of Colinton Castle. These lie 4 miles south-west of Edinburgh on a fine estate of gardens and parkland bordered on two sides by the Water of Leith and are close to the Pentland Hills. Apart from the original house (now the science block) all the buildings are purpose-built and date from the 1930s or the development programme of the 1960s, 1970s and 1980s. The environment is healthy and facilities very good (including comfortable boarding accommodation). The school adheres strongly to Scottish values and traditions, and there is emphasis on striving for excellence, a belief in the value of the individual, in hard work, integrity and good manners. The 'Scottishness' is exemplified in the wearing of a kilt on Sundays and formal occasions, the fine pipe band, and social occasions such as a Highland Ball and Scottish country dancing. There is also emphasis on the practice of Christianity; religious education is part of the curriculum. Merchiston is inter-denominational but services are based on those of the Church of Scotland. Academic standards are high and the teaching very good. A staff:pupil ratio of 1:10. Results are consistently impressive and 40–45 pupils go on to university each year (a high proportion for a small school). There are extremely strong music and drama departments involving a large number of pupils. A wide range of sports and games is available and the school has long had a reputation for excellence in these. Also a good range of extra-curricular activities with emphasis on outdoor pursuits for which the environment is ideal. A flourishing CCF in which each boy spends 2 years. A substantial commitment to local community services and an impressive record in the Duke of Edinburgh's Award Scheme.

SCHOOL PROFILE

Pupils Total over 12, 300. Day 30; Boarding 270. Entry age, 11+, 12+, 13+ and into the sixth. Pupils come from primary and preparatory schools in Scotland, north of England and Northern Ireland; also from expatriate junior schools overseas. 20% are children of former pupils.

Entrance Common entrance and own entrance exam used. Sometimes oversubscribed. No special skills or religious requirements but a breadth of interest and talents looked for. Interdenominational. Parents charged £15 per term towards text books. 30 assisted places. 8 scholarships/bursaries, 80%–15% of fees.

Parents 15+% are doctors, lawyers etc; 15+% in industry or commerce. 10+% live within 30 miles; 10+% live overseas.

Staff Head D M Spawforth, in post for 7 years. 36 full time staff, 4 part time. Annual turnover 6%. Average age 35.

Academic work GCSE, A-levels and Highers. Average size of upper fifth 63; upper sixth 63. *O-levels*: on average, 18 pupils in upper fifth pass 1–4 subjects; 18, 5–7 subjects; 28 pass 8+ subjects. *A-levels*: on average, 10 pupils in upper sixth pass 1 subject; 12, 2 subjects; 30, 3 subjects and 3 pass 4 subjects. On average, 40% take science/engineering A-levels; 30% take arts and humanities; 30% a mixture. Electronics, design, computer studies are offered to GCSE/A-level. *Computing facilities*: Purpose built computing department (2 fully equipped classrooms) used for teaching and by computer and other departments; also as an activity centre. Provision for mildly dyslexic.

Senior pupils' non-academic activities *Music*: 90 learn a musical instrument, 10 to Grade 6 or above; 33 in school orchestra, 94 in choir, 10 in pop group, 10 in close harmony group, 15 in pipe band; 1 in National Youth Orchestra. *Drama and dance*: 80 in school production, 80 in house drama productions; 100 in Scottish reels clubs. 2 go on to work in theatre. *Art*: 22 take art or design as non-examined subject; 53 GCSE art and CDT; 6 A-level. 5 accepted for Art School; 3 for design. 2 participate in Design Council Awards competition for schools. 20 belong to photographic club. *Sport*: Rugby, cricket, athletics, swimming, fencing, tennis, shooting, squash, fives, badminton, hockey, cross-country running available. 250 take non-compulsory sport. 10 represent county/country (rugby, athletics, biathlon, fencing). *Other*: 30 take part in local community schemes. 10 have bronze Duke of Edinburgh's Award, 10 have silver and 4 gold. 4 enter voluntary schemes and 2 work for national charities after leaving. Other activities include a computer club, electronics, debating, chess, bridge, video filming, driving lessons, skiing, Outward Bound (hillwalking).

Careers 1 full time and 2 part time careers advisors. Average number of pupils accepted for *arts and humanities degree courses* at Oxbridge, 3; other universities, 14; polytechnics or CHE, 3. *science and engineering degree courses* at Oxbridge, 4; other universities, 20; medical schools, 2; polytechnics or CHE, 5. Average number of pupils going straight into careers in armed services, 4; industry, 3; the City, 2; journalism/media, 2; farming, 4. Traditional school careers are law, finance, engineering, industry.

Uniform School uniform worn except the sixth.

Houses/prefects No competitive houses. Prefects, head boy, head of house and house prefects – appointed by the Head. Various committees and councils, eg food, charities, chapel.

Religion Daily morning act of worship; Sunday morning service for whole school.

Social Debates, plays, concerts, charity fundraising events, dances, Scottish reel evenings and some guest speakers organised with local girls' schools. Tours to France, Germany, Spain, Italy; also skiing; rugby tours; expeditions. Meals self service. School shops sell sports equipment, books and second-hand school wear. No tobacco allowed; sixth form club with beer bar at weekends under housemaster's control.

Discipline No corporal punishment. Pupils failing to produce homework once might expect to re-do on blue paper, obtainable only from the boy's housemaster; those caught smoking cannabis on the premises would be required to leave.

Boarding 33% have own study bedroom, 50% are in dormitories of 6 or more. Houses, of approximately 60, divided by age. Resident nurse and assistant matron; doctor on call. Central dining room. Pupils can provide and cook own food in house kitchen. 1 exeat of 3 days to a week each term. Visits to local town allowed though controlled.

Alumni association run by President of the Merchistonian Club, c/o the school.

Former pupils Rt Hon John MacGregor (Ministry of Agriculture); Lord Craigavon; Sir James Robertson; Sir Donald Acheson (Government Chief Medical Officer); Lt Gen Sir Alexander Boswell; Roger Baird (Scotland XV); Sir Eric Campbell Geddes.

METHODIST COLLEGE

The Methodist College	• Co-ed	Pupils 1568
1 Malone Road	Boys	Upper sixth 258
Belfast BT9 6BY	Girls	Termly fees:
Telephone number 0232 669558	Mixed sixth	Day £353
Enquiries/application to the Headmaster	• Day	Boarding £632
	• Boarding	HMC

WHAT IT'S LIKE

Founded in 1868, it is urban, single-site in landscaped grounds close to Queen's University and a mile from the city centre. It has two large prep schools. The principal buildings are Victorian Gothic, with suggestions of Scottish 'baronial' and hotel de ville. There are many modern buildings including a splendid chapel. It is a superbly well equipped establishment with very high academic attainments (150–160 university entrants per year). Tremendously strong in music and drama. Very high standards in sport and games. An enormous number of clubs and societies catering for virtually every need. Big commitment to local community schemes and an outstanding record in the Duke of Edinburgh's Award Scheme. Fees are very low.

SCHOOL PROFILE

Pupils Total over 12, 1568. Day 1402 (boys 773, girls 628); Boarding 167 (boys, 104, girls 63). Entry age, 5+, 11+ and into the sixth. Own prep school provides over 20%. 55% are children of former pupils.

Entrance Common entrance not used. Oversubscribed. No special skills or religious requirements. Parents expected to buy text books. 6 scholarships/bursaries available, from £400 to £300.

Parents 15+% are doctors, lawyers, etc; 15+% in industry or commerce; 15+% are teachers/lecturers. 60+% live within 30 miles; 5% live overseas.

Staff Head Dr J Kincade, in post for 14 years. 98 full time staff, 6 part time. Annual turnover 5%. Average age 38.

Academic work GCSE and A-levels. Average size of upper fifth 233; upper sixth 258. *O-levels*: on average, 41 pupils in upper fifth pass 1–4 subjects; 81, 5–7 subjects; 108 pass 8+ subjects. *A-levels*: on average, 23 pupils in the upper sixth pass 1 subject; 55, 2 subjects; 135, 3 subjects; 23 pass 4 subjects. On average, 80 take science/engineering A-levels; 70 take arts and humanities; 97 take a mixture. Russian, Classical Greek are offered to GCSE/A-level.

Computing facilities: 16 Station 480Z Network, 10 Station Nimbus network and BBC computers in various departments.

Senior pupils' non-academic activities *Music*: 90 learn a musical instrument, 45 up to Grade 6 or above, 4+ accepted for Music School; 50 in school orchestra, 300 in choir, 80 in band; 15 in City of Belfast Youth Orchestra, 8 in SE Ed & Library Board Orchestra. *Drama and dance*: 120 in school productions including musicals. 6 accepted for Drama/Dance Schools, 2 go on to work in theatre, 1 pupil from last year is musical director of plays in London. 15 AEB Drama, 16 take General Drama Studies. *Art*: 25 take A-level. 7 accepted for Art School, 1 for Art History at university, 12 belong to photographic club, 8 in art club, 11 take History & Appreciation of Art. *Sport*: Rugby, cricket, hockey, rowing, judo, swimming, fencing, squash, badminton, netball, cross-country, athletics, golf and tennis available. 270 take non-compulsory sport. Pupils have represented county and country in rugby and hockey. Others have judo belts (testing and awards). *Other*: 86 take part in local community schemes. Junior school only take bronze and silver Duke of Edinburgh's Award; 30 have gold. A few enter voluntary schemes after leaving school. Other activities include a computer club, very lively chess club (won first 3 Ulster School Leagues last year, 4th in Times British Schools Tournament 1986), driving lessons, over 60 clubs and societies.

Careers 6 part time advisors. Average number of pupils accepted for *arts and humanities degree courses* at Oxbridge, 8; other universities, 65; polytechnics or CHE, 13. *science and engineering degree courses* at Oxbridge, 9; other universities, 72; medical schools, 15; polytechnics or CHE, 12. *BEd*, 4. *other general training courses*, 20. Average number of pupils going straight into careers in armed services, 2; the church (indirectly after primary degree); a few into industry via YTP; the City, 5; civil service, 4; music/drama, 1 or 2 direct, several to music/drama schools. Careers in medicine, law, accountancy and engineering are well represented.

Uniform School uniform worn throughout.

Houses/prefects Competitive houses. Prefects, head boy and girl, head of house and house prefects – appointed by the Head in consultation with staff. Sixth form Council.

Religion Sunday evening service compulsory for boarders (in school chapel); brief act of worship at morning assemblies for all pupils.

Social Community relations co-ordinator for work in sixth forms is based in school; current affairs, debates, public speaking, Christian Union, chess and sports generally. Pupils allowed to bring own car/bike/motorbike to school. Meals self service. Small school tuck shops. No tobacco/alcohol allowed.

Discipline No corporal punishment. Pupils failing to produce homework once might expect reprimand; those caught smoking cannabis on the premises might expect at least suspension.

Boarding 40 girls, 36 boys have own study bedroom; 24 girls and 10 boys share with 1 or 2 others; 22 girls and 74 boys in dormitories of 6 or more. Houses, of approximately 11–30 are divided by age and are single-sex. Resident qualified medical staff. Central dining room. Pupils can provide and cook their own food (senior girls at supper, boys in specified rooms). 2 weekend exeats each term. Visits to local town allowed.

Alumni association Old Boys' Association, Mr Tom Hamilton, 6 Beverley

Rise, Newtownards, Northern Ireland. Old Girls' Association: Mrs Pat Arneill, 73 Skyline Avenue, Lambeg, Lisburn, Northern Ireland.

Former pupils Barry Douglas (winner of Tchaikovsky Piano Competition); James Ellis (Actor); Dr Robin Eames (Present Primate of all Ireland); George Hamilton (Sports Commentator); Jack Siggins (British Lions Manager); Roger Young (British Lion).

MICHAEL HALL

Michael Hall Rudolf Steiner School	● Co-ed	Pupils 300
Kidbrooke Park	Boys	Upper sixth 25
Forest Row	Girls	Termly fees:
East Sussex RH18 5JB	Mixed sixth	Day £750
Telephone number 034282 2275	● Day	Boarding £1650
Enquiries/application to the Secretary	● Boarding	Steiner Schools
for Admissions		

WHAT IT'S LIKE

Founded in 1925, this is the oldest, biggest and most established of the Rudolf Steiner schools in the UK. It has a fine rural site in its own parkland on the edge of Ashdown Forest and a mile from the village centre of Forest Row. It offers a very broad education to boys and girls 4–18, which is based on the educational philosophy and teaching of Steiner. The curriculum embodies cultural studies, foreign languages (for entrants a knowledge of French and/or German is an advantage), sciences, general arts and humanities, crafts, music, movement and dance. Art, music and drama are very important elements in the school life. A remedial dept is a feature. EFL also available. Steiner's fascinating educational theories, philosophy and methods need to be looked at in detail by prospective parents. The teaching is of high standard. A fair range of sports, games and extra-curricular activities is offered.

SCHOOL PROFILE

Pupils Total over 12, 300. Entry age, 6–16, seldom into the sixth form. Own junior department provides more than 20%. 5% are children of former pupils.

Entrance Not oversubscribed. Knowledge of French and/or German an advantage. No particular religious requirements. Parents expected to buy text books. Means-tested bursaries available (after first year of school).

Parents 60+% live within 30 miles; up to 10% live overseas.

Staff Head Chairman of the College of Teachers (changes annually). 44 full time staff, 9 part time. Annual turnover 10%. Average age 36.

Academic work GCSE and A-levels. Average size of upper fifth 60; upper sixth 25. *O-levels*: on average, 50 pupils in upper fifth pass 1–4 subjects; 5 pass 5–7 subjects. *A-levels*: on average 8 pupils in the upper sixth pass 1 subject; 5, 2 subjects; 3 pass 3 subjects. On average, 3 take science/engineering A-levels; 10 take arts and humanities; 2 take a mixture. Ceramics are offered to GCSE/A-level. *Computing facilities*: 5 BBC Masters (with disc and monitor) and 1 dot matrix printer. Also administration computers. Remedial provision for mildly visually handicapped and dyslexia. Also EFL.

Senior pupils' non-academic activities *Music*: 25 learn a musical instrument, 1 accepted for Music school, 2 go on to play in pop group; 25 in school orchestra, 30 in school choir. *Drama and dance*: 40 in school productions. 1 accepted for Drama/Dance school. *Art*: 120 take as non-examined subject; 35 take GCSE; 10, A-level. 1 accepted for Art School. *Sport*: Hockey, cricket, tennis, swimming, basketball, archery, sailing, rock climbing and athletics available. 25 take non-compulsory sport. Other activities include a computer club and a very lively drama section.

Careers 1 part time advisor. Average number of pupils accepted for *arts and humanities degree courses* at Oxbridge, 1; other universities, 4; polytechnics or CHE, 2. *science and engineering degree courses* at universities, 2. *other general training courses*, 4. Average number of pupils going straight into careers in the armed services, 1.

Uniform School uniform not worn.

Houses/prefects No competitive houses. No prefects, or head boy/girl.

Religion Non-denominational Sunday service in school is encouraged.

Social Some musical productions with other local schools. Art history trip to Italy, and spasmodic exchanges with sister schools on the continent. Pupils allowed to bring own bike/motorbike to school. Meals in hostel formal, self service at lunch. School shop sells second-hand clothing only. No tobacco/alcohol allowed.

Discipline No corporal punishment.

Boarding One hostel of 30 pupils, very few have own study bedroom; rooms are shared with a few others. No resident qualified medical staff. Exeats by arrangement. Visits to local town allowed.

Alumni association is run by Dr David Cram, c/o Michael Hall.

Former pupils Martyn Boysens (mountaineer); Oliver Tobias (actor).

MICKLEFIELD

Micklefield School	Co-ed	Pupils 129
Sutton Avenue	Boys	Upper sixth 15
Seaford	● Girls	Termly fees:
East Sussex BN25 4LP	Mixed sixth	Day £1030
Telephone number 0323 892457	● Day	Boarding £1820
Enquiries/application to the Headmaster	● Boarding	GSA; GBGSA

WHAT IT'S LIKE

Founded in 1910 at Reigate it moved to its present site between Newhaven and Eastbourne in 1920. The pleasant modern buildings lie in 7 acres of gardens and playing fields in a residential area of the small seaside town. The boarding houses are in the same road within a few minutes' walk of each other. A large number of developments in the last 15 years have provided excellent modern facilities. A good general education is given in a happy and stimulating environment and the school has all the advantages of being a small establishment (staff:pupil ratio of 1:12). Results are creditable. Each year a few pupils go on to a university. There are strong music, drama and art departments and a satisfactory range of sports, games and extra-curricular activities.

SCHOOL PROFILE

Pupils Total over 12, 129. Day 37, Boarding 92. Entry age, 4–6, 11 and into the sixth. Own junior school provides over 20%.

Entrance School's own assessments sometimes used. Not oversubscribed. No special religious requirements. Skills in music, drama, sports and creative arts looked for. Parents not expected to buy text books. 2 major, 2 minor scholarships, ⅔ fees to ⅓ fees. Bursaries for service children.

Parents 15+% in the armed services. 30+% live within 30 miles; 10+% live overseas.

Staff Head Mr Eric Reynolds, in post for 1 year. 20 full time staff, 14 part time. Annual turnover 10–15%. Average age 43.

Academic work GCSE and A-levels. Average size of upper fifth 30; upper sixth 15. *Computing facilities*: 1 computer laboratory, 6 Apples, 1 BBC. Provision for dyslexia and EFL.

Senior pupils' non-academic activities *Music*: 30 learn a musical instrument, 4 to Grade 6 or above; 10 in school orchestra, 25 in school choir. *Drama and dance*: 60 in school productions. 2 take grade 6 in ESB, RAD etc. *Art*: 5 take as non-examined subject; 20 take GCSE; 5 take A-level. 3 accepted for Art School. 10 belong to eg photographic club. *Sport*: Lacrosse, netball, volleyball, badminton, swimming, tennis, athletics, gymnastics, trampolining and self-defence available. 50 take non-compulsory sport. 40 take exams. Other activities include a computer club, guides, pottery and ballet.

Careers 1 full time advisor. Average number of pupils accepted for *arts and humanities degree courses* at universities, 2; polytechnics or CHE, 5. *science and engineering degree courses* at universities, 2. *BEd*, 2. *other general training courses*, 6.

Uniform School uniform worn except the sixth.

Houses/prefects Competitive houses. Prefects – elected by school; head girl – appointed by Head; head of house and house prefects. School Council.

Religion Morning Assembly. Regular Sunday services.

Social No organised local events. Annual trip abroad organised. Meals self service. School shop. No alcohol allowed. Smoking room for sixth formers.

Discipline No corporal punishment. Pupils failing to produce homework once might expect detention; those caught smoking cannabis on the premises might expect expulsion.

Boarding 20% have their own study bedroom, 10% share with one other; 12% in dormitories of 6+. Pupils divided into houses, approx 20–30, by age. Resident nurse. Central dining room. Pupils occasionally allowed to provide and cook own food. 2 weekend exeats per term. Visits to local town allowed.

Alumni association is run by Mrs A Golledge, 54 St Crispians, Claremont Road, Seaford, East Sussex.

MILLFIELD

Millfield School
Street
Somerset BA16 0YD
Telephone number 0458 42291

Enquiries/application to P H Vaughan,
tutor for admissions

- Co-ed
  Boys
  Girls
  Mixed sixth
- Day
- Boarding

Pupils 1235
Upper sixth 220
Termly fees:
Day £1010
Boarding £2455
GBA; IAPS

WHAT IT'S LIKE

Founded in 1935 by R J O Meyer, it has a fine campus of 67 acres, plus 97 acres of playing fields, with 30 boarding houses in the village of Street and in surrounding villages, in beautiful countryside. The junior school is in nearby Glastonbury. In 1984 the convent school in Glastonbury was acquired in order to create a pre-prep school. Large, diverse and complex, Millfield is an extremely well run school which enjoys a very high staff:pupil ratio (about 1:7), and this is one of its many strengths. Since 1970 a massive building programme has provided facilities which are second to none in Britain. It caters for virtually every need and displays energy, organisation and purposefulness in every activity. Academically outstanding, it sends 100–120 pupils to university each year. Over 40 sports and games are available and the school has excelled in these. In the last 20 years well over 200 pupils have gained international selection in 19 different sports. In the period 1960–84 it produced 12 Olympic competitors. Turns itself into an activity holiday centre during the summer.

SCHOOL PROFILE

Pupils Total, 1235. Day 275 (boys 170, girls 105); Boarding 960 (boys 625, girls 335). Entry age, 13+ and into the sixth. Own junior school provides one third of pupils. Under 5% are children of former pupils.

Entrance Common entrance and own entrance exam used. Oversubscribed. Good all-round academic and sporting abilities looked for. No special religious requirements. Parents not expected to buy text books. No assisted places. 160+ scholarships/bursaries, 5% of fees to 80%.

Parents 15+% are doctors, lawyers, etc; 15+% in industry or commerce. 60+% live within 30 miles; 10+% live overseas.

Staff Head B Gaskell, in post for 2 years; Principal, C R M Atkinson. 170 full time staff. Annual turnover 11%. Average age 30–35.

Academic work GCSE, A-levels, FCE and JMB. RSA exams (typewriting, shorthand and word processing). Average size of upper fifth 239; upper sixth 220. *O-levels*: on average, 80 pupils in upper fifth pass 1–4 subjects; 68, 5–7 subjects; 80 pass 8+ subjects. *A-levels*: on average, 29 pupils in upper sixth pass 1 subject; 34, 2 subjects; 123, 3 subjects; 20 pass 4 subjects. On average, 65 take science/engineering A-levels; 80 take arts and humanities; 75 a mixture. Turkish, Chinese, Malay (GCSE, A); Urdu, Astronomy (GCSE); and Philosophy (A) are offered. *Computing facilities*: Computer Science – 1 class set of 16 Amstrad PC1512, 16 BBC Masters, Word Processing: 1 set of 12. Amstrad pcw 9512 and computers in each of several academic depts, mainly BBC B. Special remedial English department; EFL provisions.

Senior pupils' non-academic activities *Music*: 286 learn a musical instrument, 64 up to Grade 6 or above, 2 accepted for Music School; 80 in school orchestra, 70 in school choir, 80 in chamber groups; 2 in National Youth Orchestra, 5 in county orchestra. *Drama and dance*: Annual plays and French play; new Dance Studio in constant use for all forms of dance; theatre seating 300. *Art*: 200 take as non-examined subject; 60 take GCSE; 30 take A-level. 8 accepted for Art School, 2 for Architecture. 20 in art society, 80+ in Millfield Activities Programme. *Sport*: Over 40 sports available. 500 take non-compulsory sport. 20 take exams. 60+ represent country/county at a variety of sports. *Other*: 96 have bronze Duke of Edinburgh's Award, 20 have silver and 14 have gold. Other activities include a computer club, debating club, driving lessons, a chess club (competitive) and many varied activities.

Careers 8 part time advisors plus 7 part time higher education advisors. Average number of pupils accepted for *arts and humanities degree courses* at Oxbridge, 9; other universities, 45; polytechnics or CHE, 14. *science and engineering degree courses* at Oxbridge, 13; other universities, 36; medical schools, 7; polytechnics or CHE, 3. *BEd*, 4. *other general training courses*, 40. Average number of pupils going straight into careers in the armed services, 2; the church, 1.

Uniform No school uniform.

Houses/prefects Competitive houses. Prefects, head boy/girl, head of house and house prefects – appointed by prefect committee and staff. School Council.

Religion Worship is compulsory on special occasions eg carol service, start of term multi-faith service plus regular services for Catholics, Jews, Muslims etc.

Social No organised local events. German/French exchange, games tours, (Germany/France/Hong Kong/Barbados – cricket). Cultural tour to Russia in 1987. Pupils allowed to bring own bike/horse to school. Meals self service. School shop. No tobacco/alcohol allowed.

Discipline No corporal punishment. Pupils failing to produce homework once might expect a warning and a deadline; those caught smoking cannabis on the premises can expect immediate expulsion.

Boarding Few seniors have own study bedroom, other seniors share; juniors in dormitories of 6+. Houses, 10–50 (most small), same as competitive houses and single-sex. Resident qualified nurse. Central dining room. Pupils can provide and cook their own food. 3 weekend exeats each term. Visits to the local town allowed.

Alumni association is run by Mr E J C Bromfield, The Millfield Society, c/o School.

Former pupils Sir John L Standing (stage and screen actor); John Sergeant (BBC parliamentary news correspondent); Charles Burton (explorer: circumnavigated world via North and South Poles); Gareth Edwards (international rugby); Duncan Goodhew and Mary Rand (Olympic Gold Medallists).

MILL HILL

Mill Hill School
The Ridgeway
London NW7 1QS
Telephone number 01-959 1176

Enquiries/application to the Headmaster

- Co-ed
- Boys
- Girls
- Mixed sixth
- Day
- Boarding

Pupils 539
Upper sixth 110
Termly fees:
Day £1425
Boarding £2160

WHAT IT'S LIKE

Founded in 1807 by a group of non-conformist Christian ministers and City merchants. In 1827 it moved to the buildings which form the central part of the main school. These, palatial, neo-classical, magnificently designed within and without, lie in 120 acres of wooded parkland in the green belt 10 miles from the middle of London. There has been much development in recent years and facilities and accommodation are first-class. Belmont, the junior school, is a few hundred yards away. A well-run school with long-established high standards, it regards hard work, self-criticism, enthusiasm and loyalty as paramount virtues. Christian services are compulsory for all. Academic results are good (50-plus university entrants per year). Strong in music, drama and art. Very broad range of games and sports (the standards are high). Substantial commitment to local community schemes. Appreciable success in the Duke of Edinburgh's Award Scheme.

SCHOOL PROFILE

Pupils Total, 539. Day 256 (boys 248, girls 8); Boarding 283 (boys 245, girls 38). Entry age, boys 13; boys and girls into the sixth. Belmont (Mill Hill Junior School) provides about 40%. 10% are children of former pupils.

Entrance Common entrance and own entrance exam used. Oversubscribed (not for boarding). No special skills or religious requirements but all are expected to attend Christian services. Parents not expected to buy text books. 10 assisted places pa. 10 scholarships/bursaries, musical and academic, up to half fees. 15% fees reduction for service children.

Parents 15+% in industry or commerce. 50% live within 30 miles; 10+% live overseas.

Staff Head Mr A C Graham, in post for 8 years. 53 full time staff, 15 part time. Annual turnover 2–4%. Average age 35.

Academic work GCSE and A-levels. Average size of upper fifth 105; upper sixth 110. *O-levels*: on average, 8 pupils in upper fifth pass 1–4 subjects; 43, 5–7 subjects; 54 pass 8+ subjects. *A-levels*: on average, 6 pupils in the upper sixth pass 1 subject; 12, 2 subjects; 78, 3 subjects; 14 pass 4 subjects. On average, 40 take science/engineering A-levels; 40 take arts and humanities; 30, a mixture. History-in-French is offered to GCSE. *Computing facilities*: 20 Archimedes Micro computers on filestore network, 30 BBC Micros, Domesday system. Private English lessons available outside the normal curriculum.

Senior pupils' non-academic activities *Music*: 85 learn a musical instrument, 30 up to Grade 6 or above; 40 in school orchestra, 60 in school choir, 20 in school jazz band. *Drama and dance*: 50 in school productions, large numbers in house plays. *Art*: 35 take as non-examined subject; 12 take GCSE; 6 take A-level. 1 or 2 accepted for Art School. 20 in art society. CDT started 1988. *Sport*: Rugby, cricket, hockey, squash, Eton fives, tennis, badminton, basketball, netball, swimming, shooting, fencing, athletics, cross-country, golf, sailing, karate and horse-riding available. 200 take non-compulsory sport. 10 take exams in eg swimming, 10 represent county (rugby, cricket). *Other*: 30 take part in local community schemes. 20 have silver Duke of Edinburgh's Award. Other activities include: an informal computer club in the computer room, CCF (Army and Navy), chess club (usually wins every competition in Barnet) and driving lessons.

Careers 8 part time advisors. Average number of pupils accepted for *arts and humanities degree courses* at Oxbridge, 5; other universities, 22; polytechnics or CHE, 10. *science and engineering degree courses* at Oxbridge, 5; other universities, 18; medical schools, 5; polytechnics or CHE, 8. *BEd*, 1. *other general training courses*, 2. Average number of pupils going straight into careers in armed services, 1; industry, 3; the City, 5; music/drama, 2; other, 23 (includes those taking year off).

Uniform School uniform worn, modified in sixth.

Houses/prefects Competitive houses. Prefects, head boy/girl, head of house and house prefects – appointed by the Head, advice accepted from upper sixth. School Council.

Religion Christian chapel compulsory for all (about 3 times per week).

Social Choir sometimes borrows girls from local school. Two exchanges with France, one with Germany; involves about 50 boys per year. Pupils allowed to bring own car/bike to school. Meals self service. School shop. No tobacco allowed. Alcohol on occasion.

Discipline Rare corporal punishment (by housemasters). Pupils failing to produce homework once might expect a warning; those caught smoking cannabis on the premises might expect expulsion.

Boarding All upper sixth have own study bedroom, most lower sixth and fifth forms share with one other; most juniors are in dormitories of 6+. Houses, of approximately 60, same as competitive houses; 1 girls only, 2, boys only and 3, mixed. Resident SRN, Doctor visits daily. Central dining room. Pupils can provide and cook own snacks. Exeats most weekends. Visits to local town allowed.

Alumni association is run by Mrs Janet Scott, c/o School.

Former pupils Dennis Thatcher; Francis Crick (Nobel prize – structure of DNA).

MILTON ABBEY

Milton Abbey School
Blandford
Dorset DT11 0BZ
Telephone number 0258 880484

Enquiries/application to the Headmaster

Co-ed   Pupils 285
● Boys   Upper sixth 54
Girls   Termly fees:
Mixed sixth   Boarding £2290
Day   SHMIS
● Boarding

WHAT IT'S LIKE

Founded in 1954, it has an exceptionally beautiful site (one that has been settled for at least 1000 years) in a large area of parkland near Blandford and the sea. The main building is a very large 18th-century country house which incorporates some of the buildings of the original Benedictine monastery and abbey of the middle ages. The magnificent medieval abbey church is the outstanding architectural feature. The main block of the school has a fine quadrangle. There are many modern additions and extensions and the accommodation and facilities are first rate. It is a C of E school with its own chaplain and the abbey church is the co-ordinating focus of the life of the community and a considerable influence on it. Worship and religious instruction are an important part of the general curriculum. Self-discipline, courtesy, self-respect and a sense of responsibility are deemed to be of prime importance in a pupil's development. A sound general education is provided and results are good. Drama is very strong; music and art flourish. Natural history has a particularly keen following. The CCF is very strong and there are close links with service units in the region. A good range of sports and games and outdoor pursuits (these include a lot of sailing). The school's local community services are lively and well-organised.

SCHOOL PROFILE

Pupils Total, 285. Entry age, 13 and into the sixth.

Entrance Common entrance exam used. Not oversubscribed. No special skills or religious requirements. Parents expected to buy text books. 8 scholarships/bursaries pa, 75–25% of fees.

Parents 10+% live within 30 miles; up to 10% live overseas.

Staff Head R H Hardy, 1 year. 32 full time staff, 9 part time. Annual turnover 3%. Average age 41.

Academic work GCSE and A-levels. Average size of upper fifth 58; upper sixth 54. *O-levels*: on average, 25 pupils in upper fifth pass 1–4 subjects; 23, 5–7 subjects; 10 pass 8+ subjects. *A-levels*: on average, 15 pupils in upper sixth pass 1 subject; 8, 2 subjects; 6, 3 subjects and 2 pass 4 subjects. On average, 27 take science/engineering A-levels; 51 take arts and humanities; 21 a mixture. *Computing facilities*: 5 BBC Bs, 1 380Z (fitted with 40/80 disc drive and inter-word inter-sheet, 2 dot matrix and 1 daisywheel printer). New computer block 1988/89. *Special provisions*: extra English and maths; also EFL for JMB test.

Senior pupils' non-academic activities *Music*: 40 learn a musical instrument, 1 to Grade 6 or above. 24 in school choir, 8 in school pop group, 6 in chamber group, 10 in theatre orchestras; 3 play in pop group and 2 go on to writing and composing after leaving. *Drama and dance*: 150 in school productions, house plays, etc; dance and drama classes but not exams. 1 accepted for Drama/Dance Schools, 1 goes on to work in theatre. *Art*: 10 take GCSE; 4, A-level; 2, A-level photography. 3–6 accepted for Art School. 15 belong to photographic, 10 to pottery, and 15+ to art clubs. *Sport*: Rugby, hockey, cricket, athletics, cross-country, sailing, canoeing, golf, tennis, shooting, swimming, fencing, basketball available. 80 take non-compulsory sport, some games or sport is compulsory. 16 pupils represent county (rugby, hockey, cross-country, athletics, cricket). *Other*: 12 take part in local community schemes. 82 taking silver Duke of Edinburgh's Award, and 2 have gold. 2 enter voluntary schemes after leaving school. 141 go on annual sponsored walk. Other activities include a computer club, strong CCF; natural history society. Many clubs. Adventure training.

Careers 2 part time advisors. Average number of pupils accepted for *arts and humanities degree courses* at universities, 4; polytechnics or CHE, 5. *science and engineering degree courses* at universities, 3; polytechnics or CHE, 2. *other general training courses*, 15. Average number of pupils going straight into careers in the armed services, 7; the church, 1; industry, 3; the City, 12; music/drama, 1; other, 8. Traditional school careers, the armed forces, agriculture.

Uniform School uniform worn throughout.

Houses/prefects Competitive houses. Prefects, head boy, head of house and house prefects – appointed by the Head.

Religion Religious worship compulsory.

Social Theatrical productions with other local schools. Modern languages trips abroad, Himalayan adventures. Prefects allowed to bring own cars, others own bike, to school. Meals self service. School shop. No tobacco allowed; alcohol allowed in sixth form club.

Discipline No corporal punishment. Pupils failing to produce homework once might expect warning and repeat work; those caught smoking cannabis on the premises could expect suspension.

Boarding 22% have own study bedroom, 50% share with up to 3 others; 18% are in dormitories of 6+. Houses, of approximately 55, same as competitive houses. Resident qualified nurse. Central dining room. 2 weekend exeats per term plus half term. Visits to local town allowed at weekends.

Alumni association run by A P Nicholson, c/o the School.

Former pupils Alastair Boyd (who parachuted off the Empire State Building).

Moira House

Moira House School	Co-ed	Pupils 280
Upper Carlisle Road	Boys	Upper sixth 40
Eastbourne	● Girls	Termly fees:
East Sussex BN20 7TD	Mixed sixth	Day £1300
Telephone number 0323 644144	● Day	Boarding £2000
Enquiries/application to the Headmaster	● Boarding	GSA

WHAT IT'S LIKE

Founded in 1875 and established on its present site in 1887. It is near Beachy Head with grounds and gardens opening on to the Downs. The buildings are well designed and comfortable and provide good accommodation and facilities. Religious education and worship are compulsory. Academic standards are high and results are good (40 university entrants per year, a high proportion for a school of this size). It enjoys a high staff:pupil ratio and has an unusual number of part-time staff. The music and drama depts are flourishing and the school particularly prides itself on its very strong careers counselling service. Good sports and games, plus an enormous range of activities. Some commitment to local community schemes.

SCHOOL PROFILE

Pupils Total over 12, 280. Day 100; Boarding 180. Entry age, 5, 11, 13 and into the sixth. Own junior school provides more than 50%. 10% are children of former pupils.

Entrance Admission by common entrance and own entrance exam. Oversubscribed. No special skills or religious requirements. Parents not expected to buy text books. No assisted places yet. 10 scholarships/bursaries per year, 75%–50% of fees.

Parents 60+% live within 30 miles; 30+% live overseas.

Staff Head Adrian Underwood, in post for 13 years. 37 full time staff, 34 part time. Annual turnover 7%. Average age 30.

Academic work GCSE and A-levels. Average size of upper fifth 50; upper sixth 40. *O-levels*: on average, 10 pupils in upper fifth pass 1–4 subjects; 20, 5–7 subjects; 20 pass 8+ subjects. *A-levels*: on average, 5 pupils in the upper sixth pass 1 subject; 5, 2 subjects; 30 pass 3 subjects. On average, 20 take science/engineering A-levels; 20 take arts and humanities. *Computing facilities*: computer centre. Provision for dyslexia; EFL.

Senior pupils' non-academic activities *Music*: 40 learn a musical instrument, 10 up to Grade 6 or above. 1 accepted for Music School; 30 in school orchestra, 40 in choir. *Drama and dance*: 80 in school productions. 10 to Grade 6 in ESB, RAD etc. 2 accepted for Drama/Dance schools. *Art*: 2 take as non-examined subject; 15 take GCSE; 10, A-level. 2 accepted for Art School. 5 belong to photographic club. *Sport*: Hockey, netball, swimming, tennis, squash, badminton, riding, sailing, windsurfing, ski-ing, judo, dance, table tennis, aerobics, cricket and golf available. 130 take non-compulsory sport. 100 take exams. 11 represent county (hockey), 1, country (triathlon). *Other*: 30 take part in local community schemes. 10 have bronze Duke of Edinburgh's Award, 5 have silver. 20 enter voluntary schemes after leaving school. 10 work for national charities. Other activities include a computer club, debate and public speaking, pottery, electronics, community service, and driving lessons.

Careers 1 full time advisor. Average number of pupils accepted for *arts and humanities degree courses* at Oxbridge, 2; other universities, 7; polytechnics or CHE, 3. *science engineering degree courses* at universities, 7; medical schools, 2; polytechnics or CHE, 3. *BEd*, 1. *other general training courses*, 10.

Uniform School uniform worn except the sixth.

Houses/prefects Competitive houses. Prefects, 2 head girls, House Councils – elected by girls and staff.

Religion Morning prayers and Sunday church compulsory; confirmation, Christian Union.

Social Public speaking, Eastbourne Festival of Music and Arts with other local schools. Organised trips abroad. Pupils allowed to bring own car/bike to school. Some meals formal, some self service. School shop. No tobacco/alcohol allowed.

Discipline No corporal punishment. Pupils failing to produce homework once will repeat their work; those caught smoking cannabis on the premises will be expelled.

Boarding 50% have own study bedroom, 50% share with others. Houses, of approximately 55, are divided by age. Resident SRN. Central dining room. Sixth form pupils can provide and cook their own food. 2 weekend and half-term exeats. Visits to local town allowed at weekends.

Former pupils Rumer Godden (novelist); Prunella Scales (actress); Joy Finzi (artist).

MONKTON COMBE

Monkton Combe School		Co-ed	Pupils 332
Monkton Combe		• Boys	Upper sixth 80
Bath		Girls	Termly fees:
Avon BA2 7HG		• Mixed sixth	Day £1675
Telephone number 022 122 3523		• Day	Boarding £2295
		• Boarding	HMC
Enquiries/application to the Headmaster			

WHAT IT'S LIKE

Founded in 1868, it lies in a very pretty village 2 miles from Bath and overlooking the Avon valley. There are most attractive buildings in Cotswold stone, and there have been many modern extensions which are very well equipped. Delightful playing fields adjoin the school. Considerable emphasis on Christian teaching and worship. Academic standards are high and results are good. There is a staff:pupil ratio of 1:10. Some 50 pupils go on to degree courses each year; a high proportion for a school of this size. Very strong in music, drama and art. A most impressive record in sports and games (a large number of representatives at county level). The CCF contingent is large and active. There are numerous clubs and societies. Creditable commitment to local community services.

SCHOOL PROFILE

Pupils Total over 12, 332. Day 44 (boys 40, girls 4); Boarding 288 (boys 250, girls 38). Entry age, boys, 13; boys and girls, into the sixth. Own junior school provides over 20%. 7% are children of former pupils.

Entrance Common entrance and own entrance exam used. Ability to contribute to the school community looked for at entry; no religious requirements but must be willing to attend Chapel. Parents expected to buy text books which can be sold back after use. 10 assisted places pa. 8 scholarships pa, 10–75% fees. 6–8 bursaries pa for children of clergy and missionaries, up to third fees.

Parents 15+% in the armed services. 10+% live within 30 miles; 10+% live overseas.

Staff Head R A C Meredith, in post for 9 years. 35 full time staff, 15 part time. Annual turnover 3%. Average age 38.

Academic work GCSE and A-levels. Average size of upper fifth 60; upper sixth 80. *O-levels*: on average, 7 pupils in upper fifth pass 1–4 subjects; 16, 5–7 subjects; 37 pass 8+ subjects. *A-levels*: on average, 8 pupils in upper sixth pass 1 subject; 18, 2 subjects; 53, 3 subjects; 1 passes 4 subjects. On average, 27 take science/engineering A-levels; 30 take arts and humanities; 22 take a mixture. *Computing facilities*: Computer laboratory of 12 machines, networked to 12 other computers in different departments. Specialist provision for EFL and dyslexia.

Senior pupils' non-academic activities   *Music*: 65 learn a musical instrument, 12 to Grade 6 or above; 26 in school orchestra, 25 in school choir, 10 in school dance band. 5/6 take music beyond school. *Drama and dance*: 60 in school productions. 1 accepted for Drama School. *Art*: 80 take as non-examined subject; 35 take GCSE; 15 take A-level. 6/8 accepted for Art School. 15 belong to eg photographic club. *Sport*: Archery, badminton, basketball, cricket, cross-country running, cycling, hockey, judo, rowing, rugby football, shooting, squash, swimming and tennis available. Pupils have represented county/country (rowing, hockey, judo, tennis, basketball, cricket). *Other*: 24 take part in local community schemes. 10 enter voluntary schemes after leaving school, 2 work for national charities. Other activities include a computer club, chess, CCF, debating (enter local and regional competitions), fishing (in local river and brook), Christian Union and Bible Study groups, war gaming.

Careers 4 part time advisors. Average number of pupils accepted for *arts and humanities degree courses* at Oxbridge, 3; other universities, 15; polytechnics or CHE, 7. *science and engineering degree courses* at Oxbridge, 3; other universities, 14; medical schools, 2; polytechnics or CHE, 6. *BEd*, 2. *other general training courses* eg agricultural, art foundation, 14.

Uniform School uniform worn, modified in the sixth.

Houses/prefects Competitive houses. Prefects, head boy, head of house and house prefects – appointed by the Head or housemaster. All new boys help with general chores.

Religion Religious worship is compulsory and encouraged.

Social Debates with other schools, sponsored Activity Day in support of a local or national charity. Ski-trip abroad each year. Pupils allowed to bring own bike to school. Meals, self service. School shop. No tobacco/alcohol allowed.

Discipline No corporal punishment. Report card system for pupils failing to produce homework. Expulsion for any offence involving drugs.

Boarding 10% have own study bedroom, 15% share with one other; 40% in dormitories of 6+. Houses, of 40–50, same as competitive houses and single-sex. 2 qualified nurses. Central dining room. Pupils can provide and cook own food. Termly exeats, 1 or 2 Saturday nights and half-term. Visits to local town allowed once a week.

Alumni association is run by A G Whitehouse Esq, 85 Hansford Square, Combe Down, Bath.

Former pupils Rt Rev G Leonard (Bishop of London); Rt Rev M A P Wood (former Bishop of Norwich); Richard Stilgoe; Martin Adeney.

MONMOUTH

Monmouth School	Co-ed	Pupils 540
Monmouth	● Boys	Upper sixth 83
Gwent NP5 3XP	Girls	Termly fees:
Telephone number 0600 3143	Mixed sixth	Day £957
	● Day	Boarding £1707
Enquiries/application to the Headmaster	● Boarding	HMC

WHAT IT'S LIKE

Founded in 1614, single-site on the edge of the town by the Wye; a very fine position. The present buildings, in the collegiate style, date from 1865 when the 17th-century school was demolished. There has been much modernisation in the last twenty years. A C of E foundation it follows the rites of the Church in Wales. A distinguished and well-run school, with a high reputation locally and further afield, it provides excellent facilities and a first-rate education on terms that few comparable schools can match. Closely integrated with the town (itself a most attractive place) there is a strong local flavour with half the pupils coming from Monmouth itself or the neighbouring villages. This close relationship between 'town and gown' has created considerable local pride in the school and has enabled many musical and sporting collaborations to flourish. Academic results are first-class, with 50–60 university entrants per year. Strong in music, drama and art. Also very strong in sports and games (especially rugby); a large number of county and international representatives. Notable emphasis on extra-curricular activities of which there is a wide range. Remarkable record in the Duke of Edinburgh's Award Scheme.

SCHOOL PROFILE

Pupils Total over 11, 540. Day 340; Boarding 200. Entry age, 11, 13 and into the sixth.

Entrance Common entrance and own entrance exam used. Oversubscribed. Good academic standard and good all-round contributors, especially in music and sport. No religious barriers. Parents not expected to buy text books. 28 assisted places pa. Scholarships/bursaries, up to 75% fees.

Parents 30+% live within 30 miles; up to 10% live overseas.

Staff Head R D Lane, in post for 6 years. 51 full time staff, 5 part time. Annual turnover 7%. Average age 40+.

Academic work GCSE and A-levels. Average size of upper fifth 84; upper sixth 83. *O-levels*: on average, 90% pupils in upper fifth pass 8+ subjects. *A-levels*: on average, 91% pupils in the upper sixth pass 3 subjects. On average, 33 take science/engineering A-levels; 35 take arts and humanities; 15 a mixture. Russian is offered to GCSE/A-level. *Computing facilities*: Computer room with 24 IBM pcs and graphics; 12 BBC and 2 Archimedes in departments.

Senior pupils' non-academic activities *Music*: 200 learn a musical instrument, 20 to Grade 6, 10 to Grade 8, a number of pupils accepted for Music School; 50 in school orchestra; 100 in choir; numerous pop groups; 50 in concert band. *Drama and dance*: 25 participate in school productions; 100 in other. 3 take exams in drama and dance. *Art*: 10 take art as non-examined subject; 70 take GCSE; 18, A-level; 6 A-level art history; 3 subsidiary art; 4 accepted for Art School; 3 for architecture courses and art history degree courses. *Sport*: Rugby, rowing, cricket, shooting, swimming, squash, badminton, sub-aqua, cross-country, orienteering, sailing, fishing, canoeing, athletics, tennis, golf, ski-ing and croquet available. 150 take non-compulsory sport. 30 take exams eg gymnastics, swimming. 27 represent county/country (rugby, rowing, swimming, tetrathlon, badminton, squash, cross-country, cricket). *Other*: 10 take part in local community schemes. 45 have gold Duke of Edinburgh's Award. 200 involved in fund raising for charity. Other activities include a computer club, photography, radio satellite club, Christian Fellowship, drama workshop, horse riding, modelling, junior debating, chess, bridge, electronics, stage craft, art club, astronomy, stamp club.

Careers 4 part time advisors. Average number of pupils accepted for *arts and humanities degree courses* at Oxbridge, 5; other universities, 24; polytechnics or CHE, 8. *science and engineering degree courses* at Oxbridge, 5; other universities, 20; medical schools, 4; polytechnics or CHE, 8. *other general training courses*, 1. Average number of pupils going straight into careers in the armed services, 4; the church, 1; industry, 2; other, 2.

Uniform School uniform worn throughout.

Houses/prefects Competitive houses. Prefects, head boy, head of house and house prefects – appointed by the Headmaster or Housemaster.

Religion Religious worship encouraged.

Social Plays, concerts, Challenge of Industry Conference with local schools. Organised exchanges with both French and Spanish schools. Pupils allowed to bring own bike to school, and car with parental consent. Meals self service. School shop. No tobacco/alcohol allowed.

Discipline No corporal punishment. Pupils failing to produce homework once might expect to have to explain why; those caught smoking cannabis on the premises could expect expulsion.

Boarding All sixth form share study bedroom (2), 33% are in dormitories of 6+. Houses, of approximately 45, divided by age group. Resident qualified nurse. Central dining room. Pupils can provide and cook their own food. 2 weekend exeats each term. Visits to the local town allowed.

Alumni association is run by H C Toulouse, 3 Monkswell Close, Monmouth, Gwent NP5 3PH.

Former pupils Lord Ezra of Horsham (former Chairman NCB); Lord Brecon; A M Jorden and E T Butler (rugby internationals); F J Davies (managing director, Rockware); R J Herd (engineer, racing car designer); G M J Worsnip (TV presenter); V G A Spinetti (actor); M W Barnes, QC; Hon C B Moynihan (Minister for Sport); David Broome (showjumper).

MORETON HALL

Moreton Hall	Co-ed	Pupils 300
Weston Rhyn	Boys	Upper sixth 50
Oswestry	● Girls	Termly fees:
Shropshire SY11 3EW	Mixed sixth	Day £1425
Telephone number 0691 773671	● Day	Boarding £2150
Enquiries/application to the Principal	● Boarding	GSA; GBGSA

WHAT IT'S LIKE

Founded in 1913 it occupies an attractive rural site. The campus is a village-like community in 78 acres of splendid grounds and gardens and the buildings are a mixture of the modern and the venerable. Extremely well equipped with modern facilities. The school looks for all-round ability and a happy purposeful atmosphere prevails. It is neither consciously progressive nor traditional in its approach. It is not academically exclusive but all girls are expected to be able to make a positive contribution to their own growth and that of the school. It is therefore a balanced community where each pupil feels valued and where growth in self-confidence develops naturally. All pupils are actively and sympathetically encouraged to achieve their best. The teaching is good (a high staff:pupil ratio of 1:9) and results are creditable (15–20 university entrants per year). The school prides itself on its careers dept which is a leader among girls' schools. Strong music and drama depts. A good range of sports and games (high standards) and a wide range of activities. 'Moreton Enterprises' gives girls in the lower sixth opportunities to learn business and entrepreneurial skills.

SCHOOL PROFILE

Pupils Total over 12, 300. Day 20; Boarding 280. Entry age, 11, 12, 13 and into the sixth. 3% are children of former pupils.

Entrance Own entrance exam used. Oversubscribed. All-round abilities looked for. No particular religious requirements. Parents not expected to buy text books. No assisted places. 4 scholarships (academic and music) for half fees. Bursaries for clergy and school teachers' children.

Parents 15+% in industry or commerce. 30+% live within 50 miles; 10+% live overseas (expatriates).

Staff Head E J Cussell, in post for 12 years. 38 full time staff, 21 part time. Annual turnover 5%. Average age 38.

Academic work GCSE and A-levels. Average size of upper fifth 55; upper sixth 50. *O-levels*: on average, 15 pupils in upper fifth pass 1–4 subjects; 20, 5–7 subjects; 20 pass 8+ subjects. *A-levels*: on average, 9 pupils in upper sixth pass 1 subject; 15, 2 subjects; 20, 3 subjects; 4 pass 4 subjects. On average, 10 take science/engineering A-levels; 25 take arts and humanities; 15 a mixture. Fashion and ceramics are offered to GCSE/A-level. *Computing facilities*: a computing centre with eight stations; computers used extensively throughout the school. Some provision made for girls who are of above average intelligence but have a specific learning difficulty.

Senior pupils' non-academic activities *Music*: 162 learn a musical instrument, 29 to Grade 6 or above; 1 accepted for Music School; 40 in school orchestra, 60 in school choir. *Drama and dance*: 100+ in school productions. 6 to Grade 6 in ESB, RAD etc, 56 spoken English (ESB, LAMDA, and festivals). 1 accepted for Drama School, 1 a BBC trainee. *Art*: 4 take as non-examined subject; 30 take GCSE; 24 take A-level. 5 accepted for Art School. 9 take history of art, 3 fashion, 7 ceramics. *Sport*: Lacrosse, hockey, tennis, netball, rounders, athletics, golf, badminton, table-tennis, aerobics, self-defence, gymnastics, dance, sailing and volley-ball available. 12 represent county in lacrosse. 80 take tennis coaching, 20 sail. *Other*: 12 take part in local community schemes. 4 have silver Duke of Edinburgh's Award and 1 has gold. 2–3 each year enter voluntary schemes after leaving school. Most pupils work for national charities. Other activities include Moreton Enterprises, driving, ice skating, self-defence, weaving, wine making plus some 50 others.

Careers 1 full time and 1 part time advisor. Average number of pupils accepted for *arts and humanities degree courses* at Oxbridge, 2; other universities, 10; polytechnics or CHE, 8. *science and engineering degree courses* at universities, 5; medical schools, 1; polytechnics or CHE, 4. *BEd*, 4. *other general training courses*, 7. Average number of pupils going straight into

careers in industry, 3; the City, 1; the civil service, 1; music/drama, 3; BBC, 1.
Uniform School uniform worn except the sixth.
Houses/prefects No competitive houses. Prefects – elected by prefects and staff. Head and second prefects – appointed by the Principal. School Council and sixth form council.
Religion Compulsory daily assembly and Sunday Church in the Anglican tradition. Some relaxation of Sunday requirements for sixth form.
Social Some music and drama with Shrewsbury School. Annual ski-ing, organised visits to Germany and France to stay with families. Pupils allowed to bring own bike to school. Meals self service. School shop. No tobacco/alcohol allowed.
Discipline No corporal punishment. Pupils failing to produce homework at any time would expect an enquiry as to why and be expected to remedy the situation at once; those caught smoking cannabis on the premises might expect expulsion.
Boarding All sixth formers have single or double bedrooms. 6 Houses of 50–55; 2 junior, 3 senior, 1 upper sixth. Resident qualified nurse. Central dining room. Sixth form pupils can provide and cook own snacks. 2–4 weekend exeats each term. Visits to local town allowed, according to age.
Alumni association Secretary is Miss D Gittins, 42 Roman Road, Shrewsbury, Shropshire.
Former pupils: Thea Musgrave (Composer).

MORRISON'S

Morrison's Academy	● Co-ed	Pupils 754
Ferntower Road	Boys	Upper sixth Yes
Crieff	Girls	Termly fees:
Perthshire PH7 3AM	Mixed sixth	Day £680
Telephone number 0764 3885	● Day	Boarding £1780
	● Boarding	HMC; GSA

Enquiries to the Rector
Application to the Director of Admissions

WHAT IT'S LIKE

Founded in 1860, it has a pleasant semi-rural 10-acre site on the lower slopes of the Knock in Crieff. Regular development over the years has produced a fine and well-equipped campus. It became fully co-educational in 1979. The primary school is an integral part of the Academy. A thorough, traditional Scottish education is provided and academic results are very good. Most pupils go on to university each year. Very strong indeed in music, and there are flourishing drama groups. A good range of sports and games (high standards achieved). About 34 clubs and societies cater for most conceivable needs. A vigorous CCF. A lot of emphasis on outdoor pursuits for which the environment is very suitable. A good record in the Duke of Edinburgh's Award Scheme.

SCHOOL PROFILE

Pupils Total over 12,754. Day 584 (boys 289, girls 295); Boarding 170 (boys 79, girls 91). Entry age, 5–12 and into the sixth. Own junior school provides over 20%.

Entrance Own entrance exam used. Oversubscribed for day places. No special skills or religious requirements. Parents not expected to buy text books. 153 assisted places. 6 scholarships/bursaries, up to half fees.

Parents 60+% live within 30 miles; up to 10% live overseas.

Staff Head H Ashmall, in post for 9 years. 68 full time staff, 4 part time. Annual turnover 1%. Average age 41.

Academic work Scottish Standard grade, Highers and A-levels. *Computing facilities*: 2 computer labs; facilities in other departments for computer assisted learning. Provisions for EFL and for pupils who are dyslexic, mildly visually handicapped etc.

Senior pupils' non-academic activities include CCF, chess, climbing, cookery, country dancing, curling, debating, Duke of Edinburgh's Award, electronics, fencing, gaelic, geography, hill walking, model-making, woodwork, orienteering, record, theatre, sailing, science, scripture union, sewing and handcraft, ski-ing and quest.

Careers Traditional school careers are medicine and law.

Uniform School uniform worn throughout.

Houses/prefects Competitive houses. Prefects, head boy and girl, head of house and house prefects.

Religion Morning prayers.

Social Discos and debates with other schools. Organised trips and exchange systems with schools abroad. Lunch self service; others formal. No tobacco/alcohol allowed.

Discipline No corporal punishment.

Boarding Various sleeping arrangements in single-sex accommodation. Central dining room. Seniors can provide and cook own supper. 3 weekend exeats each term. Visits to local town allowed.

Former pupils Sir Andrew McCance; Sir James Henderson Stewart; Dr Gavin Strang; Air-Vice Marshal MacGregor; Dr A R Belch; Dennis Lawson.

MOUNT, THE (YORK)

The Mount School	Co-ed	Pupils 274
Dalton Terrace	Boys	Upper sixth 40
York YO2 4DD	● Girls	Termly fees:
Telephone number 0904 654823	Mixed sixth	Day £1266
Enquiries/application to the Headmistress's secretary	● Day	Boarding £1857
	● Boarding	GSA

WHAT IT'S LIKE

Founded in 1831, it moved to its present site in 1857. A very pleasant compact wooded campus with splendid gardens, mature trees and playing fields. The buildings are a combination of 19th-century architecture and brand new blocks. Facilities are good. A Quaker school, it aims to develop 'the whole person' and to care for everyone as an individual. It aims, also, for academic excellence. It has all the advantages of a small school, with a good staff:pupil ratio and an unusual number of part-time staff. Each year some 15–20 leavers go on to university, others to higher education elsewhere. Very strong in music, drama and art (talent in these is looked for in candidates). Much involvement in local cultural activities and full use is made of the city's amenities. A wide range of sport and games and extra-curricular activities. Big commitment to local community services and an outstanding record in the Duke of Edinburgh's Award Scheme.

SCHOOL PROFILE

Pupils Total over 12, 274. Day 24; Boarding 250. Entry age, 11 and into the sixth. 5% are children of former pupils.

Entrance Own entrance exam used. Oversubscribed. No special skills or religious requirements, but this is a Quaker School. Parents not expected to buy text books. No assisted places yet. 10 scholarships pa for academic, music, art, drama: up to 25% fees. Bursaries: Quakers according to need; limited help to old scholars.

Parents 10+% are doctors, lawyers, etc; 10+% in industry or commerce; 10+% in the armed services, 10+% are farmers. 10+% live within 30 miles; 10+% live overseas.

Staff Head Miss Barbara J Windle, in post for 2 years. 29 full time staff, 41 part time. Annual turnover 5%. Average age 38.

Academic work GCSE, A-levels and S-levels. Average size of upper fifth 45; upper sixth 40. *O-levels*: on average, 4 pupils in upper fifth pass 1–4 subjects; 14, 5–7 subjects; 27 pass 8+ subjects. *A-levels*: on average, 5 pupils in the upper sixth pass 1 subject; 8, 2 subjects; 17, 3 subjects; 11 pass 4 subjects. On average, 15 take science/engineering A-levels; 15 take arts and humanities; 10 take a mixture. Chinese, Arabic, Swahili, Dutch and others are offered on request to GCSE/A-level. *Computing facilities*: Fully equipped room, also 4 blocks of 4 computers and 1 printer, in different subject areas of the school. Provision for dyslexic pupils and for EFL.

Senior pupils' non-academic activities *Music*: 77 learn a musical instrument, 23 up to Grade 6 or above, 3 accepted for Music School; 40 in school orchestra, 40 in school choir, 20 in school pop group; 2 in National Youth Wind Orchestra, 1 a member of Guildhall orchestra, 1 plays in pop group. 1 a concert pianist. *Drama and dance*: 60 in school productions. 6 to Grade 6 in ESB, RAD etc, 20 learn drama as an individual subject. 2 accepted for Drama Schools, 2–4 go on to work in theatre. *Art*: 35 take as non-examined subject; 8 A-level. 4–5 per year accepted for Art School (up to 90% of A-level group). 16 belong to photographic club. *Sport*: Hockey, netball, tennis, badminton, squash, swimming, rounders, horse-riding, ballet, fencing, volley-ball, athletics and gymnastics available. 80 take non-compulsory sport. 12 take exams. 1 represents country at fencing (national quarter finalist). *Other*: 65 take part in local community schemes. 50 have bronze Duke of Edinburgh's Award, 70 have silver and 6 gold. 2–6 enter voluntary schemes after leaving school. Other activities include a computer club, arts society, debating, poetry, creative writing (poet in residence 1987), several music groups, science societies, Amnesty International, community service groups, Young Enterprise, life-saving, pets group, chess club, driving lessons.

Careers 1 full time and 2 part time advisors. Average number of pupils accepted for *arts and humanities degree courses* at Oxbridge, 2; other universities, 12; polytechnics or CHE, 9. *science and engineering degree courses* at Oxbridge, 1; other universities, 4; medical schools, 1; polytechnics or CHE, 2. *BEd*, 1. *other general training courses*, 7.

Uniform School uniform worn except the sixth.

Houses/prefects No competitive houses. School prefects and head girl elected by the school. House prefects, appointed by house staff. School Council.

Religion Quaker, attendance at daily act of worship and Sunday evening meetings.

Social Debates, theatrical productions with brother school, (Bootham) and joint meeting for worship, dances. Foreign language exchanges. Trips abroad for language study, art and art history, ski-ing, religious education. Pupils allowed to bring own bike to school. Meals formal, family service. Self service, Sunday breakfast. School shop. No tobacco/alcohol allowed.

Discipline No corporal punishment. Pupils failing to produce homework once might expect discussion and completion of work; if anyone were caught smoking cannabis on the premises they would be expelled.

Boarding 16% share with 2–6 others, 15% are in dormitories of 6 or more. Houses, of 16–80; first and second years, upper sixth, remaining years. Resident qualified medical staff. Central dining room. Sixth formers sometimes allowed to cook own food. 2–5 exeats each term. Visits to local town allowed.

Alumni association is run by The Secretary, MOSA, c/o The Mount School.

Former pupils Judi Dench; Margaret Drabble; Isobel Barnett; Elaine Kellett-Bowman (Dame); A S Byatt; Jocelyn Burnell (astronomer); Mary Ure; Jenny Killick; Hilary Wainwright; Rose Neil (Ulster TV); Anna Walker (ITV Weather).

MOUNT CARMEL

Mount Carmel School	Co-ed	Pupils 385
Wilmslow Road	Boys	Upper sixth Yes
Alderley Edge	● Girls	Termly fees:
Cheshire SK9 7QB	Mixed sixth	Day £520
Telephone number 0625 583028	● Day	GBGSA; ISAI
	Boarding	

Head Mrs M Moss (4 years)
Age range 11–18; entry by own exam
Bursaries.

MOUNT ST MARY'S (EXETER)

Mount St Mary's Convent School
Wonford Road
Exeter
Devon EX2 4PF
Telephone number 0392 36770

Enquiries/application to the Headmistress

Co-ed   Pupils 290
Boys   Upper sixth 10
● Girls   Termly fees:
Mixed sixth   Day £550
● Day   ISA; ISJC
Boarding

WHAT IT'S LIKE

Established on its present site in 1949, in a quiet residential area of Exeter. It is run by the Sisters of the Presentation of Mary who have been involved in education in Exeter since the 1890s. The convent and school buildings (which are all modern and very well equipped) occupy spacious grounds with beautiful gardens and tennis courts. It is a Roman Catholic school and thus religious education, which is according to the doctrines of the Church, is an essential element of the curriculum. The aim of the school is twofold: to promote Christian values and to develop the uniqueness of the individual pupil in an atmosphere which is both academically challenging yet sensitive to her particular needs. Good examination results and facilities.

SCHOOL PROFILE

Pupils Total over 12, 290. Entry age, 11 and into the sixth. Presentation Convent, Exeter provides over 20%.

Entrance Own entrance exam used. Oversubscribed. Roman Catholic establishment but other persuasions are accepted. Parents not expected to buy text books.

Staff Head Sister Eileen Dalaney, in post for 3 years. 27 full time staff, 3 part time. Annual turnover 3%. Average age 40.

Academic work GCSE and A-levels. Average size of upper fifth 60; upper sixth 10. *O-levels*: results can be provided by the school. *A-levels*: on average, 9 pupils in upper sixth pass 3 subjects. On average, 33% take science/engineering A-levels; 33% take arts and humanities; 33%, a mixture. *Computing facilities*: Computers are used through maths; computer clubs.

Senior pupils' non-academic activities *Music*: 50% learn a musical instrument, 25% up to Grade 6 or above, 15% accepted for Music School; 20% in school orchestra, 30% in school choir, 10% in Devon Youth Orchestra and 5% take interest beyond school. *Drama and dance*: All in school productions. *Art*: 50% take GCSE; 5% take A-level. *Sport*: Netball, basketball, hockey, volleyball, tennis, badminton, rounders and athletics are available. All take non-compulsory sport. 5% pupils represent county/country in cross-country, netball and tennis. *Other*: 30% have bronze Duke of Edinburgh's Award. Other activities include a computer club, Young Enterprise schemes, a school bank, keep-fit, and community service in a local hospital.

Careers 1 full time advisor. Approximately 90% of A-level leavers go on to degree courses, a few at Oxbridge.

Uniform School uniform worn except the sixth.

Houses/prefects No competitive houses. Prefects and head girl – appointed by the staff.

Religion Roman Catholic establishment.
Social Inter-school sport; sixth form resources shared with a local independent boys' school. Organised trips abroad. Meals packed lunches. No tobacco/alcohol allowed.
Discipline No corporal punishment. Pupils failing to produce homework once might expect detention at lunchtime.
Alumni association is run by Mrs P Gorin, c/o the school.

MOUNT ST MARY'S (SHEFFIELD)

Mount St Mary's College
Spinkhill
Sheffield S31 9YL
Telephone number 0246 433388

Enquiries/application to the Headmaster

- Co-ed
- Boys
- Girls
- Mixed sixth
- Day
- Boarding

Pupils 312
Upper sixth 50
Termly fees:
Day £1155
Boarding £1692
HMC; GBA

WHAT IT'S LIKE

Founded in 1842 and run by priests of the Society of Jesus, who had a presence at Spinkhill from 1580 when priests were obliged to work in secrecy. In 1756 the manor of Spinkhill was bought by the Jesuits. The present school lies in the village and has a fine estate of playing fields and farmlands. Most pupils are Roman Catholics. There is strong emphasis on religious instruction in Catholic doctrine; Mass and some other services are compulsory for Catholic pupils. It has a good staff:pupil ratio of 1:11. Academic standards are high and results are good. Some 30–35 leavers go on to university each year. There are strong music, drama and art depts. Considerable strength in sport and games. A very good variety of clubs and societies. About a quarter of the pupils are involved in local community services and the school has an outstanding record in the Duke of Edinburgh's Award Scheme.

SCHOOL PROFILE

Pupils Total 312. Day 57 (boys 30, girls 27); Boarding 255 (boys 202, girls 53). Entry age, 13 and into the sixth. Own prep school provides over 20%. 10% are children of former pupils.
Entrance Common entrance and own entrance exam used (with interviews and IQ tests). Not oversubscribed. Sport and music skills looked for. Pupils expected, but not required, to be RC. Parents not expected to buy text books. 55 assisted places. 10 scholarships, £100 to full fees. Bursaries added to assisted places to enable such pupils to board.
Parents 15+% are doctors, lawyers, etc; 15+% in industry or commerce; 15+% in the armed services. 10+% live within 30 miles; up to 10% live overseas.
Staff Head Rev J F Grumitt, in post for 11 years. 30 full time staff, 4 part time. Annual turnover 5%. Average age 36.
Academic work GCSE and A-levels. Average size of upper fifth 60; upper sixth 50. *O-levels*: on average, 35 pupils in upper fifth pass 8 or more subjects. *A-levels*: on average 1 pupil in upper sixth passes 1 subject; 15, 2

subjects; 30, 3 subjects; 4 pass 4 subjects. On average, 20 take science/engineering A-levels; 20 take arts and humanities; 10 take a mixture. Information Technology offered to GCSE/A-level; City and Guilds Radio Astronomy offered. *Computing facilities*: about 30 microprocessors, mainly Commodore or BBC Master. Provision for EFL.

Senior pupils' non-academic activities *Music*: 30% learn a musical instrument, 8 to Grade 6 or above, 2 accepted for Music School; some in school choir; others in Sheffield Youth Orchestra; GCSE Music Lab offered. *Drama and dance*: 30% in school productions. 2 accepted for Drama/Dance Schools, 2 go on to work in theatre. *Art*: 50% take as non-examined subject; 50% take GCSE; 8 take A-level. 10 belong to eg photographic club. *Sport*: Rugby, cricket, swimming, athletics, squash, riding, hockey and basketball available. All take non-compulsory sport. Some take lifesaving exams; GCSE sports studies recently introduced. Pupils represent county/country (rugby, cricket, hockey). Winners of 1988 National Schools Sevens Open Tournament. *Other*: All have bronze Duke of Edinburgh's Award and 2 have gold. Other activities include driving lessons, and about 20 clubs from sailing to chess and computers.

Careers 4 part time advisors. Average number of pupils accepted for *degree courses in arts and humanities*, 40%; *science and engineering*, 50%; *BEd*, 2%; at Oxbridge, 2%; other universities, 23%; medical schools, 3%; polytechnics or CHE, 10%; *other general training courses*, 2. Average number of pupils going straight into careers in the armed services, 3; industry, 3; music/drama, 2.

Uniform School uniform worn in lower school.

Houses/prefects Competitive houses. Prefects, head boy, head of house and house prefects – appointed by the Head.

Religion Compulsory Mass for Catholics. Other denominations welcomed.

Social No organised local events. Exchanges with Jesuit schools in Australia, Zimbabwe and France. Day pupils allowed to bring own car/bike/motorbike to school. Meals self service. School shop. No tobacco/alcohol allowed.

Discipline Corporal punishment may be used in lower school when considered appropriate by the Headmaster taking into account parents' and DES views. Strong emphasis throughout the school on growth to self-discipline.

Boarding Sixth form have own study bedrooms; all lower school in study cubicles. Houses, approximately 50–60, divided by age and single-sex. Resident SRN. Central dining room. 2 weekend exeats each term. Visits to local town allowed for upper school.

Former pupils Rt Hon Lord Wheatley PC; Sir Martin Melvin; Air Marshal Sir Francis Fresanges; Rt Hon Sir Denis Henry; Sir David Rose; Sir Diarmaid Conroy; Major General McGuiness.

NEWCASTLE CHURCH HIGH

Newcastle upon Tyne Church
  High School
Tankerville Terrace
Jesmond
Newcastle upon Tyne NE2 3BA
Telephone number 091 281 4306

Enquiries to the Headmistress
Application to the School Secretary

Co-ed
Boys
● Girls
Mixed sixth
● Day
Boarding

Pupils 315
Upper sixth 35
Termly fees:
Day £680
GSA

WHAT IT'S LIKE

Founded in 1885 it stands in a pleasant residential district in one of the older
suburbs, close to the City centre and university. The original buildings
(completed in 1890) are well designed and there are many modern additions.
These are surrounded by pleasant gardens and grounds. The senior and
junior schools are on the same site. It caters for varying degrees of academic
ability and lays considerable stress on a Christian atmosphere and education.
Exam results are good and 20–25 pupils go on to university each year. There
are flourishing music, art and drama depts and a fair range of sports, games
and activities. Some commitment to local community schemes.

SCHOOL PROFILE

Pupils Total over 12, 315. Entry age, 4+ and into the sixth. Own junior school
provides over 80%. 7% are children of former pupils.

Entrance Own entrance exam used. Oversubscribed. No special skills or
religious requirements. Parents not expected to buy text books. No assisted
places. 10 scholarships/bursaries pa, for 50% of fees.

Parents 15+% are doctors, lawyers, etc. 60+% live within 30 miles.

Staff Head Miss P E Davies, in post for 13 years. 41 full time staff, 31 part
time. Annual turnover 3%.

Academic work GCSE and A-levels. Average size of upper fifth 68; upper
sixth 35. *O-levels*: on average, 14 pupils in upper fifth pass 1–4 subjects; 16,
5–7 subjects; 34 pass 8+ subjects. *A-levels*: on average, 4 pupils in upper
sixth pass 1 subject; 5, 2 subjects; 18 pass 3 subjects. On average, 7 take
science/engineering A-levels; 18 take arts and humanities; 5 a mixture. *Computing facilities*: computing laboratory with 11 BBC Bs, 1 Master 512, ITBM
compatible, 2 BBC Bs in Junior school, 1 in maths and 1 in physics depts.
Some remedial provisions.

Senior pupils' non-academic activities *Music*: 52 learn a musical instrument, 12 to Grade 6 or above, pupils occasionally accepted for Music School,
13 in school orchestra, 6 in school choir, 3 do country dance, 7 in madrigal
group, 10 in wind group, 4 in recorder group; 1 in Northern Junior Philharmonic orchestra, others go on to choirs, Gilbert & Sullivan group. *Drama and
dance*: 50 in school productions, 100 in other. 1 accepted for Drama/Dance
schools. *Art*: 17 take GCSE; 3 take A-level. 1 accepted for Art School. *Sport*:
50 take non-compulsory sport. 4 take exams in eg swimming. 6 represent
county. *Other*: 30 take part in local community schemes. Other activities
include public speaking, Christian Union, Friday Forum (contemporary
issues) and school newspaper.

Careers 1 part time advisor. Average number of pupils accepted for *arts and humanities degree courses* at Oxbridge, 2; other universities, 15; polytechnics or CHE, 12. *science and engineering degree courses* at Oxbridge, 1; other universities, 6; medical schools, 3; polytechnics or CHE, 3. *BEd*, 7. *other general training courses*, 6. Average number of pupils going straight into careers in industry, 2.

Uniform School uniform worn, optional in the sixth.

Houses/prefects Competitive houses. Prefects and head girl, appointed by sixth form and staff; head of house and house prefects by girls.

Religion Daily assembly. 3 church services a year.

Social Charity fair, ballroom dancing, debates with local schools. Trips for skiing, art and languages. Pupils allowed to bring own car to school. Meals formal. No tobacco/alcohol allowed.

Discipline No corporal punishment. Pupils failing to produce homework once might expect to be asked to do it.

Alumni association is run by Mrs G Bardgett, 40 Westwood Road, Brunton Park, Newcastle upon Tyne NE3 5NN.

NEWCASTLE HIGH

Central Newcastle High School	Co-ed	Pupils 553
Eskdale Terrace	Boys	Upper sixth 70
Newcastle upon Tyne NE2 4DS	● Girls	Termly fees:
Telephone number 091 281 1768	Mixed sixth	Day £622
Enquiries/application to Mrs A M Chapman	● Day	GPDST
	Boarding	

WHAT IT'S LIKE

Opened in 1895, a member of The Girls' Public Day School Trust, it has occupied the same premises in Eskdale Terrace since 1900. Numerous additions over the last twenty years include a science wing, library extension, assembly hall, computer room, lecture rooms, a sixth-form block and a gym. It serves a wide catchment area and draws its pupils from many different backgrounds; a varied social 'mix' is a feature of its philosophy. It enjoys a high reputation in the region and gets good results. Good in music and an impressive range of extra-curricular activities. Strong local support. The junior school is in Gosforth, 3 miles away.

SCHOOL PROFILE

Pupils Total over 11, 553. Entry age, 4½, 7, 9, 11 and into the sixth. Own junior department provides over 50% of pupils. A fair proportion are children of former pupils.

Entrance Own entrance exam used. No special skills or religious requirements. Parents not expected to buy text books. Assisted places. Approx 3 scholarships pa (quarter fees); also bursaries.

Parents 15+% in industry or commerce; 15+% are doctors, lawyers, etc. 60+% live within 30 miles.

Staff Head Mrs Angela Chapman, in post for 4 years. 43 full time staff, 18 part time.

Academic work GCSE, A-levels, a few AS levels. Average size of upper fifth 81; upper sixth 70. *O-levels*: on average, 80% pass 6 or more subjects. *A-levels*: over 80% pass 3 or 4 subjects. On average, 35% take science/engineering A-levels; 40% take arts and humanities; rest a mixture. Russian offered to GCSE/A-level. *Computing facilities*: A network of 8 RML 480Z microcomputers with a Nimbus 16-6 + file server, a 20 megabyte hard disk, twin floppy disk drive and 3 dot matrix printers. Regularly updated. Provisions for dyslexia – Dyslexia Institute in same street.

Senior pupils' non-academic activities *Music*: 60 learn a musical instrument, 25 to Grade 6 or above. 1 accepted for Music School; 1 or 2 play in pop group beyond school, 40 in school orchestra, 55 in school choir, 30 in chamber groups. *Drama and dance*: 20 in school productions, all at some time in drama productions; 1 accepted for Drama/Dance School. *Art*: 14 take A-level. *Sport*: Hockey, netball, tennis, athletics, rounders, swimming, gymnasium, volleyball, basketball, badminton available. Good attendance for non-compulsory sport; others have tennis coaching, hockey, netball and judo. 6 take exams eg gymnastics, swimming. 17 represent county/country (hockey, tennis, badminton, swimming, diving, athletics). *Other*: 20 help at Sheltered Accommodation. Sixth formers regularly enter voluntary schemes after leaving school. Other activities include a computer club, debating, maths, science, electronics, aerobics, judo, French, poetry, drama, chess, LATE (Looking at the Environment).

Careers 2 part time advisors and help from LEA. Average number of pupils accepted for *arts and humanities degree courses* at Oxbridge, 4; other universities, 16; polytechnics or CHE, 7. *science and engineering degree courses* at Oxbridge, 2; other universities, 8; medical schools, 5; polytechnics or CHE, 2. *BEd*, 2. *other general training courses*, 8 – predominantly nursing, physiotherapy, Arts Foundation. Other pupils go straight into careers in banking, civil service, music/drama. Traditional school careers are in medicine or law.

Uniform School uniform worn except in the sixth.

Houses/prefects 4 houses compete in sport, music and drama. Prefects, head girl and heads of house – elected by the girls. School Council.

Religion Non-denominational assembly, non-Christians can opt out. Occasional Jewish assembly.

Social Senior debates, sixth form drama and musical productions with Royal Grammar School for boys. Organised exchange to France, Germany; ski trips, trips to Greece. Pupils allowed to bring own car/bike to school. Meals self service. School shop sells uniform and tuckshop. No tobacco/alcohol allowed.

Alumni association is run by Mrs Rochester, Red Cottage, Brackendene Drive, Low Fell, Gateshead NE9.

Former pupils Miriam Stoppard.

NEWCASTLE-UNDER-LYME

Newcastle-under-Lyme School
Mount Pleasant
Newcastle-under-Lyme
Staffordshire ST5 1DB
Telephone number 0782 613345

Enquiries/application to the Principal

- Co-ed   Pupils 803
- Boys   Upper sixth 150
- Girls   Termly fees:
- Mixed sixth   Day £638
- Day   HMC; GSA
- Boarding

WHAT IT'S LIKE

Founded in 1874. The present school is a result of an amalgamation (in 1981) of Newcastle High School and Orme's Girls' School (founded in 1876) nearby. Both lie in a residential area of the potteries and have some 30 acres of grounds and playing fields. The original buildings are still part of the school. There have been a number of extensions to provide good modern facilities. The school enjoys vigorous local support. Good teaching is provided and academic standards are high. Results are impressive and 60 plus pupils go on to a university each year. The music department is very strong. A good range of sports and activities. There is a vigorous CCF and a scout troup. Some commitment to the Duke of Edinburgh's Award Scheme.

SCHOOL PROFILE

Pupils Total over 12, 803 (boys 406, girls 397). Entry age, 8, 11 and into the sixth. Own junior department provides over 20%. 20% are children of former pupils.

Entrance Common entrance and own entrance exam used. Oversubscribed. No special skills or religious requirements. Parents not expected to buy text books. 73 assisted places. 7 scholarships/bursaries, £1000–£400.

Parents 15+% in industry or commerce; 15+% are doctors, lawyers, etc. 60+% live within 30 miles.

Staff Head J W Donaldson, in post for 14 years. 84 full time staff, 12 part time. Annual turnover 8%. Average age 40.

Academic work GCSE and A-levels. Average size of upper fifth 180; upper sixth 150. *O-levels*: on average, 27 pupils in upper fifth pass 1–4 subjects; 56, 5–7 subjects; 95 pass 8+ subjects. *A-levels*: on average, 4 pupils in upper sixth pass 1 subject; 13, 2 subjects; 37, 3 subjects and 109 pass 4 subjects. Greek is offered to GCSE/A-level. *Computing facilities*: 16 BBC Econet and departmental computers.

Senior pupils' non-academic activities *Music*: 300 learn a musical instrument, 40 to Grade 6 or above, 3–4 accepted for Music School. *Drama and dance*: 4 school productions a year. 2 accepted for Drama/Dance Schools. *Art*: 40 take GCSE; 15 A-level. 20 belong to photographic club. 5 accepted for Art School. *Sport*: Rugby, hockey, cricket, cross-country, swimming, judo, shooting, netball, athletics available. Lots take non-compulsory sport. *Other*: Some pupils have gold Duke of Edinburgh's Award. Other activities include a computer club, chess, Christian Fellowship.

Careers Average number of pupils accepted for *arts and humanities degree courses* at Oxbridge, 10; other universities, 20; polytechnics or CHE, 15. *science and engineering degree courses* at Oxbridge, 6; other universities, 25; medical schools, 6; polytechnics or CHE, 15. BEd, 3. *other general* *training courses*, 8. Average number of pupils going straight into careers in the armed services, 3; the church, 1; industry, 6; the City, 1; civil service, 1; music/drama, 1.

Uniform School uniform worn throughout.

Houses/prefects Competitive houses. Prefects, head boy and girl – elected by the school. School Council.

Religion Daily assemblies.

Social 6 organised trips abroad and exchange systems with schools abroad every year. Pupils allowed to bring own car/bike/motorbike/horse to school. Meals self service. School shop. No tobacco/alcohol allowed.

Discipline No corporal punishment. Pupils failing to produce homework once might expect a repeat or detention; those caught smoking cannabis on the premises could expect expulsion.

Former pupils Sir Richard Bailey; 6 professors; 2 generals; 1 admiral.

NEW HALL

New Hall	Co-ed	Pupils 470
Boreham	Boys	Upper sixth 75
Chelmsford	● Girls	Termly fees:
Essex CM3 3HT	Mixed sixth	Day £1298
Telephone number 0245 467588	● Day	Boarding £2025
	● Boarding	GSA
Enquiries/application to the Registrar		

WHAT IT'S LIKE

Founded at Liège in 1642, then the school of the English Cannonesses of the Holy Sepulchre. The nuns were compelled to leave during the French revolution and reopened the school at its present site in 1798–99, where it is administered by nuns of the Order of the Holy Sepulchre. The main building is New Hall, formerly a Tudor palace (once the home of Mary Tudor). There was probably a house on the site before 1066. The present buildings are handsome and provide excellent facilities. The private estate of 120 acres is beautiful and there are excellent playing fields and sporting amenities. It is a Catholic school centred on a religious community and with a cosmopolitan intake. Its essential aim is that staff and pupils should experience Christian community together. Most of the pupils are Roman Catholics but others are welcomed and the school is enriched by them. The life of the school is closely associated with the liturgy of the Church, of which Sunday Mass is an important element. Religious instruction is an important part of the curriculum. A very large staff allows a staff:pupil ratio of 1:8. Academic standards are high and results impressive. Most leavers go on to university each year. There is a massive commitment to music (350+ girls learn an instrument). Very strong indeed in drama (many productions) and art. A wide range of sport and games (high standards attained). A wide variety of activities caters for most needs. A lot of social work is done by pupils locally and there is an impressive record in the Duke of Edinburgh's Award Scheme.

SCHOOL PROFILE

Pupils Total over 12, 470. Day 150; Boarding 320. Entry age, 11+, 12+, 13+, 14+ and into the sixth. Small number are children of former pupils.

Entrance Common entrance and own entrance exam used. Oversubscribed for day and sixth form places. Variety of skills looked for. Commitment to Christian values expected, large proportion are RC (although some non-Christians included). Parents expected to buy a few text books that are to be kept. Some scholarships and bursaries.

Parents 15+% in industry or commerce. 30+% live within 30 miles; 10+% live overseas.

Staff Head Sister Margaret Mary Horton CRSS, in post for 2 years. 45 full time staff, 20 part time. Annual turnover 8%.

Academic work GCSE, A-levels and LCCI Secretarial exams. Average size of fifth 84; upper sixth 75. *O-levels*: on average, 10 pupils in fifth pass 1–4 subjects; 25, 5–7 subjects; 50 pass 8+ subjects. *A-levels*: on average, 6 pupils in upper sixth pass 1 subject; 18, 2 subjects; 37, 3 subjects; 4 pass 4 subjects. On average, 10 take science A-levels; 20 take arts and humanities; 30 take a mixture. *Computing facilities*: fully equipped laboratory for full sized groups, BBCs; business studies – Wang. Special educational needs dept. Handicapped children accepted and integrated as far as possible.

Senior pupils' non-academic activities *Music*: 352 learn a musical instrument, 25 to Grade 6 or above; 1 accepted for Music School; 60 in school orchestra, 100 in school choir, 22 in school pop group; 2 in National Youth Orchestra, 5 in youth orchestra. *Drama and dance*: 150 in school productions, 80 in workshops. 40 take GCSE Theatre Arts, 20 A-level. 3 accepted for Drama/Dance Schools, 15 for BA Drama, 5 go on to work in theatre, 10 in media. *Art*: 120 take art and craft activities; 70 take GCSE art; 12 A-level, 16 take GCSE History of Art & Design, 16 take A-level History of Art. 3 accepted for Art School, 1 accepted for BA History of Art, 2 work in art galleries. *Sport*: Netball, hockey, gymnastics, cross-country, tennis, athletics, swimming, trampolining, aerobics, volleyball, badminton, squash and table tennis available. 155 take non-compulsory sport. 150 in teams. 5 represent county (athletics, hockey, netball, tennis); 1 country (athletics). *Other*: Some take part in local community schemes. Pupils take part in Duke of Edinburgh's Award, bronze, silver and gold. Some enter voluntary schemes after leaving school, others work for national charities. Other activities include a computer club, bridge club, driving lessons, public speaking, debating, voluntary service, drama, fencing and karate.

Careers 1 full time and 6 part time advisors. Average number of pupils accepted for *arts and humanities degree courses* in universities, 30; polytechnics or CHE, 10. *science and engineering degree courses* at Oxbridge, 2; other universities, 10; polytechnics or CHE, 3. *BEd*, 1. *other general training courses*, 13. Average number of pupils going straight into careers in the City, 1; other, 8.

Uniform School uniform worn; formal occasions only in sixth.

Houses/prefects Competitive houses in sport. All members of upper sixth have positions of responsibility.

Religion Compulsory attendance at Eucharist on Sundays, Assemblies, House Prayers etc.

Social Debates, choirs, social events with other schools. Trips abroad arranged most half terms and holidays. Pupils allowed to bring own car/bike/

horse to school. Meals self-service. School shop. No tobacco allowed; limited alcohol under supervision in sixth form.

Discipline No corporal punishment. Pupils failing to produce homework once might expect help from tutor; those caught smoking cannabis on the premises can expect expulsion.

Boarding Upper sixth have own study bedroom, lower sixth share; others in individual cubicles in dormitories. Houses for 50 boarders, 30 day pupils approx; vertical groups plus separate sixth form house. Resident SRN. Central dining room. Pupils can provide and cook some own food at weekends. Exeats each term – vary with age group. Weekend visits to local town allowed, dependant on age.

Alumni association c/o the Headmistress.

Former pupils Cindy Buxton (Natural History Film Maker); Ciaran Madden (Actress); Nadine Beddington (Past President ARIBA).

NORMANTON (DERBY)

Normanton School
Buxton
Derbyshire SK17 6SJ
Telephone number 0298 2745

- Co-ed
  Boys
  Girls
  Mixed sixth
- Day
- Boarding

Pupils 90
Upper sixth Yes
Termly fees:
Day £750
Boarding £1500

Head S B Smith (1 year)
Age range 10–18
Scholarships and bursaries.

NORTHAMPTON HIGH

Northampton High School for Girls
Derngate
Northampton NN1 1UN
Telephone number 0604 38095

Co-ed
Boys
- Girls
Mixed sixth
- Day
Boarding

Pupils 520
Upper sixth Yes
Termly fees:
Day £850
GSA

Head Mrs L A Mayne, first year in post
Age range 11–18, own prep from age 3; entry by own exam
Assisted places.

NORTHFIELD

Northfield School	Co-ed	Pupils 100
Church Road	Boys	Upper sixth 6
Watford	● Girls	Termly fees:
Hertfordshire WD1 3QB	Mixed sixth	Day £885
Telephone number 0923 29758	● Day	ISAI; AHIS
	Boarding	
Enquiries/application to the Secretary		

WHAT IT'S LIKE

Founded c1870, it occupied its present premises, urban and single-site, in 1944. It combines a nursery class and kindergarten. The main building is a large private house with very agreeable gardens. Modern extensions provide good facilities. A pleasant, happy school which has all the advantages of being small. It prides itself on a 'caring and supportive atmosphere' and has very small learning groups. Results are good. A decent range of sports, games and activities.

SCHOOL PROFILE

Pupils Total over 12, 100. Entry age, up to 11+ and into the sixth. Own junior school provides over 20%.

Entrance Own entrance exam used. Oversubscribed. No special skills or religious requirements. Parents expected to buy text books. Sixth form scholarships/bursaries.

Parents 60+% live within 30 miles.

Staff Head Mrs D Hilton, in post for 11 years. 7 full time staff, 19 part time. Annual turn over 4%.

Academic work GCSE and A-levels. Average size of upper fifth 20; upper sixth 6. *O-levels*: on average, 8 pupils in upper fifth pass 1–4 subjects; 8, 5–7 subjects; 4 pass 8+ subjects. *A-levels*: on average, 2 pupils in upper sixth pass 2 subjects; and 4 pass 3 subjects. On average, 2 take science/engineering A-levels; 2 take arts and humanities; 2 a mixture. *Computing facilities*: 6 computers. *Special provisions*: individual tuition when required.

Senior pupils' non-academic activities *Music*: 20 learn a musical instrument, 1 to Grade 6 or above. 8 in school choir. *Drama and dance*: At least 12 in school productions; 8 up to Grade 6 in ESB, RAD, etc. *Art*: 2 take as non-examined subject, 11 take GCSE; 4, A-level; 3 accepted for Art School. *Sport*: Hockey, netball, volleyball, badminton, tennis, rounders, swimming, athletics available. *Other*: 6 have bronze Duke of Edinburgh's Award and 2 have silver. Other activities include a computer club, sports club, charities, supporting a child in Kenya through Save the Children.

Careers 2 part time advisors. Average number of pupils accepted for *science and engineering degree courses* at universities, 2; polytechnics or CHE, 2. *BEd*, 2. *other general training courses*, 2. Average number of pupils going straight into careers in the City, 1.

Uniform School uniform worn except in the sixth.

Houses/prefects Competitive houses. Prefects, head girl, head of house and house prefects – appointed by the Head and elected by the school.

Religion Daily prayers.

Social Public speaking and road safety competitions with other local schools. Week in France for fourth and fifth forms. Pupils allowed to bring own car/bike to school. No tobacco/alcohol allowed.
Discipline No corporal punishment.

NORTH FORELAND LODGE

North Foreland Lodge	Co-ed	Pupils 180
Sherfield-on-Loddon	Boys	Upper sixth Yes
Basingstoke	● Girls	Termly fees:
Hants RG27 0HT	Mixed sixth	Boarding £1900
Telephone number 0256 882431	Day	GSA
	● Boarding	

Head Miss D L Matthews (5 years)
Age range 11–18; entry by common entrance.

NORTH LONDON COLLEGIATE

North London Collegiate School	Co-ed	Pupils 820*
Canons	Boys	Upper sixth 90
Edgware	● Girls	Termly fees:
Middlesex HA8 7RJ	Mixed sixth	Day £910
Telephone number 01-952 0912	● Day	GSA
Enquiries/application to the Headmistress	Boarding	*including junior school

WHAT IT'S LIKE

Founded in 1850 by Miss Frances Buss, the first woman to use the title 'headmistress'. In 1929 it bought 'Canons' the former home of the Duke of Chandos, a magnificent 18th-century house with fine terraces and gardens. This is the heart of the school for the sixth form. A modern school has since been built in the 30 acres of parkland. This includes a music school, a drawing school, a theatre and the junior school. A C of E foundation, it is tremendously strong in music (300 girls learn an instrument), and pretty strong in drama. An energetic, purposeful school, its facilities are very good and it provides an excellent education. A high proportion of pupils go to university. A range of sports, games and extra-curricular activities, including the Duke of Edinburgh's Award Scheme.

SCHOOL PROFILE

Pupils Total (including junior school), 820. Entry age, 7, 8, 11 and into the sixth. Own junior school provides over 30%. Approx 5% are children of former pupils.

Entrance Own entrance exam used. Oversubscribed. No special skills or religious requirements. Parents not expected to buy text books. 73 assisted places. 77 bursaries, 11 scholarships, £2700 pa.

Parents 100% live within 30 miles.

Staff Head Mrs J L Clanchy, in post for 3 years. 54 full time staff, 22 part time. Annual turnover 6%.

Academic work GCSE and A-levels. Average size of upper fifth 100; upper sixth 90. *O-levels*: on average, 100 pass 8+ subjects. *A-levels*: on average, 3 pass 2 subjects; 85, 3 subjects and 3 pass 4 subjects. *Computing facilities*: Network of 12 BBC + 4 stand alone BBC; a network of 14 Nimbus (RM) + plotters, printers, etc.

Senior pupils' non-academic activities *Music*: 300 learn a musical instrument. 2 or 3 accepted for Music School. 130 in school orchestra(s), 160 in school choir(s), 80 in chamber music groups; 20 in Harrow youth orchestra and other local orchestras. *Drama and dance*: 70–80 in school productions, about 20 participate in other productions. 1 accepted for Drama/Dance School. *Sport*: Lacrosse, netball, tennis, rounders, swimming, athletics, judo, fencing, self-defence, volleyball, badminton available. 80 take non-compulsory sport; 10 take exams. 6 represent county/country (lacrosse, netball, swimming, athletics). *Other*: 37 have bronze Duke of Edinburgh's Award, 13 have silver and 7 gold. Other activities include a computer club, driving, typing, chess, bridge, debating, Scottish dancing, pottery, photography.

Careers 2 part time advisors. Average number of pupils accepted for *arts and humanities degree courses* at Oxbridge, 10; other universities, 30; polytechnics or CHE, 8. *science and engineering degree courses* at Oxbridge, 5; other universities, 32; medical schools, 8; polytechnics or CHE, 3. *BEd*, at Oxbridge, 2. *other general training courses*, 1.

Uniform School uniform worn except in the sixth.

Houses/prefects Head girl elected by the school. School Council.

Religion Religious worship compulsory.

Social Some debates, drama, lectures with other schools. Exchange with a German school, ski-ing trips, visits to France, Russia, Italy, Greece, etc. Pupils allowed to bring own car/bike to school. Meals self service. No tobacco/alcohol allowed.

Discipline No corporal punishment. Anyone abusing any drug on the premises could expect expulsion.

Former pupils Esther Rantzen; Eleanor Bron.

NORTHWOOD COLLEGE

Northwood College	Co-ed	Pupils 265
Maxwell Road	Boys	Upper sixth 30
Northwood	• Girls	Termly fees:
Middlesex HA6 2YE	Mixed sixth	Day £884
Telephone number 09274 25446	• Day	GSA
	Boarding	
Enquiries/application to the Headmistress		

WHAT IT'S LIKE

Founded in 1878, it is single-site on the outskirts of London. The college consists of the original main building (1892) and several modern buildings erected during the last 25 years. These provide good up-to-date facilities in a pleasant environment. The school currently takes boarders but the boarding house is to close in 1990. The aim of the school is to give a thorough all-round education which enables a girl to develop her character and personality and fit her for a worthwhile career. Academic standards and results are good. 25 or more leavers go on to university or other forms of higher education each year. Girls have the opportunity to participate in music and drama. There is a good range of sports and games, a standard variety of activities and some commitment to local community schemes; the Duke of Edinburgh's Award Scheme has recently been introduced.

SCHOOL PROFILE

Pupils Total over 12, 265. Day 240; Boarding 25. Entry age, 4, 7, 11 and into the sixth. Own junior department provides over 90%. 5% are children of former pupils.

Entrance Own entrance exam used. Oversubscribed. No special skills or religious requirements. Parents not expected to buy text books. Four sixth form scholarships, £884 pa.

Parents 15+% in industry or commerce; 15+% are doctors, lawyers, etc. 60+% live within 30 miles; up to 10% live overseas.

Staff Head Mrs D Dalton, in post for 2 years. 36 full time staff, 11 part time. Annual turnover 10%. Average age 35.

Academic work GCSE and A-levels. Average size of upper fifth 52; upper sixth 30. *O-levels*: on average, 6 pupils in upper fifth pass 1–4 subjects; 21, 5–7 subjects; 25 pass 8+ subjects. *A-levels*: on average, 2 pupils in upper sixth pass 1 subject; 5, 2 subjects; 22, 3 subjects and 1 passes 4 subjects. On average, 10 take science A-levels; 15 take arts and humanities; 5 a mixture. *Computing facilities*: 12 BBCs on Econet system and 4 BBCs with peripherals in senior school. 7 BBCs in junior school.

Senior pupils' non-academic activities *Music*: 19 learn a musical instrument, 7 to Grade 6 or above; 7 in school orchestra, 14 in choir. *Drama and dance*: 55 participate in school productions; 15 in boys' schools' plays; 6 in public speaking competition; 4 in drama competition. 6 take Grade 6 GSM and D. *Art*: 12 take GCSE; 8 A-level. 2 accepted for Art School. *Sport*: Tennis, swimming, rounders, gymnastics, table tennis, badminton, squash, volleyball, netball, hockey, aerobics, golf, judo, dance, stoolball available. 25 take non-compulsory sport. 4 take exams. 9 represent county (hockey, squash, cross-country, swimming). *Other*: 40 take part in local community schemes. 7 have bronze Duke of Edinburgh's Award, 2 have silver. Other activities include a debating society, computer, science, public speaking and mathematics clubs.

Careers 10 part time advisors. Average number of pupils accepted for *arts and humanities degree courses* at universities, 5; polytechnics or CHE, 5. *science and engineering degree courses* at Oxbridge, 1; other universities, 5; medical schools, 2; polytechnics or CHE, 5. *BEd*, 2. *other general training courses*, 5.

Uniform School uniform worn except in the sixth.

Houses/prefects Competitive houses. Prefects, head girl, head of house and house prefects – appointed by the Headmistress, nominated by senior pupils.

Religion Assembly compulsory for all. Sunday church compulsory for boarders.

Social Joint productions with local independent boys' schools, debates, choral concerts. Organised ski-ing trips, Mediterranean cruises, exchange with a school in France, sailing course, hockey course. Pupils allowed to bring own car/bike to school. Meals self service. No tobacco/alcohol allowed.

Discipline No corporal punishment. Pupils failing to produce homework once might expect a detention; those caught smoking cannabis on the premises could expect expulsion.

Boarding 20% have own study bedroom, 80% share (2–5). Central dining room. Exeats each term: half term plus 4 single days (or 1 weekend and 2 single days). Visits to local town allowed.

Former pupils Dame Margaret Booth (Judge).

NORWICH HIGH

Norwich High School
Eaton Grove
95 Newmarket Road
Norwich NR2 2HU
Telephone number 0603 53265

Enquiries/application to the Admissions Secretary

Co-ed   Pupils 550
Boys   Upper sixth 80+
● Girls   Termly fees:
Mixed sixth   Day £695
● Day   GSA; GPDST
Boarding

WHAT IT'S LIKE

Founded in 1875, it is single-site in the middle of the City. The senior school is housed in a fine Georgian mansion in spacious wooded grounds and beautiful gardens. There are numerous purpose-built extensions and facilities are excellent. It enjoys a wide social spread from the whole of Norfolk and North Suffolk. Non-denominational, it provides a very good education in the grammar school tradition. Results are impressive and 30–35 leavers proceed to university each year. Tremendously strong in music (most are involved) and also strong in drama and art. High standards in sport and games. An outstanding record in the Duke of Edinburgh's Award Scheme. Full advantage is taken of the City's cultural amenities. It has a high reputation locally and is well supported.

SCHOOL PROFILE

Pupils Total over 12, 550. Entry age, 7+, 11+ and into the sixth. Own junior department provides over 20% of pupils.

Entrance Own entrance exam used. Oversubscribed. All-rounders welcome; no religious requirements. Parents not expected to buy text books. 190 assisted places. Scholarships, including music: 25–50% fees. Also bursaries.

Parents 60+% live within 30 miles.

Staff Head Mrs Valerie Bidwell. 42 full time staff, 10 part time.

Academic work GCSE and A-levels. Average size of upper fifth 90; upper sixth 75–80. *O-levels*: on average, 2 pupils in upper fifth pass 1–4 subjects; 10, 5–7 subjects; 78 pass 8+ subjects. *A-levels*: on average, 4 pupils in upper sixth pass 1 subject; 14, 2 subjects; 56, 3 subjects and 6 pass 4 subjects. On average, 19 take science/engineering A-levels; 24 take arts and humanities; 30 a mixture. *Computing facilities*: Two computer rooms – one with 480Z Research Machines, one with BBC computers. Departmental computers as appropriate.

Senior pupils' non-academic activities *Music*: 250 learn a musical instrument, 24 to Grade 6 or above. 3 go on to music degree courses. 150 in school orchestra(s), 220 in school choir(s), 6 in school boogie group, 25 in madrigal group, 4 in string quartet; 10 in brass group, 12 in woodwind ensemble; 1 in National Youth Orchestra. *Drama and dance*: 40 in school productions, 45 in company drama, 30 in drama club, 90 in pantomimes; 2 go on to work in theatre; others as leisure activity after leaving. *Art*: 30 take as non-examined subject, 20–30 take GCSE. 4 accepted for Art School; 20 belong to photographic club. *Sport*: Lacrosse, netball, life-saving, swimming, badminton, volleyball, tennis, athletics, rounders available. 60 take non-compulsory sport. 10 take exams in swimming and Royal Life Saving Society Award. 17 represent county (lacrosse, netball, swimming, tennis, athletics). *Other*: Some take part in local community schemes. 48 have bronze Duke of Edinburgh's Award, 42 have silver and 30 have gold. Other activities include a computer club, science club, stamp club, rowing club, fencing.

Careers 3 part time advisors. Average number of pupils accepted for *arts and humanities degree courses* at Oxbridge, 2; other universities, 17; polytechnics or CHE, 1. *science and engineering degree courses* at Oxbridge, 3; other universities, 11; medical schools, 3; polytechnics or CHE, 2. *BEd*, 6. *other general training courses*, 21. Average number of pupils going straight into careers in music/drama, 4; other, 1.

Uniform School uniform worn except in the sixth.

Houses/prefects Competitive houses. Prefects, head girl, head of house and house prefects – elected by staff and sixth form.

Religion Morning assembly. Parents may withdraw their children on religious grounds.

Social Debates, Young Enterprise, Theatrical Productions, BAYS with other local schools. Organised trips abroad. Pupils allowed to bring own car/bike/ motorbike to school. Meals self service. School shop sells uniform. No tobacco/alcohol allowed.

Discipline No corporal punishment. Pupils failing to produce homework once might expect to make up work promptly; those caught smoking cannabis on the premises could expect suspension, probable expulsion.

Alumni association run by Mrs E Taylor, 16 The Avenues, Norwich NR2 3PH.

Former pupils Beryl Bryden (international jazz singer); Pat Barr (novelist); Anne Weale (authoress); Jane Manning (opera singer); Jenny Lane (BBC); Ann Tyrell (dress designer); Dr Jennifer Moyle (scientist).

NOTRE DAME (COBHAM)

Notre Dame Senior School	Co-ed	Pupils 400
Burwood House	Boys	Upper sixth 20
Cobham	● Girls	Termly fees:
Surrey KT11 1HA	Mixed sixth	Day £800
Telephone number 0932 63560	● Day	
Enquiries/application to the Headmistress	Boarding	

WHAT IT'S LIKE

Founded in 1937 and run by the Sisters of the Company of Mary, an international teaching order. The main original building is Burwood House, a mansion on a fine estate. A large number of modern additions provide good facilities and equipment. Both senior and junior schools are on the same rural site, near the village. A sound general education is provided and results are creditable. Music and drama are reasonably strong; art is very strong. A number of girls go on to higher education. There is a fair range of sports and games and good facilities for these are on site.

SCHOOL PROFILE

Pupils Total over 11, 400. Entry age, 11 and into the sixth. Own junior school provides over 20%.

Entrance Own entrance exam used. Not oversubscribed. No special skills or religious requirements. Parents not expected to buy text books. No assisted places at present. 14 scholarships/bursaries, half fees to £400 pa.

Parents 15+% are in industry or commerce. 60+% live within 30 miles.

Staff Head Sister Faith Ede, in post for 1 year. 29 full time staff, 21 part time. Annual turnover 5%. Average age 43.

Academic work GCSE, A-levels, LCCI secretarial exams. Average size of upper fifth 70; upper sixth 20. *O-levels*: on average, 10 pupils in upper fifth pass 1–4 subjects; 40, 5–7 subjects; 20 pass 8+ subjects. *A-levels*: on average, 2 pupils in upper sixth pass 1 subject; 2, 2 subjects and 8 pass 3 subjects. On average, 4 take science/engineering A-levels; 6 take arts and humanities; 3 a mixture. *Computing facilities*: 3 BBC computers, 5 Sharps M280B.

Senior pupils' non-academic activities *Music*: 7 learn a musical instrument, 25 in school orchestra; 50 in choir. *Drama and dance*: 50 in school productions. 2 accepted for Drama School. *Art*: 30 take GCSE; 3 take A-level. 2 accepted for Art School. *Sport*: Netball, badminton, squash, tennis, swimming, volleyball, gymnastics available. 16 take exams. 3 represent county/country (tennis, badminton, swimming). *Other*: 12 take part in local community schemes. 36 have bronze Duke of Edinburgh's Award, and 7 have gold. Other activities include computer club, drama and debating societies.

Careers 5 part time careers advisors. Average number of pupils accepted for *arts and humanities degree courses* at Oxbridge, 2; other universities, 8; polytechnics or CHE, 2. *science and engineering degree courses* at Oxbridge, 2; medical schools, 2. *other general training courses*, 2. Average number of pupils going straight into careers in industry, 2.

Uniform School uniform worn except in sixth.

Houses/prefects Competitive houses. Prefects, head girl, head of house and house prefects – appointed by Head and staff.

Religion All girls attend Mass twice a term; assemblies reflect Christian beliefs.

Social Joint theatrical productions with local boys' school and social events in sixth form. Organised trips abroad. Upper sixth allowed to bring own car to school. Meals self service. School tuckshop. No tobacco/alcohol allowed.

Discipline No corporal punishment. Pupils failing to produce homework once might expect parents to be informed, threatening detention; those caught smoking cannabis on the premises might expect expulsion.

Alumni association run by Headmistress.

NOTRE DAME (LINGFIELD)

Notre Dame Senior School	Co-ed	Pupils 320
St Piers Lane	Boys	Upper sixth 15
Lingfield	• Girls	Termly fees:
Surrey RH7 6PH	Mixed sixth	Day £750
Telephone number 0932 63560	• Day	ISAI
	Boarding	
Enquiries/application to the Headmaster		

WHAT IT'S LIKE

Founded in 1940 by the Sisters of Notre Dame as a boarding and day school conducted by the Sisters. They withdrew from the school in 1987 and it is now a corporate charity under lay management. It combines infant, junior and senior schools on the edge of the attractive village of Lingfield (a settlement dating from 875). The pleasant buildings are well-equipped and occupy a campus which comprises about 20 acres of lawns, formal gardens, orchards and playing fields. An historic country house on site is being developed as a sixth form centre (the sixth form is expanding). The philosophy of the school is based on a firm belief in the development of 'the whole person'. Roman Catholic doctrine, morality and liturgical celebrations are an integral part of its life. There is a flourishing tradition of maximum care and support for the individual. A sound general education is provided and results are creditable. Strong in music and drama and a range of sports, games and extra-curricular activities. Some recent commitment to the Duke of Edinburgh's Award Scheme.

SCHOOL PROFILE

Pupils Total over 12, 320. Entry age, 11 and into the sixth. Own prep school provides over 20%. Some are children of former pupils.

Entrance Own entrance exam used. Not oversubscribed at present. No special skills required but pupils must be Christian. Parents not expected to buy basic text books. 2 bursaries, 50%.

Parents 15% in industry or commerce. 60+% live within 30 miles.

Staff Head Mr Gerald Davies, in post for 1 year. 25 full time staff, 14 part time. Annual turnover 5%.

Academic work GCSE and A-levels. Average size of upper fifth 66; upper

sixth 15 (but expanding). *Computing facilities*: 8 BBC computers. Provision for dyslexic pupils.

Senior pupils' non-academic activities *Music*: 53 learn a musical instrument, 14 to Grade 6 or above, 5 accepted for Music School; 14 in school orchestra, 15 in choir; 4 in local orchestras, 3 in wind bands. *Drama and dance*: 30 in school productions, 13 in drama club for GCSE. 30 take LAMDA Grade 6. 5 accepted for Drama/Dance schools, 1 goes on to work in theatre. *Art*: 300 take as non-examined subject; 25 take GCSE. 2 accepted for Art School. *Sport*: Netball, tennis, hockey, rounders, cross-country, squash, swimming, gymnastics and dance available; sailing, canoeing, rock-climbing in sixth. 200 take non-compulsory sport. 100 take exams. 10 represent county/country.

Careers 1 part time careers advisor plus visits from LEA service.

Uniform School uniform worn, modified in sixth.

Houses/prefects Competitive houses. Prefects, head girl and heads of houses – appointed in consultation with staff. School Council.

Religion Compulsory morning assembly, occasional masses and ecumenical service.

Social Drama, debates, orchestral and choral concerts with Worth School. Ski-ing holidays; exchanges arranged through AIJ. Pupils allowed to bring own bike/car to school. Meals self service. School shop selling exercise books etc. No tobacco/alcohol allowed.

Discipline No corporal punishment. Pupils failing to produce homework once might expect to repeat it plus extra work on same topic; those caught smoking cannabis on the premises would be expelled.

Alumni association run by School Secretary.

NOTTINGHAM HIGH (BOYS)

Nottingham High School	Co-ed	Pupils 825
Waverley Mount	● Boys	Upper sixth Yes
Nottingham NG7 4ED	Girls	Termly fees:
Telephone number 0602 786056	Mixed sixth	Day £700
	● Day	HMC
	Boarding	

Head D T Witcombe (18 years)
Age range 11–18, own prep from age 7; entry by own exam, including for pupils at own prep.
20 scholarships pa plus assisted places.

NOTTINGHAM HIGH (GIRLS)

Nottingham Girls' High School
9 Arboretum Street
Nottingham NG1 4JB
Telephone number 0602 417663

Enquiries/application to the Headmistress

Co-ed
Boys
● Girls
Mixed sixth
● Day
Boarding

Pupils 770
Upper sixth 95
Termly fees:
Day £695
GPDST

WHAT IT'S LIKE

Founded in 1875, single-site in the middle of Nottingham. The original Victorian houses have been modernised and there have been extensive additions to create a well-equipped school. The junior school is housed in buildings separate from but integrated with the senior school. Pupils come from a wide range of backgrounds. Religious worship is encouraged. A very good academic general education is given in both arts and sciences and results are good (the majority of girls go on to take degree courses). Strong in music, art and drama, and a good record in games and sports. A substantial commitment to local community schemes and an outstanding record in the Duke of Edinburgh's Award Scheme. Frequent collaboration with the High School for Boys in drama, debating, joint community service and Christian Union.

SCHOOL PROFILE

Pupils Total over 11, 770. Entry age: 4, 5, 7, 8, 11 and into the sixth. Own junior school provides over 20% of pupils.
Entrance Own entrance exam used. Oversubscribed. No special skills or religious requirements. 30 assisted places pa. Scholarships up to ½ fees. Bursaries in cases of financial need.
Parents 60+% live within 30 miles.
Staff Head Mrs C Bowering, in post for 4 years. 60 full time staff, 21 part time. Annual turnover, 5–10%.
Academic work GCSE and A-levels. Average size of upper fifth 112; upper sixth 85. *O-levels*: on average, 4 pupils in upper fifth pass 1–4 subjects; 21, 5–7 subjects; 86 pass 8+ subjects. *A-levels*: on average, 6 pupils in the upper sixth pass 1 subject; 16, 2 subjects; 46, 3 subjects and 13 pass 4 subjects. On average, 27 take science/engineering A-levels; 30 take arts and humanities; 30 a mixture. *Computing facilities*: 15–20 BBC computers, most of them networked. *Special provisions*: Help and guidance for dyslexic students in junior school especially.
Senior pupils' non-academic activities *Music*: 100+ learn a musical instrument, 30 to Grade 6 or above. 40 in school orchestra, 20 in school choir, 1 in National Youth Orchestra; 3 go on to a career in music. *Drama and dance*: 150+ in school productions, drama festival each year in which most participate; 20+ to Grade 6 in ESB, RAD, Spoken English and Public Speaking exams, several act with theatre groups, at present 1 with Central TV; 2 or 3 accepted for Drama School or drama degrees, 1 or 2 enter competitions. *Art*: A few take as non-examined subject, art clubs at varying ages; 30–40 take GCSE; 8+ take A-level; several take A-level fashion/fabric design. 2 or 3 accepted for Art School. *Sport*: Tennis, hockey, netball available. 200+ take

non-compulsory sport. 100+ take exams, eg gymnastics, swimming; 27 represent county (netball, hockey, tennis, swimming, shooting); 4 represent country (tennis (3), swimming (1)). *Other*: 50+ take part in local community schemes. 25–50 have bronze Duke of Edinburgh's Award, 25 have silver and 25 gold. Some take part in Conservation Group. Several enter voluntary schemes after leaving school on individual basis. Other activities include computer clubs.

Careers 2 full time staff give 12 periods/week helped by a part time member of staff 2 mornings/week. Average number of pupils accepted for *arts and humanities degree courses* at Oxbridge, 3; other universities, 30; polytechnics and CHE, 17. *science and engineering degree courses* at Oxbridge, 3; other universities, 21; medical schools, 4+; polytechnics and CHE, 2. *BEd*, 4 or 5. *other general training courses*, 2–3. The majority of students go on to degree courses, art foundation courses and occasionally retake A-levels at CFE to improve on grades. Several pupils go straight into careers in retail management.

Uniform School uniform worn except in the sixth.

Houses/prefects No competitive houses. No prefects. Head girl elected by the school. School Council.

Religion Religious worship encouraged (assembly).

Social Many debating and drama activities with Nottingham High School (Boys), also joint community service and Christian Union. Annual ski-ing holiday. Exchanges with schools in both France and Germany. Cruises. Pupils allowed to bring own cars to school. Meals self service. No tobacco/alcohol allowed.

Discipline No corporal punishment. Pupils failing to produce homework once might expect possible detention.

NOTTING HILL & EALING HIGH

Notting Hill & Ealing High School	Co-ed	Pupils 565
2 Cleveland Road	Boys	Upper sixth 65
Ealing	● Girls	Termly fees:
London W13 8AX	Mixed sixth	Day £789
Telephone number 01-997 5744	● Day	GPDST
Enquiries/application to Mrs C J Fitz	Boarding	

WHAT IT'S LIKE

Founded in 1873, suburban and single-site it lies in a pleasant and quiet residential area. The core consists of several large (formerly private) houses to which modern blocks have been added. There are playgrounds and large gardens. It has its own junior school. A sound general education is provided and, from a big sixth form, 60–70% of pupils go on to university. A good range of games, sports and activities. Good commitment to local social services. A range of enterprising European trips and tours is organised.

SCHOOL PROFILE

Pupils Total over 11, 565. Entry age, 5, 7, 11 and into the sixth. Own junior school provides over 40%. 10% are children of former pupils.

Entrance Own entrance exam and interview used. Oversubscribed. Academic ability looked for. No religious requirements. Parents not expected to buy text books. Assisted places. Scholarships/bursaries, depending on family income.

Parents 15+% in industry or commerce; 15+% are doctors, lawyers, etc and 15+% in the theatre, media, music, etc. 70+% live within the Borough of Ealing.

Staff Head Mrs C J Fitz. 33 full time staff, 15 part time. Annual turnover 5%.

Academic work GCSE and A-levels. Average size of upper fifth 75; upper sixth 65. *O-levels*: on average, 4 pupils in upper fifth pass 1–4 subjects; 47 pass 8+ subjects. *A-levels*: on average, 3 pupils in upper sixth pass 1 subject; 7, 2 subjects; 51, 3 subjects and 4 pass 4 subjects. On average, 27% take science/engineering A-levels; 46% take arts and humanities; 27% a mixture. *Computing facilities*: Specialist computer room with 8 station RM 3802 network, 5 BBCs.

Senior pupils' non-academic activities *Music*: 60% learn a musical instrument, 60% to Grade 6 or above, 2 accepted for Music School; 15 in school orchestra, 30% in school choir; comprehensive concert programme. *Drama and dance*: 25% participate in school productions. 12% belong to dance clubs; 8% and 15% (dance and drama respectively) up to Grade 6 in RAD, ESB, etc. 10% accepted for Drama/Dance School. 5% entered competitions. *Art*: 15% take as non-examined subject, 30% take GCSE; 8% take A-level. *Sport*: Netball, hockey, tennis, athletics, gym, dance, badminton, volleyball, riding, weight training, squash, golf in sixth form, table tennis available. 25% take non-compulsory sport. 5% represent county/country (gym, netball, tennis, badminton or mixture). *Other*: 20% take part in local community schemes. Each form has charity week to raise money (total last year – £4,500). Other activities include a computer club, literary society, BAYS (British Association of Young Scientists), lighting club, school shop (mini-enterprise), junior speakers club, Duke of Edinburgh's Award Scheme, photographic club, life drawing class.

Careers 2 specialist staff. Average percentages of pupils accepted for *arts and humanities degree courses* at Oxbridge, 4%; other universities, 33%; polytechnics or CHE, 6%. *science and engineering degree courses* at Oxbridge, 4%; other universities, 33%; medical schools, 6%; polytechnics or CHE, 6%. *BEd*, 3%. *other general training courses*, 2%. Average number of pupils going straight into careers in music/drama, 2%.

Uniform School uniform worn except in the sixth.

Houses/prefects No competitive houses. No prefects; head girl and deputies elected by the sixth form. School Council.

Religion Morning assembly.

Social Trips to Spain, France, Germany, Italy and Austria, ski-ing in Switzerland and activity holidays in the UK; choral tours. Pupils allowed to bring own car/bike/motorbike to school. Meals self service. School shop run by senior girls.

Former pupils Angela Rumbold; Eve Matheson.

OAKDENE

Oakdene School		Co-ed	Pupils 300
Wilton Road		Boys	Upper sixth 20
Beaconsfield	●	Girls	Termly fees:
Buckinghamshire HP9 2BS		Mixed sixth	Day £1019
Telephone number 04946 5114	●	Day	Boarding £1722
	●	Boarding	GSA
Enquiries/application to the Headmistress			

WHAT IT'S LIKE

Founded in 1911, it is single-site on the edge of the town; a compact and well-equipped campus in pleasant semi-rural surroundings, including good playing fields. Good modern facilities. A C of E school but ecumenical. A sound general education is provided and results are creditable. About 5–10 leavers go to university each year. Quite a good range of games and sports. Reasonable range of activities. It has a promising record in the Duke of Edinburgh's Award Scheme.

SCHOOL PROFILE

Pupils Total over 12, 300 (day and boarding). Entry age, 8, 11, 12 and into the sixth. Own junior department provides over 20%. 0.5% are children of former pupils.

Entrance Own entrance exam used. Not oversubscribed. No special skills. C of E; other religions accepted but should be prepared to attend assembly, RE lessons etc. Purchase of text books included in fees. 16 scholarships/bursaries, £1000–£200 pa.

Parents 15+% in the armed services; 15+% in industry or commerce; 15+% are doctors, lawyers, etc. More than 60% live within 30 miles; 10+% live overseas.

Staff Head Miss A M Tippett, in post for 1 year. 27 full time staff, 33 part time. Annual turnover 10%. Average age 40.

Academic work GCSE and A-levels. Average size of upper fifth 60; upper sixth 20. *O-levels*: on average, 20 pupils in upper fifth pass 1–4 subjects; 30, 5–7 subjects; 10 pass 8+ subjects. *A-levels*: on average, 5 pupils in upper sixth pass 1 subject; 5, 2 subjects; 10 pass 3 subjects. On average, 5 take science/engineering A-levels; 5 take arts and humanities; 10 a mixture. *Computing facilities*: 15 BBC computers. EFL provision.

Senior pupils' non-academic activities *Music*: 10 learn a musical instrument, 6 to Grade 6 or above; 1 accepted for BEd (music); 6 in school orchestra; 20 in choir. *Drama and dance*: 20 participate in school productions; 2 take Grade 6 in ESB, RAD etc. *Art*: 10 take as non-examined subject; 15 take GCSE; 4, A-level; 1 accepted for Art School; 5 belong to photographic club. *Sport*: Lacrosse, netball, athletics, tennis, swimming, rounders, badminton available. 20 take non-compulsory sport; 4 take exams eg gymnastics, swimming. 6 pupils represent county or district (athletics, lacrosse). *Other*: 15 have bronze Duke of Edinburgh's Award, 4 have silver and 2 have gold. Other activities sometimes include a computer club.

Careers 1 part time advisor. Average number of pupils accepted for *arts and humanities degree courses* at Oxbridge, 1; other universities, 4; polytechnics or

CHE, 2. *science and engineering degree courses* at Oxbridge, 1; other universities, 4; polytechnics or CHE, 2. *BEd*, 2. *other general training courses*, 8.

Uniform School uniform worn except sixth.

Houses/prefects Competitive houses. Prefects, head girl, head of house and house prefects – appointed by the Head after consultation. School Council.

Religion Weekly boarders chapel. Assembly. Boarders evening service on Sunday.

Social Dances/discos with other local schools from time to time. Organised ski trips regularly; summer adventure holiday; others occasionally. Pupils allowed to bring own car/bike to school. Meals self service. No tobacco allowed; under some circumstances sixth form may have some alcohol in a staff-controlled situation.

Discipline No corporal punishment. Pupils failing to produce homework once might expect a verbal warning and be required to hand in work the next day.

Boarding 20% have own study bedroom, 5% share (1 other); 55% are in dormitories of 6+. Houses, of 30–50 are divided by age group. Resident SRN. Central dining room. 2 exeats each term. Visits to the local town allowed.

Alumni association run by Mrs B Douglas, c/o the school.

OAKHAM

Oakham School	● Co-ed	Pupils 708
Chapel Close	Boys	Upper sixth 129
Oakham, Rutland	Girls	Termly fees:
Leicestershire LE15 6DT	Mixed sixth	Day £1117
Telephone number 0572 55238	● Day	Boarding £2139
Enquiries/application to the Registrar	● Boarding	HMC

WHAT IT'S LIKE

Founded in 1584 by Robert Johnson, Archdeacon of Leicester, it remained, until about 1960, a small and comparatively local boys' school. In the next 10 years the number of boys almost doubled and then co-education was introduced. To meet this rapid expansion the amenities were transformed and a massive building programme undertaken. There was further expansion after 1970 and it is now one of the best-equipped schools in England. It has two theatres, one of which is in the original school building. The houses are scattered in the very attractive, mellow, small country town of Oakham and extend into the countryside. There are fine gardens and playing fields. There is, inevitably, a close 'town and gown' relationship. The practice of Christianity is an essential part of the life of the community and there are regular chapel services. A happy friendly school in which a lot of attention is given to the individual. The large staff allows a staff:pupil ratio of 1:9. Academic standards are very high and results consistently good. Each year 100+ pupils go on to degree courses (15–20 to Oxbridge). It is very strong indeed in music and drama (each year there is a spring drama festival). There is a very high standard in sports and games (a large number of county and national representatives in hockey, rugby, cricket, squash and shooting). Numerous extra-curricular activities cater for most interests. There is a large and flourishing CCF for boys and girls. An exploration society has sent expeditions to Iceland, the Sahara and Papua New Guinea. A substantial commitment to local community services and a phenomenal record in the Duke of Edinburgh's Award Scheme.

SCHOOL PROFILE

Pupils Total over 12, 708. Day 270 (boys 140, girls 130); Boarding 438 (boys 260, girls 178). Entry age, 10, 11, 13 and into the sixth. 8% are children of former pupils.

Entrance Common entrance and own entrance exam used. Oversubscribed. Skills in music and art welcomed; no particular religious requirements. Parents not expected to buy text books. Assisted places pending. 35 scholarships/bursaries pa, full fees to ⅓ tuition.

Parents 30+% live within 30 miles; 10+% live overseas.

Staff Head Graham Smallbone, in post for 3 years. 108 full time staff, 30 part time. Annual turnover 3%. Average age 35.

Academic work GCSE and A-levels. Average size of upper fifth 153; upper sixth 129. *O-levels*: on average, 26 pupils in upper fifth pass 1–4 subjects; 36, 5–7 subjects; 91 pass 8+ subjects. *A-levels*: on average, 14 pupils in the upper sixth pass 1 subject; 26, 2 subjects; 79, 3 subjects and 6 pass 4 subjects. On average, 40 take science/engineering A-levels; 46 take arts and humanities; 45 a mixture. Russian offered to GCSE. *Computing facilities*: most staff and pupils have direct access to hard disk network throughout school. Some provision for dyslexia and EFL.

Senior pupils' non-academic activities *Music*: 100 learn a musical instrument, 60 to Grade 6 or above; 40 in school orchestra; 30, choir; 12, pop group; 25, concert band; 8, jazz band; 2 National Youth Orchestra. *Drama and dance*: 80 in school productions. 1 accepted for Drama/Dance Schools; 3 work in theatre. *Art*: 20 take as non-examined subject; 30 GCSE; 20 A-level. 8 accepted for Art School. 12 belong to eg photographic club. *Sport*: Rugby, cricket, tennis, netball, athletics, swimming, shooting, fencing, water polo, fives, table tennis, squash, basketball, soccer available. 150 take non-compulsory sport (at least 1 game option compulsory). 20 pupils represent county/country (hockey, rugby, cricket, squash, shooting). *Other*: 80 have bronze Duke of Edinburgh's Award, 90 have silver and 130 gold. Many other activities include computer club, chess, exploration, observing, debating.

Careers 5 part time careers advisors. Average number of pupils accepted for *arts and humanities degree courses* at Oxbridge, 9; other universities, 30; polytechnics or CHE, 15. *science and engineering degree courses* at Oxbridge, 9; other universities, 30; medical schools, 3; polytechnics or CHE, 15. *BEd*, 2. *other general training courses*, 10. Average number of pupils going straight into careers in armed services, 2; industry, 8; the City, 2.

Uniform School uniform worn except the upper sixth.

Houses/prefects Competitive houses. Prefects, head boy and girl, head of house and house prefects – elected. School Council.

Religion Regular chapel services.

Social Debating in local and national competitions. Regular German school exchange. Pupils allowed to bring own bike to school. Meals self service. School shop. No tobacco allowed; supervised licensed bar for upper sixth.

Discipline No corporal punishment. Pupils failing to produce home-work once might expect detention; those caught smoking cannabis on the premises will be expelled.

Boarding 80% share a study bedroom with 1 or 2, 20% are in dormitories of 3. 4 houses, of approximately 70, divided by age and single sex. Resident qualified nurse. 2 central dining rooms. Pupils can provide and cook own snacks. 1 termly exeat, 4 days–1 week. Visits to local town allowed in free time.

Alumni association run by Rev G Treanor, Lincoln House, Oakham.

Former pupils Thomas Merton (religious philosopher); A P F Chapman (cricketer); R Jacobs (rugby); Matthew Manning (psychic).

OLD PALACE

Old Palace School	Co-ed		Pupils 600
Old Palace Road	Boys		Upper sixth Yes
Croydon	● Girls		Termly fees:
Surrey CR0 1AX	Mixed sixth		Day £650
Telephone number 01-688 2027	● Day		GSA
	Boarding		

Head Miss K L Hilton (14 years)
Age range 11–18, own prep from age 7; entry by own exam.
4 scholarships pa and bursaries.

OLD SWINFORD

Old Swinford Hospital	Co-ed		Pupils 500
Stourbridge	● Boys		Upper sixth Yes
West Midlands DY8 1QX	Girls		Termly fees:
Telephone number 0384 370025	Mixed sixth		see below
	● Day		
	● Boarding		

Head C F R Potter
Age range 11–18; entry by own exam
Voluntary Aided school; tuition fees paid by boys' local education authority, including 25 day boys each year. Boarding fees additional. Some scholarships available.

ORATORY, THE

The Oratory School	Co-ed	Pupils 350
Woodcote	• Boys	Upper sixth 70
Reading	Girls	Termly fees:
Berkshire RG8 0PJ	Mixed sixth	Day £1538
Telephone number 0491 680207	• Day	Boarding £2198
Enquiries/application to the Headmaster	• Boarding	HMC

WHAT IT'S LIKE

Founded in 1859 to meet the educational needs of the Catholic laity. Cardinal Newman himself was very much responsible for establishing the school and his views and beliefs about education are still its driving force. It was originally founded in Birmingham, moved to Caversham after the First World War and settled at Woodcote during the Second World War. It has a very agreeable rural site with spacious grounds and purpose-built accommodation. Facilities are excellent. Religious education is an important part of the curriculum. Sunday Mass and daily house prayers are compulsory. Very good teaching is provided and academic standards are high. Some 45–50 pupils proceed to university each year; a high proportion for a school of this size. It is outstandingly strong in music and there is a considerable commitment to drama and art. A big range of games and sports is available (a lot of representatives at county level). Also a wide variety of extra-curricular activities and a strong CCF. A promising record in the Duke of Edinburgh's Award Scheme.

SCHOOL PROFILE

Pupils Total over 13, 350. Day 50; Boarding 300. Entry age, 11, 13 and into the sixth. The Oratory Preparatory School provides over 20%.

Entrance Common entrance exam and informal tests used. Oversubscribed. No special skills required. The overwhelming majority of boarders are Roman Catholic; some day boys are not. Parents expected to pay a termly flat rate charge for books. Scholarships/bursaries available, £3297–£660.

Parents 15+% in the armed services, 15+% are doctors, lawyers etc; remainder are overwhelmingly professional, commercial and industrial. 10+% live within 30 miles; up to 10% live overseas.

Staff Head A J Snow, in post for 15 years. 35 full time staff, 16 part time. Annual turnover 0–5%. Average age 40.

Academic work GCSE and A-levels. Average size of upper fifth 70; upper sixth 70. *O-levels*: on average, 22 pupils in upper fifth pass 5–7 subjects; 48 pass 8+ subjects. *A-levels*: on average, 4 pupils in upper sixth pass 1 subject; 4, 2 subjects; 56, 3 subjects and 4 pass 4 subjects. On average, 50% take science/engineering A-levels; 50% take arts and humanities. Portuguese and any foreign language (eg Arabic, Dutch) by arrangement are offered to GCSE/A-level. *Computing facilities*: 1 new computer department, comprising main teaching laboratory and 3 other rooms. Several other departments linked to school net. Provision for mild dyslexia.

Senior pupils' non-academic activities *Music*: 150 learn a musical instrument, 35 to Grade 6 or above, 1 accepted for Music School; 2 take music degrees (Oxford); 50 in 2 school orchestras, 40 in choir, 15 in string orchestra,

16 in chamber music groups; 1 in National Youth Orchestra; 2 go on to London choirs (eg RPO); 40 take music courses in holidays. *Drama and dance*: 50 in school productions. 7 took Grade 8 RAD in recent years. 1 accepted for Drama School. *Art*: 15 take as non-examined subject; 85 take GCSE; 24 A-level; 10 take other exams. 4–5 accepted for Art School; 5–6 for architecture; 2–3 for university art degree. 20 belong to school arts society. *Sport*: Rugby, cricket, soccer, lawn tennis, hockey, rowing, athletics, cross-country running, real tennis, squash, swimming, sailing, canoeing, table tennis, badminton, basketball, windsurfing, golf available. 20 take non-compulsory sport. 75 take exams eg gymnastics, swimming, life-saving. 15 pupils represent county (rugby, hockey, table tennis, squash, golf) and country (judo, shooting). *Other*: 45 have bronze Duke of Edinburgh's Award, 2 have silver (recently re-introduced). Other activities include a computer club, chess, judo, music, debating, cultural, law, science, arts, current affairs societies.

Careers 7 part time advisors. Average number of pupils accepted for *arts and humanities degree courses* at Oxbridge, 5; other universities, 26; polytechnics or CHE, 10. *science and engineering degree courses* at Oxbridge, 5; other universities, 8; medical schools, 2; polytechnics or CHE, 3. *BEd*, 2. *other general training courses*, 1. Average number of pupils going straight into careers in the armed services, 2; other, 3.

Uniform School uniform worn, modified in the sixth.

Houses/prefects Competitive houses. Prefects, school captain, house captains and house prefects – appointed by the Headmaster with Housemasters. Orderlies (fagging) only in second year.

Religion Sunday mass compulsory; weekday masses optional; daily house prayers compulsory.

Social Debates, dances, other social/educational ventures with other local schools. Organised ski trips, sailing trips, some exchanges – usually to France. Pupils allowed to bring own bike to school; exceptionally, day pupils may bring own car/motorbike. Meals self service. School tuck shop and paperback bookshop. Pupils of 16+ may smoke only in their own study. Boys over 18 may visit local inns; some social functions and informal occasions where boys between 16 and 18 may be allowed alcohol under staff supervision.

Discipline Corporal punishment very rare. Pupils failing to produce homework once might expect additional work to be set; those caught smoking cannabis on the premises could expect to be asked to leave.

Boarding 25% have own study bedroom, 35% share double studies; 20% share with 2–4 others; 20% are in dormitories of 6+. 4 senior houses and 1 junior house of approximately 70 boarders and 15 day boys are the same as competitive houses. Resident qualified nurse. School doctor lives very close to the school. Central dining room. Pupils can provide and cook own food. Exeats to suit parental convenience. Occasional visits to the local town allowed for sixth form.

Former pupils Sir James Comyn (former High Court Judge); Sir Michael Levey (former Director of the National Gallery); Mgr V F J Morgan CBE (former Vicar General of the Royal Navy); J J Hayes MP; Michael Berkeley (composer); Christopher Hurford (former Australian Government minister); Joseph Connolly (*Times* columnist); Nicholas Bicat (composer); Igor Judge QC; Paul Purnell QC; Nicholas Purnell QC; E Leigh MP.

OSWESTRY

Oswestry School
Oswestry
Shropshire SY11 2TL
Telephone number 0691 655711

Enquiries/application to the Headmaster

- Co-ed
  Boys
  Girls
  Mixed sixth
- Day
- Boarding

Pupils 375
Upper sixth 50
Termly fees:
Day £1025
Boarding £1720
SHMIS; SHA

WHAT IT'S LIKE

Founded in 1407 and one of the oldest continuous foundations in England. The agreeable well-designed red-brick buildings occupy pleasant grounds and playing fields on the edge of the market town of Oswestry and overlooking the Shropshire Plain. The junior school and pre-prep are combined nearby. Facilities are very good. A good all-round education is provided in a supportive family atmosphere and every effort is made to accommodate families' needs. Academic standards and results are good and 40–50% of leavers go on to degree courses each year. Lively music, drama and art. Sport and games are encouraged and high standards are attained (a lot of county representatives). A very large number of clubs and societies cater for every need. The CCF is vigorous and the school has an impressive record in the Duke of Edinburgh's Award Scheme.

SCHOOL PROFILE

Pupils Total (12+), 375. Day 206 (boys 117, girls 89); Boarding 169 (boys 111, girls 58). Entry age, 11+, 13+ and into sixth. 25% are children of former pupils.

Entrance Common entrance and own entrance exam used. Places generally available. No religious requirements. Parents expected to buy text books. 10 scholarships/bursaries available (including sport and music), £2300–£500.

Parents 15+% in the armed services. 60+% live within 30 miles; 10+% live overseas.

Staff Head Ian G Templeton, in post for 3 years. 31 full time staff, 4 part time. Annual turnover 5%. Average age 40.

Academic work GCSE and A-levels. Average size of upper fifth 70; upper sixth 50. *O-levels*: on average, 24 pupils in upper fifth pass 1–4 subjects; 33, 5–7 subjects; 17 pass 8+ subjects. *A-levels*: on average, 10 pupils in upper sixth pass 1 subject; 8, 2 subjects; 15, 3 subjects and 3 pass 4 subjects. On average, 15 take science/engineering A-levels; 13 take arts and humanities; 13 a mixture. *Computing facilities*: 12 networked BBC B micros plus 1 3802 Research and 3 Amstrads. Special provisions for EFL and remedial English.

Senior pupils' non-academic activities *Music*: 5 learn a musical instrument to Grade 6 or above. 1 accepted for Music School. 5 play in pop group beyond school, 30 in school orchestras, 60 in choirs, 5 in pop group, 2 in county orchestra. *Drama and dance*: Most of the school in school productions. *Art*: 30 take GCSE; 6, A-level. 4 accepted for Art School, 1 for architecture, 1 for interior design. 10 belong to photographic club. *Sport*: Boys: rugby, soccer, cricket. Girls: hockey, netball. Both: athletics, cross-country, swimming, badminton, tennis, squash available. 90 take non-compulsory sport; 20 take exams eg gymnastics, swimming. 20 represent county/country (cricket, swimming, athletics, hockey/football). *Other*: 6 have bronze Duke of Edinburgh's Award, 24 have silver and 16 gold. Other activities include a computer club, chess club, angling.

Careers 4 part time advisors. Average number of pupils accepted for *arts and humanities degree courses* at Oxbridge, 1; other universities, 4; polytechnics or CHE, 4. *science and engineering degree courses* at Oxbridge, 1; other universities, 3; medical schools, 3; polytechnics or CHE, 2. *BEd*, 4. *other general training courses*, 15. Average number of pupils going straight into careers in the armed services, 5; industry, 3; other, 10.

Uniform School uniform worn except in the sixth.

Houses/prefects Competitive houses. Prefects, head boy and girl, head of house and house prefects – appointed after consultation.

Religion Compulsory chapel. Boarders must attend unless attending own (eg Roman Catholic) church.

Social Organised exchanges in France, Germany, trips to Russia, France, Spain, Italy etc. Pupils allowed to bring own bike to school. Meals self service. School shop. No tobacco allowed. Beer allowed in sixth form club supervised by staff.

Discipline No corporal punishment. Pupils failing to produce homework once might expect a reminder then work detention for persistent failure. Should anyone be caught with drugs they would be expelled. (This has never arisen.)

Boarding 5% have own study bedroom, 50% share (1 or 2); 45% are in dormitories of 6+. Houses, of approximately 50, same as competitive houses and are single sex. Resident qualified medical staff. Central dining room. Pupils can provide and cook own snacks. 3 or 4 overnight exeats each term. Visits to local town allowed.

Alumni association run by J F Tilley, Herschell House, Whittington, Oswestry, Shropshire SY11 4DB.

OUNDLE

The School	Co-ed	Pupils 750
Oundle	● Boys	Upper sixth Yes
Peterborough PE8 4EN	Girls	Termly fees:
Telephone number 0832 73536	Mixed sixth	Boarding £2250
	Day	HMC
	● Boarding	

WHAT IT'S LIKE

It originated from the bequest of Sir William Laxton, a native of Oundle, to the Grocers' Company in 1556, and by this he re-endowed a grammar school already in existence in 1485. Its 17th, 18th and 19th century buildings (plus the many additions made in the 20th century) are scattered through the small and very agreeable township of Oundle. Thus, the school is an integral part of the town, and vice versa, and there is a close town and gown relationship. It is extremely well equipped with all that a school needs including a fine 1914–18 memorial chapel. There are 12 houses which are all independent units. Religious instruction accords with the teaching of the Church of England and there is some emphasis on regular worship. A very large staff allows a staff:pupil ratio of 1:8. The teaching is well known to be good and academic standards are high. Results are consistently impressive and large numbers of leavers go on to university (including 20 or more each year to Oxbridge) and other places of further education. There is an extremely strong music department and many of the boys are involved in numerous musical activities in the school and beyond it. There is also an excellent and very active art department. Large numbers of pupils are also engaged in dramatic activities, many of which are presented in the Stahl Theatre. Professional companies often visit to give performances. Oundle has long had a reputation for high achievements in sports and games and a wide variety of clubs and societies caters for virtually every conceivable need. The CCF (with 350 members) is one of the largest contingents in the country and it has an ambitious and enterprising programme each year. There is also emphasis on outdoor pursuits and the school runs a large adventure training section whose members have made expeditions to Ecuador, Afghanistan, Ladakh, China and Pakistan. Over 100 boys are engaged in local community services.

SCHOOL PROFILE

Head D B McMurray (4 years)
Age range 11–18; entry by own exam or common entrance.
10% of pupils from overseas. Some scholarships including art, music, continuation and sixth form.

OUR LADY'S (ABINGDON)

Our Lady's Convent Senior School
Radley Road
Abingdon
Oxfordshire OX14 3PS
Telephone number 0235 24658

Enquiries/application to the Headmistress

Co-ed
Boys
● Girls
Mixed sixth
● Day
● Boarding

Pupils 286
Upper sixth 34
Termly fees:
Day £675
Boarding £1460

WHAT IT'S LIKE

Founded in 1860 and administered by the Sisters of Mercy. It is situated in the market town on a single site with playing fields opposite. Pleasant buildings and good modern facilities. A new building programme in the 1970s provided extensive additions. There is a junior school. It has a reputation for a friendly and caring approach and aims to provide a thorough education by a combination of traditional and modern methods, in the atmosphere of a Catholic community and according to Christian principles. All boarders are Roman Catholics but day girls may be of other Christian denominations. Standards of teaching are good and so are results. Each year some girls go on to university. Very strong in music; a third of the school is involved. Some drama and art. A wide range of sports and games and plentiful activities. Some commitment to local community schemes and an impressive record in the Duke of Edinburgh's Award Scheme.

SCHOOL PROFILE

Pupils Total over 12, 286. Day 217; Boarding 69. Entry age, 11 and into the sixth. Our Lady's Convent Junior School and Manor Preparatory School provide over 20%. A very small proportion are children of former pupils.

Entrance Own entrance exam used. No special skills required. Boarders must be Roman Catholic; other Christian denominations for day girls. Parents not expected to buy text books.

Parents 15+% in the armed services; 15+% in industry or commerce. More than 60% live within 30 miles; up to 10% live overseas.

Staff Head Sister Monica Sheehy, in post for 8 years. 23 full time staff, 16 part time. Annual turnover 1%. Average age mid-40s.

Academic work GCSE and A-levels. Average size of upper fifth 50; upper sixth 34. (Sixth form increasing in size.) *O-levels*: on average, 16 pupils in upper fifth pass 1–4 subjects; 24, 5–7 subjects; 16 pass 8+ subjects. *A-levels*: on average, 2 pupils in upper sixth pass 1 subject; 6, 2 subjects; 7, 3 subjects and 1 passes 4 subjects. On average, 3 take science/engineering A-levels; 8 take arts and humanities; 5 a mixture. *Computing facilities*: Fully-equipped computer room with 12 BBC computers.

Senior pupils' non-academic activities *Music*: 33% of pupils learn a musical instrument; quite a large orchestra and 2 choirs. *Art*: 10 take GCSE; 11 A-level; 3 accepted for Art School. *Sport*: Hockey, badminton, squash, tennis, netball, gymnastics, keep fit, weight lifting, SCUBA (sixth form only), swimming, modern dance available. Almost all take non-compulsory sport. At least 2 represent county/country (badminton, hockey, squash). *Other*: 25 take part in local community schemes. 60+ have bronze Duke of Edinburgh's Award, 5 have silver and 1 has gold. Other activities include computer, French, ceramics, needlework, drama, debating, jewellery and art clubs.

Careers 1 part time advisor. Average number of pupils (based on a smaller sixth form) accepted for *arts and humanities degree courses* at universities, 3; polytechnics or CHE, 10–15. *science and engineering degree courses* at universities, 1; polytechnics or CHE, 3–6. *other general training courses*, 5–10. Average number of pupils going straight into careers in the armed services, 1–10; industry, 1–3; civil service, 3–6; music/drama, 1–3.

Uniform School uniform worn, modified in the sixth.

Houses/prefects Competitive houses. Prefects, head girl and head boarding prefect – appointed by Head following suggestions by staff. School Council.

Religion Sunday mass for boarders. All pupils join in any school service which may be held once or twice per term and assembly every day.

Social Lectures, dances, SCUBA, inter-sixth form society with other local schools. French exchange scheme organised through Dragons International and a German exchange with a school in Hanover. Pupils allowed to bring own car/bike/motorbike to school (but no parking provided). Meals formal. School shop. No tobacco/alcohol allowed.

Discipline No corporal punishment. Pupils failing to produce homework once might expect to be kept in to make it up at break, lunch time or after school; those caught smoking cannabis on the premises could expect expulsion.

Boarding Upper sixth only have own study bedroom, others, fourth form upwards, share; juniors in dormitories of 6+. Houses, of 20+ are divided into class groups. Resident qualified nurse. Central dining room. Older pupils can provide and cook own food. Exeats, any weekend except the first and last of each term. Visits to the local town allowed. Educational/pleasure trips organised regularly.

OUR LADY'S (LOUGHBOROUGH)

Our Lady's Convent School	Co-ed		Pupils 621
Burton Street	Boys		(including prep)
Loughborough	• Girls		Upper sixth 22
Leicestershire LE11 2DT	Mixed sixth		Termly fees:
Telephone number 0509 263901	• Day		Day £560
Enquiries/application to the Headmistress	Boarding		

WHAT IT'S LIKE

Established in 1845 by the Sisters of Providence – the Rosminians. It has a pleasant urban site with four independent buildings for four departments: Montessori, infant, junior and senior. The staff is both religious and secular and there is an excellent range of facilities. A Roman Catholic school, it teaches religious education in all departments according to the doctrines of the Catholic Church. A cheerful and friendly atmosphere prevails. The girls are given as much liberty as is compatible with good discipline. A strong sense of responsibility is inculcated. It provides a sound general education. Quite a good range of sport, games and activities. A substantial commitment to local community schemes and the Duke of Edinburgh's Award Scheme.

SCHOOL PROFILE

Pupils Total 621 (including prep). Entry age, 3–18 including into the sixth. Own prep school provides over 20% of pupils. 1% (variable) are children of former pupils.

Entrance Own entrance exam used. Oversubscribed. No special skills or religious requirements. Parents not expected to buy text books. 8 scholarships/bursaries, £560–£380 per term.

Parents 15+% in industry or commerce. 60+% live within 30 miles.

Staff Head Sister Mary Mark, in post for 2 years. 33 full time staff, 33 part time. Annual turnover 2%. Average age 40–45.

Academic work GCSE and A-levels. Average size of upper fifth 62; upper sixth 22. *O-levels*: on average, 46 pupils in upper fifth pass 1–4 subjects; 18, 5–7 subjects; 21 pass 8+ subjects. *A-levels*: on average, 5 pupils in upper sixth pass 1 subject; 5, 2 subjects and 6, 3 subjects. On average, 4 take science/engineering A-levels; 12 take arts and humanities; 6 a mixture. *Computing facilities*: 9 BBC computers and 4 word processors.

Senior pupils' non-academic activities *Music*: 15 learn a musical instrument, 4 to Grade 6 or above. 1 accepted for Music School; 7 in school orchestra, 15 in school choir, 6 in folk group; 2 in Leicester Philharmonic. *Drama and dance*: 40 in school productions, 5 in various productions in Leicester area; some up to Grade 6 in elocution. 1 accepted for Drama/Dance School, 1 goes on to work in theatre, 1 goes on to stage management. *Art*: 56 take GCSE; 12, A-level; 5 accepted for Art School. *Sport*: Swimming, hockey, netball, athletics, tennis, squash, badminton available (fifth and sixth canoeing, dry slope skiing). 22 take non-compulsory sport. 3 pupils represent county/country (cricket, hockey, athletics). *Other*: 28 take part in local community schemes. 25 have bronze Duke of Edinburgh's Award and 6 have silver. 1 enters voluntary schemes after leaving school. Other activities include choir, orchestra, cross-country, gymnastics, board games, debating society, science society.

Careers 1 full time and 2 part time advisors. Average number of pupils accepted for *arts and humanities degree courses* at universities, 5; polytechnics or CHE, 2. *science and engineering degree courses* at universities, 2; polytechnics or CHE, 1. *BEd*, 1. *other general training courses*, 2. Average number of pupils going straight into careers in industry, 7; civil service, 1; music/drama, 1.

Uniform School uniform worn throughout.

Houses/prefects Competitive houses. Prefects, head girl, head of house and house prefects – appointed by the Head.

Religion Daily assembly and termly services compulsory.

Social Science society, debating society with other schools. Organised trips abroad. Pupils allowed to bring own car/bike/motorbike to school. Cold lunch. School shop. No tobacco/alcohol allowed.

Discipline No corporal punishment. Pupils failing to produce homework once might expect warning; those caught smoking cannabis on the premises could expect suspension.

Alumni association is run by Mrs Rachael Morgan, 105 Leopold Street, Loughborough, Leics LE71 0DW.

OXFORD HIGH

Oxford High School	Co-ed		Pupils 600
Belbroughton Road	Boys		Upper sixth Yes
Oxford OX2 6XA	● Girls		Termly fees:
Telephone number 0865 59888	Mixed sixth		Day £625
	● Day		GSA; GPDST
	Boarding		

Head Mrs J Townsend (7 years)
Age range 9–18; entry by own exam.
Scholarships, including for music, are available.

PANGBOURNE

Pangbourne College
Pangbourne
Reading
Berkshire RG8 8LA
Telephone number 07357 2101

Co-ed   Pupils 360
● Boys   Upper sixth Yes
Girls   Termly fees:
Mixed sixth   Day £1400
● Day   Boarding £1990
● Boarding   HMC

WHAT IT'S LIKE

Founded in 1917 as the Nautical College to train boys for a career at sea. Its name was changed in 1969 and since then the emphasis has been on a more general education, but it still prepares boys for entry into the Royal Navy and other services. It retains a naval ethos and nautical tradition, and this includes the wearing of uniform. It has a very fine site indeed of 240 acres in beautiful Berkshire countryside a mile from Pangbourne village and near the river. There have been many improvements and additions in recent years and the college is now extremely well equipped. Pupils live in 6 boarding houses; after the first year they have study bedrooms. A broad general education is provided. Academic standards are high and results are good. Quite a lot of leavers go on to university and other places of further education. The college has a strong tradition of success in music and drama. There are a chapel choir, a choral society, an orchestra and a military band. Each year there is a major annual dramatic production plus a house drama festival and work by the modern theatre group. Sports and games are well provided for (the playing fields and other facilities are excellent) and these include rowing and sailing. The CCF is voluntary but there is a strong naval contingent and a Royal Marine section. Sea-going voyages are arranged each year. There is quite a lot of emphasis on outdoor pursuits for which the environment is most suitable. A good range of clubs and societies caters for most extra-curricular activities.

SCHOOL PROFILE

Head P D C Points (19 years)
Age range 11–18; entry by own exam or common entrance.
6 scholarships pa. Also art and music awards and bursaries.

PARK, THE

The Park School for Girls
25 Lynedoch Street
Glasgow G3 9EX
Telephone number 041 332 0426

Enquiries/application to the Headmistress

Co-ed   Pupils 300
Boys   Upper sixth 30
● Girls   Termly fees:
Mixed sixth   Day £756
● Day
Boarding

WHAT IT'S LIKE

The Girls' School Company Ltd was founded in 1879 and is responsible for administering this school and St Columba's Kilmacolm. The Park School lies in the middle of the city in the Park Circus Conservation Area. There are big playing fields at Anniesland and pupils also have the use of the Allander Sports Centre in Bearsden. The school is well equipped with modern facilities and a sound general education is provided. A family atmosphere, small teaching sets (the staff:pupil ratio is about 1:10) and efficient pastoral care produce good results academically and otherwise. There is much emphasis on self-discipline and acceptance of responsibility for oneself. Close liaison exists between school and parents. Each year 15–20 girls go on to university. Quite strong in music, drama and art. A good record in sports and games (a lot of representatives at county level) and a promising record in the Duke of Edinburgh's Award Scheme.

SCHOOL PROFILE

Pupils Total over 12, 300. Entry age, 5 or 12 and into the sixth.

Entrance Own entrance exam used. Oversubscribed at some stages. No special skills or religious requirements. Parents expected to buy text books. 51 assisted places. 4 scholarships/bursaries available, £342 per term.

Parents 15+% in industry or commerce; 15+% are doctors, lawyers, etc. 60+% live within 30 miles.

Staff Head Mrs M E Myatt, in post for 2 years. 31 full time staff, 15 part time. Annual turnover 4%. Average age 30–40.

Academic work O-grade, Highers, CSYS, A-levels. Average size of upper fifth 60, upper sixth 30. *O-levels*: on average, 5 pupils in upper fifth pass 1–4 subjects; 20, 5–7 subjects; 35 pass 8+ subjects. On average, 8 take science/ engineering A-levels; 6 take arts and humanities; 2 a mixture. *Computing facilities*: 20 BBC computers, disks, printers etc. Special teaching provisions as needed.

Senior pupils' non-academic activities *Music*: 17 learn a musical instrument, 5 to Grade 6 or above; 12 in school orchestra, 37 in choir; 1 in National Youth Orchestra. *Drama and dance*: 20 in school productions. 2 take Grade 6 in ESB, RAD etc. 1 accepted for Drama/Dance school; 1 goes on to work in theatre. *Art*: 60 take art appreciation as non-examined subject; 33 take GCSE; 6 A-level; 16 Higher. 3 accepted for Art School; 1 for architecture, 2 for college of textiles, 3 to technical colleges. 10 belong to art club. *Sport*: Hockey, swimming, tennis, athletics, squash, badminton, curling, judo, ski-ing, golf, aerobics, gymnastics available. 50 take non-compulsory sport. 24 represent county/country (tennis, hockey, gym, showjumping, athletics, netball). *Other*: 6 take part in local community schemes. 3 have bronze Duke of Edinburgh's Award, 3 have silver and 3 have gold. Other activities include a computer club, electronics club, theatre-goers club, debating and public speaking, Young Enterprise scheme.

Careers 1 part time advisor. Average number of pupils accepted for *arts and humanities degree courses* at universities, 8; polytechnics or CHE, 7. *science and engineering degree courses* at Oxbridge, 1; other universities, 10; medical schools, 3; polytechnics or CHE, 3. *BEd*, 1. Average number of pupils going straight into careers in the civil service, 1; music/drama, 1; other, 2.

Uniform School uniform worn throughout.

Houses/prefects Competitive houses. Prefects, head girl, head of house and house prefects – elected by the school. School Council.

Religion Compulsory daily assembly.

Social ESU debates, sport, Young Enterprise with other local schools. Organised trips abroad and exchange systems. Meals self service. School shop. No tobacco/alcohol allowed.

Discipline No corporal punishment. Pupils failing to produce homework once might expect lunch time detention, extra work and communication to parents; those caught smoking cannabis on the premises could expect expulsion.

Alumni association run by Mrs Alison Armour, 22 Norwood Drive, Glasgow G46.

Former pupils Siobhan Redmond (actress); Joanna Isles (artist).

PARSONS MEAD

Parsons Mead School
Ottways Lane
Ashtead
Surrey KT21 2PE
Telephone number 037 22 76401

Enquiries/application to the Headmistress

Co-ed
Boys
● Girls
Mixed sixth
● Day
● Boarding

Pupils 250
Upper sixth 30
Termly fees:
Day £910
Boarding £1655
GSA

WHAT IT'S LIKE

Founded in 1897, it is greenbelt with well-designed modern buildings and good facilities on a 12-acre site. Senior and junior schools combined. It is C of E by tradition but girls of all faiths are welcome. There is close co-operation between parents and staff. A sound education is given and exam results are good. Art, music and drama are popular and well supported. A decent range of sports (new sports hall), games, clubs and societies.

SCHOOL PROFILE

Pupils Total over 12, 250. Day 213; Boarding 37. Entry age, 3, 5, 8, 11, 12 and into the sixth. Own prep school provides over 80% of pupils. A small proportion are children of former pupils.

Entrance Own entrance exam used. Oversubscribed. No special skills or religious requirements. Parents not expected to buy text books. Up to 5 scholarships/bursaries per year, 30–20% of fees.

Parents 15+% in industry or commerce. 80+% live within 30 miles.

Staff Head Miss M M Dees, in post for 9+ years. 24 full time staff, 15 part time. Annual turnover up to 10%. Average age 35–40.

Academic work GCSE and A-levels. Average size of upper fifth, 52; upper sixth, 20–30. *O-levels*: on average, 5 pupils in upper fifth pass 1–4 subjects; 17, 5–7 subjects; 30, 8+ subjects. *A-levels*: on average, 5 pupils in upper sixth pass 1 subject; 5, 2 subjects; 20, 3 subjects and 1+ pass 4 subjects. On average, 10 take science/engineering A-levels; 8 take arts and humanities; 12 a mixture of both. Social biology and business studies are offered to A-level. *Computing facilities*: 7 BBC micros and 2 printers in senior school. 3 in junior school. Special provisions for mildly dyslexic, visually handicapped and EFL.

Senior pupils' non-academic activities *Music*: Many learn a musical instrument (most not at school), quite a few to Grade 6 or above. A few apply for Music School. *Drama and dance*: Many in school productions; a few up to Grade 6 in ESB, RAD. Very rare for pupils to be accepted for Drama/Dance Schools. *Art*: All pupils take as non-examined subject, 20 take GCSE; 1–5, A-level; 1–2 accepted for Art School. *Sport*: Hockey, netball, tennis, rounders, swimming, athletics, squash available. A lot take non-compulsory sport; many younger girls take exams, eg gymnastics, swimming; a few pupils represent county/country (tennis, swimming). *Other*: 15 take part in local community schemes. School supports charities. Other activities include 5 computer clubs, 20 other clubs. Duke of Edinburgh's Award Scheme recently introduced.

Careers 1 full time and 1 part time advisor. Average number of pupils accepted for *arts and humanities degree courses* at universities, 5; polytechnics or CHE, 3+. *science and engineering degree courses* at universities, 5; polytechnics or CHE, 3. *other general training courses*, 4.

Uniform School uniform worn except in the sixth.

Houses/prefects No competitive houses or prefects. Head girl – elected by sixth form. School Council.

Religion Religious worship encouraged.

Social Various organised local events. Ski-ing and other educational trips abroad. Day pupils allowed to bring own bike to school. Meals self service. No tobacco/alcohol allowed.

Discipline No corporal punishment. Pupils failing to produce homework once might expect 1 report (3 in 1 term = detention); those caught smoking cannabis on the premises could expect suspension/expulsion.

Boarding Nearly half have own study bedroom, 6 in pairs; 20 are in dormitories of 6+. Qualified nurse (at school 8–5.30), then on call. Central dining room. Sixth form can provide and cook own food. 3–5 exeats each term. Visits to local town allowed.

Alumni association is run by Mrs D Peacock, c/o the School.

PENRHOS

Penrhos College	Co-ed	Pupils 250
Colwyn Bay	Boys	Upper sixth 37
Clwyd LL28 4DA	● Girls	Termly fees:
Telephone number 0492 530333	Mixed sixth	Day £1215
	● Day	Boarding £1820
Enquiries/application to the Head	● Boarding	Independent; GSA

WHAT IT'S LIKE

Founded in 1880, it has a pleasant campus in the resort of Colwyn Bay, by the sea. Well designed and comfortable buildings with good boarding accommodation. The junior school is half a mile away. A progressive school with a happy atmosphere, it is interdenominational but basically Christian. A sound general education is provided and academic standards are good. Some 10–15 pupils go on to university each year. It is very strong indeed in music, drama and art. Considerable strength in sport and games (a number of county representatives). Its activities programmes are outstanding. Between 25–30 activities are available each term and everyone's needs are catered for. There is also a comprehensive programme for outdoor pursuits (eg sailing, canoeing, mountaineering), and a lot of overseas trips are organised.

SCHOOL PROFILE

Pupils Total over 12, 260. Day 75; Boarding 185. Entry age, 11 and into the sixth. 7% are children of former pupils.

Entrance Own entrance exam used. Not oversubscribed. No special skills or religious requirements. Parents not expected to buy text books. 12 assisted places. 5 scholarships/bursaries available, 50% of current fees.

Parents 30+% live within 30 miles; 10+% live overseas.

Staff Head N C Peacock, in post for 13 years. 30 full time staff, 13 part time. Annual turnover 1 or 2. Average age 42.

Academic work GCSE and A-levels. Average size of upper fifth 46; upper sixth 37. *O-levels*: on average, 3 pupils in upper fifth pass 1–4 subjects; 31, 5–7 subjects; 12 pass 8+ subjects. *A-levels*: on average, 3 pupils in upper sixth pass 1 subject; 6, 2 subjects; 27 pass 3 subjects. On average, 12 take science/engineering A-levels; 12 take arts and humanities; 12 a mixture. Craft Design and Technology, Graphical Communication to GCSE. *Computing facilities*: Computer room with Nimbus PCs. BBCs in laboratories and classrooms. (All first years taught keyboard skills.) Special provisions for EFL and dyslexia.

Senior pupils' non-academic activities *Music*: 60+ learn a musical instrument, 17 to Grade 6 or above, 1 accepted for Music School; 8 in school orchestra, 18 in choir, 4 in string quartet; 2 in county youth orchestra. *Drama and dance*: 24 in school productions; 100% in House plays; 50 in drama festivals. 10 take New Era, Guildhall exams. 1 accepted for Drama/Dance School; 1 goes on to work in theatre; 1 audition for Opportunity Knocks. *Art*: 17 take GCSE; 9 A-level. 2–3 accepted for Art School. 30 belong to ceramics club. *Sport*: Hockey, netball, tennis, athletics, rounders, swimming, squash, badminton available. 40% of pupils involved in climbing, canoeing, mountain walking, squash. 70% take exams. 7 represent county/country (hockey, athletics, judo). *Other*: Wide ranging service programme – old people, handicapped children; sixth form give holiday for handicapped children; inshore rescue boat. Comprehensive programme of sailing, canoeing, mountaineering etc with expeditions away from school. 25–30 other activities each term from ballet to welding; driving lessons arranged; CDT workshop.

Careers 2 part time advisors. Average number of pupils accepted for *arts and humanities degree courses* at Oxbridge, 1; other universities, 7; polytechnics or CHE, 7. *science and engineering degree courses* at Oxbridge, 1; other universities, 5; medical schools, 2; polytechnics or CHE, 3. BEd, 2. *other general training courses*, 8. Average number of pupils going straight into careers in the armed services, 1; industry, 2; music/drama, 1.

Uniform School uniform worn throughout.

Houses/prefects Competitive houses. Prefects, head girl, head of house and house prefects – some appointed, some volunteer. There is a Pupil/Staff Rules Council.

Religion Range of visiting lay and clerical people – Jesuits to Jews for Sunday service (compulsory unless specific request by parents).

Social Social functions – sports, dances etc with local boys and co-ed schools plus debates, sixth form dinner. (Not drama and music productions.) Organised ski trips, cultural trips, individual exchanges for staff and pupils from time to time. Pupils allowed to bring own bike to school. Meals self service. School shop. No tobacco/alcohol allowed.

Discipline No corporal punishment. Pupils failing to produce homework once would not receive punishment; those caught smoking cannabis on the premises could expect expulsion.

Boarding 6 have own study bedroom, all upper sixth share (2, 3, 4). None are in large dormitories. Houses, of approximately 50, are vertically organised as for competitive purposes. Resident qualified nurse. Central dining room. Upper sixth pupils can provide and cook own food. Exeats: special system of 'long weekends' at pupils' choice, 1 per term; unlimited short weekends. Visits to local town allowed.

Former pupils Lady Docker; Paula Yates.

PERSE, THE (BOYS)

The Perse School	Co-ed Pupils 398
Hills Road	● Boys Upper sixth 60+
Cambridge CB2 2QF	Girls Termly fees:
Telephone number 0223 248127	Mixed sixth Day £806
	● Day Boarding £1648
Enquiries/application to the Headmaster's Secretary	● Boarding HMC; GBA

WHAT IT'S LIKE

Founded in 1615, originally in Free School Lane, then Gonville Place (1890), it moved to its present 30-acre green field site on the outskirts of Cambridge in 1960. The whole school was constructed as new between 1958–60. It has pleasant buildings and excellent modern facilities. Further extensions were made in the 1980s. The two boarding houses are situated near the main school. It is Christian but non-denominational. It has all the advantages of being a comparatively small school. There is much emphasis on management by the boys and it runs a very efficient pastoral care scheme. Naturally, there are strong links with the university. The teaching is good, academic standards are high and results impressive. Some 45–50 leavers go on to university each year (10–15 to Oxbridge). There is a staff:pupil ratio of about 1:12. Very strong indeed in music, drama and art. The Perse has always had a notable record in sports and games (a very large number of representatives at county and national level). An excellent range of extra-curricular activities, including an unusually large and energetic CCF. Some commitment to local community services. Much use is made of Cambridge's cultural amenities.

SCHOOL PROFILE

Pupils Total over 12, 398. Day 362; Boarding 36. Entry age, 11+, 13+ and into the sixth. Own preparatory school provides over 20%.

Entrance Own entrance exam used. Oversubscribed. No special skills or religious requirements. Parents not expected to buy text books. 57 assisted places. Variable number of scholarships/bursaries, no maximum limit.

Parents 15+% are doctors, lawyers etc; 15+% in industry or commerce. 60+% live within 30 miles; up to 10% live overseas.

Staff Head Dr G M Stephen, in post for 1 year. 33 full time staff, 4 part time. Annual turnover 5%.

Academic work GCSE and A-levels. Average size of upper fifth 70+; upper sixth 60+. *O-levels*: on average, 1 pupil in upper fifth passes 1–4 subjects; 6, 5–7 subjects; 70 pass 8+ subjects. *A-levels*: on average, 2 pupils in upper sixth pass 1 subject; 7, 2 subjects; 42, 3 subjects and 4 pass 4 subjects. On average, 30 take science/engineering A-levels; 13 take arts and humanities; 12 a mixture. *Computing facilities*: 12 networked BBCs plus various others. Whole school on Econet network system from September 1988.

Senior pupils' non-academic activities *Music*: 80 learn a musical instrument, 12 to Grade 6 or above; 30 in school orchestra, 20 in choir; some pupils in own groups, small ensembles and operas; occasional pupils in National Youth Orchestra; 12 take GCSE music; 2 A-level. Occasional pupils go on to play in jazz bands; 2 Cambridge music scholarships. *Drama and dance*: 60 in school productions, most with Perse (Girls'); 150 in other productions. *Art*: 50–67% take as non-examined subject; 6 A-level; 2 history of art. 5 accepted for Art School; 4 for university. 20 in eg photographic club. *Sport*: Rugby, hockey, cricket, tennis, fives, basketball, athletics available; off site – golf, squash, swimming, cross-country available. 95 take non-compulsory sport. 36+ represent county/country (rugby, hockey, tennis). *Other*: Some take part in local community schemes. Duke of Edinburgh's Award available through Scouts. 5–10 enter voluntary schemes after school; others work for national charities. Other activities include a computer club, chess, Scouts, CCF etc.

Careers 2 part time careers advisors. Average number of pupils accepted for *arts and humanities degree courses* at Oxbridge, 6; other universities, 14; polytechnics or CHE, 1. *science and engineering degree courses* at Oxbridge, 7; other universities, 22; polytechnics or CHE, 2. Very few go into other training courses or straight into careers.

Uniform School uniform worn, modified in sixth.

Houses/prefects No competitive houses. Prefects, head boy, head of (boarding) house and house prefects – appointed by the Head after nomination. School Council.

Religion Compulsory religious worship (unless opted out).

Social Debates, discos and plays with the Perse School for Girls. Organised trips abroad. Pupils allowed to bring own car/bike to school. Meals self service. School tuckshop. No tobacco/alcohol allowed.

Discipline No corporal punishment. Pupils failing to produce homework once may not be punished.

Boarding No single study bedrooms but new house planned; most are in dormitories of 6+. Houses, of approximately 30–35 are divided by age. Resident qualified nurse, doctor on call. No central dining room. Exeats any weekend unless involved in Saturday matches. Visits to local town allowed (Saturday).

Alumni association run by Mr K Barry.

Former pupils Sir Peter Hall; 2 Nobel prizewinners; many notable university figures.

PERSE, THE (GIRLS)

The Perse School for Girls	Co-ed	Pupils 550
Union Road	Boys	Upper sixth Yes
Cambridge CB2 1HF	● Girls	Termly fees:
Telephone number 0223 359589	Mixed sixth	Day £790
	● Day	GSA; GBGSA
	Boarding	

Head Miss M R Bateman (8 years)
Age range 11–18, own prep from age 7; entry by own exam
Bursaries and assisted places.

PIERREPONT

Pierrepont School	● Co-ed	Pupils 268
Frensham	Boys	Upper sixth 20
Farnham	Girls	Termly fees:
Surrey GU10 3DN	Mixed sixth	Day £1109
Telephone number 025 125 2110	● Day	Boarding £1848
	● Boarding	SHMIS; GBA
Enquiries/application to the Headmaster		

WHAT IT'S LIKE

Founded in 1947 its main building is a house designed by Norman Shaw and built in 1876. Later additions have helped to create a compact campus on a pleasant wooded site with ample playing fields and gardens (46 acres in all). The boarding accommodation is comfortable. Religious worship in the Anglican tradition is encouraged. Academic standards are creditable and some 5–10 pupils go on to university each year. A good range of sports and games is available and standards are quite high. There is a flourishing CCF contingent and some commitment to the Duke of Edinburgh's Award Scheme since 1983.

SCHOOL PROFILE

Pupils Total over 12, 268. Day 164 (boys 150, girls 14); Boarding 91 (boys). Entry age, 11, 12, 13 and into the sixth. Very few are children of former pupils.

Entrance Common entrance and own entrance exam used. Oversubscribed at some ages. No special skills or religious requirements. Parents not expected to buy text books. 14 scholarships/bursaries, 40% to 20% day fees.

Staff Head J D Payne, in post for 5 years. 23 full time staff, 4 part time. Annual turnover 6%. Average age 40.

Academic work GCSE and A-levels. Average size of upper fifth 58; upper sixth 20. Meteorology offered to GCSE/A-level. *Computing facilities*: 12 Amstrad CPC 464s. EFL and provision for dyslexia or mild visual handicap.

Senior pupils' non-academic activities *Art*: 12–15 take GCSE; 3–5, A-level. *Sport*: Rugby, hockey, cricket, athletics, basketball, squash, badminton, volleyball, gymnastics, sailing, swimming, shooting, riding, tennis available. *Other*: Activities include a computer club, drama, CCF, Duke of Edinburgh's Award Scheme, chess, bridge, electronics, model railway, photography, orchestra.

Careers 4 part time careers advisors. Average number of pupils accepted for *arts and humanities degree courses* at universities, 3; polytechnics or CHE, 3. *science and engineering degree courses* at Oxbridge, 1; other universities, 4; medical schools, 1; polytechnics or CHE, 2.

Uniform School uniform worn except the sixth.

Houses/prefects Competitive houses. Prefects, head boy/girl, head of house and house prefects – appointed by Headmaster and housemasters.

Religion Religious worship encouraged.

Social Occasional debates with other schools. Annual ski-ing party, termly trips to France; rugby tours. Pupils allowed to bring own car/bike/motorbike to school. Meals self service. School tuckshop and bookshop. No tobacco allowed; beer or wine only in social club for 17+.

Discipline No corporal punishment. Pupils caught smoking cannabis on the premises might expect expulsion.

Boarding One-third have own study bedroom, one-third share with 1 or 2; very few in dormitories of 6+. Houses, of approximately 30–35, are the same as competitive houses. Resident SRN. Central dining room. Pupils can provide and cook own food to some extent. Number and length of exeats varies each term. Visits to local town allowed.

PLYMOUTH COLLEGE

Plymouth College	Co-ed	Pupils 620
Ford Park	● Boys	Upper sixth 90
Plymouth	Girls	Termly fees:
Devon PL4 6RN	● Mixed sixth	Day £780
Telephone number 0752 28596	● Day	Boarding £1480
Enquiries/application to the Secretary	● Boarding	HMC

WHAT IT'S LIKE

Founded in 1877, it amalgamated with Mannamead private school in 1896. It is single-site, in the middle of Plymouth and is the educational focal point of the city. In the last 25 years there has been a continuous programme of development and modernisation. Facilities (including comfortable boarding accommodation) are now of a high standard. The College preparatory department is nearby (ages 4½–11). Christian worship plays an integral part in the College's life. Academic standards are high and results are good (55–60 university entrants per year). Strong in art, music and drama. A very good range of sport and games (high standards) and other activities. Considerable emphasis on community service work and also on outward bound and adventure training. A phenomenal record in the Duke of Edinburgh's Award Scheme (35 silver, 55 gold).

SCHOOL PROFILE

Pupils Total over 12, 620. Day 520 (boys 475, girls 45); Boarding 100 (Boys). Entry age 11, boys; boys and girls into the sixth. Plymouth College Prep provides 20+.

Entrance Common entrance and own entrance exam used. Oversubscribed. No special skills or religious requirements. Parents not expected to buy text books. 173 assisted places. 12 scholarships/bursaries, £520–£50 per term.

Parents 15+% in industry or commerce; 15+% in armed services. 60+% live within 30 miles; up to 10% live overseas.

Staff Head A M Joyce. 52 full time staff, 10 part time. Annual turnover 1–2%. Average age 40.

Academic work GCSE and A-levels. Average size of upper fifth 100; upper sixth 90. *O-levels*: on average, 52 pupils in upper fifth pass 1–4 subjects; 24, 5–7 subjects; 22 pass 8+ subjects. *A-levels*: on average, 11 pupils in upper sixth pass 1 subject; 17, 2 subjects; 53, 3 subjects and 9 pass 4 subjects. On average, 40 take science/engineering A-levels; 30 take arts and humanities; 20 a mixture. Electronics and engineering are offered to A-level. *Computing facilities*: Very adequate. Special provisions for pupils who are mildly visually handicapped and EFL.

Senior pupils' non-academic activities *Music*: 39 learn a musical instrument, 19 to Grade 6 or above; 2 accepted for Music School; 6 play in pop groups, 3 in jazz ensembles; 22 in school orchestra, 3 in County Youth Orchestra; 2 in county wind band; 18 in school choir. *Drama and dance*: 70 in school productions, 3 in city productions; 1 accepted for Drama/Dance School. *Art*: 20 take as non-examined subject; 56 take GCSE; 17, A-level. 22 take A-level stage design; 12 accepted for Art School; 15 belong to photographic club; 20 belong to art club. *Sport*: Fencing, karate, judo, badminton, squash, basketball, gymnastics, rugby, hockey, cricket, athletics, tennis, swimming, sailing, canoeing, moorland walking, cross-country, soccer, golf available. 160 take non-compulsory sport. 22 represent county (rugby, hockey, cricket, athletics, squash); 1 represents country (rugby). *Other*: 35 have silver Duke of Edinburgh's Award and 55 have gold. Other activities include a computer club, chess club (British School Champion, 1986), bridge club.

Careers 2 part time advisors. Average number of pupils accepted for *arts and humanities degree courses* at Oxbridge, 3; other universities, 25; polytechnics or CHE, 16. *science and engineering degree courses* at Oxbridge, 3; other universities, 30; medical schools, 3; polytechnics or CHE, 12. *other general training courses*, 3. Average number of pupils going straight into careers in armed services, 5; industry, 12; the City, 2; civil service, 2; music/drama, 1; other, 2/3. Traditional school careers are the armed services, law, medicine, banking.

Uniform School uniform worn throughout.
Houses/prefects Competitive houses. Prefects, head boy/girl, head of house and house prefects – appointed by the Head.
Religion Religious worship encouraged.
Social Some debates, plays and orchestral events. Organised trips abroad. Meals self service. School shop. No tobacco/alcohol allowed.
Discipline Corporal punishment. Pupils failing to produce homework once might expect detention; those caught smoking cannabis on the premises could expect suspension.
Boarding 14 have own study bedroom, 80% share (2–4); 5% are in dormitories of 6+. Resident qualified nurse. Central dining room. Limited number of pupils can provide and cook their own food. 2 weekend exeats each term. Visits to local town allowed.
Alumni association run by Mr F J Jeffery, c/o the School.

POCKLINGTON

Pocklington School	Co-ed	Pupils 584
West Green	● Boys	Upper sixth 100
Pocklington	Girls	Termly fees:
York YO4 2NJ	● Mixed sixth	Day £780
Telephone number 0759 303125	● Day	Boarding £1527
Enquiries/application to the Headmaster	● Boarding	HMC

WHAT IT'S LIKE

Founded in 1514, the school was largely rebuilt in 1850 and its fine buildings are sited on the outskirts of the small market town in ample grounds. The senior school is single site; the junior dept and junior boarding house are on a separate campus. There have been extensive modern developments and facilities are very good. The standard of teaching is high and the academic results are impressive (some 55% of pupils go on to university). Quite flourishing music, art and drama depts. Good range of sports and games and high standards achieved (a lot of county players). Numerous societies and clubs. Well supported in the area.

SCHOOL PROFILE

Pupils Total over 12, 584. Day 374 (boys 340, girls 34); Boarding, 210 (boys 190, girls 20). Entry age, boys 8, 11, 13; boys and girls into the sixth. Own junior school provides over 20%. 15% are children of former pupils.
Entrance Common entrance and own entrance exam used. Oversubscribed. No special skills required. C of E School but accepts all denominations. Parents not expected to buy text books. 137 assisted places. Various scholarships for academic excellence. Bursaries awarded subject to means test, full tuition fees to £100.
Parents 15+% are doctors, lawyers, etc; 15+% in armed services, 15+% in agriculture. 60+% live within 30 miles; up to 10% live overseas.
Staff Head A D Pickering, in post for 7 years. 50 full time staff, 2 part time. Annual turnover 5%. Average age 30–35.

Academic work GCSE and A-levels. Average size of fifth 90–95; upper sixth 100. *O-levels*: on average, 15 pupils in fifth pass 1–4 subjects; 30, 5–7 subjects; 50 pass 8+ subjects. *A-levels*: on average, 7 pupils in the upper sixth pass 1 subject; 14, 2 subjects; 25, 3 subjects; 52 pass 4 subjects. On average, 40 take science/engineering A-levels; 50 take arts and humanities; 10, a mixture. CDT is offered to GCSE/A-level. *Computing facilities*: 12 BBC Micros (linked system), Amstrad, 10 Spectrums. Provision for EFL.

Senior pupils' non-academic activities *Music*: 40 learn a musical instrument, 12 up to Grade 6 or above, 28 in school orchestra, 60 in school choir, 10 in school pop group, 6 in chamber group and 36 in ensemble/band/brass group; 3 in area youth orchestra. *Drama*: 25–50 in school productions, 80 in house plays. *Art/Design*: 15–20 take as non-examined subject; 75 take GCSE or CDT; 30 take A-level or CDT. 6–10 accepted for Art School. 20 belong to eg photographic club. *Sport*: Rugby, cricket, football, athletics, tennis, hockey, cross-country, squash, basketball, volleyball, badminton, swimming, golf and fencing available. 150 take non-compulsory sport. Some take exams in swimming, karate, judo, sailing. 19 represent county (squash, cross-country, rugby, hockey and athletics), and one country (squash). Other activities include a computer club, numerous societies, and clubs from board games to electronics, woodwork to high technology.

Careers 5 part time advisors. Fully equipped careers centre. Average number of pupils accepted for *arts and humanities degree courses* at Oxbridge, 4; other universities, 25; polytechnics or CHE, 15. *science and engineering degree courses* at Oxbridge, 4; other universities, 20; medical schools, 1; polytechnics or CHE, 10. Average number of pupils going straight into careers in the armed services, 4; industry, 5; the City, 1; music/drama, 1; other, 10.

Uniform School uniform worn throughout.

Houses/prefects Competitive houses. Prefects, head boy/girl, head of house and house prefects – appointed by the Headmaster.

Religion Sunday morning service and daily assembly.

Social No organised events with local schools. Organised trips abroad to France and Germany. Pupils allowed to bring own car/bike/motorbike to school. Meals self service. School shop. Sixth formers allowed some alcohol. No tobacco allowed.

Discipline No corporal punishment. Pupils failing to produce homework once might expect to re-write it or get detention. Those caught smoking cannabis on the premises might expect expulsion, but would be helped to move to another school to make a new start if this was appropriate.

Boarding 15% have own study bedroom, 35% share with others; 50% are in dormitories of 6 or more. Houses, of approximately 50, are divided by age group and sex. Resident qualified nurse. Central dining room. Pupils can provide and cook own food. 2 weekend exeats and half term. Visits to local town allowed frequently.

Alumni association is run by M G Milne Esq, c/o School.

Former pupils Sir James Cobban CBE TD DL; Tom Stoppard; Adrian Edmondson.

POLAM HALL

Polam Hall School	Co-ed	Pupils 310
Grange Road	Boys	Upper sixth 28
Darlington	● Girls	Termly fees:
Durham DH1 5PA	Mixed sixth	Day £790
Telephone number 0325 463383	● Day	Boarding £1595
	● Boarding	GSA
Enquiries/application to the Headmistress		

WHAT IT'S LIKE

Originally a small Friends' School under personal ownership in 1884; the present school dates from 1888. The main building (and the heart of the place) is a very elegant late 18th century house in a beautiful garden and wooded part of 23 acres on the edge of Darlington. Kindergarten and junior school are combined with the main school. During the last 20 years many developments have taken place and the buildings much improved and extended. Facilities and accommodation are now excellent. Great importance is attached to pastoral life and to the creation of a happy family atmosphere. All boarders go to the parish church (or church of their own denomination) each Sunday. A good general academic education is given and a number of girls proceed to university. Very strong music and drama depts. Good range of sports, games and activities. Substantial commitment to local community service. Quite an impressive record in the Duke of Edinburgh's Award Scheme.

SCHOOL PROFILE

Pupils Total over 11, 310. Entry age, 11, 13 and into the sixth. Own junior school provides over 20%.

Entrance Own entrance exam used. Not oversubscribed. No special skills or religious requirements. Parents not expected to buy text books. Scholarships/ bursaries available, 50%–10% of fees.

Parents 10+% live within 30 miles; up to 10% live overseas.

Staff Head Mrs H C Hamilton, in post for 1 year.

Academic work GCSE and A-levels. Average size of upper fifth 58; upper sixth 28. *O-levels*: on average, 17 pupils in upper fifth pass 1–4 subjects; 13, 5–7 subjects; 27 pass 8+ subjects. *A-levels*: on average, 3 pupils in the upper sixth pass 1 subject; 5, 2 subjects; 8, 3 subjects and 9 pass 4 subjects. On average, 9 take science/engineering A-levels; 12 take arts and humanities; 3 a mixture. Statistics and stage decor offered to GCSE/A-level. *Computing facilities*: 8 BBC computers. Dyslexic and EFL provisions.

Senior pupils' non-academic activities *Music*: 150 learn a musical instrument, 10 to Grade 6 or above, 1 accepted for Music School; 15 in school orchestra, 60 in school choir, 30 in wind band; 1 in National Children's Orchestra. *Drama and dance*: 100 in school productions; 25 take modern dance; 5, ballet. 6 take Grade 6 in ESB, RAD etc. 1 accepted for Drama/Dance schools. *Art*: 2 take as non-examined subject; 20 take GCSE; 3 A-level. 2 accepted for Art School. 6 belong to eg photographic club; 10 take film animation. *Sport*: Hockey, lacrosse, netball, tennis, rounders, athletics, horse riding, swimming, golf, self-defence, basketball, volleyball available.

100 take non-compulsory sport. 45 take exams in eg swimming. 3 represent county. *Other*: 6 take part in local community schemes. 30 have bronze Duke of Edinburgh's Award and 10 gold. 15 pupils are guides.

Careers 2 part time careers advisors. Average number of pupils accepted for *arts and humanities degree courses* at Oxbridge, 1; other universities, 2; polytechnics or CHE, 2. *science and engineering degree courses* at Oxbridge, 1; other universities, 3; medical schools, 1; polytechnics or CHE, 2. *other general training courses*, 4–5. Average number of pupils going straight into careers in music/drama, 1–2; banking, 1–2.

Uniform School uniform worn except the sixth.

Houses/prefects Competitive houses. No prefects, head girl and head of house elected by school and staff.

Religion Morning assembly (reading) compulsory as is church for boarders.

Social Social functions and occasional joint musical activities with local independent schools. Organised trips abroad. Pupils allowed to bring own car/bike to school. Some meals formal, some self service. No tobacco/alcohol allowed.

Discipline No corporal punishment. Pupils failing to produce homework once might expect a late mark; those caught smoking cannabis on the premises may expect expulsion.

Boarding 2% have own study bedroom, 98% share, up to 5. Houses, of 25–40, divided by age. Resident qualified nurse. Central dining room. Pupils can provide and cook limited food. 2 weekend exeats each term. Limited visits to local town allowed.

Alumni association run by Miss E Thistlethwaite, 88 Victoria Road, Darlington.

PORTORA ROYAL

Portora Royal School
Enniskillen
County Fermanagh BT74 7HA
Telephone number 0365 22658

- Co-ed
  Boys
  Girls
  Mixed sixth
- Day
- Boarding

Pupils 350
Upper sixth Yes
Termly fees:
Day £420
Boarding £1350
HMC

Head R L Bennett (5 years)
Age range 11–18; entry by LEA exam or common entrance
2 entry and 2 leaving scholarships pa.

PORTSMOUTH GRAMMAR

Portsmouth Grammar School
High Street
Portsmouth
Hampshire PO1 2LN
Telephone number 0705 819125

Co-ed   Pupils 740
• Boys   Upper sixth   Yes
   Girls   Termly fees:
• Mixed sixth   Day   £700
• Day   HMC
   Boarding

Head A C V Evans (5 years)
Age range 11–18, own prep from age 5; entry by common entrance or own exam including for pupils of own prep.

PORTSMOUTH HIGH

Portsmouth High School
25 Kent Road
Southsea
Hampshire PO5 3EQ
Telephone number 0705 826714

Enquiries/application to the Headmistress

Co-ed   Pupils 442
   Boys   Upper sixth   70
• Girls   Termly fees:
   Mixed sixth   Day   £622
• Day   GPDST
   Boarding

WHAT IT'S LIKE

Founded in 1882, it has a pleasant premises close to Southsea Common and the sea and has been greatly extended over the years. Modern facilities are good and include a fine sports hall and excellent labs. The junior school at Dovercourt is a few minutes away. Administratively the schools form one unit. Pupils are drawn from all parts of Portsmouth and surrounding districts. The staff:pupil ratio is about 1:13. Academic standards are high and results impressive (the sixth form is increasing in size and over half go on to university each year). Music, drama and art departments are strong. A good range of sports and games (quite a few representatives at county and national level) and an adequate range of extra-curricular activities. A promising record in the Duke of Edinburgh's Award Scheme.

SCHOOL PROFILE

Pupils Total over 12, 442. Entry age, 11 and into the sixth. Own junior department provides over 20%. Small number are children of former pupils.
Entrance Own entrance exam used. Oversubscribed. No special skills or religious requirements. Parents not expected to buy text books. 29 assisted places each year. 3 scholarships/bursaries pa, half to one-third fees.
Parents 15+% are doctors, lawyers etc; 15+% in industry or commerce. 60+% live within 30 miles.
Staff Head Mrs J M Dawtrey, in post for 4 years. 32 full time staff, 11 part time. Annual turnover 4%.
Academic work GCSE and A-levels. Average size of upper fifth 84; upper

sixth 45 (rising to 70). *O-levels*: on average, 3 pupils in upper fifth pass 1–4 subjects; 9, 5–7 subjects; 63 pass 8+ subjects. *A-levels*: on average, 1 pupil in upper sixth passes 1 subject; 6, 2 subjects; 27, 3 subjects and 2 pass 4 subjects. On average, 19 take science/engineering A-levels; 14 take arts and humanities; 5 a mixture. *Computing facilities*: RML network in computer room; BBC micros. Special provision for eg EFL, dyslexia or mild visual handicap.

Senior pupils' non-academic activities *Music*: 37 learn a musical instrument in school, 25 out of school, 22 to Grade 6 or above, 2 accepted for Music School; 16 in school orchestra, 45 in choir, 16 wind band, 9 string group; 4 in county youth orchestra, 9 in area youth orchestras and bands; 2 in national scout and guide band. *Drama and dance*: 30–50 in school productions. Some pupils take Associated Board, New Era Academy or Guildhall exams; 15 participate in speech festivals. *Art*: 45 take GCSE; 15 A-level (pupils able to build a portfolio even if they are not taking A-level). 3 accepted for Art School. *Sport*: Lacrosse, netball, tennis, cricket, volleyball, badminton, table tennis, swimming, rounders available. 13 represent county/country (gym, swimming, lacrosse, netball, sailing, cricket). *Other*: 25 have bronze Duke of Edinburgh's Award, 2 have silver and 2 gold. Other activities include electronics, debating, Christian Fellowship, gymnastics, chess and board games.

Careers 4 part time careers advisors. Average number of pupils accepted for *arts and humanities degree courses* at Oxbridge, 3; other universities, 9; polytechnics or CHE, 2. *science and engineering degree courses* at Oxbridge, 2; other universities, 5; medical schools, 6; polytechnics or CHE, 2. *BEd*, 2. *other general training courses*, 2. Average number of pupils going straight into careers in industry, 1. Traditional school careers are medicine, law.

Uniform School uniform worn except the sixth.

Houses/prefects No competitive houses or prefects. Head girl and 2 deputies, elected by the school.

Religion Morning assembly unless withdrawn for religious reasons.

Social Concerts, debates, musicals, lectures with local boys' schools; BAYS, Young Enterprise etc. Exchanges with France, Germany, Spain; group cultural visits; ski-ing trips. Pupils allowed to bring own car/bike to school. Meals self service. School tuckshop. No tobacco/alcohol allowed.

Discipline No corporal punishment. Pupils failing to produce homework once might be required to do it; those caught smoking cannabis on the premises might expect immediate suspension and probable expulsion.

Alumni association run by Mrs J Gauntlett, Windy Ridge, Portsdown Hill Road, Cosham, Portsmouth, Hampshire.

PRINCESS HELENA

The Princess Helena College	Co-ed	Pupils 177
Temple Dinsley	Boys	Upper sixth 22
Preston	• Girls	Termly fees:
Hitchin	Mixed sixth	Day £1450
Hertfordshire SG4 7RT	• Day	Boarding £2000
Telephone number 0462 32100	• Boarding	GSA

Enquiries/application to the Headmaster

WHAT IT'S LIKE

Founded in 1820, the first academic school for girls (day or boarding). After a series of moves it settled at Temple Dinsley, near Hitchin. The main building is a delightful Queen Anne mansion (1712), enlarged by Lutyens in 1909. This and the Dower House lie in fine Gertrude Jekyll gardens and 183 acres of parkland. Considerable modern developments now provide first-rate accommodation and all-round facilities. It has all the advantages of a small school and a happy family atmosphere prevails. Anglican worship is compulsory mid-week and on Sundays. A good staff:pupil ratio of 1:14 (plus an unusual number of part-time staff). A good all-round education is given and results are impressive (66% of girls proceed to university). Very strong indeed in music (especially orchestral). A good range of sports, games and activities. Substantial commitment to local community schemes and an impressive record in the Duke of Edinburgh's Award Scheme.

SCHOOL PROFILE

Pupils Total over 12, 177. Day 42; Boarding 135. Entry age, 11 and into the sixth. 5% are children of former pupils.

Entrance Common entrance used. Oversubscribed. Music skills looked for. Parents expected to buy text books. 3 scholarships/bursaries per year (orchestral music and 6th form science), 75%–15% of fees.

Parents 15+% in industry or commerce. 10+% live within 30 miles; up to 10% live overseas.

Staff Head Dr D Clarke, in post for 17 years. 21 full time staff, 30 part time. Annual turnover 5%. Average age 41.

Academic work GCSE and A-levels. Average size of upper fifth 36; upper sixth 22 (expected to increase Sept '89). *O-levels*: Average of 7.5 passes per pupil. *A-levels*: Average of 2.7 passes per pupil. In a typical year, as many pupils take science A-levels as arts and humanities. *Computing facilities*: 12 computers (pupils prepared for AEB certificate in computer awareness). EFL provision.

Senior pupils' non-academic activities *Music*: 120+ learn a musical instrument, 29 to Grade 6 or above, 2–3 accepted for Music School; 30+ in school orchestra, 40 in school choir; 1 in National Youth Orchestra, 2 in National Children's Orchestra. Second in National Schools Chamber Music Competition. *Drama and dance*: 60+ in school productions. *Art*: 10 take as non-examined subject; 16 take GCSE; 8 take A-level. 2 accepted for Art School. Glass engraving, photography and ceramics. *Sport*: Lacrosse, netball, field and track athletics, cross-country, tennis, swimming, many indoor games including badminton, volleyball and squash available. 100 take non-compulsory sport. 3 represent county and 1 country (lacrosse). *Other*: 20 take part in local community schemes. 12 have bronze Duke of Edinburgh's Award, 5 have silver and 3 have gold. Few enter voluntary schemes after leaving school. A few work for national charities. Other activities include a computer club and cookery.

Careers 2 part time advisors and Cambridge Occupational Analysts. Average number of pupils accepted for *arts and humanities degree courses* at Oxbridge, 2; other universities, 7; polytechnics or CHE, 2. *science and engineering degree courses* at Oxbridge, 1; other universities, 5; polytechnics or CHE, 2. *BEd*, 1. *other general training courses*, 3–5. Average number of pupils going straight into careers in music/drama, 2; other 5–7. Traditional school careers are in science.

Uniform School uniform worn throughout, modified in sixth.

Houses/prefects Competitive houses. Prefects, head girl, head of house and house prefects – appointed by the Head, consulting colleagues and head girl. School Council.

Religion Compulsory; mid-week school assembly; Sunday, church nearby. Catholic church in Hitchin.

Social No organised local events. Exchanges with Germany and France regularly. Sixth form allowed to bring own bike to school. Meals combination of self service and formal. School shop. No tobacco/alcohol allowed.

Discipline Pupils failing to produce prep might expect an order mark; anyone caught smoking cannabis on the premises would be removed – although this has never happened; smoking cigarettes, removal after first and final warning.

Boarding 25% have own study bedroom, 17% share with one other; 5% are in dormitories of 6+. Resident qualified doctor and 2 nurses. Central dining room. 3 weekend exeats each term. Visits to local town allowed for sixth form only.

Alumni association is run by Miss Katie Marshall.

Former pupils Governesses to the children of Queen Victoria and the Kaiser; Dr Helena Wright (pioneer of birth control); Mary Allen (founder of Women's Auxiliary Police); Dorothea Lambert Chambers (six times Wimbledon champion); Kathleen Archer (MI5, who rumbled Philby); Lady Trumpington (Government minister); Cindy Shelley (actress).

PRIOR PARK

Prior Park College
Ralph Allen Drive
Bath
Avon BA2 5AH
Telephone number 0225 835353

- Co-ed
  Boys
  Girls
  Mixed sixth
- Day
- Boarding

Pupils 371
Upper sixth Yes
Termly fees:
Day £1023
Boarding £1803
HMC

Head P F J Tobin (7 years)
Age range 11–18; entry by own exam or common entrance.
7 scholarships pa. Choral exhibitions and bursaries. Founded 1830.

PRIOR'S FIELD

Prior's Field School	Co-ed	Pupils 228
Godalming	Boys	Upper sixth 20
Surrey GU7 2RH	• Girls	Termly fees:
Telephone number 0483 810551	Mixed sixth	Day £1047
	• Day	Boarding £1697
Enquiries/application to the Headmistress	• Boarding	GSA

WHAT IT'S LIKE

Founded in 1902 by Mrs Leonard Huxley, mother of Julian and Aldous Huxley. It retains links with the Huxley family which has been a guiding influence since the foundation. The main buildings, which include a Voysey house, are in a delightful and peaceful rural site of 25 acres (including formal gardens) in the green belt outside Guildford. Apart from sixth form houses, the whole school is under one roof. Being a small school it has a congenial family atmosphere and enjoys comfortable accommodation and good modern facilities. The staff: pupil ratio is about 1:8.2. Academic standards are creditable and results quite good. The majority of upper sixth formers go on to university each year. Sport is compulsory for all and reasonable standards are attained. An adequate range of extra-curricular activities. The Duke of Edinburgh's Award Scheme was started in 1988.

SCHOOL PROFILE

Pupils Total over 12, 228. Day 55; Boarding (including weekly) 146. Entry age 11+, 12+, 13+ and into the sixth. 1% are children of former pupils.

Entrance Common entrance and own entrance exam used. Oversubscribed. No special skills or religious requirements. Parents not expected to buy text books. 2 scholarships (50% to 25% fees); plus some sixth form bursaries according to ability and need (30% to 10% fees).

Parents 15+% are doctors, lawyers etc; 15+% are in industry or commerce. 60+% live within 30 miles; 10+% live overseas.

Staff Head Mrs J M McCallum, in post for 1 year. 18 full time staff, 13 part time. Annual turnover 8%. Average age 40.

Academic work GCSE and A-levels. Average size of upper fifth 40; upper sixth 20. *A-levels*: on average, 3 pupils in upper sixth pass 1 subject; 7, 2 subjects and 10, 3 subjects. On average, 5 take science A-levels; 7 take arts and humanities; 8 a mixture. *Computing facilities*: BBC computers, networked, with standard printers. Provision for dyslexia.

Senior pupils' non-academic activities *Music*: 46 learn a musical instrument, 13 to Grade 6 or above. 16 in school choir. *Drama and dance*: 15 in school productions; 4 take A-level theatre arts. *Art*: 15 take GCSE; 5 A-level art; 3 history of art A-level; 3 accepted for Art School. 7 belong to eg photographic club. *Sport*: Lacrosse, hockey, netball, rounders, tennis, swimming, athletics, basketball, badminton available; sixth form options: golf, fencing, squash, aerobics. Sport compulsory for all. 2 represent county/country (lacrosse). *Other*: 15 have bronze Duke of Edinburgh's Award (started 1988). Other activities include clubs for computers, crafts, bridge, drama.

Careers 1 part time careers advisor. Average number of pupils accepted

for *arts and humanities degree courses* at universities, 5; polytechnics or CHE, 11. *science degree courses* at universities, 4.

Uniform School uniform worn except the sixth.

Houses/prefects Competitive houses. Prefects and head girl – appointed by the Head after secret ballot of school and staff. School Council.

Religion Compulsory church on some Sundays for all Christians.

Social Ski-ing holidays and exchange with school in France. Sixth form allowed to bring own bike to school. Breakfast formal, other meals self service. School shop. No tobacco/alcohol allowed.

Discipline No corporal punishment. Pupils failing to produce homework once might expect to do it in their own time by the following day; those caught smoking cannabis on the premises might expect expulsion.

Boarding 50% have own study bedroom, 50% share with 1 or 2, occasionally 4. Houses, of 40–65, divided by age group. Resident qualified nurse. Central dining room. Sixth form can provide and cook own food. 2 weekend exeats each term. Visits to local town allowed (weekly for seniors, twice a term for juniors).

Alumni association run by Mrs R Ivison, 3 Spring Terrace, Paradise Road, Richmond, Surrey TW9 1LW.

Former pupils Baroness Warnock, Mistress of Girton; Jill Bennett, actress.

PURCELL SCHOOL

The Purcell School
Mount Park Road
Harrow-on-the-Hill
Middlesex
Telephone number 01-422 1284

- Co-ed
  Boys
  Girls
  Mixed sixth
- Day
- Boarding

Pupils 166
Upper sixth Yes
Termly fees:
Day £1150
Boarding £2220
SHMIS

Head K J Bain (5 years)

Age range 9–18; entry by interview, music audition and test.

Scholarships and bursaries awarded on musical ability. Some LEAs offer financial assistance. Caters for musical children who may or may not become professional musicians.

PUTNEY HIGH

Putney High School
35 Putney Hill
London SW15 6BH
Telephone number 01-788 4886

Enquiries/application to the Headmistress

Co-ed
Boys
- Girls
  Mixed sixth
- Day
  Boarding

Pupils 556
Upper sixth 70
Termly fees:
Day £684
GPDST

WHAT IT'S LIKE

Founded in 1893, it is single-site on Putney Hill and has the bonus of unusually beautiful gardens. The main buildings are three large late Victorian houses to which there have been important additions in recent years, including a sixth-form block, an assembly hall, a science block and a craft centre. The junior school is separate in Lytton House within the school grounds. Facilities are good. The main playing fields are on site. For hockey, pupils go to Barnes by coach. It is a well-run school, academically very competitive and with a high reputation locally. Academic results are impressive and about 40–45 girls go on to university each year. It is very strong indeed in music and also has considerable strength in drama and art. Joint social and cultural functions with King's College Wimbledon, Tiffins and Emanuel. They have a high standard in sports and games and a big commitment to local community schemes.

SCHOOL PROFILE

Pupils Total over 12, 556. Entry age, 5+, 8+, 11+ and into the sixth. Own junior department provides over 20%.

Entrance Own entrance exam used. Oversubscribed. No special religious requirements or skills (but is academically competitive). Parents not expected to buy text books. 28 assisted places pa. 5 scholarships, half to one-quarter fees.

Parents 15+% are doctors, lawyers etc. 60+% live within 30 miles.

Staff Head Mrs P A Penney, in post for 1 year. 46 full time staff, 16 part time.

Academic work GCSE and A-levels. Average size of upper fifth 78; upper sixth 70. *O-levels*: on average, 4 pupils in upper fifth pass 1–4 subjects; 27, 5–7 subjects; 47 pass 8+ subjects. *A-levels*: on average, 4 pupils in upper sixth pass 1 subject; 7, 2 subjects; 37, 3 subjects and 2 pass 4 subjects. Italian offered to A-level. *Computing facilities*: Nimbus network in computer workshop, 20 RML machines and individual computers.

Senior pupils' non-academic activities *Music*: 80 learn a musical instrument, 20 to Grade 6 or above, 2 accepted for Music School, 2 for university music degree; 1 choral scholarship; 1 teaches music privately; 30 in school orchestra, 80 in choir, 30 in school band, 80 in chamber groups; 1 in National Youth Orchestra, 3 in Stanleigh youth orchestra; some pupils in orchestras outside school. *Drama and dance*: 60 in musical productions. *Art*: 4 take A-level. 1 accepted for Art School. *Sport*: Netball, tennis, hockey (indoor and playground), badminton, volleyball, rowing, squash available. *Other*: 60 take part in local community schemes. Other activities include a computer club, music (all the time), mathematics and technology clubs; charities' events strongly supported.

Careers 2 full time careers advisors. Average number of pupils accepted for *arts and humanities degree courses* at Oxbridge, 3; other universities, 27; polytechnics or CHE, 2. *science and engineering degree courses* at Oxbridge, 3; other universities, 9; medical schools, 2. *BEd*, 1. some to music/drama at eg Royal Academy/Guildhall.

Uniform School uniform worn except the sixth.

Houses/prefects No competitive houses. Prefects and head girl – elected by staff. School Council.

Religion No compulsory worship.

Social Some joint functions with King's College Wimbledon and Tiffins.

Trips, ski-ing and exchanges with France, Germany and Italy. Pupils allowed to bring own car/bike to school. Meals self service. No tobacco/alcohol allowed.

Discipline No corporal punishment. Pupils failing to produce homework once might expect a warning; those caught smoking cannabis on the premises might expect parents to be seen immediately.

Alumni association run by Mrs Sweetingham, c/o the School.

QUEEN ANNE'S (CAVERSHAM)

Queen Anne's School	Co-ed		Pupils 375
6 Henley Road	Boys		Upper sixth Yes
Caversham	• Girls		Termly fees:
Reading	Mixed sixth		Day £1150
Berkshire RG4 0DX	• Day		Boarding £1850
Telephone number 0734 471582	• Boarding		GSA; GBGSA

Head Miss A M Scott (11 years)
Age range 11–18; entry by common entrance
Scholarships (including music) plus bursaries.

QUEEN ELIZABETH (WAKEFIELD)

Queen Elizabeth Grammar School	Co-ed		Pupils 620
Northgate	• Boys		Upper sixth 95
Wakefield	Girls		Termly fees:
West Yorkshire WF1 3QY	Mixed sixth		Day £826
Telephone number 0924 373943	• Day		Boarding £1346
	• Boarding		HMC

Enquiries/application to the Admissions
Secretary

WHAT IT'S LIKE

Founded in 1591 by royal charter, it is single-site and close to the city centre. The main building (an example of early Gothic revival) has been in use since 1854. Many extensions in the last 30 years have provided first-rate modern facilities. The junior school is in the main grounds. It has a wide catchment area and the pupils are of a wide social background. High standards of work and conduct are expected and academic results are good (50 plus university candidates per year). Increasingly strong in music (there are traditional links with the cathedral and the school provides many of the choristers), drama and art. Very strong tradition of excellence in games and sports (a lot of county representatives) and an impressive range of activities. Plentiful collaboration with Wakefield Girls' High School.

SCHOOL PROFILE

Pupils Total over 12, 620. Day 591; Boarding 29. Entry age, 11 and into the sixth. Own junior provides 20+%. 10–15% are children of former pupils.

Entrance Common entrance and own entrance exam used. Oversubscribed. No special skills or religious requirements. Parents not expected to buy text books. 154 assisted places. 6 scholarships/bursaries per year (25–50% tuition fees), 1 music scholarship £300 pa.

Parents 15+% are doctors, lawyers, etc; 15+% in industry or commerce. 60+% live within 30 miles.

Staff Head R P Mardling in post for 3 years. 56 full time staff, 2 part time. Annual turnover 5%. Average age mid-thirties.

Academic work GCSE and A-levels. Average size of upper fifth 110; upper sixth 95. *O-levels*: on average, 10 pupils in upper fifth pass 1–4 subjects; 15, 5–7 subjects; 85 pass 8+ subjects. *A-levels*: on average, 8 pupils in the upper sixth pass 1 subject; 5, 2 subjects; 4, 3 subjects; 78 pass 4 subjects. On average, 50 take science/engineering A-levels; 40 take arts and humanities; 5, a mixture. *Computing facilities*: Network of 15 BBC Compact Computers with print-out facilities.

Senior pupils' non-academic activities *Music*: 145 learn a musical instrument, 21 up to Grade 6 or above, 1 accepted for Music School; 83 in school orchestra, 66 in choir, 45 in pop group; 11 in Wakefield Youth Orchestra. 4 go on to play in pop group. *Drama and dance*: 30 in school productions. 1 pa accepted for Drama/Dance School. *Art*: 25–35 take GCSE; 18 A-level. 5–8 per year accepted for Art School, 3 for art at university. 25–40 belong to photographic club. *Sport*: Rugby, cricket, cross-country, hockey, athletics, tennis, basketball, badminton, table tennis, volleyball, swimming, gymnastics, squash and weight training available. 300–400 take non-compulsory sport. 22 represent county (rugby, hockey, cricket, athletics). *Other*: 15 take part in local community schemes. 44 have bronze Duke of Edinburgh's Award. 6 take part in voluntary hospital work. Other activities include a computer club, chess, angling, bridge, fell-walking, golf; classical, geography, and history societies; orienteering, sailing, debating, shooting etc.

Careers 3 part time advisors. Average number of pupils accepted for *arts and humanities degree courses* at Oxbridge, 4; other universities, 20; polytechnics or CHE, 5. *science and engineering degree courses* at Oxbridge, 4; other universities, 23; medical schools, 9; polytechnics or CHE, 7. Average number of pupils going straight into careers in the armed services, 3; industry, 2; banking, 3; retail management, 3. Traditional school careers are: engineering, medicine and business.

Uniform School uniform worn throughout.

Houses/prefects No competitive houses. Prefects and head boy – appointed by Head and staff. School Council.

Religion Compulsory school assembly.

Social Theatrical productions with Wakefield Girls' High School. Organised trips abroad. Pupils allowed to bring own car/bike/motorbike to school. Meals self service. School shops selling tuck and games kit. No tobacco/alcohol allowed.

Discipline No corporal punishment. Pupils failing to produce homework once might expect either a verbal warning or 'Bad Record' (a note in the pupil's school diary); suspension would be considered for those caught smoking cannabis on the premises.

Boarding All boarders go home at weekends. 5% have own study bedroom, 5% share with one other. No divided houses. Part-time doctor, matron during school hours. Headmaster's wife acts as matron after school hours. Central dining room. Visits to local town allowed.

Alumni association is run by Mr J Robin Barron, 1 Snow Hill Close, Wrenthorpe, Wakefield.

Former pupils Mike Harrison (Captain, England Rugby Union); Prof Sir Hans Kornberg (Master of Christ College, Cambridge); Kenneth Leighton; Peter Dews (playwright/theatrical producer); Ronald Eyre; Lord Marshall; Lord Wolfenden.

QUEEN ELIZABETH'S (BLACKBURN)

Queen Elizabeth's Grammar School	Co-ed	Pupils 1100*
Blackburn	• Boys	Upper sixth 175
Lancashire BB2 6DF	Girls	Termly fees:
Telephone number: 0254 59911/2	• Mixed sixth	Day £740
Enquiries/application to the Headmaster	• Day	HMC
	Boarding	*whole school

WHAT IT'S LIKE

The original foundation was 1509; refounded in 1567 under royal charter by Elizabeth. In 1882 it moved to its present site. The solid, well-designed and well-equipped buildings make a compact campus of about 16 acres in the north-west outskirts of Blackburn. Its junior school is nearby. There have been very considerable developments over the years, and a new wing costing £2 million was opened by the Queen and the Duke of Edinburgh in 1987. A distinguished school, it has high standards of teaching and impressive academic results (100–120 pupils go on to university each year). Christian in emphasis, the school is interdenominational in practice. There are close links with the cathedral. Very strong in music and art. Also much strength in sports and games. Active commitment to community services and a good record in the Duke of Edinburgh's Award Scheme.

SCHOOL PROFILE

Pupils Total 1100 (boys 1010, girls 90). Entry age, boys 8 or 11; boys and girls directly into the sixth. A few are children of former pupils.

Entrance Common entrance and own entrance exam used. Oversubscribed. No special skills or religious requirements. Parents not expected to buy text books. 273 assisted places. 20–25 scholarships/bursaries, £1000–£100.

Parents 15+% are doctors, lawyers etc. More than 60% live within 30 miles.

Staff Head P F Johnston. 85 full time staff. 9 part time. Annual turnover 3%. Average age 39.

Academic work GCSE and A-levels. Average size of upper fifth 160; upper sixth 175. *O-levels*: on average, 20 pupils pass 5–7 subjects; 140 pass 8+ subjects. *A-levels*: on average, 5 pupils in the upper sixth pass 2 subjects; 60, 3 subjects and 110 pass 4 subjects. On average, about 60% take science/

engineering A-levels; about 40% take arts and humanities. *Computing facilities*: 14 Nimbus, 22 BBCs.

Senior pupils' non-academic activities *Music*: 80 learn a musical instrument, 8 to Grade 6 or above, 3 accepted for Music School; 60 in school orchestra, 140 in choir. *Art*: 60 take art as non-examined subject; 20 take GCSE; 10 A-level; 4 accepted for Art School. *Sport*: Swimming, soccer, rugby, squash, cricket available. All take non-compulsory sport. National Independent Schools Soccer Champions (Public Schools Sixes, December 1986). 4 represent county/country (soccer, netball). *Other*: 20 have bronze Duke of Edinburgh's Award, 12 have silver and 4 have gold. Many sixth formers work for national charities. Other activities include a computer club, drama, debating.

Careers All sixth-form tutors and 3 specialist part time advisors. Average number of pupils accepted for *arts and humanities degree courses* at Oxbridge, 10; other universities, 40; polytechnics or CHE, 20. *science and engineering degree courses* at Oxbridge, 14; other universities, 60; medical schools, 28; polytechnics or CHE, 12. *other general training courses*, a few. Average number of pupils going straight into careers in the armed services, 2; the church, 1; industry and civil service, a few.

Uniform School uniform worn throughout.

Houses/prefects Competitive houses. Prefects, head boy/girl, head of house and house prefects – appointed by the Head and school.

Religion Religious worship certainly encouraged.

Social Pupils allowed to bring own car/bike to school. Meals self service. School shop. No tobacco/alcohol allowed.

Discipline No corporal punishment. Pupils failing to produce homework once might expect detention.

Former pupils Russell Harty; Bishop Peter Hall (Bishop of Woolwich); Vic Whitsey (former Bishop of Chester); Sir Kenneth Durham (former Chairman of Unilever); Professor K Miller (Head of Engineering, Sheffield University).

QUEEN ELIZABETH'S HOSPITAL

Queen Elizabeth's Hospital	Co-ed	Pupils 484
Berkeley Place	● Boys	Upper sixth 65
Clifton	Girls	Termly fees:
Bristol BS8 1JX	Mixed sixth	Day £735
Telephone number 0272 291856	● Day	Boarding £1310
	● Boarding	HMC
Enquiries/application to the Headmaster		

WHAT IT'S LIKE

Founded in 1590, a Blue Coat school along the lines of Christ's Hospital, London. It has occupied its present site since 1847. Urban, it is near the university and city centre. Its buildings are imposing and very well equipped. A selective entry school for bright boys, its academic standards are high. Generous endowment permits support of many pupils. Socially, it is comprehensive while being academically selective. Christian worship is compulsory. Very strong music department, good drama and art. Impressive academic results: 35–40 pupils go on to university each year. Strong on games side, and plentiful activities. Emphasis on outdoor pursuits. Some commitment to local community schemes and the Duke of Edinburgh's Award Scheme. It has close links with the City of Bristol and enjoys vigorous local support. Full use is made of the cultural amenities of the City.

SCHOOL PROFILE

Pupils Total, 484. Day 384; Boarding 100. Entry age, 11+, 13+ and into the sixth. Less than 10% are children of former pupils.

Entrance Bristol area entrance exam used. Oversubscribed. No special skills or religious requirements. Parents not expected to buy text books. 25 assisted places. 6 scholarships/bursaries pa, £2200–£500 pa, based on entrance exam; others related to family income.

Parents 60+% live within 30 miles; up to 10% live overseas.

Staff Head R Gliddon, in post for 3 years. 34 full time staff, 8 part time. Annual turnover 10%. Average age 35.

Academic work GCSE and A-levels. Average size of fifth 75; upper sixth 65. *O-levels*: on average, 5 pupils in fifth pass 1–4 subjects; 15, 5–7 subjects; 55 pass 8+ subjects. *A-levels*: on average, 5 pupils in upper sixth pass 1 subject; 7, 2 subjects; 38, 3 subjects and 5 pass 4 subjects. On average, 30 take science/engineering A-levels; 18 take arts and humanities; 7 a mixture. *Computing facilities*: BBC micros in the computer centre.

Senior pupils' non-academic activities *Music*: 30 learn a musical instrument, 12 to Grade 6 or above; 1 Organ scholar; 1 plays in pop group beyond school; 15 in school orchestra, 25 in choir, 6 in pop group, 25 in wind band, 8 in brass group, 12 in woodwind group; 3 in National youth choir; 3 in County of Avon School Orchestra. *Drama and dance*: 35 in school productions; 12 in joint school plays. *Art*: 15 take GCSE, 6, A-level. 2 accepted for Art School. 12 belong to photographic club. *Sport*: Rugger, cricket, swimming, athletics, tennis, squash, badminton, fencing, judo, sailing, basketball, soccer, running, hiking available. 150 take non-compulsory sport; 26 hiking. 11 represent county/country (rugger, athletics, cricket). *Other*: 20 take part in local community schemes. 14 have bronze Duke of Edinburgh's Award, 4 have silver. Other activities include a computer club, chess club (Bristol league), debates (local competitions), quiz teams (local and national competitions), drama club, film society, YHA, ATC (40 boys).

Careers 1 full time teacher. Average number of pupils accepted for *arts and humanities degree courses* at Oxbridge, 3; other universities, 14; polytechnics or CHE, 5. *science and engineering degree courses* at Oxbridge, 3; other universities, 18; medical schools, 2; polytechnics or CHE, 5. *other general training courses*, 1. Average number of pupils going straight into careers in armed services, 2; industry, 1; banking, 1.

Uniform School uniform worn, modified in sixth.

Houses/prefects Competitive houses. Prefects, head boy, head of house and house prefects – some elected, some appointed.

Religion Morning assembly, Sunday service for boarders.

Social Drama and music (choral and orchestral) with three local girls' schools; debates (Bristol Rotary Club event). Organised trip to France (French Dept and History Dept WWI), Germany (German and rugger), winter ski trip. Meals formal. School tuckshop (at break). No tobacco/alcohol allowed.

Discipline No corporal punishment. Pupils failing to produce homework once might expect a reprimand or detention; those caught smoking cannabis could expect suspension or expulsion.

Boarding 25% have study bedroom (in pairs), 35% share (6); 40% are in dormitories of 5. 2 Houses, of 40 and 60, divided by age group. Resident qualified nurse, doctor visits. Central dining room. Senior pupils can provide and cook own food. 2 weekend exeats each term plus half term. Visits to the local town allowed.

Alumni association is run by Mr R R Pope, 119 Cranbrook Road, Redland, Bristol BS6.

QUEEN ETHELBURGA'S

Queen Ethelburga's School
Penny Pot Lane
Harrogate
North Yorkshire HG3 2SG
Telephone number 0423 64125

Enquiries/application to the Headmistress

Co-ed   Pupils 205
Boys   Upper sixth 28
● Girls   Termly fees:
Mixed sixth   Day £1185
● Day   Boarding £1975
● Boarding   Woodard

WHAT IT'S LIKE

Founded in 1912 and named after the Anglo-Saxon queen who brought Christianity to the north in the 7th century, it has a fine rural site on the outskirts of the very agreeable spa town of Harrogate. Pleasant gardens and ample playing fields surround it. Beyond lies beautiful Yorkshire countryside. The buildings are well designed and spacious and the boarding accommodation is comfortable (all boarders have their own bedroom). Junior and senior schools are combined. Queen Ethelburga's has all the advantages of being small; a happy, purposeful, family atmosphere prevails. There is considerable emphasis on Christian values, and religious practice in the Anglican tradition, plus a firm belief in the merits of a single-sex education. Academic standards are very creditable and the large staff permits a staff: pupil ratio of about 1:8. Results are good and a few girls go on to university each year. The music, art and drama depts are very active. A good standard is attained in sports and games. The Parents' Association is particularly strong and the school has a high reputation locally. A commitment to local community schemes and an outstanding record in the Duke of Edinburgh's Award Scheme. Full use is made of Harrogate's cultural amenities.

SCHOOL PROFILE

Pupils Total, 205. Day 62; Boarding 143. Entry age, 7, 11 up and into the sixth. Own junior school provides over 20%.

Entrance Common entrance and own entrance exam used. Not oversubscribed. No special skills or religious requirements. Parents not expected to buy text books. 8 scholarships (including music), clergy and sixth form bursaries; 50%–20% fees.

Staff Head Mrs J M Town, appointed 1988. 21 full time staff, 13 part time. Annual turnover 10%. Average age 40.

Academic work GCSE and A-levels. Average size of upper fifth 36; upper sixth 28. *O-levels*: on average, 13 pupils in upper fifth pass 1–4 subjects; 10, 5–7 subjects; 13 pass 8+ subjects. *A-levels*: on average, 4 pupils in upper sixth pass 1 subject; 3, 2 subjects; 3, 3 subjects and 2 pass 4 subjects. On average, 4 take science/engineering A-levels; 7 take arts and humanities; 3 a mixture. Drama and textiles design offered to GCSE; Classical Studies to A-level. *Computing facilities*: Specialist computer room; machines in science, careers and English departments. Special provision for dyslexic pupils. Overseas candidates prepared for university test in English.

Senior pupils' non-academic activities *Music*: 89 learn a musical instrument, 2 to Grade 6 or above; 40 in school choir, 6 in string ensemble, 10 wind, 10 recorder ensemble. *Drama and dance*: 20 in school productions. 3 take to Grade 6 or above. 6 take ballet. 6 entered eg public speaking competitions. *Art*: 86 take as non-examined subject; 22 GCSE; 8 A-level. 2 belong to eg photographic club. *Sport*: Lacrosse, netball, gymnastics, swimming, riding, tennis, squash, badminton, rounders, athletics, ski-ing (local dry ski slope) available. 100 take non-compulsory sport. 50 take exams. 7 represent county/district (lacrosse, netball). *Other*: 35 take part in local community schemes. 37 have bronze Duke of Edinburgh's Award, 13 have silver and 15 gold. Other activities include a computer club, golf, outdoor pursuits, car maintenance, canoeing, gliding, self-defence, sailing, play reading, hospital visiting, social work in homes and charity shops, cooking, jewellery making, brass rubbing.

Careers 1 full time and 1 part time careers advisor. Average number of pupils accepted for *arts and humanities degree courses* at universities, 2; polytechnics or CHE, 3. *science and engineering degree courses* at universities, 2; medical schools, 1; polytechnics or CHE, 2. *other general training courses*, 5. Average number of pupils going straight into careers in industry, 1; retail management, 2.

Uniform School uniform worn except the sixth.

Houses/prefects Competitive houses. Prefects, head girl, head of house and house prefects. School Council.

Religion Religious worship encouraged.

Social Debates, dances, choir, literary studies outings, management courses organised with local schools. Annual visit to Switzerland, French trips and exchanges. Meals formal. School shop. No tobacco allowed; alcohol occasionally on controlled basis.

Discipline No corporal punishment. Pupils failing to produce homework once might expect reprimand; those caught smoking cigarettes on the premises might expect expulsion after warnings.

Boarding All have own study bedroom. Houses, of approximately 50, are the same as competitive houses plus sixth form house. Resident qualified nurse, visiting doctor. 2 weekend exeats each term. Visits to local town allowed, once a term (14), weekly (sixth form).

QUEEN MARGARET'S (YORK)

Queen Margaret's School   Co-ed   Pupils 261
Escrick Park   Boys   Upper sixth 18
York YO4 6EU   ● Girls   Termly fees:
Telephone number 090 487 261   Mixed sixth   Day £1135
Enquiries/application to the Headmaster   ● Day   Boarding £1820
       ● Boarding   GSA

WHAT IT'S LIKE

Founded in 1901, moved to its present site in 1949. The main building is a huge and magnificent country house built in 1758 in 50 acres of splendid parkland. A C of E foundation, its pupils come from a wide social and geographic background ('global intake'). It has many of the advantages of a small school and enjoys a good staff:pupil ratio of 1:10. There is an almost full-time remedial department. A notable feature is the big parental involvement in many areas of school life (eg organisation, cultural, work experience etc). Very strong music, drama and art and a good range of sports, games and activities. Good record in the Duke of Edinburgh's Award Scheme.

SCHOOL PROFILE

Pupils Total over 12, 261. Day 36; Boarding 225. Entry age, 11+ and into the sixth. 5% are children of former pupils.

Entrance Own entrance exam used. Oversubscribed. No special skills or religious requirements. Parents expected to buy text books occasionally in the sixth form. 9 scholarships/bursaries, plus music scholarship, from ½ fees to £300.

Parents 15+% are doctors, lawyers, etc; 15+% in industry or commerce. 10+% live within 30 miles, up to 10% live overseas.

Staff Head C S McGarrigle, in post for 4 years. 32 full time staff, 14 part time. Annual turnover 15%. Average age 40.

Academic work GCSE and A-levels. Average size of upper fifth 33; upper sixth 18. *O-levels*: on average, 8 pupils in upper fifth pass 1–4 subjects; 12, 5–7 subjects; 13 pass 8+ subjects. *A-levels*: on average, 2 pupils in the upper sixth pass 1 subject; 3, 2 subjects; 8, 3 subjects; 2 pass 4 subjects. On average, 2 take science/engineering A-levels; 14 take arts and humanities; 2 take a mixture. *Computing facilities*: A large resource centre; computers also in five departments. Almost full time remedial department and small dyslexic group.

Senior pupils' non-academic activities *Music*: 95 learn a musical instrument, 20 up to Grade 6 or above; 25 in school orchestra, 30 in choir, 35 in school bands, 70 in choral society; 5 in National Childrens' Orchestra. *Drama and dance*: 120 in school productions. 2/3 entered dance festivals. 24 in senior theatre club including running junior theatre club. *Art*: 45 take as non-examined subject; 32 take GCSE; 5 A-level. 2 accepted for Art School, 2 take History of Art (university). 11 belong to photographic club. *Sport*: Hockey, netball, lacrosse, golf, tennis, swimming, athletics, badminton, gymnastics, ski-ing, riding, orienteering, squash, martial arts and rounders available. 108 take non-compulsory sport. 125 take extra tennis; 80 ride. 70 take exams. Lacrosse: 5 pupils represent county, 5 region, and 5 go into England trials. *Other*: 35 have bronze Duke of Edinburgh's Award, and 8 have gold. 10 work for national charities. Other activities include a computer club, cookery, needlework, gardening, outreach, chess, bridge, fashion and design, driving lessons, board games, pottery and aerobics.

Careers 2 part time advisors. Average number of pupils accepted for *arts and humanities degree courses* at Oxbridge, 1; other universities, 6; polytechnics or CHE, 4. *science and engineering degree courses* at university, 1. *BEd*, 3. *other general training courses*, 6. Average number of pupils going straight into armed services, 1.

Uniform School uniform worn except sixth.

Houses/prefects Competitive houses. Prefects, head girl, heads of houses and house prefects – appointed by the Head. School Council.

Religion Compulsory C of E worship.

Social Mission work locally, debates, social events, musical events (village invited), bell ringing (local church). Organised trips abroad – ski-ing, Kenya, Paris, Greece; possible link-up with Canada. Pupils allowed to bring own bike/horse to school. Meals self service. School shop. No tobacco/alcohol allowed.

Discipline No corporal punishment. Pupils failing to produce homework might expect crisp reprimand and detention; those caught smoking cannabis on the premises might expect dismissal.

Boarding 20% have own study bedroom, 20% share with others; 60% are in dormitories of 6 or more. Houses, of approximately 50, are divided by age. Resident qualified medical staff. Central dining room. Sixth form can provide and cook own food. 1–2 weekend and half-term exeats each term. Visits to local town allowed from 13 upwards.

Alumni association is run by Mrs Judith Cooke, Old House Farm, Stubbs Walden, Doncaster DN6 9BU.

Former pupils Winifred Holtby; Joan Hall (MP); Ann Jellicoe (writer); Dorothy Hutton (RA); Elizabeth Poston (musician).

QUEEN MARY

Queen Mary School
Lytham St Annes
Lancashire FY8 1DS
Telephone number 0253 723246

Co-ed
Boys
● Girls
Mixed sixth
● Day
Boarding

Pupils 600
Upper sixth Yes
Termly fees:
Day £640
GSA; GBGSA

Head Miss M C Ritchie (7 years)
Age range 11–18, own prep from age 7; entry by own exam.
3 scholarships and 6 bursaries pa.

QUEEN'S COLLEGE (LONDON)

Queen's College
43–49 Harley Street
London W1N 2BT
Telephone number 01-580 1533

Co-ed | Pupils 390
Boys | Upper sixth Yes
● Girls | Termly fees:
Mixed sixth | Day £900
● Day | Boarding £1400
● Boarding | GSA

Head Mrs P J Fleming
Age range 11–18; entry by own exam. Weekly boarding only.
8 scholarships.

QUEEN'S GATE

Queen's Gate School
131–133 Queen's Gate
London SW7 5LF
Telephone number 01-589 3587

Co-ed | Pupils 160
Boys | Upper sixth Yes
● Girls | Termly fees:
Mixed sixth | Day £1050
● Day | GBGSA; GSA
Boarding |

Head Mrs A M Holyoak (since 1988)
Age range 11–18, own prep from age 4; entry by own exam or common entrance. Junior school pupils must pass CE to get into senior.

QUEEN'S (CHESTER)

The Queen's School
City Walls Road
Chester CH1 2NN
Telephone number 0244 312078

Enquiries/application to the Secretary

Co-ed | Pupils 420
Boys | Upper sixth 60
● Girls | Termly fees:
Mixed sixth | Day £680
● Day | GSA; SHA;
Boarding | GBGSA

WHAT IT'S LIKE

Founded in 1878, it has a pleasant urban site with gardens and playing fields on the west side of the city wall, near the Watergate. A combination of late Victorian and modern buildings. The school still uses the original assembly hall given by the Duke of Westminster in 1882 when Queen Victoria became the first patron. The junior and prep departments are housed in separate buildings in Liverpool Road. The school is interdenominational with strong Christian emphasis. A sound general education is provided and, with a staff:pupil ratio of 1:12, impressive results are obtained. A high proportion of leavers go on to university and other forms of further education each year (about 50–55 in all; between 5–10 to Oxbridge). Considerable strength in music, drama and art. An adequate range of sports and games (high standards) and a fair range of extra-curricular activities.

SCHOOL PROFILE

Pupils Total over 12, 420. Entry age, 4+, 8+, 11+ and into the sixth. Own junior school provides over 40%.

Entrance Own entrance exam used. Oversubscribed. No religious requirements. Good all-round academic ability looked for. Parents not expected to buy text books. 17 assisted places pa. Bursaries available, dependent on need.

Parents 100% live within 30 miles.

Staff Head Miss M Farra, in post for 15 years. 32 full time staff, 23 part time.

Academic work GCSE and A-levels. Average size of upper fifth 60; upper sixth 60. *O-levels*: on average, 60 pupils in upper fifth pass 5 or more subjects. *A-levels*: 2 pupils in upper sixth pass 1 subject; 3, 2 subjects; 11, 3 subjects and 42 pass 4 subjects. (Pass rate of over 90%.) On average, about one-third take science A-levels; one-third, arts and humanities; one-third, a mixture. *Computing facilities*: computer room with 11 BBC computers and network, printers etc; others in science, junior and preparatory departments.

Senior pupils' non-academic activities *Music*: Many learn an instrument; 2 orchestras, choir, wind, recorder and string groups. Strong interest in music, mainly for pleasure. *Drama and dance*: Annual production with as large a cast as possible. *Art*: Sixth form take as non-examined subject; 15–20 take GCSE; 6–10 A-level. Several accepted for Art School. *Sport*: Hockey, lacrosse, tennis, swimming, rounders, athletics available. Many take part in non-compulsory sport. Some pupils represent county/country (hockey, lacrosse, tennis, athletics). *Other*: Some senior girls take part in local community schemes and enter voluntary schemes after leaving school. Other activities include a computer club, debating, Christian Union, netball and gym clubs.

Careers 1 part time careers advisor. Nearly all pupils enter professional training or some kind of higher education; 80–85% to degree courses, 6–10 each year to Oxbridge. Fairly even spread between arts and sciences.

Uniform School uniform worn except the sixth.

Houses/prefects Competitive houses for games only. Head girl and deputies appointed by Head and staff (no prefects). School Committee.

Religion Short Christian assembly every morning.

Social Organised local events and joint functions with other schools from time to time. French and German exchanges; ski-ing trips abroad. Pupils allowed to bring own bike to school. Meals self service. Twice-weekly tuckshop. No tobacco/alcohol allowed.

Discipline No corporal punishment.

Alumni association run by Miss K M Wood, Four Winds, Stannage Lane, Churton, Chester.

QUEEN'S (TAUNTON)

Queen's College
Taunton
Somerset TA1 4QS
Telephone number 0823 72559

Enquiries/application to the Headmaster

- Co-ed   Pupils 440
- Boys   Upper sixth 60
- Girls   Termly fees:
- Mixed sixth   Day £1215
- Day   Boarding £1845
- Boarding   HMC

WHAT IT'S LIKE

Founded in 1843, a Methodist foundation, it moved to its present premises in 1846. These are single-site and semi-rural in 30 acres on the southern outskirts of Taunton. Very pleasant buildings and fine playing fields. Junior school combined. Much development in the last 25–30 years. More extensions are currently under way. Facilities are good and the school is well positioned for field work, expeditions etc to Exmoor, Dartmoor and the Quantocks. An exceptionally strong music department; good drama and art. About 75% of pupils go on to university degree courses or polytechnics. A good range of games, sports and activities. A distinguished record in the Duke of Edinburgh's Award Scheme. Vigorous local support.

SCHOOL PROFILE

Pupils Total over 12, 440. Day 240 (boys 118, girls 122); Boarding 200 (boys 152, girls 48). Entry age, 12–13+ and into the sixth. Own junior school provides 70%.

Entrance Common entrance and own entrance exam used. Oversubscribed for girls' boarding. Musical skills looked for; all denominations welcome. Parents not expected to buy text books. 14 assisted places pa. Various scholarships/bursaries, up to full fees.

Staff Head A P Hodgson, in post for 9 years. 43 full time staff, 14 part time. Annual turnover 5%.

Academic work GCSE and A-levels. Average size of upper fifth 83; upper sixth 60. *O-levels*: on average, 24 pupils in upper fifth pass 1–4 subjects; 25, 5–7 subjects; 34 pass 8+ subjects. *A-levels*: on average, 2 pupils in upper sixth pass 1 subject; 13, 2 subjects and 37 pass 3 or more subjects. *Computing facilities*: Ample. Provision for dyslexic pupils.

Senior pupils' non-academic activities *Music*: 230 learn a musical instrument, 3 accepted for Music School; 60 in school orchestra, 50 in school choir. *Drama and dance*: 50 take drama or dance. *Art*: All take as non-examined subject; 50 take GCSE; 3–4 A-level. 2 accepted for Art School. *Sport*: Rugby, hockey, netball, cricket, squash, badminton, swimming, athletics, tennis, fencing, trampolining and golf available. Many pupils represent county; 2 represent country (rugby, cricket). *Other*: 60 have bronze Duke of Edinburgh's Award, 25 have silver and 20 gold. Other activities include woodwork, dressmaking, car maintenance, home economics; archive, history, geography and computer clubs.

Careers 2 part time careers advisors. About 75% of pupils go on to degree courses at university or polytechnic.

Uniform School uniform worn throughout.

Houses/prefects Competitive houses. Prefects, head boy/girl, head of house and house prefects – appointed by the head.
Religion Part of a group of Methodist schools.
Social Organised trips abroad. Pupils allowed to bring own car/bike to school. Meals self service. School shop. No tobacco/alcohol allowed.
Discipline No corporal punishment. Pupils failing to produce homework once might expect to have to do it; discipline for those caught smoking cigarettes on the premises would depend on the circumstances.
Boarding Upper sixth have own study bedroom, lower sixth share with 2; 50% are in dormitories of 6+. Houses, of 45, same as competitive houses, are single sex. Resident qualified nurse. Central dining room. Exeats each term. Visits to local town allowed for older pupils.

QUEEN VICTORIA

Queen Victoria School	Co-ed	Pupils 270
Dunblane	● Boys	Upper sixth Yes
Perthshire FK15 0JY	Girls	Termly fees:
Telephone number 0786 822288	Mixed sixth	see below
	Day	
	● Boarding	

Head J D Hankinson (8 years)
Age range 10–18.
All pupils must be the sons of servicemen or women who have served at least 4 years in the ranks in HM Forces – parents must either be Scottish or have served in a Scottish regiment. The school is largely financed by the Ministry of Defence.

RADLEY

Radley College	Co-ed	Pupils 600
Abingdon	● Boys	Upper sixth 120
Oxfordshire OX14 2HR	Girls	Termly fees:
Telephone number 0235 20294	Mixed sixth	Boarding £2450
Enquiries/application to the Warden	Day	HMC
	● Boarding	

WHAT IT'S LIKE

Founded in 1847 by the Rev William Sewell, Fellow of Exeter College, Oxford, to provide a public school education on the principles of the Church of England. Its agreeable and well-equipped buildings (boarding accommodation is comfortable) lie in a beautiful 700-acre estate 300 ft above sea level, 2½ miles from Abingdon and 5 from Oxford. The environment is healthy. It is now one of the most successful of boarding schools for boys and has first-class facilities of all kinds. It retains strong links with Oxford and the Church of England. The chapel and religious education are an important part of the college's life. Two resident chaplains and the Warden are responsible for chapel services etc. A large and well-qualified staff (who work very hard) permits a staff:pupil ratio of 1:10. Academic standards are high and results excellent. A high proportion of leavers go on to university each year. The music department is very strong (about 150 boys learn an instrument) and there is extensive activity in drama (annual school production, shorter plays by dramatic societies, a production by the Gilbert and Sullivan society and so on). There is a fine design centre in which work of high quality is produced. Sports facilities are exceptionally good and the college is well known for its achievements in rugby, cricket, hockey and rowing (there are boathouses on the Thames, a mile away). Numerous clubs and societies cater for virtually every extra-curricular need. There is also a golf course and the college runs its own beagle pack. The CCF is a large contingent: all boys join it when aged 14½ and have to pass the proficiency exam before they leave the CCF. Considerable emphasis on outdoor pursuits and an impressive record in the Duke of Edinburgh's Award Scheme.

SCHOOL PROFILE

Pupils Total over 12, 600. Entry age, 13 and into the sixth, post GCSE very occasionally.

Entrance Common entrance and own scholarship exam used. Oversubscribed. No special skills required; C of E preferred, other denominations accepted. 20 scholarships/exhibitions, full fees to £300 pa.

Parents 15+% are doctors, lawyers etc; 15+% in industry or commerce. 10+% live within 30 miles; up to 10% live overseas.

Staff Head D R W Silk, in post for 20 years. 62 full time staff, 8 part time plus musicians. Annual turnover 6%. Average age 37.

Academic work GCSE and A-levels. Average size of upper fifth 120; upper sixth 120. *O-levels*: on average, 5 pupils in upper fifth pass 1–4 subjects; 20, 5–7 subjects; 95 pass 8+ subjects. *A-levels*: on average, 1–2 pupils in the upper sixth pass 1 subject; 5–10, 2 subjects; majority, 3 subjects and 5–10 pass 4 subjects. On average, one-third take science/engineering A-levels; one-third take arts and humanities; one-third a mixture. *Computing facilities*: well equipped computer room, facilities in depts.

Senior pupils' non-academic activities *Music*: 150 learn a musical instrument, 50 up to Grade 6 or above, 1 or 2 accepted for Music School. *Drama and dance*: Large number in annual productions. *Art*: A small number take A-level. Artist and Potter in residence. *Sport*: Rugby (school game), rowing (own boathouse), hockey, cricket, tennis, diving, sub-aqua, windsurfing, gymnastics, athletics, squash, swimming, basketball, judo, fencing, fives, rackets, sailing, golf available. All participate in some sport. Several pupils represent county/country in wide range of sports at relevant age levels. *Other*: Some take part in local community schemes. Many gain bronze, silver and gold awards in Duke of Edinburgh's Scheme. Other activities include a computer club, wide range of societies including antiques, beagling, bridge, canoeing, car, chess, classical, clay pigeon, cycling, debating, dramatic, film, history, karate, literary, magic circle, mountaineering, musical, natural history, philatelic, photographic, poetry, political, printing, scientific, Scottish dancing, trout fishing, CCF.

Careers Careers Master and committee of masters. Annual Industry Conference. Details of those going on to degree courses, or careers information, not readily available.

Uniform School uniform worn throughout.

Houses/prefects Competitive houses. Prefects, head boy, head of house and house prefects – appointed by the head. 'Chores' performed by junior boys.

Religion 4 evening services a week plus service on Sundays compulsory. Boys may choose which Sunday service to attend.

Social Debating, concerts etc with other schools. Annual ski-ing trip abroad. Pupils allowed to bring own bike to school. Meals self service. School shop. No tobacco/alcohol allowed.

Discipline No corporal punishment. Pupils failing to produce homework once might expect detention.

Boarding Most seniors have own study bedroom, a few are in dormitories of 6+ (in cubicles). 8 houses, of approximately 75, same as competitive houses. Resident qualified nurse. Central dining room. Pupils can provide and cook own food. Half term plus 1 Saturday night exeat each term. Visits to local town allowed.

Alumni association run by P H Jackson Esq, c/o the College.

RANNOCH

Rannoch School	• Co-ed	Pupils 250
Rannoch	Boys	Upper sixth 35
Perthshire PH17 2QQ	Girls	Termly fees:
Telephone number 08822 332	Mixed sixth	Day £1175
	• Day	Boarding £1990
Enquiries/application to the Headmaster	• Boarding	SHMIS; GBA

WHAT IT'S LIKE

Founded in 1959 by three masters from Gordonstoun, it has a marvellous site in 120 acres of grounds on the south shore of Loch Rannoch in a spectacular setting of highland scenery. The main building, formerly known as Dall, was built in 1855 by a chief of the Robertson clan. It is a towered and turreted mansion of Scottish 'baronial' lineage. Modern facilities, including converted farm buildings, provide excellent additional accommodation. A well-run and enterprising school, it has very strong links and contacts with the local highland community which gives vigorous support. Its 'international' spread of intake includes some 150 pupils from Scotland, 50-odd from England and about 80 from overseas (mostly the children of expatriates). It has high academic standards and impressive results. There is a staff:pupil ratio of about 1:10 and 20-plus leavers go on to universities (a large proportion for a school of this size). Chapel services are compulsory and there is quite a lot of emphasis on religious education. Strong in music, drama and art, and considerable strength in games and sports. A big commitment to local community schemes. The fine range of clubs and societies caters for many needs. The environment is ideal for outdoor pursuits and a lot are available (including fishing, ski-ing, mountaineering, camping, sailing and canoeing). The school (not surprisingly) has a most remarkable record in the Duke of Edinburgh's Award Scheme (over 300 gold awards in 20 years).

SCHOOL PROFILE

Pupils Total over 12, 250. Day 5 (boys 3, girls 2); Boarding 245 (boys 210, girls 35). Entry age, 10 onwards and into the sixth.

Entrance Common entrance and own entrance exam used. Oversubscribed. Pleasant young people looked for. No religious requirements. Parents expected to pay a small charge per session for text books. 25 assisted places. Up to 10 scholarships/bursaries, up to three-quarters of fees.

Parents Parents drawn from a wide range of occupations. 150 live in Scotland, 50 in England and 80 overseas.

Staff Head M Barratt, in post for 5 years. 25 full time staff, 8 part time. Average age 30–40.

Academic work GCSE, A-level, O-grade and Highers. Average size of upper fifth 50; upper sixth 35. 35 pupils take Highers (79% pass rate); 10–15 pupils take A-levels (95% pass rate). Geology and computer studies are offered to GCSE/A-level. *Computing facilities*: 12 BBC B master series. Provision for remedial English and mathematics.

Senior pupils' non-academic activities *Music*: Over one-third of school learn a musical instrument; 25 in school orchestra, 40 in choir, 20 in piping and drumming. *Drama and dance*: Pupils participate in 2 productions each year. *Art*: 40 take as non-examined subject; 25 take O-grade; 10 A-level and Higher. 3 or 4 go to Art School each year. 20 belong to photographic club. *Sport*: Rugby, hockey, ski-ing, athletics, cross-country, basketball, football, cricket, tennis, sailing, swimming, orienteering and golf available. Sport is compulsory but there is a range of options. 15 take GCSE in PE. Pupils make regular appearances at county/country level (rugby, ski-ing and athletics). *Other*: 30 take part in local community schemes. 45 have bronze Duke of Edinburgh's Award, 45 have silver and 25 gold. School has gained over 300 Gold Awards since 1968. Other activities include a computer club, hairdressing, archery, archaeology, auto-mechanics, bible-study, bridge, chess, clay pigeon shooting, cookery, debating, dress-making, electronics, natural history, piping, Scottish country dancing. Also ambulance, fire and mountain services, loch patrol, building, meteorological and conservation services.

Careers 1 full time and 6 part time advisors. 20+ pupils go to university each year; 10+ to college for degree courses. *other general training courses*, 5–6. Average number of pupils going straight into careers in the armed services, 2–4; some go into the church, industry, the City, civil service, music/drama.

Uniform School uniform worn throughout.

Houses/prefects Competitive houses. Prefects, head boy/girl, head of house and house prefects – appointed by the Head after consultation. Various school committees.

Religion Compulsory religious worship.

Social Very strong contact with local Highland community. Large sum raised last year to save the village hall. Organised trips abroad and exchange systems. Pupils allowed to bring own bike to school. Meals self service. School shop. No tobacco/alcohol allowed.

Discipline No corporal punishment.

Boarding All sixth form have own study bedroom, many fifth formers share.

Houses, of approximately 50, same as competitive houses and single sex. Resident qualified medical staff. Central dining room. Pupils can provide and cook own food, within limits. Exeats permitted each term, number varies. Visits to the local town allowed.

Alumni association run by Mr Colin Mackay, 8 Merchiston Gardens, Edinburgh EH10 4DD. Telephone 031 337 4591.

RATCLIFFE COLLEGE

Ratcliffe College
Syston
Leicestershire LE7 8SG
Telephone number 050 981 2522

- Co-ed — Pupils 420
- Boys — Upper sixth Yes
- Girls — Termly fees:
- Mixed sixth — Day £1160
- Day — Boarding £1700
- Boarding — HMC; GBA

Head Rev L G Hurdidge (3 years)
Age range 11–18. Boarding from age 13
Scholarships and bursaries. Grace Dieu prep school attached, taking children from age 5.

READ

Read School
Drax
Selby
North Yorkshire YO8 8NL
Telephone number 0757 618248

Enquiries/application to the Headmaster

- Co-ed — Pupils 205
- Boys — Upper sixth 9
- Girls — Termly fees:
- Mixed sixth — Day £665
- Day — Boarding £1320
- Boarding — BSA; ISAI

WHAT IT'S LIKE

Founded in 1667, it has a very pleasant rural site in the village of Drax. Teaching is on two sites, main campus for 11+, junior campus for 8–11. Boarding accommodation on three sites. All close together. Most of the buildings are early 19th century. There have been extensive modern developments in the last 30 years. Facilities are good. A small school, it is ideal for a wide range of ability, skills and interests. Strong music, drama and art depts. It gives a sound all-round education. Good range of sport, games and activities. Some involvement in local community services and the Duke of Edinburgh's Award Scheme.

SCHOOL PROFILE

Pupils Total over 12, 205. Day 60; Boarding 145. Entry age, 8+, 11+, 13+ and into the sixth. Own junior department provides 20+%. 15% are children of former pupils.

Entrance Admission by interview. Not oversubscribed. No special skills or religious requirements. Parents not expected to buy text books. 6 scholarships/bursaries, up to half tuition fee.

Parents 15+% in the armed services. 30+% live within 30 miles; 10+% live overseas.

Staff Head A J Saddler, in post for 3 years. 20 full time, 4 part time. Annual turnover 5%. Average age 35–40.

Academic work GCSE and A-levels. Average size of upper fifth 40–45; upper sixth 8–10. *O-levels*: on average, 19 pupils in upper fifth pass 1–4 subjects; 10, 5–7 subjects; 6 pass 8+ subjects. *A-levels*: on average, 3 pupils in the upper sixth pass 1 subject; 3, 2 subjects; 1, 3 subjects and 3 pass 4 subjects. On average, 40% take science/engineering A-levels; 40% take arts and humanities; 20% a mixture. *Computing facilities*: Micros in Maths and Physics. Extra help available at local Dyslexia Institute.

Senior pupils' non-academic activities *Music*: 20 learn a musical instrument, 1 up to Grade 6 or above; 15 in school orchestra, 10 in choir. *Drama and dance*: 80 in school productions. *Art*: 50 take as non-examined subject; 25 take GCSE; 5 A-level. 3 accepted for Art School. 5 belong to photographic club. *Sport*: Rugby, soccer, cricket, tennis, swimming, cross-country, athletics, badminton and table tennis available. 80 take non-compulsory sport. 10 take exams. 6 represent county/country (rugby, cricket, athletics). *Other*: 15 take part in local community schemes. 15 have bronze Duke of Edinburgh's Award. 2 enter voluntary schemes after leaving school. Other activities include a computer club, chess, karate, YFC and fishing.

Careers 1 full time advisor. Average number of pupils accepted for *arts and humanities degree courses* at Oxbridge, 1; other universities, 3; polytechnics or CHE, 2. *science and engineering degree courses* at universities, 3; medical schools, 2; polytechnics or CHE, 2. *other general training courses*, 5. Average number of pupils going straight into careers in the armed services, 15; the church, 1; industry, 10; civil service, 2.

Uniform School uniform worn except the sixth.

Houses/prefects Competitive houses. Prefects, head boy, head of house and house prefects – appointed by the Head.

Religion C of E worship.

Social Several local events organised; some trips abroad. Pupils allowed to bring own bike to school. Some meals formal, some self service. School shop. No tobacco/alcohol allowed.

Discipline No corporal punishment. Pupils failing to produce homework once might expect to repeat it.

Boarding 1% have own study bedroom, 20% share with 2 others; 60% are in dormitories of 6 or more. Houses, of 110/55/15, are divided by age. Resident qualified medical staff. Central dining room. Pupils can provide and cook their own food. 36 hour exeats on request. Visits to local town allowed for boys 15+.

Alumni association run by the Headmaster.

Former pupils John Sherwood (Olympic athlete); L V Appleyard (Ambassador to Hungary).

READING BLUE COAT

Reading Blue Coat School
Holme Park
Sonning
Berkshire RG4 0SU
Telephone number 0734 441005

Co-ed   Pupils 510
● Boys   Upper sixth Yes
 Girls   Termly fees:
● Mixed sixth Day £880
● Day   Boarding £1560
● Boarding SHMIS; GBA;
        BSA

Head Mr A C E Sanders (14 years)
Age range 11–18; entry by common entrance and own exam.
6 scholarships (including music) pa.

RED MAIDS'

Red Maids' School
Westbury-on-Trym
Bristol BS9 3AW
Telephone number 0272 622641

Co-ed   Pupils 480
 Boys   Upper sixth 40
● Girls   Termly fees:
 Mixed sixth Day £610
● Day   Boarding £1170
● Boarding GSA; GBGSA

Head Miss S Hampton (1 year)
Age range 11–18, own prep from age 7; entry by own exam.
Scholarships (including music) and assisted places. School takes interest in
the problems of children of one parent families.

REDLAND HIGH

Redland High School
Redland Court
Bristol BS6 7EF
Telephone number 0272 45796

Enquiries/application to the Headmistress

Co-ed   Pupils 385
 Boys   Upper sixth 50
● Girls   Termly fees:
 Mixed sixth Day £728
● Day   GSA
 Boarding

WHAT IT'S LIKE

Founded in 1882 in Redland Grove as a small independent school. In 1885 it moved to its present site. The main building is a handsome 18th-century mansion in pleasant gardens. The playing fields are a few minutes' walk away. The junior school is opposite. Pupils come from all areas of Bristol and Avon and from all sections of the community. The sixth form plays a considerable part in the running of the school. The teaching is good and academic standards and results are most creditable. 90% of leavers go on to higher education with approximately 60% following university courses. Flourishing music, drama and art. A full range of sports and games and a good variety of extra-curricular activities. Some commitment to local community services and an impressive record in the Duke of Edinburgh's Award Scheme. Full use is made of Bristol's cultural amenities.

SCHOOL PROFILE

Pupils Total over 12, 385. Entry age, 4–10, 11+ and into the sixth. Own junior department provides over 30%.

Entrance Own entrance exam used. No special skills or religious requirements. Parents not expected to buy text books. 83 assisted places. Scholarships and bursaries at 11+ and in sixth, £1092 to £50.

Parents 100% live within 30 miles.

Staff Head Miss E Hobbs, in post for 2 years. 38 full time staff, 15 part time. Annual turnover 10%. Average age 35.

Academic work GCSE and A-levels. Average size of upper fifth 75; upper sixth 45–50. *A-levels*: on average, 3 pupils in the upper sixth pass 1 subject; 8, 2 subjects; 33, 3 subjects and 1 passes 4 subjects. On average, 14 take science/engineering A-levels; 18 take arts and humanities; 14 a mixture. History of Art offered to A-level. *Computing facilities*: Computer room with approx 8 computers.

Senior pupils' non-academic activities *Music*: 128 learn a musical instrument, 1 accepted for Music School; 40 in school orchestra, 50 in choir, 4 in school pop group, 9 in chamber groups; 5 in County Youth Orchestra, 1 in County Youth Wind Band. *Drama and dance*: 50 in school productions; 70 in drama clubs. Occasional pupil accepted for Drama/Dance Schools or enters national competitions. *Art*: 6 take as non-examined subject; 47 take GCSE; 11 A-level; 13 history of art A-level. 2 accepted for Art School; 1 to study architecture; 1 landscape architecture; 2 history of art. 50 belong to art club. *Sport*: Hockey, netball, tennis, cricket, swimming, badminton, fencing available. 40 take non-compulsory sport. 7 represent county (hockey, netball, tennis, cricket, orienteering). *Other*: 54 involved in bronze Duke of Edinburgh's Award, 10 involved in silver and 2 gold. 10 involved in gardening and nature conservation. Other activities include a computer club, Christian Union, conservation projects, community services and clubs for gymnastics, athletics, fencing, cricket, pottery, photography, art, geographical society, drama, outdoor activities, Young Enterprise.

Careers 2 part time careers advisors. Average number of pupils accepted for *arts and humanities degree courses* at Oxbridge, 2; other universities, 13; polytechnics or CHE, 7. *science and engineering degree courses* at Oxbridge, 2; other universities, 7; medical schools, 3; polytechnics or CHE, 2. *BEd*, 4.

other general training courses, 3; catering course. Average number of pupils going straight into careers in the City, 3.

Uniform School uniform worn except the sixth.

Houses/prefects No competitive houses or prefects but sixth form executive committee; head girl – elected by staff and sixth. School Council.

Religion Daily school assembly.

Social Occasional joint meetings, musical performances and productions with other city schools. Exchanges with schools in Bordeaux and Marburg (Germany); ski-ing trips abroad; History of Art trip to Italy, Paris or Amsterdam; visits to Italy, Greece. Pupils allowed to bring own car/bike to school. No tobacco/alcohol allowed.

Discipline No corporal punishment.

Alumni association run by Mrs Jean Cooper, c/o the School.

REED'S

Reed's School	Co-ed	Pupils 280
Sandy Lane	● Boys	Upper sixth Yes
Cobham	Girls	Termly fees:
Surrey KT11 2ES	● Mixed sixth	Day £1300
Telephone number 0932 63076	● Day	Boarding £1800
	● Boarding	HMC

Head D E Prince (4 years)
Age range 11–18; entry by common entrance and own exam.
Scholarships, bursaries.

REIGATE GRAMMAR

Reigate Grammar School	Co-ed	Pupils 870
Reigate Road	● Boys	Upper sixth Yes
Reigate	Girls	Termly fees:
Surrey RH2 0QS	● Mixed sixth	Day £900
Telephone number 07372 22231	● Day	GBA; HMC
	Boarding	

Head J G Hamlin (6 years)
Age range 10–18; entry by own exam or common entrance
10+ scholarships and 20 assisted places pa, plus bursaries.

RENDCOMB

Rendcomb College		Co-ed	Pupils 233
Cirencester		• Boys	Upper sixth 50
Gloucestershire GL7 7HA		Girls	Termly fees:
Telephone number 028 583 213		• Mixed sixth	Boarding £1970
Enquiries/application to the Headmaster		Day	HMC
		• Boarding	

WHAT IT'S LIKE

Founded in 1920, it has very handsome buildings and is part of a tiny village in a superb 200-acre estate of Gloucestershire countryside. Generously endowed, it has excellent modern facilities and a very friendly atmosphere. It has all the advantages of a small school and describes itself as 'unpretentious, business-like, hardworking and caring'. A good staff:pupil ratio of 1:10. Academic results are impressive for such a small school (some 25 university entrants per year). Very strong music, drama and art depts. Big commitment to local community schemes and an impressive record in the Duke of Edinburgh's Award Scheme.

SCHOOL PROFILE

Pupils Total over 12, 233. Boys 200, girls 33. Entry age, boys 11 and 13; boys and girls into the sixth. 10% are children of former pupils.

Entrance Common entrance and own entrance exam used. Not oversubscribed. No special skills or religious requirements. Local authority boarding places; 12 academic, art, music and sport scholarships, full fees to £800. Bursaries for children of HM forces.

Parents 15+% in industry or commerce; 15% in armed services. 30+% live within 30 miles; up to 10% live overseas.

Staff Head John Tolputt, in post for 1 year. 26 full time staff, 10 part time. Annual turnover 2%. Average age 35.

Academic work GCSE and A-levels. Average size of upper fifth 40; upper sixth 50. *O-levels*: on average, 4 pupils in upper fifth pass 1–4 subjects; 25, 5–7 subjects; 10 pass 8+ subjects. *A-levels*: on average, 5 pupils in the upper sixth pass 2 subjects; 45 pass 3 subjects. On average, 18 take science/engineering A-levels; 22 take arts and humanities; 10, a mixture. Public affairs A-level offered. *Computing facilities*: 20 BBC Micros; wide range of support equipment in well-designed computer room.

Senior pupils' non-academic activities *Music*: 120 learn a musical instrument, 1 accepted for Music School; 50 in school orchestra, 42 in choir; 4 in pop group. *Drama and dance*: 60 in school productions. 4 go into rep or alternative theatre. *Art*: 60 take as non-examined subject; 10 take GCSE; 4 A-level. 2 accepted for Art School. *Sport*: Rugby, hockey, cricket, swimming, football, netball, running, athletics, squash and tennis available. 6 represent county/country (rugby, hockey, cricket). *Other*: 40 take part in local community schemes. 15 have bronze Duke of Edinburgh's Award, 10 have gold. Other activities include a computer club, bridge and film-making (winners of international awards).

Careers 1 full time and 4 part time advisors. Average number of pupils accepted for *arts and humanities degree courses* at Oxbridge, 3; other universities, 8; polytechnics or CHE, 2. *science and engineering degree courses* at Oxbridge, 3; other universities, 10; medical schools, 3; polytechnics or CHE, 2. *other general training courses*, 2. Average number of pupils going straight into careers in the armed services, 1; the church, 1; industry, 3; the City, 1; civil service, 1.

Uniform School uniform worn throughout (except by sixth form in free time).

Houses/prefects No competitive houses. Prefects, head boy and girl, head of house and house prefects – appointed by the Head and staff. School Council.

Religion Compulsory assembly twice a week, church service on Sundays.

Social Numerous social events with other schools. Exchanges with Annecy (France and Germany). Pupils allowed to bring own bike to school. Meals self service. Village shop in grounds. No pupils allowed tobacco; alcohol allowed in sixth form bar.

Discipline No corporal punishment. Pupils failing to produce homework once might expect to be kept back to do it; those caught smoking cannabis on the premises may expect expulsion.

Boarding Fifth and sixth forms have own study bedrooms, others share with up to 4. Houses, of approximately 50 will be single-sex from 1989. Resident qualified nurse and doctor. Central dining room. Pupils can provide and cook own food. Half term and 2 long weekend exeats each term. Visits to local town allowed with permission.

Alumni association is run by Christopher Wood, c/o the College.

Former pupils David Vaisey (Bodleian Librarian); Richard Dunwoody (Grand National winning jockey).

REPTON

Repton School	Co-ed	Pupils 563
The Hall	● Boys	Upper sixth 124
Repton	Girls	Termly fees:
Derby DE6 6FH	● Mixed sixth	Day £1750
Telephone number 0283 702375	● Day	Boarding £2370
	● Boarding	HMC
Enquiries to the Headmaster		
Application to the Registrar		

WHAT IT'S LIKE

Founded in 1557, the school is an integral part of the village of Repton (about 3000 inhabitants), and vice versa. The site was originally a Saxon settlement and has been occupied ever since. Over a thousand years of history is evident in the buildings and in extensive archaeological excavations. A civilised environment in which the architecture is very pleasing, as are the beautiful surroundings. It is a C of E foundation and quite a lot of emphasis is given to Anglican worship and practice. Facilities are extremely good. Academically, it is a high-powered school with very good teaching and consistently good results (85–90 leavers proceed to university each year). Very strong music and art departments, and an outstanding record of dramatic presentations of many kinds. A very wide range of sport and games is on offer and standards are high (a lot of representatives at county level). The CCF is strong and outdoor pursuits and adventure training have vigorous support. A big commitment to local community services in and around Repton and an impressive record in the Duke of Edinburgh's Award Scheme.

SCHOOL PROFILE

Pupils Total 563. Day 101 (boys 86, girls 15); Boarding 462 (boys 416, girls 46). Entry age, boys, 13+; boys and girls into the sixth. Own preparatory school (Foremarke Hall) provides over 20%. 10% are children of former pupils.

Entrance Common entrance exam used. Oversubscribed. Credit is given for extra-curricular activities. Most pupils are C of E but all denominations and religions are welcomed. Parents not expected to buy text books. 39 assisted places. 12 scholarships/bursaries pa, 75% to 20% fees.

Parents 15+% in industry or commerce; 15+% are doctors, lawyers, etc. 10+% live within 30 miles; up to 10% live overseas.

Staff Head G E Jones, in post for 1 year. 62 full time staff, 3 part time. Annual turnover 5%. Average age 34.

Academic work GCSE and A-levels. Average size of upper fifth 110; upper sixth 124. *O-levels*: on average, 8 pupils in upper fifth pass 1–4 subjects; 16, 5–7 subjects; 85 pass 8+ subjects. *A-levels*: on average, 7 pupils in the upper sixth pass 1 subject; 12, 2 subjects; 102, 3 subjects and 10 pass 4 subjects. In addition, most pupils take A-level general studies. On average, 35 take science/engineering A-levels; 55 take arts and humanities; 35 a mixture. *Computing facilities*: 22 BBC B microcomputers + disks, 6 printers, 1 RML 380, 1 Amstrad with word processors. Special provision, either inside or outside the school, for dyslexia, mild visual handicap, etc.

Senior pupils' non-academic activities *Music*: 90 learn a musical instrument, 45 to Grade 6 or above, 6 accepted for Music School, 12 to read music at university; 35 in school orchestra, 30 in choir, 10 in pop group, 70 in choral society; 2 in National Youth Orchestra. *Drama and dance*: 50+ in school productions; 120 in House plays. *Art*: 50 take as non-examined subject; 40 take GCSE; 25 A-level; 6 take history of art. 6 accepted for Art School; 2 for architecture. 15 belong to photographic club; 30 on general studies courses. *Sport*: Football, cricket, Eton fives, hockey, lawn tennis, cross-country, athletics, shooting, fencing, golf, swimming, sailing, squash, rugby football, netball, badminton available. 150 take non-compulsory sport. 400 take compulsory sport. 42 represent county/country (hockey, soccer, tennis, cricket). *Other*: 90 take part in local community schemes. 30 have silver Duke of Edinburgh's Award, 10 have gold. Other activities include a computer club, art, astronomy, canoeing, chess, debating, wildfowl, mountaineering, photography, musical, woodwork, metalwork, dramatic and academic societies, driving lessons.

Careers 5 part time advisors. Average number of pupils accepted for *arts and humanities degree courses* at Oxbridge, 15; other universities, 47; polytechnics or CHE, 17. *science and engineering degree courses* at Oxbridge, 6; other universities, 20; medical schools, 8; polytechnics or CHE, 6. *BEd*, 1. *other general training courses*, 2. Average number of pupils going straight into careers in the armed services, 1; the church, 1; industry, 3; the City, 1; music/drama, 2; other 4. Careers are widely spread but orientated towards business and industry.

Uniform School uniform worn except in the sixth.

Houses/prefects Competitive houses. Prefects, head boy/girl, head of house and house prefects – appointed by the Head and the Housemasters. No personal fagging, there are some communal services.

Religion Friday morning prayers, Sunday matins.

Social Choral society and debating with a local girls' school. Modern languages exchanges can be arranged. Overseas trips have included cricket, hockey, ski-ing, music, athletics etc. Meals formal. School shop. No pupils allowed tobacco. Sixth form, over 17, allowed limited amount of alcohol three evenings/week.

Discipline No corporal punishment. Pupils failing to produce homework once might expect extra work; those caught smoking cannabis on the premises would be required to leave the school.

Boarding 10% have own study bedroom, 10% share (2 or 3); 80% are in dormitories of 6 or more. Houses, of approximately 55–60 are the same as competitive houses and are single sex. Resident qualified nurse and doctor. No central dining room. Pupils can provide and cook own food. Exeats each term: as many Sundays as required, half term plus 1 weekend. Visits to the local town allowed sometimes, mostly for sixth formers.

Alumni association is run by J F M Walker, Latham House, Repton, Derby.

Former pupils Sir John Tooley (Royal Opera House); Robert Sangster (race-horse owner); John Stanley MP (Minister of State, Northern Ireland); Graeme Garden (TV); James Fenton (poet); Richard Heller (political journalist); Donald Carr and Richard Hutton (cricketers); Lord Ramsey (Archbishop of Canterbury); Sir J Grindrod (Archbishop of Australia).

RICKMANSWORTH MASONIC

The Rickmansworth Masonic School	Co-ed	Pupils 416
Rickmansworth	Boys	Upper sixth 43
Hertfordshire WD3 4HF	● Girls	Termly fees:
Telephone number 0923 773168	Mixed sixth	Day £943
	● Day	Boarding £1700
Enquiries to the Headmaster	● Boarding	GSA
Application to the Admissions Secretary		

WHAT IT'S LIKE

Founded in 1788, it moved from Central London in 1934 to an exceptionally fine purpose-built establishment of elegant and well-appointed buildings in 315 acres of superb grounds in the Chilterns. A very civilised environment. Extremely comfortable accommodation and first-rate facilities, including an unusually fine library. Chapel is central to the life of the school. The teaching is of a high standard with a staff:pupil ratio of 1:12. Good results and 15 or more pupils proceed to university each year. Strongish music, drama and art. Much emphasis on debating and public speaking. A feature is the school drill: a ceremonial parade cum military ballet. Good range of games, sport and activities. A fine record in the Duke of Edinburgh's Award Scheme.

SCHOOL PROFILE

Pupils Total over 12, 416. Day 190; Boarding 226. Entry age, 7, 11 and into the sixth. Own junior department provides over 20%. 5% are children of former pupils.

Entrance Common entrance and own entrance exam used. Oversubscribed for day pupils. No special skills or religious requirements but school is Anglican. Parents not expected to buy text books. No assisted places yet. 10 scholarships/bursaries for masonic families in need, £800–£500.

Parents 15+% in industry or commerce. 30+% live within 30 miles; up to 10% live overseas.

Staff Head D L Curtis, in post for 7 years. 49 full time staff, 15 part time. Annual turnover 5–10%. Average age 42.

Academic work GCSE, A-levels, RSA and Pitmans, CPVE. Average size of upper fifth 81; upper sixth 43. *O-levels*: on average, 33 pupils in upper fifth pass 1–4 subjects; 30, 5–7 subjects; 18 pass 8+ subjects. *A-levels*: on average, 7 pupils in upper sixth pass 1 subject; 13, 2 subjects; 14, 3 subjects and 2 pass 4 subjects. On average, 12 take science/engineering A-levels; 20 take arts and humanities; 11 a mixture. Sociology and politics are offered to A-level. *Computing facilities*: 2 laboratories holding about 20 working computers. Individual computers in other departments. Special provisions for mildly dyslexic pupils.

Senior pupils' non-academic activities *Music*: 30 learn a musical instrument, 6–8 to Grade 6 or above; 2 accepted for Music School; 18 in school orchestra; 39 in choir; 15 in small choral group; 12 in instrumental groups. *Drama and dance*: 40 participate in sixth form musical/G & S; 20 in school plays; 10 take RSM speech and dance exams; 1 accepted for Drama/Dance school; 2 go on to work in theatre. *Art*: 20 take as non-examined subject; 24 take GCSE; 5 A-level; 3 accepted for Art School; 15 belong to photographic club; 12 to stage scenery group. *Sport*: Hockey, netball, badminton, squash, sailing, tennis, rounders, swimming, athletics, cross-country, trampolining available. Riding can be arranged. 40 take non-compulsory sport. 6 take exams – mostly in life saving. 7 represent county/country (swimming, athletics and cross-country, tennis, hockey). *Other*: 4 take part in local community schemes. 26 have bronze Duke of Edinburgh's Award, 11 have silver and 4 have gold. 3 are Guides. 3 work for national charities beyond school. Other activities include a computer club, various cultural and academic societies, chess, bridge. Driving lessons can be arranged. Very successful public speaking teams. Chapel, Sunday School. Famous School Drill 150 years old.

Careers 1 full time advisor. Average number of pupils accepted for *arts and humanities degree courses* at Oxbridge, 1; other universities, 9; polytechnics or CHE, 7. *science and engineering degree courses* at universities, 4; polytechnics or CHE, 5. *BEd*, 7. *other general training courses*, 13. Average number of pupils going straight into careers in the armed services, 1; industry, 8; the City, 3; civil service, 6; music/drama, 2; other, 5.

Uniform School uniform worn throughout.

Houses/prefects Competitive houses. Prefects, head girl, head of house and house prefects – appointed by the Head with recommendations from staff and senior pupils.

Religion Attendance compulsory on Sundays.

Social Joint debates, theatrical productions, musicals, games etc with other schools; also with the public at large. Organised trips abroad. Pupils allowed to bring own car/bike to school. A few meals formal most self service. School shop. No tobacco/alcohol allowed.

Discipline No corporal punishment. Pupils failing to produce homework once might expect a warning; those caught smoking cannabis on the premises could expect suspension.

Boarding 32% have own study bedroom, 8% share; 60% are in dormitories of 6+. Houses, of approximately 40–48. Separate houses for juniors and for sixth formers. 2 qualified sisters and 1 nursing assistant, doctor visits. Central dining room. Seniors can provide and cook own food. 2 weekend exeats each term, plus half-term. Visits to the local town allowed weekly for juniors; more often and unaccompanied for 16+.

Alumni association is run by Mrs Susan Jones, Hon Sec OMGA, c/o the School.

Former pupils Film and TV stars, newspapers (national editor), distinguished doctor. First female president of Cambridge Union.

RISHWORTH

Rishworth School
Rishworth
Sowerby Bridge
West Yorkshire HX6 4QA
Telephone number 0422 822217

Enquiries/application to the Headmaster's Secretary

- Co-ed
  Boys
  Girls
  Mixed sixth
- Day
- Boarding

Pupils (4–18) 582
Upper sixth 40
Termly fees:
Day £925
Boarding £1735
GBA; SHMIS

WHAT IT'S LIKE

Founded in 1724, it has occupied its present site since 1826. The buildings are handsome, solid, stone-built and lie in a beautiful valley (20 miles from Manchester and Leeds) with ample gardens and grounds. There have been a lot of modern additions, including a CDT centre, which provide good accommodation and up-to-date equipment. The environment is very healthy. The original school has become the chapel and there is some emphasis on worship and religious instruction. A good deal of attention is given to the principles and practice of Christianity. A broad general education is provided and the aim is to create a social and scholastic society in which boys and girls contribute as fully as possible to each other's education. Academic standards are highly creditable and results are good. Some 10–15 pupils go on to university each year. Strong music and drama depts. A good range of games and sports, and also extra-curricular activities. Considerable emphasis on outdoor pursuits for which the surroundings are ideal. The school has an outstanding record in the Duke of Edinburgh's Award Scheme.

SCHOOL PROFILE

Pupils Total, 582. Day 377 (boys 205, girls 172); Boarding 205 (boys 128, girls 77). Entry age, 4, 7, 11 and into the sixth. Own preparatory department provides over 40%. 12% are children of former pupils.

Entrance Common entrance and own entrance exam used. Oversubscribed. No special skills or religious requirements. Parents not expected to buy text books. 8 scholarships/bursaries, full to one-third fees; 10% reductions for children of C of E priesthood or the Armed Services.

Parents 15+% in industry or commerce. 30+% live within 30 miles; 10+% live overseas.

Staff Head A J Morsley, in post for 2 years. 45 full time staff, 5 part time. Annual turnover 4%. Average age 40.

Academic work GCSE and A-levels. Average size of upper fifth 85; upper sixth 40. *O-levels*: on average, 35 pupils in upper fifth pass 1–4 subjects; 40, 5–7 subjects; 10 pass 8+ subjects. *A-levels*: on average, 7 pupils in upper sixth pass 1 subject; 8, 2 subjects; 10, 3 subjects and 15 pass 4 subjects. On average, 22 take science/engineering A-levels; 11 take arts and humanities; 7 a mixture. Drama offered to GCSE level. *Computing facilities*: 20 480 Zs, 10 BBC (1 per person in class teaching). Provision for EFL for Chinese and mild dyslexia.

Senior pupils' non-academic activities *Music*: 120 learn a musical instrument, 7 to Grade 6 or above; 20 in school orchestra, 35 in choir, 4 in school pop group; 1 goes on to play in pop group; 1 into music teaching. *Drama and dance*: 40 seniors in school productions. 3 take up to Grade 6 (ESB). 2 accepted for Drama/Dance Schools; 2 go on to work in theatre. *Art*: 5 take as non-examined subject; 35 GCSE; 6 A-level. 6 accepted for Art School. 4 belong to photographic club; others do pottery or textiles. *Sport*: Rugby, cricket, hockey, netball, gymnastics, swimming, soccer, cross country, basketball, badminton, athletics, golf, tennis, squash, sailing, volleyball, fishing available. 120 take non-compulsory sport. 250 take AAA exams. 5 represent county/country (athletics, squash). *Other*: 65–70 are taking bronze Duke of Edinburgh's Award, 25 have silver and 20 gold. Other activities include a computer club, driving lessons, CDT club.

Careers 4 part time careers advisors. Average number of pupils accepted for *arts and humanities degree courses* at Oxbridge, 1; other universities, 6; polytechnics or CHE, 4. *science and engineering degree courses* at Oxbridge, 1; other universities, 4; medical schools, 2; polytechnics or CHE, 4. *BEd*, 3. *other general training courses*, 3. Average number of pupils going straight into careers in armed services, 2; industry, 1.

Uniform School uniform worn throughout.

Houses/prefects Non-competitive houses. Prefects, head boy/girl, head of house and house prefects – appointed by Head.

Religion Religious worship encouraged; chapel attendance not compulsory in senior school.

Social Joint musical competition with local schools. 3 trips to France, 1 to Russia, 1 to Spain, 2 ski-ing trips. Day pupils allowed to bring own car to school. Meals self service. School shop. No tobacco/alcohol allowed.

Discipline Very limited corporal punishment. Pupils failing to produce homework once might expect detention; those caught smoking cannabis on the premises may expect expulsion although this has not arisen.

Boarding 10% have own study bedroom, 40% share with 2 or 3; 50% in dormitories of 6+. Houses, of approximately 16–40, divided by age and single sex. 2 resident qualified nurses, 3 local doctors. Central dining room. Pupils can provide and cook some own food. 2 or 3 weekend exeats each term. Seniors allowed weekly visits to local town.

Alumni association run by Mr Peter Marshall, President, Old Rishworthians, 98 South West Avenue, Bollington, Macclesfield, Cheshire.

ROBERT GORDON'S

Robert Gordon's College	Co-ed	Pupils 850
School Hill	• Boys	Upper sixth Yes
Aberdeen AB9 1FR	Girls	Termly fees:
Telephone number 0224 646346	Mixed sixth	Day £600
	• Day	Boarding £1300
	• Boarding	GBA; HMC

Head G A Allan (10 years)
Age range 11–18, own prep from age 5; entry by own exam.
Scholarships, bursaries and assisted places.

RODNEY

Rodney School	• Co-ed	Pupils 250
Kirklington	Boys	Upper sixth 10
Nr Newark	Girls	Termly fees:
Nottinghamshire NG22 8NB	Mixed sixth	Day £510
Telephone number 0636 813281	• Day	Boarding £960
	• Boarding	
Enquiries/application to the Principal		

WHAT IT'S LIKE

No foundation date given, but it appears to have started its life in the late 1940s. The main building is Kirklington Hall, a large country mansion with ample grounds on the edge of Sherwood Forest and close to the Dukeries. Good modern facilities. A sound education is provided and academic results are creditable. Quite strong in music and drama. An adequate range of sports, games and activities.

SCHOOL PROFILE

Pupils Total over 12, 250. 50% Day; 50% Boarding (boys and girls). Entry age, 8+ and into the sixth. A few are children of former pupils.
Entrance Common entrance and own entrance exam used. Oversubscribed. No special skills or religious requirements. Parents expected to buy text books. 2 sixth form scholarships/bursaries, £2000–£1500.
Parents 30+% live within 30 miles; up to 10% live overseas.
Staff Principal Miss J G Thomas, in post for 28 years. 18 full time staff, 12 part time. Annual turnover 1%. Average age 40.
Academic work GCSE and A-levels. Average size of upper fifth 45; upper sixth 10. *O-levels*: on average, 2 pupils in the upper fifth pass 1–4 subjects;

35, 5–7 subjects; 8 pass 8+ subjects. *A-levels*: on average, 1 pupil in the upper sixth passes 1 subject; 3, 2 subjects and 6 pass 3 subjects. On average, most take science/engineering A-levels; 3 take arts and humanities; 2 a mixture. *Computing facilities*: 12 machines. Provision for EFL.

Senior pupils' non-academic activities *Music*: 20 learn a musical instrument, 2 to Grade 6 or above, 1 accepted for Music School; 45 in school choir. *Drama and dance*: 70 in school productions; 90 take modern dance. 2 accepted for Drama/Dance schools. *Art*: All take as non-examined subject; 20 take GCSE. 1 accepted for Art School. *Sport*: Rugby, hockey, squash, swimming, football, rounders, basketball, GVC available. 15 take non-compulsory sport. 50 take exams in eg swimming. 2 represent county (rugby). *Other*: 5 have bronze Duke of Edinburgh's Award, some have silver. 60 work for national charities. Other activities include computer, rock and heather, canoeing clubs.

Careers 1 full time careers advisor. Some pupils go on to degree courses. Average number of pupils accepted for *general training courses*, 4. Average number of pupils going straight into careers in armed services, 4; industry, 3; music/drama, 1.

Uniform School uniform worn, modified in the sixth.

Houses/prefects Competitive houses. Prefects, head boy/girl, head of house and house prefects – appointed by staff. Prefect Council.

Religion Religious worship encouraged.

Social Local amateur theatre group. Organised trips abroad. Lunch self service. No tobacco/alcohol allowed.

Discipline Corporal punishment rare. Pupils failing to produce homework once might expect admonishment.

Boarding 2 have own study bedroom, 100+ share. Resident qualified nurse. Central dining room. Pupils allowed to provide and cook some of own food. 1 exeat per fortnight. Visits to the local town allowed (accompanied).

Former pupils Dame Mary Bridges; Sir Kenneth McMillan.

ROEDEAN

Roedean School
Brighton
East Sussex BN2 5RQ
Telephone number 0273 603181

Enquiries/application to the Admissions Secretary

Co-ed
Boys
● Girls
Mixed sixth
Day
● Boarding

Pupils 450
Upper sixth 75
Termly fees:
Boarding £2525
GSA

WHAT IT'S LIKE

Founded in 1885, it moved to its present site in 1898. It has a splendid position above the cliffs and overlooking the sea, between Brighton and Rottingdean. It is a purpose-built school with attractive and very well-equipped buildings on a large estate of which about 40 acres are given to playing fields and leisure activities. One of the most distinguished schools in Britain, it is well run and its very large and very well-qualified staff permits a staff:pupil ratio of 1:7. Few if any schools could match this. Academically high-powered, it gets excellent results and each year sends 52 or more girls on to university: a high proportion for a school of this size. Extremely strong in music and drama; virtually all pupils are involved in these activities. A wide range of games and sports is available and high standards are achieved. There is a big commitment to local community services. The school has an outstanding record in the Duke of Edinburgh's Award Scheme.

SCHOOL PROFILE

Pupils Total over 12, 450. Entry age, 11+, 12+, 13+ and into the sixth. 8% are children of former pupils.

Entrance Common entrance and own entrance exam used. Oversubscribed. Wide range of interests and skills looked for; no religious requirements. Parents not expected to buy text books. 6 scholarships/bursaries, 50%–12% fees.

Parents 15+% are doctors, lawyers etc; 15+% in industry or commerce. 30+% live within 30 miles; 10+% live overseas.

Staff Head Mrs Ann R Longley, in post for 4 years. 65 full time staff, 14 part time. Annual turnover 12%. Average age 36.

Academic work GCSE and A-levels. Average size of upper fifth, 80; upper sixth, 75. *O-levels*: on average, 10 pupils in upper fifth pass 1–4 subjects; 16, 5–7 subjects; 46 pass 8+ subjects. *A-levels*: on average, 8 pupils in the upper sixth pass 1 subject; 14, 2 subjects; 38, 3 subjects and 3 pass 4 subjects. On average, 16 take science/engineering A-levels; 27 take arts and humanities; 19 a mixture. *Computing facilities*: 21 computers and a fully-equipped computer room. Provision for extra English in exceptional circumstances.

Senior pupils' non-academic activities *Music*: 286 learn a musical instrument, 32 to Grade 6 or above, 2 accepted for Music School; 45 in school orchestra, 140 in choir, 25 pop group, 22 wind band, 35 in chamber groups; 1 in National Youth Orchestra. *Drama and dance*: 125 in school productions; 280, house drama; 150, verse speaking. 50 take to Grade 6 ESB, RAD etc; 3 GCSE theatre arts; public speaking 12, Rotary 6, ESU 6. 25 entered competitions (Brighton Festival). 5 accepted for Drama/Dance Schools; 5 to degree courses in media studies. *Art*: 3 take as non-examined subject; 83 GCSE; 18 A-level. 5 accepted for Art School; 1 to history of art degree course. 12 belong to photographic club; 16 take CDT. *Sport*: Lacrosse, netball, hockey, volleyball, squash, tennis, rounders, judo, swimming, fencing, badminton, athletics, riding available. 130 take non-compulsory sport. 8 take lifesaving exams. 12 represent county/country (netball, lacrosse). *Other*: 72 take part in local community schemes. 10 have bronze Duke of Edinburgh's Award, 40 have silver and 30 gold. Other activities include a computer club, driving lessons (upper sixth), debating societies, drama club, Young Enterprise business companies.

Careers 3 part time careers advisors, 1 outside specialist. Average number of pupils accepted for *arts and humanities degree courses* at Oxbridge, 5; other universities, 28; polytechnics or CHE, 2. *science and engineering degree courses* at Oxbridge, 5; other universities, 15; medical schools, 6. *BEd*, 1. *other general training courses*, 3. Wide variety of careers.

Uniform School uniform worn except upper sixth.

Houses/prefects Competitive houses. Head girl, prefects and head of house – appointed by Head, staff and sixth; house prefects – elected by school. School Council.

Religion Compulsory morning assembly and Sunday chapel except for practising members of other faiths.

Social Joint musical events, debates, quizzes, dances with local boys' schools. Exchange with school in Spain; occasional organised trips to France; annual ski-ing holiday. Sixth form allowed to bring own bike to school. Meals self service. School bookshop, tuckshop and stationery store. No tobacco/alcohol allowed.

Discipline No corporal punishment. Pupils failing to produce homework once might expect referral to tutor; those caught smoking cannabis on the premises might expect expulsion.

Boarding Sixth form have own study bedroom, upper fifth share bedroom with 2 and study with 2/3. Houses, of approximately 82, same as competitive houses plus upper sixth house. Resident qualified sister. Central dining room. Upper sixth can provide and cook own food. 2–3 Saturday night termly exeats plus half term. Visits to local town allowed.

Alumni association run by Miss A V Kent, President, The Old Roedean Association, c/o the School.

Former pupils Lynda Chalker MP; Verity Lambert (actress and director); Sarah Miles (actress); Sally Oppenheimer MP; Dame Cecily Saunders (founder of hospice movement).

ROSEMEAD

Rosemead School	Co-ed	Pupils 200
East Street	Boys	Upper sixth 17
Littlehampton	● Girls	Termly fees:
West Sussex BN17 6AJ	Mixed sixth	Day £1060
Telephone number 0903 716065	● Day	Boarding £1895
Enquiries/application to Mrs E Finch,	● Boarding	GSA
School Secretary		

WHAT IT'S LIKE

Founded in 1919, it is single-site in Littlehampton, 10 minutes' walk from the sea, 5 miles from Arundel and 10 from Chichester. It comprises agreeable modern buildings and good up-to-date facilities in large gardens. The preparatory department is close by. It has most of the advantages of a small school and enjoys an excellent staff:pupil ratio of 1:7. Academic results are quite good and some 5 pupils proceed to university each year. The atmosphere is purposeful and friendly. Good range of games, sports and activities. Adequate music and drama.

SCHOOL PROFILE

Pupils Total 200. Day 85; Boarding 115. Entry age, 11+, 12+, 13+ and into the sixth. 2% are children of former pupils.

Entrance Common entrance and own entrance exam used. Not oversubscribed. No special skills or religious requirements. Parents expected to buy text books only in sixth form. 2 scholarships/bursaries, up to £1200.

Parents 15+% in industry or commerce. 30+% live within 30 miles; 10+% live overseas.

Staff Head Mrs J Bevis, in post for 1 year. 29 full time staff, 10 part time. Annual turnover 8%. Average age 40.

Academic work GCSE and A-levels. Average size of upper fifth 45; upper sixth 17. *O-levels*: on average, 12 pupils in upper fifth pass 1–4 subjects; 30, 5–7 subjects; 3 pass 8+ subjects. *A-levels*: on average, 3 pupils in upper sixth pass 1 subject; 7, 2 subjects; 6 pass 3 subjects. On average, 6 take science/engineering A-levels; 6 take arts and humanities; 5 a mixture. *Computing facilities*: Econet Level 3 network – 8 BBC Bs + 2 BBC Master 128 + 1 Archimedes 310 Plotmate plotter – Epson dot matrix + Juki daisy wheel printers – graphics digitisers.

Senior pupils' non-academic activities *Music*: 25 learn a musical instrument, 2 up to Grade 6 or above; 15 in school orchestra, 35 in choir; 1 in National Children's Wind Orchestra. *Drama and dance*: 100 in school productions. 10 take GSM & D; 8, RAD senior grade and above. 2 accepted for Drama/Dance school. *Art*: 3 take as non-examined subject; 16 take GCSE; 12 A-level. 2 accepted for Art School. *Sport*: Lacrosse, netball, tennis, athletics, rounders, badminton, volleyball, swimming, riding, judo, ballet, squash, table tennis available. 50 take non-compulsory sport. Some represent county/country (lacrosse, tennis, netball). *Other*: 12 have bronze Duke of Edinburgh's Award. Other activities include a computer club, electronics, gym club, weight training, vehicle maintenance, folk club, chess, clog dancing.

Careers 1 full time advisor. Average number of pupils accepted for *arts and humanities degree courses* at universities, 2; polytechnics or CHE, 4. *science and engineering degree courses* at universities, 3; polytechnics or CHE, 4. *other general training courses*, 10. Average number of pupils going straight into careers in industry, 4; civil service, 1; other, 10.

Uniform School uniform worn except in the sixth.

Houses/prefects Competitive houses. Head girl and prefects (chosen by Principal and staff); head of house and house prefects by girls.

Religion Christians attend local churches.

Social Flourishing arts centre, public performances by visiting artists and master classes. School dances and reciprocal arrangements with nearby boys' boarding schools. Organised annual ski trip and trips to various parts of Europe; exchange visits to France. Pupils allowed to bring own bike to school. Meals canteen service. School thrift shop. No tobacco/alcohol allowed.

Discipline No corporal punishment. Pupils failing to produce prep once might expect to make up the work in their own time; those caught with drugs on the premises could expect expulsion.

Boarding 44% have own study bedroom, 21% share (4–6 approx); 35% are in dormitories of 6+. Houses, of 50–70 divided by age. Resident SRN and visiting school doctor. Central dining room. Sixth formers can provide and cook own food. Two weekend exeats each term. Visits to the local town allowed.

ROSSALL

Rossall School	• Co-ed		Pupils 460
Fleetwood	Boys		Upper sixth Yes
Lancashire FY7 8JW	Girls		Termly fees:
Telephone number 03917 3849	Mixed sixth		Day £1450
	• Day		Boarding £2100
	• Boarding		GBA; HMC

Head R D W Rhodes (1 year)
Age range 11–18; entry by own exam or common entrance.
20% of pupils are from overseas (including 5% foreign nationals). Academic, art and design and music awards; service bursaries. Own prep and pre-prep.

ROUGEMONT

Rougemont School	• Co-ed		Pupils 285
Kingshill	Boys		Upper sixth 32
Stow Hill	Girls		Termly fees:
Newport	Mixed sixth		Day £880
Gwent NP9 4EA	• Day		SHMIS; GBA;
Telephone number 0633 53915/211813/ 62102	Boarding		AHIS

Enquiries/application to the Admissions Secretary

WHAT IT'S LIKE

Founded in 1920, the main building was formerly the Archbishop of Wales' home. The school was established for 4–11 year olds to feed local grammar schools. The present school took shape after a parental buy-out in 1975 and a charitable trust was formed. The first sixth form opened in 1981. In effect it is three schools in one, each with its own style and identity, on two sites. High staff:pupil ratio of 1:11. Good academic results, with high pass rates in O- and A-level. Some 20–25 pupils go on to university each year. Adequate music, drama and art. Quite good sport and games (several county representatives). A most impressive record in the Duke of Edinburgh's Award Scheme.

SCHOOL PROFILE

Pupils Total over 11, 285. Boys 145, girls 140. Entry age, 3½–4½ and into the sixth. Own junior school provides over 70% of pupils. 5–8% are children of former pupils.
Entrance Common entrance and own entrance exam used. Sometimes oversubscribed. No special skills or religious requirements. Parents not expected to buy text books except specialist texts in sixth. 9 scholarships/ bursaries, maximum value full fees.

Parents 15+% are doctors, lawyers, etc. More than 60% live within 30 miles.

Staff Head F W Edwards, in post for 14 years. 54 full time staff, 5 part time. Annual turnover 3%. Average age 37.

Academic work GCSE, A-levels, RSA. Average size of upper fifth 45; upper sixth 32. *O-levels*: on average, 8% pupils in upper fifth pass 1–4 subjects; 3% pass 5–7 subjects; 72% pass 8+ subjects. *A-levels*: on average, 3% pupils in upper sixth pass 1 subject; 5% pass 2 subjects; 83% pass 3 subjects and 1% pass 4 subjects. On average, 10 take science/engineering A-levels; 7 take arts and humanities; 5 a mixture. *Computing facilities*: Computer room (20+ machines) for class work plus library machine for TTNS, PRESTEL, NERIS. *Special provisions*: EFL provision and peripatetic advisor for partially deaf, dyslexia unit recently established.

Senior pupils' non-academic activities *Music*: 15 learn a musical instrument, 3 to Grade 6 or above. 1 accepted for Music School; 3 play in pop group beyond school, 10 in school orchestra, 18 in choir, 1 in National Youth Orchestra, 3 in Gwent youth orchestra. *Drama and dance*: 20 in school productions; 1 candidate for Drama School. *Art*: 3 take as non-examined subject; 18 take GCSE; 3–5, A-level. 2–3 accepted for Art School; 12 take life class. *Sport*: Rugby, cricket, basketball, squash, netball, rounders, tennis, indoor rifle range, athletics, swimming available. 20+ (sixth form) take non-compulsory sport. 2–3 take exams eg gymnastics, swimming. 11 pupils represent county (cricket, badminton, athletics, swimming). *Other*: 5–8 take part in local community schemes. 35 have bronze Duke of Edinburgh's Award, 25 have silver and 15 gold. 4–6 are Queen's Scouts. Other activities include a computer club and 11 activities grouped under Duke of Edinburgh's Award Scheme. Choirs, ensembles, chess, drama, ballet, elocution.

Careers 2 part time advisors under direction of second master. Full membership of ISCO. Average number of pupils accepted for *arts and humanities degree courses* at Oxbridge, 1; other universities, 3; polytechnics or CHE, 5. *science and engineering degree courses* at Oxbridge, 1; other universities, 5; medical schools, 1; polytechnics or CHE, 8. *BEd*, 1. *other general training courses*, 4. Average number of pupils going straight into careers in the armed services, 1; the church, 1; industry, 1; civil service, 2; other, 1.

Uniform School uniform worn throughout.

Houses/prefects Competitive houses. Prefects, head boy/girl, head of house and house prefects – appointed by the Head, with staff consultation.

Religion Religious worship compulsory.

Social Three sets of debating competitions (Rotary, Business Women, English-Speaking Union). At least three organised trips abroad each year. Pupils allowed to bring own car/bike/motorbike to school. Meals self service. School shop. No tobacco allowed; sixth form allowed alcohol at special supervised functions.

Discipline No corporal punishment. Pupils failing to produce homework once might expect disapproval; those caught smoking cannabis on the premises could expect a warning in presence of parents.

Alumni association run by J F Williams, 5 Moyle Grove, Ponthir, Caerleon, Gwent.

ROYAL BALLET

The Royal Ballet School
White Lodge
Richmond Park
Surrey TW10 5HR
Telephone number 01-878 3929

Enquiries/application to the Ballet
Secretary

- Co-ed
  Boys
  Girls
  Mixed sixth
- Day
- Boarding

Pupils 120
Upper sixth Yes
Termly fees:
Day £1707
Boarding £2306

WHAT IT'S LIKE

Started as the Academy of Choreographic Art in 1929 by Ninette de Valois. Under the auspices of Lilian Baylis, it became The Sadler's Wells Ballet School in 1931, and the Royal Ballet School at the granting of the Queen's 1956 charter. It provides most of the soloists and corps de ballet of the Royal Ballet and Sadler's Wells Royal Ballet. Tradition of teaching can be traced back to the Academie Royale de la Danse founded by Louis XIV in 1661. Although the majority of pupils are girls, there is an increasing number of boys. School puts on an annual performance at The Royal Opera House. Dance classes are built up from one a day until pupils study dance for 17 hours a week. Curriculum includes Classical Ballet, Character Dancing, English Folk Dancing, Scottish Social and Highland Dancing, Classical Greek and National Dancing, Dalcroze Eurythmics and Drama. Although nearly all pupils go on to become professional dancers, the school aims to provide an education that will be useful for fields outside dancing as well.

SCHOOL PROFILE

Pupils Total, 120 (most board). Entry age, 11.
Entrance Audition and one year's trial. Potential talent and physical suitability looked for. Means tested DES contributions up to full fees.
Staff Director, Merle Park. Academic Principal, Nigel Grant.
Academic work GCSE and A-levels. Most pupils take 7 O-levels. Some pupils take 1 or 2 A-levels. Dance offered to A-level. *Computing facilities*: BBC microcomputers/networks. Special EFL provision.
Careers Lower school pupils graduate to Upper School (Talgarth Road) at 16+. Many then join The Royal Ballet or Sadler's Wells Royal Ballet.
Social Meals self service. Shop selling dancewear and makeup.
Boarding Qualified nursing sister, termly orthopaedic examinations for Upper School. Student counsellor, physiotherapist attends daily.
Former pupils Lesley Collier; Anthony Dowell CBE; Dame Margot Fonteyn CBE; Dame Merle Park CBE; Lynne Seymour CBE; Wayne Sleep.

ROYAL BELFAST

The Royal Belfast Academical Institution
College Square
Belfast BT1 6DL
Telephone number 0232 240461

Co-ed
● Boys
Girls
Mixed sixth
● Day
Boarding

Pupils 920
Upper sixth Yes
Termly fees:
Day £550
HMC

Head T J Garrett (10 years)
Age range 11–19, own prep from age 5; entry by own exam
Foundation and leaving scholarships.

ROYAL (DUNGANNON)

The Royal School
Dungannon
Northland Row
Dungannon
County Tyrone
Northern Ireland BT71 6AP
Telephone number 08687 22710

● Co-ed
Boys
Girls
Mixed sixth
● Day
● Boarding

Pupils 620*
Upper sixth 65
Termly fees:
Day £563
Boarding £1220
SHMIS

*whole school

Enquiries/application to the Headmaster

WHAT IT'S LIKE

Founded in 1614, in 1986 it assimilated the Dungannon High School for Girls.
Its ancient and modern buildings (the Old Building of the school is listed) lie
on the edge of the town in a fine 40-acre estate in beautiful surroundings. The
preparatory department is combined. The whole establishment is extremely
well equipped with excellent facilities and is well known to be a centre of
academic and sporting prowess; in fact, one of the most distinguished
schools in Ireland. Results are good and a large proportion of pupils proceed
to university each year. Quite flourishing music, art and drama departments.
A very good range of sport and games. Plentiful extra-curricular activities.
Quite a good record in the Duke of Edinburgh's Award Scheme.

SCHOOL PROFILE

Pupils Total (whole school) 620. Day 601 (boys 308, girls 293); Boarding 23
(boys 17, girls 6). Entry age, 4, 8 (boarding) and into the sixth. Dungannon
and Howard Primary Schools provide over 20%. 20% are children of former
pupils.
Entrance Common entrance and own entrance exam used. Not oversubscribed. No special skills or religious requirements. Parents expected to pay a
deposit of £15 for books. 7 scholarships of £150–£500 pa; 3 bursaries of £100
pa.
Parents 15+% in industry or commerce; 15+% are doctors, lawyers, etc.
60+% live within 30 miles; up to 10% live overseas.

Staff Head P D Hewitt, in post for 4 years. 44 full time staff, 4 part time. Annual turnover 1%. Average age 40.

Academic work GCSE and A-levels. Average size of upper fifth 90; upper sixth 65. *O-levels*: on average, 12% pupils in upper fifth pass 1–4 subjects; 36%, 5–7 subjects; 52% pass 8+ subjects. *A-levels*: on average, 5% pupils in upper sixth pass 1 subject; 15%, 2 subjects; 75%, 3 subjects and 5% pass 4 subjects. On average, 65% take science/engineering A-levels; 35% take arts and humanities; 5% a mixture. *Computing facilities*: 15 station RM Nimbus Laboratory (networked); 8 BBC computers; 1 RZ computer. Special help for dyslexia and EFL; facilities for handicapped also available.

Senior pupils' non-academic activities *Music*: 20 learn a musical instrument, 8 up to Grade 6 or above, 1 accepted for Music School; 20 in school orchestra, 65 in choir; 5 in National Youth Orchestra. *Drama and dance*: 80 participate in school productions. *Art*: 5 take as non-examined subject; 40 take GCSE; 10 A-level. 3 accepted for Art School. 10 belong to photographic club. *Sport*: Rugby, hockey, cricket, athletics, golf, swimming, tennis, rambling, basketball, volleyball, cross-country, indoor soccer, table tennis, weights available. 70 take non-compulsory sport. 10 pupils represent county/ country (rugby, shooting, athletics). *Other*: 5 have bronze Duke of Edinburgh's Award, 10 have silver and 4 have gold. 2 work for national charities beyond school. Other activities include a computer club, driving lessons, chess, Scripture Union, debating, photography, Blockbusters, public speaking, art, Trivial Pursuit.

Careers 4 full time advisors. Average number of pupils accepted for *arts and humanities degree courses* at Oxbridge, 1; other universities, 13; polytechnics or CHE, 6. *science and engineering degree courses* at Oxbridge, 1; other universities, 28; medical schools, 4; polytechnics or CHE, 6. BEd, 2. *other general training courses*, 3. Average number of pupils going straight into careers in the armed services, 1; the church, 1; industry, 1; civil service, 1.

Uniform School uniform worn throughout.

Houses/prefects 4 competitive houses. Prefects, head boy/girl, head of house and house prefects – appointed by the Head after recommendations of House Masters/Mistresses and sixth form.

Religion Compulsory morning assembly, Sunday morning service and Sunday evening for boarders. Exceptions made on grounds of parental wishes.

Social Debates, discos, sports meetings, quizzes, academic lectures. Annual European trip, and trips to Paris and for skiing. Pupils allowed to bring own car/bike/motorbike to school. Some meals formal, some self service. School shop. No tobacco/alcohol allowed.

Discipline No corporal punishment. Pupils failing to produce homework once might expect to have to repeat it; those caught smoking cannabis on the premises could expect expulsion.

Boarding All boarders share a modern cubicle with one other. Dormitories divided by age and sex. Resident qualified nurse/doctor. Central dining room. Exeats, every 3/4 weekends. Visits to the local town allowed.

Alumni association is run by Professor A E Long (OBA President), 29 Glen Ebor Park, Belfast, Northern Ireland. Mrs E Reid (OGA President), 15 Tannaghlane Road, Caledon, County Tyrone, Northern Ireland.

ROYAL GRAMMAR (GUILDFORD)

The Royal Grammar School
High Street
Guildford
Surrey GU1 3BB
Telephone number 0483 502424

Co-ed   Pupils 750
● Boys   Upper sixth Yes
Girls   Termly fees:
Mixed sixth   Day £1010
● Day   HMC
Boarding

Head J Daniel (11 years)
Age range 11–18, own prep from age 5; entry by own exam and common entrance.
Scholarships from full fees to £100 remission pa.

ROYAL GRAMMAR (NEWCASTLE)

Royal Grammar School
Eskdale Terrace
Newcastle upon Tyne NE2 4DX
Telephone number 091 2815711

Co-ed   Pupils 950
● Boys   Upper sixth Yes
Girls   Termly fees:
Mixed sixth   Day £650
● Day   HMC
Boarding

Head A S Cox (16 years)
Age range 11–18, own prep from age 8; entry by own exam and common entrance.
60 assisted places pa.

ROYAL GRAMMAR (WORCESTER)

Royal Grammar School
Upper Tything
Worcester WR1 1HP
Telephone number 0905 22029

Enquiries/application to the Registrar

Co-ed   Pupils 661
● Boys   Upper sixth 100
Girls   Termly fees:
Mixed sixth   Day £825
● Day   Boarding £1500
● Boarding

WHAT IT'S LIKE

Founded before 1291 (and thus one of the oldest schools in England) and given a charter by Elizabeth in 1561. Moved to its present site in 1868. Urban, single-site and near the City centre, it has fine buildings in spacious gardens. Playing fields are close by. The prep school is combined. Very good modern facilities already exist. A half-a-million pound project for more buildings is under way. In a friendly, civilised and well-disciplined environment, the

543

pupils receive a thorough education. Results are good (65–70 entrants to higher education per year). Quite strong music and drama depts; excellent computer facilities. There is a strong tradition of excellence in games, especially cricket (10 of the staff have first-class or minor counties experience). The CCF is vigorous and there is much emphasis on outdoor pursuits. Big commitment to local community schemes and an impressive record in the Duke of Edinburgh's Award Scheme. The school has a high reputation locally and is well supported. Full use is made of Worcester amenities, cultural and otherwise.

SCHOOL PROFILE

Pupils Total over 12, 661. Day 634; Boarding 27. Entry age, 8, 9, 10, 11, 13 and into the sixth (or by arrangement). 10% are children of former pupils.

Entrance Own entrance exam used. Oversubscribed. School looks for potential contributors to its wide range. Parents not expected to buy text books. 37 assisted places. 10 scholarships/bursaries, £1350 to £50.

Parents 15+% are doctors, lawyers, etc; 15+% in industry or commerce. 60+% live within 30 miles; up to 10% live overseas.

Staff Head T E Savage, in post for 10 years. 65 full time staff, 1 part time. Annual turnover 8%. Average age 35.

Academic work GCSE and A-levels. Average size of upper fifth 120; upper sixth 100. *O-levels*: on average, 11 pupils in upper fifth pass 1–4 subjects; 41, 5–7 subjects; 68 pass 8+ subjects. *A-levels*: on average, 10 pupils in upper sixth pass 1 subject; 21, 2 subjects; 56, 3 subjects; 2 pass 4 subjects. Industrial studies, Russian and electronics are offered to GCSE/A-level. *Computing facilities*: One general computer room (BBCs); one room mainly for sixth form; other machines around school; 60+ in all.

Senior pupils' non-academic activities *Music*: 25 learn a musical instrument, 9 up to Grade 6 or above; 1 accepted for Music School; 19 in school orchestra, 30 in school choir; 1 in National Youth Orchestra. *Drama and dance*: 70 in school productions. 17 to grade 6 in ESB, RAD etc. 10 now work in theatre. *Art*: 8 take A-level. 3 accepted for Art School, 1 in teacher training. 10 belong to eg photographic club. *Sport*: Athletics, badminton, basketball, cricket, cross-country, fencing, hockey, rugby, soccer, swimming, volleyball, rowing, sailing, canoeing and table tennis are available. All but 3 take non-compulsory sport. Most take exams eg gymnastics. 26 represent county (rugby, cricket, soccer, swimming, athletics, badminton, trampoline, archery etc); country (swimming, archery). *Other*: 40 take part in local community schemes. 39 have bronze Duke of Edinburgh's Award, 16 have silver and 4 have gold. Other activities include a computer club, driving lessons, CDT (school is building a car); chess, radio controlled cars, railway, outward bound (Ten Tors), CCF (Army, Navy, RAF sections), electronics club.

Careers 6 part time advisors. Average number of pupils accepted for *arts and humanities degree courses* at Oxbridge, 2; other universities, 16; polytechnics or CHE, 10. *science and engineering degree courses* at Oxbridge, 3; other universities, 18; medical schools, 2; polytechnics or CHE, 14. *BEd*, 1. *other general training courses*, 12. Average number of pupils going straight into careers in the armed services, 4; industry, 20; the City, 9; the civil service, 2; music/drama, 1; other, 2.

Uniform School uniform worn throughout.

Houses/prefects Competitive houses. Prefects, head boy, head of house and house prefects – appointed by the Head in consultation with the staff or by housemasters.

Religion Worship is encouraged.

Social Frequent links with local girls' school (Alice Ottley) especially for drama. German and French exchanges; cricket tour to Zimbabwe; trips to USSR and Strasbourg; link with school in USA being established. Pupils allowed to bring own car/bike/motorbike to school. Some meals formal, some self service. School shop. No tobacco/alcohol allowed.

Discipline No corporal punishment. Pupils failing to produce homework once might not be punished; those caught smoking cannabis on the premises might expect expulsion.

Boarding Most have own study bedroom, some share with 2 or 3 others; there is one group of 6–8. 1 house. Central dining room. Pupils cannot provide and cook own food. 2 weekend exeats and half-term. Visits to the local town allowed as required.

Former pupils Imran Khan.

ROYAL HOSPITAL

Royal Hospital School
Holbrook
Ipswich
Suffolk IP9 2RX
Telephone number 0473 328342

Enquiries/application to Director of
Greenwich Hospital, 13 Devonshire
Square, London EC2M 4TQ

Co-ed   Pupils 600
• Boys   Upper sixth 50
Girls   Termly fees:
Mixed sixth   Boarding £1158
Day   SHMIS
• Boarding

WHAT IT'S LIKE

Founded in 1712 at Greenwich, it moved in 1933 to its present exceptionally well-equipped new complex with 60 acres of beautiful grounds overlooking the River Stour at Holbrook, just south of Ipswich. It enjoys first-rate facilities and accommodation in a civilised and healthy environment. Religious worship is compulsory. A large staff allows a staff:pupil ratio of about 1:9. Academic standards are high and results good. Some 30 or more pupils go on to university each year. Very strong indeed in music and drama. It has high standards also in sports and games (a lot of representatives at county and national level). Its naval tradition (the school is open only to the children or grandchildren of seafarers) is continued in the large CCF contingent. The school has an impressive record in the Duke of Edinburgh's Award Scheme.

SCHOOL PROFILE

Pupils Total over 12, 600. Entry age, 11, 12, 13 and a few into the sixth. 15% are children of former pupils.

Entrance Own entrance exam used. Oversubscribed. No special skills or religious requirements but all pupils must be children or grandchildren of seafarers. Parents not expected to buy text books. All fees subsidised according to means test.

Parents 15+% in Armed Services. Up to 10% live within 30 miles; up to 10% live overseas.

Staff Head M A B Kirk, in post for 5 years. 63 full time staff, 5 part time. Annual turnover 4%. Average age 38.

Academic work GCSE and A-level. Average size of upper fifth 110; upper sixth 50. *O-levels*: on average, 50 pupils in upper fifth pass 1–4 subjects; 35, 5–7 subjects; 25 pass 8+ subjects. *A-levels*: on average, 6 pupils in upper sixth pass 1 subject; 15, 2 subjects; 25, 3 subjects and 4 pass 4 subjects. On average, 20 take science/engineering A-levels; 20 take arts and humanities; 10 a mixture. Electronics, industrial studies, politics offered to GCSE/A-level. *Computing facilities*: 1 room with 20 BBC computers; 6 departments have their own. Local dyslexia centre available.

Senior pupils' non-academic activities *Music*: 50 learn a musical instrument, 5 to Grade 6 or above; 30 in school orchestra, 70 in choir. *Drama and dance*: 60 in school productions. *Art*: 5 take as non-examined subject; 20 GCSE; 4 A-level. 1 accepted for Art School. 10 belong to photographic club. *Sport*: Rugby, soccer, cricket, athletics, tennis, swimming, sailing, shooting, squash, cross-country available. 100 take non-compulsory sport. 20 take exams. 15 represent county/country (rugby, swimming, lifesaving, sailing). *Other*: 25 have bronze Duke of Edinburgh's Award, 15 have silver and 6 gold. Other activities include a computer club, driving lessons.

Careers 1 full time and 1 part time careers advisors. Average number of pupils accepted for *arts and humanities degree courses* at Oxbridge, 3; other universities, 13; polytechnics or CHE, 25. *science and engineering degree courses* at Oxbridge, 2; other universities, 12; medical schools, 2; polytechnics or CHE, 20. *other general training courses*, 10. Average number of pupils going straight into careers in armed services, 15; industry, 20; the City, 2; civil service, 5; other, 15. Traditional school career is Armed Services (15–20%).

Uniform School uniform worn throughout.

Houses/prefects Competitive houses. Prefects, head boy, head of house and house prefects – appointed by Head. Sixth form committee.

Religion Compulsory worship.

Social Theatre, debates, dinner parties etc with girls' school. Organised trips abroad including ski-ing, adventure training, France (battlefields etc). Some pupils allowed to bring own bike to school. Some meals formal, some self service. School shop. No tobacco/alcohol allowed.

Discipline No corporal punishment. Pupils failing to produce homework once might expect a warning; those caught smoking cannabis on the premises might expect expulsion.

Boarding 8% have own study bedroom, 92% are in dormitories of 6+. Houses, of approximately 65, same as competitive houses. Resident qualified nurse. Central dining room. Pupils can provide and cook own food in a limited way. 1 week's exeat at half-term. Sixth form allowed visits to local town.

Alumni association run by P C Crick, c/o the School.

ROYAL NAVAL

The Royal Naval School	Co-ed	Pupils 271
Farnham Lane	Boys	Upper sixth 27
Haslemere	● Girls	Termly fees:
Surrey GU27 1HQ	Mixed sixth	Day £1232
Telephone number 042 873 5415	● Day	Boarding £1848
Enquiries/application to the Headmistress	● Boarding	GSA

WHAT IT'S LIKE

Founded in 1840 to provide for the daughters of marine and naval officers put on half pay at the end of the Napoleonic wars. Originally called the Royal Naval Female School. Nowadays two thirds of its girls are from non-naval families. In 1942 it moved to its present site in Surrey where it occupies handsome buildings in 65–70 acres of pleasant wooded grounds. Excellent modern facilities. A sound education is provided and results are good. Very strong indeed in music and drama (almost everyone is involved). Compulsory worship and prayers in the Anglican tradition. Big commitment to local community services and the police course. Good range of sports, games and extra-curricular activities. A fine record in the Duke of Edinburgh's Award Scheme.

SCHOOL PROFILE

Pupils Total, 271. Day 119; Boarding 152. Entry age, 11+ and into the sixth. St Hilary's, Godalming and St Ives, Haslemere provide over 20%. Less than 5% are children of former pupils.

Entrance Common entrance and own entrance exam used. Not oversubscribed. No special skills required. C of E school but other religions accepted. Parents not expected to buy text books. 5 scholarships, £250–£300 pa.

Parents 15+% are doctors, lawyers, etc; 15+% in industry or commerce; 15+% in the armed services. 30+% live within 30 miles; up to 10% live overseas.

Staff Head Dr J L Clough, in post for 1 year. 30 full time staff, 11 part time. Annual turnover 10%. Average age 39.

Academic work GCSE and A-levels. Average size of upper fifth 49, upper sixth 27. *O-levels*: on average, 4 pupils in upper fifth pass 1–4 subjects; 32, 5–7 subjects; 23 pass 8+ subjects. *A-levels*: on average 4 pupils in the upper sixth pass 1 subject; 7, 2 subjects; 12, 3 subjects; 1 passes 4 subjects. *Computing facilities*: BBC Micro. Visiting remedial teachers and extra coaching.

Senior pupils' non-academic activities *Music*: 117 learn a musical instrument, 8 up to Grade 6 or above; 31 in school orchestra, 79 in choir, 7 in recorder group, 1 in Surrey County Youth Orchestra/Wind Band. *Drama and dance*: 60 in school productions. 20 to Grade 6 in ESB, RAD etc. 150 in class drama, 150 house drama. 15 competitive drama festivals. *Art*: 9 take as non-examined subject; 24 take GCSE; 3–5 A-level. 3 accepted for Art School, 1 studies History of Art. 4 in art club. *Sport*: Netball, lacrosse, tennis, swimming, badminton, squash, rounders and volleyball available. 72 take non-compulsory sport. 12 take exams. *Other*: 25 take part in local community schemes. 38 have bronze Duke of Edinburgh's Award, 8 have silver and 2 gold. 10 enter voluntary schemes after leaving school, 6 work for national charities. Other activities include a computer club, electronics, cookery, driving lessons and CREST.

Careers 1 full time advisor. Average number of pupils accepted for *arts and humanities degree courses* at Oxbridge, 1; other universities, 5; polytechnics or CHE, 5. *science and engineering degree courses* at universities, 5; medical schools, 1; polytechnics or CHE, 5. *other general training courses*, 5. Average number of pupils going straight into careers in the armed services, 1; industry, 1; the City, 1; civil service, 1; music/drama, 1; other, 1.

Uniform School uniform worn throughout.

Houses/prefects Competitive houses. Prefects, head girl, head of house and house prefects – elected by the school. School Council.

Religion Compulsory morning prayers, attendance at chapel on Sundays, optional for non C of E pupils.

Social Dances, debates and social evenings with local schools. Regular school exchanges and ski-ing trips. Pupils allowed to bring own car/bike/motorbike to school. Meals self service. School shop. No tobacco/alcohol allowed.

Discipline No corporal punishment. Pupils failing to produce homework once might expect a talking to; those caught smoking cannabis on the premises might expect counselling or expulsion, depending on the circumstances.

Boarding Sixth formers have own or shared study bedroom, 25% in dormitories of 6 or more. Houses, of 41/77/35, are divided by age. Resident SRN. Central dining room. Sixth formers can provide and cook own snacks. At least 2 weekend exeats each term. Visits to local town allowed on Saturdays and during free periods.

Alumni association is run by Mrs S Hulton, Royal Naval School Society, c/o the School.

ROYAL RUSSELL

Royal Russell School	● Co-ed	Pupils 600
Coombe Lane	Boys	Upper sixth Yes
Croydon	Girls	Termly fees:
Surrey CR9 5BX	Mixed sixth	Day £900
Telephone number 01-657 4433	● Day	Boarding £1725
	● Boarding	SHMIS

Head R D Balaam (7 years)
Age range 4–18; entry by common entrance and own exam. Scholarships/bursaries.

ROYAL WOLVERHAMPTON

Royal Wolverhampton School
Penn Road
Wolverhampton WV3 0EG
Telephone number 0902 341230

Enquiries/application to the Headmaster

- Co-ed
  Boys
  Girls
  Mixed sixth
- Day
- Boarding

Pupils 339
Upper sixth 35
Termly fees:
Day £935
Boarding £1580
SHMIS

WHAT IT'S LIKE

Founded in 1850 and co-ed virtually from the outset, it moved to its present site, a large wooded area a mile from the town centre, in 1854. The main buildings are an agreeable neo-Tudor design and there are fine gardens and ample playing fields. In recent years a major programme of modernisation and extension has been going on. Accommodation and facilities are good. The junior school is close by. Christian faith and values are central to the life of the school. Daily services are compulsory and religious education is for all. The teaching is of a high standard and results are good. Some 15–20 leavers go on to university each year. The staff:pupil ratio is about 1:10. Reasonably strong in music, drama and art. An impressive range of sports and games. Quite a lot of commitment to local community services, and a fine record in the Duke of Edinburgh's Award Scheme.

SCHOOL PROFILE

Pupils Total over 12, 339. Day 168 (boys 97, girls 71); Boarding 171 (boys 99, girls 72). Entry age, 11 and into the sixth. 10% are children of former pupils.

Entrance Own entrance exam used. Oversubscribed. No special skills or religious requirements although an Anglican school. Parents not expected to buy text books. Scholarships and bursaries, for music, sport, maths and sixth form, £1580–£300.

Parents 15+% in armed services; 15+% in industry or commerce. 30+% live within 30 miles; 10+% live overseas.

Staff Head Mr P Gorring, in post for 2 years. 30 full time staff, 2 part time. Annual turnover under 5%. Average age 35.

Academic work GCSE and A-levels. Average size of upper fifth 55; upper sixth 35. *A-levels*: on average, 6 pupils in upper sixth pass 1 subject; 2, 2 subjects; 10, 3 subjects and 15 pass 4 subjects (including general studies). On average, 60% take science/engineering A-levels; 30% take arts and humanities; 10% a mixture. *Computing facilities*: 12 computers. EFL provision.

Senior pupils' non-academic activities *Music*: 20 learn a musical instrument, 6 to Grade 6 or above, 1 accepted for Music School; 30 in school choir, 8 in school pop group. *Drama and dance*: 50 in school productions. 2 accepted for Drama/Dance School. *Art*: 15 take as non-examined subject; 16 take GCSE; 8 A-level. 3 accepted for Art School. *Sport*: Rugby, soccer, hockey, cricket, tennis, fencing, basketball, squash, volleyball, shooting, athletics, badminton, rounders available. 100 take non-compulsory sport. 10 take exams. 6 represent county (rugby, fencing, shooting, hockey, athletics). *Other*: 30 take part in local community schemes. 30 have bronze Duke of Edinburgh's Award, 20 have silver and 5 gold. Other activities include a computer club, driving lessons, chess, dance, self-defence, debating, public speaking, ice skating, ski-ing, CCF.

Careers 1 part time careers advisor. Average number of pupils accepted for *arts and humanities degree courses* at Oxbridge, 1; other universities, 6; polytechnics or CHE, 9. *science and engineering degree courses* at Oxbridge, 2; other universities, 9; medical schools, 2; polytechnics or CHE, 6. *BEd*, 2. *other general training courses*, 4. Average number of pupils going straight into careers in armed services, 2; industry, 2; civil service, 1.

Uniform School uniform worn throughout.

Houses/prefects Competitive houses. Prefects, head boy/girl, head of house and house prefects – appointed by Head after consultation.

Religion Compulsory daily service, Sunday service for boarders.

Social Debating competitions and games matches with other schools. 2 trips abroad each year. Some meals formal, some self service. School shop. No tobacco/alcohol allowed.

Discipline No corporal punishment. Pupils failing to produce homework once might expect remonstration or reprimand; those caught smoking cannabis on the premises might expect suspension.

Boarding 90% have own study bedroom, 10% share. Houses, of approximately 35, same as competitive houses, single sex. Resident qualified nurse. Central dining room. Pupils can provide and cook own food. Unlimited weekend exeats. Visits to local town allowed once a week.

Alumni association run by Mr J Ingram, President ORA, c/o the School.

Former pupils Eric Idle (Monty Python); Gilbert Harding (actor); Philip Oakes (author).

RUDOLPH STEINER (EDINBURGH)

The Rudolph Steiner School
38 Colinton Road
Edinburgh EH10 5BT
Telephone number 031 337 3410

- Co-ed   Pupils 170
- Boys   Upper sixth Yes
- Girls   Termly fees:
- Mixed sixth   Day £680
- Day   Steiner
- Boarding

Head The Chairman of the College of Teachers (changes annually)
Age range 4–18; entry by interview
Founded on the educational principles of Rudolph Steiner which link the powers of thought, feeling and action in the child.

RUGBY

Rugby School
Rugby
Warwickshire CV22 5EH
Telephone number 0788 543465

Enquiries to Head Master's Secretary.
Application to the Registrar
(Mr J Inglis, 5 Horton Crescent,
Rugby, Warwickshire CV22 5DJ).

Co-ed
● Boys
Girls
● Mixed sixth
● Day
● Boarding

Pupils 720
Upper sixth 178
Termly fees:
Day £1475
Boarding £2525
HMC

WHAT IT'S LIKE

Founded in 1567 by Lawrence Sheriffe 'to serve chiefly the children of Rugby and Brownsover', it moved in 1750 to an old manor house on the site of the present School House. By the end of the 18th century it was established as a major public boarding school. Dr Arnold became Head in 1828 and added much to its fame. Substantial growth in the 19th century led to the addition of many of the buildings which give the school its distinctive character. Much more development has occurred in the 20th century, including a fully-equipped theatre, extensive and comfortable boarding accommodation, science blocks, sports facilities, a language lab, computer centres and a micro-electronics centre. It is now extremely well-equipped. There are also fine gardens, 80 acres of playing fields, plus the amenities of Rugby town a few minutes away. A traditional school, but also warm, friendly and 'open to a degree that is quite undaunting'. It is a C of E foundation and a certain amount of worship and religious education are compulsory. A large and very well-qualified staff allows a staff:pupil ratio of about 1:8. Academically, it is one of the most high-powered schools and standards are very high. Results are consistently good and each year 145–150 pupils go on to university (35+ to Oxbridge). Very few schools have a better record. The science department is a leading one in Britain and originated most of the Nuffield science now used in schools. The music, drama and art departments are tremendously strong. About a third of the pupils have some involvement in music and virtually everyone is engaged in dramatic presentations at some time or another. Everybody takes art as a non-examined subject and 145 candidates take art at GCSE. The membership of the photographic club runs to 200 pupils. Rugby has long been renowned for its achievements in sports and games of which a great variety is available. There have been numerous representatives at county level. A very large number of clubs and societies cater for virtually every need. The Tawney Society is a most important academic society for visiting speakers on political, historical and cultural topics. There is a large CCF contingent involving about 300 pupils. The school has a considerable commitment to local community services and an impressive record in the Duke of Edinburgh's Award Scheme.

SCHOOL PROFILE

Pupils Total, 720. Day 99 (boys 80, girls 19); Boarding 621 (boys 551, girls 70). Entry age, boys 13; boys and girls into the sixth. 20% are children of former pupils.

Entrance Common entrance used; interviews for 16+ intake. Oversubscribed. No special skills (music and art for scholarships); no religious requirements. Parents expected to buy text books. 28 scholarships and foundationerships (day boys), £6600–£2000 pa.

Parents 15+% are doctors, lawyers etc; 15+% in industry or commerce. 10+% live within 30 miles; up to 10% live overseas.

Staff Head O R S Bull, in post for 3 years. 86 full time staff, 14 part time. Annual turnover 5%. Average age 45.

Academic work GCSE, A-levels, Institute of Modern Linguists, City & Guilds Computing. Average size of upper fifth 145; upper sixth 178. *O-levels*: on average, 20 pupils in upper fifth pass 1–4 subjects; 45, 5–7 subjects; 80 pass 8+ subjects. *A-levels*: on average, 25 pupils in the upper sixth pass 2 subjects; 150, 3 subjects and 20 pass 4 subjects. On average, 90 take science/ engineering A-levels; 90 take arts and humanities; 15 a mixture. Design and Technology offered to GCSE; Chinese, Russian, Spanish, History of Art, Greek, Latin, Ancient History to A-level. *Computing facilities*: 65 computers (science and maths schools). Provision for extra English and handwriting.

Senior pupils' non-academic activities *Music*: 150 learn a musical instrument, 80 to Grade 6 or above, 2 take ARCO exams; 80 in school orchestra, 40 in choir, 1 in pop group, 20 in jazz band. *Drama and dance*: 550 in school and house productions, about 30 in others. 6 accepted for Drama Schools, 1 now works in theatre. *Art*: All take as non-examined subject; 145 take GCSE; 30 A-level. 4 accepted for Art School. 200 belong to photographic club. *Sport*: Rugby, hockey, cricket, athletics, swimming, squash, rackets, cross-country, fives, tennis, fencing, shooting, Association football, badminton, golf, basketball, lacrosse, sailing etc available. Most take non-compulsory sport. 3 take coaching qualifications (hockey). 20+ represent county and 3 represent country (rugby, cricket, hockey, lacrosse, cross-country, fencing, athletics). *Other*: Many help local disabled, old people, schools etc. 50 have bronze Duke of Edinburgh's Award, 10 have silver and 5 gold. 15 pa enter VSO. Other activities include computer club, chess, bridge, debating, natural history, hobbies, astronomy, CCF (300 pupils), driving lessons.

Careers 1 full time and 3 part time advisors. Average number of pupils accepted for *arts and humanities degree courses* at Oxbridge, 15; other universities, 50; polytechnics or CHE, 15. *science and engineering degree courses* at Oxbridge, 20; other universities, 60; medical schools, 10; polytechnics or CHE, 5. *other general training courses*, 5. Average number of pupils going straight into careers in armed services, 5; industry, 5; the City, 5.

Uniform School uniform worn throughout.

Houses/prefects Competitive houses. Prefects (The Levée) and head boy – appointed by Head; head of house, house prefects – appointed by housemaster. No school council but Levée takes some decisions.

Religion Compulsory 10-minute chapel 3 times/week; choice between 'Forum' (ethical discussion) or Chapel Eucharist on Sundays.

Social Musical co-operation including The Sinfonia orchestra with other local schools. 2 ski-ing trips abroad a year, 1 sports trip, natural history expeditions every other year; annual exchanges (Vienna, Madrid). Pupils allowed to bring own bike to school (other vehicles rarely). Lunch formal, other meals self service. School shops. No tobacco; sixth form bar 2 nights/week (2 pint limit).

Discipline No corporal punishment. Pupils failing to produce homework

might expect verbal reproof, 1½ hr detention for repeated offence; those caught in possession of drugs on the premises should expect immediate expulsion.

Boarding 5% have own study bedroom, 5% share with 1 other, 80% are in dormitories of 6+. Houses, of approximately 60–80 (boys), 20–40 (girls), same as competitive houses and single sex. Resident qualified medical staff. Pupils can provide and cook own snacks. 3 termly exeats (1 week, 2 weekends), unlimited Sundays after chapel/Forum. Visits to restricted area of local town allowed each lunchtime and half day.

Alumni association run by Mr I G Miller, The Knoll, Upper Stowe, near Weedon, Northamptonshire.

Former pupils Tom King MP; A N Wilson and Salman Rushdie (novelists); Marmaduke Hussey (Chairman of BBC Governors); David Croft (TV script-writer); Sir Ewen Fergusson (UK Ambassador, Paris); Robert Hardy (actor); Bishop Hugh Montefiore.

RUNTON HILL

Runton Hill School	Co-ed	Pupils 150
West Runton	Boys	Upper sixth 20
Cromer	● Girls	Termly fees:
Norfolk NR27 9NF	Mixed sixth	Day £1250
Telephone number 026 375 661/2	● Day	Boarding £1885
	● Boarding	GSA; ISIS
Enquiries/application to the Secretary		

WHAT IT'S LIKE

Founded in 1911, it has a rural seaside site in north Norfolk, between Cromer and Sheringham. The original building was a Victorian private house. The four boarding houses are grouped at the centre. Numerous modern extensions, and facilities are good. The campus is compact. The school has been kept small as a matter of policy and a happy, family atmosphere prevails. It is C of E but multi-denominational. A sound education is given and results are good (8–10 university entrants per year). The school has a tradition of music (including a music scholarship) and drama. A wide range of activities; a standard range of games and sports and strong on outdoor pursuits. A very good record in the Duke of Edinburgh's Award Scheme.

SCHOOL PROFILE

Pupils Total over 12, 140. Day 17; Boarding 123. Entry age, 11, 12, 13 and into the sixth. 1–2% are children of former pupils.

Entrance Common entrance and own entrance exam used. Oversubscribed. No special skills required. Church of England but other denominations accepted. Parents not expected to buy text books. 4 scholarships ¼–⅓ fees; some bursaries.

Parents 30+% live within 30 miles; up to 10% live overseas.

Staff Head Dr Anne Cardew, in post for 1 year. 22 full time staff, 9 part time. Annual turnover 5%. Average age 40.

Academic work GCSE and A-levels. Average size of upper fifth 33; upper sixth 15. *Computing facilities*: computers and word processing facilities.

Senior pupils' non-academic activities *Music*: 11 learn a musical instrument, 2 to Grade 6 or above; 5 in school orchestra; 26 in choir. *Drama and dance*: pupils take part in a range of productions including plays in Latin and French. 3 take drama as extra, 11 elocution and public speaking. *Art*: 3 take A-level. 1 accepted for Art School. *Sport*: Tennis, rounders, basketball, hockey, badminton, netball, squash, golf, trampolining, gymnastics, swimming available. 6 represent county (hockey, netball). *Other*: 24 have bronze Duke of Edinburgh's Award, 18 have silver and 1 gold. Other activities include a computer club, driving lessons, chess, fencing, ballet, jazz and dance clubs, jewellery making, art, mathematics and aerobic clubs all flourish.

Careers 3 part time advisors. Most pupils go on to further or higher education – 50% to degree courses.

Uniform School uniform worn excepting in the sixth.

Houses/prefects Competitive houses. Prefects, head of School, head of house and house prefects – appointed by the Head or housemistress. School Council.

Religion Compulsory morning assembly, school and church services.

Social Cromer and North Norfolk Festival of Music and Drama, Roller Disco and various discos and dances. Organised trips abroad and exchange systems. Sixth form day girls allowed to bring own car to school. Meals: lunch formal, others self-service. No tobacco/alcohol allowed.

Discipline No corporal punishment. Those caught smoking cannabis on the premises would expect expulsion.

Boarding 12% have own study bedroom, none in dormitories of 6+. 4 houses, of 24–50, same as competitive houses (separate sixth form). School doctor visits weekly. Central dining room. Pupils can provide and cook own food. Two weekend exeats each term. Visits to the local town allowed on Saturday afternoons – juniors only in groups.

Alumni association via Mrs E Reid, Secretary, c/o the School.

RUTHIN

Ruthin School		Co-ed	Pupils 180
Ruthin		● Boys	Upper sixth Yes
Clwyd LL15 1EE		Girls	Termly fees:
Telephone number 08242 2543		● Mixed sixth	Day £1130
		● Day	Boarding £1780
		● Boarding	SHMIS; GBA

Head Mr F R Ullmann (2 years)
Age range 10–18, own prep from age 6; entry by own exam.
18 scholarships available plus bursaries.

RYDAL

Rydal School
Lansdowne Road
Colwyn Bay
Clwyd LL29 7BT
Telephone number 0492 30155

Enquiries/application to the Headmaster

- Co-ed
  Boys
  Girls
  Mixed sixth
- Day
- Boarding

Pupils 357
Upper sixth 65
Termly fees:
Day £1425
Boarding £1895
HMC

WHAT IT'S LIKE

Founded in 1885, its agreeable and well-designed buildings occupy a fine site on the edge of Colwyn Bay and overlooking the Irish Sea. It has excellent facilities and accommodation. The preparatory school is combined. A Methodist school; religious services and religious education are an important part of the curriculum. The teaching is very good, academic standards are high and results are impressive (30–35 university entrants per year). Very strong indeed in drama, art and music. An excellent record in games and sports (a lot of county and international representatives). All games have a compulsory element. A wide range of activities, with some emphasis on outdoor pursuits (ideal because of the proximity of the sea and Snowdonia). Some commitment to local community schemes.

SCHOOL PROFILE

Pupils Total 357. Day 111 (boys 68, girls 43); Boarding 246 (boys 170, girls 76). Entry age, 13+ and into the sixth. Rydal prep school provides over 50%. 9% are children of former pupils.

Entrance Common entrance and own tests used. Oversubscribed. Welcomes musicians, sportsmen/women, artists. No religious requirements but the school has a Methodist foundation. Parents expected to buy text books. 7 assisted places pa. 10 scholarships, full fees to 15%. Bursaries for clergy children (40–50%) and for Service children (20%).

Parents 15+% in industry or commerce. 10+% live overseas.

Staff Head P F Watkinson, in post for 20 years. 30 full time staff, 4 part time. Annual turnover 2 or 3. Average age 40.

Academic work GCSE and A-levels. Average size of upper fifth 70; upper sixth 65. *O-levels*: on average, 17 pupils in upper fifth pass 1–4 subjects; 26, 5–7 subjects; 27 pass 8+ subjects. *A-levels*: on average, 7 pupils in upper sixth pass 1 subject; 15, 2 subjects; 36, 3 subjects and 2 pass 4 subjects. On average, 16 take science/engineering A-levels; 21 take arts and humanities; 12 a mixture. *Computing facilities*: 12 BBC microcomputers on an Econet system. Microcomputers also in physics, maths and chemistry laboratories, in home economics department and computer-controlled lathe in workshops. Special provisions for EFL and dyslexia.

Senior pupils' non-academic activities *Music*: 70 learn a musical instrument, 15–20 to Grade 6 or above, 1 accepted for Music School; 35 in school orchestra, 40–50 in choir, 10 in pop groups, 8 in wind ensemble, 8 in brass ensemble; 3 or 4 play in county youth orchestra. *Drama and dance*: 40–50 in school productions, more in house productions and behind the scenes. 1 or 2 per year accepted for Drama/Dance Schools. *Art*: 150 take as non-examined subject; 20 take GCSE; 6 A-level. 4 per year accepted for Art School. 12 belong to photographic club. *Sport*: Rugby, cricket, hockey (girls only), netball (girls only), squash, swimming, badminton, basketball, shooting, sailing, tennis, cross-country running, athletics, rounders (girls only) available. Games are compulsory, 3 times per week. 10 represent county (athletics, cross-country). *Other*: 20 take part in local community schemes. 12 have bronze Duke of Edinburgh's Award. Other activities include a computer club, chess club (Sunday Times Schools Championships and Welsh Schools Championship), judo club, debating, historical, dramatic, geographical societies, etc.

Careers 3 part time advisors. Average number of pupils accepted for *arts and humanities degree courses* at Oxbridge, 2; other universities, 18; polytechnics or CHE, 5. *science and engineering degree courses* at Oxbridge, 1; other universities, 15; medical schools, 2; polytechnics or CHE, 7. *BEd*, 2. *other general training courses*, 3. Average number of pupils going straight into careers in the armed services, 1; industry, 1; civil service, 2; music/drama, 1. Traditional school careers are law and medicine.

Uniform School uniform worn throughout.

Houses/prefects Competitive houses. Prefects, head boy/girl, head of house and house prefects – appointed by the Head after consultation. School Council.

Religion Compulsory morning prayers and Sunday morning service.

Social Debates with Penrhos College and other local schools. Exchange visits with French and German schools. Ski-ing party abroad at Easter; climbing party in summer eg to Austrian Alps. Day pupils allowed to bring own car/motorbike to school. Meals self service. Several school shops (tuck, stationery, books, secondhand clothes) and a bank. No tobacco/alcohol allowed.

Discipline No corporal punishment. Pupils failing to produce homework once would be expected to do it; those caught smoking cannabis on the premises could expect to be expelled.

Boarding 5% have own study bedroom, 85% share (2–4); 10% are in dormitories of 6+. Houses, of approximately 33, same as competitive houses and single sex. 3 resident qualified nurses plus non-resident doctor. Central dining room. Sixth formers can provide and cook own food. 2 overnight leaves per term plus any Sunday. Visits to the local town allowed.

Alumni association run by J P Pepper, Secretary of the Old Rydalian Club, c/o the School.

Former pupils Wilfred Wooller (sportsman); Professor Sir G R Elton (Regius Professor of Modern History at Cambridge); Dr Michael Thompson (Vice Chancellor of Birmingham University); Hon Sir David McNeill (High Court Judge).

RYDE

Ryde School
Queen's Road
Ryde
Isle of Wight PO33 3BE
Telephone number 0983 62229

Enquiries/application to the Headmaster

- Co-ed   Pupils 411
- Boys   Upper sixth 35
- Girls   Termly fees:
- Mixed sixth   Day £765
- Day   Boarding £1530
- Boarding   HMC

WHAT IT'S LIKE

Founded in 1921, it moved to its present site on the edge of the town in 1928. It is single-site apart from two boarding houses which are nearby. For the most part there are elegant buildings amidst fine gardens and playing fields overlooking the Solent. The grounds cover about 17 acres. There have been many additions to the buildings in recent years and the school is now very well equipped. Academic standards and results are creditable and 15+ leavers go on to university each year. Drama is very strong; there is some music and art. A good range of sports and games and a fair variety of extra-curricular activities.

SCHOOL PROFILE

Pupils Total over 11, 411. Day 344 (boys 213, girls 131); Boarding 67 (boys). Entry age, 4 onwards and into the sixth. Own junior department provides over 50%. 15% are children of former pupils.

Entrance Common entrance rarely used. Oversubscribed in some forms. No special skills or religious requirements. Parents not expected to buy text books. 5 scholarships/bursaries pa, £500–£250.

Parents 90+% live within 30 miles; up to 10% live overseas.

Staff Head P D V Wilkes, in post for 4 years. 37 full time staff, 8 part time. Annual turnover 9%. Average age 40.

Academic work GCSE and A-levels. Average size of upper fifth 75; upper sixth 35. *O-levels*: on average, 5 pupils in upper fifth pass 1–4 subjects; 30, 5–7 subjects; 40 pass 8+ subjects. *A-levels*: on average, 2 pupils in upper sixth pass 1 subject; 5, 2 subjects; 19, 3 subjects and 4 pass 4 subjects. On average, 40% take science/mathematics A-levels; 30% take arts and humanities; 30% a mixture. *Computing facilities*: Computer lab.

Senior pupils' non-academic activities *Music*: 40 learn a musical instrument, 4 to Grade 6 or above; 30 in school orchestra, 80 in choir. *Art*: 5 take as non-examined subject; 25 take GCSE; 6 A-level. 4 accepted for Art School. *Sport*: Rugby, hockey, netball, tennis, swimming, football, athletics, cricket, gymnastics, table tennis, judo, fencing available. 60 take non-compulsory sport. Other activities include a computer club.

Careers 4 part time careers advisors. Average number of pupils accepted for *arts and humanities degree courses* at universities, 8; polytechnics or CHE, 5. *science and engineering degree courses* at Oxbridge, 2; other universities, 6; medical schools, 3; polytechnics or CHE, 5. *BEd*, 1. *other general training courses*, 10. Average number of pupils going straight into careers in armed services, 3; industry, 2; civil service, 2; music/drama, 1.

Uniform School uniform worn throughout.

Houses/prefects Competitive houses. Prefects, head boy/girl, head of house and house prefects – appointed by staff. Sixth Form Committee.
Religion Compulsory religious assembly.
Social Organised trips abroad. Sixth form pupils allowed to bring own car/bike to school. Meals formal. School shop. No tobacco/alcohol allowed.
Discipline Corporal punishment rarely used. Detentions.
Boarding Fifth and sixth formers have shared study bedrooms. Houses, of approximately 20, divided by age. Resident qualified nurse. Central dining room. 2 weekend exeats per term. Visits to local town allowed.
Alumni association run by K Traves Esq, Parkwall Farmhouse, Redhill Lane, Godshill, Isle of Wight.
Former pupils Philip Norman (journalist and author).

RYE ST ANTONY

Rye St Antony School	Co-ed	Pupils 350
Pullens Lane	Boys	Upper sixth Yes
Headington	● Girls	Termly fees:
Oxford OX3 0BY	Mixed sixth	Day £750
Telephone number 0865 62802	● Day	Boarding £1400
	● Boarding	GBGSA

Head Miss P M Sumpter (12 years)
Age range 8–18; entry by common entrance

SACRED HEART

Sacred Heart School	Co-ed	Pupils 161
Beechwood	Boys	Upper sixth 25
Pembury Road	● Girls	Termly fees:
Tunbridge Wells	Mixed sixth	Day £1150
Kent TN2 3QD	● Day	Boarding £2030
Telephone number 0892 29193	● Boarding	GSA

Enquiries/application to the Headmaster

WHAT IT'S LIKE

Founded in 1915, it is single-site on the outskirts of Tunbridge Wells in 22 acres of beautiful grounds. Handsome buildings and very good modern facilities. A friendly family school which has all the advantages of being small. It is a Roman Catholic foundation and attendance at services is compulsory. Considerable emphasis on Catholic doctrine and practice. A good general education is provided and a high proportion of leavers (15–20) proceed to university. Quite strong art, music and drama departments. An excellent range of sport, games, societies and clubs. Some commitment to local community services. A creditable record in the Duke of Edinburgh's Award Scheme. Full use is made of the cultural amenities of the town.

SCHOOL PROFILE

Pupils Total over 12, 161. Day 58; Boarding 103. Entry age, 5+, 9+, 11+, 14+ and into sixth. Own prep school provides 20+%.

Entrance Common entrance exam used. Not oversubscribed. No special skills required. Roman Catholic foundation but any denomination welcome. Parents not expected to buy text books. 6 scholarships, value up to £1075; bursaries available for girls already in school in financial need.

Parents 10+% live within 30 miles; 60+% live overseas.

Staff Head Dr James A Fallon, in post for 9 years. 21 full time staff, 17 part time. Annual turnover 8%. Average age 42.

Academic work GCSE and A-levels. Average size of fifth, 38; upper sixth 25. *O-levels*: on average, 16 pupils in fifth pass 1–4 subjects; 11, 5–7 subjects; 13 pass 8+ subjects. *A-levels*: on average, 4 pupils in upper sixth pass 1 subject; 5, 2 subjects; 11, 3 subjects and 4 pass 4 subjects. On average, 7 take science/engineering A-levels; 10 take arts and humanities; 6 a mixture. GCSE computing available. *Computing facilities*: 4 BBC computers. *Special provisions*: dyslexia and EFL.

Senior pupils' non-academic activities *Music*: 30 learn a musical instrument, 20 to Grade 6 or above. 8 in school orchestra, 45 in choir; 1 in county youth orchestra; 2 students currently preparing for diploma examinations. *Drama and dance*: 10 in school productions. Some pupils taking ballet grades. Clubs for jazz dance and contemporary dance. *Art*: 6 take as non-examined subject; 24 GCSE, 6 A-level, 2 mature GCSE, 5 history of art. 2 accepted for art school. 10 belong to eg photographic club; 12 to pottery club. *Sport*: Hockey, swimming, basketball, volleyball, netball, gymnastics, badminton, cross-country, tennis, cricket, rounders, squash, aerobics, rhythmic gymnastics, riding available. 52 take non-compulsory sport. *Other*: 16 take part in local community schemes. 6 have bronze Duke of Edinburgh's Award, 10 have silver. 10 work for national charities beyond school. Other activities include a computer club, chess, bridge, science, drama, public speaking and debating. Driving lessons can be arranged.

Careers 1 full time advisor. Average number of pupils accepted for *arts and humanities degree courses* at universities, 14; polytechnics or CHE, 3. *science and engineering degree courses* at universities, 5; medical schools, 1. *BEd*, 2.

Uniform School uniform worn, modified in the sixth.

Houses/prefects Competitive houses. Prefects, head girl, head of house and house prefects elected by school (Head has power of veto). School Council.

Religion Compulsory daily worship and Sunday mass.

Social Dances, debates with other schools, occasional joint theatrical productions. Annual ball for parents and seniors. Frequent fixtures in all sports and activities. Organised trips and exchange systems with schools abroad. Pupils allowed to bring own car/bike to school. Meals self service. School shop. No tobacco allowed. Wine only at formal functions.

Discipline No corporal punishment. Pupils failing to produce homework once might expect an order mark or warning; those caught smoking cannabis on the premises could expect expulsion.

Boarding 70 have own study bedroom, 30 share with 1 other; 12 are in dormitories of 6+. Qualified nurse on call. Central dining room. Pupils can provide and cook own food. Exeats at parents'/guardians' discretion. Visits to local town allowed.

Former pupils Libby Purves.

St Albans

St Albans School
Abbey Gateway
St Albans
Hertfordshire AL3 4HB
Telephone number 0727 55702

Enquiries/application to the Headmaster

Co-ed
● Boys
Girls
Mixed sixth
● Day
Boarding

Pupils 585
Upper sixth 95
Termly fees:
Day £985
HMC

WHAT IT'S LIKE

Its origins date to the pre-Norman monastic school which, by 1300, occupied buildings near its present site and was controlled by the Abbot of St Albans. In c1570 Elizabeth granted it a charter. Late in the 19th century it moved into the Abbey Gateway. It is urban and single-site and the playing fields are a mile away. Architecturally, it comprises a very interesting mixture of buildings dating from the late Middle Ages to the 1980s. Very well equipped with modern facilities, its main aim is to develop talent and responsibility and it retains close links with the Abbey. Academic standards are high and results are good (50–60 university entrants each year). It has flourishing music, art and drama departments, a good range of sport and games and a thriving CCF. A good deal of use is made of its field study centre in South Wales. A big commitment to local community services, and an outstanding record in the Duke of Edinburgh's Award Scheme (24 silver, 42 gold).

SCHOOL PROFILE

Pupils Total over 12, 585. Entry age, 11, 13 and into the sixth. 5% are children of former pupils.

Entrance Common entrance and own entrance exam used. Oversubscribed. No special skills or religious requirements. Parents are not expected to buy text books. 150 assisted places. Up to 2 scholarships/bursaries per year.

Parents 15+% are from industry or commerce. All live within 30 miles.

Staff Head S C Wilkinson, in post for 4 years. 50 full time staff, 10 part time staff. Annual turnover 3%. Average age 38.

Academic work GCSE and A-levels. Average size of upper fifth 100; upper sixth 95. *O-levels*: on average, 10 pupils in upper fifth pass 1–4 subjects; 90 pass 5+ subjects. *A-levels*: on average 6 pupils in the upper sixth pass 1 subject; 15, 2 subjects; 70, 3 subjects; 4 pass 4 subjects. On average, 35 take science/engineering A-levels; 40 take arts and humanities; 20 a mixture. *Computing facilities*: Computer room and 20 BBC Bs & Master. Hard disk store networked to science and technology dept's computers. Portable computers. Provision for mild dyslexia.

Senior pupils' non-academic activities *Music*: 34 learn a musical instrument, 24 up to Grade 6 or above, 1 accepted for Music School, 1 for university, 10 in school orchestras, 12 in choirs, 14 in pop group, 28 in ensembles, 1 in National Youth Orchestra, 4 in district national youth orchestras. *Drama and dance*: 50 in school productions; 6 in girls' high school productions; 12 in other productions. *Art*: 4 take as non-examined subject; 20 take GCSE; 10 A-level. 1 accepted for Art School. 6 belong to photographic club. *Sport*: Association and rugby football, hockey, cricket, tennis, cross-country, basketball, badminton, sailing, golf, squash, swimming and orienteering available. 110 take non-compulsory sport. 16 represent county/country (rugby, badminton, squash, cross-country). *Other*: 60 take part in local community schemes. 24 have silver Duke of Edinburgh's Award, 42 gold. Other activities include a computer club, driving lessons, chess and bridge clubs.

Careers 2 part time advisors. Average number of pupils accepted for *arts and humanities degree courses* at Oxbridge, 7; other universities, 21; polytechnics or CHE, 10. *science and engineering degree courses* at Oxbridge, 9; other universities, 15; medical schools, 3; polytechnics or CHE, 10. *BEd*, 1. Average number of pupils going straight into careers in the armed services, 2–3; the church, 1; industry, 1–2; the City, 1–2; civil service, 1–2; retail, 3 or 4; banking, 2 or 3.

Uniform School uniform worn, except the sixth.

Houses/prefects No competitive houses. Prefects, head boy – appointed by the Head.

Religion Compulsory services unless parents request not.

Social Joint theatrical productions, oratorios, general studies, community service camp, fetes etc with other local schools. 2 or 3 skiing trips, mountaineering, exchanges to France, Germany and the USA. Pupils allowed to bring own car/bike/motorbike to school. Meals self service. School shop. No tobacco/alcohol allowed.

Discipline No corporal punishment. Pupils caught smoking cannabis on the premises could expect suspension at least.

Former pupils Professor C Renfrew (Master of Jesus College, Cambridge); Professor S Hawking.

St Albans High

St Albans High School for Girls	Co-ed	Pupils 500
3 Townsend Avenue	Boys	Upper sixth Yes
St Albans	● Girls	Termly fees:
Hertfordshire AL1 3SJ	Mixed sixth	Day £800
Telephone number 0727 53800	● Day	GSA; GBGSA
	Boarding	

Head Miss E M Diggory (5 years)
Age range 11–18, own prep from age 7; entry by own exam.
Scholarships in sixth form; 15 assisted places pa; clergy bursaries.

St Ambrose

St Ambrose College
Wicker Lane
Hale Barns
Altrincham
Cheshire WA15 0HF
Telephone number 061 980 2711

Co-ed
● Boys
Girls
Mixed sixth
● Day
Boarding

Pupils 550
Upper sixth 70
Termly fees:
Day £574

Enquiries/application to the Headmaster
or Secretary

WHAT IT'S LIKE

Opened by the Christian Brothers in 1945. For 5 years the school was run in the Community residence. Between 1960 and 1962 a school was started and there is now a modern purpose-built school in extensive parkland. It is a Roman Catholic foundation and most of the pupils are RCs. Pupils of other denominations are welcome. There is a good deal of emphasis on religious instruction and worship: Mass, prayers (public and private), retreats. A sound general education is provided and academic results are good. About 25–30 pupils go on to university each year. There is some music, drama and art. A good range of sports and games and a fair variety of extra-curricular activities. The school has some commitment to local community services.

SCHOOL PROFILE

Pupils Total over 12, 550. Entry age, 11+ and into the sixth. 10% are children of former pupils.

Entrance Own entrance exam used. Oversubscribed. No special skills; RC school but admits others. Parents not expected to buy text books. 88 assisted places. About 10 scholarships/bursaries pa, full fees to £750 pa.

Parents 15+% are doctors, lawyers etc; 15+% in industry or commerce; 15+% are teachers. 60+% live within 30 miles.

Staff Head Rev Bro T Coleman, in post for 4 years. 41 full time staff, 8 part time. Annual turnover 1–2%. Average age 30.

Academic work GCSE and A-levels. Average size of upper fifth 90–100; upper sixth 70. *O-levels*: on average, 16 pupils in upper fifth pass 1–4 subjects; 23, 5–7 subjects; 67 pass 8+ subjects. *A-levels*: on average, 10 pupils in upper sixth pass 1 subject; 6, 2 subjects; 10, 3 subjects and 34 pass 4 subjects. On average, 29 take science/engineering A-levels; 31 take arts and humanities; 4 a mixture. *Computing facilities*: well equipped laboratory.

Senior pupils' non-academic activities *Music*: 15 learn a musical instrument, 6 to Grade 6 or above. 10 in school orchestra, 20 in choir, 10 go on to play in pop group. *Drama and dance*: 30 in school productions. *Art*: 10 take GCSE; 6 A-level, 3 accepted for Art School. *Sport*: Rugby, cross-country, golf, squash, badminton, cricket, tennis, swimming available. 6 represent country (swimming, cross-country, athletics); many county representatives in all sports. *Other*: 15 take part in SVP charity work. 6 enter voluntary schemes at home and abroad after leaving. Other activities include a computer club, debating, public speaking (competition level), theatre club, art, subito, hill walking.

Careers 4 part time careers advisors. Average number of pupils accepted for *arts and humanities degree courses* at Oxbridge, 3; other universities, 9; polytechnics or CHE, 3. *science and engineering degree courses* at Oxbridge, 4; other universities, 14; medical schools, 5; polytechnics or CHE, 6. *BEd*, 3. Average number of pupils going straight into careers in armed services, 3; the church, 1; the City, 3; banking, 6.

Uniform School uniform worn throughout.

Houses/prefects Competitive houses. Prefects, head boy – elected by school and staff.

Religion Worship encouraged; mass, prayers (private and assembly), retreats.

Social Drama, theatre and swimming gala with Loreto Convent School; local festivals. Organised trips to France, Germany. Pupils allowed to bring own car/bike/motorbike to school. Meals self service. School shop. No alcohol; tobacco allowed in restricted areas.

Discipline No corporal punishment. Pupils failing to produce homework once might expect detention; those caught smoking cannabis on the premises might expect suspension, expulsion for importers.

Alumni association run by Brother Michael, c/o the School.

St Andrew's (Harrow)

St Andrew's School
Gloucester Road
North Harrow
Middlesex HA1 4PW
Telephone number 01-427 0692

Enquiries/application to Miss M Roberts or Mrs M Hudson

Co-ed
Boys
● Girls
Mixed sixth
● Day
Boarding

Pupils 166
Upper sixth 12
Termly fees:
Day £650

WHAT IT'S LIKE

There are three schools in a group: the first was founded in 1923, the junior school in 1944 and the boys' department in 1977. They are in separate areas of an urban district and the premises consist of converted houses and church halls. Basically, it is a C of E foundation, with a curious imbalance of 17 full-time staff for 400 pupils and 34 part-time. Perhaps the most unusual feature of the group is that the headmistress, appointed in 1934, remained head until 1984 when she relinquished the headship to become principal of all three schools, and she remains principal. A sound education is provided and results are creditable. Fifteen or so leavers proceed to university each year. There appears to be rather minimal music, art and drama. Some games and sports are on offer, but extra-curricular activities seem to be few. Fees are low.

SCHOOL PROFILE

Pupils Total over 12, 166. Entry age, 3 upwards including into the sixth. (Boys in junior department only.) Own junior school provides over 20%. Some are children of former pupils.

Entrance Own entrance exam used. Not oversubscribed. French or German an advantage. No religious requirements. Parents not expected to buy text books. No assisted places. Only under personal and special circumstances are scholarships and bursaries available.

Parents 60+% live within 30 miles; 10+% live overseas. Strong society of parents and friends.

Staff Principal Miss Marjorie Roberts, in post for 54 years. 17 full time staff, 34 part time. Annual turnover 1–2%. Average age 35–45.

Academic work GCSE and A-levels. Average size of upper fifth 35; upper sixth 12. *O-levels*: on average, 25 pupils in upper fifth pass 1–4 subjects; 14, 5–7 subjects; 11 pass 8+ subjects. *A-levels*: on average, 6 pupils in the upper sixth pass 1 subject; 4, 2 subjects; 6, 3 subjects; 1 passes 4 subjects. On average, 6 take science/engineering A-levels; 3 take arts and humanities; 3 a mixture. Chinese and certain Indian languages also modern Greek and Japanese are taught to GCSE/A-level. *Computing facilities*: BBC computers. Computer studies and computer science. Provision for dyslexia, mild visual handicap and EFL.

Senior pupils' non-academic activities *Music*: 8 learn a musical instrument, 2 up to Grade 6 or above. 2 accepted for Music School. *Drama and dance*: 14 in school productions. 1 exam student. *Art*: 2 take as non-examined subject; 12 take GCSE; 3 take A-level. 2 accepted for Art School. *Sport*: Tennis, netball, badminton, squash, skating, swimming, athletics, volleyball, table tennis available. *Other*: Some take part in local community schemes. 10 have awards. Some work for national charities.

Careers 1 full time and 1 part time advisors. Average number of pupils accepted for *arts and humanities degree courses* at university, 3; polytechnics or CHE, 1. *science and engineering degree courses* at university, 2; medical schools, 1; polytechnics or CHE, 1. *BEd*, 2. *other general training courses*, 10. Average number of pupils going straight into careers in the City, 1; the civil service, 3; music/drama, 1.

Uniform School uniform worn except the sixth.

Houses/prefects Competitive houses. Prefects, head girl, head of house and house prefects – appointed by the Head and staff.

Religion Christian assembly.

Social Connections with St George's Church, Harrow. Organised trips abroad annually. Pupils allowed to bring own car/bike to school. Meals formal. No tobacco/alcohol allowed.

Discipline No corporal punishment. Pupils failing to produce homework once might expect loss of house points or detention.

ST ANNE'S (WINDERMERE)

St Anne's School		Co-ed	Pupils 264
Browhead		Boys	Upper sixth 33
Windermere		● Girls	Termly fees:
Cumbria LA23 1NW		Mixed sixth	Day £1220
Telephone number 096 62 6164		● Day	Boarding £1850
		● Boarding	GSA; GBGSA;
Enquiries/application to the Headmaster			SHMIS

WHAT IT'S LIKE

Founded in 1863, it has a magnificent situation in the Lake District National Park, on a site of 80 acres with splendid views over Lake Windermere and the fells. Its pleasant and well equipped buildings are spread over two main sites. It is Christian in outlook but non-denominational. It attracts girls from all over the world and endeavours to provide a liberal and progressive education where activities such as sailing, canoeing, fell-walking, music, art, drama and voluntary service play an important part. It is a member of the Round Square Conference – a group of internationally based schools following the Kurt Hahn traditions – with whom links are forged and exchanges are made. The teaching is good and exam results are good. Some 65% leavers proceed to degree courses each year. It is exceptionally strong in its music department (virtually everyone is engaged) and also strong in art and drama. Very good range of sports and games, societies and clubs. Much emphasis on outdoor pursuits and field studies, a very big commitment to local community schemes and an outstanding record in the Duke of Edinburgh's Award Scheme.

SCHOOL PROFILE

Pupils Total over 12, 264. Day 44; Boarding 220. Entry age, 11+ and into the sixth. 3% are children of former pupils.

Entrance Own entrance exam used. Oversubscribed. No special skills or religious requirements. Parents not expected to buy text books. No assisted places. 13 scholarships, £925 to £92.50.

Parents 15+% are doctors, lawyers, farmers etc; 15+% in industry or commerce. 10+% live within 30 miles; up to 10% live overseas.

Staff Head M P Hawkins, in post for 2 years. 37 full time staff, 21 part time. Annual turnover 5%. Average age 30.

Academic work GCSE and A-levels. Average size of upper fifth 47; upper sixth 33. *O-levels*: on average, 7 pupils in upper fifth pass 1–4 subjects; 14, 5–7 subjects; 24 pass 8+ subjects. *A-levels*: on average, 3 pupils in upper sixth pass 1 subject; 9, 2 subjects; 17, 3 subjects; 3 pass 4 subjects. On average, 5 take science/engineering A-levels; 19 take arts and humanities; 7, a mixture. Italian offered at O- and A-level. *Computing facilities*: 16 Station Nimbus network; 8 station Chain network Domesday system; laser printer support. Provision for EFL.

Senior pupils' non-academic activities *Music*: 139 learn a musical instrument, 14 up to Grade 6 or above, 1 takes A-level, 2 take O-level, 8 take GCSE; 108 involved in local festival; 40 in school orchestra, 29 in flute bands, 8 in recorder club, 55 in school choir. *Drama and dance*: 100 in school productions, 50 in other. 10 up to Grade 6 in ESB, RAD etc. 40 associated speech and drama, 5 entered competitions. *Art*: 50 take GCSE; 11 take A-level. 5 per year accepted for Art School. 50 belong to photographic/art/pottery club. *Sport*: Hockey, netball, swimming, tennis, cross-country, badminton, basketball, self-defence, gymnastics, dance – various, athletics, and riding available. 120 take non-compulsory sport. 4 represent county (cross-country, netball, hurdling and sprinting). *Other*: 70 take part in local community schemes. 57 have bronze Duke of Edinburgh's Award, 22 have silver and 7 have gold. 10 enter voluntary schemes after leaving school. Other activities include a computer club, driving lessons, bridge, debating, windsurfing, sailing, canoeing, sewing, knitting, railway modelling technology, basic wood modelling, origami, macrame, drawing and archery clubs.

Careers 1 part time advisor. Average number of pupils accepted for *arts and humanities degree courses* at universities, 4; polytechnics or CHE, 5. *science and engineering degree courses* at Oxbridge, 1; other universities, 4; medical schools, 1; polytechnics or CHE, 5. *BEd*, 1. *other general training courses*, 10/12. Average number of pupils going straight into careers in the City, 1.

Uniform School uniform worn throughout.

Houses/prefects Competitive houses. No prefects. Head girl and head of house elected by the school. School Council.

Religion Morning and evening prayers. Sunday morning service.

Social Organised events with local independent schools. Exchanges with other Round Square schools and a French school. Pupils allowed to bring own car/bike to school. Meals self service. School shop. No tobacco/alcohol allowed.

Discipline No corporal punishment. Pupils failing to produce homework once can expect extra work; those involved with drugs can expect expulsion.

Boarding Head girl has own study bedroom, 20% share with others; 80% are in dormitories of 6+. Houses, of 10–122 are divided by year groups. Resident qualified nurse. Central dining room. Pupils can provide and cook own food in the senior house. 2 weekend exeats each term. Visits to local town allowed.

Alumni association is run by Mrs J Brown, 16 The Horseshoe, York.

Former pupils Dodie Smith (Author).

St Anselm's

St Anselm's College	Co-ed	Pupils 650
Manor Hill	● Boys	Upper sixth Yes
Birkenhead	Girls	Termly fees:
Merseyside L43 1UQ	Mixed sixth	Day £600
Telephone number 051 652 1408	● Day	HMC
	Boarding	

Head Rev Brother M Power

Age range 11–18, own junior from age 5; entry by own exam.
2 scholarships pa, LEA and government assisted places.

St Antony's-Leweston

St Antony's-Leweston Convent School		Co-ed	Pupils 405
Sherborne		Boys	Upper sixth 40
Dorset DT9 6EN		● Girls	Termly fees:
Telephone number 096 321 691		Mixed sixth	Day £1300
Enquiries/application to Mrs P Cartwright		● Day	Boarding £1995
		● Boarding	GSA; GBGSA; BSA

WHAT IT'S LIKE

Founded in 1891, it derives from the pioneering work of the Congregation of the Sisters of Christian Instruction (founded in 1822) which created schools in many parts of the world. It is sited 3 miles south of Sherborne in a stretch of splendid Dorset countryside. The main building is a very elegant 19th-century country house in beautiful gardens and parkland. A most civilised and healthy environment. Numerous modern extensions provide accommodation and good facilities, including labs, sports hall and arts centre. There is a brick-built church of unusual design. It is Roman Catholic, and a resident Dominican priest is the spiritual mentor. A happy, well run establishment where academic standards are high and results are good (some 20 university entrants per year). Very strong indeed in music, drama and art. Also in sports and games (of which there is a wide range) and numerous other activities. Cultural collaboration with Sherborne Boys' school, Downside and Milton Abbey.

SCHOOL PROFILE

Pupils Total over 11, 405. Day 90; Boarding 315. Entry age, 11, 12, 13 and into the sixth. Own prep school provides over 20%. 24 are children of former pupils. 1% are foreign.

Entrance Common entrance and own entrance exam used. Fully subscribed. No special skills or religious requirements, although it is a Roman Catholic School. Parents not expected to buy text books. No assisted places. Scholarships/bursaries, from ⅔–⅙ of fees.

Parents 15+% in the armed services. 10+% live within 30 miles; 10+% live overseas. 1% are foreign students.

Staff Head Mrs P Cartwright, in post for 5 years. 36 full time staff, 19 part time. Annual turnover 10%. Average age 40.

Academic work GCSE and A-levels. Average size of upper fifth 66; upper sixth 40. *O-levels*: on average, 11 pupils in upper fifth pass 1–4 subjects; 21, 5–7 subjects; 36 pass 8+ subjects. *A-levels*: on average, 6 pupils in the upper sixth pass 1 subject; 10, 2 subjects; 24, 3 subjects; 1 passes 4 subjects. On average, 16 take science/engineering A-levels; 25 take arts and humanities. Russian is offered to GCSE. *Computing facilities*: SJ Network System of 12 BBC Computers and a separate RML 380Z System. Provisions for dyslexia and EFL.

Senior pupils' non-academic activities *Music*: 55 learn a musical instrument, 24 up to Grade 6 or above, 2 accepted for Music School; 15 in school orchestra, 57 in school choir, 12 in chamber music, 20 in chamber choir, 10 in band; 4 in Dorset Youth orchestra, 2 in Dorset band, 12 in Joint Sherborne

Schools' Orchestra. *Drama and dance*: 20 in school productions, 44 in individual lessons. 4 Guildhall Grade 7, 14 LAMDA Awards. 46 in Mid-Somerset Festival, 1 in National Youth Theatre. 1 accepted for Drama School, 2 accepted for Theatre Studies. *Art*: 1 takes as non-examined subject, 64 take GCSE, 18 take A-level. 4 accepted for Art School. 27 take history of art, 5 woodcarving, 5 stonecarving, 5 sculpture/pottery. 14 belong to photographic club, 20 to pottery club. *Sport*: Hockey, netball, gymnastics, cross-country running, basketball, volleyball, badminton, squash, swimming, tennis, athletics, fencing, riding, karate available. Sixth form also have golf, archery, canoeing and yoga. 200 take non-compulsory sport. 50 take exams in gym, swimming and karate. 41 represent county/country (netball, hockey, fencing and athletics). *Other*: Some sixth year girls take part in local community schemes. 28 have bronze Duke of Edinburgh's Award, 6 have silver. Other activities include a computer club, dance department covers classical ballet, modern stage and tap dancing as well as modern educational, ballroom and country, three cookery clubs and craft club.

Careers 3 part time advisors. Average number of pupils accepted for *arts and humanities degree courses* at Oxbridge, 3; other universities, 13; polytechnics or CHE, 4. *science and engineering degree courses* at Oxbridge, 1. *other general training courses*, 15. Average number of pupils going straight into careers in the City, 1.

Uniform School uniform worn throughout.

Houses/prefects Competitive houses. Prefects, head girl, head of house and house secretary – elected by staff. School Council.

Religion Compulsory mass once a week. C of E girls encouraged to attend local church service on Sundays.

Social Joint Downside/Leweston concert held annually. Joint theatrical productions with Sherborne Boys' school and Milton Abbey School. Some pupils take part in the 1st and 2nd Joint Sherborne Schools' orchestras. Yearly trips abroad include a skiing trip, Italian architectural trip, Dieppe trip (weekend). Visits have also been arranged to Germany and the Himalayas. Pupils allowed to bring own car/bike/motorbike to school. Meals self service. School shop. No tobacco/alcohol allowed.

Discipline No corporal punishment. Pupils failing to produce homework once might expect a warning; those caught smoking cannabis on the premises might expect expulsion.

Boarding 51 (sixth form) have own study bedroom, 40 share with others (2 to a room); 204 are in dormitories of 6+. Resident nurse, school doctor holds a surgery once a week. Central dining room. Pupils cannot provide and cook their own food. 2 long weekend exeats each term, short weekends (mid-day Sat–Sun) when required. Visits to the local town allowed.

Alumni association is run by Mrs Marielle Ahern.

Former pupils Sarah Payne; Erin Pizzey.

St Audries

St Audries School
West Quantoxhead
Nr Taunton
Somerset TA4 4DU
Telephone number 0984 32426

Enquiries/application to the Headmaster

Co-ed
Boys
● Girls
Mixed sixth
● Day
● Boarding

Pupils 124
Upper sixth 13
Termly fees:
Day £1076
Boarding £1863
GSA

WHAT IT'S LIKE

Founded in 1906, it has a splendid site of 83 acres of park and woodland near the sea and the Quantocks. The main building is a handsome manor house. There are several additional buildings and the educational facilities are first-rate. An Anglican foundation, it has all the advantages of a small school. There is strong emphasis on self-reliance, responsibility and courtesy in a relaxed but well-disciplined family atmosphere. A sound education is provided and most of the sixth go on to university or polytechnic. A strong music dept, with a military band which performs regularly at national events (eg the Royal Tournament). A good range of sports and games. Activities include riding. There is also a St John's Nursing Cadet Division.

SCHOOL PROFILE

Pupils Total over 12, 124. Day 24; Boarding 100. Entry age, 4, 8, 11, 12, 13 and into the sixth. Own junior department provides over 20%. Small proportion are children of former pupils.

Entrance Common entrance and own entrance exam used. Not oversubscribed. Music skills encouraged. C of E but some other faiths are admitted. Parents expected to buy a few text books. No assisted places. Various scholarships for all-round ability, music, day girls, sixth form. Bursaries available to daughters of clergy and others in cases of need. (Values from ⅔ to ⅓ fees for boarders, up to full fees for day girls.) Service children 5% discount.

Parents 15+% in the armed services; 15+% in industry or commerce. 30+% live within 30 miles; 30+% live overseas.

Staff Head Mrs A Smith, appointed in 1988. 12 full time staff, 6 part time. Annual turnover 2%.

Academic work GCSE and A-levels. Average size of upper fifth 30; upper sixth 13. *O-levels*: on average, 14 pupils in upper fifth pass 1–4 subjects; 12, 5–7 subjects; 8 pass 8+ subjects. *A-levels*: on average, 3 pupils in upper sixth pass 1 subject; 2, 2 subjects; 6, 3 subjects; 1 passes 4 subjects. On average, 4 take science/maths A-levels; 5 take arts and humanities; 4 a mixture. *Computing facilities*: all labs, history dept, computer room, as well as prep and pre-prep. Provision for mildly dyslexic and foreign girls.

Senior pupils' non-academic activities *Music*: 50 learn a musical instrument, 8 to Grade 6 or above. Some in school choir, others in military band. *Drama and dance*: 25 in school productions. 7 to Grade 6 in ESB, RAD etc. Virtually whole school in house productions. *Art*: 18 take GCSE; 5 take A-level art. Flourishing art club. *Sport*: Hockey, netball, rounders, tennis, athletics, shooting, orienteering, badminton, volleyball, squash and judo available. 1 or 2 represent county in athletics. *Other*: Some take part in local community schemes. 1 has gold Duke of Edinburgh's Award. Other activities include a computer club, St John's Nursing Cadet division, driving lessons, small group interested in rifle shooting, riding, sailing, art clubs, music of all kinds, field club and flower arranging.

Careers 1 part time advisor. Average number of pupils accepted for *arts and humanities degree courses* at Oxbridge, 1; other universities, 3; polytechnics or CHE, 2. *science and engineering degree courses* at universities, 3; medical schools, 1; polytechnics or CHE, 1. *other general training courses*, 1. Average number of pupils going straight into careers in the armed services, a few; industry, 1; music/drama, 1. Traditional school careers: nursing, accountancy and business studies.

Uniform School uniform worn except the sixth.

Houses/prefects Competitive houses. Prefects, head girl, head of house and house prefects – appointed by the Head and housemistresses. School Council.

Religion Morning assembly and Chapel on Sundays (except for non-Christians).

Social Dances and sixth form conferences organised with other local schools. An annual ski-trip, short stay foreign girls each summer term (Swedish, German and French). Older girls allowed to bring own bike to school. Meals formal. School shops (stationery, books, chemist's, tuck). No tobacco/alcohol allowed.

Discipline No corporal punishment. Pupils failing to produce homework once might expect a warning; those caught smoking cannabis on the premises would expect expulsion.

Boarding Upper sixth have own study bedroom, lower sixth and fifth share with others; a few are in dormitories of 6 or more. Houses, up to 36, are same as competitive houses with sixth form separate. SRN on site, local doctor and resident assistant. Central dining room. Sixth formers can provide and cook own snacks. 1 fixed exeat each term (sixth form, 2). Visits to local town allowed for fifth and sixth forms.

Alumni association is run by Miss Susan May, c/o the school.

St Augustine's
(Westgate-on-Sea)

St Augustine's College
125 Canterbury Road
Westgate-on-Sea
Kent CT8 8NL
Telephone number 0843 32441/2

Enquiries to the Secretary
Application to the Headmaster

Co-ed
● Boys
Girls
Mixed sixth
● Day
● Boarding

Pupils 138
Upper sixth 17
Termly fees:
Day £910
Boarding £1720
GBA

WHAT IT'S LIKE

Founded in 1865 at Ramsgate by Benedictine monks from Subiaco, it later moved to Westgate a few miles from the Abbey of St Augustine. The junior school shares the same site. Attractive buildings and very good facilities. It is single site and semi-rural in delightful grounds, close to the Ursuline Convent School. Both boys' schools are dedicated to a Catholic education. Everyone is expected to follow a full course of Catholic instruction and to aspire to the standards of conduct, courtesy and discipline inherent in the Benedictine tradition. It has all the advantages of a small school with a staff:pupil ratio of 1:8. Academic standards are high (7–10 university entrants per year; a large proportion for a school of only 138 pupils). Strong music, drama and art; very good range of sport, games and activities.

SCHOOL PROFILE

Pupils Total 138. Day 34; Boarding 104. Entry age, 13 and into the sixth. The Abbey School, Westgate (own prep) provides over 20%.

Entrance Common entrance used. Not oversubscribed. No special skills required. Catholics preferred, but all religions accepted. Parents expected to buy text books. No fixed number or value of scholarships/bursaries, available on merit and according to special circumstances.

Parents 15+% in industry or commerce; 15+% in professions. 10+% live within 30 miles; 30+% live overseas.

Staff Head Mr K C Doherty, in post 1 year. 17 full time staff, 6 part time. Annual turnover 8%. Average age 46.

Academic work GCSE and A-levels. Average size of upper fifth 40; upper sixth 17. *O-levels*: on average, 18 pupils in upper fifth pass 1–4 subjects; 10, 5–7 subjects; 7 pass 8+ subjects. *A-levels*: on average 3 pupils in the upper sixth pass 1 subject; 5, 2 subjects; 4, 3 subjects; 2 pass 4 subjects. On average, 8 take science/engineering A-levels; 6 take arts and humanities; 2 a mixture of both. *Computing facilities*: Present system based on research machines. 480Z computers and BBC computers, all with word processing and printer facilities. Range of programming languages, access to Prestel, AMX art and Pagemaker, Microview data. Provision for EFL.

Senior pupils' non-academic activities *Music*: 12 learn a musical instrument, 10 in school choir. *Drama and dance*: 20 in school productions. *Art*: 15 take GCSE; 2 take A-level. 5 belong to photographic club. *Sport*: Cricket, tennis, athletics, golf, volleyball, basketball, swimming, hockey, badminton, association football, squash, cross-country running, rugby available. 30 take non-compulsory sport. 2 represent county in rugby. *Other*: 6 take part in local community schemes. 11 taking bronze Duke of Edinburgh's Award, 1 gold. Other activities include a computer club, snooker, library service, hobbies, electronics, art, pottery, chess, debating, drama.

Careers 1 part time advisor. Average number of pupils accepted for *arts and humanities degree courses* at Oxbridge, 1; other universities, 2; polytechnics or CHE, 1. *science and engineering degree courses* at universities, 4; medical schools, 2; polytechnics or CHE, 3. BEd, 1. *other general training courses*, 5. Average number of pupils going straight into careers in the armed services, 2; industry, 2; the City, 2; civil service, 2; music/drama, 1; other, 10.

Uniform School uniform worn throughout.

Houses/prefects Competitive houses. Prefects. Head boy and head of house and house prefects. Appointed by the head after consulting staff and senior boys. Headmaster's council.

Religion Mass on Sundays and Wednesdays. Daily evening prayer, grace at meals.

Social Dances, productions and charity concerts with the Ursuline Convent School; Thanet schools' sixth form debates. Annual ski trip with Ursuline Convent. Boarders allowed to bring own bike; day boys bike/motor vehicle to school. Meals formal. School book shop selling stationery supplies, small tuck shop. No tobacco/alcohol allowed.

Discipline Corporal punishment policy, but in practice not used. Pupils failing to produce homework once might expect to do it in their spare time; those caught smoking cannabis on the premises might expect suspension and parents informed.

Boarding 26% have own study bedroom, 67% share with others, 7% are in dormitories of 6 or more. Houses are a cross-section of the school. Resident SRN, school doctor visits weekly. Central dining room. Weekend exeats at discretion. Visits to local town allowed.

Alumni association is run by Rev Fr Augustine Coyle OSB, St Augustine's College.

Former pupils Alastair Stewart (ITN Newscaster).

ST AUGUSTINE'S PRIORY

St Augustine's Priory
Hillcrest Road
London W5 2JL
Telephone number 01-997 2022

Enquiries to Reverend Mother Prioress
Applications to Secretary

Co-ed
Boys
• Girls
Mixed sixth
• Day
Boarding

Pupils 200
Upper sixth 10
Termly fees:
Day £580

WHAT IT'S LIKE

It has an urban site in a residential area, with extensive grounds and ample playing fields. An RC school run by nuns. Academic results appear to be adequate and several pupils go on to university. Apparently minimal music and drama, but a lot of art. Adequate sports and games, minimal extra-curricular activities. No local community service or Duke of Edinburgh's Award Scheme.

SCHOOL PROFILE

Pupils Total over 12, 200. Entry age, 4–5 upwards and into the sixth. Own junior department provides over 20%. 2% are children of former pupils.

Entrance Own entrance exam used. Oversubscribed. No special skills looked for; school mainly RC but small number of others accepted. Parents not expected to buy text books.

Parents 15+% are doctors, lawyers etc; 15+% in industry or commerce. Up to 10% live within 30 miles.

Staff Head Mother Mary Gabriel. 23 full time staff, 12 part time. Annual turnover 8%.

Academic work GCSE and A-levels. Average size of upper fifth 25; upper sixth 10. *O-levels*: on average, 21 pupils in upper fifth pass 5–7 subjects; 2 pass 8+ subjects. *A-levels*: on average, 2 pupils in upper sixth pass 1 subject;

4, 2 subjects; 6, 3 subjects and 1 passes 4 subjects. On average, 2 take science/engineering A-levels; 6 take arts and humanities; 2 a mixture. *Computing facilities*: 4 or 5 computers. Provision for dyslexia, mild visual handicap etc.

Senior pupils' non-academic activities *Music*: 35 learn a musical instrument, 3–4 to Grade 6 or above, 1 accepted for Music School. 30 in school choir. *Drama and dance*: Some pupils in school productions. *Art*: All take as non-examined subject; 20 GCSE; 4 A-level; 4 accepted for Art School. *Sport*: Hockey, tennis, netball, squash, cricket, rounders available. Some take non-compulsory sport; many take exams; 6–7 represent county/country (hockey). Other activities include a computer club, debating.

Careers 3–4 part time careers advisors. Average number of pupils accepted for *arts and humanities degree courses* at universities, 5–6. *BEd*, 6.

Uniform School uniform worn throughout.

Houses/prefects Competitive houses. Prefects, head girl, head of house and house prefects – appointed by the Head.

Religion Compulsory morning assembly.

Social Organised events with other schools; some trips abroad. Pupils allowed to bring own bike to school. Meals formal. School shop selling religious items. No tobacco/alcohol allowed.

Discipline No corporal punishment. Pupils caught smoking cannabis on the premises might expect a report to parents etc.

St Bede's (Hailsham)

St Bede's School
350 The Dicker
21 Upper Dicker
Near Hailsham, East Sussex
Telephone number 0323 843252

Enquiries/application to the Headmaster

- Co-ed
  Boys
  Girls
  Mixed sixth
- Day
- Boarding

Pupils 350
Upper sixth 40
Termly fees:
Day £1260
Boarding £1970
ISAI

WHAT IT'S LIKE

Founded in 1978, it is set in the village of Upper Dicker in the countryside. The buildings and playing fields occupy four sites around this small village. The main building is 'The Dicker', a big country house with 20 acres (formerly the home of the egregious and notorious Horatio Bottomley). Nearby Camberlot Hall is one of three residences for boy boarders; in all the school covers some 65 acres. There has been constant expansion since foundation and in 9 years the school has increased in numbers from 22 to 320. Other developments are under way and its facilities are already very good. It enjoys a staff:pupil ratio of 1:8 and the academic standards are high (15–20 university entrants per year; a high proportion for a new and small school). It is strong in music, drama and art, and has a very wide range of games (particularly strong in tennis), sports and activities. There are over 60 clubs and societies providing for almost every conceivable interest. Outdoor pursuits are very popular and the school has its own riding stables.

SCHOOL PROFILE

Pupils Total 350. Day 100 (boys 70, girls 30); Boarding 250 (boys 150, girls 100). Entry age, 13+ and into the sixth. Own prep school provides about 20%.

Entrance Common entrance and own entrance exam used. Fully subscribed. No special skills or religious requirements. Parents not expected to buy text books. No assisted places. Up to 12 scholarships/bursaries (academic, musical, artistic, sporting and for all-rounders), 75% to 20% of fees.

Parents 15+% are in industry or commerce. 10+% live within 30 miles; 30+% live overseas.

Staff Head R A Perrin, in post for 9 years. 43 full time staff, 10 part time. Annual turnover 10%. Average age 39.

Academic work Pupils prepared for GCSE and A-levels. Average size of upper fifth 75; upper sixth 40. *O-levels*: on average, pupils pass 6+ subjects. *A-levels*: on average, pupils pass 2.5 subjects. Chinese, Dutch, Arabic, photography, agricultural science, office skills and information technology are offered to GCSE or A-level. *Computing facilities*: RML Nimbus network. Provision for EFL.

Senior pupils' non-academic activities *Music*: 151 learn a musical instrument, 12 to Grade 6 or above; 20 in school orchestra, 30 in school choir, 80 in choral society. *Drama and dance*: 30 in school productions, 26 in other. 17 take GCSE, 7 A-level. *Art*: 27 take as non-examined subject; 77 take GCSE; 9 take A-level. Consistent success in applications for Art School. 35 in art club, 11 in photography club, 9 in ceramics club. 6 take GCSE photography. *Sport*: Soccer, rugby, squash, tennis, cricket, athletics, hockey, netball, rounders, swimming, fencing, badminton, archery, golf, cross-country, riding, dry ski-ing, sailing, windsurfing, judo, outdoor pursuits, shooting, volleyball, basketball, gymnastics, weight training, and table tennis available. 300 take non-compulsory sport (all sport is non-compulsory). 10 take GCSE exams. 18 represent county (tennis, swimming, skiing, rugby). *Other*: 30 take part in school community work schemes. Other activities include a computer club, 60 clubs and activities, including scientific, engineering, literary, art/craft, social activities in surrounding area, musical, etc.

Careers 2 part time advisors. Average number of pupils accepted for *arts and humanities degree courses* at universities, 8; polytechnics or CHE, 7. *science and engineering degree courses* at Oxbridge, 1; other universities, 7; polytechnics or CHE, 5. *other general training courses*, 15. Average number of pupils going straight into careers in armed services, 4; industry, 4; the City, 3; music/drama, 2.

Uniform School uniform worn except the sixth.

Houses/prefects Competitive houses. Prefects, head of school, head of house and house prefects – appointed by the Headmaster and housemasters.

Religion Multi-religious School Meetings on Sundays and mid-week; plus C of E, Catholic and Free Church services.

Social Sixth Form Industrial Conference every two years with five other local schools; musical productions. Annual school ski-ing trip, French, German, and Spanish visits. Pupils allowed to bring own bike/horse to school. Meals self service. No tobacco/alcohol allowed.

Discipline No corporal punishment. Pupils failing to produce homework once might expect work detention for 1 hour; detention and gating for misdemeanours; expulsion for any drug offence.

Boarding All sixth and upper fifth have study bedrooms, usually shared with one other; 35 in dormitories of 6+. Houses, 40–70, are as competitive houses and are single-sex (2 girls', 3 boys'). School doctor visits every morning. Central dining room. 2 weekend exeats each term. Visits to local towns allowed.

Former pupils Clare Wood (Wightman Cup Player 1987).

St Bees

St Bees School	● Co-ed	Pupils 316
The School House	Boys	Upper sixth 55
St Bees	Girls	Termly fees:
Cumbria CA27 0DU	Mixed sixth	Day £1135
Telephone number 0946 822263	● Day	Boarding £2015
	● Boarding	HMC
Enquiries/application to the Headmaster		

WHAT IT'S LIKE

Founded in 1583 by Edmund Grindal, Archbishop of Canterbury. Late in the 19th century it changed from being a day grammar to one mainly for boarders. It became fully co-educational in 1976. It has a particularly fine site of 150 acres in the pleasant valley of St Bees, and is unique among schools in having not only the sea and a magnificent beach within ½ a mile, but also easy access to the entire Lake District. A very healthy environment. There are fine gardens and ample playing fields and the buildings are handsome. The original school building (1587) is now the dining hall. The principal older buildings are made of St Bees sandstone. There have been substantial developments since 1954 and the school is now very well equipped. The purpose of the school is to develop the individual talents of each pupil while providing an education based on Christian principles. Particular emphasis is placed on academic excellence and good personal relationships. Self-reliance, individuality and consideration for others are encouraged. The chapel is used frequently and worship in the Anglican tradition is compulsory. A large staff allows a staff:pupil ratio of about 1:8. Academic standards are high and results consistently good. Some 25–30 pupils proceed to university each year. Considerable strength in music, drama (all juniors receive lessons in drama as part of the curriculum) and art. An excellent range of sports and games, including Eton fives and golf (the school has its own course). Plentiful extra-curricular activities are available. There is a large and flourishing CCF, some commitment to the Duke of Edinburgh's Award Scheme and considerable emphasis on outdoor pursuits for which the environment is ideal.

SCHOOL PROFILE

Pupils Total over 12, 316. Day 149 (boys 93, girls 56); Boarding 167 (boys 101, girls 66). Entry age, 11 and into the sixth. 5% are children of former pupils.
Entrance Common entrance and own entrance exam used. Good all-round ability looked for; no religious requirements. Parents expected to buy text books. 84 assisted places. Scholarships/bursaries available.

Parents 15+% in industry or commerce. 30+% live within 30 miles; up to 10% live overseas.

Staff Head P A Chamberlain, first year in post. 36 full time staff, 4 part time. Annual turnover 3%. Average age 40.

Academic work GCSE and A-levels. Average size of upper fifth 65; upper sixth 55. *O-levels*: on average, 5 pupils in upper fifth pass 1–4 subjects; 12, 5–7 subjects; 35 pass 8+ subjects. *A-levels*: on average, 3 pupils in upper sixth pass 1 subject; 6, 2 subjects; 12, 3 subjects and 34 pass 4 subjects. On average, 17 take science/engineering A-levels; 23 take arts and humanities; 15 a mixture. Photography and Chinese offered to GCSE/A-level. *Computing facilities*: Room containing range of micro computers and associated facilities. Provision for dyslexia, mild visual handicap, EFL etc.

Senior pupils' non-academic activities *Sport*: Hockey, netball, tennis, squash, badminton, archery, gymnastics, rugby, cricket, rounders, basketball, canoeing, swimming, rock climbing, track and field, fives, golf available. *Other*: Duke of Edinburgh's Award Scheme. Other activities include a computer club, chess, drama, philately, environmental group, young farmers, debating.

Careers 5 part time careers advisors. Average number of pupils accepted for *arts and humanities degree courses* at Oxbridge, 2; other universities, 9; polytechnics or CHE, 2. *science and engineering degree courses* at Oxbridge, 2; other universities, 14; medical schools, 4; polytechnics or CHE, 5. *BEd*, 2. *other general training courses*, 2. Average number of pupils going straight into careers in armed services, 2; industry, 2.

Uniform School uniform worn throughout.

Houses/prefects Prefects, head boy/girl, head of house and house prefects – appointed by the Head.

Religion Religious worship compulsory.

Social Debates and lectures with other local schools. Trips abroad and exchanges with schools abroad. Pupils allowed to bring own bike to school. Meals formal. School shop. No tobacco allowed; alcohol only at supervised sixth form bar discos.

Discipline No corporal punishment. Pupils failing to produce homework once might expect to do it during lunchtime; those caught smoking cannabis on the premises might expect expulsion.

Boarding Houses, of approximately 70, divided by age, single sex. Resident qualified medical staff. Central dining room. Pupils can provide and cook own food. Termly exeats. Visits to local town allowed.

Former pupils Professor R A McCance; Air Chief Marshal Sir Augustus Walker; Rowan Atkinson.

St Benedict's

St Benedict's School	Co-ed	Pupils 460
54 Eaton Rise	• Boys	Upper sixth 80
London W5 2ES	Girls	Termly fees:
Telephone number 01-997 9828	• Mixed sixth	Day £865
	• Day	HMC
Enquiries/application to the Head	Boarding	

WHAT IT'S LIKE

Founded in 1902 by monks from Downside Abbey. The school is attached to the Benedictine Abbey and monastery created in Ealing and is governed by the abbot and the community. An urban site with some gardens. The buildings are mostly 20th century and provide good accommodation and facilities. The playing fields are a mile away; junior school on the same site. The education is Benedictine and inculcates the values and ethos of the order. The study of religion, Catholic and ecumenical, is compulsory. The curriculum includes classics. Academic standards are high and results are impressive (45–50 university entrants per year). Exceptionally strong in music and art. A good record in sports and games. Plentiful clubs and societies. A substantial commitment to local community schemes and a creditable record in the Duke of Edinburgh's Award Scheme.

SCHOOL PROFILE

Pupils Total over 12, 460 (boys 420, girls 40). Entry age, Boys, 11+ and 13+; boys and girls into the sixth. Own junior school provides over 20%.

Entrance Common entrance and own entrance exam used. Oversubscribed. All round and academic skills required. Pupils largely Catholic. Parents expected to buy text books. 80 assisted places. Discretionary scholarships/bursaries.

Parents 60+% live within 30 miles; up to 10% live overseas.

Staff Head A J Dachs, in post for 2 years. 51 full time staff, 10 part time.

Academic work GCSE and A-levels. Average size of upper fifth 85; upper sixth 80. *O-levels*: on average, 7–10 pupils in upper fifth pass 1–4 subjects; 12–15, 5–7 subjects; 62 pass 8+ subjects. *A-levels*: on average, 2 pupils in upper sixth pass 1 subject; 7, 2 subjects; 71, 3 subjects; 4 pass 4 subjects. On average, 28 take science/engineering A-levels; 40 take arts and humanities; 12 take a mixture. *Computing facilities*: club for 13–18, GCSE 14–16. Normal provision for dyslexia, EFL etc.

Senior pupils' non-academic activities *Music*: 240 learn a musical instrument, 7 up to Grade 6 or above; 60 in school orchestra, 60 in school choir, 15 in jazz band. *Drama and dance*: 14 in school productions. 2 accepted for Drama/Dance Schools. *Art*: 235 take art as non-examined subject; 14 take GCSE; 16 take A-level. 1 accepted for Art School. 12 in general class. 28 belong to eg photographic club. *Sport*: Rugby, cricket, squash, golf, swimming, tennis, table tennis, cross-country, and athletics available. 40–50 take non-compulsory sport. 7 represent county (rugby, golf, ski-ing, ice-skating). *Other*: 40 take part in local community schemes. 40 have bronze Duke of Edinburgh's Award, 10 have silver and 1 has gold. 50–60 enter voluntary schemes after leaving school. Other activities include chess and mountaineering.

Careers 2 part time advisors. Average number of pupils accepted for *arts and humanities degree courses* at Oxbridge, 2–3; other universities, 40+; polytechnics or CHE, 20+. *science and engineering degree courses* at Oxbridge, 2–3; medical schools, 4–6. *other general training courses*, a few. Average number of pupils going straight into careers in the church, 1; industry, a few; the City, a few; the civil service, a few; music/drama, 1–2.

Uniform School uniform worn throughout.

Houses/prefects No competitive houses. Prefects and head boy/girl – appointed by the Head.

Religion Catholic services.

Social Debating and other regional competitions. Ski trips, art visits, language trips, and exchanges. Pupils allowed to bring own car/bike/motorbike to school. Meals self service. No tobacco/alcohol allowed.

Discipline No corporal punishment. Pupils failing to produce homework once might expect to have to do it under supervision.

Alumni association is run by Mr E Shuldham, Hon Sec, Old Priorian Association, c/o school.

Former pupils 2 Cabinet Ministers.

ST BRANDON'S

St Brandon's School	Co-ed	Pupils 215
Victoria Road	Boys	Upper sixth 22
Clevedon	• Girls	Termly fees:
Avon BS21 7SD	Mixed sixth	Day £995
Telephone number 0272 872825	• Day	Boarding £1985
	• Boarding	GSA
Enquiries/application to the Headmaster		

WHAT IT'S LIKE

Founded in 1831 at Gloucester and one of the oldest independent schools for girls in England. Later it moved to Bristol and in 1946 to Clevedon. Its original purpose was to provide education for the daughters of Anglican clergy. It still does that as well as taking many others. At Clevedon it has a splendid site of 20 acres of parkland overlooking the Bristol Channel. The main school building is surrounded by well-equipped modern teaching buildings. The junior school is an integral part of the main school. Religious instruction and worship is in accordance with the teaching of the Church of England. A large staff gives a very favourable staff:pupil ratio. Academic standards are good and 15+ girls go on to university each year (quite a high proportion for a school of this size). There is great strength in music and drama (virtually everyone is involved at some time) and a high record of success in public exams in both. A good range of sports and games is provided, and there are plentiful extra-curricular activities. The school has a most impressive record in the Duke of Edinburgh's Award Scheme.

SCHOOL PROFILE

Pupils Total over 12, 215. Day 103; Boarding 112. Entry age, 5+ upwards including into the sixth. Own junior department provides over 40%.

Entrance Common entrance and own exam used. No special skills or religious requirements. Parents not expected to buy text books. Academic and music scholarships up to 66% fees; bursaries for clergy (40–50% means tested) and forces' daughters (5%–10% means tested).

Parents 50+% live within 30 miles; up to 10% live overseas.

Staff Head Mr J S Davey, in post for 10 years. 35 full time staff, 17 part time. Annual turnover 3%. Average age 42.

Academic work GCSE and A-levels, RSA Diploma. Average size of upper fifth 45; upper sixth 22. *O-levels*: on average, 11 pupils in upper fifth pass 1–4 subjects; 18, 5–7 subjects; 16 pass 8+ subjects. *A-levels*: on average, 2 pupils in upper sixth pass 1 subject; 5, 2 subjects; 14, 3 subjects and 1 passes 4 subjects. On average, 8 take science/engineering A-levels; 10 take arts and humanities; 5 a mixture. *Computing facilities*: 1 BBC Master and 1 CBM 64 in science department; BBC Bs in geography and careers departments; 4 Masters and 3 BBC Bs in computer department (2 pets). Dyslexia and EFL provisions.

Senior pupils' non-academic activities *Music*: 200 learn a musical instrument, 3 accepted for Music School; 1 for music at Cambridge; 1 participated in National Young Musician of the Year; 30 in school orchestra; 140 in 3 school choirs; 6, brass group; 2, Avon county orchestra; 2, London Guildhall Chamber orchestra; 1, Weston super Mare orchestra; 1, IAPS orchestra. *Drama and dance*: 200 in school productions; 150, house drama; 100, public speaking competition; 15 take GCSE courses; 4, A/S; 47, LAMDA exams; 150 participate in mid-Somerset festival. *Art*: 25 take GCSE; 6 A-level; 4 accepted for Art School; 10 belong to photography club. *Sport*: Netball, hockey, athletics, rounders, tennis, badminton, squash, riding (local school), golf available. 52 take non-compulsory sport. 2 represent county (under 18 netball). *Other*: 26 have silver Duke of Edinburgh's Award and 15 gold. Other activities include a computer club, chess, community service (home visits to local families), public speaking, Ichthus (Christian Union), badminton club.

Careers 1 full time careers advisor. Average number of pupils accepted for *arts and humanities degree courses* at Oxbridge, 2; other universities, 10; polytechnics or CHE, 5. *science and engineering degree courses* at Oxbridge, 1; other universities, 5; medical schools, 2; polytechnics or CHE, 2. *BEd*, 2. *other general training courses*, 3. Average number of pupils going straight into careers in industry, 2; music/drama, 2.

Uniform School uniform worn except the sixth.

Houses/prefects Competitive houses. Prefects, head girl appointed by Headmaster; head of house and house prefects elected by school. School Council.

Religion Compulsory morning assembly; church attendance for boarders.

Social Discos and competitions with other schools; local music and drama festivals, ski-ing trip, educational cruises and choir tours abroad. Sixth form allowed to bring own car/bike/motorbike to school. Meals formal. School shop. No tobacco/alcohol allowed.

Discipline No corporal punishment. Pupils failing to produce homework once might expect to repeat it in own time; those caught smoking cannabis on the premises might expect instant dismissal.

Boarding 10% have own study bedroom, 20% share with 2 others, 20% are in dormitories of 6+. Houses, of approximately 30–60, divided by age. Resident qualified nurse. Central dining room. Sixth form can provide and cook own food. Weekend exeats. Visits to local town allowed.

Alumni association run by Miss D John, 2 Bushbery, 29 Edghill Road, Clevedon, Avon.

Former pupils Katrina Douglas (ladies' golf champion).

St Catherine's

St Catherine's School
Bramley
Guildford
Surrey GU5 0DF
Telephone number 0483 893363

- Co-ed
  Boys
- Girls
  Mixed sixth
- Day
- Boarding

Pupils 440
Upper sixth Yes
Termly fees:
Day £1050
Boarding £1740
GSA

Head J R Palmer (6 years)
Age range 11–18, own prep from age 5; entry by own exam.
Scholarships and assisted places. Founded under the same charter as Cranleigh.

St Christopher (Letchworth)

St Christopher School
Barrington Road
Letchworth
Hertfordshire SG6 3JZ
Telephone number 0462 679301

- Co-ed
  Boys
  Girls
  Mixed sixth
- Day
- Boarding

Pupils 360
Upper sixth Yes
Termly fees:
Day £1100
Boarding £2000
GBA; BSA

Head Mr Colin Reid (7 years)
Age range 11–18, own junior from age 2; entry by own exam

St Clare's

School of St Clare
Polwithen
Penzance
Cornwall TR18 4JR
Telephone number 0736 63271

Enquiries/application to the Headmaster

Co-ed
Boys
- Girls
  Mixed sixth
- Day
- Boarding

Pupils 135
Upper sixth 10
Termly fees:
Day £845
Boarding £1485
GSA; Woodard

WHAT IT'S LIKE

Founded in 1889, it moved to its present premises in 1918 and passed into the hands of the Woodard Corporation in 1928. It has a fine site in a residential area on the edge of Penzance, overlooking Mount's Bay. The main building is a big converted country house in 10 acres. Numerous modern extensions and facilities, including comfortable boarding accommodation. Junior school combined. Chapel and daily services play an important part in the school's life. It is a small, happy school with a healthy environment. Students come to it from all over the UK and the world. A sound general education is given and a number of leavers go on to university. Strong drama and music departments. A range of games and activities. Emphasis on outdoor pursuits. A fair record in the Duke of Edinburgh's Award Scheme.

SCHOOL PROFILE

Pupils Total over 12, 135. Day 85; Boarding 50. Entry age, 3+ and into the sixth. Own junior school provides over 20%. 10% are children of former pupils.

Entrance Own entrance exam used. Oversubscribed. No special skills or religious requirements. Parents not expected to buy text books. No assisted places. 4–5 academic and music scholarships; clergy bursaries; reduction for service families; value up to 50% of fees.

Parents 15+% are farmers; 15+% in the armed services; 15+% in industry or commerce. 60+% live within 30 miles, up to 10% live overseas.

Staff Head Ian Halford, in post for 2 years. 16 full time staff, 22 part time (including music). Average age 40.

Academic work Pupils prepared for GCSE and A-levels. Average size of upper fifth 25; upper sixth 10. *O-levels*: on average, 4 pupils in upper fifth pass 1–4 subjects; 15, 5–7 subjects; 6 pass 8+ subjects. *A-levels*: on average, 5 pupils in the upper sixth pass 2 subjects and 5 pass 3 subjects. On average, 6 take arts and humanities A-levels; 4 a mixture of arts and science. *Computing facilities*: 7 BBC computers. Provision for pupils who are eg dyslexic, mildly visually handicapped, and EFL.

Senior pupils' non-academic activities *Music*: Many learn a musical instrument, 4 to Grade 6 or above, 20 in school orchestras; many in 3 school choirs; 4 in county youth orchestra. *Drama and dance*: Many in school productions. *Art*: 17 take GCSE; 4 A-level. *Sport*: Hockey, netball, football, gymnastics, trampolining, cricket, tennis, athletics, swimming, judo, sailing available. Many take non-compulsory sport. 2 pupils have represented county. *Other*: Some take part in local community schemes. 15 have bronze Duke of Edinburgh's Award, 4 have silver, 1 has gold. Other activities include archery, chess, judo.

Careers 2 part time careers advisors. Average number of pupils accepted for *arts and humanities degree courses* at universities, 3; polytechnics or CHE, 3.

Uniform School uniform worn except the sixth.

Houses/prefects Competitive houses. Prefects, head girl, head of house and house prefects – appointed by the head/staff and houses. School Council.

Religion Worship compulsory.

Social No organised local events. Organised trips abroad. Pupils allowed to bring own bike to school. Meals formal. School shop. No tobacco/alcohol allowed.

Discipline No corporal punishment. Pupils failing to produce homework once might expect detention; those caught smoking or drinking on the premises could expect a severe penalty.

Boarding Sixth form have own study bedroom, 70% share; 20% in dormitories of 6, not in houses. Matrons are medically trained, GP on call. Central dining room. 2 or 3 weekend exeats each term. Visits to local town allowed.

Alumni association run by Headmaster.

St Columba's (Dublin)

College of St Columba
Rathfarnham
Dublin 16
Eire
Telephone number 0001 906791

- Co-ed   Pupils 325
- Boys   Upper sixth Yes
- Girls   Termly fees:
- Mixed sixth Apply to school
- Day   HMC
- Boarding

Head (Warden) D S Gibbs
Age range 11–18; entry by own exam or common entrance.
Scholarships and bursaries.

St Columba's (Kilmacolm)

St Columba's School
Duchal Road
Kilmacolm
Renfrewshire
Telephone number 05058 2238

Enquiries/application to the Rector

- Co-ed   Pupils 300
- Boys   Upper sixth 30
- Girls   Termly fees:
- Mixed sixth Day £760
- Day
- Boarding

WHAT IT'S LIKE

Founded in 1897, its site is in the small village of Kilmacolm. The primary and secondary buildings are about a quarter of a mile apart. The surrounding countryside is delightful. The main building was erected in 1897 and there have been many extensions since. Facilities and accommodation are now very good. It became fully co-educational in 1978. Some religious services are compulsory. A sound general education is provided and results are highly creditable. About 15–20 leavers go on to university each year. There is adequate music, drama and art, and a fair range of games, sports and extra-curricular activities. The school has a promising record in the Duke of Edinburgh's Award Scheme.

SCHOOL PROFILE

Pupils Total over 12, 300 (boys 110, girls 190). Entry age, 5. Own junior school provides over 80%. 20% are children of former pupils.

Entrance Own entrance exam used. Oversubscribed. No special skills or religious requirements. Parents not expected to buy text books. 40 assisted places.

Parents 15+% are in industry or commerce. 90+% live within 30 miles.

Staff Head Andrew H Livingstone, in post for 1 year. 43 full time staff, 7 part time. Annual turnover 2%. Average age 44.

Academic work O-grade and Highers, A-level, CSYS. Average size of upper fifth 42; upper sixth 30. *O-grade*: on average, 5 pupils in upper fifth pass 1–4 subjects; 22, 5–7 subjects; 15 pass 8+ subjects. *A-levels*: on average, 2 pupils in upper sixth pass 1 subject; 6, 2 subjects; 7, 3 subjects and 15 pass 4 subjects. *Computing facilities*: New computer laboratory, complete by December 1988.

Senior pupils' non-academic activities *Music*: 15 learn a musical instrument, 3 to Grade 6 or above, 1 accepted for Music School; 15 in school orchestra, 30 in choir. *Drama and dance*: 20 in school productions. 2 take Grade 6 in ESB, RAD etc. 1 accepted for Drama/Dance School. *Art*: 10 take GCSE; 2 A-level; 6 Higher. 2 accepted for Art School. *Sport*: Rugby, hockey, tennis, lacrosse, swimming, badminton, cricket, athletics available. 40 take non-compulsory sport. *Other*: 15 have bronze Duke of Edinburgh's Award, 6 have silver.

Careers 1 part time advisor. Average number of pupils accepted for *arts and humanities degree courses* at universities, 5. *science and engineering degree courses* at Oxbridge, 1; other universities, 12; medical schools, 3; polytechnics or CHE, 3. *BEd*, 1. *other general training courses*, 2.

Uniform School uniform worn throughout.

Houses/prefects Competitive houses. Prefects, head boy/girl, head of house and house prefects – elected by fifth and sixth forms.

Religion Compulsory morning prayers 3 times a week.

Social Burns' Supper with neighbouring school. Organised trips to Paris; ski-ing; annual sixth form trip (last year to Russia). Meals self service. School tuck shop. No tobacco/alcohol allowed.

Discipline No corporal punishment. Pupils failing to produce homework once might expect additional work; those caught smoking cannabis on the premises could expect to be excluded.

St Columba's (St Albans)

St Columba's College	Co-ed Pupils 560
King Harry Lane	● Boys Upper sixth Yes
St Albans	Girls Termly fees:
Hertfordshire AL3 4AW	Mixed sixth Day £520
Telephone number 0727 55185	● Day
	Boarding

Head Br Clement (8 years)

Age range 11–18; own prep from age 7; entry by own exam.

4 open scholarships and 8 Columban scholarships (open to RCs only).

St David's

St David's School
Church Road
Ashford
Middlesex TW15 3DZ
Telephone number 07842 52494

Co-ed
Boys
● Girls
Mixed sixth
● Day
● Boarding

Pupils 250
Upper sixth Yes
Termly fees:
Day £870
Boarding £1500
AHIS; GSA;
GBGSA

Head Mrs Judith G Osborne (3 years)
Age range 5–18; entry by own exam or common entrance.

St Denis and Cranley

St Denis and Cranley School
3 Ettrick Road
Edinburgh EH10 5BJ
Telephone number 031 229 1500

Enquiries/application to the Headmistress

Co-ed
Boys
● Girls
Mixed sixth
● Day
● Boarding

Pupils 180
Upper sixth 24
Termly fees:
Day £770
Boarding £1530
GSA

WHAT IT'S LIKE

The school is a result of an amalgamation in 1979. St Denis was founded in 1855. For the first few years it was known by the name of each headmistress until the appointment, in 1908, of Miss Bourdass, a member of the staff of La Maison d'Education de la Légion d'Honneur, a school founded by Napoleon in the Paris suburb of St Denis. Cranley was founded in 1871 as Brunstane School in the Edinburgh suburb of Joppa. The present school is sited in a pleasant, residential district of Edinburgh. All buildings are on one site forming, with four boarding houses, a compact campus with fine lawns, trees, gardens and playing fields. It is quiet and spacious and well-equipped. As it is a very small school it enjoys a happy, friendly and family atmosphere. The staff:pupil ratio is 1:10. A sound general education is provided and results are good. About 10–15 pupils go on to university each year (quite a high proportion for a small school). There is quite a big commitment to music, drama and art. There is a good range of sports and games and a plentiful variety of extra-curricular activities. Quite a substantial commitment to local community services and an impressive record in the Duke of Edinburgh's Award Scheme.

SCHOOL PROFILE

Pupils Total over 12, 180. Day 80; Boarding 100. Entry age, 5–12 day, 8–12 boarding and into the sixth. Own junior department provides over 20%. 8% are children of former pupils.
Entrance Own entrance exam used. Not oversubscribed. No special skills or religious requirements but pupils are expected to participate in morning

assembly and RE classes. Parents not expected to buy text books. 15 assisted places. 4 scholarships pa including art and music, £400–£200 per term.

Parents 15+% in armed services; 15+% are doctors, lawyers etc; 15% in industry or commerce. 30+% live within 30 miles; 10+% live overseas.

Staff Head Mrs Jennifer M Munro, in post for 3 years. 18 full time staff, 7 part time plus music staff. Annual turnover 2%. Average age 44.

Academic work O-grades, Highers, CSYS and A-levels. Average size of fourth year 32; fifth year 24. *O-grades*: on average, 5 pupils in fourth year pass 1–4 subjects; 27 pass 5–7 subjects. *Highers*: on average, 3 pupils in fifth year pass 2 subjects; 9, 3–4 subjects; 9, 5 subjects and 3 pass 6 subjects. On average, 9 take science/engineering Highers; 5 take arts and humanities; 14 a mixture. Chinese and Swedish offered to exam level with university help. *Computing facilities*: 2 Apple and 5 BBC for pupil use. Provision for mildly dyslexic, remedial and EFL.

Senior pupils' non-academic activities *Music*: 30 learn a musical instrument, 4 to Grade 6 or above, 1 accepted for Music School. 15 in school orchestra, 20 in choir. *Drama and dance*: 20–30 in school productions, 3 up to Grade 6 ESB, RAD etc, 1 accepted for Drama School, 1 in Scottish Youth Theatre. *Art*: All take as non-examined subject; 16 O-grade; 3 A-level; 8 Higher; 1 accepted for Art School. 8 belong to photographic club, 12 art and craft club. *Sport*: Hockey, tennis, squash, badminton, athletics, trampolining, basketball, volleyball, swimming available. 50 take non-compulsory sport; 10 life-saving exams. 1 pupil represents county/country (ski-ing, hockey, squash). *Other*: 10 take part in local community schemes. 12 have bronze Duke of Edinburgh's Award, 6 have silver and 3 gold. 5 Ranger guides. 2 enter voluntary schemes after leaving; 20 work for national charities. Other activities include a computer club, pre-driving class, driving lessons arranged, chess, Scripture Union, geographical society, local Guide companies and Brownie packs, school community services club.

Careers 2 part time careers advisors. Average number of pupils accepted for *arts and humanities degree courses* at Oxbridge, 1; other universities, 4; polytechnics or CHE, 4. *science and engineering degree courses* at universities, 8; medical school, 1; polytechnics or CHE, 3. *other general training courses*, 8. Average number of pupils going straight into careers in armed services, 1 in three years; the church, 1 in three years; music/drama, 1. Traditional school careers are medicine, nursing and para-medicine.

Uniform School uniform worn throughout except sixth form in summer term.

Houses/prefects Competitive houses. Prefects, head girl and head of house – elected by peers, staff and Head. School Council.

Religion Compulsory morning assembly although Hindus, Muslims etc may opt out.

Social English Speaking Union debates, sporting fixtures, occasional joint production, combined careers talks, Geographical Association etc with other schools. Trips to Germany, France; visiting schools from USA, New Zealand, Austria. Meals formal. School shop twice-weekly. No tobacco/alcohol allowed.

Discipline No corporal punishment. Pupils failing to produce homework once might expect a warning; circumstances to be considered for those caught smoking cannabis on the premises.

Boarding 4% have own study bedroom. Houses, of 35 and 15 divided by age.

Day time nurse, usually one medically-trained house staff member. Central dining room. Sixth form boarders have own kitchen. 3 weekend exeats plus mid-term. Visits to local town allowed.

Alumni association run by The Secretary, St Denis & Cranley Association, c/o the School.

Former pupils Hannah Gordon, actress.

St Dominic's (Brewood)

St Dominic's School
32 Bargate Street
Brewood
Stafford ST19 9BA
Telephone number 0902 850248

Enquiries/application to Mrs L M Wilson – Secretary

Co-ed
Boys
● Girls
Mixed sixth
● Day
Boarding

Pupils 333
Upper sixth 25
Termly fees:
Day £669

WHAT IT'S LIKE

Founded in 1920 by the English Dominican Sisters and administered by them until 1975 when a board of directors took over the organisation. In 1984 the board bought the school from the Dominican order. It has a 9-acre site in the very attractive village of Brewood and its buildings, accommodation and facilities are very good. A sound general education is given, based on the Christian ethos. Academic results are good, particularly in science, and most sixth form leavers go on to degree courses. Very strong indeed in music and drama. A fair range of sport, games and activities. Successful participation in the Duke of Edinburgh's Award Scheme.

SCHOOL PROFILE

Pupils Total over 12, 333. Entry age, 4, 11 and into sixth. Own prep school provides over 50%. 25% are children of former pupils.

Entrance Own entrance exam used. Oversubscribed. No special skills or religious requirements. Parents not expected to buy text books. 10 scholarships/bursaries for sixth form, £450–£100 per term.

Parents 15+% in industry or commerce; 15+% are doctors, lawyers, etc. 60+% live within 30 miles.

Staff Head Sister Helen Weston. 30 full time staff, 7 part time. Annual turnover 10%. Average age 30.

Academic work GCSE and A-levels. Average size of upper fifth 60; upper sixth 25. *O-levels*: on average, 10 pupils in upper fifth pass 1–4 subjects; 12, 5–7 subjects; 38 pass 8+ subjects. *A-levels*: on average, 3 pupils in upper sixth pass 1 subject; 8, 2 subjects; 3, 3 subjects and 6 pass 4 subjects. On average, 15 take science/engineering A-levels; 6 take arts and humanities; 4 a mixture. *Computing facilities*: 20 microcomputers. *Special provisions*: Individual tuition available.

Senior pupils' non-academic activities *Music*: 80 learn a musical instrument, 6 to Grade 6 or above; 20 in school orchestra, 60 in school choir,

40 in folk group; 1 in National Youth Orchestra, 3 in local amateur orchestra. *Drama and dance*: 20 in school productions, 22 take GCSE drama, 120 in speech and drama class; 4 up to Grade 6 in ESB, RAD and Guildhall, 1 has ESB advanced certificate, 74 have private speech and drama study. 100 enter local festivals. 1 has gone on to holiday puppet theatre. *Art*: 26 take GCSE/O-level; 4 take A-level. *Sport*: Hockey, netball, gymnastics, table tennis, badminton available. 150 take non-compulsory sport. 20–30 take exams, eg gymnastics, swimming. 6–7 represent county (golf, tennis, swimming, horse riding). *Other*: 17 have bronze Duke of Edinburgh's Award and 6 have silver.

Careers 1 full time advisor. Average number of pupils accepted for *arts and humanities degree courses* at Oxbridge, 2; other universities, 10; polytechnics or CHE, 6. *science and engineering degree courses* at universities, 3; medical schools, 2; polytechnics or CHE, 4. *BEd*, 2. *other general training courses*, 40. Average number of pupils going straight into careers in industry, 30; civil service, 5; music/drama, 5.

Uniform School uniform worn throughout.

Houses/prefects Competitive houses. Prefects, head girl and head of house – elected by the school.

Religion Assembly compulsory. Optional mass and prayer groups.

Social Trips to France and Austria. Sixth form pupils allowed to bring own car to school. Meals formal. School tuck shop. No tobacco/alcohol allowed.

Discipline No corporal punishment. Pupils failing to produce homework once might expect detention in order to complete work on time; unethical conduct merits expulsion – no one has ever smoked.

Alumni association is run by Mr J D Walters, c/o the School.

St Dominic's Priory

St Dominic's Priory School
Station Road
Stone
Staffordshire ST15 8EN
Telephone number 0785 814181

Enquiries/application to the Secretary

Co-ed
Boys
• Girls
Mixed sixth
• Day
Boarding

Pupils 250
Upper sixth 15
Termly fees:
Day £500

WHAT IT'S LIKE

Founded in 1934 and conducted by the English Dominican Sisters, a Roman Catholic religious order. It has an agreeable urban site with gardens and well-appointed buildings. There are two main buildings: the senior school and the Croft (juniors), plus the nearby Croftside (nursery). The moral and religious training of the pupils has a high priority. There is a good deal of emphasis on religious instruction, prayer and worship. All pupils take religious studies at GCSE level. Preference is given to RCs but other denominations are welcome. The staff:pupil ratio is 1:21. A sound general education is provided and results are creditable. Ten or more pupils proceed to university each year. There is some music, and drama productions in the third year. An adequate range of sports and games and some extra-curricular activities. Some commitment to local community services and a promising record in the Duke of Edinburgh's Award Scheme. Fees are astonishingly low.

SCHOOL PROFILE

Pupils Total over 12, 250. Entry age, 4 upwards including into the sixth. Own junior departments provide over 20% of pupils. 10% are children of former pupils.

Entrance Own entrance exam used. Oversubscribed. No special skills; preference given to RCs. Parents expected to buy text books. 2 scholarships/bursaries pa, value according to need.

Parents 15+% are doctors, lawyers etc; 15+% in industry or commerce. 60+% live within 30 miles.

Staff Head Sister Mary Henry, in post for 1 year. 24 full time staff, 23 part time. Annual turnover, 2%.

Academic work GCSE and A-levels. Average size of upper fifth, 52; upper sixth, 15. *O-levels*: on average, 14 pupils in upper fifth pass 1–4 subjects; 16, 5–7 subjects; 20 pass 8+ subjects. *A-levels*: on average, 2 pupils in upper sixth pass 1 subject; 2, 2 subjects; 3, 3 subjects and 4 pass 4 subjects. On average, 3 take science/engineering A-levels; 6 take arts and humanities; 6 a mixture. Italian offered to GCSE/A-level. *Computing facilities*: Nimbus network. *Special provision*: school is close to Dyslexia Institute, to which dyslexic pupils go weekly.

Senior pupils' non-academic activities *Music*: 18 learn a musical instrument, 5 to Grade 6 or above, 1 accepted for Music School, 6 in school orchestra; 9, choir; 6, madrigal group. *Drama and dance*: Drama productions in 3rd year; Silver Award for speech and drama. *Art*: 30 take GCSE, some take A-level Textiles and go on to career in textiles, 10 accepted for Art School. *Sport*: Swimming, riding, netball, tennis, dancing, badminton, weight training, squash available. 69 take non-compulsory sport. 4 represent county (tennis, netball). *Other*: 8 take part in local community schemes. 36 have bronze Duke of Edinburgh's Award and 4 gold. Other activities include a computer club, chess club and recorder group.

Careers 2 part time careers advisors. Average number of pupils accepted for *arts and humanities degree courses* at universities, 6. *science and engineering degree courses* at universities, 4. *other general training courses*, 10. Average number of pupils going straight into careers in civil service, 4; music/drama, 2; other, 6.

Uniform School uniform worn throughout.

Houses/prefects Competitive houses. Prefects, head girl, head of house and house prefects elected by staff. School Council being set up.

Religion Compulsory morning assembly; occasional mass.

Social Organised ski-ing, French language and Italian trips abroad. Meals self service. No tobacco/alcohol allowed.

Discipline No corporal punishment. Pupils failing to produce homework once might expect extra work in lunch hour.

Alumni association run by Miss Caroline Handforth, Coppice Farmhouse, Longton Road, Stone, Staffordshire.

Former pupils Lord Stafford; Hilaire Belloc's daughters; Hilary Pepler's grandchildren.

St Dunstan's Abbey

St Dunstan's Abbey
North Road West
Plymouth
Devon PL1 5DH
Telephone number 0752 663998

Enquiries/application to the Headmistress

Co-ed — Pupils 200
Boys — Upper sixth 20
● Girls — Termly fees:
Mixed sixth — Day £775
● Day — Boarding £1305
● Boarding — GSA

WHAT IT'S LIKE

Founded in 1867, it is single-site in the centre of the town. Its fine Victorian buildings were designed by William Butterfield. There has been an extensive programme of restoration and many modern facilities have been created. Religious worship is encouraged. Academic standards are high and there is an impressive pass rate in public exams. Twelve or more leavers go on to university each year. A very strong art department; considerable strength in music and drama. Some commitment to local community schemes and the Duke of Edinburgh's Award Scheme.

SCHOOL PROFILE

Pupils Total over 12, 200. Day 180; Boarding (weekly) 20. Entry age, 5–11 and into the sixth (and where there are vacancies). Own prep school provides over 20%. 5% are children of former pupils.

Entrance Own entrance exam used. Oversubscribed in some areas. No special skills or religious requirements. Parents not expected to buy text books. 7 scholarships, ⅓–full fees.

Parents 15+% in industry or commerce; 15+% are doctors, lawyers, etc; 15+% in the armed services. 60+% live within 30 miles.

Staff Head Miss H L Abley, in post for 17.5 years. 25 full time staff, 17 part time. Annual turnover 3%. Average age 40.

Academic work GCSE and A-levels. Average size of upper fifth 42; upper sixth 20. *O-levels*: on average, 82% of pupils in upper fifth pass 8+ subjects. *A-levels*: on average, 92% pupils in upper sixth pass 3 subjects. Most take a mixture of science/engineering and arts and humanities A-levels. *Computing facilities*: 8 BBC computers. *Special provisions*: Pupils with disabilities and foreign students accepted.

Senior pupils' non-academic activities *Music*: 26% learn a musical instrument, 4 to Grade 6 or above, 20 in school orchestra, 50 in school choir. *Drama and dance*: 80% in school productions. *Art*: All pupils take art as non-examined subject until third year; 16 take GCSE; 5 take A-level; 3 accepted for Art School. *Sport*: Netball, hockey, gymnastics, tennis, athletics (badminton, squash, swimming – local sports centre) available. Various school teams take non-compulsory sport. 40 pupils per year take exams, eg gymnastics, swimming. 12 represent county (netball, hockey). *Other*: Girls take part in local community schemes, Duke of Edinburgh's Award Scheme and voluntary schemes after leaving school. Other activities include a computer club and Ten Tors.

Careers 1 full time advisor. Average number of pupils accepted for *arts and humanities degree courses* at universities, 2; polytechnics or CHE, 3. *science* *and engineering degree courses* at Oxbridge, 1; other universities, 1; medical schools, 1; polytechnics or CHE, 3. *other general training courses*, 1. Average number of pupils going straight into careers in the armed services, 1; industry, 1; the City, 1; music/drama, 1.

Uniform School uniform worn, modified in sixth.

Houses/prefects Competitive houses. Prefects, head girl, head of house and house prefects – appointed by the head and elected by the school.

Religion Religious worship encouraged but not compulsory. One compulsory lesson a week up to sixth form.

Social No organised events with local schools. Some organised trips abroad. Meals formal. No tobacco/alcohol allowed.

Discipline No corporal punishment. Pupils failing to produce homework once might expect warning/de-merit mark; those caught smoking cannabis on the premises could expect expulsion.

Boarding 3 have own study bedroom, 11 share with up to 3 others; 20 are in dormitories of 6 or more. Central dining room. Visits to local town allowed (in sixth).

Former pupils Dawn French.

St Dunstan's College

St Dunstan's College
Stanstead Road
Catford
London SE6 4TY
Telephone number 01-690 1274

Enquiries/application to the Admissions Secretary

Co-ed
● Boys
Girls
Mixed sixth
● Day
Boarding

Pupils 680
Upper sixth 75
Termly fees:
Day £940
HMC

WHAT IT'S LIKE

Founded in 1888, it is urban and single-site and has big playing fields on site. Many additions have been made to the original and striking Victorian building and modern facilities are first rate. Preparatory and junior school combined. The main emphasis in the school is on the need to develop the all-round qualities of a pupil in and out of the classroom. There is much stress on individual pastoral care and close links between home and school. The academic standards are high and results are good. A big sixth form. Some 35–40 leavers go to university each year. There is a very strong music department (musicians are especially welcome); quite strong drama and art. A good range of sport and games, with high standards (quite a lot of representatives at county level). A big CCF contingent and a very substantial commitment to local community schemes.

SCHOOL PROFILE

Pupils Total over 12, 680. Entry age, 7+, 11+ and into the sixth. Own prep school provides over 20%. 5% are children of former pupils.

Entrance Own entrance exam used and occasionally common entrance.

Oversubscribed. Musicians and genuine all-rounders especially welcome. No religious requirements. Parents not expected to buy text books. 160 assisted places. 12 scholarships/bursaries, full fees to ⅙ fees.

Parents 15+% in industry or commerce; 15+% are doctors, lawyers, etc. 60+% live within 30 miles.

Staff Head B D Dance, in post for 14 years. 60 full time staff, 6 part time. Annual turnover 5–6%. Average age 40.

Academic work GCSE and A-levels. Average size of upper fifth 95; upper sixth 75. *O-levels*: on average, 24 pupils in upper fifth pass 1–4 subjects; 29, 5–7 subjects; 41 pass 8+ subjects. *A-levels*: on average, 7 pupils in upper sixth pass 1 subject; 12, 2 subjects; 44, 3 subjects and 3 pass 4 subjects. On average, 27 take science/engineering A-levels; 31 take arts and humanities; 20 a mixture. Engineering science (as well as a separate course in physics), electronic systems are offered to GCSE/A-level. *Computing facilities*: Fully equipped computer room. Additional facilities for mathematics, physics, biology, geography.

Senior pupils' non-academic activities *Music*: 95 learn a musical instrument, 14 to Grade 6 or above, 1 accepted for Music College and 1 to university music course, 60 in school orchestra(s), 22 in school choir, 30 in wind band, 20 in chamber groups; 12 in Bromley Schools Orchestra and bands. *Drama and dance*: 30 in school productions, 15 in other productions. *Art*: 44 take GCSE; 7 take A-level; 3 accepted for Art School. *Sport*: Rugby football, cricket, swimming, water polo, athletics, basketball, rugby fives, golf, judo, sailing, tennis, shooting, squash available. Sport is compulsory. Award schemes occasionally. ASA and BAGA. 9 pupils represent county (rugby, cricket, swimming, water polo). *Other*: 84 take part in local community schemes. 8 have silver Duke of Edinburgh's Award. Other activities include a computer club, chess, bridge, Go, debating, science society, Christian Union, electronics workshop, radio, first aid (St John Ambulance), combined cadet force (army and navy) and community service groups.

Careers 2 part time advisors. Average number of pupils accepted for *arts and humanities degree courses* at Oxbridge, 5; other universities, 14; polytechnics or CHE, 8. *science and engineering degree courses* at Oxbridge, 3; other universities, 13; medical schools, 4; polytechnics or CHE, 7. Average number of pupils going straight into careers in the armed services, 2–3; industry, 2; the City, 8; music/drama, 1; other, 15. Traditional school careers are medicine, law and various forms of engineering.

Uniform School uniform worn throughout.

Houses/prefects Competitive houses. Prefects, head boy, head of house and house prefects – appointed by the Head after consultation with staff and prefects. Separate councils for middle school and sixth form.

Religion Religious worship compulsory subject to parental right to withdraw.

Social Close links for music, drama, debating, films with Bromley High School (GPDST). Visits to USA, Canada, Rumania, Russia, France, Germany and Italy have taken place. Pupils allowed to bring own bicycle/motorbike to school. Meals self service. School shop. No tobacco allowed. Wine at sixth form tutorial dinners (formal).

Discipline No corporal punishment. Pupils failing to produce homework once might expect work to be repeated, usually under supervision; those caught smoking cannabis on the premises could expect severe warning, attempt to discover source of supply, inform parents. Place boy on probation, ie a repeated offence would lead to expulsion.

Alumni association is run by Mr C L Watts, 26 Church Avenue, Beckenham, Kent.

Former pupils Prof Andrade (ex Brains Trust); Dr Walter Hamilton (former master of Magdalene College, Cambridge); Hubert Gregg (broadcaster); Michael Grade (Channel 4).

ST EDMUND'S COLLEGE

St Edmund's College	• Co-ed	Pupils 243
Old Hall Green	Boys	Upper sixth 70
Nr Ware	Girls	Termly fees:
Hertfordshire SG11 1DS	Mixed sixth	Day £1116
Telephone number 0920 821504	• Day	Boarding £1733
	• Boarding	HMC
Enquiries/application to the Headmaster		

WHAT IT'S LIKE

Founded in 1568 at Douai, Flanders, originally as a seminary. When the college was closed in 1793 during 'The Terror' the refugees fled to England and joined the Old Hall Green Academy (a school refounded in 1769) which was renamed St Edmund's College in that year. It has imposing buildings in big grounds on a fine open site near the town. St Hugh's prep school and a junior house are combined. Continuous education is thus available on one site. Numerous modern facilities include comfortable accommodation for boarders. Its prime aim is to provide the setting and the guidance to enable pupils to develop a mature Roman Catholic faith and practice. Attendance at Mass etc is compulsory. Religious instruction is an important part of the curriculum. A sound general education is given and results are good. Some 40–45 leavers go on to university each year. A strong music department, strongish art and drama. Considerable emphasis on sport and games (especially rugby) and a lot of representatives at county level. A big commitment to local community services and the Duke of Edinburgh's Award Scheme.

SCHOOL PROFILE

Pupils Total over 12, 243. Day 172 (boys 120, girls 52); Boarding 71 (boys 57, girls 14). Entry age, 7, 11, 13 and into the sixth. Own prep school provides 20+%. About 10% are children of former pupils.

Entrance Common entrance and own entrance exam used. Oversubscribed. No special skills or religious requirements but school is 80% Roman Catholic. Parents not expected to buy text books. 55 assisted places. 10 scholarships/bursaries, half to one third of fees.

Parents 15+% in the armed services; 15+% are doctors, lawyers, etc; 15+% in industry or commerce. 60+% live within 30 miles; 30+% live overseas.

Staff Head D J J McEwen, in post for 4 years. 51 full time staff, 7 part time. Annual turnover 2–3%. Average age 37.

Academic work GCSE and A-levels. Average size of upper fifth 80; upper sixth 70. *O-levels*: on average, 20 pupils in upper fifth pass 1–4 subjects; 20, 5–7 subjects; 30 pass 8+ subjects. *A-levels*: on average, 7 pupils in upper sixth pass 1 subject; 7, 2 subjects; 52, 3 subjects and 4 pass 4 subjects. On average, 50% take science/engineering A-levels; 50% take arts and humanities. *Computing facilities*: taught subject – about 35 computers. *Special provision*: very few mildly dyslexic children catered for.

Senior pupils' non-academic activities *Music*: 44 learn a musical instrument, 11 to Grade 6 or above. 1 accepted for Music School. 25 play in school orchestra, 24 in school choir; 2 play in Hertford Orchestra, 3 do diploma work. *Drama and dance*: 10+ in school productions. *Art*: 10 take as non-examined subject; 40 take GCSE art; 8, A-level. 2 accepted for Art School. 10 belong to photographic club, 10 pottery. *Sport*: Rugby, cricket, swimming, athletics, tennis, hockey, netball, squash available. 150+ take non-compulsory sport. 23 represent county/country (rugby, swimming). *Other*: 20 take part in local community schemes. 18 have bronze Duke of Edinburgh's Award, 10 have silver and 6 gold. 20 do community service. Some enter voluntary schemes after leaving school. Other activities include a computer club, driving, CCF, rifle range, horse riding, model railway, car club.

Careers 1 full time and 1 part time advisor (plus Deputy Head and House Masters and Mistresses). Average number of pupils accepted for *arts and humanities degree courses* at Oxbridge, 2; other universities, 20; polytechnics or CHE, 10. *science and engineering degree courses* at Oxbridge, 2; other universities, 20; medical schools, 5; polytechnics or CHE, 10. *BEd*, 4. *other general training courses*, 2. Average number of pupils going straight into careers in the armed services, 2; industry, 7; the City, 3; music/drama, 1. Traditional school career, medicine.

Uniform School uniform worn throughout.

Houses/prefects Competitive houses. Prefects, head boy/girl, head of house and house prefects.

Religion Compulsory religious worship.

Social Socials, sixth form conferences, careers conventions with local schools. Organised trips to France. Pupils allowed to bring own bike to school. Meals self service. School shop. Wine served at socials; otherwise no alcohol or tobacco.

Discipline No corporal punishment. Pupils failing to produce homework once might expect detention; those caught smoking cannabis on the premises could expect to be asked to withdraw.

Boarding 35% have own study bedroom, 65% share with one other. Houses, of approximately 60, same as competitive houses, single sex. Resident qualified medical staff. Central dining room. 2 weekend exeats each term. Visits to local town allowed.

Former pupils Ronald Knox; Bruce Kent.

St Edmund's (Canterbury)

St Edmund's School
St Thomas' Hill
Canterbury
Kent CT2 8HU
Telephone number 0227 454575

- Co-ed   Pupils 286
- Boys   Upper sixth Yes
- Girls   Termly fees:
- Mixed sixth   Day £1369
- Day   Boarding £1999
- Boarding   HMC; GBA

Head J V Tyson (9 years)
Age range 13–18; entry by own exam or common entrance.
Some scholarships and bursaries.

St Edward's (Cheltenham)

St Edward's School
Ashley Road
Charlton Kings
Cheltenham GL52 6NT
Telephone number 0242 526697

Enquiries/application to the Admissions
Secretary

- Co-ed   Pupils 622
- Boys   Upper sixth 45
- Girls   Termly fees:
- Mixed sixth   Day £820
- Day   ISA
- Boarding

WHAT IT'S LIKE

Formed in 1987 by amalgamating Cheltenham's two independent Catholic schools – Charlton Park and Whitefriars – which had existed for some 25 years. The new school is on 3 large sites in the outskirts of the town. The first or nursery school occupies Charlton Park junior school on the London Road. The middle school is at Ashley Manor (formerly Whitefriars School) and the senior school is located in the buildings of Charlton Park School on the Cirencester Road. All are well-equipped and have fine gardens and playing fields. All three constitute a Roman Catholic foundation run by the Carmelite Order. Christian faith is central to the school, not just as a subject but as a way of living. There is much emphasis on religious education and worship; prayers, Mass etc are compulsory. The school is open to pupils of all denominations who wish to avail themselves of a Christian education. Academic standards have been (and remain) high. Results have been good and each year 15–20 pupils have gone on to university. There is considerable strength in music, drama and art. A very good range of sports and games in which high standards are attained (a lot of representatives at county and national level). A fair variety of extra-curricular activities is available. Local community services are to be established.

SCHOOL PROFILE

Pupils Total over 12, 622. (Boys 203, girls 419.) Entry age, 4–14 and into the sixth. Own junior school provides over 20%. Less than 5% are children of former pupils.
Entrance Common entrance and own entrance exam used. Not oversub-

scribed. No special skills or religious requirements but pupils expected to attend RC services. Parents not expected to buy text books. No assisted places yet. 11 scholarships/bursaries pa, £250–£200 per term.

Parents 15+% are in industry or commerce. 60% live within 30 miles.

Staff Head Father Richard Copsey, O Carm, in post for 1 year. 70 full time staff, 15 part time. Annual turnover 4–7%. Average age 43.

Academic work GCSE and A-levels. Average size of upper fifth 140; upper sixth 45. *O-levels*: on average, 56 pupils in upper fifth pass 1–4 subjects; 34, 5–7 subjects; 39 pass 8+ subjects. *A-levels*: on average, 7 pupils in upper sixth pass 1 subject; 19, 2 subjects; 28, 3 subjects and 2 pass 4 subjects. On average, 14 take science/engineering A-levels; 35 take arts and humanities; 5 a mixture. Computer science, theatre studies, Latin offered to GCSE and A-level. *Computing facilities*: 4 BBC (first school), 12 BBC (middle school), 12 BBC, 8 Amstrad, 2 RML and assorted others (senior school). Remedial help available.

Senior pupils' non-academic activities *Music*: 55 learn a musical instrument, 24 to Grade 6 or above, 1 accepted for Music School. 30 in school orchestra, 40 in choir, 15 in madrigal and 9 flute groups, 4 in County Youth Orchestra. 3 go on to play in pop group; 20 to choirs and orchestras. *Drama and dance*: 20–100 in school productions. 12 take up to Grade 6 in ESB, RAD etc, 1 accepted for Drama School. *Art*: 6 take as non-examined subject; 65 GCSE; 9 A-level, 2 accepted for Art School. 35 belong to photographic club. *Sport*: Hockey, rugby, netball, 5-a-side football, badminton, squash, table tennis, swimming, volleyball, tennis, cricket, athletics, rounders, gymnastics, aerobics available. 100 take non-compulsory sport (teams and clubs), 5–8 take exams. 20 represent county (rugby, cross-country, athletics, badminton, squash, swimming); 6, ATC division (cross-country, rugby). *Other*: Other activities include a computer club, clubs for chess, wildlife (with nature reserve), astronomy, debating society; Duke of Edinburgh's Award scheme to be restarted soon.

Careers 5 part time careers advisors. Average number of pupils accepted for *arts and humanities degree courses* at Oxbridge, 2; other universities, 11; polytechnics or CHE, 6. *science and engineering degree courses* at Oxbridge, 2; other universities, 4; medical schools, 1; polytechnics or CHE, 2. *BEd*, 3. *other general training courses*, 11. Average number of pupils going straight into careers in armed services, 1; industry, 7; the City, 1; civil service, 1; other, 9.

Uniform School uniform worn throughout.

Houses/prefects Competitive houses. Prefects, head boy/girl, head of house and house prefects – voted by sixth form and staff, appointed by Principal. School Council.

Religion Daily assembly, mass at beginning and end of term compulsory.

Social Joint concerts with Cheltenham College, Dean Close School. Trips abroad to France, Greece etc, also skiing; exchanges to France, Germany. Pupils allowed to bring own car/bike/motorbike to school. Some meals formal, some self service. School shop. No tobacco/alcohol allowed.

Discipline No corporal punishment. Pupils failing to produce homework once might expect to repeat it; those caught smoking cannabis on the premises might expect suspension or expulsion.

Alumni association run by Mr Ablett, c/o the School.

Former pupils Lucy Soutter (international squash player).

St Edward's (Liverpool)

St Edward's College
North Drive
Sandfield Park
Liverpool L12 1LF
Telephone number 051 228 3376

Enquiries/application to the Headmaster's Secretary

Co-ed
● Boys
Girls
● Mixed sixth
● Day
Boarding

Pupils 555
Upper sixth 100
Termly fees:
Day £642
HMC

WHAT IT'S LIKE

Founded in 1900 and conducted by the Christian Brothers it is sited in a fine 30-acre wooded park in a residential district of the City and caters for a wide area of Merseyside. First-rate modern facilities are available. About 98% of the pupils are Roman Catholics (those of other faiths are accepted). A full course of religious education according to Catholic doctrine is an integral part of the curriculum. Attendance at services is obligatory. Academic standards are high and the school has a distinguished scholastic record. Some 50 leavers go on to university each year. Strong in drama; immensely strong in music – to the extent that it is almost an 'industry'. There are many well-known alumni in the musical world. Very high standards in sports and games (a large number of county representatives, especially track and field athletes). A substantial commitment to local community services and an impressive record in the Duke of Edinburgh's Award Scheme.

SCHOOL PROFILE

Pupils Total over 12, 555. (Boys 505, girls 50.) Entry age, boys, 11+; boys and girls into the sixth. Own prep school provides over 20%. 50% are children of former pupils.

Entrance Own entrance exam used. Oversubscribed. No special skills or religious requirements but 98% of pupils are Roman Catholic. Parents not expected to buy text books. 385 assisted places. 10 scholarships/bursaries, £1400–£500 pa.

Parents 15+% are manual workers; 15+% are doctors, lawyers etc; 15+% in industry or commerce. 60+% live within 30 miles.

Staff Head Rev Brother B D Sassi. 44 full time staff, 20 part time. Annual turnover 1%. Average age 45.

Academic work GCSE and A-levels. Average size of upper fifth 90; upper sixth 100. *O-levels*: on average, 14 pupils in upper fifth pass 1–4 subjects; 33, 5–7 subjects; 40 pass 8+ subjects. *A-levels*: on average, 4 pupils in upper sixth pass 1 subject; 7, 2 subjects; 20, 3 subjects and 61 pass 4 subjects. On average, 53 take science/engineering; 38 take arts and humanities, 9 a mixture. *Computing facilities*: 30 BBC computers. Provision for EFL, dyslexic and mildly visually handicapped.

Senior pupils' non-academic activities *Music*: 50 learn a musical instrument, 26 to Grade 6 or above, 3 pa accepted for Music School, 3 to play in pop group, 1–3 pa to music degree at university; 36 in school orchestra, 40 in school choir, 5 school pop group, 4 barber shop quartet, 10 other pop groups; 1 in National Youth Orchestra, 3 Merseyside Youth Orchestra, 3 cathedral choir, 6 local orchestras. *Drama and dance*: 35 in school productions; 70 in charity review. *Art*: 25 take GCSE; 11 A-level. 1 accepted for Art School; 2 for architecture. 5 belong to eg photographic club. *Sport*: Rugby, cross-country, cricket, athletics, swimming, tennis, basketball, hockey, badminton, weight-training, volleyball, climbing available. 240 take non-compulsory sport; 120, other. 30 take sport exams. 23 represent county/country (rugby, athletics). *Other*: 20 take part in local community schemes. 26 have Bronze Duke of Edinburgh's Award, 8 have silver and 4 gold. Other activities include a computer club, debating, public speaking, bridge, chess, model railway, quiz team, electronics.

Careers 1 part time careers advisor. Average number of pupils accepted for *arts and humanities degree courses* at Oxbridge, 4; other universities, 20; polytechnics or CHE, 6. *science and engineering degree courses* at Oxbridge, 4; other universities, 30; medical schools, 6; polytechnics or CHE, 3. *BEd*, 2. *other general training courses*, 1. Average number of pupils going straight into careers in armed services, 1; the church, 1; industry, 4; civil service, 4.

Uniform School uniform worn throughout.

Houses/prefects Competitive houses. Prefects, head boy and girl – appointed by the Head.

Religion Morning assembly/prayer compulsory. Daily eucharistic service is encouraged.

Social Debates, public speaking and sporting events with local schools. Frequent trips and exchanges abroad arranged by modern language departments. Pupils allowed to bring own car/bike to school. Meals self-service. No tobacco/alcohol allowed.

Discipline No corporal punishment. Pupils failing to produce homework once might be told to produce it next day; those caught smoking cannabis on the premises may expect suspension.

Former pupils Michael Williams (actor); Michael Slemen and Edward Rudd (England Rugby players) and numerous musicians.

St Edward's (Oxford)

St Edward's School
Woodstock Road
Oxford OX2 7NN
Telephone number 0865 54411

Co-ed
● Boys
Girls
● Mixed sixth
● Day
● Boarding

Pupils 580
Upper sixth Yes
Termly fees:
Day £1660
Boarding £2200
HMC

Head J C Phillips (10 years)
Age range 13–18; entry by common entrance.
Scholarships and bursaries including for the sons of Barclays Bank and for Service personnel.

St Elphin's

St Elphin's School	Co-ed	Pupils 300
Darley Dale	Boys	Upper sixth Yes
Matlock	● Girls	Termly fees:
Derbyshire DE4 2HA	Mixed sixth	Day £970
Telephone number 0629 733263	● Day	Boarding £1720
	● Boarding	GSA

Head Mr A P C Pollard (9 years)
Age range 11–18; own junior school from 3; entry by own exam.
12 scholarships pa. Special tuition for dyslexic pupils.

St Felix

St Felix School	Co-ed	Pupils 360
Southwold	Boys	Upper sixth Yes
Suffolk IP18 6SD	● Girls	Termly fees:
Telephone number 0502 722175	Mixed sixth	Day £1110
	● Day	Boarding £1800
	● Boarding	GSA

WHAT IT'S LIKE

Founded in 1897 by Margaret Gardiner, it is one of the few schools of its period actually designed and built as a school. It stands in 57 acres of beautiful gardens, lawns and playing fields near the Suffolk coast and within walking distance of Southwold. Norwich and Aldeburgh are easily accessible. It is extremely well equipped and has a chapel and a fine library. The junior school, St George's, stands in its own grounds next to the main school. There are 5 main boarding houses and 2 separate houses for the upper sixth all of which provide comfortable accommodation. Non-denominational in its foundation it welcomes girls of every religious faith. There is some emphasis on religious instruction and worship. St Felix has a strong academic bias. A large staff allows a very favourable staff:pupil ratio of about 1:7. Standards are high and results are very creditable. A lot of girls go on to university and other places of further education. Music, drama and art play an important part in the school's life. There are 2 orchestras and 2 choirs. All instruments are taught. Inter-house music and drama competitions are held regularly. A large and well-equipped art school produces work of a high standard. Many sports and games are available, as well as riding, show-jumping, sailing and canoeing. Girls regularly represent Suffolk and East Anglia in hockey, lacrosse, tennis and athletics. There is a huge range of extra-curricular activities. The school has a big commitment to local community services and each house runs its own social service project.

SCHOOL PROFILE

Head Miss M A Claydon (1 year)
Age range 11–18, own prep from age 7; entry by common entrance.
6% of pupils are from overseas. Scholarships including for music.

St Francis' College

St Francis' College	Co-ed		Pupils 240
The Broadway	Boys		Upper sixth Yes
Letchworth	● Girls		Termly fees:
Hertfordshire SG6 3PJ	Mixed sixth		Day £880
Telephone number 0462 670511	● Day		Boarding £1660
	● Boarding		GSA

Head Mrs Janise Frith (1 year)
Age range 11–18; own prep from age 4; entry by own exam.
Several scholarships and 6 bursaries.

St George's (Ascot)

St George's School	Co-ed		Pupils 275
Ascot	Boys		Upper sixth 30
Berkshire SL5 7DZ	● Girls		Termly fees:
Telephone number 0990 20273	Mixed sixth		Day £1250
	● Day		Boarding £2225
Enquiries to the Admissions Secretary	● Boarding		GSA
Application to the Headmistress			

WHAT IT'S LIKE

Founded in 1877 it has a fine site close to Windsor Great Park and opposite
the Ascot racecourse. The grounds comprise 30 acres of fields, woods,
streams and heathland and the handsome brick buildings have an elevated
position with good views. The school is well-equipped and has excellent
sports facilities. It is Christian in outlook and has its own chapel. A sound
general education is provided and academic standards are said to be high.
Music, drama and art are an important part of the curriculum. There is an
adequate range of sports and games and extra-curricular activities.

SCHOOL PROFILE

Pupils Total, 275. Day 85; Boarding 190. Entry age, 11+, 12+, 13+ and into
the sixth.
Entrance Common entrance used.
Parents Some live overseas.
Staff Head Mrs A M Griggs, from January 1989.
Academic work GCSE, A-levels.

Senior pupils' non-academic activities *Music*: Over half school learns at least 1 musical instrument; 3 choirs, woodwind ensemble, jazz and recorder groups. *Drama and dance*: Annual dramatic production; inter-house drama, declamation and public speaking competitions. *Art*: Studio and pottery workshop. *Sport*: Trampolining, fencing, table tennis, lacrosse, athletics, tennis, swimming, rounders, squash available. *Other*: Duke of Edinburgh's Award Scheme. Other activities include cookery, photography, bridge, first aid, pet-keeping, cycling, lacemaking, bird-watching, Young Enterprise, golf, riding, archery.

Uniform School uniform worn except in sixth form.

Houses/prefects Competitive houses. School Council.

Religion Compulsory morning assembly in chapel; Sunday church but non-Christians may attend own services.

Social Contact with local schools encouraged; annual ski-ing trip, occasional visits to Russia.

Boarding Resident qualified nurse; doctor visits twice-weekly.

St George's (Edinburgh)

St George's School for Girls	Co-ed	Pupils 600
Garscube Terrace	Boys	Upper sixth 59
Edinburgh EH12 6BG	● Girls	Termly fees:
Telephone number 031 332 4575	Mixed sixth	Day £780
	● Day	Boarding £1555
Enquiries/application to the Headmistress	● Boarding	GSA

WHAT IT'S LIKE

Founded in 1888 by a committee of distinguished women who were inspired by the new ideals for women's education. It has an attractive 11 acre urban site with excellent facilities and good boarding accommodation. The primary school is on the same site. Christian assemblies are compulsory for all. Academically a very distinguished school, it has high standards of teaching and consistently good results. Forty or more leavers go on to university each year, in all parts of the UK. Offers both the Scottish Highers and a 2-year English A-level course. It is very strong indeed in music, drama and art, with many successes in these fields. An excellent record in games and sports (a large number of country representatives each season). It also has an astonishing record in the Duke of Edinburgh's Award Scheme (75 bronze, 52 silver, 94 gold).

SCHOOL PROFILE

Pupils Total over 12, 600. Day 521; Boarding 79. Entry age, 5, 9, 11+ and into the sixth. Own prep department provides over 70%. 10% are children of former pupils.

Entrance Own entrance exam used. Sometimes oversubscribed. No special skills or religious requirements. Parents not expected to buy text books. 16 assisted places.

Parents 15+% are doctors, lawyers etc; 15+% in industry or commerce. 60+% live within 30 miles, up to 10% live overseas.

Staff Head Mrs Jean G Scott, in post for 2 years. 62 full time staff, 16 part time. Annual turnover 1–5%. Average age 41.

Academic work GCSE, A-levels and Highers. Average size of upper fifth 93; lower sixth (main Higher year) 80; upper sixth 59. *O-grades*: on average, 90 pupils in upper fifth pass 8+ subjects. *A-levels*: on average, 8 pupils in the upper sixth pass 1 subject; 6, 2 subjects; 20, 3 subjects and 1 passes 4 subjects. On average, 16 take science/engineering A-levels; 14 take arts and humanities; 5 a mixture. *Computing facilities*: BBC Econet with 7 terminals and 3 BBC disc machines; additional computers in primary and middle schools, and in boarding house.

Senior pupils' non-academic activities *Music*: A considerable number of girls learn musical instruments up to Grade 8 and beyond. Entries are made to both Music Schools and University Music Departments. Many take part in the school orchestra, choirs, concert band and chamber groups. Out of school a number play in the Edinburgh Youth Orchestra, National Children's Orchestra and National Youth Orchestra of Scotland. *Drama and dance*: 100 in school productions. 8 enter Edinburgh competitive festival. 1 accepted for Drama School. *Art*: 47 take as non-examined subject; 38 GCSE; 2 A-level; 16 Higher. 2–7 accepted for Art School; 2 for university Fine Art course. 50 belong to art/photographic club. *Sport*: Badminton, curling, fencing, hockey, lacrosse, squash, tennis, air rifle shooting available. 100 take non-compulsory sport. 17 per season represent country/region (lacrosse, hockey, fencing, tennis, squash). *Other*: 75 have bronze Duke of Edinburgh's Award, 52 have silver and 94 gold. Other activities include a computer club, literary and debating society, history and drama clubs, wind bands and madrigal groups.

Careers 2 part time careers advisors. Average number of pupils accepted for *arts and humanities degree courses* at Oxbridge, 2; other universities, 18; polytechnics, CHE or Scottish central institutions, 1–2. *science and engineering degree courses* at Oxbridge, 3; other universities, 15; medical schools, 4; polytechnics, CHE or Scottish central institutions, 3. BEd, 1. *other general training courses*, eg paramedical, art foundation, 8. Average number of pupils going straight into careers in the City, 1. Many pupils go on to medicine and law.

Uniform School uniform worn except the sixth.

Houses/prefects Competitive houses. Prefects, head girl, head of house and house prefects – elected by the Head. School Council.

Religion Compulsory Christian assembly each morning.

Social Balls, Scottish reel evenings, Burns' suppers, musical and dramatic productions with other local independent schools. Ski-ing trips, visits to Greece, exchanges with France and with Germantown Friends' School (Philadelphia). Pupils allowed to bring own car/bike/motorbike to school. Meals formal in boarding houses, self service in school. No tobacco/alcohol allowed.

Discipline No corporal punishment. Pupils failing to produce homework once might expect reprimand; those caught smoking cannabis on the premises might expect expulsion.

Boarding 15% have own study bedroom, 10% share with another, 75% are in dormitories of 6+. Houses, of approximately 48 and 55 are divided by age. At least 3 termly exeats. Visits to local town allowed.

Alumni association run by Mrs E Walker, Clinton House, Whitehouse Loan, Edinburgh EH9 2AN.

St George's (Weybridge)

St George's College
Woburn Park
Weybridge
Surrey KT15 2QS
Telephone number 0932 854811

Enquiries/application to the Headmaster's Secretary

Co-ed   Pupils 600
● Boys   Upper sixth 120
   Girls   Termly fees:
● Mixed sixth   Day £1285
● Day   Boarding £1854
● Boarding   HMC; SHMIS; GBA

WHAT IT'S LIKE

Founded in 1869 it moved to its present site in 1884. This is Woburn Park where there are about 100 acres of fine grounds, gardens and playing fields. Many extensions and developments have taken place over the years and the school is now very well-equipped. There are two prep schools (Woburn Hill School and Barrow Hills School) and it also draws pupils from St Maur's Convent into a joint sixth form. It is run by the Josephite Fathers who are Roman Catholic. The religious life of the school is an integral part of its existence and religious instruction and regular worship are compulsory. Academic standards are high and results impressive. Most pupils go on to university or polytechnic each year. Music, drama and art are all strong. There is a good range of sports and games (high standards are achieved) and a good range of extra-curricular activities. There is a substantial commitment to local community services through the St Vincent de Paul Society.

SCHOOL PROFILE

Pupils Total, 600. Day 350; Boarding 150; plus 100 girls in joint sixth form. Entry age, 12+, 13+ and into the sixth; girls from St Maur's Convent, Weybridge into joint sixth. Woburn Hill School, Weybridge (same campus) and Barrow Hills School, Witley, Surrey each provide over 20%.

Entrance Common entrance and own entrance exam used. Not oversubscribed. No special skills; Catholic school but other Christian denominations accepted. Parents not expected to buy text books. 30 assisted places. 2 scholarships for £642 (half day fees); bursaries at discretion of school, depending on parental circumstances.

Parents 60+% live within 30 miles; 10+% live overseas.

Staff Head Rev J W Munton, in post for 1 year. 53 full time staff, 5 part time. Annual turnover 12%. Average age 40.

Senior pupils' non-academic activities *Music*: School choir, orchestra, woodwind ensemble, other instrumental groups. *Drama and dance*: Annual play. *Art*: Art and ceramics offered at GCSE and A-level. *Sport*: Rugby, hockey, cricket, tennis, rowing, athletics, squash, sailing, golf, badminton, baske·ball, volleyball, netball available. *Other*: Duke of Edinburgh's Award Scheme. Other activities include debating, the Armadillo (learned society), Byzantian (Arts) society, photography, model making, chess.

Careers 2 part time careers advisors. Majority go on to further and higher education.

Uniform School uniform worn.

Religion Compulsory morning and evening prayers in school chapel, Sunday mass; voluntary masses.

Social Organised trips to London concerts and theatres, camping and mountaineering in Snowdonia and Lake District, sports team tours (UK and Europe); annual ski-ing trip, history of art and geography expeditions to Europe, history department tours and choir tour.

Boarding Sixth have own study bedrooms, others in small dormitories or cubicles. Resident qualified nurse, doctor visits regularly. Pupils can provide and cook own snacks. Visits to local town allowed.

Alumni association Old Georgians Association run by Father Francis Owen, CJ, Secretary, c/o the School.

St Gerard's

St Gerard's School
Ffriddoedd Road
Bangor
Gwynedd LL57 2EL
Telephone number 0248 351656

Enquiries/application to the Head

- Co-ed   Pupils 160
- Boys   Upper sixth 10
- Girls   Termly fees:
- Mixed sixth   Day £510
- Day   ISAI
- Boarding

WHAT IT'S LIKE

Founded in 1915, it is in the care of the Sisters of Mercy. Single-site and semi-rural, it has pleasant buildings in wooded grounds. A Roman Catholic foundation, it is ecumenical and its ethos is firmly based on Christian principles. A small full-time staff (10 for 270) but a lot of part-time teachers (27). Fees are low and a good general education is given. A few pupils go on to university each year. Reasonably strong music and drama; adequate sports and games.

SCHOOL PROFILE

Pupils Total over 12, 160 (girls 130, boys 30). Entry age, 3, 7, 11 and into the sixth. Very few are children of former pupils.

Entrance Own entrance exam used. Not oversubscribed. No special skills or religious requirements. Parents not expected to buy text books.

Parents 20+% are farmers; 20+% are hoteliers. More than 60% live within 30 miles.

Staff Head Sister Brigid McNally, in post for 7 years. 10 full time staff, 27 part time. Average age 41.

Academic work GCSE and A-levels. Average size of upper fifth 30; upper

sixth 10. *O-levels*: on average, 10 pupils in upper fifth pass 1–4 subjects; 9, 5–7 subjects; 9 pass 8+ subjects. *A-levels*: on average, 3 pupils in upper sixth pass 1 subject; 3, 2 subjects; 2 pass 3 subjects. On average 5 pupils take science/engineering A-levels; 4 take arts and humanities; 1 a mixture. Computer studies available at GCSE. *Computing facilities*: 3 computers available. Special provisions for EFL and dyslexic pupils.

Senior pupils' non-academic activities *Music*: 30 learn a musical instrument, 6 to Grade 6 or above; 10 in school orchestra, 40 in choir. 1 gone on to play in pop group. *Drama and dance*: 10–20 in school productions. 6 take Grade 6 in ESB, RAD etc. 2 accepted for Drama/Dance Schools; 1 goes on to work in theatre. *Art*: 10 take GCSE; 1–2 A-level. 1 accepted for Art School. *Sport*: Hockey, netball, rounders, tennis, volleyball available. 20 take non-compulsory sport. 5–10 take exams eg gymnastics, swimming. 3 in heats for senior Gwynedd team. *Other*: Activities include a computer club, orchestra, wind band, string group.

Careers 1 part time advisor. Average number of pupils accepted for *arts and humanities degree courses* at universities, 2; polytechnics or CHE, 1. *science and engineering degree courses* at medical schools, 1; polytechnics or CHE, 4. *BEd*, 1. *other general training courses*, 13. Average number of pupils going straight into careers in industry, 3.

Uniform School uniform worn, modified in the sixth.

Houses/prefects Competitive houses. Prefects, head boy/girl, head of house and house prefects – elected by the sixth form. School Council.

Religion Assembly is compulsory. Parents are given right of withdrawal.

Social Games fixtures and occasional joint ski-ing holidays with other schools. French holiday (middle school) every two years; ski-ing holiday in Italy; Russian holiday in 1988. Pupils allowed to bring own car/bike to school. Meals: packed lunches. School shop. No tobacco/alcohol allowed.

Discipline No corporal punishment. Pupils failing to produce homework once might expect a warning followed by detention and parents informed; those caught smoking cannabis on the premises could expect suspension and parents asked to come to school.

St Helen's

St Helen's School	Co-ed	Pupils 863*
Eastbury Road	Boys	Upper sixth 65
Northwood	● Girls	Termly fees:
Middlesex HA6 3AS	Mixed sixth	Day £905
Telephone number 09274 28511	● Day	Boarding £1705
Enquiries to the Headmistress	● Boarding	*whole school
Application to the Registrar		

WHAT IT'S LIKE

Founded in 1899, it has a pleasant semi-rural site of some 25 acres of gardens and playing fields 18 miles north-west of London. It comprises a preparatory department, a junior school and a senior school housed in well-equipped buildings on a compact campus. There have been extensive developments and improvements in the last 10 years. Religious teaching is in accordance with the principles of the Church of England. It has a sound academic record with consistently good results. About 30–35 pupils go to university each year (8 or so to Oxbridge). Strong music and drama; quite strong in art. A very good range of sports and games in which high standards are attained. A plentiful range of extra-curricular activities and a promising record in the Duke of Edinburgh's Award Scheme. Regular use is made of London's cultural amenities.

SCHOOL PROFILE

Pupils Total, 863. Day 699; Boarding 164. Entry age, rising 5, 7, 11 and into the sixth. Own junior school provides over 20%. Less than 10% are children of former pupils.

Entrance Common entrance and own exam used. Oversubscribed. All talents considered; no religious requirements. Parents expected to buy sixth form text books. 27 assisted places, 4 scholarships/bursaries, £905–£226.

Parents 15+% in Armed Services; 15+% in industry or commerce. 60+% live within 30 miles; up to 10% live overseas.

Staff Head Dr Y A Burne, in post for 1 year. 59 full time staff, 19 part time. Annual turnover 6%. Average age 35–40.

Academic work GCSE, A-levels. Average size of upper fifth 80; upper sixth 65. *O-levels*: on average, 6 pupils in upper fifth pass 1–4 subjects; 21, 5–7 subjects; 53 pass 8+ subjects. *A-levels*: on average, 5 pupils in upper sixth pass 1 subject; 15, 2 subjects; 40, 3 subjects and 3 pass 4 subjects. On average, 17 take science/engineering A-levels; 18 take arts and humanities; 31 a mixture. *Computing facilities*: Econet network (5J hard disk) with master 128s and ETs (16 in total), research machines, Nimbus network (12 stations) and 480Z network. Provision for dyslexia and EFL.

Senior pupils' non-academic activities *Music*: 110 learn a musical instrument, 40 up to Grade 6 or above, 1 accepted for Music School, 1 for studio recording; 22 in school orchestra, 55 in choir; 3 in Harrow Youth Orchestra. *Drama and dance*: 25–40 in school productions; 50 in house productions; 15 with other schools. 35 take Associated Board (Speech and Drama) exams. 1–2 accepted for Drama/Dance Schools; 1 occasionally to work in theatre. *Art*: 6 take as non-examined subject; 33 GCSE; 17 A-level. 6–7 accepted for Art School, 1–2 BTEC. 20 belong to photographic club. *Sport*: Netball, lacrosse, badminton, golf, judo, trampolining, gymnastics, fencing, volleyball, squash, modern dance, rounders, swimming, life saving, tennis available. 80 take non-compulsory sport. 10 take swimming exams; team entered annually for Ten Tors race. 10 represent county (lacrosse, tennis). *Other*: 45 have bronze Duke of Edinburgh's Award and 4 gold. Other activities include a computer club, French circle, one week's course for PHAB (Physically Handicapped and Able Bodied) organised by sixth form, debating, Christian Affairs Discussion Group.

Careers 1 part time careers advisor. Average number of pupils accepted for *arts and humanities degree courses* at Oxbridge, 5; other universities, 18; polytechnics or CHE, 11. *science and engineering degree courses* at Oxbridge, 3; other universities, 7; medical schools, 3; polytechnics or CHE, 3. *BEd*, 3. *other general training courses*, 2. Average number of pupils going straight into careers in industry, 2; the City, 1.

Uniform School uniform worn except the sixth.

Houses/prefects Competitive houses. Prefects, head girl, head of house and house prefects – head girl and deputies appointed by Headmistress, prefects elected.

Religion Compulsory morning assembly, weekend services for boarders, other chapel services voluntary.

Social Debates, theatrical and choral productions, local conferences with other schools. Trips abroad for languages, educational eg Greece, Russia, sporting eg lacrosse, ski-ing. Pupils allowed to bring own car/bike to school, horse locally. Meals self service. No tobacco allowed, wine for special functions.

Discipline No corporal punishment. Pupils failing to produce homework once might expect to do it later; those caught smoking cannabis on the premises might expect immediate suspension, probable expulsion.

Boarding Half upper sixth have own study bedroom, half share, below lower fifth in dormitories of 6+. Houses, of approximately 50, same as competitive houses. Sanatorium with resident qualified nurse. Central dining room. Sixth form can provide and cook snacks. Half term and 2 weekend exeats per term. Visits to local town allowed.

Alumni association run by Miss M R Selden, 26 Grove Lane, Camberwell, London SE5.

Former pupils Patricia Hodge (actress); Commandant D M Blundell, CB, WRNS; Penelope Marshall (ITN).

S Hilary's (Alderley Edge)

S Hilary's School	Co-ed	Pupils 217
Alderley Edge	Boys	Upper sixth 20
Cheshire SK9 7AG	● Girls	Termly fees:
Telephone number 0625 583110	Mixed sixth	Day £750
	● Day	GSA
Enquiries/application to the Headmistress	Boarding	

WHAT IT'S LIKE

Founded in 1876, a Woodard school, it is semi-rural and single-site in a pleasant residential area on the lower slopes of Alderley Edge, 15 miles south of Manchester. Junior and senior school share the campus and have well-designed and well-equipped buildings. Large playing fields are close by. A C of E foundation, but other denominations are accepted. Religious worship is compulsory. The school emphasises the importance of girls' education and the expectation that women can expect to fulfil several roles in their professional and family lives. It aims to develop a girl's abilities to the full, giving maximum opportunity for a university career, higher education or other avenues of professional training. There is a good staff:pupil ratio of 1:13. Academic attainments are high and a high proportion of leavers go on to degree courses. Very strong in music and drama; quite a lot of emphasis on public speaking. Adequate games, sports and activities. Some participation in local community services.

SCHOOL PROFILE

Pupils Total over 12, 217. Entry age, mainly at 4, 11 and directly into the sixth.
Entrance Own entrance exam used. Oversubscribed in Junior School. C of E school but other denominations are accepted. Parents not expected to buy text books. Scholarships/bursaries.
Staff Head Mrs J Tracey, in post for 3 years. 26 full time staff, 11 part time.
Academic work GCSE and A-levels. Average size of upper fifth 40; upper sixth 20. *O-levels*: on average, 45% pass 8+ subjects. Average of 7 passes per candidate. *A-levels*: average pass rate of 80%. On average, 7 take science A-levels; 9 take arts; 4 a mixture. *Computing facilities*: Computer suite and use of computers in subject areas.
Senior pupils' non-academic activities *Music*: 70 learn a musical instrument and take Associated Board exams. 20 in school orchestra, 80 in choir, 20 in madrigal group. *Drama and dance*: 80 seniors and 70 juniors in school productions. Guildhall exams may be taken. *Sport*: Hockey, netball, squash, tennis, rounders, swimming, volleyball, badminton, basketball available. Other activities include a computer club; public speaking; involvement in charity concerts (speech and music); various clubs.
Careers 2 advisors. Average number of pupils accepted for *arts and humanities degree courses* including Oxbridge, 8. *science and engineering degree courses* including Oxbridge, 7. *BEd*, 2. *other general training courses*, 3.
Uniform School uniform worn except in the sixth.
Houses/prefects Competitive houses. Prefects, head girl and head of house – appointed by the Head. School Forum.
Religion Religious worship compulsory.
Social Organised ski trips abroad and French trips. Pupils allowed to bring own car to school. Meals formal. School tuckshop and second-hand uniform shop.
Discipline No corporal punishment. Firm disciplinary procedures enforced.

St Hilary's (Sevenoaks)

St Hilary's School	Co-ed	Pupils 185
Bradbourne Park Road	Boys	Upper sixth 11
Sevenoaks	• Girls	Termly fees:
Kent TN13 3LD	Mixed sixth	Day £815
Telephone number 0732 453815	• Day	GSA; GBGSA
	Boarding	
Enquiries/application to the Headmistress		

WHAT IT'S LIKE

Founded in 1944, single-site and purpose-built in 4 acres of pleasant wooded grounds in a residential urban area, within easy walking distance of the station. Junior school combined. Religious worship is encouraged and religious instruction is an important part of the curriculum. With a staff:pupil ratio of 1:12, academic standards are kept high and results are good. A few girls go on to university each year. The PA is particularly strong and parental involvement is much encouraged. Adequate music and art; but, apparently, minimal drama. Adequate range of sports, games and activities. Considerable participation in voluntary community service and the Duke of Edinburgh's Award Scheme.

SCHOOL PROFILE

Pupils Total over 12, 185. Entry age, 3½, 5, 11 and into the sixth. Own junior school provides over 20%. 20% are children of former pupils.

Entrance Own entrance exam used. Sometimes oversubscribed. No special skills or religious requirements. Parents not expected to buy text books. 5 scholarships and 10 bursaries pa, up to full fees.

Parents 15+% in industry or commerce; 15+% are doctors, lawyers, etc. 60+% live within 30 miles; up to 10% live overseas.

Staff Head Mrs P Miles, in post for 10 years. 20 full time staff, 20 part time. Annual turnover 7.5%. Average age 40.

Academic work GCSE and A-levels. Average size of upper fifth 40; upper sixth 11. *O-levels*: on average, 17 pupils in upper fifth pass 1–4 subjects; 19, 5–7 subjects; 4 pass 8+ subjects. *A-levels*: on average, 5 pupils in upper sixth pass 1 subject; 4, 2 subjects; 2, 3 subjects. On average, 4 take science/engineering A-levels; 4 take arts and humanities; 3 a mixture. *Computing facilities*: 11 BBC2 Acorns in computer room plus 1 3802. Provision for dyslexia, mild handicap and EFL.

Senior pupils' non-academic activities *Music*: 13 learn a musical instrument, 2 to Grade 6 or above. 1 accepted for Music School. 10 in school orchestra, 6 in choir, pupils in school and local youth orchestras. *Drama and dance*: 2 in school productions; 1 accepted for Drama/Dance School; 1 gone on to work in theatre. *Art*: 14 take GCSE; 2 A-level. 3 accepted for Art School. *Sport*: Tennis, athletics, netball, hockey, cross-country running available. 22 take non-compulsory sport; 10 take exams eg gymnastics, swimming. 4 represent county/country (tennis, cross-country). *Other*: 22 seniors take part in local community scheme VSU. 18 have bronze Duke of Edinburgh's Award, 10 have silver. 4 enter voluntary schemes after leaving school; 6 work for national charities. Other activities include computer, art and gym clubs.

Careers 2 part time advisors. Average number of pupils accepted for *arts and humanities degree courses* at universities, 1; polytechnics or CHE, 5. *science and engineering degree courses* at universities, 1; medical schools, 1. *BEd*, 1. *other general training courses*, 7. Average number of pupils going straight into careers in the armed services, 1; industry, 7; the City, 2; civil service, 1; music/drama, 1; art/design, 1; nursing 2. Traditional school careers are in art and design.

Uniform School uniform worn, modified in the sixth.

Houses/prefects Competitive houses. Prefects, head girl, head of house and house prefects – appointed by the Head after consultation with the rest of the school. School Council.

Religion Daily assembly compulsory, worship encouraged.

Social Participation in local voluntary services unit. Organised trips abroad and exchange systems. Pupils allowed to bring own car/bike/motorbike to school. Meals formal. No tobacco/alcohol allowed.

Discipline No corporal punishment. Pupils failing to produce homework once might expect a warning and parents informed; those caught smoking cannabis on the premises could expect severe warning or expulsion.

Alumni association Friends of St Hilary's School, run by Miss M J Strudwick, 10 Sandilands, Chipstead, Sevenoaks, Kent TN13 2SP.

St Hilda's (Whitby)

St Hilda's School		Co-ed	Pupils 138
Sneaton Castle		Boys	Upper sixth 14
Whitby		● Girls	Termly fees:
North Yorkshire		● Mixed sixth	Day £723
Telephone number 0947 600051		● Day	Boarding £1344
		● Boarding	ISAI
Enquiries/application to the Headmistress			

WHAT IT'S LIKE

Founded in 1915 by Sisters of the Anglican Order of the Holy Paraclete (order and school were twin foundations). After various moves the lower and upper schools now occupy separate sites about 1½ miles apart. The former is at Carr Hall, a handsome stone manor house in 30 acres of fine gardens and grounds in the Esk valley. The latter occupies Sneaton Castle, also a handsome stone mansion (dating from 1815). Excellent modern facilities are available. The headmistress is a Sister of the Order and about 5 other sisters have various roles within the school. There is considerable emphasis on religious education, practice and worship in the Anglican tradition. A notable feature of the school is its pastoral care. It caters for a wide range of children including those with emotional difficulties due to broken homes. A good general education is provided and academic standards are high. Many leavers go on to university. Music, drama and art are quite important parts of the curriculum. A fair range of sports, games and activities. Some commitment to local community schemes and a promising record in the Duke of Edinburgh's Award Scheme.

SCHOOL PROFILE

Pupils Total over 12, 138. Day 24; Boarding 114. Entry age, girls, 4½, 8, 11, 13; girls and boys into sixth. Own junior department provides over 20%. A small number are children of former pupils.

Entrance Own entrance exam used. Oversubscribed. All special gifts are welcome; pupils preferably Christian but other faiths accepted. Parents expected to buy some text books. 15 scholarships/bursaries available, £300–£900 pa.

Parents 15+% in the armed services; 15+% in industry or commerce. 10+% live within 30 miles; 10+% live overseas.

Staff Head Sister Janet Elizabeth. 14 full time staff, 1 part time. Annual turnover 2%. Average age about 35.

Academic work GCSE, A-levels, RSA, City and Guilds. Average size of upper fifth 30; upper sixth 14. *O-levels*: on average, 6 pupils in upper fifth pass 1–4 subjects; 14, 5–7 subjects; 10 pass 8+ subjects. *A-levels*: on average, 3 pupils in upper sixth pass 1 subject; 4, 2 subjects; 5 pass 3 subjects. On average, 7 take science/engineering A-levels; 4 take arts and humanities; 1 a mixture. *Computing facilities*: Computing lab.

Senior pupils' non-academic activities *Music*: 60 learn a musical instrument, 5 to Grade 6 or above, 1 accepted for Music School; 6 in school orchestra, 30 in school choir, 6 in pop group. *Drama and dance*: 50 in school productions. Up to gold LAMDA elocution and elementary ballet. *Art*: 15 take GCSE; 3 take A-level. 3 accepted for Art School. 8 belong to eg photographic club. *Sport*: Hockey, netball, tennis, rounders, squash, table tennis, badminton, athletics, swimming available. 20 take non-compulsory sport. 6 GCSE PE. 4 have represented county. *Other*: 10 take part in local community schemes. 20 have bronze Duke of Edinburgh's Award, 10 have silver and 3 gold. 2 enter voluntary schemes after leaving; 2 work for national charities. Other activities include a computer club, driving lessons, archery, debates.

Careers 1 part time careers advisor. Average number of pupils accepted for *arts and humanities degree courses* at universities, 4; polytechnics or CHE, 1. *science and engineering degree courses* at universities, 4; medical schools, 1; polytechnics or CHE, 2. *other general training courses*, 8. Average number of pupils going straight into careers in armed services, 4; hairdressing, 1.

Uniform School uniform worn except the sixth.

Houses/prefects Competitive houses. No prefects, head girl and head of house elected. School Council.

Religion Compulsory daily prayers, Eucharist on Sundays and major holy days.

Social Debates and socials with local schools. Occasional trips to Germany; exchange with St Hilda's, Perth, WA. Sixth form allowed to bring own bike to school. Meals formal. School shop. No tobacco allowed; alcohol at High Table on Sundays.

Discipline No corporal punishment. Pupils failing to produce homework once might expect reprimand or detention; those caught smoking cannabis on the premises can expect expulsion.

Boarding 15% have own study bedroom. All boarders over 13 in single house. Resident qualified doctor. Central dining room. Sixth form can provide and cook own food. 2 weekend exeats each term. Occasional visits to local town allowed (daily in sixth).

ST JAMES (BOYS)

St James Independent School for Boys	Co-ed	Pupils 120
91 Queen's Gate	● Boys	Upper sixth 15
London SW7	Girls	Termly fees:
Telephone number 01-373 5638	Mixed sixth	Day £890
Enquiries/application to the Headmaster	● Day	ISAI
	Boarding	

WHAT IT'S LIKE

Founded in 1975, it has urban premises in handsome houses in Kensington. The junior and senior schools are 15 minutes' walk apart. It is a strongly traditional school in that it endeavours to give proper weight to all aspects of education: spiritual, mental and physical. However, it is also individualistic in approach. The study of language is based on Sanskrit which all pupils begin aged 5. At 8 they start on Greek as well. Later, Latin or a modern language is included. Philosophy is another essential subject in the curriculum and is taught to all to provide pupils with the principles of spiritual knowledge and to unite people of all races and creeds. Meditation is introduced on a voluntary basis from the age of 10. PT is compulsory for everyone every day. Drama, art and music are very important elements in the curriculum for everyone. Pop groups are absolutely banned. In the senior school physical education shifts to emphasis on team games and sports, plus outdoor pursuits such as rock climbing, sailing and mountaineering. Boxing (most unusual these days) is also regarded as a valuable physical discipline. Games are compulsory for everyone. In general, much emphasis is put on the need for good manners, good citizenship and generosity. There is quite a good range of games and societies: chess is taught by a specialist. Debating is another speciality. Academic standards are high and about 12 leavers proceed to university each year.

SCHOOL PROFILE

Pupils Total over 12, 120. Entry age, 4½ and into sixth. Own junior school provides more than 80%.

Entrance Own informal test used. Sometimes oversubscribed. No special skills or religious requirements. Parents not expected to buy text books.

Parents 60+% live within 30 miles.

Staff Head N Debenham, in post for 13 years. 24 full time staff, 6 part time. Very low annual turnover. Average age 36.

Academic work GCSE and A-levels. Average size of upper fifth 20; upper sixth 15. *O-levels*: on average, 5 pupils in upper fifth pass 1–4 subjects; 9, 5–7 subjects; 6 pass 8+ subjects. *A-levels*: on average, 5 pupils in the upper sixth pass 2 subjects; 8, 3 subjects and 3 pass 4 subjects. On average, 8 take science/engineering A-levels; 4 take arts and humanities; 3 a mixture. Sanskrit offered to GCSE level from 1991. Limited computing facilities. Provision for limited individual coaching for eg dyslexic or mild handicap.

Senior pupils' non-academic activities *Music*: About 15 learn a musical instrument, 1 or 2 to Grade 6 or above; school orchestra recently formed; whole school sings major works in 4-part harmony; ad hoc choirs formed for concerts; pop groups banned. *Drama*: School production in alternate years involving lower sixth and some others. *Art*: 8 take art as non-examined subject; 5 take GCSE; 3 take A-level. 1 or 2 accepted for Art School. 6 in art club. *Sport*: Rugby, cross country, cricket, athletics, tennis available, plus boxing and gymnastics for juniors; 15 play tennis or squash; 16 in cross country team. 2 or 3 pupils represent London in cross country. *Other*: 1 or 2 take part in Duke of Edinburgh's Award. Other activities include chess (taught by a specialist), debating (a speciality).

Careers 1 part time careers advisor. Average number of pupils accepted for *arts and humanities degree courses* at universities, 3; at polytechnics or CHE, 2. *science and engineering degree courses* at Oxbridge, 1; other universities, 6; medical schools, 1. Average number of pupils going straight into careers in armed services, 2.

Uniform School uniform worn throughout.

Houses/prefects Competitive houses. Prefects, head boy, head of house and house prefects – appointed by the Head.

Religion Compulsory daily assembly plus beginning and end of term services.

Social Joint stage productions and concerts with associated girls' school. Many organised trips abroad. Pupils allowed to bring own bicycle/motorbike to school. Meals formal. No tobacco/alcohol allowed.

Discipline Corporal punishment by Headmaster only. Pupils failing to produce homework once might expect to do it in school (at form master's discretion); those caught smoking cannabis on or off the premises can expect expulsion.

Alumni association run by Bartholomew O'Toole, c/o the School.

ST JAMES (GIRLS)

St James Independent School for Girls
91 Queen's Gate
London SW7
Telephone number 01-373 5638

Enquiries/application to the Secretary

Co-ed   Pupils 107
Boys   Upper sixth 15+
● Girls   Termly fees:
Mixed sixth   Day £870
● Day   ISAI
Boarding

WHAT IT'S LIKE

Founded in 1975, it has premises in handsome houses in Kensington. Like the boys' school next door (qv), it is both traditional and individualistic in its approach to education. Sanskrit is the basis of all language work. Greek and Latin are also introduced later. The study of philosophy and religion is an essential part of the curriculum. Each day there is gymnastic training, games or swimming. A year's riding course is given at the age of 8–9. Meditation is encouraged. Music, drama and art are regarded as vitally important parts of the curriculum and involve virtually everyone. Overall, a good general education is given and results are impressive. Twelve or more leavers go on to university each year. There is a good range of sports and games and extra-curricular activities. Some participation in local community schemes and the Duke of Edinburgh's Award Scheme.

SCHOOL PROFILE

Pupils Total over 12, 107. Entry age, 4½ and into the sixth. Own junior department provides over 80%.

Entrance No entrance exam. Sometimes oversubscribed. No special skills or religious requirements. Parents expected to buy text books in sixth.

Parents 15+% are doctors, lawyers etc; 15+% in industry or commerce. 60+% live within 30 miles.

Staff Head Miss S M Caldwell, in post for 13 years. 17 full time staff, 12 part time. Annual turnover 5–10%.

Academic work GCSE and A-levels. Average size of upper fifth 23; upper sixth 15–20. *O-levels*: on average, 5 pupils in upper fifth pass 1–4 subjects; 8, 5–7 subjects; 8 pass 8+ subjects. *A-levels*: on average, 1 pupil in upper sixth passes 1 subject; 6, 2 subjects; 12, 3 subjects and 1 passes 4 subjects. On average, 4–6 take science/engineering A-levels; 10 take arts and humanities; 5 a mixture. *Computing facilities*: RML 480Z. Provision for pupils who are eg dyslexic, mildly visually handicapped, and EFL.

Senior pupils' non-academic activities *Music*: 150 learn a musical instrument, 13 to Grade 6 or above, 1 accepted for Music School; 12 and 20 in school orchestras, everyone in school choir, small orchestral groups. *Drama and dance*: Whole school in productions. 1 accepted by Royal Ballet School. *Art*: All take as non-examined subject; 10 take A-level, 2 or 3 accepted for Art School. Art club. *Sport*: Lacrosse, netball, rounders, tennis, swimming, athletics, gymnastics, akaido available. 3 pupils represent county (lacrosse); 2 or 3 represent ISAI London North. *Other*: 2–4 take part in local community schemes. Other activities include chess and recently Duke of Edinburgh's Award Scheme.

Careers 1 part time careers advisor. Average number of pupils accepted for *arts and humanities degree courses* at Oxbridge, 1 or 2; other universities, 6; polytechnics or CHE, 2. *science and engineering degree courses* at Oxbridge, 1; other universities, 2; medical schools, 2. *BEd*, 4.

Uniform School uniform worn throughout.

Houses/prefects Competitive houses. Prefects, head girl, head of house and house prefects – appointed by the Head and staff.

Religion Religious worship compulsory.

Social No organised local events. Organised trips abroad. Meals formal. No tobacco/alcohol allowed.

Discipline No corporal punishment. Pupils failing to produce homework once might expect to do it next evening; those caught smoking cannabis on the premises would probably be dismissed.

Alumni association Friends of St James School, c/o the School.

St James's and the Abbey

St James's and the Abbey	Co-ed	Pupils 160
West Malvern	Boys	Upper sixth Yes
Worcestershire WR14 4DF	● Girls	Termly fees:
Telephone number 06845 60851	Mixed sixth	Day £1235
	● Day	Boarding £1850
	● Boarding	GSA

Head Miss E M Mullenger (2 years)
Age range 10–18; entrance by common entrance or own exam. Scholarships (including music and science) and bursaries.

St John's College

St John's College
Southsea
Hampshire PO5 3QW
Telephone number 0705 815118

Co-ed   Pupils 640
● Boys   Upper sixth Yes
  Girls   Termly fees:
● Mixed sixth   Day £610
● Day   Boarding £1250
● Boarding

Head Rev Brother Cyril (4 years)
Age range 11–18; own prep from age 5; entry by own exam. 5% pupils from overseas.
30 assisted places pa.

St John's (Leatherhead)

St John's School
Leatherhead
Surrey KT22 8SP
Telephone number 0372 372021

Enquiries/application to the Secretary

Co-ed   Pupils 440
● Boys   Upper sixth 80
  Girls   Termly fees:
  Mixed sixth   Day £1450
● Day   Boarding £1995
● Boarding   HMC

WHAT IT'S LIKE

Founded 1857, originally as a small boarding school for the sons of clergy, it moved to its present site in 1872. This is a very pleasant campus on the edge of the town and comprises 38 acres of delightful grounds dominated by the handsome late Victorian buildings to which there have been many modern additions providing excellent facilities and accommodation. The school looks for all-rounders and the aim is for academic excellence. The boys are very much involved with the running of the establishment which has an outstanding record in pastoral care. A C of E foundation where the chapel life is very active and worship is both compulsory and encouraged. Academic standards are high and results very good. A large number of leavers go on to university each year, including about 10 to Oxbridge. The music, drama and art departments are very active and as many as 150 boys are involved in theatrical presentations each year. The school has a long-standing reputation for achievement in games and sports, and games are held 5 days a week. A very substantial commitment to local community schemes and an outstanding record in the Duke of Edinburgh's Award Scheme.

SCHOOL PROFILE

Pupils Total, 440. Day 240; Boarding 200. Entry age, 13+ and into the sixth. There are some children of former pupils.
Entrance Common entrance and own tests used. Oversubscribed for day places. School looks for all-rounders; C of E school – all other religions accepted. Parents expected to buy text books. 6 assisted places. 10–15

scholarships/exhibitions (including for art and music), 75%–25% of day fees.
Parents 10+% are clergy. 60+% live within 30 miles; less than 10% live overseas.

Staff Head D E Brown, in post for 3 years. 39 full time staff, 4 part time. Annual turnover 3 or 4. Average age 37–43.

Academic work GCSE and A-levels. Average size of upper fifth 95; upper sixth 80. *O-levels*: average pupil passes 7–8 subjects. *A-levels*: most sixth form pupils get 3 or more. On average, 29 take science/engineering A-levels; 46 take arts and humanities A-levels. *Computing facilities*: 14 Nimbus RM in a lab plus sundry BBC Bs in many departments eg maths, physics, biology, chemistry, history, geography, modern languages. Classes for EFL and dyslexia.

Senior pupils' non-academic activities *Music*: 60 learn a musical instrument, 6 to Grade 6 or above, 1 or 2 accepted for Music School, a few play in pop groups; 40 in school orchestra, 50 in school choir. *Drama and dance*: 150 in 3 or 4 school productions. 2 accepted for Drama Schools. *Art*: All pupils take in first year; 24 take GCSE; 8, A-level. 3 or 4 accepted for Art School. 25 belong to photographic club; 20 to pottery. *Sport*: Rugby, soccer, hockey, swimming, fives, squash, judo, athletics, karate, table tennis, fencing, shooting available. All pupils take swimming; games 5 days a week. 6 pupils represent county (rugby and athletics). *Other*: 60 take part in local community schemes. 40 have bronze Duke of Edinburgh's Award, 30 have silver and 10 gold. A few enter voluntary schemes after leaving. Other activities include a computer club, chess, sailing, ski-ing, CCF and shooting.

Careers 3 full time careers advisors. Average number of pupils accepted for *arts and humanities degree courses* at Oxbridge, 4. *science and engineering degree courses* at Oxbridge, 5; medical schools, 7.

Uniform School uniform worn throughout.

Houses/prefects Competitive houses. Prefects, head boy (appointed by Head); head of house and house prefects (by housemasters). Some cleaning done by small boys for large boys.

Religion Religious worship compulsory and encouraged.

Social Debates, music, discussions, choir, occasional dance, rock concert and conference on industry with other schools. Organised trips/exchanges to France, Germany and Spain. Pupils allowed to bring own car/bike to school. Lunch formal, others self-service. School shop. No tobacco/alcohol allowed.

Discipline No corporal punishment. Pupils failing to produce homework once might expect lines; those caught smoking cannabis on the premises might expect expulsion.

Boarding Very few have own study bedroom, senior pupils share, juniors in dormitories of 6+. Houses, of 50–55. Resident qualified nurse. Central dining room. Pupils can provide and cook their own food. Fortnightly exeats each term. Daily visits to local town allowed (juniors with permission, seniors on trust).

Alumni association run by M E C Comer Esq, c/o the School.

Former pupils Richard Rogers; Peter Bruinvels; Tony Hatch.

St Joseph's (Ipswich)

St Joseph's College
Birkfield
Ipswich
Suffolk IP2 9DR
Telephone number 0473 690281

Enquiries/application to the Reverend
Headmaster

Co-ed   Pupils 616
● Boys   Upper sixth 85
   Girls   Termly fees:
● Mixed sixth   Day £710
● Day   Boarding £1360
● Boarding   GBA

WHAT IT'S LIKE

Founded in 1937 in the outskirts of Ipswich at Oakhill (now the prep school). In 1944 the College moved to Birkfield Lodge, a delightful Regency country house in 55 acres of wooded parkland. A very pleasant environment. Many modern extensions. Boarding accommodation and facilities are now excellent. A new CDT centre and science blocks are currently being built. A Roman Catholic school, it is conducted by the De La Salle Brothers (most of the staff are lay) and the religious education is compulsory for all. Attendance at Mass and certain other services is also obligatory. Pastoral care is particularly good and the college has the reputation of being a very happy community. A sound education in the grammar tradition is given and standards and results are very creditable (20–25 leavers go to university each year). Music, art and drama are strong departments. A wide variety of games and sports (many representatives at county level) and extra-curricular activities. Considerable commitment to local community schemes and a promising record in the Duke of Edinburgh's Award Scheme.

SCHOOL PROFILE

Pupils Total over 12, 616. Day 430 (boys 392, girls 38); Boarding 186 (boys). Entry age, 11+, boys; boys and girls into the sixth. Own preparatory school provides 30–40%. 6–8% are children of former pupils.

Entrance Common entrance and own entrance exam used. Oversubscribed. No special skills; school Roman Catholic but over 50% of pupils are not RC. Parents expected to buy some sixth form text books. 75 assisted places. Governors' bursaries available.

Parents 15+% are farmers; 15+% in the Armed Services; 15+% in industry or commerce. 30+% live within 30 miles; up to 10% live overseas.

Staff Head Rev Brother David Hennessy, in post for 1 year. 47 full time staff, 2 part time. Annual turnover 10%. Average age 42.

Academic work GCSE and A-levels. Average size of upper fifth 114; upper sixth 85. *O-levels*: on average, 42 pupils in upper fifth pass 1–4 subjects; 29, 5–7 subjects; 28 pass 8+ subjects. *A-levels*: on average, 9 pupils in upper sixth pass 1 subject; 15, 2 subjects; 31, 3 subjects; 6 pass 4 subjects. On average, 31 take science/engineering A-levels; 26 take arts and humanities; 27 a mixture. *Computing facilities*: Local area network extends campus wide; RM chain 64 net, RML Nimbus net, computers being developed as curricular tools for every subject area. EFL provision; dyslexic pupils admitted into mainstream education.

Senior pupils' non-academic activities *Music*: 20 learn a musical instru-

ment; 6 in school orchestra, 6 in school choir, 6 in school pop group. *Drama and dance*: 25 in school productions. *Art*: 90 take GCSE; 20, A-level. 4 accepted for Art School. 12 belong to photographic club; 30 to pottery and other art clubs. *Sport*: Athletics, badminton, basketball, canoeing, cross country, golf, hockey, rowing, sailing, ski-ing, soccer, squash, swimming, table tennis, trampolining, volleyball, weightlifting, windsurfing available. 80 take non-compulsory sport. 10 take exams (life-saving). 14 pupils represent county/country (rugby, cricket, badminton, athletics, squash). *Other*: 24 take part in local community schemes. 54 have bronze Duke of Edinburgh's Award, 2 have silver. Other activities include a computer club (100 members), debating, chess, public speaking, history. Frequent and varied outings for boarders.

Careers 2 part time careers advisors. Average number of pupils accepted for *arts and humanities degree courses* at Oxbridge, 1; other universities, 9; polytechnics or CHE, 5. *science and engineering degree courses* at Oxbridge, 1; other universities, 12; medical schools, 2; polytechnics or CHE, 2. *BEd*, 2. *other general training courses*, 2. Average number of pupils going straight into careers in armed services, 2; industry, 3; the City, 1.

Uniform School uniform worn throughout.

Houses/prefects Competitive houses. Prefects, head boy, head of house and house prefects appointed by the Head. No fagging but pupils have corporate responsibility for areas in common.

Religion Compulsory Sunday Mass for boarders (whole school on important occasions); weekly assembly; plus voluntary daily Mass, confessions, vigils and prayers.

Social Annual ski-ing trips abroad, French exchange, community service project in summer holidays at Togo (West Africa). Day pupils allowed to bring own car/bike/motorbike to school. Meals self service. School second hand shop. Sixth form boarders allowed tobacco/alcohol in designated room.

Discipline No corporal punishment. Pupils failing to produce homework once might expect a warning; those caught smoking cannabis on the premises can expect expulsion – without question.

Boarding Sixth formers have own study bedroom, 40% share with 2–5, 35% in dormitories of 6+. Houses, of 20–80, divided by age. Attendant qualified matron; weekly doctor's visit – local doctor on call. Central dining room. Pupils can provide and cook own food. Frequent weekend exeats. Visits to local town allowed.

Alumni association run by C Keeble, 26 Quilter Road, Felixstowe, Suffolk.

Former pupils Earl Nelson; Christopher Mullin, MP.

St Joseph's (Lincoln)

St Joseph's School	Co-ed	Pupils 200
Upper Lindum Street	Boys	Upper sixth Yes
Lincoln LN2 5RW	● Girls	Termly fees:
Telephone number 0522 43764	Mixed sixth	Day £650
	● Day	Boarding £1340
	● Boarding	

Head Mrs Anne M Scott
Age range 11–18; own prep from age 3; entry by own exam

St Joseph's (Stoke)

St Joseph's College	Co-ed	Pupils 327
London Road	● Boys	Upper sixth 31
Trent Vale	Girls	Termly fees:
Stoke on Trent ST4 5NT	● Mixed sixth	Day £597
Telephone number 0782 48008	● Day	
Enquiries/application to the Headmaster	Boarding	

WHAT IT'S LIKE

Founded in 1931 by the Christian Brothers, a religious congregation established in Ireland in 1802. It has pleasant, well-designed buildings and stands on elevated grounds comprising 10 acres. At Hanford are 15 acres of playing fields. It caters for a wide area of North Staffordshire and surrounding districts and has a long record of service to the local community. A Roman Catholic school, it is conducted by the Christian Brothers. All pupils follow the religious education programme. Academic standards and results are good. Some 12–15 leavers go on to university each year. It has a tremendously strong music department. All learn an instrument and about 220 pupils are involved in choirs and orchestras. The art department is also very strong. A very good range of sports and games in which standards are high (quite a few representatives at county level). A big commitment to local community services, charities etc.

SCHOOL PROFILE

Pupils Total over 12, 327 (boys 320, girls 7). Entry age, boys, 7+, 11+; boys and girls into the sixth. Own junior department provides over 60%. 10% are children of former pupils.
Entrance Own entrance exam used. Not oversubscribed. No special skills or religious requirements. Parents not expected to buy text books. 6 scholarships/bursaries, value £500.
Parents 15+% are doctors, lawyers etc; 15+% in industry or commerce. 100% live within 30 miles.

Staff Head Rev E S Kerrigan, in post for 4 years. 32 full time staff, 8 part time. Annual turnover 3%.

Academic work GCSE and A-levels. Average size of upper fifth 54; upper sixth 31. *O-levels*: on average, 15 pupils in upper fifth pass 1–4 subjects; 15, 5–7 subjects; 20 pass 8+ subjects. *A-levels*: on average, 4 pupils in upper sixth pass 1 subject; 5, 2 subjects; 7, 3 subjects and 13 pass 4 subjects. On average, 18 take science/engineering A-levels; 10 take arts and humanities; 2 a mixture. *Computing facilities* in labs.

Senior pupils' non-academic activities *Music*: All pupils learn a musical instrument, 6 to Grade 6 or above; 1 accepted for Music School, 3 go on to play in pop groups; 100 in school orchestra; 120 in school choir; 20 in brass and wind groups. *Art*: 240 take as non-examined subject; 40 GCSE; 4 A-level; 1 accepted for Art School. *Sport*: Rugby, athletics, cross country, cricket, squash, golf, swimming, volleyball, tennis available. 100 take non-compulsory sport. 20 take cycling exams. 12 represent county/country (rugby, cricket, athletics). *Other*: 20 take part in handicapped club. Other activities include a computer club.

Careers 1 part time careers advisor. Average number of pupils accepted for *arts and humanities degree courses* at Oxbridge, 1; other universities, 3; polytechnics or CHE, 7. *science and engineering degree courses* at universities, 10; medical schools, 2; polytechnics or CHE, 3. *BEd*, 1. Average number of pupils going straight into careers in armed services, 1; industry, 3; the City, 2; other, 4.

Uniform School uniform worn throughout.

Houses/prefects Competitive houses. Prefects and head boy – elected by staff and sixth formers.

Religion Religious worship not compulsory for non-Catholics.

Social No organised contact with other schools at present; some organised trips abroad. Pupils allowed to bring own car/bike/motorbike to school. Meals self service. Smoking by sixth formers tolerated; no alcohol.

Discipline No corporal punishment. Pupils failing to produce homework once might expect a reprimand or detention; those caught smoking cannabis on the premises would be suspended or expelled – this has not arisen.

St Lawrence

St Lawrence College
Ramsgate
Kent CT11 7AE
Telephone number 0843 587666

- Co-ed   Pupils 350
  Boys   Upper sixth Yes
  Girls   Termly fees:
  Mixed sixth   Day £1330
- Day   Boarding £1980
- Boarding   HMC

Head J H Binfield (5 years)
Age range 11–18; own junior school from age 4; entrance by common entrance or own exam. 10% of pupils from overseas
Some scholarships and bursaries available.

St Leonard's

St Leonard's School	Co-ed	Pupils 420
St Andrew's	Boys	Upper sixth 55
Fife	● Girls	Termly fees:
Scotland KY16 9QU	Mixed sixth	Day £1175
Telephone number 0334 72126	● Day	Boarding £2350
	● Boarding	GSA
Enquiries/application to the Headmistress		

WHAT IT'S LIKE

Founded in 1877, it has a single (and historic) site on the edge of the old town which is the seat of Scotland's oldest university. It is a very fine campus indeed with 30 acres of parkland and playing fields and is generally regarded as one of the leading schools for girls in Britain. It has excellent facilities and accommodation and its computer centre is reckoned to be the best in Scotland. Religious attendance is compulsory. A very large staff permits a staff:pupil ratio of 1:7. The teaching is of a high standard and academic results are consistently impressive. A high proportion of leavers (40-plus) go on to university each year. It is very strong in music, drama and art and has had many successes in these fields. Also very strong in games and sports (there are many county and international representatives, especially in hockey and lacrosse). A splendid range of extra-curricular activities and an outstanding record in the Duke of Edinburgh's Award Scheme.

SCHOOL PROFILE

Pupils Total over 12, 420. Day 63; Boarding 370. Entry age, 11+ and into the sixth form.

Entrance Common entrance and own entrance test used. No special skills or religious requirements. Parents expected to buy some text books in sixth form. 22 assisted places. 30 scholarships/bursaries available, £50–£3000 pa.

Parents 15+% in industry or commerce; 15+% are doctors, lawyers etc. 30+% live within 30 miles; 20+% live overseas.

Staff Head Mrs Mary James, first year in post. 44 full time staff, 12 part time. Annual turnover 5–10%. Average age mid–late 30s.

Academic work GCSE, Highers and A-levels. Average size of upper fifth 60; upper sixth 65. *O-levels*: on average, 50 pupils pass 8+ subjects. *A-levels*: on average, 50 pupils in the upper sixth pass 3 subjects. On average, 15 take science/engineering A-levels; 20 take arts and humanities; 25 a mixture. Very occasionally Chinese, Portuguese and Russian are offered to GCSE/A-level. *Computing facilities*: Excellent, quite outstanding computer centre – reputed to be the best equipped in Scotland.

Senior pupils' non-academic activities *Music*: 100 learn a musical instrument, approx 15 to Grade 6 or above; 10 take GCSE. 1 accepted for Music School. 35 in school orchestra, 45 in choir, 10 in jazz band, some pupils in Scottish Independent Schools Orchestra. *Drama and dance*: 25 seniors in school productions; 250 in inter-house drama festival; 12 take LAMDA Grade 6 and over (verse and prose), 28 (acting); 10–20 (ballet exams). 4 accepted for Drama School; 1 goes on to work in theatre; 1 on to speech and drama. *Art*: 10 take as non-examined subject; 15–25 take GCSE; 3–8, A-level; 9–13, A-level history of art; 7–10, Higher art and design. Up to 6 accepted for Art

School; 1–3 to university – fine art. *Sport*: Lacrosse, hockey, tennis, athletics, swimming, squash, shooting, fencing, golf, badminton, volleyball, basketball, ballet, canoeing, gymnastics, dance, judo, ski-ing available. 130 take non-compulsory sport; 1–2 fencing exams; 15–25 athletics; 6 life saving. Numerous pupils represent county and country (hockey, lacrosse, athletics). *Other*: 13 take part in local community schemes. 51 have bronze Duke of Edinburgh's Award, 30 have silver and 14 gold. Other activities include a computer club, chess club, history and arts society, geographical society, modern languages society, senior scientific society; driving lessons available.

Careers A team overseeing careers counselling; work experience/shadowing; business enterprise. Average number of pupils accepted for *arts and humanities degree courses* at Oxbridge, 4; other universities, 22; polytechnics or CHE, 11. *science and engineering degree courses* at Oxbridge, 1; other universities, 13; medical schools, 4. *other general training courses*, 12. Average number of pupils going straight into careers in the armed services, 1. No traditional school careers but law and medicine very popular.

Uniform School uniform worn until upper sixth.

Houses/prefects Competitive houses. No prefects. Head girl and head of houses – appointed by the Head and housemistresses. School Council.

Religion Girls must attend a local church on Sundays. 2 school services are arranged each term.

Social Occasional links with local schools in music, debates – more usual to join up with public schools not too far away for debates, music, classics discussions etc. Many organised trips. Recent trips in addition to annual ski-ing and trips to France have been to China, Greece and Russia. Pupils allowed to bring own car/bicycle to school. Meals formal, self service on Saturday and Sunday evenings. No school shop, very near to local ones. No tobacco/alcohol allowed.

Discipline No corporal punishment. Pupils failing to produce homework once might be expected to produce it and perhaps do some additional work; those caught smoking cannabis on the premises would be expelled immediately.

Boarding Sixth form have own study bedroom, occasionally pupils share; 50% are in dormitories of 6+. Houses, of 32–48 same as competitive houses. 2 resident SRNs, doctor visits every day. Central dining room. Sixth formers can provide and cook own food. Half-term and 2 weekend exeats each term. Visits to local town allowed.

Alumni association run by Miss B Bushnell, c/o the School.

ST LEONARDS-MAYFIELD

St Leonards-Mayfield School	Co-ed	Pupils 480
The Old Palace	Boys	Upper sixth 70
Mayfield	● Girls	Termly fees:
East Sussex TN20 6PH	Mixed sixth	Day £1290
Telephone number 0435 873055	● Day	Boarding £1935
	● Boarding	GSA; CCSS
Enquiries/application to the Headmistress		

WHAT IT'S LIKE

Started in 1863 when the Duchess of Leeds presented to the foundress of the Society of the Holy Child Jesus the property which comprised the ruins (and the surrounding land) of the 'Old Palace' of the medieval archbishops of Canterbury. These and the synod hall were restored and the school opened in 1872. Besides the original buildings there are extensive modern facilities and accommodation in delightful grounds and gardens. A Roman Catholic foundation (boarders must be Catholic) the doctrines and practice of the Church (attendance at Mass etc) are an important part of the curriculum. A high staff:pupil ratio of 1:10. Good academic standards prevail (an impressive pass rate in public exams). Music, drama and art departments are well supported. A wide range of sports, games and activities is available. The Duke of Edinburgh's Award Scheme is popular. Pupils are encouraged to participate in local community schemes.

SCHOOL PROFILE

Pupils Total over 12, 480. 70% are boarders. Entry age, 11+, 13+ and into the sixth.

Entrance Common entrance and own scholarship exams used. Usually oversubscribed. Special gifts welcomed; boarders must be Roman Catholic. Parents are expected to buy a few text books. Means-tested scholarships and bursaries, up to full fees.

Parents 35% live within 30 miles; 30% live overseas.

Staff Head Sister Jean Sinclair, in post for 8 years. 53 full time staff, 12 part time. Annual turnover varies.

Academic work GCSE and A-levels. Average size of upper fifth 80–90; upper sixth 70. *O-levels*: Average pupil passes 8 subjects. *Computing facilities*: Computer room and computers in other areas.

Religion Boarders must be Catholic; RC doctrines and practice are important.

St Margaret's (Aberdeen)

St Margaret's School for Girls	Co-ed	Pupils 231
17 Albyn Place	Boys	Upper sixth 25
Aberdeen AB9 1RH	● Girls	Termly fees:
Telephone number 0224 584466	Mixed sixth	Day £691
	● Day	Boarding £1624
Enquiries/application to Headmistress	● Boarding	GBGSA; GSA;
		HAS; SHA

WHAT IT'S LIKE

Founded in 1846 and the oldest all-through girls' school in Scotland, it is situated in Albyn Place, one of the city's finest conservation areas. Its facilities are first rate. Boarding pupils live in Glenmhor which is within walking distance. The school aims to provide an all-round modern education with a sound academic basis. A variety of sports is available.

SCHOOL PROFILE

Pupils Total over 12, 231. Day 217; Boarding 14. Entry age, 5 upwards and into the sixth. Own junior department provides over 50%. 8% are children of former pupils.

Entrance Own test and interview. No special skills or religious requirements. Parents expected to buy text books. Assisted places available. 1 internal scholarship for sixth year, £400.

Parents 15+% are doctors, lawyers etc; 15+% in industry or commerce. 60+% live within 30 miles; up to 10% live overseas.

Staff Head Miss M D Bosomworth, in post for 18 years. Miss L Ogilvie from Jan 1989. 30 full time staff, 11 part time. Annual turnover 1%.

Academic work O-grade, Highers, CSYS, A-level Music, GCSE Drama, SCOTVEC Home Economics, RSA Typewriting.

Senior pupils' non-academic activities *Music*: Orchestral groups, choirs. *Sport*: Athletics, badminton, basketball, dance, gymnastics, hockey, netball, squash, swimming, tennis, volleyball available. *Other activities* include computer club, Young Engineers' Club, drama society, debating society and Scripture Union.

St Margaret's (Edinburgh)

St Margaret's School Edinburgh Ltd	Co-ed	Pupils 537
East Suffolk Road	Boys	Upper sixth 70
Edinburgh EH16 5PJ	● Girls	Termly fees:
Telephone number 031 668 1986	Mixed sixth	Day £800
Enquiries/application to the Headmistress	● Day	Boarding £1525
	● Boarding	GSA

WHAT IT'S LIKE

Founded in 1890, it is urban with the school houses around the site within a quarter of a mile of each other. There are pleasant buildings and grounds. The nursery and preparatory departments are combined. Very good facilities and comfortable boarding accommodation are provided. A certain amount of religious worship is compulsory. The music, drama and art departments are very strong indeed. The school also has a very high reputation in sports and games (15–20 representatives at county level). The record in the Duke of Edinburgh's Award Scheme is outstanding.

SCHOOL PROFILE

Pupils Total over 12, 537. Day 462; Boarding 75. Entry age, 3, 5, 12 and into the sixth. Own prep department provides over 40%. 5% are children of former pupils.

Entrance Own entrance exam used. Sometimes oversubscribed. No special skills or religious requirements. Parents not expected to buy text books. 54 assisted places. 4 scholarships/bursaries available, full day fees to half day fees.

Parents 15+% are in industry or commerce; 15+% are doctors, lawyers etc;

15+% are academics, lecturers etc. 60+% live within 30 miles; up to 10% live overseas.

Staff Head Mrs M J Cameron, in post for 4 years. 60 full time staff, 20 part time. Annual turnover 2%. Average age 45.

Academic work O-grade, Highers, CSYS and A-levels. Average size of upper fifth 100; upper sixth 70. *O-levels*: on average, 23 pupils in upper fifth pass 1–4 subjects; 76, 5–7 subjects; 10 pass 8+ subjects. *A-levels*: on average, 22 pupils in upper sixth pass 1 subject; 10, 2 subjects; 3, 3 subjects and 1 passes 4 subjects. On average, 14 take science/engineering A-levels; 14 take arts and humanities; 3 a mixture. Dutch, Swedish and other languages as required are offered. *Computing facilities*: 2 computer labs, fully equipped. About 12 computers in individual classrooms. EFL provision.

Senior pupils' non-academic activities *Music*: 230 learn a musical instrument, 15 to Grade 6 or above, 1 accepted for Music School; 50 in school orchestra, 35 in choir; 1 in National Youth Orchestra, 3 in county orchestra. *Drama and dance*: 100 in school productions. 1 accepted for Drama/Dance School. 1 goes on to work in theatre. *Art*: 20 take as non-examined subject; 48 take O-grade; 10 A-level. 2 accepted for Art School. 50 belong to photographic club. *Sport*: Hockey, lacrosse, badminton, squash, swimming, tennis, athletics, dance-gymnastics available. 95% take non-compulsory sport; 15 take ski-ing. Pupils represent county (hockey, swimming, lacrosse, fencing, tennis). *Other*: 40+ take part in local community schemes. 45 have bronze Duke of Edinburgh's Award, 25 have silver and 25 gold. 2 enter voluntary schemes after leaving school. Other activities include a computer club, country dancing, self-defence, ski-ing. Boarders: riding, driving lessons.

Careers 1 full time and 1 part time advisor. Average number of pupils accepted for *arts and humanities degree courses* at universities, 9; polytechnics or CHE, 30. *science and engineering degree courses* at Oxbridge, 1; other universities, 8; medical schools, 2. *BEd*, 1. *other general training courses*, 10. 10 pupils a year go on to other schools for a final year.

Uniform School uniform worn except in the sixth.

Houses/prefects Competitive houses. No prefects. Head girl and head of house – elected by the school. School Council.

Religion Compulsory assembly and church on Sunday for boarders under 16.

Social Reel club, debates, productions with other local schools. Organised exchanges with France and Germany, trips of various kinds every year. Pupils allowed to bring own car/bike/motorbike to school. Meals self service. School shop. No tobacco/alcohol allowed.

Discipline No corporal punishment. Pupils failing to produce homework once might expect a reprimand; those caught smoking cannabis on the premises could expect suspension and their parents informed.

Boarding 1% have own study bedroom, 33% share (with 1); 25% are in dormitories of 6+. Houses, of 25 and 60 are divided by age group. Central dining room. Various exeats each term, up to every weekend for seniors. Visits to the local town allowed.

Alumni association run by Mrs Christine Seaton, c/o 110 Mayfield Road, Edinburgh 9.

St Martha's (Hadley Wood)

St Martha's Convent
Camlet Way
Hadley
Barnet
Hertfordshire
Telephone number 01-449 6759

Co-ed   Pupils 278
Boys   Upper sixth 15
● Girls   Termly fees:
Mixed sixth   Day £580
● Day   Boarding £1075
● Boarding

Enquiries/application to the Headmistress

WHAT IT'S LIKE

Founded in 1947, it lies opposite Hadley Wood just outside Barnet. The main building is Mount House, a very handsome 18th century country house with beautiful gardens and grounds. This has been adapted and is well-equipped. A limited number of weekly boarders are taken at the convent (Hadley Bourne) on Hadley Green about 5 minutes' walk from the school. It is run by the Sisters of St Martha, a Roman Catholic order which originated in the 17th century in the Dordogne. There is a certain amount of emphasis on religious instruction, prayer and worship. The academic standards are reasonable and results quite good. A few girls go on to university each year. Some music and art but, apparently, minimal drama. A few sports and games but no extra-curricular activities and no community services or Duke of Edinburgh's Award Scheme.

SCHOOL PROFILE

Pupils Total over 12, 278. Day 264; Boarding 14. Entry age, 11 and into the sixth. Own junior school provides over 20%. 5% are children of former pupils.

Entrance Own entrance exam used. No special skills, Catholic school accepting other faiths. Parents expected to buy text books. No scholarships/bursaries but some Catholics accepted at part fees.

Parents 15+% in industry or commerce. 60+% live within 30 miles.

Staff Head Sister M Cecile Archer, in post for 11 years. 19 full time staff, 6 part time. Annual turnover 1–2%. Average age 35–40.

Academic work GCSE and A-levels. Average size of upper fifth 60; upper sixth 15. *O-levels*: on average, 24 pupils in upper fifth pass 1–4 subjects; 17, 5–7 subjects; 7 pass 8+ subjects. *A-levels*: on average, 2 pupils in upper sixth pass 1 subject; and 4 pass 2 subjects. On average, 6 take science/engineering A-levels; 6 take arts and humanities. *Computing facilities*: computer room.

Senior pupils' non-academic activities *Music*: 40–50 learn a musical instrument, 15 in school orchestra, 30 in choir. *Art*: 23 take GCSE; 2 A-level. *Sport*: Netball, tennis, badminton, swimming, golf, squash available.

Careers 2 part time careers advisors. Average number of pupils accepted for *arts and humanities degree courses* at universities, 2; polytechnics or CHE, 3. *science and engineering degree courses* at universities, 2; polytechnics or CHE, 2. *BEd*, 1. Average number of pupils going straight into careers in industry, 3–4; civil service, 1; music/drama, 1.

Uniform School uniform worn except the sixth.

Houses/prefects No competitive houses. Prefects and head girl – appointed by the Head.

Religion Worship encouraged.
Social Some organised trips abroad. Sixth form allowed to bring own car to school. Meals self service. School shop. No tobacco/alcohol allowed.
Discipline No corporal punishment. Pupils failing to produce homework once might expect a warning; those caught smoking cannabis on the premises might expect suspension for a period.
Boarding Nearly all have own study bedroom, rest share with 2–3. Central dining room. All boarders go home at weekends. Visits to local town not allowed.

St Mary's Hall

St Mary's Hall	Co-ed	Pupils 340
Eastern Road	Boys	Upper sixth Yes
Brighton	● Girls	Termly fees:
East Sussex BN2 5JF	Mixed sixth	Day £1200
Telephone number 0273 606061	● Day	Boarding £1800
	● Boarding	

Head Miss M F C Harvey (7 years)
Age range 9–18; entry by common entrance and own exam
Scholarships; bursaries.

St Mary's Music

St Mary's Music School	● Co-ed	Pupils 31
Manor Place	Boys	Upper sixth 6
Edinburgh EH3 7EB	Girls	Termly fees:
Telephone number 031 225 1831	Mixed sixth	Day £2605
Enquiries/application to the Headmaster	● Day	Boarding £3575
	● Boarding	(means tested)

WHAT IT'S LIKE

Founded in 1880 as the choir school of St Mary's Episcopal Cathedral, in 1972 it widened its scope as a music school. It continues its choral tradition, but the bulk of its pupils are now instrumentalists. Composition, singing, counterpoint, harmony and aural training are also taught. The pupils specialise in all branches of music. The academic side is also taken care of, and an all-round education is provided. The academic work takes place in Old Coates House, next to the cathedral, dating from 1614. The musical education is done at Palmerston Place, just opposite. Good facilities and accommodation are provided.

SCHOOL PROFILE

Pupils Total over 12, 31. Day 11 (boys 8, girls 3); Boarding 20 (boys 8, girls 12). Entry age, 9–16.

Entrance Admission by audition. Oversubscribed. Good musical skills required, no religious requirements. Parents not expected to buy text books. 30 means tested aided places, 9 scholarships for choristers.

Parents 10+% live within 30 miles; up to 10% live overseas.

Staff Head J P S Allison, in post for 8 years. 5 full time staff, 33 part time. Annual turnover 1–10%. Average age mid-30s.

Academic work GCSE, O-grades, Highers and A-levels. Average size of S4-form, 6; S6-form, 6. All take arts and humanities A-levels; most get 4–6 O-grades, 2–4 Highers and 1 A-level.

Senior pupils' non-academic activities *Music*: All pupils are musicians; all are accepted for music schools. *Drama and dance*: 2–6 in school productions. *Art*: 1 takes art as non-examined subject; 2 O-grade; 2–3 A-level. *Sport*: Badminton, fencing, swimming, hillwalking available. 10 take non-compulsory sport.

Careers Advice given by teachers. All pupils are accepted for Music School or music degree course at university.

Uniform School uniform not worn.

Houses/prefects No competitive houses, prefects or head boy/girl.

Religion Compulsory religious worship.

Social Occasional activities (always musical) with other local schools. Occasional musical tours, eg choir to visit Japan in April 89. Pupils allowed to bring own car/bike/motorbike to school. Meals self service. No tobacco/alcohol allowed.

Discipline No corporal punishment. Pupils failing to produce homework once would be asked why; those caught smoking cannabis on the premises could expect expulsion.

Boarding 1 has own study bedroom, others share (1 or 2 others). Central dining room. 3 exeats each term, 3–10 days. Visits to the local town allowed.

St Mary's (Ascot)

St Mary's School
St Mary's Road
Ascot
Berkshire SL5 9JF
Telephone number 0990 23721

Enquiries/application to the Admissions Secretary

Co-ed
Boys
● Girls
Mixed sixth
● Day
● Boarding

Pupils 320
Upper sixth 40
Termly fees:
Day £1134
Boarding £1890
GSA

WHAT IT'S LIKE

Founded in 1885, it is semi-rural, single-site and purpose-built in 55 acres of very pleasant gardens and grounds. The buildings are well designed and accommodation comfortable. Very good modern facilities. It is owned and managed by the Institute of the Blessed Virgin Mary and quite a few of the staff are Sisters of the Order. A Roman Catholic foundation. All pupils *must* be RCs. The doctrines and practices of the Church (attendance at Sunday Mass etc) are an essential part of the curriculum. Academically the standards are high and results are good. Each year 10 or more leavers go on to university. Strong in music, drama and art. A wide range of games, sports and activities. Some commitment to local community schemes and a promising record in the Duke of Edinburgh's Award Scheme.

SCHOOL PROFILE

Pupils Total over 12, 320. Day 10; Boarding 310. Entry age, 10, 11 and into the sixth. 7% are children of former pupils.

Entrance Own entrance exam used. Oversubscribed. No special skills required but pupils should be Roman Catholic. Parents expected to buy text books in sixth form.

Parents 15+% in industry or commerce. 30+% live within 30 miles; 10+% live overseas.

Staff Head Sister Mark Orchard, in post for 5 years. 40 full time staff, 20 part time. Annual turnover 5%. Average age 42.

Academic work GCSE and A-levels. Average size of upper fifth 45; upper sixth 40. *O-levels*: on average, 4 pupils in upper fifth pass 1–4 subjects; 11, 5–7 subjects; 30 pass 8+ subjects. *A-levels*: on average, 1 pupil in upper sixth passes 1 subject; 2, 2 subjects; 37, 3 subjects and 1 passes 4 subjects. On average, 5 take science/engineering A-levels; 25 take arts and humanities; 10 a mixture. Italian offered to GCSE/A-level. *Computing facilities*: 8 BBC computers. Provision for mildly dyslexic pupils.

Senior pupils' non-academic activities *Music*: 50 learn a musical instrument, 10 up to Grade 6 or above, 1 accepted for Music School; 40 in school orchestra, 35 in school choir. Others in Bach Choir. *Drama and dance*: 50 in school productions. 10 up to Grade 6 ESB etc. 2 accepted for Drama School. *Art*: 40 take as non-examined subject; 30 GCSE; 15 A-level. 2 accepted for Art and Architectural School. 20 belong to eg photographic club, 20 take pottery. *Sport*: Netball, hockey, tennis, rounders, athletics, swimming, badminton, keep fit, fencing, golf, squash (in Ascot town), trampolining, karate available. 40 take non-compulsory sport. *Other*: 15 take part in local community schemes. 25 have bronze Duke of Edinburgh's Award, 3 have silver and 1 gold. 2 enter voluntary schemes after leaving. Other activities include a computer club, bridge, debating, theatre, art appreciation, music appreciation, jazz dancing, wine tasting, driving.

Careers 1 full time careers advisor. Average number of pupils accepted for *arts and humanities degree courses* at Oxbridge, 6; polytechnics or CHE, 2. *science and engineering degree courses* at Oxbridge, 1; other universities, 2. *BEd*, 1. Average number of pupils going straight into careers in music/drama, 1.

Uniform School uniform worn, except the sixth.

Houses/prefects Competitive houses. Prefects, head girl, head of house and house prefects – mixture of appointment by Head and election by school.

Religion Compulsory worship in accordance with requirements of RC church.

Social Occasional debates, sports events, theatrical performances with other schools. Organised ski-ing trips abroad; A-level French and History of Art trip to Paris. Senior pupils allowed to bring own bike to school. Meals self service. No tobacco/alcohol allowed.

Discipline No corporal punishment. Pupils failing to produce homework

once might expect detention; those caught smoking cannabis on the premises may expect expulsion.

Boarding 23% have own study bedroom, 57% share with 1 other; 20% are in dormitories of 6+. Houses, of 60, divided by age. Resident qualified nurse. Central dining room. Sixth form only can provide and cook own food. 2–4 exeats each term. Visits to local town allowed.

Alumni association run by Sister Bridget Geoffrey-Smith, c/o the School.

Former pupils Sarah Hogg; Marina Warner.

ST MARY'S (CALNE)

St Mary's School
Calne
Wiltshire SN11 0DF
Telephone number 0249 815899

Co-ed	Pupils 310
Boys	Upper sixth Yes
● Girls	Termly fees:
Mixed sixth	Day £1150
● Day	Boarding £1950
● Boarding	GSA

Head Miss D H Burns (3 years)
Age range 11–18, own prep from age 5; entrance by common entrance
Scholarships and bursaries.

ST MARY'S (CAMBRIDGE)

St Mary's School
Bateman Street
Cambridge CB2 1LY
Telephone number 0223 353253

Enquiries to the Headmistress
Application to the Admissions Secretary

Co-ed	Pupils 550
Boys	Upper sixth 50
● Girls	Termly fees:
Mixed sixth	Day £720
● Day	Boarding £1280
● Boarding	GSA

WHAT IT'S LIKE

Founded in 1898, it is sited in the City centre, overlooking the university botanic garden, within easy walking distance of museums, theatres and colleges. Excellent facilities. Basically a Roman Catholic school, but inter-denominational. It is administered by the Religion of the Institute of The Blessed Virgin Mary. Mass and other services are attended by the majority of pupils. The religious education curriculum is based on Catholic doctrine and is followed by all pupils. Within the setting of a Christian community the school provides an education of the grammar school type. Academic standards are high (92.6% A-level pass rate in 1987). Some 30 leavers go on to university each year. Talents for music, art, drama and sport are strongly encouraged. It is in fact extremely strong in drama, and very strong in music and art. Very much a local school working closely with parents. Well known in the area for its Christian teaching, pastoral care and happy and purposeful atmosphere. A wide variety of sports, games and extra-curricular activities. A very large commitment to local community schemes. Substantial participation in the Duke of Edinburgh's Award Scheme and an impressive record.

SCHOOL PROFILE

Pupils Total over 12, 550. Day 478; Boarding (weekly) 72. Entry age, 11 and into the sixth. Many pupils come from state primary schools. 5% are children of former pupils.

Entrance Own entrance exam used. Oversubscribed. Special consideration given to candidates with talents in music and art. Roman Catholic school but other Christian denominations welcomed. Parents not expected to buy text books. 115 assisted places.

Parents 60+% live within 30 miles; none live overseas.

Staff Head Sister Christina Kenworthy-Browne, in post for 11 years. 42 full time staff, 10 part time plus music and drama staff. Average age 40.

Academic work GCSE and A-levels. Average size of upper fifth 80; upper sixth 50. *O-levels*: on average, 8 pupils in upper fifth pass 1–4 subjects; 17, 5–7 subjects; 55 pass 8+ subjects. *A-levels*: on average, 4 pupils in upper sixth pass 1 subject; 6, 2 subjects; 38, 3 subjects and 2 pass 4 subjects. On average, 10 take science/engineering A-levels; 24 take arts and humanities; 16 a mixture. Greek offered to GCSE/A-level. *Computing facilities*: 2 laboratories; suite of BBC microcomputers linked by Econet with SJ level 3 fileserver; computers in science laboratories; further expansion in progress. Some physically handicapped pupils accepted.

Senior pupils' non-academic activities *Music*: 95 learn a musical instrument, 12 up to Grade 6 or above, 1 accepted for Music School; 30 in school orchestra, 63 choir, 6 guitar group, 30 in various ensembles, wind and brass groups. *Drama and dance*: 50 in school productions, 200 in school drama competition, 30 in dance display. 20 to grade 6 LAMDA, 10 in Cambridge Speech and Drama Festival. 2 accepted for Drama/Dance Schools. *Art*: 10 take as non-examined subject; 32 GCSE; 6 A-level. 3–4 accepted for Art School. 20 belong to eg photographic club. *Sport*: Athletics, badminton, canoeing, golf, gymnastics, hockey, judo, netball, rounders, squash, swimming, trampolining, tennis, table tennis, volleyball available. 50 take non-compulsory sport. 20 take exams in eg swimming. 2 pupils represent country, 4 represent county, in tennis. School won East of England cup at tennis 1987. *Other*: 100 take part in local community schemes. 20 enter voluntary schemes after leaving; 2 work for national charities. 52 have bronze Duke of Edinburgh's Award, 33 have silver and 2 gold. Other activities include a computer club, Young Enterprise (awards in 1987), debating, pottery, field work, dances. New Art, Craft and Design Centre.

Careers 2 part time careers advisors, plus outside experts. Average number of pupils accepted for *arts and humanities degree courses* at Oxbridge, 5; other universities, 18; polytechnics or CHE, 7. *science and engineering degree courses* at Oxbridge, 2; other universities, 3; medical schools, 2; polytechnics or CHE, 2. BEd, 2. *other general training courses*, 6. Average number of pupils going straight into careers in civil service, 1–2; other careers, 1–2.

Uniform School uniform worn except in sixth.

Houses/prefects No competitive houses. No prefects; duties shared by upper sixth. Head girl and group of deputies – elected by staff and sixth form. Sixth Form Council.

Religion All attend daily assembly and Christmas carol service. Mass and other services attended by majority of pupils. Roman Catholic RE curriculum followed by all pupils.

Social Combined Cambridge school choirs (major work in alternate years); debating, theatrical productions with other schools. Regular exchanges with school in Paris; Spanish, German, Italian exchanges; other excursions abroad. Pupils allowed to bring own bike to school. Meals self service. School shop. No tobacco/alcohol allowed.

Discipline No corporal punishment. There is no penal code. Pupils are expected to work hard and to respect the aims of the school. Parents would be consulted in serious cases, and decisions would depend on circumstances.

Boarding 45 have own study bedroom, 35 share (2–5 beds per room). Central dining room. Pupils return home at weekends. Visits to local town allowed, according to age.

Alumni association run by Mrs S de Backer, c/o the School.

St Mary's (Colchester)

St Mary's School
Lexden Road
Colchester
Essex CO3 3RB
Telephone number 0206 572544

Enquiries/application to the Principal

Co-ed
Boys
● Girls
Mixed sixth
● Day
Boarding

Pupils 310
Upper sixth 4
Termly fees:
Day £710
GSA

WHAT IT'S LIKE

Founded in 1908, it is the only independent girls' school in the Colchester area offering secondary education. The senior school has an urban site; that of the lower school is semi-rural, 3 miles away on a 9-acre estate. Both have pleasant buildings and adequate facilities. A sound general education is provided. Most girls transfer at 16. Quite strong music and art departments. A very good variety of sports, games and extra-curricular activities. Some commitment to local community schemes and the Duke of Edinburgh's Award Scheme.

SCHOOL PROFILE

Pupils Total over 11, 310. Entry age, 4, 11 and into the sixth. Own junior department provides more than 20%. 6% are children of former pupils.

Entrance Own entrance exam used. Oversubscribed. No special skills or religious requirements. Parents not expected to buy text books. No scholarships/bursaries but reduction for sisters.

Parents 60+% live within 30 miles; up to 10% live overseas.

Staff Head Mrs G Mouser, in post for 7 years. 30 full time staff, 23 part time. Annual turnover 6%. Average age – school says irrelevant.

Academic work GCSE and A-levels. Average size of upper fifth 56; upper sixth 4 (only began 1986). *O-levels*: on average, 14 pupils in upper fifth pass 1–4 subjects; 28, 5–7 subjects; 14 pass 8+ subjects. *A-levels*: No data yet available. All pupils taking arts and humanities. *Computing facilities*: GCSE option; small specialist room, additional facilities in maths suite. Outside coaching arranged for dyslexia and EFL.

Senior pupils' non-academic activities *Music*: 30+ learn a musical instrument, 5 to Grade 6 or above, 1 accepted for Music School; 15+ in school orchestra, 75 school choir; 2 county youth orchestra, 1 National Youth Orchestra. *Drama and dance*: 20–40 in school productions. 2 take ESB, RAD etc to Grade 6. 1 accepted for Drama/Dance school. *Art*: 20 take GCSE; 2 take A-level. *Sport*: Tennis, hockey, indoor hockey, netball, cross-country, athletics, gymnastics, badminton, squash, trampolining, weight training, self-defence, golf, swimming, keep fit available. Sport compulsory. *Other*: 10 take part in local community schemes. 15 working for bronze Duke of Edinburgh's Award. Other activities include police-run pre-driving course.

Careers 1 part time careers advisor. Most pupils have left at 16 for sixth form college.

Uniform School uniform worn except the sixth.

Houses/prefects Competitive houses. Prefects, head girl, head of house and house prefects elected by the school and staff.

Religion Daily assembly, Harvest Festival and carol services are compulsory.

Social Debates with Royal Grammar School (boys) and local independent boys' school; occasional joint productions. Annual ski-ing holiday; biennial cruise; annual language courses in France; exchanges in France and Germany. Pupils allowed to bring own car/bike to school. Meals formal. No tobacco/alcohol allowed.

Discipline No corporal punishment. Pupils failing to produce homework once might expect a stern reproach (detention and report system for frequent offenders); those caught smoking cigarettes on the premises can expect exclusion for 24 hours and letter home.

Alumni association run by Mrs J Woodland, c/o the School.

ST MARY'S (CROSBY)

St Mary's College
Crosby
Mersey L23 3AB
Telephone number 051 924 3926

Enquiries/application to the Secretary

- Co-ed
  Boys
  Girls
  Mixed sixth
- Day
  Boarding

Pupils 499
Upper sixth 70
Termly fees:
Day £612
HMC

WHAT IT'S LIKE

Founded in 1919 by the Christian Brothers. Urban and single-site, except the playing fields which are on a separate site. The first school buildings were erected in 1923–4 and there has been regular expansion and development since. There is a preparatory department and a main school and facilities are now good. It is a Roman Catholic foundation and most pupils are RCs.

However, other denominations are welcome. Considerable emphasis on religious education, prayer and worship which are all encouraged. A sound general education is provided and results are very good. Some 40 or more pupils go on to university each year. There is some music and drama, and very considerable strength in art. A good range of sports and games in which high standards are achieved. An adequate range of extra-curricular activities. A voluntary CCF is flourishing.

SCHOOL PROFILE

Pupils Total over 12, 499 (boys 475, girls 24). Entry age, boys, 11+; boys and girls into the sixth. First intake of girls at 11 in 1988. Own preparatory department provides over 20%. 40% are children of former pupils.

Entrance Own entrance exam used. Oversubscribed. No special skills required; RC school, other practising Christians admitted. Parents not expected to buy text books. 45 assisted places. 12 bursaries pa, £1800–£150.

Parents 15+% are doctors, lawyers etc; 15+% in industry or commerce. 60+% live within 30 miles.

Staff Head Rev Br P E Ryan, in post for 1 year. 42 full time staff, 11 part time. Annual turnover 5%. Average age 35.

Academic work GCSE and A-levels. Average size of upper fifth 100; upper sixth 70. *O-levels*: on average, 20 pupils in upper fifth pass 1–4 subjects; 40, 5–7 subjects; 40 pass 8+ subjects. *A-levels*: on average, 5 pupils in upper sixth pass 1 subject; 10, 2 subjects; 15, 3 subjects and 40 pass 4 subjects. On average, 35 take science/engineering A-levels; 25 take arts and humanities; 10 a mixture. *Computing facilities*: 10 RM Nimbus networked, 3 BBC Model B, 1 Commodore Pet.

Senior pupils' non-academic activities *Music*: 2 learn a musical instrument to Grade 6 or above. 20 in school orchestra, 20 in choir, 2 in other orchestras. *Drama and dance*: 40 in school productions, 10 in other. 1 accepted for Drama School. *Art*: 150 take as non-examined subject; 30 GCSE; 10 A-level; 8 accepted for Art School. 20 belong to photographic club. *Sport*: Rugby, squash, cross-country, swimming, aerobics, weight training, athletics, cricket, golf available. 60 take non-compulsory sport, 5 take exams. 9 represent county/country (rugby, athletics). Other activities include a computer club and lively chess club.

Careers 1 full time careers advisor. Average number of pupils accepted for *arts and humanities degree courses* at Oxbridge, 5; other universities, 10; polytechnics or CHE, 5. *science and engineering degree courses* at Oxbridge, 5; other universities, 20; medical schools, 8; polytechnics or CHE, 5. *BEd*, 3. Average number of pupils going straight into careers in armed services, 4; the church, 1; industry, 4; civil service, 5; other, 10. Traditional school career is medicine.

Uniform School uniform worn throughout.

Houses/prefects Competitive houses. Prefects, head boy/girl – elected by the school. School Council.

Religion Worship encouraged.

Social Joint theatrical production with local independent girls' school, debating competitions. French/German/Spanish language exchanges, ski-ing and other trips abroad. Pupils allowed to bring own car/bike/motorbike to school. Meals self service. School shop selling uniform. Tobacco allowed but no alcohol.

Discipline No corporal punishment. Pupils failing to produce homework once might expect to produce it as soon as possible; those caught smoking cannabis on the premises might expect parents to be called in.

Alumni association run by Mr T Mooney, Chairman, St Mary's Old Boys' Association, Moor Lane, Crosby.

Former pupils John Birt (Deputy Director General, BBC); Kevin McNamara MP.

St Mary's (Gerrards Cross)

St Mary's School
Packhorse Road
Gerrards Cross
Buckinghamshire SL9 8JQ
Telephone number 0753 883370

Enquiries/application to the Headmistress

Co-ed
Boys
● Girls
Mixed sixth
● Day
Boarding

Pupils 225
Upper sixth 20
Termly fees:
Day £800
GSA; GBGSA

WHAT IT'S LIKE

Founded in 1874 and originally run by the Sisters of the Community of St Mary the Virgin, Wantage, it began life in Paddington, London and moved to its present premises in 1937. The main building is a big country house in ample gardens and grounds. There have been many modern extensions to provide good facilities. The junior and senior school are separate entities on the same site on the north edge of Gerrards Cross. Non-denominational but it adheres to Anglican practice and tradition. Academic standards are good. Girls go on to degree courses each year. Good opportunities for drama, speech and music. Adequate range of games, sports and activities. A very impressive record in the Duke of Edinburgh's Award Scheme.

SCHOOL PROFILE

Pupils Total, 225. Entry age, 11 and into the sixth. Own junior school provides over 40%.

Entrance Common entrance and own entrance exam used. Oversubscribed. No special skills or religious requirements. 3 scholarships pa, £800–£200 per term plus 3 scholarships and 2 bursaries for sixth form.

Parents 15+% in industry or commerce. 60+% live within 30 miles.

Staff Head Mrs J P G Smith, in post for 4 years. 17 full time staff, 23 part time. Annual turnover 1–2%

Academic work GCSE and A-levels. Average size of upper fifth 35; upper sixth 20. *Computing facilities*: 7 BBC computers, 1 research computer, word processing etc. Provision for dyslexia, mild visual handicaps and some English language help.

Senior pupils' non-academic activities *Music*: 60 learn a musical instrument, 4 to Grade 6 or above. 28 in school orchestra, 43 school choir, 14 madrigal choir. *Drama and dance*: 70 in school productions, 110 take speech and drama, 20 in festival productions. 8 to Grade 6 ESB, RAD etc, 8 to New Era and LAMDA. 2 accepted for Drama/Dance Schools. 45 enter competitions; 10, National Youth Theatre auditions. *Art*: 28 take GCSE; 6 A-level. 1 accepted for Art School. *Sport*: Netball, rounders, hockey, athletics, tennis, swimming, gymnastics, trampolining, self-defence, squash, badminton, basketball, archery, golf etc available. 40 take non-compulsory winter tennis; 20 in gym squad and trampolining club, 20 in badminton club. 3–4 take exams. 8 represent county/country (tennis, squash, show jumping). *Other*: 25 have bronze Duke of Edinburgh's Award, 10 have silver and 4 gold. Other activities include a computer club, gardening, craft, country dancing, pet care, tap dancing, Young Enterprise group.

Careers 1 part time careers advisor. Average number of pupils accepted for *arts and humanities degree courses* at universities, 2; polytechnics or CHE, 2. *science and engineering degree courses* at Oxbridge, 1. *BEd*, 1. *other general training courses*, 12. Average number of pupils going straight into careers in industry, 2; the City, 1; music/drama, 3. Others go on to sixth form courses at other schools.

Uniform School uniform worn except the sixth.

Houses/prefects Competitive houses. Prefects, head girl, head of house and house prefects – appointed by Head and staff.

Religion Compulsory non-denominational assembly.

Social Debates, sixth form ball, Young Enterprise with other local schools; organised trips abroad. Pupils allowed to bring own car to school. Meals self service. No tobacco/alcohol/make-up/jewellery allowed.

Discipline No corporal punishment. Pupils failing to produce homework once might expect detention; those caught smoking cigarettes on the premises would be liable to expulsion. Any involvement with drugs would be regarded in the most serious light.

Alumni association run by Miss Katherine Klitgaard, c/o the School.

St Mary's (Shaftesbury)

St Mary's School
Shaftesbury
Dorset SP7 9LP
Telephone number 0747 4005

Co-ed
Boys
● Girls
Mixed sixth
● Day
● Boarding

Pupils 320
Upper sixth Yes
Termly fees:
Day £980
Boarding £1650
GSA; BSA

Head Sister Campion Livesey (3 years)

Age range 9–18; entry by own exam or common entrance. Many parents are overseas or in the Services

Scholarships (including music, art and sixth form).

St Mary's (Wantage)

St Mary's School
Wantage
Oxfordshire OX12 8BZ
Telephone number 02357 3571/2

Enquiries/application to the Admissions
Secretary

Co-ed   Pupils 300
Boys   Upper sixth 25
● Girls   Termly fees:
Mixed sixth   Boarding £2050
Day   GSA
● Boarding

WHAT IT'S LIKE

Founded in 1872 by William Butler, the vicar of Wantage, and run until 1975 by the Sisters of the Anglican Community of St Mary the Virgin. On their withdrawal it became a charitable trust. It remains an Anglican foundation and most of the pupils are Anglicans. The well-appointed buildings are on a continuous site in the middle of the small, market town. The modern facilities are of a high standard. There is a large staff creating a ratio of 1:7 pupils, plus a large part-time staff. Academic standards are high and results good. Quite a lot of leavers go on to university each year. Very strong in art, music and drama. A wide range of games, sports and activities. An impressive record in the Duke of Edinburgh's Award Scheme.

SCHOOL PROFILE

Pupils Total over 11, 300. Entry age, 11, 12 and into the sixth. Approx 10% are children of former pupils.

Entrance Common entrance used. Oversubscribed. No special skills required. Most pupils are Anglicans. Parents expected to buy some sixth form text books. 4 scholarships/bursaries, half to one-third fees.

Parents From a wide range of occupations. Up to 10% live within 30 miles; up to 10% live overseas.

Staff Head Mrs P Johns, in post for 8 years. 40 full time staff, 32 part time. Annual turnover 5%. Average age mid-thirties.

Academic work GCSE, A-levels, some Pitmans/RSA exams. Average size of upper fifth 50; upper sixth 25. *O-levels*: on average, 10 pupils in upper fifth pass 1–4 subjects; 20, 5–7 subjects; 21 pass 8+ subjects. *A-levels*: on average, 6 pupils in the upper sixth pass 1 subject; 7, 2 subjects; 10, 3 subjects and 1 passes 4 subjects. On average, 4 take science/engineering A-levels; 15 take arts and humanities; 4 a mixture. *Computing facilities*: 8 computers; first years are taught; GCSE computer studies offered. Provision for mild dyslexia and EFL.

Senior pupils' non-academic activities *Music*: 100 learn a musical instrument, 25 to Grade 6 or above; 1 accepted for Music School; some do music as part of teacher training course. 22 in school orchestra, 40 in school choir; a few in local youth orchestras. *Drama and dance*: 40 in school productions, 14 in lower fifth voluntary group; 30 take LAMDA exams. 2 accepted for Drama/Dance Schools; 5 have participated in Edinburgh Festival. *Art*: 3 take as non-examined subject; 27 GCSE, 7 A-level. 2–5 accepted for Art School. *Sport*: Lacrosse, netball, tennis (indoor and outdoor), rounders, gymnastics, swimming, basketball, volleyball, squash available. 200 take non-compulsory sport. 150, sports exams (BAGA, RLSS bronze medallion). 3 represent county/country at sport. *Other*: Sixth formers help at local primary/handicapped schools. 47 have bronze Duke of Edinburgh's Award, and 10, gold. Other activities include a computer club, science club, needlework, wind band; girls may make their own arrangements for driving lessons.

Careers 1 full time advisor plus 7/8 staff part time. Average number of pupils accepted for *arts and humanities degree courses* at Oxbridge, 1; other universities, 7; polytechnics or CHE, 9. *science and engineering degree courses* at universities, 3; medical schools, 1; polytechnics or CHE, 2. *BEd*, 1. *other general training courses*, 10. Average number of pupils going straight into a career, 1.

Uniform School uniform worn except the sixth.

Houses/prefects Competitive houses (socials): Prefects and head girl – appointed by Head in consultation with staff and girls. School Council.

Religion Compulsory daily service and Sunday eucharist.

Social Organised dances, parties, singing, drama with local boys' public schools; some activities (eg careers convention) with local comprehensive. Annual exchange with Germany, sixth formers to Paris and Florence; ski-ing trips. Pupils over 15 allowed to bring own bike to school. Meals self service. School bookshop. No tobacco/alcohol allowed.

Discipline No corporal punishment. Those caught smoking cannabis would be expelled.

Boarding 33% have own study bedroom, 5% share with 1 other, 20% are in dormitories of 6 or more. Houses, of approximately 50, are divided by age group. Resident qualified nurse; doctor visits regularly. Central dining room. Sixth form can provide and cook their own snacks. 2 weekend exeats each term plus 2 days and half term. Visits to local town allowed.

Alumni association magazine edited by Mrs D Webb, c/o the School.

Former pupils Emma Nicholson MP; Lucinda Green (3-day eventer); Dame Ruth Railton (founder, National Youth Orchestra).

St Maur's

St Maur's	Co-ed	Pupils 410
Thames Street	Boys	Upper sixth 45
Weybridge	● Girls	Termly fees:
Surrey KT13 8NL	Mixed sixth	Day £805
Telephone number 0932 851411	● Day	
	Boarding	
Enquiries/application to the Headmistress		

WHAT IT'S LIKE

Founded in 1898, it is semi-rural, single-site with spacious and pleasant grounds. The original building, now the convent, is an 18th-century country house. The main school building dates from 1897 and there have been many modern additions. The school is in the care of the Sisters of The Infant Jesus and about 50% of the pupils are Roman Catholics. Regular religious instruction and occasional attendance at Mass and other services form an integral part of the way of life. Academic standards are high as is the pass rate in public exams. 80–90% of sixth form leavers go on to degree courses. The sixth form has been run for some twenty years now jointly with that of St George's College, Weybridge, a boys' school about a mile away. Tremendously strong in music (about 50% of pupils involved). Vigorous drama and art departments. A good range of sports, games and activities. Some participation in local community schemes and the Duke of Edinburgh's Award Scheme.

SCHOOL PROFILE

Pupils Total over 12, 410. Entry age, 11+ and into sixth form.

Entrance Own entrance exam used. Oversubscribed. No special skills or religious requirements but about 50% are Roman Catholic. 15 assisted places. Scholarships/bursaries available.

Parents 15+% in industry or commerce; 15+% are doctors, lawyers etc. 60+% live within 30 miles.

Staff Head Sister Helen Wynne. Annual turnover 5%. Average age 40s.

Academic work GCSE and A-levels. Average size of upper fifth 75; upper sixth 45. *O-levels*: on average, 58 pupils in upper fifth pass 5–7 subjects; 35 pass 8+ subjects. *A-levels*: on average, 41 pupils in upper sixth pass 3 subjects. Most pupils take a mixture of science/engineering or humanities A-levels. *Computing facilities*: Nimbus; BBC. Arrangements for dyslexia and EFL can be made.

Senior pupils' non-academic activities *Music*: 170+ learn a musical instrument, 6+ to Grade 6 or above; 25–30 in school orchestra; 80–100 in choir. *Drama and dance*: Tuition for GCSE available. *Art*: GCSE and A-level available. Also ceramics A-level. *Sport*: Lacrosse, tennis, netball, swimming, gymnastics, athletics, private tennis coaching with a professional coach available all year. *Other*: Pupils take part in local community schemes and some in silver and gold Duke of Edinburgh's Award.

Careers 1 full time and 1 part time advisor. Member of ISCO. Further advisors for sixth form. Traditional school careers are law, medicine, arts.

Uniform School uniform worn throughout.

Houses/prefects Competitive houses. Prefects, head girl, head of house and house prefects – appointed by the Head after consultation with the school and staff.

Religion Compulsory assembly once a week. RE is compulsory part of the curriculum unless parents request otherwise.

Social Mixed sixth form with St George's College, Weybridge. Occasional social evenings. Several organised trips, mostly in sixth form. Pupils allowed to bring own car/bicycle to school. Meals self service. Upper sixth may smoke with parents' permission. Beer and wine allowed under staff supervision for annual sixth form ball.

Discipline No corporal punishment. Pupils failing to produce homework once or constantly arriving late might expect to be admonished; those caught endangering their own or others' lives by eg, smoking, physical violence, would be suspended or expelled following a parental interview – this has not arisen.

Alumnae association is run by the Headmistress and the Sister Superior.

S MICHAELS (PETWORTH)

S Michaels Burton Park
Petworth
West Sussex GU28 0LS
Telephone number 0798 42517

Enquiries to Mrs M E Steeves
Application to Miss P D Burtt

Co-ed
Boys
• Girls
Mixed sixth
• Day
• Boarding

Pupils 200
Upper sixth 20
Termly fees:
Day £1350
Boarding £1950
GSA; Woodard

WHAT IT'S LIKE

Founded in 1884, a Woodard school, the main building is a magnificent Georgian-style country house (1842) in splendid gardens on an estate of 150 acres at the foot of the South Downs, 3 miles from Petworth. In recent years there have been several additional buildings, and facilities and accommodation are first-rate. Girls who enter at 11 spend their first year in Wakefield House, a converted 18th-century farmhouse at the end of the gardens. A C of E foundation, chapel is compulsory on weekdays; compulsory Sunday services for boarders. There is a remarkably high staff:pupil ratio of 1:6.5. Academic standards are high and results good; 5–10 leavers go on to university each year. Most pupils are involved in music and drama. Very good range of sports, games and activities. A particularly high standard in lacrosse (a lot of county representatives). An impressive record in the Duke of Edinburgh's Award Scheme.

SCHOOL PROFILE

Pupils Total 200. Day 20; Boarding 180. Entry age, 11, 12, 13 and into the sixth. 5% are children of former pupils.

Entrance Common entrance and own entrance exam used. Not oversubscribed. No special skills required. C of E Foundation, other religions accepted provided they attend chapel. Parents not expected to buy text books. 1 or 2 academic and music scholarships and bursaries pa. Service, clergy and sixth form bursaries.

Parents 15+% of parents in industry or commerce; 15+% are doctors, lawyers etc. 30+% live within 30 miles; 30+% live overseas.

Staff Head Mrs M E Steeves, in post for 7 years. 36 full time staff, 10 part time. Annual turnover 10%. Average age 43.

Academic work GCSE and A-levels. Average size of upper fifth 41; upper sixth 20. *O-levels*: on average, 14 pupils in upper fifth pass 1–4 subjects; 14, 5–7 subjects; 12 pass 8+ subjects. *A-levels*: on average, 2 pupils in upper sixth pass 1 subject; 5, 2 subjects; 11, 3 subjects and 1 passes 4 subjects. On average, 4 take science/engineering A-levels; 6 take arts and humanities; 10 a mixture. Social biology offered to GCSE/A-level. *Computing facilities*: Computer room with 10 computers, 10 colour monitors, 10 disk drives, 2 Epson printers, 1 citizen printer, 1 printer 2000, 1 modem for Prestel. Dyslexia and EFL provisions.

Senior pupils' non-academic activities *Music*: 30+ learn a musical instrument, 10 to Grade 6 or above. *Drama and dance*: Number in school productions varies. 25 take Grade 6 in ESB, RAD etc. 1 or 2 a year accepted for Drama Schools. *Art*: 20 take GCSE; 4 A-level; 1 accepted for Art School. *Sport*: Lacrosse, netball, cross-country running, athletics, tennis, rounders, squash, badminton, swimming; 5th & 6th forms also golf, archery, yoga, windsurfing available. Most take non-compulsory sport. Nearly everyone takes Bronze medal life saving. 14 pupils represent county (lacrosse). *Other*: 35 have bronze Duke of Edinburgh's Award, 5–10 have silver. 3–4 go into GAP after leaving. Other activities include a computer club; sixth formers can learn to drive.

Careers 1 full time and 1 part time advisors. Average number of pupils accepted for *arts and humanities degree courses* at Oxbridge, 1; other universities, 5. *science and engineering degree courses* at universities, 1; medical schools, 1; polytechnics or CHE, 1. *BEd*, 1. *other general training courses*, 5.

Uniform School uniform worn years 1–5; sixth on formal occasions only.

Houses/prefects Competitive houses. Prefects – elected; head girl – appointed by the Head; head of house and house prefects.

Religion Compulsory chapel Monday–Friday. Boarders attend Sunday service.

Social Many activities, sporting, musical etc with other Woodard schools. Organised trips to France to stay with French families; ski trips; exchanges with a German school. Pupils allowed to bring own bicycle to school from 14 upwards. Meals self service. School shop. No tobacco/alcohol allowed.

Discipline No corporal punishment. Pupils failing to produce homework once might expect to have to produce it within 24 hours (detention for second offence); those caught smoking cannabis on the premises could expect expulsion.

Boarding Houses, of approximately 35, same as competitive houses. Resident qualified nurse. Central dining room. Upper sixth pupils can provide and cook own food. 2 weekend exeats per term and half term. Visits to the local town allowed.

Alumni association is run by Mrs Judy Simmonds, Tamarisk Cottage, Lake Lane, Barnham, West Sussex PO22 0AL.

St Paul's (Boys)

St Paul's School	Co-ed		Pupils 770
Lonsdale Road	● Boys		Upper sixth 156
Barnes	Girls		Termly fees:
London SW13 9JT	Mixed sixth		Day £1391
Telephone number 01-748 9162	● Day		Boarding £2209
	● Boarding		HMC
Enquiries to the High Master			
Applications to the Bursar			

WHAT IT'S LIKE

Founded in 1509 by John Colet, Dean of St Paul's. A grammar school had previously existed for centuries in connection with the cathedral and Colet probably absorbed this in the new foundation. It moved from the cathedral site to Hammersmith in 1884 and then crossed the river to purpose-built premises in Barnes in 1968. Unfortunately, a promising site was wasted by the grimly practical Clasp system. The buildings are serviceable but lack distinction. It is governed by the Mercers' Company, and has its own prep school, Colet Court (founded in 1881) on the same site. Religious instruction is in accordance with the C of E but attendance at services is voluntary. The academic reputation of the school remains formidable with the classics still prospering. A very high-powered teaching staff is strong in pastoral care (thanks to the well-established tutorial system) and produces outstanding results. Each year 130 or more leavers go on to university (some 55–60 to Oxbridge). The school is tremendously strong in music, drama and art and these departments work closely together and form an integral part of the academic and social life of the school. In music there are orchestras, choirs, jazz groups, instrumental ensembles and about 140 pupils learn an instrument. Several plays are produced each year and there are a number of minor workshop productions. The art department produces work of high quality. The school has a notable record in sports and games (there is a fine sports hall) and most pupils are involved in one or more of them. More than 30 extra-curricular activities are available.

SCHOOL PROFILE

Pupils Total over 12, 770. Day 650; Boarding 120. Entry age, 13 and into the sixth. Own prep school provides over 40%.

Entrance Common entrance and own scholarship exam used. Oversubscribed. No special skills or religious requirements. Parents expected to buy some text books. 11 assisted places pa. 153 scholarships, 100%–15% of fees.
Parents 60+% live within 30 miles.

Staff Head Canon Peter Pilkington, in post for 2 years. 74 full time staff, 28 part time. Annual turnover 3–4%. Average age 35–38.

Academic work GCSE, A- and S-levels. Average size of upper fifth 158; upper sixth 156. *O-levels*: on average, 1 pupil in upper fifth passes 1–4 subjects; 11, 7 subjects; 146 pass 8+ subjects. *A-levels*: on average, 4 pupils in the upper sixth pass 1 subject; 14, 2 subjects; 120, 3 subjects and 17 pass 4 subjects. On average, 58 take science/engineering A-levels, 84 take arts and humanities; 14 a mixture. *Computing facilities*: RM Nimbus network, 16 terminals, 12 BBC model B, 1 IBM PCAT, 2 38020 and others.

Senior pupils' non-academic activities *Music*: 140 learn a musical instrument in school, 50 outside, 50 to Grade 6 or above in school, 20 outside; 60 in school orchestra, 35 in choir, 5 in pop group, 15 in jazz groups, 40 in instrumental ensembles; 6 in youth orchestras; 10, RCM, RAM, GSM junior orchestras. *Drama and dance*: 50+ in school productions; 10–15, senior drama class. 10+ GCSE 2nd year (junior drama). 2 go on to work in theatre; 2 into National Youth Theatre. *Art*: 55 take as non-examined subject (studios open every lunchtime to interested pupils); 30 GCSE; 20 A-level; 5 take History of Art. 2 accepted for Art School. 10 belong to eg photographic club. *Sport*: Rugby, cricket, swimming, rowing, fencing, fives, athletics, tennis, sailing, judo, squash, basketball, badminton, golf, gymnastics available. 750 take non-compulsory sport. 1 pupil represents country in tennis. *Other*: 7–24 take part in local community schemes. Other activities include a computer club, aeromodelling, BAYS, backgammon, bridge, chess, Christian Union, debating, drama, electronics, military society, art appreciation, archaeological, history, classical, natural history and political societies, conjuring club.

Careers 4 part time careers advisors. Average number of pupils accepted for *arts and humanities degree courses* at Oxbridge, 30; other universities, 36;

polytechnics or CHE, 6. *science and engineering degree courses* at Oxbridge, 25; other universities, 29; medical schools, 10; polytechnics or CHE, 1. Average number of pupils going straight into careers in armed services, 1; industry, 3. Traditional school careers are medicine, law and the City.

Uniform School uniform worn throughout.

Houses/prefects Competitive houses. Prefects, head boy – appointed by Head.

Religion Voluntary worship.

Social Debates and joint theatrical productions with other schools. Organised trips abroad. Day pupils allowed to bring own bike/car/motorbike to school. Meals self service. School shop (uniform and tuck). No tobacco/alcohol allowed.

Discipline No corporal punishment. Pupils failing to produce homework once might expect a warning; those caught smoking cannabis on the premises might expect expulsion.

Boarding One-third have own study bedroom, others share with up to 6. 2 houses, of approximately 60. Resident matron. Central dining room. Pupils can provide and cook own food. Exeats every weekend. Visits to local town allowed 4.0–5.30 pm.

Alumni association run by M K Seigel, c/o the School.

Former pupils Kenneth Baker, MP; Clement Freud, MP; Admiral Treacher; Magnus Pyke; Dr Jonathan Miller; W Galen Weston; Peter Shaffer (playwright); Eric Newby (travel writer); Sir Max Beloff (writer); Sir Kenneth Dover; Professor R F Gombrich; Chris Barber (musician); John Simpson (BBC correspondent); John Cavanagh (fashion designer); Sir Isaiah Berlin among many others.

St Paul's (Girls')

St Paul's Girls' School	Co-ed	Pupils 630
Brook Green	Boys	Upper sixth Yes
London W6 7BS	● Girls	Termly fees:
Telephone number 01-603 2288	Mixed sixth	Day £1150
	● Day	GSA
	Boarding	

WHAT IT'S LIKE

Like its counterpart for boys, it belongs to the Christian Foundation originally provided by Dean Colet in 1509. The trustees are the Worshipful Company of Mercers and there are very close ties between school and Mercers. Its handsome Edwardian buildings lie in a pleasant part of Hammersmith and are outstandingly well equipped by any standards with, among other things, comfortable common rooms, first-class art rooms and workshops, excellent libraries and a fine theatre in memory of Dame Celia Johnson. Games and sports facilities are all provided on site and include an Olympic-sized swimming pool. A most distinguished and well-run school, with rules kept to the barest minimum, its atmosphere is liberal, civilised and sophisticated – even chic. The head is reputed to remind her departing sixth formers that they buy their shoes, belts and handbags in Italy, their dresses in Paris and their country clothes in London. Religious instruction is in accordance with the principles of the Church of England. A very large and extremely well-qualified staff (there are well over 30 in the music department alone) allows a staff:pupil ratio of about 1:7. Academically it is formidably high-powered, equally strong in arts and sciences. Maths, physics, chemistry and Latin are compulsory; quite a few girls study Classics. There is no streaming; all forms are of mixed ability and interests. In maths, French and Latin pupils are in sets based on ability. Considerable importance is attached to girls establishing from the outset good habits of work and learning to read and think independently. Academic results are consistently outstanding. Some 95% of leavers go on to university; 30% of these to Oxbridge. In 1985 there were 56 Oxbridge entrants. Since the appointment of the school's first director of music, the late Gustav Holst, music has been an important activity. There is a specially built music wing with a concert hall and individual sound-proof teaching rooms. The Great Hall has an organ. There are 2 orchestras, a wind band and several choirs. A high proportion of girls learn one or more instruments. A great deal of dramatic work is done each year, including workshop productions. The standards are very high. They are equally high in a wide variety of sports and games and physical education. All girls are taught self-defence in one of the martial arts. Dancing, ballet and fencing are also taught to a high level. There are numerous extra-curricular activities and numerous clubs and societies with special emphasis on art, drama and music. Computing and BAYS (British Association of Young Scientists) flourish.

SCHOOL PROFILE

Head Mrs Heather Brigstocke (14 years)
Age range 11–18; entry by own exam
Own junior school. Foundation awards including for art, music and organ.

ST PETER'S (YORK)

St Peter's School	• Co-ed	Pupils 490
York YO3 6AB	Boys	Upper sixth 100
Telephone number 0904 23213	Girls	Termly fees:
Enquiries/application to the Headmaster	Mixed sixth	Day £1191
	• Day	Boarding £2121
	• Boarding	HMC

WHAT IT'S LIKE

Founded in 627 and thus one of the oldest schools in Europe. Alcuin was a pupil and headmaster. Its first head was a saint (Paulinus). The present head (as he points out himself) has not yet been canonised. Guy Fawkes was an old boy. It is urban, single-site by the Ouse and is exceptionally well equipped in fine buildings dating from the 1830s to the present day. The prep school, St Olave's, is on the same site (75% of pupils are drawn from it). Religious worship is compulsory thrice weekly. The teaching is good and academic standards are high. About 65–70 leavers proceeed to university each year. Strong in the drama and art departments; tremendously strong music department. Wide variety of sports and games (good standards attained) and a big range of activities. There is a vigorous CCF contingent. Emphasis on outdoor pursuits. Considerable commitment to local community schemes and a creditable record in the Duke of Edinburgh's Award Scheme.

SCHOOL PROFILE

Pupils Total 490. Day 310 (boys 267, girls 43*); Boarding 180 (boys 140, girls 40*). Entry age, 13 and into the sixth. *Note: full co-education below the sixth form dates from September 1987. 75% come from St Olave's Junior School. 10% are children of former pupils.

Entrance Common entrance and own entrance exam used. Oversubscribed. No special skills or religious requirements but all attend chapel (C of E). Parents not expected to buy text books. 120 assisted places. 6–8 scholarships/bursaries, up to full tuition fees.

Parents 15+% in industry or commerce. 60+% live within 30 miles; up to 10% overseas.

Staff Head R N Pittman, in post for 3 years. 40 full time staff. Annual turnover 6%. Average age 39.

Academic work GCSE and A-levels. Average size of upper fifth 96; upper sixth 100. *O-levels*: on average, 10 pupils in upper fifth pass 1–4 subjects; 10, 5–7 subjects; 70 pass 8+ subjects. *A-levels*: on average, 5 pupils in upper sixth pass 1 subject; 5, 2 subjects; 25, 3 subjects and 65 pass 4 subjects. On average, 45 take science/engineering A-levels; 35 take arts and humanities; 20 a mixture. *Computing facilities*: Large computer department: 20 linked machines. Special provision for dyslexia.

Senior pupils' non-academic activities *Music*: 75 learn a musical instrument, 30 to Grade 6 or above; 60 in school orchestra, 60 in choir, 20 in pop group, 40 in band, 40 in ensembles. *Drama and dance*: 50 in school productions; 70 in house plays. *Art*: 30 take as non-examined subject; 20 GCSE; 10 A-level; 2 accepted for Art School. 20 belong to eg photographic club. *Sport*: Rugby, cricket, tennis, rowing, swimming, badminton, squash, netball, basketball, indoor soccer, cross-country, athletics, hockey, aerobics available. 100 take non-compulsory sport. 10 represent county/country (hockey, rugby, athletics, tennis etc). *Other*: 30 take part in local community schemes. 10 have bronze Duke of Edinburgh's Award, 10 have silver and 5 gold. Other activities include a computer club, chess, Young Farmers, debating, science, choral society.

Careers 4 part time careers advisors. Average number of pupils accepted for *arts and humanities degree courses* at Oxbridge, 4; other universities, 20; polytechnics or CHE, 5. *science and engineering degree courses* at Oxbridge, 4; other universities, 40; medical schools, 4; polytechnics or CHE, 15. *BEd*, 2. Average number of pupils going straight into careers in the armed services, 10; industry, 6; the City, 1; civil service, 1.

Uniform School uniform worn except in sixth.

Houses/prefects Competitive houses. Prefects, head boy/girl, head of house and house prefects – appointed by the Head and staff.

Religion Compulsory (3 services in the week).

Social Many holiday expeditions: Sahara, Norway, Iceland, USSR, Snowdonia. Pupils allowed to bring own car to school. Meals self service. School shop. No tobacco/alcohol allowed.

Discipline No corporal punishment. Pupils failing to produce homework once might expect a rebuke and to do it; those caught smoking cannabis on the premises would be judged according to circumstances.

Boarding Sixth form in own study bedrooms or share with 1, 2 or 3 others. Houses, of approximately 50, are vertical houses, 13–18 and are single sex. Resident SRN. Central dining room. Pupils can provide and cook own food. Exeats each weekend of 28 hours. Strictly regulated visits to the local town allowed.

Alumni association is run by Mr R D Harding, Hall Cottage, Foremarke, Repton, Derbyshire DE6 6ES.

Former pupils Parkinson (of Parkinson's Law); Norman Yardley (ex England cricket captain); Guy Fawkes.

ST STEPHEN'S (BROADSTAIRS)

St Stephen's College	Co-ed	Pupils 84
North Foreland	Boys	Upper sixth 13
Broadstairs	● Girls	Termly fees:
Kent CT10 3NP	Mixed sixth	Day £1130
Telephone number 0843 62254	● Day	Boarding £1830
	● Boarding	GSA; GBGSA
Enquiries/application to the Headmistress		

WHAT IT'S LIKE

Founded in 1867 by the Community of St John Baptist and run by Sisters of the Order until 1965. It has a fine site in a healthy environment, comprising 15 acres of grounds, including a riding school, playing fields, paddock and orchard, on the North Foreland about a mile from the middle of Broadstairs. The preparatory school is very near the main school. An unusually good staff:pupil ratio of 1:5 produces high academic standards and excellent results. Some 5–10 leavers go to university each year: a high proportion for a very small school. Most pupils are involved in music, drama and art. A very good variety of games, sports and activities. A big commitment to local community schemes and a large number of pupils participate in the Duke of Edinburgh's Award Scheme.

SCHOOL PROFILE

Pupils Total, 84. Day 19; Boarding 65. Entry age, 11+ and into the sixth.

Entrance Common entrance used. Not oversubscribed. Fluency in English required. No religious requirements. Parents not expected to buy text books. 1 assisted place. 6 scholarships pa, from £3240–£1620.

Parents 15+% in industry or commerce. 10+% live within 30 miles; 30+% live overseas.

Staff Head Miss M de Villiers, in post 1 year. 17 full time staff, 2 part time. Annual turnover 6%. Average age 41.

Academic work GCSE and A-levels. Average size of upper fifth 17; upper

sixth 13. *O-levels*: on average, 7 pupils in upper fifth pass 1–4 subjects; 6, 5–7 subjects; 1 passes 8+ subjects. *A-levels*: on average, 5 pupils in upper sixth pass 1 subject; 4, 2 subjects; 3, 3 subjects and 1 passes 4 subjects. On average, 6 take science/engineering A-levels; 7 take arts and humanities; 2 a mixture. *Computing facilities*: 2 research machines 3802 56K, double disk drive keyboard, 1 Panasonic monitor, 2 Epson MX-80F IT III printers, 5 Commodore plus/4, 64K and disk drives, printers, transformers, datasette tape drives and joysticks. EFL provisions.

Senior pupils' non-academic activities *Music*: 9 learn a musical instrument, 2 to Grade 6 or above; 2 in school orchestral group, 9 in choir, 3 in pop group. *Drama and dance*: 19 in school productions; 17 in drama club. 2 take Grade 6 in ESB, RAD etc; 2 Festival entries. *Art*: 2 take as non-examined subject; 27 GCSE; 2 A-level; 2 other exams; 1 accepted for Art School. Duke of Edinburgh's Award (photography). *Sport*: Hockey, netball, swimming, tennis, rounders, badminton, sailing, rifle shooting, horse riding available. 1 represents Kent (hockey). *Other*: 19 take part in local community schemes. 19 taking bronze Duke of Edinburgh's Award, 8 taking silver. Other activities include a computer club, bridge, community service club, film society, debating society, driving lessons, dancing.

Careers 1 full time careers advisor. Average number of pupils accepted for *arts and humanities degree courses* at universities, 1; polytechnics or CHE, 2. *science and engineering degree courses* at universities, 6; medical schools, 1 every 3 years; polytechnics or CHE, 6. *other general training courses*, 1. Average number of pupils going straight into careers in music/drama, 1. Other careers in schools abroad, sixth form colleges, as airline stewardesses, in banking.

Uniform School uniform worn throughout.

Houses/prefects Competitive houses. Prefects, head girl and heads of houses – elected by the school.

Religion All C of E or RC girls are expected to attend church on Sundays.

Social Sixth form inter-schools debates. Organised trips in the UK and abroad eg Arran, France, Germany, Holland, Russia. Pupils allowed to stable own horse at school. Meals self service. No tobacco/alcohol allowed.

Discipline No corporal punishment. Pupils failing to produce homework once might expect a debit house point and half hour detention; those caught smoking cannabis on the premises could expect expulsion.

Boarding 10% have own study bedroom, 40% share (with 1 other). Houses, of approximately 14–28 are divided by age group. Non-resident qualified nurse. Central dining room. 2–4 exeats each term. Visits to the local town allowed.

Alumni association is run by Mrs E Steed, Hon Secretary, Spratling Court Farm, Manston, Ramsgate, Kent.

St Swithun's

St Swithun's School	Co-ed	Pupils 410
Winchester	Boys	Upper sixth Yes
Hampshire SO21 1HA	● Girls	Termly fees:
Telephone number 0962 61316	Mixed sixth	Day £1210
	● Day	Boarding £1930
	● Boarding	GBGSA; GSA

Head Miss Joan Jefferson (2 years)
Age range 11–18; own prep from age 3; entry by common entrance
One major scholarship plus music scholarships.

St Teresa's Convent

St Teresa's Convent	Co-ed	Pupils 370
Effingham Hill	Boys	Upper sixth Yes
Dorking	● Girls	Termly fees:
Surrey RH5 6ST	Mixed sixth	Day £850
Telephone number 0372 52037	● Day	Boarding £1420
	● Boarding	GBGSA; GSA;
		AHIS

Head Mr Leslie Allan (1 year)
Age range 11–18; own prep from 3; entrance by common entrance or own exam
2 sixth form scholarships pa.

Scarborough

Scarborough College	● Co-ed	Pupils 320
Filey Road	Boys	Upper sixth 45
Scarborough	Girls	Termly fees:
North Yorkshire YO11 3BA	Mixed sixth	Day £1058
Telephone number 0723 360620	● Day	Boarding £1975
	● Boarding	GBA; SHMIS

Enquiries/application to the Headmaster

WHAT IT'S LIKE

Founded in 1876, it has a splendid site south of Scarborough on the eastern slopes of Oliver's Mount, overlooking Scarborough Castle and the South Bay. The main Victorian building is a fine example of its kind. In the last 25 years there have been many developments and facilities are good. It is a Christian and interdenominational establishment with high academic standards and good results (15 plus university candidates per year). The music, drama and art departments are well supported. A good record in games and sports (quite a lot of county representatives). Many extra-curricular activities cater for most needs. A flourishing CCF and some emphasis on outdoor pursuits. Some involvement in the Duke of Edinburgh's Award Scheme.

SCHOOL PROFILE

Pupils Total over 12, 320. Day 195 (boys 105, girls 90); Boarding 125 (boys 82, girls 43). Entry age, 11, 13, and into the sixth. Own prep school provides 80% of the intake at 13+. 5% are children of former pupils.

Entrance Common entrance and own entrance exam used. Sometimes oversubscribed. Pupils with high potential in music and art encouraged. The college is Christian and interdenominational. Parents not expected to buy text books. 15 scholarships/bursaries pa, £1959–£735.

Parents 15+% in industry or commerce. 60+% live within 30 miles; 10+% live overseas.

Staff Head Dr D S Hempsall, in post for 3 years. 33 full time staff, 9 part time. Annual turnover 7%. Average age 36.

Academic work GCSE and A-levels. Average size of upper fifth 85; upper sixth 45. *O-levels*: on average, 25 pupils in upper fifth pass 1–4 subjects; 25, 5–7 subjects; 34 pass 8+ subjects. *A-levels*: on average, 7 pupils in upper sixth pass 1 subject; 9, 2 subjects; 10, 3 subjects and 19 pass 4 subjects. On average, 11 take science/engineering A-levels; 22 take arts and humanities; 12 a mixture. Psychology offered to A-level; photography to GCSE. *Computing facilities*: Computer centre with network of 13 BBCs, increasing departmental usage. Qualified teacher gives individual tuition to dyslexics; some EFL provision.

Senior pupils' non-academic activities *Music*: 50 learn a musical instrument, 22 to Grade 6 or above; 2 accepted for Music School; 30 in school orchestra, 20 in choir, 10 in school pop group, 14 in sixth form choir; 1 in National Youth Orchestra. All participate in annual music competition; 15 go on to play in pop group. *Drama and dance*: 25 in school productions; 10 in drama club. 2 enter competitions. 3 go on to work in theatre. *Art*: 4 take as non-examined subject; 28 take GCSE; 9 A-level. 2 accepted for Art School. 3 belong to photographic club, 18 to art society. *Sport*: Hockey, netball, rounders: main girls' games; rugby, hockey, cricket: main boys' games. In addition: tennis, table tennis, cross-country, badminton, gymnastics, squash, riding, swimming, golf available. 50+ take non-compulsory sport. 8 represent county/country (rugby, hockey, badminton). *Other*: 10 have silver Duke of Edinburgh's Award, 1 has gold. 2 work for national charities. Other activities include a computer and microelectronics club, public speaking, theatre visits, Christian Union, Young Farmers, model railway, psychology society, science, art, child care, electronics, video, guitar, engineering, shooting, CCF, craft, photography, chess etc.

Careers 2 part time advisors. Average number of pupils accepted for *arts and humanities degree courses* at Oxbridge, 1; other universities, 8; polytechnics or CHE, 5. *science and engineering degree courses* at universities, 6; medical schools, 1; polytechnics or CHE, 2. *BEd*, 1. *other general training courses*, 22. Average number of pupils going straight into careers in armed services, 3; industry, 4; other, into farming and tourism related industries.

Uniform School uniform worn except in the sixth.

Houses/prefects Competitive houses. Prefects, head boy/girl – appointed by

Headmaster following recommendations made by Housemasters/mistresses. Head of house and house prefects appointed by Housemaster/mistress.

Religion Assemblies compulsory; additional voluntary services; bible study sessions; Christian Union.

Social Debates, industrial conferences, departmental lectures with local schools. Exchanges to France and Germany; other trips abroad, ski-ing, junior languages, CCF. Pupils allowed to bring own car/bike/motorbike to school. Meals self service. School shop. No tobacco allowed; alcohol when approved by House staff.

Discipline No corporal punishment. Pupils failing to produce homework without satisfactory reason might expect detention; those caught smoking cannabis on the premises could expect expulsion.

Boarding 20% have own study bedroom, 32% share; 23% are in dormitories of 6+. Houses, of 30–40, same as competitive houses; single sex apart from Junior House. Resident qualified nurse. Central dining room. Pupils can provide and cook own food. Exeats at discretion of house staff. Visits to the local town allowed.

Alumni association run by J M Precious, Secretary to the OSA, c/o the College.

Former pupils Ian Carmichael (actor); Brian Reading.

SCARISBRICK HALL

Scarisbrick Hall School	● Co-ed	Pupils 242
Scarisbrick	Boys	Upper sixth 20
Ormskirk	Girls	Termly fees:
Lancashire L40 9RQ	Mixed sixth	Day £570
Telephone number 0704 880200	● Day	ISAI
	Boarding .	
Enquiries/application to the Headmaster		

WHAT IT'S LIKE

Founded in 1964, it lies 3 miles from Ormskirk in a superb private estate of 440 acres comprising gardens, woodland, pastures and lakes. The main building is Scarisbrick Hall itself: a vast country mansion of 150 apartments designed by Pugin. Ornate, ostentatious and derivative, it is a good example of residential Gothic renaissance (as such, it is officially listed and protected). New buildings include a chapel, classroom blocks and a gym. There is strong emphasis on evangelical faith and practice. A surprisingly small number of full-time staff (24) for 510 pupils. Academically it appears to be well run and 10–12 leavers proceed to university each year. Some music and art but, apparently, no drama. Fees are low.

SCHOOL PROFILE

Pupils Total over 12, 242. (Boys 118, girls 124). Entry age, 4–14 and into sixth. Own junior school provides 70%.

Entrance Common entrance but mainly own entrance exam used. Sometimes oversubscribed. No special skills or religious requirements. Parents not expected to buy text books. Some scholarships (outstanding results in entrance exam, 11+ or GCSE), variable value.

Parents 15+% in industry or commerce. 100% live within 30 miles.

Staff Head D M Raynor, in post for 10 years. 24 full time staff, 11 part time. Annual turnover 5%. Average age 46.

Academic work GCSE and A-levels. Average size of upper fifth 56; upper sixth 20. *O-levels*: on average, 10 pupils in upper fifth pass 1–4 subjects; 18, 5–7 subjects; 28 pass 8+ subjects. *A-levels*: on average, 2 pupils in upper sixth pass 1 subject; 3, 2 subjects; 5, 3 subjects and 10 pass 4 subjects. On average, 7 take science/engineering A-levels; 6 take arts and humanities; 7 a mixture. *Computing facilities*: 16 computers, 16 VDUs, 3 printers, 8 single disc drives, 3×3½" disc drives, 1 dual disc drive, 1 double-sided disc drive; 1 TV, 1 video, 1 Prestel system.

Senior pupils' non-academic activities *Music*: 50 learn a musical instrument, 8 to Grade 6 or above, 1 accepted for Music School; 90 in school orchestra; 4 in Sefton or Lancashire schools' orchestra. *Drama and dance*: 3 up to Grade 6 in ESB, RAD etc. *Art*: 27 take GCSE; 3 A-level. *Sport*: Soccer, rugby union, cricket, basketball, athletics, tennis, netball, cross country, badminton, swimming available. 54 take exams in eg gymnastics, swimming. 1 represents county (athletics). *Other*: 8 have bronze Duke of Edinburgh's Award, 5 have silver (taken out of school). 3 work for national charities. Other activities include driving lessons, science society, charity fund-raising events, Christian Fellowship, orchestra.

Careers 1 part time careers advisor. Average number of pupils accepted for *arts and humanities degree courses* at universities, 4; polytechnics or CHE, 2. *science and engineering degree courses* at universities, 5; medical schools, 1; polytechnics or CHE, 2. *BEd*, 2. *other general training courses*, 1. Average number of pupils going straight into careers in armed services, 1.

Uniform School uniform worn throughout.

Houses/prefects Competitive houses. Prefects, head boy and girl, head of house and house prefects – appointed by staff.

Religion Compulsory school assembly (Christian non-denominational).

Social Trips abroad: ski-ing in the Alps, exchange with German school, visi to France. No bicycles allowed. Meals self-service. School shop selling stationery and uniform. No tobacco/alcohol allowed.

Discipline Corporal punishment (boys only) for serious misbehaviour. Pupils failing to produce homework once might expect reprimand/warning/work to be done at lunchtime; those caught smoking cannabis on the premises might expect expulsion.

SEAFORD

Seaford College
Petworth
West Sussex GU28 0NB
Telephone number 07986 392

Enquiries/application to the Registrar

Co-ed
● Boys
Girls
Mixed sixth
Day
● Boarding

Pupils 430
Upper sixth 50
Termly fees:
Boarding £1895
SHMIS; GBA

WHAT IT'S LIKE

Founded in 1884, it moved to West Sussex in 1946 and has a fine site in 320 acres of splendid wooded parkland below the Downs. Very civilised buildings (including 35 different houses for members of staff) and excellent modern facilities. A staff:pupil ratio of 1:10. A very good general education is provided and 15–20 leavers proceed to university each year. Religious worship and practice is compulsory in the school chapel which dates to pre-Norman times. The declared aims of the school are to promote all that is best in the ethos and atmosphere in an English independent school while infusing a modern and progressive spirit into all its activities. It aims to produce a civilised young man who will make the best possible use of his abilities. Good music, drama and art departments. Wide range of sport, games and extra-curricular activities.

SCHOOL PROFILE

Pupils Total, 430. Entry age, 13+ and into the sixth. 4% are children of former pupils.

Entrance Common entrance and own exam used. Oversubscribed. Skills in music and sport an advantage. Most pupils are C of E but not essential. Parents expected to buy text books in sixth. No assisted places at present. About 15 scholarships/bursaries pa (academic, art, choral, music, games, sixth form and forces), 10% to full fees.

Parents 15+% in industry or commerce. 30+% live within 30 miles; up to 10% live overseas.

Staff Head Rev Canon Charles Johnson, in post for 43 years. 43 full time staff, 15 part time. Annual turnover 4%. Average age 35.

Academic work GCSE and A-levels. Average size of upper fifth 100; upper sixth 50. *O-levels*: on average, 54 pupils in upper fifth pass 1–4 subjects; 23, 5–7 subjects; 21 pass 8+ subjects. *A-levels*: on average, 12 pupils in upper sixth pass 1 subject; 11, 2 subjects; 14, 3 subjects and 2 pass 4 subjects. On average, 17 take science/engineering A-levels; 23 take arts and humanities; 8 a mixture. *Computing facilities*: over 30 BBC computers – mixture of Masters & Model B, plus ENET network & Winchester. Provision for extra English for those with difficulties.

Senior pupils' non-academic activities *Music*: 47 learn a musical instrument, 12 to ABRSM or TCM Grades, 1 every 2 years accepted for Music School; 14 in school orchestra(s), 9 in chamber group. *Drama and dance*: 50 in school productions, 25 in drama workshop. *Art*: 14 take as non-examined subject; 48 take GCSE; 17 take A-level. 4 accepted for Art School. 25 belong to eg photographic club. *Sport*: Rugby, hockey, cross country, cricket, athletics, squash, shooting, tennis, badminton, basketball, archery, canoeing, fencing, karate, swimming, trampolining available. 200 take non-compulsory sport. 25 take exams in life saving, 15 karate. 5 represent county (hockey, windsurfing, ski-ing). *Other*: 15 take part in local community schemes. Other activities include a computer club, gun club, driving lessons, bridge, dungeons and dragons, chess, electronics, fly fishing, life saving, modern languages society, nautical, parascending, philatelic, model aircraft, creative writing.

Careers 4 part time careers advisors. Average number of pupils accepted for *arts and humanities degree courses* at Oxbridge, 1; other universities, 4; polytechnics or CHE, 5. *science and engineering degree courses* at Oxbridge, 2; other universities, 8; medical schools, 2; polytechnics or CHE, 5. *other general training courses*, 10. Average number of pupils going straight into careers in armed services, 3; industry, 15; the City, 16; music/drama, 2; other, 20.

Uniform School uniform worn (modified in sixth).

Houses/prefects Competitive houses. Prefects and head boy appointed by Headmaster; head of house and house prefects by housemasters. Junior boys do chores for the community.

Religion Religious worship compulsory.

Social Tennis, lacrosse and debates with local girls' school; social visits to sixth form club. Organised trips abroad. Pupils allowed to bring own bicycle to school (prefects can bring cars). Meals self-service. School shop. Beer and wine allowed in sixth form club; no tobacco.

Discipline Corporal punishment would be administered only after consultation with parents. Pupils failing to produce homework might expect a reprimand. Further failure would result in detention. Those caught smoking could expect a fine which would be sent to a cancer charity.

Boarding 150 have own study bedroom, 100 share; 180 are in dormitories of 6+. Houses, of 78–90, same as competitive houses. Resident qualified nurses. Central dining room. Some basic cooking facilities in boarding houses. 2 or 3 weekend exeats each term, and half term. Visits to local town allowed.

Alumni association run by D Heden, c/o the College.

SEDBERGH

Sedbergh School
Sedbergh
Cumbria LA10 5HG
Telephone number 0587 20535

Enquiries/application to the Headmaster's Secretary/Registrar

Co-ed
● Boys
Girls
Mixed sixth
● Day
● Boarding

Pupils 450
Upper sixth 90
Termly fees:
Day £1630
Boarding £2320
HMC

WHAT IT'S LIKE

Founded in 1525, it is next to a small market town with the boarding houses scattered over a big rural site in a setting of the Cumbrian hills which is superb by any standards. Excellent modern facilities and comfortable accommodation. Religious services are essentially Anglican and all attend regular worship in chapel. A first-rate education is provided and results are consistently good (55–60 university entrants per year). There is a tremendously strong music dept (250 boys learn an instrument); also very strong in drama and art. It has an outstanding record in sports and games (especially rugby and cricket) with many county representatives. All boys are involved in compulsory sport each day. Plentiful activities and much emphasis on outdoor pursuits (eg fell walking, climbing, fishing and caving) for which the environment is ideal. Frequent expeditions into the Lake District. The CCF is strong. A big commitment to local community schemes (numerous charity events) and a remarkable record in the Duke of Edinburgh's Award Scheme.

SCHOOL PROFILE

Pupils Total, 450. Day 12; Boarding 438. Entry age, 11, 13 and into the sixth. 15+% are children of former pupils.

Entrance Common entrance and own scholarship entrance exam used. Oversubscribed. Good all rounders looked for at entry; specialist scholarships available in music and art. No religious requirements. Parents expected to buy text books. 26 assisted places. 75 scholarships and 46 bursaries, up to full fees.

Parents Up to 10% live within 30 miles; up to 10% live overseas.

Staff Head Dr R G Baxter, in post for 6 years. 46 full time staff, 17 part time. Annual turnover 8.5%. Average age 40.

Academic work GCSE and A-levels. Average size of fifth 90; upper sixth 90. *O-levels*: on average, 17 pupils in the upper fifth pass 5–7 subjects; 73 pass 8+ subjects. *A-levels*: on average, 14 pupils in upper sixth pass 2 subjects; 70, 3 subjects and 6 pass 4 subjects. On average, 45 take science/engineering A-levels; 35 take arts and humanities; 9 a mixture. Design – CDT (Technology) and CDT (Design and Realisation) are offered to GCSE/A-level. *Computing facilities*: Many BBCs – 2 labs plus computers in physics, chemistry, economics, design, languages, careers, bookshop, HM office, bursary.

Senior pupils' non-academic activities *Music*: 250 learn a musical instrument, 30 to Grade 6 or above, 1 accepted for Music School; 70 in school orchestras (1st and 2nd), bands, jazz orchestra, 40 in chapel, 80 in choral society, 12 in school pop group, 15 in early music class, 150 in opera/musical; 1 in National Youth Orchestra. *Drama and dance*: 70–80 in school productions, 200 in house plays, etc. 3 accepted for Drama Schools. *Art*: Most take as non-examined subject, 40 take GCSE, 3 take A-level; 1 accepted for Art School. 20 belong to eg photographic club, 25 in art society. *Sport*: Rugby, football, cricket, swimming, water polo, tennis, fives, squash, athletics, cross-country, running, hockey, fencing, golf, basketball, badminton, table tennis, shooting, archery, yard soccer available. All boys take part in compulsory sport each day. Most do more. All 4th form do Royal Life Saving course. 15–20 pupils pa represent county (rugby, cricket, athletics, fives, hockey, shooting). *Other*: 50 take part in local community schemes. 65 have bronze Duke of Edinburgh's Award, 30 have silver and 15 gold. 30 take part in holiday for NSPCC at school. 150 take part in many other charity events. Other activities include a computer club, CCF (army and navy). All boys canoe, sail, rock climb, absail, cave, orienteer. Societies: natural history, junior and senior debating, chess, bridge, campanology, clay pigeon shooting, etc. Driving lessons arranged.

Careers 13 part time careers advisors. Average number of pupils accepted for *arts and humanities degree courses* at Oxbridge, 4; other universities, 24; polytechnics or CHE, 8. *science and engineering degree courses* at Oxbridge, 8; other universities, 16; medical schools, 6; polytechnics or CHE, 6. *other general training courses*, 2. Average number of pupils going straight into careers in the armed services, 4; industry, 3; the City, 1; civil service, 1; music/drama, 2.

Uniform School uniform worn throughout.

Houses/prefects Competitive houses. Prefects, head boy and head of house and house prefects – appointed by the headmaster or housemaster.

Religion Religious worship compulsory. Chapel every Sunday, assembly each day. House prayers in evening.

Social Organised local events with girls schools: activities (sailing, climbing etc), debates, theatre, music, dances, roller skating, dinners, English/history lectures. Many organised trips, recently include expedition to Arctic, Sahara, Iceland, ski-ing in France and Italy. Cricket: Holland and West Indies. Rugby: Canada and Portugal. Chapel choir to Belgium etc. Exchange with German and French schools. Pupils allowed to bring own bicycle to school. Meals formal, in houses. School shops selling games, books, tuck. No tobacco allowed. There is an upper sixth bar.

Discipline No corporal punishment. Pupils failing to produce homework once might expect a repeat on special paper – signed before and after by housemaster; those caught smoking cannabis on the premises could expect expulsion.

Boarding All sixth form (180) have own study bedroom, a few 5th formers share; only 3rd form are in dormitories of 6 or more. Houses, of approximately 65, are the same as competitive houses. Resident qualified nurse and doctor. Pupils can provide and cook own food. One half-term exeat per term. Visits to the local town allowed daily.

Alumni association is run by The Secretary, The Old Sedberghian Club, Malim Lodge, Sedbergh School, Sedbergh, Cumbria LA10 5RY.

SEVENOAKS

Sevenoaks School
Sevenoaks
Kent TN13 1HU
Telephone number 0752 455133

Enquiries/application to the Registrar

- Co-ed
  Boys
  Girls
  Mixed sixth
- Day
- Boarding

Pupils 852
Upper sixth 200
Termly fees:
Day £1273
Boarding £2115
HMC

WHAT IT'S LIKE

Founded in 1432 by Sir William Sevenoke, Mayor of London and friend of Henry V. As a child he had been found abandoned by the roadside near the town. By way of thank offering for his share in the victory at Agincourt he founded a school and an almshouse in the place of his origin. It is one of the three oldest lay foundations in England. The first building of note was designed by the Earl of Burlington in 1718 (now in use as one of the boarding houses). In the 20th century numerous additions have been made and the school has a compact and attractive campus (50 acres of land in all, adjoining Knowle Park) with excellent modern facilities on the edge of the town. Facilities include an international centre, an international house for sixth form boys and girls, a first-rate technical activities centre and a purpose-built theatre with sophisticated equipment. The school has its own chaplain and religious education centre called The Meeting House. Divinity is taught throughout the school and 'The Church in the School' holds a service in the local parish church. Sevenoaks is high-powered academically (the staff:pupil ratio is about 1:10) and gets consistently good results. Each year 100–110 pupils go on to university (15–20 to Oxbridge). Very few schools in Britain send more pupils to university. The music, drama and art depts are all tremendously strong and active. Each year there is the Sevenoaks Summer Festival, organised by the school and run for the benefit of the whole community of the town. Sport and games are an important part of the curriculum. There is a wide variety of these and high standards are attained (a lot of representatives at county and national level each year). An equally wide range of extra-curricular activities (about 30). The CCF is a large and flourishing contingent. Sevenoaks was one of the pioneers of school-based community services in Britain. There is now a federal unit comprising 17 local schools with 600 volunteers. About 250 of these are from Sevenoaks. The school also has a remarkable record in the Duke of Edinburgh's Award Scheme.

SCHOOL PROFILE

Pupils Total over 12, 852. Day 550 (boys 395, girls 155); Boarding 302 (boys 182, girls 120). Entry age, 11, 13 and into the sixth. Very small number are children of former pupils.

Entrance Common entrance and own entrance exam used. Oversubscribed. All special skills welcomed; no religious requirements. Parents not expected to buy text books. Applied to Assisted Places Scheme. 50 scholarships/ bursaries, full fees to £250.

Parents 15+% in industry or commerce. 60+% live within 30 miles; 10+% live overseas.

Staff Head R P Barker, in post for 7 years. 82 full time staff, 30 part time. Annual turnover 10%. Average age 40.

Academic work GCSE, A-levels, International Baccalaureate. Average size of upper fifth 130; upper sixth 200. *O-levels*: on average, 10 pupils in upper fifth pass 1–4 subjects; 60, 5–7 subjects; 60 pass 8+ subjects. *A-levels*: on average, 25 pupils in upper sixth pass 1 subject; 40, 2 subjects; 110, 3 subjects and 25 pass 4 subjects. On average, 50 take science/engineering A-levels; 75 take arts and humanities; 75 a mixture. Russian, Norwegian, Japanese offered to GCSE/A-level. Provision for pupils with disabilities if they have high academic potential and an ability to thrive in the school's environment. *Computing facilities*: Computer lab, RML network with 12 machines, PDP 11/34 mini-frame computer.

Senior pupils' non-academic activities *Music*: 308 learn a musical instrument, 3 accepted for Music School; 60 in school orchestra; 60 in choir; 60 in bands; 25 in string ensembles; 25 in chamber group; 6 in Kent Youth Orchestra; occasional pupil in National Youth Orchestra. *Drama and dance*: 130 in school productions. 6 to Grade 6; 34 take GCSE; 4 in West Kent Youth

Theatre; 110 take drama/dance classes. *Art*: 100 take as non-examined subject; 18 GCSE; 20 A-level/IB. 3 accepted for Art School. 35 belong to photographic club; 20 to other. *Sport*: Rugby, soccer, tennis, hockey, shooting, netball, basketball, lacrosse, athletics, fencing, gymnastics, weight lifting, cricket, swimming, badminton, squash, riding, cross-country running available. Twice-weekly compulsory sport; considerable participation in non-compulsory sport, all facilities used regularly. 2 represent country (rugby); 19 represent county (rugby, hockey, cross-country). *Other*: Some pupils participate in voluntary work. 22 have bronze Duke of Edinburgh's Award, 52 have silver and 39 gold. Other activities include clubs for aquarium, astronomy, bridge, chemistry, chess, Christian Fellowship, classics, computer, contacto, debating, film, geography, history, languages, life class, maths, natural history, needle club, philosophy, pottery, shooting, SSPNS, vista, war games.

Careers 1 full time and 2 part time careers advisors. Average number of pupils accepted for *arts and humanities degree courses* at Oxbridge, 7; other universities, 55; polytechnics or CHE, 10. *science and engineering degree courses* at Oxbridge, 7; other universities, 35; medical schools, 8; polytechnics or CHE, 6. *BEd*, 1. *other general training courses*, 5. Average number of pupils going straight into careers in armed services, 4; the church, 1; industry, 2; the City, 7; civil service, 2; music/drama, 3.

Uniform School uniform worn throughout.

Houses/prefects Competitive houses in Middle and Junior Divisions. Prefects, head boy/girl, head of house and house prefects – appointed by Head. School Council.

Religion Little compulsory worship; any generally accepted religious belief encouraged.

Social Occasional ventures with other schools eg Young Enterprise Scheme. Exchanges with variety of schools in France, Germany and Spain. Pupils allowed to bring own car/bike/motorbike to school. Meals self service. School shops for tuck, stationery, second-hand clothes. No tobacco/alcohol allowed.

Discipline No corporal punishment. Pupils failing to produce homework once might expect verbal reprimand; those caught smoking cannabis on the premises might expect expulsion.

Boarding 20% have own study bedroom, 70% share, 5% are in dormitories of 6+. Houses, of approximately 45, single sex. Central dining room. Pupils can provide and cook own food. 2 weekend termly exeats, and half term. Visits to local town allowed.

Alumni association run by M T M Casey McCann Esq, c/o the School.

SHAFTESBURY

Shaftesbury Independent School
Godstone Road
Purley
Surrey
Telephone number 01-668 8080

Enquiries/application to the Headmaster

- Co-ed
  Boys
  Girls
  Mixed sixth
- Day
  Boarding

Pupils 47
Upper sixth 1
Termly fees:
Day £610
ISAI

WHAT IT'S LIKE

Founded in 1976, a one-acre site with playground on the edge of the green belt. Playing fields one and a half miles away. Good solid buildings, formerly those of Purley Grammar School. A lot of money has been put into improving facilities, which are good. A Christian foundation but non-denominational. At the moment it has only 60 pupils, and the intention is to keep the number below 150. An average class of 10 pupils. After only 11 years it is already a flourishing establishment, and with impressive results. Much emphasis on personal care and attention. Very strong in music and drama (most pupils are involved). An impressive range of sport and games. Some local community service work.

SCHOOL PROFILE

Pupils Total over 12, 47 (boys 26, girls 21). Entry age, 11+ and into the sixth.
Entrance Own entrance exam used. Sometimes oversubscribed. Academic skills and other skills taken into account. No religious requirements. Parents not expected to buy text books. 6–10 scholarships/bursaries, up to £400.
Parents 15+% in industry or commerce. 60+% live within 30 miles.
Staff Head P A B Gowlland, in post for 11 years. 6 full time staff, 6 part time. Annual turnover 10–20%.
Academic work GCSE and A-levels. Average size of upper fifth 14; upper sixth 1. *O-levels*: on average, 8 pupils in upper fifth pass 1–4 subjects; 3, 5–7 subjects; 3 pass 8+ subjects. *A-levels*: on average, 1 pupil in upper sixth passes 3 subjects. Over the last 3 years, 1 took science/engineering A-levels; 1 took arts and humanities; 2 a mixture. *Computing facilities*: 3 computers, disk drives, printer, modem. *Special provisions*: Small classes cope with mild handicaps without special provision.
Senior pupils' non-academic activities *Music*: 2 learn a musical instrument, 11 in school choir which combines with other choirs for major works (Creation, Messiah, Mozart Requiem, etc). *Drama and dance*: Most participate in school productions, local and national drama festivals – several awards won; 1 recently in Grange Hill TV series. *Art*: 5 take GCSE; 1 A-level. 1 accepted for Art School in recent years. *Sport*: Football, cricket, badminton, athletics, table tennis, swimming, netball, volleyball, rounders, cross-country, athletics available. 6 take non-compulsory sport. Independent Schools Association National Finals – always have some representatives. *Other*: Some take part in local community schemes. Other activities include a computer club, Christian Union, very strong drama club, ⅓ of school in choir.
Careers 1 part time careers advisor. Average number of pupils accepted

for *science and engineering degree courses* at polytechnics or CHE, 1. Some go on to secretarial courses. Others go straight into careers in industry, the City, the civil service, banking and insurance. Traditional school careers are banking and insurance.

Uniform School uniform worn throughout.

Houses/prefects No competitive houses. Sixth form act as prefects.

Religion Everyone attends assembly.

Social Joint choral works with ISAI schools. Day trip to France every year. Pupils allowed to bring own car/bicycle/motorbike to school. No tobacco/ alcohol allowed.

Discipline Corporal punishment only by Head. Pupils failing to produce homework once might expect to produce it by next day; those caught smoking cannabis on the premises could expect suspension.

Alumni association is run by Headmaster.

SHEBBEAR

Shebbear College	Co-ed	Pupils 319
Shebbear	• Boys	Upper sixth 30
Beaworthy	Girls	Termly fees:
North Devon EX21 5HJ	Mixed sixth	Day £910
Telephone number 040 928 228	• Day	Boarding £1705
Enquiries/application to Headmaster	• Boarding	SHMIS; GBA

WHAT IT'S LIKE

Founded in 1841 by the Bible Christians, it is now under a Methodist Board of Management and works in partnership with its sister school, Edgehill College, Bideford. It has an estate of 100 acres in fine unspoilt countryside, with Dartmoor National Park to the south and the Atlantic to the west. The buildings are very pleasant and well-equipped and there have been many first-rate extensions over the last 20 years. The essential quality of the school is its blend of family atmosphere with traditional discipline and Christian ethos. It has all the advantages of a small school and a large staff permits a staff:pupil ratio of 1:10. It caters for those who need plenty of care and attention as well as for the bright. The standard of teaching is high and results are good. The art, music and drama departments are all strong and there is a good deal of collaboration with Edgehill College in drama and music and other social activities. A range of sport and games (the facilities for these are exceptionally good) and a wide range of extra-curricular activities (with emphasis on outdoor pursuits for which the environment is ideal). The college has an outstanding record in the Duke of Edinburgh's Award Scheme.

SCHOOL PROFILE

Pupils Total over 12, 319. Day 143 (boys 141, girls 2); Boarding 176 (boys). Entry age, 7, 11, 13, into the sixth, boys; occasionally girls into the sixth. Own junior school provides about 30%. A few are children of former pupils.

Entrance Common entrance and own entrance exam used. Oversubscribed for day boys at 11. No special skills or religious requirements. Parents not expected to buy text books. Scholarships for academic/artistic ability, bursaries for boarding, up to 50% of fees.

Parents 15+% in Armed Services. 30+% live within 30 miles; up to 10% live overseas.

Staff Head R J Buley, in post for 5 years. 32 full time staff, 4 part time. Annual turnover 6%. Average age 40.

Academic work GCSE and A-levels. Average size of upper fifth 60; upper sixth 30. Majority take science/maths A-levels. *Computing facilities*: Computer centre including Prestel; BBC microcomputers in some departments. EFL provision.

Senior pupils' non-academic activities *Music*: 60 learn a musical instrument, 14 to Grade 6 or above. 16 in school orchestra, 40 in choir, 8 in barbershop, 1 in County Youth Orchestra. *Drama and dance*: 70 in school musical, 12–20 in straight drama. 1 accepted for Drama School. *Art*: All lower sixth and years 1–3 take art as non-examined subject; 25 take GCSE; 2–4 A-level; 1 accepted for Art School. 12 in photographic club, 12 pottery club. *Sport*: Rugby, cricket, squash, badminton, tennis, judo, karate, swimming, cross-country, athletics, basketball, table tennis, football available. Most take non-compulsory sport, 6 rugby and 6 cricket teams. 6 represent county (rugby, cricket). *Other*: 108 have Duke of Edinburgh's Awards. Other activities include a computer club, outdoor expeditions, model railways, stamp collecting etc.

Careers Senior member of staff advises.

Uniform School uniform worn throughout.

Houses/prefects Competitive houses. Prefects, head boy (school captain), head of house and house prefects; Head appoints School Captain; housemasters appoint House Captains and prefects. Sixth form committee.

Religion Compulsory daily morning chapel; all boarders attend Sunday evening.

Social Socials, debates, quizzes, cookery and life skills classes with Edgehill College (sister school). Organised trips abroad. Pupils allowed to bring own car/bike/motorbike to school. Meals self service. School shop. No tobacco/alcohol allowed.

Discipline No corporal punishment. Pupils failing to produce homework once might expect reprimand or 2 sides of written work.

Boarding Sixth form have study bedrooms, some share. Houses, of approximately 48–55, divided by age within division of competitive houses. Resident qualified medical staff. Central dining room. Weekend exeats as arranged. Sixth form visits to local town allowed at weekends.

Alumni association run by Mr A Andrews, Ranelagh, Boughton Hall Avenue, Send, Woking, Surrey GU23 7DE.

SHEFFIELD HIGH

Sheffield High School	Co-ed	Pupils 526
10 Rutland Park	Boys	Upper sixth 65
Sheffield S10 2PE	● Girls	Termly fees:
Telephone number 0742 660324	Mixed sixth	Day £622
Enquiries/application to the Headmistress	● Day	GSA; GPDST
	Boarding	

WHAT IT'S LIKE

Founded in 1878, it moved to its present premises in 1884 and occupies a single site in spacious grounds in the pleasant suburb of Broomhill. Junior school combined at Moor Lodge. Many additions have been made to the original Victorian buildings and facilities are first-rate. It provies a sound general education and results are impressive. Some 25–30 leavers go on to university each year. A good range of sports, games and activities. Adequate music, drama and art. A promising record in the Duke of Edinburgh's Award Scheme and substantial commitment to local community services.

SCHOOL PROFILE

Pupils Total over 12, 526. (Boys 5, girls 521). Entry age, 5+, 11+ and into the sixth (and when vacancies occur). Own junior school provides over 30%. 33% are children of former pupils.

Entrance Own entrance exam used. Oversubscribed. No special skills or religious requirements. Parents not expected to buy text books. 21 assisted places. Up to 10 scholarships at age 11 and at sixth form entry, up to £311 (half fees).

Parents 15+% are doctors, lawyers, etc. 60+% live within 30 miles.

Staff Head Miss D M Skilbeck, in post for 5 years. 38 full time staff, 13 part time. Annual turnover 2%. Average age 41.

Academic work GCSE and A-levels. Average size of upper fifth 75; upper sixth 65. *O-levels*: on average, 10 pupils in upper fifth pass 1–4 subjects; 14, 5–7 subjects; 51 pass 8+ subjects. *A-levels*: on average, 13 pupils in upper sixth pass 1 subject; 9, 2 subjects; 35, 3 subjects and 4 pass 4 subjects. On average, 17 take science/engineering A-levels; 34 take arts and humanities; 14 a mixture. Russian offered to GCSE/A-level. *Computing facilities*: RML 480Z, Amstrad. Fitted computer room. Junior school BBC computer.

Senior pupils' non-academic activities (sixth form) *Music*: 20 learn a musical instrument, 6 to Grade 6 or above, 1 accepted for Music School, 1 plays in pop group; 12 in school orchestra, 10 in school choir; 6 in Sheffield Youth Orchestra, 4 in Sheffield Girls' choir. *Drama and dance*: 20 in school productions. 2 to Grade 6 in ESB, RAD, etc, 1 entered competitions, 40 in debating classes; 1 accepted for Drama School. *Art*: 2 take GCSE, 5 take A-level. 3 accepted for Art School. *Sport*: Hockey, netball, tennis, rounders, volleyball, athletics, badminton, table tennis available. 19 take non-compulsory sport. 3 take exams, eg gymnastics, swimming. 6 represent county (hockey, netball, athletics, badminton). *Other* 30 take part in local community schemes. 8 have bronze Duke of Edinburgh's Award, 4 have silver and 3 gold. Other activities include a computer club. Sixth form go out for wide range of activities eg golf, squash, ice skating. Clubs: drama, debating, Christian Union, choir, orchestra, recorder group, outdoor pursuits.

Careers 1 full time and 1 part time careers advisors. Average number of pupils accepted for *arts and humanities degree courses* at Oxbridge, 3; other universities, 13; polytechnics or CHE, 11. *science and engineering degree courses* at Oxbridge, 4; other universities, 8; medical schools, 2; polytechnics or CHE, 2. *other general training courses*, 5.

Uniform School uniform worn except in the sixth.

Houses/prefects Competitive houses. Prefects, head girl and head of house – elected by sixth form and staff. School Council.

Religion Compulsory religious assembly on four mornings out of five. Pupil involvement.

Social Games fixtures with local schools, debating with schools, joint music and drama with local boys' independent school. Ski-ing trips, exchanges and visits to France, Germany and Russia. Educational cruises. Pupils allowed to bring own car/bicycle/motorbike to school. Meals self service. School tuck shop. No tobacco/alcohol allowed.

Discipline No corporal punishment. Pupils failing to produce homework once might expect detention; those caught smoking cannabis on the premises could expect expulsion.

Alumni association Details from school.

Former pupils Margaret Drabble (journalist and writer).

SHERBORNE (BOYS)

Sherborne School		Co-ed	Pupils 648
Sherborne		● Boys	Upper sixth 130
Dorset DT9 3AP		Girls	Termly fees:
Telephone number 0935 812646		Mixed sixth	Day £1975
Enquiries/application to the Registrar		● Day	Boarding £2250
		● Boarding	HMC

WHAT IT'S LIKE

Its origins date back to the 8th century when some kind of school at Sherborne was begun by St Aldhelm. It was linked with the Benedictine Abbey whose first Abbot was probably Thomas Copeland in 1437. The school was refounded by Edward VI in 1550. The school stands on land which formerly belonged to the monastery, and the library, chapel and study block were once Abbey buildings. The Abbey itself is very fine and the whole school forms an architectural complex which is delightful and lies in the centre of one of the most attractive country towns in England. Some of the houses are dispersed in the town but all are within 5 minutes' walk of the main school buildings. There is, inevitably, a close 'town and gown' relationship. There have been numerous modern extensions and facilities are excellent (including outstandingly good libraries). It is a happy school with a strong pastoral care/tutorial system built round a traditional boarding house structure. Emphasis on religious practice in the Anglican tradition is considerable. Sunday services and twice weekly chapel are compulsory. There is a wide range of voluntary communion and other services. Theology is taught throughout the school to a high level. Academic standards are very high and results are impressive. About 85 or more leavers go on to university each year. A staff:pupil ratio of 1:9. There is a very strong tradition in music (about half the school is involved) and a wide variety of dramatic activity. A wide range of sports and games is available and standards are high (a lot of representatives at county and national level). An unusually big range of extra-curricular activities. The CCF is large (200 or more boys). Boys also help with the running of a 25-acre nature reserve near the town. There is a field centre on Exmoor. A substantial commitment to local community services.

SCHOOL PROFILE

Pupils Total, 648. Day 18; Boarding 631. Entry age, 13+ and into the sixth. 10% are children of former pupils.

Entrance Common entrance and own exam used. Oversubscribed. No special skills or religious requirements. 10 scholarships/bursaries pa, three-quarters to one-third fees.

Parents 15+% in the armed services; 15+% are doctors, lawyers etc. 30+% live within 30 miles; up to 10% live overseas.

Staff Head R D Macnaghten, in post for 14 years. 69 full time staff, 12 part time. Annual turnover 5%. Average age 43.

Academic work GCSE and A-levels. Average size of upper fifth 135; upper sixth 130. Arabic offered to GCSE/A-level. Excellent computing facilities.

Senior pupils' non-academic activities *Music*: 200 learn a musical instrument, 120 to Grade 6 or above; 1 Associate of Royal College of Organists; 1 organ and 3 choral Oxbridge scholarships this year; 75 in school orchestra, 50 in choir. *Drama and dance*: 50 in school productions; 70 in annual house plays. 2 accepted for Drama Schools. *Art*: 15 take GCSE; 9 A-level (all got grade A). 5 accepted for Art School. 30 belong to eg photographic club. *Sport*: Rugby, cricket, hockey, soccer, squash, fives, athletics, basketball, cross-country, fencing, golf, swimming, tennis, sailing, shooting available. Virtually 100% take non-compulsory sport. 2–3 pupils pa reach national level and 12, county level (rugby, hockey, cricket). *Other*: 15% take part in local community schemes. 20 work for national charities. Other activities include CCF, driving lessons and wide range of societies covering all academic fields, Christian forum, film, bridge, horticulture, typing, sub-aqua, ornithology, instrument making, chess.

Careers 5 part time careers advisors. Average number of pupils accepted for *arts and humanities degree courses* (including social sciences) at universities, 62; polytechnics or CHE, 10. *science and engineering degree courses* at universities, 24; medical schools, 4. (21 go to Oxbridge). Average number of pupils going straight into careers in armed services, 5 (most after university); industry, 3; the City, 2; music/drama, 1; other, 2. Wide range of traditional school careers, eg medicine, services, church, law.

Uniform School uniform worn, modified in sixth.

Houses/prefects Nine competitive houses. Prefects, head boy, head of house and house prefects – appointed by Head.

Religion Compulsory Sunday service and chapel twice-weekly. Wide range of voluntary communion and other services.

Social Regular concerts, debates, dances, sixth form general studies with Sherborne Girls' School and St Antony's-Leweston. Pupils allowed to bring own bike to school. Meals self service. School shop sells uniform and sports kit. No tobacco/alcohol allowed.

Discipline Corporal punishment used by Headmaster in cases of extreme dishonesty or misbehaviour. Pupils failing to produce homework once might expect repetition of similar exercise; those caught smoking cannabis on the premises might expect expulsion.

Boarding 25% have own study bedroom, 50% share; 25% are in dormitories of 6+. Houses, of approximately 70. Resident qualified sanatorium sister; local medical practitioner. Central dining room. Pupils can provide and cook light snacks and coffee/tea in houses. 2 termly weekend exeats. Visits to local town allowed.

Alumni association run by M R G Earls-Davis Esq, Hon Sec Old Shirburnian Society, c/o the School.

Former pupils David Sheppard (Bishop of Liverpool); Christopher Chataway MP; Jeremy Irons; Nigel Dempster; Generals Sir Steuart Pringle and Julian Thompson (both Royal Marines); Michael McCrum (Vice Chancellor, Cambridge); Jonathan Powell (Director, BBC1).

SHERBORNE (GIRLS)

Sherborne School for Girls	Co-ed	Pupils 463
Sherborne	Boys	Upper sixth 75
Dorset DT9 3QN	● Girls	Termly fees:
Telephone number 0935 812245	Mixed sixth	Day £1485
	● Day	Boarding £2230
Enquiries/application to the Headmistress	● Boarding	GSA

WHAT IT'S LIKE

Founded in 1899, single-site in 40 acres on a hill overlooking open country and on the edge of the very delightful town of Sherborne. Pleasant buildings and first-class accommodation. A C of E foundation, some of its services are compulsory. A distinguished and civilised establishment where academic standards and attainments are high. An exceptionally good staff:pupil ratio of 1:7.5. Some 40–45 leavers go to university each year. A tremendously strong music department; good drama and art. First-rate games facilities and a high standard in sports and games (a very large number of representatives at county level). Wide range of societies, clubs etc catering for most needs. Big commitment to local community schemes and an impressive record in the Duke of Edinburgh's Award Scheme. There is frequent cooperation with Sherborne's boys' school.

SCHOOL PROFILE

Pupils Total 463. Day 10; Boarding 453. Entry age, 12+/13+ and into the sixth. 10% are children of former pupils.

Entrance Common entrance and scholarship exams used. Oversubscribed. No special skills or religious requirements but school is C of E. Parents not expected to buy text books. 11 scholarships/exhibitions, £4460–£660 pa.

Parents 15+% in the armed services; 15+% are doctors, lawyers, etc. 10+% live within 30 miles; up to 10% live overseas.

Staff Head Miss J M Taylor, in post for 3 years. 59 full time staff, 25 part time. Annual turnover 9%. Average age 42.5

Academic work GCSE and A-levels. Average size of upper fifth 85; upper sixth 75. *O-levels*: on average, 8 pupils in upper fifth pass 1–4 subjects; 14, 5–7 subjects; 63 pass 8+ subjects. *A-levels*: on average, 3 pupils in upper sixth pass 1 subject; 7, 2 subjects; 52, 3 subjects and 3 pass 4 subjects. On average, 20 take science/engineering A-levels; 35 take arts and humanities; 10 a mixture. Russian, history of art and social biology are offered to GCSE/ A-level. *Computing facilities*: 1 British Research machine; 1 Apple and Spread Sheets; number of BBC micros. Provision for mild dyslexia.

Senior pupils' non-academic activities *Music*: 130 learn a musical instrument, 44 to Grade 6 or above, 2 accepted for Music School, 2 go on to university to study music. 30 in school orchestra, 60 in school choir, 45 in musical society (oratoria), 21 in madrigal society, 40 in opera/musical, 15 in chamber orchestra; 1 in national youth orchestra, 3 in county orchestras, 25 study chamber music, 4 take A-level music, 6 take GCSE. *Drama and dance*: 45 in school productions, 20 in senior dramatic society; 26 up to Grade 6 in ESB, RAD, Guildhall; 2 accepted for Oxford Summer School, 3 auditioning. *Art*: 32 take GCSE; 6 take A-level. *Sport*: Athletics, hockey, lacrosse, swimming, fencing, tennis, squash, volleyball, gymnastics, badminton, judo, basketball available. 29 represent county (fencing, cross-country, lacrosse, hockey, swimming, athletics, tennis). *Other*: 20 have silver Duke of Edinburgh's Award and 5 have gold. Other activities include a computer club, learning to drive, ride, canoe, sail. Lively societies: drama, debating, gym.

Careers 3 part time advisors. Average number of pupils accepted for *arts and humanities degree courses* at Oxbridge, 8; other universities, 20; polytechnics or CHE, 2. *science and engineering degree courses* at Oxbridge, 2; other universities, 12; medical schools, 3; polytechnics or CHE, 1. *other general training courses*, 5. Average number of pupils going straight into careers in the City, 1.

Uniform School uniform worn except in the sixth.

Houses/prefects Competitive houses. Head girl and vice heads appointed by Head; head of house and house prefects appointed by house mistresses. Elected upper sixth committee for administration.

Religion Religious worship compulsory.

Social Joint orchestra, joint drama, languages club, youth social services with local schools. Trips abroad and exchange systems with schools abroad. Pupils allowed to bring own bicycle to school. Meals formal; self service in upper sixth house. No tobacco/alcohol allowed.

Discipline No corporal punishment. Pupils failing to produce homework once might expect to do it in own time; those caught smoking cannabis on the premises could expect expulsion.

Boarding Upper sixth have own study bedrooms; majority of remainder in cubicles in dormitories of 6–10. 8 houses, of 45–53, all ages plus upper sixth house. Resident qualified nurse and visiting doctor. 1 night exeat per term and half term. Visits to local town allowed.

Alumni association run by Mrs Stockley, Perry Croft, Midford, Bath, Avon.

Former pupils Dame Diana Reader Harris, DBE; Maria Aitken.

SHERRARDSWOOD

Sherrardswood School
Welwyn Garden City
Hertfordshire AL8 7JN
Telephone number 0707 322281

Enquiries/application to the Headmaster

- Co-ed
  Boys
  Girls
  Mixed sixth
- Day
- Boarding

Pupils 154
Upper sixth 10
Termly fees:
Day £835
Boarding £1590
ISAI

WHAT IT'S LIKE

Founded in 1928, single-site and rural in 25 acres of delightful parkland. The main building is a fine 18th-century house shared by the junior school and the boarders. Accommodation is comfortable and modern facilities plentiful. A sound general education is provided. Music, art and drama are on the curriculum. A fair range of sport, games and activities.

SCHOOL PROFILE

Pupils Total over 12, 154. Day 99 (boys 48, girls 51); Boarding 55 (boys 33, girls 22). Entry age, 4+ and into the sixth. Own prep school provides 60%.
Entrance Parents expected to buy text books for sixth formers. 2 scholarships/bursaries, up to 1/3 fees.
Staff Head T M Ham, in post for 5 years. 21 full time staff, 5 part time.
Academic work GCSE and A-levels. Average size of upper fifth 28; upper sixth 10. Exam results not provided. *Computing facilities*: BBC Masters and B Computers and Spectrums.
Uniform School uniform worn except in the sixth.
Houses/prefects Competitive houses. Prefects, head boy/girl, head of house and house prefects – appointed by the Head. School Council.
Social Pupils allowed to bring own car/bicycle/motorbike to school.
Discipline No corporal punishment.

SHIPLAKE

Shiplake College
Henley-on-Thames
Oxfordshire RG9 4BW
Telephone number 073522 2455

Enquiries/application to the Headmaster

Co-ed
- Boys
  Girls
  Mixed sixth
- Day
- Boarding

Pupils 342
Upper sixth 40
Termly fees:
Day £1350
Boarding £2100
SHMIS, GBA

WHAT IT'S LIKE

Founded in 1959, it has a very attractive site a few yards from the Thames, 2½ miles upstream from Henley. It is based on the historic Shiplake Court. Additional buildings consist of cottages, a tithe barn and stables. First-rate facilities and comfortable accommodation have been created. In worship it follows C of E practice; church services (the village church is next to the college) are compulsory. Academic standards are high and a fair number of pupils (about 10 per year) proceed to degree courses. Strong in music, drama, art, debating and public speaking. Very good record in sports (especially rowing) and games, with a lot of representatives at county level. Five representatives in rowing at international level. Compulsory sport/games four afternoons a week. Compulsory CCF for 3 years (quite a lot of leavers go into the Army). Emphasis on outdoor pursuits and adventure training (expeditions to Himalayas, Norway and the Alps). About 50 minor extra-curricular activities available. Considerable participation in local community schemes and an impressive record in the Duke of Edinburgh's Award Scheme.

SCHOOL PROFILE

Pupils Total, 342. Day 55; Boarding 287. Entry age, 13 and into the sixth. 1% are children of former pupils.

Entrance Common entrance and own exam used. Oversubscribed (school tries to redirect boys not regarded as suitable before common entrance). C of E preferred but other religions permitted. Parents not expected to buy text books. 2 day-boy scholarships and bursary for sons of schoolmasters available, one-third to half fees.

Parents 15+% in industry or commerce. 30+% live within 30 miles, up to 10% live overseas.

Staff Head N V Bevan, appointed 1988. 36 full time staff, 2 part time. Annual turnover 2–3%. Average age 38.

Academic work GCSE and A-levels. Average size of upper fifth 75; upper sixth 40. *O-levels*: on average, 40 pupils in upper fifth pass 1–4 subjects; 10, 5–7 subjects; 2 pass 8+ subjects. *A-levels*: on average, 10 pupils in upper sixth pass 1 subject; 15, 2 subjects and 15 pass 3 subjects. On average, 15 take science/engineering A-levels; 15, arts and humanities; 10 a mixture. *Computing facilities*: 10 Amstrads, 5 BBC, 10 others; Olivetti office system; Apple for masters' common room. Provision for 16 dyslexic pupils each year.

Senior pupils' non-academic activities *Music*: 40 learn a musical instrument, 4 to Grade 6 or above, 1 accepted for Music School; 18 in school orchestra, 22 in choir, 15 in school pop group, all in school choral society; 3 play in pop group after leaving. *Drama and dance*: 15 in school productions, 35 in debating society. Occasional pupil accepted for Drama School. *Art*: 10 take as non-examined subject; 19 take GCSE art, 12 ceramics; 10 take A-level art, 2 ceramics. 3 accepted for Art School. 18 belong to eg photographic club. *Sport*: Rugby, hockey, cricket, rowing, tennis, squash, sailing, shooting, badminton, basketball, cross country, athletics, swimming available. 50% take non-compulsory sport (sport is compulsory on 4 afternoons a week). 10 represent county (rugby), 5 represent country (World Junior Rowing Championships). *Other*: 6 take part in local community schemes. 26 have silver Duke of Edinburgh's Award, and 8 gold. 3 enter voluntary schemes after leaving; 25 work for national charities. CCF is compulsory for 3 years. Other activities include a computer club, driving lessons, chess, woodwork, metalwork, pottery, silversmithing, natural history, ferreting.

Careers 1 full time and 1 part time careers advisors. Average number of pupils accepted for *arts and humanities degree courses* at universities, 4; polytechnics or CHE, 3. *science and engineering degree courses* at universities, 3; medical schools, 1; polytechnics or CHE, 2. *BEd*, 1: *other general training courses*, 3. Average number of pupils going straight into careers in armed services, 5; industry, 2; the City, 5; civil service, 1; music/drama, 1. Traditional school career is the Army.

Uniform School uniform worn throughout.

Houses/prefects Competitive houses. Prefects, head boy, head of house and house prefects – appointed by Head.

Religion Compulsory church services.

Social Conferences, joint crews for national/international regattas, drama etc with local schools. Annual expedition to Himalayas, art trip to Paris, French department trip to Paris, ski-ing trip to Alps. 50% pupils go on trip or expedition in holidays. Meals self-service. School shop. No tobacco allowed; beer allowed in junior common room.

Discipline No corporal punishment. Pupils failing to produce homework once might expect to repeat it; those caught smoking cannabis on the premises can expect expulsion.

Boarding 20% have own study bedroom, 30% share with 1 or 2; 10% are in dormitories of 6+. Houses, of 65–70, same as competitive houses. Resident qualified nurse. Central dining room. Pupils can provide and cook own food. 2 weekend and half term exeats each term. Occasional visits to local town allowed, weekly for seniors.

Alumni association run by H E Wells-Furby Esq, c/o the College.

SHREWSBURY

The Schools	Co-ed	Pupils 660
Shrewsbury	● Boys	Upper sixth Yes
Shropshire SY3 7BA	Girls	Termly fees:
Telephone number 0743 4537	Mixed sixth	Day £1550
	● Day	Boarding £2170
	● Boarding	GBA; HMC

WHAT IT'S LIKE

Founded in 1552 by charter of Edward VI, it occupies a splendid site of 105 acres on a loop of the Severn on a high bluff overlooking the old town of Shrewsbury. Its buildings, ancient and modern, are very fine indeed and include a Jacobean library. This is one of the very few important scholarly libraries in a public school and possesses valuable medieval manuscripts and the entire collection of books owned by the school in Stuart times. It is a local and national school with 8 boarding houses and 2 day-boy houses. The school house has about 100 boys, the others about 60. A sixth form annexe caters for a few senior boys where the bar and common room function as a club. New buildings include a dining hall which seats 700, a magnificent science block, a new gym, a computer room and the purpose-built Ashton theatre. Religious worship is in the Anglican tradition and all boys are expected to attend one mid-week service and one Sunday service. A large staff allows a staff:pupil ratio of 1:9. Academic standards are high and results are very good. About 95% of boys stay on for A-levels and 65% of leavers go on to university. There is a very strong tradition in music. Tuition in every orchestral instrument is available. There are 2 orchestras, a wind band, jazz band, chapel choir, concert choir and madrigal choir. Concerts are frequent and there is regular contact with local musical groups. The art school and workshops are very well equipped and many activities are catered for. Frequent dramatic productions are presented by the school and by individual houses. Facilities for sports and games are first rate and high standards are achieved. Many societies and clubs provide for most extra-curricular needs. Clubs include printing, electronics and canoe-building. Open-air activities such as hill-walking and mountaineering are encouraged. There is a flourishing CCF contingent.

SCHOOL PROFILE

Head F E Maidment, first year in post
Age range 13–18; entry by common entrance
Scholarships, including music and sixth form.

SHREWSBURY HIGH

Shrewsbury High School
32 Town Walls
Shrewsbury
Shropshire SY1 1TN
Telephone number 0743 62872

Enquiries/application to the Headmistress

Co-ed
Boys
● Girls
Mixed sixth
● Day
Boarding

Pupils 340
Upper sixth 40
Termly fees:
Day £622
GPDST

WHAT IT'S LIKE

Founded in 1885, it transferred to its present site in 1897. Over the years it has expanded steadily and various buildings have been bought. Its pleasant grounds slope down to the Severn. A sound general education is given and academic results appear to be good. About 20 leavers go on to university. A fair range of sports, games and extra-curricular activities including art, drama and music. School's own junior department is about a mile away.

SCHOOL PROFILE

Pupils Total over 12, 340. Entry age, 4, 11 and into the sixth. Own junior department provides over 50% of pupils.
Entrance Own entrance exam used. Oversubscribed. No special skills or religious requirements. Parents not expected to buy text books. 14 assisted places pa. Some scholarships/bursaries available.
Parents 15+% are doctors, lawyers etc; 15+% farmers. 60+% live within 30 miles.
Staff Head Miss E M Gill, in post for 6 years. 32 full time staff, 18 part time.
Academic work GCSE and A-levels. Average size of upper fifth 60; upper sixth 40. *O-levels*: on average, 1 pupil in upper fifth passes 1–4 subjects; 11, 5–7 subjects; 48 pass 8+ subjects. *A-levels*: on average, 6 pupils in upper sixth pass 1 subject; 5, 2 subjects; 9, 3 subjects and 20 pass 4 subjects. *Computing facilities*: 2 rooms, RML and other machines.
Senior pupils' non-academic activities A number of pupils participate in

music, drama, art and sport; details not available. Hockey, netball, tennis, athletics, swimming, badminton, rowing are available as well as chess, debating, electronics and several computer clubs.

Careers 2 part time careers advisors.

Uniform School uniform worn except the sixth.

Houses/prefects Competitive houses. No prefects; head girl – elected by staff and school. School Council.

Religion Regular non-denominational morning assembly.

Social Drama, music, debating, dances with local schools; organised trips abroad. Pupils allowed to bring own car/bike to school. Meals self-service. No tobacco/alcohol allowed.

Discipline No corporal punishment. Pupils failing to produce homework are dealt with according to the circumstances.

SIBFORD

Sibford School	● Co-ed	Pupils 327
Sibford Ferris	Boys	Upper sixth Yes
Banbury	Girls	Termly fees:
Oxfordshire OX15 5QL	Mixed sixth	Day £957
Telephone number 0295 78441	● Day	Boarding £1880
	● Boarding	Quaker
Enquiries/application to the Headmaster's Secretary		

WHAT IT'S LIKE

Founded in 1842, it has a single-site campus in a small village a few miles from Banbury. Very pleasant rural surroundings. The oldest building is a 17th-century manor house. There has been steady expansion over the years to provide very good up-to-date facilities. Its Quaker background is of great importance and the philosophy and principles of Quakerism are central to the school life. The intake is cosmopolitan. Non-academic students are particularly cared for. There are some non-examination courses and it is strong on vocational education. The Certificate of pre-Vocational Education is available for those who are not academic but have plentiful talent and skills. There is a good remedial department. A sound general training is given and the staff:pupil ratio is 1:8. A range of sports, games and activities. Some participation in local community services and the Duke of Edinburgh's Award Scheme.

SCHOOL PROFILE

Pupils Total 327. Day 73 (boys 58, girls 15); Boarding 254 (boys 159, girls 95). Entry age, 11 and into the sixth.

Entrance Oversubscribed in some areas. Creative skills particularly valued; no religious requirements. Parents not expected to buy text books. Scholarships/bursaries available to Quaker children on the basis of need.

Parents 30+% live within 30 miles; 25% live overseas.

Staff Head J A Graham, in post for 8 years. 38 full time staff, 6 part time plus visiting music staff. Annual turnover 5%. Average age 38–40.

Academic work GCSE, CPVE and A-levels in art, craft, design and technology and drama. Average size of upper fifth 65–70. Computing facilities considerable for computer assisted learning, not for computer studies. Highly sophisticated and long established (15 years) dyslexic unit; also EFL department.

Senior pupils' non-academic activities *Music*: 14 learn a musical instrument, 25 in choir, 5–6 in pop group. *Drama and dance*: 80–100 in school productions; 45 take GCSE and A-level Drama. 4–5 accepted for Drama Schools; 40 enter competitions; 2 go on to work in theatre. *Art*: 20 take as non-examined subject; 48 take GCSE; 9 A-level. 15 belong to eg photographic club; 3–4 accepted for Art School. *Sport*: Rugby, soccer, cricket (boys); hockey, netball, tennis (girls); volleyball, swimming, athletics, basketball (both) available. 230 take non-compulsory sport. *Other*: 5 take part in local community schemes. 20 have bronze Duke of Edinburgh's Award, 6 have silver.

Careers 2–3 part time advisors.

Uniform School uniform worn except in sixth.

Houses/prefects Houses are non-competitive. Head boy/girl, head of house and house prefects – appointed by the Head or house staff.

Religion Religious worship encouraged.

Social No organised events with other schools. Organised trips abroad. Pupils allowed to bring own car/bike to school. Some meals formal, some self service. School shop. No alcohol; controlled smoking in sixth form allowed.

Discipline No corporal punishment. Pupils failing to produce homework once might expect to be kept in to do it; those caught smoking cannabis on the premises could expect expulsion.

Boarding All sixth formers share a study bedroom; 12% in dormitories of 6+. Houses, of approximately 40, some single sex, some mixed. Separate sixth form house. Resident qualified nurse. Central dining room. Pupils can provide and cook supplementary food. Exeats: weekly boarding available. Visits to the local town allowed weekly from fourth form upwards.

Alumni association run by Ian Weatherhead, c/o the School.

Former pupils Paul Eddington; Sir John Berg.

SIDCOT

Sidcot School	• Co-ed	Pupils 225
Winscombe	Boys	Upper sixth 25
Avon BS25 1PD	Girls	Termly fees:
Telephone number 093 484 3102	Mixed sixth	Day £925
Enquiries/application to the Headmaster	• Day	Boarding £1760
	• Boarding	SHMIS; Quaker

WHAT IT'S LIKE

Founded in 1808, one of the oldest co-educational schools in the country, it has a very pleasant rural site of 110 acres in the Mendips, 8 miles from

Weston-super-Mare. Its buildings are an agreeable mixture of the old and modern, and there are ample up-to-date facilities. A Quaker school, the principles and philosophy of Quakerism are adhered to. A sound general education is given and about ten or so leavers proceed to university each year. Very strong indeed in the music, drama and art departments. A fair range of sport and games and plentiful emphasis on outdoor pursuits.

SCHOOL PROFILE

Pupils Total over 12, 225. Day 100 (boys 67, girls 33); Boarding 166 (boys 94, girls 72). Entry age, 9, 11, 16 and into the sixth.

Entrance Common entrance and own entrance exam used. Sometimes oversubscribed. Average intellectual ability or above looked for. No religious requirements. Parents not expected to buy text books. 30 scholarships/ bursaries and special scheme aids children from Quaker families, £300– £1000.

Parents 30+% live within 30 miles; 10+% live overseas.

Staff Head C J Greefield, in post for 2 years.

Academic work GCSE and A-levels. Average size of upper fifth 55; upper sixth 25. *O-levels*: on average, 10 pupils in upper fifth pass 1–4 subjects; 15, 5–7 subjects; 25 pass 8+ subjects. *A-levels*: on average, 8 pupils in upper sixth pass 1 subject; 5, 2 subjects and 8 pass 3 subjects. On average, 10 take science/engineering A-levels; 10 take arts and humanities; 5 a mixture. Theatre arts, economics and public affairs offered to A-level. *Computing facilities*: Computers in some departments plus a computing centre with ten machines. Special provisions for mild dyslexia and EFL programmes.

Senior pupils' non-academic activities *Music*: 80 learn a musical instrument, 5 to Grade 6 or above, 9 in school orchestra, 30 in school choir, 4 in school pop group, 5 in string ensemble, wind band and swing band; 2 in Somerset County orchestra, 1 in Wells Oration Choir, 1 in Winscombe orchestra. *Drama and dance*: 80 in school productions. 1 accepted for Drama School. *Art*: 6 take as non-examined subject, 15 take GCSE, 4 take A-level. 2 accepted for Art School, 1 for architecture. 10 belong eg to photographic club, 10 in set building, lighting, dance decorations etc. *Sport*: All usual sports available plus basketball, squash, table tennis, pool. All pupils take non-compulsory sport. 20 take swimming exams. 40 represent county (rugby, soccer, athletics, hockey, cricket, cross-country). *Other*: 6 have silver Duke of Edinburgh's Award. Other activities include a computer club and 60 clubs and societies.

Careers 2 part time advisors. Average number of pupils accepted for *arts and humanities degree courses* at universities, 2; polytechnics or CHE, 5. *science and engineering degree courses* at universities, 4; polytechnics or CHE, 2. *other general training courses*, 6. Average number of pupils going straight into careers in the armed services, 2; civil service, 1; paramedical (eg osteopathy), 1; banking, 1. Traditional school careers are in caring professions.

Uniform School uniform worn except in the sixth.

Houses/prefects Competitive houses. All sixth formers have prefectorial duties. Head boy/girl, head of house and house prefects – appointed by the Head. School Council.

Religion Boarders expected to attend Quaker Meeting for worship at least once a month.

Social Occasional joint concerts with other schools. Two or three visits abroad each year. Pupils allowed to bring own car/bicycle to school. Meals self service. School shop. No alcohol allowed; tobacco for over 16s whose parents request permission.

Discipline No corporal punishment. Punishments escalate from gating to suspension to expulsion; expulsion expected for any involvement with drugs.

Boarding Houses, of approximately 30–50 divided by age group, single sex except for junior house. Resident qualified nurse. Central dining room. Exeats any Saturday mid-day to Sunday 6 pm. Visits to local town allowed for senior pupils (14+) on Saturday afternoons.

Alumni association is run by Michael van Blankenstein, 22 Park Road, High Barnet, Hertfordshire EN5 5SQ.

SILCOATES

Silcoates School	Co-ed	Pupils 369
Wrenthorpe	● Boys	Upper sixth 45
Wakefield	Girls	Termly fees:
West Yorkshire WF2 0PD	● Mixed sixth	Day £942
Telephone number 0924 291614	● Day	Boarding £1648
Enquiries to the Headmaster	● Boarding	HMC; SHMIS;
Application to the Admissions Secretary		United Reform

WHAT IT'S LIKE

Founded in 1820 for the sons of ministers and missionaries in the Congregational Church, it is single site and semi-urban, 2 miles west of Wakefield. There are 55 acres of magnificent gardens and playing fields and many modern well-equipped buildings. Facilities are first-rate. The school has an inter-denominational approach to Christianity but retains links with the United Reformed Church. A well-run school it has high academic standards and consistently good results. About 20 pupils go on to university each year. Reasonable strength in music, drama and art. A wide range of sports and games (standards are high and there have been a large number of representatives at county and national level). Equally good range of extra-curricular activities and a fine record in the Duke of Edinburgh's Award Scheme.

SCHOOL PROFILE

Pupils Total over 12, 369. Day 262 (boys 250, girls 12); Boarding 107 (boys, 98, girls 9). Entry age, boys 7–13; boys and girls into the sixth. Own junior department provides over 20%. 7% are children of former pupils.

Entrance Common entrance and own entrance exam used. Not oversubscribed. No special skills or religious requirements. Parents not expected to buy text books. 12 scholarships, from half fees to £300; bursaries for up to half fees for good O-level results.

Parents 15+% in industry or commerce. 30+% live within 30 miles; up to 10% live overseas.

Staff Head J C Baggaley, in post for 10 years. 39 full time staff, 4 part time. Annual turnover 4%. Average age 36.

Academic work GCSE and A-levels. Average size of upper fifth 60; upper sixth 45. *O-levels*: on average, 25 pupils in upper fifth pass 1–4 subjects; 16, 5–7 subjects; 19 pass 8+ subjects. *A-levels*: on average, 4 pupils in the upper sixth pass 1 subject; 6, 2 subjects; 19, 3 subjects and 7 pass 4 subjects. On average, 12 take science/engineering A-levels; 14 take arts and humanities; 10 a mixture. *Computing facilities*: Computer centre using Amstrad, BBC and Sinclair computers; others in departments. Provision for dyslexia and EFL.

Senior pupils' non-academic activities *Music*: 28 learn a musical instrument, 15 to Grade 6 or above; 12 in wind band, 11 in choir, 6 in jazz group. *Drama and dance*: 10–30 in school productions. *Art*: 10 take as non-examined subject; 30 GCSE; 13 A-level art and design. 1 accepted for Art School. 25 belong to photographic club. *Sport*: Rugby, cricket, golf, swimming, table tennis, tennis, squash, hockey, badminton, cross-country, athletics, basketball available. 75% take non-compulsory sport. 16 take exams in gymnastics, 200 in swimming. 4 represent country (rugby); 22 represent county (rugby, table tennis, cross-country, athletics, cricket, squash, swimming). *Other*: 2 take part in local community schemes. 30 have bronze Duke of Edinburgh's Award, 20 have silver and 10 gold. Other activities include a computer club, chess, bridge, canoeing, debating, motor and film clubs, public speaking, sixth form society.

Careers 4 part time careers advisors. Average number of pupils accepted for *arts and humanities degree courses* at Oxbridge, 1; other universities, 8; polytechnics or CHE, 1. *science and engineering degree courses* at universities, 9; medical schools, 1; polytechnics or CHE, 2. *BEd*, 1. *other general training courses*, 3. Average number of pupils going straight into careers in armed services, 2; industry, 3; police force, 1.

Uniform School uniform worn throughout.

Houses/prefects Competitive houses. Prefects, head boy, head of house and house prefects – appointed by Headmaster after consultation with staff.

Religion Compulsory daily morning assembly in chapel; Sunday evening chapel compulsory for boarders, encouraged for day boys; weekly holy communion.

Social Debates with local comprehensive school. French, German, cycling, ski-ing trips; Yorkshire/Westphalia German Schools exchange. Day pupils allowed to bring own car to school; boarders, motorbike/bike. Meals self service. School shop. No tobacco/alcohol allowed.

Discipline No corporal punishment. Pupils failing to produce homework once might expect verbal warning; those caught drunk on the premises might expect suspension pending discussion with staff and parents.

Boarding 7 have own study bedroom, 25% share with 2 others; 6 dormitories of 6+. Houses are single sex. Resident qualified nurse. Central dining room. Weekend exeats at request of parents or guardian. Visits to local town allowed at weekends.

Alumni association run by John Lane, Hon Sec, 48 Sutton Lane, Byram, Knottingley, WF11 9OP.

SIR WILLIAM PERKINS'S

Sir William Perkins's School	Co-ed	Pupils 470
Guildford Road	Boys	Upper sixth Yes
Chertsey	● Girls	Termly fees:
Surrey KT16 9BN	Mixed sixth	Day £700
Telephone number 093 28 62161/60264	● Day	GSA
	Boarding	

Head Mrs A Darlow (6 years)
Age range 11–18; entry by own exam
Scholarships/bursaries.

SOUTHBANK AMERICAN

Southbank – The American International School	● Co-ed	Pupils 121
55 Eccleston Square	Boys	Upper sixth 14
London SW1V 1PH	Girls	Termly fees:
Telephone number 01-834 4684	Mixed sixth	Day £1600
Enquiries/application to the Registrar	● Day	ISAI; ECIS
	Boarding	

WHAT IT'S LIKE

Founded in 1979, located in two Georgian houses (one overlooking Eccleston Square Gardens) close to Victoria Station. It is an official centre for the International Baccalaureat. The teaching is of high standard and results are good (14+ to university each year; a very high proportion for a school of 130 pupils). EFL teaching available. Good music, drama and art. Fair range of games, clubs and societies. Full use is made of the capital's cultural amenities. It is a day school only.

SCHOOL PROFILE

Pupils Total over 12, 121. Boys 67, girls 54. Entry age, 11+ and into the sixth.
Entrance Oversubscribed. No special skills or religious requirements. Parents not expected to buy text books. 13 scholarships/bursaries, £2400 to £420.
Parents 15+% are doctors, lawyers etc; 15+% in industry or commerce. 60+% live within 30 miles.
Staff Head Milton E Toubkin, in post for 8 years. 16 full time staff, 15 part time. Annual turnover 5%.
Academic work GCSE, International Baccalaureat, US High School Diploma. Average size of upper fifth 24; upper sixth 14. *O-levels*: on average, 12 pupils in upper fifth pass 1–4 subjects, 4, 5–7 subjects, 1 passes 8+ subjects. (O-levels sat en passant for International Baccalaureat.) *A-levels*: on average 3 pupils in the upper sixth pass 2 subjects; 10, 3 subjects; 1 passes 4 subjects. On average, 14 take a mixture of both science/engineering and arts and

humanities A-levels. Danish, Norwegian, Swedish, Hebrew, Farsi, and Japanese are offered to GCSE/A-level. *Computing facilities*: 2 Macintosh, 5 BBC 'B', 4 Apple 2s. EFL provision.
Senior pupils' non-academic activities   *Music*: 12 learn a musical instrument, 1 accepted for Music School; 10 in school choirs, 6 in school pop groups. *Drama and dance*: 18 in school productions. 4 accepted for Drama/Dance Schools, 2 go on to work in the theatre. *Art*: 16 take as a non-examined subject; 8 take GCSE; 8 International Baccalaureat. 3 accepted for Art School. 9 belong to photographic club. *Sport*: Soccer, basketball, badminton, swimming, tennis, jujitsu, weightlifting available. 40 take non-compulsory sport. 3 represent county/country cross-country (golf, tennis). *Other*: 5 take part in local community schemes. Other activities include a computer club, a year book, arts forum, model United Nations and a band.
Careers 1 full time advisor. Average number of pupils accepted for *arts and humanities degree courses* at universities, 9. *science and engineering degree courses* at universities, 5; medical schools, 2. *other general training courses*, 2. Average number of pupils going straight into careers in the armed services, 2; the City, 1; music/drama, 2.
Uniform School uniform not worn.
Houses/prefects No competitive houses, prefects or head boy/girl. School Council.
Religion No compulsory religious worship.
Social No organised local events. Organised trips abroad. Pupils allowed to bring own car/bike/motorbike to school. Meals self-service. School shop. No alcohol allowed, tobacco (for over 16s) in restricted areas.
Discipline No corporal punishment. Pupils failing to produce homework once might expect reprimand and warning; those caught smoking cannabis on the premises might expect referral to school's Drugs Committee and counselling before re-admission.
Alumni association is run by Mrs Lesley Milton, c/o the School.

SOUTH HAMPSTEAD HIGH

South Hampstead High School
3 Maresfield Gardens
London NW3 5SS
Telephone number 01-435 2899

Enquiries/application to the Secretary

Co-ed
Boys
● Girls
Mixed sixth
● Day
Boarding

Pupils 520
Upper sixth 70
Termly fees:
Day £684
GPDST; GSA

WHAT IT'S LIKE

Founded in 1876, urban, single-site, it has occupied its present premises since 1882. The core is the original Victorian building. Well-equipped new buildings include a theatre and sports hall. The junior school is nearby. It is a selective and highly academic school and standards are high. The A-level pass rate in 1987 was 97.2%. Some 40–50 leavers go on to university each year. Very strong indeed in music (200 girls learn an instrument) and pretty strong in drama and art. Very good range of games and sports. Numerous activities, clubs and societies. It has flourishing local connections and a substantial commitment to local community schemes. A fine record in the Duke of Edinburgh's Award Scheme.

SCHOOL PROFILE

Pupils Total over 11, 520. Entry age, 11+ and into the sixth.

Entrance Own entrance exam used. Oversubscribed. No special skills or religious requirements. Parents not expected to buy text books. 64 assisted places. 1–3 scholarships/bursaries pa (25–50% fees).

Parents 15+% are doctors, lawyers, etc; 15+% in industry or commerce; 15+% in the theatre, music, media etc. 60+% live within 30 miles.

Staff Head Mrs D A Burgess, in post for 13 years. 32 full time staff, 15 part time.

Academic work GCSE and A-levels. Average size of upper fifth 65–70; upper sixth 65–70. *O-levels*: on average, 2 pupils in upper fifth pass 1–4 subjects; 4, 5–7 subjects; 60 pass 8+ subjects. *A-levels*: on average, 2 pupils in the upper sixth pass 2 subjects; 60, 3 subjects; 4 pass 4 subjects. On average, 20+ take science/engineering A-levels; 30+ take arts and humanities; 10+ take a mixture. *Computing facilities*: 8 BBC micros and Econet system, 2 RML 3802. Plus BST technology bus 1 day per week with 10 BBC micros.

Senior pupils' non-academic activities *Music*: 200 learn a musical instrument, 5 up to Grade 6 or above, 1–2 accepted for Music School; 60 in school orchestra, 60 in school choir, 20 in chamber music; 1 in Royal Academic Orchestra, 1 in Trinity College orchestra and 4 in jazz band. *Drama and dance*: 25 in school productions, 15–20 in other productions, 20 in dance workshops. 1–2 accepted for Drama/Dance Schools. 2 entered competitions, occasional pupil in films and national theatre. *Art*: 10 take as non-examined subject; 64 take GCSE; 20 history of art; 24 take A-level. 3–6 accepted for Art School. *Sport*: Hockey, netball, tennis, badminton, squash, basketball, trampolining, swimming, rounders, volleyball, gymnastics and dance available. 200 take non-compulsory sport. 5 represent county (netball, tennis) 1 in national training squad (tennis). *Other*: 55+ take part in local community schemes. 25 have bronze Duke of Edinburgh's Award. Numerous clubs (ornithology, science, craft) and societies (debating, political and economic). General studies programme (includes dress making, computer science etc).

Careers 1 part time advisor. Average number of pupils accepted for *arts and humanities degree courses* at Oxbridge, 9; other universities, 18; polytechnics or CHE, 3. *science and engineering degree courses* at Oxbridge, 3; other universities, 12; medical schools, 6; polytechnics or CHE, 1. *BEd*, 2. *other general training courses*, 3. Traditional school careers are medicine and law.

Uniform School uniform worn except the sixth.

Houses/prefects No competitive houses. No prefects but head girl. School Council.

Religion Non-denominational assembly is compulsory. No worship is involved.

Social Joint choral concert annually with boys' public school; joint drama productions; shared societies/speakers/debates. Trips, Russia, ski-ing, France. Pupils allowed to bring own car/bike/motorbike to school. Meals, self service. No tobacco/alcohol allowed.

Discipline No corporal punishment. Pupils failing to produce homework once might expect reprimand; those caught smoking cannabis on the premises might expect expulsion. (The policy of the council is to suspend the pupil and inform the police.)

Former pupils Rabbi Julia Neuberger; Fay Weldon (author); Miriam Karlin and Angela Lansbury (actresses); Nina Milkina and Sarah Francis (musicians).

STAFFORD INDEPENDENT

Stafford Independent Grammar School
Burton Manor
Stafford ST18 9AT
Telephone number 0785 49752

- Co-ed Pupils 150+
  Boys Upper sixth Yes
  Girls Termly fees:
  Mixed sixth Day £700
- Day ISAI
  Boarding

Head Dr J R Garrod (6 years)
Age range 11–18; entry by own exam
Founded 1982.

STAMFORD

Stamford School
St Paul's Street
Stamford
Lincolnshire PE9 2BS
Telephone number 0780 62171

  Co-ed Pupils 570
- Boys Upper sixth Yes
  Girls Termly fees:
  Mixed sixth Day £720
- Day Boarding £1450
- Boarding HMC

Head G J Timm (10 years)
Age range 13–18, own junior from age 8; entry by common entrance or from own junior
Scholarships and exhibitions.

STAMFORD HIGH

Stamford High School
High Street
St Martin's
Stamford
Lincolnshire PE9 2LJ
Telephone number 0780 62330

Co-ed	Pupils 750
Boys	Upper sixth Yes
● Girls	Termly fees:
Mixed sixth	Day £720
● Day	Boarding £1450
● Boarding	GSA; BSA

Head Miss G Bland (10 years)
Age range 11–18, own prep from age 4; entry by own exam
Some LEA places subject to tests; assisted places, one bursary for girl from Rutland.

STANBRIDGE EARLS

Stanbridge Earls
Romsey
Hampshire SO51 0ZS
Telephone number 0794 516777

Enquiries/application to the Headmaster

● Co-ed	Pupils 171
Boys	Upper sixth 6
Girls	Termly fees:
Mixed sixth	Day £1414
● Day	Boarding £2120
● Boarding	

WHAT IT'S LIKE

Founded in 1952, it is largely housed in a beautiful building of medieval origins and Tudor appearance and is of considerable architectural and historical interest. King Alfred is thought to have lived on the site and King Ethelwolf to have been buried there in the 9th century. The 13th century chapel is at the heart of the building. Made of stone and flint, it is the oldest part. The mansion lies in 40 acres of splendid landscaped grounds and gardens, with woodland and a chain of small lakes. The neighbouring countryside is largely farmland, with the New Forest 3 miles away. There is considerable emphasis on religious education and worship in the Anglican tradition. It has all the advantages of being a small school, and its most particular feature is its big remedial department staffed by a dozen teachers (some full-time, some part-time). The school tends to specialise in pupils who for various reasons have 'under achieved'. There is much emphasis on personal attention and the large staff (plus a lot of part-timers) permits a staff:pupil ratio of about 1:5. Much is achieved academically and though the sixth form is very small, several pupils go on to university each year. Music, drama and art feature prominently in the curriculum. There is an excellent range of sports and games (including fishing and riding) and a plentiful variety of extra-curricular activities.

SCHOOL PROFILE

Pupils Total, 171. Day 14 (boys 5, girls 9); Boarding 157 (boys 130, girls 27). Entry age, 13 and into the sixth.

Entrance Common entrance sometimes used. Oversubscribed. No special skills or religious requirements although C of E predominates. Parents not expected to buy text books. 10 scholarships, 33% fees.

Parents 15+% in armed services; 15+% in industry or commerce; 15+% in farming. Up to 10% live within 30 miles; 10+% live overseas.

Staff Head Howard Moxon, in post for 4 years. 30 full time staff, 16 part time. Annual turnover 4%. Average age 33.

Academic work GCSE and A-levels. Average size of upper fifth 60; upper sixth 6. *O-levels*: on average, 15 pupils in upper fifth pass 1–4 subjects; 6, 5–7 subjects; 2 pass 8+ subjects. *A-levels*: on average, 1 pupil in upper sixth passes 1 subject; 2, 3 subjects and 3 pass 3 subjects. On average, 2 take science/engineering A-levels; 5 take arts and humanities. *Computing facilities*: Computer room with 11 BBC and BBC+ with 5¼" disk drives, networked printer system, program exchange facility. Outlying departments have 12 BBC Masters with disk drives and printers; science department has BBC B and double disk drive and printer; CDT, Apple Mackintosh and printer. Special provision for dyslexia, mild visual handicaps, EFL etc.

Senior pupils' non-academic activities *Music*: 20 learn a musical instrument, 1 to Grade 6 or above. 3 in county youth orchestra, 10 in school music groups. *Drama and dance*: 30 in school productions. 1 accepted for Drama School, 1 goes on to work in theatre, 3 in youth theatre. *Art*: 30 take GCSE; 4 A-level; 5 accepted for Art School, 5 for photography. 1 belongs to photographic club. *Sport*: Swimming, squash, tennis, rugby, hockey, cricket, badminton, netball, basketball, athletics, gymnastics, judo, sailing, riding, fishing, canoeing available. 80 take non-compulsory sport, 12 take exams. 1 represents county/country (cross-country, rugby, cricket). *Other* activities include a computer club, driving lessons, chess, draughts.

Careers 1 full time careers advisor. Average number of pupils accepted for *degree courses* at universities, 4; polytechnics or CHE, 2. *other general training courses*, 1. *other further education*, 20. Average number of pupils going straight into careers in industry, 22.

Uniform School uniform worn except the sixth.

Houses/prefects Competitive houses. Prefects, head boy/girl, head of house and house prefects – appointed by the Head after discussion with housemasters. School Council.

Religion Compulsory worship.

Social Debates and speaking competitions with other local schools; some trips abroad. Pupils allowed to bring own bike to school. Meals self service. School shop. No tobacco allowed; alcohol (no spirits) at limited times.

Discipline No corporal punishment. Pupils failing to produce homework once might expect reprimand and discussion; those caught smoking cannabis on the premises might expect expulsion.

Boarding 5% have own study bedroom, 28% share, 36% are in dormitories of 6+. Houses single sex. Resident qualified nurse. Central dining room. Pupils can provide and cook own food. 3 termly exeats of a week, part-week or weekend. Visits to local town allowed.

Alumni association run by Secretary to the Wyvern Society, c/o the School.

Former pupils Paul Cox (artist); Marc Sinden (actor); Michael Blodgett (sculptor); Christopher Neame (actor/producer); Charles Balchin (TV producer).

STOCKPORT GRAMMAR

Stockport Grammar School
Buxton Road
Stockport
Cheshire SK2 7AF
Telephone number 061 456 9000

Enquiries/application to the Headmaster

- Co-ed
  Boys
  Girls
  Mixed sixth
- Day
  Boarding

Pupils 852
Upper sixth 130
Termly fees:
Day £729
HMC

WHAT IT'S LIKE

Founded in 1487 by Sir Edmond Shaa, the most prominent goldsmith of his day, the school has been in continuous existence since then under the patronage of the Goldsmiths' Company and is the second oldest secular foundation in the country. The present buildings, which lie in fine landscaped grounds, are a mile from the middle of Stockport. They have been considerably extended and improved to provide excellent modern facilities. Junior school on the same site in separate buildings. A first-class liberal education is provided and academic results are impressive (85–90 leavers go on to university each year). Very strong indeed in music, and strongish drama. High standards in sports and games (many representatives at county level) and a wide range of activities. There are close links with the town of Stockport and strong local support.

SCHOOL PROFILE

Pupils Total over 12, 852 (boys 466, girls 386). Entry age, 11 and into the sixth. Own junior school provides 30+%. 5% are children of former pupils.

Entrance Own entrance exam used. Oversubscribed. Good intelligence and balanced approach required. No religious requirements. Parents not expected to buy text books. 45 assisted places (at entry and in the sixth). Bursaries provided by the Stopfordian Trust.

Parents 15+% in industry or commerce; 15+% are doctors, lawyers etc. 90+% live within 10 miles.

Staff Head D R J Bird, in post for 3 years. 70 full time staff. 7 part time. Annual turnover 6%. Average age 35.

Academic work GCSE and A-levels. Average size of upper fifth 150; upper sixth 130. *O-levels*: on average, 10 pupils in upper fifth pass 1–4 subjects; 38, 5–7 subjects; 102 pass 8+ subjects. *A-levels*: on average, 3 pupils in upper sixth pass 1 subject; 9, 2 subjects; 14, 3 subjects and 104 pass 4 subjects (including general studies). On average, 68 take science/engineering A-levels; 52 take arts and humanities; 10 a mixture. *Computing facilities*: computer room. Special provisions as required.

Senior pupils' non-academic activities *Music*: 195 learn a musical instrument, 26 to Grade 6 or above. 2 accepted for Music School. 64 play in school orchestra, 110 in school choir, 85 in school wind bands. *Drama and dance*: 40 in school productions, approximately 10 outside school; 2 go on to work in theatre. *Art*: 40 take GCSE; 8, A-level. 3 accepted for Art School. 15 belong to photographic club, 8 to life drawing classes. *Sport*: for boys: rugby, lacrosse, cricket; for girls: netball, hockey, rounders; for both: swimming, athletics, tennis, squash. 400 take non-compulsory sport. Many represent county/country at sports. *Other*: 28 take part in local community schemes.

Other activities include a computer club, chess, drama workshops, 'Grammarrail', debating, astronomy, electronics, hill walking, mountaineering, wargames, Christian and archaeology groups.

Careers 2 part time advisors. Average number of pupils accepted for *arts and humanities degree courses* at Oxbridge, 12; other universities, 27; polytechnics or CHE, 17. *science and engineering degree courses* at Oxbridge, 10; other universities, 35; medical schools, 5; polytechnics or CHE, 9. *BEd*, 3. *other general training courses*, 4. Average number of pupils going straight into careers in the armed services, 3; industry, 2; the City, 2; other, 1. Traditional school career, medicine.

Uniform School uniform worn throughout.

Houses/prefects Competitive houses. Prefects, head boy and girl, house captains – appointed by the Head.

Religion All pupils attend daily assembly.

Social No joint events with other schools (school is socially self sufficient). Trips abroad to France, Germany, Eastern Europe and the high mountains of Europe regularly each year. Pupils allowed to bring own bike to school. Meals self service and supervised. No tobacco/alcohol allowed.

Discipline No corporal punishment. Pupils failing to produce homework once might expect extra work; those caught smoking cannabis on the premises could expect expulsion.

Alumni association run by R D H Reeman, Headmaster, c/o the School.

Former pupils Professor Sir Frederick Williams (inventor of the computer); Peter Boardman (Everest mountaineer).

STONAR

Stonar	Co-ed	Pupils 282
Cottles Park	Boys	Upper sixth 31
Atworth	● Girls	Termly fees:
Melksham	Mixed sixth	Day £1020
Wiltshire SN12 8NT	● Day	Boarding £1900
Telephone number 0225 702309	● Boarding	GSA

Enquiries/application to the Admissions Secretary

WHAT IT'S LIKE

Founded in 1921 at Sandwich, it moved to its present site in 1939. The main building is a very handsome listed 19th century country house set in 40 acres of splendid parkland. Facilities are very good and boarding accommodation is comfortable. Religious worship is compulsory in the Anglican tradition but all denominations are welcome. A large staff allows a staff:pupil ratio of 1:9 (and there is quite a large part-time staff). A good general education is provided and results are impressive. About 13 girls go on to university each year. There is a big commitment to music, drama and art. A fine range of sports and games is available and there is an excellent variety of extra-curricular activities (including riding: the school has its own stables and a number of horses and ponies). A promising record in the Duke of Edinburgh's Award Scheme.

SCHOOL PROFILE

Pupils Total over 12, 282. Day 71; Boarding 211. Entry age, 11 onwards including into the sixth. Own prep department provides over 20%. Less than 5% are children of former pupils.

Entrance Own entrance exam used. Not oversubscribed. No special skills or religious requirements. Parents not expected to buy text books. 4 scholarships plus bursaries for music, riding, art, sport; half fees to £500.

Parents 15+% in industry or commerce. 30+% live within 30 miles; 10+% live overseas.

Staff Head Mrs Susan Hopkinson, in post for 3 years. 44 full time staff, 19 part time. Annual turnover 3%. Average age 35.

Academic work GCSE and A-levels. Average size of upper fifth 45; upper sixth 31. *O-levels*: on average, 13 pupils in upper fifth pass 1–4 subjects; 16, 5–7 subjects; 22 pass 8+ subjects. *A-levels*: on average, 2 pupils in upper sixth pass 1 subject; 5, 2 subjects; 9, 3 subjects and 2 pass 4 subjects. On average, 20 take science/engineering A-levels; 52 take arts and humanities; 41 a mixture. Drama and geology offered to GCSE/A-level. *Computing facilities*: Computer studies taught to GCSE. Dyslexia and EFL provision.

Senior pupils' non-academic activities *Music*: 70 learn a musical instrument, 10 to Grade 6 or above, 1 accepted for Music School; 19 in school orchestra, 50 in choir, 14 in wind band. *Drama and dance*: 50 in school productions, 2 take to Grade 6 in ESB, RAD etc. 3 accepted for Drama School. *Art*: 33 take GCSE; 14 A-level; 5 OA-level History of Art; 2 A-level History of Art; 4 accepted for Art School; 20 belong to photographic club; 35 to art club. *Sport*: Hockey, netball, cross-country, squash, volleyball, badminton, tennis, rounders, athletics, swimming, riding available. 50 take non-compulsory sport. 10 take lifesaving exams; 10, GCSE PE. 19 represent county/country (hockey, swimming, cross-country, athletics). *Other*: Some take part in local community schemes. 20 have bronze Duke of Edinburgh's Award, 1 has silver and 6 gold. Other activities include a computer club, driving lessons, indoor riding to BHSAI, chess club, debating society, typing.

Careers 1 full time and 1 part time careers advisors. Average number of pupils accepted for *arts and humanities degree courses* at Oxbridge, 2; other universities, 6; polytechnics or CHE, 5. *science and engineering degree courses* at universities, 3; medical schools, 1; polytechnics or CHE, 4. *BEd*, 1. *other general training courses*, 3. Average number of pupils going straight into careers in armed services, 1.

Uniform School uniform worn except the sixth.

Houses/prefects Competitive houses. Prefects, head girl, head of house and house prefects – appointed by the Head. School Council.

Religion Religious worship compulsory.

Social Organised local events and trips abroad. Pupils allowed to bring own bike/horse to school. Meals self service. School shop. No tobacco/alcohol allowed.

Discipline No corporal punishment. Pupils failing to produce homework once might expect a warning; those caught smoking cannabis on the premises might expect expulsion.

Boarding Sixth have study bedrooms, rest share with 2–6. Houses, of approximately 38, same as competitive houses, divided by age. Resident qualified nurse. Central dining room. 2 weekend exeats and a week at half term. Visits to local town allowed.

Alumni association run by Mrs D Watts, 7 Salter Road, Sandbanks, Poole, Dorset.

Former pupils Katharine Schlesinger (actress); Ann Frank (BBC).

STONYHURST

Stonyhurst College	Co-ed	Pupils 431
Nr Blackburn	● Boys	Upper sixth 90
Lancashire BB6 9PZ	Girls	Termly fees:
Telephone number 025 486 345	Mixed sixth	Day £1080
Enquiries/application to the Headmaster	● Day	Boarding £2070
	● Boarding	HMC

WHAT IT'S LIKE

Founded in 1593 at St Omers, it moved to Bruges in 1762 and to Liège in 1773. Forced to leave the continent at the outbreak of the French Revolution, it established itself at the Hall of Stonyhurst (built in 1592) in 1794. It has very fine buildings in a beautiful setting in the Ribble Valley on the slopes of Longridge Fells. Its two prep schools are St Mary's Hall (at Stonyhurst) and St John's at Windsor. Extremely well equipped with modern facilities, the college is run by the Society of Jesus (a number of whose priests are on the teaching staff) and describes itself as 'a community of boys, parents, Jesuits, lay staff, old boys and friends'. It undertakes to provide instruction in Catholic doctrine and to educate boys in the principles and practice of their faith. Its large staff permits a ratio of 1:8 pupils. Excellent teaching is provided and academic standards and results are high. There are 60–70 university entrants per year (a high proportion for a school of this size) and 93% go on to degree courses. Very strong indeed in music (200 boys learn an instrument, 150 participate in orchestras) and drama. Wide range of games, sports and activities. Excellent standards in games with a number of county representatives. Considerable emphasis on outdoor pursuits for which the environment is ideal. A big CCF contingent. Very substantial commitment to local community schemes and charities and a good record in the Duke of Edinburgh's Award Scheme.

SCHOOL PROFILE

Pupils Total, 431. Day 15; Boarding 416. Entry age, 13 and into the sixth. St Mary's Hall, Stonyhurst and St John's Beaumont, Windsor provide over 50% of pupils. Approximately 25% are children of former pupils.

Entrance Common entrance and own entrance exam used. Not oversubscribed. Special skills taken into account. Pupils should be Roman Catholic although there are a few exceptions. Parents are not expected to buy text books. 26 assisted places. 10–12 academic and music scholarships and College bursaries, ⅔ fees–£500.

Parents 15+% in industry or commerce; 15+% are doctors, lawyers, etc. 10+% live within 30 miles; 10+% live overseas.

Staff Head Dr R G G Mercer, in post for 3 years. 52 full time staff, 6 part time. Annual turnover 3.

Academic work GCSE and A-levels. Average size of upper fifth 85; upper sixth 90. *O-levels*: on average, 31 pupils in upper fifth pass 1–4 subjects; 25, 5–7 subjects; 51 pass 8+ subjects. (Average number of passes, 8.3.) *A-levels*: on average, 5 pupils in upper sixth pass 1 subject; 12, 2 subjects; 57, 3 subjects and 5 pass 4 subjects. On average, 23 take science/engineering A-levels; 21 take arts and humanities; 33 a mixture. Astronomy offered to GCSE. *Computing facilities*: 6 BBC B micros in a computer room. Departmental computers; 16 AX Nimbus computers in the Design and Technology Department.

Senior pupils' non-academic activities *Music*: Approx 50% learn a musical instrument; 150 in school orchestras, 80 in choir, 20 in dance band. *Drama*: Most pupils in school productions during the year. *Art*: 18 take GCSE; 5 A-level. 4 accepted for architecture. 6 belong to eg photographic club; 5 to typography and printing. *Sport*: Rugby, cricket, swimming, cross-country, badminton, squash, tennis, golf (9 hole school golf course), fishing, shooting, indoor games (basketball etc) available. Two-thirds take non-compulsory sport. 20 take exams eg gymnastics, swimming. 12 represent county (rugby, cricket, athletics). *Other*: 29 take part in local community schemes. 17 have bronze Duke of Edinburgh's Award, 9 have silver and 3 gold. Other activities include a computer club, driving lessons, good chess club, flourishing astronomy society (school observatory), debating, political, literary and scientific societies, video film unit.

Careers 5 part time careers advisors. Average number of pupils accepted for *arts and humanities degree courses* at Oxbridge, 7; other universities, 30; polytechnics or CHE, 8. *science and engineering degree courses* at Oxbridge, 3; other universities, 23; medical schools, 3; polytechnics or CHE, 9. Average number of pupils going straight into careers in the armed services, 2; the church, 4; industry, 4; the City, 4; music/drama, 1. Traditional school careers are medicine, law, armed forces and recently social work etc but ex-pupils spread across the professions, business and industry.

Uniform School uniform worn throughout.

Houses/prefects Competitive houses for sports only. Prefects and head boy – appointed by the Headmaster.

Religion Compulsory weekly Mass, year group Mass weekly, Sunday evening service. Morning and evening prayers.

Social Exchanges with schools in Reims and Toulouse. German course in Austria. Pupils allowed to bring own bicycle to school. Meals formal and self service. School shop. No tobacco/alcohol allowed.

Discipline Corporal punishment is used as an exceptional and occasional sanction determined solely by the Headmaster. Pupils failing to produce homework once might expect some loss of free time; those caught smoking cannabis on the premises could expect expulsion.

Boarding 117 have own study bedroom; years 1 and 2 boys have own cubicle. Houses divided by age group. Resident qualified full and part-time nursing staff. Central dining room. Exeats only for special family occasions. Visits to the local town allowed, with permission.

Alumni association is run by Mr Geoffrey Wilson, Stonyhurst Association, c/o the College.

Former pupils Lord Devlin; General Vernon Walters (US Ambassador to UN); Arthur Conan Doyle; Charles Laughton; Paul Johnson and distinguished Jesuits.

STOVER

Stover School
Newton Abbot
Devon TQ12 6QG
Telephone number 0803 862402

Enquiries to the School Secretary
Application to the Headteacher

Co-ed
Boys
● Girls
Mixed sixth
● Day
● Boarding

Pupils 250
Upper sixth 15
Termly fees:
Day £888
Boarding £1626
GSA

WHAT IT'S LIKE

Founded in 1932, it lies in 64 acres of grounds, part of the original Stover Park. There are beautiful landscaped gardens and fine playing fields with splendid views across Dartmoor. A very healthy environment. The main building is a superb 18th century Palladian mansion (1777), formerly the home of the Duke of Somerset. Since foundation there have been several additions and developments, and facilities and accommodation are now very good. A relaxed and friendly atmosphere prevails and there is a policy of trying to suit the needs of the individual. Worship is in the Anglican tradition. A sound general education is provided and results are creditable. Each year a few girls go on to university. A standard range of games and sports is available, and there is a large variety of extra-curricular activities. Considerable emphasis on outdoor pursuits for which the environment is ideal, and an impressive record in the Duke of Edinburgh's Award Scheme.

SCHOOL PROFILE

Pupils Total over 12, 250. Day 108; Boarding 156. Entry age, 11 and into the sixth. 5% are children of former pupils.

Entrance Own entrance exam used, common entrance rarely. Oversubscribed. No special skills or religious requirements but strong Anglican links. Parents not expected to buy text books. 4 scholarships/bursaries pa, 50%–10% of fees.

Parents 10+% live within 30 miles; 10+% live overseas.

Staff Head Mrs W E Lunel, in post for 4 years. 15 full time staff, 14 part time. Average age 35.

Academic work GCSE and A-levels, Pitman Commercial subjects, City and Guilds practical. Average size of upper fifth 45; upper sixth 15. *O-levels*: on average, 18 pupils in upper fifth pass 1–4 subjects; 18, 5–7 subjects; 9 pass 8+ subjects. *A-levels*: on average, 2 pupils in upper sixth pass 1 subject; 6, 2 subjects; 5, 3 subjects and 2 pass 4 subjects. On average, 40% take science/engineering A-levels; 40% take arts and humanities; 20% a mixture. *Computing facilities*: Micro computers. Dyslexia provision.

Senior pupils' non-academic activities *Music*: 139 learn a musical instrument, 6 to Grade 6 or above; 30 in school choir; some play for Devon schools' orchestra and other musical groups; all musicians participate in group music. *Drama and dance*: 30% of school in productions. 6 take Grade 6 in ESB, RAD etc. *Art*: 25 take GCSE; 10 A-level. 2–3 accepted for Art School. *Sport*: Lacrosse, cross-country, swimming, tennis, netball, rounders, athletics available. 70% take non-compulsory sport eg riding, hill-walking. Many take exams. *Other*: 15 have bronze Duke of Edinburgh's Award, 5 have silver and 2 gold. Wide variety of other activities including computer club.

Careers Average number of pupils accepted for *arts and humanities degree courses* at universities, 3; polytechnics or CHE, 2. *science and engineering degree courses* at universities, 2; medical schools, 1; polytechnics or CHE, 3. *BEd*, 2. *other general training courses*, 8. Average number of pupils going straight into careers in armed services, 2.

Uniform School uniform worn except the sixth.

Houses/prefects Competitive houses. Prefects, head girl, head of house and house prefects – appointed by the Head after consultation with staff and prefects.

Religion Morning service compulsory.

Social Young Enterprise scheme with other local schools; some organised trips abroad. Pupils allowed to bring own car/bike/motorbike to school. Meals self service. School shop.

Discipline No corporal punishment. Removal of privileges is the normal sanction. Pupils failing to produce homework once might expect prep detention; anyone caught smoking cannabis on the premises would be expelled.

Boarding Head girl has own study bedroom, sixth form share; remainder in dormitories of 6+. Houses, of approximately 50, are divided by age. Resident qualified nurse. Central dining room. Sixth form can provide and cook own food. 2 weekend exeats and half term. Visits to local town allowed.

Alumni association run by Mrs M Kearney, c/o the School.

STOWE

Stowe School	Co-ed	Pupils 640
Buckingham MK18 5EH	• Boys	Upper sixth 135
Telephone number 0280 813164	Girls	Termly fees:
	• Mixed sixth	Day £1648
Enquiries/application to the Headmaster	• Day	Boarding £2355
	• Boarding	HMC; SHA;
		Allied Schools

WHAT IT'S LIKE

Founded in 1923, it lies in a magnificent park of 750 acres landscaped by Vanbrugh, Bridgman, Kent and Brown. The main building – the original Stowe House – was the seat of the Temple Family and the Dukes of Buckingham and Chandos. It is a huge and elegant country house finished in 1770 to designs by Adam. Modern facilities of every conceivable kind are outstanding. All pupils are expected to attend religious services in the Anglican tradition with special arrangements for RCs on Sundays. Academic standards are high and a large number of leavers go on to university each year. Pupils are expected to work hard and maintain a high standard of good manners. It is a well run school with a strong emphasis on personal help. Tremendously strong in music, drama and art. Wide variety of sports and games (high standards are achieved). A large number of clubs and societies (33) cater for most needs. Substantial commitment to local community schemes and the Duke of Edinburgh's Award Scheme.

SCHOOL PROFILE

Pupils Total over 12, 640. Day 20 (boys 10, girls 10); Boarding 620 (boys 540, girls 80 (max)). Entry age, 13, boys; girls and boys into the sixth. 19% are children of former pupils.

Entrance Common entrance and own entrance exam used. Any special skill is of interest. No religious requirements but pupils must attend religious services. Parents expected to buy text books. 5 assisted places (sixth form only). Scholarships, exhibitions and bursaries available up to full fees.

Parents 15+% in industry or commerce; 15+% are doctors, lawyers etc. 10+% live within 30 miles; 10+% live overseas.

Staff Head C G Turner, in post for 8+ years. Annual turnover of staff 5–10%.

Academic work GCSE and A-levels. Average size of upper fifth 115; upper sixth 135. Average number of O-levels, 7.8. Other exam results not available. *Computing facilities*: a computer room with 13 IBM PCs. Maths Dept has 4 BBCs, Design Dept has 2 BBCs and each of the following has 1 BBC: Geography, Physics, Chemistry, Biology. Special dyslexia/EFL provisions available for pupils if they are intelligent enough to be accepted.

Senior pupils' non-academic activities *Sport*: Rugby football, hockey, cricket, tennis, athletics, squash, swimming, golf, badminton, fives, cross-country running, sailing, canoeing, shooting, fencing, archery, beagling, lacrosse, netball, riding available.

Careers Approximately half the staff are involved in giving careers advice. There is an exceptional diversity of careers.

Uniform School uniform not worn, but there are dress regulations.

Houses/prefects Prefects, head boy/girl, head of house and house prefects – appointed by the Headmaster.

Religion Compulsory.

Social Industrial Conference (with Royal Latin School), public speaking with other schools. Organised trips abroad – to Nepal most years and eg across South America in 1987. Pupils allowed to bring own bicycle to school. Meals self service. School shop. No tobacco allowed. Beer/cider bar for top year with strict control.

Discipline No corporal punishment. Pupils failing to produce homework once might expect to do it again properly; those caught smoking cannabis on the premises could expect expulsion.

Boarding About 25% have own study bedroom. Houses, of approximately 60–65, have full age range in each. Resident qualified nurse and daily visits by doctor. Two central dining rooms. Pupils can provide and cook their own food. Exeats at half term only. Visits to the local town allowed.

Alumni association is run by Mr C J G Atkinson, c/o the School.

Former pupils Leonard Cheshire; Lord Quinton; 'Laddie' Lucas; David

Donne; Sir Nigel Broackes; Robert Kee; General Kitson; David Scott Cowper; Richard Branson; David Wynne; David Shepherd; David Fanshawe; Howard Goodall; Sir Nicholas Lyell.

STOWFORD

Stowford College
95 Brighton Road
Sutton
Surrey SM2 5SR
Telephone number 01-661 9444

Enquiries/application to the Principal.

- Co-ed
  Boys
  Girls
  Mixed sixth
- Day
  Boarding

Pupils 110
Upper sixth 14
Termly fees:
Day £886
ISAI

WHAT IT'S LIKE

Founded in 1975, it is one of the smaller independent schools in Britain. Single-site, in an agreeable urban residential area, it has handsome well-designed buildings in fine gardens and is well-equipped. The staff:pupil ratio is a very favourable 1:11. About 60% of the students come from the maintained sector. The school prides itself on an informal and friendly atmosphere. Academic standards and results are good, especially in science subjects. Despite having a very small sixth form, 5 or more pupils, on average, go on to university each year. There is no music or drama but the art department is strong. An adequate range of sports, games and extra-curricular activities. A promising record in the Duke of Edinburgh's Award Scheme.

SCHOOL PROFILE

Pupils Total over 11, 110 (boys 70, girls 40). Entry age, 11 and into the sixth. Local State schools provide about 60% of pupils.

Entrance Entrance by interview. Not oversubscribed. Commitment to hard work and effort demanded; no religious requirements. Parents not expected to buy text books. Scholarships from £443–£100 per term.

Parents 15+% are doctors, lawyers etc; 15+% in industry or commerce. 90+% live within 30 miles; up to 10% live overseas.

Staff Head A J Hennessy, in post for 13 years. 9 full time staff, 5 part time. Annual turnover, 15%. Average age, 40.

Academic work GCSE and A-levels. Average size of upper fifth, 30; upper sixth, 14. *O-levels*: on average, 3 pupils in upper fifth pass 1–4 subjects; 20, 5–7 subjects; 2 pass 8+ subjects. *A-levels*: on average, 3 pupils in upper sixth pass 2 subjects and 11, 3 subjects. On average, 9 take science/engineering A-levels; 5 take arts and humanities. *Computing facilities*: 6 BBC computers. Provision for EFL (including preparation for JMB test).

Senior pupils' non-academic activities *Art*: 10 take as non-examined subject; 18, GCSE; 8, A-level; 5 accepted for Art School; 10 belong to pottery club. *Sport*: Basketball, squash, badminton, football, netball, rounders, swimming, tennis available. 20 take non-compulsory sport. 4 represent county/country (swimming, cross-country). *Other*: 18 taking bronze Duke of Edinburgh's Award. Other activities include chess club, biology and small mammals club.

Careers Principal (who has industrial experience) gives careers advice. Average number of pupils accepted for *arts and humanities degree courses* at universities, 2. *science and engineering degree courses* at universities, 5; medical schools, 1; polytechnics or CHE, 6. *other general training courses*, 20. Average number of pupils going straight into careers in industry, 12; police, 1; other, 4.

Uniform No uniform for fourth form upwards.

Houses/prefects No competitive houses. Prefects, head boy/girl – elected by the school. School Council.

Religion No compulsory worship.

Social French day trips and exchanges, ski-ing, trip abroad. Pupils allowed to bring own car/bike/motorbike to school. School tuckshop. No alcohol; tobacco allowed but discouraged.

Discipline Corporal punishment rarely used. Pupils failing to produce homework once might expect lunchtime detention; those caught smoking cannabis on the premises might expect immediate suspension, professional counselling and possible expulsion.

Alumni association run by C J Grace, c/o the School.

STRATFORD HOUSE

Stratford House School
8/10 Southborough Road
Bickley
Kent BR1 2DZ
Telephone number 01-467 3580

Enquiries/application to the Headmistress

Co-ed
Boys
● Girls
Mixed sixth
● Day
Boarding

Pupils 250
Upper sixth 18
Termly fees:
Day £750
GSA

WHAT IT'S LIKE

Founded in 1912, it lies beside a station in a pleasant outer London suburb with all its buildings on one site. There are agreeable gardens. The original buildings are mid-Victorian but these have been added to and the school now has modern labs, good classrooms, a new sixth form centre and its own playing fields nearby. It specialises in academic children who lack confidence and need a small caring community in order to flourish. The teaching is good and standards and results are creditable. Some 5–10 pupils go on to university each year. Music is strong, there is a lot of drama, and art. A very good range of sports and games and a lot of clubs and societies for extra-curricular activities. There is a commitment in the sixth form to local community services.

SCHOOL PROFILE

Pupils Total over 12, 250. Entry age, 4, 11 and into the sixth. Own junior school provides over 50%.

Entrance Own entrance exam used. Oversubscribed. Musical skill an advantage; no religious requirements. Parents not expected to buy text books. 6 scholarships, up to ⅓ of fees; bursaries where needed.

Parents 15+% in theatre, media, music etc; 15+% are doctors, lawyers etc; 15+% in industry or commerce. 60+% live within 30 miles.

Staff Head Mrs A Williamson, in post for 14 years. 23 full time staff, 24 part time. Annual turnover 5%. Average age 42.

Academic work GCSE and A-levels, RSA business exams and Pitmans. Average size of upper fifth 40; upper sixth 18. *A-levels and secretarial*: on average, 2 pupils in upper sixth pass 1 subject and secretarial; 5, 2 subjects; 8, 3 subjects and 4 pass 4 subjects. Photography and engineering drawing offered to GCSE. *Computing facilities*: All departments use increasing number of computers, most with word processing facilities. Special provision for dyslexia and EFL for restricted numbers.

Senior pupils' non-academic activities *Music*: 30% learn a musical instrument. There is an orchestra, 2 choirs, 2 wind bands, string group, recorder group and guitars. *Drama and dance*: All in house productions. 10–20% in school productions. 5% accepted for Drama/Dance School, 5% work in theatre. *Art*: 18 take GCSE; 4 A-level art; 2 History of Art; 2 Technical Graphics. 2 accepted for Art School; 1 for London College of Printing. *Sport*: Netball, lacrosse, gymnastics, tennis, swimming, athletics, volleyball, badminton, table tennis, trampolining, fencing, squash, horse riding, golf available. Pupils represent county/country (lacrosse, fencing, athletics). *Other*: Half sixth form take part in local community schemes. Other activities: some 20 clubs, including a computer club, numerous drama clubs and small music groups.

Careers 1 part time careers advisor, careers lessons from third year on. Average number of pupils accepted for *arts and humanities degree courses* at universities, 50%; polytechnics or CHE, 30%. *science and engineering design courses* at Oxbridge, 5%; other universities, 5%; medical schools, 5%; polytechnics or CHE, 10%. BEd, 5%. *other general training courses*, 20%. Average number of pupils going straight into careers in industry, 5%; the City, 5%; music/drama, 5%; other, 5%.

Uniform School uniform worn throughout, modified in sixth.

Houses/prefects Competitive houses. Prefects, head girl, head, secretary and treasurer of house – elected by school and staff.

Religion Morning assembly compulsory; exceptions rare.

Social Debates and lectures at other schools; concerts and theatrical productions with Colfes Boys' School. Ski-ing trip and educational cruises abroad. Pupils allowed to bring own car/bike to school. Meals self service. School shop. No tobacco/alcohol allowed.

Discipline No corporal punishment. Pupils failing to produce homework once will get a black mark (detention for 3 black marks); those caught smoking cannabis on the premises will be expelled.

Alumni association run by Miss Jill Atkinson, c/o the School.

Former pupils Audrey Coleman (formerly hostage in Iran); Pamela Hutchison (British Ambassador during the Falklands campaign).

STRATHALLAN

Strathallan School	● Co-ed	Pupils 420
Forgandenny	Boys	Upper sixth 70
Perth PH2 9EG	Girls	Termly fees:
Telephone number 0738 812546	Mixed sixth	Boarding £2250
	Day	HMC
Enquiries/application to the Headmaster	● Boarding	

WHAT IT'S LIKE

Founded in 1912 at the Bridge of Allan, it moved to its present site at Forgandenny in 1920. The nucleus of the school is a huge and splendid 19th-century country house, on the edge of the village, in a superb estate of 160 acres. Spread round the original house are many modern additions. Facilities are first-rate. Religious practice follows the Church of Scotland, but the school is interdenominational. A high standard of teaching is provided (the staff:pupil ratio is 1:10) and results are very good. Each year 35–40 pupils go on to university. The music, drama and art departments are very strong. A good range of games, sports and activities. The CCF is well supported. Considerable emphasis on outdoor pursuits for which the environment is ideal. A promising record in the Duke of Edinburgh's Award Scheme.

SCHOOL PROFILE

Pupils Total over 12, 420. Entry age, 10+ and 13+ and into the sixth. 20% are children of former pupils.

Entrance Common entrance and own entrance exam used. Sometimes oversubscribed. No special skills required. Interdenominational. Parents not expected to buy text books. 32 assisted places. 30 scholarships/bursaries, 20%–80% of fees.

Parents Up to 10% live within 30 miles; 10+% live overseas.

Staff Head C D Pighills, in post for 12 years. 47 full time staff, 12 part time. Annual turnover 9%. Average age 38.

Academic work GCSE, A-levels and Highers. Results not provided. *Computing facilities*: A computer room for teaching awareness and others in various departments. Provision for remedial English.

Senior pupils' non-academic activities *Music*: Two orchestras (junior and senior), wind band, chapel choir; 1 pupil plays in Scottish youth orchestra; 2 accepted for university music degree. *Drama and dance*: Many in school productions. Occasionally a pupil is accepted to Scottish School of Drama. *Art*: 40 take as non-examined subject; 12 take GCSE; 11 A-level. 1–2 accepted for Art School. 12 belong to photographic club. *Sport*: Cricket, rugby, hockey, athletics, swimming, basketball, squash, badminton, sailing, canoeing available. All school take non-compulsory sport. Pupils represent county/country at various sports; eg 1 in Olympic ski-squad. *Other*: 45+ have bronze Duke of Edinburgh's Award. Some enter voluntary schemes after leaving school. Other activities include a computer club, chess, cooking, sewing (girls), design/technology/electronics, debating, play reading, fishing, clay pigeon shooting, driving lessons.

Careers 1 part time advisor. Average number of pupils accepted for *degree courses* at Oxbridge, 3–4; other universities, 34; medical schools 2;

polytechnics or CHE, 15. *other general training courses*, 5. Average number of pupils going straight into careers in the armed services, 3; industry, 2; music/drama, 1. A comparatively high proportion go in to some form of engineering.

Uniform There are dress regulations throughout.

Houses/prefects Competitive houses. Prefects, head boy/girl, head of house and house prefects – appointed by the Head after consultation.

Religion Compulsory religious worship.

Social Theatre excursions, debates, musical events with other local schools. Organised language trips to Paris; sporting trips to Canada, France, Australia; ski-ing in Austria. Meals self service. School shop. No tobacco/alcohol allowed.

Discipline No corporal punishment. Pupils failing to produce homework once might expect to have to do it – usually on Sunday afternoon; those caught smoking cannabis on the premises could expect expulsion.

Boarding All girls have own study bedroom. All boys are in dormitories of 6+, but have studies. Houses, of approximately 60, same as competitive houses and single sex. Resident qualified nurse. Central dining room. Seniors allowed to provide and cook own food. Half term and 1 Saturday night exeat each term. Visits to the local town allowed for upper sixth only.

STREATHAM HIGH

Streatham Hill & Clapham High School
Wavertree Road
London SW2 3SR
Telephone number 01-674 6912

Enquiries/application to the Headmistress

Co-ed
Boys
• Girls
Mixed sixth
• Day
Boarding

Pupils 285
Upper sixth 30
Termly fees:
Day £684
GPDST

WHAT IT'S LIKE

Opened in 1887 as Brixton Hill High School, it moved after 7 years to new purpose-built premises on Streatham Hill. In 1938 it amalgamated with Clapham High School. It has agreeable buildings in very pleasant gardens and grounds. The good facilities include a splendid library, fine labs, art studios and a CDT centre. Interdenominational; worship is encouraged. A sound, well-balanced, general education is provided. Academic results are good and the school has a high reputation in the locality. Each year 15–20 girls go on to university. There is a substantial commitment to music, drama and art. Sports and games are very well provided for (including Olympic gymnastics). There is a plentiful variety of extra-curricular activities.

SCHOOL PROFILE

Pupils Total over 12, 285. Entry age, 5, 11 and into the sixth. Own junior department provides over 20%. Very few are children of former pupils.

Entrance Own entrance exam used. Heavily oversubscribed. Musical skill looked for; no religious requirements. Parents not expected to buy text books. 153 assisted places. 18 scholarships, £684–£100 per term; also bursaries.

Parents 15+% in theatre, media, music etc; 15+% are doctors, lawyers etc; 15+% in industry or commerce. 60+% live within 30 miles.

Staff Head Miss G M Ellis, in post for 9 years. 32 full time staff, 9 part time. Annual turnover 8%. Average age 34.

Academic work GCSE and A-levels. Average size of upper fifth 50; upper sixth 30. *O-levels*: on average, 43 pupils in upper fifth pass 8+ subjects. *A-levels*: on average, 4 pupils in upper sixth pass 2 subjects; 25, 3 subjects and 1 passes 4 subjects. On average, 25% take science/engineering A-levels; 25% take arts and humanities; 50% a mixture. *Computing facilities*: Fully equipped room in main school, 4 extra machines in science department.

Senior pupils' non-academic activities *Music*: 50% learn a musical instrument, 25% to Grade 6 or above, 1–2 accepted for Music School. 10% in school orchestra, 10% in choir. *Drama and dance*: 30% in school productions. 4% go on to work in theatre. *Art*: 5% take as non-examined subject; 45% GCSE; 10% A-level; 2 accepted for Art School. 2% belong to photographic club. *Sport*: Netball, swimming, skating, tennis, squash, basketball, rounders, weights, bowls, aerobics, sports acrobatics, Olympic gymnastics available. 50% take non-compulsory sport, 20% take exams. 2 pa represent county (netball). *Other*: 5% take part in local community schemes. Other activities include a computer club, chess, debating, science club, electronics, Christian Union, cultural society.

Careers 2 part time careers advisors. Average number of pupils accepted for *arts and humanities degree courses* at Oxbridge, 2; other universities, 8; polytechnics or CHE, 5. *science and engineering degree courses* at universities, 9; medical schools, 3; polytechnics or CHE, 2. *other general training courses*, 1. Average number of pupils going straight into careers in industry, 1; music/drama, 1.

Uniform School uniform worn except the sixth.

Houses/prefects Competitive houses. No prefects; head girl – elected by the school. School Council.

Religion Worship encouraged.

Social Frequent visits to France, Austria, Italy, Greece. Pupils allowed to bring own bike to school. Meals self service. No tobacco/alcohol allowed.

Discipline No corporal punishment. Pupils failing to produce homework once might expect detention after school; those caught smoking cannabis on the premises might expect expulsion.

Former pupils June Whitfield (actress); Norman Hartnell (fashion designer); Henry Willis (organ builder).

SURBITON HIGH

Surbiton High School
(The Church Schools Company Ltd)
Surbiton Crescent
Kingston upon Thames KT1 2JT
Telephone number 01-546 5245

Enquiries/application to the Headmistress

Co-ed
Boys
● Girls
Mixed sixth
● Day
Boarding

Pupils 292
Upper sixth 35
Termly fees:
Day £780
GSA; GPDST

WHAT IT'S LIKE

Founded in 1844, a member of the Church Schools Company, it stands in a
quiet part of Surbiton in pleasant grounds. The buildings are well designed
and facilities are good. The junior and senior girls' school are in the same
road; boys' school 5 minutes away. Basically it is a C of E establishment but
all faiths are welcome. A well-run school with very creditable academic
results. About 15 leavers proceed to university each year. Reasonably strong
music and drama departments. A fair range of games, sports and activities. A
promising record in the Duke of Edinburgh's Award Scheme.

SCHOOL PROFILE

Pupils Total over 12, 292. Entry age, 5+ and into the sixth. Own junior school
provides over 50%.
Entrance Own entrance exam used. Oversubscribed. No special skills or
religious requirements. Sixth form bursaries available, half-fees.
Parents 60+% live within 30 miles.
Staff Head Mrs R A Thynne, in post for 9 years. 46 full time staff, 15 part
time.
Academic work GCSE and A-levels. Average size of upper fifth 60; upper
sixth 35. *O-levels*: on average, 7 pupils in upper fifth pass 1–4 subjects; 12,
5–7 subjects; 31 pass 8+ subjects. *A-levels*: on average, 5 pupils in upper
sixth pass 1 subject; 6, 2 subjects; 20, 3 subjects and 2 pass 4 subjects. On
average, 8 take science/engineering A-levels; 17 take arts and humanities; 8 a
mixture. *Computing facilities*: Computer room and Prestel system.
Senior pupils' non-academic activities *Music*: 25 learn a musical instrument, 20 to Grade 6 or above, 2 play in pop group beyond school; 2 accepted
for music teacher training; 1 Choral Scholarship to Oxford; 5 in school
orchestra, 15 in choir, chamber groups. *Drama and dance*: 60 in school
productions. 20 take LAMDA examinations. 1 accepted for Drama
School. *Art*: 13 take A-level; 6 take history of art. 4 accepted for Art
School. *Sport*: Gymnastics, dance, hockey, netball, tennis, athletics, rounders, swimming, badminton, squash, skating, ski-ing, weight training available. 26 take non-compulsory sport. 4 represent county (hockey, netball,
tennis, squash). *Other*: 7+ have bronze Duke of Edinburgh's Award, 15+
have silver. Other activities include a computer club.
Careers Average number of pupils accepted for *arts and humanities degree
courses* at Oxbridge, 2; other universities, 8; polytechnics or CHE, 10. *science
and engineering degree courses* at Oxbridge, 1; other universities, 5; medical
schools, 1; polytechnics or CHE, 2. *BEd*, 2. *other general training courses*, 2.
Average number of pupils going straight into careers in retail management, 1.

Uniform School uniform worn except in sixth.

Houses/prefects No competitive houses. No prefects. Head girl – appointed by Head after discussion with staff and pupils. School Council.

Religion Compulsory attendance at daily assembly.

Social Observer Mace Debating Competition with other schools. Organised trips to Russia, France, Belgium; French Department to France, Oberammergau. Pupils allowed to bring own car/bicycle to school. Meals self service. Food shop for seniors. No tobacco/alcohol allowed.

Discipline No corporal punishment. Pupils failing to produce homework once might expect a reprimand; those caught smoking cannabis on the premises could expect expulsion.

SUTTON HIGH

Sutton High School
55 Cheam Road
Sutton
Surrey SM1 2AX
Telephone number 01-642 0594

Enquiries/application to the Headmistress

Co-ed   Pupils 583
Boys   Upper sixth 62
• Girls   Termly fees:
Mixed sixth   Day £684
• Day   GPDST
Boarding

WHAT IT'S LIKE

Founded in 1884, it is one of 25 schools administered by the GPDST and uses its original building, though there have been many alterations and additions. The school now occupies what were formerly family houses in Cheam Road and Grove Road and has much purpose-built accommodation. The junior school is in three houses in Grove Road. Overall it is a pleasant campus with some games facilities on site. A sound general education is provided and results are good. Thirty or more girls go on to university each year (5–10 to Oxbridge). There is a considerable commitment to music and much strength in drama (the school has an open-air theatre built by parents and pupils). An excellent range of games and sports (high standards are achieved) and plentiful extra-curricular activities. A lot of girls contribute to local social services and the school has an impressive record in the Duke of Edinburgh's Award Scheme.

SCHOOL PROFILE

Pupils Total, 583. Entry age, 5+, 7+, 10+, 11+ and into the sixth.

Entrance Own entrance exam used. Oversubscribed. Good academic ability looked for; no religious requirements. Parents not expected to buy text books. 17 assisted places pa. 6 scholarships, 100%–5% of fees; bursaries in cases of financial need.

Parents 60+% live within 30 miles.

Staff Head Miss A E Cavendish, in post for 8 years. 33 full time staff, 16 part time. Annual turnover approx 5%.

Academic work GCSE and A-levels. Average size of upper fifth 88–90; upper sixth 62. *O-levels*: on average, 9 pupils in upper fifth pass 1–4 subjects; 16,

5–7 subjects; 65 pass 8+ subjects. *A-levels*: on average, 5 pupils in upper sixth pass 1 subject; 10, 2 subjects; 41, 3 subjects and 6 pass 4 subjects. On average, 20 take science/engineering A-levels; 22 take arts and humanities; 20 a mixture. *Computing facilities*: Computer room; chain 64 network of 480Zs (16); other computers in departments.

Senior pupils' non-academic activities *Music*: 108 learn a musical instrument, 38 to Grade 6 or above, 1–2 accepted for Music School, 1 to play in pop group; 17 in school orchestra, 28 in choir, 14 madrigal group, 1 in National Children's Orchestra, 4 Stoneleigh Youth Orchestra, 5 Junior College Orchestra. *Drama and dance*: 100–150 in 2 annual school productions; 100, sixth form revue; 150–200, senior drama competition. 25 take ABRSM, Speech and Drama; 20 Poetry Vanguard. 5 participate in festivals; 1 enters competitions. 1 accepted for Drama/Dance Schools. 1 goes on to work in the theatre. *Art*: 6 take as non-examined subject; 30 GCSE; 8 A-level; 3 accepted for Art School. *Sport*: Hockey, netball, tennis, rounders, swimming, athletics, badminton, volleyball, basketball, squash, gymnastics, indoor hockey available. 45 in school teams; 45 take sport general studies; 10 in out of school teams; 15, PE options. 3 accepted for PE college. 7 represent county (tennis, netball, hockey). *Other*: 35 have bronze Duke of Edinburgh's Award, 12 have silver and 8 gold. 40 do social service or work experience after O-levels. 4 enter voluntary schemes after leaving. Other activities include computer clubs; Christian Union, wildlife club, chess.

Careers 3–4 part time careers advisors. Average number of pupils accepted for *arts and humanities degree courses* at Oxbridge, 2; other universities, 13; polytechnics or CHE, 6. *science and engineering degree courses* at Oxbridge, 4–5; other universities, 11; medical schools, 3; polytechnics or CHE, 4. *BEd*, 1. *other general training courses*, 10. Average number of pupils going straight into careers in industry, 1; civil service, 1; other, 2–4 (including year off). Traditional school career is medicine, 8–12 pa.

Uniform School uniform worn except the sixth.

Houses/prefects No competitive houses. 2 head girls and 4–5 deputies – elected by staff and seniors. School Council.

Religion Attendance at daily assembly expected unless parents request otherwise.

Social Inter-sixth society with local schools, joint productions with Sutton Manor School. Organised trips abroad. Pupils allowed to bring own car/bike/motorbike to school. Meals self service. No tobacco/alcohol allowed.

Discipline No corporal punishment. Pupils failing to produce homework once might expect a kindly reproof; those caught smoking cannabis on the premises might expect automatic suspension.

SUTTON VALENCE

Sutton Valence School	• Co-ed	Pupils 425
Sutton Valence	Boys	Upper sixth 60
Maidstone	Girls	Termly fees:
Kent ME17 3HL	Mixed sixth	Day £1403
Telephone number 06222 842281	• Day	Boarding £2193
	• Boarding	HMC
Enquiries/application to the Admissions Secretary		

WHAT IT'S LIKE

Founded in 1576, most of its buildings are in the village and the school houses are scattered about the village. The overall site comprises about 100 acres on the slopes of a high ridge overlooking the Weald. There is excellent accommodation, delightful gardens and big playing fields. Modern teaching facilities are first-rate. The school has a reputation for close pastoral care, and the staff:pupil ratio of 1:11 helps to produce high academic standards and good results (about 20 plus university entrants per year). Flourishing music and art depts; *very* strong in drama. An impressive range of games and sports in which high standards are achieved (20 plus representatives at county level). A very large number of clubs and societies provide for most conceivable needs. Big commitment to local community schemes and a remarkable record in the Duke of Edinburgh's Award Scheme.

SCHOOL PROFILE

Pupils Total 425. Day 228 (boys 125, girls 93); Boarding 197 (boys 177, girls 20). Entry age, 11, 13 and into the sixth. 6% are children of former pupils.

Entrance Common entrance and own entrance exam used. Girls' places oversubscribed. All-rounders looked for; Anglican foundation – others accepted. Parents expected to buy text books. 46 assisted places. Scholarships for academic, music and art, value £4000–£500 pa; bursaries according to need.

Parents 15+% in industry or commerce. 60+% live within 30 miles; up to 10% live overseas.

Staff Head M R Haywood, in post for 7 years. 37 full time staff, 4 part time. Annual turnover 2–3. Average age 36.

Academic work GCSE and A-levels. Average size of upper fifth 77; upper sixth 60. *O-levels*: on average, 29 pupils in upper fifth pass 1–4 subjects; 26, 5–7 subjects; 21 pass 8+ subjects. *A-levels*: on average, 9 pupils in upper sixth pass 1 subject; 10, 2 subjects; 16, 3 subjects and 8 pass 4 subjects. On average, 16 take science/engineering A-levels; 19 take arts and humanities; 15 a mixture. *Computing facilities*: 10 BBC B's; 4 BBC Masters; 1 RM 380Z; 1 RM 480Z. EFL provision.

Senior pupils' non-academic activities *Music*: 32 learn a musical instrument, 7 up to Grade 6 or above; 25 in school orchestra; 33 in choir; 4 in senior woodwind; 3 in jazz band; 1 accepted for Music Scholarship. *Drama and dance*: 150 in school productions; 100 in house drama. *Art*: 40 take as non-examined subject; 34 take GCSE; 9 A-level; 10 belong to eg photographic club; 9 stage crew etc; 3 accepted for Art School. *Sport*: Cricket, rugby, hockey, fives, cross-country, swimming, athletics, squash, tennis, judo, fencing, golf, sailing, climbing, netball, badminton available. 420 take non-compulsory sport. Some take exams in sailing, 1; life saving, 15; judo, 15. 21 pupils represent county (hockey, netball, rugby, cricket, golf, fencing, athletics, judo). *Other*: 70 take part in local community schemes. 66 have bronze Duke of Edinburgh's Award, 25 silver and 10 gold. Other activities include 32 various clubs and societies including computer club, CCF, debating, driving, drama, community service etc.

Careers 4 part time careers advisors. Average number of pupils accepted for *arts and humanities degree courses* at Oxbridge, 3; other universities, 6; polytechnics or CHE, 4. *science and engineering degree courses* at Oxbridge, 1; other universities, 11; medical schools, 1; polytechnics or CHE, 2. *BEd*, 2. *other general training courses*, 14. Average number of pupils going straight into careers in the armed services, 2; industry, 2; the City, 2; other, 5. Traditional school careers are farming and the City.

Uniform School uniform worn throughout.

Houses/prefects Non competitive houses. Prefects, head boy/girl, head of house and house prefects – appointed by the Headmaster.

Religion Daily Chapel, Sunday service (boarders).

Social Debates, dances, industry conferences, choral activities with local schools. Organised trip to Beauvais. Day pupils allowed to bring own car/bicycle/motorbike to school. Meals self service. School shop. No tobacco/alcohol allowed.

Discipline No corporal punishment. Pupils failing to produce homework once might expect to do extra work; those caught smoking cannabis on the premises could expect expulsion.

Boarding 33% have own study bedroom, 66% are in dormitories of 6 or more. Houses, of approximately 60 aged 13–18, are single sex. Resident qualified nurse. Central dining room. 3–4 weekend exeats each term. Visits to the local town allowed, at housemaster's discretion.

Alumni association is run by Mr C R G Shaw, c/o the School.

Former pupils Sir Charles Groves; Compton Rennie; Sir Rustam Feroze; Peter Fairley; Terence Cuneo; Marie Benson.

SYDENHAM HIGH

Sydenham High School	Co-ed	Pupils 440
19 Westwood Hill	Boys	Upper sixth Yes
Sydenham	● Girls	Termly fees:
London SE26 6BL	Mixed sixth	Day £680
Telephone number 01-778 8737	● Day	GPDST; GSA
	Boarding	

Head Mrs G Baker, first year in post
Age range 11–18; own prep from age 5; entry by own exam
A few scholarships, bursaries or assisted places.

SYLVIA YOUNG

Sylvia Young Theatre School
Rossmore Road
London NW1 6NJ
Telephone number 01-402 0673

Enquiries/application to the Headteacher

- Co-ed
  Boys
  Girls
  Mixed sixth
- Day
  Boarding

Pupils 138
Upper sixth No
Termly fees:
Day £640
ISAI

WHAT IT'S LIKE

Founded in 1981, it has agreeable premises on a single site in north London. The school is committed to providing a balanced theatrical and academic curriculum to ensure that students have a wide range of career and higher education options open to them. Besides the basic academic subjects they are taught speech, singing, tap dancing, ballet, music and drama. It is a happy school with an enthusiastic staff. The pupils are highly motivated and are encouraged to express themselves and contribute on all levels. There is close communication between parents and staff and a flourishing PTA. Pastoral care is taken very seriously. Form tutors liaise closely with parents. Football is available as a sport. Spare time is spent in rehearsals for school shows and charity events.

SCHOOL PROFILE

Pupils Total 138 (boys 40, girls 98). Entry age, 7, 11.
Entrance Audition, interview, written assessment used. Oversubscribed. Potential in performing arts looked for; no religious requirements. Parents not expected to buy text books. LEA grants available.
Parents 30+% live within 30 miles.
Staff Head Maggie Melville, in post for 2 years. 2 full time staff, 16 part time. Age range 20s–50s.
Academic work GCSE. *O-levels*: on average, 10 pupils in fifth pass 1–4 subjects; 4, 5–7 subjects. *Computing facilities*: BBC 'B' micro. Remedial teaching available.
Senior pupils' non-academic activities *Drama and dance*: Some pupils in cabaret groups and charity shows. Some pupils gain ISTD Tap; ISTD Modern; LAMDA acting, verse and prose; RAD Ballet. Some pupils accepted for Drama/Dance Schools, enter competitions, go on to work in theatre or musicals. *Art*: GCSE taken. *Sport*: Football available. *Other*: Some pupils work for national charities beyond school. There is a computer club. All extra time is spent in rehearsals for school shows and charity events.
Careers 1 part time advisor. Average number of pupils going on to general training courses, 20; straight into careers in music/drama, 15. Traditional school career, theatre.
Uniform School uniform worn.
Houses/prefects School Council.
Religion Religious worship not compulsory.
Social Day trips to France. Meals self service or packed lunch. School shop. No tobacco/alcohol allowed.
Discipline No corporal punishment. Pupils failing to produce homework once might expect to complete it by the next day; those caught smoking on

th? premises could expect their parents to be called in and to be asked to leave.

Former pupils Tisha Dean (Eastenders); Frances Ruffelle (Tony Award winner 1987 – Les Miserables).

TALBOT HEATH

Talbot Heath
Rothesay Road
Bournemouth BH4 9NJ
Telephone number 0202 761881

Enquiries/application to Headmistress

Co-ed
Boys
● Girls
Mixed sixth
● Day
● Boarding

Pupils 456
Upper sixth 50
Termly fees:
Day £837
Boarding £1621
GSA;
Independent
C of E

WHAT IT'S LIKE

Founded in 1886 it moved to its present site in 1935. The premises are purpose-built on a single site in woodlands 1½ miles from the town centre and 2 miles from the coast. It has very good facilities and comfortable accommodation. A liberal education on a religious basis is provided. Academic standards are high and results good. Some 20–25 leavers go on to university each year. There are flourishing art and drama departments and a tremendously strong music department (150–200 girls learn an instrument). A very good range of sports and games (a lot of county representatives) and a fair variety of extra-curricular activities. Some commitment to local community schemes.

SCHOOL PROFILE

Pupils Total over 12, 456. Day 386; Boarding 70. Entry age, 8, 11 and into the sixth. Own junior school provides over 20%. 1–2% are children of former pupils.

Entrance Own entrance exam used. Oversubscribed. Academic and personal potential looked for. Parents not expected to buy text books. 140 assisted places. 11–12 scholarships/bursaries pa, full day fees to £200 pa.

Parents 30+% live within 30 miles; 10+% live overseas.

Staff Head Miss C E Austin-Smith, in post for 12 years. 40 full time staff, 21 part time plus visiting staff for extra subjects. Annual turnover 10%. Average age 42.

Academic work GCSE and A-levels. Average size of upper fifth 85; upper sixth 50. *O-levels*: on average, 8 pupils in upper fifth pass 1–4 subjects; 23, 5–7 subjects; 39 pass 8+ subjects. *A-levels*: on average, 5 pupils in upper sixth pass 1 subject; 8, 2 subjects; 28, 3 subjects and 3 pass 4 subjects. On average, 16 take science/engineering A-levels; 20 take arts and humanities A-levels; 11 a mixture. *Computing facilities*: 10 computers; part-time specialist staff; 1-year GCSE Computer Studies course in Lower Sixth. EFL provision.

Senior pupils' non-academic activities *Music*: 150–200 learn a musical instrument, 50 to Grade 6 or above, 1 or 2 pa accepted for Music School; 60–70 in school orchestra, 120 in school choir, 20 handbell ringers; 2 or 3 have had auditions with National Youth Orchestra; 20–30 play in Wessex, Bournemouth and Dorset youth orchestras. *Drama and dance*: 20–30 in school productions. 2 to Grade 6 in ESB, RAD. Occasional pupil accepted for Drama/Dance School or working in theatre. Girls audition for National Youth Theatre as well as for local theatres. *Art*: 35 take GCSE; 7 A-level. 1 accepted for Art School; 1 for architecture. 20 belong to photographic club, 10 to other. *Sport*: Hockey, netball, tennis, rounders, cricket, athletics, table tennis, swimming, gymnastics, sports acrobatics, modern educational dance, skills, keep fit, badminton, volleyball available; for seniors, golf, archery, riding, sailing, self defence, yoga and trampolining. 190 take non-compulsory sport. 1 represents country (tennis); 9 represent county (hockey, swimming, tennis); pupils have also represented county at fencing, cricket, netball. *Other*: 15 take part in local community schemes. 1 Queen's Guide. Other activities include a computer club, chess, dance, gymnastics and electronics clubs; science, geography, art, screen printing, conservation, history, and public speaking societies. Newly started Duke of Edinburgh's Award Scheme.

Careers 3 part time careers advisors. Average number of pupils accepted for *arts and humanities degree courses* at Oxbridge, 2; other universities, 10; polytechnics or CHE, 3. *science and engineering degree courses* at Oxbridge, 2; other universities, 8; medical schools, 3; polytechnics or CHE, 3. *BEd*, 6. *other general training courses*, 6. Average number of pupils going straight into careers in armed services, 1; civil service, 1; music/drama, 1. Traditional school careers are medicine, nursing.

Uniform School uniform worn, some licence in the sixth.

Houses/prefects No competitive houses. No prefects – all sixth formers share duties and responsibilities. 2 head girls, head of house and house prefects – democratic nomination and election, final confirmation by Head.

Religion Only Jewish and Moslem girls excused morning assembly.

Social Some dramatic activity, debates and dances with local boys' grammar school. Regular annual exchanges in Normandy, visits to Paris, Italy, USA, Israel; regular ski-ing holidays (often Italy). Pupils allowed to bring own car/bike/motorbike to school. Meals formal. Uniform exchange shop. No tobacco/alcohol allowed.

Discipline No corporal punishment. Pupils failing to produce homework once might expect rebuke and insistence on production of work the following day; those caught smoking cannabis on the premises might expect expulsion.

Boarding 7% have own study bedroom, 25% in single study cubicles, 25% double study bedrooms, 43% are in dormitories. Houses, of approximately 45. Resident qualified nurse. No central dining room. Sixth formers can provide and cook some own food, 2 weekend exeats each term plus half term. Visits to local town allowed by seniors (15+).

Alumni association run by the Head Mistress.

Former pupils Lady Faithfull; Judge Daffodil Cosgrave; Dilys Powell.

TAUNTON

Taunton School
Taunton
Somerset TA2 6AD
Telephone number 0823 76081

Enquiries/application to the Headmaster's
Secretary

- Co-ed
  Boys
  Girls
  Mixed sixth
- Day
- Boarding

Pupils 600
Upper sixth 99
Termly fees:
Day £1408
Boarding £2175
HMC; IAPS;
GSA

WHAT IT'S LIKE

Founded in 1847, it lies on the edge of the county town in spacious grounds, with open country to the north. The main buildings are mid-Victorian Gothic. The town itself is an interesting and attractive place, surrounded by splendid countryside, and very handy for Bristol, Bath, Exeter and Wells. There are 2 single-sex prep schools: Taunton Junior for boys and Weirfield for girls, close by. Continuous education from 3–18 is available. Modern extensions provide excellent accommodation and facilities, including fine libraries. It is a C of E school and some worship is compulsory. A very large staff of 134 full-timers (plus 39 part-timers) permit a staff:pupil ratio of 1:8. The teaching is good and academic standards and results are first-rate. Some 70–80 leavers go to university each year. The music and drama departments are very strong indeed. The school has considerable strength in games and sports, with many representatives at county and international level. A wide variety of activities caters for most needs. A substantial commitment to local community schemes and an outstanding record in the Duke of Edinburgh's Award Scheme (45 bronze, 40 silver, 40 gold).

SCHOOL PROFILE

Pupils Total over 12, 600. Day 300 (boys 160, girls 140); Boarding 300 (boys 180, girls 120). Entry age, 3, 7, 11, 13 and into the sixth. Own junior school provides over 20%. 30% are children of former pupils.

Entrance Common entrance used. Oversubscribed for girls' boarding places. No special skills or religious requirements. Parents expected to buy text books. 52 assisted places. 107 scholarships/bursaries, £1408–£60.

Parents 15+% in industry or commerce. 30+% live within 30 miles; up to 10% live overseas.

Staff Head B B Sutton, in post 1 year. 134 full time staff, 39 part time. Annual turnover 4.5%. Average age 45.

Academic work GCSE and A-levels. Average size of upper fifth 139; upper sixth 99. *O-levels*: on average, 36 pupils in upper fifth pass 1–4 subjects; 36, 5–7 subjects; 67 pass 8+ subjects. *A-levels*: on average, 17 pupils in upper sixth pass 1 subject; 22, 2 subjects; 52, 3 subjects and 8 pass 4 or more subjects. On average, 39 take science/engineering A-levels; 49 take arts and humanities; 10 a mixture. Greek, business studies and Spanish are offered to GCSE; Greek, ancient history, food and nutrition, design, business studies to A-level. *Computing facilities*: computer literacy taught as part of foundation year in 3rd form; computers used widely as a teaching tool from kindergarten upwards. EFL provision.

Senior pupils' non-academic activities *Music*: 155 learn a musical instru-

ment, 40 to Grade 6 or above, 1 accepted for music at university; 40 in school orchestra, 80 in choir, 4 in school pop group, 20 in chamber music group; 3 in National Children's Orchestra, occasional pupil in National Youth Orchestra; 1 choral scholar. *Drama and dance*: 150 in school productions; 6 in other. 10 take Guildhall speech and drama exams. 1 accepted for Drama/Dance School; 1 pa goes on to work in theatre. *Art*: 25 take GCSE; 8 A-level; 4 history of art. 4 accepted for Art School; 1 for BTEC course. *Sport*: Rugby, cricket, hockey, athletics, cross-country, tennis, squash, badminton, fencing, judo, canoeing, netball (girls) available. 300 take non-compulsory sport. 100 take sport exams. 24 represent county/country (rugby, hockey, cricket, netball, athletics). *Other*: 30 take part in local community schemes. 45 have bronze Duke of Edinburgh's Award, 45 have silver and 30 gold. 5 enter voluntary schemes after leaving; 2 work for national charities. Other activities include a computer club, debating, chess, scientific society, bridge, bell ringing, driving lessons, etc.

Careers 2 part time careers advisors. Average number of pupils accepted for *arts and humanities degree courses* at Oxbridge, 4; other universities, 35; polytechnics or CHE, 21. *science and engineering degree courses* at Oxbridge, 6; other universities, 26; medical schools, 3; polytechnics or CHE, 15. *BEd*, 3. *other general training courses*, 10. Average number of pupils going straight into careers in armed services, 5; industry, 10; the City, 3; civil service, 2; music/drama, 1; other, 10.

Uniform School uniform worn throughout.

Houses/prefects Pastoral non-competitive houses. Prefects, head boy and girl, head of house and house prefects – appointed by the Head after consultation with staff and head of school.

Religion 3 compulsory chapel services per week, 1 on Sundays for boarders; voluntary communion.

Social Occasional musical events with other schools. Exchanges with France and Germany. Pupils allowed to bring own car/bike/motorbike to school. Meals self service. School shop. No tobacco/alcohol allowed.

Discipline No corporal punishment. Pupils failing to produce homework once might expect to be given another chance to do so; those caught smoking cannabis on the premises might be suspended or expelled for breaking school rules.

Boarding 18% have own study bedroom, 18% share with 1 other; 10% are in dormitories of 6+. Houses, of up to 50, divided for pastoral reasons and are single-sex. Resident qualified nurses. Central dining room. Pupils can provide and cook own snacks. 2 weekend exeats each term plus half term. Unlimited visits to local town with permission, over 13.

Alumni association run by M J O Willacy, Secretary, Old Tauntonian Association, c/o the School.

Former pupils Admiral of the Fleet Lord Hill Norton; Sue Brown (1st woman Cox in Varsity Boat Race); John Jameson (Warwicks and England cricketer); Barbara Jefford, OBE (Shakespearian actress); R A Gerrard, DSO (England Rugby); Wing Cdr J R D Braham; Major F G Blaker, VC, MC.

Teesside High

Teesside High School	Co-ed	Pupils 380
The Avenue	Boys	Upper sixth Yes
Eaglescliffe	● Girls	Termly fees:
Stockton-on-Tees	Mixed sixth	Day £700
Cleveland TS16 9AT	● Day	GSA
Telephone number 0642 782095	Boarding	

Head Mrs H Coles (6 years)
Age range 11–18; own prep from age 4; entry by own exam

Tettenhall

Tettenhall College Upper School	● Co-ed	Pupils 250
Wolverhampton	Boys	Upper sixth Yes
West Midlands WV6 8QX	Girls	Termly fees:
Telephone number 0902 751119	Mixed sixth	Day £1010
	● Day	Boarding £1640
	● Boarding	HMC; SHMIS

Head W J Dale (20 years)
Age range 13–19; own prep from age 7; entry by common entrance
Scholarships.

Thetford Grammar

Thetford Grammar School	● Co-ed	Pupils 187
Bridge Street	Boys	Upper sixth 20
Thetford	Girls	Termly fees:
Norfolk IP24 3AF	Mixed sixth	Day £700
Telephone number 0842 2840	● Day	GBA
	Boarding	

Enquiries/application to the Headmaster

WHAT IT'S LIKE

Originally founded some time in the 7th century, it was refounded in the 16th and has attractive well-equipped buildings and spacious grounds in the centre of the very interesting town of Thetford. There have been extensive recent developments and facilities are very good. After a period as a voluntary controlled grammar school it reverted to independence in 1981. Since then the school has developed rapidly with full classes in all years up to and including the fourth and a fully subscribed sixth form will emerge in the next two years. A good general education is provided and results are very promising. Under the former regime 20 or more leavers went on to university each year. Music, drama and art will expand as the school burgeons. An adequate range of games, sports and activities. A promising record in the Duke of Edinburgh's Award Scheme.

SCHOOL PROFILE

Pupils Total over 12, 187 (boys 104, girls 83). Entry age, 8–11 and into the sixth. Own junior school provides over 40%. 5% are children of former pupils.

Entrance Own entrance exam used. Oversubscribed. No special skills or religious requirements. Parents not expected to buy text books. 3 scholarships/bursaries awarded at 11, full to half fees.

Parents 15+% are doctors, lawyers, etc; 15+% in industry or commerce. 60+% live within 30 miles.

Staff Head J H Woolmore, in post for 5 years. 21 full time staff, 5 part time. Annual turnover, 4%. Average age, 44.

Academic work GCSE and A-levels. Average size of upper fifth 35; upper sixth 20. *O-levels*: on average, 9 pupils in upper fifth pass 1–4 subjects; 20, 5–7 subjects; 6 pass 8+ subjects. *A-levels*: on average, 1 pupil in the upper sixth passes 1 subject; 6, 2 subjects; 11, 3 subjects; 2 pass 4 subjects. On average (last three years) 7 take science/engineering A-levels; 8 take arts and humanities; 4, a mixture. *Computing facilities*: Present provision is 3 to 4 years old and plans are in hand to re-equip and enlarge the department.

Senior pupils' non-academic activities *Music*: 5 learn a musical instrument, 1 up to Grade 6 or above; 3 in school orchestra, 3 in choir. *Drama and dance*: 20 in school productions. 1 entered competitions. *Art*: 12 take GCSE. 1 accepted for Art School. *Sport*: Rugby, hockey, netball, cricket, tennis, badminton, table tennis available. 20 take non-compulsory sport. 4 take exams. 2 represent county/country (swimming, track and field events). *Other*: 16 have bronze Duke of Edinburgh's Award, 2 have silver and 1 gold. Other activities change from term to term and include a computer club, chess, bridge, gardening, photography, nature study, weather station, play reading, fencing.

Careers 1 part time advisor. Average number of pupils accepted for *arts and humanities degree courses* at university, 1; polytechnics or CHE, 2. *science and engineering degree courses* at Oxbridge, 1; other universities, 5; polytechnics or CHE, 1. *BEd*, 1. *other general training courses*, 7. Average number of pupils going straight into careers in the armed services, 1; industry, 1; civil service, 1; other, 3.

Uniform School uniform worn, modified in the sixth.

Houses/prefects Competitive houses. Prefects, head boy/girl, head of house and house prefects – appointed by the Head. School Council.

Religion Worship in accordance with the teachings and practices of the C of E.

Social Pupils participate in the two Thetford Schools' Orchestras and in the annual Thetford Schools' Festival of the Arts and Music. Regular organised trips abroad but no exchange system. Pupils allowed to bring own bike to school. Meals self service. School shop. No tobacco/alcohol allowed.

Discipline No corporal punishment. Pupils failing to produce homework once might expect verbal reprimand; those caught smoking cannabis on the premises might be required to leave.

Alumni association is run by Mr G Carter, c/o the School.
Former pupils Humphrey Burton.

TONBRIDGE

Tonbridge School	Co-ed	Pupils 670
Tonbridge	● Boys	Upper sixth 135
Kent TN9 1JP	Girls	Termly fees:
Telephone number 0732 365555	Mixed sixth	Day £1700
Enquiries/application to the Headmaster	● Day	Boarding £2400
	● Boarding	HMC

WHAT IT'S LIKE

Founded in 1553 by Sir Andrew Judde, it expanded considerably during the 19th century to become one of the major public schools. It retains close links with the Worshipful Company of Skinners. The fine campus lies on the northern edge of the town. There are a lot of handsome Victorian buildings to which there have been numerous additions in recent years to provide first-class facilities and accommodation. Beautiful playing fields lie next to the school. A C of E foundation, there are some compulsory services and some emphasis on Anglican tradition and practice. A high standard of teaching, and academic results are extremely good. About 85 pupils go on to university each year and 30+ of these go on to Oxbridge. The music dept is tremendously strong. Art and drama are pretty strong. The school has long had a wide reputation for excellence in sports and games. There is a wide variety of these and a lot of Tonbridge boys have achieved county and international recognition. The CCF has a big contingent and there are numerous clubs and societies which cater for most needs. Very substantial commitment to local community schemes and a fine record in the Duke of Edinburgh's Award Scheme.

SCHOOL PROFILE

Pupils Total 670. Day 220; Boarding 450. Entry age, 13 and into the sixth (limited vacancies). 10–15% are children of former pupils.
Entrance Common entrance and own entrance exam used. Oversubscribed. No special skills or religious requirements (C of E foundation, but other faiths welcomed). Most parents expected to buy text books. 3 assisted places. 25 scholarships for academic, music and art, full fees to ⅙ remission; foundation Bursaries for individuals in need of assistance.
Parents 15+% are doctors, lawyers, etc; 15+% in industry or commerce. 30+% live within 30 miles; 10+% live overseas.
Staff Head C H D Everett, in post for 13 years. 67 full time staff, 4 part time. Annual turnover 5%. Average age 39.
Academic work GCSE and A-levels. Average size of upper fifth 135; upper sixth 135. *O-levels*: on average, 2 pupils in upper fifth pass 1–4 subjects; 13, 5–7 subjects; 120 pass 8+ subjects. *A-levels*: on average, 10 pupils in the upper sixth pass 1 subject; 10, 2 subjects; 83, 3 subjects; 25 pass 4 subjects. On average, 47 take science/engineering A-levels; 53 take arts and humanities;

35 take a mixture. Russian and electronics offered to GCSE and A-level. *Computing facilities*: 30 Mbyte Winchester file servers serving 3 independent but interconnected Econet networks with c.100 computers; usual word-processing, spread sheet, desktop publishing and CAD packages support most departments, plus extensive applications software. Provision for mildly dyslexic pupils with above average IQs.

Senior pupils' non-academic activities *Music*: 188 learn a musical instrument, 62 up to Grade 6 or above, 2 accepted for Music School, 2 accepted for university music degree; 32 in school orchestra, 44 play in wind bands, 27 play in chamber music groups; 47 in choir, 6 in pop group; 2 in Kent Youth Orchestra; usually 1 in National Youth Orchestra. *Drama and dance*: 40 in school productions, 30 in house plays. *Art*: 35 take as non-examined subject; 28 take GCSE; 24 A-level. 1 or 2 accepted for Art School; 1 for History of Art; 2 or 3 for architecture; 1 for landscape architecture; 1 for design consultancy. Extensive facilities open to all at any time. *Sport*: Cricket, rugby, hockey, athletics, cross-country, tennis, badminton, squash, fives, rackets, fencing, judo, golf, rowing, sailing, shooting, swimming, climbing, canoeing, sub-aqua, riding available. 180 take non-compulsory sport (200 take it seriously in top school teams). 30 take exams. 12 represent county/country in cricket. *Other*: 85 take part in local community schemes. 20 have silver Duke of Edinburgh's Award and 33 have gold. 2 enter voluntary schemes after leaving school. Other activities include a computer club, aero and radio modelling, bridge, chess, choral, Christian Fellowship, computing, debating, film, general knowledge, junior dramatic, medical group, natural history, opera, radio, plus numerous cultural societies, particularly for Upper School.

Careers 1 full time advisor (and 1 universities FE advisor). Average number of pupils accepted for *arts and humanities degree courses* at Oxbridge, 18; other universities, 45; polytechnics or CHE, 9. *science and engineering degree courses* at Oxbridge, 14; other universities, 12; medical schools, 6. Average number of pupils going straight into careers in armed services, 2 from school 4 after FE; industry, 1; the city, 5; music/drama, 1; other, 3.

Uniform School uniform worn throughout.

Houses/prefects Competitive houses. Prefects, head boy, head of house and house prefects – appointed by the Headmaster. School Council.

Religion Compulsory chapel, Sundays and 4 mornings per week.

Social Major choral performances, combined band concerts. Young Enterprise, annual lectures by distinguished speakers, girls from local schools for drama productions and dances; industry courses. French school exchange arrangement, plus smaller groups with German, Austrian and Spanish schools. Holiday exchanges, organised trips to Greece, Russia, France etc, plus orchestral/choral tours to USA/Germany etc. Pupils allowed to bring own bike to school. Meals formal. School shop. No tobacco/alcohol allowed.

Discipline No corporal punishment. Pupils failing to produce homework once might expect to do it, plus some extra, in own time; those caught smoking cannabis on the premises might expect expulsion.

Boarding 34% have own study bedroom, 3% share with 1 other; 20% are in dormitories of 6 or more. Houses, of approximately 64, are the same as competitive houses. Sanatorium sister and assistance. Pupils can provide and cook own food. 2 24-hour exeats plus half term each term. Visits to local town allowed.

Former pupils Colin Cowdrey; Frederick Forsyth; Sir Patrick Mayhew; Richard Ellison; Bill Bruford; Maurice Denham; Ben Whitrow; David Tomlinson.

TORMEAD

Tormead School
Cranley Road
Guildford
Surrey GU1 2JD
Telephone number 0483 575101

Co-ed   Pupils 520
Boys   Upper sixth Yes
● Girls   Termly fees:
Mixed sixth   Day £900
● Day   GSA; GBGSA
Boarding

Head Mrs J V Crouch-Smith (11 years)
Age range 5–18; entry by own exam.
Scholarships and bursaries.

TRENT COLLEGE

Trent College
Long Eaton
Nottingham NG10 4AD
Telephone number 0602 732737

Enquiries/application to the Headmaster

Co-ed   Pupils 587
● Boys   Upper sixth 95
Girls   Termly fees:
● Mixed sixth   Day £1142
● Day   Boarding £1950
● Boarding   HMC

WHAT IT'S LIKE

Founded in 1866, it has a secluded urban site – a compact campus of some 45 acres which includes gardens, playing fields and many fine trees (300 varieties). Its brick buildings are handsome and well-equipped. Much investment in recent years has produced first-rate modern facilities. A C of E foundation, Anglican worship and practice are encouraged and some services are compulsory. It is a well-run school with impressive standards academically. Results are excellent and 70% of leavers go on to university or polytechnic. There is an immensely strong music department. Art and drama are also very strong. Very high levels of attainment in sports and games (40 or more county and national representatives). A wide range of extra-curricular activities. There is also a massive commitment to local community services (one of the biggest in the country) and a phenomenal record in the Duke of Edinburgh's Award Scheme (60 silver, 50 gold). Full use is made of the cultural amenities of Nottingham and Derby.

SCHOOL PROFILE

Pupils Total over 12, 587. Day 296 (boys 268, girls 28); Boarding 291 (boys 251, girls 40). Entry age, boys, 11 and 13; boys and girls into the sixth. 20% are children of former pupils.

Entrance Common entrance and own entrance exam used. Oversubscribed. Looks for strengths in sport, music and the arts for entry. No special religious requirements. Parents expected to buy text books though refunds are given on resale. 25 assisted places. 32 scholarships/bursaries, for academic, leadership, art and design, music, drama, sixth form and continuation, £3900 to £450.

Parents 15+% are doctors, lawyers, etc; 15+% in industry or commerce. 60+% live within 30 miles; up to 10% live overseas.

Staff Head A J Maltby, in post for 20 years. New Head being appointed. 56 full time staff, 25 part time. Annual turnover 8%. Average age 31.

Academic work GCSE and A-levels. Average size of upper fifth 105; upper sixth 95. *O-levels*: on average, 17 pupils in upper fifth pass 1–4 subjects; 25, 5–7 subjects; 56 pass 8+ subjects. *A-levels*: on average, 5 pupils in the upper sixth pass 1 subject; 24, 2 subjects; 52, 3 subjects; 8 pass 4 subjects. On average, 28 take science/engineering A-levels; 35 take arts and humanities; 26 a mixture. *Computing facilities*: 24 BBC-B Micro systems all with printer and central applications facilities, extensive software, Prestel and weather satellite communications included. Extra English tuition and provision for mildly visually handicapped.

Senior pupils' non-academic activities *Music*: 130 learn a musical instrument, 60 up to Grade 6 or above, 4 accepted for Music School; 120 in school orchestra, 220 in choir, 5 in pop group, 200 in wind and string ensembles. *Drama and dance*: 100–150 in school productions. 6 accepted for Drama/Dance Schools, 5 go on to work in the theatre. *Art*: 45 take GCSE; 23 A-level. 10 accepted for Art School; 2 for university; 5 for poly. *Sport*: Rugby, hockey, cricket, athletics, tennis, swimming, squash, netball, basketball, rowing, shooting, judo, trampolining, cross-country, running, sailing, climbing, riding, golf and canoeing available. 40 represent county/country (rugby, hockey, cricket, athletics, squash, swimming, show jumping, netball). *Other*: 150 take part in local community schemes. 60 have silver Duke of Edinburgh's Award, 50 gold. Other activities include a wide range of clubs including computers and chess (Derbyshire league); societies ranging from archives to information technology.

Careers 8 part-time advisors. Average number of pupils accepted for *arts and humanities degree courses* at Oxbridge, 4; other universities, 19; polytechnics or CHE, 11. *science and engineering degree courses* at Oxbridge, 3; other universities, 13; medical schools, 2; polytechnics or CHE, 7. *BEd*, 3. *other general training courses*, 12. Average number of pupils going straight into careers in the armed services, 2; industry, 3; other, 4.

Uniform School uniform worn except by prefects.

Houses/prefects Competitive houses (6). Prefects, head boy and girl, head of house and house prefects.

Social Chess, basketball, cricket matches, careers convention with other local schools; local community service. Many organised trips and a wide range of exchanges abroad. Meals self service. School shop. No tobacco allowed, limited drinking in sixth form club.

Discipline No corporal punishment. Pupils failing to produce homework more than once might expect tutor to be informed and detention; those caught smoking cannabis on the premises can expect Headmaster to recommend expulsion.

Boarding 15% have own study bedroom, 25% share with others; fewer than

5% are in dormitories of 6+. Houses, of approximately 45–50, single-sex. Resident qualified medical staff. Central dining room. Pupils can provide and cook own food. 2 weekend exeats each term plus half term. Visits to local town allowed.
Former pupils: Rex Alston.

TRINITY (CROYDON)

Trinity School of John Whitgift	Co-ed	Pupils 782
Shirley Park	● Boys	Upper sixth 89
Croydon	Girls	Termly fees:
Surrey CR9 7AT	Mixed sixth	Day £990
Telephone number 01-656 9541	● Day	HMC
Enquiries/application to the Headmaster	Boarding	

WHAT IT'S LIKE

Founded in 1596 by Archbishop John Whitgift, it moved from central Croydon to its present site in 1965. This comprises a brand-new complex of buildings and playing fields in an open suburban area of 27 acres. Other playing fields nearby. It has excellent facilities and comfortable accommodation. The standard of teaching is high and so are the academic levels attained. About 70 leavers proceed to university each year. Religious worship is broadly conceived and religious education continues up to the end of the fifth year. There is a very strong musical tradition and the choirs frequently take part in national events. Considerable strength also in drama. Numerous productions in 2 well-equipped theatres. A very good record in sport and games and considerable emphasis on outdoor pursuits. A wide variety of clubs and societies cater for most needs. There is an active CCF contingent and a very active community service unit. A notable record in the Duke of Edinburgh's Scheme.

SCHOOL PROFILE

Pupils Total over 10, 782. Entry age, 10, 11, 13 and into the sixth. 5% are children of former pupils.
Entrance Own entrance exam used. Oversubscribed. No special skills or religious requirements. Parents not expected to buy text books. 138 assisted places. Scholarships/bursaries, ⅔ to ¼ fees.
Parents 15+% in industry or commerce. 60+% live within 30 miles.
Staff Head R J Wilson, in post for 15 years. 61 full time staff, 4 part time. Annual turnover 6. Average age 37.
Academic work GCSE and A-levels. Average size of upper fifth 98; upper sixth 89. *O-levels*: on average, 3 pupils in upper fifth pass 1–4 subjects; 17, 5–7 subjects; 79 pass 8+ subjects. *A-levels*: on average, 6 pupils in the upper sixth pass 1 subject; 8, 2 subjects; 70, 3 subjects; 6 pass 4 subjects. On average, 37 take science/engineering A-levels; 37 take arts and humanities; 18 a mixture. *Computing facilities*: 30 booth lab, 7 booth advanced lab, all departments equipped. Provision for dyslexia.

Senior pupils' non-academic activities *Music*: 80 learn a musical instrument, 60 up to Grade 6 or above. 2 accepted for Music School; 50 in school orchestra, 30 in choir, occasionally few in National Youth Orchestra. Many go on to professional musical activities. *Drama and dance*: 50 in school productions. *Art*: 35 take GCSE; 10 A-level. 3 accepted for Art School. *Sport*: Rugby, hockey, cricket, swimming, water polo, squash, badminton, athletics, cross-country, volleyball and sub-aqua available. Lots take non-compulsory sport. Many represent county/country. *Other*: 35 take part in local community schemes. 30 have bronze Duke of Edinburgh's Award, 20 have silver and 10 have gold. Many other activities include a computer club.

Careers 4 part time advisors. Average number of pupils accepted for *arts and humanities degree courses* at Oxbridge, 8; other universities, 45; polytechnics or CHE, 18. *science and engineering degree courses* at Oxbridge, 4; other universities, 6; medical schools, 9; polytechnics or CHE, 3. *BEd*, 1. Average number of pupils going straight into careers in the armed services, 1; industry, 2; the City, 6.

Uniform School uniform worn except the sixth.

Houses/prefects Competitive houses. Prefects, head boy and head of house – appointed by the Head and the school. Sixth form School Council.

Religion Worship encouraged.

Social Sixth form society, dramatic and musical productions with local girls' schools. Lots of organised trips abroad. Pupils allowed to bring own car/bike/motorbike to school. Meals self-service. School shop selling tuck. No pupils allowed tobacco/alcohol.

Discipline No corporal punishment. Pupils failing to produce homework once might expect no punishment; those caught smoking cannabis on the premises might expect expulsion.

Alumni association is run by The Secretary, Lime Meadow Avenue, Sanderstead, Croydon.

TRURO

Truro School
Truro
Cornwall TR1 1TH
Telephone number 0872 72763

Co-ed   Pupils 850
- Boys   Upper sixth Yes
  Girls   Termly fees:
- Mixed sixth   Day £950
- Day   Boarding £1450
- Boarding   HMC

Head B K Hobbs (2 years)
Age range 11–18; entry by own exam
Scholarships and assisted places. Own prep school, Treliske.

TRURO HIGH

Truro High School
Falmouth Road
Truro
Cornwall TR1 2HU
Telephone number 0872 72830

Co-ed
Boys
• Girls
Mixed sixth
• Day
• Boarding

Pupils 510
Upper sixth Yes
Termly fees:
Day £750
Boarding £1350
GSA; GBGSA

Head Mrs J F Marshall
Age range 11–18; own junior from age 5; entry by own exam.
Scholarships and governors' assisted places.

TUDOR HALL

Tudor Hall School
Wykham Park
Banbury
Oxfordshire OX16 9UR
Telephone number 0295 3434

Co-ed
Boys
• Girls
Mixed sixth
• Day
• Boarding

Pupils 250
Upper sixth Yes
Termly fees:
Day £1210
Boarding £1900
GSA; GBGSA;
Woodard

Head Miss N Godfrey (4 years)
Age range 11–18; entrance by common entrance.

UNIVERSITY COLLEGE SCHOOL

University College School
Frognal
Hampstead
London NW3 6XH
Telephone number 01-435 2215

Enquiries/application to the Headmaster

Co-ed
• Boys
Girls
Mixed sixth
• Day
Boarding

Pupils 580
Upper sixth 100
Termly fees:
Day £1230
HMC

WHAT IT'S LIKE

Founded in Gower Street in 1830 as part of University College London. A junior school was opened in Hampstead in 1891 and the main school moved to purpose-built accommodation in Hampstead in 1907. The school is set in pleasant grounds in a very agreeable residential area, 5 minutes' walk from Hampstead Heath; 27 acres of school's own playing fields are within walking distance. There have been extensive additions to the original handsome buildings and facilities are first-rate. The main aims of the school's philosophy and policy are the pursuit of academic excellence, a respect for and encouragement of independent thought and individual judgment, a broad curriculum and the lack of any religious barriers. A large staff permits a staff:pupil ratio of about 1:10 and academic attainments are high. About 80% of sixth formers go on to degree courses and about 20 pupils go each year to Oxbridge. The school is very strong in music and drama and provides an excellent range of activities. It also has a distinguished record in games.

SCHOOL PROFILE

Pupils Total 580. Entry age, 13+ and into the sixth. Own junior school provides over 70%. 10% are children of former pupils.

Entrance Common entrance and own entrance exam used. Oversubscribed. No religious requirements. Academic competence and an ability to contribute to the wider life of the school looked for. Parents are charged separately for text books. 10 assisted places pa for 11 year olds and 5 for sixth form. No set number of scholarships; grants and bursaries available up to full fees.

Parents Most are professional people: doctors, lawyers, etc. 80+% live within 20 miles.

Staff Head G D Slaughter, in post for 5 years. 49 full time staff, 10 part time (music). Annual turnover 4%. Average age mid thirties.

Academic work GCSE and A-levels. Average size of upper fifth 108; upper sixth 100. *O-levels*: on average, 2 pupils in upper fifth pass 1–4 subjects; 19, 5–7 subjects; 86 pass 8+ subjects. *A-levels*: on average, 3 pupils in the upper sixth pass 1 subject; 10, 2 subjects; 79, 3 subjects; 8 pass 4 subjects. On average, 40 take science/engineering A-levels; 40 take arts and humanities; 20, a mixture. *Computing facilities*: Computer room and computers in the design, maths, physics, chemistry, biology, geography and economics departments.

Senior pupils' non-academic activities *Music*: 60 in school orchestra, wind band, numerous small ensembles, pop groups. Choral society, involving parents, staff and children, numbers about 300. *Drama and dance*: All boys up to GCSE in class drama, one major school production per term. *Art*: 10 take as non-examined subject; 20 take GCSE; 4 A-level. 2 accepted for Art School. *Sport*: Rugby, rowing, football, hockey, cricket, athletics, tennis, golf, swimming, badminton, fencing, karate, basketball, fives and squash available. The vast majority play in 5-a-side football tournaments, table tennis, swimming etc. *Other*: 25 take part in local community schemes. Other activities include a computer club, a wide range of societies including chess, backgammon, politics and economics, science, geography, history, classical; driving lessons, war games, Christian Union, Jewish Society, bridge, live-action role playing society, tiddlywinks, photography etc.

Careers 5 full time and 3 part time advisors. About 80% of sixth form leavers go on degree courses. About 20 pa to Oxbridge. A few go on to teach. Roughly even arts/science spread. Very few pupils go straight into the armed services, the church, or general training courses. A number go into industry, the City, civil service; music/drama, 3 or 4.

Uniform School uniform worn except the sixth.

Houses/prefects Competitive houses ('demes'). Prefects (monitors), head boy – appointed by the Head. No head of house or house prefects.

Religion No compulsory worship.

Social Plays, choral society etc in close co-operation with South Hampstead High School. Organised trips abroad including sporting exchange with the

Lycee Marcelin Berthelot in Paris. Pupils allowed to bring own car/bike/ motorbike to school. Meals self-service. School tuck shop. No tobacco/ alcohol allowed.
Discipline No corporal punishment. Pupils failing to produce homework once might expect a warning; those caught in possession of drugs on the premises must anticipate expulsion.
Former pupils Chris Bonnington; Roger Bannister; Stephen Spender; Julian Lloyd-Webber.

UPLANDS

Uplands School
40 St Osmund's Road
Parkstone, Poole
Dorset BH14 9JY
Telephone number 0202 742626

Enquiries to Head Teacher
Application to school secretary

- Co-ed   Pupils 165
  Boys   Upper sixth 10
  Girls   Termly fees:
  Mixed sixth   Day £595
- Day   ISAI
  Boarding

WHAT IT'S LIKE

Founded in 1973, it is single site in the suburbs of Poole and has very pleasant, well-equipped buildings in ample wooded grounds. Two new wings have been built on to the original school which dates from 1895. Non-denominational but all pupils have lessons in religious studies. There are few school rules and a friendly informal atmosphere prevails (within certain strictly enforced limitations). A sound general education is provided (all pupils are expected to take 8–9 GCSE subjects). Music and art appear to be minimal but there is quite a lot of work done in drama. A good range of sports and games and extra-curricular activities. Some commitment to local community schemes.

SCHOOL PROFILE

Pupils Total over 12, 165 (boys 76, girls 89). Entry age, 11 and into the sixth. Own junior department provides approximately 50%. Under 5% are children of former pupils.
Entrance Own entrance exam used. Oversubscribed. No special skills or religious requirements. Parents not expected to buy text books.
Parents 15+% are doctors, lawyers etc; 15+% in industry or commerce. 60+% live within 30 miles.
Staff Head Miss C E Kirkpatrick, in post for 3 years. 14 full time staff, 10 part time. Annual turnover 5%. Average age 35.
Academic work GCSE and A-levels. Average size of upper fifth 40; upper sixth 10. *O-levels*: on average, 4 pupils in upper fifth pass 1–4 subjects; 27, 5–7 subjects; 8 pass 8+ subjects. *A-levels*: on average, 2 pupils in the upper sixth pass 1 subject; 7, 2 subjects and 1, 3 or 4 subjects. On average, 4 take science/engineering A-levels; 4 take arts and humanities; 2 a mixture. *Computing facilities*: computer laboratory in Technical Studies Centre.

Senior pupils' non-academic activities *Music*: 9 learn a musical instrument, 3 to Grade 6 or above. 4 in school choir, 2 in National Youth Orchestra, 2 in Wessex Youth Training Orchestra. 2 are making records and 3 now play in pop group. *Drama and dance*: 40 in school productions. 1 takes to Grade 6 ESB, RAD etc, 1 accepted for Drama/Dance Schools, 1 works in theatre. *Art*: 9 take GCSE; 2 A-level. 1 accepted for Art School. *Sport*: Rugby, soccer, hockey, netball, tennis, swimming, badminton, volleyball, basketball, table tennis, cricket, athletics available. 15 take non-compulsory sport; 10 take exams. 2 represent county (ice hockey). *Other*: 12 take part in local community schemes. Other activities include computer club.

Careers 1 full time advisor. Average number of pupils accepted for *arts and humanities degree courses* at Oxbridge, 1; other universities, 1; polytechnics or CHE, 3. *science and engineering degree courses* at universities, 1. *other general training courses*, 6. Average number of pupils going straight into careers in armed services, 5; music/drama, 2; other, 13.

Uniform School uniform worn except the sixth.

Houses/prefects No competitive houses. Prefects and head boy/girl – appointed by Head, staff and current head boy/girl.

Religion Compulsory daily assembly.

Social Occasional theatrical productions with local schools. Trips to France; ski-ing. Pupils allowed to bring own car/bike to school. Meals formal. No tobacco/alcohol allowed.

Discipline No corporal punishment. Pupils failing to produce homework once might expect verbal warning; those caught smoking cannabis on the premises might expect expulsion.

Former pupils Iona Brown (violinist); Mary Donaldson.

UPPER CHINE

Upper Chine School	Co-ed	Pupils 253
Church Road	Boys	Upper sixth 15
Shanklin	● Girls	Termly fees:
Isle of Wight PO37 6QU	Mixed sixth	Day £895
Telephone number 0983 862208	● Day	Boarding £1725
Enquiries/application to the Headmistress	● Boarding	GSA

WHAT IT'S LIKE

Founded in 1799, it moved to Shanklin in 1914 and has a delightful site of 30 acres close to the sea, with very beautiful gardens and grounds. Pleasant buildings and very comfortable accommodation in the outskirts of Shanklin Old Village. The junior school is combined. A large staff permits a ratio of 1:8 pupils. A happy, friendly family atmosphere prevails and there are all the advantages of a small school. Academic standards are good. Eight or more leavers go on to university each year. Virtually everyone is engaged in music and drama and the school is fortunate in having a purpose-built theatre. Sports and games are very strong and there is a wide variety of activities. A big commitment to local community schemes and a fine record in the Duke of Edinburgh Award Scheme.

SCHOOL PROFILE

Pupils Total, 253. Day 73; Boarding 180. Entry age, 11–13 and into the sixth. 2% are children of former pupils.

Entrance Common entrance and own entrance exam used. Not oversubscribed. No special skills or religious requirements, but strong in sport, music and drama; most are C of E. Parents expected to buy text books (most are second-hand). 6 scholarships/bursaries, £895 to £70.

Parents 15+% in the Armed Services. 60+% live within 30 miles; up to 10% live overseas.

Staff Head Miss Brenda A Philpott, in post for 6 years. 22 full time staff, 8 part time. Annual turnover 5–10%. Average age 35–40.

Academic work GCSE and A-levels. Average size of upper fifth 40; upper sixth 15. *O-levels*: on average, 7 pupils in upper fifth pass 1–4 subjects; 14, 5–7 subjects; 19 pass 8+ subjects. *A-levels*: on average, 2 pupils in the upper sixth pass 1 subject; 4, 2 subjects; 8, 3 subjects; 1 passes 4 subjects. On average, 6 take science/engineering A-levels; 5 take arts and humanities; 4, a mixture. Theatre arts are offered to GCSE and A-level. *Computing facilities*: 11 Stations BBC computers linked with PRESTEL. Provision for mild dyslexia and EFL.

Senior pupils' non-academic activities *Music*: 120+ learn a musical instrument, 6 up to Grade 6 or above; 40 in school orchestra, 120 in choir, all in biennial house competitions. *Drama and dance*: 75 in school productions, all in biennial house drama competitions. 10 take Grade 6 in ESB, RAD etc. 1 accepted for Drama/Dance Schools, 1 works in the theatre. *Art*: 5–10 take as non-examined subject; 15–20 take GCSE; 4 A-level. 1 or 2 accepted for Art School. *Sport*: Hockey, netball, badminton, squash, rounders, tennis, swimming, sailing, windsurfing and judo available. 20 take non-compulsory sport. 60+ take exams. 2/4 represent county/country (hockey, netball). *Other*: Many take part in local community schemes. 30 have bronze Duke of Edinburgh's Award, 6 have silver and 2 gold. Other activities include a computer club, public speaking, debating and driving lessons.

Careers 1 full time advisor. Average number of pupils accepted for *arts and humanities degree courses* at universities, 3; polytechnics or CHE, 2. *science and engineering degree courses* at Oxbridge, 1; other universities, 4; medical schools, 1; polytechnics or CHE, 2. *other general training courses*, 3. Average number of pupils going straight into careers in the armed services, 1; music/drama, 1.

Uniform School uniform worn throughout.

Houses/prefects Competitive houses. Prefects, head girl, head of house and house prefects – elected by the Head, staff and sixth formers. School Council.

Religion Morning assembly and compulsory Sunday service.

Social Debates, informal talks, matches etc with other local schools. Trips to France. Day girls allowed to bring own car/bike/motorbike to school. Formal lunch and breakfast, self service supper. School shop. No tobacco/alcohol allowed.

Discipline No corporal punishment. Pupils failing to produce homework

once might expect to do it later; those caught smoking cannabis on the premises might expect expulsion.

Boarding All sixth formers have own study bedroom, 2–4 share with others. Houses, of approximately 28–48, divided by age. Resident qualified nurse. Central dining room. Sixth form can provide and cook own food. 2-night exeats each term. Visits to local town allowed.

Alumni association is run by Mrs Margaret Ward-Booth, 22 Winchester Gardens, Andover, Hampshire.

UPPINGHAM

Uppingham School
Uppingham
Rutland LE15 9QE
Telephone number 0572 822216

Enquiries/application to the Headmaster

Co-ed
● Boys
Girls
● Mixed sixth
Day
● Boarding

Pupils 680
Upper sixth 160
Termly fees:
Boarding £2300
HMC

WHAT IT'S LIKE

Founded in 1584 by Robert Johnson, it lies in the centre of the small and attractive market town of Uppingham. The town itself is a conservation area and many of the school buildings are listed. The buildings and playing fields (of which there are 56 acres) spread right across the town, providing a close 'town and gown' relationship. The original 16th century school room is now the art school. There are many well-designed modern buildings and not a few from the period of the great 19th century headmaster, Edward Thring, who provided a variety of musical, sporting and practical activities then virtually unknown in comparable schools. It is a C of E foundation and worship in the Anglican tradition is compulsory. A large staff allows a staff:pupil ratio of 1:9. The standards of teaching are high and academic results are very good. Some 85–90 leavers go on to university each year. There is much musical activity involving about half the school. Among the many excellent modern facilities is a theatre where many dramatic presentations are staged. The school has long had a high reputation for its achievements in sport and games, and there is a very active CCF. A wide range of extra-curricular activities is available. The community service unit is one of the largest in the country.

SCHOOL PROFILE

Pupils Total over 12, 680 (boys 600, girls 80). Entry age, boys, 13; boys and girls, into the sixth. 17% are children of former pupils.

Entrance Common entrance used. Not heavily oversubscribed. No special skills required. C of E foundation, others accepted. Parents expected to buy some sixth form text books. At least 12 scholarships/bursaries, ⅔ to ¹⁄₁₀ fees.

Parents 20+% are doctors, lawyers, etc; 25+% in industry or commerce; 30+% in agriculture and related activities. 10+% live within 30 miles; up to 10% live overseas.

Staff Head N R Bomford, in post for 6 years. 75 full time staff. Annual turnover 5%. Average age 41.

Academic work GCSE and A-levels. Average size of upper fifth 120; upper sixth 160. *O-levels*: most pass over 5. *A-levels*: most pass at least 3. On average, 35+% take science/engineering A-levels; 35+% take arts and humanities; the remainder take a mixture. *Computing facilities*: A computer centre and computers in other departments. Limited help for dyslexics.

Senior pupils' non-academic activities *Music*: 50% learn a musical instrument, 30% up to Grade 6 or above; 100 in school orchestra, 40 in choir, 200+ in concert choir. Number of Oxbridge organ and choral awards (5 in 1987). *Drama and dance*: 120 in last major production. *Art*: 20 take GCSE; 10 A-level. Some accepted for foundation courses. *Sport*: Most sports available other than rowing. *Other*: Some pupils take part in local community schemes. Computer centre open most hours of the day; CCF, debating etc.

Careers 3 part time advisors (higher education and industrial consultant). Average number of pupils accepted for *arts and humanities degree courses* at Oxbridge, 10; other universities, 33; polytechnics or CHE, 12. *science and engineering degree courses* at Oxbridge, 10; other universities, 32; medical schools, 3 or 4; polytechnics or CHE, 13. *other general training courses*, 10. Average number of pupils going straight into careers in the armed services, 6; other, 10–15.

Uniform School uniform worn throughout.

Houses/prefects Residential houses. Prefects, head boy/girl, head of house and house prefects – appointed by Headmaster or housemaster.

Religion Attendance at chapel compulsory.

Social French exchange. Meals formal. School shop. No tobacco allowed, occasional bar for upper sixth.

Discipline No corporal punishment.

Boarding 14 houses, of approximately 50 (13–18), are single-sex. Resident qualified nurse. Limited exeats. Visits to local town allowed.

Alumni association is run by W M Bussey Esq, c/o the School.

URSULINE HIGH

Ilford Ursuline High School	Co-ed	Pupils 420
Morland Road	Boys	Upper sixth Yes
Ilford	● Girls	Termly fees:
Essex IG1 4QS	Mixed sixth	Day £720
Telephone number 01-554 1995	● Day	GSA; GBGSA
	Boarding	

Head Miss Penelope Dixon (4 years)
Age range 11–18; entry by own exam.
2 scholarships and 25 assisted places pa, also bursaries.

VICTORIA COLLEGE (BELFAST)

Victoria College
Cranmore Park
Belfast BT9 6JA
Telephone number 0232 661506

Enquiries/application to the Headmistress

Co-ed
Boys
● Girls
Mixed sixth
● Day
● Boarding

Pupils 743
Upper sixth 80
Termly fees:
Day £410
Boarding £1070

WHAT IT'S LIKE

Founded in 1859 by Mrs Margaret Byers, it is one of the longest established girls' schools in the British Isles. Since 1972 it has occupied its present site at Cranmore Park in beautiful grounds in a secluded and quiet residential area in south Belfast, a very pleasant environment. The school operates on two campuses 4 minutes' walk apart. The purpose-built buildings are modern and compact and very well equipped. Drumglass House, an elegant Georgian building, is the boarding establishment. There are excellent sports and games facilities in the grounds. A non-denominational school, it works a selective system and academic standards are high. Results are impressive and 60–70% go on to university each year in Great Britain and Northern Ireland. Strong in music, less strong in drama. A very good range of sports and games (a large number of county and national representatives) and an equally good range of extra-curricular activities. There is a big commitment to local community services. The college has a phenomenal record in the Duke of Edinburgh's Award Scheme: probably without equal in any British boys' or girls' school.

SCHOOL PROFILE

Pupils Total over 12, 743. Day 685; Boarding 58. Entry age, 4, 11 and into the sixth. 30% are children of former pupils.

Entrance Oversubscribed. No special skills or religious requirements. Parents not expected to buy text books. 2 scholarships for boarders, up to £300. Non-fee-paying status for pupils who satisfy residential qualification and pass selection tests.

Parents 15+% are doctors, lawyers etc; 15+% in industry or commerce. 60+% live within 30 miles; up to 10% live overseas.

Staff Head Mrs B M Berner, in post for 12 years. 54 full time staff, 14 part time. Annual turnover 4%. Average age 37.

Academic work GCSE and A-levels. Average size of upper fifth 100; upper sixth 80. *O-levels*: 7 pupils in upper fifth pass 1–4 subjects; 17, 5–7 subjects; 91 pass 8+ subjects. *A-levels*: 3 pupils in the upper sixth pass 1 subject; 6, 2 subjects; 66, 3 subjects and 4 pass 4 subjects. 40% took science/engineering A-levels; 45% took arts and humanities; 15% a mixture. Italian offered to GCSE/A-level. *Computing facilities*: 5–6 machines in each of 2 computer rooms; network to be installed in new library and resource centre. Provision for EFL.

Senior pupils' non-academic activities *Music*: 120 learn a musical instrument, 30 to Grade 6 or above, 20 accepted for Music School. 30 in school orchestra, 60 in choir. *Drama and dance*: 14 in school productions, 12 in other. 20 work in the field. *Art*: 35 took GCSE (1988), 3 A-level. 3 accepted for

Art School, 5 for degree courses in history/appreciation of art, conservation, architecture. *Sport*: Hockey, tennis, athletics, netball, fencing, gymnastics, trampolining, swimming and life-saving, squash, badminton, dance, keep fit available. 240 take non-compulsory sport; 30 take exams. 11 represent county/country (hockey, tennis, fencing, squash, athletics, table tennis). *Other*: 60 take part in local community schemes. 85 have bronze Duke of Edinburgh's Award, 60 have silver and 60 gold. Other activities include computer club, social services group, peace and reconciliation movement, Guides, traffic education, driving lessons.

Careers 3 part time advisors (staff), 1 local officer. Average number of pupils accepted for *arts and humanities degree courses* at Oxbridge, 2; other universities, 27; polytechnics or CHE, 6. *science and engineering degree courses* at Oxbridge, 1; other universities, 27. *BEd*, 3. *other general training courses*, 4. Average number of pupils going straight into careers in armed services, 2; industry, 1; other, 5. Medicine, law and sciences most popular careers.

Uniform School uniform worn throughout.

Houses/prefects Competitive houses. No prefects. Head girl and head of house – elected by sixth form, confirmed by staff. School Council.

Religion Compulsory non-denominational assembly unless parents request otherwise.

Social Sport, debates, conferences, quizzes, lectures, concerts, plays with other schools. Some organised trips abroad. Meals formal in boarding house, self service in school dining hall. Tuckshops on each campus. No tobacco/alcohol allowed.

Discipline No corporal punishment. Pupils failing to produce homework once might expect a warning and to produce work next day; those caught smoking cannabis on the premises might expect warning of dangers, counselling and contact with parents.

Boarding 40% have own cubicle, 30% are in dormitories of 6+. 1 boarding house. Resident qualified medical staff. Central dining room. Pupils can provide and cook own food in small groups. Fortnightly exeats. Visits to local town allowed when local conditions permit including theatre and cultural events; seniors indirectly supervised at weekends; juniors supervised.

Alumni association run by Hon Secretary, 1 Malone View Avenue, Belfast 9.

Former pupils A few local TV personalities.

VICTORIA COLLEGE (JERSEY)

Victoria College	Co-ed	Pupils 492
St Helier	● Boys	Upper sixth 64
Jersey	Girls	Termly fees:
Channel Islands	Mixed sixth	Day £356
Telephone number 0534 37591	● Day	sixth free
Enquiries/application to the Headmaster	● Boarding	Boarding £1665
		HMC

WHAT IT'S LIKE

Founded in 1852 it has an impressive site on a spur overlooking the town of St Helier with fine views over the bay to the south. There are parkland, gardens and playing fields. The original Victorian buildings (including the Great Hall) are still used, and there have been numerous modern additions. The prep school (in new buildings) was opened in 1966 and this is sited at the south end of the College lawn. A well-run school it has high academic standards and gets good results. About 20–25 pupils go on to university each year. Strong in drama and art. A wide variety of sports and games is available and high standards are achieved (quite a lot of representatives at county and national level). The College has a flourishing CCF and a large number of pupils take part in a wide range of activities. A good record in the Duke of Edinburgh's Award Scheme.

SCHOOL PROFILE

Pupils Total over 12, 492. Day 465; Boarding 27. Entry age, 11 and into the sixth. Own prep provides over 60%. 25% are children of former pupils.

Entrance Common entrance and own exam used. Not oversubscribed. No special skills or religious requirements. Parents not expected to buy text books. 5 scholarships/bursaries pa, up to full day fees.

Parents 15+% are doctors, lawyers etc; 15+% in industry or commerce; 15+% in finance. 60+% live within 30 miles; up to 10% live overseas.

Staff Head M H Devenport, in post for 20 years. 43 full time staff, 5 part time. Annual turnover 7%. Average age 41.

Academic work GCSE and A-levels. Average size of upper fifth 90; upper sixth 64. *O-levels*: on average, 12 pupils in upper fifth pass 1–4 subjects; 24, 5–7 subjects; 54 pass 8+ subjects. *A-levels*: on average, 12 pupils in the upper sixth pass 1 subject; 15, 2 subjects; 28, 3 subjects and 5 pass 4 subjects. On average, 23 take science/engineering A-levels; 22 take arts and humanities; 19 a mixture. *Computing facilities*: Laboratory and machines in all major departments. Provision for EFL.

Senior pupils' non-academic activities *Music*: 26 learn a musical instrument, 14 to Grade 6 or above; 19 in school orchestra, 15 choir, 4 brass ensemble, 5 string quintet; 15 in Jersey Youth Orchestra, 8 Jersey Youth Wind Band; 6 go on to play in pop group. *Drama and dance*: 30 in school productions; 80 in house plays. 1 now works in theatre. *Art*: 10 take as non-examined subject; 49 take GCSE; 18 A-level. 6 accepted for Art School; 2 for other art courses. 10 belong to eg photographic club. *Sport*: Soccer, rugby, squash, shooting, athletics, cross-country, hockey, sailing, cricket, swimming, golf, tennis, basketball, fives, fencing, karate, archery, badminton available. 175 take non-compulsory sport. 25 take exams. 11 represent county/country (rugby, squash, hockey, cricket, shooting). *Other*: 50 take part in local community schemes. 30 have silver Duke of Edinburgh's Award. Some work for national charities after leaving. Other activities include computer club, chess, CCF, marine biology.

Careers 2 part time advisors on staff, one Jersey State advisor available. Average number of pupils accepted for *arts and humanities degree courses* at Oxbridge, 1; other universities, 12; polytechnics or CHE, 13. *science and engineering degree courses* at Oxbridge, 2; other universities, 6; medical schools, 3; polytechnics or CHE, 4. *other general training courses*, 7. Average number of pupils going straight into careers in armed services, 3; industry, 2; local finance, 16; local civil service, 2.

Uniform School uniform worn throughout.

Houses/prefects Competitive houses. Prefects, head boy, head of house and house prefects – appointed by senior staff with pupils' advice. School Council.

Religion Daily Christian assembly; parents may request withdrawal.

Social Debating contests with local schools; Jersey Youth Orchestra and Theatre, local Eisteddfod; annual dramatic production with Girls' College. Regular French exchanges. Pupils allowed to bring own car/bike/motorbike to school. Meals formal for boarders, self service for day pupils. School shops sell tuck, 2nd hand uniform. No tobacco/alcohol allowed.

Discipline No corporal punishment. Pupils failing to produce homework once might expect extra work; those caught smoking cannabis on the premises might expect suspension or expulsion.

Boarding One-third have own study bedroom, remainder in dormitories of less than 6. Houses divided by age. Resident qualified matron, doctor on call. Central dining room. Seniors can provide and cook own snacks. Exeats any weekend. Visits to local town allowed for 15+.

Alumni association run by Dr Jonathan Osmont, Florence House, 39 Cleveland Road, St Helier, Jersey CI.

Former pupils Kenneth More; Air Vice Marshal Alcock; Ambassadors Sir Martin Le Quesne and Sir Arthur De La Mare; Sir William Haley (former Editor, *The Times*); Sir Peter Crill (Bailiff of Jersey).

WADHURST

Wadhurst College	Co-ed	Pupils 230
Wadhurst	Boys	Upper sixth Yes
East Sussex TN5 6JA	● Girls	Termly fees:
Telephone number 089 288 3193	Mixed sixth	Day £1070
	● Day	Boarding £1800
	● Boarding	GSA; GBGSA

Head Miss D Swatman (16 years)

Age range 9–18; entry by own exam and common entrance.

Scholarships (including for music and science) and bursaries (daughters of the clergy or missionaries). Special provision for limited number of dyslexic pupils.

WAKEFIELD HIGH

Wakefield Girls' High School
Wentworth Street
Wakefield
West Yorkshire WF1 2QS
Telephone number 0924 372490

Co-ed   Pupils 750
Boys   Upper sixth Yes
● Girls   Termly fees:
Mixed sixth   Day £710
● Day   GSA; GBGSA
Boarding

Head Mrs P A Langham (1 year)
Age range 11–18; own prep from age 4; entry by own exam including for
pupils at own prep.
Bursaries and assisted places.
Joint activities with Queen Elizabeth Grammar (Boys).

WARMINSTER

Warminster School
Warminster
Wiltshire BA12 8PJ
Telephone number 0985 21208/213358

Enquiries/application to The Master

● Co-ed   Pupils 307
Boys   Upper sixth 40
Girls   Termly fees:
Mixed sixth   Day £1065
● Day   Boarding £1775
● Boarding   SHMIS; IAPS

WHAT IT'S LIKE

Founded in 1707, it has a semi-rural site on the edge of the very attractive old
town and facing open country. It was formed in 1973 by the amalgamation of
the Lord Weymouth School (formed in 1707) and the school of St Monica
(founded in 1874). Its handsome and well-equipped buildings lie in beautiful
gardens and grounds. The school has long-established and close links with
the town and the locality where it enjoys strong support. The junior school is
combined on a neighbouring site. Thus continuous education is available
from age 5. Warminster is a small friendly school whose declared aim is to
develop the potential and recognise the value of all pupils. A large staff
allows a staff:pupil ratio of 1:8. Academic standards are high and results
good. About 30–35 leavers go on to university each year. More than half the
school are involved in music and about 85 pupils learn an instrument. A
similar number are engaged in dramatic activities and there is an unusually
strong art dept. A high reputation in sport and games (a large number of
representatives at county level). A big CCF contingent, a wide variety of
extra-curricular activities, a substantial commitment to local community
schemes and an outstanding record in the Duke of Edinburgh's Award
Scheme.

SCHOOL PROFILE

Pupils Total over 12, 307. Day 87 (boys 50, girls 37); Boarding 220 (boys 115,
girls 105). Entry age, 8, 11, 13 and into the sixth. Own junior school provides
over 50%. 10% are children of former pupils.

Entrance Common entrance and own entrance exam used. Oversubscribed. No special skills or religious requirements. Parents not expected to buy text books. 20 scholarships/bursaries for sixth formers, £1775 to £200 per term.

Parents 15+% in Armed Services; 12+% in industry or commerce. 10+% live within 30 miles; 10+% live overseas.

Staff Head D M Green, in post for 4 years. 43 full time staff, 4 part time. Annual turnover 8%. Average age 34.

Academic work GCSE and A-levels. Average size of upper fifth 60; upper sixth 40. *O-levels*: on average, 12 pupils in upper fifth pass 1–4 subjects; 30, 5–7 subjects; 18 pass 8+ subjects. *A-levels*: on average, 5 pupils in the upper sixth pass 1 subject; 12, 2 subjects; 21 pass 3 subjects. On average, 18 take science/engineering A-levels; 13 take arts and humanities; 8 take a mixture. Environmental studies are offered to GCSE/A-level. *Computing facilities*: A new computer centre, computers and word processors in most departments. Dyslexic Unit staffed by specialised teachers (for about 10% of pupils).

Senior pupils' non-academic activities *Music*: 85 learn a musical instrument, 12 up to Grade 6 or above, 2 accepted for Music School; 40 in school orchestra, 30 in choir, 10 in pop group. 4 go on to play pop. *Drama and dance*: 180 in school productions. 10 to Grade 6 in ESB, RAD etc. 1 accepted for Drama/Dance Schools, 2 go on to work in the theatre. *Art*: 280 take as non-examined subject; 36 take GCSE; 10 A-level. 5 accepted for Art School. 20 belong to photographic club. *Sport*: Football, cricket, hockey, netball, athletics, cross-country, basketball, squash, volleyball, fives, golf, riding available. 250 take non-compulsory sport. 20 take exams. 25 represent county/country (hockey, football, athletics, cross-country, basketball, squash). *Other*: 20 take part in local community schemes. 45 have bronze Duke of Edinburgh's Award, 30 have silver and 12 gold, 120+ in CCF. 5 enter voluntary schemes after leaving school. Other activities include a computer club, driving lessons, over 40 different clubs and societies.

Careers 1 full time (visiting) and 3 part time advisors. Average number of pupils accepted for *arts and humanities degree courses* at Oxbridge, 1; other universities, 4; polytechnics or CHE, 4. *science and engineering degree courses* at other universities, 6; medical schools, 1; polytechnics or CHE, 3. *BEd*, 1. *other general training courses*, 20. Average number of pupils going straight into careers in the armed services, 4; the church, 1; industry, 3; the City, 1; civil service, 1; music/drama, 1.

Uniform School uniform worn except the sixth.

Houses/prefects Competitive houses. Prefects, head boy and girl, head of house and house prefects – appointed by the Head or house staff. School Council.

Religion Daily assembly and Sunday morning chapel.

Social Drama, debates, social service, mini-Enterprise. Annual exchanges with schools in France, Germany and Spain, ski-ing. Pupils allowed to bring own car/bike to school. Some meals formal, some self service. School shop. No tobacco/alcohol allowed.

Discipline No corporal punishment. Pupils failing to produce homework once might expect detention; those caught smoking cannabis on the premises might expect expulsion.

Boarding Sixth and fifth forms have own study bedroom, 5% are in dormitories of 6 or more. Houses, of approximately 35–50, are divided by age and are single-sex. Resident qualified medical staff. Central dining room. Pupils can provide and cook own food. Exeats at half term and any weekend. Visits to local town allowed.

Alumni association is run by Mr G C Straughan, Mead Cottage, The Ley, Box, Corsham, Wiltshire.

Former pupils F Jaeger, C J Benjamin, E J Baddeley (actors); Ian Macdonald (racing driver); Thomas Arnold (headmaster).

WARWICK

Warwick School	Co-ed Pupils 700
Myton Road	● Boys Upper sixth 100
Warwick CV34 6PP	Girls Termly fees:
Telephone number 0926 492484	Mixed sixth Day £840
	● Day Boarding £1705
Enquiries/application to the Headmaster	● Boarding HMC

WHAT IT'S LIKE

Founded in c914 in the reign of Edward the Confessor (the putative patron), it occupied its present site, on the banks of the Avon south of the town, in 1879. The main building is an arresting example of the rococo Tudor style and other buildings have developed round it in an E-shaped pattern. There are several impressive Victorian buildings and a variety of much more recent ones. In the last 10 years about a million pounds have been spent on improved boarding and academic facilities. All these are now first-rate. Large playing fields lie alongside. A C of E foundation, in which attendance at chapel is compulsory with considerable emphasis on religious education. There are longstanding and very close associations between the school and the town and there is vigorous local support. Academic standards and achievements are of a high order: some 55–60 leavers go on to university each year. The music, drama and art departments are very strong. The school boasts a remarkable number of clubs and societies (50 in all) which cater for almost every conceivable need. There is an excellent range of sports and games (about 800 pupils are involved in these) and high standards are attained (20 or more representatives at county level). Another notable feature is the substantial commitment to local community schemes.

SCHOOL PROFILE

Pupils Total over 12, 700. Day 650; Boarding 50. Entry age, 7, 8, 11, 13 and into the sixth. Warwick Preparatory School provides over 20%.

Entrance Own entrance exam used. Oversubscribed. No special skills or religious requirements. Parents not expected to buy text books. 160 assisted places. 80 scholarships, bursaries for tuition or boarding fees and choral scholarships, £400–£120.

Parents 15+% in industry or commerce. 60+% live within 30 miles; up to 10% live overseas.

Staff Head J A Strover. 67 full time staff, 7 part time. Annual turnover 2%. Average age 40.

Academic work GCSE and A-levels. Average size of upper fifth 130; upper

sixth 100. *O-levels*: on average, 30 pupils in upper fifth pass 1–4 subjects; 40, 5–7 subjects; 60 pass 8+ subjects. *A-levels*: on average, 5 pupils in upper sixth pass 2 subjects; 30, 3 subjects and 65 pass 4 subjects. On average, 40 take science/engineering A-levels; 40 take arts and humanities; 20 a mixture. *Computing facilities*: Computer laboratory with 16 BBCs; most departments have their own computer. Special English class for overseas boys.

Senior pupils' non-academic activities *Music*: 50 learn a musical instrument, 25 to Grade 6 or above, 1 accepted for University Music Course; 25 in school orchestra, 50 in choir, 5+ in pop group, 10 in madrigal group; 4 in local orchestra, 4 in local madrigal group; 3 in orchestra, choir, madrigal group beyond school. *Drama and dance*: 40 in school productions; 10 in others. *Art*: 36 take as non-examined subject; 45 take GCSE; 10 A-level. 3 accepted for Art School, 3 for architecture. Art club/airbrush club available for all boys; art appreciation in general studies programme as option for all sixth form. *Sport*: Rugby, hockey, cricket, football, tennis, cross-country, squash, badminton, basketball, fencing, judo, aikido, archery, shooting, canoeing, sailing, athletics available. Most take non-compulsory sport. 20 represent county (rugby, cricket, hockey, swimming, tennis). *Other*: 130 take part in local community schemes. 200 in CCF. Other activities include 50 different societies eg chess, a computer club, debating, music, drama, photographic, media studies, bee-keeping, horticulture.

Careers 5 part time careers advisors. Average number of pupils accepted for *arts and humanities degree courses* at Oxbridge, 8; other universities, 19; polytechnics or CHE, 10. *science and engineering degree courses* at Oxbridge, 7; other universities, 22; medical schools, 6; polytechnics or CHE, 5. *BEd*, 1. *other general training courses*, 13. Average number of pupils going straight into careers in the armed services, 2; industry, 2; the City, 2; music/drama, 1; other, 5. Traditional school careers are engineering, medicine, law.

Uniform School uniform worn, modified in the sixth.

Houses/prefects 6 competitive houses. Prefects and boarding house prefects – elected; head boy appointed. School Council.

Religion Compulsory Chapel.

Social Joint concert with King's High School for Girls; also joint plays and society meetings. Organised trips to Canada, USA, Germany, France. Pupils allowed to bring own car/bicycle/motorbike to school. Meals self service. School shop. No tobacco/alcohol allowed.

Discipline No corporal punishment. Pupils failing to produce homework could expect detention; those caught smoking cannabis on the premises could expect expulsion.

Boarding 10% have own study bedroom, most of the rest share with one other; youngest in dormitories of 4–6. Houses, of approximately 55–20 are divided by age. No resident medical staff. Central dining room. Sixth formers can provide and cook own food. 2 weekend exeats each term, plus half term. Visits to the local town allowed daily from the age of 13.

Alumni association is run by Mr P E Bailey, Secretary, Old Warwickian Association, 24 Park Road, Leamington Spa, Warwickshire.

WELLINGBOROUGH

The School	• Co-ed	Pupils 413
Wellingborough	Boys	Upper sixth 62
Northamptonshire NN8 2BX	Girls	Termly fees:
Telephone number 0933 222427	Mixed sixth	Day £1136
Enquiries/application to the Headmaster	• Day	Boarding £1857
	• Boarding	HMC

WHAT IT'S LIKE

Founded in 1595, it occupied its present site in 1881. This is an attractive, compact campus (on the south side of the town) with pleasant buildings, lovely gardens and ample playing fields (about 50 acres in all). There have been many developments in the last 20 years and the school has first-rate facilities. Chapel services and teaching are in accordance with the principles of the Church of England. A well-run school, it provides a sound general education with good academic results. About 30 pupils go on to university each year. Music, drama and art are regarded as particularly important disciplines and activities; music is especially strong. An excellent range of sports and games in which high standards are achieved (a lot of representatives at county and national level). There is also a good variety of extra-curricular activities. Some commitment to local community services and a promising record in the Duke of Edinburgh's Award Scheme.

SCHOOL PROFILE

Pupils Total, 413. Day 338 (boys 247, girls 91); Boarding 75 (boys 58, girls 17). Entry age, 13 and into the sixth. Own junior school provides 65%. 8% are children of former pupils.

Entrance Common entrance and own entrance tests used. Oversubscribed. All skills welcomed; Christian environment (C of E, chapel services). Parents expected to buy sixth form text books. 60 assisted places. 12 scholarships/bursaries (including sport), one-sixth to full fees.

Parents 15+% are doctors, lawyers etc; 15+% in industry or commerce. 60+% live within 30 miles; up to 10% live overseas.

Staff Head G Garrett, in post for 15 years. 34 full time staff, 8 part time. Annual turnover 10%. Average age 40.

Academic work GCSE and A-levels. Average size of upper fifth 90; upper sixth 62. *O-levels*: on average, 20 pupils in upper fifth pass 1–4 subjects; 30, 5–7 subjects; 40 pass 8+ subjects. *A-levels*: on average, 5 pupils in the upper sixth pass 1 subject; 8, 2 subjects; 14, 3 subjects and 32 pass 4 subjects. On average, 24 take science/engineering A-levels; 24 take arts and humanities; 14 a mixture. *Computing facilities*: Network with 2 rooms, file server, 12 BBC Masters and 12 BBC B machines. Provision for mild dyslexia and EFL.

Senior pupils' non-academic activities *Music*: 46 learn a musical instrument, 19 to Grade 6 or above, occasional acceptance for Music School, pop group or university; 22 in school orchestra, 4 in choir, 18 wind band; 2 in National Youth Orchestra, 12 in county bands and orchestras. *Drama and dance*: Annual play/musical, house drama festival, public-speaking competition. *Art*: 10–12 take as non-examined subject; 28 take GCSE art/ceramics; 8 take A-level. 2–3 accepted for Art School. *Sport*: Football, cross-country, hockey (girls), netball, tennis, rounders, rugby, cricket, swimming, shooting, badminton, athletics (track and field), basketball, volleyball, fencing, weight training, riding, golf (own 9-hole course) available. 280 take non-compulsory sport. 21 represent county (girls' hockey, badminton, athletics; jogging, cricket, tennis, cross-country, athletics, table tennis); 1 represents country (table tennis). *Other*: 80 currently involved in Duke of Edinburgh's Award Scheme, 16 have bronze, 5 have silver and 1 gold. Other activities include computer club, driving lessons (in town), debating, chess.

Careers 1 part time careers advisor, house masters/mistresses also assist. Average number of pupils accepted for *arts and humanities degree courses* at Oxbridge, 3; other universities, 12; polytechnics or CHE, 3. *science and engineering degree courses* at Oxbridge, 2; other universities, 12; medical schools, 3; polytechnics or CHE, 2. *BEd*, 2. *other general training courses*, 2–3. Average number of pupils going straight into careers in armed services, 2–3; the church, 1 occasionally; industry, 6; civil service, 3; others (GAP etc), 12.

Uniform School uniform worn throughout.

Houses/prefects 9 competitive houses (3 boarding, 6 day). Prefects, head boy/girl, head of house and house prefects – appointed by Head after consultation.

Religion Compulsory morning chapel service (C of E).

Social Sporting and cultural competitions with local schools. French visits (guardian scheme), exchange through Dragons International, German exchange (Anna-Schmidt Schule, Frankfurt), 2 annual ski-ing parties; trekking (Himalayas) alternate years. Lunch formal, others self service. School shop. No tobacco allowed; beer/cider only in licensed sixth form club.

Discipline No corporal punishment. Pupils failing to produce homework once might expect to do it for next morning, detention for repeated offence; those caught smoking cigarettes on the premises can expect parents to be contacted and possible expulsion, depending on circumstances.

Boarding 10% (upper sixth) have own study bedroom, 10% (girls) share with 1 other, 80% are in dormitories of 6+. 3 boarding houses, of approximately 30 boys, 20 girls, same as competitive houses and single sex. Qualified nurse resident when required; doctor visits 3 times/week. Central dining room. Pupils can provide and cook own food in limited facilities. 2 termly exeats, Saturday afternoon to Sunday evening. Visits to local town allowed from 13 (after lunch or before 6.15).

Alumni association run by Mr R W S Burrell, c/o the School.

Former pupils David Wilson-Johnson (baritone); Ray Whitney MP; General Sir Peter Hudson (formerly Deputy C-in-C, UK Land Forces); Richard Coles (Communards pop singer).

WELLINGTON COLLEGE

Wellington College
Crowthorne
Berkshire RG11 7PU
Telephone number 0344 772261

Enquiries/application to the Registrar

Co-ed
● Boys
Girls
● Mixed sixth
● Day
● Boarding

Pupils 818
Upper sixth 165
Termly fees:
Day £1570
Boarding £2160
HMC

WHAT IT'S LIKE

Founded in 1853, by public subscription in memory of the Duke, granted a royal charter in that year. The monarch is the Visitor and appointments of governors and changes in statutes are approved by Buckingham Palace. By 1872 it had become a major public school. Its original grand and imposing buildings were designed by Shaw who, with remarkable foresight, provided each pupil with a bed-sitting room. Its chapel was designed by Gilbert Scott. Many additional buildings now provide excellent accommodation and facilities. The college lies in an estate of 400 acres and has fine gardens and superb playing fields. The prep school has its own grounds nearby. The spiritual and religious life of the college is of considerable importance and pupils are encouraged to commit themselves fully as Christians. High standards of teaching prevail and academic results are first rate. Some 95–100 leavers go on to university each year. The music dept is immensely strong (orchestras, choirs, 10 bands, and 370–400 pupils learn an instrument). Very strong, too, in drama (9–12 productions per year, plus visits by professional companies), and also in art. The college has a high reputation in games and sports of which a wide variety is provided. There are many clubs, societies and extra-curricular activities. The CCF is a big contingent and the college maintains its traditional links with the army (many Wellingtonians have been distinguished soldiers). There is a major commitment to local community schemes, involving some 300 pupils, a higher proportion than almost any other school.

SCHOOL PROFILE

Pupils Total 818. Day 122 (boys 114, girls 8); Boarding 696 (boys 655, girls 41). Entry age, boys, 13; boys and girls into the sixth. 16% are children of former pupils.
Entrance Common entrance used. Oversubscribed. No special skills or religious requirements. Parents expected to buy text books in the sixth form only. 34 assisted places. 11 scholarships/bursaries, ⅔ fees to £510.
Parents 15+% in the armed services; 15+% in industry or commerce. 30+% live within 30 miles; up to 10% live overseas.
Staff Head Dr D H Newsome, in post for 8 years. 82 full time staff, 5 part time. Annual turnover 4%. Average age 38.
Academic work GCSE and A-levels. Average size of upper fifth 170; upper sixth 165. *O-levels*: on average, 5 pupils in upper fifth pass 1–4 subjects; 25, 5–7 subjects; 130 pass 8+ subjects. *A-levels*: on average, 8 pupils in the upper sixth pass 1 subject; 15, 2 subjects; 117, 3 subjects; 22 pass 4 subjects. On average, 73 take science/engineering A-levels; 65 take arts and humanities; 24 take a mixture. Plans to offer Arabic to GCSE/A-level. *Computing*

729

facilities: Computer department with BBC microcomputers.. Provision for mildly dyslexic.

Senior pupils' non-academic activities   *Music*: 376 learn musical instruments, 50 up to Grade 6 or above, small number accepted for Music School; 50 in school orchestra, 65 in choir, 10 in bands. *Drama and dance*: 30+ in school productions. 6 take AEB A-/O-level. 2–4 accepted for Drama/Dance schools, 2–4 go into rep or alternative theatre. 12 take lighting course; 12, sound course; 18, general studies; 26 in theatre club. *Art*: 44 take as non-examined subject; 50 take GCSE; 53 A-level; 12, History of Art. 3 accepted for Art School, 4 for architectural courses. 15 belong to photographic club. *Sport*: Rugby, cricket, hockey, athletics, archery, basketball, fencing, cross-country running, fives, golf, karate, rackets, sailing, shooting, ski-ing, soccer, squash, sub-aqua, swimming, tennis available. Vast majority of pupils take non-compulsory sport. 3 represent county/country in hockey. *Other*: 300 take part in local community schemes. Other activities include a computer club, driving lessons, astronomy, bridge, chess, debating, natural history, opera, pottery, printing, travel/expeditions.

Careers 4 part time advisors. Average number of pupils accepted for *arts and humanities degree courses* at Oxbridge, 8; other universities, 55; polytechnics or CHE, 15. *science and engineering degree courses* at Oxbridge, 14; other universities, 18; medical schools, 3; polytechnics or CHE, 4. *other general training courses*, 10. Average number of pupils going straight into careers in the armed services, 15; the church, 1; industry, 8; the City, 12; civil service, 2; music/drama, 1; other, 15.

Uniform School uniform not worn.

Houses/prefects No competitive houses. Prefects, head boy and girl, head of house and house prefects – appointed by Headmaster and housemasters.

Religion Worship encouraged.

Social Local events include choral/orchestral events, debates and occasional dances. German exchanges, Chamber choir to France/Germany, Modern Language Department to Paris. Pupils allowed to bring own bike to school. Meals self service. School shop. No tobacco allowed but a junior common room for the sixth form.

Discipline No corporal punishment. Pupils failing to produce homework once might expect extra school or detention; those caught smoking cannabis on the premises might expect removal from the school.

Boarding All have own study bedroom. Houses, of approximately 55 for boys, 1 for the 50 girls. Resident Sister. School doctor visits daily. Central dining room. 2 week-end exeats each term plus half term. Visits to local town allowed with housemaster's permission.

Former pupils Too numerous to mention.

WELLINGTON (AYR)

Wellington School	Co-ed	Pupils 335
Carleton Turrets	Boys	Upper sixth 50
Craigweil Road	● Girls	Termly fees:
Ayr KA7 2XH	Mixed sixth	Day £730
Telephone number 0292 269321	● Day	Boarding £1545
	● Boarding	GSA; GBGSA
Enquiries/application to the Headmaster		

WHAT IT'S LIKE

Founded in 1849 to educate 'young ladies of quality' in French, history, music, art and embroidery. By 1900 it had a considerable reputation and had grown. In 1923 it moved to its present site Carleton Turrets, a split site, semi-rural, with all buildings within a few minutes' walk of each other. Ayr itself is a very attractive town, with two theatres and several museums, close to the sea. The school includes a junior department and a kindergarten. Good sporting facilities on site. A well-run school it has high academic standards and results are impressive. About 15–20 pupils go on to university each year. Strong in music and drama. There is a vigorous sporting tradition with a large number of representatives at national and county level (especially hockey). There is also a strong careers department and a DTI/IOD Work Shadowing Scheme for 17 year olds. A wide range of extra-curricular activities is available. An impressive record in the Duke of Edinburgh's Award Scheme (60 girls).

SCHOOL PROFILE

Pupils Total over 12, 335. Day 270; Boarding 65. Entry age, 3, 10, 12 and into the sixth. 20% are children of former pupils.

Entrance Common entrance and/or own entrance exam used. Usually over-subscribed. Ability in English, maths, music and sport looked for; no religious requirements. Parents expected to buy some text books (most covered by small hire charge). 40 assisted places. Bursaries for senior boarders, variable value.

Parents 15+% in armed services; 15+% are doctors, lawyers etc; 15+% in industry or commerce; 15+% are teachers. 60+% live within 30 miles; 10+% live overseas.

Staff Head A J Grigg, in post for 5 years. 47 full time staff, 17 part time. Annual turnover 4–5%. Average age 35.

Academic work O-grades, Highers, CSYS; O- and A-levels in special cases. Average size of upper fifth 66; upper sixth 50 (sixth form of 95). *O-grades*: on average, 12 pupils pass 1–4 subjects; 41, 5–7 subjects; 9 pass 8+ subjects. *Highers*: on average, 6 pupils pass 1 subject; 18, 2–3 subjects; 15 pass 4 subjects; 9 pass 5+ subjects. Spanish, Latin and Russian offered at Higher and CSYS levels. *Computing facilities*: 9 stand alone systems in computer room, 7 in departments; pupils may use machines under supervision at lunchtimes. Provision for dyslexia and EFL.

Senior pupils' non-academic activities *Music*: 43 learn a musical instrument, 10 to Grade 6 or above. 40 in school orchestra, 85 in choir; string quartet; 16 in recorder and madrigal groups. 1 in National Youth Orchestra, 3 in other orchestras. *Drama and dance*: 90 in school productions. 30 take

LAMDA Grade 6 or above; 3 accepted for Drama Schools; 50 take individual speech and drama (elocution). *Art*: 2 take as non-examined subject, 5 take Higher; art club. *Sport*: Hockey, netball, athletics, tennis, swimming, archery, badminton, golf, gymnastics, trampolining, squash, self-defence, riding, short tennis, skating, ski-ing available. 7 pupils represent county at sport, 5 represent country (hockey, swimming, judo, cross-country). *Other*: 50 have bronze Duke of Edinburgh's Award, 6 have silver and 2 gold. Other activities include chess, Girls' Venture Corps, debating, first aid, Scripture Union, ballroom dancing.

Careers 1 full time, 2 part time advisors. Average number of pupils accepted for *arts and humanities degree courses* at universities, 4; polytechnics or CHE, 5. *science and engineering degree courses* at Oxbridge, 1; other universities, 10; medical schools, 1; polytechnics or CHE, 4. *other general training courses*, 8. Average number of pupils going straight into careers in armed services, 2; civil service, 2; banking, 2.

Uniform School uniform worn throughout.

Houses/prefects Competitive houses. Prefects, head girl, head of house and house prefects – appointed by Head with staff advice. School Council.

Religion Daily assembly (Jews excepted), boarders attend Sunday church of their choice. Most attend Church of Scotland.

Social Debates, ESU, dances, trivial pursuit challenges, sport, music and drama festivals with other schools. Annual French school exchange, trips to Germany, Russia, ski-ing. Pupils allowed to bring own car/bike/motorbike to school. Meals self service with formal seating. School shop. No tobacco/alcohol allowed.

Discipline No corporal punishment. Pupils failing to produce homework once might expect verbal admonishment. Taking of drugs would result in instant expulsion.

Boarding Houses, of approximately 30–50, are divided by age. Central dining room. Sixth form can provide and cook own food. 2 exeats and half term each term plus 2 other weekends for sixth form. Visits to local town allowed Saturday morning, those under 16 accompanied.

Alumni association run by Mrs W Laughland.

Former pupils Dr Elizabeth Hewat (theologian and historian); Miss Elizabeth Kyle (author); Miss Kirsty Wark (presenter, BBC TV).

WELLINGTON (SOMERSET)

Wellington School	• Co-ed	Pupils 670
Wellington	Boys	Upper sixth 80
Somerset TA21 8NT	Girls	Termly fees:
Telephone 082 347 4511	Mixed sixth	Day £720
Enquiries/application to the Headmaster	• Day	Boarding £1350
	• Boarding	HMC

WHAT IT'S LIKE

The school first came into existence on its present site as a private school in 1837 and was refounded in 1879. In 1908 it was re-organised under the

Charitable Acts. It lies on the southern side of Wellington at the foot of the Blackdown Hills. It has pleasant well-equipped buildings in gardens and about 24 acres of playing fields. Academic standards are high and results good. About 45–50 leavers go on to university each year. Music and art are strong; drama very strong indeed with a great deal of activity involving large numbers of pupils. A big range of sports and games in which high standards are achieved (a large number of representatives at county and national level). Considerable commitment to local community schemes. A flourishing CCF and much emphasis on Outward Bound activities. A good record in the Duke of Edinburgh's Award Scheme.

SCHOOL PROFILE

Pupils Total over 12, 670. Day 418 (boys 219, girls 199); Boarding 252 (boys 168, girls 84). Entry age, 11+ and into the sixth.

Entrance Common entrance and own entrance exam used. No special skills or religious requirements. Parents not expected to buy text books. 40 assisted places (5 at sixth form). Some scholarships.

Parents 15+% come from Armed Services; 15+% are in industry or commerce. 30+% live within 30 miles; up to 10% live overseas.

Staff Head J MacG K Kendall-Carpenter, in post for 15 years. 52 full time staff, 5 part time. Annual turnover 4–5%. Average age 39.

Academic work GCSE and A-levels. Average size of upper fifth 160; upper sixth 80. *O-levels*: on average, 35 pupils in upper fifth pass 1–4 subjects; 36, 5–7 subjects; 76 pass 8+ subjects. *A-levels*: on average, 6 pupils in the upper sixth pass 1 subject; 12, 2 subjects; 50, 3 subjects and 12 pass 4 subjects. On average, 40 take science/engineering A-levels; 23 take arts and humanities; 22 a mixture. *Computing facilities*: purpose-built room with 25 BBC 2 Acorn computers, graph plotter and printers. Provision for EFL (JMB course) also individual tuition.

Senior pupils' non-academic activities *Music*: 53 learn a musical instrument, 24 to Grade 6 or above, 5 go on to play in pop group, 3 go on to further music courses. 19 in school orchestra, 10 in choir, 10 in ensembles (brass, woodwind), 2 in county youth orchestra. *Drama and dance*: 40 in school productions, 250+ in house play festival. 10 take to Grade 6 ESB, 5 Poetry Society exams, 20–30 in theatre workshops. *Art*: 2 take as non-examined subject, 66 take GCSE, 17 A-level. 2 accepted for Art School, 1 for university. 12 belong to photographic and 15 to art club. *Sport*: Rugby, hockey, cricket, athletics, cross-country, netball, rounders, swimming, badminton, squash, tennis available. Most take non-compulsory sport; some take life-saving exams. 30+ represent county/country (rugby, hockey, athletics, cross-country, netball). *Other*: 40 take part in local community schemes. 25 have bronze Duke of Edinburgh's Award, 15 have silver and 1 gold. 3 work for national charities. Other activities include computer club (open during free periods), folk band, corps of drums, literary society, dynamic chess club, others for film, natural history, modellers, ancient and modern linguists, railway, travel, war games and Young Farmers; CCF, adventure training, first aid, ecological conservation, horticulture, car maintenance, canoe construction and use.

Careers 1 full time and 2 part time advisors. Average number of pupils accepted for *arts and humanities degree courses* at Oxbridge, 2; other universities, 20; polytechnics or CHE, 6. *science and engineering degree courses* at

Oxbridge, 2; other universities, 25; medical schools, 2; polytechnics or CHE, 10. *other general training courses*, 18. Average number of pupils going straight into careers in armed services, 6; industry, 11; the City/finance, 5; civil service, 4; music/drama, 1; other, 42. Traditional school careers are engineering, industry.

Uniform School uniform worn throughout.

Houses/prefects Competitive houses. No prefects; school captains/vice captains appointed by Headmaster; house captains by housemasters.

Religion Daily chapel services; C of E worship encouraged; RI for all unless parents wish otherwise.

Social Public speaking competition with other schools. Exchanges with Lillebonne, France (town twinning) and Immenstadt. Day pupils allowed to bring own car/bike/motorbike to school; boarders, bike only. Meals self service. School tuckshop. No tobacco/alcohol allowed.

Discipline Corporal punishment used. Pupils failing to produce homework once might expect to produce it within 24 hours; those caught smoking cannabis on the premises might expect immediate suspension, subsequent expulsion.

Boarding Houses, of approximately 59, same as competitive houses and single sex. Resident qualified nurse, doctor on call. Central dining room. Pupils can provide and cook own food. Exeats of 24 hours at discretion of house staff. Visits to local town allowed after school.

Former pupils David Suchet (actor); Jeffrey Archer (author); Keith Floyd (gourmet/broadcaster); Brigadier Shelford Bidwell (military historian); Michael Green (ITN correspondent); Prof Ellis Baker (pharmacologist); Judges John Baker and David Williams; Kenneth Steele (former Chief Constable, Avon & Somerset).

WELLINGTON (WIRRAL)

Wellington School
Wellington Road
Bebington
Wirral L63 7NG
Telephone number 051 645 2332

Enquiries to the Headmaster
Application to the Secretary

- Co-ed   Pupils 300
- Boys   Upper sixth 14
- Girls   Termly fees:
- Mixed sixth   Day £635
- Day   ISAI
- Boarding

WHAT IT'S LIKE

Founded in 1953 by its former headmaster, it has an urban site in the Wirral. Pleasant buildings and about 4 acres of grounds and 15 acres of playing fields. It aims to provide a liberal education in the arts and sciences for boys and girls of average or above average ability, and to educate them in a Christian environment. There is a staff:pupil ratio of 1:12. Results are creditable and 5–6 pupils go on to university each year. Some music, drama and art. An adequate range of sports and games. No community services.

SCHOOL PROFILE

Pupils Total over 12, 300 (boys 240, girls 60). Entry age, 11 and into the sixth.
Entrance Common entrance and own entrance exam used. Not oversubscribed. No special skills or religious requirements. Parents expected to buy text books. 5 scholarships/bursaries, £635–⅓ fees.
Parents 15+% are doctors, lawyers etc; 15+% in industry or commerce; 15+% are lecturers and accountants. 80+% live within 30 miles.
Staff Head C L Kirch, in post for 2 years. 15 full time staff, 6 part time. Annual turnover 10%. Average age 37.
Academic work GCSE and A-levels. Average size of fifth 45–50; upper sixth 14. *O-levels*: on average, 4 pupils in fifth pass 1–4 subjects; 38, 5–7 subjects; 3 pass 8+ subjects. *A-levels*: on average, 1 pupil in the upper sixth passes 1 subject; 3, 2 subjects; 8, 3 subjects and 2 pass 4 subjects. On average, 7 take science/engineering A-levels; 4 take arts and humanities; 3 a mixture. Computer department.
Senior pupils' non-academic activities *Art*: 30 take GCSE; 3 A-level. 2 accepted for Art School. *Sport*: Rugby, soccer, netball, basketball, cricket, swimming, athletics (track and field), squash, golf, table tennis available. *Other*: Duke of Edinburgh's awards taken through ACF unit. Other activities include rifle, chess, film, drama, needlework clubs, debating and railway societies, Army Cadet Corps.
Careers 1 part time advisor. Average number of pupils accepted for *arts and humanities degree courses* at universities, 2; polytechnics or CHE, 2. *science and engineering degree courses* at universities, 4; polytechnics or CHE, 6. Average number of pupils going straight into careers in armed services, 1; industry, 10; the City, 4; civil service, 9; other, 7.
Uniform School uniform worn except the sixth.
Houses/prefects Competitive houses. Prefects, head boy/girl – appointed by Head.
Religion Worship encouraged.
Social Inter-school debates. Some organised trips abroad. Pupils allowed to bring own car/bike/motorbike to school. Meals self service. School shop. No tobacco/alcohol allowed.
Discipline Corporal punishment allowed. Caution system operates for eg pupils failing to produce homework.
Alumni association run by Mr Jeremy Stephens, 75 Church Road, Bebington, Wirral.

WELLS CATHEDRAL

Wells Cathedral School	• Co-ed	Pupils 481
Wells	Boys	Upper sixth 56
Somerset BA5 2ST	Girls	Termly fees:
Telephone number 0749 72117	Mixed sixth	Day £898
	• Day	Boarding £1598
Enquiries/application to the Headmaster	• Boarding	HMC; GBA; SHA; SHMIS

WHAT IT'S LIKE

Founded in the 12th century, the school has one of the finest sites in Europe, on the edge of Wells and a little to the north of the cathedral. It occupies all but one of the medieval and 18th-century buildings of 'the Liberty'. By virtue of its outstanding historical and architectural interest the cathedral, the bishop's palace, the Vicar's Close and 'the Liberty' are an important conservation area. The site includes a number of lovely walled gardens and an area of parkland used for playing fields. The school houses are scattered in the town. The school is exceptionally well equipped with modern facilities and accommodation, including excellent laboratories, libraries and a big music school. A large staff permits a staff:pupil ratio of about 1:11, plus over 40 part-timers most of whom are peripatetic music teachers. Academic standards are high and results good. About 25–30 leavers go on to university each year. One of the school's great strengths is music. Many pupils are involved in choirs, orchestras and bands. A large number learn an instrument. As it is an ancient church school there are close links with the cathedral. Worship in the Anglican tradition is both compulsory and encouraged. The drama department is also strong. There is a broad range of games and sports available and a very large number of extra-curricular activities: 27 clubs and societies cater for most needs. The CCF has a big contingent and there is a sizeable community service group. A promising record in the Duke of Edinburgh's Award Scheme.

SCHOOL PROFILE

Pupils Total over 12,481. Day 217 (boys 121, girls 96); Boarding 264 (boys 141, girls 123). Entry age, 11 and into the sixth. Own junior school provides over 20%. Under 1% are children of former pupils.

Entrance Common entrance and own entrance exam used. Oversubscribed. No special skills or religious requirements. Parents expected to buy text books. 66 assisted places. Approx 8 scholarships/bursaries per year, £600–£200 per term.

Parents 15+% in the armed services. 30+% live within 30 miles; 11+% live overseas.

Staff Head J Baxter, in post for 2 years. 60 full time staff, 2 part time. Annual turnover 5%. Average age 38.

Academic work GCSE and A-levels. Average size of upper fifth 73; upper sixth 56. *O-levels*: on average, 16 pupils in upper fifth pass 1–4 subjects; 29, 5–7 subjects; 28 pass 8+ subjects. *A-levels*: on average, 8 pupils in upper sixth pass 1 subject; 10, 2 subjects; 28, 3 subjects and 3 pass 4 subjects. On average, 15 take science/engineering A-levels; 30 take arts and humanities; 12 a mixture. Botany offered to A-level. *Computing facilities*: Specialist computing area and specialist staff (1); computers for each laboratory in Science Department.

Senior pupils' non-academic activities *Music*: 95 learn a musical instrument, most to Grade 6 or above; 11 accepted for Music School, 5 to university music courses; most play in school orchestra, 80 in choir, 10 in concert band, 35 in wind ensemble, 16 in big band; 1 in National Youth Orchestra. *Drama and dance*: 76 in school productions; 55 in house drama; 13 in sixth form theatre arts course. 6 take Grade 6 in RAD, 6 DES (1). 3 accepted for Drama/Dance schools; some pupils enter competitions. *Art*: 28 take GCSE; 13 A-level. 4 accepted for Art School. *Sport*: Athletics, badminton, basketball, canoeing, caving, cricket, cross-country, dance, gymnastics, golf, hockey, horse-riding, judo, netball, roller hockey, skating, rounders, rugby, sailing, soccer, squash, swimming, table tennis, tennis, volleyball available. 120 take non-compulsory sport. 12 pupils represent county (hockey, cricket, rugby, basketball). *Other*: 12 have bronze Duke of Edinburgh's Award, 5 gold. 30 in community service group. 5 enter voluntary schemes after leaving school. Other activities include a computer club and there are currently 27 activities available on 1 afternoon a week. Pupils choose and can interchange, mostly on a termly basis. They cover a wide range of subjects from chess to car maintenance section.

Careers 1 part time careers advisor. Average number of pupils accepted for *arts and humanities degree courses* at Oxbridge, 3; other universities, 12; polytechnics or CHE, 13. *science and engineering degree courses* at Oxbridge, 3; other universities, 7; medical schools, 3; polytechnics or CHE, 3. *other general training courses*, 2. Average number of pupils going straight into careers in the armed services, 2; industry, 1; the City, 1; music/drama, 1; retail trade, 1. Traditional school careers are in music and the services.

Uniform School uniform worn throughout.

Houses/prefects Competitive houses. Prefects, head boy/girl, head of house and house prefects – appointed and elected by staff and school.

Religion Compulsory worship.

Social Debates, prefects' conferences, sport, sixth form fund raising with other local schools. Organised trips abroad and exchange systems. Day pupils allowed to bring own car/bicycle to school. Meals self service. School shop. No tobacco/alcohol allowed.

Discipline No corporal punishment. Pupils failing to produce homework once might expect to do it again; those caught smoking cannabis on the premises could expect expulsion.

Boarding 1% have own study bedroom, 70% share (with 1 or 2); 5% are in dormitories of 6 or more. Houses, of approximately 27–54, are divided by age group (middle and senior) and are single sex. Resident qualified nurse. Central dining room. Pupils can provide and cook snacks. 2 exeats each term of 1.5 days. Visits to local town allowed with permission – 16+.

Alumni association is run by J Robertson, Chairman – Old Wellensians, The Fosse House, Oakhill, Nr Bath.

Former pupils Brian Beazer; Malcolm Nash; Danny Nightingale.

WENTWORTH MILTON MOUNT

Wentworth Milton Mount	Co-ed	Pupils 350
College Road	Boys	Upper sixth Yes
Boscombe	● Girls	Termly fees:
Bournemouth	Mixed sixth	Day £820
Dorset BH5 2DY	● Day	Boarding £1400
Telephone number 0202 423266	● Boarding	GBGSA; GSA

Head Miss Margaret Vokins (6 years)
Age range 11–18; entrance by common entrance or own exam
Scholarships and bursaries (daughters of ministers and lay members of URC) available.

WESTBOURNE

The Westbourne School for Girls Ltd	Co-ed	Pupils 210
1 Winton Drive	Boys	Upper sixth 42
Glasgow G12 0PY	● Girls	Termly fees:
Telephone number 041 339 6006	Mixed sixth	Day £792
Enquiries/application to the Headmaster	● Day	
	Boarding	

WHAT IT'S LIKE

Founded in 1877, it has a pleasant site in the west end of the city and 3 miles from its centre. It comprises two main buildings and combines junior and senior schools. A full range of up-to-date facilities is available. A well-run, purposeful school with a large staff enabling a staff:pupil ratio of about 1:11. Academic standards are high and results good. About 15–20 girls go on to university each year. There is considerable strength in music, art and drama. A fine range of games and sports is provided and good standards are attained (not a few county representatives). Also a good variety of extra-curricular activities. The school's record in the Duke of Edinburgh's Award Scheme is impressive.

SCHOOL PROFILE

Pupils Total over 12, 210. Entry age, 2½, 5, 12 and into the sixth. Own prep department provides over 20%. 24% are children of former pupils.
Entrance Own entrance exam used. No special skills or religious requirements. Parents expected to buy text books. 60 assisted places. 6 scholarships/ bursaries available, £450–£300.
Parents 15+% in industry or commerce; 15+% are doctors, lawyers, etc. 60+% live within 30 miles.
Staff Head Mr J N Cross, first year in post. 26 full time staff, 5 part time. Annual turnover 2%. Average age 40.
Academic work O-grades, Highers, CSYS and A-levels. Average size of upper fifth 45; higher grade 42. *O-levels*: on average, 8 pupils in fourth pass

1–4 subjects; 12, 5–7 subjects; 25 pass 8+ subjects. *Highers*: on average, 3 in fifth pass 1 subject; 8, 2 subjects; 8, 3 subjects and 23 pass 4 subjects. On average, 15 take science/engineering Highers; 16 take arts and humanities; 13 a mixture. *Computing facilities*: Senior computing – SCOTVEC computing modules and use in other classes including word processing. Special provisions for mildly handicapped and EFL.

Senior pupils' non-academic activities *Music*: 50 learn a musical instrument, 10 to Grade 6 or above. 3 accepted for Music School. 6 in guitar group and 15 in ensembles after leaving school; 28 in school orchestra, 25 in choir, 6 in Glasgow Youth Choir, 6 in Scottish National Orchestra Junior Chorus, 3 in Scottish Opera, 1 choir girl of the year runner-up 1987. *Drama and dance*: 60 in school productions; 35 in opera; 12 stage and dance movement; 2 accepted for Drama/Dance Schools; 1 goes on to work in theatre. *Art*: 6 take as non-examined subject; 18 O-grade; 12, Higher. 4 accepted for Art School; 6 for architecture. 10 belong to photographic club. *Sport*: Hockey, tennis, athletics, swimming, squash, badminton, volleyball, netball, basketball, gymnastics, Scottish country dancing, ethnic dancing, ski-ing, skating available. 75 take non-compulsory sport; 50 take exams eg gymnastics, swimming. 8 represent county/country (athletics, hockey, tennis, golf, squash, swimming). *Other*: 41 take part in local community schemes. 13 have bronze Duke of Edinburgh's Award, 7 have silver and 18 gold; 8 enter voluntary schemes after leaving school; 15 work for national charities. Other activities include a computer club, chess club, literary and debating society, public speaking, Scripture Union.

Careers 1 part time advisor. Average number of pupils accepted for *arts and humanities degree courses* at Oxbridge, 2; other universities, 10; polytechnics or CHE, 6. *science and engineering degree courses* at universities, 3; medical school, 5; polytechnics or CHE, 4. BEd, 2. *other general training courses*, 9. Average number of pupils going straight into careers in the armed services, 1; the City, 2; music/drama, 2; trainee management, 2. Traditional school careers are in medicine, law, marketing with languages.

Uniform School uniform worn throughout.

Houses/prefects Competitive houses. Prefects, head girl, head of house and house prefects – voted by the Head, staff and school. School Council.

Religion Compulsory religious worship.

Social Inter-school debates, quiz competitions, drama and musical productions. Organised annual ski trips; trips to France and Germany. Pupils allowed to bring own car/bike to school. Meals self service. School shop. No tobacco/alcohol allowed.

Discipline No corporal punishment. Pupils failing to produce homework once might expect to have to produce the work the following day; those caught smoking cannabis on the premises could expect parents to be sent for and Chairman of Board of Governors consulted.

Alumni association run by The Secretary, Old Girls' Club, c/o the School.

Former pupils Vivien Heilbron, Lorna Heilbron, Joyce Deans (drama and TV); Fiona Kennedy (TV singer); Dr Ruth Jarrett (Aids Researcher, Glasgow University); Dr Myra Nimmo (Commonwealth athlete); Kirsten Borland (town planner).

WEST BUCKLAND

West Buckland School
Barnstaple
Devon EX32 0SX
Telephone number 05986 281

Enquiries/application to the Headmaster's Secretary

- Co-ed
- Boys
- Girls
- Mixed sixth
- Day
- Boarding

Pupils 378
Upper sixth 31
Termly fees:
Day £845
Boarding £1555
HMC

WHAT IT'S LIKE

Founded in 1858, it lies on the south-west edge of Exmoor, 10 miles from Barnstaple, on a 60-acre site. The handsome 19th-century buildings (with many modern additions) contain the school, except for the girls' junior house. It is an Anglican foundation and Christian teaching and principles underlie much of its life. It has developed a strong sense of community and there is much emphasis on everyone participating in the life of the school. The need for success is also emphasised. A sound general education is provided and results are good (10–15 leavers go on to university each year). There are very active music, drama and art departments. A lot of emphasis on sports and games (standards are high; numerous county representatives). The CCF contingent is flourishing and outdoor pursuits are popular. A most impressive record in the Duke of Edinburgh's Award Scheme.

SCHOOL PROFILE

Pupils Total over 12, 378. Day 243 (boys 149, girls 94); Boarding 135 (boys 104, girls 31). Entry age, 7 and into the sixth. Own junior department provides 20+%. 3% are children of former pupils.

Entrance Common entrance and own entrance exam used. Oversubscribed. No special skills or religious requirements. Parents not expected to buy text books. 14 assisted places pa. 6 scholarships/bursaries pa, £900–£175.

Parents Parents come from a broad mix of occupations. 60+% live within 30 miles; up to 10% live overseas.

Staff Head Michael Downward, in post for 9 years. 43 full time staff, 10 part time. Annual turnover 5%. Average age 36.

Academic work GCSE and A-levels. Average size of upper fifth 68; upper sixth 31. *O-levels*: on average, 26 pupils in upper fifth pass 1–4 subjects; 23, 5–7 subjects; 18 pass 8+ subjects. *A-levels*: on average, 5 pupils in upper sixth pass 1 subject; 6, 2 subjects; 6, 3 subjects and 10 pass 4 subjects. On average, 13 take science/engineering A-levels; 11 take arts and humanities; 7 a mixture. *Computing facilities*: BBC models on Econet, 12 centrally, 5 about the school. Special EFL department.

Senior pupils' non-academic activities *Music*: 26 learn a musical instrument, 15 to Grade 6 or above. 8 in school orchestra, 24 in choir, 13 in madrigal group; 2 join university choirs. *Drama and dance*: 25 in school productions; 1 accepted for Drama/Dance School. *Art*: 14 take as non-examined subject; 22 take GCSE; 2, A-level. 1 accepted for Art School. 5 belong to photographic club; 4 to others. *Sport*: Rugby, netball, cross-country, hockey, basketball, fencing, squash, cricket, tennis, athletics, rounders and others available. 130 take non-compulsory sport. 18 take exams. 16 represent county/country (rugby, cricket, athletics). *Other*: 10 have bronze Duke of Edinburgh's

Award, 45 have silver and 15 gold. 2 enter voluntary schemes after leaving school; 1 works for national charities. Other activities include a computer club, archery, bell ringing, chess, Christian Union, debating, shooting and others.

Careers 2 part time advisors. Average number of pupils accepted for *arts and humanities degree courses* at Oxbridge, 1; other universities, 3; polytechnics or CHE, 2. *science and engineering degree courses* at Oxbridge, 2; other universities, 6; polytechnics or CHE, 4. *other general training courses*, 2. Average number of pupils going straight into careers in the armed services, 3; industry, 3; civil service, 1; other, 4.

Uniform School uniform worn throughout.

Houses/prefects Competitive houses. Prefects, head boy and girl, head of house and house prefects – appointed.

Religion Morning assembly/Sunday service compulsory; lively voluntary Christian Union in lunch hour.

Social No regular events organised with local schools. Annual ski training and mountain expeditions. Annual exchanges with schools in France/Germany. Pupils allowed to bring own car/bike/motorbike to school. Meals formal. School shops selling tuck, basic equipment and second-hand. Sixth form pupils allowed tobacco/alcohol in restricted location.

Discipline No corporal punishment. Pupils failing to produce homework once might expect to have to complete it; those caught smoking cannabis on the premises could expect to be withdrawn.

Boarding Most upper sixth have own study bedroom; 15% share (3 to a room); 75% in dormitories of 6+. Houses, of 90+ (including day pupils), same as competitive houses, single sex. Resident qualified nurse. Central dining room. Pupils can provide and cook own food. Exeats to suit individual needs. Visits to local town (10 miles away) allowed weekly at 13+. Special bus runs on Saturdays.

Former pupils R F Delderfield (playwright and novelist); Brian Aldiss (science fiction writer); John Ashworth (Vice-Chancellor, Salford University).

WESTFIELD

Westfield School	Co-ed	Pupils 220
Oakfield House	Boys	Upper sixth 25
Oakfield Road	● Girls	Termly fees:
Gosforth	Mixed sixth	Day £782
Newcastle upon Tyne NE3 4HS	● Day	Northumbrian
Telephone number 091 285 1948	Boarding	Educational
		Trust

Enquiries/application to the Headmaster's Secretary

WHAT IT'S LIKE

Founded in 1959, it is suburban with the senior school on a 5-acre site and the junior on a separate one, one-quarter of a mile away. Agreeable buildings and good modern facilities. A sound basic education is given and results are creditable. Each year a few pupils go on to university. Flourishing music, art and drama departments. A good standard in sports and games (quite a lot of county representatives) and an impressive range of activities. A very promising record in the Duke of Edinburgh's Award Scheme.

SCHOOL PROFILE

Pupils Total over 12, 220. Entry age, 3–13 and into the sixth. Own junior school provides over 50%. 15% are children of former pupils.

Entrance Own entrance exam used. Not oversubscribed. No special skills or religious requirements. Parents not expected to buy text books. Up to 10 scholarships/bursaries pa, 25–90% of fees.

Parents 15+% in industry or commerce; 15+% are doctors, lawyers, etc. 60+% live within 30 miles; up to 10% live overseas.

Staff Head Mr J S Taylor, in post for 2½ years. 28 full time staff, 5 part time. Annual turnover 5%. Average age 41.

Academic work GCSE and A-levels. Average size of upper fifth 50; upper sixth 15 (expected to increase to 25 next year). *O-levels*: on average, 12 pupils in upper fifth pass 1–4 subjects; 25, 5–7 subjects; 13 pass 8+ subjects. *A-levels*: on average, 2 pupils in upper sixth pass 1 subject; 2, 2 subjects; 8 pass 3 subjects. On average, 2 take science/engineering A-levels; 7 take arts and humanities; 3 a mixture. Textiles and theatre arts offered to GCSE/A-level. *Computing facilities*: Commodore, BBC, word processing. Provision for special learning difficulties.

Senior pupils' non-academic activities *Music*: 10 learn a musical instrument, 2 to Grade 6 or above; 7 in school orchestra, 10 in choir, 5 in opera club. *Drama and dance*: 30 in school productions, 28 in workshops etc. 4 take Guildhall Grade 7, 6 Grade 5; others participate in local amateur/operatic societies. *Art*: 48 take GCSE; 4 A-level. *Sport*: Netball, hockey, swimming, tennis, trampolining, gymnastics available. 40 take non-compulsory sport. 20 take exams. 15 represent county/country at various sports. *Other*: 20 have bronze Duke of Edinburgh's Award, 5 have silver and 2 gold. 5 work for national charities beyond school. Other activities include a computer club, croquet, fashion, field work, French, gardening, history, magazine editing and production and many others.

Careers 2 full time and 1 part time advisors. Average number of pupils accepted for *arts and humanities degree courses* at Oxbridge, 1; polytechnics or CHE, 6. *science and engineering degree courses* at universities, 1. *BEd*, 4. *other general training courses*, 10. Average number of pupils going straight into careers in industry, 10; civil service, 2.

Uniform School uniform worn except in the sixth.

Houses/prefects Competitive houses. Prefects, head girl, head of house and house prefects – appointed jointly by the Head and school. School Council.

Religion Religious worship compulsory.

Social Social activities with various boys' schools. Organised trips to France, Germany, Russia, USA ('twin' school in Massachusetts). Pupils allowed to bring own car/bike/motorbike to school. Meals self service. School shop. No tobacco/alcohol allowed.

Discipline No corporal punishment. Pupils caught smoking cannabis on the premises could expect expulsion.

Alumni association run by Mrs Ann Guthrie, c/o the School.

WEST HEATH

West Heath School
Ashgrove Road
Sevenoaks
Kent TN13 1SR
Telephone number 0732 452541

Enquiries/application to the School
Secretary

Co-ed
Boys
● Girls
Mixed sixth
● Day
● Boarding

Pupils 148
Upper sixth 15
Termly fees:
Day £1430
Boarding £2110
GSA; SHA

WHAT IT'S LIKE

Founded in 1865, it has pleasant, well-designed buildings and excellent facilities and accommodation in a rural site of 32 acres of woodland and grassland on the edge of town. A large full-time staff (24, plus 29 part-timers) permits a staff:pupil ratio of 1:6. A sound general education is provided and results are good. About 10–12 pupils go on to university each year; a high proportion for such a small school. Very strong indeed in music (virtually everyone is involved) and good in art. Adequate sport, games and activities. A promising record in the Duke of Edinburgh's Award Scheme.

SCHOOL PROFILE

Pupils Total over 12, 148. Day 11; Boarding 137. Entry age, 11/12; occasionally into the sixth form. 15% are children of former pupils.

Entrance Common entrance exam used. Generally oversubscribed. No special skills or religious requirements but school is wholly Christian. Parents expected to buy text books. 4 internal scholarships and bursaries for daughters of old girls, £300 pa maximum.

Parents 10+% live within 30 miles; up to 10% live overseas.

Staff Head Mrs D Cohn-Sherbok in first year in post. 24 full time staff, 29 part time. Annual turnover 5%. Average age 40.

Academic work GCSE and A-levels. Average size of upper fifth 24; upper sixth 15. *O-levels*: on average, 5 pupils in upper fifth pass 1–4 subjects; 10, 5–7 subjects; 5 pass 8+ subjects. *A-levels*: on average, 2 pupils in upper sixth pass 1 subject; 6, 2 subjects; 6 pass 3 subjects. On average, 2 take science/engineering A-levels; 9 take arts and humanities; 3 a mixture of both. *Computing facilities*: 9 computers.

Senior pupils' non-academic activities *Music*: 60 learn a musical instrument, 20 to Grade 6 or above. 3 accepted for Music School. 30 in school orchestra, 30 in choir, 5 in pop group. *Drama and dance*: 10 in school productions. *Art*: 10 take as non-examined subject; 20 take GCSE; 5, A-level. 3 accepted for Art School. 5 belong to photographic club. *Sport*: Lacrosse, tennis, hockey, netball, swimming available. 70 take non-compulsory sport. 5 represent county/country at various sports. *Other*: 20 have bronze or silver Duke of Edinburgh's Award. Other activities include debating.

Careers 2 members of staff advise. Average number of pupils accepted for *arts and humanities degree courses* at Oxbridge, 1; other universities, 10; polytechnics or CHE, 2. *science and engineering degree courses* at Oxbridge, 1. *other general training courses*, 5.

Uniform School uniform worn for morning classes and games, except in the sixth.

Houses/prefects No competitive houses. Prefects, head girl and house prefects – elected by the school.

Religion Compulsory attendance at services.

Social Debates with local schools. Organised ski-trips abroad. Senior pupils allowed to bring own bike to school. Meals formal. School shop. No tobacco/alcohol allowed.

Discipline No corporal punishment. Those caught smoking on the premises could expect expulsion after a warning and a fine.

Boarding Lower sixth have own study bedroom, upper sixth are in bungalows in the grounds; others in dormitories of 6+. Central dining rooms. Sixth form can provide and cook own suppers. Exeats each term: 2 nights and half term. Visits to the local town allowed for seniors.

WESTHOLME

Westholme School	Co-ed	Pupils 401
Blackburn	Boys	Upper sixth 45
Lancashire BB2 6PS	● Girls	Termly fees:
Telephone number 0254 53347	Mixed sixth	Day £590
Enquiries/application to the Registrar	● Day	GSA
	Boarding	

WHAT IT'S LIKE

Founded in 1923, the upper school is semi-rural and single-site. Its two prep departments are on two other sites. The well-designed and pleasant buildings stand in attractive gardens and grounds. Facilities are good and there has been continual development over the last 30 years during which time there have been 15 major additions. Its liberal and sound education is based on Christian principles and practice. Standards are good academically and 25 or more pupils go on to university each year. Strong in music, drama and art. Adequate games and activities. A promising record in the Duke of Edinburgh's Award Scheme.

SCHOOL PROFILE

Pupils Total over 12, 401. Entry age, 11 and into the sixth. Own prep department provides over 20%. 10% are children of former pupils.

Entrance Own entrance exam used. Oversubscribed. No special skills or religious requirements. Parents not expected to buy text books. 100 scholarships/bursaries, £295–£90 per term.

Parents 15+% in industry or commerce; 15+% are doctors, lawyers, etc. 60+% live within 30 miles.

Staff Head Mrs Lillian Croston, appointed April 1988. 31 full time staff, 15 part time. Annual turnover 4%. Average age 39.

Academic work GCSE and A-levels. Average size of upper fifth 104; upper sixth 45. *O-levels*: on average, 9 pupils in upper fifth pass 1–4 subjects; 19, 5–7 subjects; 74 pass 8+ subjects. *A-levels*: on average, 5 pupils in upper sixth pass 1 subject; 4, 2 subjects; 6, 3 subjects and 30 pass 4 subjects. On average, 10 take science/engineering A-levels; 28 take arts and humanities; 7

a mixture. *Computing facilities*: A network of 16 BBC Master computers; a network of 16 Radio Shack computers as dedicated word processors. 2 Research Machines 380Z. 2 Apple computers.

Senior pupils' non-academic activities *Music*: 25 learn a musical instrument, 20 to Grade 6 or above; 25 in school orchestra, 40 in choir; 50 participate in musical productions at school; 3 in Lancashire Schools' Symphony Orchestra. *Drama and dance*: 30 (including understudies) in school productions. 22 take ESB Certificate in spoken English for higher education. 2 accepted for Drama/Dance Schools. *Art*: 50 take GCSE; 5 A-level; 12 A-level history of art. 2 accepted for Art School. *Sport*: Badminton, tennis, hockey, volleyball, netball, rounders, athletics available. 40 take non-compulsory sport. 6 represent county (badminton, tennis, athletics). *Other*: 6 have bronze Duke of Edinburgh's Award, 8 have silver and 10 have gold. Other activities include a computer club, public speaking societies, film club, cookery club, pony club.

Careers 2 full time advisors. Average number of pupils accepted for *arts and humanities degree courses* at Oxbridge, 1; other universities, 20; polytechnics or CHE, 8. *science and engineering degree courses* at Oxbridge, 1; other universities, 3; medical schools, 4; polytechnics or CHE, 3. *BEd*, 3. Average number of pupils going straight into careers in banking, 2.

Uniform School uniform worn except in the sixth.

Houses/prefects Competitive houses. Prefects, head girl, head of house and house prefects – appointed by staff and pupils. School Council.

Religion Compulsory morning assembly.

Social Joint concerts and joint general studies lectures with local schools. Organised trips abroad and exchange systems. Pupils allowed to bring own car/bike/motorbike/horse to school. Meals self service. No tobacco/alcohol allowed.

Discipline No corporal punishment. Pupils failing to produce homework once might expect lunchtime detention; those caught smoking cannabis on the premises could expect expulsion after interview with parents.

Alumni association run by Mrs E Gibson, c/o the School.

WESTMINSTER

Westminster School	Co-ed	Pupils 610
17 Dean's Yard	● Boys	Upper sixth 145
London SW1P 3PB	Girls	Termly fees:
Telephone number 01-222 5516	● Mixed sixth	Day £1550
Enquiries/application to the Registrar	● Day	Boarding £2350
	● Boarding	HMC

WHAT IT'S LIKE

Founded by Elizabeth I in 1560. For some centuries before the Reformation, the Benedictine monks of Westminster Abbey had run a small school for boys, but when the monastery was dissolved in 1540 Henry VIII ensured that education was continued at Westminster by including provision for 40 scholars in the constitution of Westminster Abbey. This provision was confirmed by his daughter in 1560, establishing at the same time links between the School and Christ Church, Oxford and Trinity, Cambridge. As the School prospered, the scholars were soon outnumbered by the non-scholars or Town Boys as they were called. From the beginning of the 17th century the School became well known and it remains one of the most distinguished in the country. It has a unique site beside the Abbey and Parliament and is renowned for its respect for learning, its individuality and nonconformity, and in more recent times its system of weekly boarding. It is blessed with many fine buildings (some of great architectural merit) which are elegant and beautiful within as well as without. The buildings are enhanced by pleasant gardens. The main playing field is at Vincent Square. Recently 7–9 Dean Bradley Street was bought to create a massive new science building. The School is already one of the best-equipped in Britain. It naturally has close links with the Abbey which is used regularly for worship. A large staff (plus a large part-time staff) allows a very favourable staff:pupil ratio. A very high-powered school academically, it achieves consistently excellent results and sends each year 120 or more pupils to university (about 60 of these go to Oxbridge). The music, drama and art departments are well-known for their excellence and there is a great deal of musical and dramatic activity. There is a wide range of sports and games (in which high standards are achieved) and a very wide variety of extra-curricular activities. Much use is made of the cultural facilities of London. Many distinguished speakers address clubs and societies. A flourishing Expeditions Society organises many events.

SCHOOL PROFILE

Pupils Total, 610. Day 392 (boys 333, girls 59); Boarding 218 (boys 193, girls 25). Entry age, boys, 13+; boys and girls into the sixth. Westminster Under School provides about 20%. 5% are children of former pupils.

Entrance Common entrance and own sixth entrance exam used. Oversubscribed. Skills in sport, music, art looked for; no religious requirements. Parents expected to buy text books. 4 assisted places pa for Under School pupils. 8 scholarships pa, half boarding fee; some sixth form bursaries.

Parents 15+% are doctors, lawyers etc. 60+% live within 30 miles; up to 10% live overseas.

Staff Head Master David Summerscale, in post for 3 years. 62 full time staff, 30 part time. Annual turnover 4%. Average age 35.

Academic work GCSE and A-levels. Average size of upper fifth 115; upper sixth 145. *O-levels*: on average, 15 pupils in upper fifth pass 5–7 subjects; 100 pass 8+ subjects. *A-levels*: on average, 5 pupils in upper sixth pass 2 subjects; 129, 3 subjects and 31 pass 4 subjects. Russian offered to A-level. *Computing facilities*: 20 BBC computers.

Senior pupils' non-academic activities *Music*: 180 learn a musical instrument, 18 to Grade 6 or above, 2 accepted for Music School; 30 in School orchestra, 40 in choir, 4 in jazz group. *Drama and dance*: 85 in School productions. *Art*: 80 take as non-examined subject; 25 take GCSE; 12 A-level. 6 accepted for Art School. 15 belong to photographic club; 30 take ceramics. *Sport*: Athletics, cricket, fencing, fives, football, martial arts, netball, shooting, squash, rowing, swimming, tennis etc available. A number of pupils represent county/country in a range of sports. *Other*: 20 take part in local community schemes. Other activities include debating, chess, computer, bookbinding.

Careers 2 part time advisors. Average number of pupils accepted for *arts and humanities degree courses* at Oxbridge, 35; other universities, 40. *science and engineering degree courses* at Oxbridge, 25; other universities, 20; medical schools, 8. Average number of pupils going straight into careers in armed services, 1; music/drama, 2.

Uniform School uniform worn by boys throughout. Girls have dress regulations.

Houses/prefects Competitive houses. Prefects (monitors), head boy (Captain of School), heads of house and house prefects (monitors) – appointed by Head Master.

Religion Compulsory morning service in Westminster Abbey 3 times/week. Weekly assembly in School Hall.

Social Joint events with other schools organised occasionally. Annual German exchange, group visits to Spain, Russia, Greece. Pupils allowed to bring own bike to school. Meals formal (lunch), others self service. School shop. No tobacco/alcohol allowed.

Discipline No corporal punishment. Pupils failing to produce homework once might expect to produce it next lesson; threat of detention for future offence. Those caught smoking cannabis on the premises would expect expulsion.

Boarding 40% have own study bedroom, 40% share with 1 other, 20% are in dormitories of 6+. Houses, of approximately 70, are the same as competitive houses and are single sex. Resident qualified nurse, visiting doctor. Central dining room. Exeats every weekend. Visits to town allowed.

Alumni association run by S E Murray, c/o the School.

Former pupils Peter Ustinov; Michael Flanders; Donald Swann; Lord Havers; Nigel Lawson; Antony Howard; Dominic Harrod; Andrew Lloyd-Webber; Dan Topolski; Henry Tizard; Sir Andrew Huxley; Sir John Gielguid; Sir Adrian Boult etc.

WESTONBIRT

Westonbirt School	Co-ed	Pupils 230
Tetbury	Boys	Upper sixth 40
Gloucestershire GL8 8QG	● Girls	Termly fees:
Telephone number 066688 333	Mixed sixth	Day £1375
	● Day	Boarding £2140
Enquiries to the Head	● Boarding	GSA,
Applications to the Registrar		Allied School

WHAT IT'S LIKE

Founded in 1928 on the Cotswold estate of Sir George Holford. Westonbirt House is the main building: a magnificent Renaissance style mansion – in effect a rural palace – which lies in 500 acres of fine gardens and parkland. More beautiful surroundings it would be difficult to find. Over the years it has been adapted and new buildings have been added. The orangery has been converted into a theatre and concert hall. Facilities and accommodation are first class. The ethos tends towards a good all-round education which develops individual talents – whatever they may be. Religious services (held in the village church) are Anglican and are compulsory. Academic standards are very creditable and results good. About 15 pupils go on to university each year. Very strong in music, art and drama. An adequate range of games, sports and activities. A promising record in the Duke of Edinburgh's Award Scheme. School runs a thriving Young Enterprise Company.

SCHOOL PROFILE

Pupils Total 230. Day 13; Boarding 217. Entry age, 11+, 12+, 13+ and into the sixth. 4% are children of former pupils.

Entrance Common entrance and own entrance papers used. Sometimes oversubscribed. Aptitude at music, drama, art, and sport helps. School is C of E and all are required to attend services. Parents not expected to buy text books. 7 scholarships/bursaries, 15–90% of fees.

Parents 10+% live within 30 miles; 10+% live overseas.

Staff Head Mrs Gillian Hylson-Smith, in post since 1986. 33 full time staff, 4 part time. Annual turnover 8–10%. Average age 39.

Academic work GCSE and A-levels. Average size of upper fifth 48; upper sixth 40. *O-levels*: on average, 8 pupils in upper fifth pass 1–4 subjects; 13, 5–7 subjects; 28 pass 8+ subjects. *A-levels*: on average, 5 pupils in upper sixth pass 1 subject; 5, 2 subjects; 29, 3 subjects and 2 pass 4 subjects. On average, 12 take science/engineering A-levels; 20 take arts and humanities; 8 a mixture. Theatre studies offered to A-level. *Computing facilities*: Careers room computer. Room set aside for computing in all aspects. *Special provisions*: individual coaching available.

Senior pupils' non-academic activities *Music*: 28 learn a musical instrument to Grade 6 or above; 1 accepted for Music School; 22 in school orchestra; 48 in choir; 15 in chamber groups. *Drama and dance*: 2 to Grade 6 in ESB, LAMDA etc. *Art*: 3 take art as non-examined subject; 25 take GCSE; 10, A-level; 1 accepted for Art School; 14 take photography; 25 belong to photographic club. *Sport*: Lacrosse, netball, tennis, swimming, athletics, badminton, squash, cross-country available. 25 take non-compulsory sport. School clubs: ballet (6), squash (40), tennis (20). 20 take exams in life saving, trampoline. 10 pupils represent county at lacrosse. *Other*: 2 take part in local community schemes. 20 have bronze Duke of Edinburgh's Award, 6 have silver.

Careers 1 part time advisor plus the Head (who has a postgraduate diploma in careers education and guidance). Average number of pupils accepted for *arts and humanities degree courses* at Oxbridge, 2; other universities, 13; polytechnics or CHE, 6. *science and engineering degree courses* at universities, 3; medical schools, 2. *other general training courses*, 10. Average number of pupils going straight into careers in industry, 2.

Uniform School uniform worn except in the sixth.

Houses/prefects Competitive houses. All sixth form have prefectorial duties. Head girl, head of house and house prefects – appointed by the Head after consultation with staff and girls.

Religion Compulsory daily prayers and Sunday service.

Social Music and discos with Bristol Boys' day schools and other independent schools. Organised French ski-ing trip. Pupils allowed to bring own car/bike/motorbike to school. Meals formal, except supper. School shop. No tobacco/alcohol allowed.

Discipline No corporal punishment. Pupils failing to produce homework once might expect detention; those caught smoking cannabis on the premises could expect expulsion.

Boarding 26% have own study bedroom, 2% share with one; very few are in dormitories of 6+. Houses, of approximately 40, same as competitive houses. Resident qualified nurse and visiting doctor. Central dining room. Sixth form pupils can provide and cook own food. 3 exeats each term, 1 or 2 nights. Visits to the local town allowed about every fortnight.

Alumni association c/o The Registrar, Westonbirt.

WHITGIFT

Whitgift School	Co-ed	Pupils 730
Haling Park	● Boys	Upper sixth 108
South Croydon	Girls	Termly fees:
Surrey CR2 6YT	Mixed sixth	Day £1040
Telephone number 01-688 9222	● Day	HMC
Enquiries/application to the Headmaster	Boarding	

WHAT IT'S LIKE

Founded in 1596 by John Whitgift, Archbishop of Canterbury. After steady decline in the 18th century it was reborn in North End, Croydon. In 1931 it moved to its present site in Haling Park: 45 acres of wooded parkland, formerly the estate of Lord Howard of Effingham. These are exceptionally beautiful surroundings for an urban day school. The buildings are well-designed and well-equipped (including a sixth form centre, good libraries and a superb sports hall). Further buildings are due for completion in the 1990s; these are to comprise a centre linking design and technology with science and fine arts, together with a new library and computer centre. One of the fundamental aims of the school is to balance an excellent academic record with a wide range of co-curricular activities. A friendly and happy school, it has an ecumenical approach to religious worship. Academically high-powered it achieves very good results and sends 70 or more pupils to university each year (including 20 to Oxbridge). Very strong in music, drama and art. Very high standards, too, in sports and games of which there is a wide variety. A flourishing CCF and outdoor pursuits scheme. A plentiful range of extra-curricular activities, a substantial commitment to local community services and a good record in the Duke of Edinburgh's Award Scheme.

SCHOOL PROFILE

Pupils Total over 12, 730. Entry age, 10, 11, 13 and into the sixth.

Entrance Common entrance and own entrance exam used. Oversubscribed. No special skills or religious requirements. Parents not expected to buy text books. 91 assisted places. Whitgift Foundation provides large number of scholarships/bursaries (1 for music); 6 exhibitions.

Staff Head D A Raeburn, in post for 18 years. Annual staff turnover 10%.

Academic work GCSE, A-levels. Average size of upper fifth 125; upper sixth 108. *O-levels*: on average, 8 pupils in upper fifth pass 1–4 subjects; 22, 5–7 subjects; 95 pass 8+ subjects. *A-levels*: on average, 5 pupils in the upper sixth pass 1 subject; 10, 2 subjects; 55, 3 subjects and 35 pass 4 subjects. *Computing facilities*: Computer, 14 VDUs; centre open during free time.

Senior pupils' non-academic activities *Music*: Well supported; high standard of tuition in orchestral instruments, piano, organ by 3 full-time, and many visiting staff; many instrumental/choral groups; opera performed most years; own concert hall. *Drama and dance*: Several productions a year; major play often tours abroad. *Art*: Pottery, sculpture, lithography, stage design and photography offered. 5 take A-level. 3 accepted for Art School. *Sport*: Rugby, hockey, cricket, swimming, athletics, cross-country, fencing, squash, fives, basketball, badminton etc available. *Other*: Many take part in local community schemes. Other activities include computer, chess, debating, current affairs, clubs, CCF, adventure training, cycle touring.

Careers Careers advice from many of the staff. Average number of pupils going on to *degree courses* at Oxbridge, 20; other universities, 50; medical schools, 5; polytechnics or CHE, 15. Traditional school careers in science, technology and business administration.

Uniform School uniform worn throughout.

Houses/prefects Competitive houses. Prefects, head boy, head of house and house prefects – appointed by Head or housemasters. School Council.

Religion Compulsory twice-weekly morning assembly.

Social Joint functions with local girls' schools; sailing and climbing journeys. School exchanges (France, Germany), ski-ing trips. Pupils allowed to bring own car/bike/motorbike to school. Meals self service, seniors; formal, juniors. No tobacco/alcohol allowed.

Discipline No corporal punishment.

Former pupils Reg Prentice; Martin Jarvis; Raman Subba Row.

WILLIAM HULME'S

William Hulme's Grammar School	● Co-ed	Pupils 800
Alexandra Park	Boys	Upper sixth 103
Manchester M16 8PR	Girls	Termly fees:
Telephone number 061 226 2054	Mixed sixth	Day £867
Enquiries to the Headmaster	● Day	HMC
Application to the Bursar	Boarding	

WHAT IT'S LIKE

Founded by the Hulme Trust and opened in 1887, it has an urban site 2½ miles south of Manchester city centre. Steady expansion and development have taken place throughout the 20th century, with many additions in the last 25 years. It is now extremely well-equipped. Non-denominational, it has high academic standards and good results. About 50–55 pupils go on to university each year. There is some music and art, and a good deal of drama. A wide range of sports and games in which high standards are attained (not a few representatives at county and national level). Extra-curricular activities are numerous. A voluntary and flourishing CCF and some commitment to the Duke of Edinburgh's Award Scheme. Considerable use is made of a field study centre in Wensleydale and also of the cultural amenities of Manchester.

SCHOOL PROFILE

Pupils Total, 800 (boys 740, girls 60). Entry age, 11+ and into the sixth. (Girls admitted at 11 from September 1988.)

Entrance Own 11+ entrance exam used. Oversubscribed. No special skills or religious requirements. Parents not expected to buy text books. 35 assisted places pa. Scholarships/bursaries, value £1000.

Parents 60+% live within 30 miles.

Staff Head P D Briggs, in post for 1 year. 50 full time staff, 8 part time. Annual turnover 8%. Average age 41.

Academic work GCSE and A-levels. Average size of upper fifth 115; upper sixth 103. *O-levels*: on average, 19 pupils in upper fifth pass 1–4 subjects; 42, 5–7 subjects; 54 pass 8+ subjects. *A-levels*: on average, 9 pupils in upper sixth pass 1 subject; 13, 2 subjects; 46, 3 subjects and 15 pass 4 subjects. On average, 46 take science/engineering A-levels; 33 take arts and humanities; 8 a mixture. *Computing facilities*: 13 BBCs (Econet with 20MB filestore), 4 Amstrad PCW 8256.

Senior pupils' non-academic activities *Music*: 8 learn a musical instrument. 12 in school orchestra, 16 in choir, 3 in string group. *Drama and dance*: 30 in school productions, 80 in house plays. *Art*: 20 take as non-examined subject, 10 GCSE, 4 A-level. 1 accepted for Art School. 5 belong to eg photographic club. *Sport*: Rugby, lacrosse, hockey, netball, cricket, tennis, swimming, badminton, squash available. 20 take non-compulsory sport (badminton). 10 pupils represent county (rugby, lacrosse, cricket, squash), 1 represents country (speed skating). *Other*: 20 have bronze Duke of Edinburgh's Award and 10 silver. Other activities include usual clubs and societies, also computer, Outward Bound, climbing, chess, video unit.

Careers 2 part time advisors (Head of Careers and Director of Studies). Average number of pupils accepted for *arts and humanities degree courses* at Oxbridge, 2; other universities, 15; polytechnics or CHE, 6. *science and engineering degree courses* at Oxbridge, 3; other universities, 21; medical schools, 5; polytechnics or CHE, 5. Average number of pupils going straight into careers in armed services, 1; the City, 1; other, 2.

Uniform School uniform worn, modified in sixth.

Houses/prefects Competitive houses. Prefects, head boy – appointed by Head; head of house and house prefects – appointed by housemaster.

Religion Daily non-denominational Christian assembly; weekly Jewish religious assembly.

Social Debates, discussions, lectures, dances with local independent girls' school. Annual German exchange; trips to France, Spain; sports tours to USA, Canada, West Indies. Pupils allowed to bring own car/bike/motorbike to school. Meals self service. School book and tuck shops. No tobacco/alcohol allowed.

Discipline No corporal punishment. Pupils failing to produce homework once might expect to do work next day and a discussion on learning to be prompt; those caught smoking cannabis on the premises might expect expulsion.

Alumni association run by G Eric Barnes, 5 Rossall Close, Hoghton, Preston, Lancashire PR5 0LB.

Former pupils Sir Robert Mark; Air Chief Marshal Sir Joseph Gilbert; Judge Michael Blackburn; John Lee MP.

WIMBLEDON HIGH

Wimbledon High School	Co-ed	Pupils 450
Mansel Road	Boys	Upper sixth 55
London SW19 4AB	● Girls	Termly fees:
Telephone number 01-946 1756	Mixed sixth	Day £789
Enquiries/application to the Headmistress	● Day	GSA; GPDST
	Boarding	

WHAT IT'S LIKE

Founded in 1880 it has an agreeable urban site with large gardens. The junior and senior departments are on one campus. The main playing fields are 10 minutes' walk away on the site of the original All England Lawn Tennis Club. The school has a reputation for excellent academic standards and a high regard for pastoral care. It draws its pupils from a wide area and a variety of backgrounds. Academic results are consistently good and each year 45–50 pupils go on to university. Music, drama and art are all strongly supported. An adequate range of sports and games and extra-curricular activities. Some commitment to local community services and the Duke of Edinburgh's Award Scheme.

SCHOOL PROFILE

Pupils Total over 11, 450. Entry age, 11+ and into the sixth. 10% are children of former pupils.

Entrance Own entrance exam used. Oversubscribed. No special skills or religious requirements. Parents not expected to buy text books. 62 assisted places. Scholarships (1 pa plus sixth form), half fees.

Parents 15+% are doctors, lawyers etc; 15% in industry or commerce. 60+% live within 30 miles.

Staff Head Mrs R A Smith, in post for 6 years. 44 full time staff, 33 part time (including 20 music). Annual turnover 10%. Average age 40.

Academic work GCSE and A-levels. Average size of upper fifth 60; upper sixth 55. *O-levels*: on average, 5 pupils in upper fifth pass 5–7 subjects; 55 pass 8+ subjects. *A-levels*: on average, 2 pupils in the upper sixth pass 1 subject; 5, 2 subjects; 44, 3 subjects and 4 pass 4 subjects. On average, 14 take science/engineering A-levels; 23 take arts and humanities; 20 a mixture. *Computing facilities*: 8 480Z research machines, 3 BBC computers. Provision for mild physical handicaps.

Senior pupils' non-academic activities *Music*: 120 learn a musical instrument, 38 to Grade 6 or above; 30 in school orchestra, 40 in choir, 15 in jazz band; 6 in National Youth Orchestra. *Drama and dance*: 50–60 in official school productions, 40 in informal productions; 12 take A/O-level drama and theatre arts. 1 works in theatre, 2 in National Youth Theatre, 2 applying for drama courses. *Art*: 40 take as non-examined subject in sixth form; 61 take GCSE; 16 take A-level. 2 accepted for Art School. *Sport*: Hockey, netball, tennis, rounders, squash, badminton, volleyball, table tennis, swimming, gymnastics available. 40 take non-compulsory sport. 4 represent county/country (hockey). *Other*: 20 take part in local community schemes. 16 have bronze Duke of Edinburgh's Award; at least 1 enters voluntary schemes after leaving. Other activities include computer club, modern dance.

Careers 2 part time careers advisors. Average number of pupils accepted for *arts and humanities degree courses* at Oxbridge, 4; other universities, 35; polytechnics or CHE, 1. *science and engineering degree courses* at Oxbridge, 4; other universities, 5; medical schools, 6; polytechnics or CHE, 1. *BEd*, 1. *other general training courses*, 4 (nursing).

Uniform School uniform worn except the sixth.

Houses/prefects No competitive houses. No prefects but sixth form committee elected by staff and pupils. Head girl chosen by Headmistress from committee.

Religion Daily non-denominational religious assembly.

Social Debating society, drama, choir and orchestra with King's College School. French and German exchanges, ski-ing, sixth form art visits to Italy, hockey to Holland, choir to Canada. Sixth form allowed to drive to school but no parking available in grounds. Meals self service. No tobacco/alcohol allowed.

Discipline No corporal punishment. Pupils failing to produce homework once might expect verbal warning, possibly a note in homework diary; those caught smoking cannabis on the premises might expect immediate suspension, probably subsequent expulsion.

Alumni association run by Mrs Jean Appleby, 1 Ridgeway Place, London SW19 4EW.

WINCHESTER

Winchester College
College Street
Winchester
Hampshire SO23 9NA
Telephone number 0962 54328

Enquiries to the Headmaster or the Registrar
Application to the Registrar

Co-ed   Pupils 660
● Boys   Upper sixth 130
   Girls   Termly fees:
   Mixed sixth   Day £1950
● Day   Boarding £2600
● Boarding   HMC

WHAT IT'S LIKE

Founded in 1382 by William of Wykeham, Bishop of Winchester and Chancellor to Richard II. It lies at the edge of the City and close to the water meadows. It has the longest unbroken history of any school in the country and has been in continuous occupation of its original buildings for 600 years. Most of them are still used for the purpose for which they were designed, and they are virtually without rival among school buildings for their venerability and beauty. The Scholars still live in the 14th-century 'College' as it is known. The medieval buildings are open to visitors. Other buildings date from the 17th, 18th and 19th centuries, plus some recent structures. Accommodation and facilities are first rate. They include exceptionally good libraries, a theatre and a music school. Intellectually and academically, Winchester is one of the most distinguished schools in Britain and standards are very high. A large staff permits a staff:pupil ratio of 1:8. Between 110–120 pupils go on to university each year, and these include 40 plus to Oxbridge. A tremendously strong music department involves a majority of the school; two-thirds of the pupils learn a musical instrument and there are several choirs and orchestras. There are numerous school and house dramatic productions involving 200 or more boys. The art department is also very strong. Thirty different sports and games are available (including Winchester football which is peculiar to the College). High standards prevail in sport and games and there have been many representatives at international and county level. A very large number of extra-curricular activities are available. The College also has an impressive commitment to local community schemes.

SCHOOL PROFILE

Pupils Total 660. Day 35; Boarding 625. Entry age, 13 and into the sixth (if room). 11% are children of former pupils.

Entrance Own entrance exam used. Oversubscribed (registration from age 8; preselection at 11 conditional upon passing entrance exam; late applicants on waiting list). Academic ability and other interests looked for. No religious requirements. 5 assisted places pa. 15 scholarships pa, £4980–£7800 plus some 6 music awards, average value £1300.

Parents 15+% are in industry or commerce; 15+% are doctors, lawyers etc. 10+% live within 30 miles; up to 10% live overseas.

Staff Head J P Sabben-Clare, in post for 3 years. 83 full time staff, 8 part time. Annual turnover 3%.

Academic work GCSE and A-level. Average size of upper fifth 130; upper sixth 130. *O-levels*: on average, 125 pupils in upper fifth pass 8+ subjects. *A-levels*: on average, 5 pupils in upper sixth pass 2 subjects; 85, 3 subjects and 40 pass 4 subjects. On average, 40 take science/engineering A-levels; 40 take arts and humanities; 50 a mixture. *Computing facilities*: 16 BBC micros and Archimedes connected by a network system plus computers belonging to masters.

Senior pupils' non-academic activities *Music*: Two-thirds of pupils learn a musical instrument, most to Grade 6 or above; 3–4 accepted for Music School plus instrumental/choral awards to Oxbridge; 100 in school orchestra, 150 in choir, 20 in pop group, string quartets, brass quintets, wind quintets, composition (10 pupils); 7 in National Youth Orchestra. *Drama and dance*: 200 participate in school and house productions. 1 accepted for Drama/Dance School. *Art*: 25 take art as non-examined subject; 24 take GCSE; 18 A-level. 2 accepted for Art School; 2 for architecture. 20 belong to eg photographic club; 100 to art society (for talks). *Sport*: Athletics, badminton, basketball, canoeing, cricket, fencing, fishing, fives, gymnastics, hockey, judo, karate, rackets, rowing, sailing, shooting, soccer, squash, steeplechase, sub-aqua, swimming, tennis, trampoline, volleyball, water polo, weight and circuit training, Winchester College football available. 300 take non-compulsory sport; 120 compulsory PE. 40 take exams in swimming. 4 pupils represent country at rowing; 28 represent county (judo, water polo, athletics). *Other*: 100 take part in local community schemes. 2 have gold Duke of Edinburgh's Award. 30 enter voluntary schemes after leaving school. Other activities include a computer club, archaeology, astronomy, bell-ringing, chess, classics, debating, drama, film, modern language play reading, music, natural history, philately, photography, printing, science. The Empson Society has lectures on literature, the Toynbee Society on historical and philosophical subjects.

Careers 4 part time advisors. Average number of pupils accepted for *arts and humanities degree courses* at Oxbridge, 24; other universities, 42; polytechnics or CHE, 1. *science and engineering degree courses* at Oxbridge, 16, other universities, 28 (of which 8 read medicine); polytechnics or CHE, 1. Average number of pupils going straight into careers in the armed services, 2; the City, 1; music/drama, 2; other, 10.

Uniform School uniform not worn, but dress regulations.

Houses/prefects Competitive houses. Prefects, head boy, head of house and house prefects – chosen by Housemasters after consultation with prefects; approved by the Headmaster.

Religion Compulsory religious worship.

Social Debates, music, drama; mostly with St Swithun's School. Organised trips abroad eg ski-ing; art trips to Italy; exchange with a Paris Lycée. Pupils allowed to bring own bike to school. Meals formal. School shop. No tobacco/alcohol allowed.

Discipline No corporal punishment. Pupils failing to produce homework once might expect a reprimand from teacher and work to be produced; those caught smoking cannabis on the premises could expect rustication; expulsion if selling it.

Boarding 15% have own study bedroom, 80% are in dormitories of 6+. Houses of 55, same as competitive houses. Resident matron. No central dining room. 4-day weekend exeats in summer and Easter terms; 10 days exeat in winter term. Visits to the local town allowed.

Alumni association run by P S W K Maclure.

Former pupils Viscount Whitelaw; Sir Geoffrey Howe; Douglas Jay; Peter Jay; Lord Penney; Sir Jeremy Morse; George Younger; Field-Marshal Lord Carver; Professor Freeman Dyson; Howard Angus; William Mann; Tim Brooke-Taylor; Brian Trubshaw; Richard Noble.

WITHINGTON

Withington Girls' School
Wellington Road
Fallowfield
Manchester M14 6BL
Telephone number 061 224 1077/8820

Enquiries/application to the Headmistress

Co-ed
Boys
● Girls
Mixed sixth
● Day
Boarding

Pupils 400
Upper sixth 65
Termly fees:
Day £740
GSA

WHAT IT'S LIKE

Founded in 1890, it is urban single-site, housed in a pleasant late 19th-century building with big playing fields nearby. There have been a lot of additions over the years and modern facilities are excellent. Academic standards are high and results good. There are 40–50 university entrants each year. Extremely strong music and drama departments and a fine range of activities. The school has a high reputation for its achievements in sport and games (there are quite a lot of representatives at county level). A promising record in the Duke of Edinburgh's Award Scheme. The school enjoys vigorous local support and has a very big commitment to local community services.

SCHOOL PROFILE

Pupils Total over 12, 400. Entry age, 11 and into the sixth. Own junior school provides 40% of pupils. 3–4% are children of former pupils.

Entrance Own entrance exam used. Oversubscribed. All round ability and excellent potential looked for. No religious requirements. Parents not expected to buy text books. 80 assisted places. Bursaries available in cases of need, assessed individually.

Parents 15+% in industry or commerce; 15+% are doctors, lawyers etc. More than 60% live within 30 miles.

Staff Head Mrs Margaret Kenyon, in post for 2 years. 34 full time staff, 5 part time. Annual turnover, 5–7.5%. Average age, 38.

Academic work GCSE and A-levels. Average size of upper fifth 66; upper sixth 65. *O-levels*: on average, 1 pupil in upper fifth passes 1–4 subjects; 9, 5–7 subjects; 56 pass 8+ subjects. *A-levels*: on average, 2 pupils in upper sixth pass 1 subject; 5, 2 subjects; 31, 3 subjects and 25 pass 4 subjects. On average, 25 take science/engineering A-levels; 18 take arts and humanities; 22 a mixture. Greek offered to GCSE/A-level. *Computing facilities*: Specially designed room with a 12 station Nimbus network and several stand alone machines.

Senior pupils' non-academic activities *Music*: 55 learn a musical instrument, 30+ to Grade 6 or above; 2–3 accepted for Music School; 40 in school orchestra, 80 in choir, 40 in wind band, 6 in National Youth Choir, 25 in Northern Youth Orchestra, 20 in Stockport Youth Orchestra, 10 in Trafford Youth Orchestra. *Drama and dance*: 150 in school productions, 10 in Contact Theatre, 6 in Royal Exchange Theatre (helpers); 2 take up to Grade 6 ESB, RAD; 4 IBTA, NATB elementary ballet awards. 2 accepted for Drama/Dance Schools (including university courses). 1 goes on to work in theatre approx every 5 years. *Art*: 12 take GCSE; 7, A-level; 2–3 accepted for Art

School. *Sport*: Hockey, lacrosse, netball, badminton, table tennis, volleyball, tennis, cricket, rounders, aerobics, trampolining, self defence, basketball available. 150 take non-compulsory sport. 5 do county training. 10 pupils represent county (tennis, lacrosse, hockey). *Other*: 100+ take part in local community schemes. 12 have bronze Duke of Edinburgh's Award, 9 have silver and 1 gold. 100+ work for national charities. Other activities include a computer club, active scientific society (many outside speakers), electronics, bridge, ski-ing, hiking, active modern language society.

Careers 1 part time advisor. Average number of pupils accepted for *arts and humanities degree courses* at Oxbridge, 7; other universities, 17; polytechnics or CHE, 5. *science and engineering degree courses* at Oxbridge, 5; other universities, 14; medical schools, 8; polytechnics or CHE, 3. *BEd*, 2. *other general training courses*, 1. Average number of pupils going straight into careers in the City, 1. Medicine is single most popular profession.

Uniform School uniform worn modified in sixth.

Houses/prefects Competitive houses. All upper sixth form are prefects. Head girl, 2–3 deputies chosen by Headmistress after consulting with sixth form and staff. House captains (and vice) elected by house.

Religion All encouraged to take part. Monday assembly compulsory; separate Jewish assembly once weekly.

Social Girls are invited to lectures at Manchester Grammar School and audition for plays there. Organised ski-ing trips, adventure holidays at Club Corrèze for 13 year olds. French/German trips for GCSE candidates. Pupils allowed to bring own car to school. Meals self service. No tobacco/alcohol allowed.

Discipline No corporal punishment. Pupils failing to produce homework once might expect a verbal reminder; those caught smoking cannabis on the premises could expect expulsion.

Alumni association run by Mrs Marjorie Rawsthorn.

Former pupils Judith and Sandra Chalmers.

WOLDINGHAM

Woldingham School	Co-ed	Pupils 450
Woldingham	Boys	Upper sixth 60
Caterham CR3 7YA	● Girls	Termly fees:
Telephone number 0883 49431	Mixed sixth	Day £1245
	● Day	Boarding £2055
Enquiries/application to the Admissions Secretary	● Boarding	GSA; GBGSA

WHAT IT'S LIKE

Founded in 1842 by the Society of the Sacred Heart. In 1946 it moved from Roehampton to Woldingham, Surrey. Today it is under lay management and is part of the international network of Sacred Heart Schools in the trusteeship of the Society and run according to its educational aims and philosophy. Its site of Marden Park was originally created by Sir Robert Clayton in the 17th century. The original mansion was destroyed by fire; the present 19th century Senior School building is set in magnificent grounds and gardens.

The junior house is a modern building with accommodation for some 160 girls. Much has been achieved in recent years. Developments include an assembly hall, 120 sixth form study-bedrooms, 9 labs, 3 art studios, a computer centre, an indoor swimming pool and, recently, a purpose-built Science and Technology Centre. The school is a Roman Catholic school in the ecumenical tradition. Its primary purpose is to provide a sound education which will help girls to become mature and committed Christians who can make independent decisions in their careers and personal lives. All pupils take religious studies at GCSE level. Emphasis is placed on participation in the Church's liturgical year. Girls are expected to play a full part in the running of the school and responsibilities and privileges are introduced at an early stage. A large and carefully-selected staff allows a very favourable staff:pupil ratio of about 1:9. Academic standards are high and results impressive. Some 30+ pupils go on to university each year. A very big commitment to drama and art. A good range of sports and games and an equally good range of extra-curricular activities. A promising record in the Duke of Edinburgh's Award Scheme.

SCHOOL PROFILE

Pupils Total, 450 (the majority are boarders). Entry age, 11 and into the sixth. 20% are children of former pupils.

Entrance Common entrance used. Oversubscribed. No special skills required; RC and other Christian denominations preferred. Parents expected to buy text books. 5 academic scholarships at 11+, 13+, 16+, value £1000.

Parents 15+% in industry or commerce. 10+% live within 30 miles; 40+% live overseas.

Staff Head Dr P Dineen, in post for 4 years. 51 full time staff, 6 part time. Annual turnover 7%. Average age 35.

Academic work GCSE and A-levels. Average size of upper fifth 70; upper sixth 60. *O-levels*: on average, 8 pupils in upper fifth pass 1–4 subjects; 30, 5–7 subjects; 30 pass 8+ subjects. *A-levels*: on average, 4 pupils in upper sixth pass 1 subject; 4, 2 subjects; 40, 3 subjects and 2 pass 4 subjects. On average, 20 take science/engineering A-levels; 25 take arts and humanities; 15 a mixture. *Computing facilities*: computers are used increasingly across the curriculum. In addition there is a computing room which is standardising on BBC Masters. Some special provision can be arranged for able girls who are handicapped by dyslexia and similar conditions.

Senior pupils' non-academic activities *Music*: 312 learn a musical instrument, 10 to Grade 6 or above, 2 accepted for Music School. 98 in school orchestras, 220 in choirs, 50 in pop groups. *Drama and dance*: 100 in school productions. 3 to Grade 6 in ESB, RAD etc, 2 accepted for Drama/Dance Schools. *Art*: 30 take GCSE, 12 take A-level, 5 accepted for Art School, 50 belong to eg photographic club. *Sport*: Hockey, netball, rounders, tennis, track and field, gymnastics and dance, squash, swimming, badminton available. 12 represent county/country (tennis, athletics, hockey). *Other*: 20 have bronze Duke of Edinburgh's Award, 5 have silver and 5 gold. Other activities include horse-riding, chess, driving lessons.

Careers 3 part time advisors. Average number of pupils accepted for *arts and humanities degree courses* at Oxbridge, 2; other universities, 12; polytechnics or CHE, 12. *science and engineering degree courses* at Oxbridge, 2; other universities, 8; medical schools, 3; polytechnics or CHE, 8. *BEd*, 2. Average

number of pupils going straight into careers in the City, 5; music/drama, 2.
Uniform School uniform worn throughout.
Houses/prefects Competitive houses. Prefects, head girl, head of house and house prefects – shortlisted by sixth, selected by senior staff. School Council.
Religion Compulsory Mass on Sunday; encouraged other days.
Social Some debates and dances with local schools. Visits to Russia (history), Italy (history of art), Austria (ski-ing and choir), France, Spain and Germany (languages). Pupils allowed to bring own bike (from third year), car (sixth form) to school. Meals self service. School shop. No tobacco/alcohol allowed.
Discipline No corporal punishment. Pupils failing to produce homework once might expect tutorial help; those caught smoking on the premises might expect suspension; involvement in drug-taking would incur immediate expulsion.
Boarding 30% have own study bedroom, 17% share, 20% are in dormitories of 6+. Not divided into houses. 2 resident qualified nurses, 2 doctors, dentist and physiotherapist in attendance. 2 central dining rooms. Exeats each weekend from noon. Visits to local town allowed (14+) Saturday afternoons.
Alumni association run by Miss L Ferrar, 14 Abercorn Place, London NW8 9XP.

WOLVERHAMPTON GRAMMAR

Wolverhampton Grammar School
Compton Road
Wolverhampton
West Midlands WV3 9RB
Telephone number 0902 21326

Co-ed
● Boys
Girls
● Mixed sixth
● Day
Boarding

Pupils 620
Upper sixth Yes
Termly fees:
Day £790
HMC; GBA

WHAT IT'S LIKE

Founded in 1512 by Sir Stephen Jenyns, a member of the Merchant Taylors' Company and Lord Mayor of London in the year of Henry VIII's coronation for the 'instruction of youth in good manners and learning'. The school was originally in the middle of Wolverhampton and in 1875 moved to its present fine 20 acre site on Compton Road. The original buildings are handsome and there have been many modern additions to create first-rate facilities for a school which has a high reputation locally. Pupils come in from a wide catchment area, including Stourbridge, Kidderminster, Bridgnorth, Stafford and Walsall. Girls were admitted to the sixth form from 1984. The school is non-denominational but many of the staff and pupils are practising Christians. There is some emphasis on worship and practice in the Anglican tradition and religious education is part of the curriculum at all levels. A sound general education is provided by a well-qualified staff (staff:pupil ratio of about 1:12) and academic standards and results are consistently good. Of 900 leavers in the last 10 years, 550 have gone on to universities and other places of further education. Over 90 of these were Oxbridge entrants. Music is very strong. There are choirs, orchestras, a brass band and a choral society (numbering 200). Public performances are frequent. There is a good deal of emphasis on drama with four main productions each year. The art department is also strong and work of a high standard is produced. A wide range of sports and games is provided. Facilities for these are first rate and the school is outstanding at soccer, fives and athletics. There have been a number of representatives at county and regional level. A plentiful variety of clubs and societies exist for extra-curricular activities. A flourishing scout group involves a number of boys in outdoor pursuits, including Outward Bound and sailing courses. Full use is made of the cultural amenities at Stratford, Birmingham and Wolverhampton.

SCHOOL PROFILE

Head P H Hutton (10 years)
Age range 11–19, entry by own exam.
Assisted places and bursaries.

WOODBRIDGE

Woodbridge School	● Co-ed	Pupils 521
Woodbridge	Boys	Upper sixth 75
Suffolk IP12 4JH	Girls	Termly fees:
Telephone number 0394 385547	Mixed sixth	Day £1060
Enquiries/application to the Headmaster	● Day	Boarding £1840
	● Boarding	HMC

WHAT IT'S LIKE

Founded in 1577, it lapsed during the Civil Wars and was refounded in 1662. It occupied premises in Seckford Street and in 1864 moved to its present beautiful site overlooking the River Deben. For 300 years it was the boys' grammar school for the area and became co-ed in 1974. It possesses fine buildings (old and modern) on a delightful campus of gardens and playing fields covering some 45 acres and is 5 minutes' walk from the centre of the most interesting town of Woodbridge. There has been steady expansion and in recent years there have been added a sixth-form centre, a superb sports hall, a music school, an art block and a technology block. It is now very well-equipped. Woodbridge Abbey is the junior school nearby. A C of E school, it is ecumenical in spirit and practice, with some emphasis on worship and religious instruction. A sound general education is provided and academic standards are high. 85% of sixth form go on to higher education (university, polytechnics etc) each year. There is considerable emphasis on pastoral care and constant contact with parents. The school has a good range of sports and games and standards in these are quite high (a good many representatives at county level). A wide variety of extra-curricular activities is available and the school has a promising record in the Duke of Edinburgh's Award Scheme.

SCHOOL PROFILE

Pupils Total over 11, 521. Day 406 (boys 216, girls 190); Boarding 115 (boys 75, girls 40). Entry age, 11+ and into the sixth. Own junior school provides over 20%.

Entrance Common entrance and own 11+ exam used. Oversubscribed. No religious requirements but potential to cope with 10 GCSEs and 3 A-levels looked for. Parents not expected to buy text books. 101 assisted places. 60 scholarships/bursaries, £1060–£265.

Parents 60+% live within 30 miles; up to 10+% live overseas.

Staff Head Dr David Younger, in post for 3 years. 43 full time staff, 6 part time. Annual turnover 10%. Average age 40.

Academic work GCSE, A-levels. Average size of upper fifth 75; upper sixth 75. *O-levels*: on average, 1 pupil in upper fifth passes 1–4 subjects; 23, 5–7 subjects; 51 pass 8+ subjects. *A-levels*: on average, 12 pupils in upper sixth pass 1 subject; 14, 2 subjects; 43, 3 subjects and 6 pass 4 subjects. On average, 60% take science/engineering A-levels; 30% take arts and humanities; 10% a mixture. *Computing facilities*: Computer room, 26 BBC Micros. Provision for those with mild visual handicap.

Senior pupils' non-academic activities *Music*: 50 learn a musical instrument, 24 to Grade 6 or above, 3 accepted for Music School. 40 in school orchestra, 36 in choir, 20 in chamber music group, 40 in band, 2 in youth orchestra at Snape. *Drama and dance*: 30 in school productions. *Art*: 10 take as non-examined subject; 26 GCSE; 11 A-level; 3 accepted for Art School. *Sport*: Hockey, rugby, cricket, netball, tennis, athletics, swimming, sailing available. 50 take non-compulsory sport. 14 represent county/country (shooting, hockey, rugby). *Other*: 10 have bronze Duke of Edinburgh's Award, 10 have silver. Other activities include computer club, chess, CCF (Army/RAF), rifle club, modern dancing, Christian Union, drama, music, fencing.

Careers 1 full time careers advisor. Average number of pupils accepted for *arts and humanities degree courses* at Oxbridge, 2; other universities, 18. *science and engineering degree courses* at Oxbridge, 3; other universities, 21; medical schools, 4; polytechnics or CHE, 9. *BEd*, 1. *other general training courses*, 4. Average number of pupils going straight into careers in armed services, 3; industry, 1; the City, 1; civil service, 1; other, 3.

Uniform School uniform worn throughout.

Houses/prefects Competitive houses. Prefects and head boy/girl – appointed by Head, house prefects and head of house by housemasters.

Religion Compulsory daily assemblies (C of E).

Social Debates, sporting activities, sixth form disco; visits abroad with local schools. Pupils allowed to bring own bike to school. Meals self service. School shop. No tobacco/alcohol allowed.

Discipline No corporal punishment. Pupils failing to produce homework once might expect either to produce it next day, or stay for further period after school; those caught smoking cannabis on the premises might expect suspension or expulsion.

Boarding 20% have own study bedroom, 20% share, 60% are in dormitories of 6+. 4 houses (of 15–55), divided by age, single sex. Resident matron in each house. Central dining room. Sixth formers can provide and cook snacks. 3 weekend exeats in 4. Visits to local town allowed daily.

Alumni association run by Mr J A Leslie, c/o the School.

Former pupils Rt Hon Sir Edward Du Cann.

WOODHOUSE GROVE

Woodhouse Grove School
Apperley Bridge
Bradford
West Yorkshire BD10 0NR
Telephone number 0532 502477

Enquiries/application to the Headmaster

- Co-ed
  Boys
  Girls
  Mixed sixth
- Day
- Boarding

Pupils 498
Upper sixth 80
Termly fees:
Day £998
Boarding £1635
HMC; Methodist
Group

WHAT IT'S LIKE

Founded in 1812, the main school and Brontë House (the junior department) have fine buildings in spacious grounds in the Aire Valley near Leeds and Bradford. Excellent all-round facilities and comfortable boarding accommodation are provided. A Methodist foundation, it attempts to provide a caring community and each pupil is encouraged to develop individual talents to the full. Religious worship in the Anglican tradition is compulsory. Academic standards are high and results good. Some 25–30 leavers go on to university each year and the same number to polytechnics. It is very strong in music, especially instrumental music. Sporting facilities are first rate and the standards in sport and games are high (several county representatives). There is some commitment to local community services and it has a promising record in the Duke of Edinburgh's Award Scheme.

SCHOOL PROFILE

Pupils Total over 12, 498. Day 366 (boys 273, girls 94); Boarding 132 (boys 102, girls 29). Entry age, 11, 13 and up to 24 each year into the sixth form. Own junior school provides over 20%. About 8 or 9% are children of former pupils.

Entrance Common entrance and own entrance exam used. Oversubscribed. Instrumental music (orchestral scholarships) or sport looked for. No religious requirements but school is Methodist. Text books provided by the school. 130 assisted places. About 80 academic and music scholarships each year, up to £2500 pa.

Parents 15+% are in the armed services. 60+% live within 30 miles; 10+% live overseas.

Staff Head D A Miller, in post for 16 years. 40 full time staff, 25 part time. Annual turnover 3%. Average age 41.

Academic work GCSE and A-levels. Average size of upper fifth 80; upper sixth 80. *O-levels*: on average, 11 pupils in upper fifth pass 1–4 subjects; 48, 5–7 subjects; 21 pass 8+ subjects. *A-levels*: on average, 7 pupils in upper sixth pass 1 subject; 10, 2 subjects; 39, 3 subjects and 18 pass 4 subjects. On average, 41 take science/engineering A-levels; 22 take arts and humanities; 11 a mixture. Geology and CDT offered to GCSE/A-level. *Computing facilities*: Computer studies GCSE and A-level plus acquaintance courses taught on Commodore 64/128 machines. Several departments use BBC machines. About 30 pupils in dyslexia unit. EFL provision.

Senior pupils' non-academic activities *Music*: 144 learn a musical instrument, 18 to Grade 6 or above, 2 accepted for Music School, 1 plays in pop group beyond school; 56 in school orchestra, 40 in concert band, 30 in choir,

10 in pop groups; 1 in National Youth Orchestra or European Youth Orchestra. 12 have played with National Children's Orchestra and local orchestras/bands. *Drama and dance*: 20 participate in school productions. 52 take Guildhall School exams. *Art*: 15 take as non-examined subject; 15 take GCSE; 16 A-level. 4 accepted for Art School. 14 belong to photographic club. *Sport*: Rugby, cricket, netball, hockey, tennis, squash, athletics, cross-country, badminton, basketball, table tennis, swimming available. Almost all take non-compulsory sport. 15 take RLSS. 9 represent county/country (rugby, lacrosse, cricket, hockey, athletics). *Other*: 15 take part in local community schemes. 12 have bronze Duke of Edinburgh's Award, 2 have silver and 2 have gold. Other activities include a computer club, chess club and matches, vigorous cycling club, Understanding Industry course for lower sixth each year. Driving lessons available.

Careers 5 part time advisors. Average number of pupils accepted for *arts and humanities degree courses* at universities, 11; polytechnics or CHE, 12. *science and engineering degree courses* at Oxbridge, 3; other universities, 14; medical schools, 2; polytechnics or CHE, 14. *BEd*, 4. *other general training courses*, 5. Average number of pupils going straight into careers in the armed services, 3; the church, 1; industry, 4; the City, 1; civil service, 1; music/drama, 2; 3, other.

Uniform School uniform worn except in the sixth.

Houses/prefects Competitive houses. Prefects, head boy/girl, head of house and house prefects – appointed by the Head.

Religion Morning prayers compulsory.

Social Regular exchanges with France and Germany. Meals self service. School shop. No tobacco/alcohol allowed.

Discipline No corporal punishment. Pupils failing to produce homework once might expect a warning.

Boarding Upper sixth have own study bedroom, lower sixth share; about half in dormitories of 6+. Houses of 50, in vertical groups and single sex. Resident qualified nurse(s). Central dining room. At least two weekend exeats each term. Visits to the local town allowed with permission.

Alumni association is run by G H Knowles, Hon Secretary, Old Grovian Association, c/o the School.

Former pupils Lord Woolley (President NFU); Sir Noel Stockdale (Chairman Asda); Alan Cuckston (harpsichord); Steven Burnhill (rugby international); Kenneth Hind (MP Ormskirk 1983–).

WORCESTER COLLEGE FOR THE BLIND

Worcester College for the Blind
Whittington Road
Worcester WR5 2JU
Telephone number 0905 354627

- Co-ed   Pupils 85
- Boys   Upper sixth Yes
- Girls   Termly fees:
- Mixed sixth   see below
- Day   HMC
- Boarding

Head Rev B R Manthorp
Age range 11–18; entry by assessment
Specialist school for the blind or those with seriously defective sight. Aided and administered by the RNIB. Fees subsidised by the RNIB and normally paid by pupils' LEA.

WORKSOP

Worksop College
Worksop
Nottinghamshire S80 3AP
Telephone number 0909 472391

- Co-ed   Pupils 390
- Boys   Upper sixth Yes
- Girls   Termly fees:
- Mixed sixth   Day £1310
- Day   Boarding £1950
- Boarding   HMC; Woodard

Head Mr A H Monro (2 years)
Age range 13–18; entrance by common entrance; own prep school
Scholarships including music and art.

WORTH

Worth School
Paddockhurst Road
Turners Hill
Crawley
West Sussex RH10 4SD
Telephone number 0324 715 207

- Co-ed   Pupils 320
- Boys   Upper sixth 68
- Girls   Termly fees:
- Mixed sixth Boarding £1975
- Day   HMC
- Boarding

Enquiries/application to the Headmaster

WHAT IT'S LIKE

Founded by Downside Abbey in 1933 as a prep school for Downside. In 1957 Worth was made independent and autonomous and in 1959 the upper school was opened for boys of 13+. By 1964 the school had reached the full age range of 13–18. Worth inherits many of the traditions of Downside but has developed its own life and distinctive spirit. The original buildings consist of a late 19th century country house built by Lord Cowdray which is set in an estate of 500 acres of parkland. Monastery and school are closely connected. Many of the lay staff live in houses on the estate so that, as far as possible, monks, lay staff and boys form one community. A well-equipped, energetic and well-run school, Worth lays considerable stress on religious instruction, worship and prayers; the school is informed by the belief that people's growth in faith and commitment to Christ is the fundamental basis of their education and future careers. A large staff (of whom a dozen or so are Benedictine monks) permit a staff:pupil ratio of 1:8. Academic standards are high and results consistently good. Each year 40 or more pupils go on to university (a high proportion for a school of this size which has had a sixth form for only 24 years). It is very strong indeed in voluntary service, drama and art. There is a wide range of sports and games and an excellent variety of clubs and societies which cater for most extra-curricular activities.

SCHOOL PROFILE

Pupils Total over 12, 320. Entry age, 9, 13 and into the sixth. Own junior department provides over 20%. 3–4% are children of former pupils.

Entrance Common entrance used; own exam for transfer from Worth junior house. Oversubscribed. Sport and musical skills looked for; pupils should be RC. Parents expected to buy A-level text books. 6 scholarships/bursaries, 50%–15% of annual fees.

Parents 15+% in armed services; 15+% are doctors, lawyers etc; 15+% in industry or commerce. 60+% live within 30 miles; 20+% live overseas.

Staff Head Father Stephen Ortiger, in post for 5 years. 52 full time staff, 20 part time. Annual turnover 2–4%. Average age 40.

Academic work GCSE, A-levels. Average size of upper fifth 70; upper sixth 68. *O-levels*: on average, 3 pupils in upper fifth pass 1–4 subjects; 15, 5–7 subjects; 48 pass 8+ subjects. *A-levels*: on average, 2 pupils in upper sixth pass 1 subject; 3, 2 subjects; 58, 3 subjects and 4 pass 4 subjects. On average, 20 take science/engineering A-levels; 30 take arts and humanities; 15 a mixture. *Computing facilities*: 30 in 2 computer rooms (junior and senior). Help with learning difficulties.

Senior pupils' non-academic activities *Music*: 60+ learn a musical instrument, 4 to Grade 6 or above, 1 accepted for Music School every other year. 60 in school orchestra, 25 in choir (member of RSCM), 10 in school pop group, 18 in string band, 15 in swing band. *Drama and dance*: 70 in school productions. 1 accepted for Drama/Dance School every other year; occasional pupil goes on to work in theatre. *Art*: 20 take as non-examined subject; 45 take GCSE, 20 take CDT GCSE, 3 A-level. 3 accepted for Art School; 15 belong to photographic club. *Sport*: Rugby, football, cricket, tennis, squash, fencing, sailing, judo, karate, athletics, swimming, orienteering, cross-country, weight-lifting, basketball, indoor hockey available. Most take non-compulsory sport. 15 take lifesaving exams. Pupils represent county/country (rugby, cross-country, fencing). *Other*: 200 take part in local community schemes. 65 have bronze Duke of Edinburgh's Award, 45 have silver and 6 gold. 5 enter voluntary schemes after leaving, 25 go with handicapped to Lourdes, 3 work with national charities, 3 with charities in India. Other activities include a computer club, voluntary service (old/disabled), social and development projects, and a wide range of sporting and academic hobbies and societies.

Careers 4 part time careers advisors. Average number of pupils accepted for *arts and humanities degree courses* at Oxbridge, 4; other universities, 17; polytechnics or CHE, 3. *science and engineering degree courses* at Oxbridge, 3; other universities, 16; medical schools, 6; polytechnics or CHE, 3. *BEd*, 1. Average number of pupils going straight into careers (many after further education) in armed services, 15; the church, 2; industry, 1; the City, 10; civil service, 2; music/drama, 1. Traditional school career, medicine.

Uniform School uniform worn throughout.

Houses/prefects Competitive houses. Prefects, head boy, head of house and house prefects – appointed by Head and housemasters.

Religion Sunday Mass compulsory; voluntary weekday house Mass/evening prayers.

Social Plays with girls' schools, debates, choral society, sixth form dances. French exchange, skiing, annual Lourdes pilgrimage. Meals self service. School shop. No tobacco allowed; limited alcohol for seniors at school functions.

Discipline No corporal punishment. Pupils failing to produce homework once might expect to have to get up early and do it before school, or in detention.

Boarding Most sixth formers have own study bedroom, 10 sixth formers share (1 other). Resident qualified nurse; doctor visits regularly. Central dining room. Basic allowance of 3 weekend exeats per term, up to 5 may be earned. Sunday visits to local town allowed (14+).

Alumni association run by Kevin Taggart, c/o the School.

WREKIN

Wrekin College	● Co-ed	Pupils 385
Wellington	Boys	Upper sixth 65
Telford	Girls	Termly fees:
Shropshire TF1 3BG	Mixed sixth	Day £1540
Telephone number 0952 40131	● Day	Boarding £2250
Enquiries/application to the Headmaster	● Boarding	HMC; Allied School

WHAT IT'S LIKE

Founded in 1880, it has a fine campus on an estate of about 100 acres stretching out to the Shropshire Plain and backed by the hills of the Wrekin and Ercall. The well-designed and attractive buildings are well dispersed among lawns and gardens with very fine playing fields close by on the edge of the market town. Modern facilities and accommodation are first rate. A

C of E foundation, but interdenominational. Anglican practice and worship is encouraged. The pastoral care system is of a high order. Academic standards are high and results are good. Some 20–25 leavers go on to university each year. Music, art and drama departments are very vigorous indeed. Sports and games (there is a wide variety) are an important feature. All take part in some compulsory sport. There have been many county and international representatives. An impressive range of extra-curricular activities. Some commitment to local community services.

SCHOOL PROFILE

Pupils Total, 385. Day 60 (boys 45, girls 15); Boarding 325 (boys 200, girls 125). Entry age, 13 and into the sixth. 15% are children of former pupils.

Entrance Common entrance and own entrance exam used. Oversubscribed. No special skills or religious requirements. Parents not expected to buy text books. No assisted places yet. 20 scholarships/bursaries, £1366–£510.

Parents 15+% in industry or commerce. 10+% live within 30 miles; up to 10% live overseas.

Staff Head J H Arkell. 37 full time staff, 12 part time. Annual turnover 6%. Average age 35.

Academic work GCSE and A-levels. Average size of upper fifth 80; upper sixth 65. *O-levels*: on average, 12 pupils in upper fifth pass 1–4 subjects; 43, 5–7 subjects; 26 pass 8+ subjects. *A-levels*: on average, 5 pupils in upper sixth pass 1 subject; 6, 2 subjects; 46, 3 subjects and 5 pass 4 subjects. On average, 12 take science/engineering A-levels; 13 take arts and humanities; 40 a mixture. Pottery is offered to GCSE/A-level. *Computing facilities*: 12 in one room and several elsewhere – physics, economics etc. Special unit, with two specialist teachers, for dyslexic pupils and EFL.

Senior pupils' non-academic activities *Music*: 52 learn a musical instrument, 12 to Grade 6 or above; 2 accepted for Music School; 1 plays in pop group beyond school; 28 in school orchestra; 46 in choir; 8 in pop group; 20 in jazz band; 4 go to summer schools. *Drama and dance*: 25 participate in school productions – 3 a year. Drama and dance taught to all junior girls. 1 or 2 a year go on to work in theatre. *Art*: 20 take art as non-examined subject; 30 take GCSE; 25 A-level; 1 pottery; 5 a year on average accepted for Art School; 6 belong to photographic club. Photography offered to GCSE. *Sport*: Rugby, hockey, cricket, netball, athletics, swimming, squash, fives, fencing, shooting, canoeing, sailing, abseiling, climbing, cross-country, 5-a-side soccer available. Most take non-compulsory sport and all take part in some compulsory sport. 3 pupils represent country at gymnastics; 38 represent county (hockey, rugby, athletics, squash, swimming, fencing). *Other*: 15 take part in local community schemes. 3 have silver Duke of Edinburgh's Award, 1 has gold. Other activities include a computer club, chess club, driving lessons. All juniors take self defence. Many seniors take a course in financial skills (mortgages, hire purchase etc).

Careers 2 full time advisors and 1 part time from commerce/industry. Average number of pupils accepted for *arts and humanities degree courses* at Oxbridge, 2; other universities, 14; polytechnics or CHE, 8. *science and engineering degree courses* at Oxbridge, 1; other universities, 6; polytechnics or CHE, 4. *BEd*, 3. *other general training courses*, 10. Average number of pupils going straight into careers in the armed services, 2; industry, 5; music/drama, 1. Sixth formers attend interview preparation course.

Uniform School uniform worn except by girls in sixth.

Houses/prefects Competitive houses. Prefects, head boy and girl, head of house and house prefects – appointed by the Head.

Religion Religious worship.

Social Choral works with several local schools. 4 organised trips abroad at Easter holidays (eg canoe trip up Moselle). Meals self service. School shop. No tobacco allowed; alcohol in supervised sixth form bar.

Discipline No corporal punishment. Pupils failing to produce homework once might expect to do it again; those caught smoking cannabis on the premises could expect expulsion.

Boarding 20% have own study bedroom, 40% share (with one other); 20% are in dormitories of 6+. Houses, of 65 same as competitive houses, single sex. Resident qualified nurse and doctor. Central dining room. Pupils can provide and cook own food. 2 overnight exeats and half term. Visits to the local town allowed.

Alumni association run by The Reverend K D Minty, c/o the College.

Former pupils Sir Peter Gadsden (Lord Mayor of London, 1980); Brian Epstein (Beatles manager); Cyril Holmes (Olympic athlete and rugby player); many generals, judges and eminent doctors. Harry Andrews (actor); Noel Murless (Keeper of Queen's racehorses).

WROXALL ABBEY

Wroxall Abbey School		Co-ed	Pupils 150
Warwick CV35 7NB		Boys	Upper sixth Yes
Telephone number 0926 87220		● Girls	Termly fees:
		Mixed sixth	Day £1070
		● Day	Boarding £1800
		● Boarding	GSA; ISAI

Head Mrs I D M Iles (8 years)

Age range 11–18; own junior from age 8; entrance by common entrance or own exam

Scholarships and bursaries. Dyslexia provision.

WYCHWOOD

Wychwood School		Co-ed	Pupils 160
74 Banbury Road		Boys	Upper sixth 20
Oxford OX2 6JR		● Girls	Termly fees:
Telephone number 0865 57976		Mixed sixth	Day £875
		● Day	Boarding £1490
Enquiries/application to the Headmistress		● Boarding	GSA

WHAT IT'S LIKE

Founded in 1897 it is urban and single site on the Banbury Road half a mile from the middle of Oxford. It comprises four main houses and sundry other buildings. Modern facilities are good. Worship in the Anglican tradition is compulsory for the first three years. The school council plays a large part in the daily organisation. The atmosphere is friendly and relaxed. Academic standards are high and results are good. Some 8–10 leavers go on to university. A strong music department (virtually everyone is involved). Drama and art are also strong throughout the school. Full use is made of Oxford's cultural amenities. Adequate sports, games and activities. Some involvement in local community schemes.

SCHOOL PROFILE

Pupils Total over 12, 160. Day 80; Boarding 80. Entry age, 11 and into the sixth. Crescent School, Oxford and Manor Prep, Abingdon provide over 20%. 5% are children of former pupils.

Entrance Own entrance test used. Not oversubscribed. Interesting children with any special talent looked for at entry. No religious requirements. Parents expected to buy text books for pupils in sixth form.

Parents 30+% in industry or commerce; 30+% are doctors, lawyers etc. 50+% live within 30 miles; up to 10% live overseas.

Staff Head Mrs M L Duffill. 14 full time staff, 12 part time. Annual turnover 1%. Average age 40.

Academic work GCSE and A-levels. Average size of upper fifth 28; upper sixth 20. *O-levels*: on average, 6 pupils in upper fifth pass 1–4 subjects; 17, 5–7 subjects; 6 pass 8+ subjects. *A-levels*: on average, 5 pupils in upper sixth pass 2 subjects; and 10 pass 3 subjects. On average, 4 take science/engineering A-levels; 10 take arts and humanities; 2 a mixture. Photography and theatre studies are offered to GCSE. *Computing facilities*: BBC Masters, 1 machine to 2 pupils in a class. Some provision for dyslexia, visual handicap and EFL.

Senior pupils' non-academic activities *Music*: 145 learn a musical instrument, 25 to Grade 6 or above. 1 accepted for Music School. 50 in school orchestra, 50 in choir, others in chamber groups and take singing lessons; 1 in National Youth Orchestra; 6 in county orchestra; 4 in Thames Vale Orchestra. *Drama and dance*: 50 in school productions eg Shakespeare, Salad Days, The Boyfriend, The Importance of Being Earnest. *Art*: 80% take GCSE; 6, A-level. 4 accepted for Art School. 10 belong to photographic class. *Sport*: Badminton, squash, tennis, swimming, netball, hockey available. 25 take non-compulsory sport. 3 represent county/country (tennis, swimming). *Other*: 15 take part in local community schemes. Other activities include a computer club, debating society, Christian Union, science club.

Careers Average number of pupils accepted for *arts and humanities degree courses* at Oxbridge, 1; other universities, 4. *science and engineering degree courses* at universities, 4. *other general training courses*, 8. Average number of pupils going straight into careers in the City, 1; civil service, 1.

Uniform School uniform worn except in the sixth.

Houses/prefects No competitive houses. No prefects but councillors selected by the school. Head girl – appointed by Head. School Council.

Religion Church attendance compulsory in first three years.

Social Theatre, operas, lectures etc organised. Use of the city and university facilities. School exchange with Madrid. First and fourth year have week's visit to Normandy. Field trips in UK. Pupils allowed to bring own bike to school in third year. Meals formal. School tuckshop, opens twice a week. No tobacco/alcohol allowed.

Discipline No corporal punishment. The school has a well tried and proven system of Majors which the girls promoted and therefore adhere to. A pupil caught drinking, smoking or going out of school without permission could expect to be sent home immediately.

Boarding Upper sixth have own study bedroom, Lower sixth share (2 or 3); all others in dormitories of 6 or less. Central dining room. Sixth form can provide and cook own food at specified times. 2 exeats each term plus four days. Visits to city allowed by fourth form and above.

WYCLIFFE

Wycliffe College	● Co-ed	Pupils 337
Stonehouse	Boys	Upper sixth 75
Gloucestershire GL10 2JQ	Girls	Termly fees:
Telephone number 045 382 2432	Mixed sixth	Day £1455
	● Day	Boarding £2240
Enquiries/application to the Headmaster	● Boarding	HMC

WHAT IT'S LIKE

Founded in 1882 by G W Sibly, the first headmaster. It became a public school in 1931, by which time the Sibly family had given it a distinctive character which included vigorous championing of vegetarianism and a 'sturdy Protestant independence'. It enjoys a very fine 60-acre, semi-rural site in the Gloucestershire countryside and is within easy range of Gloucester, Cheltenham, Bath and Bristol. The buildings – a mixture of late Victorian and modern, and some typically Cotswold – are loosely scattered over a campus which has magnificent gardens and playing fields. A very healthy environment. Much development has taken place in the last 20 years and the school is very well equipped. The junior school is close by on a 27-acre site. It is interdenominational and there is considerable emphasis on religious instruction and worship (the fine chapel was built by pupils and members of staff in the 1950s). A well-organised school in which there is much enterprise and energy. The teaching is good and academic results are impressive. Each year 35–40 pupils go on to university (a high proportion for a school of this size). There is much strength in music, drama and art. An excellent range of sports and games and an equally good range of extra-curricular activities. The school has a massive commitment to local community schemes and a remarkable record in the Duke of Edinburgh's Award Scheme.

SCHOOL PROFILE

Pupils Total, 337. Day 130 (boys 95, girls 35); Boarding 207 (boys 154, girls 53). Entry age, 13 and into the sixth. Own junior school provides over 20%. 8% are children of former pupils.

Entrance Common entrance and own scholarship exams used. Not oversubscribed. Musical skills looked for; no religious requirements. Parents not expected to buy text books. 34 assisted places. 10 scholarships/bursaries, 50%–5% of fees.

Parents 15+% are in industry or commerce. 30+% live within 30 miles; 10+% live overseas.

Staff Head A P Millard, in post for 1 year. 35 full time staff, 7 part time. Average age 36.

Academic work GCSE, AS, A-levels. Average size of upper fifth 64; upper sixth 75. *O-levels*: on average, 17 pupils in upper fifth pass 1–4 subjects; 23, 5–7 subjects; 24 pass 8+ subjects. *A-levels*: on average, 5 pupils in upper sixth pass 1 subject; 17, 2 subjects; 49, 3 subjects and 4 pass 4 subjects. On average, 20 take science/engineering A-levels; 37 take arts and humanities; 18 a mixture. *Computing facilities*: 12 Applemac in purpose-designed rooms, 2 BBC, laser printer and image writer. Provision for EFL and those with difficulty in English.

Senior pupils' non-academic activities *Music*: 80 learn a musical instrument, 36 to Grade 6 or above, 1 accepted for Music School, 1 for university music course. 25 in school orchestra, 30 in choirs, 5 in school pop group, 20 in concert band, 12 in stage band. 3 in county youth orchestra. *Drama and dance*: 30 in school productions, 10 in weekly workshops. 1 accepted for university drama course. *Art*: 8 take as non-examined subject, 17 GCSE, 23 A-level. 5 accepted for Art School. 30 belong to eg photographic club. *Sport*: Rugby, rowing, soccer, hockey, tennis, cricket, athletics, swimming, badminton, cross-country, basketball, squash available. 2 represent country in lacrosse, judo (bronze medallist); several represent county (rugby, cricket). *Other*: 100 take part in local community schemes. 20 have bronze Duke of Edinburgh's Award, 50 have silver and 10 gold. Other activities include a computer club, scouts (and venture scouts), CCF (Army/RAF), car mechanics, drama, sub-aqua, metalwork, woodwork, electronics, video-making, pottery, debating, Young Enterprise, gymnastics, model-making.

Careers 1 full time and 1 part time careers advisors. Annual Careers Day. Average number of pupils accepted for *arts and humanities degree courses* at Oxbridge, 3; other universities, 20; polytechnics or CHE, 12. *science and engineering degree courses* at Oxbridge, 3; other universities, 10; medical schools, 2; polytechnics or CHE, 6. *BEd*, 2. *other general training courses*, 4. Average number of pupils going straight into careers in armed services, 1; the church, 1; the City, 1.

Uniform School uniform worn throughout.

Houses/prefects Competitive houses. Prefects, head boy/girl, head of house and house prefects – appointed by Head.

Religion Worship encouraged. Compulsory daily chapel, Sunday service for boarders. Resident Chaplain.

Social Debates, quizzes with local schools; ski-ing, language, rugby, rowing trips abroad. Pupils allowed to bring own car/bike/motorbike to school. Meals self service. School shop (stationery, sports equipment, toiletries). No tobacco/alcohol allowed.

Discipline No corporal punishment. Pupils failing to produce homework once might expect extra work period; those caught smoking cannabis on the premises might expect expulsion.

Boarding 25% have own study bedroom, 35% share, 40% in dormitories of 6+. Houses, of approximately 45, are same as competitive houses and are single sex. Resident qualified nurse/doctor. Separate house dining rooms.

Pupils can provide and cook own food. Termly exeats (4 days). Visits to local town allowed in free time.
Alumni association run by Major P L Rawll, Bursar's Office, c/o the College.
Former pupils Jeremy Nicholas and Mike Gwilym (actors); Simon Coombs MP; Air Vice Marshal Michael Graydon.

WYCOMBE ABBEY

Wycombe Abbey School
High Wycombe
Buckinghamshire HP11 1PE
Telephone number 0494 20381

Enquiries to the School Secretary
Application to the Headmistress

Co-ed
Boys
● Girls
Mixed sixth
Day
● Boarding

Pupils 468
Upper sixth 80
Termly fees:
Boarding £2400
GSA

WHAT IT'S LIKE

Founded in 1896, it is near the centre of High Wycombe. The main building is a very large mansion in 160 acres of fine grounds. Exceptionally good modern facilities and comfortable boarding accommodation are provided. Academic standards are high. It is a C of E school with its own chapel. All pupils are required to attend daily prayers and a Sunday service. Scripture lessons are also obligatory. The music, drama, and art departments are extremely strong. A fine range of sports, games and activities is available. Standards in games are high (20 or more representatives at county level). There is a big commitment to local community schemes and the school has a promising record in the Duke of Edinburgh's Award Scheme.

SCHOOL PROFILE

Pupils Total over 12, 468. Entry age, 11, 12, 13 and into the sixth.
Entrance Common entrance exam used. Special skills are always of interest. No religious requirements, but school is C of E. Parents expected to buy some text books. 10 junior, 3 sixth form scholarships/bursaries, two-thirds–full fees.
Parents 15+% are doctors, lawyers, etc. Up to 10% live within 30 miles; up to 10% live overseas.
Staff Head Patricia M Lancaster, in post for 14 years; (From January 1989), Mrs J M Goodland. Annual turnover of staff 1%.
Academic work GCSE and A-levels. Average size of upper fifth 80; upper sixth 80. *O-levels*: on average, all pupils in upper fifth pass 5 or more subjects. *A-levels*: on average, 1 pupil in the upper sixth passes 2 subjects; 79 pass 3 subjects. *Computing facilities*: equipped computer room.
Senior pupils' non-academic activities *Music*: 368 learn a musical instrument, 60 to Grade 6 or above, 1 accepted for Music School; 90 in school orchestra, 170 in choir; some in National Youth Orchestra. *Drama and dance*: 200 in school productions; 30 take Grade 6 in ESB, RAD etc; 1 accepted for Drama/Dance School. *Art*: 40 take GCSE; 5 A-level; 20 belong to photographic club. *Sport*: Lacrosse, netball, tennis, squash, golf, rounders,

fencing, gym, trampolining available. Most take non-compulsory sport or participate in matches. 20 represent county/country (tennis, lacrosse, squash). *Other*: 80 take part in local community schemes. 30 have bronze Duke of Edinburgh's Award, 10 have silver and 5 have gold. Many involved in fund raising for charities. Other activities include 2 computer clubs, dining, cookery and bridge clubs, Caledonian, fine art, debating and play reading societies, driving lessons.

Careers 1 full time advisor. Traditional career, law.

Uniform School uniform worn except in the upper sixth.

Houses/prefects Competitive houses. Prefects, head girl, head of house and house prefects. School Council.

Religion Religious worship compulsory.

Social Caledonian Society, choir, debating society, public speaking and dining clubs with boys' schools. Organised choir trip to Berlin, ski-ing, cultural visits. Meals formal. School shop. No tobacco allowed; alcohol only on certain occasions.

Discipline No corporal punishment.

Boarding Pupils divided into different houses for sleeping, 43 in each.

Former pupils Dame Elizabeth Butler Sloss; Lady Elspeth Howe (Equal Opportunities, wife of Sir Geoffrey Howe).

WYNSTONES

Wynstones	● Co-ed	Pupils 134
Whaddon	Boys	Upper sixth 25
Gloucester GL4 0UF	Girls	Termly fees:
Telephone number 0452 22475	Mixed sixth	Day £600
	● Day	Boarding £930
Enquiries/application to the College of Teachers	● Boarding	Steiner

WHAT IT'S LIKE

It has an agreeable semi-rural site with well-equipped buildings and gardens. Its programme is based on Rudolf Steiner principles and the education is concerned with the inner developmental stages of the child. In the Kindergarten, the main emphasis is on the development of the will, through play and group activities such as games, songs, verses, stories, artistic and practical work. In the lower school the emphasis is on the education of the heart – the life of feelings – to awaken imagination and a sound social sense. In the upper school the emphasis shifts to the development of clear thinking and the exercise of healthy critical judgment. Academic results are quite good and a few pupils go on to university each year. There is much emphasis on musical activity and a good deal of drama and art. A full gym, sports and games programme is available and there are some extra-curricular activities. The school has a promising record in the Duke of Edinburgh's Award Scheme.

SCHOOL PROFILE

Pupils Total over 12, 134. Day 125 (boys 66, girls 59); Boarding 9 (boys 5, girls 4). Entry age, 6–7 and into the sixth.

Entrance Entrance by interview. Sometimes oversubscribed. No special skills or religious requirements. Parents expected to buy text books. No scholarships/bursaries.

Parents 60+% live within 30 miles; up to 10% live overseas.

Staff Head, Chairman, College of Teachers (changes annually). 25 full time staff, 20 part time. Annual turnover 2%. Average age 40.

Academic work GCSE and A-levels. Average size of upper fifth 30; upper sixth 25. *O-levels*: on average, 23 pupils in upper fifth pass 1–4 subjects; 5 pass 5–6 subjects. *A-levels*: on average, 10 pupils in upper sixth pass 1 subject; 4 pass 2 subjects; all in arts and humanities. *Computing facilities*: 2 computers. (School's approach to teaching does not include it as a learning aid for other subjects.) Provision for special needs within Steiner educational philosophy, artistic, speech and movement therapy.

Senior pupils' non-academic activities *Music*: 30 learn a musical instrument, 6–8 to Grade 6 or above, 1 accepted for Music School every second year; 27 in school orchestra, all attend choir and regular lessons on appreciation and composition; 5 play in local orchestra. *Drama and dance*: 20 in school productions; 2 take exams. 1 accepted for Drama/Dance School; 3 go on to work in theatre. *Art*: 66 take as non-examined subject; 12 take GCSE; 4, A-level; 1–2 accepted for Art School; 2 belong to eg photographic club. *Sport*: Basketball, tennis, hockey, softball available. 20 take non-compulsory sport: 3 represent county/country (basketball, rugby). *Other*: 15 have bronze Duke of Edinburgh's Award, 2 have silver and 1 gold; 3 gain other awards. 5 enter voluntary schemes after leaving; 1 works for national charity. Other activities include woodcraft, lapidary, jewellery, photography, printing; small school farm.

Careers 1 part time careers advisor. Average number of pupils accepted for *arts and humanities degree courses* at universities, 3; polytechnics or CHE, 1. *science and engineering degree courses* at universities, 2. *BEd*, 1. *other general training courses*, 2. Average number of pupils going straight into careers in music/drama, 1; other careers, 1.

Uniform School uniform not worn.

Houses/prefects No competitive houses or prefects.

Religion Non-denominational Christian assemblies/festivals.

Social Sporting functions with local schools. Organised trips abroad with other Rudolf Steiner schools. Pupils allowed to bring own car/bike/motorbike/horse to school. Meals self service. No tobacco/alcohol allowed.

Discipline No corporal punishment. Pupils failing to produce homework once might expect to stay in after school; those caught smoking cannabis on the premises would have no future at Wynstones.

Boarding In local, selected private family homes of school parents.

Alumni association run by Mrs Faith Hall, c/o the School.

YARM

Yarm School
The Friarage
Yarm
Cleveland TS15 9EJ
Telephone number 0642 786023

Enquiries/application to the Headmaster's
Secretary

Co-ed   Pupils 365
● Boys   Upper sixth 50
Girls   Termly fees:
● Mixed sixth   Day £850
● Day
Boarding

WHAT IT'S LIKE

The original Yarm Grammar School was founded in 1590. In 1977 the pupils were transferred to the new Yarm comprehensive. In 1976 it had been decided to re-found the school on an independent basis. The new one opened in 1978. The major buildings are located at the Friarage, an 18th-century mansion on 14 acres of pleasant grounds alongside the River Tees. Excellent modern facilities are provided. Academic standards are high. About 50% of the sixth form (a high proportion for a school of this size) go on to university each year (this number includes about 6 to Oxbridge). The music, drama and art departments are strong. There is a wide variety of sports and games and an excellent range of activities. The school enjoys a good reputation in sport and games and has produced a number of county representatives. In the Duke of Edinburgh's Award Scheme it has an outstanding record.

SCHOOL PROFILE

Pupils Total over 12, 365 (boys 350, girls 15). Entry age, boys, 10+, 11+; boys and girls directly into the sixth form.

Entrance Common entrance or own entrance exam used. Usually oversubscribed. No religious requirements. Parents expected to buy some text books in sixth form. 40 scholarships/bursaries at all age ranges, up to 33% of fees.

Parents 15+% in industry or commerce; 15+% are doctors, lawyers, etc. Most live within 30 miles.

Staff Head R Neville Tate, in post for 10 years. 33 full time staff, 12 part time. Annual turnover 5%. Average age 39.

Academic work Pupils prepared for GCSE and A-level. Average size of upper fifth 60; upper sixth 50. *O-levels*: on average, 24 top pupils in upper fifth pass 9 subjects. Overall average 7.4 subjects/pupil. *A-levels*: Average number of passes/candidate, 3.1. On average, 50% take science/engineering A-levels; 35% take arts and humanities; 15% take a mixture. *Computing facilities*: Computer room (maths dept) plus use of computer facilities/ computer aided learning/word processor in modern languages, physics, chemistry, biology and careers depts (19 BBC plus printers / disks etc). Computer aided design facility. All pupils take City and Guilds course in computer competence.

Senior pupils' non-academic activities *Music*: 15% learn a musical instrument, 14 to Grade 6 or above; 5% in school orchestra; 8% in choir; 1 pupil in National Youth Orchestra; 3 in other orchestras; 1 pupil on average accepted for music school. *Drama and dance*: 10–20% in school productions each year; 1 pupil on average accepted for drama/dance school. *Art*: 60% take art as non-examined subject; 12–15 take GCSE, 4–6 A-level; 2 on average accepted for art school; 18 belong to eg photographic club. *Sport*: Rugby, hockey, cricket, athletics, rowing, tennis, squash, cross-country available; limited activity in ski-ing, swimming, golf, badminton and 6-a-side football. 80 take non-compulsory sport. 16 represent county (rugby, hockey, cricket, tennis, squash). *Other*: 90+ have bronze Duke of Edinburgh's Award, 20+ have silver and 20+ gold. Other activities include a computer club (junior and senior), CAD and computer graphics clubs, chess (Inter School teams), maths (Inter School contests), some rock climbing and expedition work, photography, war games, walking, metalwork, plastics moulding, radio control car club, electronics, debating, cooking, extra curricular art and design, expedition activity (eg India 1986, Egypt 1985, Peru 1988).

Careers 2 part time careers advisors. Average number of pupils accepted for *degree courses* at Oxbridge, 20%; other universities, 30%; polytechnics or CHE, 40%. Average number of pupils going straight into careers in industry, 8% of sixth form; armed services, 4%.

Uniform School uniform worn modified in the sixth.

Houses/prefects Competitive houses. Prefects, head boy, head of house and house prefects – appointed by the Head. School Council.

Religion One compulsory chapel service per week.

Social Joint concerts and orchestral occasions with local choral society and Polam Hall girls' school (Darlington). About 4 or 5 organised trips abroad each year plus exchanges. Sixth form pupils allowed to bring own bicycle to school. Meals self service. Uniform shop and tuck shop run as company by pupils. No tobacco/alcohol allowed.

Discipline Corporal punishment by Headmaster only. Pupils failing to produce homework once might expect verbal rebuke.

Alumni association is run by G E Thompson, c/o The Friarage, Yarm, Cleveland.

YORK COLLEGE

York College for Girls
62 Low Petergate
York YO1 2HZ
Telephone number 0904 646421

Enquiries/application to the Headmistress

Co-ed
Boys
● Girls
Mixed sixth
● Day
Boarding

Pupils 212
Upper sixth 20
Termly fees:
Day £873
GSA/Church
Schools
Company

WHAT IT'S LIKE

Founded in 1908, it is right in the City centre in the shadow of the Minster. Its very attractive buildings incorporate 15th-century, Georgian and Victorian architecture, plus a big modern wing. The junior school is nearby and the playing fields are 7 minutes away. It follows Anglican tradition and worship and keeps close links with the cathedral. A balanced all-round education is provided and academic standards are high. Some 12+ leavers go on to university each year. It is tremendously strong in music and drama. About

50% of pupils learn an instrument and most are involved at some time or another in dramatic productions. A good range of games and sports is available and there are plenty of activities. There is a massive, 100% commitment to local community schemes. Involvement on such a scale is rare.

SCHOOL PROFILE

Pupils Total over 12, 212. Entry age, 4 and into the sixth. Own junior department provides over 20%. Less than 10% are children of former pupils.
Entrance Own entrance exam used. Not oversubscribed. No special skills. Anglican school but accepts pupils of all religious persuasions. Parents not expected to buy text books. 1–3 scholarships/bursaries pa, one-third to full fees.
Parents 15+% in farming. More than 60% live within 30 miles.
Staff Head Mrs J L Clare, in post for 6 years. 26 full time staff, 8 part time. Annual turnover 5%. Average age between 30 and 40.
Academic work GCSE and A-levels. Average size of upper fifth 40; upper sixth 20 (increasing). *O-levels*: on average, 9 pupils in upper fifth pass 1–4 subjects; 10, 5–7 subjects; 14 pass 8+ subjects. *A-levels*: on average, 1 pupil in upper sixth passes 1 subject; 1, 2 subjects; 1, 3 subjects and 4 pass 4 subjects. On average, 4 take science/engineering A-levels; 4 take arts and humanities; 4 a mixture. *Computing facilities*: Computer room. Maths and geography have their own computers. Computer studies offered at A-level.
Senior pupils' non-academic activities *Music*: 50% learn a musical instrument. *Drama and dance*: School tries to involve everyone at some time. *Art*: 25% take GCSE. 1–2 accepted for Art School. *Sport*: Tennis, rounders, swimming, hockey, badminton, netball, squash, athletics, cross-country, fencing, gymnastics available. Over 50% take non-compulsory sport. 2 or 3 represent county/country at various sports. *Other*: Everyone takes part in local community schemes. Other activities include a computer club, choir, orchestra, chess, weight training, art club, drama club, needlework, dance.
Careers 1 full time advisor. Average number of pupils accepted for *arts and humanities degree courses* at Oxbridge, 2; other universities, 5. *science and engineering degree courses* at universities, 3.
Uniform School uniform worn except in the sixth.
Houses/prefects No houses. No prefects. Head girl and deputy – elected by the staff and sixth form. School Council.
Religion Daily assembly. Termly eucharists in the Minster. Saints Day communion in own chapel.
Social Organised trips abroad and exchange systems. Pupils allowed to bring own bike/motorbike to school. Meals self service. No tobacco/alcohol allowed.
Discipline No corporal punishment. Pupils failing to produce homework once might expect a 'returned lesson' or a disorder mark; more serious offences could expect parental involvement and possible expulsion.
Alumni association run by Mrs G Sharper, Secretary OGA, Manor Garth, Church Lane, Skelton, York.
Former pupils Dame Janet Baker.

SPECIAL
FEATURES
INDEX

SPECIAL FEATURES INDEX

Name of School	Boys/ Girls/ Co-ed	Day/ Board	Termly fees Day/ Board	Financial help	Intake age/ Own prep	Special strengths	Special provisions	Religion	Affiliations
AVON									
Badminton	Girls	Day Boarding	£1150 £2050	Schols 20	7	Music, Sport, Drama, Art		Inter-denom	GSA
Bath High	Girls	Day	£620	Asst places Schols	5			Non-denom	GPDST GSA
Bristol Cathedral	Boys Mixed sixth	Day	£747	Asst places 25+ pa Schols	10			C of E	HMC CSA
Bristol Grammar	Co-ed	Day	£740	Asst places 350 Schols 7	11 Own junior	Sport		Inter-denom	HMC
Clifton	Co-ed	Day Boarding	£1600 £2350	Asst places 34 Schols 24	13 Own prep	Music, Art	EFL	Christian Jewish	HMC
Clifton High	Girls	Day Boarding	£720 £1450	Asst places 52 Schols 43	10 Own junior	Drama, Art, Sport		Christian	GSA
Colston's (Boys)	Boys Mixed sixth	Day Boarding	£1100 £1825	Asst places 90 Schols 8	13 Own prep	Sport	Dyslexia	C of E	HMC SHMIS

780

School	Gender		Fees	Places/Scholarships	Entry age	Subjects	Support	Religion	Association
Colston's (Girls)	Girls	Day	£705	Asst places 150 Schols 60 Bursaries	10	Music, Art		Christian	GSA
Grosvenor High	Co-ed	Day	£590	Schols 2 pa	11 Own junior		Dyslexia EFL	Christian	ISAI
King Edward's (Bath)	Boys Mixed sixth	Day	£681	Asst places 18 Schols 2 pa	11 Own junior			C of E	HMC
Kingswood	Co-ed	Day Boarding	£1400 £2160	Asst places 37 Schols 6 pa	11 Own prep	Art, Sport	Visiting specialists	Methodist	HMC
Monkton Combe	Boys Mixed sixth	Day Boarding	£1675 £2295	Asst places 10 pa Schols 8 pa Bursaries 8 pa	13 Own junior	Sport, Art	EFL Dyslexia	Christian	HMC
Prior Park	Co-ed	Day Boarding	£1023 £1805	Schols 7 pa Exhibitions Bursaries	11	Music		RC	HMC
Queen Elizabeth's Hospital	Boys	Day Boarding	£735 £1310	Asst places 25 pa Schols 6 pa	11			Christian	HMC
Red Maids'	Girls	Day Boarding	£610 £1170	Asst places Schols	11 Own junior (7)			Non-denom	GSA GBGSA
Redland High	Girls	Day	£728	Asst places 83 Schols Bursaries	4	Art		Christian	GSA

Name of School	Boys/ Girls/ Co-ed	Day/ Board	Termly fees Day/ Board	Financial help	Intake age/ Own prep	Special strengths	Special provisions	Religion	Affiliations
St Brandon's	Girls	Day Boarding	£995 £1985	Schols Bursaries	5	Music, Drama	Dyslexia EFL	C of E	GSA
Sidcot	Co-ed	Day Boarding	£925 £1760	Schols Bursaries	9	Sport	Dyslexia EFL	Quaker	SHMIS
BEDFORDSHIRE									
Bedford	Boys	Day Boarding	£1200 £2058	Asst places 76 Schols 32 Bursaries	11 Own prep (7)	Music, Sport		Christian	HMC
Bedford High	Girls	Day Boarding	£780 £1530	Asst places Bursaries	7	Sport	EFL (sixth form)	Christian	GSA
Bedford Modern	Boys	Day Boarding	£733 £1365	Asst places 135 Bursaries 30 pa	11 Own prep (7)	Sport	Dyslexia EFL Mild handicap	C of E	HMC IAPS
Dame Alice Harpur	Girls	Day	£641	Bursaries Asst places	11 Own prep (7)			Christian	GSA
BERKSHIRE									
Bearwood	Boys	Day Boarding	£1200 £2050	Schols 25+ Bursaries	11	Music, Sport	Dyslexia EFL	C of E	GBA SHMIS

782

School	Type	Day/Boarding	Fees	Scholarships/Bursaries	Age	Specialities	Extra	Denom	Assoc
Bradfield	Boys Mixed sixth	Day Boarding	£1836 £2450	Asst places 3 Schols 15 pa Bursaries	13	Music, Drama, Sport		C of E	HMC
Brigidine	Girls	Day	£595	Bursaries 2 pa	11	Drama	Yes	RC	GBGSA
Crookham Court	Boys	Day Boarding	£745 £1470	Bursaries	11		Dyslexia EFL	Christian	ISAI
Douai	Boys	Day Boarding	£1210 £1923	Schols 10	11		Dyslexia EFL	RC	HMC
Downe House	Girls	Day Boarding	£1330 £2050	Schols	11			C of E	GSA
Eton	Boys	Boarding	£2585	Schols 155 Bursaries 120	13 Own junior (10)	Sport, Art, Music, Drama		C of E	HMC
Heathfield (Ascot)	Girls	Boarding	£2300		11			C of E	GSA
Leighton Park	Boys Mixed sixth	Day Boarding	£1500 £2145	Schols Bursaries	11	Music, Drama, Art, Sport	Extra English Dyslexia	Quaker	HMC
Licensed Victuallers' (Slough)	Co-ed	Day Boarding	£957 £1767	Schols Bursaries	13 Own junior (4)			Non-denom	ISAI
Luckley-Oakfield	Girls	Day Boarding	£950 £1500	Schols	11			C of E	GSA GBGSA
Maidenhead	Girls	Day	£851	Schols 4	3	Drama	Yes	RC	

783

Name of School	Boys/ Girls/ Co-ed	Day/ Board	Termly fees Day/ Board	Financial help	Intake age/ Own prep	Special strengths	Special provisions	Religion	Affiliations
Pangbourne	Boys	Day Boarding	£1350 £1975	Schols 6 pa Bursaries	11			C of E	HMC
Queen Anne's (Caversham)	Girls	Day Boarding	£1050 £1700	Schols 6 Bursaries	11			C of E	GSA GBGSA
Reading Blue Coat	Boys Mixed sixth	Day Boarding	£880 £1560	Schols 6 pa	11			C of E	GBA SHMIS
St George's (Ascot)	Girls	Day Boarding	£1250 £2225		11			Christian	GSA
St Mary's (Ascot)	Girls	Day Boarding	£1134 £1890		10		Dyslexia	RC	GSA
Wellington College	Boys Mixed sixth	Day Boarding	£1570 £2160	Asst places 34 Schols 11	13	Drama, Music, Art	Dyslexia	Christian	HMC
BUCKINGHAMSHIRE									
Charmandean	Girls	Day Boarding	£756 £1381	Schols (sixth form)	11 Own prep (8)			C of E	ISAI
Oakdene	Girls	Day Boarding	£1019 £1722	Schols 16	12 Own prep (8)		EFL	C of E	GSA

School	Type	Day/Boarding	Fees	Scholarships	Entry age	Activities	Special needs	Religion	Associations
St Mary's (Gerrards Cross)	Girls	Day	£800	Schols 6 pa Bursaries 2	11 Own junior	Drama	EFL Dyslexia Mild handicap	Christian	GSA GBGSA
Stowe	Boys Mixed sixth	Day Boarding	£1648 £2355	Asst places 5 pa Schols Exhibitions Bursaries	13	Sport	Dyslexia EFL	C of E	HMC SHA Allied
Wycombe Abbey	Girls	Boarding	£2400	Schols 13 pa	11	Sport, Music		C of E	GSA
CAMBRIDGESHIRE									
King's (Ely)	Co-ed	Day Boarding	£1485 £2330	Schols 50	13 Own junior		Yes	C of E	HMC
Leys, The	Boys Mixed sixth	Day Boarding	£1605 £2160	Asst places 7 Schols 18	13 Own prep	Drama, Art	Dyslexia EFL	Methodist	
Perse (Boys)	Boys	Day Boarding	£806 £1648	Asst places 57 Bursaries	11 Own prep	Art, Sport		Christian	HMC GBA
Perse (Girls)	Girls	Day	£775	Asst places Bursaries	7			Non-denom	GSA GBGSA
St Mary's (Cambridge)	Girls	Day Boarding	£720 £1280	Asst places 115	11	Drama Young Enterprise	Physical handicap	RC	GSA

Name of School	Boys/Girls/Co-ed	Day/Board	Termly fees Day/Board	Financial help	Intake age/Own prep	Special strengths	Special provisions	Religion	Affiliations
CHANNEL ISLANDS									
Elizabeth College	Boys	Day Boarding	£420 £1170	Schol 1 pa	7 11			C of E	HMC
Ladies' College (Guernsey)	Girls	Day	£320	Direct grant	3			Christian	GBA GSA
Victoria College (Jersey)	Boys	Day Boarding	£356 £1665	Schols 5 pa	11 Own prep		EFL	Christian	HMC
CHESHIRE									
Grange	Co-ed	Day	£600		11 Own prep			Christian	ISAI
Hammond	Co-ed	Day Boarding	£640 £1770	LEA	11	Classical ballet specialist		C of E	ISAI
King's (Chester)	Boys	Day	£544	Asst places 100 Schols	11 Own junior (8)		Visual handicap	C of E	HMC
King's (Macclesfield)	Boys Mixed sixth	Day	£825	Asst places 35 Schols 5	11	Sport	Yes	C of E	HMC

School	Gender	Day/Boarding	Fees	Scholarships/Bursaries	No.	Special	Religion	Assoc.
Mount Carmel	Girls	Day	£520	Bursaries	11		RC	GBGSA
Queen's (Chester)	Girls	Day	£680	Asst places 17 pa Bursaries	11 Own junior (4)		Christian	GSA GBGSA SHA
S Hilary's (Alderley Edge)	Girls	Day	£750	Schols Bursaries	4		C of E	GSA
CLEVELAND								
Friends' (Great Ayton)	Co-ed	Day £795 Boarding £1715		Schols	7	EFL	Quaker	GBA
Teeside High	Girls	Day	£650		4		Non-denom	GSA
Yarm	Boys Mixed sixth	Day	£850	Schols 40	10	Sport	Christian	
CORNWALL								
Duchy Grammar	Co-ed	Day £690 Boarding £1350		Schols 6	7	EFL	Christian	ISAI
St Clare's	Girls	Day £845 Boarding £1485		Schols 4–5 Bursaries	3	Yes	C of E	GSA Woodard
Truro	Boys Mixed sixth	Day £760 Boarding £1400		Asst places Schols	11 Own prep		Methodist	HMC
Truro High	Girls	Day £680 Boarding £1320		Asst places Schols	5		C of E	GSA GBGSA

Name of School	Boys/ Girls/ Co-ed	Day/ Board	Termly fees Day/ Board	Financial help	Intake age/ Own prep	Special strengths	Special provisions	Religion	Affiliations
CUMBRIA									
Austin Friars	Co-ed	Day Boarding	£772 £1414	Schols 13	11	Sport	EFL Dyslexia	RC	SHMIS
Casterton	Girls	Day Boarding	£1067 £1767	Asst places 43 Schols 48	8	Hockey	Dyslexia	C of E	GSA
Lime House	Co-ed	Day Boarding	£675 £1500	Schols 12 pa	4	Drama, Art	Dyslexia EFL	Christian	ISAI
St Anne's (Windermere)	Girls	Day Boarding	£1220 £1850	Schols 13	11	Drama, Music, Art	EFL	Christian	Round Square GSA GBGSA SHMIS
St Bees	Co-ed	Day Boarding	£1135 £2015	Asst places 84 Schols Bursaries	11		Yes	C of E	HMC
Sedbergh	Boys	Day Boarding	£1630 £2320	Asst places 26 Schols 75 Bursaries 46	11	Sport		C of E	HMC
DERBYSHIRE									
Mount St Mary's (Sheffield)	Co-ed	Day Boarding	£1155 £1692	Asst places 55 Schols 10	13 Own prep (8)	Music, Drama, Sport	EFL	RC	HMC GBA

School	Type	Day/Boarding	Fees	Scholarships	Age	Extras	Special	Denomination	Affiliations
Normanton (Derby)	Co-ed	Day Boarding	£750 £1500	Schols Bursaries	10		Dyslexia EFL	Non-denom	ISAI
Repton	Boys Mixed sixth	Day Boarding	£1750 £2370	Asst places 39 Schols 12 pa	13 Own prep	Music, Sport	Dyslexia EFL	C of E	HMC
St Elphin's	Girls	Day Boarding	£900 £1600	Schols 12 pa	3			C of E	GSA SHA
DEVON Allhallows (Lyme Regis)	Co-ed	Day Boarding	£980 £2100	Schols	13			C of E	HMC
Blundell's	Boys Mixed sixth	Day Boarding	£1250 £2100	Schols 50	13			Non-denom	HMC
Edgehill	Girls	Day Boarding	£845 £1610	Asst places 20 pa Schols	11	Music	Remedial	Methodist	GSA
Exeter	Boys Mixed sixth	Day Boarding	£830 £1530	Asst places 30 Schols Bursaries	11 Own prep	Music, Drama, Sport		C of E	HMC
Grenville College	Boys	Day Boarding	£875 £1735	Schols Bursaries	10		Dyslexia EFL	C of E	GBA Woodard SHMIS
Kelly College	Boys Mixed sixth	Day Boarding	£1220 £2100	Schols 17 Exhibitions Bursaries	11			C of E	HMC GBA

Name of School	Boys/Girls/Co-ed	Day/Board	Termly fees Day/Board	Financial help	Intake age/Own prep	Special strengths	Special provisions	Religion	Affiliations
Maynard	Girls	Day	£720		10 Own prep (7)			Non-denom	GSA GBGSA
Mount St Mary's (Exeter)	Girls	Day	£550		11 Own prep	Music		RC	ISJC
Plymouth College	Boys Mixed sixth	Day Boarding	£780 £1480	Asst places 173 Schols 12	11 Own prep	Music, Art, Sport		Non-denom	HMC
St Dunstan's Abbey	Girls	Day Boarding	£775 £1305	Schols 7	5	Netball		Christian	GSA
Shebbear	Boys	Day Boarding	£910 £1705	Schols Bursaries	11 Own prep (7)		EFL	Methodist	SHMIS GBA
Stover	Girls	Day Boarding	£888 £1626	Schols 4 pa	11		Dyslexia	C of E	GSA
West Buckland	Co-ed	Day Boarding	£845 £1555	Asst places 14 pa Schols 6	7	Sport	EFL	C of E	HMC

DORSET

School	Type	Day/Boarding	Fees	Scholarships	Entry	Extras	Special needs	Religion	Affiliation
Bryanston	Co-ed	Day Boarding	£1534 £2300	Schols 20	13	Music, Drama, Art, Sport		Christian	HMC
Canford	Boys Mixed sixth	Day Boarding	£1540 £2220	Schols 13+ pa	13			C of E	HMC Allied
Clayesmore	Co-ed	Day Boarding	£1615 £2295	Schols 20 pa	13 Own prep	Sport	Remedial EFL	C of E	SHMIS
Croft House	Girls	Day Boarding	£1320 £1900	Schols 5 Bursaries	11		Individual tuition	C of E	GSA
Hurn Court	Boys	Day Boarding	£810 £1420		10		Dyslexia Specific learning problems	Inter- denom	ISAI
Milton Abbey	Boys	Boarding	£2290	Schols 8 pa	13	Art, Sport	Remedial EFL	Christian	SHMIS
St Antony's- Leweston	Girls	Day Boarding	£1300 £1995	Schols	11 Own prep	Music, Drama, Art, Sport	Dyslexia EFL	RC	GSA GBGSA
St Mary's (Shaftesbury)	Girls	Day Boarding	£980 £1650	Schols	9			RC	GSA
Sherborne (Boys)	Boys	Day Boarding	£1975 £2250	Schols 10 pa	13	Music, Drama, Sport		C of E	HMC

Name of School	Boys/ Girls/ Co-ed	Day/ Board	Termly fees Day/ Board	Financial help	Intake age/ Own prep	Special strengths	Special provisions	Religion	Affiliations
Sherborne (Girls)	Girls	Day Boarding	£1485 £2230	Schols Exhibitions	12	Music, Drama, Sport	Dyslexia	C of E	GSA
Talbot Heath	Girls	Day Boarding	£837 £1621	Asst places 140 Schols Bursaries	8	Sport	EFL	C of E	GSA
Uplands	Co-ed	Day	£595		11 Own junior			Christian	ISAI
Wentworth Milton Mount	Girls	Day Boarding	£820 £1400	Schols Bursaries	11			Non-denom	GSA GBGSA
DURHAM Barnard Castle	Boys Mixed sixth	Day Boarding	£772 £1442	Schols	11 Own prep	Sport		Christian	HMC
Durham	Boys Mixed sixth	Day Boarding	£1535 £2302	Schols	11	Sport	Yes	C of E	HMC
Durham High	Girls	Day	£710	Schols 3 pa	11 Own junior		EFL	C of E	

792

School	Type	Day/Boarding	Fees	Scholarships	Entry	Special	Needs	Religion	Assoc
Polam Hall	Girls	Day Boarding	£790 £1595	Schols	11 Own junior		Dyslexia EFL	Christian	GSA
ESSEX Brentwood	Co-ed	Day Boarding	£975 £1708	Asst places Bursaries Schols 12 pa	11 Own prep	Sport	EFL	Protestant	HMC
Chigwell	Boys Mixed sixth	Day Boarding	£1101 £1645	Asst places 60 Schols 6	11 Own prep (7)		EFL	Christian	HMC
Eton House	Boys	Day	£455		10 Own prep (5)		Mild handicaps	Christian	ISAI
Felsted	Boys Mixed sixth	Day Boarding	£1704 £2207	Asst places 38 Schols 16	13 Own prep			C of E	HMC
Friends' (Saffron Walden)	Co-ed	Day Boarding	£1085 £1816	Asst places 80 Schols 4	11		Extra English	Quaker	SHMIS
New Hall	Girls	Day Boarding	£1298 £2025	Schols Bursaries	11	Music, Drama, Art	Edu- cational needs Handicaps	RC	GSA
St Mary's (Colchester)	Girls	Day	£710		11 Own junior (4)		Dyslexia EFL	C of E	GSA

Name of School	Boys/ Girls/ Co-ed	Day/ Board	Termly fees Day/ Board	Financial help	Intake age/ Own prep	Special strengths	Special provisions	Religion	Affiliations
GLOUCESTERSHIRE									
Cheltenham (Boys)	Boys Mixed sixth	Day Boarding	£1785 £2380	Schols Bursaries	13 Own junior	Drama, Music, Sport		C of E	HMC
Cheltenham (Girls)	Girls	Day Boarding	£1420 £2120	Grants	11			C of E	GSA
Dean Close	Co-ed	Day Boarding	£1400 £2200	Schols Bursaries	12 Own junior			C of E	HMC
Hatherop Castle	Girls	Day Boarding	£920 £1800	Schols 5 pa	10			Christian	GBGSA ISAI
King's (Gloucester)	Co-ed	Day Boarding	£980 £1655	Schols 15	13 Own prep (4)		Dyslexia	C of E	SHMIS CSA
Rendcomb	Boys Mixed sixth	Boarding	£1970	Schols 12 Bursaries LEA	11			Christian	HMC
St Edward's (Cheltenham)	Co-ed	Day	£820	Schols 11 pa	4	Sport	Remedial	RC	ISAI
Westonbirt	Girls	Day Boarding	£1375 £2140	Schols Bursaries	11	Lacrosse	Individual coaching	C of E	GSA Allied

					Art, Music	EFL	Inter-denom	HMC
Wycliffe	Co-ed	Day £1455 Boarding £2240	Asst places 34 Schols 10	13 Own junior			Inter-denom	HMC
Wynstones	Co-ed	Day £600 Boarding £930		6		Yes	Non-denom	Steiner
HAMPSHIRE Atherley	Girls	Day £789	Schols 5–6	11 Own junior (4)		Dyslexia EFL Mild visual handicaps	C of E	GSA CS Co Ltd SHA
Bedales	Co-ed	Day £1714 Boarding £2438	Asst places 5 pa Bursaries	13 Own junior (3)	Music, Drama, Art	Dyslexia	Non-denom	HMC
Churcher's	Boys Mixed sixth	Day £917 Boarding £1770	Asst places 19 pa Bursaries	11			Non-denom	HMC SHMIS
Ditcham Park	Co-ed	Day £930	Schols 2 pa	11 Own junior (5)		Remedial Dyslexia	Non-denom	ISAI
Embley Park	Boys Mixed sixth	Day £1075 Boarding £1780	Schols Bursaries	11		Dyslexia EFL	Christian	ISAI
Farnborough Hill	Girls	Day £878	Asst places 179 Bursaries 21	11			RC	GSA

Name of School	Boys/ Girls/ Co-ed	Day/ Board	Termly fees Day/ Board	Financial help	Intake age/ Own prep	Special strengths	Special provisions	Religion	Affiliations
King Edward VI (Southampton)	Boys Mixed sixth	Day	£800	Asst places 40 pa Schols Bursaries	11			Non-denom	HMC GBA
Lord Wandsworth	Boys Mixed sixth	Day Boarding	£1450 £1920	Asst places 75 Schols 26 Foundation Awards	11			C of E	HMC
North Foreland Lodge	Girls	Boarding	£1900		11			C of E	GSA
Portsmouth Grammar	Boys Mixed sixth	Day	£700		11 Own junior (5)			Non-denom	HMC
Portsmouth High	Girls	Day	£622	Asst places 29 pa Schols 3 pa	11 Own junior	Music, Sport	EFL Dyslexia Mild handicap	Christian	GPDST

School	Type	Fees	Awards	Entry	Special subjects	Special needs	Religion	Association
St John's College	Boys Mixed sixth	Day £610 Boarding £1250	Asst places 30 pa	11 Own junior (5)			RC	
St Swithun's	Girls	Day £1210 Boarding £1930	Schols	11 Own junior (3)			Inter-denom	GSA GBGSA
Stanbridge Earls	Co-ed	Day £1414 Boarding £2120	Schols 10	13	Art, Drama	Yes	C of E	GBA
Winchester	Boys	Day £1950 Boarding £2600	Asst places 5 pa Schols 15 pa Music Awards 6	13	Music, Water polo, Rowing		C of E	HMC
HEREFORD & WORCESTERSHIRE								
Alice Ottley	Girls	Day £775 Boarding £1525	Schols	11 Own junior			C of E	GSA GBGSA
Bromsgrove	Co-ed	Day £1089 Boarding £1717	Schols Bursaries	13 Own junior (8)	Drama, Sport	Yes	Christian	HMC
Hereford Cathedral	Co-ed	Day £850 Boarding £1487	Asst places 40 Schols 5	11 Own prep			C of E	HMC
King's (Worcester)	Boys Mixed sixth	Day £889 Boarding £1506	Asst places 34 pa Schols 20	13 Own prep (8)	Sport	Mild visual handicaps Dyslexia	C of E	HMC

Name of School	Boys/ Girls/ Co-ed	Day/ Board	Termly fees Day/ Board	Financial help	Intake age/ Own prep	Special strengths	Special provisions	Religion	Affiliations
Lawnside	Girls	Boarding	£1830	Schols 6 pa Bursaries	11			C of E	GSA GBGSA
Malvern (Boys)	Boys	Day Boarding	£1560 £2150	Asst places 58 Schols 20	13	Music		C of E	HMC
Malvern (Girls)	Girls	Day Boarding	£1280 £1920	Schols 10 pa	11	Music, Sport, Art		C of E	HMC GSA
Royal Grammar (Worcester)	Boys	Day Boarding	£825 £1500	Asst places 37 Schols 10	11 Own junior (8)	Drama, Sport		Christian	HMC
St James's & The Abbey	Girls	Day Boarding	£1235 £1850	Schols Bursaries	10			C of E	GSA
Worcester College for the Blind	Boys	Day Boarding	LEA RNIB subsidies		11		Specialist school for the blind		HMC
HERTFORDSHIRE									
Aldenham	Boys Mixed sixth	Day Boarding	£1530 £2430	Asst places 35 Schols Bursaries	13	Sport	Extra English	C of E	HMC

School	Sex	Day/Boarding	Fees	Scholarships / Places	Entry age	Drama/Dance specialist	EFL / Extra help	Denomination	Association
Arts Educational (Tring)	Girls	Day Boarding	£918 £1545		9	Drama/Dance specialist		Inter-denom	SHMIS
Berkhamsted (Boys)	Boys	Day Boarding	£1100 £1924	Asst places 5 pa, Schols 10–12	13, Own junior (7)	Sport	EFL Extra English	C of E	HMC
Berkhamsted (Girls)	Girls	Day Boarding	£878 £1596	Schols	5			Non-denom	GSA
Bishop's Stortford	Boys, Mixed sixth	Day Boarding	£1440 £2020	Asst places, Schols, Awards	13, Own prep (7)			Non-denom	HMC
Haberdashers' Aske's (Boys)	Boys	Day	£1122	Asst places 40 pa, Bursaries 12 pa	11, Own junior (7)	Music, Drama, Art	Dyslexia	Christian	HMC
Haberdashers' Aske's (Girls)	Girls	Day	£693	Asst places 127, Schols, Bursaries	11, Own junior (5)	Music		Christian	GSA
Haileybury	Boys, Mixed sixth	Day Boarding	£1600 £2500	Schols 15, Bursaries	13	Music, Drama, Sport	EFL	C of E	HMC
Northfield	Girls	Day	£885	Schols	11, Own junior	Art	Individual tuition	Christian	ISAI
Princess Helena	Girls	Day Boarding	£1450 £2000	Schols 3 pa	11	Music	EFL	C of E	GSA

Name of School	Boys/Girls/Co-ed	Day/Board	Termly fees Day/Board	Financial help	Intake age/Own prep	Special strengths	Special provisions	Religion	Affiliations
Rickmansworth Masonic	Girls	Day Boarding	£943 £1700	Bursaries Schols	11 Own junior (7)		Dyslexia	C of E	GSA
St Albans	Boys	Day	£985	Asst places 150 Schols 2	11		Dyslexia	Christian	HMC
St Albans High	Girls	Day	£800	Asst places 15 pa Schols	11 Own prep (7)			C of E	GSA GBGSA
St Christopher (Letchworth)	Co-ed	Day Boarding	£1100 £2000		11 Own junior (2)			Non-denom	GBA
St Columba's (St Albans)	Boys	Day	£520	Schols 12 pa	11 Own junior (7)			RC	
St Edmund's College	Co-ed	Day Boarding	£1204 £1871	Asst places 55 Schols 10	13 Own prep (7)		Dyslexia	RC	HMC
St Francis' College	Girls	Day Boarding	£880 £1660	Schols Bursaries	11 Own junior (4)			RC	GSA
Sherrardswood	Co-ed	Day Boarding	£835 £1590	Schols 2 pa	4			Non-denom	ISAI

800

School	Type	Fees	Scholarships	Entry	Specialisms	Support	Religion	Assoc.
HUMBERSIDE								
Hull High	Girls	Day £730 Boarding £1100	Schols	11 Own junior (4)			C of E	CSCL GSA
Hymers	Boys Mixed sixth	Day £605	Asst places 135 Schols	11 Own junior (8)	Music		Christian	HMC
Pocklington	Boys Mixed sixth	Day £780 Boarding £1527	Asst Places 137 Schols Bursaries	13 Own junior (8)	Art, Sport	EFL	C of E	HMC
ISLE OF MAN								
Buchan	Girls	Day £718 Boarding £1435	Schols	11 Own junior (4)			Non-denom	GSA
King William's	Co-ed	Day £1350 Boarding £1900	Schols Bursaries	8			C of E	HMC
ISLE OF WIGHT								
Bembridge	Co-ed	Day £864 Boarding £1560	Schols 6 Bursaries	13 Own prep (7)		Learning difficulties	Christian	SHMIS
Ryde	Co-ed	Day £765 Boarding £1530	Schols 5 pa	4			Christian	HMC
Upper Chine	Girls	Day £895 Boarding £1725	Schols 3 Bursaries 3	11 Own junior	Drama	Dyslexia EFL	C of E	GSA

Name of School	Boys/Girls/Co-ed	Day/Board	Termly fees Day/Board	Financial help	Intake age/Own prep	Special strengths	Special provisions	Religion	Affiliations
KENT Ashford	Girls	Day Boarding	£839 £1466	Asst places 41 Schols 6	11 Own junior	Dance/drama, Art	Yes	Non-denom	GSA
Bedgebury	Girls	Day Boarding	£1100 £1856	Schols 15 pa	8	Art, Sport	Dyslexia EFL	C of E	GSA
Benenden	Girls	Boarding	£2150	Schols 12	11	Drama, Sport	Yes	C of E	GSA
Bethany	Boys	Day Boarding	£1245 £1865	Schols 10 pa	11		Dyslexia	Christian	SHMIS
Cobham Hall	Girls	Day Boarding	£1725 £2585	Schols Bursaries	11	Music, Art, Drama	Yes	Inter-denom	GSA GBGSA
Combe Bank	Girls	Day Boarding	£980 £1680	Schols	11 Own prep (3)		Dyslexia	RC	GSA
Cranbrook	Co-ed	Day Boarding	Free £920	Schols	13			Non-denom	SHMIS Woodard
Dover College	Co-ed	Day Boarding	£1370 £2080	Schols Bursaries	13 Own prep (3)			C of E	HMC GBA

802

School	Sex	Day/Boarding	Fees	Scholarships	Entry	Subjects	Special	Religion	Assoc
Duke of York's	Boys	Boarding	£200	MoD	11		Only sons of army personnel admitted	C of E	GBA
Kent College (Tunbridge Wells)	Girls	Day Boarding	£1045 £1765	Schols 7 Bursaries	11		Dyslexia	Christian	GSA
King's (Canterbury)	Boys Mixed sixth	Day Boarding	£1715 £2450	Schols	13			C of E	
King's (Rochester)	Boys Mixed sixth	Day Boarding	£1019 £1699	Asst places 54 Schols 99	13 Own junior (5)	Music		C of E	HMC
Sacred Heart	Girls	Day Boarding	£1150 £2030	Schols 6	5	Music, Art	Dyslexia EFL	RC	GSA
St Augustine's (Westgate-on-Sea)	Boys	Day Boarding	£910 £1720	Schols	13 Own prep		EFL	RC	GBA
St Edmund's (Canterbury)	Co-ed	Day Boarding	£1369 £1999	Schols 35	13 Own junior			C of E	HMC GBA
St Hilary's (Sevenoaks)	Girls	Day	£815	Schols 5 Bursaries 10	11 Own junior (3)		Dyslexia EFL Mild handicap	Christian	GSA GBGSA

Name of School	Boys/Girls/Co-ed	Day/Board	Termly fees Day/Board	Financial help	Intake age/Own prep	Special strengths	Special provisions	Religion	Affiliations
St Lawrence	Co-ed	Day Boarding	£1330 £1980	Schols Bursaries	11 Own junior (4)			C of E	HMC
St Stephen's (Broadstairs)	Girls	Day Boarding	£1130 £1830	Asst place 1 Schols 6	11		EFL	Christian	GSA GBGSA
Sevenoaks	Co-ed	Day Boarding	£1273 £2115	Schols Bursaries	11	Rugby, Music, Drama	Mild handicap	Inter-denom	HMC
Sutton Valence	Co-ed	Day Boarding	£1403 £2193	Asst places 46 Schols Bursaries	11	Sport	EFL	C of E	HMC
Tonbridge	Boys	Day Boarding	£1700 £2400	Asst places 3 Schols 25 Bursaries	13	Music, Art	Dyslexia	C of E	HMC
West Heath	Girls	Day Boarding	£1430 £2110	Schols 4 Bursaries	11	Music		Christian	SHA GSA
LANCASHIRE Arnold	Co-ed	Day Boarding	£679 £1360	Asst places 55 Schols 8	11 Own junior	Music, Drama, Art, Sport	Dyslexia	Christian	HMC

School	Sex	Day/Boarding	Fees	Awards	Entry		Subjects	Denomination	Affiliations
King Edward VII (Lytham)	Boys	Day	£650	Asst places 30 pa Schols 2 pa	13 Own junior (7)			Non-denom	HMC
Kirkham Grammar	Co-ed	Day / Boarding	£675 / £1255	Asst places 10 pa Schols 10	11	Yes	Drama, Sport	Christian	SHMIS
Queen Elizabeth's (Blackburn)	Boys Mixed sixth	Day	£740	Asst places 273 Schols 20–25	8		Music	Non-denom	HMC
Queen Mary	Girls	Day	£640	Schols 3 pa Bursaries 6 pa	11 Own junior (7)			Non-denom	GSA GBGSA
Rossall	Co-ed	Day / Boarding	£1450 / £2100	Schols Bursaries	11 Own prep			C of E	HMC GBA
Scarisbrick Hall	Co-ed	Day	£570	Schols	4–14			Non-denom	ISAI
Stonyhurst	Boys	Day / Boarding	£1080 / £2070	Asst places 26 Schols 12 Bursaries	13 Own prep			RC	HMC
Westholme	Girls	Day	£590	Schols 100	11 Own prep			Christian	GSA
LEICESTERSHIRE Leicester Grammar	Co-ed	Day	£630	Schols 8 pa	10		Music	C of E	

Name of School	Boys/ Girls/ Co-ed	Day/ Board	Termly fees Day/ Board	Financial help	Intake age/ Own prep	Special strengths	Special provisions	Religion	Affiliations
Leicester High	Girls	Day	£700	Schols	10 Own junior (6)			C of E	GBGSA GSA ISAI
Lough-borough High	Girls	Day Boarding	£650 £1150	Asst places Schols Bursaries	11 Own junior			Non-denom	GSA GBGSA
Oakham	Co-ed	Day Boarding	£1117 £2139	Schols 35 pa	10	Music, Art, Sport	Dyslexia EFL	Christian	HMC
Our Lady's (Lough-borough)	Girls	Day	£560	Schols 8	3	Art		RC	
Ratcliffe College	Co-ed	Day Boarding	£1160 £1700	Schols Bursaries	11 Own prep (5)			RC	HMC GBA
Uppingham	Boys Mixed sixth	Boarding	£2300	Schols 12+	13	Music	Dyslexia	C of E	HMC
LINCOLNSHIRE St Joseph's (Lincoln)	Girls	Day Boarding	£650 £1340		11 Own prep (3)			Christian	

Stamford	Boys	Day Boarding	£720 £1450	Schols Exhibitions	13 Own prep (8)		C of E	HMC
Stamford High	Girls	Day Boarding	£720 £1450	LEA Asst places Bursaries	11 Own junior (4)	Non- denom	GSA

LONDON
INNER LONDON, NORTH

Francis Holland (Regent's Park)	Girls	Day	£840	Schols	11	C of E	GSA GBGSA
Lubavitch (Boys)	Boys	Day	£450	Schols	11 Own junior (2)	Jewish	ISAI
Lubavitch (Girls)	Girls	Day	£445	Schols	11 Own junior (2)	Jewish	ISAI
South Hampstead High	Girls	Day	£684	Asst places 64 Schols 3	11	Non- denom	GPDST GSA
University College School	Boys	Day	£1230	Asst places 10 Schols Grants/ Bursaries	13 Own junior	Non- denom	HMC

INNER LONDON, SOUTH

Name of School	Boys/Girls/Co-ed	Day/Board	Termly fees Day/Board	Financial help	Intake age/Own prep	Special strengths	Special provisions	Religion	Affiliations
Alleyn's	Co-ed	Day	£1080	Asst places 196 Schols 15	11			C of E	HMC
Blackheath High	Girls	Day	£684	Asst places Schols Bursaries	11 Own junior (4)			Non-denom	GSA GPDST
Christ's College	Boys	Day Boarding	£655 £1245	Schols 2	4		EFL	Non-denom	ISJC ISAI
Colfe's	Boys Mixed sixth	Day	£905	Asst places 222 Schols 30 pa	11 Own junior (7)	Music, Rugby, Drama	Mild dyslexia	C of E	HMC IAPS
Dulwich	Boys	Day Boarding	£1070 £2140	Asst places 58 Schols 40	8			C of E	HMC GBA
Emanuel	Boys	Day	£896	Asst places 322 Schols Bursaries	10	Rowing, Music, Drama		C of E	HMC
Francis Holland (Sloane Square)	Girls	Day	£987	Schols 5 pa Bursaries	11 Own junior (4)		Dyslexia EFL	C of E	GSA

School	Type	Day/Board	Fees	Scholarships/Assisted places	Entry	Special	Dyslexia	Denom	Assoc
James Allen's	Girls	Day	£990	Asst places 150 Schols 17 pa	11 Own junior	Music, Drama		Non-denom	GSA
Putney High	Girls	Day	£684	Asst places 28 pa Schols 5	11 Own junior	Music		Non-denom	GPDST
Queen's Gate	Girls	Day	£1050		11 Own prep (4)			Non-denom	GSA GBGSA
St Dunstan's College	Boys	Day	£940	Asst places 160 Schols 12 pa	11 Own prep (7)			Christian	HMC
St James (Boys)	Boys	Day	£890		4		Yes	Non-denom	ISAI
St James (Girls)	Girls	Day	£870		4		Yes	Non-denom	ISAI
Southbank American	Co-ed	Day	£1600	Schols 13	11	Drama	EFL	Inter-denom	ISAI ECIS
Streatham High	Girls	Day	£684	Asst places 153 Schols 18 Bursaries	11 Own junior (5)			Non-denom	GPDST
Sydenham High	Girls	Day	£680	Schols Bursaries	11 Own junior (5)			Non-denom	GSA GPDST

809

Name of School	Boys/Girls/Co-ed	Day/Board	Termly fees Day/Board	Financial help	Intake age/Own prep	Special strengths	Special provisions	Religion	Affiliations
Westminster	Boys Mixed sixth	Day Boarding	£1550 £2350	Asst places 4 Schols 8 pa Bursaries (sixth form)	13 Own prep	Music, Sport		C of E	HMC
INNER LONDON, EAST									
City of London (Boys)	Boys	Day	£1165	Asst places 25 pa Schols 15 pa	10			Non-denom	HMC
City of London (Girls)	Girls	Day	£850	Asst places 104 Schols 3 pa	11 Own prep (7)	Music, Drama, Art, Sport	Yes	Christian	GSA
Italia Conti	Co-ed	Day	£1250		9	Drama/dance specialist		Inter-denom	ISAI
INNER LONDON, WEST									
Godolphin & Latymer	Girls	Day	£998	Asst places 170 Schol Bursary	11	Art		C of E	GSA
Latymer Upper	Boys	Day	£920	Asst places	9			Non-denom	HMC GBA
Queen's College (London)	Girls	Day Boarding	£900 £1400	Schols 8	11			C of E	GSA

School			Fees	Awards	Age	Specialism	Physiotherapy	Religion	Assoc.
Royal Ballet	Co-ed	Day Boarding	£1707 £2306	DES	11	Ballet (specialist school)			
St Paul's (Girls)	Girls	Day	£1150	Foundation awards	11			C of E	GSA
OUTER LONDON, NORTH									
Arts Educational (London)	Co-ed	Day	£1132	Asst places Schols Bursaries	11 Own junior	Drama (specialist school)		Non-denom	
Bancroft's	Co-ed	Day	£972	Asst places 70 Schols	11	Sport		C of E Jewish	HMC SHA
Buckingham	Boys Mixed sixth	Day	£735	Schols 3 (sixth form)	11		Yes	Christian	
Channing	Girls	Day	£1050	Schols Bursaries	11 Own junior (5)			Christian	
Cranbrook College	Boys	Day	£530		5				ISAI
Harrow	Boys	Day Boarding	£1860 £2480	Schols 20	13	Art, Sport, Music		C of E RC Jewish	HMC

811

Name of School	Boys/ Girls/ Co-ed	Day/ Board	Termly fees Day/ Board	Financial help	Intake age/ Own prep	Special strengths	Special provisions	Religion	Affiliations
Heathfield (Pinner)	Girls	Day	£789	Schols	11 Own junior (7)			C of E	GSA GBGSA GPDST
Highgate	Boys	Day Boarding	£1305 £2270	Asst places 21 Schols 10 Bursaries 30	12 Own junior	Sport		C of E	HMC
John Lyon	Boys	Day	£830	Asst places 118 Schols	11			Christian	HMC GBA
King Alfred (Hampstead)	Co-ed	Day	£1104	Bursaries 5 (sixth form)	4	Art, Drama	Remedial	Non-denom	GBA
Merchant Taylors' (Northwood)	Boys	Day Boarding	£1365 £2100	Asst places 20 pa Schols 14 Bursaries	11		Warnock	C of E	HMC
Mill Hill	Boys Mixed sixth	Day Boarding	£1425 £2160	Asst places 10 pa Schols 10 Bursaries	13 Own junior		Extra English	Christian	HMC
North London Collegiate	Girls	Day	£910	Asst places 73 Schols 11 Bursaries 77	11 Own junior (7)			C of E	GSA

Northwood College	Girls	Day	£884	Schols 4 (sixth form)	11 Own junior (4)			Christian	GSA
Purcell School	Co-ed	Day £1150 Boarding £2220		Schols Bursaries LEA	9	Music specialist		Non-denom	SHMIS
St Andrew's (Harrow)	Girls	Day	£650		3		EFL Dyslexia Mild handicap	C of E	
St Helen's	Girls	Day £905 Boarding £1705		Asst places 27 Schols 4	11 Own junior (5)	Art	Dyslexia EFL	C of E	
St Martha's (Hadley Wood)	Girls	Day £580 Boarding £1075			11 Own junior			RC	
Sylvia Young	Co-ed	Day	£640	LEA	7	Specialist stage school	Remedial	Non-denom	ISAI
Ursuline High	Girls	Day	£720	Asst places 25 pa Schols 2 pa Bursaries	11			RC	GSA GBGSA
OUTER LONDON, SOUTH									
Baston	Girls	Day £780 Boarding £1425		Schols 3	11 Own junior (3)	Art, Sport	EFL	C of E	ISAI

Name of School	Boys/Girls/Co-ed	Day/Board	Termly fees Day/Board	Financial help	Intake age/Own prep	Special strengths	Special provisions	Religion	Affiliations
Bishop Challoner	Boys Mixed sixth	Day	£695	Schols 6	11 Own junior (4)			RC	ISAI
Bromley High	Girls	Day	£684	Asst places Schols 3 pa	11 Own junior (4)			Non-denom	GPDST GSA
Commonweal Lodge	Girls	Day	£790	Schols 3 pa	5		Yes	Christian	GSA
Croham Hurst	Girls	Day	£777	Schols 16	11 Own junior (4)		Dyslexia EFL	Christian	GSA
Croydon High	Girls	Day	£789	Asst places 24 pa Schols 4 pa	11 Own junior (5)	Music, Sport, Drama		Christian	GPDST
Eltham College	Boys Mixed sixth	Day Boarding	£1029 £2194	Asst places 102 Schols 19 pa	11 Own junior (7)	Music, Sport		Christian	HMC
Farrington	Girls	Day Boarding	£977 £1785	Bursaries 4	11	Art, Sport	Dyslexia EFL	C of E	GBGSA
Hampton	Boys	Day	£880	Asst places 150 Schols 8	11	Music, Art, Sport	Some	Non-denom	HMC

School	Sex	Day/Boarding	Fees	Scholarships/Bursaries	Entry	Special subjects	Special provision	Religion	Associations
Holy Trinity (Bromley)	Girls	Day	£638	Schols 3	11 Own junior			RC	GSA GBGSA
King's College (Wimbledon)	Boys	Day	£1100	Asst places 9 pa Schols 12 pa	13 Own junior	Sport, Music		C of E	HMC
Kingston Grammar	Co-ed	Day	£880	Asst places Schols 10 pa Bursaries	11		Dyslexia Visual handicaps	Christian	HMC
Lady Eleanor Holles	Girls	Day	£820	Bursaries Schols	11 Own junior (7)			C of E	GBGSA GSA
Marymount	Girls	Day Boarding	£1675 £2842	Bursaries	12		IB EFL	Non-denom	
Old Palace	Girls	Day	£650	Schols 4 pa Bursaries	11 Own junior (7)			C of E	GSA
Royal Russell	Co-ed	Day Boarding	£900 £1725	Schols				C of E	SHMIS
St Paul's (Boys)	Boys	Day Boarding	£1391 £2209	Asst places 11 pa Schols 5 Bursaries	13 Own prep	Music		C of E	HMC

Name of School	Boys/Girls/Co-ed	Day/Board	Termly fees Day/Board	Financial help	Intake age/Own prep	Special strengths	Special provisions	Religion	Affiliations
Stratford House	Girls	Day	£750	Schols 6 Bursaries	11 Own junior (4)		Dyslexia EFL	Christian	GSA
Surbiton High	Girls	Day	£780	Bursaries (sixth form)	5			C of E	GSA GPDST
Sutton High	Girls	Day	£684	Asst places 17 pa Schols 6 Bursaries	11 Own junior (5)	Sport		Christian	GPDST
Trinity (Croydon)	Boys	Day	£990	Asst places 138 Schols	10	Music	Dyslexia	C of E	HMC
Whitgift	Boys	Day	£1040	Asst places 91 Schols Bursaries	10			Non-denom	HMC
Wimbledon High	Girls	Day	£789	Asst places 62 Schols	11 Own junior (5)		Mild handicap	Non-denom	GPDST GSA
OUTER LONDON, EAST									
Forest School	Co-ed	Day Boarding	£1050 £1529	Asst places Schols	Girls 11 Boys 7			C of E	HMC GBA

School	Type		Fee	Scholarships / Assisted places	Entry	Specialism	Special needs / EFL	Denom	Assoc
OUTER LONDON, WEST									
Ealing College	Boys Mixed sixth	Day	£695	Schols (sixth form)	11			Non-denom	
Notting Hill and Ealing High	Girls	Day	£789	Bursaries Asst places	11 Own junior (5)			Non-denom	GPDST
St Augustine's Priory	Girls	Day	£580		4	Art	Yes	RC	
St Benedict's	Boys Mixed sixth	Day	£865	Asst places 80 Schols	11 Own junior			RC	HMC
GREATER MANCHESTER									
Bolton (Boys)	Boys	Day	£796	Asst places 300 Music 1 pa Bursaries	11 Own prep (8)	Music	Wheelchair access	Christian	HMC
Bolton (Girls)	Girls	Day	£775	Asst places	11 Own prep (5)			Non-denom	GSA GBGSA
Bury Grammar (Boys)	Boys	Day	£621	Asst places 30 Schols 1 pa	11 Own junior	Sport		Christian	HMC
Bury Grammar (Girls)	Girls	Day	£621	Asst places 35 pa Schols 1 pa	11 Own junior (4)	Sport, Art	Minor learning problems	Christian	GSA

Name of School	Boys/ Girls/ Co-ed	Day/ Board	Termly fees Day/ Board.	Financial help	Intake age/ Own prep	Special strengths	Special provisions	Religion	Affiliations
Cheadle Hulme	Co-ed	Day Boarding	£835 £1735	Asst places 20 Schols 4	11 Own junior (7)			Non-denom	HMC
Chetham's	Co-ed	Day Boarding	£2466 £3185	Asst places 242	7	Music specialist		Non-denom	SHMIS
Hulme Grammar (Boys)	Boys	Day	£725	Asst places 220 Schols 6 pa	11 Own prep		Yes	Non-denom	HMC
Hulme Grammar (Girls)	Girls	Day	£665	Asst places 35 pa Bursaries	11 Own prep			Non-denom	GSA
Jewish High	Girls	Day	£675		11			Jewish	
Manchester Grammar	Boys	Day	£830	Asst places 290 Bursaries	11			Christian	HMC GBA
Manchester High	Girls	Day	£720	Asst places Bursaries	11 Own junior (4)			Non-denom	GBGSA GSA
Manchester Jewish Grammar	Boys	Day	£670	Means tested fees Council bursaries	10			Jewish	

School	Sex	Day/Boarding	Fees	Places/Schols	Entry	Specialisms		Religion	Assoc
St Ambrose	Boys	Day	£574	Asst places 88 Schols Bursaries	11	Sport		RC	
Stockport Grammar	Co-ed	Day	£729	Asst places 45 pa Bursaries	11 Own junior	Sport	Yes	Christian	HMC
William Hulme's	Co-ed	Day	£867	Asst places 35 Schols Bursaries	11			Christian Jewish	HMC
Withington	Girls	Day	£740	Asst places 80 Bursaries	11 Own junior	Music, Drama, Sport		Christian Jewish	GSA
MERSEYSIDE Belvedere	Girls	Day	£695	Asst places 159 Schols Bursaries	11 Own prep (4)	Drama		Non-denom	GPDST
Birkenhead	Boys	Day	£675	Asst places Schols	13 Own junior (4)			Christian	HMC
Birkenhead High	Girls	Day	£622	Asst places 40 pa Schols Bursaries	11 Own junior (4)	Drama, Sport, Music		Christian	GPDST
Huyton	Girls	Day £816 Boarding £1852		Schols Bursaries	2			C of E	GSA GBGSA

Name of School	Boys/ Girls/ Co-ed	Day/ Board	Termly fees Day/ Board	Financial help	Intake age/ Own prep	Special strengths	Special provisions	Religion	Affiliations
Liverpool College	Boys Mixed sixth	Day Boarding	£769 £1422	Asst places 175 Schols Bursaries	11 Own prep (5)	Sport		C of E	HMC
Merchant Taylors' (Crosby)	Boys	Day	£820	Asst places 185 Grants 50	13 Own prep (7)	Sport	Dyslexia Visual handicap Deafness	Non-denom	HMC
Merchant Taylors' (Girls)	Girls	Day	£735	Asst places 164 Schols 7	11 Own prep (4)			Non-denom	GSA
St Anselm's	Boys	Day	£600	Asst places Schols 2 pa LEA	11 Own prep (5)			RC	HMC
St Edward's (Liverpool)	Boys Mixed sixth	Day	£642	Asst places 385 Schols 10	11 Own prep	Music, Athletics	Dyslexia EFL Visual handicaps	RC	HMC
St Mary's (Crosby)	Co-ed	Day	£612	Asst places 45 Bursaries 12 pa	11 Own prep	Art, Sport		RC	HMC
Wellington (Wirral)	Co-ed	Day	£635	Schols 5	11			Christian	ISAI

MIDLANDS WEST

School	Co-ed	Day/Boarding	Fees	Bursaries	Entry		Denomination	Associations
Coventry	Co-ed	Day	£630	Bursaries	11 Own junior (7)		Non-denom	HMC GBA
Edgbaston High	Girls	Day	£730		11 Own junior (3)		Non-denom	GSA
Holy Child Senior	Girls	Day / Boarding	£760 / £1260	Schols Bursaries	11 Own junior (3)		RC	GSA GBGSA
King Edward's (Birmingham)	Boys	Day	£810	Asst places 280 Schols 20	11		Christian	HMC
King Edward VI (Birmingham)	Girls	Day	£808	Asst places 185 Schols 25	11		Non-denom	GSA
Old Swinford	Boys	Day Boarding		Voluntary aided 25 LEA places pa	11		C of E	
Royal Wolverhampton	Co-ed	Day / Boarding	£935 / £1580	Schols Bursaries	11	EFL	C of E	SHMIS
Tettenhall	Co-ed	Day / Boarding	£1010 / £1640	Schols	13 Own prep (7)		Inter-denom	HMC SHMIS
Wolverhampton Grammar	Boys Mixed sixth	Day	£790	Asst places Bursaries	11		Non-denom	HMC GBA

Name of School	Boys/Girls/Co-ed	Day/Board	Termly fees Day/Board	Financial help	Intake age/Own prep	Special strengths	Special provisions	Religion	Affiliations
NORFOLK									
All Hallows (Ditchingham)	Girls	Day Boarding	£950 £1505	Schols	5		EFL	C of E	GSA SHA
Cawston College	Boys	Day Boarding	£905 £1575		11		Specific learning problems	C of E	Woodard
Eccles Hall	Boys	Day Boarding	£885 £1740		10		Specific learning problems	Non-denom	ISAI
Gresham's	Co-ed	Day Boarding	£1480 £2180	Asst places 5 pa Schols	13			C of E	HMC
Hethersett Old Hall	Girls	Day Boarding	£805 £1405		11 Own prep (8)			C of E	GSA
Langley	Boys Mixed sixth	Day Boarding	£989 £1904	Bursaries	11			Non-denom	GBA
Norwich High	Girls	Day	£695	Asst places 190 Schols Bursaries	11 Own junior (7)	Music, Drama, Art, Sport		Non-denom	GSA GPDST
Runton Hill	Girls	Day Boarding	£1250 £1885	Schols 4	11	Sport		C of E	GSA

School	Type	Day/Boarding	Fees	Scholarships	Entry age	Specialisms	Religion	Associations
Thetford Grammar	Co-ed	Day	£700	Schols 3 pa	11 Own junior (8)		C of E	GBA
NORTHAMPTONSHIRE								
Northampton High	Girls	Day	£850	Asst places	11 Own junior (3)		C of E	GSA
Oundle	Boys	Boarding	£2250	Schols	11		C of E	HMC
Wellingborough	Co-ed	Day Boarding	£1136 £1857	Asst places 60 Schols 12	13 Own junior	Sport	C of E Dyslexia EFL	HMC
NORTHUMBERLAND								
Longridge Towers	Co-ed	Day Boarding	£825 £1625	Schols 6 pa Bursaries	4	Art	Christian	SHA ISAI
NOTTINGHAMSHIRE								
Nottingham High (Boys)	Boys	Day	£700	Asst places Schols 20 pa	11 Own junior (7)		Non-denom	HMC
Nottingham High (Girls)	Girls	Day	£695	Asst places 30 pa Schols Bursaries	11 Own junior (4)	Drama, Sport	Non-denom Dyslexia	GPDST

Name of School	Boys/ Girls/ Co-ed	Day/ Board	Termly fees Day/ Board	Financial help	Intake age/ Own prep	Special strengths	Special provisions	Religion	Affiliations
Rodney	Co-ed	Day Boarding	£510 £960	Schols (sixth form)	8		EFL	Christian	
Trent College	Boys Mixed sixth	Day Boarding	£1142 £1950	Asst places 25 Schols 32	11	Music, Drama, Art, Sport	Extra English Visual handicap	C of E	HMC
Worksop	Co-ed	Day Boarding	£1310 £1950	Schols	13 Own prep			C of E	HMC Woodard
OXFORDSHIRE									
Abingdon	Boys	Day Boarding	£920 £1830	Asst places Schols	11			C of E	HMC GBA
Bloxham	Boys Mixed sixth	Day Boarding	£1420 £2115	Schols Bursaries	13			C of E	HMC Woodard
Brown & Brown	Co-ed	Day Boarding	£900 per subject £840+ tuition	Schols 5	15	Art, Drama	Dyslexia EFL	Non- denom	CIFE Assoc of Tutors
Carmel College	Co-ed	Day Boarding	£1355 £2500	Asst places 91 Schols 120	11	Art	EFL Dyslexia Slow learners	Jewish	SHMIS

School	Type	Day / Boarding fees	Scholarships	Entry age	Special	Denom.	Associations
Cherwell Tutors	Co-ed	Day £2000 / Boarding £3000	Schols 3	16	Dyslexia EFL	Non-denom	BAC CIFE
Headington	Girls	Day £850 / Boarding £1570	Schols Bursaries	10 Own prep (4)		C of E	GSA GBGSA
Magdalen College School	Boys	Day £810 / Boarding £1580	Asst places 24 pa Schols 5 pa Bursaries	11	Choir school	C of E	HMC CSA GBA
Oratory	Boys	Day £1538 / Boarding £2198	Schols Bursaries	11 Own prep	Art, Music Dyslexia	RC	HMC
Our Lady's (Abingdon)	Girls	Day £675 / Boarding £1460		11 Own junior		RC	
Oxford High	Girls	Day £625	Schols	9		Non-denom	GPDST GSA
Radley	Boys	Boarding £2450	Schols Exhibitions	13	Sport	C of E	HMC
Rye St Antony	Girls	Day £750 / Boarding £1400		8		RC	GBGSA
St Edward's (Oxford)	Boys Mixed sixth	Day £1660 / Boarding £2200	Schols Bursaries	13		Non-denom	HMC
St Mary's (Wantage)	Girls	Boarding £2050	Schols 4 Bursary 1	11	Music, Drama, Art Dyslexia EFL	C of E	GSA

Name of School	Boys/ Girls/ Co-ed	Day/ Board	Termly fees Day/ Board	Financial help	Intake age/ Own prep	Special strengths	Special provisions	Religion	Affiliations
Shiplake	Boys	Day Boarding	£1350 £2100	Schols 2	13	Sport	Dyslexia	C of E	SHMIS GBA
Sibford	Co-ed	Day Boarding	£957 £1880	Bursaries	11	Drama, Art	Dyslexia EFL	Quaker	
Tudor Hall	Girls	Day Boarding	£1210 £1900		11			C of E	GSA GBGSA Woodard
Wychwood	Girls	Day Boarding	£875 £1490		11	Music, Art	Yes	C of E	GSA
SHROPSHIRE Adcote	Girls	Day Boarding	£1050 £1770	Schols (sixth form)	8		Dyslexia EFL	C of E RC	GSA
Ellesmere	Boys Mixed sixth	Day Boarding	£1420 £2020	Schols Bursaries Exhibitions	11			C of E	HMC Woodard
Moreton Hall	Girls	Day Boarding	£1425 £2150	Bursaries Schols 4	11	Lacrosse, Art	Learning difficulties	C of E	GSA GBGSA
Oswestry	Co-ed	Day Boarding	£1025 £1720	Schols	11	Sport	EFL Remedial English	Christian	SHMIS

Name	Type	Fees	Scholarships	Entry age	Special subjects	Special needs	Religion	Affiliations
Shrewsbury	Boys	Day £1550 / Boarding £2170	Schols	13			C of E	GBA HMC
Shrewsbury High	Girls	Day £622	Asst places 14 Schols Bursaries	11 Own junior (4)			Non-denom	GPDST
Wrekin	Co-ed	Day £1540 / Boarding £2250	Schols 20	13	Sport, Art	Dyslexia EFL	C of E	HMC Allied
SOMERSET								
Bruton (Sunny Hill)	Girls	Day £750 / Boarding £1350	Asst places 25 Schols 3	11 Own junior	Hockey, Drama	EFL	Christian	GSA
Downside	Boys	Day £1338 / Boarding £2026	Schols 10 pa Bursaries	13		Dyslexia EFL Physical and visual handicap Dietary needs	RC	HMC
King Alfred (Bridgwater)	Boys	Day £600 / Boarding £1190	Schols (senior)	11			Inter-denom	ISAI
King's (Bruton)	Boys Mixed sixth	Day £1635 / Boarding £2290	Schols 8	13 Own junior		Dyslexia	C of E	HMC
King's (Taunton)	Boys Mixed sixth	Day £1520 / Boarding £2050	Schols	13 Own prep (7)			C of E	HMC Woodard

Name of School	Boys/Girls/Co-ed	Day/Board	Termly fees Day/Board	Financial help	Intake age/Own prep	Special strengths	Special provisions	Religion	Affiliations
Millfield	Co-ed	Day Boarding	£1010 £2455	Schols 160	13 Own junior	Music, Sport, Art	EFL Remedial English	Multi-faith	GBA IAPS
Queen's (Taunton)	Co-ed	Day Boarding	£1215 £1845	Asst places 14 pa Schols	12 Own junior		Dyslexia	Methodist	HMC
St Audries	Girls	Day Boarding	£1076 £1883	Schols Bursaries	11 Own junior (4)		Dyslexia EFL	C of E	GSA
Taunton	Co-ed	Day Boarding	£1408 £2175	Asst places 52 Schols Bursaries	11 Own prep (3)	Sport	EFL	C of E	HMC GSA
Wellington (Somerset)	Co-ed	Day Boarding	£720 £1350	Asst places 40 Schols	11	Sport	EFL	C of E	HMC
Wells Cathedral	Co-ed	Day Boarding	£898 £1598	Asst places 66 Schols 8 pa	11 Own junior	Music, Drama, Sport		C of E	HMC GBA SHA SHMIS
STAFFORDSHIRE									
Abbots Bromley	Girls	Day Boarding	£1200 £1790	Schols Bursaries	11 Own junior (7)			C of E	Woodard GSA GBGSA

	Type	Day/Boarding	Fees	Places/Schols	Entry	Subjects	Special	Religion	Assoc.
Denstone	Co-ed	Day £1540 Boarding £2118		Asst places 110 Schols 78 Bursaries	13 Own prep	Music, Sport	Yes	C of E	HMC Woodard
Newcastle-under-Lyme	Co-ed	Day £638		Asst places 73 Schols Bursaries	11 Own junior (8)			Christian	HMC GSA
St Dominic's (Brewood)	Girls	Day £669		Schols 10	11 Own junior (4)	Drama	Individual tuition	RC	
St Dominic's Priory	Girls	Day £500		Schols 2 pa	4	Art	Dyslexia	RC	
St Joseph's (Stoke)	Boys Mixed sixth	Day £597		Schols 6	11 Own junior (7)	Sport		RC	ISAI
Stafford Independent	Co-ed	Day £700			11				ISAI
SUFFOLK									
Culford	Co-ed	Day £1160 Boarding £1785		Asst places 50 Schols 4	11 Own junior (8)		Yes	Methodist	HMC
Felixstowe	Girls	Day £1136 Boarding £1865		Schols	11	Music, Drama, Dance, Art	EFL	C of E	GSA
Framlingham	Co-ed	Day £1125 Boarding £1755		Schols 8	13 Own junior	Art	Yes	C of E	HMC

Name of School	Boys/ Girls/ Co-ed	Day/ Board	Termly fees Day/ Board	Financial help	Intake age/ Own prep	Special strengths	Special provisions	Religion	Affiliations
Ipswich	Boys Mixed sixth	Day Boarding	£900 £1360	Asst places Schols	11 Own prep (7)			C of E	HMC GBA
Ipswich High	Girls	Day	£622	Asst places 29 pa Bursaries Schols 3–4 pa	11 Own junior (4)	Music, Drama, Art		Non-denom	GSA GPDST
Royal Hospital	Boys	Boarding	£1158	Means tested fees	11	Sport	Open only to the sons or grand-sons of seafarers Dyslexia	Christian	SHMIS
St Felix	Girls	Day Boarding	£1110 £1800	Schols	11 Own prep (7)			Inter-denom	GSA
St Joseph's (Ipswich)	Boys Mixed sixth	Day Boarding	£710 £1360	Asst places 75 Bursaries	11 Own prep	Sport	EFL Dyslexia	RC	GBA
Woodbridge	Co-ed	Day Boarding	£1060 £1840	Asst places 101 Schols 60	11 Own junior (5)	Sport	Mild visual handicap	C of E	HMC

SURREY

School	Type	Day / Boarding	Scholarships	Entry age	Specialist	Dyslexia / EFL	Denomination	Associations
Box Hill	Co-ed	Day £1135 Boarding £1935	Schols 10	11				Round Square SHMIS ISAI GBA
Bush Davies	Co-ed	Day £1200 Boarding £1700		11	Drama specialist		Christian	
Caterham	Boys Mixed sixth	Day £964 Boarding £1755	Schols	8			United Reform	HMC GBA
Charterhouse	Boys Mixed sixth	Day £2133 Boarding £2585	Asst places 10 pa Schols 32 Bursaries	13	Music, Sport, Art		Christian	HMC
City of London Freemen's	Co-ed	Day £1055 Boarding £1579	Schols	13 Own prep			C of E	SHMIS
Cranleigh	Boys Mixed sixth	Day £1640 Boarding £2350	Asst places Schols	13 Own prep			C of E	HMC GBA
Dunottar	Girls	Day £680	Schols 4	11 Own prep			Non-denom	GSA
Elmhurst	Co-ed	Day £1250 Boarding £1710		9	Dance specialist		C of E	GSA
Eothen	Girls	Day £879	Bursaries	12 Own prep (3)		Dyslexia EFL	C of E	GSA Church school

Name of School	Boys/ Girls/ Co-ed	Day/ Board	Termly fees Day/ Board	Financial help	Intake age/ Own prep	Special strengths	Special provisions	Religion	Affiliations
Epsom College	Boys Mixed sixth	Day Boarding	£1500 £2150	Asst places 10 Schols 30	13	Music, Sport	Mild disability	C of E	HMC
Ewell Castle	Boys Mixed sixth	Day	£880	Schols	3		EFL	Non-denom	SHMIS GBA
Frensham Heights	Co-ed	Day Boarding	£1370 £2290	Schols	11			Non-denom	GBA SHMIS HMC
Greenacre	Girls	Day Boarding	£535 £1125	Schols Bursaries			EFL	Christian	
Guildford High	Girls	Day		Schols (sixth form)	11 Own prep (5)			C of E	GSA CSCL
King Edward's (Witley)	Co-ed	Day Boarding	£1310 £1780	Asst places 15 Bursaries	11	Art		C of E	HMC
Notre Dame (Cobham)	Girls	Day	£800	Schols 14	11 Own junior	Drama		RC	
Notre Dame (Lingfield)	Girls	Day	£750	Bursaries 2	11 Own prep	Music, Drama, Sport	Dyslexia	RC	ISAI

Parsons Mead	Girls	Day £910 Boarding £1655	Schols 5 pa	11 Own prep (3)		Dyslexia EFL Mild visual handicap	C of E	GSA
Pierrepont	Co-ed	Day £1109 Boarding £1848	Schols 14+	11		Yes	C of E	SHMIS GBA
Prior's Field	Girls	Day £1047 Boarding £1697	Schols 2 pa Bursaries	11		Dyslexia	Christian	GSA
Reed's	Boys Mixed sixth	Day £1300 Boarding £1800	Schols Bursaries	11			C of E	HMC
Reigate Grammar	Boys Mixed sixth	Day £900	Asst places 20 Schols 10+ Bursaries	10			Non-denom	HMC GBA
Royal Grammar (Guildford)	Boys	Day £1010	Schols	11 Own prep (5)			C of E	HMC
Royal Naval	Girls	Day £1232 Boarding £1848	Schols 5 pa	11	Drama	Remedial	C of E	GSA
St Catherine's	Girls	Day £1050 Boarding £1740	Asst places Schols	11 Own prep (5)			C of E	GSA
St David's	Girls	Day £870 Boarding £1500		5			C of E	GSA GBGSA
St George's (Weybridge)	Boys Mixed sixth	Day £1285 Boarding £1854	Asst places 30 Schols 2 Bursaries	12 Own prep			RC	HMC SHMIS

Name of School	Boys/Girls/Co-ed	Day/Board	Termly fees Day/Board	Financial help	Intake age/Own prep	Special strengths	Special provisions	Religion	Affiliations
St John's (Leatherhead)	Boys	Day Boarding	£1450 £1995	Asst places 6 pa Schols 15	13		EFL Dyslexia	C of E	HMC
St Maur's	Girls	Day	£805	Asst places 5 Schols 1 Bursaries	11		EFL Dyslexia	RC	
St Teresa's Convent	Girls	Day Boarding	£850 £1420	Schols 2 pa (sixth form)	11 Own prep (3)			RC	GSA GBGSA
Shaftesbury	Co-ed	Day	£610	Schols Bursaries	11		Mild handicap	Non-denom	ISAI
Sir William Perkins's	Girls	Day	£700	Bursaries Schols	11			Non-denom	GSA
Stowford	Co-ed	Day	£886	Schols	11	Art	EFL	Non-denom	ISAI
Tormead	Girls	Day	£900	Schols Bursaries	5			Non-denom	GSA GBGSA

School	Type		Fees	Scholarships	Entry	Features	Preparation	Religion	Associations
Woldingham	Girls	Day Boarding	£1245 £2055	Schols 5	11	Sport, Art	Preparation for US College entrance Remedial	RC	GSA GBGSA
SUSSEX EAST **Battle Abbey**	Girls	Day Boarding	£1040 £1670	Schols 1 pa	11	Small school, family atmosphere Drama, Art	Dyslexia Extra English Learning difficulties	Christian	GSA
Brighton College	Co-ed	Day Boarding	£1415 £2150	Asst places 20 Schols 14	13 Own junior	Art, Sport, Music, Drama		C of E	HMC
Brighton High	Girls	Day Boarding	£622 £1868	Asst places 35 pa Schols Bursaries	11 Own junior (5)			Non-denom	GPDST GSA
Charters-Ancaster	Girls	Day Boarding	£850 £1650	Schols 4 Bursaries	3	Music, Drama, Art	Dyslexia Extra English	Christian	GSA GBGSA
Eastbourne	Boys Mixed sixth	Day Boarding	£1550 £2100	Schols	13			C of E	HMC GBA
Hamilton Lodge	Co-ed	Day Boarding	£2325 £3100	LEA	7		Specialist school for the deaf	Non-denom	

Name of School	Boys/ Girls/ Co-ed	Day/ Board	Termly fees Day/ Board	Financial help	Intake age/ Own prep	Special strengths	Special provisions	Religion	Affiliations
Legat Ballet	Co-ed	Day Boarding	£965 £1595	Schols	10	Ballet specialist	Dyslexia Learning difficulties EFL	C of E Catholic	
Mayfield	Boys	Day Boarding	£1355 £2070	Schols Bursaries	10	Sport	EFL Dyslexia	RC	ISAI
Michael Hall	Co-ed	Day Boarding	£750 £1650	Bursaries	6	Languages	Visual handicap Dyslexia EFL	Non-denom	Steiner
Micklefield	Girls	Day Boarding	£1030 £1820	Schols 4 Bursaries	11 Own prep (4)		Dyslexia EFL	Christian	GSA GBGSA
Moira House	Girls	Day Boarding	£1300 £2000	Schols 10 pa	11 Own prep (5)	Sport	Dyslexia EFL	Christian	GSA
Roedean	Girls	Boarding	£2250	Schols 6	11	Music, Drama, Art, Sport	Extra English	Christian	GSA
St Bede's (Hailsham)	Co-ed	Day Boarding	£1260 £1970	Schols 12	13 Own prep	Tennis, Art	EFL	Non-denom	ISAI
St Leonards-Mayfield	Girls	Day Boarding	£1290 £1935	Schols Bursaries	11			RC	GSA CCSS

School	Type		Fees	Scholarships/Bursaries	Age	Specialities	Special needs	Religion	Affiliations
St Mary's Hall	Girls	Day / Boarding	£1200 / £1800	Schols 62 Bursaries	9			C of E	
Wadhurst	Girls	Day / Boarding	£1070 / £1800	Schols Bursaries	9		Dyslexia	C of E	GSA GBGSA
SUSSEX WEST									
Ardingly	Co-ed	Day / Boarding	£1830 / £2340	Schols 25	13 Own prep (7)	Music, Drama, Art		C of E	HMC Woodard
Burgess Hill	Girls	Day / Boarding	£1020 / £1790	Schols 17 pa	11	Drama	EFL Dyslexia	C of E	GSA
Christ's Hospital	Co-ed	Boarding	Means tested	Hospital endowments for all	10	Music, Drama, Art	Dyslexia	C of E	HMC
Farlington	Girls	Day / Boarding	£1100 / £1800	Schols 6 pa	9	Music	Dyslexia	C of E	GSA
Hurstpierpoint	Boys	Day / Boarding	£1770 / £2280	Schols 20	13 Own junior	Sport, Music		C of E	Woodard
Lancing	Boys Mixed sixth	Day / Boarding	£1530 / £2250	Schols Exhibitions	13			C of E	HMC Woodard
Lavant House	Girls	Day / Boarding	£970 / £1635	Schols 6	11 Own prep (8)		Dyslexia	C of E	GSA GBGSA AHIS
Rosemead	Girls	Day / Boarding	£1060 / £1895	Schols 2	11	Drama		Christian	GSA

Name of School	Boys/ Girls/ Co-ed	Day/ Board	Termly fees Day/ Board	Financial help	Intake age/ Own prep	Special strengths	Special provisions	Religion	Affiliations
S Michael's (Petworth)	Girls	Day Boarding	£1350 £1950	Schols 2 pa	11	Lacrosse	Dyslexia EFL	C of E	GSA Woodard
Seaford	Boys	Boarding	£1895	Schols 15 pa	13	Art	Extra English	C of E	SHMIS GBA
Worth	Boys	Boarding	£1975	Schols 6	13 Own prep (9)		Learning difficulties	RC	HMC
TYNE & WEAR Dame Allan's (Boys)	Boys	Day	£733	Asst places Schols 8 Bursaries	10	Sport		C of E	HMC
Dame Allan's (Girls)	Girls	Day	£696	Asst places 20 Schols 8	10			C of E	GSA
La Sagesse	Girls	Day	£698	Asst places 175 Schols 6 pa	11	Drama	Dyslexia	RC	GSA
Newcastle Church High	Girls	Day	£680	Schols 10 pa	4		Remedial	C of E	GSA
Newcastle High	Girls	Day	£622	Asst places Bursaries Schols 3 pa	11 Own junior (4)		Dyslexia	Non- denom	GPDST

School			Fees	Scholarships	Entry	Sport	Learning difficulties	Denomination	Association
Royal Grammar (Newcastle)	Boys	Day	£650	Asst places 60 pa	11 Own junior (8)			Non-denom	HMC
Westfield	Girls	Day	£782	Schols 10 pa	13 Own prep (3)	Sport	Learning difficulties	Christian	Northumbrian Educational Trust
WARWICKSHIRE									
King's High (Warwick)	Girls	Day	£670	Asst places 35 pa	11			Non-denom	GSA GBGSA
Kingsley	Girls	Day Boarding	£700 £1360	Schols 4 pa	8			C of E	GSA
Rugby	Boys Mixed sixth	Day Boarding	£1475 £2525	Schols 28 pa	13	Drama, Sport, Art	Extra English	C of E	HMC
Warwick	Boys	Day Boarding	£840 £1705	Asst places 160 Schols 80 Bursaries	13 Own prep (7)	Sport	EFL	C of E	HMC
Wroxall Abbey	Girls	Day Boarding	£1070 £1800	Schols Bursaries	11 Own junior (8)		Dyslexia	C of E	GSA ISAI
WILTSHIRE									
Cranborne Chase	Girls	Day Boarding	£895 £2150	Schols	11	Drama, Art	Dyslexia	Christian	GSA

Name of School	Boys/Girls/Co-ed	Day/Board	Termly fees Day/Board	Financial help	Intake age/Own prep	Special strengths	Special provisions	Religion	Affiliations
Dauntsey's	Co-ed	Day Boarding	£1260 £2084	Asst places 55 Schols Bursaries	10	Music, Art, Sport	Yes	Christian	HMC
Godolphin	Girls	Day Boarding	£1115 £1875	Schols Bursaries	11			C of E	GSA
La Retraite	Girls	Day	£650	LEA	11 Own junior (3)			RC	GSA
Marlborough	Boys Mixed sixth	Day Boarding	£1676 £2235	Schols	13	Music, Art, Sport	Dyslexia	C of E	HMC SHA
St Mary's (Calne)	Girls	Day Boarding	£1150 £1950	Schols Bursaries	11 Own junior (5)			C of E	GSA
Stonar	Girls	Day Boarding	£1020 £1900	Schols 4 pa	11 Own prep	Sport	Dyslexia EFL	C of E	GSA
Warminster	Co-ed	Day Boarding	£1065 £1775	Schols Bursaries	13 Own prep (8)	Music, Drama, Art, Sport	Dyslexia	C of E	SHMIS

YORKSHIRE NORTH									
Ampleforth	Boys	Boarding	£2330	Schols Bursaries	10	Music, Drama, Art	Yes	RC	HMC
Ashville	Co-ed	Day Boarding	£888 £1633	Schols Bursaries	13 Own prep (7)	Drama, Art, Sport	Dyslexia EFL	Methodist	HMC
Assumption	Girls	Day Boarding	£900 £1615	Schols 2	11 Own junior (8)	Art	Dyslexia EFL	RC	GSA
Bootham	Co-ed	Day Boarding	£1173 £1899	Schols 12 Bursaries	11		Dyslexia EFL	Quaker	HMC
Giggleswick	Co-ed	Day Boarding	£1498 £2245	Schols Bursaries	13	Art		C of E	HMC
Harrogate College	Girls	Day Boarding	£1210 £1815	Asst places 40 Schols 50	11		Dyslexia Deafness	C of E	GSA
Hunmanby Hall	Girls	Day Boarding	£975 £1820	Schols 9	5	Drama, Sport	Remedial EFL	Methodist	GSA
Mount (York)	Girls	Day Boarding	£1266 £1857	Schols 10 pa Bursaries	11	Music, Art	Dyslexia EFL	Quaker	GSA
Queen Ethelburga's	Girls	Day Boarding	£1185 £1975	Schols 8 pa Bursaries	11 Own prep (7)		Dyslexia EFL	C of E	Woodard
Queen Margaret's (York)	Girls	Day Boarding	£1135 £1820	Schols 9	11	Art, Sport	Remedial Dyslexia	C of E	GSA

Name of School	Boys/Girls/Co-ed	Day/Board	Termly fees Day/Board	Financial help	Intake age/Own prep	Special strengths	Special provisions	Religion	Affiliations
Read	Boys	Day Boarding	£665 £1320	Schols 6	8	Art	Dyslexia	C of E	ISAI
St Hilda's (Whitby)	Girls Mixed sixth	Day Boarding	£723 £1344	Schols 15	11 Own junior (4)			C of E	ISAI
St Peter's (York)	Co-ed	Day Boarding	£1191 £2121	Asst places 120 Schols 8	13 Own junior		Dyslexia	C of E	HMC
Scarborough	Co-ed	Day Boarding	£1058 £1975	Schols 15	11 Own prep		Dyslexia EFL	Christian	GBA SHMIS
York College	Girls	Day	£873	Schols 3 pa	4			C of E	GSA CSCo
YORKSHIRE SOUTH									
Sheffield High	Girls	Day	£622	Asst places 21 Schols 10 pa	11 Own junior (5)			Christian	GSA GPDST
YORKSHIRE WEST									
Ackworth	Co-ed	Day Boarding	£1038 £1790	Schols 35	11	Music, Drama, Sport	EFL Dyslexia	Quaker	SHMIS

School	Type	Day/Boarding	Fees	Asst places/Schols	Entry	Special		Denom	Assoc
Batley	Boys Mixed sixth	Day	£693	Asst places 247 Schols 5–10	11	Music		Christian	GBA
Bradford (Boys)	Boys Mixed sixth	Day	£766	Asst places 30 Schols 5	11			Christian	HMC
Bradford (Girls)	Girls	Day	£637	Asst places 60 Bursaries	11 Own junior	Art, Sport		Christian	GSA
Fulneck (Boys)	Boys	Day Boarding	£770 £1455		13 Own prep (8)	Small school, family atmosphere		Moravian	SHMIS
Fulneck (Girls)	Girls	Day Boarding	£685 £1297		4			Moravian	GSA
Gateways	Girls	Day	£620	Schols 8	13 Own junior (4)	Art	Dyslexia	Non-denom	GSA
Leeds Grammar	Boys	Day	£720		8			C of E	HMC
Leeds High	Girls	Day	£772	Asst places 20 pa Schols Bursaries	4			Non-denom	GSA

Name of School	Boys/ Girls/ Co-ed	Day/ Board	Termly fees Day/ Board	Financial help	Intake age/ Own prep	Special strengths	Special provisions	Religion	Affiliations
Queen Elizabeth's (Wakefield)	Boys	Day Boarding	£826 £1346	Asst places 154 Schols 6 pa	11 Own junior	Art, Sport		Non-denom	HMC
Rishworth	Co-ed	Day Boarding	£925 £1735	Schols 8 pa	11 Own junior (4)	Art, Drama	EFL Dyslexia	C of E	SHMIS GBA
Silcoates	Boys Mixed sixth	Day Boarding	£942 £1648	Schols 12	13 Own prep (7)	Sport	EFL Dyslexia	United Reformed	HMC SHMIS
Wakefield High	Girls	Day	£710	Asst places Bursaries	11 Own prep (4)			Non-denom	GSA GBGSA
Woodhouse Grove	Co-ed	Day Boarding	£998 £1635	Asst places 130 Schols 80	11 Own junior (8)	Music	Dyslexia EFL	Methodist	HMC
WALES CLWYD Howell's (Denbigh)	Girls	Day Boarding	£1250 £1900	Asst places Schols Bursaries	11 Own prep (7)			Anglican	GSA GBGSA
Penrhos	Girls	Day Boarding	£1215 £1820	Asst places 12 Schols Bursaries	11		EFL Dyslexia	Inter-denom	GSA

School	Type	Day/Boarding	Scholarships	Entry	Extras	Denomination	Affiliation
Ruthin	Boys Mixed sixth	Day £1130 Boarding £1780	Schols 18 Bursaries	10 Own junior (6)		C of E	SHMIS GBA
Rydal	Co-ed	Day £1425 Boarding £1895	Asst places 7 pa Schols 10 Bursaries	13 Own prep	EFL Dyslexia	Methodist	HMC
DYFED							
Llandovery	Co-ed	Day £953 Boarding £1595		11		C of W	HMC
GLAMORGAN SOUTH							
Howell's (Llandaff)	Girls	Day £732 Boarding £1588	Asst places 190 Schols 16	11 Own junior (7)	Music	Non-denom	GPDST
GWENT							
Haberdashers' Monmouth	Girls	Day £800 Boarding £1420	Schols	11 Own junior (7)		C of E	GSA
Monmouth	Boys	Day £957 Boarding £1707	Asst places 28 pa Schols	11	Sport	C of E	HMC
Rougemont	Co-ed	Day £880	Schols 9	3	Sport	EFL Deafness Dyslexia	Christian	SHMIS GBA AHIS

Name of School	Boys/ Girls/ Co-ed	Day/ Board	Termly fees Day/ Board	Financial help	Intake age/ Own prep	Special strengths	Special provisions	Religion	Affiliations
GWYNEDD St Gerard's	Co-ed	Day	£510		11 Own prep (3)		EFL Dyslexia	Christian	ISAI
POWYS Christ College	Boys Mixed sixth	Day Boarding	£1220 £1610	Schols Bursaries	11			C of E	HMC
SCOTLAND CENTRAL Dollar Academy	Co-ed	Day Boarding	£694 £1512		12 Own junior (5)			C of S	HMC GBA ISBA
Queen Victoria	Boys	Boarding	MoD.		10		Open only to the sons of Scottish service personnel	Non-denom	
FIFE St Leonard's	Girls	Day Boarding	£1175 £2350	Asst places 22 Schols Bursaries	11 Own prep	Drama, Art, Sport		Christian	GSA

School	Type	Day/Boarding	Scholarships	Entry	Extras	Support	Religion	Affiliations
GRAMPIAN Gordonstoun	Co-ed	Day £1526 Boarding £2376	Asst places 21 Schols 25 Bursaries	13 Own prep	Music, Drama, Outward bound, Art, Sport		Christian	HMC
Robert Gordon's	Boys	Day £600 Boarding £1300	Asst places Schols Bursaries	11 Own prep (5)			Non-denom	HMC GBA
St Margaret's (Aberdeen)	Girls	Day £691	Asst places 14 Schols 1 pa	5			Non-denom	GSA GBGSA
HIGHLAND Fort Augustus	Boys	Day £960 Boarding £1570	Asst places 25	11			RC	GBA
LOTHIAN Daniel Stewart's	Boys	Day £772 Boarding £1492	Asst places Schols Bursaries	12 Own prep (3)			Non-denom	HMC
Edinburgh Academy	Boys Mixed sixth	Day £1040 Boarding £2100	Asst places 7 pa Schols 5	10 Own prep (5)	Art	Learning support	Christian	HMC
Fettes	Co-ed	Day £1465 Boarding £2180	Asst places 28 Schols 15	10	Art	Dyslexia EFL	Christian	HMC GBA ISBA

Name of School	Boys/ Girls/ Co-ed	Day/ Board	Termly fees Day/ Board	Financial help	Intake age/ Own prep	Special strengths	Special provisions	Religion	Affiliations
George Heriot's	Co-ed	Day	£785	Asst places 220 Schols 30 Foundationers 70	12 Own junior (5)	Rugby	EFL Dyslexia	Christian	HMC
George Watson's	Co-ed	Day Boarding	£772 £1442	Asst places 237 Schols Bursaries	12 Own junior (3)	Drama, Sport, Music	Remedial	Christian	HMC
Loretto	Boys Mixed sixth	Day Boarding	£1470 £2350	Asst places 22 Schols	13 Own junior		Dyslexia Cystic fibrosis	Inter- denom	HMC
Mary Erskine's	Girls	Day Boarding	£770 £1500	Schols 4	12 Own junior (5)			Non- denom	GSA
Merchiston	Boys	Day Boarding	£1480 £2300	Asst places 30 Schols 8	11	Sport, Art	Dyslexia	C of S	HMC
Rudolf Steiner (Edinburgh)	Co-ed	Day	£680		4			Non- denom	Steiner
St Denis and Cranley	Girls	Day Boarding	£770 £1530	Asst places 15 Schols 4 pa	12 Own junior (5)		Dyslexia EFL	Christian	GSA

School	Type	Day/Boarding	Fees	Places/Scholarships	Entry	Own prep/junior	Sport/Music	EFL	Religion	Association
St George's (Edinburgh)	Girls	Day Boarding	£780 £1555	Asst places 16	11 Own prep (5)	Sport, Music		Christian	GSA
St Margaret's (Edinburgh)	Girls	Day Boarding	£800 £1575	Asst places 54 Schols 4	12 Own junior (3)	Sport	EFL	Christian	GSA
St Mary's Music	Co-ed	Day Boarding	£2605 £3575	Schols 9 Means tested places 30	9	Music specialist		Christian	

STRATHCLYDE

School	Type	Day/Boarding	Fees	Places/Scholarships	Entry	Own prep/junior	Sport/Music	EFL	Religion	Association
Belmont House	Boys	Day	£750	Asst places 15 pa	12 Own junior (5)	Sport	EFL	C of S Jewish	IAPS
Craigholme	Girls	Day	£665	Asst places 20 Bursaries	5			Christian Jewish	SHA
Fernhill	Girls	Day	£550	Asst places 45	12 Own primary			RC	
Glasgow Academy	Boys	Day	£705	Asst places 40 Schols	4			Christian	HMC
Glasgow High	Co-ed	Day	£800	Asst places 58 Schols 5 pa	10 Own junior (4)			Christian	HMC
Hutchesons'	Co-ed	Day	£660	Schols Bursaries	5	Music		Christian	HMC

Name of School	Boys/Girls/Co-ed	Day/Board	Termly fees Day/Board	Financial help	Intake age/Own prep	Special strengths	Special provisions	Religion	Affiliations
Kelvinside	Boys	Day	£819	Asst places 50 Schols 4 pa	4	Sport	Mild handicaps	Christian	HMC GBA
Laurel Bank	Girls	Day	£830	Asst places 60+ Schols Bursaries	4		Some	Christian	
Lomond	Co-ed	Day Boarding	£785 £1815	Asst places 44 Schols 15	5	Sport	Yes	Christian	
Park, The	Girls	Day	£756	Asst places 51 Schols 4	12 Own junior (5)	Art, Athletics	Yes	Christian	
St Columba's (Kilmacolm)	Co-ed	Day	£760	Asst places 40	5			Christian	
Wellington (Ayr)	Girls	Day Boarding	£730 £1545	Asst places 40 Bursaries	12 Own junior (3)	Drama, Sport	Dyslexia EFL	C of S	GSA GBGSA
Westbourne	Girls	Day	£792	Asst places 60 Schols 6	12 Own junior (2)	Music, Art	EFL Mild handicaps	Christian	
TAYSIDE Dundee High	Co-ed	Day	£678	Asst places 150 Schols 30	12 Own junior (5)	Sport, Music, Drama	Dyslexia	Christian	HMC

850

Glenalmond	Boys	Boarding £2450	Asst places 36 Schols Bursaries	12	Sport		Episcopalian	HMC GBA
Kilgraston	Girls	Day £740 Boarding £1430	Asst places Schols	8		EFL Deafness Visual handicap	RC	
Morrison's	Co-ed	Day £680 Boarding £1780	Asst places 153 Schols Bursaries	12 Own junior (5)		Dyslexia Visual handicap EFL	Christian	HMC GSA
Rannoch	Co-ed	Day £1175 Boarding £1990	Asst places 2 Schols 10 pa	10	Art, Sport	Remedial	Christian	SHMIS GBA
Strathallan	Co-ed	Boarding £2250	Asst places 32 Schols 30	10		Remedial English	Inter-denom	HMC
NORTHERN IRELAND CO ANTRIM								
Friends' (Antrim)	Co-ed	Day £283 Boarding £550	LEA	11 Own prep (4)		EFL Mild handicaps	Quaker	
BELFAST Belfast Academy	Co-ed	Day £500	LEA	11	Sport		Non-denom	HMC

Name of School	Boys/ Girls/ Co-ed	Day/ Board	Termly fees Day/ Board	Financial help	Intake age/ Own prep	Special strengths	Special provisions	Religion	Affiliations
Campbell College	Boys	Day Boarding	£802 £1794	Schols Bursaries	13 Own prep	Music	Dyslexia Extra-English EFL	Protestant	HMC
Christian Brothers'	Boys	Day	£400	Schols	11			RC	
Hunterhouse	Girls	Day Boarding	£273 £813		11 Own prep		EFL	Christian	Voluntary Grammar
Methodist College	Co-ed	Day Boarding	£353 £632	Schols 6	11 Own junior (5)	Music		Methodist	HMC
Royal Belfast	Boys	Day	£550	Schols	11 Own junior (5)			Non-denom	HMC
Victoria College (Belfast)	Girls	Day Boarding	£410 £1070	Schols	11 Own prep (4)	Music	EFL	Non-denom	
CO DOWN Bangor Grammar	Boys	Day			11 Own junior (5)			Non-denom	HMC GBA

CO FERMANAGH Portora Royal	Co-ed	Day £420 Boarding £1350	Schols 2 pa	11	Rowing		C of E	HMC
LONDONDERRY Coleraine	Boys	Day £325 Boarding £908	Bursaries	12	Art	EFL	Christian	HMC
CO TYRONE Royal (Dungannon)	Co-ed	Day £563 Boarding £1220	Schols 7 Bursaries 3	4		Dyslexia EFL Handicaps	Christian	SHMIS
EIRE St Columba's (Dublin)	Co-ed	Day Boarding	Schols Bursaries	11				HMC

INDEX

INDEX